The Choynski Chronicles

A Biography of Hall of Fame Boxer
Jewish Joe Choynski

Christopher J. LaForce

Win By KO Publications

Iowa City

The Choynski Chronicles

A Biography of Hall of Fame Boxer Jewish Joe Choynski

By Christopher J. LaForce

(ISBN-13): 978-0-9799822-8-6

(hardcover: 50# acid-free alkaline paper)

Includes appendix, endnotes, bibliography and index.

Cover design by Christopher J. LaForce and Gwyn Snider ©

Manufactured in the United States of America

Win By KO Publications
Iowa City, Iowa
winbykopublications.com

Dedication

I dedicate this book to my late father, Joseph Henry LaForce. His only brother, my late uncle Napoleon Gabriel LaForce, nicknamed him "Kid," as in, "Kid" LaForce. "Mon Oncle Gaby" apparently fancied that my Dad would grow up to become a boxer. My father (and his sister, my Aunt Yvonne) was a big fan of another Jewish entertainer, Al Jolson, which interest I share. Also – to my mother, Elma Brainard LaForce. She raised our large family (I am one of 14 offspring), while caring for my invalid father (who died in 1974 of Multiple Sclerosis). Her encouragement and nurturing instilled in me a sense of values and a love of the Lord.

Original Joe Choynski artwork © 2013 by Christopher J. LaForce.

Contents

Foreword

By Herbert G. Goldman

It is with distinct pleasure that I write this admittedly brief foreword to this first and fine biography of Joseph Bartlett Choynski, first light heavyweight boxing champion of the world.

Joe is something of an anomaly as a boxer. He went the distance – and gave hell to – some much larger men, notably Jim Jeffries, whom he held to a 20-round draw. He knocked out the great Jack Johnson, yet was stopped in seven rounds by welterweight Joe Walcott, whom he outweighed by 24 pounds (168-144) and towered over by nine inches. Middleweight Kid McCoy was another nemesis. So was Bob Fitzsimmons, another light heavyweight whose knockout loss to huge Jim Jeffries in 1899 inspired Lou Houseman to create the light heavyweight division. (More on that anon.)

Choynski was not short on guts, but he was vulnerable when not on the defensive. Had he been more durable, he would rank among the greatest fighters of all-time. Joe, nonetheless, is among the most storied. His battle on the barge with James J. Corbett is the stuff that legends are, and have been, built on. He belongs among the fabled names of what was once called Boxing's "Golden Era" – the days of Corbett, Jeffries, Sharkey, Johnson, McCoy, Tommy Ryan, Walcott, Gans, and Dixon.

Almanacs have long listed Jack Root as the first world light heavyweight boxing champion, and boxing fans – a rather conservative lot – have been reluctant to accept that this was not the case. Here, however, are the facts:

Old boxing record books listed George Gardner as the first world light heavyweight champion by virtue of his knockout over Jack Root in what was allegedly the first world light heavyweight championship bout in 1903. Root, who had become a wealthy man in the motion picture exhibition business after his retirement, would frequently stop by the offices of The *Ring* magazine en route to Europe, and buttonhole the staff – including founder-editor Nat Fleischer, with tales of his life inside the ring. Root claimed, quite rightly, that his bout versus Gardner was not for the vacant world title, but that he, Jack Root, had been defending champion. Jack claimed to have won the vacant title earlier that year when he outpointed Charles (Kid) McCoy in a 10-rounder in Detroit his manager, Lou Houseman, had billed for the world light heavy-weight title. Houseman was thus the creator of the class and Root, his charge, the first world champ of the division. Fleischer accepted this in his annual Ring Record Books, and almanacs soon followed suit.

A tremendous flood of research in the past 20-odd years has since debunked this bit of "history." Lou Houseman was indeed the founder of the light heavyweight division, but he founded it in 1899, not 1903. Houseman had been hired to arrange a series of top boxing contests for a fair in Dubuque, Iowa, that year. He billed several for regional titles and one for a new world crown – Joe Choynski versus Jimmy Ryan of Australia for the "light heavyweight championship of the world" on August 29, 1899. Houseman's inspiration for this new and needed weight division was the 167-pound Bob Fitzsimmons' loss of the world heavyweight title to huge Jim Jeffries the previous June 9. Choynski outscored Ryan over 20 rounds and was acclaimed the first light heavy champ.

The assertion that Choynski "did not seriously see himself as the light heavyweight champion" does not hold up against the fact that his bout against Jim Hall on September 25, 1899 – less than six weeks after his defeat of Ryan – was billed as a defense of his world light heavyweight title. Joe also defended the new title in a rematch against Ryan at the Broadway Athletic Club (A.C.) in downtown New York on October 20. Choynski held the title until January 12, 1900, when he was stopped in four rounds (a very controversial outcome, as we'll see inside the book) by Kid McCoy, also at the Broadway A.C. While no title billing for this contest has been found in contemporary sources, the obituary of the bout's referee, Johnny White, in the *New York Herald* of January 15, 1920, said the fight was for "the light heavyweight title."

In fact, the light heavyweight division was not fully accepted by the public until Paul Berlenbach popularized it in a series of defenses in the mid-1920s. Small wonder that early reference sources do not contain a complete history of its beginnings. Choynski, for his part, did little to assert his role as the first champ of the division following his retirement from boxing. His battles against Corbett, Jeffries, and Johnson were of far more interest to newspapermen and fans. Not so with Jack Root, a far less storied fighter. Root's reign as world light heavy champ was his big claim to fame. And why not make himself the first champ – especially when few would contradict him after Choynski's death in 1943. (Root died 20 years later.)

The story of Joe Choynski, though, is far more than the start of the light heavyweight division. It's the story of the son of Jewish immigrants from Poland who forged a legend with his fists and paved the way for other Jewish boxing champs from Abe Attell to Benny Leonard, Benny Bass, Maxie Rosenbloom, Barney Ross, and others. It is the story of a remarkable man (who became, successively, boxing instructor at the Pittsburgh Athletic Club, a chiropractor, and an insurance agent after his retirement from boxing), his times, and the fabulous world of boxing in a truly storied era. This biography has long been needed. Now we have it, thanks to Christopher LaForce.

Acknowledgements

I have been fortunate to have had the assistance of many knowledgeable and helpful people. Without the generous contributions of photos, articles and other material, a "cradle-to-grave" biography of Joseph Choynski would have been more difficult and incomplete.

To the descendants of the Choynski family, I thank David Fleishhacker for the many photographs he sent, from his late mother Janet's collection. For information of other types, I also thank David, his brother, Mort (Mortimer Fleishhacker III passed away on October 25, 2011) and their sister, Delia. They are the grandchildren of Joe's brother, Herbert.

Two who have contributed the most to this project in terms of photos and material have been Albert and Harriet Draper, who reside in Santa Rosa, California, Sonoma County. Al's wife is the former Harriet Coe, niece of Joe Choynski, youngest daughter of Edwin Walker Coe, and last surviving member of the generation following Joe and siblings. Besides sending a ton of photos, documents and anecdotes, they gave valuable perspective and encouragement. Much of the material sent by the Drapers and Fleishhackers is being published here for the first time.

I thank the following, for material and information: Timothy C. "Tim" Coe, grandson of Edwin Coe, Don Coleman of the U.K., Thomas Lipinski of N.Y. State, IBRO Director Dan Cuoco and member, Tony Triem.

My good friend Tracy Callis of Roanoke, Virginia, who proofread the manuscript, gave much encouragement, many suggestions and wrote a blurb for the book. Tracy is not only a fellow member of the International Boxing Research Organization (IBRO), but also on the staff of www.cyberboxingzone.com. He has written or co-authored several books on the subject of boxing. Tracy's record of Choynski's fighting career on the Cyber Boxing Zone site was of much help.

My good friend Bob Petersen of Lane Cove, Australia, Professor emeritus of the University of Sydney. In 2003 his fine biography of Peter Jackson came out, entitled "Gentleman Bruiser." A revised edition was published in 2011 by McFarland & Company, Inc., entitled, "Peter Jackson." Bob sent me a veritable cornucopia of newspaper clippings, book excerpts and photos. He also gave much advice along the way.

The late Harry Shaffer, former IBRO member and owner of Antiquities of the Prize Ring, who passed away June 7, 2012: for the wealth of archival data and material this generous soul sent me, as a courtesy to an associate.

Fellow IBRO member and friend Tony Gee of London, England, for many important items, including British newspaper accounts of Joe's 1892 England sojourn. Tony supplied the 1949 photograph of the headstone of

Joe and Louise Choynski, and varied, valuable information. Tony is among the world's leading experts on the bare-knuckle era and especially noted for his work, "Up To Scratch." He is currently writing a book about Scottish bare-knuckle fighters. Tony's parents, Hazel and Leonard, for the research they did and help they gave. Leonard Gee died of cancer on May 29, 2010.

Herbert G. Goldman, for writing the Foreword for this book. He was Managing Editor of The *Ring* from the late 1970s through the '80s, joined *Boxing Illustrated* in 1987 and eventually became Editor-in-Chief. He is the biggest proponent for Joe Choynski as the first light-heavyweight champion of the world, a stance I support. Mr. Goldman has penned lauded biographies of entertainers Al Jolson, Fanny Brice and Eddie Cantor.

Ron Jackson of Oklahoma, who should by now have a certain book of his own in print, entitled "Fight to the Finish." It covers the Jim Corbett-Joe Choynski rivalry up to 1889, in particular the legendary fight on the barge. I exchanged information with Ron and he sent me, among other items, Robert Singerman's work on the life of I.N. Choynski, entitled, "The Journalism of I.N. Choynski, He Flatters None and Displeases Many."

Mark Palmer of Cincinnati, Ohio. He visited Walnut Hills Cemetery for me, taking photographs of the cemetery and burial site of Joe and Louise Choynski. Mark writes about amateur wrestling, wrestling history, and is a Staff Writer at www.revwrestling.com. He and Bob Petersen are co-authoring a book on early wrestling history and its great practitioners.

Mark T. Dunn of Bloomington, Illinois, who published his wonderfully-researched biography of "Parson" Davies in 2011, entitled "Chicago's Greatest Sportsman, Charles E. 'Parson' Davies." Mark exchanged much useful information with me, provided terrific photos and drawings of "The Parson," and took photographs of Joe Choynski's final residence for me.

Adam Pollack has written a series of excellent books on the heavyweight champions of Joe Choynski's day. He started with his book on John L. Sullivan and has continued through his latest, Jack Johnson. Adam shared photos and industry expertise with me. (Oh, and he's also my publisher, through his own publishing company, Win By KO Publications)!

Greg Lewis of Wales and his wife, Moira Sharkey, formerly of Ireland, for material and information on Tom Sharkey. They have written a book on musician Bruce Springsteen and the first, full biography of "Sailor" Tom Sharkey, entitled, "I Fought Them All." A nice work!

My friend, Rob Snell of England has a terrific website, www.boxingbiographies.com, which was helpful.

David Chesanow provided many valuable Choynski items and a lot of useful advice on the publishing industry. David is a professional copyeditor, as well as a collector of Choynski memorabilia and effects.

Jack Giordano, born in Canastota, New York (location of the International Boxing Hall of Fame) has for several years resided in

Redwood, New York, birthplace of Tommy Ryan. Jack gave information on Ryan and a tour of tiny Redwood. He and wife, Judy, were gracious hosts.

To Stephen Gordon, Mike DeLisa, Tracy Callis and the rest of the gang at cyberboxingzone.com, and to John Sheppard and the staff of Boxing Records at boxrec.com, for their accurately compiled records.

My quest for the elusive record of Joe's chiropractic schooling ended when, on a hunch, I contacted the National University of Health Sciences (NUHS), in Lombard, Illinois. Two persons, Public Relations Specialist Tracy Litsey and President James Winterstein, D.C., advised that Choynski attended The Universal College of Chiropractic in Pittsburgh, Pennsylvania for 18 months and graduated on May 5, 1920.

My chiropractor, Dr. Max Rouslin of Asheville, North Carolina, made me aware of Dr. Richard Vanrumpt (1904-1987), who graduated from the National College of Chiropractic in 1923 and who, like Joe, was a former pro boxer. An important chiropractor, Vanrumpt developed the Directional Non-Force Technique. Max introduced me to "McTeague," the 1899 novel by Frank Norris, which became an MGM motion picture in 1924 under the name "Greed." (Max is also the best chiropractor I have known. If you are passing through Asheville, visit his "Max-Well Chiropractic" office!)

Writer and Journalist Lenn Zonder of New Haven, Connecticut, for valuable background on Yale, New Haven and its Jewish community, and I.N. Choynski's early years in the United States.

Tony Barton of Australia, whose uncle was the grandson of Australian heavyweight champion, Joe Goddard. He sent photos of Goddard and some rare and heretofore unpublished information on his great-grandfather.

George Rugg, curator of the Hesburgh Libraries at the University of Notre Dame (Indiana), and to The Joyce Sports Research Collection there. George provided a slew of archival clippings, documents and prints.

Bill Schutte of Whitewater, Wisconsin, from whom I was able to purchase some rare photos of Joe Choynski and other key figures.

Q. David Bowers, for permission to quote his 1986, *Nickelodeon Theatres and Their Music*. To the Greenville (South Carolina) Library system, especially the Hughes Main and local Taylors (Burdette) branches, for processing my inter-library loan requests. If I have overlooked anyone, I express sincere regret and ask that you forgive me.

Finally (but *not least*) – To my dear wife Amy, who patiently endured my computer time, proofread the manuscript and made thoughtful and useful suggestions, particular for the first chapter. To my children, Shannon, Ryan and Jessica, who were also understanding. I love you all very much! To my wonderful family of 12 siblings (and sister, Jane, who died in 1979), who have given so much love and support in my life.

Introduction

Boxing speaks to the most elementary, visceral impulses. To deny this is to reject our origins and basic programming. The instincts for protecting family and self are part of humanity's evolution. No matter how we might try to obscure these primal urges with the mantle of civilization, to obliterate them is impracticable. From the era of the ancient Greeks and Romans, with their cestus, myrmex and sphairai, humans have engaged in contests of more or less "controlled strife." Early tribal chieftains achieved their status by being the most formidable at physical combat. Whether it is boxing, (genuine) wrestling or MMA (mixed martial arts), I have always been intrigued by the idea of the greatest fighter on the planet. While such shows as Spike's (defunct) *Deadliest Warrior* also hold fascination, there is something about *unarmed* combat that is for me the most meaningful.

One of my first memories of Boxing came in the 4th Grade at Madrid-Waddington Elementary School in Northern New York State. On a table, I saw an issue of *Sports Illustrated*, opened to an article on the training camps of Muhammad Ali and Joe Frazier. This was leading up to their epic clash of March 8, 1971, commonly referred to as, "The Fight." After reading of the contrasting styles and training camps of both (Ali's camp was in the hot climate of Miami Beach, Florida, while Frazier's was in the frigid locale of New York's Catskill Mountains), I became a lifelong aficionado of pugilism. In 1977, I began an intensive study of the technique and history of Boxing and have been an historian since. I was the only southpaw in the Massena (New York) Boxing Club, set up in the basement of St. Mary's Catholic Church, Massena. It was there that I trained and boxed with stops and starts, from 1978 until 1984, when I relocated to Dover, New Jersey and attended the Joe Kubert School of Cartoon & Graphic Art.

I first became aware of Joe Choynski when, in the early 1970s, I was perusing the family *World Book* encyclopedia. I read of "Gentleman" Jim Corbett's "invention" of the left hook in his legendary tilt on the barge with the subject of this biography. At the time, Joe was to me just another boxer with a funny last name, an also-ran. I have since learned much about Joe, though in some ways he remains a bit of a mystery.

As I began in High School (11th Grade) to collect clippings, books, video and other boxing-related items, I became more aware of Joseph Choynski, the storied puncher, "near-champion" and feared opponent of the heavyweights. His fistic ledger revealed that he had battled, on essentially even terms, the most respected fist-fighters of his day. The era of Choynski and his contemporaries, known variously as The Victorian Era, Gaslight Era and The Gilded Age, was also the first Golden Age of heavyweights of the Marquis (or Marquess) of Queensberry era. The other Golden Age was from the late 1960s through late '70s, featuring Ali, Frazier, George Foreman and a young Larry Holmes. They had a fine supporting cast: Ken Norton, Jerry Quarry, George Chuvalo, Jimmy Young, Jimmy Ellis, Oscar Bonavena, Earnie Shavers, Ron Lyle and others.

Choynski's heavyweight contemporaries encompassed the likes of James J. Jeffries, the indestructible "California Grizzly," "Fighting Blacksmith" Bob Fitzsimmons and "Gentleman Jim," James J. Corbett, champions all. Top contenders of the day were the tenacious wolverine, "Sailor" Tom Sharkey, "Irish Champion" Peter Maher, "Corkscrew" Kid McCoy, Gus Ruhlin, "The Akron Giant," Australians Joe Goddard, Frank "Paddy" Slavin and "The Black Prince," Peter Jackson. They were a mix of greats and near-greats, who would likely give champions of all generations a stiff argument. After seeing Choynski's results against these titans (he traded punches with all but Slavin), I accorded "Chrysanthemum Joe" a special place on the podium, up with the rest of the "pantheon."

Piecing together a coherent timeline and detailed chronology of the life of Joseph Bartlett Choynski has been quite a challenge. In doing so, the author has needed to become, in essence, a bio-archeologist, sifting through the fragmentary rubble and potsherds of extant information. Choynski was largely a private individual away from the ring and theater, especially reticent regarding his spouse, Louise. They tended to keep their private life distinctly separate from their public personas and away from the intrusion of the media. He is a tough subject, which is in good part why there has never been a full biography done of him to date. Although Joe was usually a natty dresser in public and led a cultured lifestyle, ostentatious he was not. Because of this, his life record was not as extensive as, say, Jim Corbett, John L. Sullivan or many others of Joe's ilk. Distinct from a subject like, say, Mark Twain, Joe did not keep journals or write a lot about his adventures and life events. Also, in consequence to the time frame in which Choynski lived, there are virtually no relatives, friends or acquaintances still alive from which to glean first-hand information.

I felt that the type of person most qualified to write a biography of Joe would be an historian who shared his Jewish heritage, as he might have more insight into the man that Joe Choynski was. I do not share that heritage, as I was raised a Roman Catholic, but I have always been fascinated by and have a deep respect for Judaism. It was, in large part, my friend Bob Petersen who convinced me that I could, and should, write the story of Joe's life. I hope I have done his story justice.

I spent the first 15 months or so, beginning around September, 2007, gathering all I could find on Joe Choynski, his family, opponents and such. I collected nearly 8,000 items, comprising photos, book excerpts and other material. More than 4,000 of these were archived newspaper articles which I amassed from websites such as <u>newspaperarchive.com</u>, <u>fold3.com</u>, <u>cdnc.ucr.edu</u>; <u>genealogybank.com</u>, <u>paperspast.natlib.govt.nz/cgi-bin/paperspast</u>, <u>loc.gov/chroniclingamerica</u>, <u>digitalnewspapers.org</u>, <u>fultonhistory.com</u>, <u>kdl.kyvl.org</u>, <u>texashistory.unt.edu</u> and others, compiling a comprehensive storehouse of data to draw upon.

During my research, I found that the historical data on Joe Choynski contained more than its share of inaccuracies and discrepancies. On more than one occasion, for instance, Herbert Choynski, of the United States Army at the Presidio in San Francisco, was apparently the party erroneously referred to in newspapers as "Joseph B. Choynski" in the rank of Corporal or other military class.[1] There were multiple cases of mistaken identity in several papers, referring to cousins or other relatives of the Choynskis or Ashims. There were, in addition, multiple variations in the names of the siblings of Louise Miller-Choynski, from one Federal Census to another. These are but a few examples of the many discrepancies I found. Unfortunately, when I converted my already massive 8" x 11" version of the manuscript to 6" x 9" for book form, the page count shot up to an unmanageable 1,200 pages! Sadly, I needed to cut out much of the writing I had done on Joe's siblings and other relatives, much detail of fight accounts and such, in addition to dozens of photos I wanted to include. I originally started chapter one with my narrative of the Corbett-Choynski barge battle from the 1942 Warner Brothers film, *Gentleman Jim* (Bob Petersen's idea). Alas, it was also cut, out of necessity.

I have omitted most material of questionable veracity. A prime example is a story from *Parade* magazine (UK), December 30, 1961. It told of a down-on-his-luck Joe, who, living in Chicago in 1922, was employed as a bodyguard for Frank Reed, owner of a night club called "The Jack of Diamonds." A lieutenant for mobster Dean "Dion" O'Banion, named Al Lacey, was trying to strong-arm Reed into paying "protection" money to O'Banion. When Frank told Lacey to beat it, Choynski offered to bounce Al, but was ignored by everyone. Joe was referred to as a bum and an old hobo. Dion told Lacey to give Reed 48 hours, before they would harm Frank's girlfriend, Katie. Reed had Joe stay by Katie's side until it all blew over. On the 4th day, six of Dion's "top strong arm boys" showed up at the night club, while Reed was away. As the goons approached Katie, Joe bravely stepped in front of the singer, yelling for her to run to her room. Choynski held them off as long as he could, falling and rising five times. When police arrived, they found poor Joe lying in a pool of his own blood, four of the mobsters lying unconscious nearby. The other two had fled the scene, but not before "stamping" on Joe's hands, "so he could never fight again," and left without Katie. Instead of being grateful, Reed dropped Joe from his payroll. He wanted bums, not heroes who could "get in the way of his limelight." The real Joe was living between Pennsylvania and California in 1922, working as instructor at the Pittsburgh Athletic Association, then in California as a chiropractor and fitness instructor.

I have done my best to avoid the pitfalls of hero worship, and to give a fair, unbiased accounting of a life. Joe was a good man, but, like all, had his flaws, or warts, if you will. I have attempted to capture as closely as possible the scope of his personality, the negative and the positive, goodness and imperfection. I hope I have largely succeeded. Further, I have, wherever possible, used primary source and contemporary material, as well as reliable secondary source information. As a personal choice, I have avoided the ethnic slurs and racial stereotypes commonly used in Joe's time. While these terms may have reflected the bigotry of that era, I find them distasteful and have kept the quotation of them to a minimum. Beyond this, I have tried to satisfy both the boxing historian, who expects great detail, and the casual fan, who, by and large, wants a biography to read like a novel. I have made a concerted effort to cite and credit all sources that I have obtained information from, and if I have overlooked any such sources, please email the author at calaforce@bellsouth.net and let me know. I will amend errors I am made aware of, in future editions.

The research for the Joe Choynski story has in itself been an education for the author. Not only has it revealed much data heretofore lost to the passage of time, but has opened new portals and paths to side history and characters of which I had no inkling before. My attempt to "unearth" some of the details of Joe's life have been frustrating. The same applies to his spouse. I put together life and career of Louise from her death certificate, burial information and newspapers such as the *New York Clipper*.

As the 18th century scribe, John Evelyn, wrote, "It is not imaginable to such as have not tried, what labour an historian who would be exact is condemned to. He must read all, good and bad, and remove a world of rubbish before he can lay the foundation." This applies more to "legendary" figures and those so removed in time that reliable documentation is lacking. In the absence of incontrovertible evidence, one occasionally speculates, using the best information possible, and lets the reader decide some things for themself. On the other hand, the uncovering of the details of Joe's life and the research involved, has been mostly a rewarding and enjoyable experience. I feel honored and privileged to have been able to tell his story. It is my hope that you, the reader, will derive as much pleasure from it as I have had in writing it.

Round One

A Chrysanthemum Sprouts

Sadly, Joe is mostly remembered today by boxing historians and die-hard aficionados. He fought in the heavyweight division at a time when it was chock-full of great champions and contenders, yet in our day, Joe, at 168 pounds, would only be a super-middleweight. A bit too heavy to battle his era's middleweights (the division's limit then set at 154 or 158 pounds) and there not yet existing a firmly established light-heavyweight (175 pound) division, Choynski was forced to fight the big men. The heavyweights, though much lighter on average than today's behemoths, still ranged from about 180 to 220 pounds. Thus handicapped, Joe was nonetheless able to gain admirable results. He was probably the first true "boxer-puncher" stylist of the heavyweight class, the first important Jewish boxer in the history of the United States, and in addition, the first light-heavyweight champion. Moreover, Joe was the premier Jewish-American to become an athlete of international standing.

Joseph Bartlett Choynski's first glimpse of the world came on Sunday, November 8, 1868. The family home was at 118 Natoma Street, where they had lived since at least 1866, in the area of San Francisco known as "South of the Slot." The narrow groove for cable cars that ran along Market Street formed the line of demarcation, separating this district from that known as "North of the Slot," which was generally for the affluent. As it was the custom of the day, it is reasonable to assume that the family doctor performed a home delivery. Unfortunately, any details of Joe's birth have been lost to history. There are no family or other records, no anecdotes passed down to elucidate who attended the event, Joe's birth weight or time of birth. The majority of medical records and general documentation did not survive the earthquake and fire of 1906. It is known that the family physician in 1857 and 1863 was a Dr. C. Bruns, whose office was at 611 Washington Street. It is likely he who delivered Joe.[1] Sadly, no photographs exist of Joe in infancy or childhood. The earliest known image dates from around 1886, when he was not quite 18.

1868, a Time of Reconstruction

The nation was still healing from the deep wounds of the Civil War. African-Americans, former slaves, were struggling in this environment of new-found "freedom," where so many avenues were still blocked. Many moved north, where "the American Dream" was slightly more attainable.

Beyond the western frontier, opportunities were more plentiful and "class boundaries" less pronounced. San Francisco is a city with a history unique from any other in the United States. Pulitzer Prize-winning journalist Herb Caen referred to it as "Baghdad by the Bay," meant to reflect its eclectic, multicultural nature. (He also coined the term "beatnik" in 1958). The first denizens of the area were Native Americans with a common language, the Ohlone, or Costanoan. The major tribe was the Yelamu.[2]

Over the centuries, several explorers either sailed past or stopped in the area, including Juan Rodriguez Cabrillo in 1542-43, English mariner and privateer Francis Drake in 1579, and Sebastian Vizcaino in 1602. None, however, discovered "the Golden Gate" or what is now San Francisco. In November, 1769, Don Gaspar de Portola of Spain led an expedition overland from the south over the Montara hills, sighting the Gulf of the Farrallones. He dispatched Sergeant José Francisco Ortega, who came upon the vista of San Francisco Bay. 1770 saw the arrival of Padre Junipero Serra, head of the Franciscans, to establish a mission in the name of St. Francis of Assisi, the patron of his order. On October 8, 1776, Mission San Francisco de Asis (later renamed Mission Dolores) was opened. When Mexico overthrew Spanish rule in 1821, the new government colonized the settlement, secularized the missions and confiscated most of their money. Under its authority, the cannons and other defenses fell into disuse.

The city was known then as Yerba Buena, after the fragrant herbs on its shores. At first the United States had no designs on the area, but eventually desired the bay for its unequalled potential as a whaling port and for trade. President Andrew Jackson offered the Mexican government $3,500,000 for it, but the offer was rejected. American fur traders and others began trekking west from frontier states around 1841. The Jackson administration incrementally stepped up forays into the region. In 1845, Captain John C. Frémont began leading attacks against the Mexican military presence there. After several skirmishes and a brief flirtation with a makeshift flag for the "Republic of California," consisting of a red star and a grizzly bear, American flags were hoisted over Monterey and Yerba Buena. In 1847, Yerba Buena's name was officially changed to San Francisco, at which time there were about 500 inhabitants. The Treaty of Guadalupe Hidalgo made California the property of the United States on February 2, 1848.[3]

The Gold Rush

James W. Marshall, a pioneer from New Jersey who came west via the Oregon Trail, was constructing a large lumber mill in January, 1848 at Coloma, California, for a rancher named Captain John Sutter. This was at the south fork of the American River, about 30 miles from San Francisco. When Marshall and hired hands were enlarging the millrace, a ditch to bring water through the saw-mill, he spotted several gold nuggets at the bottom of the ditch. The next day, Sutter attempted to swear the workers to secrecy. That didn't last long, of course, and when word did get out, it resulted in the great gold mania of 1849. The tide of humanity would increase the population of San Francisco in one month, from some 420 persons to 2,000. Within several months it climbed to 15,000.

On January 30, 1849, the Pacific Mail Steamship Company's lone side-wheeler, the *California*, dropped anchor on the West coast of Panama on the return trip around Cape Horn from New York. There, she found a teeming mass of gold hunters who had braved the trek across the Isthmus of Panama, the threat of yellow fever and other hazards. Many lost their lives waiting for a ship that had a vacancy. On February 28, the *California* became the first vessel to round Cape Horn and sail into San Francisco Bay under its own power. The steamship's rated capacity was 100 persons; she was carrying several times that. The Pacific Mail Steamship Company, in order to meet the demand of the Argonauts,* eventually increased the number of steamships in its fleet to 29. Within the next decade, the company would transport 175,000 passengers to California.

* The nickname given to those joining the California gold rush, especially by sea. They, like Jason and the Argonauts, "sought the golden fleece."

Several hundred ships were abandoned in the harbor by their crews, who flocked to the gold mines and streams seeking fortune. The bay soon became a graveyard filled with their empty, rotting hulks. Some were converted into storage and makeshift hospitals, but most decayed or were dismantled. A large portion of the city was living in tents, as there were not enough buildings to house the mass of humanity. There were also few, if any docks, and many made on the order of $20 a day transporting ships' passengers and cargo ashore, a large sum in that era.[4]

One factor making San Francisco and the West so unique is that the Jewish element arrived at essentially the same time as other settlers. They were of great importance in building this new community. Many who otherwise might have behaved with prejudice were willing to accept as equals, those showing a propensity for hard work. The populace of the young, eclectic city arrived from all points of the globe. It was probably the most tolerant city in the nation, perhaps the world. Men of the Jewish faith were free to pursue, if they wished, "muscular Judaism," which included boxing and other physical endeavors. This began with the second generation, however, as the impoverished pioneers from Europe were not accustomed to American sport – or, mostly, to sport of any kind.

Historians described men of the day as wearing everything from double-breasted jackets and swallow-tail coats to serapes and bear skins. When women began to arrive in significant numbers, the style of dress improved commensurately. By 1853, the population had exploded to about 42,000, the number of houses and businesses multiplying, as well. Competition for shipping became fierce, so between 1850 and 1854, 160 clipper ships were built. They could make the trip from New York to California in three or four months, two or three months quicker than earlier ships. When the Intercontinental Railroad reduced the transport of goods and people down to a matter of a week or so, the clippers began to fade from the picture.

Colonel Jonathon Stevenson was appointed by the U.S. government to head a special regiment near the end of the war with Mexico. Their task was to join the occupation and make the inhabitants of San Francisco "feel that we come as deliverers." Instead, many of these men strong-armed the citizens, entering saloons, restaurants and other places, helping themselves to whatever they desired. They became known as the "Hounds," due to their penchant for "hounding" Mexicans, Chileans and other foreigners there seeking fortune. At roughly the same time, immigrants from Australia arrived, many of them criminals. These were referred to as "Sydney Ducks" and they contributed to the growing element of lawlessness and rampant violence. The first Vigilance Committee organized in 1851 to combat this felonious tidal wave. Just as an earlier, less formal committee of San Franciscan vigilantes had largely banished the "Hounds," so the Vigilance Committee drove out or hanged many of the "Ducks."[5]

1851 saw a new Gold Rush, in Australia. In 1858, new digs for gold prospectors were the Canadian northwest and Colorado's Pike's Peak. It was certainly an era for the discovery of mineral wealth in diverse regions. In 1859, what began as a gold strike in nearby Nevada became the Silver Rush. The so-called "Comstock Lode" was the single biggest mineral strike in American history. The ensuing mineral madness caused many Californians to migrate to the Washoe region of Nevada. The Gold Rush that started along the Klondike River near Dawson City, Yukon, Canada between 1896 and 1898, resulted in about 12½ million ounces of gold being harvested. The 1849 Gold Rush of California, however, resulted in the creation of San Francisco as a major metropolis.

This young city spawned many colorful and seedy characters, not the fewest of which were from the section known as the "Barbary Coast." The area was located on the eastern shore of the peninsula and named (circa 1860) after the North African coast (and the Berbers), where Arab pirates plundered ships in the Mediterranean. Frisco's Barbary Coast grew to encompass an area including parts of Pacific, Montgomery, Washington, Kearny and Stockton streets, Columbus Avenue and Broadway. This notorious haven of vice was loaded with brothels, saloons and gambling dens. "Debauchery, pollution, loathsome disease, insanity ... dissipation, misery, poverty, wealth, profanity, blasphemy and death are there."[6] This is where the term "to shanghai" was said to have originated. "When there was a shortage of sailors for departing ships, any able-bodied man who wandered into the wrong saloon or drank with the wrong companion, could wake up with a mysterious hangover aboard a ship."[7] These men would be given doped liquor, then cracked over the head, dropped through a trap door into the cellar, and transferred to an ocean-bound ship.

"Give it a wide berth, as you value your life," wrote *The New Overland Tourist* of the Barbary Coast in 1878. The block bounded by Kearny, Montgomery and Broadway was referred to as "Devil's Acre," and the Kearny Street side of the block, "Battle Row." The word "hoodlum," also said to have been coined here, referred to "the young ruffians who roamed the Coast armed with bludgeons, knives or iron knuckles. It is thought that the word comes from 'huddle 'em!' the cry of the boys as they advanced on a victim." Police patrolled the area in pairs, such was the danger. Turtleneck sweaters and derby hats were commonplace. Banjos, pianos and brass horns were part of the night life. One of the popular tunes of the day was "There'll Be a Hot Time in the Old Town Tonight."[8]

One intriguing personality was Philo Jacoby. Born in 1837 in what is now Lebork, Poland, Jacoby became that generation's Pacific Coast Renaissance Man. In 1863 he founded *The Hebrew*, a Jewish weekly that ran until 1923. In 1876, at the Centennial Exposition in Philadelphia, Philo won the title "Champion Rifle Shot of the World," the best of a field of 20,000 competitors from across the globe. He toured Europe, defeating the best sharpshooters from Austria, Germany, Prussia and Switzerland, and was presented by Emperor Franz Joseph of Austria with a gold medal. Jacoby also gained renown as a strong-man and athlete. He was among the first members of San Francisco's Olympic Club, where he performed such feats as bending crowbars and breaking cobblestones with his bare hands. The mass of trophies and medals Philo received over the years was astounding.[9]

Many famous writers were born or gained fame in the city, including Bret Harte, Robert Ingersoll, Mark Twain, Joaquin Miller, "The Byron of Oregon," Ambrose Bierce, Robert Frost and Jack London. Bierce, for one, exchanged letters with Joe's father. Gene Tunney, one of two world heavyweight kings to retire (permanently) as champion, attributed London's classic boxing novel, *The Game* as a major influence in his decision to retire at his peak. The other, Rocky Marciano, read *The Game* at Gene's recommendation, and Gene believed it influenced him, as well. The Wells Fargo Company, a banking and express business, was founded in 1852 and headquartered at 114 Montgomery Street. Montgomery, the main financial district, became known as "The Wall Street of the West." The Montgomery Block was the locale of many notable artists and writers in the 1880s, including Frank Norris. It is today the site of the Transamerica Pyramid.[10]

On October 1, 1868, the worst earthquake the city had seen to that point in history occurred. A slip on the Hayward Fault caused the earth to shake violently, resulting in property damage of some $300,000, close to $5 million in today's currency. The quake registered a magnitude of about 7.0 on the Richter scale. Tremors and aftershocks continued for several days following the initial temblor. A "grand display of meteors" was seen just prior to Joe Choynski's birth, as well, part of the Leonid shower.[11] Some might deem this appropriate in a metaphoric sense, presaging as it did the genesis of a child who would one day gain renown as an explosive puncher, one who frequently produced "fireworks" in the ring.

During the October quake, heavy damage was sustained to edifices near the Choynski home at 118 Natoma Street. The Gas Works Coal Shed,

Herbert, I.N. and Miriam Choynski, circa 1868

located 3½ blocks away at the corner of Fremont and Howard, required $10,000 to $12,000 to repair, in 1868 dollars. The street in front of Mission and Fremont, about 3½ blocks from the Choynski domicile, sunk two or three feet. Their home was likely rendered uninhabitable, as the early months of 1869 found baby Joe and family in a house his father purchased at 524 Howard Street. They resided there until sometime in 1875, when I.N. moved them to Geary Street, where the Antiquarian Bookstore would be located. The bookstore became something of a landmark. Here and at their home, such literary figures as Joaquin (Cincinnatus H.) Miller, Bret Harte, Robert Ingersoll and Mark Twain would visit and debate various topics.[12]

At the end of 1868, the West was about to be joined to the eastern United States by the Transcontinental Railroad. The Union Pacific Railroad was about 175 miles from Salt Lake City, Utah and roughly 400 miles from joining the Central Pacific Railroad.[13] On May 8, 1869, the ceremonial golden spike completing the route was driven at Promontory Summit, Box Elder County, Utah, forever altering travel and business in the United States. Whereas the first Pony Express rider arrived in San Francisco from Missouri in 1860, the mails, goods and people would now arrive much more quickly and frequently. Joe's native city has endeared itself to inhabitants and visitors. Boxing manager Willus Britt, uttered, circa 1909: "I'd rather be a busted lamppost on Battery Street, San Francisco than the Waldorf-Astoria!"[14] The era of Joe's youth in California is the stuff of legends. Horse-drawn conveyances were common, but in 1873 there first appeared what is probably the most enduring symbol of San Francisco, the cable car. Cable cars still run in the City by the Bay.

Roots of the Choynski Tree

It is my belief that Joe's surname is the most misspelled in the history of Boxing (even through 2013, the era of the Klitschkos and other former Eastern-bloc fighters). I have seen the name misspelled as Choyinski, Choyanski, Choyunski, Choyniski, Choinski, Choynsky, Choinsky, Chynski and about any combination possible. The most obvious pronunciation, though incorrect, would be "CHOYN-skee." Other versions have been "Choy-YEN-skee" or "Choy-IN-skee," "Show-IN-skee," "Ko-EN-skee" and "Ko-YEN-skee." In 1942, Joe was a "consultant" for the Hollywood version of James J. Corbett's career, "Gentleman Jim." His name in the movie was phonetically spoken, "Ko-IN-skee," and Joe never contradicted it. The "Barbados Demon," Joe Walcott, fought Choynski late in Joe's career. In an interview from his days as a porter for Madison Square Garden, Walcott pronounced Joe's name, "Ko-IN-skee." The late Mort Fleishhacker, Herbert Choynski's grandson, also advised me that the family pronounced the name, "Ko-IN-ski."

Joseph Bartlett Choynski's paternal family record goes back to Prussia. The ancient village of Choyno or Chojno is where Isidor Nathan Choynski was likely born and where the surname originates. An internet search for a "Choyno" in latter-day Europe reveals little of value, but "Chojno" produces better results. There are no less than six "Chojnos," all located in Poland. Jewish historian, Robert Singerman, wrote: "Evidence suggests he (Joe's father) was born in Chojno, an estate a short distance due west of Strasburg (Polish, Brodnica), West Prussia, probably in 1834." Modern Brodnica, Poland was formerly known as Strasburg. Chojno is a village in the district of "Gmina Bobrowo" in Brodnica County, (north-central) Poland, near a small lake and forest. The forest is likely that over which the 'Rittergutsbesitzer (Lord of the Manor) of Choyno' presided.

Napoleon Bonaparte instituted the census in the "modern world," requiring that every family have or establish a surname. Janet Choynski Fleishhacker, daughter of Herbert Choynski, said the family took their surname during the time of Napoleon in Poland. The name "Choynski" comes (indirectly) from the Polish word "Choinka," referring to an evergreen tree, or by extension, a forest of them. Christian Poles use the term "Choinka" for a Christmas tree. The suffix "-ski" means "of or from," "-ska" being the female form, i.e., Choynska for a woman's surname. "-ski" is now used for both genders. Choynski, therefore, may mean "of Choyno," or in a more semantical sense, "of the forest."

The earliest validated records of Jewish settlement in Poland come from late in the 11th century, though they likely arrived earlier. The influx was mostly due to persecution in Western Europe, which gained in force during the Crusades. In 1349, Jews flocked in massive numbers from Germany to Polish Prussia to escape persecution over the "Black Death." For centuries it seems they were scapegoats for every tragic event. Choynski forebears apparently came into early Poland from Germany, as attested by I.N. Choynski's writings. A massive arrival of Jews began in the 16th century. The merchant middle-class they comprised were granted enough freedom and protection by the kings of Prussia that they eventually outnumbered Jews of other European countries. Here, Hebrew literature proliferated, and the fame of Polish rabbis spread throughout the continent. Mordechai Nathan Choynski was among their number. Prussian armies were defeated by Napoleon in the battles of Jena and Auerstedt. In 1807, due to the Treaty of Tilsit, Prussia lost most of Poland and became a satellite of France. Field Marshal Blücher was instrumental in the defeat of Napoleon at Leipzig (1813) and Waterloo (1815). Prussia reclaimed its territories, joined the German Confederation and withdrew from central Poland, for the creation of Congress Poland under the sovereignty of Russia.[15]

Janet Fleishhacker stated in a 1974 interview, that in recognition for deeding some land in Prussia for a university to be established, the Choynski antecedents were allowed to take the surname Choynski, "which means 'son of the woods' in Polish ... a rather distinguished name ... Catholic ... as well as Jewish ... all Jewish names were adopted ... (they) were not allowed to have their names in the old days." She was told by the family that this occurred "at the time of Napoleon in Poland." This places the event somewhere from 1807 to 1814. Napoleon visited nearby Brodnica in 1807. The earliest known mention of a Choynski ancestor was the land-owner Janet spoke of, likely Joe's great-grandfather. Joe's father, I.N., wrote that all of his ancestors had been "starving rabbis," with the sole exception of his "grandsire, the 'Rittergutsbesitzer (Lord of the Manor) of Choyno,' the original family name." The Edict of October 9, 1807 dissolved the archaic feudal system and granted people of all classes the right to own landed property. This included burghers and peasants, as well as nobility.

Due to persecution in that place and time, it was rare for Jews to own land. The term "manor" in this case implied a house with farm buildings. Whether the Choynskis relinquished their property under duress or willingly is uncertain, but a book written in 1876 may shed some light. It explains that the Law of September 14, 1811 "took half or a third of the land possessed by the tenants of Prussia and handed it over to the landlords. The land occupied by these tenants was land on which ... the lord of the manor had no right of re-entry." It forced "the lord of the manor to sell his manorial overlordship for one-half." It may have been this law that took much of the Choynskis' landed property from them.[16]

Joe's paternal grandfather, Mordechai Nathan Choynski, was born circa 1811 in Choyno, West Prussia. It was probably his sire, the 'Rittergutsbesitzer of Choyno,' who deeded the tract of land. Mordechai married Rosalie, born in Graudenz, Prussia. Her maiden name and birth date are unknown, but it is believed she was about two years older than him. Mordechai was a rabbi and Talmudist. The couple had five children: Ernestine, Moses, Rosa, Isidor and Jesajas (Isaiah). In 1845, all were registered in Strasburg. The exact dates and order of birth are uncertain, except for Isaiah and Isidor. They

Rosalie and Mordechai Nathan Choynski

are the only two *confirmed* as immigrating to the United States. (Moritz, allegedly a brother, did, as well). Mordechai died in Graudenz in 1883.[17]

Joe's uncle, Isaiah W. Choynski, was born in October, 1844 or 1845 (his headstone says 1844) and died in San Francisco in 1919. The 1900 Federal census shows Isaiah immigrating to the U.S. in 1865 or 1866. He was a merchant, journalist and newspaper editor. The 1898 Directory shows him as a journalist at the *San Francisco Chronicle*. Isaiah married Fanny Warschauer (1851-December 4, 1935) in 1869. The Warschauers for years ran a large boarding house at 44 3rd Street, and operated the Windsor House at Market and 5th. Though most sources show Isaiah and Fanny having only two children, Milton L. and Harry, they actually had four. In order of birth: Solomon, born 1871, Aaron, March, 1873, Harry, in 1876 and Milton, December 4, 1874. The latter, a noted attorney, died March 21, 1956. Harry, on January 11, 1918, was promoted to Vice-President of the Anglo and London Paris National Bank. The 1880 census lists a Samuel Choynski, born in 1869, and Philip Choynski, born 1874, living in Isaiah's household.

Their father's birthplace was Prussia, their mother's, Posen.[18] They were probably nephews, sent over by one or more of Isaiah's siblings.

An 1862 issue of the *Marysville Daily Appeal* said I.N. "is a staunch Union man of Republican antecedents, has a brother in the Union army, and no affinity with those who denounce that brother as an 'abolition minion'. Like all of his Polish countrymen, he is true to freedom." Isidor said a brother of his took part in the Battle of Bull Run ... under General William S. Rosecrans.[19] He didn't name the sibling, but it was thought to be Isaiah, no other brother having been confirmed living in the United States. I.N. didn't specify if this was the first Battle of Bull Run (Manassas, July 1861) or the 2nd Battle (August 1862). As Rosecrans' Civil War career ran from 1861 to 1865, Isaiah, if he served, had to have immigrated to the States earlier than 1865. My research failed to substantiate a war record for him.

The other relative immigrating to America was Moritz B. Choynski, apparently I.N.'s brother. He was born in 1841 in Kempen, Prussia. Moritz enlisted as a Corporal in New York City on August 27, 1961. On October 11 he mustered into B Company, first Regiment, New York Engineers. During his Civil War service he was reduced in ranks to Private, for reasons unclear. Moritz was promoted January 1, 1863 to "Full Artificer," and mustered out on September 9, 1864 at Crow's Nest, Virginia. He was likely the brother Isidor referred to. Moritz next appears in 1871, occupied as a carpenter at 116 2nd Street in Sacramento, California, apparently through 1873. He was listed as a "mobile carpenter" and Cabinet Maker at 44 Spring Street in Los Angeles in 1874. By 1883, he was in Seattle, Washington, where he would reside, the remaining few years of his life.[20]

Moritz died June 24, 1891 in Seattle. June 25 *Seattle Post-Intelligencer*: "The well-known character, Moritz Choynski, was found dead in his cabinet shop, at the rear of the Plymouth Congregational church ... The rumor that he had come to his death by violent means, that ... everything about the shop was in a badly disarranged state, resulting from some sort of a fracas, quickly spread ... Coroner Horton was called to the case. Choynski ... apparently having fallen over a carpenter's saw horse, his head, just above the forehead ... struck a sharp piece of board. Dr. Horton and Prosecuting Attorney Miller held ... the death ... purely accidental ... the probable result of an epileptic fit, to which, it was said, he was subject."

"Moritz ... a much pitied man ... about 45 ... had ... experienced some bitter trouble, else ... afflicted with disease ... as to make him sour and misanthropic ... a very isolated man; still ... true to his friends. He ... shot Peter Bauman ... on May 10, 1889 ... in the Pantheon saloon ... Bauman had borrowed a screw-driver from him. Choynski, with his ... chronic crabbed manner, demanded the return of (it) ... Choynski went into the saloon with a note, couched in not very amiable terms ... to Bauman, to hand to the barkeeper, and after taking a drink, Bauman approached him. Choynski retreated backward, beckoning Bauman not to follow him ... drew a small revolver and shot at Bauman, the bullet taking effect near Bauman's right eye. The grand jury indicted Choynski for assault with a deadly weapon ... but he got Mr. Eben Smith to defend him, he having been defended once before by Mr. Smith in an assault and battery case ... The jury brought in a verdict of simple assault, Choynski being fined $25."

"Choynski ... has behaved in a very peculiar manner lately on the streets and has rambled about at all hours, seeming to wander aimlessly ... pre-occupied with some mental trouble. Mr. Smith thinks he was a native of Germany, because he had frequently referred during the trial to his mother in Germany to whom he was in the habit of sending money whenever he could, his remissness in this respect often making him morose ... *He also made reference repeatedly to a cousin in San Francisco, and it was generally reported that he was of kin to Joe Choynski, the prizefighter, but this opinion has never seemed to be more than mere conjecture.* (Emphasis by author, LaForce). He was unmarried and lived in his little shop, and in his trade he was very skillful ... The life and manner of the deceased was of ... a nature as to excite suspicion that at an early day there had been an estrangement of some kind in the Choynski family in the old country, but this has never been proved ... he came to the States when very young, and during the war served in the Union army. He came to this city about 12 years ago and was a member of Stevens post, GAR (Grand Army of the Republic)."

June 26 *Post-Intelligencer*: "The funeral of Moritz Choynski will take place at Bonney & Stewart's parlors today ... (He) will be buried in the cemetery of ... Ohaveth Sholem ... William Kierski ... informed (that) the GAR had intended to have Choynski buried in the Grand Army cemetery. According to Mr. Kierski, Moritz Choynski was a native of Kempen, Prussian Poland, *and had a brother in San Francisco, Mr. I.N. Choynski, the publisher of a weekly, called Truth, and Joe Choynski, the pugilist, was a nephew.* (Emphasis is mine). Choynski lived in Los Angeles a long while previous to coming to Seattle, and, it is said, he was married to a Spanish woman there. His mother is still alive in Prussia." So ended a sad, ill-fated life.

Joe's father, Isidor Nathan (I.N.) Choynski, was born either in 1834 or 1835. The 1880 United States Federal Census gives the year as 1834. Joe's death certificate lists his father's birthplace as "Germany," other sources, as Graudenz, Prussia. Graudenz belonged to Poland until 1772, when it became part of Germany, so if Isidor was born in Graudenz, both are correct. I.N. gave a clue, however, when he wrote in 1885, "You can reach my birthplace within five minutes, by telegraph, by the Strasburg watch."[21] Modern Strasburg, Germany is some 185 miles from Chojno, "as the crow flies." Modern Brodnica's old German name in West Prussia was Strasburg, though, the name he would have known it by. Modern Chojno, about four miles west of Brodnica, is most likely his birthplace. I.N. admits he was not a "good boy," but "the biggest and sauciest." At nine, he recalls being punched in the back by a rabbi, who told Isidor he would never amount to anything. I.N., in his youth, made a westerly path into Germany, where he would have "seven meals a week at seven different houses," in trade for tutoring children of the Jewish German families.

Isidor graduated from a gymnasium, or high school in Prussia, of which he wrote, "Gymnastic exercises were as religiously and rigidly enforced as any of the studies in the curriculum."[22] I.N. possibly attended a University in Prussia; as an adult, he was said to have spoken "17 languages, including Sanskrit." A typical European University of that time taught Modern Greek, German, Sanskrit, Hebrew, English, French, Italian, Chinese, Arabic and Turkish. He knew Latin and was fluent in Yiddish, as well. I.N. likely left West Prussia in 1849, based on him writing in 1883, that he had not seen his parents in 34 years. Isidor was often mistaken when recalling dates, but more than one article says he arrived in America at age 14![23] In 1848, revolutions broke out across Europe and many Jews fled, including Isidor. It is uncertain whether political turmoil, unfair conscription for Jewish men or just seeking a better life prompted Isidor to leave.

During a trial in 1890, as the defendant on extortion charges, I.N. testified that he had come to the States in 1851. This indicates he may have laid over as long as two years in England. Ellis Island did not open as an entry and processing point for immigrants until 1892. Before that, it was Manhattan's Castle Garden. Prior to August, 1855, passengers entering the U.S. would disembark at any available wharf on Manhattan. Information taken on immigrants was skimpy, consisting of their name, occupation, age, gender and ethnic background. I.N. likely disembarked at the docks on South Street or the pier at the end of Hubert Street.[24]

Isidor came over with his knapsack, "the likeness of my parents," ritual prayer garments, ibn Pakuda's "Duties of the Heart" and his childhood friendship memento book. "But I brought with me, in my heart of hearts, Judaism, pure and undefiled ..." The latter would not remain with him. Later in life, Joe's father would become, as described by Robert Singerman, "an embittered misanthrope." In early 1886, Isidor described himself as an "agnostic or pessimist – take it either way ..." A young I.N. once wrote, "I do abuse the Jews wherever I get a chance, because they shall be the best, the pure cut diamonds ... I have ever been, jealous of the good name of the Jews ..." and "I never take a microscope ... to detect foibles in our people, and if I do, now and then, cut deep, I want to cure the sore."[25] How ironic, that a man so severely critical of others for being less than paragons of piety, would himself develop atheistic tendencies.

I.N. made his way to New Haven, Connecticut shortly after landing in Manhattan. New Haven is about 80 miles from New York City and the home of Yale University, known then as Yale College. Choynski has long been referred to as the first Jew to graduate from Yale, but research indicates that he did not. The author investigated independently, before learning of others' research. Lenn Zonder of New Haven and Robert Singerman could not substantiate that he attended Yale College, either. Yale's Chief Research Archivist told Singerman in 1977 that I.N. may have attended lectures or courses for the public on Saturdays. As the years passed, his "automythological graduation from Yale" may have arisen from such unofficial attendance. Harvey Ladin, President of the Jewish Historical Society of New Haven, said Yale instructors "often gave courses to local people for a small fee, and this supplemented their meager salaries."[26] I.N.'s son, Edwin, stated that his father received a teaching certificate from Yale prior to becoming a teacher in Poughkeepsie. I.N. wrote, "I was there, and did some tall peddling during

I.N. Choynski, circa 1850s

recess in order to keep myself in shoes." He also wrote of his second cousin, Adolph Asher, "who when a toddling boy watched me as I was musing under the shades of the stately elms which surround the grave Alma Mater at Yale." There can be little doubt that I.N. received important education at New Haven's halls of learning.

Within six months of his arrival, family tradition has I.N. teaching English in Poughkeepsie, New York. He recalled being a schoolmaster in Monroe, New York, and an "itinerant basket peddler" around the Hudson River valley with a cousin, Israel Morris Goldreich. Choynski and Goldreich came to New York together on the same ship. Next, they allegedly decided to travel on a vessel for San Francisco. According to Goldreich's grandson, H. Phillip Levy, the two were separated on the way to the shipping office to purchase tickets for the journey. Upon returning to their housing quarters, they discovered that Israel visited the wrong steamship company and inadvertently booked passage to Australia. Goldreich refused to exchange the ticket for one bound for Frisco, determined that God was calling him to the Antipodes. This seems implausible. The only way to Australia from New York at the time was to London, then Cape Town, South Africa, on to

Australia. The *S.S. Aorangi* did that route many times – but only after 1883.[27] Goldreich arrived in Australia in 1859. He had a distinguished, 36-year career as a Rabbi in Ballarat, where he passed away in 1905.

I.N.'s initial stop on the West coast, apparently, was Oregon. Edwin said: "Coming to California, he went to Philadelphia. There, he took a ship to the Isthmus. In the Pacific, the Captain missed the port of San Francisco and the passengers were landed in Oregon. There he lived for two years and in 1854 came to San Jose, California." I.N. recalls teaching in the school of Rabbi Herman Bien, in the basement of Temple Emanu-El, in 1856 or '57.[28] He served as Assistant Clerk on the Oregon State Legislature, from May 16 to June 4, 1859, and settled permanently in California sometime around 1859. His naturalization documents are from September of that year. He was said to have been a member of the 2nd Committee of Vigilance, reorganized in 1856.[29] Isidor's first known writings were for San Francisco's *Weekly Gleaner*. The paper was founded in January, 1856 by editor, Rabbi Julius Eckman, and is responsible for the bulk of existing knowledge of early San Francisco Jewish history. Beginning July, 1860, I.N. was co-editor. He sprinkled his prose with Yiddish and Hebrew idioms. Family tradition says he wrote the occasional editorial for the *San Francisco Chronicle*, when requested by founders, Charles and Michael De Young, and was an editor for the *Alta California*, as well.

In February, 1860, I.N. and Solomon Sanders opened the Vanderbilt "Billiard" Saloon at the corner of Sacramento and Leidesdorff. Choynski's residence that year was listed as "Jackson & Stockton."[30] The city's Jewish populace numbered about 5,000, and I.N. soon became one of its most prominent, despite the fact that Jews of Bavarian, or German, origin tended to have feelings then of superiority over those of Polish descent. He was initiated into the Freemasons Progress Lodge, and in April, became President of the Hebrew Young Men's Literary Association (HYMLA). I.N. was an eloquent orator, lecturing at many venues.

On July 12, 1860, occurred what was perhaps the first meeting between I.N. and Harriett. July 14 *Alta California*: "The semi-annual ball of the Hebrew Young Men's Literary Association ... night before last at Tucker's Academy of Music, proved an eminently ... pleasant affair ... the banner presentation on behalf of the Hebrew young ladies ... a beautiful piece of work ... in white and blue satin, with gold lettering – was gracefully tendered by Miss Hattie Ashim and Miss A. Wiener, the former making an admirable little address, very appropriate, and charmingly spoken. The ... response (was) by the President, Mr. Chosynski (sic)." I.N. showed he was also capable of writing fiction, authoring "*The Jewish Exile; or Life's Trial*" for the *Weekly Gleaner* in 1860. It gave an account of the voyage of one Siegmund from Eylau to the United States by way of Hamburg and Frankfurt, Germany, to Liverpool, England. This was likely his own path to America.

In November, he left the *Gleaner* to manage the *San Francisco Abend* (Evening) *Post*, a new, pro-Republican German-language paper.

Isidor began stumping for Republican Presidential candidate Abraham Lincoln in the 1860 campaign. He was assigned to influence German-born voters, Jew and Gentile, as a fellow immigrant. When Lincoln was elected U.S. President that year, many of his loyal constituents won appointments. It has been stated by a myriad of sources that I.N. Choynski was "Collector of the Port" of San Francisco, even by his son, Joe. Technically, the title was "Inspector." In an April 8, 1861 letter from Salmon P. Chase (6th Chief Justice of the U.S.) to Lincoln, Chase gave a list of his recommendations for "Appraisers at San Francisco," which included "J.N. Choyuski." Isidor was part of the

I.N. Choynski, circa 1870s

committee that organized Frisco's grand inauguration ball for Lincoln, held March 4 at Platt's New Music Hall on Montgomery Street.[31]

Choynski was appointed an Inspector at the Customs House on June 26, 1861. He did not hold the post for more than a year, due to the corruption scandal involving Ira P. Rankin and others in the department. This brought about Rankin's removal as head of the Collector's Office in 1862, along with other appointees. I.N.'s salary as Inspector of Customs was $3.75 per day, a tidy sum for the period. In 1862 at San Jose, Isidor was nominated for the Union County legislature, finishing 3rd in a tight race. The following year, he declined a nomination for an Assembly position at the Copperhead County Convention. A document dated November 13 by James W. Nye, Governor of the Nevada Territory, appointed Choynski a "Commissioner for California," for a term of two years. This gave I.N. the right to own mines in the Nevada Territory.[32]

In November, 1862, when Harriett was pregnant with their first-born son, Herbert, Isidor left for Aurora, Nevada with his father-in-law, Morris, seeking fortune in the gold and silver fields. The first mining outfit the pair opened, in January, 1863, was given the name "Hattie Mining Company." "Hattie" was one of two nicknames I.N. had for Harriett, the other being "Ducky." In several letters he sent home to her from Nevada (13 of which survive), he referred to her alternately in these terms. In a letter dated

February 8, I.N. wrote: "I go daily to examine the quartz lode in the *Hattie*, it is a fine claim, and I love to examine the stratas (sic) in the shaft, as it bears your name." By May 17, Isidor's outlook had changed:

"My dearly beloved wife, Have just received your affectionate epistle,

Morris B. Ashim

together with the cartes de visite which please me much, especially the one without the bonnet. Ducky, I too have been sick, and only left my bed this afternoon; the chills, stomach and headache have played the very deuce with me ... the last three days, but I am now on a par with most men in this camp. Dad is doing well, but the sudden change from a high life in the city to one in a rude mountain camp has nearly prostrated me, but thanks to a wise Providence and my strong frame I shall be all right again in a day or two. The weather is hot and the grub bad ... I have to pay $12 per week, though I can eat nothing, and if I could the fare in the restaurants here consists chiefly of pork and beans and my palate rebels against such unwholesome food. I fared much better here last winter, but I must be content as I am making a living here for you and my boy. So the little fellow crys (sic) at you! Well, well, he is showing his colors rather early."

"Ducky, warm steam baths may be had at North Beach, you know the place. Do not neglect to follow the precepts of Dr. Bruns ... When will you be through sewing those invincible short dresses? Harriet, I wish you would send me a pinch of my tea in ... your letters; I only want enough to last me about a month. I don't use much of it, and you can well put a trifle in a couple of letters. Falk has the key to the post office ... Dad sends love. My love to the family. Your (sic) affectionately, Isidor - P.S. Dad says that as soon as he will strike a rich claim he will come home, no sooner."

By May 29, I.N.'s attitude had devolved further: "I am tired out; have been over steep hills, descended into shafts, broken up quartz, and performed all sorts of manual labor." June 1: "I am very busy; have to superintend in person some 20 different mines and then pay the workmen their wages, measure shafts, &c. I tell you the market looks very dull ..." I.N. and Morris started up or were officers in no less than 11 mining companies after "Hattie," none of which prospered. The names were

Ashim, Corinthian, Schiller, Victoria, Silver & Luna, Gortha, B.B. Mining Co., Happy Day, Rich Spot, West Ophir and Durand. The first were quartz mines, but later silver and gold, as well. I.N. somehow found time to write articles for *the Daily Alta California* and *San Francisco Bulletin*.[33] By the time he left Nevada, I.N. had lost most of his money. He returned to San Francisco broke and disillusioned. To keep the family afloat, I.N. sold newspapers on the street. He gathered enough money to establish, on December 20, 1863, "The Antiquarian Book Store," at 146 2nd Street.

Choynski's store stocked such old and new literature as The *Overland Monthly*, *People*, *Comic Monthly*, *Literary Companion*, *New York Clipper*, *New York Mercury and Dispatch*, *Harper's*, *Right Way*, *Police Gazette*, *Boston Investigator*, *Demorest's Monthly*, *Godey's Lady's Friend*, *Every Saturday*, *Our Boys and Girls*, *World*, *Galaxy*, *Banner of Light*, *Home Journal*, *London Court Journal*, *Le Monde Illustré*, *Round Table* and *Albion*. He received most via mail steamer. An 1871 advertisement read, "Dealer in pictures, cutlery, fine stationery, etc. A large stock of ancient and modern books. Agent for all books and magazines from the Eastern States and Europe ... printing and book binding ..." An 1874 ad declared he was an "Importer of ... school books, novels ... fancy goods, at wholesale and retail. Old books bought, sold and exchanged." I.N., Harriett and infant Herbert lived for a time at 540 Mission. His business address was "2nd near Howard."[34]

On June 24, 1864, Morris Ashim died, one obituary giving his age as 46. Soon afterward, Isidor quit the Freemasons, a result of disputes with its hierarchy, and its alleged antisemitism. I.N. accused them of preventing Jewish members from achieving high positions within the ranks. In late 1866, he joined its Jewish counterpart, B'nai B'rith. He became Master of Progress Lodge in 1869, and President of San Francisco District Grand Lodge Number 4, in 1874 and 1875. This was the coordinating center for all lodges on the west coast. It was "the highest office in the community ... of the Jewry of the western states." He established five new lodges, over a territory that included California, Oregon and Nevada. At this time (1874), I.N. and family were living at 127 O'Farrell.[35]

In 1874, Isidor began writing for The *American Israelite*, founded by Rabbi Isaac Mayer Wise, "The Father of Reformed Judaism." He was paid a penny per line. It is here that he began using the pseudonym, "Maftir." The term signifies the last person to read from the Torah on the Sabbath or holidays, thus, he who has the last word. I.N. certainly had the last word in his column, which was very critical toward anyone and anything that did not fit his notion of Judaic perfection. On multiple occasions, his editors, Rabbi Wise and Rabbi Julius Eckman, felt the need to apologize to their readership for comments he made. It was, in part, this need to criticize those in authority, that prompted I.N. to establish his own paper in 1877, The *Antiquarian*. He founded another periodical, *Public Opinion*, in 1878 or

1880, which replaced The *Antiquarian* in December, 1880.

A letter dated February 1, 1887 was sent by I.J. Aschheim,* possibly a relative of Harriett's, to B'nai B'rith's monthly magazine, The *Menorah*. He speaks of a controversy between members of B'nai B'rith's Constitution Grand Lodge, and I.N.'s mockery of the ensuing arguments: "Our darling brother, I.N. Choynski. To say this agitation proved a veritable bonanza for our friend, does not half express it. Individual liberty or governmental restriction ... preservation of the Order, all are matters which concern him but very little. He is pre-eminently a journalistic trapeze performer and contortionist ... always in search of a large field. This controversy from his standpoint was a first-class comedy, in which he was called upon to play a star engagement, and no matter who was hit, he took full elbow room for his stale jokes. The man is harmless, and we assure our brethren in the East that his opinion is by no means *Public Opinion*, and *Maftir* is not Torah."

* Aschheim is listed as Secretary of B'nai B'rith District Number 4.

Robert Cowan, who had, since his youth, known Isidor, called him "a large man and a picturesque character ... it was his fancy to wear a huge stovepipe hat, the brim of which was invariably pressed flat, a distinctive mark affected only by three of his contemporaries." Around 1863, I.N. specialized in schoolbooks, but later, had "Infidel, Liberal and Spiritual(ist) books always on hand." The 1864 *City Directory* shows the family dwelling at 34 Geary, and I.N., manager of the *Weekly Gleaner*. He opened a branch "newspaper and stationery" store in June, 1868 at 107 Sansome Street, in a section of the new "Orient" restaurant. Years later (so papers claimed in 1912), a young Joe Choynski "worked in his father's cigar store in Canal Street, San Francisco." The 1868 *Directory* shows that Isidor had opened an "antiquarian bookstand" on the Southwest corner of 4th and Jessie. The 1873 *Directory* shows this and the 2nd Street location still open. Data on his credit was compiled by agents for R.G. Dun & Company, for 1870 to 1878, revealing that Choynski was "habitually tardy" in paying bills, and all of his creditors had extreme issues collecting from him. When I.N. was dunned for his debts, he became "impertinent & abusive."[36]

"With General John F. Miller and Agapeus Honcharenko, he also began publication of the *Alaska Herald* in 1868, which continued until 1873. He was a fluent writer, fertile, venomous and sardonic." Probably the two most important pamphlets Isidor would publish were *California of the Padres, or, Footprints of Ancient Communism* by Elizabeth Hughes, and *The Antiquarian Spelling Book*, both in 1875. The former was a commentary on the Christian Padres, who forcibly converted local natives into Christians. The *Spelling Book* resulted in it being written, that "Jewish education on the west coast started with Choynski." If not entirely true, the statement is nonetheless flattering. He published a similar book in 1879, *Kinne's Comprehensive Spelling-book*. In 1875, the family dwelling was at 44 3rd Street. His brother Isaiah was a bookbinder, located at 511 Market, but also living at 44 3rd Street. By 1879, the bookstore had relocated to 34 Geary. An ad read: "Dealer in Rare Books and Prints. The Choicest Collection of Rare and Curious Coins, American and European. Magazines from time immemorial."[37] On November 22, 1876, Isidor testified to the United States Senate for resumption of the recently-discontinued "fast mail" via railroad. It may be noted, with some irony, that I.N. blamed not only the Chinese, but railroad monopolies, for the "ruin" of California.[38]

Isaac Mayer Wise (whom I.N. called "The Western Pope") visited San Francisco in 1877. He wrote about the congregations there, particularly Temple Emanu-El and Temple Sherith Israel, the latter attended for some time by the Choynski family. (Emanu-El was established by German Reform Jews and Sherith Israel, by Polish and Orthodox Jews). He reported in the September 14 *American Israelite*, "Jewish literature is provided for that community by I.N. Choynski, who moved his valuables into a new and elegant store (34 Geary), where he sells good books and writes bitter reports of things generally. He flatters none and displeases many."[39]

Joe's father was an original "shock jock," but also referred to as "the West's foremost Jewish journalist of the 19th century." As an anti-establishment hang-out, his bookstore was said to have attracted "Irish political exiles and intellectuals." I.N. told Julius Eckman in 1872 that Harriett desired to give her kids a Jewish education, so Eckman gave her advice. Isidor left the Sherith Israel congregation in 1879, but Harriett continued to be observant. She kept a kosher house, fasted on Yom Kippur and probably attended synagogue. She also had a deep interest in poetry and music. Joe, Maurice and Miriam married gentiles, and though Herbert was

Rabbi Julius Eckman

the only one to marry another Jew, he was an atheist. After I.N.'s death, Harriett said "money didn't mean anything to him," his pet phrase being, "Let's spend it all and go to the poorhouse together."[40]

Robert Cowan: "To many people Choynski was gruff and uncompromising, but to (me) he was always affable and pleasant ... Christmas-time, 1879, I ... entered Choynski's shop, then on Geary Street. I said, 'I am told you have Frost's Indian Wars of the United States ...' 'I have it,' he replied, 'but it is upstairs among the second-hand books, and I haven't time, this Christmas trade is keeping me too busy to ... hunt it out. Come back after the 1st of January.' 'What will be the price?' 'Three dollars,' he replied ... soon after New Year's Day, I returned to his shop ... We went upstairs, and ... found the book on the shelf. I handed him the three dollars. He handed one dollar back. 'You ... said the price was three dollars ...' I said. 'Yes ... but *you came back*! No one in this town ever comes back. The book will cost you two dollars.' From that time on ... he was always a good friend ... His eldest (sic) son Joe was the famous boxing ring champion, and of him and his pugilistic accomplishments the father was quite proud. After a lingering and most painful throat affliction Choynski died January 24, 1899."[41] In 1880, I.N. published a famous cartoon, depicting anti-Chinese labor leader and "sand-lot orator," Denis Kearney, in prison and taunted by several Chinese men. I.N. was also anti-Chinese, denouncing them as "heathenish," "crafty," "depraved" and engaging in illicit activities. He, like many Californians of the day, resented and hated the Chinese for taking jobs that Caucasians would otherwise have obtained.

In June, 1881, I.N. visited southern California with daughter, Miriam. Among the cities they stopped at were Los Angeles, Santa Barbara and San Diego. He called San Luis Obispo "one of the most thriving towns in California ... 3,000 inhabitants ... 23 Jews (families), all ... engaged in business ..." Isidor earlier had a branch of his Antiquarian Book Store there, which he sold in 1878 to local manager, Albert Pinkus.[42] This author inadvertently helped save the town's Sauer Bakery building, in which I.N.'s store had been located. The old, two-storey adobe at 848 Monterey was rented by several businesses simultaneously. By an amazing coincidence, I contacted Alex Gough on November 25, 2007, one day before San Luis Obispo's Cultural Heritage Committee held a crucial meeting to decide the fate of the building, which the developer wanted to tear down. Alex owns and operates Adobe Realty in his Sauer-Adams adobe, the Sauer family's original bakery and home, around the corner from I.N.'s branch store. Alex said my "input was very valuable at the ... meeting ..." He shared the photo and historical information I provided, with local historian, Dr. Dan Krieger, who "made an excellent presentation ... based on the Choynski family, the Sauers and other key facts. The committee ... backed up by a half dozen architectural historians ... came around and the vote was five to one in favor of saving the properties ... the wrecking ball is held in abeyance." The developer "agreed to retain and restore as much ... as he ... can ... the Sauer Bakery ... will look much as it did in the photo you sent me."

Isidor didn't develop a national following without reason. When he left the *American Israelite* in 1883, that paper wrote: "The determination ... by ... 'Maftir,' to ... retire from the journalistic field, has caused a feeling of widespread regret on the part of the readers ... shared by the publishers ... His letters have for nearly two decades been ... of this paper ... one of its most interesting features. We have at times found ourselves forced to differ with him, but have always admired his honest ability and fearlessness. Many a sham and humbug will feel easier hearing that 'Maftir' will no longer be on hand to expose him." Singerman is probably correct in suspecting that the real factor leading to I.N.'s departure was his trashing of everything Masonic. Rabbi Isaac Mayer Wise was a 32nd Degree Scottish Rite Mason. He wrote a June 16, 1882 editorial, apologizing for Isidor's criticism of Masonry, and promised, "the offence shall not be repeated." Shortly after leaving the paper, I.N. became editor of San Francisco's *Jewish Times*, writing biographical sketches of various Jews of the Pacific coast. Sadly, no issues appear to have survived. Nor did his sharp pen only strike at Freemasons or fellow Jews. He attacked Catholics and other Christians, as well, referring to Jesus as "the hanging one," for instance, and Christmas as the "anniversary of the birth of the little Joker." For this, he was castigated and rebuked by many of his Jewish peers. "Maftir" suggested that if Mary, who he referred to as "Mrs. Christ" and Joseph, who he called "the second-hand carpenter," had more children, these siblings should have their birthdays celebrated as good money makers, as well.[43] I.N.'s bookstore did a very good trade at Christmas-time, and his sarcasm could be called hypocrisy.

Another "Maftir" article, around November 27, 1885, read: "When a boy ... in the town where I delighted to run bare-footed ... my father's coat, turned and dyed and made to order to fit me, was just large enough to fit a boy twice my age; but then, those were economical ... times, and my mother – bless her soul ... now 76 ... was desirous to have me grow and prosper ... with maternal solicitude, wanted me to outgrow the garment, but the thing fell under the pressure before I got old enough ... my father cannot tell a stitch from a stratagem, though my cousins (in New Haven) can ... my coat ... upon the return of which, from the thief who stole it from my tailor, Levy ... is not my coat at all. ... I hung the thing in my office, waiting till some fine, rainy day ... The rain came and ... I tried to put in one arm, and would you believe it, the thing was too small for my 3rd boy? (Joe)"[44]

The 1884 *City Directory* shows Isidor's bookstore at 7 Powell Street. It was here that he published his four-sheet, weekly paper, *Public Opinion*." An 1885 ad described his stock as the "Largest collection of old and rare publications on the Pacific Coast." The 1886 *Directory* shows Joe, for apparently the first time, as a "candy maker," living at 1209 Golden Gate Avenue. I.N.'s store had moved to 33 or 39 6th Street. An 1889 *Directory* shows it at 137 Taylor, also the location of *Public Opinion*. Isaiah and family were living at 2434 Bush Street, where they resided for years. From 1892 to 1894 the bookstore was at two locations, 137 Taylor and 427 McAllister streets, but in 1898, it was at 1209 Golden Gate Avenue, the family home, and its final location. This apparently resulted from trouble in June, 1893, while I.N. was hospitalized with cancer (see chapter 9). Debts had forced him to combine residence and business.[45] Maurice had moved out by 1895, to 789 Mission; Herbert had long since left the nest.

An October 30, 1886 article by author, "Wendell," was entitled, "Maftir Taken to Task": "I have long observed in the erratic 'Maftir' an unhappy propensity to deride and ridicule everything that passes within the scope of his biased vision ... the frosts of many winters have silvered his hair, and this ... may account for his ... eccentricities. It has been aptly stated that the ratio of our infirmities increase with our years ... Maftir is rapidly nearing the standard of three score and 10 ... with the greatest reluctance I ... pose as a critic, and launch myself into a controversy with the erudite and august Maftir, as I am ... a foeman unworthy of his steel ... the latter is very lax in his religious ideas, tinged with ... egotism ... a poor precedent on which to educate the growing generation of Israelites in the creed of Judaism. His morbid longings and morose disposition urge him to continually lament the corrupted state into which the world has fallen. It recurs to me why his prolific brain and facile pen do not devise ... measures of escape from this abject condition, and, Moses-like, lead us out of the wilderness. That Maftir can be a terse, engaging writer, and is the possessor of considerable literary acumen, is an indefeasible fact, but he should ... rehabilitate his malevolent nature. Yet there is time for reform."[46]

The April 24, 1898 *San Francisco Call* published a strange article, "Character Told In The Shape Of The Hat You Wear." Shown are outlines of the craniums of 14 prominent men, among them, Isidor. "Craniologists claim that a man receives ideas ... and impressions from the external world with the left lobe of the brain, but originates ideas with the right. One thing very marked in ... heads is a certain mark of nationality or race. Those of Irish extraction invariably have square foreheads, indicating leadership. Those of German extraction have a larger posterior brain than forehead, showing that they enjoy good food and drink, and also a trait of generalship. A Jewish head shows a large, rounding forehead, well proportioned with the back of the head, straight on the sides ... Isador (sic) N. Choynski is the father of Choynski, of pugilistic fame, and also an editor. His head is uncommonly large and well balanced, showing by the large forehead and straight sides the philosophical tendencies of the Jewish race and the force of moral convictions." So went some beliefs of the age.

Public Opinion had a circulation of from 3,000 to 3,500 through the 1890s, but dropped to about 1,000 in 1899, the year I.N. died. Herbert took over the reins, and by 1900 raised the circulation to 5,000. The July-December, 1899 *Menorah* carried an article by the IOBB (International Order of B'nai B'rith): "I.N. Choynski, a prominent worker in the cause, died ... The (IOBB) President ... said, 'Many ... still prominent in the Order remember him in the prime of his mental vigor, a giant both physically and intellectually. Powerful in discussion, keen and incisive in his logic, fearless

in the expression of his opinion, he exerted an influence second to none.' "
Janet Fleishhacker told the same story her son, Mort, related in August,
2007: "He was called 'I.N.,' never 'Isidor' ... They used to say my father
(Herbert) was equally feisty and difficult, but a marvelous man ... whom I
worshipped. As a young man ... still going to school, he used to work
occasionally in the bookstore. People would come in and say, 'Is I.N. in?'
He would say, 'Yes,' and they would say, 'Where is he?' 'Who?' 'Choynski,'
'Oh, he's gone out.' 'But, you said he was in.' 'I did not.' They'd say, 'You
said I.N. was in,' and he'd say, 'Veil, it *is* in.' "[47]

Joe's mother, the former Harriett Ashim, was born January 13, 1843,
either in London or Liverpool, England. She was the eldest of four children
born to Morris B. Ashim and
Rachel Bartlett. The other siblings
were Louis, born in 1844, Rose,
1847 and Benjamin, around 1854.
Morris was born to a Jewish family
in Posen, Prussia, either in 1897 or
1818 (a vast discrepancy, varying by
source). Rachel, a gentile
(Protestant), was born in London,
in 1808. Morris moved to London,
where he met Rachel. In order to
wed Morris, Rachel converted to
Judaism. Her maiden name was
likely the source of Joe's middle
name. She is not to be confused
with Rachel E. Ashim, Solomon's
wife. Morris, described by the
District Grand Lodge of B'nai
B'rith as "a true and upright man,"
served as President of San Francisco's Hebrew Benevolent Society in 1857.
That year, he also became founding treasurer of the Chebra Bikur Cholim
u-Kedisha Society (to aid the sick, distressed or terminally ill) and was
President of the city's International Order of B'nai B'rith.[48]

Harriett Ashim-Choynski

Harriett came to the United States with her family in 1850. They settled
for a short time in Kentucky, probably Louisville, before moving West.
Exactly how that journey unfolded is uncertain, as multiple versions have
survived. One source has the Ashims making the long trek westward across
the American frontier, through St. Louis, Missouri, via covered wagon.
According to an interview with the elderly Harriett in the January 12, 1924
San Francisco Bulletin, the family battled Indians on the site of Salt Lake City.
In 1974, Herbert's daughter, Janet, told a different version, at odds with the
above. She had been told by her family and Harriett, that the Ashims came

to the States when she was eight or nine years old. Harriett was a cripple, having fallen around that time and broken her hip on the marble steps of a public building. She had a bad limp the rest of her life.

The Ashims took a ship from Louisville, Kentucky to the Isthmus of Panama, where they traversed the 50-some miles westward. The 9-year-old Harriett became separated from her family on the west coast. They located her after great difficulty, boarded the clipper ship and completed the voyage to San Francisco. This version is much more detailed, and the more likely of the two. Also, as the book *Our City, the Jews of San Francisco* noted, "Those Jews who came cross-country with wagon trains could be counted on the fingers of one hand." Another source said the Ashims took a covered wagon *to* Kentucky, presumably from New York, subsequently journeying by boat to Panama. They arrived in San Francisco on September 8, 1850, the day before California became a State.[49] The October 21, 1852 *New York Times* shows that "Ashim, Mrs., and 3 children" left the Port of New York on the 20th aboard the Steamship *Star of the West*, bound for California. The ship's first stop was San Juan, Nicaragua, which has river access from east coast to west, and is two nations above the usual Panama route. It is not clear which of the Ashims made this voyage, but Harriett would have been nine years old that year. The *San Francisco Directory* shows that Morris had a clothing store at 139 Front Street in 1852.

Rabbi Julius Eckman was born in Rawicz, Prussia in 1805, graduated from a Berlin university and arrived in America in 1846. Considered too gentle for the rigors of the American pulpit in this era of the "great warfare of reform," Eckman held brief appointments in places like Mobile, Richmond, New Orleans and Charleston, as one of the few English-speaking rabbis in the country. In July, 1854, he was elected the first rabbi of San Francisco's Congregation Emanu-El, a position that lasted only one year. Julius soon gained a long-term appointment for the city's Temple Sherith Israel, but his passion was education. He established the West's first Jewish religious school, on Sutter Street near Stockton (Street), which he named "Hepzibah" ("My delight is in her"). Harriett was one of Eckman's students and they developed a lifelong friendship. She became the chief assistant at his free Sabbath school, and the Rabbi always held her in the highest esteem. At the time of her marriage to I.N., Eckman wrote in his *Weekly Gleaner*, that Harriett "is the only pupil ... connected with our religious school, from its opening in July, 1854, to this day: first as a pupil and afterwards as a faithful, untiring teacher."[50]

The first known mention of a Choynski or Ashim in California involves fighting. July 12, 1857 *Daily Alta California*: "Yesterday ... during the free performance at the Circus ... A boy ... Lewis Ashim, took a hold of Edward A. Chambers' cap, and refused to give it back ... Words passed ... Ashim picked up a large piece of rock and cut Chambers' head with it, inflicting a severe, but not dangerous, wound. Ashim was arrested, and followed to the station-house by at least a hundred of the boys." This was probably Harriett's brother, Louis. His action might have been a result of "Jew-baiting." On April 14, 1847, Simon Ashim "of Houston, Texas," Morris' brother, married Mathilda Jacobi. In 1858, he was briefly thrown into debtors' prison, in Charleston, South Carolina.[51] Afterward, Simon vacated the state, moving first to Georgia, and later, San Francisco.

The Ashims owned a bakery in San Francisco, at the corner of Commercial and Leidesdorff. Most of the clan lived at 717 Eddy Street. Morris' and Simon's younger brother, Solomon, resided in Ormsby County, Nevada in 1862. In '62 and '63, the clothing store, owned by Morris, was located in Carson City. Aaron Fleishhacker's General Store was in the same town.[52] Aaron, who came to California in 1853 and later to Nevada, made a fortune in various ways. He grubstaked John Mackay, who soon hit the "Big Bonanza," the richest strike of the Comstock Lode. Between 1863 and '74, the three Ashim brothers lived in such Nevada towns as Aurora, Carson City, Eureka, Reno and Virginia City.

On August 22, 1873 a flood destroyed the Ashim & Brother dry goods store in Pioche, Nevada. Damage was from $4,000 to $5,000. Around 1872, two of the brothers built a shop in Eureka, run by their wives. Four columns in a June 1, 1878 paper listed the inventory of Mathilda's grocery and mercantile. Her Epicurean Restaurant was at the corner of Buel and Bateman. A terrible fire on April 19, 1879 consumed about 300 buildings. One of the first devoured by the inferno was Ashim's restaurant. Their loss was $6,000; insurance coverage, only $3,500. Eureka's loss was close to a *million* dollars.[53] The Ashims moved back to Frisco soon after.

Simon was born in Prussia in 1822 or 1823, and died May 23, 1886. He is buried at Hills of Eternity Memorial Park, Colma, California, along with Mathilda, who died in 1912. A May 29, 1886 obituary reads: "Simon ... one of the Pioneer merchants of California, having come here in '51 from Charleston, S.C., where he married a sister of Col. Nathaniel Jacobi, a wealthy importer. Mr. Ashim leaves a widow and four children ... Barach J. Ashim ... a United States gauger (for the IRS) in this city, and George Ashim ... a clerk with the Post Office ... His two daughters are Mrs. McNichol (Rebecca) and Miss May Ashim. Their father came ... from Russia when about 18 ... and settled in Texas. He then went to Charleston, S.C. ... came to the Pacific Coast, where he carried on a general mercantile business in California, Nevada, Idaho and Montana, accumulating a large fortune, which he subsequently lost. Mr. Ashim was a strictly honest and upright businessman ... a kind husband and father ... a staunch Democrat ... His father, in Russia, was the first manufacturer of asphaltum roofing material, owning a patent ... This business is now owned by a wealthy brother ... in that country. Ashim ... was 63 years old."

While in Charleston, Simon ran a clothing store and owned four black slaves. A *Call* obituary gives his children as: "Miriam Rosalie ("May"), born September 29, 1863 in Carson City, Nevada; Barach J.; E. Leopold and Rebecca, both born in South Carolina; the latter ... probably 1853; George, born in St. Helena, California and Benjamin 'Bart,' born 1854." Simon fought for the Confederate side during the Civil War. Barach, referred to variously as Baruch, Barack and Bark, became a pharmacist, born in 1851 or 1852. The 1870 Census shows Solomon, 37, born in Russia, wife, Rachel, age 30, and a son, Henry, nine, born in New York.[54]

Barach Jacob Ashim is a notable character. In 1861, before Nevada attained statehood, President Lincoln selected the "Old Grey Eagle," James W. Nye, as that Territory's first Governor. Orion Clemens, older brother of Mark Twain (Samuel Clemens), was appointed Nye's Secretary. Sam traveled to Nevada with Orion, where he tried his hand at gold mining. No success was achieved, but in September, 1862, he was employed as a reporter for the *Territorial Enterprise* (Virginia City, Nevada). Here, he began

Barach Ashim (lower right) with Mark Twain (far left)

using the pseudonym, "Mark Twain" (a term denoting the "two fathom mark" on the side of a Mississippi steamboat). While covering Nevada's 1st and 3rd constitutional conventions, Twain was unable to keep pace with the speakers. Around 1864, he visited the school of William B. Lawlor in Carson City, where he met a student proficient in shorthand, Barach (nicknamed "Barry") Ashim. Clemens hired Ashim as his personal transcriber. He was so impressive, members of the Legislature paid him a bonus for his efforts. The teen "appears to have been Nevada's first Jewish public employee ..."[55] In August, 1873 or '74, Barach and five others left Eureka, Nevada for Panamint, California. About 100 miles from Panamint, their water ran out. Becoming separated on the barren terrain, all made it to the border town of Lida, Nevada, except Barach. He was too weak to flee when a band of "Panamint Indians" (probably Shoshone) "discover him." They gave him water, fed him gourds and saved his life.

In March, 1875, in Darwin, California, near Death Valley and the Nevada border, Barach confronted a Croatian immigrant named Nikola "Nick" Perasich. Nick, who had a reputation for swindling people, owned a restaurant in Panamint. He fled for Darwin, owing Barach, a Panamint storekeeper, $47.50. Perasich was known as a "quarrelsome, brow-beating fellow," who once tried to bribe his Greek cook, Constantine, into feeding his Mexican partner, Cervantes, a cake containing glass shards. When Constantine refused, Nick fired him, refused to pay him back wages, and when the cook tried to collect, pistol-whipped him, nearly to death. Ashim, armed with a Whistler six-shooter, caught up with his debtor on the 10th at a restaurant in Darwin. Seated at a table next to Perasich was H. Petrovich, Nick's partner in the Panamint restaurant. Nick went for his pistol, telling Barach he would pay "when he returned to Panamint." Barach left the restaurant, but returned the next day with Tom Carroll, "an Irishman and ruffian from Pioche." Ashim again demanded Nick pay up.

Shots were fired, but events transpired so quickly, it took days to sort it all out. The *Panamint News* was quoted:"A man ... said: 'Pay me the $47.50 you owe me, you s—of a b----!' and ... began shooting with a self-cocking pistol. The man ... is ... Ashim, of the firm of Ashim & Brother ... accompanied ... by ... Carroll, of Darwin ... Ashim walked up to E.A. Reddy's saloon and gave himself up. He was taken to Independence by Reddy ..." March 28 *Panamint News*: "Sheriff Moore says the evidence ... shows the affair on Ashim's part was not so cold-blooded as first reported ... Perasich ... attempted to draw his revolver, when Ashim fired, hitting Perasich in the back of the right hand. Perasich turned partially around and threw up his left arm ... Ashim ... hitting him in the left side. Perasich was next shot in the right side of the head ... by Ashim or Carroll ..."

Barach stated at the trial that he fired his pistol only to frighten Perasich, who was "coming at him," and his bullet entered the wall behind Nick. The bullet was indeed found embedded in the wall ... proving Barach's testimony. He claimed his second shot was aimed at Perasich's shooting hand. Nick slumped lifelessly to the floor, two bullets imbedded in his chest. During the gunfight, Nick's partner, Petrovich, drew his own pocket pistol, but accidentally shot off two fingers of his own hand. Tom Carroll skipped town and was never seen again. Vigilantes formed a posse to locate Carroll, who some said was hired by Ashim to kill Perasich, while citizens of Darwin demanded that Barach be lynched. Criminal lawyer Pat Reddy snuck Ashim out in his "buggy," to the custody of Sheriff Moore of Independence (California). Barach paid $15,000 bail and got out of town just in time. Two of Perasich's brothers, Elias and Peter, heard of the murder and hurried from Carson City to Darwin, too late to find Ashim, who fled to San Francisco and laid low for six months.

Barach arranged to meet his mother, Mathilda, and sisters Rebecca and Miriam at Carson City's Ormsby Hotel, and proceed with them to his trial in Independence. Mathilda entered the hotel and was recognized by a Dalmatian (Croatian) waiter. Upon Barach's 5 a.m. arrival, a friend warned him that Elias Perasich was hiding behind the dining room door, with a shotgun. Ashim high-tailed it down the road. A stagecoach took aboard Mathilda and daughters. The Perasich brothers tried to board, but were refused by the driver, who saw the men were "armed to the teeth." The pair chased the stagecoach on foot. Barach saw them and dived into a cornfield. As the stage passed near, Barach leaped out and sprinted toward it.

Elias Perasich fired a shot that whizzed by Ashim's head. Barach was pulled in through a window of the stage by his mother and a sister. A bullet ripping through the back of the coach narrowly missed Barach, who made his escape. Witnesses at the trial testified that Carroll initiated the gunplay, fired the fatal shots, and even took a potshot at waiter-owner John Sullivan, whom he missed. Elias and Pete camped out by the north road out of town, waiting to get Ashim. The one-armed lawyer, Pat Reddy, took a stage leaving on the north route. The Perasichs, thinking Ashim inside, stopped it and demanded Barach step out, finding themselves looking into the business end of the lawyer's pistol. They gave up the chase and left town. Ashim either fled Independence via the south road, or witnessed the confrontation from the loft of Reddy's stable, waiting until dark to head out on Pat's "faithful buggy."[56] Barach died July 22, 1913.

The only known photographs of an Ashim, aside from Joe's mother, Harriett, are of her father, Morris, and cousin Barach. The March 6, 1875 passport application of Solomon "Sol" Ashim gives his birth date as January 15, 1833, but adds: "Stature: 6' ½". Forehead: high. Eyes: gray. Nose: prominent. Mouth: mustache. Chin: dimple. Hair: dark brown. Complexion: medium. Face: oval." Joe did not inherit his stature solely from his father's side. By August 11, 1859, Simon was in San Francisco, where Morris and Solomon had opened a dry goods store on the northeast corner of Leidesdorff and Sacramento streets. It was a combination auction and commission facility, under the name, "Ashim & Brother," later modified to "Ashim Brothers." An April, 1860 ad said they carried "Hats ... Fine and Heavy Clothing, Gents' Furnishing Goods ..."[57]

Janet Choynski Fleishhacker told how Harriett Ashim met I.N. Choynski. She was a "serious student ... more interested in books than anything else." Harriett, in her late teens, was at her home, and Rabbi Julius Eckman made a call. She was writing a report for school on President James K. Polk. Eckman said he would "introduce you to a young man who can tell you more about President Polk than you can find in all those books you're reading, and brought to her the man who became my grandfather." In 1861, Harriett graduated from the General High School of San Francisco, one of 11 females and only two males from this first class of 13 students. Harriett married I.N. on March 20, 1862, Rabbi Julius Eckman officiating. The couple's first home was at 237 Tehama Street.[58]

In December, Joe Choynski's grandmother, Rachel Ashim, died in San Francisco. The notice said, "Friends will attend her funeral tomorrow at 10 o'clock, a.m., from her late residence, 34 Geary Street." It appears the Ashims resided at this address prior to the Choynskis. One article said, of Isidor and his weekly *Public Opinion*: "He may have taken in subscriptions, but mostly, it was said, he took in his subscribers. He sent his paper for a year and then went and collected three dollars. The postal law allowed that as long as a paper was received and the publisher not notified through the post office to discontinue it, the receiver was liable for the price. Mr. Choynski made the price high enough to pay him for the trouble of collecting. He ... said in his paper that every time Joe was going to fight, papa and mamma prayed he would get licked." Evidence indicates, however, that I.N. was proud of his son's ability to handle himself. He died of throat cancer on January 24, 1899, age 64, and on the 26th was buried, like most of the clan, in the Ashim-Choynski Plot, Hills of Eternity Memorial Park, Colma.[59] Colma is the only necropolis in the United States, housing the deceased of San Francisco, which were relocated due to a shortage of land within the city and fear of the spread

Herbert Choynski, age 12

of disease. The dead in Colma outnumber the living by a factor of nearly 1,000 to 1. The town, nicknamed "The City of Souls," contains about 17 cemeteries, its motto being, "It's great to be alive in Colma."

Joe Choynski had four siblings: Herbert, Miriam, Maurice and Edwin. Herbert I. Choynski was born January 8, 1863. He was a clerk at I.N.'s bookstore at age 17, and volunteered for the Army during the Spanish-American War, eventually becoming a Colonel. His daughter, Janet, said he had a tremendous desire to be appointed to the Academy at West Point. It was virtually unheard of for a Jew to receive such an appointment then, and Herbert was bitterly disappointed when not selected. (Isidor petitioned U.S. President James Garfield in 1881, to appoint his son to a cadetship at West Point. He apparently never received a response). She said of Herbert's law practice: "He ... had no hesitancy ... telling judges what he thought of them ... He was a great espouser of causes, particularly the underprivileged ... had many black clients and was always concerned that the black people exploited their own very badly. My mother ... said he

underestimated his own talents ... not charging ... adequate fees ... He had ... Jewish clients ... in the kosher meat business and could have ... asked a very substantial fee for his services, but was perfectly content to take meat ... instead. He was a strong activist against any kind of double dealing ..."[60]

A leading defense attorney and "pugnacious political lawyer," Herbert was best known for helping expose the corruption of San Francisco boss, Abe Ruef (rhymes with "goof"). Ruef hired Herbert to represent him soon after the scandal broke, but released him shortly thereafter, as "Choynski made no effort to placate Ruef. On the contrary, he gave out interviews ... charging that Abe had received $500,000 for the

Herbert Choynski, mid to late 1890s

trolley permit, and each Supervisor ... given $4,000 to $5,000 for his vote." A 1918 paper referred to Herbert as "the shrewdest criminal lawyer of the state."[61] In 1906, he married Ethel Berger (September 7, 1879 - January 10, 1969). She is buried in the Ashim-Choynski Plot. Herbert died May 1, 1936.

Ethel's brother was Samuel Berger, the United States' first Olympic Games Boxing gold medalist. Janet: "My uncle ... was like my older brother. My father paid for his tuition ... to Hitchcock Military Academy ... mother ... raised him ... as ... me ... strict ... Sam ... was a fine athlete ... died of cancer at age 42 (author: age 40) ... a member of the Olympic Club at age 16 ...

won the first gold medal in boxing ... St. Louis in 1904 ... real gold ... The medals are not solid gold today. Uncle Sam was ... a great friend of Arthur Brisbane ... for the Hearst papers, and many ... writers of that era ... interested in social reform ... He ... had a fine library ... Karl Marx's Communist Manifesto ... books on social problems." Janet was Herbert and Ethel's only child (September 13, 1908 - September 12, 1987). She was married twice. First, on May 1, 1929, to Mortimer Fleishhacker, Jr. (1907-1976), San Francisco financier and philanthropist. The widowed Janet married William Bates in 1985. Janet and Mortimer had three children, born in San Francisco: Delia (Joan Delia), born September 20, 1930, Mortimer III, September 5, 1932 and David Fleishhacker, May 30, 1937.[62]

Miriam Choynski, 1881

The second child of I.N. and Harriett was Miriam, born May 23, 1864. It has been noted through the years, that Miriam never married, but in fact, she did. She wedded a gentile (but not gentle) mariner, Captain Henry G. Williams, on January 3, 1889 in Oakland. He was a colorful character, piloting a steamship for the Pacific Mail Steamship Company, carrying mail to and from the San Francisco area. Williams had been in their employ since the Civil War, first stationed in China. Returning to the United States, H.G. operated as a blockade runner for the Confederate government until captured by Union forces on the Mississippi River. He took an oath of allegiance to the North, whom he served for the duration of the war. After this, he returned to the Pacific Mail Steamship Company, eventually becoming their Pilot Commissioner. Williams first made his fortune in 1877, after he left $600 with a mining broker during the big stock boom, before going to sea. Upon his return, Henry had $70,000 to his credit in the Bank of California. He invested in real estate and had an income of $900 a month, which he "spent like a prince."

The Captain was also a boxing patron and reportedly took a tip from

Joe Choynski in 1892, to put his money on John L. Sullivan over Jim Corbett. In doing so, Williams lost $10,000. Miriam divorced him after about six months, causing I.N. to ban her from his house, saying, "Never

Miriam, circa 1881

cross my portals. My daughter is lost to me." She was welcomed back by her mother, after Isidor died. The 1904 *City Directory* shows "Miss M. Choynski" back at 1209 Golden Gate Avenue. Williams took $1,500 in jewels from Miriam when they parted. The seaman had three wives before he died on June 19, 1901, all divorcing him for various reasons, including abuse. In 1900, H.G. was sentenced to six months in the County Jail for beating his 3rd wife, Amelia, because she dared ride her bicycle without his permission. He also allegedly tried to drown her in a bathtub, pulled her around the house by her hair, "dislocated her fingers by ... bending them backward," hurled a kitchen

Captain H.G. Williams, circa 1901

clock and a lighted lamp at her, and beat her senseless. Williams had at least one illegitimate child, a daughter named Marie.[63]

Janet said Miriam attended Madame Ziska's Academy for Young Ladies and was the apple of her father's eye. He "worshipped this beautiful daughter and nothing was too good for her ... contrary to my husband's family who did not believe in ostentation of any kind, he adorned her with diamond earrings ... spoiled the life out of her. But no young man who came to court her was good enough ... She made the ... mistake of eloping with someone who had been brought to the house by a mutual friend. He was an older man, a seagoing man and ... a Christian besides. Apparently, it was a disastrous marriage ... the most dreadful disgrace ... I was a grown woman before I knew Aunt Miriam had ever been divorced. But ... today, we don't think those things so serious." In late 1881, "Maftir" penned:

"The winter is ... the most enjoyable of our seasons ... neither cold enough for an ulster nor too warm for a duster ... I expect to give some parties this winter – no poker parties. I have a daughter, the only one the Lord ever vouched-safe unto me, and if some honest mechanic will take her off my hands, I will give him my blessing, all the dowry I have to give ... what shall I do with a 17 year old girl who wears 18 button gloves? Won't I get it though when that Bath reads this article in the *Israelite*, as she is bent upon either a lawyer or banker or some other Jew with a wholesale store."[64] Miriam, known to her nieces and nephews as "Auntie Mame" or "Mamie," never remarried and died February 2, 1953 in San Francisco.

Maurice Asham Choynski was often referred to as Morris, and nicknamed "Chauncey," a corruption of the Choynski surname. The 3rd child of I.N. and Harriett was born April 1, 1866. As an adult, he moved to Chicago, where he owned and operated several nickelodeon motion picture theaters. The January 12, 1924 *San Francisco Bulletin* referred to him as the "Chicago movie theatre magnate." Maurice married Sarah J. Collins, a Catholic, on November 27, 1902 in Allegheny, Pennsylvania. He opened the 2nd motion picture theater in the Windy City's history on January 1, 1906, with Henry Cohen and Daniel

Maurice Choynski & Harriet Coe, 1940

L. Noon. Maurice missed inaugurating the 1st theater by a mere seven days, that honor going on December 25, 1905 to Aaron J. Jones. In 1910 and 1911, his theater was located at 318 South Halsted, Chicago. Maurice was an activist, like Isidor and Herbert, as indicated in 1916: "The ... producers' branch of the National Association of the Motion Picture Industry ... went on record as favoring federal censorship ... Their action caused no little excitement. Maurice Choyinski (sic), one of the Exhibitor-Directors ... called upon ... lawyers, and asked them ... whether ... the enactment of a federal censorship law would do away with all and any other forms of censorship. Both answered emphatically in the negative and having got this answer, Choyinski made a strong plea against federal censorship."[65]

In 1916 and '17, Maurice and business partner, Nathan Wolf (or Wolff), filed suit against the Selig Polyscope Company and Essanay Film Manufacturing Company for conspiracy to injure the plaintiffs' business.

The defendants claimed to have contracted to print and distribute film advertising posters to theater proprietors, at a high price, in what was akin to extortion. Choynski and Wolf charged that they had entered into no such contract, and were awarded a judgment of $2,000. The Selig Polyscope Company, which closed in 1918, was best known for launching the movie careers of Tom Mix and Roscoe "Fatty" Arbuckle. Maurice was described in July, 1916 as "lean and tall, witty and forceful." He visited San Francisco in 1940 at age 74, and saw the Golden Gate International Exposition with his wife, Sarah, Edwin's wife, Florence, and youngest daughter, Harriet. The latter met him then for the first time, recalling in 2009, "I was 14 years old when I met Morrie ... he was a very sweet man, and it seemed as if I had always known him. Perhaps because he looked like my father – only much taller." Maurice died June 11, 1944 in Chicago, Illinois.[66]

Edwin Walker Choynski (or EWC, later Eddie Coe), was born May 27, 1879 (not May 5, as generally stated). He was a teamster on the

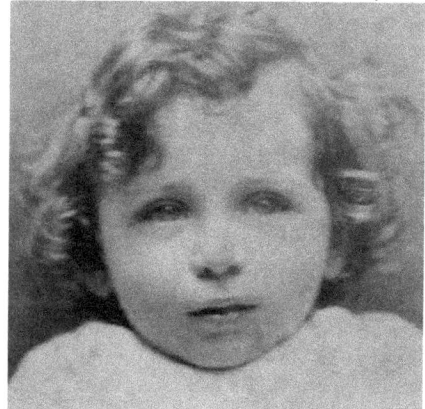

Embarcadero, later a noted stockbroker, writing a financial column in the *San Francisco Call*. Edwin was a life-long member of the Olympic Athletic Club. Herbert was also a member, at least in 1913. EWC was the shortest of the four boys, family tradition saying he stood 5' 8". Joe was at least 5' 10½" and Maurice and Herbert were about 6' tall. On November 20, 1913, Edwin married Florence Dibert (or Diebert, a Christian). They had three children. Florence, (September 1, 1914 - November 6, 2002), Edwin Joseph (March 22, 1917 - 2006) and Harriet Marie, born January 9, 1926, who married Albert J. Draper on June 5, 1954.

Edwin Choynski, age 1, 1879

Harriet said Edwin began his education at Lincoln Grammar School and finished at Lowell High School. "There were the years (as) a teamster and tours of mining camps in Nevada and Alaska. Then, he became an accountant, and ... bought a seat on the Mining Exchange. I went to ... St. Cecilia's Catholic school. The nuns inspired me to be a missionary and I tried to convert him, but he had his own beliefs ... though he never attended any formal church. I remember, during World War II finding him on his knees (probably for his ... two children at the fronts). He retired in his late fifties ... and continued to go to the Stock Exchange every day after selling his seat ... Afterwards, he went to the Olympic Club to play handball and swim. He fell out of a tree one day and his Paget's disease turned into cancer that required amputation of one leg. Then, he seemed to lose interest in a prosthesis, so he remained relatively inactive until his death, at 78." Edwin died January 1, 1958 in Atherton, California and is buried at Hills of Eternity, in Colma.[67] His son, Edwin Joseph ("Tim") Coe, performed at the 1940 Golden Gate Exposition, in Billy Rose's Aquacade, with swimming celebrities Esther Williams, Gertrude Ederle and Johnny Weissmuller. During World War II, Tim became a Captain in the first Air Commando Group. Colonel Philip "Flip" Cochran was the flying instructor, and the inspiration for the character Colonel "Flip" Corkin, in the famed Milt Caniff comic strip, "Terry and the Pirates." Florence Coe worked with General Patton on the front in a M.A.S.H. hospital.

Edwin, age 4, 1883

Harriet Coe Draper at Ashim-Choynski plot, Hills of Eternity Memorial Park, 2006

I.N. Choynski (1860-1865) (top), Miriam
Choynski (1891) (right) and Herbert
Choynski (circa 1890) (bottom right)

Round Two

Young Joe in Old San Francisco
(1868 – October 1888)

The Choynski household of Joe's youth was an intellectual one; printed matter abounded. Not only was I.N. extremely well-read and articulate, but the rest of the family, including Joe. Their home, in fact, became something of a salon, a venue for debate. Famous writers visited and shared views with I.N., both at his home and bookstore. These literary luminaries were the free thinkers and rebels of the period, such as Robert "The Great Agnostic" Ingersoll, Joaquin "Poet of the Sierras" Miller, Henry George, Bret Harte and Samuel L. Clemens, a.k.a. Mark Twain. They were very much like I.N. Choynski, himself. Isidor's early writings criticized others for failure to attend temple regularly, and other transgressions. He later became, as he described himself, "somewhat of an atheist." I believe he was influenced by the agnostic (or atheistic) philosophies of men like "Infidel Bob" Ingersoll, who said: "Is there a supernatural power ... a supreme will that sways the tides and currents of the world – to which all causes bow? I do not deny. I do not know – but I do not believe. I believe the natural is supreme – that there is ... no power worship can persuade or change – no power that cares for man." Clemens, who suffered more than his share of tragedies, was also called an agnostic. Joaquin Miller was known for his poetry, long hair, red shirt, unpolished boots, tramp-like appearance and eccentricities.

Joe wrote: "These men and other celebrities, including famous actors, were frequent guests in my father's home. My mother, a gifted woman of English birth, entertained them royally. I knew them well." "He (I.N.) numbered among his personal friends Joachin (sic) Miller, Bret Harte, Mark Twain and Bob Ingersoll. These noted men often visited at our home and I listened in on many of their conversations with my dad, imbibing much of their philosophy."[1] It is unlikely that Joe met Twain in San Francisco; it must have been later. Clemens spent time in the city between May, 1864 and December, 1867, often staying at the Occidental Hotel. He left before Joe's birth and allegedly never returned. There were four Jewish sub-communities in the locale at that time: Fillmore-McAllister, the San Bruno Avenue area, West Oakland and South of Market. Joe's family lived in the latter. There existed in Petaluma, a "rural Jewish colony composed of chicken farmers ..." Joe later owned his own chicken farm in Illinois. The household had a piano by 1863 or 1864, and, as Joe was later said to have sometimes "played a waterlogged piano," he probably learned on this one.[2]

Henry George allegedly wrote his famous economic treatise, *Progress and Poverty*, in the back of I.N. Choynski's "Antiquarian Bookstore." It proposed a single, land value tax to fund the United States government. Published in 1879, it became an international best-seller. Among those strongly influenced by his work were Leo Tolstoy, George Bernard Shaw and Sun Yat Sen. The board game Monopoly was supposedly based on Henry's principles. I.N. purportedly aided George when he was "down on his luck" and his family near starvation, loaning him a sum totaling $2,500. Isidor kept notes of the debt. George headed East without repaying I.N., though he was now prosperous. When Harriett made a trip to New York in 1886, she presented George with the notes, to collect on them. "Not only did the author ... fail to settle his indebtedness but he got the notes into his possession and that is the last Mr. Choynski has heard of them. He, however, has photographs of them, and, as the *Star* maintains, is ready with proofs of George's dishonesty."[3] No more was heard of the issue.

A brief letter Joe wrote to his father from summer camp in June, 1878, age 9½, gives a brief glimpse of him at that time: "Dear Pa, I have had lots of fun. I've rode the horse and saw the locomotive draw the logs and went out hunting with Henry and shot nothing and on his way home he saw a couple of deer and shot at them but missed them. And lost one of his cartridges and then we went home. from Joe Boe Choynski."[4] Though little exists to tell us what young Joe did on a typical day, a letter written to him in May, 1891 by younger brother, Edwin, reveals some of what that the (nearly) 12-year-old did. Edwin composed the missive while "The California Terror" was in Australia, and references a loss to Joe Goddard:

"My dear brother Joe, I did not write before because I thought you would win your fight and come home. I am very sorry you lost ... I hope you are all right and won't get sick. I had a daisy time in the week vacation. I went out somewhere with the boys every day. Friday ... about 12, got their lunch and we all went for a hard day's travel to the Cliff House. We started at 20 minutes past eight and it was about half past 10 when we got out there. Howard Welsh brought along his big dog and he nearly caught a rabbit and a squirrel on the way ... we ... walked a mile from the Cliff House to the beginning of the turn where there was a large pond not very deep, but clear water ... There was nobody there but ourselves and we decided to go in swimming. So all got undressed to go in. Howard Welsh and another boy were the only ones who knew how to swim so all the rest of us tried, but we had more fun chasing for oranges. Before 12 we put something over and waited till us (sic) thought it time to eat lunch. After we were through we waited another half hour and went in again. About 3 o'clock we ... started for home. On the way Howard Welsh caught a wounded sea gull and brought it home. When we were home ... we started a game of Talli-hi-ho ... That same night I went with Mama to the Baldwin (theater) to see

The Little Tycoon. Today in school we had a substitute and had a daisy fun. I hope to have a fine time tomorrow, April Fool's Day. Washington's Birthday was fun and we had vacation Monday but ... no procession."

Edwin mentioned "Aunty and Uncle Walker," family friends, who he got his middle name from. The Choynski family spent summers at the

Edwin Choynski and Howard Welsh, on roof at 1209 Golden Gate Avenue, 1895

Walker Ranch in Sebastopol, California.[5] Edwin had visited the first Cliff House, built in 1863, which Joe trained near. It burned on Christmas Day, 1894. There were three versions, all built on the same site. Millionaire Adolph Sutro had the Victorian (2nd) Cliff House built in 1895, in the style of a French chateau. It survived the earthquake and fire of 1906, but burned down the following year. Sutro's daughter, Dr. Emma Merritt, constructed the 3rd Cliff House, which opened on July 1, 1909 and is still a popular restaurant and tourist attraction.

A description of young Joe's neighborhood was given in the 1948 book, *This is San Francisco*: "Along the narrow alleys that paralleled Market and Mission ... Natoma, Jessie, Stevenson ... The smells ... of stew meat cooking and potatoes boiling, the gashouse and factory smoke, washing on the line; and ... sounds ... drinkers singing snatches of songs over their tall steams, babies crying in packing-case cradles, women gossiping over backyard fences in the brogue of the Irish, in Dutch, in Yiddish, in Polish."

The Choynski household was sufficiently affluent to employ servants. In an *American Israelite* article from between 1879 and 1881, I.N. wrote, sarcastically: "Miss Bridget O'Flagherty gave my wife notice that she was going to quit. Bridget is a very good girl. She never went out oftener than seven times a week, and as we live near the Cathedral, she never missed morning mass. But, she is good, clean and all that, and would never ask her mistress more than twice to read her the news, at the breakfast table, at the 'ould sod.' But, Bridget ('Bid') got her back up one morning because the young lady – a neighbor – who called upon our daughter, rang the bell instead of coming, unannounced, through the kitchen by way of the back gate, and not disturb her while washing the dishes. Servantgalism is a factor ... of no small dimensions, and a Bid understands how labor regulates capital ... We got a Chinaman. The first day he ate up all our sweetmeats and the second day he mashed our costly soup tureen. We set him adrift and got another Chinaman but he would not stay. Another heathen was ordered from the Chinese intelligence office, and he too, would not remain ... Thus, we tried eight children of the moon who, when they took their bearings in the kitchen, left without saying a word."

"The boss of the kettledrum ... explained: When a Chinaman leaves a house where he has been discharged – no matter how just the cause – he writes ... hieroglyphics upon some portion of the wall, but most generally scratches them in the sink, so his successor from the Celestial Empire may take warning and not work for unbelievers who will not allow their dishes to be broken, their preserves to be eaten up and their jewelry stolen by the long-nailed, long-sleeved Chinese." The boss of the "Chinese intelligence office" located and erased the scrawl in the Choynski kitchen, and sent another servant. I.N. adds: "Russian girls" work cheaply, "six dollars a week with board and lodging thrown in, and only two evenings in the week to themselves ... Why don't Russian girls come rushing into our state?"

1879 saw the invention of the incandescent bulb, or filament lamp, by Thomas Edison (in America). It brought an end to the Gaslight Era, which had dominated Joe's youth. In 1880, the I.N. Choynski domicile at 127 O'Farrell had a 37-year-old servant from Ireland named Kate Liddy. Janet Choynski Fleishhacker wrote that Isidor enjoyed a daily breakfast of gefilte fish and a pint of champagne,[6] an explosive combination! Around 1884, the family moved to 1209 Golden Gate Avenue.[7] It was evidently a duplex, as the October 2, 1884 *Alta California* reported that an Isaac L. Lang was arrested at his 1209½ Golden Gate Avenue home, for embezzlement.

It is uncertain which schools Joe attended; he seemingly never revealed this. It is known that Miriam and Edwin attended Lowell High School. Maurice graduated in May, 1881 from South Cosmopolitan Grammar School, the same month and year that Miriam graduated from The Girls' High School.[8] Lowell was known as The Boys' High School, when Joe might have been there. In 1875, the school had moved into a new three-story building on Sutter Street, between Gough and Octavia. At least one of

Joe's cousins, Aaron Choynski, graduated from Lincoln Grammar School, at the corner of 5th and Market, a magnificent structure.[9]

Joe: "I can't remember when I had my first fight. But, if you know anything at all about old San Francisco, you must understand that we were always fighting. First, we battled for the championship of our block. Next, we fought to see which kid would be the king-pin of his school. Ultimately, of course, we had gang fights." In 1919, journalist-cartoonist Ed Hughes claimed that Joe enjoyed "fights as spectator and participant at a picnic ground at North Beach, an isolated section of Frisco. Altho (sic) billed as amateur exhibitions, these ... were genuine fights ... Towheaded Joe 'came thru' several of the tournaments and laid the foundation for his spectacular exploits in the ring." The veracity of this is unproven.[10]

By age 20, Joe had made the decision to tread his own, unique path. Most California Jews, after the Gold Rush, encouraged a lifestyle of education, sports being little known in their circles. Still, there existed an element that admired proficiency in self-defense. As one Jewish writer put it, "It is no secret there are those who feel strongly ... that they would swap the greatest inventor or artist of the race, in return for a man who could prove himself the greatest fighting machine in the world."[11] "Joe Boe," as Isidor sometimes called him,* discovered he not only had a great talent for fisticuffs, but eventually, that he wanted to make it his life's work. At the time, "prizefighting" was looked upon by many as beneath contempt, a ruffian's sport. Indeed, there were many instances of fixing and the sport was followed closely by gamblers, with little regulation or supervision. Still, Joe set out intrepidly on the course he chose, the only one of the Choynski men not to have pursued a strictly "intellectual" occupation.

* Had Joe changed his surname to Coe, as his mother, sister and a brother did in 1921, he might have been referred to as "Joe Boe Coe!"

Joe left school at age 16. He mentions hanging around the docks and learning tricks, like soaking one's face in brine to toughen the skin. Joe said he picked up this tip from Chinese friends, adding: "As a boy, I was tall and slender, with a mop of blonde hair. This was always flopping. It gave me a wild appearance, and thus hung on me the soubriquet of 'Chrysanthemum Joe.' This clung to me through life." Jim Corbett recounted, in 1897: "My old friend Joe Choynski had become a professional pugilist. Joe and I had gone to school together and we had fought each other again and again after school without any science, but with a good deal of ginger."[12] Jim began in 1872 at St. Ignatius, a parochial school, but was expelled for fighting a bully, "Fatty" Carney. He later attended Sacred Heart College, but was again expelled, this time for an altercation with one of the schoolteachers, a Catholic Brother. It is unlikely that I.N. would have allowed his children to attend a Catholic school, and Joe said he never saw Corbett until he was 16 (chapter 27). Most likely, Joe attended the public schools closest to his residence, which changed over the years, and went to several schools.

Joe wrote, for the December, 1932 *Ring*, "California's Golden Age of Boxing": "When I was a boy, California furnished a romantic setting for many contests that made ring history ... the entire Pacific Coast swarmed with fighters, some from other parts of our country, others from Australia, the reason ... I presume, the extraordinary popularity of John L. Sullivan. Sullivan was the idol of every boy in our city. I doubt there was one section of San Francisco ... that didn't boast of at least one fistic aspirant. In the Mission section, the hairy-chested, hard-boiled mugs ... tried to emulate the ... Strong Boy. Sailors aplenty were among the scrappers. These tattooed, burly-shouldered fellows, fearless, full of fight, kept the local battlers busy and many scraps, often impromptu affairs, were replete with action. Those were the days when San Francisco ... was the nation's capital of boxing. The streets ... swarmed with fistic celebrities ... each had ... hangers-on. Finish fights were the rule ... The modern 10-round two-step was considered worthy only of preliminary lads. Two- or three-ounce gloves were used when the knuckles were upholstered at all, and fights with skin-tight gloves or bare knuckles were frequent. There was no padding on ring floors. When your bean hit the boards you felt it – if you remained awake."

Not least among the ethnic rivalries in the city was that involving the Irish and the Jews. That between the Corbetts and Choynskis has been well documented. Joe: "There was jealousy and keen competition. You fought well, or you didn't. And if you didn't – well, that was just too bad. You took a licking as often as a seal takes a bath. My mother hated fighting. But I didn't. I loved it. Like Bob Fitzsimmons, I acquired much of my strength in a blacksmith shop; also in a candy factory – by rolling and carrying 300-pound barrels of sugar up three flights of stairs ... I did a lot of 'pulling' on 50-pound batches of gooey candy. If those things won't develop a man's back, legs, and arms, nothing will! Hence, my punch. But, in spite of all this, I knew little or nothing of real fighting when I had my first clash with James J. Corbett. Corbett, on the other hand, was even then regarded as a wizard. He was fast as light and keen as a razor ... I had my following, and Jim had his. We were born to clash."[13] The era saw the transition from the old, bareknuckle, London Prize Ring rules, to the new, gloved, Marquis of Queensberry code. Sullivan would defend his Prize Ring crown against Jake Kilrain on July 8, 1889, but Joe and Jim were strictly glove fighters.

The candy factory where Joe worked was said to be George F. Roberts & Company, located since at least 1874 at 1301 Polk, on the northwest corner of Polk and Bush streets. In 1889 it is listed at 1301 Powell, likely a misprint of the Polk address. The 1890 *City Directory* shows the factory at a new location, 101 Post. The blacksmith shop where he worked may have been the one owned by Joe's friend, Edward Matthew Graney, or the shop owned by Ed's father, George G. Graney, an immigrant from Ireland who taught his son the trade.[14] The December 3, 1896 *San Francisco Call* called Graney "Joe Choynski's friend and backer since the Mission lad first quit his candy manufacturing bench for the ring."

Joe, in 1932: "The enormous strength I acquired in my blacksmith and candy factory toil may be judged by a throw I made of the 16-pound hammer when still a youth. One day ... I was watching the famous Scotch athlete, Tom Carroll, then champion hammer-thrower, practicing in a sand lot. This was the Carroll who taught Bob Edgren to throw the hammer. Carroll was over 6' tall and weighed over 200 pounds. He would hurl the weight and we youngsters would return it for another heave. Once the hammer fell near me and I picked it up by the wooden handle used in those days and flung it back almost to the feet of the champion, a distance of nearly 90 feet, which was the record in those days. I will never forget the look of amazement on Carroll's

Joe Choynski, allegedly 1886

face. After staring at me a few seconds he exclaimed, 'My word!' and strode away. My first boxing was with fellow employees at the candy factory. I had all the worst of it at the start, but quickly discovered a way to handle my left. It must have come naturally, for I had never seen a real boxer in action. One of my pals of that time was Eddie Graney, who later became famous as a fighter and bookmaker. Graney and I joined the Golden Gate Athletic Club, where our dues were $1 a month each. There we had plenty of boxing with other sturdy youths, eager, like ourselves, to master glove science."

"My natural quickness and strength soon gave me supremacy over all the club boxers. Occasionally some amateur from other clubs visited the Golden Gate gym and they all found me too tough ... Gradually I acquired a reputation around the gymnasiums and street corners of San Francisco, second only to ... Jim Corbett, and this led ultimately to my finish fight with (him). Jim was two years older ... and had been for several years building up more than local fame. Corbett had been tutored at the swell Olympic Club under Walter Watson, an eminent boxing instructor, who had come over from England seeking the job as instructor at the New York Athletic Club. Mike Donovan was also after the job, and it was arranged to have a glove battle ... to decide the matter. This meeting resulted in a victory for Donovan, and he got the position. Watson then accepted an offer from the San Francisco club. He was a graduate pupil of the great Jem Mace, which means he was master of boxing science ... at these clubs California's future greats were tutored." A 1922 paper claimed, incorrectly, that Joe and Jim used to "fight at least once a week" at the Olympic Club.[15]

Ed Graney was born July 24, 1868 on Clara Street in San Francisco. The June 29, 1913 *San Francisco Call* claimed: "On May 7, 1887 ... Graney, James J. Corbett and Joe Choynski were made honorary members of the California Athletic Club, and all joined the Golden Gate Club, of which Corbett became boxing instructor. The Golden Gate Club was located in Stevenson Street near 3rd ... in this club Eddie Graney did his first boxing of note ... the first ... to put on the gloves with Young Griffo, upon the arrival of that ... marvel from Australia ... also first to don the mittens with Bob Fitzsimmons, when the New Zealand horseshoer arrived ... Graney ranked as the best trial horse of the club and boxed with new men of all classes, invariably acquitting himself with credibility." Corbett was known to have taught at the Olympic Athletic Club, not the Golden Gate A.C.

Corbett recalled, for the October 2, 1915 *Boston Journal*: "Do you know ... Joe ... would have been the greatest fighter in the world if the Choynskis had lived more than four blocks away from the Corbetts? Yes, sir, Joe was unfortunate in that I lived too near him. I grabbed all the fire that might have been his. Joe spent so much of his early career trying to whip me, he let fame duck around the corner on him. It was just a feud between the Corbetts and the Choynskis. It started when some one of the Choynski clan banged one of the Corbett clan on the jaw over a game of marbles. Tom (Corbett) and Joe were in it at the start. I took up the Corbett end and Joe the Choynski side ... We were both good boxers for kids and ... the honor of Hayes Valley depended on the result of every bout. Joe was so good with his fists that I was forced to take the matter of self-defense seriously."

"I used my father's stable for a gymnasium and a horse stall for a ring. I always seemed to improve just enough to beat Joe, although some of the sand lot decisions were mighty close. In the barge fight ... When it came ring time, they told me one man would have to select a pair of driving gloves. That's where I fooled them. I took the larger gloves and let Joe have the skin tight pair. They didn't seem to realize that you can't jar a man half as much with tight gloves as you can with pillows. The tight ones will cut, but they won't jar. It's twice as hard to knock a man out with driving gloves as it is with the regulation pair ... it was up to Joe to cut me if he could. That fight took a lot out of Joe. I don't suppose either of us would have been heard of, pugilistically, had it not been for that row over the marbles, but Joe would have been far more famous had I not always blocked his way." This is the only time a game of marbles was mentioned in the rivalry, begun by a "my brother can beat your brother" challenge. Jim later said he first met Joe at the Corbett home.

"At that time, my older brothers and those of Joe Choynski, worked in the same department in the City Hall ... the tax collector's office. Just how the argument concerning boxing came up between Joe's brother and mine, I don't know. But, one night at the supper table, my brother Frank said ... 'Jim, there's a boy named Choynski coming over here to box with you, and I want you to box better than ever before in your life. Go out to win, Jim.' Frank's request seemed to me a bit strange, but I didn't question it. We were mighty

Jim Corbett, 1893

fond of each other, and what Frank asked me he got – if it was in my power to give. So I just said: 'All right, Frank: I'll show the best I've got.' "

"Soon after supper, the doorbell rang – the Choynski boys had come. I went out into our yard, and there, for the first time in my life, saw Joe Choynski, who was to become my great rival. He was a wonderful looking youngster, blond haired, pink cheeked, extremely intelligent, clean cut and beautifully built. He appealed to me ... as a young Hercules, and he certainly was the finest looking kid I'd ever had for a ring foe ... I whispered to my brother, Frank: 'Who is this kid?' 'Well, he's a champion – so his brothers say ... the best boxer in his neighborhood, and his brothers think he is a lot better than you, Jim. Now, I want you to prove to-night that he isn't.' ... we all walked to the 'arena' ... the livery stable my father kept ... The buggies were pushed back from the center of the driveway, so as to leave a little square in which we could box. The buggy seats served as a 'grandstand,' with my father's horses ... as bleacher spectators. The only light ... from gas jets on the wall, at a point somewhat removed from the 'ring.' "

"When the gong – an old dishpan – was banged, Joe and I went at it, hammer and tongs. There wasn't any initial 'fiddling.' Neither of us knew much about the science of the game in those days. All we knew was that the other fellow should be hit – and we certainly did hit. Standing in the center of the ring, we slugged, toe-to-toe. It was a biff-bang, biff-bang, with no quarter given and none asked. Perhaps one or another of our brothers hit the dishpan when the first three minutes of boxing was completed. I don't know, because I didn't hear it. If Joe heard it, he ignored it. Both of us were too intent upon swatting the other to think about resting for a full minute. So we kept at it, pounding away with all the power that was in us, hitting sometimes, missing often, but ever aggressive."

"The bout had gone along about seven minutes or so ... growing a little more furious each minute, when I succeeded in pushing a right-hander against Joe's jaw. It stunned him a bit and he backed away. I followed ... shooting in rights and lefts, as best I could in my unskilled way. And, finally my efforts were successful, because the constant battering stopped Joe – and I was the winner of the bout. As Joe and his brothers were leaving the stable, my brother, Frank, yelled to Joe's brother: 'Hey, Herbert, do you think my brother is the champ now?' 'No!' shouted Herbert Choynski. 'Your kid's good, alright, but Joe can beat him. And he'll do it some day – you just watch and see if he don't.' 'You'll find Jim Corbett ready any time Joe wants to meet him again,' was Frank's retort."

In 1930, Joe said he "was born to fight. One day, like a bolt from the blue, I got an invitation from Corbett ... to come to the Corbett livery-stable for a little set-to. Up to this time, I had never seen (him). He had been tutored at the exclusive Olympic Club ... I ... in the streets and on the sandlots. There is plenty of difference." I believe not enough has been made of this difference in training. Corbett has been portrayed as the amateur and Choynski as the professional, which is extremely misleading. Joe was a pro in only the most technical sense, with but a fraction of Jim's experience. Corbett often sparred with the best professionals in the country when they visited San Francisco. He had the finest fistic schooling and used the Olympic club's gym frequently, working out several times a week, whereas Joe's training was spotty. This first meeting occurred in 1884. In 1927, Joe said the Corbett family lived upstairs over the stable.[16]

"I went to the stable accompanied by my brother Maurice. Corbett and I started boxing ... among the horses ... it didn't take me long to tumble that he had stumped me as far as science goes. We fought with bare knuckles. Corbett's speed dazzled me. He moved like a flash of lightning. The 1st ... was fast as thought. Before the initial session was over, I realized I would have to pick up many pointers if I hoped to hold my own with Corbett. He danced around ... like an apparition. He gave me a boxing lesson for two rounds. I was busier than a bird-dog. When I wasn't ducking ... I was trying to dodge the flying heels of the excited horses. There was no referee and no decision, but I gave Corbett credit for out-boxing me. We shook hands and parted. But I knew there was going to be bad blood between us. My brother, Maurice, worked at the City Hall. So did Corbett's brother, Harry.

They took up the feud. Maurice issued a challenge ... through Harry. It was arranged that we should meet at the Dog Pound."

Jim wrote, for the June 15, 1917 *Syracuse Herald*: "The victory I had achieved ... in my father's livery stable failed to convince Joe's brother that I was Joe's superior in boxing. And so his brother and mine continued their arguments ... for many months. Finally, Joe's brothers, making light my ability in their youthful way, said to my brother Frank: 'Oh, well, it's no trick to win a bout with gloves. But, in a bare knuckle contest, a man's fight, Joe could give your brother Jim an artistic beating.' 'Joe can have his chance, any time he wants it!' retorted Frank ... a match was arranged, bare knuckles ... to the finish the next Sunday morning."

Jim promised his father he would walk to the Choynski home (1209 Golden Gate Avenue) and tell Joe he was pulling out of the fight, so as not to risk his job at the Nevada Bank. Jim arrived with that intention, but when Maurice answered the door, he (according to Corbett) wouldn't let Jim see Joe. Maurice said something to the effect of, "Oh, Joe's here, all right. He's not the type to back down when he says he'll fight. When you see him this afternoon, he'll knock you all over the lot." Jim's temper flared, and he told "Chauncey," "Bring him out now, and I'll show you." Corbett wrote, in his assisted autobiography, *The Roar of the Crowd*, "the five of us walked three or four miles to the sandhills beyond the limits of the town, stopping at a little hollow, where we peeled to the waist."

"The only spectator was a man out for his Sunday afternoon walk with a baby in his arms, and there he sat, enjoying this free entertainment, little realizing, I suppose, that of those two slugging 'kids' one was later to be a near champion, the other champion heavyweight of the world!" Some later accounts give the location as "on the bench near the famous Cliff House." In 1913, Corbett told Robert Ripley (of "Believe It Or Not" fame) that the pair met "about the sand hills out toward the Cliff House." In 1917, Jim gave the locale as "about three miles ... outside the city. Soon we came to a little valley." In his 1927 memoirs, however, Choynski said of the "Dog Pound," it is "now at Lake-street in the Presidio."[17]

Joe: "I went to the Dog Pound with Maurice and Frank Nichols. Corbett ... had ... eight or 10 members of his Hayes Valley 'gang' with him. This didn't look so good. Jack Gallagher was timekeeper. There was no referee. We went ... with bare knuckles. Again, I was dazzled by Corbett's speed. That lightning-like left ... tapped my beezer before I could think. His feet were twinkling like a tap dancer's. Blows came so fast I couldn't begin to dodge them. I stopped plenty. Then, with no secret hope that I could even land the lick, I started a mighty heave for Corbett's head. It landed, biff! on his temple – and Corbett toppled to the ground. That thrilled me! Instantly, Gallagher called 'time.' ... my friend Frank Nichols set up a yell: 'Run, Joe – you and Maurice – you've got no chance here now!' I knew he referred to Corbett's gang. After that knockdown of their favorite, I wouldn't have even a dog's chance, here in the Dog Pound. So, Maurice and I started to pull out. But here, Corbett jumped up ... sore as a goat. He paid no attention to me. He leaped at Maurice. 'You're responsible for this!' he yelled, and ... handed poor Maurice a peach of a wallop on the nose! To this day, I don't know why he took it out on my brother."

Jim said, in 1894, that he punched Maurice "for having made me break my promise to my father." *The Roar of the Crowd*: "I also had the satisfaction of putting out for the count his older brother, who was much bigger and stronger than I."[18] "Joe and I went at it hammer and tongs ... from the start ... this was a bare-fist fight ... the blows stung harder than ... the first time with gloves. Right at the start ... Joe hit me a terrific ... punch on the jaw that nearly knocked me out. But, I rallied ... and went after Joe. After about seven minutes of mixing it, I hooked one to Joe's chin ... victory was mine." The 3rd clash would come in 1889. In 1930, Joe names Maurice Choynski and Harry Corbett as the two who worked at City Hall. Jim sometimes gives the pair as Herbert Choynski and Frank Corbett. Boxing historians usually name them as Herbert and Harry, a combination of the two. It appears, though, that Herbert and Frank were the rivals at City Hall. In 1892, Jim wrote: "Frank is a clerk in the Assessor's office in 'Frisco."[19]

Upon Jim's return, his parents expressed concern that reports of the fight getting back to the bank might jeopardize his occupation as a clerk. "Then I hurried back to the house and, dodging my folks, slipped up to my room to clean up the marks of the battle; but the two boys with me were so excited over the outcome that they rushed into the stable and told my father I had whipped Choyinski (sic). He came up to my room and said, rather sadly, 'Jim is it true that you had a fight with Choyinski, after what you promised me?' 'Yes, Dad,' I confessed, 'but I couldn't help it. If you had heard the names they called me, you'd have fought, too. If I had backed out, I would have been a coward. I licked him and his brother, too.' 'What!' retorted Dad, 'not only Joe but that big fellow (Maurice) who goes past the door every morning?' 'Yes, Dad, the two of them.' " Corbett, like Jim Jeffries and Jack Johnson, was prone to exaggeration and braggadocio, so he may have embellished somewhat. Jim said his father, Patrick, uttered, "You licked – the *two* Choynski boys? Aah! To hell with the bank!"[20]

The Olympic Club, which Jim joined in 1884, was founded in 1860. Still going, it is the oldest athletic club in the United States. The exact dates of his first two bouts with Joe are unknown, but occurred sometime in 1884 or 1885. The 3rd took place March 23, 1887 at the Olympic Club. It was the last bout of the evening, set for five rounds, having been arranged by "Professor" Watson. Jim was originally to have faced Joe McAuliffe, a 6' 3" bruiser nicknamed "The Mission Giant," but for some reason the match fell through. Fighting preliminary were Watson, Tom Cleary and Dewitt Van

Court. Joe: "I was asked by Corbett to take the place of the Mission Giant, appear before the gents, in tights and everything. This made me laugh. I told Corbett I had never been in a ring, and that I owned no tights. Corbett said he'd get me a pair. And he did. But, he got 'em so tight I was afraid to bend. They were three sizes too small. Corbett was well seconded. He had Billy Delaney and Walter Watson in his corner. They provided no seconds for me. I guess Corbett made a monkey out of me for the first two rounds. His speed was indecent. I didn't know it then but I realized later that I was in there with the fastest thing in heavyweights the ring has ever developed."

"That left hook shook me repeatedly for two or three rounds. Then, feeling pretty sure Corbett couldn't stow me away, I sailed in and cut loose with everything I had. I forgot the swell club ... the clustered gentlemen and the influence of Corbett, and pegged away ... for all I was worth. I kept this up for the 3rd, 4th and 5th rounds ... although Corbett knocked me down, I doubted whether he could knock me out. I was strong, but untrained. I guess I fooled him. Corbett was, of course, in perfect condition. He had been training every day – often spending hours on the development of one punch – while I knew nothing of gyms, and spent my time wielding a sledgehammer and wrestling with 300-pound sugar barrels. So I was pretty badly winded when we finished the five-round bout at the Olympic. There was no referee, but I agreed that Corbett out-pointed me."

"In the shower-room ... some fellow poked his head in the door and pitched a pair of five-dollar gold pieces on the floor ... I had never seen the man before. Then Corbett came in. He asked: 'Did Brown give you some money?' I showed him the gold coins. Corbett grabbed one of the fives. 'Half of it is for me,' he snapped, and I let it go at that. For the first time, I began to see the real possibilities in scientific boxing. Corbett ... was far advanced along those lines. I ... began a concerted effort to master ... the finer points ... I had relied on my strength and fine recuperative powers. Now I began an earnest study of footwork. I developed my left ... feinting and countering. But ... I had no shrewd trainers ... as Corbett had."[21]

In 1892, Joe claimed: "It was not a fight in any sense of the word, and so far as Corbett's defeating me, I had so much the better of it that at the finish some of the spectators jumped into the ring and carried me out on their shoulders. I was only 17 ... had never before sparred in public ... I should not then have done so but the man who was to have sparred with Corbett disappointed and Corbett ... asked me to appear. 'You'll get $10,' he said, 'and it will only be a friendly set-to.' I told him I didn't want the money, as I desired eventually to join the club as an amateur. In the 1st round Corbett knocked me down once or twice and I thought to myself that there is not much friendliness about this, so I started in to punch, and from that time got the better of it. Just before the commencement of the last round I heard someone whisper to Corbett, 'Go in and knock him out,

Jim.' 'All right,' said Corbett, 'I'll put him out in this round.' "

"This nerved me and I went for him. After the fight someone threw me two five-dollar pieces ... Corbett rushed up ... in his impulsive, gushing manner and said, 'Did you get that, Joe? ... The money' 'Yes' ... he took one of the coins and said, 'Give me this' ... rushed off again ... saying ... 'So long, Joe; see you again soon.' From that time we did not meet in the ring until our actual fight ... on a barge." The bulk of the card was "between (Watson's) pupils of the Acme Club of Oakland and the Olympians. Corbett scoring a clean knockdown in the 1st ... another in the 2nd. In the 3rd, both administered ... heavy hitting, and ... ended with Choyinski clinching to avoid punishment. In the 4th honors were easy ... the 5th ... Choyinski ... caught Corbett on the cheek, receiving a stinger in return on the forehead. Short-arm fighting followed, Choyinski going down several times to get away ... (it) ended in some very hard-hitting ... in favor of Corbett."[22]

Jim Corbett, 1893

Joe mentions tilts with men named Jack McCauley, O'Sullivan and J. O'Connell, but these have not been found in newspaper reports. The November 27 *Police Gazette* echoes a McCauley bout, but gives no date. The September 12, 1896 London *Mirror of Life* said he fought Jack McAuley (sic) and Pat Sullivan two rounds each, sometime in 1887. In 1937, Joe said: "Jack Lynch charged me like a wild bull in the 1st round ... at the Golden Gate Club. I sidestepped and knocked him dead in his tracks. When he woke up he roared, 'Say, young feller, what in hell's your name?' 'I'm Joe Choynski' ... 'Ye-uh,' he replied, 'but what's your real name?' "

Joe faced Tom Moran on July 22 in the North Beach Athletic Club, on the corner of Green and Stockton streets. The club was described by the *Alta California* as a dingy room with "only five or six rough pine benches and a patched up ring." Choynski went under the alias "Joe King," probably to avoid his mother finding out about the "contest to a finish between Joe Choynski ... of the Golden Gate Athletic Club, and Moran, the would-be fighter of the Beach. Never has a more ridiculous exhibition been given in this city. Moran was made a holy show of ... completely licked by the first blow struck. Despite ... given 22 seconds to respond to the call of time and six minutes rest between the 1st and 2nd rounds, he ... quit before the 2nd round was finished." *Police Gazette*: (calling him Ed Choynski) "Choynski is still in his teens, but notwithstanding his youth, he has gained a well-earned reputation for being a game and dashing boxer. Moran is short, strong and muscular, and when stripped ... to strangers would have been the favorite."

"The 1st round opened with a few preliminary feints from both ... In less than 10 seconds ... Moran was on his back under the ropes, impelled ... by a terrific blow in the face. He scrambled to his feet, apparently none the worse ... Choynski pounced in ... with the agility of a cat, and with a straight shot on his nose, sent him to the floor again in such a used-up condition that, after a 20-second rest, he had to be assisted to his corner. The round lasted just 22 seconds. Moran was encouraged by his friends into opening the 2nd round, but his lively antagonist quickly made him measure his length on the floor, and the fight was given to Choynski. Moran did not get in a blow. Tom Barry ... before the exhibition commenced, announced to several members of the club that if Moran failed to appear he would do up Choynski just for pastime ... when the bout was over, Barry was ... told that Choynski would be pleased to meet him. The well-known pugilist ... said he did not want to fight a second-hand man, and an offer of $30 from the club, win or lose ... for four rounds was no inducement ..."[23]

Joe took on Joe Connolly (or Connelly), on the night of September 7 at the Golden Gate Athletic Club. Located at 109 Stevenson Street,[24] it was organized January 29, 1887, and the next year would have a membership of 500. It became the primary venue Joe was identified with. The first event was a running high-jump from a springboard, 15 feet from a string stretched 6' 4" above the ground, cleared by A.H. Lean. Next came a contortion act, two trapeze artists and a four-round boxing contest. This was followed by a parallel bar exercise by the Eintracht Club and a Greco-Roman wrestling match. The Connolly fight was the club's first heavyweight championship. At 10:30 p.m., Joe entered the ring, with seconds, J.B. Howard and C.J. Tillson. Connolly and handlers, Jim Toland and Frank Connolly, soon followed. Jack Hall, newly-arrived from Sydney, refereed. The fighters went right at it, the *Alta California* calling the 1st about even. Connolly started the 2nd frame with a rush, getting in two shots to Joe's head. Choynski battered the Irishman all over the ring. Connolly dropped to the floor to avoid punishment. In the 3rd and final round, Connolly came out gamely, with a "highly colored eye." Joe caught him with a stinging left in the neck or eye. The *Police Gazette* said he followed with a right uppercut. Connolly was deposited on the ring floor, unable (or unwilling) to rise, even after the 10 seconds were counted. Choynski was the heavyweight champion of the Golden Gate Athletic Club.[25]

As noted earlier, I.N. Choynski was proud of his son, even as he understood that esteem for a prizefighter's abilities wasn't universal. In the September 23, 1887 *American Israelite*, he wrote: "We are coming father Abraham!* The boys of the Jewish persuasion are getting heavy on their muscle. Many ... are training to knock out J. L. (John L. Sullivan), and it may come to pass. It is almost an everyday occurrence to read in our papers that a disciple of Mendoza ... has knocked out the best of sluggers, who point with pride to their ancestors ... This week a youngster, who calls himself J.B. Choynski, 19 years old, native of this city, weighing 160 pounds, fought for the championship and gold medal with one named Connelly (sic), and the lad with the Polish name knocked the well-knitted Irish lad of much experience, out in three rounds, and carried off the medal ... triumphantly. The Choynski is a candy-maker, works every day and does not go into training; but has bones like unto Tubal Cain."[26]

* From the 1862 Civil War marching song, "We Are Coming, Father Abraham." The "Abraham" refers to President Abe Lincoln.

"I knew that boy's grandfather quite well – he is dead several years, but if the pious, learned grandfather could lift his head from the grave and look upon the arena where mostly the scum of society congregate, and behold his grandson slugging and sparring and fighting and dodging ... he would hang his head and exclaim ... What is this horrible show for?" So, while Isidor could feel pride in his son's victories, he realized that "old school" Jews would have experienced revulsion at one of their own as a "box-fighter." I.N. described his sons as "four great, big, stalwarts, who are Turn Verein‡ fellows, and are, I think, able to knock Sullivan out ... in a single round." He certainly held a high opinion of his boys!

‡ A turnverein is a German athletic club, originally for tumblers (gymnasts), but which later included other sports and physical activities.

Indeed, none of Isidor's sons were afraid to use their fists. June 8, 1892 *San Francisco Chronicle*: " 'John Doe Schancy, alias Choynski,' was entered on the city prison register yesterday. The prisoner was Morris Choynski, a brother of Joe, the prize-fighter. He was ... charged with battery of S. Jacobs, a pawn-broker, who claims Morris gave him a terrible beating ... the outcome of a business dispute. A friend ... deposited $40 and he was released." No more was found of the incident. On October 17, 1907, Herbert Choynski was entangled in a bloody brawl with two former associates (chapter 22). Edwin's love of boxing was exceeded only by Joe's. As an affiliate of the Olympic Club, Edwin boxed amateur exhibition bouts, at which he was fairly adept. Evidently, Isidor did not share in the pugilistic prowess of his progeny, as attested by the following: "The Canyonville

(Oregon) school in early days had a well-earned reputation of being hard to manage. I.N. Choynski ... tried it one winter, but he lacked Joe's skill as a fighter, and the boys knocked him down and out." Another account said: "Later, the directors employed I.M. (sic) Choynski. He taught one term and was employed to teach a second term, but the big boys put him out of the schoolhouse through the window and ran him off."[27]

Next for Joe was Billy "Forty" Keneally. The skirmish occurred on November 29, for the heavyweight championship of the Golden Gate club, and the club's new gold medal: "in the shape of a solid gold shield, with a figure of a heavy-weight ... studded with 10 diamonds. It is as handsome a trophy as has ever been given in this city by an athletic club." The medal cost the club $150. Joe received it on October 7, when he sparred with a man named Goldsmith. Munis Leo presented the medal on behalf of the club and it was stipulated that Choynski should defend it for three months, against any member that cared to challenge for it. Walter Watson trained Keneally, who dwarfed Joe in size.[28] "The fight was a slaughter-house exhibition ... Kenealy was a blacksmith and, at that time, knew no more of the ... inwardness of boxing than a kangaroo does of the Koran. For all that he sent Choynski down at the outset, and had him all but out." Time was called at 10:30 p.m. *Police Gazette*: "The heavy-weight amateurs were introduced by the Master of Ceremonies. Professor (William) Miller of Australia was unanimously chosen referee ... The seconds ... Professor Walter Watson and George Maxwell of the Olympic Club for Kenealy and Paddy Carroll and Edward Greeney (sic) for Choynski." The following account is derived from several contemporary papers.[29]

Round 1 – *Police Gazette*: After cautious sparring, Kenealy landed a light left to the chest. Joe countered with a left to the face, but Billy rushed him to the ropes, and "planted some heavy stingers with his left on Choynski's face and body." A left to the jaw staggered Joe, and he "fell to the floor to avoid punishment. On regaining his feet Kenealy rushed ... again, but hit wild and missed many good opportunities for a finish blow ... Choynski was exhausted from a heavy jab ... from his opponent at close quarters. (Joe) ... managed to avoid several blows ... by Kenealy at his neck. Finally the latter forced Choynski to the ropes and knocked him down ... by a right-hand ... on the neck ... Choynski got up and avoided another of Kenealy's swinging blows by ducking." *Alta California*: Near round's end, Billy "threw Choynsky (sic) heavily upon his back ... the call of time alone saved Choynsky."

Round 2 – *Police Gazette*: "Kenealy rushed savagely ... and struck wild. Choynski ... gained his wind and stopped Kenealy several times when the latter rushed him. Kenealy (felt) the effects ... and his excitement cooled off ... his hitting was more effective and he knocked Choynski down four times in this round. The latter fought very gamely, however, and although appearances indicated the contest was Kenealy's, Choynski invariably came up to the scratch when time was called. (Billy) could have won ... if he had followed up ..." *Alta California*: "Kenealy ... caught Choynsky full in the face, staggering him, and followed ... with a knockdown blow."

Round 3 – *Police Gazette*: "Choynski ... moved to the center of the ring ... fresh as a lark ... 'He has gained his second wind!' 'He will win now, sure!' and such ... were heard from all quarters ... Kenealy ducked cleverly from a punishing blow ... at his face ... clinched to avoid an upper cut ... Choynski feinted with his left and planted a heavy right-hand blow straight from the shoulder on Kenealy's nose which drew the claret in abundance. Kenealy was dazed ... Choynski sent in right and left in quick succession with great force on Kenealy's face, neck and body. The latter commenced to show signs of weakness; but, although ... groggy, he managed to get a round-arm blow on Choynski's neck, which brought the latter to his knees. Both men clinched several times ... The round finished in Choynski's favor." *St. Louis Post-Dispatch*: "Kenealy bowled Joe over three times, but in his ignorance kept away ... and allowed him to pull himself together. This Choynski did in good shape, and gave such a battering to the blacksmith that they had to pour water over the latter to keep him awake for the 4th round." The *Alta California* saw things differently: "Choynsky ... scored two knockdowns in quick succession ... the blood flowing freely from both ..."

Round 4 – *Police Gazette*: "Quick hitting and stopping. Choynski ... hit Kenealy several times in the face. One upper cut swelled Kenealy's left eye tremendously. The latter was ... dazed and staggered around the ring ... awaiting a good opening, Choynski swung his left with full force and caught his opponent in the jugular. The blow was decisive. Kenealy dropped to the floor, leaning for support against the ropes, and when time was called he was unable to get up." The *St. Louis Post-Dispatch* differed: "Both men were literally dead to the world. Kenealy's nose, eyes and mouth were bleeding, and both men were gore to the waist. Choynski ended it all by a lucky right-hander, which sent the blacksmith into dreamland." *Alta California*: "Kenealy scored a knockdown. After some terrific fighting, both ... clinched repeatedly ... both were badly cut up, and fell from exhaustion. Kenealy ... received a knockdown which ended the ... fight ..."

A 1915 paper gave the weights as 152 pounds for Joe, 187 for Keneally, a disparity of 35 pounds! That rag, however, seems to give very light stats for Joe in his fights, and exaggerated avoirdupois for his opponents. *Police Gazette*: "Kenealy weighed 165 pounds and Choynski 162 pounds. This was Kenealy's first appearance in a contest for supremacy. Choynski has won several ring contests; in fact, he was never conquered. He has defeated Jack McCauley, P. O'Sullivan, J. O'Connell, and his most important contest was a draw with Jim Corbett at a resort outside of the city limits. Choynski states that Kenealy is by far the best man he ever met (Author: Probably because Joe was angry at Corbett), and were it not for his limited experience in contests to a finish, he thinks that he would have been defeated ... It was the best and gamest battle ... witnessed in this city for many years."[30]

I.N. Choynski contradicted the experience level of Keneally, whilst proudly praising his son, in the December 16, 1887 *American Israelite*: "The young Jew got away with blacksmith (William) Keneally, who is 32 years of age and has been a boxer of many years' standing. The Choynski boy fairly wiped the floor with the Irish gentleman and finished him in four hard contested rounds. The Jews, who take little stock in slugging, are glad there is one Maccabee among them, and that the Irish will no longer boast that there is not a Jew who can stand up to the racket and receive punishment according to the rules of Queensberry. Joe Boe is marching about town ... with his diamond badge pinned to the lapel of his vest ..."

Joe: "I weighed less than 150 pounds but ... won with ... ease. Later I ... defeated such promising heavies as Jack McCauley, Pat O'Sullivan, Jim Hall (colored) and a fellow they called 'The Tipton Slasher.' Now they matched me with Billy ('Forty') Keneally ... Corbett's sparring partner. He weighed 180 ... hard as Bessemer steel. I was to meet Kenneally in an amateur inter-club tournament, but ... club officials called me on the carpet. My amateur standing had been challenged. This fellow Brown was there, though I didn't recognize him until someone asked: 'Mr. Choynski, didn't a man named Brown give you money for boxing Corbett at the Olympic?' I replied: 'A man I didn't know threw two five-dollar gold pieces into the shower-room, but Jim Corbett came in and took one of them!' This stopped them cold."

Corbett, in *The Roar of the Crowd*, says he was raised with "Forty" Keneally and, of the moniker, "Forty": "He was given this nickname because a horse that could go in 2:40 in those days was considered pretty fast, and Keneally was a good sprinter and could travel in quick time himself." Choynski: "So I went after the 180-pound Keneally. I thought I (had) a cinch. But those are the fights that fool you. It was a dog-fight; the rough-and-tumble Keneally almost scoured the chrysanthemum off my dome before I got going good. He pounded me to the floor in the opening round and when I got up I was reeling like a merry-go-round. But I weathered the storm, and we slugged it out until the 4th. Then I nailed Keneally with a left ... reminiscent of the blacksmith shop. Whereupon, Corbett's big sparring partner dropped out for the night. They didn't have to count over him. What they needed was smelling salts."[31]

In 1888, Joe engaged in a series of short, gloved "sparring exhibitions," in which participants boxed, sometimes for points, but didn't try to knock each other out. On the evening of February 14 in the Golden Gate club, he boxed three rounds with Jack (or John) McCaulley (or McCauley), at a benefit for Paddy Carroll, a pug who recently injured an arm boxing at the California A.C. Ironically, Joe sparred defensively because he injured his right arm while boxing the night before. There were four other bouts,

Greco-Roman wrestling, a trapeze act and club-swinging. The club staged its April exhibition on Friday the 13th, which included a three-round spar between Choynski and Joe Bowers. Boxer Frank Glover declined to referee the Joe Mahan-George Smith main event, so Joe did so. Jim Corbett, also present, commended Joe on his control of the fight.[32]

In April, Australian heavyweight champion Peter Jackson arrived in the States. He trained at the Golden Gate club and traveled with Paddy Gorman.[33] On June 26, Joe sparred for the first time with Peter, "four spirited rounds," on the Tom Cleary-"Young Mitchell" Pacific Coast middle-weight title card. An apparently apocryphal tale sprung up at this time. In 1888 or 1889, both posed outdoors for photographs at Barney Farley's roadhouse in San Mateo, in boxing stances. Someone allegedly asked Jackson to show his left uppercut. Peter, who had been trained by Larry Foley to throw straight from the shoulder, supposedly glared at the speaker and said he never heard of the blow. In truth, Jackson used uppercuts and "half-arm" punches, or hooks.[34]

Peter Jackson and Joe Choynski, at Barney Farley's

Choynski was timekeeper for the July 20 Jack McCauley-Edward Cuffe battle at the Golden Gate club. Its August 7 exhibition featured Joe against Cuffe. He was in the corner of Dan Mahoney vs. Jerry Haely. On the evening of August 13 at the Olympic club, Joe seconded Young Brady against Joe Soto. Jim Corbett refereed, and Ed Graney boxed on the card. The next night, Joe tackled a newcomer, George Bush. The *Alta California* called it "a trial exhibition ... testing Bush's qualifications as a pugilist." The 1st frame saw George land a right swing over Choynski's eye that sent him to the floor. He rose, telling Bush the punch was a beauty and made him see stars. The men exchanged punches to the bell. In the 2nd heat, Joe pounded Bush and had him ready to go as time was called. "In the 3rd and last round honors were about even ... it was the general opinion that George was a good one and a hard hitter, but ... out of condition."[35]

On September 28, Joe had a trial against a neophyte named Jim Hall (not the Australian), said to have "recently arrived from Tulare. He is very anxious for a match with Turner, the colored pugilist from Stockton. Hall is also a colored man ... about 165 pounds. In the 1st and 2nd rounds Choyinski (sic) touched his man gently, giving Hall a good opening ... encouraging and drawing him on, but Hall is awkward in handling himself and continually changes position with his dukes. In the 3rd ... Hall let go a wicked swinging right that caught Choyinski in the jaw. This ... raised the fire in Choyinski and he let go ... right and left, catching Hall every time in the face ... dazing him and the call of time was all that saved him ... being put to sleep."[36]

On the October 26 Joe McAuliffe-Mike "The Ithaca Giant" Conley card, Choynski fought a "heavy-weight iron-molder" named W. Cantwell. The *Chronicle* called him Frank Cantwell, saying he was repeatedly floored in a "slogging match." The *Mirror of Life* said "Jem Contwell." *Alta*: The fight "was first-class and nearly ended in a knock-out, as Joe landed some heavy blows in the 4th ... sending blood flying in all directions ... knocked down two or three times, Cantwell was ... willing to quit when time was called." Billy Jordan was

Peter Jackson, 1888

"master of ceremonies." In these pre-public-address-system days, Billy's booming bellow could be heard all over an arena. A 1944 article said Frank P. Cantwell was a bicycle enthusiast from Tacoma, Washington, who later organized the Tacoma contingent of Jacob Coxey's "Army."[37]

Joe was originally to be the temporary boxing instructor at the Golden Gate Athletic Club in the absence of regular instructor, Con Riordan (sometimes, Riordon). Con likely had given Joe some tutoring in the sport. Ed Cuffe took Riordan to Centerville, California to train him for a bout against George Bush. Bush was getting into trim at Joe Dieves' place, and the fight was slated for the same club. Cuffe instead chose Choynski to train him.[38] Yet another change of plans would soon begin Joe's career as a professional boxer, and end his time as a "simon-pure."

Round Three

The Professional
(November 1888 – April 1889)

A monumental event was on the horizon for our subject, his first match in the punch-for-pay ranks. It took place on the night of November 14, against the same George Bush he boxed a "trial" with in August. Joe's pro debut has been handed down as an impromptu event and indicated as such by him; one incited by occasion rather than premeditated choice. There is at least one dissenting voice, however. In a 1943 *Police Gazette*, a Centerville, California senior signing his letter only as "Old Timer" offered his (alleged) first-hand account of Joe's 1st pro fight: "It was probably staged ... for the benefit of the ... customers. However, I and others knew Joe was going in as a principal that night, prior to the fight." "Old Timer" incorrectly refers to Ed Cuffe (of Buffalo, New York) as "Joe Brooks." "Joe (Choynski) came to Centerville during his vacation to train Joe Brooks ... for a fight, I think, at the Golden Gate Club. Before leaving for San Francisco, he told some of the boys that Brooks had a small insect bite on his hand and wanted the fight postponed. Joe said Brooks was afraid of his opponent, and ... 'If he refuses to fight, I'll go in there and lick him, myself.' He did."

On the 14th, the Golden Gate Athletic Club put on their monthly fight card, the main event to be Bush vs. Cuffe. The gymnasium was filled to overflowing, but club President Steinbach announced that, due to a sore left hand caused by blood-poisoning, Ed Cuffe would not be able to fight. A Dr. Chaignau had "lanced the afflicted spot and declared it impossible for Cuffe to abide by his contract. Cuffe advanced and exhibited his injured hand, and as he is a plucky fellow who has afforded sport to the club before, a shower of silver fell in the ring from charitably disposed members willing to tide the unfortunate fellow over his period of ill luck."[1]

Choynski, having just arrived from a "wedding supper" for one of his friends at the candy factory, volunteered to fight Bush in Cuffe's place. "The spectators gave three rousing cheers for Choynski, who afterward appeared in the ring accompanied by his seconds, Paddy Gorman and Young Granger." Other papers called Granger "George Greaney" or "Smithy." This was almost certainly Ed Graney, the blacksmith.[2] Bush's cornermen were Sam Fitzpatrick and Tom Keefe (or Keep). Fitzpatrick (born Samuel Fitch in Maitland, Australia) would soon become the trainer of Peter Jackson and later, of Jack Johnson. Billy Jordan refereed and "Professor" Walter Watson was a timekeeper. The *San Francisco Chronicle* said both men wore black tights and no shirts; Bush was taller but looked a bit flabby. Choynski's muscles stood out in bold relief.

Joe: "Then oddly, as such things happen, I turned professional. But ... it all happened so suddenly that I scarcely knew how the trick was turned. Eddie Graney ... knew nothing of the affair. I think he was even more surprised than I was. Bush, who stood 6' 3" tall, had come to the Golden Gate to condition George Godfrey for a battle with ... Peter Jackson. Graney and I waited for the two giants to appear, but there was a delay. Suddenly, the announcer yelled: 'I am sorry, but there has been a hitch in the arrangements. Ed Cuffe has a poisoned hand, and the club physician will not allow him to ... fight.' There was bitter disappointment. Part of the crowd began booing, but others demanded: 'A substitute. Get a good man and give us a fight!' Eddie Graney looked at me. 'But where'll they find a substitute?' he demanded.

"Tuxedo" Eddie Graney, circa 1903

'There's nobody –' I jumped up. 'Oh, yes there is!' I said ... on the spur of the moment, I agreed to turn professional and take on a man as big as a piano-box! They thought I was crazy, and I suppose I was a little balmy at the moment, but I had made my announcement and I meant to stick to it. The crowd ate this up. The sportsmen gave me a rousing cheer as I started for the dressing-rooms. They hated disappointments as much as I did."

"Well, here we were in our corners – and I felt somewhat of a thrill. Yes, and ... a little guilty, too! My first professional fight! What an hour it was! Then, the wedding we had attended rose up to taunt me, and I thought, with horror, of the cake, ice-cream and port wine in my stomach! 'This fight,' I said to myself with ... conviction, 'has got to end quickly. If that giant ever hits me in the lunch – good bye, wedding feast!' The Maine giant looked terribly big standing over there, big and hairy and full of fight. I guess he rated me as a joke, a skinny little apparition to be pushed over with a wave of the hand. The bell banged ... Bush must have been in a hurry. He began rushing me and plastered my chrysanthemum with sledgehammer rights. One caught me on the beezer and the claret was flowing freely. But, I had enough red-ink on board to satisfy all the customers. I took four swats to give one. Then, I laced the giant's bread-basket, swarmed him against the ropes, and was beating him like a drum as the gong rang. The crowd was wild. I could hear 'em roaring like Yosemite Falls."

"Two minutes ... sufficed to finish the task ... After some of the hottest and fastest milling of my whole ring career, I found the giant's whiskers with a sugar-barrel right and he decided the unpadded floor was the right spot for him. He didn't get up until long after the cheering subsided. For prostrating this mammoth I received the purse of $900. But the fans were so tickled over my demonstration they insisted on passing the hat. This netted me $760 more. When I went home and showed my mother all this wealth, she scolded me. I think she wanted to cry, for it seemed terrible to her for me to become a fighter; but I consoled her and eventually she was reconciled to the idea." Another version has him forgetfully leaving the money on the kitchen table, his mother finding it and asking her son where it came from. Joe supposedly told her, in an attempt to cover up, that he was merely taking care of the winnings of a boxer he was training. It was only the following morning, after Harriett read about the boxing match in the papers, that Joe admitted to the pro fight. Edwin's wife, Florence, claimed in later years that "Before a fight his mother became upset, behaving like a crazy woman, but the rest of the family overrode her objections."[3] A combined fight description follows:[4]

Round 1 – *Alta California*: Joe "stood with his legs well apart and body inclined backward. He looked cool and confident, but Bush, who sparred at long range and kept his body bent as if suffering from incipient colic, did not look thoroughly at home within the roped inclosure." Joe led off with a left to the neck or nose. George retaliated with an open-handed right to the neck. "Choynski ... forced the fighting and made several left-hand blows, which were of the mixed upper-cut and swing order, but Bush, who wore an anxious look, avoided them by ducking low and clinching. About the middle of the round Bush lowered his head and made a rush, ala (Mike) Conley ... hands down ... and Choyinski (sic) sent in a terrific left-hander straight from the shoulder that caught Bush on the side of the nose, under the left eye, sending him to the floor in a dazed condition." The *Chronicle* and *Police Gazette* said a crashing right to the head floored George and had him bleeding badly. Bush got up and rushed, head down, forcing Joe to the ropes, but took a wicked left uppercut, dropping him a 2nd time. "He arose ... very groggy and the call of time only, saved him from a settler."

Round 2 – Bush ducked a left and rushed again with his head down, "forcing (Joe) to the ropes and taking some heavy undercut punishment."

Joe pushed him away ... Bush sent in an effective left-hander on Choynski's chin ... cross-buttock(ed) Choynski (Author: a London Prize Ring throw, illegal under Queensberry Rules), both going to the floor under the ropes." When they separated, Joe landed a pair of lefts to the nose and a crushing right that caught Bush in the eye and sent him "down into his corner with hands astride of the rope," where he was counted out. The *Chronicle* said Bush was on "his hands and knees, with his head under the lower rope of the ring ... and his seconds had to lift him ... into his chair. The match was for a club trophy ..." The *Police Gazette* said George sustained "a broken nose and the loss of a front tooth." Joe's knockout victory in his first pro fight and the money he earned left an indelible impression on him.

On November 29, Joe was at the Oakland Olympic Grounds, 14ᵗʰ and Center streets in Oakland, as a Field Marshal for the Pacific Coast Amateur Association's Field Day. About 2,000 people attended, among them Jim Corbett, who was also a marshal. Represented were four of the six athletic clubs belonging to the Association: the Olympic Athletic Club, Golden Gate, Acme club, and the University of California A.C. The Field Day was essentially a track meet with a one-mile match bicycle race thrown in. It is claimed in *The Legendary Mizners* (1953): "Corbett was apparently spoiled by hero-worshippers. Joe Choynski once told Will Irwin it was an unwritten law of the Olympic club that anybody who played handball, checkers, billiards or any other game with the Professor (Corbett) had to lose to him in order to humor the young wizard."[5] Choynski states (in 1927) that his subsequent opponent, or at least his next fight of note, was against Frank Glover of Chicago. The next time Joe traded punches in the ring, though, was December 26, 1888, against a newcomer named J.E. McDonald. (The September 12, 1896 *Mirror of Life* calls him "Jem McDonald," while the December 26, 1922 *Oakland Tribune* says, Harry McDonald.) It was a three round try-out for McDonald, "his first trial before an audience."

Alta California: "J.E. McDonald, a recent arrival from Indiana, who tips the beam at 185 pounds and stands over 6' high, was given an opportunity ... to show his qualifications ... Choyinski (sic) forced matters and was sent to the floor twice, but he got in his left on McDonald's eye and ... a stinging right-hander on the jaw that dazed the big fellow. Choyinski could have ended the trial here by knocking his man out if he had felt so inclined. In the 2ⁿᵈ ... the men sparred lightly, both being badly winded ... McDonald tried to get at Choynski's head with his heavy right, but the latter's clever ducking saved him some knockdown blows. Choyinski ... was able to get home whenever he pleased. In the 3ʳᵈ and last round McDonald tried to knock out Joe, but (Joe) ... always in condition, proved ... too clever a boxer for the Indiana man – who has got a great deal to learn ..."[6]

The clash with Glover occurred February 26, 1889 in San Francisco. Several papers referred to it as Choynski's "first appearance in the ring as a professional," although the Bush fight, according to Joe, held that distinction. He referred, however, to the Glover fight as his pro debut on at least one occasion. Joe was being trained by Australian boxer, Tom Meadows, at Joe Dieves' training quarters on San Leandro Road (Alameda), while "Frank Glover has been taking his exercise in Berkeley." Glover showed up "fit as a fiddle." His birth name, according to at least one source, was Frank John Heisenberg. "Glover has quite a reputation as the 'Chicago stock-yard fighter.' "[7] Joe said: "Glover was a big man, and a good one, but I was putting all I had into my professional fights – blacksmith sledges, sugar-barrel wedges, candy-pulling muscles and everything."

On February 25, a group of local sportsmen visited Choynski's training quarters at Joe Dieves' ranch. They said Meadows had whipped Joe into top condition. Glover was trained and handled by Pete O'Brien. "Unlike Choynski, Glover has a record that has won ... him the reputation of ... a first-rate ring tactician."[8] Frank's record shows several obscure victims, but he twice defeated Tommy Chandler, a useful heavyweight who had swapped blows with John L. Sullivan and Jack Burke. Glover claimed he was cheated out of victory in a six round loss to Burke.

FRANK GLOVER.

On the night of the 26th, Frank Glover entered the ring, attended by trainer Billy Delaney and Jim Carr. Choynski was seconded by Tom Meadows and Ed Graney. Hiram B. Cook refereed. Glover wore dark blue tights and black boxing shoes. He had good muscular definition and looked well trained. Joe entered the ring smiling, wearing black tights and checkered running shoes. The weights were given as 175 to 165 in favor of Glover. The pair wore what were described by *The San Francisco Call* as "huge" four ounce gloves. At 9:50 p.m. the fighters shook hands and time was called. Another blend of contemporary accounts follows:[9]

Round 1 – The *Call* said "Joe boxed in his usual peculiar style with his hands wide apart and open and his eyes on his opponent's feet or gloves. Both were smiling and pleasant." Only a few light taps were landed. Choynski, in his faded memory of 1930, contradicted contemporary accounts of a sedate 1st frame: "Frank ... had come West in the ... belief that he could whip the terrible Joe McAuliffe ... it took McAuliffe 49 rounds to stop him. Then, they offered Glover a consolation match – with me ... there was not much consolation ... for our Chicago friend. But I made a mistake in the opening round. I hit Glover too hard. Or I didn't hit him hard enough, I don't know which. Anyway, I knocked him clear through the ropes and into the laps of the customers. They hoisted him back, after some difficulty and a lapse of time, and after this he covered up like a crafty gopher when the cats are stalking the fields. So ... I had to risk breaking my hands in an effort to convince him ... for thus consoling Glover I received $1,750 – and the boys began calling me the best man on the West Coast."

Round 2 – Choynski got a vicious left into Glover's "wind" that left a red mark. Frank worked him into a corner and threw hard, Joe ducking cleverly. Glover swung both hands, but Joe kept ducking and counter-punching with left and right. He staggered the Chicago man, who "began to look serious, while Joe grinned and edged toward him."

Round 3 – Choynski shot a hard left jab to the nose and a steaming right that floored Frank and drew blood. "Glover, upon arising, tried his rushing tactics and got in several blows, but Joe was cool and stood him off." "Choynski did some great leg work ... dodging two ... vicious leads with back jumps ... getting back in time to get in right and left before Glover recovered his balance ..." Joe was using Corbett-like tactics.

Round 4 – The session saw light sparring. Toward the close, Glover got in a good right, either to Joe's nose, jaw or under his eye. "Glover fiddled his hands nervously, while Choynski was slow and cool ..."

Round 5 – *Police Gazette*: "Smiles were traded ... Choynski ... sending his ... to lighten the gloom on Glover's homely mug ... went at the visitor ... banging him right and left ... with irresistible force. His guard was broken down, and his most desperate efforts to ... shield his battered face were futile. He lolled on the ropes and was terribly punished ... When he tried to clinch Choynski held him off with one hand and continued to pound him with his right. No man could stand up under such a fusillade ... and Glover was finally compelled to wriggle ... to the floor to avoid being knocked out ... he was bleeding freely, and Choynski went ... to finish him. He had very little time ... Glover only took three or four of the terrible right-handers before he again sought the shelter of the floor. The ... betting, which had been ... in favor of Glover, took a grand flop in the other direction." The *Alta California* and the *Call* said that at one point, the men clinched on the ropes and both fell to the floor. "The spectators were wild ... when they saw how the Californian fought. Choynski sailed into his quarry again and had Glover almost at his mercy when time was called."

Round 6 – "Glover, though weak, was game ... tried to rush, but ... ran against Joe's gloves ... that made him stagger ... as the gong sounded Joe ... his left ... sent the blood flying from Glover's ... damaged mouth," "landed a good punch on Glover's ribs, and ... got the best of some infighting that compassed the only battling during the round. Glover went to his corner with a very dickey left eye, a bloody nose and fear in his heart."

Round 7 – *Call*: Glover looked weary and scared. Choynski sailed in with both hands and pounded Frank until "the latter ran like a rabbit around the ring to avoid Choynski's dangerous right. Glover tried to get home that swinging right-hand blow he cherishes so fondly, but Choynski was on guard and got cleverly out of danger's way. Glover did not get in one good blow." *Police Gazette*: "Choynski scored hit after hit ... winding up with a tooth-loosening right-hander that started Glover to running ..."

Round 8 – *Call*: "Joe trying to get Glover to lead or rush, but failed ... he followed ... without striking back, stopped blow after blow with apparent ease ... Choynski was evidently saving his strength." *Police Gazette*: "Both were tired ... the round was the one dull one of the fight."

Round 9 – A confident Joe punished his foe "on his ... swelled mouth and closed eye" with repeated jabs "of the (Peter) Jackson stripe ..." "Glover ... getting very weak, managed to get home one good right-hand swing on Choynski's neck, which did not seem to bother ... much." *Police Gazette*: A right bloodied Glover's mouth, and he "was chased about the ring ... taking smash after smash ... The Chicago pug's homely features were dyed a bright red ... the claret pouring in streams from ... nose and mouth."

Round 10 – Joe drove Glover around the ring with straight lefts and rights. "Glover was too weak to strike back, but he took his punishment ... and reeled around like a drunken man." *Police Gazette*: "The only question in anybody's mind ... was Choynski's ability to keep his wind long enough to inflict the vast deal of punishment Glover seemed capable of taking. He ... cross-countering Glover on his insane rush, and giving him a blow on the mouth with his right that started the Chicagoan's teeth to falling out and the blood to flow ... Glover could save himself only by clinching ..."

Round 11 – Glover seemed stronger and better than previously. "Choynski appeared to be a little tired and remained on the defensive." "He got three repeaters in succession on Joe's neck and followed it up by one in the wind. It looked now as if Joe was exhausted and the turning point in Glover's favor had arrived." *Police Gazette*: "The sparring ... was all Glover's way, but he was beyond capability of punishing, and Choynski only laughed as he took the blows intended to break his jaw on the point of his shoulder. He made no returns and was evidently gathering strength for a final effort."

Round 12 – *Alta California*: "Glover got ... his right on Joe's ear, and made a swing with his left for Joe's neck, but the latter ducked and Glover went bang against the ropes ..." *Call*: "Joe ... forced matters and continued to jab his left into Glover's face ... Glover was dazed and staggered, but tried to land his right. Joe merely ducked toward him ... In a wrestle both fell, Choynski on top. Glover ... held on so hard that it took all the referee's strength to get him away. Time saved him again."

Round 13 – *Call*: "Choynski followed ... with a series of blows ... all over Glover's face, making his features (very bloody). Glover took his punishment ... and although barely able to stand ... tried hard to drop his right alongside of his antagonist's ear, but the blow invariably went over the Californian's head and landed softly on his back. Choynski continued to jab his rapidly failing quarry at long range, and when time was called the boy from Chicago was all but a defeated candidate." *Alta California*: "Glover got in a swinging right on Joe's neck and smiled with satisfaction; but what a smile! It even made Joe smile to see such a face as Glover presented."

Round 14 – Choynski was pale and weary, but came out to finish Frank. *Call*: "After feinting once or twice the California boy punched Glover in the mouth, and he ... went groggy ... Joe swung his mighty right and Glover fell like a log." When Frank got up ... Joe crashed "a terrible punch under the ear," driving him to the mat again. The game Glover pulled himself up once more, slowly. *Alta California*: "Joe went for him ... and both men went to the floor, where Glover clasped Joe ... Joe wriggled away ... rushed Glover and both men fought desperately, Glover going down four times in succession. Upon getting up for the 5th time Joe sent in a right ... that caught Glover square in the face, knocking him through the ropes, his head striking the iron railing ... about two feet from the ropes, where he remained ... unconscious ... Glover was terribly punished about the face, while Joe showed only a few lumps on his forehead."

Police Gazette: "The California boy ... dropped his sledge-hammer right on Glover's jaw. The blow would have stopped an ox. Glover was lifted clear off his feet ... thrown between the ropes ... he landed ... on the small of his back on the middle rope ... the spring of the rope dropped his head heavily on the hardwood floor. He was totally unconscious ... dead to the world. Cold water and other restoratives ... applied without avail; finally his trainers had to carry him ... to his dressing room ... insensible ... over half an hour before he recovered sufficiently to take a hack to the Hamman baths."

Papers said Glover "lost half his teeth and his face was badly bruised." "Choynski received little damage and later in the evening was to be seen at the walking match." The *Philadelphia Inquirer* observed that Joe outfought Frank at long-range and dominated the infighting, and his only mark was a "slight contusion over the left eye." The *Chicago Tribune* said it was *under* the eye. Glover said "his legs gave out and he could not get out of the way. 'I got them cramped from running ... a few days before the match, and they were sore and stiff when I entered the ring.' The victor is broad-shouldered and tapers into comparative slimness. He is muscular, active, and sanguine. Speaking to 'Pittsburgh Phil' a few days ago at the Baldwin (Joe) said: 'I don't have to fight unless I want to, but I'll fight as long as there is anything in it until somebody licks me. I think I can lick anybody, and I will think so until somebody licks me.' While he speaks thus confidently ... he does it in a quiet way, and is not given to talking fight. He is intelligent and good-natured, and it is not to be wondered that he is remarkably popular."

The day after the tilt, Referee Patsy Hogan said, "California has found a man in Joe Choynski who is worthy of the name of a first-class pugilist. As a fighter, he is a cool and collected student of his opponent, a straight and effective hitter, a good judge of distance and a dead, game man. His battle with an experienced man like Glover ... proves every word I say ... Glover ... was the worst looking object that ever left a prize ring. He had some of his teeth knocked out, his nose was flattened, both eyes nearly closed, and he was over half an hour coming round after ... knocked out."[10] The March 4 *Alta California* speculated on another match between Joe and Jim: "... the vast improvement shown by Choynski during the past year is expected to more than overcome the differences which formerly existed."

Famous American Referees

Referees: Johnny White, Tim Hurst, Sam Austin, Malachy Hogan and George Siler

On March 13, Joe and Australian boxer friend, Paddy Gorman, were at the Golden Gate Athletic Club to second "Sailor" Brown against "Young Mitchell." Mitchell was Jonathan L. Herget, best friend to Peter Jackson. In the 1890s he would run "Mitchell's Tamale Café," on the corner of Golden Gate Avenue and Taylor Street. Herget had a highly successful career as "Young Mitchell." He was seconded by "Professor" Walter Watson and Martin Murphy. The fight was for $1,500 and the "middleweight championship of the coast." Mitchell kayoed Brown in the 21st round.[11]

The California Athletic Club was one of several venues looking to select

Joe's next opponent. Jim Corbett said it was a Jewish organization, his own Olympic club being a Christian association. Club President L.R. Fulda speculated: "We might match Jim Fell against him but for (Fell's) habit of getting mad and striking the referee. If anyone ever tried anything like that here we would put a couple of special officers at work on him with their clubs."[12] The April 22 *Alta California* said the California club had matched Joe to fight Dave Campbell in June. Campbell was a useful fighter from Oregon who on December 8 held Corbett to a 10-round draw. For some reason, the fight between Choynski and Campbell never materialized. The Club's Board of Directors offered a purse of $3,000 for Corbett to fight Choynski in their building, but Jim was already under contract with the Olympic club. The Olympic would not allow professional contests to take place within its walls, nor let its members or instructors take part in professional clubs. Corbett therefore refused to fight a pro bout with Joe. Instead, he sought to challenge Joe in a private fight for a stake of $1,000.

On April 26, Peter Jackson fought Patsy Cardiff at the California Athletic Club, where Choynski was now boxing instructor. On the undercard, Joe boxed a short exhibition with Con Riordan. Cardiff fought the great John L. Sullivan to a draw several years before, when Sullivan broke the radius of his left arm. Riordan would box an exhibition with Bob Fitzsimmons on November 17, 1894 at Jacobs's Theater in Syracuse, New York, slump into unconsciousness and die the next day. Several sources show the Choynski-Riordan exhibition as a four-rounder, but the next day's *Alta California* said it was three. Joe's next fight was a rematch with his nemesis, Corbett. This time, though, it would be a clandestine affair before an audience comprised of the sporting fraternity and mixed personage.

James John Corbett was born September 1, 1866, more than two years before Joe. He was one of 10 children born to Patrick and Catherine Corbett, six boys and four girls. Jim's younger brother Joe would gain some fame as a Major League Baseball starting pitcher, from 1895 to 1904. He played for the Washington Senators, Baltimore Orioles and St. Louis Cardinals, his Orioles winning the League championship in 1896. Eldest brother Frank worked for a time at City Hall with Herbert Choynski, and brother Harry, older than Jim by two years, became owner of a famous gambling hall and saloon in the city, where a majority of bets on boxing matches occurred. Jim thought innovatively about boxing and refined defensive tactics. He would be known for ability to evade and slip punches, especially those aimed at his head. It was like his head was on a swivel; he could swing it in a circle with lightning speed to avoid blows.

In December, 1925, 28-year-old soon-to-be heavyweight champion, Gene Tunney, sparred with a 59-year-old Jim Corbett on top of the Putnam Building in Manhattan's Times Square. After completing their three two-minute rounds, Gene told writer Grantland Rice: "I honestly think he's better than Benny Leonard. He still had bewildering speed. It was the greatest thing I've ever seen."[13] He said, in the short while he was with old Jim, he learned plenty. While this has a bit of a patronizing tone about it, Tunney was specific enough about the punches and combinations Jim threw, to show he was impressed. Also, rating Jim above Tunney's great stablemate, Leonard, was a high compliment. Corbett, Gene said, mixed up his punches better than anyone he had ever seen, "with the possible exception of Sugar Ray Robinson," who is generally considered the best "Pound-For-Pound" boxer of all time. Gene conversed with Corbett about the sport and said Jim could expound on the "Sweet Science" better than anyone else he knew. "The Fighting Marine" added that Corbett would chart the positions of the feet in the ring for different situations, planning evasive tactics. Jim Corbett is still considered by many, the "father of scientific boxing," and is one of the legendary greats of the Marquis of Queensberry Era. He was arguably the fastest overall heavyweight of all time with hands, feet and reflexes, including even Muhammad Ali.

After Choynski's victory over Glover, the public was again divided in its choice of Joe or Jim Corbett as the best heavyweight on the West coast. The drums beat louder for the two to engage in a finish fight. Joe claimed that the California Athletic Club offered the pair a $20,000 purse to fight in their building. At other times, he and most sources said the offer was $10,000. Either was a sizable fortune in 1889. Corbett held out for a private fight, for a side bet of only $1,000, in order to appease the Olympic Club, his sire, and because he did not as yet desire to turn professional. Local papers like the *San Francisco Examiner*, *San Francisco Chronicle* and *Alta California*, in addition to the California A.C., fanned the flames, exaggerating and fabricating insults that Jim and Joe supposedly hurled at each other. Nat Fleischer even claimed in 1942 that the "Jew vs. Gentile" factor was stressed so by local papers, that the city and the law feared a "racial riot." Jim said his father, Patrick, eventually compromised with him, saying, "Jim, don't go in the club and fight for money. Go out in the hills and fight him for nothing. My boy, I don't want you to be a prizefighter. That settles it." Pa Corbett wanted a "better life" for his offspring, and Jim's job in the bank was the path that Patrick saw for his son to attain this.[14]

The June 8, 1889 *San Francisco Evening Post* claimed, "Choynski had a setto in Alameda with Peter Jackson, and gave the brunette a very hard rub. Jackson complimented Joe on his prowess, and having heard some talk of rivalry between Choynski and Corbett, remarked that Joe could do up Jim in five rounds. Choynski's friends noised Jackson's words about until Corbett heard them. He promptly asserted that the best way to settle the question was for Choynski and himself to don the mittens." The Jackson "setto" probably occurred while Joe was training for the Glover fight, at Joe Dieves' San Leandro Road training quarters in Alameda.

Corbett said he and Joe met the next day at the sporting-editor's office of an unspecified newspaper. Jim arrived with renowned sportsman, Porter Ashe, "and Judge Lawlor, now Supreme Court Judge of the state ... who sent Abe Ruef to prison." Joe was accompanied by Ed Graney, wealthy cigar merchant Mose Gunst (Morgan Arthur Gunst), and noted horse-man, Tom Williams. Here they negotiated the details of the fight. Papers played it up as a clash, not only of Corbett and Choynski, but also California Club vs. Olympic Club, professional vs. amateur, Gentile vs. Jew, capital (bank) vs. labor (candy factory), even Hayes Street vs. Golden Gate Avenue. This was the most widely anticipated bout of fisticuffs in California to that time.[15]

Bob Vernon, "the well known sporting writer," claimed in the February 27, 1910 *San Francisco Call*: "I was in 'Frisco when that match was made ... in the barroom of the old Baldwin annex, and a bunch of us were there talking over things, when Joe Choynski's brother, who was near the gang, resented some remark that Jim had made. Jim reached over and slapped Choynski in the face with his glove and told him to beat it. Mr. Choynski did beat it, and a few minutes later returned with his brother, Joe ... Well, sir, in a second, that place resembled a riot. Jim was trying to get at Joe, and vice versa. They agreed finally to fight the thing out on the private ..." This is another intriguing, though unverified – and questionable, claim.

The California Athletic Club said they were vehemently opposed to any "Corbett-Choynski prize-fight" and that Joe had just resigned as instructor at their club. Judge Lawlor and Ed Graney comprised the committee to select the site of the match, a place where they could avoid police interference. Corbett said he left the following morning for Sausalito (then called "Saucelito") to set up training camp, and Joe headed in the other direction, to a town about 10 miles from San Francisco. Due to the meanderings of memory, he and Joe couldn't even agree on this in their memoirs. Choynski recalled that Corbett trained at the Olympic Club and that he prepared in Sausalito. Joe wanted skin-tight or "kid gloves," but Jim wanted two-ounce gloves, the general standard for Queensberry bouts at the time. "Gentleman Jim" won the coin toss and got his choice.[16]

The site finally settled on for the clash was a barn in Fairfax, Marin County, described by Joe as a picnic grounds on the other side of the bay from San Francisco. A 1976 article wrote: "Insiders knew the fight was to be staged in a falling-down barn on a deserted milk ranch in the hills three miles north of San Anselmo station, near Fairfax." Corbett said police would often show up at his training camp as well as Joe's, hoping to overhear something that would give away the clandestine fight location. On the night before the event, two detectives were sleeping in the open lot across the street from Jim's quarters, ready to follow the Corbett entourage the next morning. Instead, a young man named Hall MacAllister, Jr. "borrowed" his mother's enclosed carriage, pulled by an expensive pair of trotters. The group slipped out the back door in pitch darkness and drove the horses and "finely appointed" carriage through the back lots, making good their escape to the vacant summer home of MacAllister's mother.[17]

May 19 *Alta California*: "A report was current on the streets yesterday, that Choynski and Corbett, with a party of friends, had been seen going on board the Sausalito boat, and that the much-talked-of fight would come off in a spot previously selected about eight miles out. To the initiated the gossip of the street conveyed no news for the simple reason that they were aware both men have been training within a short distance of one another, Choynski at Ferguson's place at Sausalito, and Corbett a little further out, at Tamalpais." This, according to the May 12 edition, was "at the base of Mt. Tamalpais, in the southern end of Ross Valley, Marin County, where the air is of the purest, and the climate is not subjected to the severe fogs prevailing further down the valley. The reporter found Corbett pushing the billiard balls around the table in a great effort to defeat his trainer, Fred Hansted, better known as Professor Young Dutchy, one of the best all-around (sic) athletes and sparrers in the business."

"When questioned as to his ... mode of training Jem (an old nickname for James) answered in his usual jocular way, 'The Professor here calls me at 6 a.m. by pulling me feet first out of bed. Then he treats me to a cold sponge bath, and quickly dries me off. I then do an exercise for a few minutes with a pair of two-pound dumb bells, after which I am well rubbed down, and then start out for ... a mile walk ... 7:30 a.m. ... I return and feel able to digest a jelly doughnut with monkeywrench sauce.* My breakfast consists of a porterhouse steak, dry toast and a couple of soft-boiled eggs, washed down with a cup of tea, without milk or sugar. A short rest and we start out on a little trip over the hills, returning home after having covered 12 or 15 miles. I then jump into a shower bath, am well rubbed down with alcohol to prevent catching cold, and after a little rest, have lunch, which consists of a bit of fowl and calves' foot jelly and a bottle of ale."
* Apparently, an 1800s slang reference to Irish coffee.

"After lunch I generally rest awhile, passing the time away until 3 o'clock reading or discounting the Professor a game of billiards. At 3 p.m. I swing clubs, raise the dumbbells and then take six three-minute rounds at the bag. After this I use the skipping rope for a few minutes, jumping 300 or 400 times, the last few being done as quickly as possible. The Professor then takes me out and gives me the plunge from his patent bath, rubs me down well, and works on me until I am well cooled off. I rest until supper, which is pretty much the same as breakfast. I retire at night about 9 o'clock, previous to which I use the dumbbells for a few minutes.' " On May 27, it was told that "Young Dutchy" needed to leave camp due to the illness of his wife and the reins were handed over to Corbett's regular trainer of the future, Billy Delaney. Someone named Peter McIntyre assisted.

Middleweight George LaBlanche, "The Marine," helped Joe train at Sausalito, while preparing for his own bout against Mike Lucie. They did their roadwork "in the valleys north of Sausalito, where the temperature is much higher than on the southern and wind-swept slopes." They also ran along the beach, and said they were prepared to travel south to Mexico if needed, to avoid police interference. *Chronicle*: "The air is heavy with rumors about the ... fight and the place is kept a profound secret lest the police interfere." Early on the morning of the 30th, the teams of Corbett and Choynski headed for the fight site. Jim said his entourage rode for about an hour before reaching the barn at Fairfax, where they found "about a hundred people waiting for us. We were hustled into the farmhouse nearby and into a room without any of the usual training equipment – nothing but an old bed, and that without mattress or blankets. They told me Choyinski had arrived and was in another room of the house."[18]

The fight was on May 30, Decoration Day (now Memorial Day). On the week of the fight, the famous actor, Nat Goodwin (Nathaniel Carl Goodwin, Jr.), was playing at San Francisco's Baldwin Theater. He was a huge boxing fan "and in Choynski he saw his ideal of the real fighting man." Nat swung a towel in Joe's corner during the fight. On the day, he did what normally would have been unthinkable – he called in "sick." Goodwin allegedly paid a messenger a $50 tip to take a telegram all the way to San Rafael and from there send it to the Baldwin Theater. The message to theater manager, Al Hayman, read: "Taken seriously ill. Cannot appear today. Dismiss the matinee audience." Choynski said, "Nat couldn't be bothered with theaters when a real prize-fight was on the boards."[19]

Contemporary papers said: "Over 150 spectators are on the ground(s)." "For several days past, tips such as San Bruno, San Pablo station, Ocean House Road ... have been given out as the battleground. This was done to throw the hangers-on off the track. It was about 9:10 when the party, by way of Sausalito, reached the battleground, and 9:30 when those by way of Tiburon closed the side gate that opened off the main road that led to White Hill and to the old and deserted farm of Pete Austin." May 31 *Chronicle*: "After an uneasy glance at ... the uninvited crowd, the party took a glance at the surroundings, both architectural and natural. The former were in dilapidated barns and two highly ornamental shanties. The natural objects of interest were the steep and well-wooded hills that rise on either side of the valley beyond San Rafael. A more secluded spot and one apparently better suited for the purpose in view could not have been chosen. The place is about two miles north of Fairfax and hemmed in by the hills so that the most clamorous demonstration could scarcely attract outside attention."

The May 31 *Chronicle* noted: "The pugilists ... were resting in the shanties near the barn." This slightly contradicts other statements, which said Joe and Jim rested in two separate rooms of the deserted farmhouse. "The ring had ... been pitched in the barn loft, the approach to which was a rickety and narrow stairway. The barn appeared ... a most unsubstantial structure to uphold the large crowd ... Already the uninvited mob had kindly taken possession of the loft and assigned themselves to the best points of view. This arrangement was ... upset by the invited guests, who had banded together and assumed the governing power, beginning by issuing a verbal writ of ejectment to every spurious angler, pseudo hunter and fictitious cowboy ranged around the ring. The edict was obeyed and the loft cleared. The ... authorized spectators ... came upstairs, minus weapons, which consisted of two pistols and sundry flasks of bourbon ... the referee announced he would allow no technical fouls, but would facilitate a fight to a finish ..." The weights were Corbett, 185 pounds, Choynski, 165.[20]

"The principals and ... seconds had been on the ground for fully an hour before the friends arrived, and should have been ready long before ... the 24

Joe Choynski, circa 1889

foot ring had been pitched the day before in the upper part of the barn ... The floor ... sprinkled with resin ... many of the boards removed from the sides ... to give ... fresh air. It was ... 25 minutes after the 125 persons had been admitted ... before the principals (appeared). It was ... 10:27 when ... Corbett stepped into the ring, clad in flesh-colored tights ... belt of apple-green silk interwoven with red (most papers said red, white and blue). He ... wore low hose and brown shoes ... was ... about 183 pounds. Joe Choynski followed ... seconds later ... He wore black tights ... a black belt. His legs were covered with long, black hose attached to his tights. Choynski ... weighed 162 ..."[21]

Joe said the press often exaggerated his weight, to make contests appear less one-sided. "I was 20 years old and weighed 155. Corbett was 22 and outweighed me 15 pounds, possibly more. Although we limited the 'crowd' to 20 men, 10 on a side, fully 100 crept through the dawn to the barn ... The time was set for six o'clock. There had been a lot of wrangling, and I think it was nearer 10 o'clock before we struck the first blow. Patsy Hogan, the pugilist, was referee. The timekeeper was T.T. Williams (a prominent newsman, not Tom Williams, who owned the barge, *Excell*). Corbett, looking debonair as usual, turned pink when he saw Jack Dempsey in my corner ... recovered ... and offered to bet Dempsey $500 he could whip me. Mose Gunst backed me for $1,000. The Olympic Club backed Corbett."[22]

Jim: "In those days a great many men in San Francisco still carried guns, and usually we were not worried about it, so I was surprised when Judge Lawlor said ... 'Jim, there is a lot of feeling over this fight, and I am afraid ... someone may pull a gun. Don't you think we had better search them before they are allowed in the barn?' Someone went to Choyinski's (sic) room ... he agreed, and a few minutes later ... Lawlor returned, his arms piled ... with more guns than I had ever seen in one place ... all loaded. I was told the same thing happened in Choyinski's room, so there was no one in the barn armed." *Call*: "Some had razors, some pistols and others, bowie knives. A few pairs of scissors were found among the tailors of sporting proclivities. Such a collection of frontier armaments could not have been found anywhere ... outside of Buffalo Bill's Wild West show."[23]

Graney: "I enjoyed my most thrilling experience (that) night ... to avoid ... bloodshed, every man ... was asked to deposit his gun in charge of a man selected for ... keeping guard ... Johnny Hammersmith, Mose Gunst and myself were appointed a searching committee ... it became our delicate duty to examine pockets in quest of shooting irons. Mose ... and I started toward old Ned Foster, and we hadn't taken three steps before Ned whipped out a gatling gun that looked big enough to sink every ship in the navy. For a moment, I didn't know whether he was going to shoot ... and I don't mind telling you, I was pretty scared. So was Mose, for Ned walked up to him in a threatening manner, but quietly turned over his gun ... enough revolvers were found to stock an army of Central American Revolutionists." In 1916, Graney said they had spectators deposit their guns in an old wheelbarrow near the entry door. Some had been carrying two guns.[24]

Judge Lawlor told Jim the Choynski camp (actually, Mose Gunst) hired Jim's friend, "Nonpareil" Jack Dempsey for $1,000 (the middleweight, not related to the heavyweight champion), to work Joe's corner. This left Jim nonplussed, as he said Choynski and Dempsey were not well-acquainted. Jack explained that it was only for the money. Jim told him, on the way to the barn, "That's all right, Jack. You can't *make* him whip me ... we went up the stairs and found the ring pitched in the center of the loft and possibly a hundred men ... from high-class gamblers to prominent bankers ..." Jim evidently overlooked the vast number of "common folk" in the throng. He said that just before the referee's instructions, his friend, Porter Ashe, the millionaire racehorse gambler, gave him $500 and told him to bet with

Choynski on himself to win. Joe didn't have any money with him.

Call: "Instead of the regulation wooden buckets, the seconds ... carried old oil cans filled with water, and ... bottles ... emptied of liquor on the road from Sausalito ..." Graney recalled, in 1913, that in Joe's corner were Dempsey, Nat Goodwin and himself, while behind Jim were Billy Delaney and Jim Carr. "Tom H. Williams of racetrack fame and Porter Ashe, well known attorney, were Jim's bottle holders." Eddie said the space in the barn was "about 24' to 36'," while the February 2, 1952 *Sausalito News* said 26' by 29'. Referee Patsy Hogan instructed that they would fight under Marquis of Queensberry rules, and the fray commenced. In 1917, Corbett said "someone rang a milkman's bell that had been brought along to serve as a gong ..." May 31 *Chronicle*: "A decorous silence ... fell on the motley crowd in the rickety, old loft as the two stalwart lads stepped up to the scratch for the 1st round. Their gloves were ... mere coverings of kid and a few hairs inside by way of apology for stuffing." Joe: "At last, with the hay pushed back in the dusty loft, we ... began the opening scenes in the strangest fistic drama this nation has ever recorded." A blended report follows:[25]

Round 1 – The fight began at 10:40. They sparred at long range, Jim the aggressor. "He stood ... with his left lightly poised ... that of the practiced ... boxer ... cleverer sparrer and the nimbler on his feet. His attitude made him look much ... taller ... as Choynski spread his feet more and leaned back further. (Joe) is anything but a showy boxer, but his style ... is effective. He exerted himself very little on his feet, and slowly moved round on the defensive with his long left well extended and his muscular right ready for a smash ... shot his left in ... on Jim's ribs." Corbett feinted, backed Joe into a corner and "returned ... with compound interest ... a swift left ... and a (right) rattler on his jaw ... the first effective hit of the fight ..."

Joe recalled, in 1930: "Corbett had 'kneaded' his gloves until the knuckles were almost bare. I could feel his hard, bony hands against my face. I crashed a hard right to his head ... scoured his ribs with lefts. We ... exchanged long, looping punches that cut and scarred. All around us ... the hum of excited voices. Here, in this misty barn, were the two dandies of Market Street, the fashion-plates of the Golden Gate – determined to cut each other to ribbons because of a grudge. Up to this time, the men of San Francisco had never seen Corbett's face marred. But I marred it, and he marred mine. The crowd ... was fairly quiet, but Corbett's partisans grew noisy as he began landing more often ... once, when he floored me briefly, they roared right out, whereupon, Nat Goodwin scored them roundly. 'Do you want the sheriff on us? ... Keep still, you idiots. Choynski will give him plenty!' In the 1st round honors were fairly even. We both bled."

Corbett: "We fought ourselves into a clinch and Choyinski (sic) said, 'Jim, let's break away nice and gentlemanly.' Then, all in a flash, the conversation I had with him about a year before came into my mind, when he told me of the time he had won his fight with 'Nigger' Wilson and ... others, and ... would say the very same thing ... two or three times, then shoot his right over ... no sooner had he come out with this 'break ... gentlemanly' idea than I shot over *my* right, hitting him on the chin and dropped him for a count of five. There was almost a riot, and it was a good thing that those guns were lying on the beds in the farmhouse!"

Round 2 – *Alta California*: "Both men ... smiled at each other. Corbett said ... 'Joe, give me a rush.' Choynski did ... flying at him like an enraged tiger. The infighting ... was very exciting. Corbett ... sent in a terrible smash with his left ... on Choynski's jaw, partly dazing him. Choynski slipped and went to the floor in a heap, rolling over. He was up ... in an instant ... and the men grappled, fighting desperately. Choynski ... got in a good right-hander on Corbett's neck, and ... a left-hander on the chin, which broke the skin, just as time was called." The *Reno Evening Gazette* differed: "There was the hardest kind of slogging, Corbett employing rushing tactics and hitting fiercely. He caught Choynski on the mouth, which drew blood, and Choynski appeared groggy when the round closed."

Chronicle: "The 2nd ... was ... a corker ... a series of fast and savage rallies ... no spectator could follow the blows. Corbett took the aggressive ... with his left again and got in return a smash on the chin which drew first blood ... The ... men were slogging regardless of science, each trying to knock the other out, without ... any thought to his own danger. Corbett ... showed to best advantage with his superior weight and quickness, and ... his right on Joe's ear with such effect that the fight looked as if it might end then ... The clinch which followed ... was as savage as the slog, and though the referee kept yelling 'Break,' 'Break,' Corbett kept his right going on every available inch of Joe's anatomy, and Joe responded to the best of his ability. By a prodigious effort the referee literally pried the ... men apart, but they were not half-arm distance when ... they rushed into ... another savage clinch ..."

"The referee yelled 'Break,' and Choynski's seconds called 'Foul,' but the Professor's blood was up, and he was not to be denied until the referee ... tore the men apart ... furious hostilities were resumed, both ... fighting so close that the battle was more of a scuffle than a boxing match. Choynski suddenly went down, being half pushed and half struck down, and the belligerent Professor ... banged himself against the ropes in his fervor for blood. Choynski was up immediately and rushing at Corbett, another clinch ... Corbett continued to use his right on Joe's ribs ... disregarded the rules about punching his man when ordered to break ... was cautioned by the referee. He had much the best (sic) of the round and Joe ... walked back to his corner with a big, blue welt rising on his ribs ..." Choynski (1930): "In the 2nd I took a short fall. I was up quickly and feeding Corbett that right."

Round 3 – *Alta California*: "A mark about 2½" long and discolored, was seen on Choynski's left ribs. Many claimed it was from a blow ... Others ...

that (he) got the mark in his roll on the floor ... little work was done, both ... sparring." *The San Francisco Bulletin* disagreed: "Choynski appeared very groggy. He was inclined to clinch. Corbett hit him several hot ones in the jaw and neck, throwing him against the ropes. Corbett ... very confident, while his opponent ... dazed. The round ended with a lively encounter."

Chronicle: "Choynski's seconds read him a severe lecture on the pugilistic sin of losing his temper and Corbett also got the office to keep cooler, so the 3rd round was an unemotional spar ... The Professor tried several times with his left to hit Choynski, who was very shifty, and the leads fell short." Choynski: "But, grudge or no grudge, we kept joshing each other. I would tell Corbett where to hit me – then try to make him miss. He would dance around me, in that tantalizing way of his and dare me to land a blow on his chin. And I did. With returns! Here, however, I want to dispel a common error. I have heard men say that Jim Corbett could not hit effectively. *Jim Corbett had plenty of punishing power.* (The emphasis is Joe's). He could hit a man and make it hurt. But he was always extremely cautious. He was like Tommy Ryan in that respect. He never tore in and risked things. It was this extreme caution that lost him his memorable battle with Fitzsimmons."

Round 4 – Corbett: "In hitting him on the head, I knocked my right thumb out of joint. So things kept up until the 6th(?) when the Sheriff climbed up into the loft ..." Jim penned this in the 1920s, and the years were not entirely kind to his memory. The fight was halted in the 4th. In the June 27, 1917 *Syracuse Herald*, Jim said he injured his thumb in round three. *Alta California*: "Choynski obeyed orders ... to keep away, but was finally compelled to lead to get out of a corner ... Corbett followed up close and twice tried to land on Choynski's face, but was parried off, Choynski fighting on the defensive. In backing away he partly turned, and aiming his right in a threatening manner, cast his eyes down, as if to draw Corbett on."

"Just before time was called for the 5th round the lookout ... noticed two double-teams coming up the road with persons waving their hands and pointing backward. A second later (he) recognized Sheriff Healy of Marin County ... coming up the road on a dead gallop ... 100 yards away ... time was called and both men stepped up to the center. The referee said, 'Boys, back to your corners; this contest is postponed. Gentlemen, stay where you are; there is nothing to be afraid of.' A few seconds later Sheriff Healy came up the stairs, and after taking in the situation, said to Corbett, who was sitting in his corner, 'Young man, put on your coat.' A friend stepped up and said, 'Sheriff Healy, allow me to introduce you to Mr. Corbett.' The men shook hands, and the crowd and principals slowly left."

"The ring was ... taken down and sent to the broad-gauge depot, where it was expected an engine and car could be procured to take the parties into an adjoining county (Sonoma), but ... the Superintendent would not consent, he said it would be compounding a felony. After an hour's delay, the referee concluded to postpone the fight for 10 days, and the crowd took the 3:25 train from San Rafael by way of Sausalito with Choynski on board for home. Corbett took his team at San Rafael and drove over the mountains to Tamalpais Villa, where he will remain until called by the referee. The principals ... were in the city last night, and their appearance on the street caused considerable talk. It was the general opinion that there would be no more fighting between them and all bets ... declared off."

The *Chronicle* differed: "The native sport on the roof ... shouted that the dreaded functionary was approaching. Hostilities were suspended ... and a pair of very large, soft and innocent-looking pillows were (sic) tossed ostentatiously at the middle of the ring to indicate that a pacific bout of fisticuffs was going on at a harmless picnic. The alleged placaters showed marvelous alacrity in skipping down the stairs, and when the sheriff galloped up, the loft was deserted and the ring stakes leveled. Everything seemed to indicate that there was a most law-abiding picnic in progress and the gentlemen with fishing poles were inquiring anxiously if there were any trout streams in the neighborhood. This did not wholly blind the sheriff ... he informed them quietly but firmly they had better pack up and get over the county line if they desired to conduct a prize-fight to a finish. The lectured coterie cordially thanked the official for his friendly advice and made tracks for the depot ... The referee, seconds and Corbett came over with the party. Choynski went back to his training quarters at San Rafael with his trainers." The June 5 *Oakland Tribune* said Joe returned to his training quarters at Joe Dieves' on San Leandro Road.

Corbett: "When we reached the station, (we) found it crowded. The people in all the little towns around had read the ... papers telling about the fight ... The crowds would have followed us ... over the county line, and the police would have been on our tracks again; therefore, we decided to go back to our training quarters. Before we left the ring, the referee had ordered Choyinski and myself to take care of our gloves, to make sure the next time we met we'd have them with us, for boxing gloves had to be made to order to fit a boxer's hand and could not be secured at a moment's notice." In 1933, retired San Francisco Fire Department Captain William J. "Forty" Keneally recalled that "Nat Goodwin ... was so scared at the news that the Sheriff was there he slid down the haymow and stuck fast in the manger. All arms ... were confiscated and I remember I had one of the guns and kept it until I gave it to Jim years later as a souvenir."[26]

June 2 *Alta California*: "Choynski was in town Friday, and his friends were not chary of their remarks regarding the manner in which the fight had been arranged. A pretense of the utmost secrecy was made for several weeks ... yet when the eventful day arrived a couple of hundred fellows trailed the contestants to the stable ... The Sheriff, if rumor does not belie him, gave the party every show for having a good time and getting full value for their money by keeping ... in the background ... some miles away ... until he thought ample time had elapsed for the battle to be decided ... Meantime ... both Choynski and Corbett had been taking a rest after the jolting they had experienced over the rough roads, and the time thus spent is what put the Sheriff out in his kindly calculations ... Choynski may have been letting his opponent do all the fighting in order that he might to an extent exhaust himself, and if the fight had continued Choynski would have taken advantage of Corbett being winded to ply him hard and fast."

On May 31, local papers carried the thoughts of the principals. Choynski, while admitting he got the worst of the encounter, still felt he could defeat Corbett and that the fight was too short to decide a victor. Joe said he had been feeling out his rival and "trying to draw him into a rush. He ... can't hurt me. I know I can last longer than he can, and ... I have been in the ring before." Jim said he was surprised by the running tactics of Joe, observing that his opponent appeared nervous, missing and coming up short with punches on multiple occasions. He said it was obvious that "Little Joe" was counting on a haymaker, short right at close quarters to finish things, but wasn't able to land it. One of the papers said Joe had suffered a cut lip, swollen nose and his right ear had a lump behind it, while Corbett only sustained a scratched chin and a slightly swollen thumb.[27]

On the same day the "barn fight" took place, Joe's father was arrested on three charges of libel and one of attempted extortion. He was booked at the City Prison on a warrant issued by Judge Hale Rix. The charges were made by L. Lincoln of the Keystone Watch Company of Philadelphia, which had an office in Frisco's Flood Building. According to I.N., an agent had several months earlier come into his office with an ad he wanted published, for a $15 fee. Isidor instead agreed to accept a watch of the same value from the watch company in payment. For this he was given 15 "tickets," worth $1 apiece, which were to be redeemed for the watch.

When he eventually went to redeem the tickets and collect the watch, Choynski said he was told by Keystone that they no longer had any $15 watches. They wanted him to take another watch of a higher cost and pay the difference. I.N. refused, saying the company at least needed to redeem the tickets and give him $15 in cash. They declined, even after he offered to accept 25¢ on the dollar for the tickets. Next, I.N. wrote Keystone a letter, inquiring, "Why does not your agent call and redeem those 15 tickets? You cannot expect me to pay twice the value of the watch and give you space beside." The letter contained a threat to publish Mr. Lincoln as a fraud, if he did not make good on the transaction. Shortly thereafter, Choynski published an article in his "*Public Opinion*," saying that Lincoln was "one whom any jury would convict of highway robbery without a trial." Bail for "Maftir" was set at $1,500.[28] The charges were dropped – for the present.

Round Four

Corbett and the Bloody Battle on the Barge
(May 1889 – July 1889)

Corbett: "For the next few days the committee was busy looking for another place for the continuation of the bout. It took them about a week to locate one, and by that time my thumb was in very bad condition and very sore. Finally, Porter Ashe and Judge Lawlor 'phoned me one evening, to come to San Francisco as they had the place all arranged." He and Delaney took a carriage, with curtains drawn, along bumpy roads to a waiting ferry boat. This conveyed the pair to a locomotive, leased for the occasion. "That night they put me on a train for a little country town called Benetia (sic). From the station I was taken to the fine country home of Wilson Mizner, the author of 'The Deep Purple' and other famous plays ... They told me we were to fight on a barge in the middle of the Bay the following morning at eight o'clock ... telling me to go to sleep at once and get a good rest. Can anyone in his wildest moments imagine a fellow going to sleep in a strange bed, with about 25 chaps outside ... some of them right outside my window, and all talking about the fight and thinking they were whispering, but getting so excited that I could hear every word they said? I did not close my eyes all night, but I didn't say anything to them about it for I knew they would worry more than I had." Jim said the heat that night was terrible, making it all the more impossible to sleep. Rumors had the fight taking place at the Farrallones, Goat Island or elsewhere. Many rumors were intentionally passed around to throw the law and other undesirables off the trail. The *Post* said the Sheriff of Solano County had either gone on a fishing trip up the coast, or away on business.

Corbett said he graduated at this point in training "from egg and sherry to steak." His handlers had a steak and a few crackers for him to eat, and Jim's pal, "Forty" Keneally, cooked the steak in the nearby field on a fire they had built. "No one in the world wanted me to win more than my friend 'Forty,' for he had been given one of the worst beatings he ever had in his life by ... Choyinski. Naturally Kenneally ... would have given up 10 years of his life rather than not be on hand to see me defeat Choyinski! I have always, even in bad moments, had a sense of humor (possibly it's the Irish in me). As we were starting (for the barge), I looked around at all the boys, who were very nervous by now, and said with a solemn face, 'Someone must stay here and watch this house until we get back – someone that I can trust. Forty, you're that man. You stay here and watch this house until the fight is over.' His eyes grew bigger and bigger, and I shall never forget the look on his face! He always stuttered when he got excited and, to add to his eloquence, his mouth was at the moment filled with bread!"

Keneally said he was Jim's friend, but would cut off his own right arm before he would miss the fight. "I eased up on him ... told him he could go, and his face was all grin." The party set out in a rowboat for Carquinez Strait, between the towns of Martinez and Benicia. Benicia was famous for long being the home of former bareknuckle legend, John C. Heenan, born 1835 in Troy, New York, but who as a youth came to Benecia's Navy Yards to work. In his 1925 memoirs, Corbett said also with them was "a dear, loyal little friend of mine ... Gene Vancourt ..." This was Eugene Salter Van Court, a former pro baseball player, umpire and instructor at the Olympic Athletic Club. He was the brother of De Witt Van Court, Los Angeles Athletic Club trainer and a close friend (later a second) of Jim Jeffries.[1]

The venue would be the grain barge *Excell,* owned by wealthy race-horse owner and gambler, Tom Williams, a backer of Corbett. The barge was not self-powered, hence, it was towed into the bay by a steamer or tug, and anchored. The *Sea Queen* was a new tug, built earlier that year (1889). It was 100' long, 22' wide and 12' deep, capable of transporting a large number of spectators to the fight, and became famous for carrying the principals. "Prizefighting being illegal in California, no sheriff in the near counties would sanction the conflict. But in the definition of the law, was (sic) any of these bays ... open to tidewater from the Pacific, and therefore seas, within the jurisdiction of any landlubberly sheriff? The question, if brought up in court, might take months to settle ... the fight would (be) a private affair, unadvertised and shrouded so guardedly that only a few millions on the Coast were aware of the secret." Choynski wrote: "We arrived in the little town of Benicia after nightfall on the 4th of June. We were to meet on the barge at sunrise the next day. I went to bed early, but not to sleep, for I kept thinking of the fight. I was working out a plan to beat Corbett. I arose early. I thought I knew what I was going to do. But, sad to relate, fighters often listen to the advice of others."

"At that hour, hacks were clattering around the city front, and pedestrians stumbling along through lumber and freight piles. The denizens ... surprised by the untimely invasion, emerged from their ... haunts to scrutinize the strangers, and for half an hour the Stygian gloom and loneliness of the neighborhood vanished." "A ... fog, black and clammy, had drifted upon San Francisco and except for the wan street-lamp and the lanterns of the helpful policemen, the darkness at the Vallejo Street dock was that of a coal-bin at midnight. Not for large sums would any of the 300 persons waiting for the tugs *Sea Queen* and the *(Joseph H.)Redmond* have been anywhere else. They had two o'clock-in-the-morning courage, tickets in their pockets, most precious tickets, and money to bet on their respective heroes. It was a motley gathering, some in cloak and top hat, others in turtle-neck sweater and derby, all a bit tense, but good-humored and chaffering." One paper said 150 people waited at the wharf for a boat.

"The exclusive invited guests were told to be at the Vallejo street wharf at 1:30 a.m. ... Among them was Jack Dempsey ... who had been engaged by Mose Gunst to look after Choynski." The *Sea Queen* reached the rendezvous at 5 a.m. It "had a fair sized load on board at the hour, and another tug was chartered to follow her, and carried 50 more. All who had been invited and many more were on board, but the outsiders did not fare quite so well as they did at the fight last week. The gallant captain of the *Sea Queen*, a rather hard looking fellow with a Scotch accent, went around with a lantern and routed the interlopers out. Four were dragged out of the long boat, three raked off the roof behind the funnel, two were dug out from under a coil of spare cable, and still there were several overlooked ..."

"The other patrons on the dock were helped aboard six felucca-rigged boats from Fishermen's Wharf which ... 'had abandoned their nightly quest of the finny denizens of the deep for passenger transport.' The fleet had dirty weather of it, the tide being contrary, the fog almost impenetrable by searchlight. At four o'clock the tugs passed the lights of Mare Island, then Crockett at the opposite bank, with sirens howling in a fog grown denser. They should have had 50 feet of water under keel, but at Glen Cove they stuck fast in mud. There was nothing for it but to continue by rowboats into Southampton Bay, two miles ahead in the darkness. One of the boats upset, but it was righted after immense effort, and the voyagers ... were hauled aboard, half drowned. Small comfort awaited them on the barge. Patrons from Benicia and Martinez ... had the ringside chairs. Lanterns were strung up, and by their light carpenters were building a sort of grandstand, a catwalk fixed to the front of the wheelhouse, which, this being a bay-barge, was 12 feet high. The boat, green-painted, was moored in two feet of water between Dillon Point and the city dump of Vallejo. A vendor punted over with hot tamales and coffee, which were engulfed while the crew stretched canvas to ward off the chill winds with its threat of pneumonia."

"At 6 a.m. carpenters had completed the ring, and a sail had been hoisted (beneath the wheelhouse) as a protection for the fighters." The morning wind on the river was cold and raw. A level floor had been nailed down over the old planks of the barge. Many uninvited spectators tried to climb up the high sides of the barge. It was said that famous playwright and Benicia native, Wilson Mizner, "had the knuckles of one hand smashed with a boat hook as he tried to climb on the barge, and was forced to watch the fight from the rowboat in which he had arrived."[2]

Corbett wrote, in 1917: "A half dozen rowboats took our party to the barge, while a small fleet of the same kind of skiffs augmented by a tug, transported the Choynski party and the 250 spectators to the boat anchored in the bay ... As we neared the barge, I noticed that it had a flat pilot house. I don't know why the comparison came to my mind, but the nearer we got to it, the more it seemed like a gallows. And try as I might, I couldn't get that impression out of my mind. As soon as we arrived on the barge, I went into the pilot house and dressed for the battle. To show how little I knew then about the proper toggery for such a fight, I put on rubber soled shoes – an error that I was to regret bitterly before the fight reached its end."

The barge, *Excell*, from June 6, 1889 San Francisco Chronicle

Jim, in *The Roar of the Crowd*: "Everybody we knew seemed to be there ... the same crowd that attended the ... struggle in the barn." June 6 *Chronicle*: "A few minutes after 6 o'clock Choynski reached the barge and, mounting to the wheel-house with his seconds, began to strip for the battle. At 6:15 a.m. Corbett ... in one of the adjacent steamers, was rowed ... to the barge. He had his ring costume under his ordinary clothes, and while Choynski was ... upstairs, he stood by the ringside chatting with the referee and his brothers. It was exactly 6:25 a.m. before ... Referee Hogan stepped into the ring. Choynski climbed down the lofty wheel-house and Corbett began to divest himself of his store clothes, and the crowd closed in on the ropes, expecting the fight to begin ..." While at least two of Jim's brothers attended, there is no indication that Joe's brothers were there. The *San Francisco Post* said there was a 30 minute delay, as the resin had been forgotten.

Choynski: "By 6:30 a.m., we were on the rough flooring of the barge. Jack 'Nonpareil' Dempsey and Eddie Graney were with me again. Corbett had (Walter) Watson and Delaney. We were hemmed in by a wall of 60 men. Soon the barge was out in the bay. No fear now of police interference. At 6:48 a.m., time was called." A 1976 article quoted Hogan: "It was claimed last time these two men met, I showed favor to one man. This I deny, and I have come here to see fair play, and I will now make the following rule. In addition to the Marquis of Queensberry, which I will strictly follow, in the case of a clinch I will order the men to break away, which they must do, and step back one pace and clear. If you do not follow these instructions, I will call a foul." Corbett's hand showed up black and bruised. 206 spectators were said to be present. The *Excell* was able to carry at least 15,000 sacks of grain, so 206 people might have stood on the barge.[3]

"They got on the scales. Gentleman Jim weighed 182 pounds, (his) opponent 10 pounds lighter. The ... Queensbury code was read. Nat Goodwin ventured the jest that aboard ship, London Turf rules would not be admissible. Then a hitch occurred. The articles called for provision by the fighters of their own two-ounce gloves (or three-ounce, sources differ). Corbett brought three-ounce mitts; Choynski arrived gloveless." It was accused that Joe or one of his group had thrown his pair overboard to try and force a bareknuckle fight, knowing Jim's hands were injured. There was a lot of argument and discussion as what to do next. Corbett would not consent to a bareknuckle bout with his right thumb dislocated. "A Calistoga vineyardist tossed a pair of driving-gloves." In 1909, Bob Edgren wrote: "Captain Griffith, a racing man, passed up his driving gloves. Joe offered to let Corbett use them. 'Use them yourself or use bare knuckles,' said Corbett. Choynski put the gloves on. They were so tight that he couldn't close his fists. He wanted to cut the fingers off but Corbett objected."[4] Graney agreed, in 1913: "Captain Griffith, who owned the great pacer, Flying Jim, gave Choynski his driving gloves and the fight proceeded ..."

Graney claimed, in the 1920s: "I have heard it said on numerous occasions ... Choynski's seconds, the Nonpareil in particular, deliberately 'lost' Choynski's gloves. Sometimes the story is that Dempsey, learning that Corbett had injured his right hand in the barn fight, tied a rock to Choynski's gloves and threw them in the bay, realizing his man would have a decided advantage were the fight to be a bare-fist affair. Here is what actually happened: When the barn fight was stopped by the sheriff of Marin County, Dempsey and myself tossed Choynski's gloves into the center of the ring to be taken care of by Patsy Hogan ... Otherwise, they might have been tampered with. What was to prevent someone from putting a horseshoe or a cobblestone in one of the gloves? Of course, neither side would have stooped to such unsportsmanlike tactics, despite the hard feeling aroused by the contest ... In the excitement ... Hogan neglected this part of his duties, and Choynski's gloves were picked up as a souvenir by one Jack Arnold, a profound admirer ... who said afterward he wanted to present them to his infant son, born just one month before! This is the real explanation of why (Joe) was without boxing gloves ... on the barge."[5]

Corbett related, in 1913, that Joe said the gloves "were lost in escaping the police in the barn." Jim didn't believe him. He added, in 1917: "Just as I was emerging from the pilot house ... Delaney ... pulled me to one side and whispered excitedly, 'I just heard ... Dempsey tied a stone to Joe's gloves and dropped them overboard, when they were on their way out here on the rowboat. They are playing that trick to make you fight with bare hands ...' We went to (Joe) ... 'Where are your gloves?' I demanded ... Joe looked at Dempsey, and Jack ... said 'Oh, we lost them overboard.' " In 1892, Jim contradicted this: "We met and fought (in Fairfax) until the police interfered, and then in the scramble it was discovered that one set of gloves were (sic) lost. I knew my hands were pretty well gone and I agreed to give Choynski the benefit of kid gloves, while I kept the five ouncers ... to protect my hands as much as anything ..." In 1916, Corbett claimed to have told the Choynski crowd "to go ahead and use any sort they wished, providing they weren't copper riveted." One (1976) source described Joe's gloves as "A pair of large, red ... thin kid driving gloves ..."[6]

Evidently there was another such pair available, as part of the agreement was that Jim could switch to skin-tight gloves any time he chose. These had

three heavy seams on the back down the center, which left welts on Corbett's body. Jim was soon sorry he consented to the driving gloves, but the Choynski camp said Jim's gloves became so soaked with sweat and blood, they increased the impact of his punches. Corbett wrote, years later: "As we stood ... in the broiling sun (we didn't get started until noon) little did I figure this was to be the toughest battle that I ... ever ... was to fight ... I was to receive more punishment than ... in all my other battles put together; more in fact, than I have ever seen inflicted on any other prize fighter ..." Joe and virtually all the papers said the clash began about 6:45 a.m. Among those in attendance was 12-year-old TAD (Thomas Aloysius Dorgan), later to become a great boxing journalist-cartoonist. The June 6 *San Francisco Post*

The grain barge, *Excell*, during the fight

said at the beginning of the fight, it was cold and the men were blue, but by round 17, the weather was getting hot.

Graney, in 1914, agreed with Corbett, that the same handlers at the barn battle resumed their roles on the barge. They were a bit off the mark. Paddy Gorman, for instance, seconded Joe on the barge. Ed said it was anchored in Suisun Bay, at the confluence of the Sacramento and San Joachin Rivers, which is "spot on." On March 19, 1914, A man named W.J. Fitzpatrick, described as "a pioneer hotel keeper of Benecia ..." gave this version: "I witnessed part of the fight. Few, if any, watched ... all the way through, because there is a limit even to the brutality of human beings. I helped build the ring ... the night before the scrap. Corbett and Choynski fought with bare fists, with the exception that Choynski wore a pair of driving gloves with heavy seams on the back and the fingers cut out. Corbett wore heavy, hard leather bands around his hands, with a buckle in each palm. Open hand slaps counted with Corbett."[7] Fitzpatrick's description was mostly accurate, but in error as far as the fighter's hand coverings went. Now, the fight, combining mostly contemporary reports:[8]

Round 1 – Joe: "Corbett, 20 pounds heavier and considerably taller ... kept working me around so the bright morning sun would be full in my eyes. Then he swung down on me, reaching for ribs and mouth, but I began driving my left at his head and heart. We hit hard, with no thought of the small bones in our hands, and time and again we injured those delicate bones. The crowd was deathly still. There wasn't much sound – only the sloshing of the water and the terrible impact of the gloves. It was grim business. Back in my corner ... Dempsey began drumming it into me that I must keep away from Corbett. No fighting man ever received worse advice from another." Jim: "We started off in the whirlwind fashion of the bout in the barn ... Choynski, knowing I had a bad right hand, started rushing me from the start, and I had to win with my left hand alone. A sturdier, tougher fellow than Choynski never stepped into a ring and I had my work cut out for me. As he came toward me I would 'bat' him with my left, right in the face ... The first two rounds I had his face looking like a piece of liver." "Both ... did not move a foot from the center of the ring." Most papers said little or no damage occurred in the first two frames. The *San Francisco Chronicle* favored Jim, while the *Alta California* did the same for Joe.

Round 2 – *Alta California*: "Just before time was called ... Tom Williams said in Corbett's corner, 'In case we change gloves and kids don't fit we want bare knuckles.' Dempsey ... said, 'Oh, no; that don't go; it is a State's prison offense' ... (Joe) forced the fight, getting in his left on Corbett's face ... Corbett ... caught Choynski lightly on the ear. Choynski ... a left-hander on Corbett's neck." Jim said, in this round, he "framed it with Bill Delaney ... to bluff Joe into believing my right hand was in prime condition ... Delaney ... yelled: 'Let him have that right now, Jim – let him have it quick.'

(Author: If this sounds like a campy way to telegraph a ruse, you're not alone). I shot it up at Joe's head, figuring the yell from Delaney would be warning for him to duck it out of the way. And it did. My heavy swing whizzed over Joe's head ... Joe, who earlier had been careless of that right hand ... watched it closely." At another time, Jim said he began the ruse in the 10th round. June 6 *Chronicle*: "The Professor was wary and dangerous with his left. Jim stepped in ... and caught a right-hander on the ribs that left some strawberry marks ... a left-hander ... on the same spot and ... a telling right on the ribs ... (Jim) started ... some left hand work ... sparring at long range was quickly followed by a rally, some hot exchanges and a clinch."

Choynski: "I went out ... determined to follow instructions and fight cautiously. But in my heart I felt Dempsey was wrong. Then, strangely, Corbett and I suddenly began joshing each other again. As the blows thudded ... we set up a current of banter that continued for many rounds. As Corbett would launch a blow he'd yell: 'All right, Joe – let's see you stop this one!' And ... I would bark: 'Okay, Jim – both together now!' Then we'd smash the blows home and our heads would jerk backward and upward ... The first five rounds were wicked. Blood flowed freely. Corbett winced as his hands back-fired. I groaned inwardly as I felt my own knuckles cracking. Men at ringside began shouting hoarsely. Sea gulls, wheeling high, swooped now and then as cigar butts and bits of bloody cotton were tossed upon the pitching waters of the bay. I am no judge ... but from what I could gather ... we were putting up some of the most beautiful boxing and slugging ever seen in a ring. After I got wise to the 'morning-sun' racket, I vied with Corbett to get a 50-50 break on the glare. I ... had to keep that blaze out of my puffed eyes. If you have ever looked into the California sun, morning or evening, you can appreciate my position. There is nothing brighter in America. Corbett ... was slippery as an eel. The moment I'd swing him around into the glare, he'd wiggle away, and ... I was squinting like a Chinaman. Then the hail of blows would break over me like gun-fire."

Round 3 – Corbett: "He started to duck and I landed on his forehead with my left and broke this, too! I knew it was hurt ... how badly, in the excitement, I couldn't tell; but as the rounds went by it got so sore ... each time it landed it hurt me almost as much as it did Choynski ... (Joe) would get in a terrific blow every little while. He was kind of sweet on hitting me in the left eye with his right hand, and he had my face 'busted up.' So the fight went on at this terrific pace ... my left ... was throbbing ..." Joe was floored once, one paper saying from "a smashing left full on the stomach," another, from a push-punch. Joe got up smiling, and Jim "got a smash in the mouth for his pains." He landed "a light counter that made Choynski's mouth bleed, but did not show a mark, himself." First blood for Corbett. *Chronicle*: "Corbett ... forced his man ... Choynski caught it hot on the jaw with both hands. He shook his head grimly when the men stepped back ...

his lips already began to swell. The round was strongly in favor of Corbett, and from this on he took a lead." *Alta California*: "Corbett ... swinging in his long left, catching Choynski on the jaw, the latter going down. (He) ... was up in a second ... got in ... his left on Corbett's ear. Corbett sent in a straight left that caught Choynski square on the nose. Choynski said, 'That was a good one.' (He) returned the compliment ..."

Round 4 – Papers disagreed as to Jim's dominance. *Oakland Tribune*: "Choynski ... was wild and short. Corbett hit him a straight smash in the face and ducked beautifully. The round amounted to nothing, but showed Jim's superiority as a boxer. Joe could not reach him with any force." *Alta California*: "Choynski led first ... got in on Corbett's cheek and again in the stomach ... on Corbett's throat ... a good one on (Jim's) ribs, leaving its mark." *San Jose Mercury News*: "Corbett did most of the leading, getting in a number of effective blows." *Chronicle*: "Corbett took the aggressive ... led his left ... short, and caught ... a hot right on the ribs ... he got a left in the stomach ... but returned ... a straight counter on Joe's mouth that brought the blood ... Corbett put in another straight left on Joe's mouth, and from this on began to jab his man with the left on jaw and nose."

Round 5 – *Chronicle*: "Choynski came up in a rollicking way ... and did some good work, but Corbett ... scored a flush hit with a left on his nose that brought the blood in a deluge over his neck and chest. Choynski kept trying for a knock-out with his right, but Corbett was cautious, and though Joe got some good right-handers in on Corbett's body, no damage was received ..." January, 1957 *Westways* magazine: "Choynski's head was impregnable ... as round and hard as a cannonball. Such a head was not known to the Fancy in San Francisco until the rise of Tom Sharkey. By the 5th ... Corbett, the bluestocking favorite, was looked upon as quite his opponent's equal ... as resolute and more than a shade the cleverer boxer. If the art of boxing is to hit and not be hurt, Corbett had yet something to learn. His hand had gone limp after its impact on Choynski's flinty skull ... his face, bore herring-bone patterns imprinted by the vintner's gloves. But he was now finding himself. For three years he had been training in the gymnasium fitted up by John W. Mackay, the Comstock nabob, in the cellar of the Nevada Bank, and boxed with sluggers from the Mission. He had devoted his talent to a mastery of the wearing-down process."

Round 6 – *Oakland Evening Tribune*: "Joe went for the body and Jim's left went on Joe's mouth ... Joe got in a beauty on Jim's stomach and another on his ribs but Jim only smiled." *Alta California*: "Choynski came up smiling, while Corbett's face was set and determined. Choynski ... rubbed Corbett's face, who said, 'That was pretty light.' Corbett sent in his left and caught Choynski under the jaw. The men now talked in a friendly manner, Corbett saying, 'Joe, you have got your eye on that bottle.' Choynski sent in his left and got in a rib-tickler on Corbett, saying, 'Don't get rattled, Jim.' "

Round 7 – *Alta California*: "(Jim's) ribs and shoulders showed the marks of Choynski's blows. (Joe) led with a terrible swinging left, Corbett ducking

Battle on the barge, June 6, 1889, S.F. Chronicle

and Choynski going half way round from the force of the blow." *Oakland Tribune*: "Joe slipped and Jim got in two smashes on his mouth." *San Jose Mercury News*: "There was some hot work ... give and take." *Chronicle*: "Jim got ... left on Choynski's nose and brought another deluge of blood."

Round 8 – Choynski, on advice from his seconds, "jumped at Corbett and tried to land his right, going to the ropes from the force of his own blow." Corbett sent his superior left over Joe's guard, on the nose, sending a gory stream onto the pine boards. Jim pressed him, and when Choynski tried to jab with the left, delivered a flush hit on the stomach, flooring Joe. A June, 1919 *Police Gazette* wrote: "Corbett came out with a rush and slammed Choynski to the floor with a heavy right to the face. Choynski staggered to his feet, his nose broken and both eyes puffed. From then on until the end he took a terrific beating."

Round 9 – Corbett repeatedly connected with the jab on the nose and mouth. Joe swung wildly and seemed rattled. *Oakland Tribune*: "Jim made a fine left lead in the ribs after the right on the jaw and knocked Choynski down." *Chronicle*: "The Professor's white drawers were all dippled (sic) with the blood of his punished adversary and clots of gore began to make the floor ... slippery." Choynski: "Before we reached the 10th I was thoroughly convinced that Dempsey was dead wrong about me keeping away from Corbett. In the first place, it tired me out to play Corbett's own game ... Corbett trained in a gymnasium every day ... spent hours perfecting his footwork. It was his regular practice to work with fast men each day from 4-6 or from 8-10. As for that left-hand body punch ... it was perfection itself, as it should have been, as for months he spent an hour a day practicing that one blow. I should have kept on top of Corbett ... slugged him to a standstill. Had I done this, I feel sure I would have stopped Jim ..."

Round 10 – Corbett: "About the 10th round I discovered I had foolishly put on the wrong kind of shoes, the rubbersoled sort that amateurs wear in a gymnasium. They are all right there, but when you get out on a hard floor in the hot sun and they begin to blister your feet ... you are going through something! Each of my soles was one great water blister. With these bothering me so, and Choyinski still so full of fight, I thought less of sparing my right hand; so I fixed it up with ... Delaney, to call out every once in a while, 'Jim, it's time you used your right now.' ... I would ... 'telegraph' the blow, purposely. I didn't really want to hit him, but ... make him afraid of that hand ... This threat made Choyinski ... go to my left, and gave me a chance to use a little left hand hook which they knew nothing about in those days; in fact it had not been used before – nor had I myself used it before. It was just discovered through my great need. In using this left hook I found ... I could save the two knuckles that were hurt (3rd and little finger) by hitting with the side of the hand and 3rd knuckle."

In later years, Corbett said: "I should have given some credit to Joe ... and called it the 'Choynski.' But I guess I was still mad at Joe, so it got called the 'left hook,' and that's what it has been through all the years since ... the first new blow in pugilism since pugilism was young."[9] *Chronicle*: "Choynski's lips began to protrude like an African's ... His cheeks were also swollen and his right eye black and closing. He had lost all his smile, but was game." *Alta California*: "Choynski ... got in a good one on Corbett's ribs with his left. Corbett swung his left and caught Choynski on the neck and again on the nose, the blood spattering all over both men." *Oakland Tribune*: "The blood poured from his (Joe's) mouth and it looked as if only the call of time saved him. He was badly beaten and Jim was unhurt."

Round 11 – Joe landed rights to Corbett's nose and left eye. This got Jim's left going, and the blood flowing heavier from Joe's nose. He was choking on the blood and spitting mouthfuls of it. "He got in on Corbett's ribs as time was called." Jim: "By this time Choynski's face was badly cut up, especially at mouth and nose, and he was a free bleeder. There was not so much blood spilled from me except a little from the mouth, for I never bleed easily. However, my eye was nearly closed and there was a swelling around the cheekbone. The 'claret' from Choyinski ... spattered the spectators ... we found ourselves slipping around the deck in our own blood. By this time the sun was very high in the sky and hot, and I could see that its rays, beating down pitilessly on Choyinski's raw face, troubled him a great deal." The heavy seams on Joe's gloves left three angry welts on

Jim's skin every time they landed. "I looked like a zebra – not striped with yellow, but with red, and the sun made these wounds pain horribly. We did not stall much or wrestle ... blow succeeded blow fast and furiously. Probably a great deal of this fight could be characterized as slugging, since, though I did use my head ... and was quick and fast, I was still an amateur and had not yet gained the scientific skill one gains through experience ... I learned more about fighting in this contest than I ever knew before." In truth, Jim already had at least one pro fight, in Salt Lake City in 1886.

Round 12 – *Chronicle*: "A clinch ... and the men went down, Choynski ... rushed ... but could not land his right, and Corbett jumped away laughing." *Alta California*: "Choynski ... got in on Corbett's ribs, following ... with one in the throat. Corbett sent in that invincible left on Choynski's nose ... four repeaters in the same place. As time was called, Choynski was going to his corner with head down and blood spurting from his nose." In the November 26, 1908 *Salt Lake Evening Telegram*, Delaney claimed that "Choynski had Corbett so bad at the end of the 12th that Jim went over and sat down in Joe's corner." Jim: "Now, this flat boat had just two pillars, about two feet in thickness, rising from the sides with a little platform or deck upon them and a little pilot or lookout house in the center above. By accident I found the spot where this gave just enough shadow to cover one man from the sun ..." "The spot struck the ring nearest my corner ... The sun was beating down so that even the boards seemed baked, and the resin sizzled under our feet. Finally, about the 12th or 15th round, I hit upon the scheme of getting in the shade. It was big enough to protect me from the rays of Old Sol, and you bet it was a great relief. Dempsey was quick to discover my tactics, and informed Joe ... The ... idea of landing a knockout punch suddenly switched to that of a shadow tag. I was a shade shiftier than Joe, and I won out. Had I lost hold on that spot, there would have been no other outcome for me than defeat. Of all the little things that have changed the course of a battle, this probably was the most unique."

Round 13 – *Oakland Tribune*: "He (Joe) made several hard rushes, but did no harm. This was the best round Joe fought, but ... too late. Joe puffed heavily." June 5 *San Jose Mercury News*: "Both slipped and fell ... Jim picked Joe up. The latter appeared to be himself again and forced the fighting." *Chronicle*: "Joe ... looked weak ... a horrible sight ... Corbett tried to knock him out and both were covered with the blood of the one." *Alta California*: "Corbett opened on Choynski's nose. Choynski, game as a lion ... got in on Corbett's cheek twice ... forcing Corbett to the ropes and getting in on Corbett's eye. Both went down in a clinch, Corbett on top. He got up and also helped Choynski to rise. Choynski again rushed Corbett to the ropes and got in several light blows to the face as time was called." In the January 12, 1931 *Chillicothe Constitution-Tribune*, Corbett recalled the 25th (sic) round as the one in which he helped Joe to his feet. Jim claimed, "I just wanted to get another sock at him while he was still dizzy."

Round 14 – Joe rushed and landed some good shots to the face, dazing Corbett with a right. Jim countered with a stiff jab that brought the gore. "About 40 sports turned away and walked to the stern of the barge, unable to stand the sight of blood." "Corbett's eye was black and Joe's face and body a mass of blood. He looked pitiful and weak. He could barely stand or see." *San Jose Mercury News*: "Corbett could have finished him, but his second advised him to keep away, as through his bloody visage Joe still looked dangerous." *Chronicle*: "Choynski ... was ... forced on the ropes and nearly knocked out. Corbett's strength failed at the critical moment and both were very weak at the call of time and red from head to foot."

In 1917: Jim said, "Joe started another of his bull-like rushes. I shot a left jab ... and he met it full on the forehead. I had broken the other knuckles of my left hand ... and the pain had caused me to faint – standing up." "Everything growing hazy in front of me ... there I stood with arms by my side, and there was an awful silence for a few seconds. Choyinski looked at me and thought I was pulling some trick. But a few seconds later, his supporters realized I was not faking, that I was in a position to be licked, and I heard a terrific shout from them ... I got a horrible punch on the right eye. All I could sense was ... the blows Choyinski rained on me ... I was not 'out' ... just groggy and instinctively kept my head rocking with his blows and managed to keep my chin out of danger ... my hands still at my side. If just one had landed there, I would have been down and out for the count. The round ended at last, and I can remember my seconds leading me to my corner – I didn't know where it was – and sitting me ... in my chair."

Another time, Jim said, "Suddenly I heard ... a warning from Delaney – and a second later, the most terrific blow that ever hit me landed flush on my mouth. By some strange twist of fate that blow, instead of flooring me, seemed to clear my dazed brain, and a second or so later the bell rang ..." In 1913, Corbett said he landed a straight left on Choynski's head and broke his thumb, and "at the same time, Joe caught me a wicked left on my eye that cut and closed it." In *The Roar of the Crowd*, Jim said, during this round his brother Frank was looking for Harry, and "found him at the stern of the boat, his head over the gunwale and looking into the water, crying." When Frank asked what Harry was doing, he said he couldn't bear to see Jim licked. Frank punched Harry in the nose, feeling he had "deserted" Jim in his greatest time of need (not that Harry could have helped). In 1911, Delaney recalled, "In the 14th, the referee ... asked (Jim) if he wasn't willing to have the thing called a draw. 'Not on your life,' replied Corbett."[10]

Round 15 – *Oakland Tribune*: "Still Joe was up cheerfully. Jim smashed him again and again and threw him on the ropes. Corbett began to weaken and if Choynski had a blow in him he should have won ... a ... remarkable change." *San Jose Mercury News*: "The bloodiest round ... Joe was forced over the ropes knocking others down with him." *Chronicle*: "The excitement ... was intense. Both ... so weak a child could have pushed down either. Choynski, bleeding profusely and shaky on his legs, staggered around and struck wildly at Jim, while the latter, pale with exhaustion, reeled ... and lacked the strength to do any more than lift his crimson gloves. It was a close shave for the Professor, and when time was called it looked like anybody's fight." *Alta California*: "Corbett ... forcing Choynski to the ropes ... held him by repeated blows to the face, Choynski's body and head hanging far over into the crowd. Corbett reached over and gave him ... his left ... straightened Choynski up, who ... fought desperately and gamely ..."

Delaney asked Corbett just before the start of the 15th if he was all right; Jim said he would "pull through." Joe came at him hard; Corbett was groggy and clinched until his head cleared. Next, as a ploy to show Joe that he had recovered, Jim feinted and tried a fancy sidestep. He had not regained his equilibrium, though, and nearly fell on his face. "Picture a drunken man reaching for a post and you have me then!" Choynski's killer instinct kicked in and he rushed with renewed determination. Corbett admits he was "well on the way to defeat." He clinched at every opportunity and managed to survive the round. Joe's strength was greatly depleted by the punishment and blood loss he had endured. This and the wildness of his punches allowed Jim to last to the bell. Joe: "As I slouched to my corner at the end of the 15th Graney saw I was tiring rapidly. Here Graney shoved Dempsey away from me. Eddie bawled: 'To blazes with this cautious stuff, Joe! Corbett's cutting you to pieces at long range. Now, go in there and fight him. *Fight him!* That's your game.' " In 1917, Jim said the altercation between Frank and Harry occurred in this frame, saying he heard a commotion and peered between Choynski's arms in a clinch.

Round 16 – Contradictions abounded. Joe: "I began the kind of fight I should have launched in the opening rounds. I ploughed into Corbett and started throwing rights and lefts from every conceivable angle. I think this amazed Jim. He had seen me tiring ... thought I was all set for the killing. In the face of a terrific lacing, I ... put a lot of steam into those punches. Corbett felt them, all right ... he wore a cane for three weeks after that battle ..." Jim said he came out with all his old pep and, as much as the intense sunlight was bothering his face, he knew it caused more discomfort to Joe's. *Oakland Tribune*: "Joe slipped down in his corner and took his 10 seconds. After a little sparring in Jim's favor, Joe gave him an awful smash in the nose." *San Jose Mercury News*: "The fight opened a very brutal phase ... Corbett landed very nearly when and where he liked." *Chronicle*: "Corbett looked terribly distressed and Choynski's face was all out of shape, his cheeks being puffed up and his eyes closing and his lips protruding until they stuck out beyond the line of his nose. Corbett ... crowded his man, and as Choynski got away he stepped into his bloody corner and slipped in his own gore. He was up when six seconds were counted (Hogan evidently called it a knockdown) and resumed fighting, showing more strength in his arms than Corbett, who was still too weak to punish."

Round 17 – Choynski said his eyes were nearly closed and he was having trouble seeing Corbett. "During the last few rounds we were both on the verge of exhaustion ... sick from the movement of the boat, the terrific strain and the smeary blood." Corbett said Choynski took a trick out of his own book, beating him to the shady spot and waiting for Jim to come to him. "... most of our fighting was done near those pillars." "Each round after the 14th, when it looked as if I were headed for defeat ... when I would clinch with Choyinski in a certain part of the ring, I could hear someone repeating the Lord's Prayer. Finally it came to me that the owner of the voice must be praying for me because my opponent was of another religion, and one that does not use that prayer. So in one of these rounds (toward the end of the fight) ... Choyinski's back was against the ropes and I could look right over his shoulder at a little old fellow whose lips were moving in prayer. I recognized him as a little Irishman by the name of Tom Riley (or Reilly), a friend of our folks, and no one ever knew how he got there. But there he was, leaning on the ropes with his eyes shut, little spatters of blood on his face, praying!" In 1917, Jim thought this occurred in the 15th.

Oakland Tribune: "Joe gained in strength ... but still threw his blows away. It began to get hot ..." *Chronicle*: "Another even round ... Corbett improved toward the close." *Alta California*: "Corbett got in several times on Choynski's nose ... the game Choynski swung his left and reached Corbett under the left eye, the crowd saying, 'Good boy, Joe.' " Tim McGrath, later a manager of Joe's, said he was at the fight. He recalled that, in this session, Corbett gave Joe "the hardest body beating man ever took. Everybody was yelling for the sponge to be tossed into the ring to save Choynski."[11]

Round 18 – *Chronicle*: "The 18th round practically settled the fight, for Corbett improved while Choynski got another smash on the nose that further weakened him ... This time he bled so profusely that gore was spattered over the spectators as he moved around the ring and spat out mouthfuls." *Alta California*: "From the 18th to the 21st round Corbett continued to punish Choynski terribly in the face. His left glove was as red as the pair of red kids that Choynski wore." June 26 *Police Gazette*: "Corbett almost went down from a terrific left hook to the eye ..."

Round 19 – *Oakland Tribune*: "Smash in Joe's stomach went Jim's left at the start of the round and then once more on that sore, sore nose."

Round 20 – Choynski: "Then Jack Dempsey, seeing me bleeding so freely and thinking I was all in, whispered to Graney. I couldn't hear the words but I knew ... He wanted me to quit! It was the 20th round, I shoved Dempsey away. Then I pulled Eddie Graney's head down ... let Graney tell it: 'Dempsey held a sponge in his hand. He was worried about Joe. He suggested to me that he throw in the sponge. Here Joe pulled my head down near his bloody lips and spoke the words I shall never forget: *Don't throw in the sponge, Ed!* he pleaded. *I'm not licked yet. I'm fighting my own fight now. Please don't stop it. Let him kill me, but don't say I quit!* Those were the words of an iron man of the ring, a man who didn't know the meaning of the word fear, and I am proud that I was behind him that unforgettable day in June! So I told Dempsey to get out his knife. And we trimmed Joe Choynski's lips!' After this it was only a matter of time. I summoned all the strength I had and again took the offensive." Bob Edgren, in 1909, said this occurred in the 22nd round. *Oakland Tribune*: "Corbett ... seemed ... stronger again. A finer show of dogged courage than Choynski's was never seen." *Chronicle*: "The flow of blood nearly choked Choynski, but he ... looking for a right-handed swing and managing to keep the Professor off from finishing him."

Round 21 – *Chronicle*: "Choynski got desperate and rushed the Professor to the ropes. He tried it again but Corbett ducked and as Choynski dashed against him he lurched back and fell on the floor, slippery with blood. He got up on time and fought to the end gamely."

Round 22 – *Oakland Tribune*: "Joe got one in the stomach ... but kept on as desperately and gamely as ever." *Chronicle*: "The 22nd, 23rd and 24th rounds were all in favor of Corbett, who kept his man bleeding. By spurts Choynski rushed ... and tried infighting, at which he was most effective. He still struck viciously, but missed with his left oftener than he hit, as Corbett ... was nimble on his legs ... evading his rushes. The most exciting incident of these rounds was the attempt of one spectator to throw another overboard after a windy squabble about the merits of the men. The weaker disputant held on with a desperate grip to the deck of the barge and thus avoided a bath." *Alta California*: "Choynski got in a backhand slap on Corbett's face. The latter sent in his left on Choynski's nose ... and ... was about to finish him, but (Joe) drew himself up and said, 'Oh, no, you don't,' as time was called."

Round 23 – *Oakland Tribune*: "Joe's face was a purple mask and Corbett's, clean and determined. It was monstrous and brutal ..."

Round 24 – *Oakland Tribune*: "Joe made a desperate rally, which Corbett saved by a clinch ... (Jim) hit him twice with his left ... and hit again. Joe became groggy and could hardly stand. He got an awful stab in the nose and another that made him reel ... Jim was tired ..."

Round 25 – Joe made a savage rally, rushing Corbett to the ropes and landing punches with both hands to the ribs and head. It was short-lived, however: "(Joe) ... was repulsed and ran, head down; Corbett following him and upper-cutting him on that sore face and nose three times before he raised his head." "Jim chased him around the ring and butchered him. It was murderous. Joe could hardly stand, and a tap made him reel. Corbett almost hit him at will, but was not strong enough to knock him out. Joe's face was like chopped liver steeped in blood."

Round 26 – *Chronicle*: "Choynski's seconds gave him a swig of brandy ... in a last effort to revive the battered fighter ... (he) caught some ugly left-handers as Corbett pressed him to the ropes, keeping the sun all the time in ... eyes that were rapidly closing." *Alta California*: "Corbett ... cheek ... puffed and ... lips swelled ... sent in a hard one on Choynski's wind and time was called." Jim recalled (in 1925) that "Choyinski was rapidly tiring ... from exertion, but also from the great loss of blood ... and I ... had been suffering the tortures of the damned from the hot sun, my blistered feet, the raw welts all over my body and the pain from my left hand ... We were sorry-looking sights ... when we came up for the 28th round."

Round 27 – Joe's seconds "gave him a stiff pull at the brandy bottle between rounds. He came out with a terrible, do-or-die rush and Corbett clinched ... then floored (Joe) with a left to the eye. Jim kept ... the sun in his eyes at all times ..." "He got up in seven seconds and ... Corbett struck him again with his left (to the chin) and Joe fell helplessly to the ground. He partially arose in a dazed condition in 11 seconds but could not retain his feet. Corbett was declared the winner. Choynski was in a very dilapidated condition and it was some time before his second succeeded in resuscitating him. His face presented a horrible appearance ..." Delaney recalled, 22 years later, "In the 28th and last round, with both weak as kittens, Corbett palmed Joe with his left hand flush on the face. The jar stood Choynski up stiff; then he fell over on his back, dead to the world. He didn't move after hitting the floor. At the count of 10, Corbett collapsed completely. I never had up to that time, and never have since, seen so much cleverness, endurance and gameness displayed, as ... in that bloody battle."

Chronicle: "Choynski ... rushed Corbett ... to the ropes and hit him a hot right on the head. He tried ... again, but ... went down with a right-hander on the neck ... he did manage to struggle to his feet and rush ... He was too weak ... to do any more ... the Professor crowded him ... to the ropes and floored him again with a left and right delivered in close order on both sides of his head. The right-hander sent the game lad down for the last time, and he rolled over on his back, beaten and disheartened, a ... disfigured and pitiful object. He struggled to regain his feet but had only got on one knee when the 10 seconds ... elapsed. He got to his feet, however, and struggled to his corner, where his victorious opponent shook hands with him ..."

Choynski: "The end came in the 27th. I couldn't see Corbett, but I got close ... and staggered him with a final barrage of rights and lefts. Then his weight and science tipped the scales, and I was the one to be counted out, one knee on the deck and one hand on the ropes. I was exhausted. But I had done my best." Most sources say the final frame was the 27th, but Corbett said: "The end ... came in the 28th round. I saw the condition Choynski was in and felt that one good left hand hook would finish him ... Delaney kept shouting, 'Now, Jim, cut loose with that right hand ...' I ...

swung 'haymakers' at Choynski, intending to miss ... Again and again I swung the right, deliberately missing ... and watched him duck in an arc towards ... my left. I called on that last reserve, swung my right hand, and as he came over more slowly than ever to the left, put everything that I had in the world into my left – whole fist now, not caring whether I would smash every bone in that hand, because I meant it to be the final blow – and timed it so perfectly that, as he reached the end of the arc, it landed squarely on the vital point of the jaw and down he fell." In 1894, Jim recalled: "In desperation I swung at his jaw and accidentally hit him with my wrist. He dropped like a log, clean out. I would not do the same thing again for a mint of money, as the blow broke my wrist."

In the *Syracuse Herald*, Jim said the finale was round 28, but contradicted the accidental nature of the wrist blow: "With all the power of my body behind it, the wrist of my left hand crushed flush against his jaw ... because two knuckles of my left hand were smashed, and the only effective blow I could deliver was a left-hand swing, landing with the forearm. Joe tottered ... then toppled ... in the shade of the deckhouse. That blow took ... my last ounce of strength. Had Joe ... arisen ... before the count of 10 ... he could have won that fight with the next punch ... I helped the referee to count out Joe. I ... wabbled, alongside of him, chanting the fatal formula ... and as ... 'ten' was reached and there came to my pain dulled brain the realization that the fight was over, I collapsed, but I didn't fall ... Delaney and 'Forty' Keneally ... leaped through the ropes as I was toppling over, grabbed me and dragged me to my corner, a victor in a contest called by many 'the most furious and bloodiest in the modern history of the ring.' "

In 1924, Jim said: "When the slowly counting referee reached 'ten' he slapped me on the back, and I would have fallen if Delaney had not caught me and carried me to my corner." He also alleged that at age 8 he had been "tubercular." This was poppycock, as symptomatic tuberculosis (referred to then as consumption), was incurable – and fatal – in that pre-antibiotic era. In February, 1941, Harry Pegg, Editor of the *Veteran Boxer*, claimed, "Joe writes that ... Dempsey was intoxicated; kept telling Joe to stand up and keep away from Corbett ... was out to see Corbett win ... Had Choynski defied Dempsey and used his own style of fighting, Dempsey would have stepped in the ring, and Joe would have lost on a foul ..." *Daily Alta California*: "It was 8:40 o'clock when referee Hogan declared Jim Corbett the winner, and cheers were given for both men." A (circa 1969) *Police Gazette* said "He (Choynski) was a terrible sight when his seconds carried him out of the ring and laid him on some sailcloth." *Westways* magazine, January, 1957: "Weeping, he (Joe) was lowered over the side into his boat."

The June 26 *Police Gazette* also said Joe's nose had been broken. *Chronicle*: "At 9:35 the *Sea Queen*, having taken the principals ... on board, started on the return trip. Choynski's face continued to swell. He was taken into the captain's cabin and attended to by a surgeon. His injuries were all bruises on the head, which will quickly heal. Corbett ... The left side of his face was much swollen and his ribs sore, but his most painful injury was the fracture of the bones in his left hand. A large crowd awaited the arrival of the *Sea Queen* ... and the pugilists were fairly mobbed as they tried to force their way to a couple of hacks ..." A 1976 article said: "As the *Sea Queen* maneuvered for a landing at the Vallejo Street pier, Corbett saw his father standing on the dock. When the deckhands lowered the gangway, (he) was the first man aboard. Grabbing his son in his arms, he hugged and kissed him affectionately. The old gentleman was excited and it took Jim a while to calm him down. The fighters were then driven to the Hamman Baths, where they spent the next seven hours soaking their bruises."[12]

The April 12, 1892 *San Francisco Call* quoted Joe: "Corbett hit ... upper drive on the nose, which split my nostril and laid open an artery ... I bled so profusely that ... the barge was almost covered with blood. In spite of this ... I had Corbett so badly punished in the 15th ... he wanted to quit, and almost cried because his backers wouldn't permit him to ... Tom Williams, the well-known horse-owner ... had to actually push him into the ring when time was called ... Notwithstanding the terrible amount of blood I was losing, I still think I could have won the fight but for an attack of cramps in my leg, which prevented my coming up to time within ... 10 seconds. In 12 seconds ... I had crawled to the ropes and dragged myself up, for my leg wouldn't support me, but ... too late ... I was never knocked out, though."

Corbett's wife, Olive, said, in 1895: "I was badly worked up that night. I staid at home, as always ... and waited in fear and trembling for the news. When Jim came in, I nearly fainted. One side of his face was all cut up. That was the only time he was punished at all." Corbett related his life story to Nat Fleischer in 1933, who published it in his 1942 biography "Gentleman Jim." In his failing recollections, Jim said Choynski "was at his best. I don't think he ever again put up such brilliant exhibition of scrapping as he did that eventful day." Corbett admitted, though, that "Memory of it comes drifting back to me like a mist. Nothing is quite clear."[13]

W.J. Fitzpatrick added, in 1914: "After each round ... their seconds would dig (sic) buckets of ocean water from the bay and douse it upon them. The art of seconding, like fighting, was in a crude state ... The fight was so absolutely brutal that few men could watch it through. Many turned their faces from the ring and gazed out over the peaceful water. I left in disgust after a few rounds. I returned ... when the fight ended. The men were on the floor a great deal, and the ring was slippery with blood. I hope never to see such a thing again. Everybody was glad when the fight was over. Corbett won the fight, but not until his face, chest and arms had been cut and slashed ... in a dozen places. Choynski fared even worse. His face was beaten to a pulp and his body ... a mass of bleeding cuts when the 27th round came, and ... could no longer do more than stand upon wobbly legs, and so dazed, his brain could not direct his arms to continue the fighting."[14]

Billy Delaney: "Several times the referee wanted to ... declare the fight a draw, but neither man would stand for it. They insisted on fighting on when

... neither had much left but confidence. It was anybody's fight right along ... Both of Corbett's hands were broken in the 20th and the blood from cuts over his eyes almost blinded him. In the 25th ... Corbett bled like a pig and was fading fast." Joe said he had no alibis, that he'd had in his day "150 fights, losing but 8 or 10," and had always given his opponents full credit for their performances, win or lose. Porter Ashe won $8,000 betting on Jim, while cigar merchant Mose Gunst lost $10,000 on Joe. Ashe started a subscription for Choynski. He and Tom Williams each chipped in $100 to start it off and referee Patsy Hogan passed the hat. Ashe also organized a benefit for Choynski. The ring was taken down and readied to be shipped back to the Golden Gate

Joe Choynski sketch

Club, whence it had been borrowed. In later years, Graney was quoted as stating, "That fight ... was the greatest battle I ever saw. No two men alive today could even hope to duplicate it."[15]

Corbett wrote in 1932 that he went to Choynski's cabin and shook his hand, "turning the old feud into a friendship which has lasted ever since. He is now instructor in the Pittsburgh Athletic Club, and every time I go to that city he and his wife have dinner with me." Jim said he spent seven hours in the Turkish bath, "my blistered feet in two pails of hot water, and my hands in two other pails of the same hot liquid, hot towels in addition on my zebra-striped face." The *Alta California* said the tugs arrived at the Vallejo Street dock at 11:45. On the trip back aboard the *Sea Queen*, a Dr. Stanton examined Corbett's hands, finding the second bone in the back of Jim's left hand broken and the right hand badly swollen at the wrist. "Corbett ... was found ... in some distress from a pounding on the ribs and a subsequent traumatic pleurisy ... both wrists were fractured."

Later that night, Corbett visited Choynski at the Hamman Baths. The two shook hands and chatted in a show of mutual respect. While at the

Baths, Joe told an *Alta California* reporter that he never realized he had so many friends until after this grueling battle. They had provided for his mundane wants and offered financial assistance. "Both men displayed (a) gameness and cleverness never looked for by their most ardent admirers. While Choynski suffered defeat, he has gained more reputation and friends than he could in winning a dozen battles from such men as Glover, Bush, Cuffe ... If he still intends to follow the ring as a profession, he has a bright career before him which is not the least dimmed by this his first defeat."

Paddy Gorman, Choynski's second, had not left Joe's bedside during his recovery. "Choynski sustained serious injury to the left nostril which promises to be a source of future disquietude, if not of danger, the hemorrhage being so great at times as to cause excessive weakness." Joe said he would return to Joe Dieves' training quarters at San Leandro Road to recuperate. Corbett told the *Alta California* that he sat at the Hamman Baths for nearly 24 hours. "I couldn't move hand or feet for nearly two days, and it was weeks before exertion did not bring intense agony. But, bad as was my condition, I think Joe's was worse. He was forced to remain in the bath for three full days, and ... after he got out he was a fearful sight ... Choynski hit me harder in those 28 rounds and battered me more than Jeffries, Fitzsimmons, Sharkey, Sullivan and all the others put together. It was that fight with Choynski that led me to become a professional boxer." At another time, Corbett said he spent two days in the Hamman Baths.[16]

So severe was the brawl on the barge, it is a wonder the two boxers' careers weren't ended before they fully got underway. Many a tale has been written of the brouhaha, and with much hyperbole. One can find stories describing how Joe's shredded, bloody lip was hanging down over his chin. Dangling by a mere thread, the remainder of the lower lip was mercifully snipped away with scissors by Joe's second, Jack Dempsey. The clash itself took place on "the splintered deck of an ancient barge ..." as though the *Excell* was some antediluvian remnant of Atlantis or Sumerian relic, that had washed up in the Bay of San Francisco. The stark brutality of the fight was real enough, no embellishment or fabrication was needed.

In the days following the bout, speculation ran high as to how the outcome might have changed if different tactics had been used. Some felt Joe might have prevailed if he had "made a hurricane fight" from the start. "The opinion was expressed by pugilistic experts that Choynski was handicapped by having skin gloves. The professional boxers agree that the two-ounce fighting gloves administer the greatest punishment." Bob Edgren offered, in 1921, that "Choynski always said Corbett had the better gloves, as he could hit with full force and not injure his hands. On the other hand, the admirers of Corbett called attention to the fact that he entered the ring with his right hand disabled and soon injured his left by breaking the bones in the back of it. Despite these handicaps he punished his man heavily and showed beyond all question that he was much the cleverer boxer."[17] The article ventured the belief that Joe would have lost anyway, as he was overmatched. Choynski would go on to improve his boxing skills and fighting prowess, though, possibly more than Corbett. A few years later, Joe would still have been an underdog due to a dearth in weight, but it would have been a very compelling and exciting match-up.

A rumor made the rounds that Choynski was dying. A Sacramento paper said the tale of his impending demise from internal hemorrhaging was without foundation. This story may have stemmed from Joe's nasal damage and bleeding. Both men attended the Golden Gate Athletic Club's monthly exhibition, on the evening of June 19. "During the intermission Jim Corbett and Joe Choynski came in together and took seats in the gallery, where they conversed in the most friendly way and were chums throughout the exhibition. Choynski every once in a while went through some illustrations in punching while talking to Corbett." They watched the main event, between "colored welterweights" Charlie Turner of Stockton and Wiley Evans of Boston, won by Turner on a grueling KO17. In this fight, referee "Young Mitchell" (Johnny Herget) applied the rule that Patsy Hogan initiated in the barge battle, namely, when the fighters were ordered to break a clinch, they must let go and each take a step back.[18]

On June 27, the new Atlas Athletic Club held its first show, in the Eureka Turn Verein Hall at 706 Powell Street. Ed Graney was on its Board of Directors, and Joe refereed. An early bout was between two one-legged men, J. Maguire and Joe Nolan, who wore no prosthetic limbs during the fray. Graney, called "champion amateur lightweight of the coast," boxed Paddy Smith. At 10:15 p.m. the main event commenced, a finish fight between 125-pounders, Young Frenchy of Texas and Joe Graham of San Francisco. Joe refereed and Graney held the watch. It was customary for each fighter to have a designated time-keeper, and the club often appointed their own. Frenchy kayoed his adversary in the 3rd heat.[19]

The July 8 *Denver Republican* said "Joe Choynski has announced that he has positively retired from the ring and accepted a position in an insurance office in San Francisco. He was forced to have a surgical operation performed upon his nose a few days after his battle with Jim Corbett ..." The exact nature of the procedure is uncertain, but as Joe rarely had trouble with nosebleeds later, it was likely a cauterization of internal blood vessels. The crushing loss no doubt had a bearing on Joe's announcement, but he was not yet 22, and retirement didn't last long. He was at the California A.C. on the night of the 12th to second featherweight Johnny Griffin of Braintree, Massachusetts against Billy Murphy of Australia. Graney was a timekeeper. After two rounds it looked as though Griffin would win by knockout, but he ran into a well-timed right and was counted out.[20]

On July 15 at Mechanics' Pavilion, a benefit was tendered for Joe, called, "undoubtedly the most attractive of its kind ever presented at any athletic entertainment." An astounding assortment of boxers and wrestlers performed that evening, in addition to a "grand military band of 40 pieces." Between 2,100 and 2,500 were present, "including many ladies, with their escorts." Billy Jordan was the announcer. The Golden Gate band played between fights, which saw such matches as "Young Mitchell" and Billy Shannon, Billy McCarthy and Billy Murphy, Paddy Gorman and Mike Lucie, and Graney vs. Paddy Smith. Wrestling matches in both Greco-Roman and Catch-as-catch-can styles, and an exhibition in club swinging by "Professor" Hatch of the California Athletic Club were also featured.

Next came the event of the evening, four rounds between Corbett and Choynski, or as the *Alta California* said, "these boys now meeting as the best of friends, with the same impartial referee, Patsy Hogan ..." Joe walked away from the benefit $1,600 richer. They boxed "four friendly rounds, which were loudly applauded ..." and put on the best display of the night, but once again, Jim had the edge on Joe. "The men displayed the greatest good humor and forbearance throughout, eliciting frequent applause. Corbett was greeted with merriment at the start by tapping Joe on the nose before they had fairly finished shaking hands. In the succeeding rounds he led with right and left, reaching Choynski's nose and ears frequently, while the latter's blows were divided between Corbett's chest and eyes." Both were given a rousing round of applause and the decision given to Corbett. It was stated that the latter insisted on being paid for his appearance. While there is nothing wrong with this, Jim having received little for their preceding clash, it perhaps runs contrary to what the June 8 *Alta California* stated, that, when asked by Porter Ashe to perform at the benefit, Corbett "says he is willing to do anything for his old rival, now that they have again become friends." This would be the last time the fighters engaged in a real contest together. Part of the barge, *Excell*, still remained afloat in Southampton Bay near Benecia as late as March, 1933.[21]

In 1925, Jim said of Joe: "In my estimation one of the gamest and best fighters that ever lived, though a ... bit too light for the heavyweight class. He was really as good as most champions I have seen, and this ... covers a period of nearly 50 years." In 1930, Joe said, "Corbett would never meet me again. Why not? I don't know. I challenged him repeatedly. But he would have no part of me."[22] Many a young boxer would have given up thoughts of a ring career after such a loss. The man who gave Corbett the fight of his life was made of tougher stuff, though, and went on to fistic greatness. The grudge match on Williams' grain barge was important for many reasons. If Jim hadn't won, he likely would not have taken up the sport in earnest, and his name would not be in the record books as the first Queensberry rules heavyweight champion. In any case, the fighting careers of these two storied pugilists might be said to have been launched with the barge.

Round Five

Building on a Reputation
(August 1889 – August 1890)

Sausalito was fast becoming a favorite training spot for local fighters, as attested by the July 27 *Alta California*: "At present Choynski, Paddy Gorman (an Australian), LaBlanche (the Marine) and Billy Murphy are all quartered over there." They frequently took "a nine or 10 miles run along the winding road that borders the bay at Sausalito." While others seemed to have fights lined up, Joe was struggling to find opponents. Some negotiated themselves out of a fight, like Joe Bowers, who demanded $1,500 and insisted Choynski come down to 160 pounds, neither of which could be done. The battle with Corbett had scared away prospective opponents.

On August 2, the new Atlas Athletic Club hired Joe and Ed Graney as instructors.[1] It was common then for the term "instructor" to encompass not only one who gave boxing lessons, but coached other athletics, as well. Further demonstrating how popular athletics had become, yet another club opened in early August, the California Cribb Athletic Club. It was located in Mowry's Hall, on the corner of Grove and Laguna streets and had 1,060 members. The club held its first entertainment on the evening of August 6, with "Young Mitchell" as master of ceremonies. Among the bouts was a four-rounder between Choynski and newcomer Gus Keen, of New York. The spar was a try-out for Gus, and, while Joe "succeeded in making Keen feel very tired before the wind-up ..." he didn't try to knock out him out.[2]

August 27 saw our subject on the undercard of a legendary middleweight battle between George "The Marine" LaBlanche and "Nonpareil" Jack Dempsey. LaBlanche, a Canadian (real surname, Blais), who had been a United States Marine, scored a monumental upset, knocking Dempsey out in the 31st round. Jack had dominated to that point, but in the last heat, LaBlanche suddenly spun around, left arm extended, crashing his fist into Dempsey's nose. Jack landed nose-first on the canvas, dazed. He just failed to beat the count and George was declared winner by knockout. He was not crowned middleweight champion, however, as the "pivot punch" was later ruled to be illegal. Dempsey had a KO13 over LaBlanche in 1886. Choynski's bout was an exhibition against Billy McCarthy, that evidently went four rounds. It is not indicated if this was the superb Australian middleweight, or another of the same name. All that was written is: "Billy McCarthy and Joe Choynski followed, Choynski going down in the 2nd round and sliding on his ear under the ropes, filling the ear with resin." Whether Joe slipped or was knocked down is uncertain.

The California Athletic Club put on a September 24 show, witnessed by their 1,800 members. On the card, Choynski "played with Thomas McCarty for a little while." No more about the spar was given. The main event was a featherweight match between Tommy Warren of California and English champion, Frank Murphy of Birmingham (England). Joe was Murphy's timekeeper and Jim Corbett performed that task for Warren. The final decision was a No Contest in 68 rounds! The October 7 *Chronicle* said Joe had sparred the previous week with Billy Hennessy, who was training for an October 16 fight against the "colored Stockton middle-weight," Charlie Turner. "And the latter did so well with the big man that Hennessy's stock went up many points. The sports reason that if a tall, powerful man like Choyinski found it so hard to reach Hennessy, a small man like Turner will be outclassed." Joe was likely toying with Billy. On the night of the 14th at the Pacific Athletic Club, Joe boxed a three-round exhibition with Fred Woods. The monthly exhibition of the Golden Gate A.C. on October 16 saw Hennessy and Turner battle with 5 ounce gloves. Choynski was a timekeeper for one of the fighters. Turner floored Hennessy repeatedly in the later sessions, finally knocking his opponent out in round 45![3]

Joe was a timekeeper again on October 25, when the Occidental Club featured a match between 127-pounders Jack Delancey and "Australian" Jimmy Murphy. In the 1st heat, Murphy pushed Delancey through the ropes. Fortunately, Choynski was there and caught him, preventing a possible injury. Although Delancey fought back desperately, Jimmy scored a kayo in the 11th. Company F, First Regiment of the National Guard, celebrated their 31st anniversary on November 16, 1889 at their Armory, on the corner of Market and 10th. "The celebration took the form of a literary and musical entertainment, interspersed with ... exhibitions of the manly art. Among the professors who showed their skill were Joe Choynski and E. (Alec) Greggains, Ed Graney and Paddy Smith ..." No details were given, but it's likely that Joe and Greggains, close to the same weight, sparred each other. On the 24th, the Lurline Club gave an entertainment that included boxing, wrestling, swimming, rowing and singing. "Joe Choynski and Hanley, Ed Greeney and Professor P.H. Gray ... gave some excellent exhibitions of the manly art ..." Two nights later, Joe was at the Pacific Athletic Club for their athletic show. The club was located on Mission Street near 20th. "A number of noted boxers attended, and among those who donned the mittens were Joe and Ed Graney."[4]

As was often the custom, a benefit show was given for an athlete in financial need. On November 30 at the Golden Gate Club, the recipient was boxer Mike Lucie. The resort was filled to overflowing and the Committee of Arrangements included Dempsey, LaBlanche, Graney, Choynski and "Young Mitchell." Several exhibitions took place, among them Choynski and Billy Hennessy, Joe McAuliffe and Con Riordan, Graney and Young Huntington, concluded by a set-to between beneficiary Mike Lucie and Denny Costigan.[5] Costigan would die in November 1900 of consumption (tuberculosis). He was a local sports figure and close friend and second of fellow consumptive, Jack Dempsey.

The December 13 *Alta California* reported Jim Corbett's resignation from the Olympic club. His reasons: "Before ... my last fight with Choynski, the managers of the California Athletic Club tried to induce me to have the fight in their rooms. They made me a good offer, which perhaps I should have accepted. They agreed to give me $2,000, even if I were defeated, and to engage me as instructor at a salary of $250 a month. The Directors of the Olympic Club knew this proposition was made ... and told me it would be money in my pocket not to accept it. They finally persuaded me to remain with them. The result was that I did not even have all of my expenses paid. Had I accepted the offer of the California Athletic Club, I might now be $7,000 or $8,000 ahead. The Olympic Club still owes me some of my salary ..." Jim said when his friend, President Harrison, resigned due to Jim's unfair treatment by the club, he terminated his own membership. Choynski had taught boxing for a short time at the California A.C., yet that club displayed hypocrisy by denying any interest in a Choynski-Corbett fight.

On the evening of the 20th, Choynski was in Joe Connelly's (or Connolly's) corner, for his KOby4 loss to Thomas McCarthy, at the Golden Gate club. Joe and Graney seconded Paddy Smith, against Danny Needham, at the Occidental A.C. on December 23. Danny's handlers were "The Ithaca Giant," Mike Conley, and Pete McCoy. Smith and Needham each weighed 137 pounds; Frank Glover refereed. A rugged, give-and-take battle ended in the 17th, when Smith caught a swinging right on the jaw from Needham. After the fight, the 180 to 200 pound Conley sarcastically "remarked that Choynski 'had better go round and tell people again that Needham was no good as a fighter.' This excited Joe, who had been ... tipping him (Smith) as a sure winner. Choynski whipped off his coat and offered to fight Conly (sic), and but for the interposition of a policeman there would have been an impromptu knock-out. Choynski is now talking of putting up a forfeit to fight Conly, but has not yet done so." A fight with Conley never materialized, although Mike came out with a challenge to fight Joe "before any of the clubs for a purse and will wager $1,000 or $2,000 on the outside and in case there is no purse offered will meet him on the turf for the same amount." The last reference was to a bareknuckle encounter, which Joe is never known to have engaged in.[6]

On December 26, bicyclist "Senator" Morgan received a telegram from Choynski. Joe referenced the Jim Corbett-Dave Campbell fight, which would occur on the 28th in Portland. The yellow-haired Californian wrote, "I challenge the winner of the Corbett-Campbell contest. Letter leaves today, Corbett answer on arrival." Corbett handily out-scored Campbell, but had been contracted to knock him out, so the bout was ruled a 10 round draw. No reply from Corbett, or Campbell, for that matter, was forthcoming. Joe was having a difficult time getting another fighter to face him in the ring. It was said, however, that around this time, Corbett occasionally sparred Choynski at the Golden Gate Athletic Club.[7]

The January 3, 1890 *Chronicle* declared, "Joe Choynski has at last obtained a match. His opponent is a 6' 4" resident of Portland, Or., who is known as 'McClarney, the Irish Giant'. This may be another of the ... 'scientific point' fakes as ... Corbett and Campbell ... at Portland. Choynski's exhibition will come off on the 18th, and he has gone north much more expeditiously and joyously than if he were hunting a real fighter." On the 21st the men signed articles for a 10 round fight under Queensberry Rules, for a 65-35, winner-loser split of the boxers' share of the receipts.[8] The January 22 *Brooklyn Eagle* said Joe had just been signed to fight " 'Billy Wilson, the colored champion of the Northwest,' by the Golden Gate Club, for a purse of $1,500 ... $250 ... to the loser." That bout would follow shortly. The match with James (or Frank) McClarney occurred January 25 at the Mechanics' Pavilion in Portland, resulting in a KO2 win for Joe. January 26 *Portland Oregonian*: "There had been considerable speculation regarding the outcome ... for, while the ability of Choynski was well known ... the fistic skill of the 'Giant', who overmatched his opponent in size, reach and weight, was comparatively an unknown quantity ..." The January 28 *San Francisco Bulletin* said "between 1,300 and 2,000 people" were present.

After preliminaries, which included sparring and "Girard Leon and his trained donkey ... to advertise Sicher & Mayer's Schiller cigars ... a detachment of about 15 of Portland's most stalwart officers ... entered the building. The spectators ... excused them, for even the blue-coated minions of the law occasionally like to see good sport. It was 20 minutes past 10 o'clock (p.m.) when the two contestants entered the ring." Choynski, attired in a flesh-colored suit, was followed by his second, James Geoghan, timekeeper Dave Campbell, bottle-holders and attendants. McClarney followed immediately after, attired in a light-colored waist with dark tights and seconded by John H. Clarke. "George Williams acted as his time-keeper. Ash M. Hamilton, the well-known turf exchange man, was referee."

Round 1 – *Portland Oregonian*: McClarney struck out at Joe several times, but he cleverly evaded all, and landed three punches with "lightning rapidity" on his taller adversary's nose. Frank "made a vicious lunge at Choynski," but fell short. Joe quickly countered with "a stinging blow on the side of the head, which sent him against the ropes and to the floor. It ... might have been a knockout if not for the ropes. McClarney had not got in a blow, and it became evident that he had no business in the ring with a man of Choynski's cleverness." The January 28 *San Francisco Bulletin* disagreed: "Both sparred carefully a minute and a half before ... Choynski secured the first point in a blow on the chest. McClarney got back on Joe's ribs. Choynski struck McClarney a right hander on the ear that almost knocked him off the stage. McClarney recovered ... as time was called."

Round 2 – *Oregonian*: "McClarney, bent on finding a good place to land his right, walked around Choynski several times ... It was evident to those who know Choynski's tactics that he was watching a chance to get in one of those 'double header engine' blows, which Corbett sometimes speaks of. McClarney struck out for him but the blow again fell short, and Choynski countered by landing his right on the side of the Giant's head. This blow was followed by another on McClarney's right ear and by a 3rd on the jaw, which knocked him down. He fell heavily, his head striking with great force against the floor. The 'Giant' arose ... a trifle groggy. He advanced toward Choynski ... After a few feints, Choynski sent in two red-hot, straight-from-the-shoulder blows – right and left – on the giant's neck and jaw. The giant fell heavily to the floor, his head striking with a thud." That was all. The *Bulletin* said "The whole affair lasted but 6½ minutes."

Joe, from 1930: "I agreed to take on another mammoth, Mike (sic) McClarney, an Irish giant of 6' 2", who had been flattening all comers around Portland, Oregon. McClarney weighed close to 200, but was fast. For two minutes of the opening round he tore after me like an enraged bull. Once he bashed me a mighty bender behind the ear. I saw ferris wheels and whirligigs, but somehow I ... didn't go down ... I belted the Irish giant so hard I knocked him through the ropes. He tore down a post as he fell out into the audience. The big crowd in Exposition Hall had never seen a man knocked out before. They thought McClarney was dead, and ... immediately made a mad scramble for the exits. Somebody yelled for an undertaker ... it was a pulmotor they needed ..." January 27 *Oregonian*: "W.R. Vice, one of the pillars of the California Athletic Club, who came up with Choynski from San Francisco on his way to the Sound, was seen by an *Oregonian* reporter yesterday. He said: 'Did I expect to see Choynski win? Well, I should say so. There is no man in San Francisco I place more confidence in than Choynski. For his size he is the equal of any man in the ring.'"

Although not found in his boxing record, Joe said ("I Fought 'Em All"): "Next they took me down the river – the Willamette – to tackle a gigantic lumberjack. He had been flattening the challengers so fast the promoters couldn't dig up victims for him. His friends collected $1,000 to bet he could take me. In the open, at Three-Mile House, this powerful lumberjack ... donned three-ounce gloves. He had muscles like iron and looked as if he might stun a gorilla ... He looked down on me and grinned. I guess he thought, 'It won't be long now.' This fellow ... dashed at me like a bulldog ... after a cat. I tapped him one, and spun him around. He let out a hoarse bellow and plunged in. To this day I can see those bulging arms swinging. I knew I must not let him connect. So I ducked and smashed a right hook to his whiskers. He tumbled as if he had been smashed with a beer-mallet. I left him sprawled under the trees in the midst of his dumbfounded friends." In 1927, Joe said he and others "went by team" (horse-drawn transport) down the Willamette River to Three Mile House. "He (McClarney) was a fierce-visaged and powerfully-muscled fellow ..."

Joe returned to San Francisco on February 11. Reports had him signed to fight old-time pugilist Jim Fell in Portland, but the match fell through (no pun intended).[9] Fell was born in England around 1856. February 17 *Chronicle*: "Fell is a typical Yorkshire countryman, and has all the broadness of the accent of that class, despite the fact that he has been a number of years in America. He was boasting the other night that he owned more real estate than any pugilist in America. 'I have foor big lots at Grawnd Rapids, Mich.,' said he, 'with a 'ouse on 'em as I built by foighting. I licked one fellow to pay for the loomber an' anoother to pay the carpentering an' plawstering. I've got the 'ouse moost finished now except the windies an' the doors, an' I'll have to foight this man Joe Michikinsky to get them in.' 'You mean Joe Choynski,' suggested a listener. 'Ya-as, Joe Chymikinsky. That's 'im as I'm after,' said the imported slogger, and that was the nearest he has ever come to pronouncing Joseph's somewhat Polish cognomen."

Joe now prepared for Billy Wilson, "the colored champion of the Northwest." "(He) ... is considered in Boston, where he originally hails from, good enough to fight (George) Godfrey, so Choynski has no easy game. The purse is $1,500." Another paper called Billy, "a hard hitter and a fairly scientific boxer. He has been giving sparring exhibitions here (Sacramento) for a couple of weeks past at a variety theater. Wilson and Choynski met at the Golden Gate Club and signed ... for a finish fight ..." Joe (1930): "Billy Wilson, an enormous black fellow, began hurling challenges at Peter Jackson. (He) hailed from St. Paul ... had piled up a formidable list of

Billy Wilson, "The Black Demon"

heavyweight casualties. All the heavies on the West Coast were dodging Wilson. Nonpareil Jack Dempsey ... said (Billy) had enough stuff to whip

John L. Sullivan. Therefore, when I announced ... cheerfully, that I would take on this excess baggage from St. Paul, Jack Dempsey raised his hands in horror. 'He'll murder you!' said Dempsey. 'Well,' I replied, 'as far as I can observe, Wilson has two hands and a pair of legs. If he had any more, they'd only be in his way ...' A chap who had once conditioned me for a fight, joined Wilson's staff and proceeded to show him how to meet my attack. He beat it into Wilson's head that he must be on guard against my terrible right. So Wilson spent most of his time building up a plan to avoid my right ..."[10] In 1927, Choynski identified this "chap" as "Spike" Connelly.

On February 21, Isidor was arrested on charges of attempted extortion. "Obadiah Livermore, a real estate agent ... charges that Choynski attempted to blackmail him out of money to suppress a scurrilous article ... proposes to push the case to the bitter end and show that he will not be blackmailed ..."[11] February 27 *Alta California*: "The preliminary examination of I.N. ... was begun yesterday before Police Judge Rix. About three weeks ago, Mr. Livermore received the following note: 'It will be to your interest and that of the writer to call and see yours respectfully I.N. Choynski.' (He) sent A.N. Hungerford and E.A. Leigh to see the writer. When they entered Choynski's office, he presented a manuscript written by a 'reputable citizen', who alleged that he saw a 13-year-old girl enter Mr. Livermore's office and remain there for a long time. On learning this, Mr. Livermore said the editor of *Public Opinion* could go ahead with any exposure he had to make."

"The next (edition) contained a 'Valentine' signed 'Obadiah,' the substance of which was the girl story. A marked copy of the paper was sent to the real estate agent. Two days later Mr. Livermore received a letter ... 'You will please take the matter ... and relieve me of any further responsibility. Will go to press to-morrow. I.N. Choynski.' Mr. Livermore again sent his friends ... to ask who the 'reputable citizen' was ... giving such information. Choynski drew forth (a) manuscript, and said it was all right. It would take just '100 big American dollars' to silence the matter, $75 for the reputable citizen' and $25 for his trouble. Choynski offered no defense and Judge Rix held him for trial in the Superior Court in $1,000 bonds."

Leigh (Livermore's bookkeeper) and Hungerford, a relative, testified with Obadiah on February 27. The "obnoxious valentine" published by Isidor was read in court. I.N. told Rix he did not care to enter any testimony on his own behalf, and the Judge set bail. On March 21, yet another suit was filed against I.N.! Three counts of libel and one count of attempted extortion. The accuser was L. Lincoln of the Keystone Watch Company, who sought $25,000 in damages from the article I.N. published in 1889, calling Lincoln a fraud. Bail was set at $500 per count, or $2,000.[12] Livermore's suit evidently encouraged Lincoln to file litigation. Once more, though, Lincoln apparently dropped his charges, as no more was heard of that case. The Livermore suit would not resume until July.

Billy Wilson went into training at the "Fourteen-mile House" and Joe, again at Barney Farley's "hostelry" in San Mateo, "which so far has not turned out a single loser ..." Wilson stood from 5' 9½" to 5' 11", and his record included wins over Mervin Thompson, "The Cleveland Thunderbolt," "Professor" Hadley and McHenry Johnson, all prominent black fighters. A Sacramento daily wrote: "Wilson ... weighed 187 and was in good condition. Choynski was in perfect trim at 169." The fight was held at the Golden Gate Athletic Club on March 26, and Mike Lucie refereed. The contestants entered the ring at 9:00 p.m. and time was called at 9:07.[13] Wilson was rumored to weigh about 200 pounds and appeared not to have trained hard. He was seconded by Billy "Spike" Hennessy, who Choynski referred to as "a friend and admirer of mine, and a noted conditioner ..." and John Naughton of Sacramento. Several state officials came from Sacramento to back Wilson. Joe was attended by Ed Graney and brothers Charley and J. Tillson, and he gave his weight as an inflated 180 pounds. The report that follows is derived from primary and other sources:[14]

Round 1 – The *Chicago Herald* called Wilson "the more powerful hitter and an equally clever boxer ..." *The Inter-Ocean* said he "drove Choynski around the ring with powerful left-handers on the ribs and once sent him sprawling under the ropes with a light tap." To avoid the rushes of the "St. Paul bull," Choynski danced from corner to corner ... Joe ... found Wilson's left eye with a right-hander that knocked him down." Joe floored his foe either 3 or 4 times, depending on the source. Wilson was saved by the gong. *Sacramento Daily Record-Union*: "Wilson showed himself to be remarkably quick, and started to force Joe. The latter would either retreat or duck, and ... suddenly turning ... drive his heavy right on Wilson's nose, which started bleeding ... Wilson ... was badly jabbed, and towards the end of the round was knocked down with a heavy blow in the mouth ..."

Joe, from 1930: "The 1st round, opening at a killing pace, found the enormous black veering off ... in an effort to dodge my right ... always ... to the left. But he crowded me at times and we landed some slashing blows. I knew at once that ... Dempsey had not been joshing about Wilson. He had long arms, knew how to use them, and he gave me plenty to think about. His blows carried ample power. Suddenly, during a deadly mix-up near my corner, I slipped just as he laced me with a stinging uppercut. It seemed to knock my head loose from my shoulders. This wallop dazed me, but I bounded up, without the aid of a count, and began trying to even the score. Above the uproar I heard the cries of Wilson's trainer ("Spike" Connelly) – imploring him to look out for that right of mine ... he stepped in close and banged a left to my stomach. (Author: A foolish way to avoid a right!) Suddenly, I saw my chance. I threw every possible ounce of weight behind my left and smacked a hook to the big fellow's jaw. Wilson fell as if he had run head-on into a Market Street trolley. The fight was over in less than one round. Wilson had avoided my right – but they hadn't figured on my left, with its punishing hook." The left hook actually came in the 2nd frame.

Round 2 – Accounts disagreed. *Daily Inter-Ocean*: "Wilson ... drove his opponent against the ropes, but his blows were wild and Choynski sent him to the floor with a left ... on the jaw. Wilson partly arose, but fell back and was counted out. The fight was brief and unsatisfactory, only two good blows being exchanged by either man." "He started ... rushing at Choynski, and the latter stopped him repeatedly by left-hand jabs in the mouth. Wilson tried several swings and wild lunges ... One blow caught Choynski on the breast and the receiver slipped and fell on his knees. The local man finally smashed Wilson a firm left-hander on the nose and William went down very neatly. He came up and slight taps sent him down five times. The last time Wilson went to lumber he got a fairly good jab on the mouth, which would have caused (other top) men ... to smack their lips and come up for more. Wilson remained down in a nice, easy position ... flat on his back, with his legs and arms spread out, while the seconds were being called off. Wilson did not feel ... pained mentally when the fight was awarded in favor of Choynski. Neither man was injured in the least." *Sacramento Daily Record-Union*: "Wilson ... was very cautious. Choynski was the first to lead, but Wilson ducked, and, throwing out his right shoulder, threw Joe heavily. Joe was up in a moment ... jabbing away on Wilson's bleeding nose. Wilson seemed to lose heart ... being almost unable to touch Choynski. Joe finally got in a heavy smash on Wilson's mouth which took the latter off his feet, his head rebounding from the floor, where he was counted out."

Although many contemporaries considered the left hook that knocked Wilson out to have been among the most powerful punches ever delivered, the *Chicago Herald* believed the fight was fixed, at least on the part of Wilson: "... today the betting was 100 to 50 in favor of Choynski, which led to the rumor that the fight had been fixed by gamblers ... The result showed this suspicion to be correct." If the supposed fix was common knowledge, only the *Herald* caught wind of it, no other paper mentioning it. Rather, commonly noted was the overweight appearance of Billy. The detailed article in the unnamed paper said: "Wilson looked like a man who had been enjoying the good things of this life for some months. He appeared to be very much fatter than the ordinary pugilist ..." Wilson would later maintain that he had been drugged, but wasn't generally believed.

Graney signed on April 5 for Joe to fight Jack Davis, a Canadian of Welsh descent. "Davis, who is highly recommended by Patsy Fallon, the well-known sport now visiting here, has telegraphed his willingness to meet the tall, young coast man, and the men should make a very close finish. Davis is at present teacher of boxing at the Gate City Athletic Club of Omaha and stands 5' 10" in height, weighs 175 pounds, and among other scalps dangling from his pugilistic belt is that of John P. Clough, whom

Davis defeated twice."[15] John P. Clow, alias John Moore, was from Denver, Colorado and one of the better heavyweights of the day. He was shot to death on December 9, 1890, the result of a disagreement over a horse.

The April 9 *Rocky Mountain News* wrote that "Choynski is already in training ... He is a tall, powerful, gamey fellow, a glutton for punishment, a hard hitter and a shifty big fighter. His long reach is his great defensive." The April 14 *Alta California* offered: "Jack Davis ... will leave Omaha for this city today. In the opinion of old ring-goers he is reckoned as a dummy who was spoken of as a clever fellow by one of (lightweight champion) Jack McAuliffe's backers. 'A record of Davis,' says a New York paper, cannot be found in the East, but he will have one doctored up to show his friends in San Francisco." The same paper reported that Joe's future manager, "Parson" Davies, Peter Jackson and combination, had a narrow escape from death. Davies noted that he, Jackson, sportswriter W.W. Naughton, Jack Ashton, Sam Fitzpatrick and the rest of the company, was staying at the Louisville Hotel, Louisville (Kentucky), when a tornado swept through. "One side of the hotel was sheared off by the fury of the storm. Luckily, the party was on the other side of the house and escaped injury."

Joe refereed a bout between Charlie Turner and Denny Kelliher (or Kelleher) of Boston on April 25 at the Golden Gate A.C. Both men tipped the scales at between 153 and 155 pounds. The 3rd round was one of the wildest and most exciting in the city's history, the fighters taking turns flooring each other. The bell saved Kelliher from a knockout. Turner dominated rounds four through 10, but in the 11th, Choynski cautioned Turner for choking Kelliher. Choynski didn't need to render a decision, as in the 13th, Kelliher floored Charlie for the count with a right cross.[16]

On May 10, Bob Fitzsimmons arrived in San Francisco on the *Zealandia*. Among the first to greet him was Choynski. In his memoirs, Joe remembers their initial meeting, though he mistakenly recalls it occurring in or prior to March: "One day while I was training for the Wilson match, I had my first sight of Bob Fitzsimmons, who had just arrived from Australia, poorly dressed and almost friendless, carrying all his possessions in a carpet bag. As I was getting ready to punch the bag, Tom James, steward on the Pacific Steamship, *Zealandia*, said, 'Joe, I want you to meet Bob Fitzsimmons.' Fitz shook hands awkwardly and mumbled, 'Pleased to meet you.' I thought Fitz was the least impressive fighter I had ever seen. But, he came out at my invitation ... trained there ... I quickly decided he was a finished boxer even then. Much more so ... than ... in later years, when he changed his style completely and went in whole-heartedly for slugging. He was a pleasant chap in those days, willing to do anything asked of him ..."[17]

Freddie Bogan, a "crack Californian lightweight" training with Joe at this time, gave his flawed account years later, of Bob's first day in America: "It was in 1890 and I was loafing around the Golden Gate Athletic Club of San

Francisco, as I was accustomed to do ... when about three o'clock in the afternoon the present world's champion applied for a match. All of us boys stood around and laughed at his appearance, for he was a sight. He was attired in a Seymour coat, a pair of high water trousers, a little cap and a dirty looking soft shirt. He carried a little black hand satchel with a rope handle, and one who has seen his hump-shouldered and knock-kneed figure can imagine what a queer looking individual he must have been. The club matchmaker looked him over and told him that there might possibly be a chance to match him with Wiley Evans for a date several weeks off, but he did not know what kind of a match he would make with Evans."

"Everyone who applied for a fight at one of these clubs and was not

Bob Fitzsimmons, undated, but circa 1892

known had to be tried out ... when Fitz was told this, he retorted, 'I don't have to be tried out. I had a good record in Australia and am good enough for this country.' With that, he ... walked away and I did not see any more of him for several weeks. He applied for ... horseshoer at Eddie Greaney's blacksmith shop the next day, but was told there was no room for him. Two years afterward he won a $2,000 wager for the horseshoeing championship from Greaney. Several days later I went out to the Cliff House, which was seven miles from 'Frisco on the Mission road, and which was known as one of the best training resorts in the country. Joe Choynski was also there, getting ready for a fight with Corbett, as was 'Reddy' Gallagher ... preparing for a battle with Billy McCarthy."

"Well, one day Gallagher was taken sick and ... in walked Fitz with a letter from President Fulda of the California Athletic Club, saying he had substituted the Australian in place of Gallagher, against McCarthy. Fitz worked along with us for several days and we paid little attention to him, except that we smiled at his peculiar ideas about training. When he put on heavy sweaters in the morning for a run, he would go out and take a slow walk, and we thought this was because he could not run a long distance, so one day Choynski suggested that we invite him out for a run and try to kill him off. Much to our surprise he accepted the invitation, and away we started. Our idea was to carry him at a rapid pace to the sea beach, six miles away, and then back at our very best and make him cry 'enough.' "

"Choynski and I would take turn about setting the pace, and we were feeling the effects of the rapid gait long before we had reached the ocean. I kept watching Fitz's face, expecting to see signs of distress, but instead there was that same, steady expression of satisfaction and absolutely no rapid breathing. Choynski noticed it too, and I could tell he was perplexed, but neither of us had wind to talk, and away we jogged through the sand hills down to the beach, and then right back on the return journey. On the way back Fitz kept asking questions in regard to the scenery, but the answers he got were jerky and few. He was tireless, and his long legs strode faster and faster. He was now setting the pace, with Choynski and me ready to drop, but too proud to quit, and we were never so glad to see anything in our lives as when the Cliff House burst upon us at a turn of the road. While we were being wiped down, the Australian coolly wiped himself off with a towel and remarked that the pace had been 'bloomin' fast.' "

"After dinner we were frisking around lazily in the gymnasium, when Fitz proposed to Joe that they don the gloves. The latter assented and they started off ... Choynski ... was a clever hitter and weighed about 165 pounds in good condition. That day, we all saw Fitz tip the scales at 147. I never saw a prettier bout in all my life. When they had gone a couple of rounds I ran upstairs, took off my gymnasium apparel and donned my street clothes. Right here I want to claim the distinction of being the first person in America to herald Bob Fitzsimmons as the coming middleweight champion. I went at once to see my friend, Mose Gunst, who was a very wealthy man, and always bet heavily on prize fights. When I told him that the newcomer from Australia would beat McCarthy sure, he laughed, for at that time the young Irishman was considered a great fighter ... Gunst sent for Choynski and asked his opinion ... and when Joe told him the same thing, he decided to take the short end of the betting. Well, everybody knows what a punching the present champion gave McCarthy ... the referee stopped the bout in the 9th to save the man's life."[18] Many historians have wondered how Fitz made the remarkable improvement he did, between the time he left Australia and several weeks hence. In my opinion, the training and sparring Bob took part in with Joe had something to do with it.

The Jack Davis fight was set for May 26 at the Occidental Club. The May 10 *St. Louis Post-Dispatch* said, "Choynski is a hurricane fighter and no one can stop him but a stiff left-hand jabber. His nose bleeds very freely from slight hits and it is said that he lost his fight with Jim Corbett as much from weakness caused from loss of blood as anything else. He is a good deal cleverer now than he was then and it may not be so easy to get on to his boko.* If Davis defeats him he will be a wonder indeed." Joe finished his training at Barney Farley's (on San Bruno Road), while Davis did the same in Alameda. The feeling was that Davis, though a bit of an unknown quantity, could make things interesting for Choynski, if not pull off an upset. Through at least May 22nd, Joe sparred with Fitzsimmons, while "Ruby Robert prepared to fight Frank Allen ..."[19]

* Boko – 1800s British and Australian slang for the nose.

On the afternoon of May 23, Joe and a friend named Frank Wilkinson were involved in a severe horse and buggy accident. Frank was driving Joe to the Golden Gate Club to see the Ellingsworth-Kelliher fight. The horse pulling the buggy was "a high-spirited two-year-old. About two miles this side of Barney Farley's, the colt got his head and was bowling along at a furious rate, when the wheels struck against some obstruction." The May 25 *San Francisco Call* said the horse had been "startled by the report of a 'dead soldier,'* which dropped from the buggy and smashed on the road." Frank was unable to halt the startled equine. "Turning a sharp curve, the buggy cramped and pitched the driver and pugilist into a ditch." The latter got off very lightly, a lively shake-up and a bruised knee being the extent of his injuries. Wilkinson, however, was severely injured. Two or three of his ribs were broken and he was otherwise badly bruised. Choynski walked back to Farley's for help and Wilkinson was taken to St. Luke's Hospital for treatment. He may possibly die of his injuries." "... expected to die of his injuries" was a common, sensationalist phrase from the era. Frank survived.

* An empty beer, liquor or wine bottle.

Reports said Joe was too badly injured to keep his bout with Jack Davis. He iced his sore knee, however, and was there on fight night, as President Jackson of the Occidental Club had been assured. "Choynski was thrown from a buggy ... and injured his knee-caps and shins severely. To hide the injury ... he wore stockings reaching to the knees. Davis is said to be feeling salubrious and his trainer, Dr. Weathereye, is very confident he will surprise Co-in-sky before the 1st round is finished."[20] As it turned out, Davis not only acquitted himself well, but according to some accounts, nearly knocked Joe out. Choynski weighed 165 pounds, Davis, 170. Joe entered the ring at 9:00 p.m., followed by seconds Ed Graney and Charley Tillson. *The Bee* said "the Tillison Brothers and Ed Greene." Davis entered 10 minutes later, with Doc Weathereye (the *Chronicle* said Weatherbee) and Billy Shannon. The referee was Frank Crockett. A composite fight report follows.[21]

Round 1 – *Chronicle*: "(Davis) was remarkably quick on his feet and clever with his fists. There was no perceptible difference in ... height ... but in reach of arm Choynski had a noticeable advantage. This ... was more than compensated for by Davis' superior agility on his legs and great strength, Choynski with all his muscular development looking small in comparison." Davis rushed Joe several times, but Choynski ducked, danced away and evaded, belying Jack's allegedly superior mobility. "Davis ... landed a right

that floored Joe, and Jack fell on top of him." Both were up instantly and just before the bell, Joe smacked Jack in the mouth with a staggering left that made him totter. Other reports said the opposite: Davis missed a few punches, then "ran Joe around the ring. The latter slipped and fell, was up in an instant and caught Davis, landing a hard one on his neck, sending him down with his heels in the air, tripping Choynski as the latter

Jack Davis, circa 1891

passed him. Davis got up groggy, and Choynski landed a left-hander on his nose. Choynski forced the fight, but the Omaha man fought desperately and struck hard. He went to his corner groggy."

Round 2 – Joe countered with still lefts to the head, feinted a left and smashed a right to the neck. Davis made a wild rush, forcing Joe to a ring-post. The *Call* and *Alta California* both said Joe slipped to the floor, the *Chronicle* and *Fresno Republican* calling it a knockdown. The *Chronicle* said Davis rushed at Joe, and "planting left and right on the head, Choynski went down on hands and face, but evidently not much hurt, for he was up at once and got in another shattering left on the mouth ... the round ended in a clinch, very evenly." "Davis ... continued his rushing tactics, landing a heavy body blow which knocked Choynski to the floor ... furious fighting on both sides, Davis showing great strength, while Choynski evened up matters with his superior science in ducking and getting away." The *Call* added, "Davis worked his shoulders and left arm in a peculiar way and charged at Choynski. Joe ducked and Davis went bang against a post ... Choynski ... landed on his opponent's mouth." *Omaha Bee*: "Choynski had everything his own way in this round, though there was little execution ... Davis ... was strong and willing and he kept Joe on the run ..."

Round 3 – *Chronicle*: "The 3rd ... proved (Davis) a dangerous infighter, possessed of a wicked right." Early in the frame, Jack slipped to the floor. Upon arising, Choynski sent him staggering into the ropes, either with a single left or a succession of lefts and a potent right. Joe's corner screamed for him to finish his man, so he tore in with both hands to the head. "Davis met the onslaught with a will, and (landed) a tremendous (right) cross-counter on Choynski's left ear that dropped him to his hands and knees. He was no sooner up than ... floored again, apparently for good, but the gong sounded in the nick of time, and the local man was carried to his corner ..." *Alta California*: "The California boy went down in a heap, dazed. He rolled over and got on his knees ... when the gong rang ... Eddie Greaney ... with the aid of the other seconds, rushed him to his corner, where the liveliest work on record was done to bring a man around." The *Call* saw only one knockdown, from a Davis uppercut. *Fresno Republican*: "Choynski was knocked to the floor twice ... with a hard left to the wind." *Omaha Bee*: "Toward the close of the round ... Davis smashing Joe on the neck and sending him in a heap ... He got up groggy and was floored again by the time three seconds elapsed." Some articles written months later felt that Joe would have been counted out, "had the time been properly called."[22]

Round 4 – *Chronicle*: "Davis was cautioned by the referee for clinching his man by the neck and trying to throw him off his hip. Davis seemed to have the fight, and Choynski went to the floor three times but pulled through ..." Joe caught Davis coming in, with a straight left to the head, then at least three more like it. Jack was groggy. "The referee ... got a staggerer on the ear from Davis, who was so rattled he could not distinguish the neutral official." *Call*: (Davis) "... again charged, only to meet a right-hander on the jaw which would have brought an ordinary pugilist to the boards. The blow only staggered Davis and as he reeled backwards. Choynski dashed in ... and was caught with another swinging blow on the jaw. The blow ... (brought) Choynski to his knees. When he regained his pins, Jim Corbett, who had a prominent seat in the gallery, shouted, 'Joe, keep your head and jab him with your left!' "

"Choynski smashed Davis a wicked left on the mouth ... brought the Omaha man to his knees. When the latter got on his pins again he ... rushed at the referee, who was within striking distance. Crockett ducked quite cleverly away from a swing which might have brought him to the lumber had it reached its mark ..." *Fresno Republican*: "Davis landed his left on Choynski's mouth, knocking him again to the floor. Joe rose perceptibly groggy ... Davis landed a heavy one on Choynski's eye, flooring him. Choynski's recuperative powers here stood him in good stead, and while on the retreat he landed his right and left heavily on Davis' neck." *Rocky Mountain News*: "... both men had to be led to their corners."

Round 5 – *Call*: "Choynski had received ... advice from Graney to keep away from his powerful antagonist and content himself with his clever system of jabbing. Davis tried several rushes, but Choynski invariably got out of harm's way by dodging to either side. Occasionally Joe would drop in his left and send Davis' head back on his shoulders. Choynski had the best of this round by reason of his cool fighting." *Fresno Republican*: "Choynski recovered his wind and with scientific leading landed two blows to Davis' one. At the close, Choynski landed a heavy right-hander on the neck, knocking Davis to the ropes in a demoralized condition."

Round 6 – *San Francisco Call*: "Choynski ... jabbed or countered Davis each time the latter rushed. Joe displayed better tactics ... The Omaha boy caught Choynski a pretty stiff right on the back of the neck and clinched as the round closed. *Fresno Republican*: "Both were vicious and landed heavy right-handers on the stomach. Choynski now used his left almost entirely ... jabbing Davis in the neck and wind repeatedly. The Omaha man was plainly getting very fatigued and Joe's science was telling."

Round 7 – Choynski dodged his adversary, allowing Davis to rush headlong into the ropes. Joe staggered him several times, with left-handers and a hard left-right. "Omaha Jack" finished the frame bleeding freely from nose and mouth and spitting copious amounts of blood. The Fresno paper said Davis landed two lefts to the face, but Joe dominated.

Round 8 – *Chronicle*: "Choynski ... tried his old trick of rushing round the ring until a favorable chance came, when he turned like a flash and knocked his pursuer senseless with a right on the jaw. The gong sounded as Davis lay on the floor and he was carried to his corner and partly braced up for the 9th round." *Call*: "Davis came to the center of the ring showing signs of grogginess, while Choynski ... betrayed a weakness in the legs ... Davis finally rushed ... received a smash on the nose which sent him back several feet. As he ... moved toward the Californian, the latter saw a good opening and as quick as a flash he swung his right. The mitten caught Davis on the point of the chin and he dropped limp on the floor, his forehead striking the redwood ... when the 8th second was shouted the gong sounded ..." *Fresno Daily Morning Republican*: "Davis ... met with a heavy right and left on the mouth, knocking him to the floor. On rising, the dose was repeated, and at the sound of the gong he was on the floor, unable to move."

Round 9 – *Call*: "The good work done by the Omaha man's seconds in sponging and hand-rubbing did not thoroughly revive their charge, but ... he staggered from his chair and gamely faced his opponent." Joe stabbed at Davis' face and a smashing one-two "twisted him clean around, and he fell face downward on the resined floor. When the official timer shouted 'ten seconds' – Choynski sprang from his corner and assisted Davis' seconds to place the game fighter in the chair." *Alta California*: Jack just beat the count, but "was sent back again into his corner from a hard left-hander that caught him on the chin. He again staggered to his feet, but fell, face down, before taking three steps. Choynski stepped forward and, with the assistance of Eddie Greaney, carried Davis, in a helpless condition, to his corner." The *Chronicle* claimed there were *four* knockdowns: "Choynski speedily knocked him down four times, the last being a finisher." Aftermath – *Chronicle*: "He remarked to Choynski after he regained consciousness, 'You did well for a little fellow.' Choynski's knees were badly hurt by the falls."

Call: "All present voted the contest by a long shot, the best fight ... ever ... under the auspices of the Occidental Club ... Davis, either from the fall or blow he received in the 8th round, had his nose broken. With the exception of a lump above the left cheekbone and a few insignificant abrasions ... Choynski escaped without a mark." The May 28 *Milwaukee Evening Wisconsin* had a humorous addendum: "One of the latest fads of the San Francisco ladies is to go to the sparring scrimmages dressed in male attire. One of them went to see the Choynski-Davis affair, disguised in her big brother's derby hat, summer trousers, and sack coat. She watched the preliminaries without exhibiting unusual emotion, but when the heavyweights began to battle like a pair of enraged bulls, she, like a true female, gave a spasmodic shriek and fell in a dead faint." This not only illustrates the male chauvinism of the age, but brings into question the reporter's truthfulness, i.e., utilizing the stereotype of the swooning female.

Choynski worked Fitzsimmons' corner, at Bob's request, in his May 29 fight against Australian middleweight, Billy McCarthy. The fight ended in a bloody, brutal, knockdown-filled, 9th round kayo for Fitz. Billy was said to have been handicapped by a dearth in reach. Joe: "Fitz, at that time, had no conception of his latent ability. In fact, he lacked confidence ... was easily discouraged, and seemed ready to quit on the slightest pretext. It was in the 1st round ... when Fitz injured his right thumb on McCarthy's head. Fitz immediately became downcast. He wanted to quit. 'Nonsense,' I objected, 'you don't even need a right hand to whip this man. Go on in there and jab his head off with your left. Then all you've got to do is hook him. And the fight's over!' Fitz was doubtful, but I felt sure he could do as I said; and he did. The result was Fitz knocked McCarthy out with his left. Fitz, of course had a lot of things peculiarly his own, especially his footwork. This was one of the most significant points in connection with his most amazing work in the ring ... I paid close attention to his footwork."

Bob also became known for his masterful ability to create openings by feinting, and his famous "shift." He would feint not only with his hands, but with the head, feet, knees and other body parts. The "shift," is where Fitz would suddenly switch the position of his feet, bringing his left foot back at the same time he brought his right foot forward. This gave him a southpaw's leverage with a sudden, crushing left hand, and took out many an unwary foe. Another unique trait was his ability to strike a devastating punch from any position, and while off balance.[23] The June 3 *San Francisco*

Call reported: "Joe Choynski has presented his friend Eddie Greaney (sic) with a very handsome chain and locket. On the latter is the ... letter 'G' set in diamonds, and on the reverse ... engraved 'Joe to Ed.' Greaney prizes the gift highly and takes pleasure in showing it to his acquaintances. Choynski will leave for the springs to-day to be gone three weeks." Today, such a gift from one male to another might be looked upon as "more than mere friendship," but in that era it was fairly common as a token of esteem.

Joe took a short vacation to Aetna Springs, a resort in the Napa Valley area of California. He left San Francisco on June 3 and arrived at the springs sometime before the 14th. Choynski was back in Frisco by June 30 and about to accompany Fitzsimmons to New Orleans, where Lanky Bob would fight Arthur Upham at the New Orleans Athletic Club.[24] Joe sparred a four round exhibition with Bob on July 9 at the California Athletic Club, located at New Montgomery and Howard streets. This was called a friendly go, especially since Police Captain Short was in attendance to make possible arrests if any slugging commenced. The short bout was described as "an exhibition of fancy tapping that was loudly applauded." Bob later engaged in a "catch-as-catch-can" wrestling match, which he won.[25] Still unable to nail down a fight of his own, after numerous rumored matches fell through, Choynski left the next day, the 10th, for New Orleans, with Fitz and Jimmy Carroll. Carroll (born James Fleming in London, England), was a noted lightweight boxer who for a time was Bob's manager and trainer. Jim Corbett was on hand to witness the July 27 fight, which was sort of a "coming-out party" for Fitz in the United States. Bob's opponent, Arthur Upham, was no match for "The Lanky Cornishman," and was knocked cold in the 5th round. Choynski returned home, leaving Fitzsimmons in New Orleans, where on January 14, 1891 Bob beat a consumptive Jack "Nonpareil" Dempsey for the world middleweight championship.

The extortion trial of I.N. Choynski began, and was not going in his favor. He took the stand on his own behalf, and, as The July 17 *Alta California* put it, "His testimony was a long, rambling statement, interlarded with many things not bearing on the ... trial." Isidor said he received information from the publisher of one of the city's weekly newspapers, alleging that Obadiah Livermore engaged in "improper relations with a young girl." I.N. said he "did not believe the story ... and he wanted to wash his hands of it. On redirect examination, he said two items relating to the matter ... had been published in his paper. He did not write them, however, and did not know how they got in. He said it was very easy for items to slip in that way, and it might happen in any printing office." I.N.'s credibility rating must have dropped a few degrees upon this "revelation." On July 17, the jury returned a verdict of guilty. Choynski's bail was increased from $2,000 to $5,000 and his attorneys voiced their intent to appeal to the Supreme Court. The conviction for sending a threatening letter with intent to extort money was a felony under state law, punishable by up to five years in prison. The next evening, I.N. was released on $5,000 bail. On August 12, after several delays, Choynski was given a sentence of three years in Folsom Prison for one count of attempted extortion and three counts of libel. "The court refused to sign a statement of probable cause (that there was a basis for appeal), but granted a stay of execution until the 18th ... The prisoner was remanded to the custody of the Sheriff."[26]

On July 28, Joe asked a contact in England, Marcus Mayer, to match him with Jem Smith or Charley Mitchell, at either the Ormonde or Pelican clubs in London. This availed him naught. The closest to real action Joe had was a sparring exhibition with an Ed Lynch, on August 3. It was held at San Francisco's Ariel Rowing Club's South End Boat-house, for their annual "Jollification." Boxing, boat racing, singing, dancing and music were featured.[27] Then, as Joe put it: "Soon after I knocked out Wilson, boxing in California was shut down because of the death of some ham-and-egg fighter in a ring ... and I decided to go to Australia. Chats with Fitzsimmons about the Antipodes had aroused my interest. I had often marveled at the uniformly remarkable boxing skill of Australian fighters. They were invariably artists with the gloves, especially in their footwork. I was curious to discover the reason for (their) fistic pre-eminence ... Fitzsimmons, coming from a country blessed with such great teachers as Jem Mace and Larry Foley, had a bag of tricks any man might study with profit. Australia, with a civilized population less than that of the city of Chicago, has developed some of the finest fighting men the ring has ever seen."[28]

California papers noted: "Joe Choynski, the notorious prizefighter, has become weary of San Francisco since the ... athletic clubs ... have fallen into disrepute, and announced his attention to leave by the next steamer for Australia. He ... has heard there is a pugilistic boom in Sydney, and wants to match himself with some of the bruisers of Australia." "(Joe) has a poor opinion of the prospects of fistic sport in this city, and has consented to join Tom James of the *Zealandia* in a voyage for the benefit of his health and pocket." In 1914, *New Zealand Truth* sportswriter, E. Neville Forder (pen name, "Boxer Major"), claimed that a Captain H.G. Morse, a pilot for the Oceanic Steamship Company, "induced Joe to try his luck in Sydney ..." Morse was called "one of the most genial, popular and able commanders who ever sailed the seas," and "a bluff, warm-hearted sailor ..."[29]

On August 14, Joe took on wrestler Evan "Strangler" Lewis in a wrestling match! He would receive (a measly) $5.00 for every minute he was able to resist being thrown by "The Strangler." The match occurred at the Orpheum Theater.[30] August 15 *San Francisco Chronicle*: "Joe Choynski, the pugilist, made his first public appearance as a wrestler at the Orpheum last night. It took Evan Lewis just eight minutes to gain a fall, and then not until Joe was half-choked by a three-quarter Nelson lock. By the performance

Choynski won just $40." This was a respectable performance for a boxer against *any* professional wrestler, more so when considering that Lewis would go down in history as the first American heavyweight wrestling champion. Evan stood only 5' 9", but was 180 pounds of rock-hard muscle and had perfected the "strangle-hold," a variation of what in MMA (Mixed

Martial Arts) is referred to today as the "rear naked choke." He first won the American Freestyle (then called "Catch-as-Catch-Can") title in 1887 over Joe Acton, and in 1893 added the World Freestyle and American Greco-Roman championships, against Ernest Roeber. Lewis had just won the "Collar and Elbow championship" from Roeber on May 18, 1890. Over the course of his career, the grappler defeated the likes of Tom Cannon, Martin "Farmer" Burns, Edwin Bibby and Matsada Sorakichi. Later,

Evan "Strangler" Lewis, 1888

legendary mat star, Ed "Strangler" Lewis (real name Robert Friedrich), took his name after Evan, who is, unfortunately, little-remembered today.[31]

As far as the state of Joe's current boxing technique went, The August 23 *Police Gazette* opined: "Choynski is an all-round out-fighter, but he is lost at close quarters." The August 20 *San Francisco Chronicle* relayed the story that Joe was set to take on rival, Jim Corbett, the following afternoon. This would also be a best-two-out-of-three Catch-as-Catch-Can wrestling match. The August 21 *Alta California* refuted the rumor: "The report that Messrs. Corbett and Choynski are to wrestle in the rooms of the Olympic Club is erroneous. No such event is to come off. The statement was unauthorized by any officials of the club." The stage was now set for Joe to take leave of his native soil and seek his fortune in the land of "Oz."

Round Six

Down Under (The Australian Tour)
(September 1890 – October 1891)

The *S.S. Zealandia* was one of five 3,000-ton steamers owned by the Oceanic Steamship Company, headquartered in San Francisco. Built in 1875, it was a four-masted vessel, 376 feet in length. The other steamships in the Oceanic Line were the *Alameda, Australia, Mariposa* and the *Umatilla*. These grand ships set sail from the Folsom Street wharf, and conveyed passengers and mail to and from the United States, Hawaii, New Zealand and Australia. From the U.S., they landed in Honolulu, Auckland and Sydney. Joe would have purchased tickets at the 327 Market Street office of J.D. Spreckels & Brothers, General Agents for the Oceanic Company. J.D. (John Diedrich) was a son of sugar magnate Claus Spreckels, an important figure in San Francisco history, who made a fortune importing and processing sugar cane from the Hawaiian Islands.

On the morning of August 23, 1890, Choynski boarded the *Zealandia*. "A large number of ... friends assembled on the dock and gave him a hearty farewell." "Several representatives of the sporting fraternity were at the wharf to see him off. He expects to get a match with Joe Goddard ... In that event he will get Sam Fitzpatrick, who is with Peter Jackson, to train him. Joe will remain in the Antipodes about four months (then) ... a trip to England before returning home." The *Zealandia* left the dock about 12:00 noon, bound for Australia by way of Honolulu, Hawaii.

At 10 a.m. on the 30th, the ship took land at Honolulu, on what is today called the "Big Island." The archipelago, commonly referred to then as the "Sandwich Islands," was named so by Captain James Cook in the 1770s to honor his sponsor, John Montagu, 4th Earl of Sandwich. Joe said he was sea sick, from the time he left the port of San Francisco until within a few hundred miles of Honolulu. Upon disembarking, our subject "was challenged by a strapping big 200-pound bruiser named Wilson to fight him to a finish. Choynski had but 10 hours' stay in the city, and although ... out of condition he accepted the 'defi', and covered a wager of $250 ... placed on Wilson ... Choynski writes to ... Ed Graney, that he had a picnic and knocked the big fellow out in half a round." In an 1894 article he refers to Wilson as "an oarsman and boxer of repute ..." In his memoirs, Choynski described his opponent as "The marshal of the kingdom, a big, fine-looking half-caste, the Tahitian champion oarsman ... learned boxing from an English instructor ... He was a giant in proportions and knew just enough boxing to fall into a right hook in the 1st round. When he awoke, he swore the ground came up and hit him. The king ordered a dance of his finest girls in my honor and served champagne."

Contemporary Hawaiian papers wrote: "Joe Choynski ... known as the 'California Boy' ... will give an exhibition at the Commercial billiard parlor at 3 o'clock (p.m.), free to all." Another called it the Commercial Hotel, adding: "Two local amateurs confronted Joe. Although the notice ... was very short, the crowd ... was moderately large. Mr. Jim Welch (served as guide) to Mr. Choynski during the latter's brief stay ..." Joe misspelled the name of the Hawaiian sovereign, King (David) Kalakaua, as "Kalaukea." Kalakaua, called "The Merrie Monarch," had reigned since 1874, but on January 20, 1891, a few months after meeting Joe, he was visiting San Francisco for medical treatment. He died there, in the Palace Hotel, the last reigning king of the Hawaiian Islands. The marshal of the islands, from July 1, 1890 to March 9, 1891, was Charles Lewis Kamohoalii Hopkins, whose father, John Gordon Hopkins, had come from England in 1845. He may have had his son trained in the British style. The next marshal was Charles Burnet Wilson, whose surname matches Choynski's opponent. Joe may, in later years, have mistaken Wilson for his real antagonist, Hopkins.

The *Zealandia* left that evening. It stopped briefly at Auckland, New Zealand, arriving at Sydney, New South Wales, Australia on September 19.[1] After disembarking, "a delegation of sportsmen escorted me to my hotel. They were deeply interested in my strange clothing, especially my starched shirts and collars, which they had never seen before. I received an offer to meet Jim Fogarty, a leading Australian heavyweight ... better known by the reassuring title of the 'Jawbreaker'. The purse offered was £100 (pounds). I laughed and told them I would not fight for less than three times that ... They nearly fainted, but finally agreed to my terms ..." Soon after arrival, Joe was offered $75 to fight an unidentified man to a finish.[2]

Joe said Larry Foley "conducted the school for training the great fighters of the Antipodes. He, with Mick Dooley, was cleverest of them all. He had been a pupil of the matchless Jem Mace. What a man Mace was! All over the pugilistic world, I have found his influence. He invented the head-shift. In Australia they paid high tribute to Mace. They told me it was virtually impossible for a boxer to hit Mace's head. He must have been a marvel ... in his prime."[3] Jem "The Gypsy" Mace is generally considered Britain's last bareknuckle champion. After his active fighting career, he traveled the world, spreading boxing and his fighting techniques to such countries as New Zealand and Australia. Although Sydney then had several large and popular fight venues, it was Foley's "White Horse Hotel," at 527 George Street, which became the primary boxing center in Australia. Behind the hotel, Foley built a quaint structure capable of holding up to 600 persons, crammed in like so many brisling. It was constructed of timber, covered with sheets of corrugated roofing iron and nicknamed the "Iron Pot."[4] Joe likely visited the White Horse Hotel during his sojourn to Australia.

"While training for Fogarty my bag-punching attracted wide attention in Sydney. The Australians had never seen a small bag, using only the heavier ones, and they were captivated. Soon after my demonstration they sent to the States for small bags. These were considered marvelous." Choynski may have been the first to introduce the "speed" bag on the island-continent. The day after putting ashore, he refereed a lightweight bout between Jim Barron and Jim Saxon, Barron trashing his foe in the 1st stanza.[5]

On the 22nd, at Sydney's new Australian Athletic Club, Jim "Jawbreaker" Fogarty knocked out Charlie Dunn with a jolting right that left Dunn unconscious for five minutes. Taking in the festivities were Choynski and Tom James, "the popular chief steward of the *Zealandia* ..." Dunn was beaten, but not before staggering Fogarty with several stiff lefts to the face, drawing blood. The observant Joe would have noted that Jim was open to a good left. "Dunn was trained to the hour ... Fogarty was ... not ... His stomach was round as an alderman's ... his flesh soft, but healthy-looking. He stood straight up, and danced about on his feet like ... he were setting to partners." Tom James doubled as a globe-trotting boxing agent for John D. Spreckels, who was a member of the California Athletic Club.[6]

No further mention of the deadly Chrysanthemum's activities came, until the November 7 *Tacoma Daily News*: "The namesake of young Mitchell, who arrived from Australia on the *Zealandia*, says ... Since he arrived in the colonies Choynski has been very careful not to show what he knows about fighting. Mitchell says Joe boxed at several exhibitions and he was amused at his tactics. Joe would let his opponent punch him about the ring, and would quit at the end of the set-to apparently winded and a little groggy. Evidently he is trying to mislead those about him." This was John Herget, who fought as "Young Mitchell." Joe was part of a "monster athletic and boxing tournament" at Larry Foley's Gaiety Theater on November 18, a fund-raiser to benefit "the widows and children" of the Mercantile Marine Officers' Association strikers. Among the fistic luminaries present were "Young Griffo," Mick Dooley and Peter Jackson. The latter was visiting his adopted homeland from the States. Sparring exhibitions likely occurred. Joe and Peter would soon begin a sparring association of their own.[7]

On November 24 the Fogarty match came off at the Australian A.C., located in Darlinghurst, a suburb of East Sydney. The huge structure, later called the Darlinghurst Rink, had recently been opened, as "a venture of a small syndicate of Jews." They paid Larry Foley a fat sum for the use of his name as the ostensible manager. Famous amateur boxer, George Searle, was the club's premier referee. Umpires shortly afterward were Joe's friend, Frederick Egerton Diamond and Steve O'Donnell. The former, for on the order of 30 years, was the Australian correspondent for the *National Police*

Gazette. Years later, Neville Forder of the *New Zealand Truth* said, without giving much detail, that a well-known Australian sportsman and fellow (former American) Jew named Phin Thompson "took Joe under his wing and gave him a ... home nearly all the time he was in Australia ..."[8]

Joe ended up fighting Fogarty for £250. The *San Francisco Chronicle* said the purse was $1,200 and the *Grey River Argus*, 50 sovereigns. Fogarty was shorter than Joe by a few inches, but had an advantage of 10 to 20 pounds in weight. Born April 1, 1863 at Wattle Flat, Central Tablelands, New South Wales, Jim was said to have earned the nickname, "Jawbreaker," due to the mandibles he busted with his right hand. In 1886, he knocked out "Australian" Billy Smith in two rounds, but Fogarty's most important victory was in 1887, when a KO29 lifted the Australian middleweight crown from the head of Billy McCarthy.[9]

The crowd was large and "of good social standing." On the card, featherweight champion, "Young Griffo," toyed with a fighter named Nicholson, billed as the featherweight champion of New Zealand. Griffo, real

Jim "Jawbreaker" Fogarty, 1887

name Albert Griffiths, was a boxing savant. Largely unschooled, he had possibly the greatest natural skills and defense in the history of the sport. His undoing was alcoholism, but a nonchalant attitude and general disregard for training didn't help. The previous September 2, he defeated "Torpedo" Billy Murphy for the world featherweight title via TKO15 (Technical Knockout). Griffo immigrated to the United States in 1893, and fought great champions like George Dixon and George "Kid" Lavigne, allegedly making them look foolish.

Choynski: "The night of the fight came around and I was ... in my dressing room when in walked the 'Jawbreaker'. 'I propose that we save a score,' said Fogarty. 'I don't get you,' says I. Then Fogarty explained that 'saving a score' was the Australian way of proposing a loser's end of £20, instead of fighting winner take all, as the articles of agreement stipulated. I agreed that the loser should have something. The fight with Fogarty went the scheduled 10 rounds. I jabbed him almost out and did not receive a scratch in return." Contemporary accounts do not give the slated distance, but have Jim quitting at the end of the 10th, before the finish. On the same night, shortly before this fight, Choynski seconded Jim Ryan in a match against Con Sullivan. Larry Foley was in Sullivan's corner.[10]

Into the ring first "came Fogarty, in white pants, attended by Davis, Malone and Con Sullivan. He was followed immediately by ... Joe Choynski, who wore pink tights ..." (100-some years ago, pink was considered a man's color). Joe was attended by Sam Fitzpatrick, Jack Bateman and "Martin Denny, coming champion lightweight." The referee was George Searle, and the weights, 13 stone, 5 pounds (187 pounds) for Fogarty, 12 stone (168 pounds) for Joe. December 26 *Sydney Referee*: "The contest was of great significance, as it gave the Australian sporting fraternity an idea of the fighting abilities of the American contingent." The following report is comprised primarily from the *New Zealand Truth* and *Sydney Referee*.[11]

Round 1 – December 26 *Sydney Referee*: "Choynski ... had a loose, easy, confident style of sparring, whilst the Australian looked bunched up and nervous ... it was fully two minutes before a blow was struck. Fogarty was first to lead, getting home heavily on the mouth with the left, and Joe stood ... for a second and then smiled ... as if to say, 'You bad little boy to do that' ... once more the long, funny-looking chap from the Golden Gate poked his left glove within two inches of the Australian's smelling apparatus and grinned merrily ... Fogarty ... let go his right for the ribs, but Joe squirmed away ... Joe put his left glove on the mouth and the right on the ear and slipped away from Fogarty's right cross as quick as a half-fledged emu going for a morning worm. Then he turned and sauntered up ... with a languid air of a city dude ... Joe would draw back the left arm as if ... to shoot it straight and hard at the belly, and Fogarty would jerk back that deadly right ... to smash across, and Joe would fool him and walk round, picking his nose with his right glove, and as corners were called, he was ... sauntering round the stage with a pensive expression ... which led one to believe his thoughts were away in 'Frisco with the girl he left behind him ..."

November 30 *New Zealand Truth*: Choynski towered over Fogarty, "but the shorter man made the other look small beside the enormous development of limbs, quarters and shoulders ... not that Joe is a chick, having a full chest and very fair arms and legs. They sparred ... Fogarty in his usual shapely style, Choynski loose and ugly American fashion, the right keeping guard in a way that Australian boxers abhor ... His style seemed to confuse Fogarty; for one moment the left would be held up for inspection ... close to Fogarty's classic features; the next it would drop limply down by its owner's side. Choynski shot a stiff left on the nose and Jim sent the right pretty hard round the back rib, and was away before Choynski's right could land ... Choynski sneaked close and sent the left flush on the nose ..."

Round 2 – *Referee*: "Joe went out with his long arms dangling at his side ... Fogarty countered once hard on the chin with the left ... and Joe went up to pat him on the back, remarking ... 'Good boy, Jim'. Jim let go his right for the jaw, but the Californian ... as cool as the North Pole, quietly iked (sic) his shoulder and the blow glanced harmlessly past." *Truth*: "Joe feinted with the left and Fogarty got a hot left on the mouth ... and the right hit hard on the visitor's ribs. Choynski jabbed his right across the ear ... Fogarty looked savage and let go the right at the ribs. Joe met and stopped him with a smash with his dangerous left in the teeth, and then like a flash, he swung it, as Australian's do their right (author: this is known as "hooking off the jab"), and caught Fogarty a crashing blow on the right point of the chin, sending him reeling half way across the ring, and bringing a dazed, stupid look to his eyes. Instantly following up, Choynski shot another hard left on the nose, and blood showed as he backed away ..."

Round 3 – *Truth*: "Walking up with a pleasant look on his features, Choynski popped a little left on the chest, and ... biffed it hard on the belly, and Fogarty began to cough and retch ... Choynski served out two ringing left hooks on the jaw ... and Fogarty flew across the ring and ... put his hand down to avoid falling ... Joe ... stabbed two dandy lefts where they'd most interfere with his man's digestion. Then a hook under the chin lifted Fogarty in the air, and he was sick at the stomach ... while Choynski was fresh and smiling on corners." *Referee*: "The American ... cuffed Fogarty under the ear with his long left hand when and where he wanted ... sidled round and ... Fogarty went after him, then Joe put on a bored ... expression and poked him in the belly ... making him grunt and groan ... A grin ... went round amongst the spectators ... Joe ... cuffed him on the jaw, and had him doing a sort of back-heel Highland fling for the rest of the round."

Round 4 – *Truth*: "Fogarty kept breaking ground. Joe kidded his man, and, as he poked out his long left at the body, Fogarty grabbed his glove and held it while he tried to get the right on. Fogarty was cautioned ... Choynski biffed him twice in the tender stomach ... Fogarty perspired freely ... while he ... could not hit Choynski with either hand, the American's coolness and cleverness being simply astounding."

Round 5 – *Truth*: "The visitor began kidding and bustling. Fogarty tried left and right, but both were calmly stopped, while Joe put the left smartly on his eye ... Fogarty sent the left pretty hard on the nose and Choynski felt that organ gingerly ... then sent Fogarty's head back with a left flush on the nose, repeating ... twice more. Fogarty got a hard right home on the ribs ... copped a stiff left on the nose in return ... left and right came like flashes from Choynski on nose and mouth, and Fogarty bled freely as he went to his corner." *Referee*: "Joe let go a dandy left ... without shifting his feet, wriggled his body out of danger ... Then he plunged (his left) fair in on the naval twice ... It was a regular pantomime and a continuous giggle went about the audience ... twice Fogarty tried for the jaw with his right ... but Joe simply turned half around from the hips up ... and let the blow slide."

Round 6 – *Truth*: "He (Fogarty) received two slashing lefts ... sending his head back. Fogarty led desperately at the jaw with the right, but Choynski's long left met him in the face, and the right battered on the ear." *Referee*: "The men clinched and at the word, 'break', they came away splendidly, the American being loudly cheered for his manly style of getting back with his hands held apart. Over and over ... a vote of praise ... for his gentlemanly conduct ... Choynski hit our man just when he pleased ... though his blows did not seem to possess the piledriving power of our heavyweights ... there was power enough ... to utterly demoralize the jaw-cracker."

Round 7 – *Truth*: "Three times Choynski got flush on the dial, and Fogarty crossed, only to land back of the shoulder. Four times ... Joe's dandy left stopped full on Fogarty's mouth and nose, the last staggering him all but prone ... that tireless weapon fell again in turn, and Fogarty was in trouble on the ropes when the bell rang. Choynski's cool certainty of landing, and his gentle smile and walk around, only to return and land again – the calm way in which he would watch 'that right hand' threatening, and either get just beyond its reach or lift his shoulder to taking it, were little short of phenomenal." *Referee*: "Once more the American eagle was flapping its wings – bang – biff in the face of the poor kangaroo."

Round 8 – *Truth*: "Joe served out two splendid lefts ... Several more ... on the mouth and ... just touched his man's chin with a right meant for an extinguisher ..." *Referee*: "Joe led on the chin with his long-range left, and Jim put his right on the ribs twice ... Joe cuffed him under the ear, poked him on the nose, sauntered away meditating and came back and did precisely the same thing over and over again, until the giggle outside the ropes broke into a 10-dollar grin, and ... the grin gave place to a series of open laughs, which made the Californian look reprovingly at his friends in the chairs, as much as to ask them to be good for a little while longer."

Round 9 – *Truth*: "The Sydney man backed constantly, looking fagged and beaten. The long left of the American kept landing, and Fogarty was hawking and spitting blood. Totally confused and unable to hit ... apparently afraid to ... get close, Fogarty kept receiving left stabs and hooks till corners." *Referee*: "One ... four, five, as quick as a man could count, the left hand of the Golden Gate representative fell on the frontispiece of our man ... hung over on the ropes ... Joe ... stepped away and let his man come out of a very tight spot, and the crowd cheered him for his magnanimity ... at the end of the round it was the Indian Ocean to a dish of dirty water that the flag that we love so dearly was going to be hauled down."

Round 10 – *Truth*: "All over the ring Choynski drove his foe, stabbing and hooking alternately with the left, till Fogarty was stained with carmine ..." Joe belted him into a corner, in a stupefied state, and "Fogarty went down to a tap on the bugle. He got up ... backed along the ropes ... and the bell sent him very cronk to his corner. Hardly had he got to his chair, than ... a word from him, his seconds ... skied the sponge ... There was a storm of hoots and groans, in response to which Fogarty walked to the ropes and said: 'Gentlemen, it is no use me going on, getting punched to pieces by a man I can't hit.' 'You might have tried a bit harder, anyway,' (said) a disgusted backer of the Sydney bruiser ..." *Referee*: "The American ... fought with the utmost fairness ... Never once did he infringe the rules that bind a man to honor and fair play, and the Stars and Stripes never waved over a more manly fellow ... our lad

Joe Choynski woodcut, June, 1890

was met in a 24 ft. ring ... (an) impartial referee ... the Australian ... was fairly ... whipped ... Young Denny looked after Choynski during his training, and did it like the thorough tradesman he is."

November 25 *New Zealand Truth* ("Cestus"): "Had (Jim) known it, he had the fine American beaten early in the battle. That heavy right ... landed once, and after the fight Choynski told me he thought ... the top of his head had been knocked loose, and was being kept in its place by the hair. With this information ... Fogarty could have won easily, for his opponent was dazed, and sparred mechanically all through one round; but it was not the luck of the Irish lad to know how much damage he had done." This was the only report having Joe in any trouble during the fight. The *Truth*'s Neville Forder: "Joe simply fooled with the great jaw-breaker. He gave him his shoulder time and again ... always out of reach of that terrible right. He banged and battered and hooked ... with that ... left ... his coolness was little short of marvelous."[12] The January 10, 1891 *Police News* said Joe was the first foreigner to defeat an Australian on his own turf, with the exception of English lightweight, Ben Seth, whose victim was a mere featherweight.

Peter Jackson visited Australia from August 21 to September 26, when he returned to America on the *Mariposa*. In an interview shortly after his return to San Francisco, the "Black Prince" said: "There are three athletic clubs running in Sydney, the Sydney Gymnastic Club, the Australian and the California Athletic ... The Australian club, where Choynski and Fogarty boxed, is a new institution. It has for instructors Larry Foley, Billy ("Shadow") Maber and Jock Molloy, while the Sydney Gymnastic includes on its staff of teachers Mick Dooley and George Dawson, the lightweight champion ... there were several matches spoken of for Joe (Choynski). Among those ... Owen Sullivan, Mick Dooley, Jack Perry, Ned Ryan and Harry Laing. Laing is a half Maori and the champion of New Zealand ... now in Australia looking for matches."[13] The January 25 *Wheeling Sunday Register* said Harry was anxious to fight Joe. Choynski was not destined to face Laing, a good, strong heavyweight, but would have no great trouble getting matches Down Under. He wrote a letter home to Ed Graney, saying he hadn't felt lonely since he arrived in Australia. Graney: "He did not train very hard for his fight with Fogarty owing to the hot weather, which was very hard for him to get used to. Joe says the police were against the club in which they fought, and for that reason he was very careful. Two days after his match with Fogarty, he appeared with Jack Fuller in a short set-to in full dress. The proceeds ... went to the relief of the orphans of Sydney."[14]

On the last day of 1890, it was reported that "Choynski and Joe Goddard are matched to fight for £350. Choynski had all his goods packed ready to start off to California by the *Zealandia*, but the match with Goddard stopped him."[15] That optimism was curtailed, however, as the January 10, 1891 *Wanganui Herald* read, "J.B. Choynski ... has been laid up with a bad attack of cholera, and is just recovering ..." If indeed he had cholera (the July 20 *Melbourne Sportsman* called it "incipient dysentery"), this, coupled with the intense summer heat of Australia, would have made Joe's dehydration dangerous and debilitating. He recovered in short order.

I.N. Choynski was granted a certificate of probable cause by Supreme Court Chief Justice Beatty, in order to appeal his extortion conviction. Judge Shafter set bail, in the amount of $5,000. The appeals process took about two years, but in 1892, the California State Supreme Court ruled that the instructions given to the jury had been "too broad." The Court therefore ordered a retrial, which apparently never occurred. Many records were lost in the great earthquake and fire of 1906, but this appears to be the last heard of the case, and I.N. remained free.[16]

When Bob Fitzsimmons defeated "The Nonpareil," the usual suspects lost a small fortune placing bets on Dempsey. "Among the local losers Mose Gunst heads the list, as usual. While Mose is a good judge of a 'sure thing' in horse-races, he is a complete 'hoodoo' on square prize-fights ... The most prominent local winners are J.D. and Adolph Spreckels ... reported to have cleared $6,000." Other winners were "Parson" Davies, $3,000, and Chief Steward James of the *Zealandia*.[17] "Ed Graney ... the manager and backer of Joe Choynski, had taken the measure of ... Dempsey and Fitzsimmons, and his excellent judgment ... imparted to ... his friends, saved the latter from losing many dollars." Graney copped Fitz to knock out Jack in 13 rounds or less. The fight ended on a KO in the 14th.

"Graney said: '... from what I had seen of a private six-round contest ... at Barney Farley's between Fitzsimmons and Choynski, I could not bet on Dempsey whipping a man who should be in the heavy-weight class. Any judge ... who has seen Choynski fight must acknowledge that he has a long reach and can hit a pretty heavy blow ... Joe did not have a shadow the best of the mill. Fitzsimmons landed on him many times, and the force of his blows convinced Choynski that (Fitz) could handsomely defeat any middle-weight, not barring the famous Dempsey.' "[18] The date and details of the "private six-round contest" are not known.

While Choynski was a great fighter, Fitz was one-in-a-million. He would go on to stop "Gentleman" Jim Corbett on March 17, 1897 to win the world heavyweight championship, then drop down a division and cop the light-heavyweight crown from George Gardner on November 25, 1903, at the age of 40. Bob is still considered by some historians the greatest "pound-for-pound" boxer in history! He was a "freak of nature," a much harder puncher than his weight would dictate, with the craftiest boxing skills and outstanding recuperative powers. The January 22 *Chicago Herald* said Joe could easily drop down a few pounds and Fitz add a few, to meet at a mutually-agreed weight. The *Police Gazette* said on the 31st, "Fitz is willing, and Choynski, who is in Australia, has been cabled to."

Choynski had been training at Bondi, under the guidance of Sam Fitzpatrick, with "Young Griffo" quartered in the same house. "Goddard prepared for the struggle at Mortlake ... (but) had done most of his preliminary training at South Melbourne." "Sam Fitzpatrick will remain in the Colonies until after the ... fight ... Goddard ... made matters so ... interesting for Peter Jackson a few months ago." That fight was ruled an eight round draw, though the majority felt that Goddard earned the verdict. Jackson may have underestimated him, and allegedly had not been keeping in top shape. Goddard proved what an incredibly tough, relentless fighter he was, coming back from being floored and giving Peter more than he wanted. "Goddard is ... perhaps the most terrific rusher that breathes to-day, and ... few men living ... can take a grueling as he can ... he will be on top of the Golden Gate lad all the journey, if not at the finish." Goddard, nicknamed "The Barrier Champion," had defeated Jim Fogarty.[19]

Joseph John Goddard (some historians erroneously believe his real name to be James Bradley) was born November 25, 1857, not November 28, 1861, as often listed. The place was Pyramul, New South Wales. His parents were the former Margaret Shannon of Sydney and William Goddard, born about 1818 in London, England. William was transported to

Australia as a convict in 1838, earning his freedom in 1848 as part of an expedition to Cape York Peninsula, the furthest tip of Queensland. Of the 13 who set off, only William, party botanist William Carron and their aboriginal guide, Jackey, who saved the two white men, survived, making it the greatest exploration disaster in Australian history.[20]

Bill Doherty, soon to become Australian middleweight and heavyweight champion, wrote, in his 1931 classic, *In the Days of the Giants*: "Goddard, as far as I knew – and I knew him well – never had any tuition in boxing. He graduated into the game from the great school of life ... navvy camps and tents of bushwhackers ... ballast pits and forests where he had earned his living ... Goddard was 28 before he ... pulled on a glove professionally. He never had any science, but his success ... owing to his magnificent fighting spirit and superb physique." Joe (1930): "Goddard, an iron man if one ever lived,

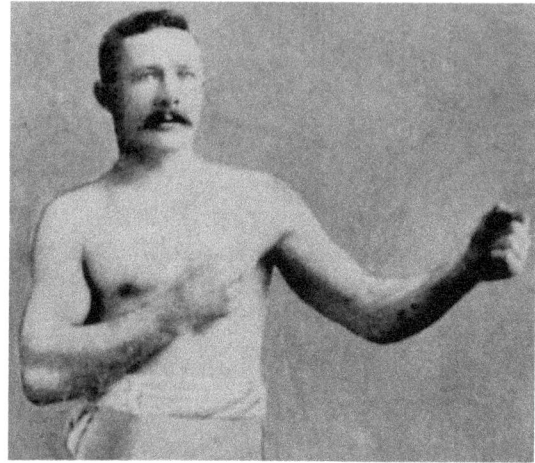

Joe Goddard, "The Barrier Cyclone"

outweighed me 50 pounds. He had flat muscles like steel. Nobody in all Australia had been able to pound him down and keep him down. He was rough as a longshoreman, almost impervious to a knockout punch and his head was like cast-iron." Goddard wasn't one to draw the "color line," either, fighting several black men, including Joe Butler, "Starlight" (Edward Rollins), Bob Armstrong, Peter Felix and Peter Jackson.

"He was rated, and rightly, with such great heavies as John L. Sullivan, Frank Slavin and Peter Jackson. At that time I think Goddard could have beaten Sullivan, all things considered. The huge Barrier Champion always claimed that a man could not be knocked out – but rather, that they quit! He judged all men by himself! Training for this battle I bumped into some of the hottest weather I've ever experienced. It was unbelievably hot. I have never before or since, worked under such a grinding handicap. The newspapers said the temperature went up at times to 120° (Fahrenheit), and I believe it. It certainly gets hot in Australia in the summer time. Joe Goddard was a bone-crusher. I found this out the moment I climbed in the ring with him at Sydney." (Actually, Melbourne). "Goddard, with his formidable knockout record and unscrupulous ring tactics, was a menace that no man could afford to hold cheaply ... he was fast and prodigiously strong, with a head like a lion." Regarding Joe's opinion of Goddard being Sullivan's superior around 1891, he expressed the opposite sentiment shortly before he departed Australia, as will be seen later.

Australian writer (Alfred Greenwood) "Smiler" Hales wrote, in 1892: "A grim, ghastly warrior is Goddard. He makes no fancy passes. He indulges in no dainty work, but with a frowning brow and clenched teeth he stalks up to his foe ... leaps ... upon him, bearing down his guard and smashing both hands home ... God help the other fellow when Goddard gets to close quarters, for once there, his mighty arms ... never cease ... Bang, smash, everything goes with him. He has but one motto, viz. – to win ... quickly. Punishment does not scare or stop him; it only seems to madden the man and make him more eager for the conflict. I saw Dunn catch him on the point so hard ... the blow lifted Goddard clean out of the ring. He was up and fighting again in nine seconds. Choyinski (sic) split his chin to the bone right on the point and dropped him like a dead man; not once, but (twice), but he was up and after his man for more of the same ..."

"Mickey Dooley lashed the chin point almost off him with his great right hand, and down fell the 'Barrier' boy ... but he climbed up and belted the immortal soul out of Dooley and won out. Smashed in the face until his nose is broken and his cheek-bone is laid bare, he smiles that old, grim smile of his, and bracing himself for the shock, charges on once more. He is a grizzly warrior ... game, with the she-wolf's courage ... with the strength of an ox. Had he started in the game in his youth, so as to have become cleverer, he would have whipped all creatures ... in Australia ... the punch that can make Goddard dream of 'home and mother' will have to be hard enough to split California's big trees. He will not sell a battle. In the ring he is a six-foot lump of ugliness, showing no mercy, expecting no quarter. He fights like a fiend. Out of the ring he is quiet, level-headed and inoffensive." The *Star* said that when he met Dooley the 2nd time, "many said big Joe was more than 10 sec. on the floor on one occasion."[21]

Goddard was an "old man," said to be age 28. He was actually 32! This was an advanced age for a pug with his fighting style. When he lost to Sharkey, Jeffries and Maher, the "Barrier Cyclone" was criticized, yet critics didn't realize he was 40 years old! That Joe started so late, helped dictate that he is today a largely forgotten fighter. It is my opinion that he never received his just due. The bruiser who faced Choynski was a formidable adversary. "The Fighting Navvy" is credited with the famous Australian phrase, "A round or two for a pound or two," a battle cry he used to entice challengers in a traveling tent show, early in his career.

A reporter visited Choynski at his Bondi training camp on February 5 (February 7 *Australian Star*). "The weather was wet, and a cold, bleak wind blowing ... the Cliff Hotel, where ... Choynski was taking ... exercise in the Gymnasium ... with his trainer, Fitzpatrick, and ... champion featherweight,

Griffo ... The American ... was engaged landing out a suspended air-bag, which was knocked against the level-boarded ceiling again and again with terrific force ..." The next day, the reporter met Goddard at his Mortlake camp. Big Joe, staying at Sturt's Palace Hotel, told the scribe, "I don't want to be clever, because I can beat all these clever fellows."

On the night of February 10 at the Sydney Amateur Gymnastic Club, the two Joes clashed. A capacity crowd packed the hall to its rafters. The fighters wore lightly-padded mitts of four or six ounces (reports differ) and the purse was either £350 or £500 ($1,750, according to the February 21 *Police News*). They would battle in a 24-foot ring. February 10 *New Zealand Truth*: "The audience was a select one ... members of Parliament ... some of the Cabinet, doctors, lawyers, clergymen, magistrates, artists, journalists, merchants and men of independent means ... The deservedly popular referee, Mr. Sydney J. Broomfield, kept the crowd well in hand ... Just as the clock pointed to 8:35 (p.m.), a thundering round of applause announced Goddard had entered the ring. He was attended by the retired champion, Larry Foley ... Herbert Goddard (his younger brother, also a fighter) and (trainer) Jack Marshall. Joe took the hoodoo corner ..."

"When two minutes later Choynski ... appeared, applause was deafening and attested to the young Californian's popularity. Jack Fuller, Sam Fitzpatrick and Jack Bateman were behind the American ... Choynski held out his hand, which Joe shook heartily." The *Truth* gave the weights as 187.6 pounds, Goddard, 155.68, Choynski (13.4 stone to 11.12 stone). This sounds very low for Choynski, but given his bout with cholera (or dysentery) and the heat, it makes sense. The *Melbourne Sportsman* said Goddard's weight was 14 stone, 6 (202 pounds), Choynski's, 12 stone (168 pounds). Nearly every paper gave Goddard a 28-pound edge. "The Barrier champion lifted both hands and bowed to the audience. He was attired in black knee breeches, with a handkerchief round his waist. Foley tossed Fitzpatrick for ... corners ... the former won." Choynski wore "full-length pink tights." "At 8:45 the men stood up to the ring of the electric bell ..."[22] A blended report of mostly contemporary accounts follows:[23]

Round 1 – Choynski darted in and out, feinting, his left arm well forward. Goddard rushed in, throwing both hands. "The Californian electrified the house by going away ... like a dream, with a rapid side-step." The "grisly fighter from the silver fields ... crowded ... Choynski and gave him a right rib-bender that made him squirm ... the next instant the Golden Gate lad had turned at bay and fought like a devil, his teeth hard set ... left and right found Goddard's face at such a rate that the grim and unbeatable Barrier lad ... reeled from the furious onslaught, but ... dashed back at his man ... the exchanges fell like hail on a window. Crash – Choynski's right hand speeds ... from the shoulder true and strong, and down in a huddled heap goes the pride of the backblocks! He was up in a second, and the fight was fiercer than ever. Then Choynski broke ground, and his footwork was wonderful. Again and again he slipped aside as the giant bore down upon him, and cheer after cheer greeted his masterly work. Goddard got home a heavy left on the chin, and repeated it ... Choynski ... banging his left four times hard home on the dial, and crossing with the right, got fairly on the jaw-point. The bell rang and both men were actually shaking in their shoes as they went to their corners, so fierce had been the pace."

Barrier Miner. "The Australian caught the Californian ... turning, with a blow on the ribs, which sent him down for a few seconds. When on his feet ... he started feinting and slipping away ... the burly miner ... lashed out right and left. Choynski at length landed Goddard on the chin, taking him clean off his feet. Blood was issuing freely from Goddard." Another version said big Joe drove "Little Joe" to the ropes, and Choynski fell through them. "No sooner was he up than he clinched ... and Goddard shoved him down again. Choynski got up roused, slipped Goddard's left to the head, then crossed the 'Barrier Cyclone' heavily on the ear with the right. Late in the round ... Choynski shot the left hand on the nose and meeting the rush, timed his man to the inch, shooting the right from the hip upwards and across. It landed with terrific force under Goddard's chin, knocking him clear off his feet, cutting to the bone and dropping the giant heavily to the boards. He got up before 10 seconds ... and faced his man, half-stunned, blood trickling over his chest. They exchanged hard lefts on the mouth, but the bell rang ..." Two American papers, quoting a report conveyed overseas on the *Mariposa*, said Goddard "took his 10 seconds and was carried to his corner, the call of time saving him from a knockout."

Choynski: "He rushed me ... I saw my chance, caught him wide open, and floored him with a crashing blow that split his massive chin. And right there was where I won the fight – and lost it! I knocked all the fight out of Goddard in that 1st round – only to bump into one of the most aggravating deals a man can get ... there was the referee to consider. The Australian ring was 24 feet each way, with the referee standing outside the ropes, not inside ... as in America. And it so happened that when the great Barrier Champion went down, the referee was on the opposite side of the ring ... before he started counting, *he ran all the way around the ring!* (Emphasis is Joe's). Talk about your Chicago counts! (referring to the 1927 Dempsey-Tunney "Long Count" fight). Joe Goddard was on the floor at least six seconds before the referee went to work. Then he took the full 10, which gave him at least 16, and finally hoisted himself up ... I was bitterly disappointed ... but what could I do? The crowd gave me a mighty cheer."

A.G. Hales, claiming to be an eyewitness to the brawl, wrote (*Black Prince Peter*, 1931): "Scarcely had they put up their hands ere Goddard feinted and rushed; Choynski went up on his toes, and his left arm came up and across. The blow split Goddard's face as though an axe, not a glove, had fallen on it, and the big Australian came thundering to the floor as if his neck were broken. It looked all over. Men wondered how ... the American could find the power to lift that mass of brawn and bone off its pins and hurl it headlong to the earth with a blow. Goddard turned slowly on his face and began to claw his way on to his feet. He was up just in time. Then Choynski went for him like a wolf. Crash! ... The big fellow ... was down, head over heels ... bleeding from a gash over the eye, another gash ran from the corner of his cast-iron mouth to the chin, there was another horrid split on the cheek bone under the eye, and one ear was dripping blood. He got up, and a straight punch with all the American's weight behind it fell on his chin, and sent him kicking on to his back in his own corner. I do not think that in the whole history of the ring a man ever got so much terrific hitting in so short a space of time as Goddard got."

Bill Doherty (*In the Days of the Giants*): "The most sensational I have ever witnessed. Among the welter of terrible punches traded on that historic occasion one punch of Choynski's stands out unforgettably clear in my memory ... when he floored Goddard with a right to the chin in the 4th round ... a masterpiece, delivered by a master ... everything a knock-out blow should be, straight as a sword-thrust, perfectly timed, perfectly placed, with all the speed and power and weight behind it a trained and skillful athlete could command ... Goddard crashed to the boards and lay still ... not a man in the building but was sure ... the fight was all over 'bar shouting' ... But just because he was Joe Goddard, before the count of 10, Joe struggled to his feet. By all the rules and traditions of the game such a punch should have kept the strongest man down and out for keeps. It was illogical, impossible, unheard of, that after being hit in such a fashion a man should rise and fight again – but in the career of Joe Goddard and in the man himself, there was much ... unheard of ... and seemingly impossible ... the look of him as he made toward Choynski was something to strike terror into the soul of the boldest ... he was on the American ... striking him with frightful, flailing, downward blows ... like nothing so much as the savage, raking paw-strokes of a wounded lion." As "unforgettably clear" as that right was, Bill was mistaken as to the round it occurred in.

Round 2 – Choynski: "Now began one of the fiercest onslaughts of my career. Goddard was infuriated because I had flattened him. Only the long count saved him. He launched furious rushes, one after the other, and threw himself against me like an express train. Each time he rushed I ducked, and his enormous body would ram with shocking force against my elbow or shoulder. Then the referee ... ordered me not to do this, asserting that it was foul for my shoulder or elbow to collide with Goddard's body! It was all right for Goddard to batter me down, using any kind of tactics, bonecrusher and otherwise, but when it came to defense, I must play the game their way! But I complied. I was determined to live up to their rules.

So I traded wallops with Goddard. Talk about thrills! The crowd was standing from the first exchange. The *Sydney Referee* described the battle as 'the most terrible ever seen in Australia.' " "Choynski brought the right across heavily on the jaw, turning Goddard around, badly stunning him and nearly causing the Aussie to fall off his feet. The former New South Wales miner ... crashed a left against Choynski's teeth, and then, closing in, grappled with the smaller man and threw him. Choynski's second, Bateman, tried to claim a foul, but the referee refused. At the bell, both fighters were staggering with weakness ... Choynski was bleeding at the mouth and had a lump over his left eye, while Goddard was covered in blood."

Sydney Referee: "Choynski uppercut with both hands, and the big fellow smashed in his sledge-hammer blows like rain ... the men clinched ... Choynski stepped neatly out of the melee, and bang went his right, and Goddard reeled backwards ... But ... in a second ... left and right fell his flail-like blows on the Golden Gate lad ... both toppled to the floor, but each rose swiftly. Goddard rushed and met a grand left flush in the mouth, but it didn't stop (him). Smash ... went his powerful fists on chest and neck and ribs. Then Choynski hooked him again and again in the face with the left, over went his right, and down went Goddard on his knees, but amidst a howl of wonder, he was up and at his man. Now the conflict waxed fiercer and fiercer; the pride of race and lust of battle spurred 'em both and they swarmed in for a knockout. Again Goddard was sent to the boards, but his mighty lion-heart did not quail ... he broke down Choynski's guard and forced the lighter lad in front of him ... He beat him to the floor and fell on him. A foul was claimed but not allowed ..."

Round 3 – *Barrier Miner*: "Goddard ... chased his opponent round the enclosure. Choynski suddenly turned and punished Goddard, who ... had both ... eyes cut ..." *Truth*: "Goddard sprang at his man, sending both hands and all his weight, but Choynski ducked superbly and clinched. Then ... no scribe could count or describe the blows. Choynski gave no ground, his punches were well timed and most effective while Goddard's were more frequent, but ... round-house ... American Joe dropped ... Australian Joe with a single, stunning right cross to the left eye. It re-opened a cut that Mick Dooley first laid open in an earlier encounter. He retaliated and created a slight cut over Choynski's eye. Goddard's weight forced the other Joe to the boards, and he fell heavily on ... him. Upon arising ... the Aussie forced Choynski over the top rope on the small of his back and used his massive bulk to crush him down on the ropes. The referee again made no attempt to force Goddard off, as ... he should have. When ... Joe finally did pull back, Choynski slid with a limp thud to the floor, where he lay for a five-count ... to the astonishment of all, he sprang to his feet and rushed in, dealing out fast and good lefts to body and face. The Barrier Cyclone was nearly helpless ... Choynski tried to marshal his resources for the knockout.

He turned the Australian around with a heavy right to the chin and Goddard staggered halfway across the ring, but would not fall. An ordinary man would have caved in ... but not lion-hearted, iron-jawed Joe. At the bell, both stood ... exhausted, weak and bleeding.

"Like two whirlwinds the men went at each other ... with sickening force fell the crushing blows. Larry Foley told Goddard: 'Fight for his body, He's too slippery with his head.' It was well for the Barrier lad that he had that prince of seconds behind him, for never in this world did a man need wise counsel more in time of desperate need. Smash! Full on the point went Choynski's left hook, followed by a heavy chop on the chin – and down crashed Goddard. Up he got ... Locked in a clinch, the men swayed like trees in a storm; both fell. When they arose, Goddard was bleeding freely from nose and mouth and a gash over one eye. Choynski did not show a mark, but his body ... must have felt as if the posts of the gate of hell had fallen on him. Repeatedly the gallant lad ... showered lefts and rights on the iron frame ... but the Barrier man is seemingly invulnerable! ... Choynski trying, with that peculiar hook ... to lay Goddard down ... for a moment, it looked as though America had the battle won ... Choynski got his back to the ropes ... Then, as (when) fought Owen Sullivan, Goddard ... hurled his gigantic frame against Choynski ... by sheer strength crushed his body over the ropes. Poor Joe ... slipped down and looked as if every rib in his body was broken. We thought the life had been crushed out of him. 'Foul!' rose the cry, but the referee refused to allow it ... Choynski rallied ... battered Goddard until he was almost helpless ... arms hanging at his sides. Choynski dashed in his left four times, so fast and so hard ... Goddard's hands again fell. He stood in the center of the ring, rocking on his feet and smiling in a sickly manner. Time was called and he staggered to his corner."

Round 4 – Goddard made a better recovery than Joe. He forced the lighter man heavily into the ropes and swung furiously with both fists. The punches were not particularly heavy, but the sheer volume wore on Choynski. The majority of Goddard's blows were to the "wind," ribs and over the heart. Winded, Goddard stepped back and swung a potent right uppercut to the mouth that dropped Joe. The San Franciscan was up at "four," and Goddard pegged away, driving Choynski around the ring. Finally, the former candy-maker, totally worn out, reeled toward Goddard and fell limply to the floor. "Goddard stood glaring at him, panting painfully, his knees rocking under him ..." Five seconds elapsed, but to everyone's surprise, Joe rolled over and pulled himself to his feet. As they staggered toward each other, the bell ended the round. Amid frantic cheers, the exhausted pugilists were half-carried to their corners. Both were bloody, but Goddard's face was almost unrecognizable.

About 30 seconds had elapsed, when Sam Fitzpatrick walked to the middle of the ring and threw up the sponge, signaling capitulation. Goddard stood, his brother Herbert raised him up and carried him to the center of the ring, accompanied by wild cheers. Choynski sat limp and despondent in his corner. Goddard strode over and shook his hand heartily. As the Australian staunched the flow of blood from his cheek, chin and left eyebrow with a towel, he made a brief speech. Part of the dialogue was an expression of sorrow for Choynski, beaten and so far from home. He also made a declaration to the effect that his victory was due to his being the heavier man. Ironically, Goddard also gave thanks for the "fair play" he received from the officials. It's unfortunate that Joe, the foreigner, couldn't say the same! *Sydney Referee*: "The American youth ... kept coming up for more, and managed to stay to the call of time. But, he was clean exhausted and unable to respond for the 5th round. Goddard was declared the winner, and so ended one of the greatest exhibitions of gameness and terrific punching ever witnessed by a Sydney fight crowd!"

"Boxer Major" (Neville Forder), *New Zealand Truth*: "Interviewing the men below stairs, I found Choynski lying on a stretcher, being attended to by his seconds and Bateman and Fuller expressed great disgust at the sudden surrender. His lips were pretty badly burst and he was cut slightly over the left eye, but otherwise he had no marks, and said it was his legs that refused duty. But for that he could have gone on indefinitely ... 'He was too heavy for me, and wore my strength out,' said poor Joe. He was then hurried away to get a hot bath. Goddard came down later, strong as a horse, laughing and assisting to dress himself. His face was badly marked ... He stood ... like a grand young giant ... shook hands all round and went off in a cab for a hot bath ... the form shown ... places him right on the top rung of the ladder ... In the absence of Jackson and Slavin he is our champion, and ... no man living could be imported who could down Rusher Joe." In 1917, Goddard was quoted as saying, "I didn't know 'ow ... or where 'e 'it me, but 'e knocked me down so much that I lost track. Then I 'it 'im, and, lookin' around the ring, I found that I 'ad won the bloody fight."

The prevalent opinion was that the chink in Joe's armor was his legs. Like Bob Fitzsimmons, he had a well-developed and heavily muscled upper torso, but disproportionately thin lower limbs. Still, judging from eyewitness accounts, had it not been for a weight discrepancy of nearly 30 pounds, Choynski would have beaten his man down. Part of the aftermath of this encounter was another call for a "light heavyweight" division, as, per a February 1891 publication: "It is as we have always said – a first-class man of over 185 pounds, in condition, will (barring accidents) invariably defeat any man who weighs less than 175 pounds. As the case now stands, a man of 160 pounds is obliged to fight men ... 30 to 50 pounds heavier ... Then, why not have a class from 158 (the current middleweight limit) to 175 pounds, and give such men a show?"[24] The light-heavyweight division would not receive universal acceptance until at least 1904, though I contend that Joe Choynski was its first titleholder. More on that later.

On March 19, the steamship *Mariposa* landed at San Francisco after a 24-day journey. Choynski was not among its 151 passengers. A number of sporting men expectantly waited at the Folsom Street wharf to see Joe and Goddard, who was rumored to be returning with him. The *Mariposa*, seven days out from Hawaii, brought news of tremors on the Big Island and that the cone of the Halema'uma'u crater of the volcano Kilauea had disappeared. Sam Fitzpatrick was aboard. He said that Choynski would not return until after his May match with Mick Dooley, that Goddard's weight advantage over Joe had been 39 pounds, and that the Australian took 15 stitches in his face after the fight. "Had it not been for a severe attack of sickness the Californian was nursing for several weeks after he signed articles to fight Goddard, the latter never would have won."[25]

On April 17, a San Francisco friend of Choynski's, Charley Asher, received a letter from Joe, saying if he defeated Dooley in his next bout, he would attempt to secure a rematch with Goddard.[26] Triumphing over Dooley was no foregone conclusion. In 1886, Mick stopped a young Bob Fitzsimmons in four rounds. While Dooley stood about 6' tall, he only weighed 165-175 pounds. He was perhaps Australia's most skillful boxer, but because he often fought men much heavier than himself, Mick was occasionally knocked out. He was kayoed by Peter Jackson in 1886 and by Frank Slavin in 1887 and 1888. In 1890, Dooley fought Goddard twice. In their first tilt, it was anyone's battle up to the 21st frame, when Joe stopped him. Mick blackened both of Goddard's eyes, however, and according to Bill Doherty, had come "within an ace of getting the verdict." He also floored the Barrier man several times but, like Choynski, could not quite keep him down. The May 25 *Melbourne Sportsman* said Dooley broke his left hand in the 4th round, a tremendous handicap. Doherty recalled seeing Choynski employ a "semi-crouch" on several occasions.

Around May 15, Joe, in a letter home, said he had become inured to the Australian climate and was rounding into "really tip-top condition."[27] An Aussie scribe wrote: "Choynski and ... Dooley ... The fight is in everyone's mouth in Victoria. The clever, shifty, cunning American is a great favorite with the Vics, as he is here, on account of his nice, quiet, inoffensive style of pegging along through life. There's no bluster about Joe. He trains hard, and always has a quiet, confident way with him that pleases the lovers of a good athlete. He's as mild as milk outside the ring, though a terrific pace maker in it. Our Mick jogs along the same as of old, putting in good work and getting well. He is the pet of all who tumble against him, from the newsboys to the merchants, for he behaves like a level-headed man in season and out of season. He too, will have a mighty big following in Melbourne ... The ... club will be full to the doors ... and one of the cleverest battles ever fought will be witnessed or I am much mistaken."[28]

On the 16th, Joe umpired a fight at the California Club (also known as "Yankee Sam's Hall") on Castlereagh Street in Sydney, between a Maxwell and Burke. Although the custom in Australia was for the arbiter to remain outside the ring, he repeatedly had to enter the ring to separate the combatants. "The rules of the game were disregarded, all pretence to a scientific display was apparently forgotten and the men simply punched and slogged viciously and persistently for a round and about three-quarters." Maxwell was floored for the count in the 2nd round.[29]

In 1915, an Edward Gorman claimed to have grown up with Mick Dooley. His letter to Neville Forder, published in the February 26 *New Zealand Truth*, said, and Forder agreed, that Mick often experienced extreme nervousness, "doubt and funk," before a big fight. Forder: "He was easily depressed and always seemed to think the world and luck were against him ... Dooley's pessimism made him go into a fight with ... conviction that he was going to be licked. Not that Dooley could not ... fight hard when he got warmed up ... let us remember that four rounds at Foley's ... when Larry kidded both Mick and Peter Jackson to have a lash. Dooley fought like a very demon throughout those four rounds, and wasn't so far behind the mighty black at the close, despite the latter's

Mick Dooley

advantage in height, reach and weight." Dooley apparently performed better in impromptu clashes, when he had little time to fret and worry.

The Dooley fight occurred May 25, 1891 at the Melbourne Athletic Club in Victoria, for a purse of £300. "A fortnight or so before the match, both men arrived from Sydney by the express. Choynski ... with Mr. Harry Thompson, went down to Mooney's Royal Hotel on the Esplanade, St. Kilda, Frank Slavin's old training quarters. Within easy distance of the baths and with capital walks in the vicinity, it is not to be wondered that Choynski and Mr. Thompson continued to 'feel good.' A ball (punching bag) was rigged up at the baths, and at this Choynski did regular work. There are few more proficient than he at this ... When we called at the Royal Hotel yesterday afternoon, Choynski was lying down reading the paper. While we were having a whiskey and a smoke Joe walked into the parlor. A shake of the hand all round ... to a query, he described himself fit. 'No, I haven't been working at the baths. I had my ball hung up at yonder boat-shed, where the ceiling is higher. I have often gone for a walk to Brighton and back ... a plunge into the sea, and I feel fit for anything ... if I don't win ... I shall have to quit the game. But I think I'm going to win ...' " Dooley trained at the Foundry Hotel, under Charley Werry's direction. Joe said, years later: "Dooley's wonderful skill was not much greater than my own by that time, for I had profited by my study of the boxing of Australians, adapting much of it to my American knowledge."[30]

Tom Burrows put on an exhibition of Indian club swinging. He became known as Australia's most proficient exponent of that art. "Professor" William Miller* had the hall decorated with flags of many nations, a multitude of trophies and a large, Australian flag hung over the eastern end of the ring. Present were racing men, doctors, lawyers and members of other local clubs. The fighters were weighed before entering the 24-foot-square ring. Joe, wearing light blue, tipped the scales at 172 pounds. Dooley, wearing the dark blue of the Sydney Amateur Gymnasium, weighed 169. He was accompanied by Peter Newton, Jack Fuller and Charley Werry, while Joe was attended by Harry Thompson, Jack and Martin "Buffalo" Costello. The boxers wore two-ounce gloves, made especially for them. The referee was W.R. Virgoe. The following is another amalgamated account:[31]

* Miller was a multi-sport prodigy who won competitions in weightlifting, boxing, wrestling, gymnastics, fencing and long-distance walking. He was one of the best all-round athletes in history.

Round 1 – Choynski adopted rushing tactics, driving a left to the body and a quick right to the jaw. Dooley countered with a staggering straight right to the head. They traded body blows, then stepped around cleverly and feinted. While Dooley was noted for his quickness afoot and left jab, Joe gave him little opportunity to use them. He drove Mick to the ropes with a fierce attack and roughed him up. In a furious rally, Dooley landed a heavy right under the ear, Joe countering with a left square on the mouth. About a minute in, Mick was weak in the legs and went down. After rising, he tried to land the right, but Choynski nimbly stepped away. Just before the bell, Joe landed a hard right to Dooley's head. He won the frame.

Round 2 – The round and fight ended with sudden quickness. Dooley lashed out, but Choynski drove him into a corner with a sharp right to the body. He cleverly avoided two punches, then landed a left to the mouth and a sizzling right to the jaw, dropping his foe. Dazed, Mick took less than his allotted seconds before rising. Joe charged in, doubled him up with a left to "the mark" (solar plexus) and crashed a quick, tremendous right, just under the ear. The blow knocked Dooley clean off his feet and dropped him as if he'd been shot. The 10-count was a mere formality; the veteran was out cold. Joe helped carry the helpless Dooley to his corner. Contemporary accounts were unanimous in saying it had been one of the shortest fights on record. What was not unanimous were the versions of the 2nd heat.

The May 25 *Melbourne Sportsman* said Joe dropped Mick three times in the round. That paper and the *Police News* claimed two days later that Dooley went down twice in the 2nd, each time from a right to the head. The round lasted 1 minute, 11 seconds. The American's victory not only secured him the rematch with Goddard, but, according to the May 27 *San Francisco Chronicle*, he had also beaten Australia's light-heavyweight champion.

In his dressing room, Joe was interviewed by reporters, and fans scrambled to see who would get his shoes as souvenirs. Martin "Buffalo" Costello, Joe's American second and a noted fighter, himself, pulled one of Joe's shoes off as a keepsake. A "private" fan acquired the other. Joe seemed to dislike so much attention, though he chatted pleasantly. He said he expected to score an early knockout, as he was very fit and went aggressively for the win. It was some time before Dooley was aware he had lost the bout, and fully 30 minutes before reporters could get a coherent response from him. He was marked and cut up. Mick buried his head in his hands, and said this would be his last ring battle, although he went on to fight another nine years, with mixed results.

Though not widely-documented, Joe boxed a four round bout on June 3 with "Buffalo" Costello, at the Melbourne A.C. Martin was originally from Buffalo, New York, hence the nickname, but had been living and fighting in Australia since 1887. This match has been referred to as both an exhibition and a No Decision.[32] Writing to Ed Graney from the Melbourne suburb of St. Kilda, Joe said, "I have several good offers to stay in this country; one ... to take charge of a hotel. They also want to make a bookmaker out of me, but I prefer old Frisco. Griffin ('Young Griffo') is very anxious to go to America and has asked me to take him with me, when I return."

Next for Choynski was a "tune-up" against Owen Sullivan, on June 20 at the Melbourne club. He contracted to stop Owen within 8 rounds, for a purse of £100. An Adelaide paper said both men weighed 12 stone, 4 pounds (172 pounds), which sounds light for Sullivan. The latter lost to Goddard in 1889 on a KOby11, but the next year battled him to a D10. Next, Owen stopped Jim Hall in 11, followed with a 44-round loss to New Zealand heavyweight champion, Harry Laing, but in his last fight, had a W8 over Peter Petersen. Bill Doherty described Sullivan as "a tall, lanky, raw-boned Irishman, an irrepressible humorist, a spendthrift, absolutely unpolished in his manners, and a man of little education."

Joe was again seconded by Harry Thompson and "Buffalo" Costello. Sullivan was attended by Charley Taylor, Martin Denny and a man named Boland. W.R. Virgoe was the umpiring official, as in the Dooley fight. Joe said Owen stood 6' 5" and "not only of gigantic proportions, but he was one of the clever boxers of the Larry Foley school. My friend who wagered I would stop Sullivan in four rounds was considered 'balmy', and I confessed I believed he ... acted rashly. But I knocked Sullivan out in the 1st round with a punch to the ribs. He had to be carried from the ring and was 'out' for an hour. We were afraid he was going to die. It was a week before he could leave his bed." Joe's memory was a bit hazy, as reports said it lasted into the 2nd frame, and described the action like this:[33]

Round 1 – "Choynski went in to make the pace and just escaped a wicked right from Sullivan. The American continued to bore in and got home three times on the face and body. Owen replying with a good one on the chin, sending Choynski's head well back. Quick exchanges ensued, ending in Choynski being brought to his knees with a right on the jaw. He was up like a cork, and with fire in his eye, rushed at Sullivan and dealt him a right-hander under the heart with such terrific force that he came to the boards heavily and many thought the fight was over. He came up to time, however, and mixed things ... till the gong sounded." Two papers said Joe floored his foe twice, one asserting, with body shots.

Round 2 – "Choynski went to the attack and got home twice with the left on the body and ... a right on the jaw. Sullivan, though apparently weak, managed to put in a flush left, and was immediately ... floored with a right. He took his 10 sec. and struggled manfully to his feet, only to be ... knocked down with a heavy right on the jaw. This time he was counted out, although he tried hard to regain his feet. When taken to his corner he was quite dazed. The blow under the heart in the 1st round settled the contest. Joe Goddard was present ... and looked in splendid fettle." Choynski gained £75 as the winner, Sullivan taking £25 as the loser.

Choynski said he went to the race track the next day and "was nearly floored when strangers would introduce themselves to me and tell me they won on me and offer to divide their winnings with me. Who ever heard of such a thing in America? Another delightful custom was how they paid over the stakes. A banquet was held the day after the fight, to which the principals, their seconds, managers and members of the press were invited. Complimentary things were said, and the fighters were given their money."[34] Joe soon began training for the Goddard rematch, confident he could beat his "maniacally tough" adversary this time, being fully adapted to the Australian clime and Goddard's fighting style.

The Melbourne Athletic Club made an offer of $5,000 to "Gentleman" Jim Corbett, to face the winner of this fight. Corbett refused, saying he could make more on the minstrel stage and that neither man was in his class as a fighter. This was a bluff. Jim didn't want to risk his status as a leading contender for John L. Sullivan's heavyweight title, against opponents of their caliber. After he retired from the ring, Corbett admitted that he was keenly aware of the danger both Choynski and Goddard posed. Instead, Jim won the championship from Sullivan on September 7, the following year in New Orleans, on a 21-round knockout. He would make but one successful defense of the title, a 3rd round kayo of washed-up Brit, Charley Mitchell, who was scarcely more than a middleweight.

The July 17 *Philadelphia Inquirer* wrote that, at Choynski's request, the fight would take place under *"Police Gazette* rules," a variation of the Queensberry code. They necessitated a finish fight, among other things. The *Oakland Tribune* and *San Francisco Call* that day related, "Choynski and Martin Costello have taken to the drama and recently appeared ... in a play called Men of Muscle. It is a sort of burlesque on Sullivan's Honest Hearts and Willing Hands. Choynski says his engagement will expire when the vessel with Sullivan on board is sighted." The August 1 *Police Gazette* added that "Choynski's opening lines are 'Dere comes fader (father).' It seems that on the first night he forgot them, but the audience kindly overlooked the lack of memory and gave the Californian a hearty reception. Joe has somewhat changed since his residence in the colonies, for he now cultivates a moustache and side chops, and is quite English, you know."

When John L. Sullivan arrived in Australia on July 20, Choynski was said to have been there to greet him. If he was, then Joe not only did so on the day of his second encounter with Goddard, but somehow traveled the roughly 1,000 kilometers (some 620 miles) from Melbourne to Sydney. Unlikely, at best. Joe supposedly told John L. (quite prophetically): "They'll pay to the limit to see you scrap, John, there is not another nation on earth so fight-crazy, but I'm afraid they won't fall for the stage stuff!"[35]

At last the night arrived, July 20, 1891. That day's *Melbourne Sportsman* remarked that Choynski had been weakened by incipient dysentery in his first fight with Goddard, but managed to strengthen his legs some with special exercises at St. Kilda, where he prepared again. Goddard took his training first at the Foundry Hotel, but finished at a site on the Esplanade at Queenscliff, a seaside resort. "Smiler" Hales was one of the scribes who came down from Sydney to see the battle. William Miller had the Melbourne Athletic Club decorated for the occasion, as he did for the Choynski-Dooley bout. Trophies and international flags were on display, along with portraits of "old-time and modern fighters," which included likenesses of Frank Slavin and Joe Goddard. The Stars and Stripes was hung prominently above one corner of the ring, the Australian flag over the opposite corner. The fighters wore specially-made gloves, stuffed with hair and covered with chamois kid. Comments were made of the difficulty many had, with the proper pronunciation of Choynski's surname, variously saying "Choinski, with a soft 'Ch', 'Koneskee', 'Shoynskee', while there was a smile at the man who happened to get it right with 'Ko-in-skee.' "

This was again for the heavyweight championship of Australia. Attendance was nearly 1,000, which might be considered low, except that admission was unusually high. The *South Australian Register* said the fees were 10 shillings to club members, 20 shillings for athletic members, and £3 for honorary members. Several youths who could not afford admission climbed up on the galvanised iron roof, where, armed with large roofing shears, they cut and peeled back several sections. From their perch, the larrikins peered through to the ring below. Authorities of the club attempted to dislodge the freeloaders by spraying a fire hose until they were drenched, but didn't gain the desired effect. Water from the hose came down through the recently-cut openings in the roof, drenching paying spectators inside. Club management soon called a halt to the hosing operation, and the "deadheads" remained on the rooftop.

The fighters' weights were given as 185½ pounds for Goddard, 173, Choynski, showing the latter added several pounds since their last meeting.

Joe Goddard, "The Fighting Navvy"

In fact, Joe weighed the most of any fight in his career. The main event followed an exhibition of "American axe swinging" and preliminary bouts, including American Joe McAuliffe vs. Tom Duggan. Jack Marshall, Herbert Goddard and Larry Foley followed the Barrier man into the ring (the *Melbourne Sportsman* said Tom Duggan, instead of Foley). Choynski was attended by Harry Thompson and Martin & Jack Costello. W.R. Virgoe again refereed. The men fought for a purse of £400, £75 of it to the loser. At least one post-fight report said Joe "never landed once with any effect,"[36] but others declared it one of the most terrific punch-ups in the history of Australia. Odds before the fight were about 6 to 4, Goddard, but at the end of two rounds, *"Two to one on Choynski,* was huskily whispered by an erstwhile backer of the Barrier Boy." A blended report follows:[37]

Round 1 – At 9:20 p.m., "Professor" Miller told the men to shake hands and come out fighting. Choynski ducked a left from Goddard, which went over his shoulder. There was a quick exchange, Joe getting in a hard left to the mouth, Goddard countering with a mule-kick left-right to the jaw. "Frisco Joe" began dancing around the ring, Goddard in hot pursuit. He smashed a left to the face, but Choynski countered with a double-left to the mouth that drew blood. The Australian connected with a short, right hook that floored "Chrysanthemum Joe," but he quickly regained his feet. Now came a terrific exchange of blows and fierce infighting interspersed with repeated clinching. The pace was torrid. The crowd protested when Goddard landed a couple of punches after the bell. Both went to their chairs, blood pouring from Aussie Joe's nose and mouth.

Round 2 – The men traded bombs, and soon both were bleeding from the nose. Choynski was fast and clever on his feet, but his adversary's quickness coming forward forced the smaller man to fight back. Goddard slipped and fell from the follow-through of some wild punches. Upon arising, he resumed his effective aggression. He was out-landing "The Frisco Flash" until Joe side-stepped and crashed a right on the Cyclone that sent him "reeling 10 paces back from the shock." Big Joe came back for more and smashed in left and right, "flail-like blows" to Choynski's neck, chest and ribs. His quarry gave it back with a double dose, forcing Goddard against the ropes and hooking him repeatedly with the left. Joe dropped the Australian to his knees with a crashing right. The American looked like a winner, especially when he followed with another blockbuster that nearly floored Goddard again. The Barrier champion would not be denied, though, and swarmed all over his foe, finally knocking Choynski down. At least one report said he fell on the latter, and a claim of foul was made, but rejected (again!) by the referee. More clever ducking followed from the visitor, who opened an old cut under Goddard's eye. Both went to their corners huffing and puffing and bathed in blood.

Round 3 – Here, the accounts are somewhat at odds. *Melbourne Sportsman*: "The Fighting Navvy" resumed his rushing ... Using "extremely clever dodging tactics," Joe frequently caused the haymakers of the "Barrier Boy" to cut harmlessly through the air. Despite furious attempts by the New South Wales terror to bludgeon his man, the battling "Maccabee" used his boxing skills, defense and power to good advantage. Goddard did land one good right to the short ribs that doubled Joe over for a moment, but he was soon back on his bicycle. "Goddard's bloody face presented a terrible aspect, and drops of gore every now and then flipped on the reporter's paper. Choynski ... (got) the right on Goddard's head with a smack that sounded all over the gymnasium." *Melbourne Argus*: "A heavy body blow brought Choynski to the ground, but he rose almost immediately, and forcing the fighting got home heavily on Goddard's jaw and fairly floored him for the second time. A fierce rally followed, in which the referee vainly endeavored to part the two men, but eventually superior weight told, and Choynski went down again." It wasn't possible that the pair could go 10 rounds at such a tempo. They traded for all they were worth and stood exhausted a short while, arm weary and completely punched out.

Referee: Choynski went for a knockout, looking like a winner, but "pegged away in vain. Flesh and blood would have quitted beneath the powerful blows he landed, but the Barrier man is iron and road metal with a heart of steel." Once more, Goddard used the illegal tactic of hurling all of his bulk over Joe, bending him back over the ropes as though trying to break his spine. Although the crowd was composed of his countrymen, a cry of "Foul, Foul!" went up, only to be ignored by the partisan ref. The same referee as their last fight, same result. *Call*: "Choynski had somewhat the best of the 3rd round, and would probably have been victorious had it not been for a couple of weakening punches in the stomach and ribs. Goddard was ... the worst disfigured, but Choynski retired after the hurricane engagement to his chair, completely exhausted." The *Melbourne Argus* said Goddard's "right eye was almost closed, his cheek bloody and his body bore several marks." Choynski could barely walk to his corner.

Round 4 – Goddard came out strong, bleeding freely from nose and mouth. He pounded the body but received terrific counter-punches to the head. The *Sportsman* had by far the best and most complete account of the session: "Goddard missed a vicious swinging left ... The American lad dashed in and, amidst tremendous cheering, planted left and right on Goddard's face. The latter was compelled to break ground. Choynski was on top of him in an instant. Forcing him against the ropes, Goddard ducked to avoid a left hook and getting his head between the American's legs, lifted him clean off his feet and slid him gently down his back. Choynski, by way of acknowledgement for being let down so lightly, at once shook hands with Goddard and returned thanks."

They waged a furious battle. Choynski drove Goddard across the ring, chipped him on the jaw with the right and dropped him near the ropes. The crowd thought their Joe was done, but he just beat the 10 count. Frisco Joe tore in, but the bigger man landed rib-roasters and a heavy clout on the jaw. The Aussie "Blizzard" had depleted the last of Choynski's reserves. His strength gone, the brave Jewish lad "continued ... pegging away stubbornly. They ... swap punches with both hands, the crowd cheering the 'Yank' for his gameness. Goddard, though ... shaky on his pins, made a vicious rush, poked the left in on the body and planted the right on the head ... Choynski turned to break away and fell from sheer exhaustion flat down on his face ... no sign of his making an effort to rise. The severity of the contest had told its tale. The timekeeper ticked off the 10 seconds, but still Choynski was stretched out on the floor ... Choynski's seconds carried him to his chair. Amidst great and prolonged cheering Goddard was declared the winner. He then walked over and shook hands with his opponent, and was carried on the shoulders of his seconds out of the ring."

The *Call* quoted a report brought on the *Mariposa*: "Goddard kept piling in hot shots on the American's body and face, until he finally landed on the latter's chin, sending Choynski down. Joe arose, but was knocked down three times before counted out. All ... say it was the most stubborn and wicked ever witnessed in ... the colonies." Most papers said Joe was counted out, but the *Sydney Referee* disagreed: "Again and again he sent Choynski to the floor, though more than once was sent reeling all ways at once by daisy bashes on the chin. Choynski broke up completely, and though ... grandly handled in his corner, could not respond for the 5th round ..."

July 23 *South Australian Register*: "Choynski showed ... complete exhaustion, due to the heavy body blows ... another left ... in the ribs sent him to earth. He rose again ... but in a staggering fashion, and Goddard ... knocked him down again with two blows, one on the body, and one on the neck, as he fell. Choynski dropped by the ropes ... without moving ... Goddard was declared the winner ..." Choynski only said, years later, "Our second fight was pretty much a repetition of the first, only more grueling, and Goddard defeated me in four rounds. The same sort of rulings by the Australian referee defeated me."[38] He had to be assisted off the stage. "Goddard, on the contrary, was so fresh he vaulted over the ropes to shake hands with his defeated antagonist." The pair would battle once more, in the United States, under rules more favorable to Choynski.

Sportsman: "Choynski's lips were split and his torso showed vivid marks from the multitude of punches ... His legs once again were thought to have failed him. Goddard's left eye was cut and swollen ... Goddard jumped about in high glee, waving his hands above his head in frantic excitement. He walked about in an ecstasy of delight ... his actions ... uncontrollable. He was quickly rushed into his dressing room and literally held down in the couch, whilst his seconds got his clothes on and wiped off ... the gore ..." The "Barrier Boy" later discovered his right hand had been injured at some point in the fight. He said, "I will fight as long as I can stand. I will have to be dead beat before I show the white feather." In Choynski's room, it was recommended he take a cab for a hot bath at the White Hart Hotel, but he kept saying he was all right. When he went to stand up, Joe was still groggy and was assisted. One of his seconds produced a "little phial, from which escaped a brandified odor, he applied it to the lips of the defeated, who gulped a drop of the stimulant and seemed to brace himself up wonderfully. Gaining a sitting position, he put his hands to his temples, spread the fingers out, covered his eyes and again gave way to a little sob."

Will Lawless, who wrote for the *Sydney Referee* under the pseudonym, "Solar Plexus," was quoted in the December 11, 1927 *San Antonio Light*, saying the cannonading clout in round one that gashed Goddard's cheek "was the hardest punch he ever saw a man stop in his 40 years as a ringside reporter." When Choynski returned to Frisco, he told his friends: "The rabbits have cauliflower ears and the canary birds bark like bulldogs in Goddard's neighborhood. No one in this country will stop him." The June 11, 1911 *Sandusky Register* interviewed Barney Holmes, a veteran Australian boxer who said he was at the fight. "I was in a hotel next to the ... Melbourne A.C. ... We could look from our window right into the ring ... In the 3rd round Choynski landed a hard right to Goddard's jaw and put him down and out. My brother and I, who were each holding a watch, timed it to 16 seconds before Goddard rose. He eventually knocked Choynski out ... Choynski was robbed of the heavyweight championship of Australia."

William Miller said it was the greatest contest ever in that club, while Martin Costello had never seen such a "hurricane" fight in all his life. *Referee*: "Choynski ... proved a man of whom America may well feel proud. He gave away 2 stone 6 pounds and it was that which licked him. Choynski is reckoned a wonder in America, and against men his own weight, so he is." Many persons, including old-time fighters, said it was the severest fight they had ever seen. *New Zealand Truth*: "Goddard is said to have shown a lot of improvement in foot, hand and head-work, and the reporters agree he now hits straight with the left and reserves the right for actual business." "Australian" Jimmy Ryan, a future Choynski victim, in the November 27, 1899 *Sandusky Star*: "Ryan ... thinks Goddard, when good, was the best the world ever saw. But then, Ryan is inclined to like the slugger against the clever man. 'I tell you how good Goddard was ... You know how good, hard-hitting, game fellow Joe Choynski was ... He could hit like a Krupp hammer and was right clever, too. Well, he fought Goddard in Sydney, and, though he knocked him out time and again, Goddard put him out in four rounds. Joe thought it was wrong and tried again."

"In the 4th round he put Goddard down three times with terrific drives ... One of the three raps kept Joe down nine seconds, but when the round was over, he was fighting as strong as when he began. The records credit Goddard with a knockout, but the fact is Choynski gave it up after that round. Joe was unhurt, but he knew he had hit Goddard hard as he could ever hope to, and felt it was useless to continue. He just held out his gloves and said to his seconds, *Take 'em off. It's no use hitting that bronze statue.* Choynski is as game a fellow as ever pulled on a glove, but there is nothing so discouraging as to find your best blows landing well and not counting.' " At this point, Goddard would have had a fine chance with any boxer on the planet. It is a sad fact that the underrated Barrier champion is today largely forgotten. As a final post-script it is fair to note that, while Goddard was at the apex of his prime in these two bouts, Choynski had yet to attain his peak. "The Frisco Flash" was only 22 and would go on to better things. In a modern setting, with contemporary rules and arbiters, neither bout would have lasted as long as they did. From descriptions of the blood gushing from Aussie Joe's face, it is probable that the referee and ringside doctor would have stopped the fight in favor of Choynski.

July 27 *Pittsburgh Press* (dateline, San Francisco): "News of Joe Choynski's defeat ... was received ... with great sorrow, as ... many friends and admirers here ... looked upon him as a sure winner ... One consolation, he gave the big fellow a good, hard battle and fought gamely to the last. Joe

Choynski is today one of the best 180 pound men in the ring, and to agree to a match with a man over 200 pounds was a very foolish bit of work ... Eddie Graney, the amateur featherweight ... cried like a child when he received the news of Joe's defeat. Choynski's father, who publishes a weekly paper in this city called *Public Opinion*, said, when he heard of his son's defeat: 'It serves him well right; I hope it will make a man of him,' However, Joe's father was also opposed to him participating in a contest, and Joe and his father would occasionally have a set-to in the backyard. Choynski, who is very proud, will probably stay in Australia until he can bring back laurels enough to more than counter balance his recent defeat." This quip by Joe's sire shows his mercurial persona, vacillating between fatherly pride and chastisement.

The *Alameda* was expected to bring home not only Joe, but Goddard, Billy Murphy and "Young Griffo," when it arrived "next Thursday week." Such was not the case. "The steamship *Alameda* arrived this morning, 24 days from Sydney ... The *Alameda* passed the ... *Mariposa* at Auckland, July 18. John L. Sullivan and a theatrical troupe were aboard the *Mariposa* on the way to Sydney. It was reported that Sullivan indulged in liquor ... at Auckland, to such an extent that Captain Haywards of the *Mariposa*, had ... to confine him to his cabin." Choynski said he might fight Woolf Bendoff in South Africa, before returning to the States.[39] He arrived in Broken Hill, New South Wales on August 20. "There was a flutter in sporting circles this morning when it was known that Joe Choynski, the great American pugilist, had arrived in town ... Choynski comes under management with Mr. D. Green, of the Royal Mail Hotel, for ... giving an exposition of the 'gentle' art of boxing ... Saturday evening ... at the Skating Rink."

"There were only a few persons at the railway depot in the early morning to bid Choynski welcome, but during the day, with Mr. Dave Green as cecerone (sic) (cicerone), he has been doing the rounds of the town, visiting its lions and being introduced to many ... Choynski is a man to whom nature has been somewhat kind in her gifts ... whose facial appearance and physical development would cause every nine persons out of 10 who met him on the street to remark upon the same. In manner he is genial and unobtrusive ... there is nothing in his behaviour or appearance suggestive of the professional pugilist as ordinarily depicted. (Joe) was educated at one of the local public schools in Frisco, after leaving which he learned the trade of confectioner. The manufacture of lollies, however ... did not suit him altogether, for at an early age he evinced a fondness for the pugilistic art ... He is 5ft. 11in. high, and weighs, in condition, 12st. (168 pounds). Choynski is accompanied by Mr. Donohue, a Melbourne sporting man, and has taken up quarters at the Grand Hotel."

Choynski was back at the Skating Rink in Broken Hill on the night of August 22, to spar Dave Green, an old boxing instructor. *Barrier Miner*:

"There was no lack ... in ... enthusiasm or numbers, when Joe ... made his appearance ... there were many whose faces are rarely ... seen outside of the walls of a church or lecture room ... his own countrymen, of whom there is a considerable sprinkling on the Barrier, turned up in large numbers to do him honor. An agreeable innovation was ... the presence of a piano on which a lively air or two was played during the intervals. If boxing is ... a brutal sport, then it is appropriate that music should not be wanting to 'soothe the savage breast.' Jerry Marshall acted as master of the ceremonies, and his announcement that Choynski would referee the 10st. (stone) amateur competition was received with vociferous applause ..."

"Choynski is certainly the most gentlemanly-looking boxer that has yet happened this way, there being nothing in his address, manners, or language which would discredit either a bank manager or a lawyer, but much which many of these gentry might imitate with great advantage to themselves." *Adelaide Advertiser*: "Joe Choynski appeared ... before a big crowd ... who gave the visitor a hearty reception ... then Choynski and Dave Green gave a delightful sparring exhibition. Green does not seem a bit less handy with the gloves now than he was in the days gone by when he used to teach Adelaideans a few wrinkles of the ring, and, as Choynski remarked at the conclusion of the bout, he is still capable of teaching a lot about the noble art."[40] The duration of the bout wasn't mentioned.

An incident occurred back in the U.S. that would soon take on some meaning in Joe's life. At Mount Clemens, Michigan on August 23, two of the most noted figures in the realm of pugilism had a bloody confrontation. Australian boxer, Jim Hall, and his manager, Charles "Parson" Davies, had been visiting the mineral springs in town and were in the bar-room of their hotel, when an inebriated Hall quarreled with his "pilot." He swung viciously at Davies with a bottle, but a "bystander" grabbed his arm. Shaking his arm free, Hall attempted again to clobber the "Parson" with the bottle. This time, Davies grabbed a lemon knife on the bar, and dodging Hall's swing, stabbed Jim in the right side of his throat. The wound missed Hall's jugular vein by about ¼" but cut a gash from chin to ear that bled profusely. " 'You've done me, Charlie, but stay with me,' exclaimed Hall as the blood spurted in a horrible flow from the wound. The room after the fracas presented a gory appearance. Hall will recover."[41] Jim Hall was a notorious and nasty drunk, as will be further seen.

The *Mariposa* arrived back in San Francisco on September 5, also without Joe. It was delayed by a severe storm between Sydney and Auckland, which caused massive flooding in Melbourne and elsewhere. The waves stove in the pilot house and smoke room, nearly washing several persons overboard. The flooding likely had an effect on Joe's travel in Australia, where he wasn't fighting, but keeping busy. He "just finished a successful sparring tour and was about to be tendered a grand benefit by ...

friends." "Choynski has made more friends in Australia than any American who ... ever visited this country ... according to the *Sydney Referee*, has given up his trip to Africa and will return to California on steamer *Alameda* if he does not get a match." "Choynski ... was offered another match with Joe Godard (sic) for £1,000, to take place within six months, which he accepted. But Godard (sic) would not sign ... said he did not intend to fight again for a long time." On October 9, Choynski refereed the finals of the Zealandia Athletic Club tournament.[42]

Sullivan and his play, "Honest Heart and Willing Hands," received a cool reception in Australia. The Aussies wanted to see him fight, not act. Goddard challenged him to a fight, but Sullivan said he was under contract to tour with the play, and not allowed to fight. He showed the absurdity of this claim when he proposed that Joe instead fight Sullivan's sparring partner, Jack Ashton. Jack was somehow not bound by contract to refrain from ring combat, yet John L. was? Sullivan hoped that Ashton, a useful heavyweight, would defeat Goddard, eliminating him as a threat. "The Champion of the Barrier district," however, beat Ashton in eight rounds, either by decision or knockout (sources vary). Soon after, Sullivan and his entourage high-tailed it out of Australia, taking Joe Choynski with them.

Joe Choynski, circa 1891

Let Joe tell it: "My last public appearance in Australia was an exhibition bout with Steve O'Donnell, another remarkably clever boxer, 6' 2" tall, who afterward became Jim Corbett's sparring partner. Steve had every natural advantage except courage. The next day I ran into John L. Sullivan on the street and he invited me into an ale house to have a drink. As an actor he was a great heavy-weight. He told me he was tired of the poor patronage his show had attracted and suggested that, as I was about to return home, we book passage on the same ship. I readily agreed. Just before I departed for home after 14 months in Australia, a banquet was given for me ... and I was presented by the sports of Melbourne with a silk purse containing 200 sovereigns. They begged me to remain ... but I was getting homesick. The *Sydney Referee* ... gave me a fine eulogy ... by Smiler Hale ... (it) contained more compliments ... than I care to quote."

Joe said the banquet occurred at the Crystal Palace in Melbourne on September 14, and the Melbourne club presented him with a farewell gift of $250. In a touch of irony, making the presentation was W.R. Virgoe, who refereed the 2nd Goddard contest and, according to Joe, handicapped his chances of winning. The benefit concluded with a three round spar between

Choynski and Goddard, who had turned down a 3rd fight with the former. One paper said the Sydney sports threw their own banquet for Joe on October 28. It must have meant September 28, as the *Alameda* returned to California on October 30. About 70 of New South Wales' leading sports were present, including Will Corbett, founder of the Sydney Athletic Club.[43] Joe told the gathering he expected to return to Australia in about a year and a half, but this would be his only visit to the island continent.

His "eulogy" follows: " 'You go home by the *Alameda*, Joe?' 'Yes, and Sullivan, Ashton ... and all the 'Honest Hearts and Willing Hands' company ... I guess we'll have a good time. I intend to come back to Australia and settle down in Melbourne as a book-maker, for I have a big fancy for that city, where I have a host of good and solid friends, who have treated me in a manner which I can never forget nor attempt to repay ... say Dooley hits mighty hard with his right hand. He let go at me once and I turned my back sharply, and right between my shoulders there seemed the clear dent of his four knuckles; it could be seen for weeks after the battle. Goddard was my *black crow.* ' 'Never mind, Joe, you evened up on Owen Sullivan.' 'Yes, and I was glad I hit him as hard as I did, for he said some nasty things about me before the fight.' 'You have an old score to settle with Jim Corbett, have you not?' 'Yes, and I intend to settle it. *Pompadour Jim* can fight, but he don't like it. I'll punch the head off that fellow before I'm through ... I'd rather whip him than be able to do up John L. Sullivan. Good day, Smiler.' "[44] As A.G. "Smiler" Hales never let truth get in the way of a good tale, it can be questioned whether those were Joe's exact words, regarding Corbett.

Joe allegedly told Hales, when asked if he thought "The Boston Strong Boy" could land his legendary right on the clever Peter Jackson: "You have never seen Sully fight, Smiler. His right arm don't (sic) do any swinging; it comes across like a flash of lightning with a jerk, and if it misses he's so quick you can't get your head out of range before it's back, ready for another shot at your jaw, and how it does fly, ping, ping. I think he'll land on Jackson right enough if he meets him ... People in this country don't understand the color line, and therefore they can't grip Sullivan's prejudice against Jackson properly, but you may rest easy that John is afraid of no man breathing. Personally, I wish he would fight Jackson, for I know how long the fight would last, and who would win it."

As for Goddard, Choynski said, "I don't think he'd have a ghost of a show with Sullivan. Sullivan is quicker than I am, and he hits with terrible power. If I'd a 10th of Sullivan's force I'd have beaten Goddard both times ... but I hadn't it. I think, honestly, that John would smash him down with very little trouble."[45] Joe's opinion is diametrical opposed to what he expressed in "I Fought 'Em All," that Goddard would have taken the 1891 version of John L. He was perhaps playing up to Sullivan here, caught up in the friendship he had established with "the great man." Joe continued: "A

168

great crowd was at the pier to bid farewell to John L. Sullivan and myself as we sailed for America, where I had in store for me more important fighting than I had dreamed of at that time. On the boat Sullivan told me I had two great hands and a bright future. (He) and I were together most of the time on our voyage home from Australia. He was an affable and interesting companion – not at all the surly and drunken brute which many picture him. I found Sullivan very intelligent. And by the way I also found that he was a skillful boxer as well as a tremendous hitter." Joe said he and Sullivan walked the deck arm in arm as John L. told him stories.

"When we arrived at the Samoan Islands, King Mateefa*, who had learned that we American fighters were on the ship, sent us an invitation to visit him. The king was a magnificent physical specimen, 6' 4" tall, weighing 300 pounds and a perfectly proportioned athlete. He was almost nude and tattooed from waist to head. Mateefa, however, was a university-trained man, and spoke English perfectly. As he shook hands with Sullivan, he remarked with a laugh, 'Why, you are not such a big man; I would not be afraid to fight you myself.' " The *Alameda* landed in the port of Apia, the capital of Samoa, on the north coast of Samoa's second largest island, Upolu. It was one of the few times in that era when a ship of the White Star Line (Oceanic Steam Navigation Company) stopped off at Samoa, rather than Fiji. A secondary source said that, "twice each week," Joe and John L. "boxed on the boat's stern and Sullivan made Choynski promise to meet him in at least one exhibition after they arrived home." Joe kept his word.

* Author – "King Mateefa" (Actually, Mata'afa, a title meaning "Paramount Chief") was Mata'afa Iosefa, one of two men in the Samoan Islands at that time (1891-1893) who laid claim as ruler of their people. The other was Malietoa Laupepa, who was described by missionaries as only about 5' 9" tall and 180 pounds.[46] Photos reveal Iosefa as a tall man. Robert Louis Stevenson arrived in Samoa in 1890 and wrote about the rival leaders.

Round Seven

"Parson" Davies
(October 1891 – April 1892)

The Pacific Mail steamship *Alameda*, carrying Choynski and Sullivan, returned to San Francisco early on October 30. "Joe Choynski was welcomed home in warm style by his many friends, Eddie Greany (sic) being the first to climb up the side of the steamer. Half a dozen times Joe's chums have gone out to meet the Australian steamers, and been disappointed. When they found him at last they nearly shook his hand off. He speaks very warmly of the treatment he received from his colonial friends. He weighed in his clothes yesterday 179 pounds, so he gained no weight in the colonies. As soon as Choynski could get away from his sporting friends he drove home to his mother, whom he had not seen for 14 months, and ... the wandering lad received a joyously tearful reception. He brought home a load of presents for his fond parent, and was reminded ... that he was back just in time to celebrate his 23rd birthday. Last evening the San Franciscan was around to see his friends, and there was much inquiry after Australian sporting news."[1] Several opponents were mentioned for Joe, such as Joe Lannon, George Godfrey, Bill Keough, the "Nevada Giant," Patsey Farrell, a Pittsburgh policeman, and Fitzsimmons.[2]

"Joe Choynski bobbed up serenely on this morning's steamer ... looks bigger ... stronger and much improved in every particular. He sports a light mustache, and ... his head was covered by a neat bell-top hat. He ... fairly bubbled over with joy as he beheld the familiar house tops and hill-tops of his native city. 'Glad to get back, Joe?' asked the (San Francisco) *Post* man ... 'You bet,' said Joe. 'How did they treat you down there?' 'Fine! The people are great ... I couldn't ask for better treatment than they gave me. It's a great sporting country, too.' " Choynski was said to have returned with $28,000 in his pocket. The *San Francisco Examiner* called Joe's topper a tall, silk hat, and his clothing, of the latest Australian cut. Both Joe and Sullivan were more hirsute upon returning than when they left the States, Joe with his "sandy-hued mustache" and Sullivan, with a set of mutton-chop sideburns. After complaining to reporters about his treatment Down Under and about Australia altogether, John L. checked into the Baldwin Hotel.[3]

Ed Graney was scheduled to defend his "horseshoeing" championship against world middleweight boxing champ, Bob Fitzsimmons, also a noted and proficient blacksmith. On October 24, however, while at work in his shop, Graney suffered a nasty kick in the face from a horse. October 30 *St.*

Louis Post-Dispatch: "At first it was thought he would die from congestion of the brain, but the young blacksmith's splendid constitution pulled him through and he is now on the road to recovery. The Pacific Athletic Club of San Francisco has taken the matter in hand and a purse of $500 will be hung up for the contest to take place in (their) fighting arena. The contest, instead of ... for 100 shoes, will be reduced to 50, so that it can be finished in one night. Each man will make 50 light shoes and will have two heifers, 'one to fire' and 'one to strike.' Fitzsimmons, in his prime, is said to have had a record of making one dozen ¾" x ⅜" shoes in 20 minutes ... three dozen in an even hour ... considered by experts to be first-class work." An account of the match wasn't found, but lightweight Freddie Bogan wrote in 1898 that it was for a wager of $2,000, and Fitz won from Graney.

The Pacific club also offered a purse of $5,000 for a fight between Joe and Corbett. It was said that both accepted the match, but it would soon come out that "Gentleman Jim" wanted no part of a Choynski fight. Three of the local clubs were bidding for Joe, and all he was asking for was an opponent close to his own weight. The evening of November 4 saw him at the California Athletic Club, along with Sullivan. Watching the club's weekly entertainment, both were asked to make a speech. "The Boston Strong Boy" said he was "ready to meet the best man in the world in a contest to a finish, and you will hear from me before another year." "Choynski ... blushingly remarked that he had done his best to uphold the reputation of his country when in a distant land, and it would be his aim to do his utmost to win every match he would engage in."[4]

With renewed frustration at not clinching an immediate match back home, Joe told the November 6 *St. Louis Republic*: "I have a mind to give up fighting altogether. While in Australia I had several good offers made me to enter the bookmaking business. Just before leaving Melbourne splendid inducements were offered me to remain there, and since I have returned home I have regretted that I did not go into business. I am likely to remain in San Francisco several months before getting a match, while if I should return to Australia, I should be doing a comfortable business in less time than that. I will remain here probably a couple of months, and then if nothing turns up I think I will go back to Melbourne and start a book." Another venue trying to locate a good opponent for Joe was the Olympic Club of New Orleans, where the first generally recognized heavyweight championship under Marquis of Queensberry Rules would be fought the following year, between James J. Corbett and John L. Sullivan.

On November 5 at the Pastime Athletic Club, Joe refereed "a six-round go between an ebony-hued arrival from New South Wales named O'Brien, and James Kelly of San Francisco ..." He was "presented with a beautiful floral piece shaped like a horseshoe, and to demands for a speech made a few remarks. Peter Jackson, Jack Ashton and the Black Pearl ... to calls for speeches all, with the exception of Peter ... made a few incoherent remarks and buried themselves in the crowd. Jackson tried to speak but failed, and created a great deal of laughter by thanking the club for Choynski's floral piece, which he thought had been presented to him." Hmmm. Might there have been some drinking involved? The next day, "Bob Fitzsimmons presented Joe Choynski with a handsome diamond ring ... Bob and Joe have been close friends ever since the champion came to this country."[5]

A little-known but important spar took place on November 13 at Barney Farley's. The next day's *San Francisco Chronicle* wrote: "An event which local ring-goers would have paid $5 a head to see took place ... at Barney Farley's and cost nothing ... a lively four-round go between Bob Fitzsimmons and Joe ... When Fitz first came from Australia Choynski tried him out and found the long middle-weight so clever ... It was all Choynski could do to tap Fitzsimmons occasionally. The middle-weight champion put on the gloves yesterday with Joe to see if the San Francisco lad had learned any new wrinkles at the antipodes, and speedily discovered that his stock of ring knowledge had been augmented considerably."

"They had scarcely put up their hands when Fitz 'feinted' in a careless way and to his surprise the heavy-weight countered on his ribs in a style that made his auburn locks a shade paler. 'My word, but that was pretty swift,' gasped Fitz, and he let out a dozen links to keep pace with his speedy opponent. Choynski was with him every time, and though the rounds were friendly ones they showed that Choynski is a lot more clever in every way than when he went to Australia. 'You'll do,' was Fitzsimmons' remark as he pulled off the gloves, and to the few spectators he confided the assurance that 'Joe has improved a hundred per cent since I sparred him before.' " At this stage Joe was still referred to as a 'heavy-weight' and Bob as a 'middle-weight,' but in reality, the two were close to the same weight. Soon they would each weigh between 165 and 170 pounds, as Fitz moved up to tackle the "leviathans." The *Chronicle* said a match was set for Joe, as, "Billy Woods, who is to fight Joe Choynski in the Pacific Club, will arrive from Denver to-day. Choynski has already gone into training at Barney Farley's, with the ever-reliable Sam Fitzpatrick looking after him."

The Pacific Athletic Club's main event at their monthly exhibition on the 20th, was between lightweights George "Kid" Lavigne and Joe Soto. "Joe Choynski, who had his colonial mustache removed, refereed the match." The "contest" lasted into the 31st session, as Soto shamelessly fled from Lavigne. In that round, "Choynski stepped to the center of the ring and announced that Soto had given up the fight on account of his hands having given out, and a physician who examined his dukes after he had entered his dressing-room reported that no bones were broken, but that his fists were very much swollen from hitting his opponent's head."[6]

A benefit was tendered for ex-heavyweight London Prize Ping Rules champion Paddy Ryan, at the Pacific club on the night of November 26. Slated to perform were Choynski, Billy Woods, Binny, the "Black Pearl," Alec Greggains, Joe McAuliffe, Con Riordan, Harry Maynard, Fitzsimmons and others. The final match was a four-rounder between the beneficiary and John L. Sullivan, who took Paddy's bareknuckle crown in 1882. On September 21, Woods fought "Omaha" Jack Davis, and Woods "ran like a thief." However, he was credited with a knockout in 12 or 13 rounds. The *Chronicle* said, "He is splendidly built, and ... very active for a big man. He can use both hands, has a good position and with experience ought to make a fine fight." Harry Corbett (Jim's brother) took a lot of Choynski money at odds of 2 to 1 in his favor. The purse was $4,000.[7]

The evening of December 17 saw Joe fight the longest scrap of his career. "The affair lasted 34 rounds and was brilliant in spots ... when Woods consented to go in and mix things ... Then, Woods was well hammered, while Choynski, who, if he learnt nothing else in Australia, certainly acquired the faculty of protecting himself, came out of each passage at arms without a scratch. The ... fight was uninteresting ... on account of Woods' keep-away tactics." Joe said, "Con Mooney, dog-fighter and rat killer, picturesque character and a life-long friend of Bat Masterson, was at ringside. He kept telling Woods I had weak legs ... for him to stay away and tire me out."[8]

"Denver" Billy Woods

Billy was undefeated, the only "blemishes" on his record being three draws, one with Mike Conley. He had superb stamina, knocking out several opponents in long-duration fights, one in the 39th round. Joe referred to Woods as a Scotch heavyweight from Denver who stood about 6' 1" and was a "perfectly built athlete." This was a fight to the finish. The weights were given as 181 pounds for "Denver" Billy Woods, 172 for Choynski. Billy's seconds were Mike Murphy and Patsy Hogan. Joe had Sam Fitzpatrick and Ed Graney in his corner. The referee was either Mike Ryan or Mike Sullivan (the *Rocky Mountain News* and *Denver Republican* differed). Upon Woods' entry into the ring, Choynski walked over to greet him and the two wished each other a Merry Christmas. There were about 4,000 in attendance. The following is a blend of nine reports:[9]

Round 1 – Choynski kept his left shoulder raised "in the style so familiar to ... his former fights." He feinted with the left as Woods circled and kept his distance. Joe avoided a pair of lefts and gave Billy the shoulder. Woods missed another left, and Joe countered with a left hook to the jaw. He pursued Woods, and, by crouching and making rapid feints with both hands, worked him into a corner. The Denverite lowered his head and rushed for the open, but Joe shook him with a left to the chin. Again Billy tried to escape and Joe hammered him. Woods staggered backward and fell to the floor, blood pouring from his nose and mouth. Two contemporary articles said the knockdown blow was a left to the head; others described it as a right. A December 20 article called it a shot to the ribs. Joe reminisced: "In the 1st session Woods floored me. I got up and floored him. The gong rang, with Woods taking the count." Billy was saved by the bell.

Round 2 – Joe began as the aggressor, pursuing Woods, who slipped down. Billy came back, however, with a fusillade of blows to the face. Scoring overall was apparently about even. Woods was still bleeding from mouth and nose and Joe may have slipped once, as well.

Round 3 – The bias of Woods' local *Colorado Sun* began to show, as it continued to say Billy did most of the leading. All other reports (even the other Denver publications) agreed that Joe pressed the fight. A few indicated the scoring punches as about equal, but the December 17 article said Joe "pinned him unerringly with his left on mouth and nose." His aggression took the round, and Billy backed away at round's end.

Round 4 – Joe made a slow chase after Woods, who smiled and backed away. When cornered, Billy ducked and charged to freedom. Once, Joe grazed the top of his skull with a left hook that would have spelled finis, had it landed square. He cornered Woods and landed quickly to the head, neck and jaw. Billy ducked, covered his face and sidled out to ring center. Joe missed a swing and slipped to the floor. When he rose, Woods made a stand, swinging at his tormentor with both hands. Joe remained cool and countered with stiff jabs. Billy tried a couple of right swings to the head, but encountered Joe's elevated shoulder. Woods did manage a pair of jabs to the mouth and a good right to the ribs just before the bell, Joe appearing tired. December 18 *Morning Call*: "Choynski ... dashed at Woods, and ... a rally, out of which Woods came with a very bloody nose."

Round 5 – Choynski pursued Woods, but finally tired of it, dropping his hands at his sides. He stood stock still, in a gesture meant to shame his opponent into fighting. Billy just smiled and maintained a wide berth. Joe's ploy did have an effect, though, as the assemblage hooted the Denver man, who finally made a rush. He missed a pair of lefts and fell from Joe's right counter to the jaw. The punch landed from too far out to do much damage.

Round 6 – Woods landed a left on Choynski's head. Joe retaliated with two lefts to the nose that sent Billy reeling and drew blood. The latter parried a couple of shots and landed two or three glancing blows.

Round 7 – Billy retreated and Joe followed. Once more, the San Franciscan grew tired of chasing his reluctant opponent, dropped his arms and stood still, a look of disgust on his face. The only blows worth mentioning were a right to the head by Woods and a Choynski counterpunch to the nose. Woods stopped to catch his wind, then the bell.

Round 8 – Choynski chased the back-pedaling Woods. This time, though, he went into a crouch, led with a left and crashed a right to the neck. Woods dropped to the floor. After Billy rose, Joe landed a pair of lefts to the face. Woods' had a blackened right eye at the bell.

Round 9 – The visitor's eye was swollen and bleeding, and he clinched several times to avoid Joe's attack. Little was done in the round.

Rounds 10 through 12 – Nothing occurred, except Woods, an internationally known cyclist, demonstrated a strong pair of running legs.

Round 13 – The session was a good one for Joe, a disaster for Woods. Billy started out okay, landing a left hand to the neck, then Choynski punched Woods onto the ropes and "fairly butchered him." He hammered a couple to Billy's head, causing the latter to stoop and grab him around the legs. The former candy-maker shoved him away and pounded with both fists, sending blood in all directions. Woods crouched and covered his face with the gloves, to no avail. Joe bludgeoned him with left uppercuts until his victim was forced to fight back. One of these uppercuts raised a lump "as big as a goose egg" over Woods' right eye. A couple of times Billy dropped to the floor to avoid the assault, but toward the close of the round he landed a couple of punches. Unfazed, Joe staggered him with powerful counters and sent "Denver" to his knees. At the bell, Woods' cornerman, Mike Murphy, wanted to lance the lump over his eye, but Billy refused.

Over the next 12 rounds, little occurred. Woods ran in an attempt to prolong the fight and wear Choynski down. When Joe landed, Billy merely put up his guard, refusing to fight back and open himself to more punishment. He dropped to his knees if Joe had him in any trouble. At the end of 20 heats, both appeared fresh, except that Woods' face was badly marked up. Choynski had done all the forcing and was far ahead on points, while Billy continually clinched. In the 22nd, a wild rush by Woods sent Joe to the mat, but he came back with a "crashing right-hander" that sent Billy across the ring, into the ropes. At the end of 25, Woods was badly cut.

Round 26 – Woods, in a clinch, pushed Choynski back over the ropes. Toward the end of the frame, Joe hammered a left-right that sent Billy reeling, and he landed to the face again.

Round 27 – Joe dropped his foe with a left-right and had him in distress several times. Billy clinched to save himself and occasionally retaliated, with errant punches. He got one good left to Joe's ribs and nearly threw him with a hold around the waist, drawing a caution from the ref.

Round 28 – Woods landed a good straight left to Choynski's chin, with little effect. Joe tried several times to corner Billy, but the latter twice fell through the ropes in a desperate attempt to evade his pursuer.

Round 29 – They exchanged a couple of lefts at long range.

Very little happened in the 30th and 31st frames.

Round 32 – The *Fresno Weekly Republican* said Woods caught Joe in the back as the latter broke ground, nearly sending him to the floor. Billy clinched, but Joe landed a left-right to the head. The *Rocky Mountain News* said that, while both men were used up, Woods had the better of it.

Round 33 – The pair took the round off as a breather, simply walking around each other. Joe landed one glancing left to the head.

Round 34 – The fighters were so exhausted they could barely lift their arms. Even so, Choynski forced Woods to the ropes. Billy stooped with arms around his head and tried to escape. Joe feinted, then launched a haymaker left to the neck and Billy crashed to the floor. He slowly rolled over and barely beat the count, but "The Terror" tore in, drove a left to the mouth and a right to the ear. Woods fell on his back, made a game effort to rise, but dropped again to his hands and knees and was counted out.

The consensus was that Woods was a failure and Choynski failed to meet his friends' expectations. Joe remembered, "I did not get home until 2 a.m. after the fight, at which time I walked 10 miles out to Barney Farley's roadhouse, just to taper off on my training. Some reporters there saw me and learned that I had hiked 10 miles after fighting 34 rounds. They told (Con) Mooney my legs were so 'weak' that I could walk from San Francisco to Los Angeles and still lick a carload of men like Woods." Farley stated, "I was never so surprised in me life as I was at 5 o'clock this morning, when Choynski an' Sam Fitzpatrick walked into me house near the industrial school. They had walked all the way from town. Shure they did not walk fur economy, but bekuse of the habit they have of walkin' out there. Joe, you know, wint to see his folks after the fight, and thin he came out ter see me. There's nuthin' the mather wid the b'y but a little rid spot over one eye. I think he fought foine, don't cher know. He was in no hurry shure an he might 'a done his man up quicker." " 'Choynski fought the poorest battle of his life,' was the style in which Mose Gunst summed up the contest. It is the general impression that had the ring been two or three blocks in area Woods would have worn his man out by pedestrian superiority."

On December 20, Choynski boxed a three round exhibition with heavyweight champion, John L. Sullivan. John was performing in a play called "Broderick Agra," but attendance was sparse. This was the final performance of the play in that city. While John earlier boxed long-time sparring partner Jack Ashton in the sparring sequence, he faced Joe on closing night. Joe: "John L. ... was showing at the Bush Street theatre to small audiences. He asked me to box three rounds with him on Sunday night. The exhibition ... drew a packed house. Sullivan was grateful ... for this ... and we remained warm friends until his death. I discovered in that ... bout ... that he was decidedly on the toboggan. He was slowing up and his wind was bad. I felt glad he had not fought in Australia for if he had, the championship would have left America." This was as close as Joe would get to a *heavyweight* title shot – a sparring match with a reigning champion.

The men wore regulation fighting togs, and while not a serious bout, Choynski made "earnest attacks" and was a "willing" participant. It was described as a spirited exhibition, with Sullivan displaying some of his old speed. What began as "light sparring" had by round two become a series of rather aggressive exchanges. John L. was breathing heavily, his lack of wind showing. While the *San Francisco Examiner* said Sullivan in the 3rd stanza was "inclined to be gracious," others disagreed. There is little doubt it was Joe who eased up, being kind to the aging, out-of-condition champion. The 3rd and final round was "business-like" and the pace had slowed. Isenberg wrote that it "was little but grappling and half-speed punches ..." Though it was generally understood that a heavyweight champion could lose his title if knocked out during an exhibition, Joe made no effort to do so. A secondary source from 1955 said, "The great champion

John L. Sullivan, circa 1890

sparred three rounds with Choynski ... without landing what even resembled a solid blow. Choynski, on the other hand, darted in and out, sneaking many a good shot into John's blubbery middle."[10]

The next day, Joe received a telegram from the New Orleans Olympic Club, offering him $7,500 to fight "Irish Champion," Peter Maher. "Choynski has made no response ... as he believes, like a majority of local sports, that Maher is not anxious for a fight." Maher was inconsistent in his training habits and performances, but was not afraid to fight. Peter and Joe would have not one but three ring battles. Another paper said on January 17, that the club made similar offers to many name fighters, "as a rule without much success." It said Charley Mitchell and Frank Slavin refused to fight Jim Corbett for purses of $12,000 and $15,000, respectively. "Corbett refused to meet Maher for a $10,000 purse on the ground that Maher had never fought a first-class man. Corbett was offered $8,000 to meet Bob Fitzsimmons, but refused to meet a middle-weight. Then, a $7,500 purse was offered for a fight between Fitzsimmons and Maher, but 'Fitz' declined ... considering him a second-rater. The next offer was a $10,000 purse for a fight between Maher and Joe Choynski. (Maher's manager, Billy) Madden could not make a match without the consent of the Sage of Dublin (Tony Sage). This was received tonight, and the fight between Maher and Choynski will surely take place."[11]

While Corbett was known for avoiding fights against top opponents unless it paved the way for a title shot or served as a low-risk, easy payday, there were apparently extenuating circumstances involved in many of these "offers." $10,000, $12,000 and $15,000 were tremendous amounts of money at that time and not to be easily cast aside. Without explaining, Maher's backer, Tony Sage, cabled a message to Madden to refuse the fight, stating he would not put up the money for Peter to fight Choynski.[12]

The January 5, 1892 *Morning Call* read: "Joe Choynski, while sojourning in the colonies, became very much infatuated with bicycling, and it is said that before he took his departure for his 'Frisco home he was seriously contemplating a challenge to Billy Jordan, the heavy-weight bicycle champion of the Coast. Since his arrival he has made several rounds of the park on his rubbered steed, and had it not been for an accident which happened (to) him on Saturday, the majority of his friends here would, perhaps, never have known that he was a member of the wheeling fraternity. Joe, it appears, was speeding along Golden Gate Avenue on his return from a visit to Young Jumbo, when he heard a sweet voice crying out, 'Is that you, Joe, dear?' It was Choynski's best girl, who was following on behind on horseback. The young pugilist turned so quickly when he heard the loving query that his wheel lost its bearings and dashed slap-bang against a trough which was at the time filled to overflowing. The rider took a magnificent header and landed head first in the trough. When he recovered his equilibrium his position can be imagined as he gazed wet-eyed to see where his lady friend had gone. She was an interested spectator, however, and on seeing that Joseph was uninjured laughed heartily and cried, 'Ta, ta, Joe, dear; I did make you take water, didn't I?'"

The "Young Jumbo" referred to was apparently the "pugilistic sporting oracle" of San Francisco, known only as "Young Jumbo," and for his inaccurate athletic missives.[13] It is a shame the identity of Joe's girlfriend is lost to history, as this is a rare mention of a romantic interest of his. Joe might have done better had he taken a line from Harry Dacre's hit song of that year, "Daisy Bell," and taken his lady friend on a tandem bike, or, "bicycle built for two." The *Call*'s January 8 edition noted: "Billy Jordan says that owing to a severe attack of gripology, which he has been nursing for some weeks, it will be impossible for him to accept Joe Choynski's challenge to ride a three-mile bicycle race against a Pacific Ocean fog."

Choynski's bicycle riding had an historical element. According to the October 20, 1893 *Idaho Daily Statesman*, Joe was the first pugilist of note to take up the activity. "Jim Corbett is the last boxer to adopt a bicycle in training. Joe Choynski was the first fighter to use a bicycle, and the chances are that it will become even more popular." It seems Joe was a key figure in "cross-pollinating" the sport of boxing, introducing the "speed bag" to Australia and possibly, the bicycle to United States boxers, from Australia. Former opponent, "Denver" Billy Woods, may have preceded Joe in the cycling aspect, however. There were primarily two types of bicycles in the 1890s. The first was the "ordinary" bicycle, that funny-looking contraption with the massive front wheel, which most people think of when referring to bikes from that era. The other was the quadrant, or safety bicycle, which appeared remarkably similar to modern bicycles. The quadrant bike was almost certainly of the type owned by Joe.

The California Athletic Club announced an extremely ambitious series of fights within its confines: "A resolution authorizing ... a series of purses to settle ... the heavy-weight championship. Slavin, Mitchell, Sullivan, Jackson, Maher, Choynski, Goddard and McAuliffe are ... selected as candidates. The purses are not to be less than $7,500 each and may be raised to the club's entire income, less expense month by month, until the championship has been settled. It has also been decided to offer a purse to Fitzsimmons and Choynski for a finish fight."[14] This plan never came to fruition. The January 15 *Oregonian* said the Pacific club had given up all hope of matching Joe with an opponent. "It has telegraphed all over the country for a man to meet him, and received only two replies. George Godfrey telegraphed that he had retired ... but if the club would give him $5,000 he would ... Joe Lannon replied ... 'Will meet Choynski for $5,000 and expenses.' Both offers were rejected as being too high." Joe was having the same trouble getting matches as before he left for Australia.

On January 15, Choynski was at the California club, where he had a "warlike conversation" with "Colonel" Larry Flanigan, a noted supporter of Joe McAuliffe. Choynski accused Flanigan of "having circulated a report that he (Joe) was angered because McAuliffe did not include him in his challenge to all heavy-weights. The exchange of words was very warm for a time and Choynski ... refused to shake the hand of the 'Colonel,' both broke away on bad terms. The wound is still open."[15] On January 31, Joe refereed a roller skating hurdle race at the Mechanics' Pavilion's Olympian Rink, said that date's *Morning Call*. It was billed as the "Beginning of the greatest 24-hour contest of modern times – Californians against the world."

A six-rounder between Joe and Frank Slavin of Australia was proposed for the California A.C., but Charley Mitchell, Slavin's manager, cabled a telegram telling club President L.R. Fulda that Frank's schedule would not allow it. The dispatch was shown to Choynski, and as Joe had also left the challenge open to Mitchell, the question was why Charley didn't say if he was willing to fight.[16] On the night of February 9, according to the next day's *Call*: "Joe made a great hit last evening at a 'hop' ... at Odd Fellows' Hall. His particular friend, Eddie Graney, said that Joe captivated all the pretty ladies with his mushroom whiskers, and that it was utterly impossible to secure a smile from any of the maidens fair while Joseph was in sight. Choynski is acknowledged to be a fair fighter, but last evening inducements of the most flattering kind could not induce him to 'break away' when time was called." Small as he was, Joe had problems enticing heavyweights to face him, and was contemplating going east to see the Fitzsimmons-Maher fight and try to secure fights for himself.

On the 18th, George Dawson, holder of the *Referee* Australian lightweight 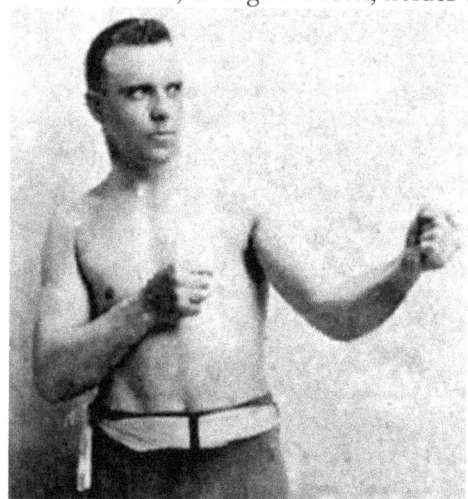 championship belt, arrived on the steamer, *Mariposa*. He was described as a quiet, unassuming fellow and would shortly become a noted trainer for Bob Fitzsimmons. "On landing he was at once taken in hand by Joe Choynski, at whose house on Golden Gate Avenue he will probably stay for a few days. 'Smiler' Hales ... said, 'a larger crowd went to see Dawson off than bid farewell to Sarah Bernhardt some months before.' " Frisco welterweight Danny Needham, a friend of Choynski's, asked Joe to accompany him to New Orleans as a cornerman for his bout with Tommy Ryan. "Choynski is booked to leave ... to-day for New Orleans. He has been suffering from a slight attack of la grippe. He will carry East several marks and bruises on his hands and body which he received a week ago, the result of a stiff header from the saddle of a bicycle." Alec Greggains traveled with them as another handler.[17] The fight was on the undercard of the Fitz-Maher go, but would be cancelled. Choynski and Greggains would instead train Fitzsimmons. Alec was a good, game boxer who later became a noted boxing promoter, manager, and proprietor of the San Francisco Athletic Club, which he opened around 1885.

Alec Greggains

By February 26, Choynski was already in New Orleans with Greggains, and Fitz was training in nearby Bay St. Louis, Mississippi. Bob requested them as seconds, and to assist in training for Maher. Choynski's role would prove to be critical, some would say, legendary. Joe, in his memoirs: "Peter

Maher was making a lot of noise at this period and I tried to get a fight with him in New Orleans. But the Louisiana promoters thought I was too tough for Maher. So they decided on ... Fitzsimmons ... Fitz was not highly rated in those days and he himself did not then realize his real ability. Fitz asked me to second him and I went to New Orleans. He was doubtful about the outcome. But I insisted he could beat Maher and I was right for he turned the trick in 12 rounds." Fitz sparred four rounds each with Choynski and Greggains on February 28 and more with them on the 29th.[18] The March 1 *Milwaukee Evening Wisconsin* noted that Choynski, although a participant in the Fitz-Maher bout, put out a challenge to meet the winner.

On March 1, Bob was still in Bay St. Louis, training under Jimmy Carroll, a good English lightweight who became an excellent trainer. Maher had just arrived in New Orleans, but his handler, Billy Madden, who first gained fame as manager and trainer of a prime John L. Sullivan, snuck Maher into the city under cover. The exact reason for the subterfuge is unknown. March 2 *Philadelphia Inquirer*: "On rising yesterday, he (Fitz) tipped the beam at 175 pounds. Seven miles work on the country roads and rattling bouts ... with Joe Choynski and Alexander Greggains, who are his guests, took off five pounds but still left the big New Zealander strong and well. Fitzsimmons has been training up instead of down ... allowed a greater variety of food and drink than in ordinary training, and while he has done a great amount of hard work daily, he was not forced to wear sweaters, and so gained weight and size while he gained strength."

The first Fitzsimmons-Maher fight occurred the night of March 2, 1892 at the New Orleans Olympic Club. The purse was $10,000, huge for the era. Legend has it that Bob was saved from a knockout in the 1st round by the clever intervention of Joe Choynski. Multiple papers had reporters there. The club was decorated for the occasion in "carnival-colored drapery and flags of all nations." In preliminary bouts, Charley Mitchell outshone Arthur Upham; Frank Slavin boxed Felix Vaquelin and sparred Mitchell. Maher entered the ring with Billy Madden, Gus Tuthill, Jack Fallon and Dan Holland. He wore his usual light brown mustache and looked muscular and fit. His demeanor was described as confident, but not happy, in fact, one of "viciousness." Peter had a superstition against fighting on Ash Wednesday, and unsuccessfully tried to obtain another date for the fight. Fitzsimmons followed, with Jimmy Carroll, Choynski, Greggains and "Professor" Jimmy Robertson. Carroll said his charge and the entire party had spent the day playing piano and singing. Bob entered the ring wearing trunks, shoes and a smile (*Picayune*). He walked over to Peter, shook his hand and everyone else's, then went to his corner and squatted."

Fitz and Maher both stood about 5' 10½" to 5' 11½". Boxers of that era were often measured with their shoes on, so only an anthropometrist's or physician's measurements could be trusted. The Harvard anthropometrist and physical culture expert, Dr. Dudley Allen Sargent, is a fine example. He took measurements of John L. Sullivan, Fitzsimmons, Jim Jeffries, Tom Sharkey, Jack Johnson and others. The actual heights of these men were about an inch less than generally reported. The weights were given as Maher, 178 pounds, Fitz, 165, although the *Topeka Weekly Capital* said Bob weighed between 168 and 170 pounds all week. His shoulder and back muscles were highly developed by the blacksmith's sledge. The club's official timekeeper was R.M. (Reuben) Frank. "Professor" John Duffy refereed. He explained the rules and handed out the gloves, which were white. The bell called the men from their corners at 9:15 p.m. The following is a composite from several primary sources:[19]

Round 1 – Maher started with his left well extended. "He showed ... he knew how to deliver all the blows, but his principal difficulty was getting in position to use (them). Fitzsimmons stooped a little, kept his body flexible, left out far in front and his right moving around, mostly for protection. For a man of his length and build, his quickness in ducking ... and getting away was marvelous." Maher shot out three lefts, one grazing Bob's nose. As Peter led again with the left, Fitz shot in a right to the neck that was half push, but sent his foe to the "grass." It was a slip, but angered the Irishman, who upon rising, rushed at the Cornishman. Bob danced around Maher and made him miss, halting his flight to plant a staggering left-right to the face. The right badly cut Peter's bottom lip, and the wound became a factor in the fight (this, before the advent of the mouthpiece).

Now, the puncher from the Land of Erin became vicious and the two traded shots. Fitz ended the exchange with a stiff left to the mouth, and a clinch. Maher shook him off and forced Bob to the ropes. There, he landed a left to the ribs and a short, powerful right to Bob's temple that the *Picayune* said knocked him nearly through the ropes. Some accounts said Bob was floored. He was clearly groggy, "the color had left his cheeks" and Peter moved in for the kill. Just then the bell rang, probably saving Bob. Fitz said, almost two months later: "He made a desperate lunge and caught me on the ear. I fell on the ropes as the gong struck. Choynski was right there, and he picked me up and carried me to the corner. When I hit Peter with my right hand I broke my thumb. I never used that hand but once more in the fight, when I got in a pivot blow."

Moses Koenigsberg covered the fight for the (New Orleans) *Daily Truth*. In 1915 he would launch King Features Syndicate for the William Randolph Hearst empire. He wrote: "Maher moved in. A terrific left hook sent him sprawling on his haunches. His nose and both lips were split. Blood was gushing ... in streams. Peter sat for a moment in utter bewilderment, his arms entwining his knees. Quicker than the eye could follow, the ... Irish fighter straightened as if jerked by a spring. His right ... described an arc from the floor to Fitzsimmons' forehead. The smash drove Bob staggering backward ... to the ropes. There he hung draped over the upper strand. His glazed eyes turned unseeing across the arena. His arms dangled behind him outside the ring. His toes upturned, he teetered on his heels ... entirely defenseless. Again John Duffy missed his cue. The ... rules provide that a fighter hanging helpless on the ropes shall be considered down. The referee must begin counting the decisive 10 seconds. Instead, Duffy stood motionless, in a daze. The crowd was in a roaring frenzy."

"Maher tore across the ring toward Fitzsimmons. Madden raced after him around the ropes, shouting, 'Keep away, Peter! Keep away! Don't foul him!' Maher's right hand, poised for a mighty punch, fell to his side. Madden ... bellowed to Duffy, 'Count him out! Count him out!' Maher's seconds took up the call. Peter walked toward the referee ... then the gong sounded. Above the uproar rose a shrill voice. 'That's a fake!' it piped. 'The round isn't over.' A scrimmage eddied around Reub Frank, the official timekeeper. In the center, a crowd of men in tuxedos were yelling about 'a bloody outrage.' They were members of Squire Abingdon Baird's party. Their seats were close to the timekeeper's bell. Several of them charged that a blooming bounder had struck the gong with a walking-stick. Reub Frank, in agitation, admitted that 'something went wrong with the clapper.' Angry men ... stop-watches in their hands, swore that 30 seconds had been cut off the prescribed three minutes."[20] Note that nothing was mentioned before or afterward, of Choynski as a party to any bell-ringing.

Joe dragged the "Fighting Blacksmith" back to his corner. There, Bob's seconds revived him with brandy (allowed in that era) and smelling salts (ammonia). Several versions over the years say Joe used an old trick of biting Bob's ear to bring him around (ugh!). Fitz had an ability to recuperate in the one minute rest better than perhaps any fighter who ever lived, and he came out for round two in fair shape. Around March 13, "Professor" Mike Donovan received a letter from the son of Pat Kendrick, who Mike called the only man ever to give him boxing lessons. Kendrick's son, also called Pat, was at the fight and said: "When Maher knocked Fitzsimmons down in the 1st ... with a right-hand smash in the ribs the Australian was doubled up and almost 'out'. The friendly bell saved his bacon ... Carroll and ... Choynski ... brought him together again. Fitz had badly dislocated his right thumb in delivering the blow that floored Maher, but the mishap was unknown in the Irishman's corner ... had he gone at Fitz in thunderbolt fashion he would have very likely got the $9,000 end of the purse ..."

Round 2 – Maher had blood streaming from his lip, and both started with caution. Peter sunk a heavy right to the ribs, Fitz ducking a follow-up right to the jaw. Each landed to the ribs. Bob drove a left to the ear and a right to the mouth that increased the flow of blood. The Irishman retaliated with a heavy punch to the ear. Both landed right and left but "Lanky Bob" staggered his adversary with a series of potent left jabs to the mouth. Peter landed more frequently, but Bob was the more clever fighter.

Rounds 3 and 4 – Fitz did a stick-and-move, using nice footwork and a damaging left jab. Peter bled heavily from his bottom lip. Bob was avoiding a slug-fest, in retrospect, due to the broken right hand he sustained at the start. Over the course of the fight, Maher landed some good shots with both fists, but Bob was clearly out-boxing and outscoring his rival.

Round 5 – Bob slowed, Maher landing an assortment of power punches.

Round 6 – Peter landed enough to make the session about even.

Round 7 – In this heat, Fitz landed an illegal right "pivot-blow," like the one LaBlanche used to knock out "Nonpareil" Dempsey. "The forearm hit full against the neck and chin and shook Maher up ..." Peter's corner shouted "Foul," but referee Duffy refused to allow it. Maher became very aggressive, though both men connected with good punches.

Round 8 – Although Maher was losing a lot of blood down his chin, he swallowed as much again, making him sick. He also bled heavily from the nose, which interfered with his breathing. Fitz evaded much of Peter's attack by skillful side-stepping, and nearly floored his opponent with a sharp left to the nose. Maher appeared weak at the bell.

Rounds 9 through 11 – Fitz held the edge, landing stiff jabs. Otherwise, each connected with heavy swings, though without causing serious damage.

Round 12 – Bob kept his hard left in Maher's face. Peter appeared to be in pain, but tried rushing Fitz on several occasions, to no avail. His wild swings missed their mark. At round's end, they returned to their corners and Maher told his handlers he'd had enough. They threw in the towel to signify admission of defeat. Referee Duffy pointed to Fitzsimmons as the winner. Bob's corner opened the brandy bottle and congratulated their man. Fitz visited the Maher corner and offered Peter some brandy, which he accepted. *Picayune*: He "shook the Irishman's hand and was ... dragged to the outer ring, shaking the hands extended almost clear around the square."

Aftermath – It is perhaps telling that no primary source mentions Choynski ringing the bell early to save Fitzsimmons. It is only later that these stories came out, mostly from secondary sources, and several individuals are named as the culprit. It appears likely that Joe was credited for something he didn't do. As the general story goes, he saw that Bob was about to be knocked out, and, at a point near the official timekeeper, climbed into the ring and surreptitiously kicked the bell. All parties, thinking the round had ended, ceased hostilities. The official timekeeper (R.M. Frank) supposedly tried to yell that the frame had not ended, but could not make himself heard. He finally shrugged his shoulders and rang the bell again after the minute's rest elapsed. To this author's knowledge, Frank never validated nor refuted that a furtive bell ringing had occurred. Here is a synopsis of some later stories I gathered, regarding the short 1st heat:

Probably the account closest to the event in time was the December 29,

1894 *San Francisco Chronicle*. Ex-Fitzsimmons trainer Jimmy Carroll, who held a grudge against "Long Bob" for some reason, spread the tale that he (Carroll) saved Fitz from a sure knockout. The author of the article denied any involvement of Carroll's, writing that "Joe Choynski engineered that job and carried it out unadvised and unassisted. When the Irishman's big fist slammed up against the Australian's ostrich-like boko (nose), the only cool head in Fitzsimmons' corner was on Joe Choynski's shoulders. For the nonce Carroll didn't know whether he was going or coming. Jimmy may have done good work on his man when he was in his corner, but it was Choynski's quick wit and strong arms that got him there." It isn't noted who the writer was or if he had been at the fight.

The *Alaska Citizen* wrote in 1912 that, in the 2nd frame (actually the 1st), Maher knocked Fitz "clean through the ropes. The Cornishman seemed to be done for, and ... Joe Choynski ... had his wits about him, and ripping off the leg of a chair he struck the gong a resounding whack. The referee, believing the round was over, stopped counting, and Fitz was ... revived quickly, and acting under Choynski's orders, fought Maher at long range thereafter ... when the 12th round ended, Peter said, 'I can't go on. The red-headed divvle has blinded me entirely.' " In 1914, a scribe for a Duluth, Minnesota paper (who I suspect was the same who wrote for the *Alaska Citizen*) also said that Choynski used the leg of a stool in round two, to reach over the timekeeper's shoulder and strike the gong.

The *Salt Lake Telegram* claimed, in 1917, that Fitzsimmons' timekeeper, "George Clark, leaning over the timekeeper's shoulder, hit the gong with a heavy cane." October 30, 1899 *Denver Post*: "George Clark ... deducted a whole half minute from the 1st round when he saw the condition Fitz was in. Many claim it was Choynski that hit the bell. Very true he did. But George Clark broke the rope and attracted Choynski's attention. Joe, believing the round was really over, hit the gong ... jumped in the ring and carried Fitz back to his corner. All this transpired while Billy Madden ... was looking on, and yet did not discover that his man was robbed of the decision and a purse of $10,000." "Parson" Davies also pointed the finger at Clark, saying, "George Clark of Chicago ... had $3,000 bet on Lanky Bob and when he saw Maher floor his man, he lost his head and rung the gong 14 seconds before the round was ... over. Fitz was dead to the world ..."

Another 1917 article read: "Joe Choynski's presence of mind and sheer nerve in a pinch saved Bob ... If you doubt this statement, have the boy page John 'Tex' Dunn, matchmaker of the Broadway Sporting club of Brooklyn ... Jawn: 'Do you know Maher had Fitz out in the 1st round ...? Well ... I know ... I was the master of ceremonies that night ... (Author: In reality, Edward Curtis was master of ceremonies, per the March 3, 1892 *St. Paul Globe*). Bob was on the floor, ready for the shutter when Joe Choynski, his chief second, jumped into the ring, kicking the bell with his foot as he went, to end the round. It was a nervy, quick-witted trick on Choynski's part, but no one was any the wiser.' " This was hardly the first time someone had the cojones to impersonate another, in this case, an M.C.

1925 *Oakland Tribune*: "In New Orleans ... Maher had the Cornishman on the floor. Bud Reno (author: probably Bud Renaud), a gambler, hit the gong and saved Fitz from a knockout ..." In 1943, journalist Joe Williams said: "John B. Kirkman, veteran follower of the ring, writes it was Spider Kelly who pulled the gong ... Legend had it the late Joe Choynski was the culprit."[21] John "Spider" Kelly was arguably the greatest cornerman of his generation, but he is not known to have been present at ringside.

In 1926, referee Billy Roche penned, "In the 2nd round Peter nailed Ruby Robert with a polthogue* that dropped him as if he had been pole-axed. He was on the floor when the bell came to his rescue, and to his dying day Maher insisted that Joe Choynski, Fitz's chief second ... reached over and hit the bell to cut the round short." At least one sketch from the period shows the arena's bell mounted about six feet up on a pole near the ring. This indicates that only a man with a cane could have pulled off a furtive bell strike. To further cloud the issue, though, the November 28, 1900 London *Mirror of Life* alleged that Choynski himself stated, "(Reub) Franks had his hand on the bell rope just as Fitz was knocked out. I took in the situation, and, striking Franks on the arm, rang the bell, then jumped through the ropes and carried Fitz back to his chair as limp as a rag."
* A polthogue is Irish slang for a stiff punch.

Gilbert Odd wrote, in 1976: "Pat Donohue, who held the watch for Maher, declared strongly against the curtailed round, but by then it was too late ... according to George T. Pardy, a Chicago sports editor ... 'The trick was turned by a Chicago saloon-keeper with a big bet on Bob, who reached over with a heavy walking cane and banged the gong, cutting the round short.' " Mose Gunst, who was at the tilt, only said, "He (Maher) was whipped simply because he is faint-hearted. Fitzsimmons also showed the white feather and gave indications of a willingness to jump the pit ... he was within an ace of going out in the 1st round, and the call of time alone saved him ... had Maher struck him 10 seconds before he did he would have been counted out."[22] The entire truth about the fight will never be known.

Ringside reporter Moses Koenigsberg: "Joe Choyinski (sic) did not share in the Fitzsimmons party festivities. He ... worked assiduously on Fitz in his corner, but after the battle, when the gaiety began, he ... sulked outside the dressing-room. 'This puts the bee on me,' he grumbled. 'That guy is so yellow that jaundice wouldn't change his looks. Yet he's got the gall to lap up this bushwa as if it was coming to him.' Mr. Choyinski at times indulged a predilection for idiomatic expression ... his allusion to an insect ... signified a stinging impatience ... 'What do you mean?' I asked, tactlessly passing over the lucidity of his statement. 'You heard me. What do you want? A blackboard and some white chalk to make pictures?' 'You win,' was my hurried answer. 'What you said was ... clear; but what happened ...?' "

" 'All this bull about Fitzsimmons. He tried to quit. We had a hell of a time getting him up for the 2nd round. He was out when we carried him to his corner. It took several whiffs of the ammonia to get the birdies out of his noggin. Then he blubbered to Carroll, 'It's no use, Jimmy. He's too hard for me.' Carroll told him Maher was all in and ordered him to ... finish the Irishman. Fitz kept whining, 'He's too blooming hard for me.' That wallop that Peter lifted from his feet sure buffaloed Bob. When the gong rang ... Bob wouldn't budge. Carroll was crazy. I had a needle ready and I jabbed it into Bob's rump. That's why you saw him come bouncing out.' Choynski left the building with me. He had given me an exclusive story."

Choynski: "At Bay St. Louis, where Bob trained ... a banquet was arranged in his honor after his victory. Fitz told me he had never made a speech in public, and wouldn't know what to say when the toastmaster called on him. I suggested he get someone to write ... a speech. He ... hired a lawyer friend to do the work. Then he got me to help him rehearse. We stayed up nearly all night several nights practicing in Fitz's hotel room. Fitz had his talk down letter perfect. On the night of the banquet all present got gloriously full of wine and there were no speeches from anybody."[23] As a final post-script to the fight, Maher attempted suicide by jumping out the window of the train bringing him and the Fitzsimmons party from New Orleans. Ten miles from Charlotte, North Carolina on March 5, Peter, likely under the influence of alcohol, was so distraught that he "sprang from his seat and made a rush for the open window." Fitz and others grabbed him and physicians administered an opiate so Maher could sleep.[24]

On March 4, papers said a fight had been "arranged at the Merchants' club" for $5,000 a side between Joe and Jim Corbett.[25] The *St. Louis Post-Dispatch* noted, "Choynski does all fighting and no talking, while Corbett does all talking and no fighting. He has matured considerably since he met Corbett ... has the advantage of much experience ... become a much more skillful boxer ... the same is true of Corbett ... except Corbett has not had as many real fights ... Choynski ... is said to be very gentlemanly, and the best educated man in the ring." The next day, however, Jim declared that "he authorized no one to make a match ... with Choynski and ... will not fight him, having already beaten him four times. Corbett expresses willingness to meet Fitzsimmons or the winner of the Jackson-Slavin match."

The men who arranged the "fight" were Brooklyn turf-man, Phil Dwyer, who represented Jim, and "celebrated New Orleans sport," Bud Renaud, who backed Joe. The *Post-Dispatch* said the agreement had been drawn up and signed at the Central club. "Mr. Corbett ... is back in his old attitude of wanting to fight any man in the world except a man ... willing to fight him. If Choynski is so easy a mark for Corbett, why does not the latter take advantage of this opportunity to win a large amount of money with so little trouble? If Corbett had any prospect ... with any other fighter by defeating whom he would gain greater fame, his objection would be well taken, but Choynski is the best man, Charley Mitchell excepted ... in a position to meet him for months to come."[26] The truth is, Corbett put all sorts of barriers in Fitz's way until he could avoid him no longer. He did the same with Peter Jackson, avoiding a rematch with Jim's title on the line at all costs. Nor did the "Pompadour" pugilist ever get in the ring with Choynski again, and he never fought Frank Slavin. While Corbett was a great boxer, he was a quirky sort who often shied away from stiff competition. The history of mental illness in his lineage may have been a factor in his quirkiness.

On March 10 at the St. Charles Theatre in the "Big Easy," Choynski sparred an unspecified number of rounds with Fitzsimmons. Joe was said to have "made a favorable impression, being very clever and strong. Neither used his right hand, but sparred scientifically with the left." Afterward, Joe went four rounds with Alec Greggains. He didn't give up easily, in trying to get Corbett back in the ring. As Joe told it: "Although I had never had a manager, I decided now that I should get some smart fellow to handle my engagements. 'Parson' Davies was managing Peter Jackson and Jim Hall. I signed on with Davies. The 'Parson' had me go to Chicago, and ... put me to work at the old Battery, 'knocking out all comers.' The 'Parson' advertised a purse of $100 to any man I could not stop in four rounds." In 1927, Joe said of these challengers, "Big, bull-necked, iron-jawed fellows jostled each other for the chance. Night after night a fresh victim was led in and carried out. Some of these bullies were tough nuts."[27] Joe would make Chicago his primary residence for the next several years. The key factor, of course, was that Davies operated out of the Windy City.

March 11 *Chicago Daily Inter-Ocean*: "Joe Choynski ... will go East to try to force a match with Corbett. He claims Corbett only whipped him once, when he was an inexperienced boy of 19 and knew nothing about boxing, that he has improved a great deal since and is ... anxious to try conclusions again." On the 13th the paper said: "Joe Choynski ... arrived in Chicago last night ... weighs now, out of condition, about 183 pounds, and is the smallest big man ever seen. He will remain here a week and may go on to New York in an effort to force Corbett into another match."

Charles Edward Davies was born in Antrim, Ireland, near Belfast, on July 7, 1851. The family was Catholic and originally from Galway. "The Parson" gave autobiographical information over the years, much of it inaccurate. This was likely due to the failings of memory, lack of childhood records, and his parents passing away when he was young. Thanks to Mark T. Dunn of Bloomington, Illinois, we have a much more accurate view of Davies and his family.[28] Charles said he lost his mother at age 7, and immigrated to the United States (New York City) at age 12 with his father,

Paul, who died the following year. Actually, Paul R. Davies died December 25, 1867 and is buried in the Pinkerton plot at Graceland Cemetery, Chicago. The family had a long, close relationship with the Pinkertons, founders of the Pinkerton Detective Agency. Paul had been chief clerk for their Chicago office. "The Parson" became a close friend of Billy Pinkerton. Charles: "I was left an orphan and the world looked large to me. I had gone to school little and my chances ... anything but encouraging."

The "Parson" had several brothers, the oldest being Henry W. "Harry" Davies, born in 1843. Others were George F. (1848), Vere, born about 1857 and William H. Davies, birth year unknown. Charles had at least two sisters, though information on them is lacking. For his education, Davies read newspapers, but never returned to school. He got work "around the New York clubs," and, as he recalled, "I finally came to Chicago, where my brother George had a saloon ... So I went to work for him. Another brother, Harry, was working for the Pinkertons in New York. I ... got interested in sports. John Ennis made me think he could beat Dan O'Leary in a 100-mile walking match. Ennis ... quit after going 15 miles and $500 I had ... invested in the race was wiped away ... I ...

A young Charles "Parson" Davies

drifted back to New York and promoted a big walking match between O'Leary, Ennis, Charles Harriman ... and others. It was here I got my nickname of 'Parson' ... W.K. Vanderbilt ... was responsible ..."

Davies moved back to Chicago and made it his home for many years, owning liquor stores and saloons by the names of "The Store" and "The Champion's Rest." He soon entered the domain of boxing. As early as 1882, Charles was managing pugilists like bareknuckler Jim Elliott, later guiding the career of Peter Jackson, "The Black Prince" of Australia. Others he piloted were bantamweight champion Jimmy Barry, welterweight and middleweight champ Tommy Ryan, Bob Armstrong, Jim Hall, Patsy Cardiff, Charley Mitchell, Jake Kilrain, Jack Burke, "The Irish Lad," Paddy Ryan, John L. Sullivan and James J. Corbett. Davies also managed professional wrestlers such as Evan "Strangler" Lewis, William Muldoon, Matsada Sorokichi and Dan McLeod. Lewis was the first to become a champion under his management. When the wrestling game became the domain of criminals, Davies dropped the sport forever. "I won't have anything to do with it, now that it is crooked," he told a friend.

Davies resided in Chicago from about 1871 to 1898, when he went to New Orleans. Dunn: "I believe he essentially got run out of Chicago by 'Bathhouse' John Coughlin and 'Hinky Dink' Kenna." They were First Ward aldermen known as the "Lords of the Levee," who led the corrupt "Gray Wolves" of Chicago. "The Parson" also got into horse racing in later years in New Orleans. He charged a managerial fee of 50% of his fighter's earnings, 25-50% considered standard in the day.

Davies was never a "man of the cloth," but received his nickname due to the "clerical cut of his clothes and the severe, placid expression his face always wears." He was given the nickname by William K. Vanderbilt when, during a walking exhibition in Madison Square Garden in 1879 (then called Gilmore's Garden) featuring Dan O'Leary, Vanderbilt allegedly pointed at the man in the "frock coat and silk hat" and inquired, "Who's that minister talking to O'Leary?" Upon being told, "He isn't a clergyman, he's the manager of a stable of walkers ..." W.K. Vanderbilt reportedly remarked that he looked more like a parson than a sporting manager. Frank Davidson, reporter for the *Chicago Times*, overheard the statement and the sobriquet stuck.

Charles "Parson" Davies, circa 1890

Davies never liked the nickname, preferring to be called Charles or Charlie, but he eventually accepted it. He started out sporting a black beard, besides the high collar. He later shaved off the beard. "Parson" Davies was called by many the greatest boxing manager of his day, though there were many greats, such as William Brady and Tom O'Rourke. One source said he "had no peer as manager, matchmaker, promoter of combats, maker of new champions." "He was the image of courtesy and Chesterfieldian manners – an Irishman of the old school, though without a trace of 'brogue.' He never married ..." Davies' word was his bond; he was respected by all.[29]

John L. Sullivan arrived with Duncan Harrison's company the day after Choynski, and his play opened to a packed house at the "People's." He told a Chicago reporter he would be able to get back into the ring for one final time "the last week in August or the first week in September." Sullivan would fight Corbett on September 8 for the heavyweight championship. He named possible opponents and his opinion of them. Corbett was named as the most likely prospect, but he had nothing good to say about Jim or any other fighter – with the sole exception of Choynski. Of Joe, John said: " 'As clever and game a little gentleman as I ever saw. He's a willing and good two-handed fighter, a gentleman in and out of the ring and a fellow whose friendship I am proud to claim.' Mr. Harrison added glowing words of praise ... at the mention of Choynski's name."[30]

Author Charles Hermann mistakenly recalled meeting Joe in 1891; it was probably 1892. He wrote: "Joe Choinski (sic) was also a fine character. I first saw him in Chicago in 1891. He dressed like a dude, and looked nothing like a fighter on account of his clothes and hat which was adorned with a conspicuous band. For that reason, roughnecks often made slurring remarks ... one afternoon ... three alleged toughs made some such remarks about Joe. He heard what they said and stopped and requested an apology. Instead, they came at him. He hit one and down he went; then another ... The 3rd threw up his hands and said, 'I don't want any of it.' I said, 'Joe, what's the trouble?' He replied, 'I've been insulted.' Those three were really big, tough guys. While the two were getting up, the 3rd asked me, 'Who is that bloke?' I told him and all three were profuse in apologizing. Joe ... told them, 'I'll not accept your apology. Had I been some ordinary gentleman you would have made a sucker out of me. Just behave as you should is all I ask of you.' I know of two other similar occurrences – one on Michigan Avenue and the other while Joe was riding a bicycle in Lincoln Park. A truck driver didn't like Joe's regalia and started abusing him. Joe pulled him off his dirt truck and taught him a lesson. Joe Choinski was always a perfect gentleman and never looked for trouble. He told me he felt he was doing a good service in teaching ruffians how to behave."[31]

On March 14, an offer was wired for Choynski to fight the "Colored Heavyweight Champion," George Godfrey, of Boston. A purse of $3,000 was guaranteed before the Gladstone Club of Providence, Rhode Island. Joe said he was holding out for $4,500. Negotiations continued and Joe would fight "Old Chocolate" before the year was out. Alec Greggains, on his way back to San Francisco from New Orleans, was full of ill will toward Bob Fitzsimmons and Jimmy Carroll. His beef was that, after performing so well in their capacity of cornermen for Fitz, "Neither Greggains nor Choynski received a cent for acting as seconds, and members of the local sporting fraternity who have heard of this are not slow in deprecating the parsimonious pugilist (Fitz). Greggains ... said though Carroll and Fitzsimmons made lots of money from their exhibition last week they did not give him a nickel. He appeared twice during the evening."[32] In his old age, a bitter Choynski would refer to Fitz as ungrateful, and worse.

On the 19th, Joe attended the world billiard championship, held at the Central Music Hall in Chicago. Specifically, it was for the "14-inch balk line billiards" title. He saw 25-year-old Frank Ives defeat defending champion Jacob "The Wizard" Schaefer by a final score of 800 points to 499. It was considered a big upset, as Schaefer had been champion since 1878 and considered the best player in the history of the sport.[33] Davies' troupe entertained on March 29 at the Detroit Rink in Detroit, Michigan. Choynski boxed Jim Hall four rounds with gloves, "both men showing up in good shape. Hall especially appeared to advantage. His flesh looked firm and ruddy, his blows were strong and well aimed, and his guard Choynski was unable to get through with effect ... Davies ... made a cool $1,000 out of the exhibition." They were back at Battery D in Chicago on April 2. John (or Jack) Dalton, was scheduled to face Joe. "Choynski vs. Dalton, Hall vs. Martin ... and Hall vs. Choynski filled out the programme. Captain Fitzpatrick of the Central and a squad from the same station were in attendance, and ... put a stop to anything that looked like bloody work by stopping the initial bout after 15 seconds of boxing."

"Joe ... and ... Hall ... punched each other lightly with six-ounce mittens ... It was a friendly set-to, but the 2,000 spectators had a chance to judge of the quality of the men. Choynski was clever and so was Hall. There were a few lively exchanges, but the fighters feared the police might interfere and worked slowly. Hall probably outpointed Choynski a trifle. Later on, Choynski sparred three rounds with Jack Dalton."[34] Joe wrote, in "I Fought 'Em All": "I settled his hash in three rounds." In the 1920s and 1930s, Joe wrote most of his memoirs, highlights of his life and career. He was often confused in the chronology of events. Here, he thought the Dalton match took place after he'd begun playing in "Uncle Tom's Cabin."

On the night of April 3, Joe, Hall and Davies arrived in Philadelphia. Hall was to box a four-rounder the next night at the Ariel Club against New York's Jim Glynn. Joe would second him and face either "Denver" Ed Smith or "a noted heavyweight," the following Saturday. On the 4th, Hall faced a tall, thin chap named "Jack Flood of Richmond," as Glynn failed to show. Hall and Choynski entered the ring to a rousing cheer. Hall took out the outgunned Flood in only 49 seconds.[35]

On April 5, Davies and team were still in Philly, where they "put in a busy day ... visiting the clubhouses of various athletic organizations and other places of interest ... in the evening they attended the theatre." On April 6 Hall stopped Jack Haughey in the 2nd round. It was reported on the 8th that "Hall and ... Choynski will spar all comers at Niblo's, New York next week ..." Joe and Jim had matches on the 9th, each scoring a 1st round knockout. Hall took out Mike White of Pottsville and "Little Joe" faced Joe (not George) Godfrey. The crowd of 2,000 also witnessed a mishap outside the ring. "The circus seats at the southern end of the hall ... crowded with several hundred people, gave way under the immense weight and fell with a crash. Luckily no one was seriously hurt, only three persons ... slightly bruised." Joe Godfrey was noted mostly as cannon-fodder for the likes of Jake Kilrain, Peter Maher and Bob Fitzsimmons. Choynski: "Joe Godfrey had been promising me great things for quite some time – but to promise is one thing; to execute is quite another. I finished him off with a lightning right to the cheek ... in the first minute of the 1st round."[36]

Fitz was to appear in a play at the People's Theater, where he would (appropriately) portray a blacksmith. "Fitzsimmons could make some friends by making amends for a slovenly trick at New Orleans after his last fight. Alex Greggains and Joe Choynski worked like beavers in his corner and bolstered him up when he was almost out after the 1st round ... he bought Choynski his breakfast the next morning, and affected that he had done his duty. Greggains did not even receive that much. Fitzsimmons left Choynski stranded in the Crescent City, and but for 'Parson' Davies would have been in a bad way." It is uncertain if "The Parson" bailing Joe out influenced his signing with him. "The position of sparring instructor in the new Chicago Athletic Club is being eagerly sought for by several prominent pugilists. It was supposed some time ago that Billy Myer had been chosen ... the announcement seems to have been premature. Joe Choynski is the latest aspirant ... he has some strong support among lovers of athletics ... Myer and Choynski belong to the better grade of pugilists, are quiet and unassuming in their ways and amply qualified to fill the position ...." Joe would be chosen for the job, but it would not happen until 1895.[37]

Choynski and team arrived in New York City on the 10th or 11th. Joe and Jim sparred each other at Niblo's Theater on April 11 and Joe got it good. "Monday night Jim Hall nearly knocked out his sparring side partner, Joe Choynski ... A short, half-arm jab caught Joseph on the point of the chin, and he was very groggy for a moment. It was not intended, of course." The Australian was a superb fighter when not under the influence of alcohol. He and Choynski would eventually face off in two ring battles. The men stayed at the Metropolitan Hotel and performed in conjunction with the Henry burlesque company. They sparred each other again on the 13th.

April 12 *San Francisco Morning Call*: "A letter was received yesterday by a prominent member of the California Athletic Club from a friend in New York ... The writer ... had a long conversation with Choynski regarding his fights with Corbett, and of the latter Joe spoke: 'Corbett's last statement that he would not fight me again because he had already defeated me three times is a deliberate lie, and directly I see him I will tell him so to his face and pull his nose unless he contradicts it. Corbett has never met me in a ring but twice in his life and has only defeated me once. The first time we met was at one of the ordinary exhibitions of the Olympic Club, at which ... Corbett was boxing instructor.' " Joe detailed the exhibition and barge fight, saying he barely failed to beat the count in the latter battle, due to leg cramps. "I have no right to complain ... though. It's the fortune of war, and I should never have a word to say against Corbett but for the false statements he has made and the manner in which he has tried to belittle me.

To show you the kind of man he is, I will give you a further instance."

"After our fight I had a benefit tendered me, and Corbett promised to do all he could for me, free. It was arranged that he and I should spar the wind-up, but before the night came Corbett demanded $300 to appear ... this took me by surprise, but it was agreed that he should be paid the $300 ... when the time came he first complained about the smallness of the ring, which was an 18-foot one, and then said he had a letter saying I had been in training to fight him and absolutely refused to go into the ring until I had been before the directors of the club and solemnly promised that it would be purely only a sparring exhibition. This is the sort of man Corbett is, and anyone in California will confirm what I say. He blames me for having forced him into the professional ring and says that but for me he would still be an amateur. Long before he first met me he had fought (Jack) Burke ... and ... exhibited with a sparring combination in Salt Lake City, where he fought McDonald. Therefore I fail to see how this fight with me made a professional of him ... I don't say these things because Corbett defeated me. Joe Goddard did the same and I have not the slightest feeling against him. ... I want to prove to you the fallacy of his statements concerning me ..." Joe still harbored a grudge against Goddard, too, as will be seen later.

Shortly after midnight on April 13, an incident occurred involving the Davies troupe (The *New York Herald* said, around 3 a.m. on the 14th). In the café of Niblo's Garden, at the Metropolitan Hotel, were gathered Davies, Choynski, Hall, Peter Maher, Billy Madden, Gus Tuthill, Jere Dunn (the gambler who shot pugilist Jimmy Elliott to death in 1883) and Steve Brodie, who claimed to have jumped off the Brooklyn Bridge in 1886. Allegedly, 42 quarts of champagne were consumed in celebration of the signing of the Fitzsimmons-Hall fight. As these "kindred spirits" partied, in walked ex-pug and trainer Eddie Conners. For some reason, he had it in for Maher and made an insulting remark about the religious medal on Peter's vest. The latter responded with "sulphurous vehemence," and Eddie called him a "bleeding coward," for quitting against Fitz. Maher advanced toward the smaller Conners, who pulled out a dirk knife and "jumped at Maher." Jim Hall shoved Peter out of range, and Davies shattered a champagne bottle on Conners' head. Conners dropped unconscious to the floor, his scalp bleeding. The party "broke up with wonderful rapidity."[38]

Kansas City Star: "Jim Hall was the only one who stayed to play good Samaritan. He had been 'done up' by the 'Parson' himself a few months ago, and remembered how it felt. So he called a cab and took Conners to a drug store near the Bowery where the wounds were dressed. Conners was then driven to the house of a friend nearby, where physicians were called. Davies went to Philadelphia yesterday and none of the other members of the party would admit that he knew anything about the scrap. Brodie had 'gone home' just before it occurred; Choynski was 'up stairs asleep,' Maher admitted he was too full to remember anything ... Madden and Hall had just 'gone out to get a breath of fresh air,' and Dunn had 'gone home early.' "

April 15 *Philadelphia Inquirer*: "Davies ... was seen at the Continental Hotel yesterday, and ... said, 'This New York story is false and unjust. In the first place, Conners, who is pictured as a consumptive, is a lusty Bowery tough and employed as a bouncer in a variety hall on that thoroughfare. The only indication of consumption ... is ... when he stacks up against liquor that someone else pays for. In that case, his consumption is very noticeable.' " Charles detailed how ... In walked Conners, who picked a fight with Peter and pulled a knife ... According to Davies, Choynski forced Conners to put the knife back in his pocket. In a melee that ensued between Conners and others, he sustained his injuries and was ejected from the hotel by the proprietor, clerks and bartenders, who Davies directed the reporter to contact if further proof was needed. Conners recovered.

Hall and Choynski boxed exhibitions with each other almost every night at Niblo's, but on the 19th, Joe took on "Jerry Slattery, a New York slugger of some note." "During the two rounds he lasted, Slattery's head hit the stage seven times and he concluded to quit." One paper said the knockout occurred about two minutes into the 2nd. Back in Philadelphia, Davies arranged fights between Hall and Billy Leedom and between Joe and "Denver" Ed Smith. The original date of April 23 couldn't be met, as his boxers couldn't arrive back in time from New York. Charles postponed the Smith fight until the 30th, and Hall-Leedom to May 2, but matched Smith and Leedom against each other on the original date. Still in the "Big Apple," Joe scored a knockout at 14 seconds of the 2nd round over Charles McCarthy on the 21st, after an initial knockdown by Joe. One source said it was held at Clermont Rink, New York City.[39]

On April 22, Joe kayoed a Tom Ryan (not *the* Tommy Ryan) in the 2nd heat, at Niblo's.[40] Back in Philly on the 30th, he finally met "Denver" Ed Smith at the Ariel Club. Smith was born Edward Corcoran, on March 17, 1865 in Birmingham, England. He made a name as a fighter in that country, moved to the States in 1884, and in 1888 settled in Denver, Colorado. Smith was known as a "cyclone fighter," referred to now as a "swarmer." He lost in a respectable five rounds against Peter Jackson in 1890. In 1893, Ed scored a notable upset, stopping the iron man, Joe Goddard, in the 18th round. At 5' 10½", he weighed about 175 pounds.

May 1 *Philadelphia Inquirer*: "The first three rounds were very tame, Choynski having the better of it. In the 4th ... the Californian went in for blood, and Lieutenant Gillingham called a halt after Choynski had struck Smith on the chin with a straight left-hander which caused the 'cyclone' to drop on one knee. The blow was not really a knockout, but it badly dazed the Denver lad." The May 8 *Chicago Daily Inter-Ocean* dissented: "Some good authorities who saw the Smith-Choynski contest emphatically state that

Smith had the better of his man from start to finish. Jack Fogarty (a Philly promoter) says that Smith should have been awarded the fight." Choynski wrote, in 1930: "I took no chances on his evil ring procedure. I stood off, chopped him to ribbons, and then laid him out for the pulmotor squad. He lasted a little over two rounds." Joe's fading memory showed.

"Denver" Ed Smith

On "May Day," Fitz and party arrived in Philly. The May 2 *Philadelphia Inquirer* said Davies registered at the Continental Hotel about the same time. "There was quite a congregation of sports assembled in the reading room of the Continental Hotel last night. Fitzsimmons sat at one end of a long table, and close by was his manager and trainer, Jimmy Carroll ... David Trattel, manager of Fitzsimmons' combination; Captain (H. Walter) Schlichter of the Philadelphia Amateur Swimming Club ... Billy Carroll, the comedian; Joe Choynski, Professor J.H. Clark, Ed Smith of Denver ..." The Fitz-Hall fight was not set, after all. Fitz said, "If Hall don't (sic) fight me in September, when the Olympic Club offers us a purse of $12,000, he will never have another chance, for I shall ignore him. Hall's excuse that he is going to England to see the Jackson-Slavin fight is no excuse at all. That fight takes place on May 30, and after that he will have over three months to train." It wasn't mentioned if Jim Hall was in attendance. After this meeting, Davies, Choynski and Hall prepared to set sail for England. There, they would join Peter Jackson, who was already in training to meet Frank Slavin, in a fight that would prove among the best in boxing history.

Round Eight

The British Tour and Old Chocolate
(May 1892 – January 1893)

At 12:00 noon on May 4, the 455-foot-long steamship *Germanic* departed New York harbor, carrying 98 cabin passengers. Among them were Davies, Hall and Choynski. The ship belonged to the White Star Line (Oceanic Steam Navigation Company). Other ships in its fleet were the *Adriatic*, *Baltic*, *Doric*, *Majestic*, *Teutonic* and the *Britannic*. (In 1910, the White Star Line would have an ocean-liner built named the RMS *Titanic*, which infamously sank in 1912). The *Germanic* was primarily steam-driven, but had four masts rigged with sails for back-up.[1] She ran a regular route between New York and Liverpool, England, where the trio landed on May 12 or 13.[2]

The England of 1892 was a land in the midst of the Victorian Era. This was named for the reign of Queen Victoria, which lasted from 1837 to 1901. The time saw a great expansion of culture, wealth and scientific knowledge, but also of excess. It was an age of invention, philosophy and introspection, featuring ostentatious architecture, furniture and other expressions of an expanding middle class, and an upper class feeling its oats. The nation was struggling to maintain the dominance it held over approximately 25% of the world. Men wore top hats, bowlers, bow ties and facial hair of all sorts and styles. The sack, or lounge coat, was quickly replacing the frock coat. Women wore corsets, bustle dresses and clothing which featured a high neck, wasp waist and puffed sleeves. This is the England visited by Joe Choynski, his manager and associates.

May 13, 1892 *San Francisco Call*: "Davies ... Hall ... Choynski and Fred Johnson have arrived in England, and Davies will visit Peter Jackson and see that he gets into condition for his match with Slavin. Hall will get ready for a sparring tour and ... a possible match with Ted Pritchard, and Choynski will prepare for his exhibition tour." Fred Johnson was a featherweight (122-pounder). To accommodate the crowds who would view his fighters in action, Davies rented London's Novelty Theatre, on Great Queen Street. On May 16, he attended a fight card at the National Sporting Club, which had opened its doors the previous year. When asked to make a speech, Charles told the audience, "We are here for Boxing, not Speech-making." He then proclaimed that Hall and Choynski were ready to fight "any man in England" in their weight class. The next day, the trio dined at the club, where it was announced that Lord Lonsdale would be timekeeper for Peter. This was Hugh Lowther, 5th Earl of Lonsdale, the club's first President, later donor of the prestigious Lonsdale belts.[3]

May 21 (London) *Sporting Life*: "To disavow all knowledge of 'The Parson' is to admit oneself unknown in the world of sport ... during his last sojourn in England he endeared himself to all who had the pleasure of his acquaintance, not only in Great Britain, but also in the Emerald Isle. Landing in England on the 13th inst., after a satisfactory voyage in the *Germanic*, Davies ... Hall ... and ... Choynski ... immediately repaired to Brighton on a visit to Peter Jackson. After ... Davies repaired to the County Cricket Ground, Hove, and ... met (Ted) Pritchard ... discussed ... matters relative to a match with Pritchard and Hall ... Davies took his leave of Pritchard and trainer (Sam Blakelock)." Davies had expressed ... that Hall would only be able to drop as low as 163 pounds for a fight ... Ted replied that "he had decided not to give any weight away after his last match ..."

"Questioned as to Choynski, the gallant young Californian, 'The Parson' said that up to the present he had failed to find him a customer. His weight accounted for the difficulty, as he is a little too heavy for a middle-weight, though Davies entertains strong hopes of obtaining a good match for him before leaving England. 'The Parson' remarked that ... Choynski ... Above all ... yearned for a contest in this country ... Davies has forwarded a letter to America offering to match Choynski to fight George Godfrey, the coloured pugilist, to a finish before the Coney Island or Olympic Clubs."

"Parson Davies has this week arranged for a series of exhibition contests at the Novelty Theatre ... Hall and Choynski will appear on Monday next and following evenings in the celebrated play of 'Tom and Jerry,' and Davies offers £10 to any English pugilist Hall and Choynski cannot stop or best in four rounds (Queensberry Rules). This is not made in a spirit of braggadocio, but purely from business motives. Hall and Choynski will be on stage every night at 10 o'clock, and anyone who desires to compete can communicate with Davies through the *Sporting Life*. Several have already accepted the offer, and the Parson feels sure that the public will be well satisfied with the entertainment ..." This was the story of Choynski's career, that he was too heavy to fight middleweights but too light to be a true heavyweight. Pickings would be slim for Joe in the United Kingdom. He would have to content himself with sparring and challenge bouts, and assisting Jackson and Hall in training for real fights.

On May 22, the *Chicago Tribune* reported that Davies had watched Jackson punch the bag non-stop for two hours and was satisfied "The Black Prince" was in "splendid condition." His opponent-to-be, Francis Patrick Slavin, considered one of Australia's three best heavies, was helping his brother, Jack, prepare for a June 2 bout at the Ormonde Club against Con Riordan. "The match between Pritchard and (Jack) O'Brien will probably take place the same week. This is rather a large dose of pugilism even for London, and it is not at all unlikely that Scotland Yard will bestir itself in the matter." Ted Pritchard, only 5' 9" and a middleweight, had in March scored an 8th-round knockout of Jack Burke. In July, he came back from two knockdowns in round one to upset English Heavyweight Champion, Jem Smith, on a 3rd-round TKO (technical knockout). Jem would avenge the loss in 1892 by dispatching his foe in two frames. Pritchard, unlike many British fighters of the period, was no push-over.

Joe's first match in London occurred at the Novelty Theatre on May 25. May 26 *Sporting Life*: "Last night's attraction ... a trial of skill between Joe ... and Jack Hart, of Smithfield, who is entered for Frank Hinde's 11 stone 4 lb (158 pounds) Competition at the Central Hall, Holborn. It was the best of four rounds, for £10 ... The ... programme opened with the play, 'My Sweetheart' ... after which came a scene from 'Tom and Jerry.' ... 'Parson' Davies elaborated upon ... conditions of the contest and receiving an enthusiastic reception. He officiated as timekeeper, and Mr. R. Watson referee ..."

Joe Choynski, circa 1892

Round 1 – "Choynski shot the left, following ... with a stinging right ... which made Hart look uncommonly serious. He tried to counter Joe, but the latter slipped him ... several left-handed belly punches and a stinging right staggered Hart, who had ... difficulty maintaining his equilibrium. Choynski gave him time to pull ... together, but was soon busy with the left until, fearing the collapse of his opponent, was compelled to ease up. Just before the end of the bout (round) Hart looked like falling ... to enable him to obtain a rest, the 'Parson' called 'Time!' and Jack almost reeled to his corner."

Round 2 – "It was apparent that Hart had quite enough of the companionship of the Australian (sic), who played very light. (The *Sporting Life* scribe evidently mixed up the country of Joe's origin with that of Jim Hall's). Occasionally Jack reached Joe's face, and from start to finish Choynski relied wholly and solely on his left hand, with which he hit Hart *ad lib.*, administering an occasional body blow which unmistakably bothered his adversary. It was interesting to see how easily Choynski sent in his left quite as often as he pleased, with a one, two, three, four, and away, and finally completely used up, Hart dropped into his chair."

Round 3, and last – "Joe made the pace, and Jack caught him round the waist to avoid. Choynski allowed him to retreat out of harm's way ... then ... hit him with the left ad nauseam. Clearly Hart was very weak, and it was surprising to see how early in the contest Choynski, with the left, completely demoralised him. Towards the end Jack was entirely useless, and after boxing until all the strength was belted out of him, retired, leaving the £10 still on the nail, possibly for Jem Haines to capture if Jem Hall does not bar his progress." Hall was scheduled to fight Haines, although his boxing record shows him knocking out a Kit Mahoney that night in round four. A later report has Hall fighting Kit on June 4. Among the fistic celebrities there were Charley Mitchell, who claimed the English heavyweight crown, Tom Williams, "champion of Australia" and wrestler/boxer Gus Lambert.

The following night (May 26), Joe took on a stiff named William Patmore, stopping him in the 2nd session. May 28 London *Sporting Life*: "Choynski made very short work of the Barking representative, W. Patmore, last evening ... In the 1st round Joe completely demoralized the Englishman and several times knocked him down. Patmore on each occasion feebly rose and at the end of the first bout (sic) was perfectly useless. In the 2nd he fared worse, and Choynski treated him with great leniency. Patmore staggered to and fro, and at last held out his hand, much debilitated. There were present Tony Sage (of Dublin), (Referee) Charley Mitchell ... To-night the week's entertainment terminates ... Jem Hall and the Brothers Short will give a heavy-weight juggling exhibition. Other boxers are invited to attend, and Charley Mitchell ... as referee. No one will be barred ... In addition, the play of 'My Sweetheart' will be performed, also a score from 'Tom and Jerry,' and Tom Cribb's Parlour."

Joe's final "fight" on his English sojourn occurred two nights later, on May 28, 1892. He faced a pug named Morris Horrigan. The preliminary entertainment was followed by speeches from "Parson" Davies and Referee Charley Mitchell. Next, came a match between Jim Hall and one Albert Pierce. Hall floored his antagonist multiple times in the two frames it lasted, Pierce's gameness being loudly applauded. The main event was a different matter. The *Sporting Life* noted: "Joe Choynski opposed one Morris Horrigan, but the last named seized upon the slightest pretext for shuffling off the stage. Directly he faced Joe, and the latter gave him a hook ... with the left, though not hard. It fairly frightened Horrigan, who raced around the stage and at last embraced the Australian (sic). In consequence of this, Horrigan fell and childishly claimed a foul, though Choynski tried all he knew to keep him upon his feet. He, however, knew that he was safer on the ground, and on standing up took off his gloves. Mitchell and Davies entreated him to continue, and offered him £5 to have one more round, but Horrigan declined and made all haste from the stage, glad to be free from Joe Choynski, who was much disappointed at the turn affairs had taken." This 1st-round victory thus ended the only "meaningful ring action" that Joe would see across "the Pond." Would that he could have at least faced opponents with the courage that Hall's last adversary showed!

On May 30 at London's National Sporting Club (NSC), the Peter Jackson-Frank Slavin contest was held. It was for the Australian heavyweight crown, and, some said, the "British Empire" championship, as well. They fought for a purse of $10,000 and the hall was packed to capacity with 3,000 spectators. The NSC was located at 43 King Street, Covent Garden in London. It was given as a "command" (to protect the reputations of the aristocracy) that names of those attending NSC events should not be made public, but it was revealed that among the number of celebrities present were "Buffalo" Bill Cody and J.D. Spreckels. There were also present "earls and baronets, military officials of the highest rank ... celebrated actors, distinguished doctors, eminent authors, noted painters, illustrious lawyers and conspicuous men-about-town." Choynski described Slavin as, "a powerfully built fellow with a head like a gargoyle."

At 11:30 p.m., Slavin entered the ring with Tom Burrows, Tom Williams and brother, Jack Slavin. His weight was given as 185 pounds. Charley Mitchell was barred from the arena, due to "ungentlemanly conduct" on a previous night. Jackson followed soon after, weighing 192; his cornermen: Choynski, Davies and either Harry Smith of London or Jim Young. The battle took place in a 20-foot square ring, rather than the standard 24-foot. The smaller ring favored a rushing bruiser like Slavin. Lord Lonsdale was Jackson's timekeeper. The referee was B.J. "John" Angle, and the men "fought with gloves somewhat under four ounces in weight." The contest was scheduled for 20 rounds, "though if there had been no knockout ... the referee had the right to order as many more rounds as he pleased to decide which was the better man."[4]

Peter Jackson, circa 1890-1894

The 1st round saw Jackson keep his left in front of Slavin's face. Peter landed three quick body blows, causing Frank to wince. Peter drew "first blood" in the 2nd with a "straight punch full on Slavin's mouth and nose." "The Black

Prince" landed an assortment of shots through the first six rounds, lefts and rights to the head, neck and body which finally caused his antagonist to stagger. Peter frequently caught Frank "coming in," thus increasing the impact of his punches. "Paddy" managed to get home some rib-roasters, especially toward the close of round three. The heat in the club was stifling. The 5th was an excellent give-and-take session, Frank's best to that point, although the edge was generally given to Peter.

In the 6th, Slavin cornered Jackson and landed two punches to the heart, Peter countering with left and right to the head. One account said Frank was saved by the call of time. At the start of the 7th, Slavin grit his teeth "like a fiend," tore after Jackson with his remaining strength and landed "some telling blows." It was a dying gasp, as Peter kept the jab in his face and some potent rights. In the 8th, Frank's left eye was swollen nearly shut, making it hard to avoid Peter's right. Still, he led at the start and only the black's adroit evasive tactics carried him from trouble. Jackson was perspiring freely and both were weakening, but Slavin more so. Odds before the fight, about 6 to 4 Slavin, were 6 to 4 in favor of Jackson at the end of this frame. The St. Croix native crashed straight lefts into Slavin's face in round nine, and a heavy right cross just before the bell.

Round 10 – "Jackson landed a swinging right ... on Slavin's throat, sending him against the ropes." Peter, a master of the "old one-two," began throwing a combination right to heart, left to jaw, over and over again. "Slavin ... fainting and bleeding ... staggered from one side of the ring to the other, but would not go down. Jackson ... thrice turned to the referee to ask, 'Must I hit him again?' " Angle reportedly replied, either, "You must knock him out to win" or "Box on." "With one reluctant, concluding chop, 'Black Prince Peter' dropped his adversary in a corner, unable to rise. The time was 1 minute and 25 seconds of round 10."

"After 18 seconds more had elapsed, Slavin's cornermen came for him and dragged his limp form to the stool ... It was another three minutes before he gave any signs of life." "At the close of the fight (Slavin's) ... eyes were tightly closed, his face badly swollen and discolored, and the body covered with blood. Jackson, too, lost some blood and showed marks of the encounter, but he was in a comparatively fresh condition ..." "Old and expert sportsmen like Angle, Pleisse, Sir John Astley, Lord Lonsdale and the Marquis of Queensberry say they never saw a better fight or as good a one between two big men." This was Jackson's last* and greatest, victory. He went on the downgrade after this fight, giving in to drink and dissipation and later, to tuberculosis. Slavin, for his part, was never the same fighter, in fact, he went into an immediate career nosedive.

* Aside from a meaningless November 28, 1892 W4 over Denny Kelliher.

Joe Choynski: "Slavin was an aggressive fighter, but Peter was too clever for him. Jackson would jab his left to the head and follow with a hard right to the body. As Slavin rushed, the clever black man would step away as easy as if he were showing a new dance step to a pupil. They set a fast and exciting pace for six rounds. From the 7th round to the end Slavin was groggy. At the close of the 11th (Joe evidently meant "the 9th"), Jackson said to me ... 'I'm getting very tired.' He had almost worn himself out trying to knock Slavin down. A groggy man is often harder to knock down than one in good shape. They hang on and on. I advised Jackson to move Slavin to a position near the ropes, wallop him with everything he could put into a punch, then push him hard against the ropes and step back. My expectation was that Slavin would fall on the rebound. Slavin fell off the ropes and was counted out. He was too weak to rise. Jackson became a popular idol in England, and enjoyed himself so well he undermined his health."

On June 1, Jackson was at the Epsom racetrack, taking in the Derby with members of the National Sporting Club and George Godfrey, who was visiting. While not certain, Choynski likely was there. On the 2nd, Joe was at ringside in London's Ormande Club to witness the Jack Slavin-Con Riordan fight. In 1893, it was commented: "He (Joe) declares it to be, barring his own fights, the most exciting experience he ever had. Jem Smith, who he says is as fat as an alderman, was the cause of it. In one of the rounds, Slavin was forced to the ropes and, in an instant, Smith, who had money on Riordan, slipped his hand over the ropes, and getting a good grip on Slavin's belt, held him there while Riordan beat a tattoo on his face and ribs. At last, Slavin cried out to (Charley) Mitchell that he was in trouble, and the blusterer sized up the situation at a glance. 'Let go!' he yelled, as he frantically waved his fist under Smith's nose; 'Give the kid a chance for his life.' 'I be doing nothin', you know, Chawley,' was Smith's rejoinder. The rest of the sentence was drowned in a roar of abuse that came from the audience. A riot was stopped by the timely interference of the police."[5]

Joe and gang had a June 4 boxing show at the Novelty Theatre. "Handled by a clever manager ... Choynski and Hall are doing well in this country, gaining both reputation and money. Of course, they go against picked men, but their showing over a 3rd or 4th class man is so marked that people are beginning to believe both are world beaters. Last evening ... A customer turned up to have a try at the £10 offered ... a middle weight named Kit Mahoney ... Compared to the Englishman, Hall looked like a giant. In the 3rd bout (round) ... All the steam was out of Mahoney ... 4th round ... a heavy right on the chin put him out in the first minute."[6] It appears these are the only fighters that dared to challenge the visitors.

It was reported on June 5: "Jackson has had several good offers to remain in England. A syndicate of brewers and distillers has offered to furnish the colored champion with $150,000 to open a mammoth saloon in London. Jackson will not consider the offer, as he is bound to return to America with 'Parson' Davies. Jim Hall has taken up with Charley Mitchell and Pony Moore, who will find the money for Hall in his fight with Ted Pritchard. 'Parson' Davies will not have anything to do with the fight, as he thinks that Hall has made a very foolish match with Pritchard, confining himself to 160 pounds. Davies thinks the lowest that Hall should fight at is 163 pounds, but he says Hall can get to the stipulated weight and make a good fight. Hall will train at Mitchell's place at Brighton ... Joe Choynski is still waiting for a job, and he is likely to wait. None of the English boxers care to 'take him on,' not even Jem Smith. When George Godfrey arrived here from Boston, it was thought that some of the clubs would make up a purse for the two Americans, but they took no notice of the colored Bostonian, who will probably return to the States at once."[7] Godfrey did return to America, but he and Joe would meet in the ring soon.

James "Jem" Smith was born January 21, 1863 in Shoreditch, London, England and was a transition fighter, participating in London Prize Ring and Marquis of Queensberry rules fights. He only stood about 5' 8½", but often weighed over 200 pounds. Smith was not terribly fast, mobile or even a great hitter, but was stocky, muscular and a good wrestler, with lots of strength, durability and stamina. The wrestling ability stood him in good stead during bareknuckle fights, but sometimes got him in trouble in gloved encounters. In a fight against Peter Jackson in November, 1890, Jem, knowing he was losing, purposely back-heeled his opponent in round two with a "cross-buttock," Prize Ring fashion. He was disqualified. June 6 saw a little-reported event: Jackson and Slavin boxed a five round exhibition at Central Hall in High Holborn. Joe Steers refereed. Godfrey and old Jem Mace were presented on the stage and cheered by the crowd of 4,000.[8]

A Chicago paper wrote: "Peter Jackson is starring in the provinces, but Hall and Choyinski (sic) are lying on their oars awaiting ... Davies' orders. The 'Parson' has had several offers to star his troupe on the continent, but as there is very little money in the project, it is ... probable that the Americans will return to New York at an earlier date than was at first intended. Jem Smith, who still holds the title of champion of England, has not replied to Joe Choyinski's (sic) challenge, and none of the clubs are overanxious to put up a purse for the two Americans." In a desperate attempt to lure Smith into a ring, Choynski made an offer "to stop any man in England in four rounds." This was aimed, in particular, at Jem, who refused the defi. As the *Wheeling Register* put it: "Mr. Smith declines to accept it, because so doing would interfere with his regular summer's work ... that of physical protector (bodyguard) of a bookmaker."[9]

Australian hard-rock, Joe Goddard, was now in California, training for his fight with Joe McAuliffe, which he would win via KO15. Penned the *San Francisco Call*: "Speaking of knockout blows, Goddard said he has heard considerable talk of men being knocked out by a straight punch on the point of the jaw. 'Do you see this mark?' and the Barrier champion pointed to a long distance counter sign right under the point of his chin. 'Choynski gave me that as a token of his hitting powers, and I guess if there was any such thing as a man being knocked stiff when hit on that point, I would not be here now to inform you of the fact. The blow was very heavy and it knocked me on the flat of my back, but I was up in time and returned the compliment with double force. I am ready to fight any man in the world and I can't see where science cuts any figure in prize-fighting as long as a man can win his fights by awkwardness ... and good, stiff punching."[10]

Choynski: "I challenged Ted Pritchard, middleweight champion of England ... The English laughed at my presumption, whereupon I offered to bet £1,000 I would knock out Pritchard in four rounds. The Britons thought me 'balmy' ... Pritchard wanted none of my game. Jim Hall, however, was honored by a match with Pritchard and ... Slavin, and Hall stopped them both. Among the British sporting characters I came to know in London was ... Squire Abingdon, one of the wealthiest men in England. One day, the London papers carried the news that Abingdon had given a famous actress and professional beauty a black eye, and she had fled to Nice to compose her nerves. I was chatting with Abingdon and Charley Mitchell in his hotel suite, just off Piccadilly, when the Squire ordered his secretary to send £2,000 to the lady and tell her to come back. Mitchell ... asked, 'What do you want her back for?' 'Oh,' replied Abingdon, 'it's worth that much to give her another punch in the eye.' "

"I appeared at the Novelty Theatre ... in a play called 'Punch and Judy'. We had a bar-room scene which called for a three-round bout. The management provided a different opponent for me each night by offering £20 to any man who lasted three rounds. Many husky aspirants with iron jaws tried for the purse. Some got through the 1st round. Night after night powerful fellows, full of fight and hope, were pitted against me. There would be a rush or two, a loud stamping of feet on the stage floor, a feint, over would go a left hook or a right cross with a thud to the chin or temple, and another inert body would be dragged off. I knocked out ... a score of heavies. I recall only two or three men – Mike Horrigan, full of tattoo marks, and Albert Hall of Canning Town, who went past the first two rounds. They were hitters themselves and gluttons for punishment. What a hammering those beef-eaters took before they stayed down."

"One fellow, a gigantic truck gardener who enjoyed a fistic reputation in his rural community, offered to refund the £20 if I would let him make a showing by staying the limit. He agreed not to try to hurt me. During the 1st round I was pasting him on the arms and shoulders, purposely avoiding vulnerable spots. Suddenly he let drive as murderous a right punch as I ever ducked. It almost scorched my hair as it screamed past my head. I promptly snapped a terrific left hook to his jaw and, although the bell rang when he was taking the count, he was still out when the time came for the 2nd round.

When he was finally able to speak he swore we had all conspired to bash him on the head from behind." Choynski, like most tourists, purchased souvenirs while in London. Among these was a copy of *The Scapegoat* by Hall Caine, published earlier that year (1892).[11] If Joe's memory was correct, some 35 to 45 years later, then the identity of these other victims have been lost to history, there being no other record of them, it seems.

Davies outlined his plans in a missive to a Chicago paper: "July 18 I shall start on a tour with Peter Jackson. The tour would have been weeks ago, but Peter's right hand was broken in his fight ... We have any number of good engagements, and I cannot tell when we shall be home. I sincerely hope ... in time to see the Sullivan-Corbett fight. Joe ... is anxious to get on with George Godfrey when he returns to America." Then, "Eddie Greaney (sic) was seen by a *Call* reporter last night ... the last he heard from his bosom friend, Joe Choynski, was that he had a bad cold and was going to Germany to the springs. 'Directly Joe gets back to London ... I'll bet I cover Joe Goddard's deposit within 24 hours ... It's an old saying that *the 3rd time does it*, and I think if the match comes off, Joe will about make up for his defeats.' " From England, Joe applied for the recently-opened position of athletic instructor for the Chicago Athletic Association, joining other prominent boxers, past and present. "Jem Mace of London ... retired champion pugilist of the world ... made application to the board of governors of the Chicago ... association ... The receipt of this letter was a great surprise to everybody connected with the club. Among others who have applied for the place are Jim Hall, Joe Choynski and Billy Meyer."[12]

The group's first stop from England was Paris, France. They began a tour of Germany, when, after passing through Belgium, they arrived in Aachen on July 9. Davies, Choynski and gang made their way to Berlin by the 11th, but at some point visited Switzerland, as Joe related in "The Days of Finish Fights." He wrote a letter from Germany on July 27 to "a friend" in New York, stating that Jackson's hand was still in bad shape. He penned an epistle to an Ohio paper, saying his "trip has been delightful ... Our German, Davies' and mine, is not up to the standard, but we manage to make ourselves understood at meal times." In a couple of weeks they were back in London, for a short tour of provincial England. On July 30 it was noted, "Richard K. Fox (owner, *Police Gazette*) sent the following cablegram ... 'London, July 29: Joe Choynski has accepted the challenge of Jem Smith, the English champion ... to fight ... either in England or America in any club that will offer the largest purse, the fight to take place in February."[13]

Davies tried hard to seal a fight with Jem, but it was not to be. August 4: "The attempt to arrange a match in London yesterday between Choyinski (sic) and Jem Smith ... proved a failure. The meeting place was the *Sporting Life* office, and among those present were Warren Lewis of New York, Richard K. Fox, Charles E. Davies (and) Charley Mitchell ... Smith was accompanied by his backers. Choyinski (sic) proposed to fight Smith for £200 a side in the Coney Island Athletic Club. Smith refused to go to America. Richard K. Fox informed Smith that he would ... guarantee him $1,000 if he didn't receive fair play either in the Olympic or Coney Island Club. Smith would not ... arrange any match other than ... in England."[14]

August 9 *Salt Lake Herald-Examiner*: "Jim Smith has backed down from his proposal to fight Choynski. The English champion wants the Californian to wait four months for a fight. Parson Davies offered to guarantee a big purse besides matching his man for $5,000. This does not suit those who like to have a mob at ringside." The statement referred to bareknuckle encounters of the past in England and Europe, where toughs cut the ropes and invaded the ring when their countryman was about to lose a fight. A couple of prime examples were the Heenan-Sayers championship battle in 1860 and the Frank Slavin-Jem Smith title bout in 1889. Thus, the one big fight that Joe could have had overseas never materialized.

On August 7, Davies said "he would match Joe Choynski to fight eight three-minute rounds with James Daly, Corbett's trainer, at the fighting carnival ... in September ... 'If the Olympic club will offer a reasonable purse, Choynski will sail at once for New Orleans, and I will not ask for expenses money for him. The reason that I stipulate eight rounds is that there is not time for Choynski to train for a finish contest on that date. If he does not make this match we will sail for America on the *City of Rome*, August 25." Daly confirmed that he and Choynski had agreed to fight, but had not yet signed articles. He was assisting Corbett in his training for the Sullivan title tiff, and said Jim referred to Choynski as a "cyclone."[15]

On the 15th, a benefit was held for Frank Slavin at the Trocadero Music Hall, Joe and Davies attending. "The programme was greatly strengthened by the services of nearly every artiste in London. A 'parlour' was formed on the stage, including Charley Mitchell, Charlie White, Jack Lewis, Pony Moore, Peter Jackson, 'Parson' Davies, Joe Choynski, Jem Mace ... A.G. Bettinson ... Arthur Cooper ... Jousiffe, J. Goode and Jack Slavin. Mr. Richard Warner presented (Frank) Slavin with a check for £175, with a few remarks, eulogising his pluck, to which Frank Hinde responded. Frank is a born orator and fairly fetched the audience, he stating that Slavin made no excuses for his defeat; he simply met a better man, but though beaten he was by no means disgraced. It is a pity that other of the boxing fraternity cannot take a defeat in a similar sportsmanlike manner."[16]

Joe concluded: "There being no immediate matches in sight, 'Parson' Davies and I decided to return to America for the Corbett-Sullivan fight ... I also challenged Jem Smith, the English heavyweight champion, but Jem ignored my challenges until just before I was sailing for home, when he suddenly accepted with the proviso that he be given six months to train. But why should I? I could whip a dozen men in that space of time! And a lot of them bigger than Smith. I asked him if he would pay my expenses while I tarried for him to prepare. Of course, he declined." Joe said they also decided to return home "for fear of the 'flu' epidemic which was prevalent in Europe." Hall knocked out Pritchard in the 4th round on August 20, laying claim to the English middleweight crown. He would never again, however, be a part of "The Parson's" stable. Davies told him

that no man needed two managers – Hall had chosen Mitchell and that was that.[17] Peter Jackson would stay behind in the land of John Bull another two months, remaining under Davies' management.

A Chicago paper claimed, of the Pritchard fight: "It ... took place at 'Squire' Abington's (sic) place near Brighton. This fact ... coupled with others ... gives strength to the rumor that Pritchard was going to win ... by hook or crook. The fact that there was only one of Hall's friends at ringside ... shows there was something more than accident in the arrangements when Jim Wakely, Phil Lynch and Charley Johnson were left behind. Davies is Hall's manager and should have been (there), while Choynski ... came from America ... to be Hall's second if any match was made in England. That these two men are sore is certain ... Abington had all his chosen henchmen around him in case ... needed.

Joe Choynski, undated, Chicago

They were the pick of the Birmingham division and comprised Jack Baldock, Jimmy Carney, Bill Smith and Sam Blakelock ... instrumental in preventing Frank Slavin beating Jem Smith at Bruges. That Pritchard did not win ... the immense superiority of Hall ... so pronounced and sudden that nothing short of murder could have deprived him of the victory."[18]

Choynski, Davies and Warren Lewis left England on August 25, aboard the steamship, *City of Rome*. The vessel was part of the Inman Line, measuring 586 feet in length, 52 feet in width and weighing 8,826 tons. At the time of its first launch in 1881, it was the 2nd largest steamship in the world. It was a handsome ship, having as a figurehead, "a full-length figure of one of the Roman Caesars," and a clipper bowsprit. "The promenade deck seems almost endless. The lower deck on each side ... affords room ... for carriages to drive, while from the upper decks the water seems very far below. The drawing-room is ... handsomely finished ... opens ... to the main saloon below. The latter resembles the dining-room of a hotel in ... size, but is elaborately fitted-up." The vessel was lighted with ornate, silver electric lamps. Like the *Germanic*, the *City of Rome* had four rigged masts and three tandem steam engines.[19] It would have been quite a voyage home.

Daly probably pulled out of the fight with Joe because Corbett needed his full attention for the Sullivan bout. One report said, "Choynski will meet anybody for eight rounds at New Orleans during the fighting carnival, if an opening can be found. It is said the Parson returns some $25,000 better off than when he sailed, as a result of his luck at betting in the English metropolis."[20] On the evening of August 14, an un-named San Francisco relative of Joe's nearly drowned. "A party of four in a Whitehall boat was capsized off Meiggs' wharf about eight o'clock ... The shouts ... attracted the attention of the *Merchants' Exchange* marine reporter ... who ... went to the rescue. The men were clinging to the upturned boat for dear life when taken into the *Exchange* boat. They gave their names as Heaney, Slaven, Riley and Choyinski (sic), and said they were returning from a pleasure trip to Sausalito ... Choyinski was the worst off of the party, as he swallowed a quantity of bay water, which made him very sick. The ... four soaked men were sent home to dry." It was not revealed who this was, but the next time one of Joe's kin suffered a mishap, the results would be far worse.

Late on September 2, the *City of Rome* arrived at Quarantine, Staten Island, New York, by way of Glasgow, Scotland.[21] The areas of quarantine were located on the east side of Staten Island at Swinburne and Hoffman Islands, but the area around and including the quarantine stations was named Quarantine. There was a large outbreak of Asiatic cholera that year, brought mostly from Europe, and the *City of Rome* was one of several ships detained in an attempt to prevent the spread of the deadly disease. The two-masted steamer, *Moravia*, landed in New York harbor just a few days earlier (August 30), and was found to contain a virulent strain of cholera on board, which resulted in 22 deaths during its trip from Germany. The following day, United States President Benjamin Harrison released an edict stating that any ship arriving at any harbor from an infected port would be placed in quarantine for not less than 20 days.[22] This was the fate of Choynski and Davies' steamer. Ultimately, none of the other ships there were found to have cholera aboard, only the *Moravia*. Still, Charles and Joe faced the prospect of missing the September 7 Sullivan-Corbett title fight.

September 3 *Chicago Inter-Ocean*: "Nothing has yet been heard from Peter Jackson, Joe Choynski and the 'Parson,' but they are thought to be in quarantine on the *City of Rome*. The betting is $35 to $20 that the shrewd 'Parson' manages ... to get around the authorities and make his way to New Orleans in time to witness the contest." September 10 *Deseret Weekly*: "A large party of friends are on board the *'Black Bird,'* waiting to take Parson Davies, Jackson and Choynski up to New York if they can get permission from the health authorities to land them from the *'City of Rome.'* " Joe, from his memoirs: "When we arrived at New York we found ship passengers were being held in quarantine at Fire Island because of the scourge abroad ... Realizing we would miss the fight if ... detained in quarantine, the 'Parson,' Warren Lewis, a well-to-do New York saloon-keeper and I escaped from the ship at night and went ashore on a tug, which New York friends provided for us." The September 4 *Chronicle* contradicted this: "The release of the *City of Rome* from quarantine was received with joy by ... Davies ... Jackson ... Choynski and Warren Lewis, the backer of Jim Hall ... Friends had tried in vain to release them in the afternoon. All but Jackson started at once for New Orleans." It is unlikely that the ship was released early from its Presidentially-imposed, "mandatory" 20-day quarantine.

Joe: "The 'Parson' and I chartered a Pullman with ... friends and started for New Orleans. At Washington our car was hooked on to the same train Corbett was on, and I had my first chats with him since he and I fought. Contrary to published accounts of his extreme nervousness before that battle, I found him entirely composed and confident of victory. Had he been as calm in his meeting with Fitzsimmons there might have been a different result."[23] On September 4 at 9:30 a.m., the train pulled into Greensboro, North Carolina and more than 1,000 people were at the station to greet Corbett. He had slept little to that point in the journey, "having been disturbed at the different stations by people who climbed up to the windows of his private car and cheered him ... then the train sped ... southward. Corbett began his morning exercise in the baggage car by throwing the medicine ball with Daly and Dillon. Davies and ... Lewis were ushered into his car ... and were delighted with (Jim's) appearance."

"At 11 o'clock the most interesting event of the hour occurred. Joe Choynski ... Corbett's rival since boyhood ... who has not seen or spoken to him for three years, was brought in, accompanied by Mike Donovan and several others. Choynski and the big Californian glanced at each other for a moment ... then shook hands heartily. They talked a long while over old times and surprised all by the enthusiastic way ... they spoke of their many battles. Corbett and Choynski exercised together for 20 minutes or more, throwing the medicine ball, etc. Choynski congratulated Corbett on his appearance and gave the opinion that Sullivan would have a hard fight." September 5 *Chronicle*: "After a lot of palaver and negotiation through 3rd parties, Choynski consented to go into Corbett's car and make up. This decision was reached after hours of wavering. Jim sent word to Joe that he was willing to let bygones be bygones if Joe was, and Joe ... replied, 'Me, too.' Choynski proceeded to Corbett's car, looking a little sheepish, and the two saluted each other with 'Hello, Jim!' and 'How are you, Joe?' "

"Choynski asked, in rather an aggrieved tone, 'Why did you say you licked me that last time?' and Corbett replied: 'I licked you four times, and licked you good. You ought not to mind me saying so. If you think I didn't, you can say as many times as you like that you licked me. I won't feel sore.' After this they tossed the ball to each other for 15 to 20 minutes, and Choynski perspired freely, while Corbett was as dry as a chip." At this time, Corbett would have been in the best shape of his life, while Joe had only been sparring. "A correspondent asked Corbett what the quarrel was about, and he said: 'Choynski and I have fought at least 50 times when we were boys in California. I was the only chap anywhere around that he couldn't lick. Every time he whipped a new man and got a little extra reputation he would want to have another go ... with the hope of defeating me. We met four years ago and I licked him, but he wouldn't own up and got sore. That's what started the quarrel.' " The *Inter-Ocean* said Joe gave Corbett "a wishbone, saying it was brought from Europe with him, and he hoped it would bring him good luck." The *San Francisco Chronicle* quoted Joe Goddard saying, as to a Choynski-Fitzsimmons bout, that Joe "would kill Bob. Why, I never knew of a fellow punching as hard as he does."

Inter-Ocean: "Salisbury (North Carolina) was reached at noon. There was a large crowd assembled to see Corbett. He coaxed Choynski to impersonate him at the open door of the baggage car, as they stood close together. The crowd could not tell which of them was Corbett. Charlotte, North Carolina was reached at 1:00 p.m. Corbett's car was uncoupled from the special and side-tracked. Corbett and party propose to stay 24 hours at Charlotte." The "special" carrying Choynski and gang continued on to the "Big Easy." Joe: "Three days before the bout I watched Sullivan punch the bag. I had hoped to find him fit ... I knew at once he was fearfully slow. Fitzsimmons or Maher would have beaten him then in two or three rounds. One incident of that fight I have never seen recorded in print, in the 21st round – the last – Sullivan suddenly bent forward and stuck out his jaw ... to hit. I suppose he wanted to show his extreme contempt for Corbett's blows. The old gladiator was arm and leg-weary. Corbett, of course, had fought intelligently. He was in perfect condition, waiting for the inevitable collapse of the once mighty champion. While in New Orleans I seconded Jack Skelly in his fight with George Dixon, for which I received $500 and Jack McAuliffe against Billy Myer, for which I received $1,000."[24] This was fantastic money for a cornerman. Joe figured in two of the three title fights comprising the historic New Orleans three-day "fistic carnival."

An amusing anecdote about John L. Sullivan was related by Captain Tebeau, a baseball and sporting figure of the day: " 'The Parson says he happened to stroll into the Young Men's Gymnastic Club on the Sunday morning in September last on which John arrived in New Orleans. Sullivan was indulging in a plunge bath and a crowd was grouped around the tank, sizing him up. When he crawled out, Joe Choynski, who had just stripped for a bath, walked over and shook hands with him and asked him how he felt. *O, pretty good, but I have a nasty pain in the stomach*, said John. *You see, Joe, it was like this. I eat a couple of chickens' eggs coming down on the train and I can feel them crawling around in me now, and I think, by gawd, they've got gaffs on.*' "[25]

The first night of the carnival was September 5 and saw world lightweight champion, Jack McAuliffe, defend his diadem against Billy Myer. In McAuliffe's corner were Choynski and "Professor" Robertson. The referee was John Duffy. Myer was floored several times and rendered unconscious in the 15th by Jack's heavy right. The next night, world featherweight champion George Dixon, a Canadian, put his title on the line against an American, Jack Skelly. It was noted that attendance was sparser than the night previous, influenced by the bigotry of the day, being that Dixon was black. It was also mentioned in a novel sort of way that "Negroes were admitted to a section of the hall. There were about 400 negroes present." It was said to be Skelly's first pro fight, and against a champion! Choynski was in Skelly's corner, other squires (varying by source) being "Professor" John Robinson, Jimmy Carroll and Johnny Griffin. Papers couldn't even agree on who refereed, one saying it was John Duffy, another, Captain William Barrett. Dixon dropped Skelly in rounds three and six, bloodying and beating his opponent all over the ring. George knocked Jack down and out with a hard right in the 8th round.[26]

Weakened by alcoholism, inactivity and general dissipation, Sullivan managed to last until the 21st frame before exhaustion and "Gentleman" Jim Corbett's punches laid him down for the count. A new champion was crowned and generally considered, in the United States at least, the first heavyweight champion under Marquis of Queensberry rules. A short time later, Joe and Davies left New Orleans. The "Parson" arrived in Chicago on September 25, to attend to various matters, but Choynski was sent on to Atlantic Heights, New Jersey, to begin training for the Godfrey fight at the "Navesink Highlands." "The 'Parson' is busy arranging a tour for Peter Jackson, who will arrive in this country in October. The 'Parson' will give most of his time within the next month to ... Choynski ... with ... Jackson, McVey, and Davies to train him, should not lack anything in that line."[27]

Navesink Highlands, located just east of the sleepy village of Navesink, New Jersey, in the midst of picturesque "hills on high, undulating ground, which gently slopes to the Shrewsbury River ..." was a peaceful, secluded area amid many trees and open areas. Joe was at the Coney Island Athletic

Club on September 26, to second undefeated Jimmy Lynch of New York against Johnny Griffin of Braintree, Massachusetts. For the 122-pound (featherweight) championship of America, the fight was won by defending champ Griffin on a KO5. Referee Al Smith and Choynski were both cheered loudly upon entering the ring.[28] The October 8 *Brooklyn Eagle* said Joe's efforts were all that allowed Lynch to fight on after round three.

Choynski went into active training on October 2. Mose Gunst returned to the States from Havana, Cuba and landed in New York. He stopped to see Joe in New Jersey and pronounced him looking well. Mose next checked in at Chicago. *Inter-Ocean*: "Mose Gunst ... the embodiment of all that is fair and square in pugilism ... en route to the Golden Gate ... is probably the most famous patron of pugilism alive. It is mainly due to Gunst that the big athletic clubs of the world exist, for ... he first conceived the idea of organization and method, where men could meet, and under the protection, not espionage of the law, settle questions of supremacy." It was told how Mose often placed loads of money on a loser, strictly out of sentiment for that fighter. He did win a small amount on Corbett to beat Sullivan, only betting a "pittance," due to his dislike for Corbett.[29]

George "Old Chocolate" Godfrey was training for the clash near his home in Chelsea, Massachusetts. He is not to be confused with the "George Godfrey" (The "Leiperville Shadow"), who fought in the 1920s and '30s, a heavyweight whose real name was Feab Smith Williams. The original George Godfrey was born March 30, 1853 on Prince Edward Island, Canada. In his prime, he stood 5'10" or 5'10½" tall and weighed between 170 and 175 pounds. As a boy, he moved to the Boston, Massachusetts area and learned to box. He soon gained a reputation as a clever, tough and game pugilist. Godfrey shared the same "stomping grounds" as John L. Sullivan and for a time was considered possibly his equal as a fighter. Sullivan, in fact, pulled out of a scheduled September, 1881 fight with George at the last minute and, thereafter, declared that he was too good (that is, "superior") to fight a black man. The era was, of course, noted for its bigotry, but John was more biased than many.

Godfrey began his professional career around 1879 and had many fights and victories under his belt by the time he was matched with Joe. Godfrey defeated such good black heavyweights as "Professor" Charles Hadley, McHenry Johnson, "The Minneapolis Star," Billy Wilson and C.A.C. "Black Thunderbolt" Smith. George was eventually considered the United States "Black" or "Colored Heavyweight Champion," and, in some quarters, the heavyweight champion of New England. There was no shame in losing on a 19th-round technical knockout in 1888 to Peter Jackson, in a fight for the world Black heavyweight championship. George beat such noted white heavies as Joe Lannon (D6, D15, KO4), Jack Ashton (KO14), Patsy Cardiff (KO16) and "Denver" Ed Smith (KO23). In 1891, he was stopped in 44 frames by Jake Kilrain, but for the Choynski fight, Godfrey was coming off straight wins over Lannon and C.A.C. Smith.

George was described as "a thrifty soul" who owned "considerable property" around Boston. He was a family man and invested his money wisely, one report saying he owned four houses. As preliminary, and unorthodox, conditioning, he was digging cellars in "Bean Town." Like a later Massachusetts fighter, Rocky Marciano, Godfrey started very late in the game, about 26 years old. As many other such fighters, he was a late-bloomer, still good enough to box a D15 with Nick Burley in 1896. For the Choynski contest, the Bostonian would be 39 years old, but in great shape and a dangerous foe.[30] Meanwhile, Joe was rounding into top form with Martin "Buffalo" Costello. October 16 *Brooklyn Eagle*: "Choynski varies his work with long bicycle road work and can be seen taking 10 mile spins every afternoon. The roads and surroundings at the highlands ... the finest he ever saw for training purposes ... The big Californian ... is ... anxious to win his contest with the colored champion, as he feels sure he can get another crack at Joe Goddard. Choynski is a very pleasant fellow and his open countenance and winning smile make friends for him very fast."

On October 17, he and Costello set out on a run "with riding whips and sweaters. They will come back when they have covered about 12 miles of sandy roads ... the Californian ... would never dream of fighting for fighting's sake. He goes into the ring only because there is a chance to make money ... He can, with difficulty, be tempted into expressing an opinion. He looks upon Godfrey as ... simply an obstacle in the way of a handsome purse ... a man ... his senior by many years. 'Do you think it is right to hammer a man who is over 40?' asked a visitor: 'I wish he were over 80 and had only one leg,' was Choynski's quick response. 'The man who fights for glory ought to lose no time in going to glory.' " By such statements, which he stuck to through most of his career, Joe contradicted what he wrote in his memoirs: "My mother hated fighting. But I didn't, I loved it." "Such remarks ... may ... superinduce the notion that Choynski is a hard, cold-blooded, calculating individual, whose excessively sordid soul never rises above mercenary motives ... who, for a dollar would batter a man out of all semblance to humanity. On the contrary. Choynski is as cheery a specimen as ever went into training for a fight. No story he tells loses its point in the telling and the songs he sings will bear repetition more than once."

The "Parson" said: " 'Godfrey ought to be the favorite in the betting, if records count for anything.' John McVey is helping Choynski to train. At a little distance from the Choynski quarters is a cottage which shelters ... John Cattanach. Cattanach holds the wrestling championship of the New England states, but is somewhat of a novice as a pugilist. He has the shoulder of a giant and his muscular development from the waist upward is that of a Hercules. From Choynski, he has received many points likely to be of service ..."[31] Joe would win a KO2 over Cattanach in 1895. John McVey was a former trainer of Jim Corbett, usually known as Jim McVey.

Press Agent John Eckhardt of the Coney Island A.C. invited newsmen to visit Joe's training quarters. He was housed in a two-storey cottage on the Shrewsberry River, "immediately facing the Atlantic Ocean and only a step from the water's edge. Choynski and his trainers were sitting on the veranda when reporters arrived. Choynski's daily programme is to rise with the sun and after ... a light breakfast, take a spin on his bicycle for a dozen miles or so. A bath follows, a good rubbing and a hearty breakfast. After a short rest a half hour's practice with dumb bells and an interval of punching the bag ... After dinner a brisk walk of about 15 miles over the rough country roads with Costello finishes the day's work. Yesterday he gave an exhibition of his skill in fighting the bag, displayed remarkable quickness in his actions." The October 22 *Sporting Life* (Philadelphia) said Joe biked five miles every morning. One paper said: "The harder part of the training is done in a barn a short distance up the road ..." Joe took a turn at the wrist-strengthening machine and threw the medicine ball for 20 minutes.

George Godfrey, circa 1888-1892

Godfrey was hoping to make enough from the fight to invest in a new electric railway, soon to be built in his native Chelsea. His house on Spencer Avenue was "well-furnished, especially his two sitting rooms. In one is a tiny Chickering piano and on the walls are crayon portraits of himself, wife, mother and father. The latter is still alive and lives at Prince Edwards (sic) island. His picture shows him to be a rugged looking Englishman, while his mother was a fine appearing colored woman. George's wife is a very pleasant white woman and their seven children show by their appearance that they have never wanted for anything ... all healthy looking and neatly dressed." George's training routine was similar to Joe's, except Godfrey didn't believe in punching the bag, feeling it wasn't a good exercise.[32]

The October 21 *Brooklyn Eagle* said of Choynski: "He is one of the best hearted men in the business. Two other fighters who will have gloves on their hands before long are indebted to him for all sorts of practical illustrations of the art of hitting and getting away. His patience is inexhaustible and his good nature equal to any strain." Joe went on his daily "12-mile tramp" carrying a riding whip. This was probably as a protection against dogs. The *Eagle* declared that Bob Fitzsimmons had just left New Orleans for New York and would "offer his services to train Joe Choynski for his coming fight." Negotiations between the Hall and Fitz camps had stalled and Bob hated to be idle. He didn't join in Joe's training, however. It was announced that, just before the fight, on the 29th, the nearby Red Bank (New Jersey) Opera House would host a benefit for Joe. Davies had arranged it, and Fitz appeared at this, as did Peter Jackson, who volunteered to referee the bouts involved. He had just arrived at Quarantine (Staten Island) the morning of the 26th, after returning from Europe.[33]

A large crowd was present at the Opera House, including persons from all over Monmouth County and the Atlantic Highlands. Peter Jackson was introduced and made a brief speech. "There were a number of set-tos between local boxers, and then the famous pugilists appeared. Each set of boxers sparred three rounds of three minutes each ... in this order: Jack Quinn, the Scottish lad and Thomas Clark; John McVey and Buffalo Costello, and Choynski and Jack Cattanach of Providence. Before the last bout Parson Davies stepped upon the stage and announced that Choynski was in the pink of condition, due to this climate and his kind treatment ... the Providence boy was able to land only two or three blows in the three rounds, while Choynski apparently had no difficulty to hit when and where he pleased. The proceeds of the entertainment were about $500."[34]

The October 29 *New York Sun* joked: "Admirers of pugilism were discussing the merits of Godfrey and Choynski yesterday when one ... remarked: 'Godfrey is clever and tricky, but Chownskee is young and strong.' 'Ha! Ha! Ha! Chownskee is good,' laughed the red-nosed sport with the big diamond. 'You mean Chewingskye' ... 'How's a feller to know who yer talking about? Choosinski is his name.' The debate was reaching a point where fists were clinched, when suddenly Parson Davies hove in sight, and the question was submitted to him ... 'The young man's name,' said the Parson with his most suave smile, 'is pronounced as though spelled Ko-in-sky, with the accent on the second syllable.' Thereupon peace descended upon the debaters and the Parson pursued his unruffled promenade."[35]

The day before the fight, the *Brooklyn Eagle* described George: "Godfrey is, like his cunning opponent, a fast and furious fighter. He takes punishment well and his gameness goes unquestioned. Although the oldest prize fighter in the ring to-day, Godfrey figures among the quickest and cleverest of them. He is wonderfully energetic and full of agility. In action he is apparently a youth, so quick does he dodge a swing and dart like a flash at his foe. He ... says ... he must have that $5,000 purse for the education of his children and their future support." The loser's end would be $1,000 or $2,000, varying by source, still decent money for the era.

On the morning of the fight, October 31, both boxers were "on the ground at Coney Island ... secluded even from their most intimate friends." "Joe Choynski is at Mrs. O'Brien's house on the boulevard and Godfrey has put up at the residence of a friend not more than 15 minutes' walk from the Casino. Choynski has undergone a physical examination at the hands of Dr. J.H. Van Mateo of Atlantic Highlands. The doctor pronounced Choynski ... in the best of condition. His wind ... perfect and his strength extraordinary for a man his size. Godfrey is in equally good trim ..." Betting was about even. Each was a boxer-puncher, capable of skillful exchanges or slugging. George's right was dangerous; Joe launched bombs with both fists.[36]

Fight night – Among the notables at the Coney Island Athletic Club were Peter Maher, Bob Fitzsimmons, Joe Goddard, Jack McAuliffe, Billy Rocap and Joe Butler. The weights were given as 168 pounds for Choynski, 175 for Godfrey. "Standing room was at a premium, the largest crowd of sporting people who ever attended a fight in this vicinity being jammed in the building. Peter Jackson was present and was cheered to the echo as he entered his private box." "7,000 people sat around the stakeless ring and cheered ... the gladiators." The men entered the ring at 10 p.m. with their attendants. Joe's squires were "Buffalo" Costello, McVey, Jimmy Carroll and "Parson" Davies. Godfrey's seconds were Sam (or Frank) Steele, Jim Godfrey (George's brother), Jack McGee and Professor Williams of Brooklyn. This was a fight to the finish for a purse of $5,000. Choynski's ring garb elicited much comment, as he wore pink trunks and flesh-colored tights (some reports said red clothing). Godfrey's fighting togs consisted of black tights and stockings (some accounts said "blue"). Johnny Eckhardt, club secretary, was chosen as referee. The following combines more than a dozen different sources, mostly contemporary and primary:[37]

Round 1 – Godfrey was watchful and stationary, while Choynski advanced and retreated. He "presented his side to his adversary and kept his long left out at almost full arm's length." Joe had the reach advantage. He dodged a punch from George and countered with a left jab to the face. After some light exchanges, the younger man got in a hard left to Godfrey's jaw. Late in the round, as George was pursuing him, Joe slipped down on his hands and knees. His opponent stood over him, "with his left on Joe's back, ready to strike. Eckhardt separated them and the gong sounded."

Round 2 – Godfrey "grinned in a self-satisfied way as he ... feinted at the Californian." "Choynski smiled as he advanced to the middle of the ring ..." The pair stalled and fiddled for nearly a full minute, until Godfrey led. Choynski was clever on his feet and dodged the attack. George was the aggressor, but fell short with his punches. Joe got in a good left, and it was commented how much he resembled Jim Corbett in style and tactics, "for his grace and rapidity of movement, for the accuracy with which he judges distances, and for the celerity he displays in keeping out of harm's way." George landed inconsequential punches, including one to the back of Joe's head in a clinch. Choynski began an attack to his foe's gut.

Round 3 – Joe cleverly ducked George's swings and drove shots to the stomach. At one point, he slipped under Godfrey's left arm and his rushing opponent bounced off the ropes and turned, a look of intense surprise on his face. Choynski stuck the straight left and nimbly evaded counters. He landed so many jabs that Godfrey's left eye began to swell shut. Joe then staggered him with a clout to the neck. George got in some stiff shots, a right opening a cut over Joe's left eye, but the latter easily won the heat.

Round 4 – Each waged a defensive battle. George missed the many lefts he attempted and Joe, the powerful rights he launched. Nat Fleischer wrote, in "Black Dynamite," "Godfrey punished Joe around the body severely in the 4th ..." The (Philadelphia) *Sporting Life* said: "Choynski drove his left in on the negro's eye with an iron-like jab. In an instant the yellow skin around his eyebrow turned to a dirty purple. Still there was no blood. Godfrey kept batting his eyes like an owl. Choynski seemed uncertain on his feet. Every time he rushed and missed he would almost go through the ropes."

Round 5 – Some papers said Godfrey cut Joe's left eye in the session. Joe staggered George with a left hook, but he came back with a right to the left eye that sent his man against the ropes. The Californian rebounded and landed another left that was heard all over the building. "The blood running down in Joe's eye seemed to bother him, and he frequently wiped it off." He had decidedly the better of this furious heat. The *Chronicle* said Choynski's seconds cut his swollen left eyelid between rounds, to extract some of the blood. Fleischer: "In the 5th, a short, snappy hook closed Godfrey's right eye ... immediately after this the colored boxer slashed Choynski with a right chop that cut the Californian over his left optic."

Round 6 – Joe had a cut, swollen left eye and blood trickling from his mouth. He landed a left to Godfrey's jaw, but George trumped him with a good one to the neck. He followed Choynski around the ring and got a couple more to Joe's nose before the bell. Both went laughing to their corners and were roundly cheered for their scientific, hard-hitting battle. It was Godfrey's round. *Sporting Life*: "The 6th round was a marvel of science. Time after time the negro drove in with vindictive whirl, and time after time the white ducked under his flying fist and away. The hard, iron knot at the end of the Californian's left arm was driven repeatedly into the negro's stomach, the negro grunting with each blow."

Round 7 – It was evident that Choynski was boxing more than he had in previous battles, utilizing the jab instead of letting both hands go with abandon. When he did throw the right, he made it count. Godfrey began with a rush, which Joe mostly avoided, although he took a punch to the midsection. Joe countered with a left to the mouth that caused George's lip to bleed, and a short time later, doubled him over with "a corker on the stomach." He got in a right to Godfrey's ear and cleverly eluded when the latter thought he had him cornered. The older fighter got in "some swing blows," Joe avoiding others by judicious clinching. Both did some "dancing" in this frame, landing a pair of potent lefts to the gut and another to the face. The body blows caused Godfrey to leap off his feet in pain. He just missed Joe with a strong uppercut. The *Colorado Sun* said it was Godfrey's round, but most papers gave Choynski the edge.

Round 8 – Joe landed a left to the solar plexus. They exchanged punches to the body and head, then George drove a right cross to the head that dropped Joe on his butt. He rose to one knee and took six or more seconds before getting up. He came right back at Godfrey and the two exchanged heavily to the gong. Two reports said the knockdown was at least a partial slip. Fleischer noted, though, "Godfrey's best round was the 8th, when he floored Choynski with a right on the jaw, and Joe, after taking a seven count, was visibly weak and glad to hear the bell." *Sporting Life*: "Choynski swung his right on Godfrey's jaw and the latter staggered. (Joe) jumped in to finish him, but Godfrey gave him a rap that sent him to his knees. Then both men sprang to their feet and went at it like wild men ... the round ended with the men locked in a death-like grip on the ropes."

Round 9 – Joe started with a smile. He was the aggressor, landing a stiff punch to "the bread basket." George tried to advance, but Choynski quashed this by feinting to the body. The former candy-maker finally threw his right with consistency, but staggered Godfrey with a left to the chin, another to the short ribs, and pelted George's stomach, making him wince.

Round 10 – Godfrey rallied, getting Choynski against the ropes. He landed heavily to Joe's swollen eye, drove in a good uppercut and landed to the body. Joe replied with hard lefts to body and head, and a right that snapped his foe's head back. One report said Joe had the better of the infighting and rode with several punches. The *Colorado Sun* said it was the best round of the fight and George clearly won it. Fleischer: "In the 9th and 10th Choynski opened up with both batteries. He nailed Godfrey with right and left swings that staggered the colored pugilist and made him clinch ..."

Round 11 – Both had their left eyes swollen shut. Godfrey drove a left to the pit of the stomach, but "Little Joe" landed his long, accurate left jab to the head and body. One made a resounding crack to the midsection. A stiff jab sent Choynski's head back, but Joe doubled over his foe with a body punch. He pounded the Bostonian all over the ring until the bell saved him. Fleischer: "Joe slipped to the floor during an exchange at close quarters in the 11th, and as Godfrey rushed him when he rose, connected with a left hook to the jaw that spun 'Old Chocolate' around."

Round 12 – Joe landed lefts to the chest and face. He suddenly went to the canvas, either tripping over Godfrey's feet, or George hitting him in the back of the head as he turned. Joe was all right and continued out-scoring his opponent. He landed one particular stomach punch that made Godfrey writhe in pain. George appeared groggy, but just as the gong sounded, landed a bomb flush on Joe's head and floored him. He got up okay and would have won the frame, if not for the knockdown(s).

Round 13 – Steele and McGee worked frantically between rounds, but Godfrey was fading fast. Choynski was told by his corner to try and end matters. He met his opponent in ring center and landed a quick punch or two. A sharp exchange followed, Joe getting the better of it. At some point, Choynski ducked low under Godfrey's attack, but slipped to his knees and crawled to safety. Some in the crowd laughed, while others hissed. Joe landed left and right to the torso, a left to the jaw, then made George leave his feet again with one hellacious shot to the stomach. He answered with a straight left that split Choynski's lower lip, but Joe had the final word with a punch to the closed left eye of his adversary. Fleischer: "The hopes of Godfrey's backers brightened in the 13th, when George landed a right on the jaw, and Choynski dropped. But the fact was that the blow was only a glancing one that caught Joe off balance, and he did not even take a count before rising. Choynski was pounding steadily now, landing often on Godfrey's stomach and kidneys, alternating with cutting jabs to the face, and before the 14th round ended the colored man was groggy and holding."

Round 14 – This was a slow frame, Choynski marshalling his resources for a finish, George slowing due to weakness. Joe landed numerous lefts to the face and body. The round ended with Joe forcing his man to the ropes. *Sporting Life*: "At the beginning of the 14th round Choynski's lips were puffed out, his swollen eye causing him to arch his brows in the effort to keep it open. Godfrey's eye looked like the ball of a red chrysanthemum."

Round 15 – Godfrey made a desperate charge, but Choynski stepped adroitly out of range, feinted and landed hard lefts to stomach and head. The last punch caused George to stagger. He was completely blinded in the left eye by this time. Joe retreated, George in furious pursuit. The younger man turned suddenly and planted a stiff left in the face. Quick as a flash, Joe stepped to Godfrey's blind side and shot a pile-driving right below the left eye. George dropped to the mat like a hogshead, on his right side, completely out. Eckhardt's 10-count was a mere formality, but once finished, Joe picked up Godfrey and carried the brave warrior to his corner. The fight ended at one minute and 11 seconds of the round. It took several minutes for George's handlers to revive him. "The great crowd ... howled and stamped and clambered over the benches in great avalanches of humanity ..." "The crowd separated, but before all hands left the building

Choynski admitted that the blow which knocked out Godfrey had broken three of his knuckles."[38]*Sporting Life*: "Choynski was comparatively fresh ... His left eye was swollen and his lip slightly cut. Godfrey was badly used up. His left eye was closed from the swelling, his left cheek lacerated, and there half a dozen painful bruises and puffings on his neck and shoulders."

Choynski recalled: "Godfrey ... was a good man, remarkably clever and a hard puncher, but he had a way of taunting an opponent in the hope of infuriating him. I slashed Godfrey unmercifully in the first five rounds, but took many a blast ... in return, and ... it seemed a question who would win. In the 14th round Godfrey began taunting me, but I kept my head and let him rave. Every time he'd let out a taunt, I'd unleash a haymaker. Godfrey didn't like it. So, in the 15th he made a big mistake, and it cost him the fight. He called me a vile name! I guess he thought this would make my blood boil. Well, it did ... but luckily I knew enough to keep my liver in its place till the first wild rage had passed. Then, coolly and somewhat deliberately, I squared the account. I busted Godfrey in the stomach and then cracked him on the jaw. The gentleman of the insults went down – and out. It doesn't pay to say things like that to a fellow who can keep his wits about him. Personally, I never made it a practice of saying insulting things to any man. With the exception of one occasion, I refrained from saying unkind things in the ring. I did speak sharply to Joe Goddard ... but that was in retaliation. He had used me unfairly in our Australian fights."[39]

The win was not expected to garner Choynski a shot at the title, but it cemented his status as a top contender. In 1888, it took the virtuoso heavyweight, Peter Jackson, 19 rounds to accomplish what Joe did in 15. Godfrey's only other loss since his career began in 1879, came in 1891, when the much heavier Jake Kilrain stopped him in round *44*. George said his head struck a lead pipe protruding from the wall, resulting in that knockout. Jim Corbett "won a pile of money" on Choynski, and wired various friends before the fight to wager on Joe. Among those who won betting on Joe were actor Maurice Barrymore, Joe Goddard, Steve Brodie and Mose Gunst.[40] The October 20, 1893 *Idaho Daily Statesman* claimed that Choynski wept when he wasn't allowed to keep his gloves as souvenirs. It also claimed, "After the Goddard-Maher fight it required four men to get the gloves away from Goddard, and he said: 'Toik yer purse, but gi' me the gloves. 'Ang your rules; I want the gloves.' " He didn't get them.

Soon after the fight, Choynski returned to the Navesink Highlands to train with Peter Maher, who was preparing to meet Joe Goddard. Tony Sage of Dublin, Ireland, Maher's former backer, wrote a letter to Dave Holland (Maher's manager), saying: "One piece of advice. Peter should not be left alone one minute by himself. McGrath or someone you have confidence in should sleep in the same room with him in case he might be foolish enough to take a drink of water, which to him is nearly as bad as beer." The McGrath mentioned was Irish bantamweight boxer Joe McGrath, one of Maher's training companions.[41] Tony's "Sage advice" may have been tongue-in-cheek, as Peter was indeed fond of beer and good old Irish whiskey. Maher was an inconsistent performer and sometimes lazy in training, but could blast out opponents with the best of all time. No one hit a harder punch for his weight, or perhaps *any* weight, in the long history of boxing. His right was an especially potent weapon.

Choynski signed to fight at the Ariel Club in Philadelphia against a good, black fighter named Joe Butler. Many white boxers in this age drew "the color line," either due to bigotry, or as a convenient way to avoid a confrontation with a boxer they feared losing to. Choynski, however, showed throughout his career and life that he was no bigot. He faced fighters of any weight, race or religion, and befriended Chinese when many ostracized them. Also training with Joe at the New Jersey pugilistic colony were "Buffalo" Costello and Joe McGrath. The November 14 *Brooklyn Eagle* said the manner in which "Parson" Davies handled the camp at Navesink and the success of Choynski against Godfrey, attracted other boxers, trainers and managers there. "Mr. Davies is not a trainer to the extent that he takes a part in the day's performance, but he permits very little to escape him and is quite apt to know just what is going on and to have something to say about it if there is anything pointed to be said."

The November 19 *Police Gazette* noted: "The victory ... over ... Godfrey ... was a popular one ... owing probably to the fact that Choynski has made a legion of friends in all parts of this country by his gentlemanly ways. Choynski fights similar to Corbett, and can undoubtedly strike a harder blow than the California wonder, but he is not as scientific. Choynski had never before fought in the East and ... critics were eager to see how he would perform. On several occasions during his battle with Godfrey, he fought like an amateur. Choynski could dance away, slip, fall and duck safely while in front of Godfrey. But, what would have been the result had he tried that style ... with Bob Fitzsimmons or Jim Hall? Choynski's victory gained him golden opinions, but many first-class judges ... believe he has plenty of room for improvement. Choynski has no doubt improved since he fought Goddard in Australia, but the improvement is not enough, in my opinion, for him to defeat Goddard, and I understand that it is on the slate for Choynski to try, should Goddard defeat Maher on December 8 in the Coney Island Athletic Club." Improve he would, but it would be a while before he got his nemesis, Goddard, back in a ring.

Choynski was at a hotel in Philadelphia on November 18, accompanied by Peter Jackson. Newly-crowned kingpin Corbett was there, as well, and Jackson met him in the lobby. Gracious, as nearly always, Peter congratulated Jim and shook his hand. Corbett's muttered response was unintelligible. About this time, Joe made the first mention of wanting to star on stage in a play, preferably one written for him. His wish would happen soon, but the press found the notion ridiculous when he first expressed it.[42] Back at training camp, the "California Terror" gave pointers to "Buffalo" Costello, during his own preparation. The November 22 *Brooklyn Eagle* stated, "It is difficult to understand why ... one should have the advantage over the other, but ... Costello is becoming quite a marked favorite ... training with Choynski probably accounts for some of his strength with the betting fraternity. Choynski, who is the soul of good nature, is always perfectly willing to tell a training companion everything he knows."

Joe's next bout was against C.A.C. (Charles) Smith. He recalled, in 1927: "There followed another campaign of meeting all comers, this time at old

Niblo's Garden, New York, (part of) Sam T. Jack's burlesque show. One night I would maul some aspirant and the next night Hall would be the executioner, except when some ... formidable-appearing foe would be scheduled; then Hall would plead illness. Not one ... succeeded in going

C.C. "Thunderbolt" Smith

the route ... there appeared a gigantic colored fighter, C.C. Smith, who had more than a local reputation as the 'Black Thunderbolt.' It was Hall's turn to save the $100, but Jim developed an illness ... management was panicky and was for having the 'Black Thunderbolt' blackjacked in the alley or arrested ... anything to save the money. I suggested they give me the chance and wait until the 3rd round before starting the 'win, tie or wrangle' stuff." In 1897, Smith would give Peter Maher a rough six round battle, losing on points. He defeated Frank Craig, Mervine Thompson and Steve Taylor.

The fight was held at Philadelphia's Ariel Club on November 21, and, as Joe elaborated: "Davies was afraid the Thunderbolt would annihilate me, but I told the Parson that lightning was more potent than thunder. So I turned on the current – the lightning struck Smith and he fell like a blasted tree." The *Philadelphia Inquirer* said: "Joe Choynski was the attraction at the Ariel Club last night, and stopped C.C. Smith, the colored Thunderbolt, in the 4th round. All through the contest Choynski had things his own way." On the night of the 23rd, Joe was back at the same club, taking on Denny

Kelliher in a four-rounder. "Kelleher (sic) was no match for Choynski and in the 2nd round he got a punch in the jaw that left him practically knocked out. The referee stopped the fight then and gave it to Choynski."[43]

Our subject's next contest at the Ariel A.C. was to have been with Joe Butler on November 26, but Butler's manager "objected." The latter had a match scheduled against a Fred Williams and the manager evidently didn't want the fight jeopardized by an injury, either to Mr. Butler's body or reputation. A replacement was found – Jack Fallon (John W. Fallon), a local heavyweight of good reputation who stood 5' 11" and weighed 190 pounds. He was known as "The Brooklyn Strong Boy," a sobriquet doubtlessly borrowed from John L. Sullivan. Any similarity to the "Boston Strong Boy"

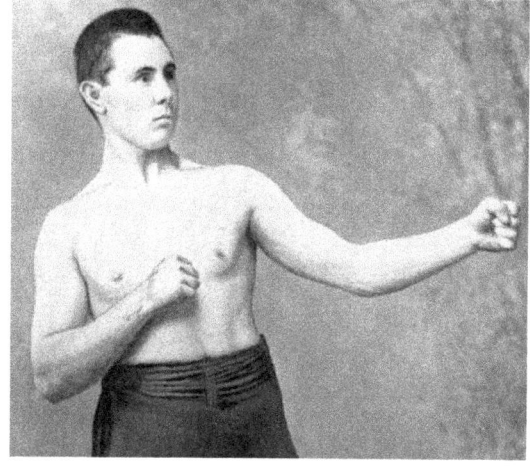

Jack Fallon, "The Brooklyn Strong Boy"

ended with the nickname, as Joe stopped his foe in the 4th and final session. Fallon had little notice for the fight and was described as "big and fat," but gave a very credible showing, as witnessed by 4,000 people.

"Fallon ... smashed Choynski in the face several times in the first three rounds. At the end of the 3rd ... the Brooklyn man was growing very tired. In the 4th round Choynski landed four times in succession on Fallon's face and knocked him under the ropes with a left-hander on the jaw. Fallon struggled to his feet, fell down again and was counted out." Another paper said, "Fallon ... held his own for the first three rounds, but in the 4th ... Choynski landed savagely on his ... stomach and put him out by a blow on the jaw." Next, Joe Butler sparred an exhibition of "three friendly rounds" with Joe. He did well, considering he was only a middleweight. The previous September 21, Butler twice floored a surprised Joe Goddard in a three round bout that was stopped by police to rescue the latter.[44]

"Buffalo" Costello had his rematch with Alec Greggains on November 28 at the Coney Island A.C. The scheduled fight to a finish became a marathon contest. In Costello's corner were Billy Delaney, Jimmy Carroll and Choynski. The fight started around 10:00 p.m., but for some reason Joe didn't join until 11:00, wherein he "assumed command in Costello's province." The men opened "hostilities" with cautious sparring. In the 2nd, Costello drew "first blood." The rest of the fight interspersed action with lulls in activity. Alec scored a few knockdowns, while Costello bloodied his foe more than once. In round 46, "the electric lights burned blue, sputtered and went out, leaving the men to battle in semi-gloom." The bout continued by gas-light. Costello was said to have broken his right hand, in round 40 or 51. The fight became tedious, and Referee Eckhardt declared a draw at the end of the 80th frame. The match lasted five hours and 20 minutes. The purse was split evenly.[45]

When Joe stated his intent to act on stage, many boxers had already done so, like J.L. Sullivan, Corbett and Peter Jackson. "Joe Choynski ... believes he is built for an actor. He intends ... to have a play written around himself, and star under Parson Davies' management." Their itinerary called for a grand reception in San Francisco, "under the auspices of ... the California and Pacific Athletic clubs. Choynski ... will be

Joe Butler

Jackson's sparring partner on their tour west, which will commence about the holidays."[46] Meanwhile, Jack Fallon was granted a rematch (of sorts) on December 3. He would win a purse if he lasted four rounds with Joe. Jack gained the money, but also notoriety as a coward. "Fallon ... received $50 ... because ... Choynski failed to stop him, at the Grand Theater ... Fallon did a good deal more falling than fighting ... thus saving himself ... 'A man like ... Fallon is a disgrace to the profession and the sooner he retires from the ranks the better ...' said Choynski." Fallon retired from the ring in 1894 and was noted that year as a member of the Gravesend, Long Island police force, where he was described as "a model officer."[47]

On the 8th, Joe attended the Joe Goddard-Peter Maher pier six brawl at the Coney Island A.C., one of the great slug-fests of all time. The bruisers went toe-to-toe with all the power they could generate, and by the time it ended in the 3rd heat, the carnage was horrific. Maher was floored four times, but slashed open deep cuts over Goddard's eye and cheek and badly staggered his foe. Only Peter's depleted strength saved Goddard from being stopped at the close of the 2nd. The Australian finally beat down the Irish Champion in the 3rd, and Joe's 12 pound edge in weight didn't hurt his cause any.[48] Goddard challenged Corbett to a championship fight afterward, but Jim wanted no part of him, as he admitted years later.

Choynski arrived back in Chicago on December 20, "to fill an engagement ... at Battery D December 29. The handsome San Franciscan looks heavier than on his last visit ... Choynski will be the guest of Joe

Ullman, Frank O'Brien and Sam Myers." An offer was made to Maher to face Joe on the 29th and his "backer," Dave Holland, expressed satisfaction at the terms. Peter, though, wired that he couldn't make it, as he had promised to second his countryman, Joe McGrath in a fight.[49] In his stead, Choynski would box Bob Ferguson and Mike Boden on the same night! On December 24, Joe was at the Chicago Stock Exchange for the Board of Trade's annual public reception. "Business cares and dignity had been thrown to the wind, and as the fusillade of corks became more furious cares were thrown aside and happiness held full sway ... Secretary Elkins ... determined to see there was (sic) no Rugby foot-ball tactics employed and a semblance of order was preserved. The Stock Exchange receptions have a reputation which does not inspire a timid man of weak physique with much enthusiasm in accepting ... their invitations. One guest ... seemed ... indifferent to the chances of being handled roughly. A ... blonde-haired ... man with a brown mustache ... Joe Choynski ..." The "Hungarian Band" provided music; there was singing and dancing. Free silk top hats were handed out, though the order was given that they should not in drunken revelry crush them this year. Joe was a guest of one of the brokers.[50]

Joe tipped the scales at 169 pounds on the evening of December 29. His opponents, Bob Ferguson and Canadian, Mike Boden, were reported to weigh 203 and 188 pounds, respectively.[51] Joe faced each in a four round bout, Detective Captain Shea being present to ensure order was kept. First up was Ferguson. "The Californian fiddled around the 1st round, opening up only near the close, and with the left, that some wiseacres contend is useless to him, had the big Stock Yards man a-going when time was called. In the 2nd the little heavy-weight dropped Ferguson twice with short-arm rights, then mercifully let up on him. That usefully developed left of Choynski in the 3rd shot out clean cut and hard five times straight. In the 4th, Ferguson was dropped with a right-hander to the point of the jaw, and after 50 seconds, stopped cold." Following a short, two-bout intermission, Choynski took on Mike "The Canuck" Boden.

"The Californian could do nothing with the foul tactics of Boden, contenting himself by an occasional hooker (sic) and a deal of strong elbow work. Boden stayed the four rounds out and this was ample glory ... though he was made a 'monkey of.' " As John L. Sullivan, Jack Dempsey and Mike Tyson learned, some opponents will not be knocked out in a short, allotted time, if they are only there to survive. The *Chicago Tribune* said the pair "fought four savage rounds." Choynski floored Boden in the 2nd and 3rd, but Mike continually clinched to save himself. He was "groggy and practically knocked out" in round three. It was more of the same in the 4th, Boden hugging for dear life each time he was struck. In 1905, Jim Corbett said: "Mike Boden ... had a national reputation of taking everything in the punch line in a graceful manner. He could stop a mighty swing with his jaw and smile. He never went down for the count, that any of his antagonists remember. He was a physical freak. There would never be another man like him. Joe Grimm occupies the distinction Boden did a score of years ago."[52] The April, 1943 *Ring* said Boden was a southpaw who previously had been a wrestler. The *Ring* scribe called him a "rough-and-tumble thug."

On December 31, Joe and Davies left for San Francisco to attend the January 7 testimonial for Joe and Peter, by their friends in the city. Choynski would be stopping at Salt Lake City, Utah, to contest a four-round fight with "a local man" on January 2. "The local sports are well acquainted with Jackson, Corbett ... nearly all noted pugilists ... but this is the first visit of 'Brave Joe' ... Choynski deserves the title by which he is known the world over. The fair-haired Hebrew is a great favorite here, and one reason ... is because he is a westerner. His admirers are talking of giving him a reception tomorrow night, after he gives his exhibition at the People's theatre, for which a programme of unusual interest has been prepared. The feature of it will be a set-to between (Joe) and Frank Fitzgerald."[53]

Another item on Joe's agenda was to train George Dawson for a fight with Tommy Ryan. Dawson was the former lightweight champion of Australia and later, a trainer of Bob Fitzsimmons. Davies said that Joe "has several engagements ... the training of Dawson is only a minor consideration. Dawson took particular pains to see Choynski was well treated when ... in Australia, and the Californian is ... anxious to do all he can for Dawson."[54] Joe and Davies arrived in Salt Lake City the morning of January 2. "They were met at the depot by Colonel Kelly, who escorted them to the Knutsford and looked after their comfort during the day. In the morning the party took a drive over the city, visiting Fort Douglas and other points of interest, and in the afternoon the noted pugilist went out to the Springs with Colonel Kelly and enjoyed a bath." Joe was asked, " 'Have you any matches ahead ...?' 'No. I am going back to San Francisco, my home, to see my folks. I have been away for a long time, you know.' "

The exhibition at People's Theatre occurred on the night of the 2nd: "It was 10:30 (p.m.) when ... The men gave a very pretty set-to, one which appeared to satisfy everyone. Choynski proved himself a master of the manly art. Fitzgerald is a novice with the mitts, and the bout gave the Californian a good opportunity to display his ability. There was no hard hitting, of course, for both men went at each other in a lively manner from start to finish. Joe's style of sparring is peculiar to himself, and is very pleasing. At the end of the four rounds the men were given an ovation, and Choynski seemed highly pleased with his reception ..." Fitzgerald was referred to as the cleverest man with the gloves in all of Utah.

Ogden Standard: "Of Choynski only pleasant words can be written. Quiet, modest, gentlemanly and sociable ... While babies will never be thrown into spasms by his face, it is also a sure bet that the girls will never rave over his beauty. His countenance has a decided Hebraic cast, and like ... Jim Corbett, he wears his hair *a la* Pompadour." Joe recounted his matches with Goddard, saying he had "The Barrier Champion" beaten on several occasions, once having him out for 16 seconds. The referee wouldn't begin a count until he had walked around the ring from the opposite side, standing outside the ring. The bell saved Goddard at the count of nine.[55]

The pair arrived in San Francisco on January 4. "I never felt better," Joe said. "I weigh about six pounds more than I ever did before ... You know as much about my past as I do. As to my future, that rests entirely with the parson, who ... is managing my affairs. I will probably remain here about a month and ... go to New Orleans ... The long trip has done me good. While on the continent (England) I was treated for a disorder of the stomach, and I return to this country feeling 50 per cent better. Everywhere I was treated well, especially in London, where I did very little in the fighting line to merit recognition, but you see Peter Jackson stands ace high there and anyone in his company can expect good treatment. My reason for going to New Orleans is to see the fight between Hall and Fitzsimmons, and ... to get a match with the winner. Fitzsimmons and I were formerly great friends and a match ... never thought of, but friendship should not stand in the way of business in these times of big purses." Various papers said "Choynski still suffers from an injured knuckle on his right hand ... received in the battle with Godfrey and ... was not improved by his exhibitions in Chicago."[56]

The Pacific Athletic Club had a seating capacity of 5,000, but sold more than 6,000 tickets for the testimonial, so popular were the boxers. Club President Harrison announced he was offering "$5,000 for a finish contest between Joe ... and either Peter Maher ... or Jim Daly ..."[57] On the night of January 10, the testimonial was held instead at the Orpheum Theater across from O'Farrell Street, which had a greater seating capacity. "All local sports attended the Jackson-Choynski testimonial ... There were no knockouts or bloody affrays, but scientific boxing and wrestling bouts ... the 10-round bout between Choynski and the colored champion of Australia was the event of the evening. Both men showed up well ... Choynski has greatly improved since he left here a year ago. He has boxed a great deal with Jackson lately and their exhibition was good." The audience stamped, whistled and howled until long after 8:30 p.m., when the first entertainers were announced. There was a four-fighter battle royal and a jump-rope exhibition, among other displays. Choynski was presented with a floral horseshoe.[58] The same day's *San Francisco Morning Call* noted that "Joe ... is taking some exercise preparatory to his exhibition contest with Peter Jackson on Tuesday evening next, the 17th inst. at the Wigwam. The benefit is sure to attract a large gathering ... next week." No further mention is found of a January 17 exhibition; it may not have occurred.

While in the city, Davies, Jackson and Joe took a horse-drawn coach out to Barney Farley's road house in San Mateo. There, on the front steps, each holding his hat, they had their photos taken along with such boxing figures as John Herget, George Dawson, Sam Fitzpatrick and W.W. Naughton. The best date found for the photo is January 11. That evening, Joe was part of a "road party," along with Davies, Jackson, Dawson, Naughton, Fitzpatrick and "a dozen of Peter's buddies. In a carriage pulled by four grays ... (they) went on an excursion along El Camino Real out Millbrae and San Mateo way, about where the San Francisco International Airport is today. They consumed boiled chickens, oysters, big yellow peaches and lots of alcohol ... sang themselves hoarse. Peter and Herget 'supplied the clown comedy portion of the outing.' It was a happy day."[59]

Davies received two offers from New Orleans for Joe to fight Jim Daly. The Crescent City A.C. offered $7,000 and the Olympic Club, $7,500. "Davies says Choynski is anxious for a match for the highest purse ... and a side wager, but will fight for a purse alone if Daly does not wish to risk a side wager."[61] January 19 *Brooklyn Eagle*: "A funny state of affairs has come about in San Francisco ... Goddard arrived yesterday with a great how de do, accompanied by Billy Madden. Goddard has come, it is said, with a challenge for Peter Jackson on his tongue. There is no doubt both Jackson and Choynski would consent to fight Goddard if they did not have prospects of better matches, but ... they do not like to be dogged about by the barrier champion, who is always challenging somebody."

"When it was learned that Goddard would be in the city about the same time as Choynski, 'Parson' Davies ... at once began negotiations with Daly for a match, but was still in a bad fix, for Jackson was on his hands and he knew that Goddard would be after him. Now there is no man whom Jackson would rather meet than Goddard, except Corbett. Corbett would give him a chance to place himself at the top of his class, the place he has struggled hard for, for years. Goddard would add no glory to his record and in fact might lessen the chances of victory with Corbett. So ... Davies got him an engagement in Los Angeles ... Choynski, finding he would be here alone, also talked of going to Los Angeles. Goddard ... also attached his name to articles ... in Chicago for a fight with ("Denver" Ed) Smith. So, in case Goddard's broad challenges ... be taken up and he be not satisfied with the situation he could ... bow ... out of California. Goddard would prefer someone else than Jackson, and Choynski prefers someone ... less ... than the barrier man ... Meantime all are ... not within talking distance." Big Joe fought Ed Smith in New Orleans on March 3, and was stopped in the 18th round. It is dubious that Choynski was trying to avoid a confrontation.

Round Nine

Uncle Tom's Cabin
(January 1893 – March 1894)

Davies and Jackson arrived in Los Angeles on January 19 or 20. On the night of the 20th, "Peter sparred four rounds with Frank Childs, the local colored heavyweight." Childs was a talented boxer known as "The Crafty Texan," after his birth state. From 1894 he fought out of Chicago, and, like Choynski, was too small to be a true heavyweight. Over his career, Frank defeated men like Bob Armstrong, Joe Walcott, Joe Butler, "Klondike" Haines (or Haynes), Billy Hanrahan and "Mexican" Pete Everett.

When he arrived at his hotel, Davies found a telegram from Lincoln R. Stockwell, a prominent San Francisco theater manager who was managing the Alcazar Theater, on O'Farrell Street. Stockwell offered Davies $2,500 for a two-week engagement, for Peter Jackson to star in his latest play, a production of "Uncle Tom's Cabin." This was based on the 1852 novel by Harriet Beecher Stowe, which did more to ignite public opinion against slavery than any other element. The production would begin on February 8. The offer was specifically for Davies and Jackson to portray the Auctioneer and Uncle Tom, respectively. "He (Stockwell) also agrees to furnish a company of 40 people and to route it to Chicago if the show proves a success ... Davies will return to San Francisco tomorrow and give Stockwell a definite answer Saturday. The 'Parson' says there is no reason why Jackson should not succeed on the stage. His qualifications are at least equal to those of Sullivan or Corbett. Should the offer result in engagement, Davies will go direct to Chicago to arrange for the placing of the show on the boards in that city during the World's Fair."[1]

Davies' acceptance was not long in coming. If Jim Corbett had truly been willing to fight Jackson, under reasonable conditions (not in the deep South, for instance, as Corbett insisted on), the first really undisputed *world* heavyweight championship could have been established. As it was, Jim was insincere, merely giving lip service to a desire to risk his title against Peter. Davies, lacking a compelling opponent for his charge, was quick in grabbing this new opportunity. The next day the "Parson" finalized the deal, but it took a bit longer for Peter to acquiesce. " 'When I asked him what he thought of it,' said Davies, 'he held up his hands and backed away from me. His eyes dilated, and he could not have looked more rattled if I had unfolded a scheme for robbing a bank. 'What's the matter,' I asked. 'Don't you like the idea?' 'Not much,' gasped Peter. 'I'd rather fight twice a night than act once a year.' 'But there is nothing particularly difficult in the part of Uncle Tom, and there are lots of people who don't care a button for fighting, who would like to see you in some kind of play. Just think the matter over. The lines are simple and about the hardest thing you have to do in the whole business is to die.' 'Yes,' chimed in Peter in lugubrious tones, 'and directly I close my eyes some fresh fellow up in the gallery will begin to count me out.' " Stockwell, a noted actor and comedian, asked Peter to accept the role, and he said yes, if L.R. would coach him in acting. Stockwell would enact the role of Lawyer Marks. Stockwell's theater would be closed for a week to prepare the scenery and rehearse.[2]

It might be considered ironic for someone like Peter Jackson to portray Uncle Tom. Although an unassuming, rather quiet person, Peter was not a submissive type. Aside from his obvious occupation in the violent sport of boxing, Jackson had to be tough in that age of extreme racial bigotry. The "Black Prince" was born on the Caribbean island of St. Croix on September 23, 1860, near the town of Christiansted.[3] As a child, he took to seafaring, and in 1879 found himself in Sydney, Australia. This became his home for the next nine years, before he made his way to the States, in 1888. In the Land Down Under, he faced a relatively minor amount of racism, but in America found it difficult to break

Peter Jackson, early May, 1893

the "color line." Jackson gained recognition as Australian and British Heavyweight Champion, but because of his race, would never be given a chance to add the American and "world" title to his résumé. Neither John L. Sullivan nor Jim Corbett would risk their crowns to his formidable fists. One modern writer went as far as to state that Jackson's role as Uncle Tom hurt his boxing career, alleging he would nevermore be considered seriously as a contender for the championship.[4] It is doubtful if Peter's role as Tom was taken seriously enough to have an adverse impact. Besides, a unique feature of this rendition of "Uncle Tom's Cabin" was a boxing exhibition between him and Choynski. In these exhibitions, Jackson never showed as anything but a dominant fighter, though he was now a bit past his peak.

While Davies was having no luck getting Jim Daly in the ring for Choynski, he did get him a fight: "Tommy West, the plasterer, who fought Billy Smith an 11-round draw, is going to stand up before Joe Choynski for four rounds, and has not the least doubt but that he will win the $1,000 (sic) Joe offers to any man he cannot stop ... West claims he will not pursue any 'Tug Wilson' tactics, but will give as good as he gets." The reference was to "Tug" Wilson, real name Joe Collins, one of the few to survive the same four round challenge against John L. Sullivan. He did so by constant clinching and falling to the floor with little or no provocation. Joe's fight with West took place February 6 at the Pastime Athletic Club in Portland, Oregon. "The Pastime Club has kindly allowed Choynski the use of the rooms, and his manager, the genial 'Parson' Davies, has fixed the price of admission at $1 to all parts ... except the press stand."[5]

On the night of the "fight," a large crowd saw Tommy West prove himself a liar. As reported by two local papers and the *Oregonian*, West fell repeatedly to elude Joe's punches. "1,200 men ... hurled execrations at Tom West, putative pugilist, because he declined to stand up to be knocked down by Joe Choynski. It was on the card that Choynski would forfeit $100 if he failed to 'stop' West in four rounds, but (Joe) neither knocked out his antagonist nor lost the money; all owing to West's reluctance to receive bodily punishment and Referee Jack Dempsey's decision that he outraged the rules for such contests, made and provided by the noble Marquis of Queensberry. The decision was given in the 3rd round, when West had squatted in the squared circle 38 times by actual count and Choynski failed to deliver a clean blow. The latter clearly demonstrated his willingness and ability to put West to sleep ... however, and the verdict elicited no logical protest." This was essentially a WDQ3 (disqualification) for Joe.[6]

A secondary source said that, sometime after the "Uncle Tom's Cabin" show closed in 1894, "To anyone who could last three minutes against either Jackson or Choynski went a prize of $500. Only once, in Louisville, Kentucky, did the Parson have to pay off. A 230 pound miner challenged Choynski, and although he was dropped flat on his back four times, managed to be erect on his wobbly feet for the full time."[7] Exactly when this occurred and against whom was not divulged, but if it happened, the bulk of the miner alone makes his "survival" more understandable.

The first stage rehearsal was held February 12 at Stockwell's Theatre, at 11 Powell Street, opposite the Baldwin Hotel. Before "half a dozen newspaper men and as many members of the theatrical *profesh*," Jackson and Davies ran through acts three and four. Those present gave a good review of the performances of Peter and "The Parson," especially the latter. Jackson started out a bit nervous, but overcame it as the act progressed. Stockwell sent the company on a week-long tour as a dry-run, to Santa Rosa and Oakland. 62 people were required for the production.[8]

Choynski and Ed Graney arrived in Chicago on or about February 26. Joe was still finding it difficult to obtain boxing matches, and to make matters worse, it was announced on the 28th that the California club had closed its doors as a result of a ring fatality. A boxer named William Miller died shortly after a fight with Dal Hawkins, causing all local clubs to cancel their scheduled fights and for boxing to be banned indefinitely in San Francisco. Joe and Ed arrived in New Orleans on the 27th. They were to second, on the 29th, Tommy Ryan and George Dawson, respectively.

Joe was still campaigning actively to get the Fitz-Hall winner into the ring with him. A Chicago paper said: "A high-class man from California who declined to be quoted, declares that in a private meeting at San Francisco, Choynski made Fitz quit with a punch in the stomach in two minutes; Choynski has boxed a lot with both Fitzsimmons and Hall; and his opinion has a good deal of influence. With Choynski came Sol Smith, who is matched to fight George Dixon in the Coney Island Club, with Abrahams (Abrams) as his manager." The veracity of Fitz quitting cannot be validated, especially since the alleged eyewitness remained anonymous.

Opening night for "Uncle Tom's Cabin" was February 27, at Stockwell's Theatre. The marquee spelled out in lights, only the words, "Uncle Tom." There were a significant number of African-Americans present, including a contingent from the Lotus Club, most occupying one of the proscenium boxes. The company played to a nearly packed house, which included a large number of women. The play was well received, one paper observing: "The 'gods' were a little restless in the early stages of the play. To them, the fighter was the attraction ... Even the bloodhounds in the 1st act did not rouse the audience to the highest pitch of enthusiasm, and Liza's perilous passage of the ice floe was only a mild sensation. Mr. Stockwell had mounted the play in such an excellent manner, however, that the house soon began to recognize the fact that the performance did not rely on any one feature for its successful progress ... in the 3rd act Uncle Tom first came upon the stage. Little Eva, mounted upon a Shetland pony, was escorted in by Uncle Tom, and ... lifted to the ground. He knew his lines perfectly and he spoke them far more intelligently than many an actor of wide experience seems able to do. He has a sing-song tone that almost forces a smile from the listener at times, but he is so evidently in earnest and so conscientious in his work that the audience were not inclined to be critical."[9]

Choynski didn't second Ryan, after all. Due to an injury, Tommy was forced to cancel his bout with Dawson. Instead, on the night of March 2, Joe was in the corner of grappler Evan "Strangler" Lewis, facing Ernest Roeber for the world heavyweight wrestling championship. The site was New Orleans' Olympic Club. A "canvas was spread over the river clay forming the floor ..." In the corner with Joe were Duncan McMillan and

Dr. J.J. Davis of Chicago. The "Strangler" was a bit soft due to a dearth of training, the result of an illness to his wife. Still, he was able to gain three out of five falls and won the match.[10] The following night, Joe saw the Goddard-Smith battle, and a rather stunning upset. At ringside were many celebrities, including "Bat" Masterson and notorious gate-crasher James "One-Eyed" Connelly. Smith and Goddard started at a terrific pace. Both fell near the end of the 6th, barely able to rise at the bell. "Denver" pummeled and floored his man in round seven, Joe returning the favor in the 8th. Momentum swung to and fro. Smith was saved by the bell ending the 13th and 14th heats, but hammered Goddard's jaw in the 18th and scored a clean knockout.[11]

"Uncle Tom's Cabin" poster, undated, author's collection

Frisco Joe seconded lightweight Mike Daly of Bangor, Maine on the evening of March 7 against Paterson, New Jersey's Austin Gibbons. Also in the corner were Alex Greggains, "Professor" John Donaldson, Captain Bill Daly and Ned Merrigan. The bout came off at the brand-new Crescent City Club and saw Gibbons finally apply the finisher in the 31st round.[12] Choynski was at the Fitzsimmons-Hall fight the next evening. In the 4th frame, Bob landed a crushing right to the chin that knocked his foe unconscious for several minutes. Fitz had a knack of catching opponents with a thunderbolt when they least expected it. Referee "Professor" John Duffy said, "Hall had the best of the bout until he was knocked out. He is cooler, the more scientific and by far the heavier hitter, and had he not been overconfident matters might have been different." Historically, Fitz was considered the heavier puncher. Nonetheless, it was nearly unanimous that the "Lanky Cornishman" landed a "chance blow," or, lucky punch. Choynski: "I ... am anxious to fight the winner. Hall, I believe, grew a trifle careless about his guard and that caused his defeat. Both are wonderfully clever men and ... evenly matched." In 1930, Joe said Hall gave "the freckled Australian a sweet cuffing for three rounds. Then Fitz caught him with a sledge-hammer right ..."[13] Bob, Britain's first world heavyweight champion, had recently become an American citizen.

The two met up again on the 9th. Fitz was "fresh and rosy, attired in the height of fashion, with shining silk tile (hat) upon his head and an immense cane in hand ... Hall stuck to his old clothes, and was somewhat sober of mien ... Fitzsimmons said he had not been celebrating, but spent the day quietly with his family. 'Hall is a very good man ... much better ... than ... in Australia ... fully 50 per cent better. He has improved in ... out-fighting and in-fighting. He is far cleverer and ... stronger ... but I am a bit cleverer. He is not as tricky as I am ... my principal advantage, and every advantage counts. As far as hitting goes, I guess I can hit as hard as he can.' "

"Choynski is the greatest light heavy-weight to-day ... not as clever as Hall or I, but can hit as hard as any of us. Goddard whipped him because Goddard is big and strong, a very hard puncher, and able to stand and give punishment; and Choynski threw away every chance he had by going right at him and fighting Goddard in the latter's own style. I know that Choynski tipped Hall to win in 10 rounds, but I think none the less of him on that account. Every man is entitled to his opinion. The only thing I blame him for is coming to my house and making the statement. At the same time, I saw Choynski intended to challenge the winner, and, as I had announced I would not go out of my class again and was his friend besides. I calculated that he was trying to get me angry in order to get on a match. There will be no match unless Choynski comes to my weight."[14]

The March 11 *Bird O' Freedom*, a black newspaper out of New South Wales, Australia, quoted an article from the January 29 *San Francisco Chronicle*: "Jackson had made the suggestion that it would be necessary to have muscular men to take the parts of Sambo and Quimbo. The characters named are slaves, and it is their duty to carry Uncle Tom from the stage after (Simon) Legree strikes him down. As Peter weighs considerably over 200 pounds, there is some reason for his solicitude ... but 'Parson' Davies has come to the rescue with a scheme which ... will ease Jackson's mind and at the same time add a new attraction to Stockwell's production ... The Parson's plan is to have Joe Choynski represent Sambo, and to telegraph East for (William) Muldoon, or some other professional strong man, to come and be the Quimbo of the play. If the scheme is pushed through, Jackson will be well-supported in more ways than one."

Looking back over the gulf of time, Choynski said: "In Chicago 'Parson' Davies got Peter Jackson and me together and told us we were to become actors. 'We are going to play *Uncle Tom's Cabin*,' said Davies. 'Peter will be Uncle Tom, Choynski will play George Shelby and I will play the auctioneer. We will write a prologue to introduce a boxing match, and Uncle Tom will put on the gloves with Shelby.' Needless to say, this was 'way out of character for Uncle Tom, but ... a huge hit with the audience. Peter Jackson asked me after the 'Parson' had gone out if I thought the old fellow had gone 'balmy.' I nearly fainted and Jackson swallowed two quarts of Scotch." Choynski now steps a bit out of character, himself, as he maligns Peter, saying (it took) "Peter Jackson half a day to write his name, but he was possessed of high intelligence and learned his lines ..."

"Peter ... was Uncle Tom – with that English accent of his. I got many a scream out of that one ... but I had no love for the footlights, and welcomed every chance to 'put on an understudy' ... go out and add to my knockout record in the ring." Joe (1927): "I sweated off 40 pounds in struggling through the first performance. Little Eva was played by Anna Laughlin, who later made a big hit with Montgomery and Stone in 'The Wizard of Oz.' It was a scream to hear Peter Jackson with his Australian accent intoning the lines of the old southern slave ... in reply to Simon Legree's question, 'Don't you belong to me body and soul?' "No, marsa, me body, hit belongs to you, but me soul, hit belongs to the guid Lawd.' I am sure Harriet Beecher Stowe turned over in her grave then. But, we played ... to packed houses."[15] Stowe actually didn't die until July 1, 1896. She isn't known to have mentioned Stockwell's rendition of her novel.

By March 12, Choynski had joined the troupe. "Manager Stockwell has had good luck with ... Jackson and ... Davies in 'Uncle Tom's Cabin.' He has had such a steady run for two weeks that he proposes to give the public a 3rd, during which he will add several new features to enhance the interest, including 'three friendly and scientific rounds' by ... Jackson ... and ... Choynski." "Stockwell wrote a letter last Monday to the Hawaiian Islands, proposing a combination with his pugilist and the ex-Queen. It seems he is really confident of a successful season ... Some of Jules Tavernier's volcano panorama would be utilized for scenery, and a breath of spice and palm could be wafted across the stage by several ex-residents." The March 17 *Morning Call* said the Saturday matinee would be the last performance of the season for "Uncle Tom's Cabin," and would feature "The Black Lottie Collins in her 'Ta-Ra-Ra Boom-De-Ay' ..." Collins' real name was Bessie Carr, and she had made the song famous. Attendance that "final week" was so high, Stockwell had a change of plans in ending the play just yet.[16]

"The large attendances ... have warranted management to continue ... one more week. Several new novelties will be added (including) ... a sparring match in three rounds for scientific points between Jackson and ...

Choynski ... between the 2nd and 3rd acts. After the run ... has ... completed ... the entire production will be taken east, playing in all principal ... cities. Local sports are all agog over the coming of Peter Jackson and 'Brave Joe' Choynski ..." *Call*: "Joe Choynski ... will be included ... ostensibly to fill a small part, but really ... to appear as Peter Jackson's sparring antagonist. Both pugilists will hold themselves in readiness to respond to any challenges ... Choynski is ... in hopes that Fitzsimmons will accept the 'defi' issued ..."[17]

Joe Choynski, circa 1893

The final show in Frisco was March 19: "Davies advanced to the footlights and said: 'Ladies and gentlemen ... We are going away to-night and bring with us one of your boys, a good one, Joe Choynski. We hope to return within 12 months with honors ...' Jackson and Choynski ... boxed three ... pretty and exceedingly harmless rounds ..." Davies' plan was for a tour down the coast to San Diego, back to Frisco, then Ogden and Salt Lake City, Utah, en route to Chicago for the World's Fair. There, they expected to make a stack of money with "Uncle Tom's Cabin," boxing and wrestling. "Strangler" Lewis was expected to join Davies' specialty combination.[18]

The trio's first stop was Salt Lake City, on March 31. "Peter Jackson ... 'Brave Joe' Choynski, as game a man as ever donned a mitten and 'Parson' Davies ... The party made Colonel Kelley's resort on State street their headquarters, and here a *Herald* reporter met them." He asked how Jackson liked the stage: " 'Well, I have only had six weeks experience, but I like it very well. My tour extends to Chicago, where I open at the Haymarket theatre on April 7. There is nothing in this talk about me playing

(Shakespeare's) Othello. No one knows better than I what a long step it is from Uncle Tom to the Moor. I don't pretend to be an actor. I am somewhat fitted for the part I play now and am doing my best to learn and advance. I hope to find other small parts suited to my limited ability. Dumas' *Man and the Hour* has been suggested ...' 'Brave Joe' Choynski, whose great battle with George Godfrey some time ago stamped him as one of the best men in the world in his class, travels with Jackson as his sparring partner. 'I have no definite plans for the future,' said Joe. 'I am willing to meet either Ed Smith or Bob Fitzsimmons, and hope to get a match with one ... soon.' 'Parson' Davies is as blithe and chipper as ever ... 'A week ago,' said the Parson, 'I offered to back Choynski against Fitzsimmons for $5,000, but have not been able to get any reply. Of course I think Joe can beat Bob, or I shouldn't put my money up on him.' "[19]

The company were in Cheyenne, Wyoming on April 4. By the 8th, they were in Kansas City, Missouri, to open a week-long run at the Gilliss Opera House. Matinee prices were 50¢, 35¢ and 25¢.[20] April 10 *Kansas City Star*: "The Australian negro is not only infinitely the superior of the lamented Sullivan in dramatic ability, but ... a better actor than Corbett. Jackson is ... conscientious and the careful ... preparation for the stage is apparent in every line he speaks and every move he makes." The article commented on Peter's deep, resonant voice, but added: "The chief fault in Jackson's acting is his elocution. He has yet to learn the importance of distinct enunciation. In the emotional scenes, the black is hardly equal to the demands of the occasion, but nevertheless is as good as most of the Uncle Toms the stage has seen in recent years. Perhaps most interesting ... is the acting of 'Parson' Davies. The Parson plays ... an auctioneer and appears in only one scene. His friends and admirers have always known that the Parson was versatile, but ... never had an idea his versatility was of so wide a range. It is not too much to say that Davies is as good an actor as is ... found in the entire cast, and it is possible that he leads his ... Eva, played by little Anna Laughlin, is excellent ... despite her youth, a very good actress."

"Between the 1st and 2nd acts Jackson and Choynski ... spar three friendly rounds, of which the sporting editor of the *Star* had this to say: 'The set-to ... lacks the surroundings offered by the glove contest which closes the Corbett show. There are (sic) no ring, no seconds and no crowd of people on the stage to arouse the audience to excitement, but it is a clever exhibition of scientific boxing by two masters of the art. Peter towers over Choynski and has the advantage of weight and reach, but the set-to at times becomes spirited and they mix it up in a lively fashion. Peter's style of boxing is very different from Corbett's. He is wonderfully shifty on his feet and his arms work like pieces of machinery and the spectators cannot but be impressed with the feeling that he is a clever two-handed fighter and possessed of enormous punishing power. Choynski is ... an expert boxer, but Jackson's superiority is plainly apparent ...' " Just as Joe's sojourn to Australia helped develop his boxing skill, his constant sparring with Jackson could only have further cultivated his fistic acumen.

A local paper on April 14 said, "The company has played each night this week to a crowded house of which the colored people of the two Kansas Citys and suburban towns formed a considerable part. Mr. Jackson plays his part splendidly and may develop into a leading actor ... as he already is in the pugilistic world." An *American Citizen* (Kansas City, Kansas) reporter visited Jackson at Room 330 in the Midland Hotel on April 10. He was sitting at a desk, wearing a "spring suit of English tweed and patent leather gaiters, while a light smoking cap of plaid material was upon his head." Davies was also there, but Joe's whereabouts wasn't noted. Regarding his Uncle Tom role, Peter said he could not help "feeling humiliated at some of the situations, as he is compelled to submit to a licking, be sold on the block and die in the last act every night."[21]

The *Omaha Bee* went as far as to call the Stockwell production, "The greatest Uncle Tom's Cabin show ever organized." It said the company would arrive on the 19th, for an engagement of three nights at Omaha's Farnam Street Theater. "But Peter, the Midnight Mars, is not the sole attraction ... with him come the peerless Charles E. Davies ... his manager, and genial, indomitable Joseph Bartlett Choynski ... panting to get a whack at ... Fitzsimmons' jaw ... The 'Parson' will do the auctioneer, while Joseph ... the role of Haley, the slave driver. Peter, they say, is nearly as good an actor as he is a fighter, which is speaking volumes ... it will be a treat to see Gentleman Peter, for he is a gentleman, maugre his sable skin, in a character dear to the American heart, but greater ... to see him in gladiatorial togs tackle the doughty ... Choynski in their three-round go ... They make a great set-to and the audience never fails to enthuse to an incandescent pitch, when the two ... 'mix' matters in the finale."[22]

The Bee covered opening night, April 20: "Despite the disagreeably inclement weather the house was packed from top to bottom, save a few vacant seats in the parquet. There were many ladies present and they attested their appreciation ... Mrs. Stowe's great novel has a firm grip on the American public ... Of course, the dear old play has been worked into a laughing burlesque by barn storming combinations, with their double Uncle Toms, triplet Topsies, twin Evas and half dozen Marks ..." The critic sang the praises of Jackson, adding, "But ... his co-laborers in a common cause ... 'Parson' Davies ... and Joseph Bartlett Choynski, one of the exemplars of the prize ring, come in for an abundant measure of praise. The 'Parson' is extremely clever, as he is in the ordinary rut of everyday life ... Choynski as Haley, the slave driver, plays his part with a discrimination and a judgment that suits the part to a T. Next in kindly esteem comes little Anna Laughlin as Eva. She is an infantile prodigy and no exaggeration. Sweet and pretty as a rosebud, evincing all the qualifications that go to constructing the finished artist. She is painstaking, careful and studious, with a marvelous enunciation in a wee bit of a thing, and altogether fair and lovely to look upon. Altogether the company ... is 'way above mediocre ...'"[23]

The child actress, born October 11, 1885 in Sacramento, California, went on to star in vaudeville, but would gain fame as Dorothy Gale in the stage version of Baum's "The Wizard of Oz," from 1903 to 1905. Laughlin later starred in early motion pictures, doing so until 1915. She gave birth to one child, the noted radio singer, Lucy Monroe. Tragically, Anna would commit suicide on March 6, 1937. Her daughter, Lucy, sang "The Star-Spangled Banner" at every New York Yankees opening day and every Yankees World Series between 1945 and 1960.[24]

April 21 *Omaha Bee*: "The ... bout between Jackson and Choynski ... is a feature ... it would be culpable to neglect. The two ... appear in full ring costume, and after being introduced by Mr. Davies, become neighborly to an extent that enkindles in the heart of pugnacious Young America a most vociferous enthusiasm. As Peter smashes Joe and Joe comes back across with a swinging right, they fairly get up in the loft and howl, and when the two ... 'mix' in the wind-up the scene ... defies description. Of course, the bout is purely friendly and scientific, and the man would be egotistical ... who presumed to have received a line in either man's mode of fighting by this highly interesting exhibition."[25] The cast appeared at Pope's Theatre in St. Louis, Missouri from May 1 through May 7, 1893, featuring matinees on Wednesday and Saturday. "A pugilistic 'Uncle Tom' is a variation in her famous work that Harriet Beecher Stowe probably never contemplated ... Jackson is not engaged for his histrionic ability, but as a prize-fighter, his standing is assured." "Peter will spar with Joe Choynski, which would be a glory to the vision of Harriet Beecher Stowe."[26]

In a bit of pretense, the *Call* wrote: "The piece will be freshened a good deal in an incidental way. New specialties, ballads, etc., will be introduced, and the Jubilee singers will make the auditorium ring with free-and-easy choruses, such as were supposed to have been sung in the cane fields of Louisiana when the *'good old times'* prevailed before the war. Mr. Peter Jackson will step aside from his religious and sentimental business in 'Uncle Tom' for the nonce and give us an idea of the difference of the times now and then by ... three 'friendly and scientific' rounds with *Professor Johnson*. The anomaly is laughable and not startling ... but that ought to reincarnate Harriet Beecher Stowe to utter an indignant protest." The "Professor Johnson" was almost certainly a misprint, as Joe was Jackson's sparring partner, and no Johnson is elsewhere mentioned in their camp.

As can be seen, there were differing opinions on the aesthetics of the character Uncle Tom taking part in fisticuffs, but many felt it demonstrated how far things had come since the days of slavery. This was misleading, however, as boxing (and for a short time, Major League baseball) was one of the few sports in which a comparatively reasonable amount of freedom was given to blacks by whites. James Naismith invented basketball in December, 1891, but it would only begin being played, on a college level, in 1892. American Football evolved from what is now association football (soccer) and rugby, but not until 1892 did the sport see the first "professional" football player, William Walter "Pudge" Heffelfinger. A form of gridiron football similar to today's was being played on a college level in the 1870s, but it was one in which blacks were excluded from.

Choynski, meanwhile, was "just spoiling for a fight ... Denver Smith and Bob Fitzsimmons are the two principal men for whom Joe is gunning, and neither ... seems to be anxious to arrange a fight with Parson Davies' protégé. Under Jackson's tutelage, Choynski has become a dangerous man, and he promises to make a game fight with any pugilist of his weight in the country." The party pulled into Chicago on the morning of May 7. Jackson and Davies were interviewed by *The Inter-Ocean*. "The Parson" said their contract for the season with L.R. Stockwell would expire two weeks hence ... As for Davies, "I shall remain in Chicago during the Fair, and at its close, may again take to the boards."[27] The "Fair" was officially known as the "World's Columbian Exposition," but commonly called the "Chicago World's Fair." It celebrated the 400th anniversary of Christopher Columbus' arrival in the New World. It was mentioned that an effort was being made on the part of Davies to match Choynski with Peter Maher.

That night, the troupe opened at the Haymarket Theatre, on West Madison Street. One review was critical of Jackson's acting ability: "Sporting editors say he is a pretty good man in their line ... pity the same compliment cannot be paid him in the dramatic columns. But, as a curiosity of dramatic art, Peter Jackson ... is well worth the price of admission. He comes on in the opening of the first act and disappears until the 3rd act except when he puts his big fists in sheep-covered pads and goes through some combative motions with Joe Choynski, after ... a panygeric (sic) (panegyric) delivery by ... Davies." Tickets cost from 15¢ to $1.50.[28]

The combination opened at the New Windsor Theatre, beginning with a matinee on May 14. As an interlude, though, Bob Fitzsimmons stated, "My mind is so unsettled that I don't know who I will fight ... there's Joe Goddard; he wants to fight me. I consider Joe Choynski the best man of his weight in the country, and I would like to meet him. If I defeat him I cannot gain any more reputation than I have now. I see he has posted $1,000. That's the way to do business. I'll fight Choynski providing I get a good offer from the clubs. His offer to bet $5,000 on the outside suits me all right. I won't say anything definite just now. I will wait until next week and then I will attend to everybody who wants to fight me."[29]

The troupe played the Windsor through the 20th, when they closed their season. The next evening at the Westminster Hotel, "The Parson" gave a dinner to celebrate the season. "Covers were laid for 24 ... Jackson and Joe Choynski made brief speeches, and 'Parson' also got in a word or two. Jackson leaves next Tuesday for New York, whence he will sail for England and the West Indies. Choynski and Davies will make Chicago their permanent headquarters. Parson said ... Peter was going to England to perfect himself in the negro dialect."[30] Joe served as a second for "Buffalo"

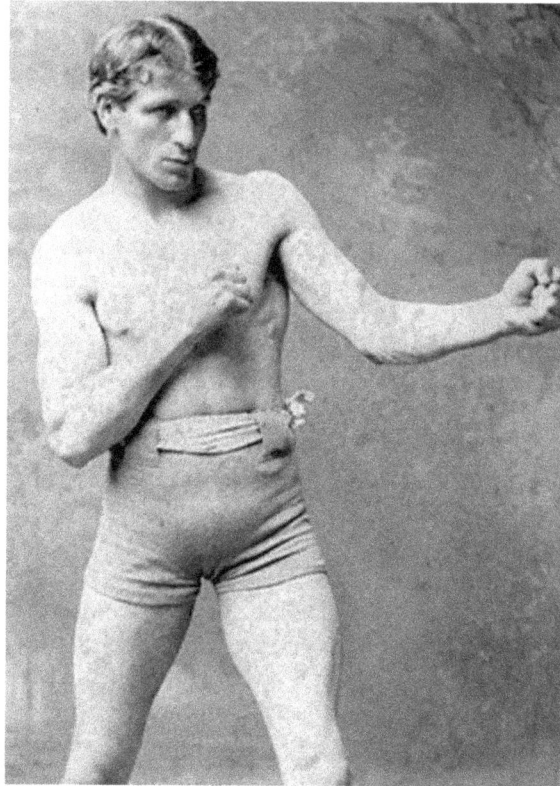

Joe Choynski, undated

Costello against "Denver" Billy Woods, on May 12 at Roby, Indiana. That state recently passed a bill allowing "gymnastic exhibitions of athletic science," in this case, boxing. The new Columbian Athletic Club was built for the occasion, by Dominick O'Malley of New Orleans and Louis M. Houseman of Chicago. The last named will be an important factor in Joe's life. The new arena was "lit by 25 electric lights," with 50 kerosene lamps for "an emergency." Through the supervision of A.G. Spalding & Bros., a "stakeless" ring was erected, held together by wires and iron piping. Choynski, called "the ablest second that ever swung a towel," joined Sam Fitzpatrick and Tom Tracey in Costello's corner. Referee George Siler was the sole arbiter. It was a good fight up until round 21, then it became "a walking match." The fight was finally stopped and declared a "No-Contest" in the 57th frame.[31]

It was next revealed that "Isidor N. Choynski ... is lying in a critical condition at the German Hospital, having undergone an operation for cancer. Besides having had an aggressive and painful cancer removed from his side, Choynski, Sr. is liable to have the furnishing of his establishment at 427 McAllister Street summarily removed to the unsympathetic cobbles by the Sheriff. Choynski's landlady said he has not been assiduous in showing the color of rent money for months and she brought court proceedings to compel him to vacate the McAllister-street premises. She states that the writ was issued last Monday and the Sheriff will move on the works in a day or two. Choynski has an 'antiquarian bookstore,' and it is the contents ... the Sheriff will distribute on the McAllister-street cobbles ... according to the landlady ... will take place to-morrow. Choynski is not expected to leave the hospital for two weeks, and his establishment has been closed since his removal to the hospital."[32] That month, Isidor wrote to California Senator Stephen White, asking for employment, either with the State Immigration Commission or as a clerk. The financial panic of 1893 resulted in the closure of a number of local businesses, and Isidor commented on his own hardships. In the April 13 and June 1, 1893 *American Israelite*, he said his business was bankrupt.[33] It appears that I.N. lost his McAllister location, but likely had someone rescue his wares.

Joe left Chicago for New York on the night of June 15, in another attempt to get Fitzsimmons in the ring.[34] Bob, who always kept his real weight a guarded secret and rarely let anyone see him get on the scales, was still claiming that Choynski was above his own weight class. On these grounds, the "Lanky Cornishman" refused to fight him. Actually, they weighed nearly the same at this point and henceforth. Fitz wasn't really afraid, but according to many sources, including Joe, was still developing the confidence that would ultimately take him to three world titles.

In early June, Fitz went to New York City to fight Dominick McCaffrey. McCaffrey had to cancel due to a head injury, but still a fight between Bob and Joe didn't materialize. Judge Newton of the Coney Island A.C. obtained Choynski's signature to articles of agreement and offered a rich $15,000 purse, which it was expected, Fitz would accept. Davies offered to spice up the pot with a $5,000 side bet, but Bob was not ready to do business. "I have repeatedly said I would never go out of my class again if I could help it, and I am going to keep my word as far as Choynski is concerned. I don't see what right he has to fight me, anyway. He is a 4th rate man and if he wants a fight in such a bad way, why don't he tackle some of the good men, such as Butler, O'Donnell, etc. ... I won't fight for $15,000. From $40,000 to that amount is a very big drop, isn't it? ... If I go out of my (weight) class it will be to fight Corbett. I have written several letters to 'Parson' Davies regarding Choynski, but I never received an answer. I'll bet the 'Parson' as much as he wants ... If they give me a big purse and Choynski can get down to weight (158 pounds), I'll sign articles and agree to be in the ring ... within three weeks' time"[35] $15,000 was a large purse, and no fighter was being paid $40,000 at that time. Fitz knew well that Joe could never get down to 158 pounds, certainly not with any vitality. Bob had gone very quickly from calling Joe the best fighter for his weight, to labeling him "a 4th rate man."

Davies briefly took Australian featherweight, "Young Griffo," into his fold – for about two weeks, around June 15 to the 28th. Charlie brought him to St. Louis to fight Tommy Tracey, but Griff went missing. Davies found him in a bar, on a binge, and only with great difficulty forced the inebriated pug into the ring. Griffo quit in the 1st round, causing "The Parson" to divest himself of the Antipodean. *Trenton Times*: "Parson Davies has decided to leave the management of Griffo to Ed. Alexander, who brought the Australian over ... he considers that two stars like Jackson and Choynski are enough for one man to handle." Griffo was always difficult, if not impossible, to control. On the 26th in Roby, Indiana, Joe witnessed Peter Maher KO4 Val Flood at the Columbian Athletic Club.[36]

While waiting for *any* opponent to face him, Joe bided his time as a second and trainer in Roby. His next charge was California friend, Solly Smith. Smith's adversary was John T. Griffin of Massachusetts, for what many papers called the featherweight championship of the world, though with less than universal recognition.[37] Joe joined Sam Fitzpatrick and Seward Smith in the corner. On the morning of the fight, July 10, after Solly ran five miles through Lincoln Park, he moved on to the wrestling mat, a staple of many boxers' training in that era. He engaged Choynski in "a full half hour catch-as-catch-can. Joe remained wholly on the defensive ... giving the little fellow ... opportunity for limbering up his muscles ..." One paper said they wrestled for an hour. At the Columbian A.C., Smith and Griffin each weighed less than 122 pounds. Griffin used an artistic left jab to close Solly's eyes over the first three rounds. Choynski pushed an apparently beaten Smith out for round four, where, tottering along the ropes, he countered a body shot with a wild right, winning by knockout.[38]

Joe was occasionally asked to play different roles in the play, as shown when the July 13 *Maitland Mercury* wrote: "In 'Uncle Tom's Cabin,' as delineated by Peter Jackson and his company, the part of Legree is taken by Joe Choynski, 'Parson' Davies is for the nonce an auctioneer, and 'Peter the Great' is the venerable and hardly used negro. A ludicrous alteration of ... Beecher Stowe's plot is that Tom does not sing hymns to Little Eva, but indulges in an eight round contest with the brutal overseer."

The Columbian Athletic Club made Fitz an offer of $17,000 to fight Joe within their edifice. Bob took little time in wiring back his refusal. Davies took him to task, telling reporters: "I am surprised Bob will let the $17,000 purse ... get away ... It appears ... he is acting very queerly in this matter. Fitzsimmons has stated repeatedly that he believes Jim Hall can whip Choynski. He whipped Hall easily enough, and yet ... refuses to meet Choynski at 165 pounds. There is not a bit of sense in any of Fitzsimmons' arguments. He declares he will not go out of his class to fight. He went out of his class to meet Peter Maher, did the same ... when he met Jim Hall at New Orleans and is willing to do it again to meet Corbett. Yet he won't give the seven pounds to Choynski and win the $17,000, which to him would be like picking it up on the street, the way he figures out Choynski's ability. There is not a fighter in his so-called class he could get a $2,500 purse to whip. Bob had better meet Choynski and win ... if he can, as blacksmiths are a drug on the market and the pugilistic theatrical attraction is not what it is cracked up to be." Bob repeated that he would only fight beyond the middleweight limit if Corbett risked his heavyweight crown, and would "never fight again for a purse less than $25,000."[39]

On July 23, Choynski left for Cedar Lake, Indiana to train lightweight Paddy Smith for a fight against "Young Corbett" (George Green). Jim Corbett, himself in training for a heavyweight title defense against Charley Mitchell, laid off a short time to handle his namesake. Hence, Corbett and Choynski were in opposing corners. Speaking of Mitchell, "Jolly Cholly" was a heavy underdog to Corbett, and should have been, being little more than a middleweight and one of the last of the bareknuckle era. While most of the eastern cognoscenti picked Corbett in a walkover, several experts in the west, including Choynski, chose Charley to win. In Joe's case, it was likely more spite than anything, considering his rivalry with Jim.[40]

Joseph Bartlett Choynski
San Francisco, California

A July 25 article said "The Parson" was "considered the shrewdest manager of pugilists in the world" and the coming season of "Uncle Tom's Cabin" would begin in September. The production would carry "20 colored jubilee singers and 18 live bloodhounds." Davies was in New York to negotiate with Fitzsimmons, but also to meet Peter Jackson, returning on the *Teutonic* from a visit to England. The *Police Gazette*, quoting an unspecified edition of the *Chicago Sporting Gazette*, wrote: "Choyinski (sic) is the *recognized light heavy-weight champion of the world*, and, without a doubt, the master of any 175 pound man now in the ring. He and Fitzsimmons have measured each other's strength on more than one occasion in private, and Choyinski's eagerness in seeking a match and Fitzsimmons' oft-repeated refusal to meet him, should prove conclusively in what esteem the men hold each other."[41] This may have been the first time in which Joe was referred to as the world light-heavyweight champion. He would later vanquish specific opponents to substantiate the assertion. Surely, the title was not yet universally recognized, but the "quasi-division" was credible enough to have a distinct name and consideration in many quarters. The need for a division to bridge the gulf between 154-pound middleweights and 180+-pound heavyweights, was acknowledged by most.

On the 29th, Joe proclaimed Paddy Smith fit. "The peculiarity of Smith's training ... he has not donned a glove or put up a hand to box with anybody ... is ... unheard of ... though the explanation Smith gives is not wholly without logic. 'All the boxing I do will never make me any more clever. Nine out of every 10 men who train for a fight step into the ring with hands that have been injured ... training. If I break my hand ... I want it to be on the jaw of the man I fight, not on the head of a trainer.' " Smith spent his time walking, running 100-yard sprints and playing quoits. It wasn't until the night before the fight, that Joe put on the gloves with Paddy. They boxed four light rounds. Paddy (Patrick) was the brother of "Denver" Ed Smith, and though training was unorthodox, it didn't hurt him here.

The finish fight occurred at the Columbian A.C. on the night of July 31. Smith was seconded by Joe, Dan Murphy and Billy Pool, while "Young Corbett" was squired by Billy Delaney and "Professor" John Donaldson. George Siler refereed. Jim Corbett sat in Green's corner but did not take an active role. Choynski's charge won the marathon bout on a KO28. On August 14, Joe saw the Dan Creedon-Alex Greggains middleweight battle at the same venue. Also present were Davies, Mose Gunst and wrestler Evan Lewis. Creedon was hailed as Australian middleweight champion, Greggains, billed as champion of the Pacific Coast. Alex was stopped in the 15th round.[42] Thus ended Joe's theatrical off-season.

As Davies prepared for the 2nd season of "Uncle Tom's Cabin," there were a few additions and changes. None, however, held the importance in Joe's life as one in particular. As Joe told it: "Romance came into my life ... In September the company met at Mount Clemens, Michigan, to rehearse for the season. There were several new members in the cast. The hotel management asked 'Parson' Davies to arrange a little entertainment. Among the new members was Miss Louise Anderson Miller, who had come to play Topsy. She contributed a song, and it seemed to me I had never heard such a wonderful voice. We became acquainted and were married in June of the following year at Cincinnati ..." "I can't say what she saw in me, but I knew she was the one woman for me. Time proved I was correct."[43]

Louise wasn't the only "girl" interested in Joe. Around this time, when the crew were in Erie, Pennsylvania awaiting a train for Akron, Ohio, an incident occurred, reported by a Hawaiian paper: "An Elopement Foiled.

Two pretty girls appeared at the Erie Depot and asked for the time of the train for Akron. The father of one of them appearing, they scampered off. He refused to give his name, but said his daughter had become infatuated with Joe Choynski, the prize-fighter, who has been filling an engagement with Jackson at Cincinnati. Shortly afterward, the train left with Jackson, Choynski and Parson Davies, but without the girls."[44]

On the night of August 31, "Uncle Tom's Cabin" was resumed at the Newark, Ohio Music Hall. They featured in Cincinnati on September 4 through 7 at Havlin's Theatre, staying at the Gibson House. They appeared for a one-night stand at the Olean Opera House on the 14th. Davies played dual roles, that of the Auctioneer and George Harris, the escaped slave. Jackson, of course, reprised his role as Uncle Tom, and Choynski, as George Shelby. Between Acts 1 and 2, Peter and Joe put on their obligatory three round spar. The public, for the most part, were paying to see this as much as, if not more than, anything else. Also featured was jubilee singing and wing and buck dancing.[45] The combination played from September 18 through 20 at the H.R. Jacobs Grand Opera House in Syracuse, New York. The September 17 *Syracuse Courier* said they had competition. The nearby Weiting Opera House featured its own version, with two Topsies, two Marks, two Evas and two Uncle Toms, a gimmick many troupes around the country used. Stockwell's device was the utilization of boxing celebrities and notable props, such as live bloodhounds.

On the 19th, the *Courier* noted: "The bout ... was a spirited and scientific exhibition. Choynski is a clever man ... and gave Peter many a hard dig, which the colored man lost no opportunity of returning ... Davies ... never acted but once before the present play ... at a benefit ... in Frisco, when Jim Corbett was in the same cast. First, he played the auctioneer in the present play, but three weeks ago started to play the part of 'George Harris' and now plays both characters. When Choynski was introduced ... many noticed the wonderful likeness ... the Frisco boy bears to 'Joe' Dunfee of this city, who has ... acquired some fame as a pugilist. Choynski is a little taller than our 'Joe' but his head and face are strongly remindful of Dunfee. Jackson ... was very clever as 'Uncle Tom.' Indeed, he is more of an actor than Corbett or Sullivan. Parson Davies acted ... acceptably, and Joe Choynski was no mean actor." A 1902 Iowa paper said Choynski had, at least once, played the arch-villain, Simon Legree, in the play.

The crew wrapped up their Syracuse stop with a matinee on the 20th. "Jackson and 'Joe' Choynski sparred three 'friendly and scientific rounds' ... Choynski was mostly engaged in keeping a damaged nose out of the way of Jackson's gloves, and Jackson was busy letting him do it. However ... both showed great quickness, and often ... would duck with great ... celerity. Choynski is about the same build as ... Dunfee ... but does not seem to have the hitting power of the local man. He is much quicker, however. The show itself is much above average, 'Parson' Davies being an exceedingly clever actor." The northern New York Joe was born August 15, 1868. He was a useful middleweight, losing a KOby2 in 1895 to Dan Creedon, but crushing "Denver" Billy Woods in two, the same year. Dunfee fought a lot of no-name fighters, but won a lot more than he lost. He is usually listed at 5' 11", the same height as Choynski. Dunfee was muscular, but "shoulder-bound" and rather slow. Governor Matthews of Indiana issued four warrants on September 27, for charges of participating in prizefighting in Roby. "The requisitions were on the Governor of New York for Solly Smith, John Griffin, Joe Choynski and Dan Creedon. Benjamin Hays left for New York ... to arrest the men." He never got Joe.[46]

The company played Kingston, New York on October 2 and New York City from October 15 through 22. A strange incident occurred in the "Big Apple." "Joe Choynski ... considered well nigh invincible among pugilists ... was ignominiously knocked out on the night of Thursday, October 19. Joe's humiliation was indescribable, but ... nothing as compared with the distress he felt for the loss of $1,500 stolen from him. The story ... just leaked out ... 'Choynski ... when he finished his part at the theater went ... with an acquaintance to a resort where several beverages were imbibed. In one of these ... was a stick of chloral, and it knocked Joe out as quickly and as hard as he had ever put to sleep an amateur boxer. The acquaintance was named George Stevenson. The chloral ... did the knocking out and Stevenson did the rest. A few hours later, someone who knew Joe ... saw him staggering aimlessly through Union Square and a cab was called and the fighter, still half comatose, was removed to his hotel. Parson Davies was informed that his pugilist was on a toot, which rather staggered (him), knowing Joe was not addicted to strong drink ... rather than incur notoriety, Joe preferred to let the money go. Stevenson is alleged to have sailed to Europe with the money Saturday. Police are not content to let the matter drop, and have closed the resort where the robbery was committed.' "[47]

Some papers corroborated the story, but others accused a 2nd man. *San Francisco Chronicle*: "The police are looking for a complaintant (sic) to press the charge against John Grady, one of the criers in the horse show in Madison-square Garden ... arrested yesterday while ... donning his uniform. He is suspected of being implicated in the robbery of Joe Choynski. His (Joe's) story of being robbed was to the effect that he met some friends, who brought him to the resort at 104 East 14th Street, where he was given drugged drink, which made him unconscious. When he came to himself the following day he discovered he had been robbed of $1,400 in money, a diamond stud and a diamond ring. The detectives say there is some doubt whether the man who was robbed was Choynski."

"The police declare that Grady is an old jail bird, but he pretends to be a member of the Young Men's Christian Association. Since the alleged robbery he has been missing and his mustache has been shaved off. The detectives say Grady admits he was drinking with a man named 'Joe' in the resort, but he stoutly denied having a hand in the robbery. Justice Voorhis remanded Grady." So goes another example of the contradictory accounts from different papers. Perhaps Stevenson and Grady were in "cahoots." When the case came up in court, Joe did not show at the Essex Market Police Court. "As no one else appeared to make any charge, Justice Voorhis discharged Grady."[48] Like a handful of celebrity athletes in his time and many who came later, Joe tried to maintain a sparkling clean public image. He presented himself as a teetotaler, and though he didn't drink excessively, Choynski did enjoy a nip of the nectar. While he skipped the court proceeding, Joe was able to box the next day.

"Uncle Tom's Cabin" played at New York's Park Theatre at Broadway and 35th Street, the week of Monday, October 16. Davies was negotiating for Joe to battle Australian heavyweight, Steve O'Donnell. The final arrangements were to have taken place at the office of Richard K. Fox of the *Police Gazette* on October 19, between Davies and O'Donnell's backer, Mike Haley. Joe and Davies were there as scheduled, with a $500 forfeit, to sign for $5,000 and the largest purse offered. "Neither Haley or O'Donnell appeared. Davies: 'Haley was bluffing. I called him and that's all there is in it. Choynski is ready to sign articles when Haley puts up a forfeit.' "

A mixed review of the company's October 17 performance read: "The metropolitan debut of Peter Jackson as a dramatic artist served at the Park Theatre last night one of the most brilliant groups of colored ladies and gentlemen ever seen at any public function. Wealthy janitors, urbane caterers, barbers of polished manners and sleeping car porters ... thronged the lobby between the acts and eagerly discussed the play and the merits of the actors. A venerable kalsominer (whitewasher) who is the recognized authority on all matters of act in the vicinity of 27th street, and to whose summer school, near Canarsie, is due the recent renaissance of whitewashing as a form of decorative art, remarked at the final fall of the curtain that he 'never see nothing better,' and there was none to dispute his opinion. In Parson Davies' version of Uncle Tom's Cabin, there are no bloodhounds and no death of Sinclair, but no other familiar feature of the play is missing, and there is even a donkey for Little Eva to ride."

"There is a Topsy ... a very Louise Miller ... a remarkably good Shelby and George Harris ... played by Joe Choynski and Parson Davies, respectively, while Mr. Jackson walks through the piece as Uncle Tom in a saddened and decorous manner ... Uncle Tom submits to all sorts of ill treatment ... his admirers in the auditorium would like nothing better than to see him put Legree asleep and knock out the brutal slave trader. But, the only time he uses his fists is between the 2nd and 3rd acts, when he puts on the gloves with ... fellow artist, Joe Choynski, while Mr. Davies as master of ceremonies ... surprised ... by his talent as a comedian. The deathbed o' Little Eva was viewed by a moist-eyed audience. There is no doubt ... the child's demise was hastened by the ... singing of the Oakland Quartet."

The combination played November 4 to SRO (standing room only) at the Opera House in Lowell, Massachusetts. Stockwell was no longer part of "Uncle Tom's Cabin." He was in New York City, starring in the play, "Maine and Georgia." Davies' troupe rolled into Holyoke, Massachusetts on November 14 for a one-night stand. The next morning they arrived in New Haven, Connecticut and stopped off at the new Hotel Monopole. *New Haven Evening Register*: "Apropos of Choynski, Mr. Davis (sic) said this morning that a short time ago the *New York Morning Advertiser* printed a story in which it was stated that he was lured into a place in New York October 13 last, drugged by a woman and robbed of a lot of money. The story, Mr. Davies said, was a pure fake. Choynski got a letter this morning from Carey Walsh, the man who keeps the saloon where the affair is said to have occurred, in which he said he was going to sue the paper for libel. Choynski also thinks of bringing suit." This was probably a misconstruing of the robbery on October 19, or more yellow journalism. The troupe's itinerary between October 23 and November 8 (Joe's 25th birthday) brought them to such cities as Augusta, Bangor and Lewiston, Maine; Manchester, Portsmouth, Laconia, Concord and Nashua, New Hampshire; Lawrence, Haverhill, Lynn, Taunton and Fall River, Massachusetts.[49]

On November 9, the company was in Newport, Rhode Island. From there, it was Woonsocket on the 11th and New Haven, Connecticut on the 15th. The troupe stopped off in New York around the 13th; they were spotted that day at the Grand Horse Show at Madison Square Garden. On November 27, Joe and Peter boxed an exhibition at the Fulton Opera House in Lancaster, Pennsylvania. A young Johnny Houck witnessed the event. Johnny was the brother of Leo Houck (originally, Hauck), a claimant to the world middleweight title and later boxing coach at Penn State University. Johnny became a noted local historian, corresponded with Choynski for years, and met him a few years prior to Joe's death.[50]

In late November, the company appeared in Hartford, Connecticut, where Harriet Beecher Stowe had been living the past 23 years. She was disabled, and "as a courtesy Davies sent her an invitation to occupy a box at the production. Some of Ms. Stowe's friends ... were scandalized by what they considered the corruption of her play (by) a sparring match. They attempted to organize a protest and circulate a petition in opposition to the show, but their efforts came to nothing." *Kansas City Star*: "Joe ... a coming aspirant for heavyweight honors, (is) in a class between middleweights and men of Corbett and Jackson's weight, height and reach ... a stiff puncher, particularly clever in infighting and remarkably quick on his feet ..."[51]

On December 4, the troupe played to SRO at the National Theatre in

Philadelphia. The *Philadelphia Inquirer* said the three rounds between Peter and Joe, "while ... friendly ... were lively enough to give the house a good line on the ability of the two ... Davies as the Auctioneer ... sustained (his) part in a highly creditable manner. Little Annie Laughlin was an ideal Eva, her emotional episodes being ... free from the many disagreeable qualities of voice and manner usually possessed by stage children. The Topsy of Miss Louise Miller was bright and original." Choynski, Jackson and Davies went to the Walnut Street Theatre on the 13th to watch Charley Mitchell box Billy Woods. A nightly Choynski-Jackson exhibition was described thus: "In a sparring match lately between Peter Jackson and Joe Choynski, the former tapped the Hebrew just 69 times in one, two-minute round. Peter can tap pretty severely, too, when he likes ..." Next, the team set out for Worcester, Massachusetts where they appeared December 14 and 15.[52]

Choynski wrote a December 16 letter from Worcester to an Australian friend, F.C. (sic) Diamond (probably *Police Gazette* correspondent, Frederick E. Diamond). He said Jim Hall, sparring in various theaters with Steve O'Donnell, was "at his old tricks, and has been arrested for knocking the windows out of a cab. It's awfully cold here ... the streets are covered with ice ... it is 11 degrees below zero ... probably colder still before long." Joe expressed acrimony toward Fitz, writing: "Bob Fitzsimmons is dead broke and has made up with his wife ... you know he applied for a divorce. She was not good enough for him when he had money, and now his 'other' girl has no use for him. He will probably be back in Sydney some day shoeing horses for a living. Give my kind regards to all Australian friends."[53]

The "Uncle Tom's Cabin" tour opened December 18 at Jacob's Theatre, on the East Side of Manhattan, playing through the following Saturday. On the afternoon of the 22nd, in "The Parson's" theatre dressing room, a deal was negotiated for a Choynski-Steve O'Donnell fight, between Davies and Jim Hall, who was acting for Steve. Choynski and O'Donnell were chatting pleasantly with each other. It was to be a finish fight, either in Jacksonville, Florida or New Orleans, Louisiana, using the smallest gloves allowable. A St. Louis paper said it only took Davies about five minutes to cement the deal.[54] As 1893 ended, a future accounting could show that Choynski and Davies had challenged Bob Fitzsimmons, Peter Maher, Jim Daly, "Denver" Ed Smith and Steve O'Donnell, all to no avail. The deal with O'Donnell fell through. Not until 1899 would he and Joe face each other in a ring.

Will Corbett, sporting editor of the *Sydney Referee*, ruminated and recalled items from 1892 for the April 2, 1919 issue: "W.W. Naughton wrote: 'Those who have seen Jackson recently in his Uncle Tom sparring bout with Choynski say Peter is as speedy and dexterous ... as ever ... Peter's sparring with Choynski was a revelation. His handling of himself was far superior to even Corbett's vaunted science. Personally, while some of the wise men of the East are going into ecstasies over Corbett ... declaring he is

50 years ahead of the age he lives in, I consider Jackson the superior ... of any man that lives. Corbett is more showy and has lots of little stabs and twirls ... purely his own, but judging ... style from a standpoint of legitimate blows and guards, Peter suits me better. I am making ... deductions from boxing as taught by the old masters, just as ... a fencer would do in passing an opinion upon the merits of a bout with the foils.' "

"The *New York Herald* published this ... from the pen of a well-known medical man: 'In Uncle Tom's Cabin, a set-to is introduced ... in which Joe Choynski does his level best ... to respond to the fast and furious onslaught of ... Peter Jackson. It would be impossible to give a more satisfactory illustration of hard and fast fighting than is supplied by these ... all critics ... without prejudice are forced to admit that no man was ever better balanced on his legs or a better judge of distance than Peter Jackson ... Where men are noted for their shiftiness – the absurd word intended to describe extraordinary agility in getting away out of reach – step, or leap-back, Jackson simply bends backward his head, or, if necessary, his upper body ... the true scientific evasion, and it is wonderful how unerringly he withdraws just beyond reach ... securing the ... advantage of getting in the most telling returns. That his lung power is of the best is proven by the perfect calm of his breathing during his hot work with Choynski and after it.' "

On January 1, 1894, the company was in Worcester, Massachusetts, where Jackson and Choynski's lively three rounds were "cheered to the echo," and the audience demanded an encore. While Peter's superior height and reach allowed him to dominate, landing to the face and ribs, Joe electrified the assemblage at times by cleverly getting inside on his opponent. On the 15th, the combination passed through Pittsburgh, Pennsylvania en route to Baltimore, Maryland. Their ultimate destination was Jacksonville, Florida, to attend the Corbett-Mitchell title bout. The men rode a special train comprised of 10 cars and were joined at Quaker City, Pennsylvania by such as Pony Moore (Mitchell's father-in-law), "Nonpareil" Dempsey, "Brooklyn" Jimmy Carroll and John Eckhardt.[55]

While in Baltimore on the night of January 21, the party celebrated with two other theater companies. Around midnight, they left Harris' Academy of Music in downtown Baltimore and headed by stage to the Halstead Road House near Pimlico. The revelers left the roadhouse at 3:00 a.m., after a night of dining and drinking, "The Parson" atop the stage with the driver. About 6:00 a.m. "the stage was at the corner of Centre and Cathedral streets when it took a corner too quickly and overturned. Davies and the other passengers were thrown from the stage; Davies had his hand badly sprained and mashed and took a large chunk of flesh out of one knee."[56]

The Corbett-Mitchell fight was held at Jacksonville's Duval Athletic Club on January 25, and the crowd saw "Gentleman Jim" overwhelm Mitchell on a 3rd round knockout. "Jolly Cholly," who was noted for infuriating opponents with verbal abuse, really got Corbett's goat with the vituperation and invective he hurled. Mitchell aroused Jim's ire to the point where, in round two, he floored Charley, then hit him while he was still down, as Mitchell continued his stream of vitriol. Fortunately for Corbett, Referee "Honest" John Kelly overlooked this clear breach of the rules and did not give the fight and title to the Englishman on a foul. "Pompadour Jim" discarded his usual stick-and-move style and slugged his foe with a fury he had rarely, if ever, shown before. The 32-year-old Mitchell, who had fought only a handful of short bouts the past several years, was little more than a soft touch for the heavyweight champion.

The combination resumed "Uncle Tom's Cabin," at Pittsburgh's Grand Opera-House. Jackson was still convinced he would get his chance at Corbett, but it was not to be. In this author's opinion, Jim really had no intention of fighting "The Black Prince." They played at Dolan's in Logansport, Indiana on February 3. On the 4th and 5th, they performed at the Academy in Milwaukee, Wisconsin. Meanwhile, Corbett, in attempting to dodge a fight with Fitz, told Bob he needed to beat Choynski before Jim would consider his challenge. Corbett, well aware of Joe's repeated challenges to Fitz, was also resting on his laurels, starring in plays and languishing as a pugilist. The company played Kalamazoo, Michigan on February 13, and the week of March 4 saw them at Harris' Bijou Theater in Washington, D.C. "Prior to their appearance in their respective parts, Peter Jackson and Joe Choynski will spar three scientific rounds which will give the spectators an idea of pugilism at its best, with none of the disgusting details of the prize ring ... some very complimentary things have been said of Jackson's impersonation of the old slave, for which part he does not have to make up. A contingent of colored singers and dancers add to the realism as well as the amusement of the plantation scenes ..."[57]

The *Post*'s review of the March 5 show revealed it had one of the biggest audiences in the history of Harris' Bijou Theater. "There was the general desire to see Peter Jackson, the man who will whip Corbett, if anybody ... Then ... the curiosity to see ... Davies and Joe Choynski, about whom so much has been written in the newspapers ... The evident desire has been to avoid any sacrifice of the legitimate interest of the play to the pugilistic features ... It is quite possible that a great many ladies understood for the first time last night what there is about a gloved contest that possesses so much fascination for the masculine mind. Jackson's three-round bout after the first act with Choynski was a very spirited one and reflected credit on both participants; for it can be no small matter to engage day after day in contests with so much ginger in them. It was purely a friendly display of science, but no amount of amicability or skill could obviate the fact that an encounter of that kind with a man of Peter Jackson's muscle is a pretty severe physical test ... Louise Miller is the mischievous and ingenuous

Topsy, and created much merriment ... The Oakland quartet afforded much entertainment in their songs, jubilees, and buck dancing. Little Annie Laughlin gave a pretty performance ... of Eva."[58]

The tour continued with stops at Richmond, Indiana on March 15 and a performance at the Decatur, Illinois Grand Opera House on the 17th. The depot was crowded with admirers when the company's train came in, and a large throng stood outside the hotel and Opera House, before and after the show. At show time, "The gallery was filled and the balcony nearly so." The usual three-round go followed, although the first two frames were tame enough to bore the crowd. The 3rd was better and pleased the spectators, who had come primarily to see the spar. "And after the boxing was over there were plenty of empty seats all over the house." One poor review came from the *Decatur Morning Herald*: "If anything, it was worse than rotten. There was not much attempt at acting. The ... cast seemed to understand that the audience was there to see Jackson ..." He was staying at the St. Nicholas Hotel, and Joe likely was, too. Peter was interviewed after the show in his dressing room. He told the reporter he was disappointed to hear that Corbett "had business to attend to" in June and would not be able to fight him for the world championship, after all. Peter was a humble, unassuming person, who did no "smack-talking," made no excuses and refused to do so when prodded. They left that night for St. Louis.[59]

Joe Choynski, June 15, 1894

The company opened in St. Louis with a matinee at Pope's the following afternoon, where they played a full week. The *St. Louis Post-Dispatch* referred to earlier performances in Toronto, Ontario and Buffalo (New York), where hundreds of people had to be turned away. Its review on the 18th commended Jackson on his "intelligent and sympathetic" interpretation of Uncle Tom, Davies on "arousing no end of uproarious merriment" as the auctioneer. "Little Eva and Topsy ... are ... in unusually competent hands ..." The three-rounder after act one was described as "the most spirited display ever given under the usual friendly and scientific classification." On March 19: " 'Uncle Tom's Cabin, without blood-hounds and minus a donkey, but with the colored pugilist Peter Jackson, concealing his physical strength and revealing his dramatic as Uncle Tom ... (played) to fair houses."

April 30 found the combination in Beantown. May 1 *Boston Morning Journal*: "The Boston Theatre last evening ... introduced for the first time to a Boston audience as an actor, Mr. Peter Jackson ... hitherto known ... as the champion heavyweight pugilist of Australia, and Mr. Davies ... also made his bow ... as a seeker of histrionic fame ... one of the most successful handlers of athletes in the country. Aside from this was the more interesting fact that Mr. Jackson would appear in a friendly set-to of three rounds with Mr. 'Joe' Choynski ... this was the means of calling out a large audience of sporting people to witness his ability and cleverness as a scientific sparrer ... Jackson had things all his own way, as the Californian was simply 'not in it.' the play itself ... Mr. Jackson's interpretation of Uncle Tom is really good, with the exception of one important particular – that of intonation. Did he speak but a little more distinctly, he would be the ideal Uncle Tom, for his carriage, demeanor and expression throughout seemed to fill the part exactly. Mr. Davies, as George Harris and the auctioneer, was good, while Geo. R. Caine, as Phineas Fletcher and Simon Legree, was excellent, his interpretation of the latter character being so well done that he was roundly hissed. The Topsy of Louise Miller was most warmly received ..."

May 1 *Boston Daily Globe*: "One misses much of the slavery element which made the old drama so exciting, but then one gets a sparring exhibition by two renowned pugilists and things are evened up. 'Time!' called the parson, as he backed to the rear of the stage ... there was science ... but it was the science of not hitting, at least, not hitting hard. The 1st round was a neat bit of byplay. Joe danced and Peter feinted. They tapped each other good humoredly ... as the parson called 'time.' The 2nd round was full of business, and the blows fell hard and fast in the air, but it was amusing to see Peter avoid hitting Joe and smiling sweetly as Joe tried to hit him. In the 3rd round, several fine face blows were got by both men, and Joe looked as if he was getting the worst of it. When Peter ducked, Joe swept the air in a big circle and almost whirled himself off his feet. At the close ... there was a spurt and a fire of blows, but no one was hurt, and the men shook hands amid the laughter and cheering of the audience. Eva is excellent and Topsy, who don't 'like cream-colored n_ggers,' is immense. The scenery is good and the dancing and singing on the Red river plantation is a show by itself." The show ran all week.

A critical review from an unidentified Boston paper: "One who saw the whole performance could not help wondering why ... The story had been so changed that one step further would not have been surprising ... For instance, Uncle Tom could have accompanied George Harris in his flight and boxed three rounds with the pursuers, knocking them out instead of having them shot. He could have amused Little Eva with a sparring match instead of singing gospel hymns to her ... At the close, he could have a 'fight to the finish' with Legree and bring the performance to a pleasant termination. Certainly, changes like these would have been no more startling than some that were given. The version differed considerably from the traditional form of the play, as the Vermont scenes and St. Clair's death were omitted, the part of Topsy was made a comparatively unimportant one, and there was introduced so much singing and dancing by negroes that the performance lasted an unusually long time ... Peter Jackson was moderately effective at Uncle Tom ... Charles E. Davies was amusing in the auction scene, and Louise Miller was a clever Topsy. The scenery is very good, particularly the plantation scene." The writer who penned this was evidently lost to the fact that the play was designed mostly as a vehicle for exhibiting Peter Jackson, and to a lesser extent, Joe Choynski.

The company disbanded on or about May 24, after a two-week engagement in Chicago.[60] Thus ended the 2nd and final season of "Uncle Tom's Cabin." It had a lucrative and successful run, and resulted in Joe meeting his future wife, Louise. In the March 19, 1919 *Sydney Referee*, Will Corbett claimed that Louise portrayed "Little Eva" at some point. This has not been substantiated. The *Referee* has an unnamed paper summing up the demise of the production: "Uncle Tom's Cabin has become a chestnutty drama to the public, which had ... tired of pugilistic actors." The latter was not literal truth; Jim Corbett, for example, did extremely well on the stage, while still active as a boxer. March 31 *Sporting Life* (Philadelphia, Pennsylvania): "It is said Joe Choynski will become a resident of Cincinnati and abandon the ring. The story is that Joe is in love with a pretty girl, and that is the only condition upon which she will consent to marry him. Joe is perfectly willing, but wants one more fight. It is said this is the story back of his challenge to fight anybody in the world, barring Corbett and Jackson." The "pretty girl" is, of course, Louise, but Joe came nowhere near ending his boxing career at this time. The first known mention of the impending marriage came in The May 22 *Milwaukee Evening Wisconsin*. It simply said he "was soon to marry Miss Lutie Miller, an actress living in Cincinnati."

Round Ten

The Battling Blacksmith
(April 1894 – January 1895)

In 1927, Joe Choynski noted: "As I write these recollections I find myself constantly remembering knockouts that had entirely escaped my memory ... of men of little or no ring knowledge – strong, tough fellows with plenty of confidence and ambition, but no match for one of my skill and wallop. Most of these fellows I recall only as oxen led to the slaughter. I have forgotten their names in most cases and my record book does not mention them. I take this occasion to apologize to those big fellows I stowed away whose names are omitted from this history. By this time I had fully mastered ring science. I developed an unerring judgment at distance and had become expert in hitting a moving target. I had studied and analyzed the work of every skillful boxer I had seen and adapted their best features ... As an actor I was a great middleweight, and I preferred the roped arena to the stage. Still, I believe I was as good at acting as any of my fistic contemporaries who went on the stage, as Sullivan, Fitzsimmons, Jeffries or even Corbett, who stuck at the grease paint longer than any of them." Joe's next opponent would not be an "oxen led to the slaughter."

Negotiations were finally underway between the camps of Bob Fitzsimmons and Choynski. "Ruby Robert" wrote Davies a letter stating his willingness to battle Joe "for a purse and as large a side bet as may be desired." The change of heart stemmed from his intention to earn a shot at Corbett's heavyweight crown. Jim stipulated that Bob needed to defeat Choynski before he would be granted a title shot. Joe had $5,000 of his own money to put up as a side bet. The *Boston Journal* said, " 'Parson' Davies was seen at the Quincy House yesterday afternoon, and ... said ... 'I don't think we shall have any trouble in arranging a match with Fitz. Fitz is an easy man to make a match with and lives up to his agreements. Joe is not at present in a very good condition. He is not sick, but you know that traveling about as we have for the past season is likely to affect a man. These frequent changes, poor dressing rooms and all that goes to make up the work of a prosperous theatrical company has worn Joe out ... he has run down to 160 pounds. One place is as good as another ... provided the money is there, and that is what we are out for, rather than for glory.' "[1] The latter phrase was repeated by Choynski, himself. While he may have enjoyed fighting in his youth, financial reward was now Joe's prime motivation.

The New Orleans Olympic Club promptly offered a $6,000 purse to host the fight. Joe and Bob met in New York City on May 8. On the 9th, Choynski and Davies returned to Chicago. One paper said all involved had come to terms on a finish fight "at catchweights," meaning the fighters could enter the ring at whatever weight they bore at the time. The stipulation was that a purse be put up by some club for $15,000 or more. Articles had not been signed yet. Davies told a reporter, "I am all at sea in respect to my movements. Our season with 'Uncle Tom' is closed. I could have made any number of contracts for the show, but did not feel justified ... in view of the possibility of making matches for Jackson and Choynski. I shall remain here several days with Choynski ... we shall go to England. Corbett seems in no hurry to arrange a fight. The match between Choynski and Fitzsimmons is no nearer a fixed event than ... some time ago."[2]

Years later, Joe wrote: "I had not the slightest doubt as to my ability to knock Fitzsimmons down — and out. Fitzsimmons was one prize-fighter I never underestimated. He had developed into a two-fisted bearcat and every boxer who knew anything at all had the utmost respect for his wallops. It will be remembered that I had known Fitz ever since his arrival in San Francisco. I had seconded him. I had watched his footwork. He was no closed book to me. No man realized more fully than I did the full extent of the dynamite he carried in his gloves. Most of (his) opponents entered the ring scared out of their wits. I have told how nervous Corbett was. McCoy never could be induced to fight Fitz. Peter Maher, who had tasted defeat at the hands of Fitz, had to be almost carried into the ring for his 2nd fight with Ruby Robert. Even Jeffries, in his first bout with the Australian, gave every appearance of doubt and dread until the last two rounds."[3]

The Fitzsimmons fight was set for June 18 at the Boston Theater. By the 9th, Choynski was training at Lake Quinsigamond, in Worcester County, Massachusetts. This would become his favorite training spot. It was said, "authorities ... will stop the bout if it takes on the aspect of a brutal battle." The next evening at the Front Street Opera House in Worcester, Joe sparred two rounds each with local heavyweight Martin Whalen and Tommy West, a trainer. Joe "easily demonstrated his superiority." "Little Joe" had the misfortune to sprain one of his thumbs while sparring with Whalen, but it did not prevent him from exhibiting at the "Eyrie" on the afternoon of the 17th. Joe "had stopped training and is now laying up weight. He will enter the ring weighing close to 163 pounds, about six pounds less than his opponent. 'Parson' Davies will go down to Boston on the 8 o'clock train today and Choynski and Griffo will go down at noon."[4]

According to author Gilbert Odd, Choynski tried hard to get the Antipodean to put his world middleweight title on the line. Fitz's manager, Martin Julian, wanted no part of it. When Joe allegedly pointed out that, if not for him Bob would have been knocked out by Peter Maher, "Lanky Bob" supposedly replied: "You're a cunning bastard. If you would bring off a trick like that to save me, what would you get up to take my championship?" Although there were rumors that the two fighters secretly agreed to take it easy and essentially spar eight rounds to a draw, I have not found any hard evidence to support it. Some accounts in the months and years following, have Choynski pulling a double-cross by sucker-punching Fitz. Joe flatly denied this being anything but a legitimate fight.

Davies wrote to the *New York World*: " 'Joe has been waiting two years for this chance ... A few months back he was ill, but a short rest did wonders ... When he began training he weighed about 160 pounds, and had lost no flesh to speak of. I think he will fight at about 162 pounds. Joe will surprise the sporting world, unless Fitz has improved 50 per cent over his form with Maher and Hall.' ... a decision will be given on points if both ... are on the deck when the 8th round closes. The betting is 100 to 75 on Fitzsimmons."[5] "On the deck" meant on their feet. June 23 *Sporting Life* (Philadelphia): "The men were to fight eight rounds and if both ... able to go on ...

Bob Fitzsimmons, 1899

the contest should be declared a draw. The pivot-blow was barred."

In 1927, Joe wrote, with faulty memory: "Among the hundreds of men I had the honor of knocking out was Bob Fitzsimmons. I floored Fitz for the count in the 3rd round ... but was robbed of the decision. The record books do not credit me with this knockout; they tell you the fight was stopped in the 3rd round by police interference and ... called a draw. But, of the hectic 3rd ... when Fitz took the count, the record books are silent. I want to state in advance that I don't think Bob ... was a party ... whereby I was robbed. He was crafty, could snap a murderous jolt from any position without being 'set' ... that made him unique among fighters ... a graduate of the Australian school of boxing. Clearly, it would be suicidal to tear recklessly into such a two-handed killer, as one might against boxers like Corbett or McCoy. Extreme caution would be necessary. I ... felt I knew his bag of tricks. It had been interesting to me, a fellow knockout artist, to observe Fitz purposely leading short to lure a foe closer and make him careless so Fitz could hand him the works. I can see the crafty gladiator now as he stood opposite me that night waiting for the bell, his little semi-bald head set down low under the protection of his high shoulders, his eyes gleaming brightly like blue flames as he studied me."

Many sources incorrectly say the bout occurred on Bunker Hill Day. That celebration takes place June 17. It was a short, but memorable struggle in the Boston Theater on the 18th. 3,000 witnessed the only real fight between the two. The ring was pitched near the stage footlights, the scenery in back lending a picturesque quality. Referee Charlie White said (in 1911) the ring was the unusual octagonal model Tom O'Rourke used when he managed George Dixon. The ropes of this enclosure were lower than in a regulation ring. Fitzsimmons' camp objected, but were told it was too late to acquire a traditional model.[6] The unusual shape of this "non-squared circle" increased the possibility of a boxer backing into the ropes, rendering him off-balance and momentarily vulnerable. This was said to have been a factor this night. A blend of mostly contemporary reports follows:[7]

Bob Fitzsimmons, 1891

Choynski entered the ring first, accompanied by Davies, Tommy West, Ned McAvoy and Mick (or Nick) Dunn. Bob followed, attended by Charlie White, Jimmy Handler, Sam Kline and Fred Voght. The weights were given as 175 pounds, Fitz and about 162 for Joe. Reports were virtually unanimous in saying Bob looked heavier than Joe. The *Police Gazette* said Joe weighed "fully 15 or 20 pounds less than the Australian. What Fitzsimmons weighed could not be learned." Joe had overtrained, reducing his weight to the point of weakness. The weight factor is something not addressed in other books. He was attired in red tights with a red, white and blue sash, while Fitz "wore his usual color, cardinal, and had a belt made of tiny silk American flags sewn together ..."[8] The fight was set for eight rounds, five ounce gloves being used, and Captain Bill Daly refereed. The timekeeper was Dan Murphy. Captain Warren and Sergeant Sullivan of

Station 4 and other policemen were in attendance, to stop the fight if things became too violent. Time was called at 9:40 p.m.

Round 1 – The men circled and sparred for an opening. Fitz jabbed out a left that Joe ducked. He landed a light right, but "The Frisco Flash" snapped his head back with a pair of jabs. They exchanged a few love taps before the round closed. Joe: "I can see Lanky Bob ... now, as he ... studied me closely, his little eyes squinting, but he tried no goat getting. I guess he respected me ... I certainly had no intention of rushing in ... and stopping a haymaker. The 1st and 2nd rounds, while fairly even ... some stiff punches. Both of us were shaken, but no great damage done. Once, after he stung me with a stiff jolt on the nose, Fitz drawled: 'Ow'd you like the smell of that 'oof?' I don't know why he said this. It was the only time I had ever heard him speak to an opponent in the ring ... I retorted: 'Do you think you're shoeing horses now, Bob?' " The *Boston Herald* said Joe ducked under Bob, stood and lifted him off his feet in a show of strength.

Round 2 – Fitz landed two jabs to the face. The San Franciscan smiled, rushed and countered with a right and hard left to the ribs. There followed some "fast and furious" infighting. Joe was not prospering at this, so he backed to long-range. He ducked a pair of vicious lefts and countered with his own. Bob sank a strong right to the body. Choynski answered with a good left to the face. One report had Bob backing his foe to the ropes and grazing him with a right uppercut. A dissenting account said Joe backed the Cornishman to his corner and got in a "neat left uppercut." Charlie White wrote that Bob "brought that steel forearm of his down hard on Joe's neck, causing Choynski much pain." *Sporting Life*: "Before the 2nd ... was finished, Fitzsimmons missed seven right-handed swings, and was jabbed in the face as many times ... men who had bet two to one on Fitzsimmons wished they had not been so rash." Joe looked a bit weak at the bell. Looking back through time, he wrote, "We went to our corners at the end of the 2nd. As I sat resting I saw him watching me. His peculiar little eyes glittered. Then came the 3rd round – and the fireworks began."

Round 3 – Joe: "We had been fiddling and feinting ... when Bob ... began shuffling his feet ... edging his left foot steadily forward. This was a characteristic Fitzsimmons manoeuvre ... getting ready for a swift double lead, as quick as lightning. I knew I could expect a left for the body or head ... followed by a darting crusher ... Quick as a flash I decided to break up this play with an offensive. I started a swift right, purposely high, and stopped it instantly as Bob worked the Jem Mace head-shift – then crashed a paralyzing left over his ear with all my strength. Bob ... tumbled flat on his back with a heavy crash, as if he had been thrown from a catapult. Right there was when the jobbing was done. Captain Jack Dalton (actually, Bill Daly) began counting: 'One – get back, Choynski – two – keep away, Choynski – three, four – Choynski, there will be no counting while you are close – five, six – don't come near, Choynski–' and so on through the travesty, the same old army game, designed to rob a fighter of a clean-cut victory. Just before his 'ten' was reached – it must have been nearly twice that – the bell rang! But according to my timekeeper, that round was just one minute and 45 seconds old! Fitz was helped to his corner ... they worked over him desperately. I was informed later that the bell had been rung on the orders of Captain Glori, a Newark, New Jersey police officer ... acting as manager for Fitzsimmons. Feeling I had Fitz where another minute or two would give me time to flatten him, I offered little protest. The short round and long rest benefited Fitz. When he came out for the 4th he was almost himself again. The man had amazing stamina."

Corbett gave a version for the November 6, 1919 *Fort Wayne News and Sentinel*, he says he quoted from Choynski, though he didn't note from what year. It may have been an earlier recollection, as Joe got the referee's name right. "I caught Fitz on the chin with an awful right hander ... Fitz reeled and ... hit the floor ... as completely out as any man in prize ring history. I knew it would be a ... lot more than 10 seconds before he would ... get on his feet ... Captain Bill Daly was refereeing ... he began running around in circles. He did not start to count – seemed too bewildered. Finally, I yelled at him to toll off the seconds. Daly paid no heed ... the crowd ... cheering wildly for me, howled at Daly, 'start that count.' ... only then did Daly get busy. But ... permitted many seconds to lapse between each toll. Every new count seemed to give him pain. After he reached five, he made a new count only every 10 seconds. All the while, Fitz lay dead on the floor."

"At last the count reached nine. Daly waited – and waited some more. It seemed an eternity ... then Daly looked appealingly at the timekeeper, whereupon the timekeeper rang the bell ... I know the round was shortened by at least a full minute, because I had my own timekeeper at that fight, and he checked up all the time. The club timekeeper gave me the worst of it right afterward, by letting nearly two minutes elapse before he called us together for the short round." Most athletes, when they fail to succeed, make excuses. Joe sometimes did the same. As no modern witness was there, it will never be certain if events transpired the way he remembered. The *Boston Globe* said the crowd was so raucous, police sent the boxers to their corners with 15 seconds remaining in the round. The June 7, 1899 *Waterloo Courier* said Fitz was "saved by the bell." A blended report follows:

Choynski was short of wind. He missed a couple of lefts and Bob "grazed the back of his head with a terrible right-handed swing." Joe slipped down, took eight seconds and rose. Fitz feinted and launched a wicked left at the head. Joe made a clever sidestep and quick as a flash, smashed his own left on Bob's jaw. The middleweight champion crashed to the floor, landing on all fours, then rolled onto his back, badly dazed. Most accounts said the punch was a left, including Joe's memoirs, but at least six reports claimed it was a right to the jaw. Most reports had Fitz down for nine seconds. Both were bleeding, according to the *Police Gazette*.

New York World: "The scene ... cannot be described. Daley counted off, _very slowly_, eight seconds and Fitz got on his feet." This supports Joe's claim of a long count. "All sorts of advice was hurled at the plucky Californian, so much indeed, that it rattled him. He tried to steady himself for a finishing, but Fitz would clinch, and Choynski expended a great deal of his strength trying to keep him off. This ... continued for fully half a minute, when the New Zealander showed signs of recovery. Towards the close of the round, he feigned fatigue, and when a good opportunity presented itself, let his right go with full force, just grazing the back of Joe's head. This was a place where condition told, and Fitz kept swinging away with both hands. Then, he began clinching, and *10 seconds before the bell was due*, the police ordered the men to their corners." The latter backs Joe's claim of a short 3rd round, though not by the margin he put forth. That Fitz might have been aided by a long count, though, is seldom mentioned. "Choynski's opportunity was gone ... Joe was fagged out, and a minute's rest was not as much service to him as to the thoroughly conditioned Fitz by 50 percent."

Above the din, Bob somehow heard the referee's count, and regained his feet at nine. The crowd stood, screaming. He was shaky, bleeding from nose and mouth, and reeling about. Joe pursued Fitz and "forced him around the ring, landing both hands at will." His punches, though, were lacking in power and Bob clinched his neck at every opportunity. "Joe's seconds called to him to steady himself and had he done so, he ought to have finished Fitz in a minute. He was so eager, though, ... that he went at his man helter-skelter." Daly broke them apart numerous times. Toward the end, Bob was actually was the stronger of the two. Papers agreed that Choynski had weakened himself by overtraining and losing too much weight. He shot his bolt in trying to free himself from Bob's clutches and lacked the power to put over the coupe de grâce. "The round came to a close with both men just staggering around, trying hard to get in a final blow, which seemed ... all that was needed to finish either one."

Joe (1927): "Fitzsimmons later gave an ... account to Bob Edgren (author: an immensely talented artist and writer) of how he felt when I knocked him down in the 3rd round. 'The first thing I saw ... was what looked like all the chairs in the gallery coming over on me like a waterfall. I tried to get out of the way and found I could not move. It never struck me that I was on the floor and had been knocked down. Pretty soon the chairs stopped falling. I didn't hear the referee counting anything. Then somebody sang out, *I told you Joe would lick him in one punch*. That kind of roused me. I saw Choynski dancing around as I got to my feet. I wasn't sure yet that I was (illegible) him, but as he came in I ducked just in time; I ducked again. I couldn't think yet. The 3rd time he came in, my head began to come back to me.' " In other versions, Bob said it was "Parson" Davies' voice he heard saying, "I told you Joe would lick him ..." which brought him to his senses. The reality? It is highly unlikely that Bob could have overheard Davies (or anyone else) over the raucous, screaming crowd.

March 4, 1905 *Denver Post*: Fitz recalled: "In the 2nd (Joe) ... crossed his right and left on the jaw and I went down in a heap. The floor seemed to be moving up to me, and I remember putting out my hand, as though to stave it off ... I began to gain my senses, and just as eight was counted I got up and rushed Choynski into a clinch. I was still a trifle dazed, but held on for a second, and then when I stepped back, Choynski tried to nail me with his left hand. I ducked the lead and stepped in, myself, letting go my left hand square in the face. The blow caught Choynski on the nose, breaking it in two places. The round was a fierce one, and I was glad to get through it." He told the January 17, 1909 *Weekly Dispatch* (London, England): "I feinted. I thought I stepped aside but found I had stepped on the rope. In the struggle to save myself I blacked my eye. Then he gave me left and right, and down I went." Fitz erred in saying this was the 2nd frame. August 24, 1918 *New Zealand Truth*: "I said to myself, *Bob Fitzsimmons, you're going to get married. You bet the thousand dollars you borrowed from John D. Spreckels on yourself, and ... you are on the floor knocked out by Joe Choynski. Get up!* The queer part ... was I thought up was down and down was up. They told me afterwards how the crowd laughed when they saw me rooting my head into the canvas as I tried to get up. Finally I did, and don't remember going any further. They called it a draw. It was the hardest punch I ... received in all my life."

Charlie White, 1911: "By clever ducking, Joe made Bob miss a couple, then got in a blow to Fitz's neck. It did not appear to have much force, but was hard enough to send Bob (back). Here is where the octagonal-shaped ring was the cause of what Bob's trainer had foreseen. As Bob fell back, he came up hard against the ropes. Had the ring been of regulation shape, he probably would have had plenty of space. As the rebound off the ropes shot Fitzsimmons forward, Joe half turned and caught him under the ear with a right hand hook, and Bob went down like a ton of brick. Rolling over with a sickly smile, Bob struggled to his knees at the count of four. Choynski was still standing over him, and Bob suddenly reached out and clasped Joe around the knees, burying his face in his opponent's stomach. As Joe tried madly to free himself ... Fitzsimmons drew himself up slowly, his face still buried in Joe, and at the count of eight regained his feet, and had his arms tightly wrapped around Joe's shoulders and neck, while Choynski wasted all his strength and wind whaling harmlessly away at Bob's back. Both were covered with blood, but (Bob) was getting stronger every moment ... police threatened to stop the fight, and the seconds rang the bell, cutting the bout short by 10 seconds, but the men were so intent on finishing each other they did not hear the gong and had to be separated."

Round 4 – "Fitz's wonderful recuperative power ... asserted itself. While Choynski was leg-weary and slow ... the Australian ... hit him two on the face and jaw and floored him ... when he arose repeated the dose. Twice more did Fitzsimmons floor him, but each time the Californian staggered to his feet. The battle was getting gory and Police Captain Warren, followed by a squad of officers, entered the ring and told Daly the mill must stop if the spectators did not cease ... yelling. This ended the round ... about 30 seconds short." Most papers agreed the 4th was cut short by 30 seconds. Charlie White said (1911) that following the 3rd knockdown, Joe's seconds threw water on him until they were stopped by the referee.

"Fitz forced the fighting, landing left jabs on the face and right on the ribs. Fitz sent him down with a left and right on the wind and jaw. The call of time alone saved Choynski ..." *Boston Post*: "Choynski was knocked down five times in the 4th ... Choynski was lying helpless on the floor and could not have risen in 10 seconds, but just as he went down the bell rang and Joe was dragged to his chair and revived." (Philadelphia) *Sporting Life* (and *Police Gazette*): "Before the count of 10 was finished, the badly used-up Californian staggered to his feet and escaped another knockdown by clinching. The referee parted them. And just as the gong rang, the Australian's right came around, landing full on the jaw. This certainly would have ended the fight in a knock-out, for Choynski had to be lifted to his chair. He sat up erect, but his head flopped over like a person with a broken neck. Good care revived him just in time to stagger up to the call of time." In November, 1919, Jim Corbett quoted Joe Choynski as stating: "He (Fitz) came out in fair fighting condition. I went after him, determined to put him to sleep for a half hour, but Fitz was canny. He clinched and stalled along all through the 4th, and I couldn't reach him with a vital blow."

(*New York World* and *St. Louis Republic*): Fitz, though wild at times, drove Choynski all over the ring. Joe was "a past master at avoiding punishment, and he slipped to his knee several times before he was fairly knocked down. Each time he took ... at least nine seconds. These tactics annoyed Fitz, who seemed bent on finishing up his job in a hurry. When he finally sent Joe down with a right-hander on the jaw, however, the vicious look on his face disappeared, and he offered to help his opponent to rise. Joe was in great distress. His nose was bleeding profusely and his long locks were sadly disheveled. Still he kept on, ducking the other's wicked blows ..." At one point, Bob dropped Choynski near Joe's corner. After six seconds, Joe used the ropes to haul himself up. Joe: "He realized ... how near I had come to cooking his goose and began fighting like a tiger. We slugged, clinched ... and clinched again. We were both bloody. The 4th finished in an uproar."

Round 5 – Fitz rushed Joe to the ropes and whipped a terrific left to the jaw that was a bit high, but floored his weakened adversary for a nine-count. He staggered to his feet with Bob in pursuit. Another left dropped the Frisco fighter once again. Joe pulled himself upright by clinging to the ropes, whereupon he clinched. Daly separated the men, and Fitz floored his foe with yet another left to the jaw. "As he essayed to rise Capt. Warren again made his appearance and this time said that under no conditions would he allow the battle to continue. According to the articles, which read that if both men were on their feet and willing to go on at the finish of the stipulated eight rounds it should be declared a draw, there was but one decision for Daly to make, and the fight was declared a draw."

The *Boston Post* said one minute and 40 seconds had elapsed when the fight was halted by police, adding: "Fitzsimmons had Choynski on the ropes and ready to give him the last punches. They weren't clinched, although Choynski was holding. Referee Daly went over and separated the men. This he shouldn't have done, in the opinion of many ... These ... claim he saved Choynski from defeat ... Sergeant Sullivan, followed by a half dozen bluecoats, leaped on the stage, with Captain Warren outside the ring. The edict went forth that the battle should stop, and according to the articles was declared a draw ... Choynski used a straight left ... a good deal, and with effect ... He was cleverer than Fitz." Corbett claimed in 1919 that Joe said: "I got after him again in the 5th, balked him in his stalling efforts, and was bearing him around the ring. I had him at a point where he was sure to go down with a few more blows. Then, the police ... stopped the fight, and the referee, to the amazement of the crowd, declared ... a draw." Compared with contemporary reports, this version holds little water.

New York World: "Choynski was a sorry sight as he pluckily squared off ... His eyes, which have always gone back on him, were fast going now ... he resorted to all the tricks ... to save himself, and slipped with great frequency. Some of his descents may not have been intentional, for Fitz's seconds threw great quantities of water on the smooth board floor ... An uppercut sent Choynski down. He took all the time he could ... and arose, only to be punched sprawling again with a right-hander on the jaw. Fitz then began using his shoulders, as only experienced fighters know how, and Joe's remaining strength was fast being exhausted. The blood from Joe's nose covered his chest, and just as he clinched Fitz the police stepped in and stopped the contest. Twenty seconds remained of the round (putting the elapsed time at 2 minutes, 40 seconds) ... Daly ... was bound to declare it a draw ... Finally, after a spread-eagle speech, he announced his decision ... an immensely popular one, although there was not a good punch left in the Californian." The spectators cheered the fighters "and hissed Daly and Captain Warren, satisfied ... that Fitz was the greatest ring general ever seen in Boston, and Choynski ... as game a man as ever stepped into a ring."

The June 9, 1895 *Brooklyn Daily Eagle* claimed: "Those within the sacred circle declared at the time that the backers of the two men arranged that they should give an interesting and apparently meritorious exhibition for eight rounds, secure a draw with both men on their feet, and divide the gate receipts. Then Parson Davies ... got Choynski in the best possible shape ... and told him to go in and win if he could. Choynski carried out his instructions to the letter, and it was only when Fitzsimmons found himself going in that 3rd round that he realized that Joe was fighting and not exhibiting. Then he too, took a share in the sport, with the result indicated." This article perpetuates the idea that the fighters had an agreement going in to take things easy and collect their pay, and that Joe "double-crossed Bob" by trying to win. Choynski vehemently denied there was any "agreement" and Bob mentioned no such thing at the time. The "pre-arrangement" was likely a myth some reporter cooked up in the interest of selling a story, with help from Fitz, who at times claimed there was a prior agreement.

(Choynski, 1927): "Fitz caught me ... I went to my knees. He could hit. But I was up and at him, with the blood spattering, when the bell banged and police stopped the fight. It was recorded as a draw. But it was not a draw. I had won – and was robbed. But I don't mean to say that Fitz was a party to the jobbing. Nor am I 'beefing' about it at this late date. I am merely presenting facts as they occurred." The June 20 *Boston Post* quoted Joe: "I do not see any newspaper mention of the interference by them (police) at that time. When I sent Fitzsimmons to the boards ... with a lefthander on the jaw, I thought the jig was all up. He probably thought so about me in the 5th round, when police interfered again. He thinks that he would have won, I suppose, if the officers had let him alone. Well, I think I'd have won if they had let me alone." According to the June, 1919 *Police Gazette*, Fitz said, in his dressing room, "It's all right. I noticed there were no policemen handy, though, when I was all but out." No, but just possibly there was a friendly referee and a friendly bell-ringer.

Joe: "I was walking near Faneuil Hall in Boston a day or so after when suddenly I encountered Lanky Bob, himself. We shook hands and leaned against a doorway for a chat. Fitz's right eye was in mourning (blackened) and he wept, feeling his right cheekbone as we talked. 'This is 'ot enough for Haustralia,' he commented. I recalled the terrible heat in Sydney when I was training for Joe Goddard. This led to a discussion about old friends of Bob's I had met in Melbourne and Sydney." "The weather was terribly hot. 'That was some bloody wallop you 'anded me, Choynski!' he said. 'I know it,' I replied. 'But there's one thing I want to ask you, Bob: How did you ever manage to get up?' His reply was characteristic. 'I was thinking of what Rose would say,' he said. Rose was his wife, and more than once her benign influence helped Bob Fitzsimmons. And this time the thought of her pulled him off the floor when defeat started him in the face. I admired his spirit. But I could not then forget the raw deal I got."

The fight was generally felt to be a Fitzsimmons victory, as police ended the bout with Joe in dire straits. The controversy took a long time to subside. "Parson" Davies: "Joe was not himself ... anyone who witnessed the fight will bear me out ... if he had been, he would have finished Fitzsimmons in the 3rd round. We have no excuses to offer ... but I guarantee the next time the men meet, Joe will certainly be in better shape."

Joe Choynski and "Parson" Davies at Lake Quinsigamond, MA, June, 1894

Wheeling Register: "It would be interesting to know what Champ Corbett thinks of the performance of this apparently indomitable and irresistible whirlwind (Fitz) and of the prospect of meeting him."[9] A tongue-in-cheek Jewish editorial in the July 2 *Kansas City* (Missouri) *Times* said: "The glory hath departed from Israel!, says the *American Israelite*. Brother Joe Choynski failed to stand up for eight rounds before Fitzsimmons. The fight was called a draw, but Joseph was completely used up at the end of the 5th ... when police interfered. The fight was 'not for Joseph,' and the banner of Judah was trailed in the dust. There may be some consolation in ... a rumor to the effect that Peter Jackson is said to be of pure Jewish ancestry."

June 20 *Brooklyn Eagle*: "Joe ... looking none the worse ... paid the ... Associated press a visit last evening accompanied by Parson Davies ... When questioned about the battle Choynski said Fitzsimmons had promised him another chance and he would wait until that was over before talking about the night's contest ... Choynski weighed in two hours before the battle at 159 pounds, 1 ounce, while good judges claim Fitzsimmons weighed not ... less than 170." Mirroring the previous report, on June 22, Choynski and Davies visited the offices of the *Police Gazette*. Its reporter said that, other than a black eye, Joe did not show any effects of the battle. "The Parson" claimed his charge would have beaten Bob, if not for being overtrained. He said Choynski "only weighed 159½ pounds, when he should have weighed 175 pounds." As the men fought as heavyweights, there was no upper weight limit and they were not required to weigh in.

Joe wasn't satisfied that Fitz was his superior as a fighter and wanted a rematch, "at catchweights ... Choynski claims ... he overtrained ... too anxious to be in first-class condition, and after the 3rd round, when he had Fitzsimmons knocked out, he became suddenly weak."[10] Finishing 2nd to Bob was nothing to be ashamed of. "Ruby Robert" is even today considered near the top of the all-time "pound-for-pound" ratings. After winning the world middleweight title from Dempsey in 1891, Bob annexed the heavyweight championship in 1897 and completed his unprecedented triple crown by adding the world light-heavyweight diadem, in 1903.

The following year, Fitz told the *Brooklyn Daily Eagle*: "I was never so nearly going down and out in any fight before as I was on that occasion. The ring, as you remember, was an octagonal one and I had never fought in such a ring before. (Author: few fighters had!) Choynski ... followed me up to the corner ... I stepped aside to let one of his blows slip past me. I misjudged the distance and he gave me a hard clip over the right eye which dazed me, following it up with a smash on the jaw with his right that fairly had me going. I knew enough to keep at close quarters till the gong gave me a chance to recover and then ... I was all right and had matters pretty much my own way.' " Bob sometimes altered details of the clash over the years. March 24, 1912 *Washington Post*: "We were to have boxed six rounds ... a draw if both ... were on their feet at the end of the 6th. I knocked Choynski out six different times in four rounds; the last time he was out for 30 seconds. Why didn't the referee count him out? He must have clicked off the seconds with an hourglass. John L. Sullivan sat at ringside and said it was a blooming shame the way they robbed me. The police stopped the fight the last time I knocked Choynski stiff. 'Parson' Davies and his mob dragged Joe out of the ring, and he never came to for six hours. He fainted three times that night and collapsed the first time he tried to leave his room ... The Choynski affair convinced me there was only one way for Fitz to win – knock 'em in the head and kill 'em stone dead."[11]

Finally, a May 5, 1895 article offered: "Fitz was more than fortunate in Boston with Joe Choynski. The latter had more than held his man even in all the boxing, until he saw his chance and smashed Bob on the jaw with his left. Fitz was dazed, and Joe's right, a little too far back to be instantaneously effective, sent him to the stage on all fours ... with great difficulty he was able to get on his feet ... within ... 10 seconds. He was as groggy as a drunken sailor, but Choynski was too eager to give him the croup (sic) de grace. Fitz had both of his arms up guarding his jaws ... had Choynski steadied himself and given him one good punch on the 'mark' all would have been over. Instead, he was foolish enough to let Fitz close with him and clinch ... as they separated Fitz, who was now banging his arms about like the wings of a thrashing machine, landed on Joe's jaw and sent him to the floor. He is a far better general ... and he did not repeat the mistake the Californian made. But ... seemed unable to put him out."[12]

Choynski (1927): "After the Fitzsimmons fray, I took on two tough fellows who had been upsetting the plans of ambitious heavies. One was Frank Childs, the other Billy Stift. I stopped both in three rounds, at Chicago. I also stopped Mike Brennan in two rounds at Chicago; Jim Chamberlain, colored, in one round at Louisville; Ed Black in three rounds at Detroit ... Mike Queenan, in three rounds at Kansas City, and numerous other contenders ..." Only two of these appear on Joe's verified record, Stift and Childs. The former boxed exhibitions of unknown duration with Joe on November 5, 1894 and November 13, 1895, while Childs lost in six rounds to "The Hebrew Hammer" on December 1, 1902, both in Chicago. Each had wins over formidable fighters. Joe was likely referring to some of the bruisers he fought in Chicago on a "stay four rounds and win a purse" basis. It is considered a near-certainty that some fights are missing from his record, the case with most fighters from the early days of the Queensberry Era. The author has located a few of these fights.

The evening of July 26 saw Joe referee the Tommy Ryan-"Mysterious" Billy Smith world welterweight championship. It was held at the Twin City Athletic Club in Minneapolis, Minnesota and went the scheduled 20 rounds. Smith was the aggressor, chasing Ryan all over the ring, but unable to land his wicked right. Tommy remained on the defensive, landing left and right to the head with frequency, closing Smith's eye and drawing "first blood." A Decatur paper said he broke Smith's nose, as well. "Toward the last Smith slipped in the water in his corner and Ryan dazed him with a left in his jaw. From that time on he apparently had Smith at his mercy and yet was unable to knock him out." Choynski gave his decision to Ryan, though some felt a draw would have been a better call. Joe declared in 1914 that this was the most difficult fight he ever refereed, saying Ryan "managed to nose out a victory" by "better strategy and generalship."[13] Choynski and Ryan would soon become stablemates under Davies. Billy complained to the August 25 *Police Gazette* that Choynski "was bought by sporting men, and he could not have won with an ax." Although Smith and Ryan fought each other a recorded seven times, the best "Mysterious" could do was two draws, a No Decision and an 18-round No Contest in 1895. He lost three times to Ryan, including a 4th round knockout defeat in 1902.

While returning to Chicago on July 27, Choynski and Davies narrowly escaped calamity. Entering the city of Portage, Wisconsin aboard the Chicago, Milwaukee & St. Paul No. 6 train, there was a deadly collision. "The train struck an engine ... projecting far enough over the main track to cause a serious accident. Engineer A.H. Chadwick did not have time to save himself. All the passengers received bruises, but none was seriously hurt." At 3:00 a.m. on August 22 in Louisville, Kentucky, "Jim Hall ... training here for a fight with Joe Choynski, came near being killed ... He was shot at five times by his backer, Bob Gray, proprietor of the Pickwick café. The two were out on a spree and had been making the rounds of the saloons since midnight. Gray was very drunk and spending his money too freely to suit Hall, who tried to stop him and seized Gray. In an instant Gray had drawn his revolver and began firing. It was such a close range that the powder singed Hall's clothing. He retreated into the alcove near the door, and fortunately was unhurt. One of the bullets, however, passed through his coat on the right hand side, barely missing the flesh. Gray continued shooting until his revolver was empty. Hall immediately hustled his drunken friend into a coupe that was waiting, and together they left the place. After disposing of Gray, Hall began on another spree and drank all day. He is sober this morning and both men declare they are friends."[14]

On September 15, Joe defeated a Harry Miller in three rounds in Cincinnati. He battled Mike Boden, "The Canuck," at Tattersall's (in Chicago) on the 17th. This was another contest where Joe would knock out his opponent in four rounds or forfeit a purse. He went three rounds with Mike back in December, 1892. Boden, known as the "Trial Horse," found this 2nd meeting a trying ordeal. Choynski went right in at the first bell, intent on taking his bulky adversary out quickly. He floored him twice in round one, the first time by a hard right to the nose, drawing blood. Mike went into a crouch, but "The California Terror" raked his man with uppercuts to the face and stomach. The Chicago resident by way of Canada managed to survive the frame by clinching, but was bloody and staggering at the gong. In round two, the San Franciscan "made a chopping block of Boden's face," landing powerful uppercuts, one of which put his adversary through the ropes. Upon exiting the ring, Boden's body became entangled with Joe's, tripping him as time was called. In the 3rd, the Californian uppercut to the stomach. "Choynski went savagely at Boden ... and fought him around the ring, punching him without rest or mercy. Boden could not return a blow, and did not try to guard or dodge them. Choynski landed 32 blows in two minutes and Boden at last fell against the ropes, where he hung helpless and almost unconscious. (Referee) Carroll counted him out without a stir from the helpless man ..." and declared Joe the victor.[15]

April, 1943 *Ring* magazine: "Joe was a first-class wrestler, nor was he averse to 'fighting fire with fire.' When Boden tried foul tactics Choynski did the same, with improvements of his own. Referee Malachy Hogan openly yelled at Joe to — 'give that dirty dog a taste of his own medicine!' and Joe complied joyously. His speed made Boden look foolish, in no time he had Mike bleeding profusely from mouth and nose, at close quarters the bout became a regular cat and monkey session, with nothing barred. Boden fell several times without being hit, no doubt to be disqualified, but Hogan didn't interfere. In the 3rd ... Boden was battered from rope to rope, without being able to land a punch. At last he clutched Choynski desperately around the waist and hung on, refusing to break. Joe coolly fitted his left elbow into his opponent's throat, below the Adam's apple, and brought his right down like a hammer on top of the other glove. Boden gurgled, choked, relaxed his grip, sank to the floor, and lay there until counted out. It was by no means an ethical victory, but ... spectators cheered Choynski enthusiastically ... highly pleased at seeing Boden beaten at his own fouling game."

There must have been a dark cloud hanging over the latter half of 1894, as it was now Joe's turn to face an encounter with a gun. He and Davies were in Jackson, Michigan on September 21, where Choynski was to box 10 rounds with Joe Tansey, a Chicago native. That afternoon in Joe's hotel room, Davies was writing articles of agreement for an October 8 fight (which never occurred) between Choynski and Jim Hall at Tattersall's. As he put it: "Joe is always poking about. He looked in a small drawer of the bureau ... and there found a 44 Remington bulldog revolver. I saw him looking at it, but presently with a bang the cartridge exploded and Joe cried out, 'I am shot in the hand!' " The gun was accidentally discharged by Joe, the bullet passing through his right hand and shattering the metacarpal bone of the first finger. The bullet imbedded halfway in the wall, where it was dug out by "The Parson." A physician was called and presently a Dr. Wright arrived ... and dressed the wound. Several papers said it would take months for the wound to fully heal, one adding, that in all probability, "the California boy will never be able to enter the ring again." Others said the injury might "eventually disable him for life." This was mostly sensationalism, although the wound was career-threatening. Dr. Wright, after dressing the damaged hand said, "Joe's future as a pugilist depends on the union of the bones of the hand. It's a dangerous wound."[16]

On the 27th the pair arrived back in Chicago, where they sought out a local doctor. He removed the splints and bandages from Joe's hand and found it to be in "a terribly swollen and inflamed condition." The doctor told the men "it would be many months before he would again have the use of his hand and no ill effects would follow, providing proper care was taken." Joe was understandably upset, though he had no one to blame but himself. An October 3 telegraph stated that Joe was to referee the October 16 Tommy Tracey-Billy McCarthy fight in Madison, Illinois. No further mention is found of this, so the hand injury may have necessitated him begging out. An October 25 dispatch from Cincinnati noted: "The cheap prizefighters will have to go. The officials view with suspicion the multiplying boxing clubs and influx of unwelcome guests. Frank Maciewski, Joe Choynski's cousin, was picked up today and told to get something to do or get out of town. Others will be compelled to go. Charley Slusher of

Louisville was put behind bars."[17] Maciewski, the fighting cousin of Choynski, who went four rounds with American lightweight champion Austin Gibbons in 1892 and lost in nine to New Zealand bantamweight "Torpedo" Billy Murphy in 1895, is only mentioned one other time, as is known, by Joe himself (see chapter 15).

An October 14 article, "The Knockout Blow, What Is It?," read: "Joe Choynski has settled many a foe by jabbing uppercuts under the chin. Joe favors a short swing, preferably with the left, as more apt to catch men unawares, but his specialty is a lightning uppercut. 'That sort of a blow,' says Choynski, 'checks a foul fighter, scares a timid boxer, and stands off a clinch. It must be quickly given and is not really a knockout, but ... staggers ... and paves the way for a final swing or jab.' " This "jabbing uppercut" sounds like a variation of the left hook, which Joe was an early exponent of. *New York Illustrated News*: "His ambition at present is to ... sail for England under the management of 'Parson' Davies and get a go with the 'Harlem Coffee Cooler'."[18] This was Frank Craig, a good, black middleweight and light-heavyweight whose résumé was loaded with the best boxers of his day. Joe never fought Frank Craig.

Tommy Ryan, 1890s

Despite the prognosis that it would take several months for his hand to heal, it was announced on November 1 that Joe had regained use of the mitt and would spar daily with Tommy Ryan, at Duplessis' gym in Chicago. Ryan was preparing for a fight with Jack Dempsey in December at New Orleans. Tommy Ryan was born Joseph Youngs (or Younges) on March 31, 1870 in the tiny glass-making hamlet of Redwood, New York. He was now living in Chicago and had become a member of Davies' stable of fighters. *Oakland Tribune*: "In order to give both Ryan and Choynski work and afford amusement for spectators, Professor Duplessis has arranged to give a boxing programme at the gymnasium every afternoon." Although unverified, Joe was said to have boxed an exhibition of unknown duration with Billy Stift, on November 5. On the 6th, he helped prepare former opponent Billy Woods for his fight with Jim Hall at Tattersall's.[19] A man of Joe's size who punched with his force, usually had brittle bones of the hand, like Fitzsimmons. Joe did suffer from this, to an extent. Muhammad Ali also had delicate hands, while George Foreman and Sonny Liston had the fortuitous physiology of durability, with fists like iron mallets.

Pugs and Pigskin – On Saturday, November 10, Joe and a group of boxers took in a college football game between Chicago and Lake Forest (Illinois). Amusing coverage follows: "The crowd ... contained one group ... probably never before seen on a college football field. Wrapped in their heaviest overcoats the prizefighters of Chicago watched and wondered ... Their mission was one of investigation and comparison, as one ... expressed ... (featherweight) Tommy White conceived the ... visit to the football field ... brought Frank Garrard, Lou Agnew and little Charley Mason; Harry Gilmore and tiny Jimmy Barry arrived together with Arthur Schultz ... Casper Leon came up from Roby ... Frank O'Neil journeyed in from Lyons. Big Joe Choynski came late and had Joe Bertrand and Sid Huntington in tow. Every man in the party was well dressed and clean shaven. At 3:30, the football players came on the field. 'Big, husky fellows,' said Frank Garrard. 'They seem to be in great condition.' A Chicago man kicked off the ball, and big Hayner caught it. He started up the field, and six men intercepted him. Two flopped him on his head, one pushed his face into the sod, and the rest fell over him in a heap. Jimmy Barry's eyes stuck out. 'Can you throw a man and then fall on him that way?' 'Hot stuff,' said Lou Agnew ... 'What sort of rules are these, anyway? ... that guy hit the fellow in black sleeves twice below the belt ... then threw him!' 'London Rules, I guess,' said Choynski. 'Under London Rules you can throw your man.' "

"Chicago gained the ball on four downs ... Rice of Lake Forest broke through and tackled the Chicago runner. Somebody kicked him in the shoulder, and little Jimmy Barry threw up both hands and cried: 'The sneaking brutes!' A punt was muffed ... and Hirschberger of Chicago burst through for a gain of 20 yards. 'Good boy!' said Charley Mason. 'He used his head on one fellow and his knees on another, though. How many fouls can a man make in this game, anyway?' Johnson of Lake Forest caught Flint of Chicago around the neck and squeezed his throttle till he was black in the face. 'Why don't the referee yell for them to break?' asked Joe Bertrand. 'A man who chokes another in the ring gets hissed by the crowd.' Things grew hotter in the 2nd half. It was dark and the Chicagoans began to roll up points. Exasperated by their sure defeat, the Lake Forest men began to slug. The prizefighters looked on in horror. There was a crash and the rival Captains – Allen and Hayner – reeled back from a collision and fell heavily. A surgeon came from the crowd. 'Thoughtful of the management,' said Sid Huntington. 'Wonder if they have an undertaker ready, too!' Joe Choynski ... was counting off the seconds. He muttered 'ten' and stopped. 'Both those fellows (are) knocked out,' he said. 'Why don't they take them away and take care of them?' Bleeding from several scratches, the prostrate gladiators rose and resumed hostilities. 'Great guns!' cried Casper Leon. 'Do they let men go back and play after a fall like that? A prize ring referee would never let fighters go on when they were punished that way.' "

"A pitched battle was going on at the north end of the field and fists fell like blacksmiths' hammers. Whenever the referee turned his back there was a fight. The players did not seem to care, but the astounded prizefighters actually shuddered. Harry Gilmore broke out a moment later, when seven Lake Forests jumped on Roby of Chicago and eight of Roby's colleagues overwhelmed Jewett, the big colored half back. 'Those fellows,' said the ex-lightweight, 'do things that simply would not be tolerated in the prize ring. If a fighter uses such tactics he is barred from the ring and his name is hated by all sporting men.' A shrill squeak from the referee announced that time was up. The players, spangled with red scratches, broke for their dressing rooms. There had been little slugging, and the men had, as a rule, played like gentlemen. But the pugilists failed to see it just that way. When the fray was over and the fighters were started for home, Tommy White voiced the sentiments of the delegation. 'Prize fighting is brutal and must be stopped by law. Football is gentlemanly and must be upheld and encouraged. But as to the humanity or inhumanity of boxing and football, we can only say – see both games – then judge as to which is the more brutal.' " In 1896, Joe rendered this opinion: "The very makeup of the players – their leather head cases, ear, eye, nose and mouth protectors, the fact that their whole bodies were thoroughly padded – proves that each and every one of them expects to be injured." In 1895, a reference was made to the Corbett-Fitzsimmons fight. A cartoon showed a (gridiron) football player lying on his back on the playing field, an opposing player stomping on him with his spikes. It was suggested that "As football players, they could pull off the big mill without danger of legal interference."[20]

James J. Jeffries, who reigned as world heavyweight champion from June 9, 1899 until retiring undefeated in May, 1905, witnessed his first college football game on November 11, 1899. He also commented on the hypocrisy involved with those who campaigned against boxing for its brutality, while promoting or condoning football. "I never looked at so much lively slugging and roughing in all the years I've been in the fighting business. If I had to take my choice between having a man punch me as hard as he could or run 10 yards and jump on me with his shoulder against my stomach, I think I'd take the punch ... But I don't kick about it as lots of these football supporters kick against fighting. I notice that under these football rules they give a knocked-out man three minutes to recover and get (back) into the game. It means he has a chance to get hurt 18 times as much at football as ... at fighting. Under Queensberry rules a man who can't go on fighting within 10 seconds after he is knocked down is out of the game. That's a merciful rule. Next time the good people make a roar about prize-fighting I'll know what is their idea of a pleasant, easy, safe sport."[21]

In a November issue of the *Philadelphia Item*, Choynski wrote on the topic, "How Did You Ever Become A Boxer?" "The question ... has been asked me so often that I have concluded to write a short sketch of my career. At the age of 17 I started in to learn to box, just for my own amusement ... I entered for an amateur heavyweight ... finally winning the Pacific coast championship. I then decided to give boxing up, as I had the refusal of a position in a San Francisco bank. At the same time the California Club directors were after me to meet Frank Glover, of Chicago, for a $1,500 purse." I found two articles claiming that young Joe held the position of "cash boy," either in a bank or department store in Frisco.[22] "My people were ... against professional boxing, so I went as an unknown ... a few days before the contest it was known that I was to go against a man of Glover's reputation, and being my first professional contest, (Joe usually calls the earlier George Bush fight his pro debut) the knowing ones had me defeated before it came off. The $1,500 seemed a big sum to me and easily won, so I concluded to try my luck at boxing, thinking it much easier and far more remunerative than working in a bank."

"I ... conceived the idea of going to Australia for pleasure and to pick up any business that might turn up. The climate was such, however, that I was never very well. Mr. Davies and I ... went to England, where I offered $50 to any one whom I could not stop in three rounds. With Mr. Davies I visited all the principal countries of Europe ... on pleasure ... I boxed Bob Fitzsimmons a draw in Boston last June, and had him out in the 3rd round when police stopped it. We continued ... and he had the best ... when police stopped it again. I hadn't a mark on me, while Fitz had several; he should have won easily, as I was in no condition to meet any one. I only weighed 158 pounds, and my proper weight when well is 170 pounds. I would like a return contest with Fitzsimmons if it could be arranged. I stopped Mike Boden in Chicago a couple of months ago – something no man has ever done ... I was matched to meet Jim Hall ... but I shot myself in the right hand. It is now as strong as ever and I have every confidence in it. I would like very much to meet Steve O'Donnell or Maher. I am a candy-maker by trade but have not followed it for several years."

On December 8, Joe and Davies arrived in New Orleans to assist Tommy Ryan for his fight with Dempsey. Ryan was training at "Captain Smith's place." Also there were Jimmy Barry, "Kid" McCoy and Jim Hall. A group photo from this time was taken, presumably at "Captain Smith's." Choynski wrote a caption years later, saying: "Yours, sitting at left. Tommy Ryan and bird. Jimmy Barry: Bantam, under bag, and his 'detective' friend. Kid McCoy, behind Barry. Ryan training to meet Dempsey the Nonpareil:

postponed – met in NY, Ryan won: Dempsey (illegible) referee stopped it. We all knew Jack was in. Ryan did not attempt to hit him. McCoy (illegible) Superintendent???" On the 13th, after sparring with Choynski, Ryan said he was in fine condition.[23]

Two days later, his fight with Dempsey was cancelled, for reasons that were sketchy. The fight was rescheduled and held at Coney Island in January, 1895. Ryan and Choynski began a sparring engagement on December 19 in Chicago. A few days

L-R, front, Unknown, Joe Choynski, Tommy Ryan, Jimmy Barry, Barry's detective friend; back, Unknown, Johnny Lavack, Unknown, Kid McCoy. December, 1894, Ryan training for Dempsey. Joe's hand wound is visible.

later, Davies announced plans for a trip to England, in search of fights. He sent a cablegram to Atkinson of The London *Sporting Life*, wagering $2,500 that Ryan could defeat any fighter in England of from 140 to 144 pounds. Another $2,500 was for a match between Choynski and any heavyweight in England, Peter Jackson excepted and Frank Craig preferred, for the heavyweight championship of England. "In case the latter does not accept, this challenge (is) open to England's boxing champions ..."[24]

Beginning the new year, Davies leased the cottage at Asbury Park, New Jersey, where Jim Corbett trained for the 1892 John L. Sullivan bout, and had it "fitted up for training quarters ... He has with him Tommy Ryan, Joe Choynski, Jimmy Barry, Bob Armstrong ... and Harry Pigeon, Ryan's trainer." Barry, the 105-pound champion, was to be matched against Kid Madden on the card. Jimmy became a Hall of Famer. Joe Choynski said, in 1927: "Barry ... the greatest fighter I ever saw. He had everything: speed, science, stamina, ring generalship, courage and uncanny punching power. There were many great bantams in that day, but Barry outclassed them all ..."[25] Armstrong was a recent addition to Davies' stable. He was a large, strong fighter, later referred to as "the greatest sparring partner who ever lived," due to his uncanny ability to mimic the style of any boxer.

Davies' secretary, Harry Glickauf, scouted two of Armstrong's bouts late in 1894. Sometime early in 1895, Davies' had Choynski box a few rounds with Bob, as a tryout. Charlie told Joe not to spare Armstrong, so "The Terror" was tough on him. "Choynski was a master scientist as well as a cruel puncher, and he let himself out at top speed in the three rounds they sparred. Knowing every trick and move in the game, it was inevitable that Choynski should outbox and punish the Negro youth, but Bob stood the gaff heroically and, when the bout was over, Choynski showed the effects of the visitations of Armstrong's straight left by a cut lip and a distinct swelling under his right eye. But the net result proved that Armstrong was worth developing, and so Joe stated candidly to Davies."[26] In early January, Ryan was training with Choynski for a May 27 rematch with "Mysterious" Billy Smith, at Coney Island. Tommy apparently wasn't aware yet of his rescheduled bout with Dempsey. "Choyinski (sic) has been doing light exercise prior to going into active training for his 25-round 'go' with Jim Hall, which comes off June 17 ... At present he weighs 163 pounds. 'Bob' Armstrong ... seems ... the making of a clever boxer. He is 21 years old ... 6' 4" ... 210 pounds, and a finely-proportioned fellow."[27]

Joe had a gig to pose and show off his muscles at the National Cycle Show in Chicago, beginning January 7 "in the 'twin armories' on the Lake Front ... Cycle shows have been held before in the East, but this is the first attempt ... in the West ... Postmaster Hesing will ... make a brief speech showing the rapid development in the manufacture of bicycles, and the important part they are destined to play in the transmission of mails and on the battlefield. The 2nd Regiment Armory Building will be devoted exclusively to exhibits of ... the wheel ... In the Battery ... tires and bicycle accessories ... at 3 o'clock each day a grand concert will be given by the 2nd Regiment Band. On the stage ... each afternoon and evening, will be given living pictures about which there will be nothing indelicate, although several female figures will be pressed into service. Joe Choynski ... will appear to show the muscular development advanced by constant use of the wheel. Zimmerman will appear as the champion cyclist, and John S. Johnson as the champion skater. Sanger and other famous cyclists will lend their aid ..." The show ran all week, from 1:00 p.m. to 10:30 p.m.[28]

"Choynski has found that life as a 'living picture' is not all it is cracked up to be. Joe, when not boxing, spends a good part of his spare time ... sailing about the town on a high-priced bicycle. When managers of the Chicago cycle show were casting about for subjects for their living pictures, it was suggested that the famous boxer would make a good one, being of excellent form and ... good looking. Joe ... consented to pose at so much per. How much was it worth to the cycle show? Well ... about $5 a day for two performances. 'What, $5 a day!' almost screamed the big Californian.

'Why, I wouldn't disarrange my scarf for that amount. You had better send for Fitzsimmons; He'll do it for $2.50 just to spite me, or ... telegraph to Texas for Corbett. He'll do it for nothing if he knows it was offered to me.' The ... show people hastened to placate the indignant boxer, and after a discussion, Joe's ruffled feathers were smoothed down, and he left the building a full-fledged 'living picture' – but the price has not been divulged."[29]

The penultimate night of the cycle show was the 11th, and Joe received hearty applause. Afterward, he left for New York to second Tommy Ryan. In early January, long-time friend and backer, Mose Gunst, was appointed Police Commissioner of San Francisco, a move that surprised many and scandalized some. The cigar merchant had, after all, been deeply involved in prize-fighting. Born in New York in 1854, Gunst moved to Frisco in 1873. He began in the cigar trade in 1877, becoming wealthy. Mose started in boxing as the backer and advisor of John L.

Mose Gunst: Circa 1892 (top); With San Francisco Police Department, 1896 (bottom)

Sullivan, after "The Strong Boy" and manager, Billy Madden, had a falling out. Gunst soon took a fancy to other pugilists, such as Joe Choynski. He became a director and matchmaker for the California A.C., and was involved in gambling houses. "He is a Hebrew by birth, an atheist by election. Of inordinate vanity, he has always managed to crowd his name into print, and to his own efforts as much as any other ... is due the fame he enjoys." Ironically, it was said that Gunst would devote his time to combating that "evil" known as gambling.[30]

Ryan and Choynski left for New York on January 13, and finished training at the new Manhattan Athletic Club. The referee was famed baseball umpire, Tim Hurst. *Inter-Ocean*: "Ryan ... is an adept at bag punching ... many ... claim he is the superior of ... Corbett and Fitzsimmons. Ryan is willing to meet either in a competition of this kind ... Davies will back him for ... $500 to $1,000."[31] An article wrote of wealthy businessmen and youths of "leisure" who, while not daring to publicly patronize boxing, boxed in gyms to stay in shape. It said these men "would rather be handy with the gloves than shine in society. Joe Choynski, a quiet and well-behaved boxer, has visited all the good athletic clubs and put on gloves with ... the blue-book families. He said ... some of the best men he ... met were ... gentlemen who take up gymnasium work for fun ... and to ... condition ... some ... if they chose to give up stock speculation or the law, might ... become champions. Most ... would not attend a ... prize-fight, but when the champion pugilist visits the club he is ... made welcome. Pugilism is in great disfavor at present, but ... the man who has shown skill, strength and generalship within the padded ropes commands ... respect among a class of men not commonly known as ring-followers."[32]

On January 18 at the Seaside Athletic Club, the Ryan-Dempsey fight was one of the few in that time scheduled for 15 rounds to a decision, knockouts allowed. Often, the bout was halted by the law if violent blows were thrown. Limited-distance bouts were scheduled from four to 45 rounds. Referee Hurst would decide who was ahead in the fight, if it was stopped short by police. The stipulation was winner take all, primarily to present to the public the illusion that the boxers were desperate to win, rather than train and fight for no compensation. In reality, a secret agreement was often reached to split the purse 60-40 or 75-25.[33]

Dempsey's performance was so pathetic, Hurst ordered the men to their corners in the middle of round three, awarding the welterweight championship to Ryan. Jack's ineptitude was probably due to consumption. The next day, "a representative of the Atlantic Athletic club had a talk with (Joe at Coney Island, about) a match with Peter Maher. Choynski said he would meet Maher ... but ... not ... within two months ... Choynski's hand is not strong yet ..."[34] The *Chicago Inter-Ocean* said, on the 20th: "The following dispatch ... from Charles E. Davies ... Coney Island, N.Y., Jan. 19 ... 'Ryan and myself remain East several weeks. Have numerous engagements offered. Choynski left for Chicago today. He marries Miss Louise Miller, of my last season's 'Uncle Tom' company, January 26 in Cincinnati.' "

Round Eleven

Lutie Miller

Louise Anderson Miller was born in Cincinnati, Ohio, one of nine children to Thomas S. Miller and the former Mary Susan Gossin. The date was March 3; the year: 1871, according to her death certificate and headstone, but 1870, from the 1870 United States Federal Census. Mary was born October 29, 1826, also in Cincinnati, to Henry Gossin and Susan Bowman. The records pertaining to Thomas are sketchy and the overall family records have more than their share of discrepancies. He was born somewhere in Virginia, either in 1823 or 1824, probably the latter. Thomas moved to Ohio sometime before 1850, and met Mary Gossin. They married in July, 1845. Their first child, Florence, was born in 1849 in the vicinity of Cincinnati. Strangely, while her proper name appears in several Censuses, Florence is listed as "Isabell" in the 1880 version. The 1850 Census lists Thomas' occupation as Wagon Maker, and the three are living in Sycamore Township (Olde West Chester), Hamilton County, Ohio.

The Miller's second offspring, Amanda M., didn't arrive until 1852. She is referred to as Amanda in all but the 1870 Census, where she is called "Mallie." The 1853 Williams' Cincinnati City Directory gives the family address as 523 Sycamore and lists Thomas as a laborer. Jennie B. Miller was born in either 1855 or 1856, followed by Julia C. in 1858. The 1857 Directory shows a T.S. Miller, probably Thomas, as a clerk for the County Treasurer's Office, no residence given. Continuing the string of inconsistencies, Julia is referred to in the 1870 record as "Kittie." Ella was born in 1860. That year's Census shows the family living in the "East Half, 15th Ward, Cincinnati," where Thomas is still a Clerk. The value of their "real estate" was a meager $150 and their "personal estate" valued at $450. As Ella is not listed in that record, created in June, she was born in the 2nd half of the year. Next in line was Etta T. Miller, born November 4, 1861.

After six daughters in a row, Mary gave birth to the couple's first son in 1864, whom they named Thomas H. Miller. A 2nd son, Albert, followed in 1866, after which came the birth of Joe's future spouse, Louise. She first appears in the 1870 Census as Louise or "Louisa," the cursive script of the census taker being almost illegible. Her age is given as 3/12, as the directive was "Age at last birthday. If under one year, give months in fractions ..." This places her birth in March, 1870. (The 1880 Census gives her name as "Lulu"). In 1870 the family was living in "Cincinnati South's 16th Ward" and Thomas (the father) was a Laborer. Mary is "Keepinghouse" and the two oldest daughters, Florence and Amanda ("Mallie") are seamstresses.[1] 1880 saw the family living at 298 George Street in Cincinnati.

Little was known about Louise Miller before this book was written, and less about her family. She told Joe that she began singing, acting and performing at the age of *four*.[2] At some point in her childhood, Louise was given the nickname, "Lutie." In this manner she was most commonly referred to in reports of her stage performances. It turns out there was similar talent in her family, as sisters Ella and Etta also became successful theater personalities. Other "Millers" prominent on the stage were Julia, Kittie, Albert, Jennie and Mary. A famous actress known as Florence Miller performed in Cincinnati in March, 1894 and in Walnut Hills at Kissel's Garden on June 26, 1894. It has not been verified, though, that any of these were members of Lutie's family. Etta was the first of the three sisters documented as a theatrical entertainer. In October and November, 1877, she performed in various parts of Illinois with "The Golden Troupe," headed by Martin and Bella Golden. She did the same with George Kendall's Dramatic Company, from late 1881 through early 1882.[3]

Etta's career was not without drama behind the curtain, as well. On January 11, 1885, she charged her manager with attempted rape. The *New York Clipper* reported on the 13th: "Sheldon Bateman, manager of the 'Romany Rye' Company playing here last week, was arrested night before last as he was about to leave town with his company. He is charged by Miss Etta Miller, a stage-struck damsel, with an attempt at rape, and at the hearing to-day was held for court in default of 1,000 dollars bail. The impression prevails to some extent that he is as much sinned against as sinning. There was a pseudo newspaper man named W.P. Pinkerton a party to the case, sailing under the alias of Livingston. There is a warrant for his arrest, but he has skipped the town and Bateman is left to stand the brunt. He has not yet secured bail, in quest of which I noticed him in the Opera-house last night, in charge of a detective."[4] No more is found of the case, so whether Etta dropped the charges, someone was convicted or if the case remained unsolved, is a mystery. Not surprisingly, Etta's name is never again found associated with Bateman or his Romany Rye Company.

September 29, 1883 marks Lutie Miller's first known appearance as an entertainer. The event took place at D.W. Andre's Opera House in Connersville, Indiana, in the war drama, "A Soldier of the Union; or, a Woman's Devotion." She captivated her audience. The October 18 *New York Dramatic Mirror* said: "Little Lutie Miller, a beautiful child of 11, elicited great applause by her exquisite singing and dancing. She was repeatedly recalled." A 2nd performance followed on October 1. It is clear that from an early age, Louise was a natural performer.

On June 13, 1885, the *Clipper* reported from Cincinnati the first mention found of Ella as an actress. "Ella Miller, soubrette, is lying very ill at her house in this city." The nature of the ailment wasn't revealed, but she recovered. Ella's name dominated the headlines for a time, as far as the family goes. She was in Parkersburg, West Virginia just before November 20, 1885, in a play entitled, "Ten-mile Crossing." Soon after, she had her own troupe, as revealed by the *Clipper*: "The Ella Miller Co. disbanded last week ..."[5] Sometime between then and July, 1886, Ella's younger sister, Etta T. Miller, married fellow thespian Frank L. Lewis. The July 24, 1886 *New York Clipper* featured an article by Louis Pierce, manager of the Octagon Comedy Company, which read: "Wanted ... Full Dramatic Company, for a season of 40 weeks, first-class, singing soubrette. Would be pleased to hear from old friends, Etta Miller Lewis ... please write." Etta kept her name as "Etta Miller" for a few years yet, before going by "Etta T. Lewis."

Lutie is next found at the Grand Central Theatre in Covington, Kentucky on January 23, 1886, in a company run by a P.J. Williams. She is 16. On December 9, she was involved in an amusing incident: "We know a young man in this city who thinks himself a great masher. (He) holds the credentials of a well-known dramatic and sporting paper ... The other evening when as Dolly Dutton, Miss Lutie Miller, who plays with the Standard Company at the Opera House, sang her flower song and threw button-hole boquets to people in the audience, this smooth, no-flies-on-him, dramatic correspondent was sitting in the front row. He ogled and smiled and tried in every way to attract the attention of the singer, but the boquets 'didn't come his way.' His disappointment was laughable, but not so much as this surprised and injured sir, when he told a friend the story and said, 'I don't see why she threw all the flowers to old, gray-headed men.' These would-be mashers will try their wiles on the wrong actress some time, and one of the 'awful' topical songs which can score anybody in the audience, selected by the singer, will make them drop with a d-l a-g t-d."

"The Blondell & Bowers company played 'Fanchon' at the Opera House last night to a good house. Miss Miller, the soubrette of the company, took the leading role, and with the exception of the shadow dance, played it well. Miss Miller is a versatile actress and appears equally well in parts as widely different as Moselle in 'Nevada' and Fanchon. To-night, the company appears in the great Irish drama, Colleen Bawn, with Miss Miller as 'Eily O'Connor.' " "One of the best of all Irish plays ... It will be finely rendered by the Standard Theatre Company, with S.D. Blondell and Miss Lutie Miller in the roles of Denny Mann and Eily O'Connor."[6] The term "soubrette" signifies a petite actress and soprano singer, described as young, saucy, mischievous, coy and often flirtatious.

On December 11, Louise appeared at the same venue in "The Little Detective." "Miss Lutie Miller did the character parts incident to the impersonation of the leading role in the 'Little Detective' at the Opera House last night. Miss Miller played her several parts well, being particularly taking as the dude. Mr. Blondell and Mr. Harris upheld the comedy element in a most happy manner, Mr. Blondell as Patsey Burnstein, a Jew, and Mr. Harris as Ikey Schwartzkoff, a German. Mr. George Peckham, the genial flute player of the Newark Orchestra, has been having a horrible time ... this week. 'Peck's' head is, as every theatre-goer knows, almost devoid of hirsute appendage, and shines in the footlights' glare like a billiard ball. Miss (chievous) Lutie Miller ... sings several songs in which kissing and bald headed men figure prominently, and when she needs an apt illustration she is wont to step to the front of the stage, and demonstrate her vocal lectures with Mr. Peckham as a subject ... of a hearty laugh, but we understand he is getting awful tired of acting the rob, of a 'horrible' example."[7]

The *Newark Daily Advocate* said: "The Standard Theatre Company ... in part of comedy talent is one of the strongest seen here at cheap prices, and left an impression ... that will be of much service to them upon their return ... Messrs. Blondell and Harris, and Miss Lutie Miller are enough in themselves to pack the house ..." The company closed a four-night engagement at the Mansfield, Ohio Opera House on New Year's Day, 1887, the *New York Mirror* noting, "The soubrette and life of the company is Lutie Miller."[8] January 8 *Daily Advocate*: "The favorite Standard Theatre Company No. 1, with the charming little soubrette, Lutie Miller, will play a return engagement at the Opera House of one week, commencing Monday, January 17. For that engagement they will present 'Joshua Whitcomb,' 'Streets of New York,' 'Cousin Joe' and other plays and farces in addition to the excellent repertoire when the company was last here."

On the 14th the Newark paper noted, "Miss Lutie Miller, the universal favorite of dozens of cities, will be seen in new songs and dances, and will, we are confident, largely increase her list of admirers among Newark theatre goers. Monday evening the great New England rural comedy 'Joshua Whitcomb' will be presented with L.D. Blondell as Uncle Josh and Lutie Miller as Little Dot (sic), the crossing sweeper." January 17 saw the team begin their solid week of plays at the Opera House, with a change of bill each night. Announcing the Standard Company as the "Strongest Dramatic Company on the Road," the paper's ad of the 15th focused on only one player. It billed "The charming soubrette, Miss Lutie Miller!" and said she "Will appear in new characters, with new songs and dances." Ticket prices were only 10¢, 20¢ and 30¢.[9] A Frank Lewis is mentioned as part of the acting contingent, and is probably the husband of sister Etta.

"Vivacious Lutie Miller as Tot, the crossing sweeper, broke everybody all up. She sings and dances better than she did before, and is so pretty and natural that she doesn't seem to be acting at all, but merely impersonating a pure, girlish character, all her own. To-night the company will play their *piece de resistance*, the 'Little Detective,' in which Miss Miller assumes six characters." "This piece has proven one of the greatest favorites in the company's repertory, and is always demanded a 2nd time during a week's engagement." Most reports name Louise's character as "Little Tot, the crossing sweeper," so "Dot" was evidently a typo.[10] The paper's review on the 19th said, "The Standard Theatre Co. gave a pleasing rendition of Lotta's favorite comedy, the 'Little Detective' ... last night. Little Lutie Miller, in the character part of the dude, one of six changes, 'just paralyzed' everybody. Mr. Blondell and Mr. Harris, as Ikey and Jakey, the Jewish and German crooks, were very funny. Mr. (R.W.) Raymond played the villain elegantly."

No review is found for Wednesday night's (January 19) "Streets of New York," but the following evening, they "gave a fine rendition of Boucicault's great Irish drama, the 'Colleen Bawn' ... The stage setting of the 4th act, representing the lake, was very pretty. The moonlight effect, as Myles La Copaleen (Mr. Harris) rescues Eily O'Connor (Miss Miller) from the water, was beautiful and called forth rounds of applause. Miss Lutie Miller, as Eily O'Connor ... was very taking. To-night, the great melodrama, Nevada, with Mr. Blondell as the darky, Jupe, and Miss Lutie Miller as Moselle." The "Streets of New York" was also a creation of legendary playwright Dion Boucicault (1820-1890). After Friday's performance of "Nevada," "Messrs. Blondell, Bower and Lewis and Miss Lutie Miller visited Cincinnati friends ... Sunday."[11] July 16 *New York Clipper.* "Lutie Miller goes with Esther Lyons' Co. next season. She is a clever little soubrette." The August 27 *Clipper* said Ella would leave on the 30th for Pittsburgh (Pennsylvania) to join Peter Baker's "Chris and Lena" Company.

By September 12, Louise had left the Standard Theatre Company and joined a troupe called the "Early Birds." They made their New York debut that afternoon at the London Theatre, "at which time the house was packed to suffocation. You couldn't move ..." After the first several acts, of singing, acting, banjo and a trapeze performer, the paper noted, " 'She,' a burlesque on the present Haggard craze, introduced the whole company. The bright music, credited to Fred Solomon, goes nicely. The show ... should prove a remunerative undertaking. Next week, the Night Owls."[12]

The September 28 *Hamilton Democrat* tells of the first and one of the rare occasions when Lutie's older sisters, Ella and Etta, performed together. "Blondell & Bowers' Standard Theatre Company No. 1 will appear for one week at Globe Opera House (Hamilton, Ohio) commencing Monday, Oct. 3d ... Lizzie Evans' Maud Muller, Lotta's Little Detective, The Western Border Drama, Nevada and many more, introducing songs and dances at every performance. Miss Etta Miller, the charming soubrette, is a sister to Ella and Lutie. Ella Miller will also be here with the company." Other notables were Daisy Pryor, L.D. Blondell, Dick Raymond, Frank Lewis and manager Cooney Bowers. (They) "traveled all through Ohio, Pennsylvania and West Virginia ... pronounced by press and public the best popular price company on the road." Louise traded spots with Ella, as the latter joined the Standard troupe, while "Lutie" was now with Baker's "Chris and Lena" combination. "Mr. Pete Baker, the German comedian, began his engagement at the Windsor Theater last night in 'Chris and Lena.' The performance was well received by a large audience. Lutie Miller, a good singer and dancer, made a very favorable impression." It was announced on October 8 that "Peter F. Baker ... proposes to make a trip to Germany with Chris and Lena next summer. He will be accompanied by ... Lutie Miller ... and Manager Thomas R. Perry."[13] The trip didn't happen.

Ella and Etta began a five night stand with Standard Theatre Company No. 1 at Wallace's Opera House in Newark, Ohio, premiering the evening of November 15. They starred in "Lotta's Little Detective," "Moselle," "Maud Muller," "Under the Gaslight" and "Streets of New York." Moselle was the main character in the play "Nevada," and the role of "Dandy Dick" was played by Ella. A November 9 ad noted: "Miss Ella Miller, the charming, singing and dancing soubrette ... will be remembered in Newark – playing ... last season with Pete Baker's Chris & Lena Co., assuming the character of Lena. Miss Etta Miller, sister to Ella ... will ... sing some of the most popular songs of the day." It also noted, "Miss Ella Miller, of Lancaster, O. killed an immense blacksnake in her bedroom." Tough actress! The *Newark Advocate* said the ladies, along with Cara Pryor, were "three of the best singing and dancing soubrettes on the stage." A Frank Lewis (apparently Etta's husband) was (still) with the company. The November 11 *Advocate* said "Miss Ella Miller, the charming soubrette ... played her last engagement in Newark with Pete Baker's Chris & Lena Company."[14] The *Newark Advocate* covered the week's performances, Ella and Etta in various roles. "Among some of the new features (were) Miss Ella Miller, as Dan the newsboy, introducing songs and dances."[15]

Louise was still starring with the Pete Baker Company in "Chris and Lena." In January and February, 1888, they played in such cities as Milwaukee, Wisconsin, Joliet, Illinois and Kansas City, Missouri. "Lutie Miller is a charming little soubrette with a sweet voice and made quite a hit as Lena." "Pete Baker is about as fine a German character-actor as struts the boards to-day. He can make more fun standing still than a dozen other character-actors can by strutting. His supporting company is good, especially Lutie Miller ... The engagement is proving a grand success."

"Last evening ... The role of Lena was very acceptably filled by Lutie Miller, who sings nicely and dances gracefully. The songs of ... Miss Miller, were ... frequently encored. Mr. 'Pete' Baker is ... one of the veterans of the stage, though ... 20 years in the profession has scarcely left a trace on his well-rounded features. 'Chris and Lena' is to him what 'Rip Van Winkle' is to Joe Jefferson and 'Davy Crockett' is to Frank Mayo. It has been a good many years and ... many thousands of miles since he first appeared as the jolly German. He has produced 'Chris and Lena' in all the leading cities of

Europe, South America, Australia and New Zealand."[16]

The company were in New Orleans, Louisiana, the week of March 23. Review extracts: "The Lena of Miss Lutie Miller is a very pleasing performance. This little lady has a good and powerful voice, is a graceful dancer, and puts into her role all the vivacity and *naïveté* it requires. Her imitation of the German accent is as natural as possible. One of the hits of the evening was a burlesque of the Sullivan and Mitchell prize-fight ... The *Daily Picayune.*" "Chris and Lena is a musical comedy in four acts and has been played by Mr. Baker over 2,000 times. Miss Miller is a charming soubrette, and is possessed of a sweet voice. She rendered a number of new songs, and was the recipient of considerable applause. - *Times-Democrat.*" They were requested to remain another week.[17]

The next report wasn't until May 20, 1888, when they played Jacobs and Proctor's Opera House in Utica, New York. "The *Cleveland Plain Dealer* says: A good house laughed at the German dialect comedy of P.F. Baker ... The principal improvement ... is ... that Lena is no longer played by a female impersonator, not a welcome sight to an average audience, but by a handsome and talented young actress, Miss Lutie Miller, who became quite a favorite shortly after her first appearance. She is a good singer and knows how to make herself liked. Mr. Baker has discarded most of his old songs and introduced ... new ones. 'I'm Sorry You're Going Away,' 'Happy and Free,' and his old hunter's and fireman's songs." "P.F. Baker closed a successful season of 42 weeks June 30 at Buffalo, New York. 'Chris and Lena' will be laid away for the present. Next season, 'The Emigrant' will be revived with new costumes, music and scenery." July 14 *New York Dramatic Mirror*: "Lutie Miller ... is spending the Summer with her parents in Cincinnati. The lady has signed with Mr. Baker for next season."[18]

Our little leading lady is next found at Harris' Theatre in Pittsburgh, Pennsylvania, where Baker's troupe opened its season on September 3, to a SRO crowd. A local paper said: " 'The Emigrant' has been almost entirely rewritten by Mr. Baker, and is now a much better play than 'Chris and Lena' Miss Miller ... rendered good support ..." "Baker as Ludwig von Vinkelsteinhausenblauser, the Emigrant, was funny enough to make people's sides ache. The tableaux, 'The Mill On Fire,' 'Capture of the Gamblers,' 'A Dark Surprise' and 'Hlainy Unmasked' almost set the gallery wild with delight." "Baker is ... a versatile comedian and has an excellent voice. In his burnt cork impersonation he is especially clever (as Aunt Jeremiah, "an aged Afro American woman"), and his ' 'scuse me, did I say howdy?' never failed to elicit applause." "Of the ladies, Miss Lutie Miller as Lizzelle, a German girl ... (is) also entitled to mention. The costumes are the handsomest ever seen in a play of this calibre."[19] There were other reviews, all positive. October 2 *Chicago Tribune*: "The soubrette, Miss Lutie Miller, adds much to the fun that Mr. Baker creates." The November 27 *New York*

Clipper suddenly announced out of Cincinnati, that "Lutie Miller, of P.F. Baker's Co., is seriously ill at her home in this city." Nothing is mentioned about the nature or duration of the illness, but it goes without saying that she recovered. This ended, however, her stint with Pete Baker.

The January 16, 1889 (Cincinnati) *Sporting Life* featured a story from January 9: " 'The ball players who make Cincinnati their home represent all sorts of trades and professions, to which they can return when Father Time will present them with increasing years, Charley-horse, game legs and lame arms. The butcher, the baker and the candlestick maker do not prance on the field, but they are among the few trades not represented by 'the boys.' Red Bittman of the Buffalos and Jake Stenzel of Columbus are carriage blacksmiths ... Bob Clark of the Brooklyns and 'Mox' McQueery of Syracuse used to be hucksters in the old days." "Only two have theatrical ambitions – 'Cooney' Bowers and John Nichoff. They are organizing a company to star Miss Lutie Miller, a Cincinnati girl, 'in the provinces' ..."

The January 18 *Newark Daily Advocate* found Louise in her own company, appropriately named, "The Lutie Miller Company." "Miss Lutie Miller ... the past two years starring with Pete Baker's Chris & Lena Company, will appear at Wallace's Opera House for three nights ... on January 24, 25 and 26, at ... 15, 25 and 35¢ and will represent the following well known plays: Is Marriage a Failure, and her favorite character, The Little Detective. Miss Lutie Miller will be supported by a powerful company, including the only J.K. Emmitt's rival, B. Robinson. Thursday night will be ladies night. Miss Miller has kindly agreed to admit the ladies of Newark free Thursday, thereby introducing her company."

The edition of the 22nd said, "Thursday night ... Miss Miller has many warm admirers in Newark and she will receive a warm welcome. She will endeavor ... to please all with her excellent singing and dancing, in one of her favorite characters, 'The Little Detective.' Mr. G. Robinson ... will sing some of the most popular warbling songs of the day. He has had at least 10 different offers to travel with the largest minstrel companies on the road, but refused all of them, accepting an engagement with the Lutie Miller Co." A nice testimonial to the popular Louise! The following day's paper, referring back to the "Baker era," wrote: "Miss Lutie Miller, while playing an engagement at Boston with Pete Baker's Chris and Lena, received not less than 40 beautiful florals from her many lady admirers during the play one evening. She received several calls, and floral after floral was thrown upon the stage. One lady in her excitement threw her glove."

"Saturday afternoon (January 24), Miss Lutie Miller will give a grand matinee at the Opera House for the benefit of the school children ... only 10¢ admission will be charged. Teachers who accompany the school children will be admitted free ... There will be a packed house ... to-night (Friday), to greet the charming soubrette, Miss Lutie Miller and her splendid company in the great play, 'The Little Detective.' Mr. G. Robinson ... one of the greatest comedians living, will ... appear at each performance. Charming songs and dances, laughable comedy and thrilling tragedy. Miss Lutie Miller will sing all the latest songs. Miss Etta Lewis, the pianist for Miss Lutie Miller, is one of the best in the profession." This was Lutie's sister.[20] January 25 *Newark Advocate*: "Miss Lutie Miller opened at Wallace Opera House last night to standing room, in the beautiful Irish play, 'Kathleen Mavourneen.' Mr. G. Robinson ... advertised as the warbler of the United States, really proved himself such last night. Miss Miller to-night ... assumes six different characters, introducing new songs and dances."

The next day's paper noted, " 'The Little Detective' was a great hit and Miss (Lutie) Miller ... wonderful. Mr. G. Robinson, the warbler, is said to be superior to anything in that line ... the fine playing of her pianist is one of the enjoyable features. This evening the great play, 'Is Marriage a Failure' ...'' The company played in other parts of Ohio through early February, when the February 9 *Ohio Democrat* said, "Lutie Miller closes her engagement here this evening." On the 24th it was revealed from Bellaire, Ohio that "Miss Lutie Miller is laid up with an injured foot at Cincinnati, the result of running against the point of a pick while playing in this city." The March 1 *New York Mirror*, dateline Bellefontaine, Ohio, said, "The Kindergarten co. passed through here last week. Lutie Miller, of this co., met with an accident at Kenton, severely spraining her ankle. Her sister will take her place until she recovers."[21] This must have referred to Etta.

"Lutie Miller ... joined Harry William's 'Kindergarten' Co. at Louisville, Ky., April 13, taking the part of Ivy Magee ... Manager Williams reports ... that the season will not close until about the middle of June." The actress from the "Queen City" is not found in the press again until January 26, 1890, and sister Etta is with her. According to the *New York Clipper*: "Lutie Miller, the Cincinnati soubrette, will commence an acting tour at Lancaster, 27, 28, under 'Cooney' Bowers' arrangement. Her repertory includes 'Rem Rounds' 'Is Marriage a Failure' and 'The Little Detective.' In her company are Dave Baldridge ... and Etta Lewis – nearly all Cincinnati folk." The troupe played near her home during that month's 3rd week: "Globe Opera House, Saturday, February 22, Return engagement of the funniest of all musical comedies, The Kindergarten ... Presented by Howell & Geberts Company of comedians, including ... Miss Lutie Miller as Ivy Magee ... New Music! Special Scenery! Novel Dances, our own grand orchestra. Kindergarten band concert at noon. Admission, 25 and 50¢."[22]

Ella joined Pete Baker's Company around February 17: "In 'The Emigrant.' Ed. Barton and Ella Miller (a sister of Lutie Miller) have joined Mr. Baker, and Miss Miller is now playing Agnes." As for Louise, her next known gig was with an unnamed troupe on May 12. "The performance of 'The Wages of Sin' at Harris' Bijou Theatre last night was well attended ...

The play is one of the strongest of modern melodramas ... Miss Lutie Miller is a soubrette who sings well, and possesses a vivacity that made her impersonation of Julianna Boggs admirably sparkling."[23] The June 14 *New York Clipper* wrote: "Ella Miller, soubrette, and Earl Atkinson have closed with the John Dillon Co. The first named will spend the rested (?) term at her home, Walnut Hills, near Cincinnati." The Miller clan had lived in the suburb of Walnut Hills for many years, as Joe and Louise would later. The 1891 and '92 Williams' Cincinnati Directories list "Miller, Lutie – Manager, Ernst & Miller, 651 Gilbert Av., home, 637 McMillan." This was perhaps the managerial entity created for the Lutie Miller Company.

On November 11, Louise reprised her role as Ivy Magee with the Kindergarten Company, in Carbondale, Pennsylvania. On the 14th, it was announced that she "was taken ill at Danville (apparently Danville, Pennsylvania) and had to leave the company. Manager W.P. Howell at once left for New York to get a substitute for Miss Miller's part." The nature of Lutie's latest ailment isn't known. The company played on the 13th at Lea's Opera House in Port Jervis, New York to a crowded house, but "The part of Ivy Magee was taken by Mabel Haven, Lutie Miller being indisposed."[24]

Louise is not heard from again until May 17, 1891, when the *Sunday Herald* (Washington, D.C.) wrote that "the charming and fascinating soubrette, Miss Lutie Miller" would play the lead role of "Little Nugget" in the "farce-comedy" play of the same name, the next night at Harris's (Bijou Theatre), in the nation's capital. She would perform "bewitching songs, dances and medleys." The May 30 *New York Mirror* said she "replaced Drusie Gilmore as soubrette of the Little Nugget co. during the ... Cawthorn Brothers engagement ...' " Lutie next turns up on February 11, 1892, playing in far away Dallas, Texas. " 'Ole Olson,' a farcical comedy dealing with Swedish life, was presented for the first time ... at the opera house last night ... witnessed ... by a ... kindly appreciative audience ... the plot ... is adapted only to the exigencies of laughter and amusement. Mr. Robert L. Scott as Ole Olson was original and quaintly humorous."[25]

Louise was evidently with the combination for some time, as the April 15 *Carroll* (Iowa) *Sentinel* noted. "Ole Olson at Music hall ... was largely attended ... As a sort of all round jim crow performance the entertainment would have been passably good if that horrible bore of an Ole could have been kept off the stage ... give us Irish, German, American, Negro or any ... kind of character, but spare us from any more Ole Olson impersonations. Little Miss Lutie Miller in her soubrette role was good and she, in company with Mrs. O'Flannigan could have given a far more clever performance by themselves than they did weighed down as they were by the Ole Olson and his horrible impersonations of the Swedish language." And that was it for Lutie, the last known record of her stage career or doings before she joined L.R. Stockwell's troupe in "Uncle Tom's Cabin," in August, 1893.

Etta Lewis's thespian career appears to have ended around 1895. Ella, though, appears several times more. On May 14, 1892: "Edward E. Oakes, Treasurer of the Marlande Clark Company, playing at Harris's Theatre, left town rather suddenly after the performance last night, taking with him $85 of the company's money. Miss Ella Miller, a member of the company, went with him, and the supposition is that they have eloped." No Ella Oakes was found in any contemporary record, though, nor any indication that they married. On the 21st, it was noted out of Pittsburgh: "Manager Oaks ... and Ella Miller left the city after the performance, and have not since been heard from. Florence Gerald ... acting manager ... put the police in possession of the facts." Ella turns up only three days later without Oakes: "The roster of the Carolyn Gage Co.: Kent Thomas ... Ella Miller ... Carolyn Gage."[26] She is next heard from more than a year later. The December 17, 1893 *New York Clipper* noted: "Ella Miller has signed with W. Kent Thomas to play the soubrette ... in 'A Double Wrong.'"

On Friday, January 25, 1895, in Cincinnati, Ohio, Joe took out a marriage license to wed Louise Anderson Miller. "His wife to be is three years his junior ..."[27] The big event occurred the following day, although, as both wanted it, quietly. Papers from various parts of the country mentioned the wedding: "Joseph Choynski ... was married at 6 o'clock this evening to Miss Louise Miller, who

Joe Choynski and Louise Miller, wedding photo, January 25, 1895

has made quite a success as an actress and who is familiarly known as 'Lutie.' The ceremony took place at the bride's residence at Walnut Hills."

"Choynski ... married ... Miss Louise Miller, a pretty brunette ... The Reverend Sydney Strong of the Congregational Church officiating. The bride was attired in a traveling costume of light gray, with hat and gloves to match. None but their intimate relatives were present. Congratulatory telegrams were sent from all parts of the country. Presents were received from 'Parson' Davies, several Chicago Board-of-Trade men and others. The couple left for Chicago to-night, where they will reside. Choynski will go on the Board of Trade there." "At the house of the bride's parents on Walnut Hills, Miss Louise Miller married ... Joe Choynski ... a very quiet affair, only immediate friends of the family having been invited." The Miller home was at 637 McMillan Street. Thomas and Mary would move shortly afterward to 35 Mitchell Avenue.[28] Lutie's father, though, had not long to live.

A word on Sydney Dix Strong (1860-1938). The pastor who married Joe and Louise made a significant impact on the religious and political climate of his day. He graduated from Oberlin College in 1881 and became a leading practitioner of the "social gospel," authoring many books on religion. His peers at Oberlin wrote, in 1905: "Sydney D. Strong ... in College a first-rate scholar, a good baseball pitcher ... capable editor of The *Review* ... an all around useful, popular man." *Oberlin Alumni magazine*: "There

Reverend Sydney Strong

is no Congregational Pastor west of New York who wields a greater influence ... As a writer for children, a trenchant yet kindly critic of the infirmities of the ... church ... with one passion to make the gospel go to the ends of the earth, he has ... honored his Oberlin training." While not a "fire and brimstone" type, neither did Strong "tickle the ears" of his flock. January 23, 1906 *Paducah Sun*: "The 'Kirmess Sermon,' in which Dr. Sydney Strong, pastor of the 2nd Congregational Church of Oak Park compared society women of Chicago to half-naked, sensualized heathen women of Africa ... When Dr. Strong delivered his scathing rebuke to Chicago's exclusive set, his services were valued at $3,000 a year. The trustees ... voted him an increase of $1,250 a year."

Strong was appointed to the Walnut Hills Congregational Church in 1892. In 1897, he was called to the larger parish of Oak Park, Illinois, a suburb of Chicago, being pastor there until 1906, when he moved to Seattle, Washington. In 1908, Sydney was appointed to that city's Queen

Anne Congregational Church, held that office until 1921 and remained in Seattle until his death. Here, Strong became most outspoken, as a pacifist and opponent of war, making him unpopular during World War I. He died in 1938. Sydney's controversial daughter, Anna Louise Strong, was born in November, 1885, the eldest of three children. Like her parents, Anna attended Oberlin College. She later became concerned with child welfare and was pro-labor. Anna was present in Seattle at the 1916 Everett Massacre, as a reporter. Several members of the IWW (Industrial Workers of the World) were gunned down by the Everett mill's armed guards. Deeply affected by this, Anna developed the philosophy that capitalism was flawed and a source of many ills. While her father had leanings toward Socialism, she became an overt proponent of Communism.

From 1921 to 1940, Anna spent most of her time in the U.S.S.R., and met Josef Stalin. She visited China in 1925, and became friendly with Chairman Mao Tse-tung. In 1930, Strong helped found The *Moscow News* in the Soviet Union, and in 1932, married Soviet official Joel Shubin. Anna's passport was revoked by the U.S. government from about 1949 until 1958, when she returned to China. She died there in 1970, and is buried in the National Memorial Cemetery of Revolutionary Martyrs in Beijing.[29]

No. 885. Walnut Hills Congregational Church, Locust St., Cin.

Walnut Hills Congregational Church

Walnut Hills Congregational Church, where it stood in the time of Joe and Louise, at 934 Locust Street, was completed in 1885. At the earlier George Street Presbyterian Church, Lyman Beecher was Pastor between 1844 and 1847. He was also the father of Harriet Beecher Stowe and Henry

Ward Beecher, a noted Congregationalist minister. Louise joined Walnut Hills Congregational Church on January 4, 1891 along with a James Albert Miller, possibly be her older brother, Albert. On April 10, 1892, her mother, Mary S. Miller and sister, Mrs. Etta Lewis, joined the church. Louise's brother, Thomas H. Miller, became a member on April 1, 1894, followed by Anna Louise Strong, on April 14, 1895. As several siblings joined the church shortly before the marriage of Joe and Louise, they likely attended the wedding. Unfortunately, there exists no list of the ceremony's attendees. We don't know which of Joe's siblings made the trip to Walnut Hills, although it is confirmed that Edwin was unable to attend.[30]

There is no evidence that Joe Choynski was an observant Jew, or, for that matter, an observant Christian. Nor does he appear to have officially joined the Congregational Church. Conversely, it is not known that Joe was an atheist. He may simply have had an ecumenical or more universal view of a deity. Louise had a niece who also became a noted singer and actress. Edna Spence, born in June, 1886, is listed in the 1900 Federal Census as living with Joe and Louise. It is not known which of Lutie's siblings she was the daughter of. The Census only tells that she and her mother were born in Ohio, her father, in England. There are numerous mentions of a Miss Edna Spence (or Spencer) in film and vaudeville over the years, through at least 1932. It is not confirmed that this was Lutie's niece, however.[31] As will be seen, Joe and Louise performed in vaudeville with an unnamed niece, after Joe's retirement from boxing. This was probably Edna.

Ella's career continued for several more years. She was noted as part of Jules Walters' "A Money Order" Company in 1895, but isn't heard from again until October 1, 1898, when she is listed with L.J. Carter's "Remember the Maine" Company. February 19, 1901 finds Ella in "the thrilling American play, *The Trapper's Daughter*, Miss Ella Miller, the winsome little soubrette, assuming the title role ... a complete acting company ... orchestra ... mechanical effects ... donkeys, dogs, burros, goats, cowboys ... etc. Col. V.C. Cody, the celebrated rifle shot, will give an exhibition of fancy rifle shooting in front of the theatre at 7:30 p.m." On August 3 she turns up with Fred Raymond's Company, which offered such plays as "Missouri Girl" and "Old Arkansaw." The last time she is heard of is March 8, 1902: "Ella Miller is no longer connected with the "Old Arkansaw" Co., having been called home on account of illness."[32] It is not known who was ill.

Round Twelve

Dan Creedon
(January 1895 – July 1895)

While Joe and Louise enjoyed their honeymoon, Charles Davies was negotiating fights for his stable of boxers. On January 30, he was said to have matched two of his fighters against each other, Joe and "Tommy Ryan of Troy, New York for $100 a side. The fight will be pulled off at Frankton, Indiana. Two ounce gloves will be used. Choynski must be shy of funds otherwise he would be after bigger game."[1] There is little doubt the match was meant strictly as a payday, as it is unlikely either fighter would have been told by Davies to try and defeat the other. A No-Decision or draw would have been in their best interests, so as not to damage the prospects of either down the line. Joe would indeed have been "looking for bigger game," although Ryan held his own with "Kid" McCoy, another great middleweight who fought the best heavyweights of the generation to a standstill. The Choynski-Ryan match never came off, though.

The January 31 *Brooklyn Daily Eagle* noted, "(Sam) Fitzpatrick (said) if a match is made between (Young) Griffo and ("Kid") Lavigne he will, on the recommendation of Parson Davis (sic) take the Kid to Worcester, Massachusetts, to train ... Lake Quinsigamond, which is on the outskirts of Worcester, is one of the prettiest little sheets of water in the country, with capital roads ... hotel accommodations and splendid boating ... Choynski trained there last year for his fight with Fitzsimmons and he fell so heartily in love with the spot that he declared his intention of training Jackson there if Corbett could ever be induced to meet the colored heavyweight."

Next up for Joe was the fine middleweight, Dan Creedon. Dan was born in Invercargill, New Zealand in June, 1868 and stood about 5' 9". On February 4, "Col. Hopkins ... received a proposition ... to match Choynski against Dan ... Creedon's backer ... says if Choynski will weigh in at 162 pounds Creedon will meet him at about 156 ... for a 10-round mill ..." Hopkins said: "The Californian is a rusher ... When ... permitted to make his own pace, Choynski will sail in and either whip his man or get whipped himself, in about 10 rounds. That's exactly what Creedon wants. Let a man come at him and I know how he'll stop him. They can't smother Dan with any of those cyclone rushes, and the man that tries ... will soon find this out to his sorrow. Choynski is a light heavy-weight and can get within five or six pounds of the middleweight limit. That's all we ask ... Choynski should be eager to meet Creedon for there ... is more glory in besting him than the

'Coffee Cooler', who has twice met defeat at Dan's hands."[2]

"The five greatest ball-punchers in the pugilistic profession are Jim Corbett, Tommy Ryan, Bob Fitzsimmons, Young Griffo and Dan Creedon. Parson Davies claims that Ryan is the best of the lot ... Corbett gives nightly exhibitions of ball punching in his play, and he is very expert. Bob Fitzsimmons alternates his fist blows with jabs from his elbows, and can make the ball 'bark' each time he uses them on it. Griffo, too, is good at this elbow work, as is also Creedon." On the 14th, Davies issued invitations for a bag-punching exhibition by Ryan at 5 pm at the new Manhattan Athletic Club. "Ryan gave a wretched exhibition last week and it was given out that he was sick. There were those, however, who thought that the astute parson was hiding his cards in order to get a bag punching contest on with Corbett, Fitzsimmons or some other big 'un. Parson Davies and his two clever protégés, Joe Choynski and Tommy Ryan have engaged passage on the steamship *Majestic*, which sails for England on the 27th inst."[3]

On the night of February 25, Joe saw his first ring action since his wedding. At the Waverly Theatre in Chicago, under the auspices of the Triangle Athletic Club, a boxing show was held. *The Chicago Inter-Ocean* said "2,000 sporty citizens witnessed," while the *Omaha World-Herald* said it was "before 500 people." Quite a disparity. Tommy Ryan won an easy four-rounder over "Shorty" Ahearn. Joe then took on a massive black fighter named Jim (or Jack) Douglass. It was a "sparring exhibition" scheduled for three rounds, and the first recorded bout of Douglass's career. *The Inter-Ocean* said "Douglass weighed close to 300 pounds, and came on the stage with an abnormally developed frontispiece." The *Chicago Tribune* called him "a big negro with a ponderous stomach," and the *Sandusky Register* said Jim weighed 250 pounds. "In the 1st round Joe caught him a hot one under the ear, and Douglass stopped to take stock of his features, Choynski ... standing off with arms akimbo ... a right jolt from Choynski to the broadened nose jarred Douglass ..." Joe was clearly going easy on his "opposition." In the 2nd, "he got Douglass to chasing after him and hit him four fast raps in the countenance ..." Joe punched Jim groggy, and the latter "was saved from a knockout by the interference of the referee."

In the final round, Choynski saw he was facing a dazed target. Joe "planted a blow on Douglass' chin that took out all the fight left in him and completed the time by patting him playfully on the chin." Joe "mercifully refrained from putting him out." One paper said, "before the 3rd round was over with, the 'Parson' ordered the bout done with."[4] In 1927, Choynski recalled: "One night I met a big, colored fellow named 'Pluch' Douglas at the Triangle Club, Chicago. In the 1st round I jolted 'Pluch' to the floor. The referee counted slowly up to eight. Then he said, 'Ain't you going to fight no more?' The big negro opened his eyes, raised up on one elbow and replied, 'Yes, sah, I suttinly is – but not tonight.' "

On March 1, Davies postponed the European tour, as he received a letter from Colonel Hopkins, saying he was ready to "match Creedon against Choynski six rounds and Tracy (sic) against Ryan eight rounds ... Boston, Coney Island or Chicago ..."[5] March 3 *Chicago Inter-Ocean*: "Ryan and Choynski are training again. Some day both of these boxers will turn up so stale that it won't be much of a job for any scrub fighter to knock them out." Davies arranged exhibition bouts for the 11th at Kansas City, Missouri's Auditorium Theater, matching Joe and Tommy in "four round scientific set-tos." Ryan, called "a pocket edition of Champion Corbett for cleverness in boxing," would also put on a bag-punching exhibition. "Choynski is a favorite in Kansas City, where he has frequently been seen as the sparring partner of Peter Jackson." A Kansas paper said "Choynski excels Creedon, being longer in arm and body, has more stamina and quite as much science. Creedon is a good, stiff puncher, but Choynski ought to out-point him in cleverness." Dan was described as "clever, a terrific hitter, can take a great deal of punishment, and his fighting is of the rushing, aggressive style ... possessed of a bull-dog like ferocity in the ring"[6]

Chicago Daily Inter-Ocean: "Choynski has two inches the best of Creedon in height, but the New Zealander makes up for this with one of the longest reaches a fighter was ever blessed with. For his inches Creedon is the longest-armed fighter today ... on proportionate measurements excels Peter Jackson ... He has suffered but one defeat in this country, the two-round fight with Fitzsimmons at New Orleans last September. His wins over such ... as Dick Moore (twice), 'Buffalo' Costello, Alec Greggains and Frank Childs make Creedon a dangerous man ... and Choynski will have to use his head to win." Creedon's wingspan measurement wasn't specified, but Choynski's reach (fingertip-to-fingertip) was 75½" to 76" in length. Tom Tracey, Ryan's scheduled antagonist, was called the foster brother of Dan Creedon. Choynski and Ryan arrived in Kansas City on March 10 and quartered themselves at the Milland Hotel along with the "Parson."[7]

On the evening of March 11, 1,000 fight fans attended the boxing show at the Auditorium. "The bout between Choynski and Mike Madden was disappointing, the latter being in no shape and not causing Choynski to exert himself. In the 4th, Choynski beat a tattoo on Madden's face and made him call enough." A bout between Tommy and a local boxer named Emmett Melody "was a stiff go ... Ryan ... had the better ... on the whole."[8] The March 13 *Kansas City Times* said Davies, "The Admirable Crichton of Queensberry,"* would, upon returning to England, assume management of (what little remained of) Peter Jackson's career. Davies felt that Frank Slavin's recent victory over Frank Craig would give Slavin the confidence to challenge Jackson again. "Joe Choynski is kind of sore because the Cooler went out so early ... He figured on getting a fight out of 'the Cooler' when he reached England, but poor Craig is a drawing card no longer." They were to tour England and Ireland, bring Jackson back to the U.S. and match him against Steve O'Donnell. The *Times* noted that Peter had "taught the art of the folded fives in Sydney, Australia" to Slavin and O'Donnell. He had become despondent, though, in not getting a title fight against John L. Sullivan or Jim Corbett, taken to drink and dissipated. He would soon begin feeling the effects of consumption (tuberculosis), which would take his life in 1901. The trip to England was ultimately cancelled.

*After James Crichton (August 19, 1560 – July 3, 1582), a Scottish polymath. It was another way of calling Davies a "renaissance man."

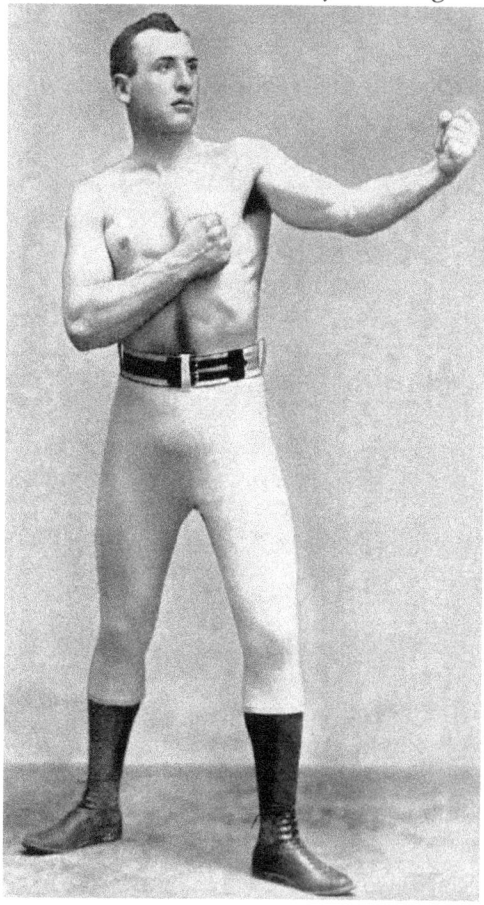

Dan Creedon, of New Zealand

Peter Jackson wrote "Professor" Mike Donovan a letter from Glasgow, Scotland, saying he had "made arrangements in London and the provinces, and so far I am doing very well. I shall remain here until April. I see by the (London) *Sporting Life* that Charley Davies has offered to back Choyinski (sic) against me. I can't quite make it out. I'm sure it can't be true." There were some rumblings along those lines, Joe and the "Parson" perhaps desiring to get a fading Jackson's name on "The Frisco Flash's" résumé, while offering Peter a nice payday. Nothing came of it. Davies, Choynski and Ryan arrived back in Chicago on March 13, and continued on to a training camp they had set up at nearby Lyons, Illinois. There, Joe, at least, would prepare for his contest at Tattersall's. The *Inter-Ocean* said Joe would train there, but "Tom will do his exercising in a local gymnasium."9

Ryan faced Tracey on the 20th. "No decision was reached ... because the managers ... were apprehensive of police interference with the Choynski-Creedon fight ... if the affair ... was carried to the extreme. But ... Tracey was badly whipped ... Referee Liber said: 'In the 7th ... when Tracey was on the floor, Parson Davies ... told me to call the contest off because it was becoming too brutal, and in the next round I did so. Tracey had no earthly show to win, and I simply did what Ryan's manager demanded.' Ryan was very angry ... declaring he had been robbed of a decision ... fairly won."[10]

The next night, Joe took on Creedon, before a crowd of 6,000. George Siler refereed. The dust-up went the distance, and though prior agreement dictated a draw in that case, Joe dominated. Had a decision been based on merit, he would have been an easy winner. "Choynski had all the best of it, except in one round. He knocked Creedon down twice, brought the blood in a stream from his nose and had his man tired and very groggy when the 6th round closed. Choynski weighed 161 pounds and although Creedon's weight was not given, he looked to weigh fully as much."[11] This was *much* too light for Joe, if accurate, and would have weakened him.

"Tattersall's ... was ... covered with sawdust and tanbark. (Joe) was attended by Charley Essig, Al Shrosbree and Lou Agnew, Vere R. Davies (Charlie's brother) acting as timer. Creedon, looking a bit fat about the waist and weighing ... close on to 170 pounds ... Jack Costello, a brother of the 'Buffalo,' now a fugitive from justice in Canada, acted as Creedon's timekeeper." "Creedon acknowledged his master last night in Joe Choynski. Not in so many words, but at the end of the 6th round, as he lay on the floor of the ring ... he looked over at Joe and shook his head, as though to say, 'I'm apparently not equal to the task.' " The first half of the contest, Creedon "stayed out in front and Choynski was busy keeping his stomach out of harm's way and avoiding the vicious right hand swings ... The last half ... was entirely in favor of Choynski ..." A blended account follows:[12]

Round 1 – Creedon rushed his man to the ropes. Joe slipped cleverly out of range, landing a left to the mouth. Dan dug a left to the body, Joe countering with a stiff jab. Seeing Creedon's dangerous right, Joe stuck to straight lefts. He drew first blood from a cut on the bridge of Dan's nose.

Round 2 – Choynski evaded several of Creedon's swings, with clever footwork and artful dodges. The "Chrysanthemum" clouter showered his foe with stinging lefts to the face and the heart, with the odd right thrown in. Dan's nose bled, and he was badly winded at the bell.

Round 3 – This was perhaps Creedon's round, though they traded heavily. He landed a hard right to Joe's mouth and drove him to the ropes with a kidney shot. Dan landed a flurry in the corner at the bell. *The Inter-Ocean* dissented, saying Joe took the frame with a load of jabs and hooks.

Round 4 – Another close one, most papers feeling Dan had "a shade the best." Joe jabbed his proboscis, causing the blood to flow again. "Creedon uppercut Joe and swung his right for (the) body, but Joe side-swiped him and a clinch followed." Dan reached the "bread-basket" several times, Joe landing often with an educated left. He tried to land a right-hand crusher, but couldn't quite find the spot. Creedon was covered with blood.

Round 5 – "Creedon worked hard for the stomach," landing a nice left-right. "Joe got angry and slammed three good ones into Creedon's battered visage." "Choynski forced and hopped about his man like a goat. His left was still strong and unerring in its aim." Joe drove a powerful right to Dan's heart, that "took all of the fight out of him," and floored him with a left (or a right). Dan "was down four seconds, when the gong ended the round."

Round 6 – Creedon's bleeding nose appeared to be broken. Joe landed almost at will, dropping his rival with a terrific right. Dan rose at nine, but was weak. He survived by clinching repeatedly. "Referee George Siler told the audience to judge which was the better man." "These, of course, on the showing made, shouted for Choynski, and though the official records won't show it, Choynski gained a victory." Siler was required to declare a draw, the fighters having completed the route on their feet.

Said Joe, in 1930: "Creedon was clever and made every effort to side-step my hard blows. And he could hit. I felt any number of his blows. Only Creedon's marvelous defensive work enabled him to last the six rounds." A paper quoted Dan, saying to Joe on the 29th: " 'Had I known you weighed less than 175 pounds, I would never had agreed to meet you.' ... Creedon explained that he supposed he was going up against a heavyweight, by whom it would be no disgrace to be defeated. Choynski weighed exactly 165¾ pounds when he faced the stocky Australian ... the lighter man by almost eight pounds ... Tommy Ryan did not appear in Choynski's corner Thursday night ... the welterweight champion took to his bed after his go with Tracey and has been there ever since. His old enemy, tonsillitis, has given him great trouble for the past two years, and his condition was greatly aggravated by working in the cold building Wednesday night."[13]

On March 24, an ominous event occurred. At about 6:00 p.m. in his home at 216 State Street in Chicago, Davies was dictating a telegram to his secretary Harry Glickauf, to send to Coney Island's Seaside Club. Glickauf suddenly noticed Davies had ceased dictating. He glanced over at "The Parson," seated in his chair, and saw that Davies' body had gone rigid. It would be discovered that Davies had been accidentally poisoned by strychnine. His biographer, Mark T. Dunn, believes the severe eye problems Charlie experienced later in life resulted from this poisoning.

Dr. Francis McNamara of 277 State Street, the physician for Davies and several fighters, including Choynski, wrote Davies a prescription for phenacetine, a drug used as an antineuralgic. Due to its carcinogenic properties, it is no longer marketed, but was commonly used in the 1890's. When Charlie went to a drug store to refill the original prescription, someone made the error of filling it with strychnine. Davies took what he thought was phenacetine, around 4:30 p.m. "The rigid appearance ... was caused by the ... strychnine ... a potent stimulant of the spinal cord, increases the secretion of gastric juices and heightens sensory awareness." It also causes painful spasms. "Eventually his muscles will tire, and he will not be able to breathe. Long-term effects of strychnine poisoning may result from brain damage caused from low oxygen levels or kidney failure."

Dr. McNamara and a Dr. Smedley were summoned, and Davies was treated ... He was comatose for nearly an hour. "The two doctors stayed with Davies until 11:00 p.m. when they pronounced him out of danger of death. It may be that some of the illnesses ... Davies suffered during the remainder of his life were caused in part by the long-term effects ... In retrospect Charlie's poisoning was a watershed event in his life." On March 25, Choynski and Charley Essig seconded Lou Agnew at the Triangle Club in a fight with Arthur Schultz, who Agnew knocked out in the 5th round.[14]

Soon afterward, Joe began training Jimmy Barry for his "American Bantamweight Championship" fight with Casper Leon, "The Sicilian Swordfish." "Barry ... to box 15 rounds with ... Leon, the clever Italian midget, at the 2nd Regiment Armory ... is training faithfully under ... Choynski ... conceded to be one of the best trainers and seconds in the profession. Joe is a perfect glutton for work and keeps Barry on the jump ... After a 10-mile walk ... Choynski put his charge through ball punching, wrestling and other ... exercising, and at the finish Barry remarked that it was the hardest day's work he had ever done to get himself into condition." "Joe ... with his wonderful knowledge of the game, was the best man Barry could have been placed under. Barry ... has ... headquarters at McGurn's Court ... in company with his seconds, Joe Choynski, William McGurn, Paddy Fitzgerald and Charles Essig ..."[15] The Barry-Leon battle came off that night, the 30th. This was also pre-arranged as a draw if the bout went the distance, but Jimmy gave Casper a beating. "In the 14th ... Barry hammered the Italian all over the ring and the referee, Malachi Hogan, had to tell him to get up, even after the police were in the ring." The bout was officially a draw. The next afternoon, Joe and Tommy Ryan gave a boxing and ball-punching exhibition at the Clark Street Theater.[16]

Davies left for New York on May 2 to complete final arrangements for two fights, Choynski-Jim Hall and a Tommy Ryan-"Mysterious" Billy Smith rematch. "Ryan, Choynski and Barry will leave Saturday night, and ... do their training at the seashore a few miles from New York, where the Parson will secure a cottage." The camp was at Asbury Park, New Jersey. Joe was scheduled to second Jake Kilrain on the night of May 6 in a fight against Steve O'Donnell, but it is uncertain if he did or not. Kilrain (real name John Joseph Killian) was knocked out in round 21 by O'Donnell.[17]

The May 10 *Brooklyn Eagle* complimented Davies on the discipline of his training camps. The Griffo-Lavigne fight had been postponed from May 14 to the 30th, ostensibly due to the "excessive drinking of young Griffo and his refusal to train properly. He will be sent to Asbury Park to train under Parson Davis' (sic) eye, as no one else has been able to keep him down to his work." In truth and while little known, Griffo was an alleged pedophile, and had fled a Coney Island arrest warrant, filed at the request of the Society for the Prevention of Cruelty to Children. The purported victim was a 9-year-old boy named Gottlieb. Around the 19th, Davies wrote Glickauf from Asbury Park, stating, "Ryan has entirely recovered from the effects of the recent operations on his throat and nostrils and is confident of defeating ... Smith ..." Charlie said his three fighters were all in good condition, their current weights being: Choynski, 162 pounds, Ryan, 141 and Barry, 106½. Joe and Davies attended the May 20 Peter Maher-Bob Marshall fight at Sea Beach Palace, Coney Island, New York. Peter floored his outgunned foe four times, stopping him in 45 seconds.[18]

A San Antonio paper commented on Hall's raging alcoholism and dissipation, and his interaction with Joe: "Choynski these days is too much for the tall Australian, no matter ... the condition of the latter. Choynski has been coming right along, while Hall has been 'sick' and other things. Once upon a time Jim Hall had the proud distinction of being noted as one of ... Davies' string of fighters ... Choynski was of the parsonage too and ... while in this capacity the pair often flew together, not too hard ... just tolerable; each always imagined he might lick the other if they were not of the same flock ... Hall got it into his head that he could lick Joe, and Joe got the same thing, only reversed, in his own nut. At that time they would have made a great fight. Jim is laboring under a hallucination."[19]

The *Brooklyn Eagle* commented on the Ryan-Smith fight: "These men have met on three previous occasions ... The first two encounters were declared draws and the last one was decided in Ryan's favor, much to the disappointment of Smith, who claimed that the referee, Joe Choynski, was too friendly (toward Ryan) to suit him. As a rule clever boxers are not heavy punchers, but Ryan is an exception, for he can punch as hard as many a heavyweight. He has been in training for the past four weeks down on the farm at Asbury Park ... accompanied on his road runs by big Joe Choynski, which is assurance that Ryan will step into the ring the night of the contest fit to battle for his life." The pair sparred at least one exhibition during this time, at Dead Lake, New Jersey, near Asbury Park.[20]

At the Seaside Athletic Club at Coney Island, New York, on the evening of the 27th, the 20-round Ryan-Smith fight occurred. "Tommy Ryan of Chicago was whipped tonight by 'Mysterious Billy Smith,' in turn whipped the mysterious one, and finally was 'articled' out of the decision in a police finish. Ryan followed with Joe Choynski, Jimmy Barry and Harry Pigeon behind him. In the 18-round battle which ensued Ryan put up, paradoxically though it may seem, the poorest fight of his life and the best one ... Smith hit Ryan more often, possibly, than the Chicago boy was ever landed on before in his fistic career. In the 10th round it looked as though it were all over with the Westerner. Apparently defenseless and unable to retaliate, he was pounded all over the ring. In this round 'Parson' Davies, seeing his man wavering, did a little cheating with the watch and 'did' Smith's timekeeper out of full 15 seconds. This saved Ryan, who was a sight. His face was covered with blood from his badly battered nose ..."

"Choynski worked over Ryan as only Choynski can. Large portions of red liquor were administered and Ryan came to. He was weak ... but evaded the bull-like rushes of Smith from this time to the close of the 16th round. In the 17th ... the Chicagoan drew on his reserve force, and such recuperative power was never witnessed in any land. Following a short ... right jolt to Smith's jaw he danced in with right and left till Smith was saved only from a knockout by the (bell). Ryan ... rushed Smith in the 18th ... Two minutes had gone by and Smith (was) mercilessly beaten and ... helpless ... his body leaning on the ropes, when the police interfered and Referee Hurst had to call it a draw." Spectators included actors Maurice Barrymore and Nat Goodwin, Old West figure "Bat" Masterson, William Brady, Jim Corbett, Jim Hall, Tom O'Rourke and notorious "Brooklyn Bridge jumper" Steve Brodie.[21] Choynski's skills as a second were key in Ryan's comeback.

Joe Choynski, 1897 pose

Next, Joe faced Jack (John L.) Cattanach, a Rhode Island native, at Baltimore, Maryland's Front Street Theater on June 3, under the aegis of the Eureka club. Cattanach was a heavyweight who battled many top fighters. He was stopped by Steve O'Donnell in August, 1893, in 1897 by Joe Butler (KOby1), George Byers (KOby2, 1899) and Tom "Stockings" Conroy (KOby3). June 3 *Baltimore Sun*: "Joe Choynski ... drove out the Pimlico road and through Druid Hill Park yesterday with Parson Davies and (manager of Joe Gans and others)

A.L. Herford. The star boxers will go on at 10:15 o'clock, and (Jake) Kilrain will be referee. Choynski is 26 years of age, weighs, in condition, from 165 to 170 pounds and lacks half an inch of being six feet tall. His trade is candymaking but, like Corbett, he became a bank clerk in San Francisco and gave that up for boxing ..."[22]

The *Milwaukee Evening Wisconsin* referred to Joe as the champion light-heavy weight and to the bout as a sparring contest. "Cattanach had Frank Farley in his corner, and Ernault Gephard attended Choyinski (sic)." The crowd sweltered under the heat of the gas jets that illuminated the arena. Jack was an easy mark for Joe, who played with his victim in the 1st round, "tapping him when and where he pleased ... The spectators hissed and yelled *fake*." *Omaha World-Herald*: "Cattanach had gone down twice without being punched hard enough to disconcert a fledgling. He was possessed of neither science nor courage." Joe showed disgust, and "early in the 2nd round responded to calls for a knockout. He tapped the Rhode Islander in the jaw, and he remained on the floor until counted out. Then he sneaked away amid the jeers of the crowd." "Once he went down when Choyinski led and missed him, and every time ... arose reluctantly. His hollow victory over Cattanach last night proved one of four things, namely, that Cattanach is no fighter, that he was in no condition to go into the ring ... was too greatly scared to make a showing, or, in ring parlance, he 'laid down.' Referee Kilrain ... tried to tell the spectators that Choyinski far outclassed Cattanach, and had consequently stopped him easily."[23] The *Daily Kennebec Journal* noted: "Joe Choynski unwittingly in a fake fight at Baltimore."

The famous turfman, Phil Dwyer, was organizing a benefit for the consumptive Jack Dempsey, to take place at Madison Square Garden. He started a subscription list for "The Nonpareil" with a donation of $500. The proceeds ... were to be sent to Mrs. Dempsey at their home in Portland, Oregon. Dempsey (real name John Edward Kelly, from County Kildare, Ireland), would be dead by November 1. "Jim Corbett, Bob Fitzsimmons, Peter Maher, Steve O'Donnell, Joe Choynski, Jim Hall, Tommy Ryan, Jimmy Barry, Dan Creedon and Jack Fogarty have volunteered to spar, and the men will be paired to get the best results."

On the night of June 8, thousands gathered in the Garden to witness the Dempsey benefit. Festivities commenced with a three-round spar between the once-great featherweight, George Dixon, known as "Little Chocolate" and Jack Lynch. Next up was Choynski, who likewise boxed a three-round exhibition with sparring partner, Bob Armstrong. This was followed by three-rounders between Australian's Jim Hall and Mickey Dunn, then "Kid" McCoy and Harry Pigeon. Next, Peter Maher sparred Peter Burns of Harlem over the same distance. Heavyweight champion Jim Corbett boxed a trio of rounds with John McVey. Middleweight king Bob Fitzsimmons engaged in a three-round spar with Frank Bosworth. "The last bout of the evening was ... John L. Sullivan and Jack Dempsey. When the ex-champion appeared in the ring ... there were cries of 'speech.' John L. made a short speech ... 'Mr. Dempsey and myself will now give one exhibition, and we will do the best we can, although we are two *has-beens*.' " He and the "Nonpareil" then gave their three-round finale.[24]

The June 9 *Newark Daily Advocate*'s tribute to bicycling included: "Joe Choynski ... who recently bested the wheel in a four-round bout, says that learning to ride is worse than taking part in a 50 round fight with bare knuckles." "How long the bicycle fad will last in society's circles is a much discussed theme. In time there may be hitching posts with padlocks and chains, outside shops, or boys to hold wheels. At present ... the crowded streets are not safe for ladies. While bicycling demands ... a bath and change after it, it will be a luxury, like horseback riding, and how long it will ... be enjoyed as a treat remains to be seen. – *Chicago Times-Herald*."[25]

On the 16th, the *Chicago Inter-Ocean* noted that Davies had measurements taken of Choynski and Bob Armstrong, while they were at Asbury Park: *Joe Choynski* – right wrist, 7¼"; left wrist, 7¼"; left fist shut, 11¾"; right fist shut, 12"; left forearm, 11¼"; right forearm, 11¾"; biceps left forearm, 12½"; biceps right forearm, 12½"; biceps expanded right forearm, 14¾"; biceps expanded left forearm, 14¾"; 12½"; neck, 17¼"; chest, 40½"; chest expansion, 43"; waist, 30"; left thigh, 21½"; right thigh, 21¼"; left calf, 13½"; right calf, 14"; length of reach (arms extended), 76½"; age, 26; height, 5' 11¾"; fighting weight, 168 (pounds).

Bob Armstrong – right wrist, 7¾"; left wrist, 7¾"; left fist shut, 12½"; right fist shut, 13"; left forearm, 12½"; right forearm, 12½"; biceps left forearm, 13"; biceps right forearm, biceps expanded right forearm, 14"; biceps expanded left forearm, 14½"; 12¾"; neck, 13½"; chest, 41¾"; chest expansion, 44"; waist, 32½"; left thigh, 23"; right thigh, 23¼"; right calf, 13¾"; left calf, 13½"; length of reach (arms extended), 79¼"; age, 21; height, 6' 3¾"; fighting weight, 193 (pounds).

On the 19th, at the Opera House in Red Bank, New Jersey, Choynski gave a ball punching exhibition and sparred with Bob Armstrong. This was part of a show, featuring Jimmy Barry, Harry Pigeon, "the famous trainer and welter-weight, and many other well-known athletes." A benefit for old John L. was held on June 27. The June 24 *Philadelphia Inquirer* wrote: "Five or more of the leading boxers of the day will engage in a bag-punching for the championship at John L. Sullivan's benefit at Madison Square Garden ... Fitzsimmons offers to box any man in the world on that occasion. Choynski comes out with the same proposition. Peter Maher will take on one, two or three men ..." On the night, however, "a letter from Fitzsimmons was read, expressing his sorrow at not being able to be present. The bag punching contest between Joe Choynski of San Francisco, Harry Pigeon of Canada and Jack Cornell of New York was well appreciated, and the San Francisco man easily outclassed the others. Exhibition sparring followed between ... Choynski and Bob Armstrong; Peter Maher ... and Peter Burns of Maine; Steve O'Donnell of Australia and Tom Burns of Denver. At 11:10 o'clock the last and biggest event on the programme was in order ... between Champion Jim Corbett and John L."

Corbett grasped Sullivan's hand and said: "It will always be a pleasure ... to assist my friend John L., and he has only to command me at any time. The men boxed three short rounds ..." Fitz needed to cancel, as his manslaughter trial in Syracuse, New York began on the 24th, stemming from the death of Con Riordan the previous year. Joe telegraphed his opinion to an unnamed paper, saying he didn't agree that Fitz only landed a light blow on Con. "Bob hits too hard in play ... without intending to hurt people. He is too awkward and too powerful to gauge a blow and reduce its force, but he is not naturally brutal ... earnest and fierce enough when boxing, but is a kindly, well-meaning fellow." Bob was eventually acquitted. *New York Times*: "The bag punching by 'Joe' Choynski attracted much attention, and he was heartily applauded, but things were different when he took on the colored man George (sic) Armstrong for his punching bag. (Bob) was a trifle too much for 'Joe,' and the rounds had to be chopped off very short." They sparred six rounds. Among the bouts were "Kid" McCoy "of Minneapolis" and Billy Vernon, "The Haverstraw Brick-maker."[26]

Bob Armstrong, 1899

Corbett was also training in Asbury Park, for the Fitzsimmons fight. "After breakfast Jim ... takes his bicycle for a 10-mile spin ... Oftentimes he pays a short visit to Parson Davies, who has a 'farm' about a mile west of

Asbury Park. The Parson has a fine collection of 'pugs' on hand just now, including Jimmie Barry, Joe Choinski (sic) and Bob Armstrong ... Bob ... has strength and willingness ... but ... is a long way from being scientific. Joe Choynski ... like a midget beside him, can punch holes in him. Bob is good natured, but sometimes a ... nasty jab makes him hot, and ... onlookers chase around for clubs to defend themselves. Jim ... cheers the big negro on in his work by telling him he is a wonder."[27]

On the 4th of July, Davies wrote a letter from Asbury Park, stating: "Joe Choynski and wife left last week for Cincinnati, where the couple will pay a short visit. Sullivan's benefit ... netted him about $4,200. Through the kind offices of Al Smith, Corbett and I shook hands and are now on friendly terms ... on the day of Sullivan's benefit. Yesterday (Jimmy) Barry and I called on Corbett ... he and Barry played a game of handball with Delaney and Corbett's brother, defeating them by three points. They are coming over to ... play another friendly game in our handball court, and we will probably have another large lady audience, such as was present yesterday. We stay here until July 13 and then go on to Boston for Barry's match (with a Dave Ross) ... I intend making another effort to get O'Donnell to meet Joe." On the 6th, the "Parson" sent a certified check for $1,000 to Al Smith at the Gilsey House in New York, as a forfeit to bind a match with Steve O'Donnell. Davies specified that if the O'Donnell challenge was rejected, the 2nd preference for an opponent for Choynski would be Jim Hall.[28]

Corbett was interviewed by the July 7 *Wheeling Register* regarding O'Donnell, who was Jim's sparring partner and highly thought of by him. He said: "Joe Choynski is foolish to meet O'Donnell ... That challenge is all a bluff in my opinion. Any man who knows anything about sports knows that O'Donnell is about to get a match with Peter Maher. Parson Davies is well aware of that ... he knows O'Donnell won't break that match to fight Choynski."[29] Davies' sincerity was genuine, although, not until 1899 would Joe and Steve "cross swords." Shortly before this, Davies and Tommy Ryan parted company, as revealed by the July 8 *Chicago Daily Inter-Ocean:* "Parson Davies has had a run of poor luck with his men on the last Eastern trip. The Smith-Ryan contest at Coney Island barely paid the cost of preparing the welter-weight champion for battle. Then came the split between the 'Parson' and his man. This was no surprise to those who are acquainted with the relative temperaments of manager and fighter. On top of this, the Choynski-Hall fight petered out after Davies' man had incurred all the expense of a diligent course of training." The next noteworthy event of Choynski's ring career would have significant overtones.

Round Thirteen

The First Light-Heavyweight Champion
(August 1895 – March 1896)

Joe and Louise were in Cincinnati (actually its suburb of Walnut Hills), as the *New York Clipper* of July 13 and July 30 noted, to celebrate the 50th wedding anniversary of Thomas and Mary Miller. "Joe Choynski and his wife, formerly Lutie Miller, are here to attend the golden wedding of the latter's parents." An August 9 dispatch said Joe and Jim Hall were "matched for a glove contest to a finish for the light heavyweight championship of the world to take place between October 26 and November 5." Such a division had long been proposed, even needed, and Joe had been referred to, as early as July 29, 1893, as the light-heavyweight champion. On August 20 in Louisville, Kentucky, Joe scored a 2nd round knockout over a minor player named Dick Wilson, nothing more being found of the bout. The August 27 *Brooklyn Daily Eagle* wrote, "Joe Choyinski (sic), the light heavyweight champion, arrived in Chicago from Louisville, Ky. last evening, and boarded a train a few hours later for Boston. Choyinski is to meet George Godfrey ... before the Suffolk Athletic club of Boston, Mass. Thursday night. Joe says he is in fine condition and, having defeated George in 15 ... a few years ago, naturally expects to repeat the trick."[1]

The men were to fight that night (other accounts said the 29th), along with a Joe Walcott-Dick O'Brien fight, as part of a boxing carnival, but it was called off. O'Brien was arrested by Boston police on a charge of prize-fighting, which prompted directors of the club to "postpone the event indefinitely. Godfrey, Connolly and Garrard were at the rink ready to go on. Choyinski ... in a hotel near at hand, was represented by Parson Davies. The action of the police was not unexpected by the carnival management. The contests ... were purely in keeping with scientific boxing ... the same that have been held in Boston in the past, and in no way could be termed other than scientific bouts ..." The law was making a test case of the Walcott-O'Brien bout, to see whether "in giving such exhibitions, the club was acting with its charter or not ... should the decision be favorable to the club, the events scheduled for to-night will be pulled off some time within a week ..."[2] While the legal outcome is not known, the rematch with Godfrey never happened. The September 5 *Call* reported it was "almost certain the next match held at Colma will be between Sharkey, 'the demon of the navy,' and Joe Choynski, the old war-horse ... Choynski has written to a friend in this City that he will journey to California and fight Sharkey or any other heavyweight, if anything like reasonable inducements are offered ... Sharkey does not seem anxious to fight anybody at present ..."

On the night of September 2, at a hall in Washington (now Broderick), California (Yolo County), a notable fight came off. The next day's *Los Angeles Herald* reported a "slugging match" for a purse of $50: "The contestants were Morris Choynski and Billy Lynch. it is said Lynch was completely knocked out in the fourth round. The fighters wore six-ounce gloves." The only "Morris" Choynski known to be living in California was Joe's brother, Maurice, although he moved sometime that year to Pittsburgh, Pennsylvania. If this *was* Maurice, then Joe wasn't the only member of the family to have boxed professionally!

Tom O'Rourke, manager of such greats as George Dixon, Joe Walcott and "Sailor" Tom Sharkey, discussed a collaboration with Davies. The plan was to begin a tour in Philadelphia at the Winter Circus on September 17, after which they would visit other major northern cities, before doing a route of southern venues. O'Rourke would have Dixon, Walcott and a Joe Elms in his string, while Davies would take Choynski, Barry and Armstrong. The team would wind up their southern visit in Dallas, Texas at the boxing carnival being held there. Then, they would head back to New York and embark for the United Kingdom on December 15. Tommy Ryan was to join them in England, from where the group would sail for the Cape country of South Africa, where boxing was booming. They would be gone about two years. The attraction was to be known as the National Athletic Club of America, and would feature wrestling, bag punching, weightlifting and other athletic exercises in addition to boxing. Davies went into minute detail about the venture and added, "I have arranged to have Tommy Ryan train at San Antonio, and he will go there about four weeks before his fight with Smith. He is living in Syracuse, having gone into the saloon business with Tom Cawley, a local boxer. He says that he has a nice place and is doing very well."[3] The name of the saloon was "The Champion." Actually, Ryan would not fight another bout under Davies' management.

On September 16, Joe's father-in-law, Thomas S. Miller passed away, less than two months after he and Mary celebrated their golden anniversary. Joe and Louise were back in Cincinnati for the funeral. The cause of death was listed as "sclerosis of liver." Thomas was 71 or 72 years old. He was buried at Walnut Hills Cemetery. Records show his interment date as "Sep 20, 1892," but the year is a typo. Actress daughter Etta Lewis signed as "nearest relative." He would eventually be joined there by Mary, daughters Etta and Louise, and Joe. On the 29th, the *Chicago Tribune* said, "Joe Choynski, the light heavyweight champion" had arrived in the Windy City the night previous, looking "fine as silk." The paper commented on his bad luck in getting fights. Joe didn't know "whether he is a 'Jonah' or not," but was "willing to test it" by making matches with any boxer in his class.

The September 16 *Daily Inter-Ocean* made its case that Joe and Ryan overtrained. "Tommy Ryan, in a letter ... dated Mount Clemens (Michigan) states he is now taking matters easy at the Michigan watering place, and ... will start in training actively for the Smith fight in about two weeks. Tommy ... appears to have come to his senses. Overtrained and drawn down to a point approximating collapse, the welter-weight champion has not entered the ring right for a year. His has been an eternal grind, a wearying, strength-sapping, endless training, which has reduced his speed and stemmed his powers of endurance ... With nothing on, Tom has been known to keep himself on 'edge' for months with his bag-punching, wrestling, sprinting and rope-skipping. The result has been that he has been 'ready for a fight at the drop of the hat' whenever called upon. Like Choynski, Ryan is an inordinate worker. Both men are forever at it, 'to keep in shape.' The system is wrong. A scrapper should allow himself rest." Choynski was indeed a "workaholic" in regard to training. To blame many of his setbacks on overtraining, though, might be stretching the point a bit.

September 25 *Inter-Ocean*: "Fitzsimmons would like ... Choynski as a second to back him up in the fight with Corbett. No one knows better than Fitz the qualities that are responsible for Choynski's reputation as the best second that ever wielded a towel over a man in the ring (a reference to the Maher fight). The fair-haired Californian had not heard personally from Fitzsimmons on the subject. 'I would not be adverse to seconding Fitz,' said Choynski last night, 'but I would most seriously object to playing 2nd fiddle to anyone in Fitz's corner. If I am to second him I want to have sole charge of him in the ring, and not stand like a dummy, subject to the advice of any other man he may have in his corner. I do not want some *pudding-head* to tell me what to do and how to do it.' Choynski admits he was a sick man on the day he was to have fought Godfrey, but contends he could have remained the full limit of the 20 rounds. He states ... Davies gave up some money in order to call the fight off, and this at a point where it was impossible to proceed with it. Had Davies waited an hour longer the club would have been compelled to pay Choynski his training expenses."

Shortly before this, Davies began managing the two old bareknuckle pugs, John L. Sullivan and Paddy Ryan, promoting them on tours. Not surprisingly, the two old sots gave Davies a lot of angst. Alcohol and pugilism (hell, alcohol and anything!) seldom mix well. The "Parson" was having a run of bad luck all around, his most recent matches being cancelled, either by sickness or politics. Also, the planned "Tour de United States," combining his and O'Rourke's stables had to be scrapped, due in large part to an indictment against Joe Walcott in Boston for prizefighting. Instead, Davies planned to take Sullivan and Ryan on a tour, beginning in early October. Charlie commented to the *Daily Inter-Ocean* on rumors that an injury to Jim Corbett's knee (supposedly on a fall from his bicycle) might prevent him from defending his heavyweight crown against "Freckled Bob" Fitzsimmons. Davies said he would be more than willing to have Choynski stand in against Bob if "Gentleman Jim" pulled out of the fight.[4]

Dr. John Wilson Gibbs, physician and anthropometrist, made a statement to several papers regarding Corbett's courage, or rather, lack of it. Gibbs treated at different times, Sullivan, Corbett, Peter Jackson, Jim Hall, Fitzsimmons and Choynski, and as he put it, "I have made a thorough study of them all." He said Corbett was a coward, giving examples to support the statement. First, he recalled how, when Jim came to him "for treatment a few months prior to his contest with John L. Sullivan," he "was possessed of an abnormally high-strung nervous system."

"As a crisis ... would approach, Corbett would become so nervous he ... seemed on the verge of prostration. With an adversary ... he knew positively he could defeat he would not experience this ... the moment he faced an opponent whose courage and skill he had reason to respect he would be overwhelmed with extreme nervousness ... I am told on the best authority that Corbett became so nervous and frightened as the train bearing him and his party approached the scene of ... battle between Sullivan and himself he was overcome with diarrhea and fell away ... from 186 to 178 pounds ... when he knew Sullivan was a physical wreck and in no shape to do battle. The formidable name of Sullivan alone terrified him. At the opening ... he was painfully nervous and had to be braced up by mysterious 'tonics.' " This contradicted stories of Corbett's gamesmanship just before the fight, supposedly tricking the superstitious John into entering the ring first.

"When Corbett fought Joe Choynski ... he wanted to 'quit' ... in the 21st round, saying his hands pained him so that he could go no further. He was even about to pull his gloves off when his trainer and second, Billy Delaney ... said: 'My God, Jim, don't quit now; see, you've got him all but finished. A few more punches will do the trick.' " Gibbs showed a negative bias toward Jim; that, or he was seeking publicity. Many took exception to the doctor's assessment of Corbett, at least one eyewitness saying Jim was as cool before the Sullivan fight as any man had ever been in a ring.[5] There was nothing to suggest that Gibbs was a qualified psychologist.

The first stop for Davies' tour was People's Theater in Toledo, Ohio. Besides Sullivan and Paddy Ryan, the combination included Joe Choynski. "The Parson" wrote, in a letter to Harry Glickauf, that "Choynski's ball punching met with hearty applause, and he was voted an artist in that line." On October 10, Davies and gang left for Pittsburgh, Pennsylvania, to meet with John J. Quinn, backer of Peter Maher, and arrange a fight between the Irishman and Joe. The plan was for a finish fight the following spring, winner take all. At Pittsburgh's Bijou Theater, a SRO crowd saw the troupe. On the 18th in Jersey City, New Jersey, the quartet played to another packed house. Davies said they had nothing further planned, but he was trying to arrange stops in New York State, with Detroit, Michigan to follow.[6]

Choynski told the October 20 *St. Paul Daily Globe* that he picked Corbett to defeat Fitzsimmons. Joe, having traded punches with both, said Jim was more clever and elusive, and Bob's only chance would be to bore in and triumph by superior infighting. Of the type of fighter able to succeed in this manner, i.e., Goddard or Slavin, Joe felt that, while Bob had the necessary strength, he was delicate around the head, unable to take it sufficiently in that area. It wouldn't be the first time "Game Joe" would be wrong in picking a winner. To be fair, though, many felt that Corbett had Fitz knocked out in round six, but for a slow count by the referee.

The sparring tour continued, but Joe was the only one of Davies' boxers to participate. "The Parson," Sullivan and Ryan had departed, and Davies remained on tour with them until January. "Joe Choynski, who fills a week's engagement at Sam T. Jack's, beginning next Sunday (November 1), has been hard pressed to find a suitable sparring partner. Will Mayo, the tall fellow who fought Henry Baker at Roby and knocked out Herman Bernau a few days ago, was finally secured and will box Choynski whenever no ambitious local man can be induced to go against the Californian." The entertainment was held at Chicago's Madison Street Opera House. November 3: "Joe Choynski, the most popular of local boxers, will appear at each performance. Mr. Choynski will head a troop of athletes – boxers and wrestlers – and will spar with Will Mayo, punch the bag and meet all ambitious young men in friendly competition."

The next day, Joe put on a bag punching exhibition. November 4 *Chicago Inter-Ocean*: "Mayo and Choynski had two bouts yesterday ... friendly contests for points and the blows ... mere taps. Some pretty sparring was displayed ... and Choynski had plenty of opportunities to display his ability." They repeated the performance nightly. On November 6, "There were two lively bouts ... The first was a three-round go between Will Mayo and Burt Leslie, both Chicago men. Mayo had all the best of it. In the 2nd bout, Tom Silverthorn, a husky blacksmith of New York, stood in front of Choynski for three rounds. Choynski made a monkey of his man, landing at will, while Silverthorn was unable to touch him." Real fights were not always obtainable, due to the quasi-legal climate of the day. Joe, while not quite languishing, was also not polishing his skills against top-flight talent.

Around this time, there was a falling out between Joe and Tommy Ryan, largely due to a clash of personalities. Ryan declared on November 9 that he would fight Joe "at any time and place the latter may desire." "The challenge grew out of a personal quarrel and some remarks made by Ryan in Chicago." Around the end of September, a Chicago paper wrote: "Whatever may be Choynski's opinion of Tommy Ryan as a fighter, he certainly has not a very high regard for him as a man. Ryan's innate self-conceit and ungrateful actions to those who have befriended him in the past are two qualifications that would not serve to commend him in the eyes of a man of Choynski's stamp. For little Jimmy Barry, though, Choynski expresses the greatest admiration ... 'Barry is a fighter from the top of his head to the sole of his feet, and ready to go up against anything that he may be pitted against at the shortest kind of a notice. It seems to make no difference to him whether there is any money in sight or not.' "

November 7 *Inter-Ocean*: "Although Choynski and Ryan are under the same management, they have no love for each other. Joe accuses Tom of having a swelled head and says he is not as good a boxer as he would have people believe, and Tom says similar things of Joe. Ryan ... to convince Joe he is his superior, will box him four, six or eight rounds any night during Choynski's present engagement at Sam Jack's." On the night of November 9, Mayo, boxed Silverthorn. The 2nd go was between Choynski and Al Tulrock. Joe "... hitting him whenever and wherever he pleased."[8] The November 11 *Milwaukee Evening Wisconsin* wrote, of the new Illinois Athletic Club: "Joe Choynski has practically been decided upon as the athletic instructor for the recently organized athletic and social club of the bank clerks in Chicago." Joe's appointment would last several years and lead to similar positions. So popular was the Sam T. Jack show, it was booked to play in the city "indefinitely," and expanded to include "Lewis and Fields, parodists; Grace Celeste, dancer, and ... Sergeant McCue of the regular army, in cavalry, trumpet and bugle exercises." Joe attended that evening's Peter Maher-Steve O'Donnell match at the Empire A.C. in Maspeth, Queens, New York, and saw Maher blitzkrieg his hapless foe in one round.[9]

The *Daily Inter-Ocean* of the 14th featured an article on bag punching. Besides a brief history of the device, it illustrated how recent bag punching exhibitions caught on so well in Chicago that they were considered "better than boxing" and perhaps threatened to replace it. Quite an exaggeration. "Professor" Mike Donovan (legendary middleweight champion and instructor, father of famed boxing referee, Arthur Donovan, who himself sired noted NFL player, Art Donovan) is often credited with inventing the first "speed" punching bag. It is also attributed to Pete McCoy, a trainer of John L. Sullivan, though a Simon Kehoe was granted a U.S. patent for a version in 1872. Mike stated in "Donovan's Science of Boxing" (1893) that he began use of it while training for an 1878 fight against William McClellan. He initially bounded a round, rubber foot-ball "alternately with the right and left hand from the floor to the ceiling ..." but later suspended the ball from the ceiling. The bag was popularized by Pete McCoy in John L. Sullivan's training camp for the 1882 Paddy Ryan bout, the first specimen being no more than an association football suspended from the ceiling. The soccer ball in that era resembled a medicine ball, though much lighter. Use of the heavy bag originated much earlier, though just when isn't known. They were much lighter than modern heavy bags.

"The question of who is the champion bag puncher is almost as difficult ... to decide as football supremacy. It seems ... Tommy Ryan has the best claim to the title. Ryan is very clever ... with his feet and ... hands, and adds all the quickness which has distinguished his work in the ring. Joe Choynski is another claimant to the rank ... extremely clever and rapidly improving in his work with the ball. A reporter for the *Inter-Ocean* found the big Catalonian (sic) in his dressing room at Sam T. Jack's Theater ... waiting to do his act with the bag. Choynski said that, although he had been using the bag ever since he had been boxing, he had only been using it for exhibition purposes a few months. He does nothing but straight punching and does

Billy Stift, 1902

but little work in juggling the ball. The blows he uses are straight from the shoulder and are clean, knock-out blows. He has several platforms, one ... built under his supervision, cost him but $3.50."

"Corbett is an excellent bag puncher, although he does not pay so much attention to it as some ... He moves all around the ball like a cat, and rains in his blows from all sides. Jimmy Barry, Fitzsimmons, Mellody ... Jimmy Handler ... and Tommy McKeever ... are among the prominent men at the bag. Fitzsimmons has a clever trick for concluding his performance. Like Choynski, he ends with a number of heavy swings and in the last of these, by a peculiar blow, breaks the rope and sends the ball spinning into the balcony ..." A statement said that baseball writer Billy (William A.) Phelon would box Joe at Sam T. Jack's that night, November 16, "the outcome of some bantering talk a few days ago." Phelon was among the top sportswriters of his generation. He had earlier been a famous amateur baseball player and boxer. Billy undertook to stay three rounds with Joe, "a wine supper and numerous side bets" being at stake. Choynski had a friendly set-to on the night of the 13th with Billy Stift, a hard-punching heavyweight.[10]

The November 14 *Chicago Daily Inter-Ocean* noted: "Joe Choynski has a large order on hand at Sam T. Jack's today. In the afternoon, he will box Charley O'Connor, well known as an esthetic sport around town. At night he meets Frank Childs, the big, colored fighter, and expects a warm tussle." That evening, Joe met the once-formidable Childs and toyed with him for two and a half rounds. "Nearing the close of the last round, Joe shot in a short-arm right to the point of the jaw and Childs went to earth. He got up like a man looking for solace on Queer street, and Choynski let him off with a light tap. Tonight, wee Willie Phelon, feuilletonist, is to go up against Choynski. They are to box three rounds. The members of the unattached press will hold a memorial meeting tomorrow morning. Willie will have lived 22 useful years when his taking off occurs."[11]

To the humorous quip was added this sober notice from Syracuse, New York by a still-rancorous Tommy Ryan: "I did not run away from Chicago after making a bluff, as one paper had it. I will come back and ... meet Choynski a limited number of rounds, and I have every reason to believe I can best him."[12] The fight never materialized, but Joe's bout with Phelon apparently did. Writing for *Baseball Magazine* in 1914, Phelon declared: "Choynski could put simply annihilating force into a single blow, and could flash it in with startling speed. Wow, but how Joe could hit 'em! I KNOW ... I FELT ONE ... when I was young, I dreamed of the ring and its glories, ... donned the gloves, and I capered round a lot of stevedores and hamfats, and ... was advanced to the glory of a bout with Joe Choynski. Joe's legs were not specially good; he was too light for the big men, and didn't have quite the foxy skill and wary tactics of Fitzsimmons; but he could drive them over like a bullet, and when he smote they reeled, they fell. He'd have raked the white hopes (of Johnson's era) like a gatling gun."

On the 17th, the *Kansas City Star* printed Choynski's reply to Ryan's defi. Joe said Ryan was so far out of his weight class, a fight between the two was "out of the question." "I am doing pretty well in my own class, and Ryan can keep himself busy looking after welterweights. He is in Syracuse and I ... in Chicago, too far away to talk business. However, I am going to Buffalo (New York) Sunday night to take part in the J L Sullivan-Paddy Ryan entertainment, and while there will speak to 'Parson' Davies ... if Davies can arrange ... a six or eight round bout at Syracuse, I will convince Ryan he is barking up the wrong tree." Ryan, throughout his career, demonstrated he was a tough nut, not afraid of anyone. While training 220-pound heavyweight great Jim Jeffries, Ryan often went at him as if trying to knock his head off, many feeling he was jealous of Jeff's larger frame and status. Tommy thought he would have been a great heavyweight if he had been blessed with Jim's size. He was probably right. At times Ryan showed a cruel streak, as when he clubbed fellow Syracuse boxer and hulking heavyweight, Ed Dunkhorst, in the nose with a croquet mallet.[13]

Davies told *The Inter-Ocean* that the president of New York's Empire

Athletic Club, J.C. Kennedy, received a telegram from J.J. Quinn, manager of Peter Maher, saying "he ... preferred a match with Bob Fitzsimmons to one with Joe Choynski." Davies: "I am at a loss to understand Mr. Quinn's statement, inasmuch as he promised Joe ... and myself in Pittsburgh a short time ago that, in the event of ... Maher defeating Steve O'Donnell, Joe should have the first contest with Maher, stating ... it was not necessary to sign an agreement. A few hours after Maher had defeated O'Donnell, Mr. Quinn reiterated his statements ... Kennedy ... is prepared to arrange such a contest ..."[14] By December 1, Davies was in St. Louis, saying he would "bring ... his entire troupe ... to take part in the benefit. The party was to include "John L. Sullivan, Paddy Ryan, Joe ... Ryan and (Jimmy) Barry.

Rumors abounded that an injury to the right hand of bantam Jimmy Barry had ended his boxing career. He broke the hand five weeks earlier in a fight with "Kid" Madden, and it had been in a cast since. In refuting the rumor, a writer for the December 3 *Inter-Ocean* visited Dr. F.W. McNamara, the physician used by Davies. McNamara treated Joe when he had need for medical attention, and treated Barry's injury. The doctor advised that "the fracture was in the bone which connects with the index finger and has healed very neatly. Choynski suffered the same injury, although a pistol shot, and not a blow on an opponent's head, was the cause ... Joe put out a 250-pound colored pugilist with a blow from that same hand soon after, and never caused himself a moment's pain."

On December 4, "The Parson," accompanied by Empire A.C. president, Jim Kennedy, met J.J. Quinn at Green's Hotel in Philadelphia, where he tried to clinch a match between Joe and Peter Maher. Quinn made it clear that he would make no such agreement, as Maher would consider no opponent except Fitzsimmons, for the "world title." Corbett had recently announced his retirement and "conferred" the heavyweight championship on Maher, a thing he had no clear right to do. Peter, to his credit, refused the appointment, wanting to fight for the crown against the consensus top contender, Fitz. Quinn offered, " 'If Choynski wants a fight, I will match Jim Hall against him.' This match was made at once, catch weights at Maspeth, on January 13, next." Prior to leaving for New York, Davies made a rather silly statement, based on the idea that the championship had defaulted back to Sullivan, in the event of Corbett's retirement: "I do not propose that Choynski shall be declared out of the championship class, and as John L. Sullivan is now champion of the world again, I shall challenge him on behalf of Choynski. Sullivan will not fight again and he will retire in favor of Choynski, and the winner of the Fitzsimmons-Maher fight will be compelled to challenge Joe for the championship."[15] This was all mooted by the fact that Corbett eventually reclaimed his title as heavyweight champion and defended (unsuccessfully) against Bob Fitzsimmons.

Joe, Sullivan, Paddy Ryan and Davies arrived in Chicago on the night of

December 8. The four "returned to the Hotel Imperial after a drive of 10 miles behind one of William C. Bailey's high steppers. This was ... shortly after 5 o'clock (p.m.). Bailey had piloted the big fellow into the café and thrown a bowl into him, which appeared to thaw the ex-champion out a bit." He proceeded to call Corbett and Fitzsimmons "a couple of rats," saying they had "done more to injure the sport of boxing than any 10 men you can pick out." He said Jim "thinks more of the arrangement of his hair than he does of his reputation." The gist of Sullivan's rant was that the fighters should do less yakking and more smacking. He called Tommy Ryan "a cur." John often showed a bitter, angry side. He admitted his bigotry, saying, "I do not like colored people, would never consent to fight them, and yet I have a regard for them if they show they are right."

"Harry Weldon, erudite sporting editor of the *Cincinnati Enquirer*, has the following to say about the proposed match between ... Ryan and Joe Choynski: 'Parson Davies, who is managing the two ... will not let them fight ... Ryan is conceited enough to think he can whip Choynski. It would take the latter about three rounds to make Tommy get the pipe ideas out of his head.' " By this time, Davies was only loosely affiliated with Ryan.[16] On December 27, Joe was at San Francisco's People's Palace Theatre, as part of the benefit for the late Jack Dempsey's widow and two orphaned daughters. "Crowds stood in the doorways and aisles. All prominent politicians and sporting men of the city were on hand. Billy Jordan was master of ceremonies." Joe sparred with "Spider" Kelly, Tom Sharkey with Billy Geogan, and Alex Greggains boxed Joe King. "Young Mitchell" was presented with "two huge floral pieces and made a little speech."[17]

Shortly afterward, the *Galveston Daily News* ran a story, questioning the courage of Peter Maher. Several fighters levied accusations that Maher quit in the 12th round against Fitz and in round three of his first fight with Goddard. Choynski disagreed: "I don't say Peter Maher is a quitter ... I impugn no man's courage. What chastity is to a woman, 'heart' is to a fighter. To say he lacks this quality is to put a dagger in his reputation. Unquestionably, Maher is a great fighter. How great, I wish he would give me a chance to find out. I have challenged him to battle, and he cannot ignore that challenge ... Fitzsimmons and Goddard ... may want a fight with Peter ... but I claim first call, as I was first in the field to challenge."

"I don't take much stock in Maher's defeat of O'Donnell. The latter appeared like a dead man the moment he got in the ring. His much vaunted skill appeared to have vanished. How he could possibly have let Maher cross him with a right-hander early in the conflict and put him out, passes my comprehension. If Maher would try that with me, I'll promise to jolt his head and neck for him. A dummy, not to say a clever man, ought to have been able to stop Maher's rush with a straight left-hander or step out of harm's way. Technically, Maher is not world's champion. Corbett had no more right to hand over the title to him than I have to deed away to a friend a house of which I have only a lease. He could only retire and let the belt and title be fought for. The press and public, however, seem inclined to bestow the title on Peter, so we will let it go at that. He will have to fight for it, anyway, so it is all the same in the end."[18]

The January 3, 1896 *St. Louis Republic* bore the news that, "George Schwegler, the champion amateur boxer of the New York Athletic Club, has been prevailed upon by his clubmates to put on the gloves in a limited round contest with Joe Choynski. The mill will take place some time this week before a selected crowd. Schwegler is a fast and skillful boxer, but hardly in Choynski's class." This bout never came to fruition, which was probably a good thing for Schwegler. Joe was, if not in search of a division, badly in need of one. He was too heavy to get his weight down to fight middleweights, but as there was no firmly established 175-pound, or light-heavyweight, classification in at least the first half of Choynski's career, he fought by necessity fighters who far outweighed him. Today he is often considered to have been a heavyweight, but only because he fought in the unlimited division by mandate. Fights at "catch-weights" with 160-pounders didn't happen much for heavier fighters.

For the first time (that is known), Joe was to engage in a fight billed for the "light-heavyweight championship." "Manager Kennedy of the Empire Club at Maspeth, Long Island, has arranged a good bill ... The star bout ... between Jim Hall ... and Joe Choynski ... should prove an exciting one. They will box 20 rounds at catch weights for the light heavyweight championship of America. Hall is in training at Pittsburgh, while Choynski is doing his work at a Chicago gymnasium. 'Parson' Davies ... says the only fault he has to find with Choynski is that he may overtrain. Joe likes work and can take any amount of punishment ... should Choynski win, he will match him against ... Maher or Fitzsimmons." On the 11th, Joe left for New York to complete preparations at the New York A.C. for Jim Hall, at whose request the bout's date was changed from the 13th to the 20th. Just before departing his south-side training quarters in Chicago, Joe was weighed, in his clothes, at 182 pounds. At the New York club, Choynski sparred daily with the club's instructor, legendary middleweight, "Professor" Mike Donovan. Joe said: "I feel better at the present moment than I have for two years, and never felt more confident of winning a contest than I do this one."[19]

When Hall first arrived in America (1891), he was described as "One of the shiftiest, quickest men ever ... from Australia, as light on his feet as a kitten, with a right hand ... as the left foot of a mule. He ducks like a bantam, hits like a heavyweight, and combines with both the profound knowledge of attack and defence accorded to but a few boxers in a century." He was considered "as good a fighter in his class as could be wished," but after the knockout loss to Fitz, Jim indulged in alcohol. Lately, though, "his admirers insist his training has been consistently good ... he is now in the best of condition and ready to make the fight of his life. Be that as it may, he will find in Choynski a man whose habits are correct and whose physical condition is perfect ... The plucky fighter (Joe) will carry all the Chicago coin, no matter what odds prevail."[20]

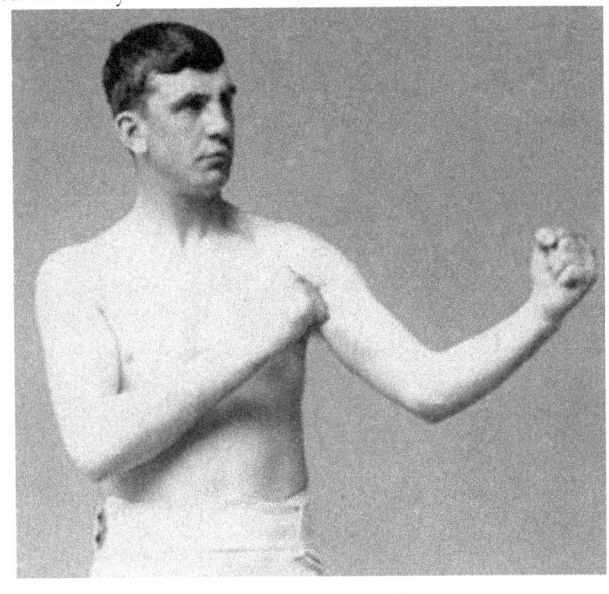

Jim Hall, of Australia

January 17 *Brooklyn Daily Eagle*: "Choynski ... finishing up his training at the New York Athletic Club, is a busy boxer ... having himself tried out by the boxing members of the New York club ... a great many members ... are clever with the gloves ... every one ... wanted a bout with the big Californian the first day he made his appearance ... Joe is a big, good-natured fellow, and of course he did not like to refuse the ambitious boxers. The 1st day he boxed three men, the 2nd day six, and yesterday ... a dozen, and undoubtedly would have kept on increasing had the Californian accepted all offers made to him. 'I suppose I would have had the whole club after me if I had remained here another week,' laughingly remarked Choynski yesterday afternoon, after he got through boxing with the club's instructor. Professor Donovan, in speaking of the contest, had this to say: 'In my mind it will be one of the best contests ever seen in the Empire arena. They say Hall is in good shape and I am positive that Choynski is; that is all that is necessary for a first class contest. I am of the opinion that, barring accident, Choynski will surely win.' "

January 19 edition: "In all ... previous contests, the big Californian has shown great vitality, as well as recuperating powers. Choynski has a left ... hook that has made more than one aspirant for pugilistic honors fall by the way side. He is a favorite ... from the fact that he is such a careful man in the ring, never taking any desperate chances that might cause him to lose the contest. Hall, on the other hand, is generally given credit for being an all around good fellow, who likes good living. This aside, he is credited with being a clever fellow, a good ring general and a scientific fighter. The

Australian will have the advantage ... in the way of reach and height ...'"

One paper noted on January 20: "Keen interest is being shown in the 20-round contest ... between ... Jim Hall and Joe Choynski ... the recognized heavy-weight (sic) champion. Choynski has been in New York for a week ... working under the best generals and preparatory instructors that the pugilistic world has ever seen. A telegram to Al Smith from Connolly, Hall's manager and backer, says that Hall could not possibly be in better trim. Hall says that if defeated, he will forever retire from pugilism, while Choynski, if victorious, declares his intention of forcing Corbett into another battle." An edition of The *Ring* (circa 1960) said, "When Choynski entered the ring against Jim Hall, two of his ribs were broken due to an accident he suffered in the 'gym' at the New York Athletic Club the day before the fight." Joe related, in 1930, that he "went into the ring handicapped by several broken ribs. These were given me by Dody Schwangler ... an amateur, a favorite pupil of Mike Donovan ... I was pulling my punches and offering no defense. This was an exhibition. Suddenly, Schwangler landed a crazy heave that shattered several of my ribs. Hall thought he had my goat. As I passed him, he said, 'There goes that Choynski fellow. I'll make a monkey of him. He can't hit me with a sack full of beans.' " It was later claimed Donovan pupil, Fred Winthrop, inflicted the damage. Mike also attested to the incident, but didn't name who he called a former champion from Yale.[21]

That night, a packed house of 4,000 to 5,000 saw a hotly-contested fight at the Empire A.C. As usual, varying weights were given for the contestants. Joe was generally said to be 161 pounds, while Jim's avoirdupois ranged from 160 to 166. As the fight was at "catch-weights," the men didn't need to make a certain weight. Joe was first to enter the ring, "with the usual tawny Chrysanthemum hair which distinguishes him in all his fights." He was attended by Tom O'Rourke, "Kid" McCoy and Casper Leon; Davies was also there. "The Parson never takes any active interest in his protégé's corners." Hall's seconds were Sam Fitzpatrick, Jack Fogarty of Philadelphia, Benny Murphy and Tim Scanlon. Well-known baseball umpire, Tim Hurst, refereed and the announcer was Charley Harvey. A blend of nearly a dozen primary reports follows, with secondary sources added.[22]

Round 1 – The men dispensed with the customary handshake, likely due to the ill feeling between them. After initial "fiddling," they went to work, with little harm done. Joe ducked a pair of rights, stepping nimbly out of range. He landed two lefts to Jim's stomach and one to the mouth. They exchanged lefts to the body. Joe landed a hard left, to end the round.

Round 2 – They sparred for an opening. Jim was especially defensive, though he landed several stiff jabs to the nose. Joe drove a right over the heart, took a measuring left from Hall, but ducked the follow-up right, meant to be a crusher. Joe landed a hard left smash to the "wind" just before the bell. The round was about even, or a bit in Choynski's favor.

Round 3 – Joe made Hall's body the target of some authoritative lefts and pursued him about the ring. He was trying to get Hall to drop his guard, but he was on to the scheme. Jim preferred to either bend his torso back out of the way, ala Peter Jackson, or take the punch, rather than expose his head. He drove a right over the heart, but Joe countered with a straight left to the body. Hall landed one sharp jab to the head, but the crowd found the proceedings tame, and they hissed.

Round 4 – Opinions differed. The *Boston Herald, San Francisco Call* and London *Mirror of Life* said Hall had a small edge, landing on Joe's ribs and head, the last saying he raised a lump over Joe's eye. The *Brooklyn Eagle* and a *Police Gazette*, circa 1921, said Joe got the better of it, with a body attack. The latter wrote, "Punch after punch, hard enough, it seemed, to bore a hole, found their way into the pit of the Australian's stomach, leaving (it) bruised and almost bleeding. Hall's straight lefts found their way to the neck, but the blows seemed to lack the power of muscle behind them."

Round 5 – Choynski smashed a hard right to the ribs. Jim shot a straight left for the face, but Joe countered, bringing "his right glove over with crushing force on the side of his opponent's head. The latter was stunned for an instant, but stepped into a clinch ... Hall's left found ... the Californian's nose and the blood spurted ... in a stream." Jim landed smart jabs and a few rights, but Joe was wild. He slipped to the canvas, but rallied to close the heat with a good body shot or two. Hall's round. *Brooklyn Daily Eagle*: "Hall('s) ... defensive work was particularly fine. Choynski ... swung round with the force of his attempt ... Hall rushed ... to seize his advantage, but the wily Californian slipped to his knee ... As Choynski turned ... and tried to sprint near the ropes, Hall's heavy left was flung out flush in his face ... Choynski went to his corner with blood flowing profusely."

Round 6 – Joe connected with left and right to the head, but got some hard jabs to the nose. He landed to Hall's stomach, Jim countering with a hard right to the face that briefly staggered him. Just before the bell, Joe dropped Hall to his knees from a hard right to the head, and Jim took six seconds before rising. Joe was bleeding profusely at the close. *New York Sun*: "Hall landed left and right on Choynski's nose and the latter rushed his man to the ropes, where both fell, Joe on top. When they got up, they began slugging until both were clearly tired." *Brooklyn Daily Eagle*: "Hall's long reach now came into play. He kept Joseph at long range for a while and jabbed him repeatedly; Choynski ... mixed it up roughly ... however, and Hall was obliged to break ground before the ... onslaught."

Round Seven – Joe's mechanics were lacking and he looked awkward, although he landed a heavy punch to the body. His defense looked porous, "missing many a chance to get away from an incoming straight punch." Hall was slow in taking advantage of some "capital openings." Once, while Joe was ducking, Hall caught him with a good right uppercut to the chin and a hard left to the jaw. Jim ... was shifty on his feet and elusive, continuing to land the stinging left jab and at least one right to the face.

Round 8 – Joe drove a left to the body, a right to the head and chased Hall around the ring. He landed some good lefts to the face, but was wild with many punches. Jim landed the jab frequently and a few good rights to the head, thereby taking the round. A lone paper, *The San Francisco Call*, said it was Hall who chased Choynski around the ring.

Round 9 – Hall landed a hurting left to the body. Joe lowered his arms for a second to guard the busted ribs. Hall capped him with a short right to the jaw, flooring Joe. (The *Brooklyn Eagle* said it was "a half-arm punch right over the heart.") The latter took eight seconds from referee Hurst, but climbed to his feet. He was dazed and Hall connected with another right, straight to the chin. Again Joe fell, and it looked bad for him. Two papers said Joe fell the 2nd time from weakness or from missing a punch. Choynski said in 1930, that his ribs felt as if they were sticking through his skin. He took an eight or nine-count before rising, and Hall pursued for the knockout. Joe kept away and defended, but got in a left to the face and right to the stomach. Jim landed three lefts, but he was tired and unable to finish Joe. The latter clinched and was said to have been "saved by the bell." The crowd made a thunderous cheer in seeing Joe survive the round. The *Mirror of Life* disagreed, feeling that Hall, after the 2nd knockdown, stayed his attack, either through mercy or seeking an opportunity for a finisher. "He was hissed loudly by the spectators for not taking advantage of the situation and putting Choynski out." It was the turning point of the fight.

Round 10 – Joe said in 1930, that he went to his corner at the end of the 9th "feeling pretty low. Tom O'Rourke, in my corner, looked at me inquiringly. I muttered: 'Don't worry, Tom. I'm not finished. I'll cut loose the next round.' And I certainly did. Hall was the most astonished man on Long Island when I came out fighting." Hall, thinking he only needed another punch or two to finish Joe, got a shock. "Choynski's prime condition began to assert itself, and he delighted and surprised his supporters by smashing Hall viciously and repeatedly on the ribs." "Hall winced, and spoke to Choynski in tones inaudible, but was evidently not pleased at the telling blow the Californian had dealt him." "Hall sent his left in the stomach twice ... while Choynski delivered a hard double blow in side and jaw." Hall seemed tired, but cool, as he tried to keep his distance and land the jab. This was a close round, but likely in Joe's favor.

Round 11 – Choynski targeted the body with a series of vicious shots, but in his zeal got a bit careless and Jim landed two stabbing lefts to the mouth and nose that started the blood flowing again. He landed a clean right to his adversary's jaw, but there was now a lot less steam behind his hardest punch. Joe landed a swinging right to the jaw near the end of the round that floored his rival. Hall was on one knee when the bell sounded.

Round 12 – Choynski aggressively pursued Hall. He landed two shots to the torso and a right to the mouth. This riled the Australian, who started trading haymakers with his tormentor. They went toe to toe, Joe smashing in hard body shots and Hall getting a right-hand scorcher to Joe's jaw (or nose) that staggered him a bit. Both were dead tired. The *Brooklyn Eagle* said Jim briefly "had Choynski at his mercy near the ropes," but this was the sole reference giving him even a brief advantage in the round. Joe shot a powerful right to the head that floored his rival. The *Police Gazette* said Joe scored a 2nd knockdown to end the round. The *San Francisco Call* and the *Mirror of Life* said the count was interrupted, at four, by the bell. The spectators cheered wildly as the men went to their corners.

Round 13 – Joe came rushing out and staggered Hall with a wicked left to the bread-basket. (The London paper said, to the neck). He swung left and right, until a left (or right) to the jaw dropped Jim. He clambered to his feet at nine and clinched. They traded vicious blows in ring center. Joe took after his man and threw a fusillade of punches the likes of which the crowd had not seen before. He was bleeding profusely again, but threw a stiff left and a full, swinging right blockbuster on the chin, sending Hall crashing to the deck. "The latter fell on his side, rolled over on his back, and remained there while the referee struck the air with 10 strokes." The round lasted one minute and 15 seconds. As soon as Hurst declared Choynski the winner, "Joe ran over and tried to help his beaten adversary to his feet. Hall was unable to rise and had to be carried to his corner. His seconds worked over him for 10 minutes ... then led him to his dressing room."

Joe and Davies arrived back in Chicago on the morning of the 22nd, "with the scalp of Jim Hall braided in their watch chains." "The only marks on his (Joe's) face are two red spots on his lips, which Joe claims are cold sores, and a scratch on the eye ... Both men denied the charges made by some of the writers at the ringside, that it was a lay-down, in strong terms. Choynski said that without doubt Hall fought his best clear through, but the steady punching in the stomach wore him out. 'Parson' Davies said Joe fought the gamest, pluckiest fight he ever saw in a ring. He had decided that all was over when he saw his man fall prostrate, and when he fell a 2nd time he was certain of it. By pure nerve, Joe pulled himself together and won out. He said he should certainly challenge the winner of the Maher-Fitzsimmons fight." The November 16, 1896 *Brooklyn Eagle* said Joe's broken rib "made him ... so slow of foot." An undated issue of the *Police Gazette* reprinted its 1896 report: "The fight ... was the best the big men had offered in quite some time. They fought unlike heavyweights, and the 5,000 spectators got the worth of their money sevenfold."

The January 26 *New York Recorder* said "it was the largest crowd" and "greatest glove contest yet witnessed in the Empire's arena ... Choynski displayed the most remarkable gameness and recuperative power. Beaten, as everyone ... present thought, he went in and finished Hall, to the surprise and amazement of even the oldest veteran ... Choynski was handled splendidly by ... O'Rourke, who ... told Joe to play for the body." Joe: "The press dispatches had me almost out in the 9th ... that I was down nine seconds, fell when I attempted to regain my feet, and the gong saved me, all of which does me an injustice. I admit I did go down, but I was up in a flash, and fought Hall hard for the remainder of the round, which I should judge was about 15 seconds." Joe added that, "although he was in the best possible condition, he only weighed 155 pounds the day of the fight," not a likely scenario. "That he had trouble with his stomach while ... training, and his doctor advised him to abstain from all liquids and to eat sparingly, which accounted for his light weight. 'I took particular pains to fight for his body,' he said, 'knowing that to be his weak spot ... when I weakened him with body punches, I shifted for his head and settled him.' " Choynski said he received the scratch over the eye while boxing with Mike Donovan.

Hall arrived in Pittsburgh the same day, also hardly looking the worse for wear. "A little discoloration under the left eye was the only evidence to show he had engaged in a ring contest. Hall promptly called on his intimate friends and told them not to believe the story that he had 'laid down,' and they accepted his declaration." Jim said he had the fight all his way for 10 rounds, but his stamina and body gave out after that. "I hurt my shoulder in a clinch in the 4th round. Then, when Choynski played for my wind I guarded with my hands. His blows struck my wrists and forearms and so deadened them that finally I could not raise my arms to my face. Even now I cannot put on my clothes without assistance. We were both tired to death near the end. Choynski bled freely, and when his long hair fell down over his eyes and became saturated with blood, he looked like a sheep at slaughter."[23] The damage Joe inflicted on the arms of Hall sounds similar to what Rocky Marciano did to Roland LaStarza in 1953.

In Joe's era, it seemed every other fight was suspected of being fixed. Some were, of course, but the preponderance of evidence and eyewitness reports doesn't corroborate a high number being so. Paranoia and yellow journalism likely had more to do with it than anything else. One paper wrote, "The exhibition was so slow in the early rounds that it conveyed the impression there was a job." A few papers said, because Hall "dominated for 12 rounds, then suddenly collapsed," this pointed to a conspiracy. The truth is, ringside reports did not say this at all. To the contrary, they were unanimous in saying that Hall began fading about the 10th round, while Choynski began to come on and do most of the damage. Would Hall go a punishing 13 rounds to take a dive? I don't think so, keeping in mind that Choynski was, at best, only a slight favorite in the betting. This is not a fight where a tremendous amount of gambling money was to be had.[24]

A St. Louis scribe with the pen name, "Macon," wrote: "The minute's rest, the dose of brandy and the ministrations of his seconds did wonders for Choynski, and he walked to the scratch for the 10th round determined to do or die. He had been told while sitting on his chair that the only chance he had ... was to get close to his man. Said O'Rourke ... 'He knows more in a minute than you know in an hour, his arms are inches longer than yours, and he'll knock your head off if you don't do as I tell you!' (Author – this sounds like O'Rourke's melodramatic and controlling style.) Joe ... dashed right in between Hall's guard, and his assault was so sudden ... that he landed several sharp blows on Hall's head before he fully comprehended the situation. Choynski ... has wonderful recuperative powers ... In the 12th, he (Hall) got a clout on the side of the head that sent him to the floor. He took his time getting up, and ... looked at Choynski almost appealingly. In the 13th and last round, Hall was roughly handled. Choynski kept right at him and twice sent him down. The 2nd time, Hall rolled over on his back. While Hurst was checking off the 10 seconds, he once made a faint effort to get up, but his head fell back ... Choynski, as usual, was overtrained. He only weighed 159½ pounds and he was under a doctor's care before he came here. Hall's weight was given as 166 pounds, but he looked 10 pounds weightier. He looked a full stone (14 pounds) bigger than Joe ..."

"At times both ... were slower than cold molasses. Had it not been for the watchful care and constant advice – often shouted ... of Tom O'Rourke, I don't think Choynski would have lasted eight rounds. He is a tremendously hard hitter ... game as a pebble, but ... a poor ring general, and as soon as he gets into trouble he loses his head as completely as the veriest novice. The idea of his challenging the winner of the Maher-Fitzsimmons fight is absurd, and as for ... being able to go up successfully against Jim Corbett ... as ridiculous as a pipe dream."[25] "Macon" didn't think as highly of Joe's generalship and savvy as most ring cognoscenti of the day. As to the alcohol in Joe's corner, the January 26 *Brooklyn Eagle* read: "Fitzsimmons is considered to be the most abstemious man in pugilism. *Choynski's favorite beverage is claret and the best at that. While in Worcester some time ago, Choynski sent all the way to Boston for his favorite brand of wine. When he is in training, Parson Davies sees to it that he has the best.* Peter Jackson has the reputation of ... the largest capacity for whiskey among the fighters."

Jimmy Barry left for El Paso, Texas on the 28th to train for his February 18 fight against Johnny Murphy. Promoter Dan Stuart was preparing training quarters "for him near the scene of the mills." Joe was sent by Davies the next day, to have charge of Barry's training and be his chief second. "Barry's departure was unexpected, or Choynski would have left with him last night. Joe stayed over to pick up the things that Barry left, and will arrive ... in time enough to get the bantam in working order. Choynski's presence behind the little Chicagoan will be an additional assurance of victory. If there is any speedy recovering, such as the Californian understands so well himself, he is just the ... man to direct the reviving process. 'Parson' Davies will be on hand to put on the finishing touches."[26] Fitzsimmons was already at his El Paso training camp with his pet lion, Nero, and company, preparing to take on "Irish Champion" Peter Maher. Barry, who was to fight on the undercard of a boxing carnival there, arrived February 2, taking up quarters with lightweight and welterweight Jack Everhardt. With him were Joe Vendig, Jim Hall and Johnny Murphy.

Several papers said Choynski would also be in Fitz's corner on the night of the Maher fight. Jim Hall had already left for Los Cruces to assist Maher in his training. Dan Stuart's carnival was to consist of boxing, bull fights, cattle roping, horse races and a game of football between teams from El Paso and Dallas, Texas.[27] Unfortunately, the law chased the Fitz-Maher fight out of such diverse places as New Orleans, Louisiana, Hot Springs, Arkansas, Dallas and El Paso. Ultimately, the match would occur near Langtry, Texas, where Judge Roy Bean, organizer of the bout, had his famous (or infamous) "Jersey Lilly" saloon. To avoid interference from the law, the ring was pitched just on the Mexican side of the Rio Grande near a high cliff. But, there was no undercard, and Barry returned to Chicago.

Hot topics of the time were the revision of boxing's rules and setting of weight classifications. How a champion would respond to challenges and how often he was expected to defend his title were other key points in the discussion. An important sporting convention was to take place in El Paso on or about February 16, coinciding with the boxing carnival. "It is proposed to call together all the fighters, fighters' managers, and sporting writers, quartered in El Paso on the day set for the congress ... Dan Stuart agrees to furnish the opera house here for the occasion ... It is proposed to organize, among other things, an American sporting league, with officers ... Another thing that action will be taken on is a division of the heavyweight class. It is held, and with good cause, that the man who weighs 159 pounds, and who, under the present scale is a heavyweight, like Choynski, for instance, should not be subject to challenge by a man weighing 200 pounds. It is probable that some medium line, possibly 175 or 180 pounds, will be fixed upon. No occasion like the one in view is likely to present itself in many years for action of this kind ..."[28] Unfortunately, the convention never occurred, either. The beginning of the light-heavyweight division is somewhat cloudy and its full acceptance, gradual. Interestingly, though, the one name used as an example of its dire need, was Joe Choynski.

Joe would not have attended the festivities in El Paso, anyway. Beginning February 1, several papers related, dateline Chicago: "Joe Choynski ... is seriously ill at his home here. 'Parson' Davies telegraphed him to join the Sullivan troupe and take the place of the disabled ex-champion. When he returned ... after his fight with Jim Hall, his friends noticed that he was not all right physically, and his illness is attributed to the punishment he received from Hall." The *Lowell Sun* wrote that Davies "and several members of his aggregation" passed through St. Louis, Missouri on the 2nd, en route to El Paso. "He stated ... that Choynski is in no condition to make any more matches for the present, for he is suffering from an abscess in the ear and ... over-training. Choynski, who expected to challenge the winner of the Maher-Fitzsimmons fight, will not be able to go into training for four or five months, so the 'Parson' declares." Another publication said Joe had a bad head cold.[29] After years of fighting, one would think Joe would have learned not to over-train.

On February 7, President Grover Cleveland signed the Catron Bill into law, making prizefighting a felony "on all soil over which the Federal government has exclusive jurisdiction." The bill was rushed through legislation, primarily to prevent the Fitzsimmons-Maher fight from taking place within the United States and its territories. Offenders would be not only the fighters, but anyone ... assembling ... to witness a fight." This was one of several laws enacted over the years which either legalized boxing or made it an illicit activity, and was a serious setback for the sport. It was mitigated somewhat by the Horton Law, signed by the Governor of New York in April, legalizing boxing in the state until 1900, when the Lewis Law repealed it. In an effort to keep his stable of fighters working, Davies, just prior to departing for El Paso, "forwarded a challenge to London to have a battle arranged between Joe Choynski and Dan Creedon ... before the National Sporting Club during Derby week ... the latter part of May ... according to a dispatch from London to the *Police Gazette*, Creedon has accepted ... The ... Club will give a purse of $2,500 ..."[30]

Davies arrived in San Francisco on March 6, his first visit there in three years. "This time he is the manager of John L. Sullivan and Paddy Ryan, who will appear next week in 'The Wicklow Postman' ... 'We were delayed almost two weeks,' said the 'Parson,' 'by the accident to Sullivan. He has the strength of 10 men. Imagine a man weighing 280 pounds thrown off a train traveling 40 miles an hour. We picked him up and he was senseless. His clothes were on fire, as some matches he had in his pocket ignited when he fell. He was cut and bruised frightfully ... not a bit of his body the size of your hand that did not have a scar or bruise. We sewed a long cut in his scalp on the train with piano wire. We had to wait until he recovered. He doesn't speak any lines, but just boxes at the end of the show with Paddy Ryan.' " Davies didn't mention that John had been on a drinking binge when the accident occurred. "I have Joe Choynski in Chicago with his wife. If all boxers were like Joe, they would be an honor to the profession. I think Congress went too far when it suppressed prize-fighting. If it were only as expeditious in passing other laws as ... in prohibiting fighting, the country would be very much better off than it is to-day."[31]

It was announced March 19 that Frisco's new National Athletic Club would feature an eight-round bout on April 16, between Joe and Alec Greggains. The article then added: "The proposed match between ... Greggains and ... Choynski has fallen through. At 11 o'clock last evening ... Davies, J. Gibbs and Tom Sharkey held a private conference, and Sharkey was substituted for Greggains. The agreement entered into ... is the same as drawn up against Greggains; that is, Choynski to win must stop Sharkey in eight rounds."[32] It is one thing to pay an opponent a sum if he can stay a given number of rounds in a "handicap" match; it is another entirely to be given a loss on your record if you beat the hell out of an adversary but fail to knock him out. Such a thing would not be countenanced today, and it

"Kid" McCoy

was probably foolish for Davies to accept such conditions with a brutally tough heavyweight like Sharkey. "The Walloping Tar," as Tom was sometimes called, was early into a pro career. He was still crude and fairly easy to hit, which is why Davies gambled that Choynski would be able to take Sharkey out before the expiration of eight rounds.

The bout didn't occur until the middle of April. Meanwhile, a match was pulled off at the Grand Central Palace in New York, with "Kid" McCoy. Born Norman Selby in 1872 or 1873 on a small farm in Moscow, Indiana, McCoy would become perhaps the most colorful boxer of his era, and one of the deadliest. He had superlative boxing skills, remarkable speed, an incredibly stiff punch, and a devious, plotting mind. Legend has him originating such corny tricks as pointing to an opponent's feet, saying, "Hey! Your shoe's untied!" and knocking the poor sucker out when he glanced downward. A horde of 3,500 to 5,000 expected to see a competitive fight. Instead, due to police interference, they got an effete exhibition. The contest, originally a six-rounder at catchweights, was reduced to a four-round spar, with rounds of only one minute each.

March 21 *Police Gazette*: "There were four other bouts ... in all but one,

Capt. Delaney called a halt. The crowd had shouted themselves hoarse in derision over the interference in the preliminary bouts, and when the principals in the main go appeared, they were somewhat humored over the prospects of a red-hot fight. After the men had shaken hands, a long consultation was held in the centre of the ring ... and when Johnny Dunn announced that the men could not pull off the bout on its merits, a howl went up. The crowd started to leave the hall, but the men stayed and boxed four short rounds." Referee "Brooklyn" Jimmy Carroll announced he would "render no decision, owing to the stand taken by police." *Brooklyn Eagle*: "After the bout, Choynski ... said he had come ... to fight McCoy six rounds on its merits ... although he and McCoy had always been friends, friendship ceased as soon as they entered the ring ... the audience could not possibly be more disappointed over the outcome ... than he was."[33]

March 25 *Chicago Inter-Ocean*: "Joe Choynski, 'the cavalier of the prize ring,' returned to Chicago yesterday ... tells a rather interesting story of the part Fitzsimmons took in the proceedings. It appears the heavyweight champion got to McCoy's ears before the arrival of Choynski, and told him to beware of 'friendly bouts' with the conqueror of Jim Hall. 'He will agree to box you in friendly fashion ... just as he did with me, and then when he sees an opening, he will put a knockout onto you.' This disturbed McCoy some, and as soon as Choynski stepped off the train, the 'Kid' took him off to one side and asked him what he was going to do about it, at the same time divulging the source from which he gathered his fears. 'I told him,' said Choynski, in telling the story yesterday, 'that I was not going to allow him to make a fool of me, and that I would allow him to set his own pace as to a knockout. As a matter of fact, I was engaged to box with him in a friendly manner, yet this did not carry with it an agreement to permit myself to be *gone over with* by McCoy. I went on and boxed him just as I told him I would.' 'How did McCoy manage to whip Ryan,' Choynski was asked. 'That is something I cannot explain. I have every reason to dislike Ryan, yet I am at a loss to account for McCoy's victory over the ex-Chicago man.' "

Choynski and McCoy fought three more times, each occasion highly eventful and not without controversy. Joe departed a few days later for San Francisco, where another chapter in his career would open. Joe was about to engage in a series of bouts against some of the top heavyweight bruisers of this, the first "Golden Age" of the Marquis of Queensberry Era.

Round Fourteen

Taking on the Sons of Erin
(April 1896 – November 1896)

The March 31 *San Francisco Call* said Joe was expected by April 2, and would be "met on the arrival of the overland train at 16th-street station, Oakland, by a number of his old friends ... In all probability, Choynski will train ... at Barney Foley's (sic) hostelry near Ingleside." On April 4, he arrived in the City by the Bay. "The doughty young boxer brings his ... bride ... Joe Choynski, boxer, wrestler and all-round master of physical culture, arrived last night by the 8:40 train from Chicago. He was met at Oakland by his sister, his brother Herbert ... other members of the family, Edward Greany (sic), Mrs. Greany and a number of other friends. The champion's delight at seeing once more the hills of his native City was most affecting. Standing on the steamer's deck, he supported his lovely ... bride with one arm ... with the other he indicated a number of the City's landmarks, which seemed most endeared to his memory. On arriving in the City, more friends were waiting ... and the young high priest of the manly art and his fair lady were escorted to their ... quarters with every demonstration of welcome. The champion now weighs about 162 pounds, and has made quite a record during his absence ... On the 16th ... he will meet ... Tom Sharkey ..."[1]

"Choynski ... agreed to knock Sharkey out in eight rounds or forfeit the purse. The town is wild over the match ... betting will be about 2 to 1 on Choynski ... Davies ... just left here with Sullivan and the show ..." The bout would be held at the People's Palace, an old cyclorama at the corner of Mason and Eddy streets, under the auspices of the National A.C. "Sharkey easily disposed of every opponent he has faced ... since he took to pugilism as a business ... The fighting seaman is a magnificently built fellow, whose staying powers are unquestionably great ... Sharkey went to his old quarters at the Cliff House, where he has trained hard and fast ever since ... Choynski ... was in tolerably fair condition when he landed ... he concluded that all he required to fit him for a sharp engagement was a little bag-punching and some long-distance walks in the suburbs. He ... has never felt better in his life ... Mr. Davies states that he will arrive here on the 14th inst. ... his return will be welcomed by his many friends."[2]

On the evening of April 9, a private bout was held within the confines of the Olympic Athletic Club. *Chronicle*: "Some ... members of the Olympic Club were treated last evening to a very interesting two-round bout between Joe Choynski (California's favorite boxer) and M. Van Buskirk, the champion heavyweight ... of the Olympic Club." This was Theodore Van Buskirk, "The Marysville Hercules." For a time he was considered the amateur heavyweight champion of the Pacific Coast, later recording professional victories over an aging Joe Goddard and "Mexican" Pete Everett, and drawing with Henry Baker and Jack Stelzner. "Manager Kennedy arranged the meeting between the two big 'uns after he promised Choynski that not more than a dozen people should witness it. It was about 9 p.m. when Van Buskirk entered the room generally used by the gun club ... dressed in his best boxing clothes and looked every inch a fighter ... when Joseph put in an appearance in ring costume, those who had not seen him before manifested surprise at his build. They expected to see a whopping big fellow, with legs like a Trojan and a back similar to that of a prize bull. They were sadly disappointed ... as Choynski carries rather slender nether limbs, but from his hips up he is a magnificent specimen of the athlete. He showed by a somewhat haggard face that he has been exercising for some time 'on the quiet,' and needs only light exercise to fit him for a battle royal. Eddie Graney was referee and timekeeper."

"Van Buskirk was taken by surprise when Choynski went right in for business. There was no fiddling or tomfoolery ... The men boxed two short rounds ... The Olympian made a good stand, considering he had a master mechanic before him, but Choynski, in the language of the ringmaster, 'put it all over him' ... rights and lefts landed on Van Buskirk's nose and body ... Choynski has improved wonderfully since his departure from this City, three years ago. He is ... quick as a flash, and uses ... right and left alike. His foot work is ... good ... he carries heavy-weight goods which sound rather loud when they drop on any ... spot. Van Buskirk, when compared with Sharkey, is slow ... consequently it would be foolish ... to draw a line on what Choynski can do with his next opponent by taking the bout of last evening as a criterion."[3] Sharkey was noted for his very quick feet, able to get around, in and out on an adversary in an astounding manner.

A pre-fight note: "Joe Choynski had better look out for his head. Tom Sharkey is after it with two big mitts and expects to make the capture in a walk. The pride of the navy ... looks as fit as a fiddle. He is confident ... that not only will Choynski be unable to put him out ... but the San Francisco whirlwind will have all he can do to worry through the contest. 'I'll fool some of these people who think I am going to run away,' said Sharkey yesterday ... I'll knock his head off, sure.' Great, flexible bunches of muscles stood out on the back and over and beneath the shoulders; The great, deep chest stood out like a mountain, showing the wonderful wind of the pride of Mare Island. Below, in the locality where aldermen and retired pugs nurse great rolls of fat, was a ... hollow, hard as nails, a wall of muscle. It took ... hard work to bring Sharkey around to this condition ... though he only took a rest of a week after ... Greggains. Danny Needham ... and Tim

McGrath ... the past 20 days ... have worked like beavers to make their man fit ... at the training quarters in the pavilion at Seal Rock house."

"Up at 6 o'clock every morning, the ex-marine took a lively walk on the sandy beach before breakfast ... a 10-mile run ... through the Park and back, followed by a hard rub. Some mornings, just to vary the monotony and scare the seals, Sharkey, at the end of his run, would spin out to the end of the Olympic pier, dive off into the ocean and swim through the breakers to the Seal Rocks, then into shore. That's ... over a stiff quarter of a mile in the roughest kind of water, but it develops lung power ... noonday lunch, (then) to the training quarters. There, every afternoon, he pounded the bag fast and furiously for eight rounds, after which he eased up a little with dumbbells. Then he

Tim McGrath (left) and Tom Sharkey (right)

donned the mitts with Danny Needham, the two going at it hammer and tongs style for four rounds. Dumbbells, Indian clubs, skipping rope and a rub-down ... a rest ... till dinner. In the evening a smart walk on the beach ... He will weigh 171½ pounds, three more than Choynski. He has a chest measurement of 45" ... his waist looks waspish at 31". He is 17¾" around the neck and his biceps measure 14½". From tip to tip of his outstretched arms is just 72½", which does not give Choynski much ... advantage ..." *The Kansas City Star* said Tom's chest measured 47".

Tom: " 'I do not pretend to say I can whip Choynski, but I have all the confidence in the world of fooling ... those fellows who think I am the kind of a man Choynski can do with as he pleases. After the fight is over, there will be many know-it-all sports who will have good reason to cuss their luck for betting against Sailor Shark.' Choynski: 'I have never seen my ... opponent box ... therefore cannot presume anything. I put him up as being a 2nd Goddard, but on a smaller scale. If he can stand the same kind of punishment I gave the Australian, he will surprise me very much ... but I will fight Sharkey on different lines, as I have a contract ... to stop him in eight rounds or less." Joe was training at Barney Farley's roadhouse.[4] Thomas Joseph Sharkey was born in Dundalk, Ireland on November 26, 1873, one of 10 children. He left home as a youth and joined the United States Navy in 1892, being stationed at Honolulu, Hawaii. There, he learned to box and became the best fighter among his peers. Tom was discharged after three years in the Navy, and turned professional soon after.[5]

This is a good juncture to expound on the subject of boxing styles. There are four basic styles: *Classic Boxers*, *Sluggers*, *Swarmers* and *Boxer-Punchers*. There are multiple, if not infinite, variations of these styles, as individuals combine various elements into their own, unique method of combat. The classic boxer utilizes the "textbook" science of the sport and its four basic punches, the left jab, left hook, straight right (or right cross) and the uppercut. These can be thrown to the body or head and are often used in quick combinations. Classic boxers are strong in terms of defense, counter-punching and strategy, and usually have good mobility. The slugger is self-explanatory; they concentrate on raw punching power and thus, usually have not bothered to develop a lot of accuracy or skill.

The swarmer by definition is a volume puncher, scoring points and wearing down opponents with flurries of blows. Usually a strong infighter, in the lighter divisions, a swarmer is generally a light puncher, but among heavyweights, the best have also been heavy strikers. There have not been many, but examples of top heavyweight swarmers are Tom Sharkey, Rocky Marciano, Joe Frazier and Joe Goddard, before he came to the States. Notable among those lacking a potent punch in the division, was Tommy "Hurricane" Jackson, a contender during the reigns of Marciano and Floyd Patterson. Jackson was also an exception because he was tall (about 6' 3") and had a long reach (80"). The style is usually dictated by the short height and stubby arms of the fighter, which necessitates him getting in close. The prime of a swarmer is rather brief, as the volume of punches and pace he must maintain tends to burn him out in a relatively short time. The boxer-puncher combines a good amount of boxing skill with a strong punch, the ratio of skill to power varying from one fighter to another.

Often, these styles are not purely defined. For instance, John L. Sullivan had terrific hand and foot speed for a slugger and sometimes swarmed all over his adversaries. Jim Jeffries and Sonny Liston are often classified as sluggers, but both possessed enough boxing ability to probably rate as boxer-punchers. The three swarmers, Sharkey, Marciano and Frazier, each had a strong enough punch to possibly qualify as sluggers. Classic boxers like Jack Johnson and Larry Holmes hit hard enough, when they wished, to likely rate as boxer-punchers. As to how the various styles perform against each other, there is a tendency for the "rock/paper/scissors" effect to hold force. Though only a trend, this is how it works: The classic boxer usually avoids the heavy punches of the slugger, to either win a decision or "wear the stone down with a trickle of water," and stop his man late.

The slugger will, more often than not, knock out the swarmer, using his heavy bombs to exploit the latter's weakness to counterpunches. This was best exemplified by a vintage George Foreman blasting the shorter (and shorter-armed) Joe Frazier into helplessness. Jim Jeffries twice defeated Tom Sharkey via decision, first over 20 rounds, then 25. Had Jeff not had very sore hands in their initial encounter and a badly injured left in their 2nd, there is little doubt he would have stopped Tom, or at least won by a wider margin. The swarmer will, all things being equal, maintain such a grueling pace and hurl so many punches, that the classic boxer cannot avoid enough to emerge victorious. As examples: Marciano stopped classic boxer Roland LaStarza in 11 rounds in a 1953 title defense, Frazier halted Eddie Machen in 1966 in 10 and, while still at his peak, won a 15-round verdict over Muhammad Ali. How the boxer-puncher fares against the other three styles depends largely upon the amount and ratio of skill and power he possesses, as well as individual strengths and weaknesses.

Another factor to consider in comparing a fighter with those of other time periods, is the matter of punching technique. Early (Marquis of Queensberry era) books on boxing instruction and method show practitioners throwing punches with the back of the fists facing outward (thumb on top), rather than turning the fist over on impact, as is done today, with the back of the hand facing upward. Without this last-second twist of the wrist and the snap it imparts, substantially less power is generated. When compared to the same blows thrown in modern times, perhaps 10-15% power was lost in a left jab, 15-20% in a straight right. The hooks demonstrated in these old photos were thrown in arcs too long to retain the effectiveness they are designed to carry. Only a short, tight hook, with proper hip sway and transfer of weight from the back foot to the front, imparts full punching force. The sloppiness of these punches puts their target beyond the point of optimum power and can open up the striker to counterpunches. Even the uppercuts thrown by boxers of that time appear wider and launched from further out than in later decades. As this punch was meant to be thrown during infighting or in close, an incorrectly executed uppercut leaves one open to a counter.

During the 1910s, fighters appeared to be throwing these punches correctly, by and large. From the beginning of the Queensberry era to the 1910s, something led these pugilists to evolve the major blows of their profession. Perhaps someone like "Kid" McCoy, with the sharp twist he gave his "corkscrew" punches, contributed to this evolution. Joe Choynski also threw a version of the modern left hook. The transition to what we see today seems rather instantaneous, rather than incremental, whatever the cause.[6] Still, to a large extent a punch is a punch, and the stamina and toughness of a boxer means about as much as anything.

Some archetypes and proponents of each boxing style through the years: *Classic Boxer*: Jim Corbett, Willie "Will o' the Wisp" Pep and Pernell "Sweet Pea" Whittaker. Muhammad Ali is a standard entry, though in truth, his style was not "text-book," as he would lean away from punches and use other, unorthodox tactics. Still, Ali was a great and effective boxer, with his phenomenal speed and agility. *Slugger*: Earnie Shavers, David Tua, (young) George Foreman. *Swarmer*: Harry Greb, Henry Armstrong. These two fought in the lighter divisions and, while lacking in punching force, came at their foes like human buzz-saws. Punch counters would go crazy, trying to follow the number of blows they threw. *Boxer-Puncher*: Bob Fitzsimmons, Tommy Ryan, Sam Langford, Joe Louis, "Sugar" Ray Leonard, "Sugar" Ray Robinson, Tommy Hearns and Wladimir and Vitali Klitschko.

How does this apply to the Sharkey fight? As stated, Tom is generally considered a swarmer, an early-day Rocky Marciano, though calling him a slugger might not be off the mark. To note a couple of differences, however, Rocky favored his right, which he dubbed "Mary Ann," while Sharkey's best punch was a left hook. Marciano was a rather slow starter, whereas Tom usually came charging out of the gate. Choynski was a boxer-puncher, probably the first of the new Queensberry era's heavyweights. He blended equal parts skill and punching power, though he sometimes slugged when he should have boxed, leaving himself open. Joe was just reaching his boxing prime, while Tom had not yet attained his peak.

On the night of April 16, a crowd of 2,500 to 3,000 witnessed the first of three clashes Joe and Tom would have together. Tom, wearing an ulster, entered the ring at 10 p.m., with seconds Needham, McGrath and "Spider" Kelly. Choynski followed soon after, with Ed Graney and J. Carkeek. The *Chronicle* said his handlers were Graney, Young Agnew and Charles Tillson. "Sharkey looked in fine condition, but was drawn down considerably in flesh. His eyes looked dull from a course of hard training. He said he felt 'O.K.,' and would fight for his life. Joe Choynski, with his football bangs ... wore a confident look and smiled when the large audience gave him a hearty reception." The man "mutually chosen to referee the match" was Albert (or Arva) King, an arbiter who doesn't appear to have been heard from again. King cautioned the boxers not to resort to foul fighting. Next is an amalgam of seven fight reports, including two local. The blow-by-blow for rounds two through seven are from the *San Francisco Chronicle*.[7]

Round 1 – Sharkey had an anxious look as he met Choynski at ring center. On instructions from "Spider" Kelly, Tom backed away and maintained a defensive tact. The *Chronicle* disagreed with the majority, saying Tom not only showed no desire to retreat, but landed the first punch. Joe began punishing his squat foe with the signature left, mostly to the face. He showered Sharkey with lefts, then landed a sharp hook to the jaw, sending him through the ropes and out of the ring. He somehow scrambled back, to resume the fracas. "The California Terror" beat his adversary all over the ring, Tom clinching and falling repeatedly. Near the end of the round, Joe corralled his opponent in the southeast corner, which started a rally. He shot a stiff, right uppercut to the chin of the Irish Gob. Tom missed a wild left, but immediately cranked another punch that allegedly caught Choynski square in the groin, just before the bell. "The receiver doubled up like a jack-knife ... and his second, Eddie Graney, ran to his assistance."

"The attendants of Sharkey jumped into the ring, and pandemonium reigned ... Captain Birdsall ... ordered everybody, excluding the contestants, outside the ropes." (Some papers said "Police Lieutenant Birdsall"). Joe was helped to his corner. So intense was his pain that he nearly fell through the ropes. At first, Birdsall was adamant that he would call a halt, but was finally convinced to allow the fight to continue, after Joe was granted a 20-minute rest. The apparent point of contention was whether or not the low blow was intentional. Joe's corner were satisfied it had not been, and did not claim a foul. "Choynski evidently received a hard and painful blow, which he acknowledged was unintentional ... spectators were growing impatient ... when Choynski rose from his seat and signified to the referee ... that he was ready to proceed, a wild cheer shook the rafters ..."

Round 2 – Sharkey remained defensive. Joe drove a right counter that nearly sent Tom through the ropes, left jabs to body and head, and another right. "From the 2nd to the 7th ... (Joe) frequently caught Sharkey on the neck with left-handers ... the sailor was sent on all fours at least a dozen times, but ... always on the retreat when hit ... to stop a fighter who battles on the defensive in a limited round contest is a contract ... few ... can ... accomplish, especially if ... physically the equal of his opponent."

Round 3 – Joe missed a left jab and Sharkey countered with a right to the nose. Choynski landed a left, then a right uppercut to the jaw. He continued the assault, Tom getting one good punch in to the heart. The killer Chrysanthemum out-punched his rival to the gong.

Round 4 – "Choynski got a left on Sharkey's wind, knocking him against the ropes and down." When Tom rose, Joe landed a left to the body, three to the mouth, and a strong right to the jaw. The former candy-maker battered his foe's right ear with a succession of lefts, threw him against the ropes, and floored Tom with another to the mouth. Sharkey rested on one knee until the timekeeper tolled "seven." The scrappy sailor landed a couple of light blows, but Joe cracked another left to the jaw at the call of time.

Round 5 – Joe sent in light lefts to Tom's face and torso. After a punch or two, a clinch would follow. This was a frame composed of mutual rest.

Round 6 – "Choynski forced Sharkey around the ring and tried to knock him against the post, landing twice on his neck." Each landed well to head and body. Late in the round, a flurry by Joe caused Tom to cover up. "Close infighting was followed by a heavy left on Sharkey's jaw ..."

Round 7 – Joe led with the left, but was twice countered to the face. After a clinch, "Choynski feinted with his left and landed his right on Sharkey's ribs, following with light lefts on the head and face. Choynski ... led again with his left, which Sharkey ducked and countered, landing squarely on the left jaw and staggering Choynski."

Round 8 – "Choynski had one of those reckless smiles on his face, while the jaws of the sailor were clinched tight ... determined to do or die." "Sharkey dropped on his knees several times to avoid being knocked out, and for this mark of cowardice was hooted ..." Tom landed some, but Joe pounded him terribly, especially to the head. Sharkey was groggy, but showed a chin of granite. "Choynski pelted him at will ... the first half of the round, it appeared ... all day with the marine, the crowd cheering might and main. 'Clinch, clinch,' came the cry from Sharkey's corner ... he ... clinched on every opportunity, the false cries of time helping him toward the end ... Choynski ... was willing ... but his blows were wild and lacked ... steam. He repeatedly attempted to uppercut ... invariably going over (the) head ... the call of time sounded to save (Tom) ... There were cheers for the sailor; his seconds went wild ... the crowd rushed to the platform ... Choynski and Sharkey, both smiling, shook hands ... and parted."

San Francisco Call: "The general opinion ... was if Sharkey had not run away from ... Choynski would have won ... Neither ... bore any marks of punishment." *Rocky Mountain News:* "Joe knocked Sharkey down repeatedly and had him all but out when the call of time ... ended the fight." Other papers agreed. December 2 *Davenport Republican:* "The Cornishman's (Fitz's) backers ... say ... Choyinski (sic) had the sailor all but out when Sharkey disabled him with a foul punch, which took away all of Joe's stamina." In Sharkey's 1917 memoirs, "Fighters I've Met," he had a different take: "I knew the minute I saw him that he had bitten off more than he could chew. Choynski ... had little thin legs, and wore his hair bushy, like Paderewski.* I wanted to laugh when I saw him. The idea of a little thin, dudish fellow like that stopping me seemed ridiculous ... But I didn't laugh. Tim McGrath told me I was not to underrate Choynski – that he was one of the hardest hitters in the world. And ... in my corner that night, with McGrath, was Spider Kelly. I had heard about the Spider long before I ever arrived in San Francisco; people ... told me that he was a great second, and ... still a crackerjack of a fighter. I spoke to Kelly about Choynski. 'He doesn't look tough,' I said; 'bet I can break him in two.' 'Never mind how he looks,' said the Spider, 'you'll find him tough enough. Look out for his left. If he hits you with it on the right spot we'll be taking you home in a hearse.' "

"The second the gong sounded I found that Kelly had the right dope. Choynski had a sure enough left. I could feel it whizzing past my ears. I did a bit of thinking in the 1st round. Back in Honolulu, a man named Fred Nealon, who trained me for some of my fights, depended on a left-hand punch. 'When he leads,' said Nealon, 'duck a little to the side and step in with your right. Hold your arm stiff and dig your glove into his ribs.' Every time Choynski lead (sic) I stepped in and caught him. I didn't mind his other punches. I caught them on the neck and face. But every time he tried to use his straight left I beat him to it with my right. The fight had been going less than two minutes when I sent Choynski through the ropes with one of my rib roasters. What followed cannot be easily described. I thought Hades had broken loose and that I was right in the center of it all."

* Ignacy Jan Paderewski (1860-1941) was a brilliant composer and pianist, a Prime Minister of the Republic of Poland, noted for his wild hair.

"Ed Graney ... jumped in through the ropes and claimed a foul ... Spider Kelly jumped in through the ropes and started to lead me to my corner. 'You've licked him!' roared the Spider, 'come away! Get out!' Alva King ... didn't know what had happened. Graney's attitude frightened him. He ran around the ring asking questions, with Graney jumping in front of him and yelling 'Foul! Foul!' Meanwhile Choynski had been dragged to his corner and was recuperating. It was a terrible mess. Everybody in the crowd was standing up and yelling – you couldn't hear yourself think. Graney ran to Mose Gunst. Mose then was Police Commissioner, and, with an officer at his side, had been sitting in the press row, just outside the ring. 'Mose!' screamed Graney, 'Mose! Choynski has been fouled!' Whether Gunst was responsible for what happened after ... I don't know, but ... Choynski was given from 15 to 20 minutes to recuperate."

"When we were ordered to fight again Choynski was just as fresh, if not as confident, as when he started. Graney, so I learned afterwards, laughed at the way he had 'buffaloed' the referee, and ... admitted Choynski had not been fouled. He explained ... it was all a part of the game, and thought if a second could fool or bluff a referee it was his business to do so. I also learned that Graney, after having the fight stopped in order to get Choynski his rest, was instrumental in getting it started again. He said the people ... paid their money to see a fight and it wouldn't be right to deprive them of the fun. Now that it's all over I can laugh ... But I was a mad sailor at the time. I couldn't understand that Eddie in saving his man, who had ... been knocked out, had accomplished a wonderful piece of work ... that I held Choynski to an eight-round draw did not help my feelings. Nor ... that the papers next day all agreed that Choynski could hardly have gone two rounds more. All I knew was Choynski had agreed to stop me ... instead I ... stopped him, and ... had been bamboozled out of the decision."

Bob Edgren wrote of Joe, in the March 13, 1915 *Syracuse Herald*: "Of all his family, he was the only one who turned his attention to a non-intellectual pursuit ... he used his inherited intelligence to such good effect that, although only four or five pounds above the middleweight class, he fought well against all of the greatest heavyweight champions of his time. Sharkey started every fight with one trick. He feinted with his left as he ran in, then swung his left, and if it failed to land at once was followed with a swinging right, delivered almost instantly after the left. He tried it on Choynski. To his astonishment, (Joe) stepped in the moment he feinted with the left, and hit him fairly on the nose. He went for Choynski with a bull-like rush ... his swings beat the air. Choynski timed Sharkey perfectly, caught him off his balance after he'd missed a swing, and putting every ounce of strength into what was intended for a knockout blow, struck him squarely on the jaw. Sharkey's heels left the floor and flew ceilingward. He turned half over in the air, shot between the ropes head first, and fell in the front row of seats, on top of three reporters, breaking the reporters' table. Up jumped the crowd, craning necks to see what had become of the sailor. Sharkey was floundering on the floor, out of sight. Choynski men were claiming their wagers. There was ... much congratulating of Choynski, alone in the ring except for the referee, who was counting ..."

"But at seven came another sensation. Sailor Sharkey ... was running rapidly around the ring, looking for a place to climb back in. He pushed excited spectators out of the way, scrambled to the platform, hurled himself headlong through the ropes as the referee reached 'eight,' and ... charged ... across the ring at Choynski. Almost before he had time to put up his hands, Sharkey was upon him, furiously eager for revenge. Choynski, cool again, determined, crafty, caught Sharkey off balance in the midst of one of his wild rushes, and again knocked him through the ropes with a right-hander on the jaw. This time Sharkey struck the floor, bang, right on top of his head. Choynski watched warily to see if he'd stay down, and a look more of weariness and annoyance than surprise crossed his face, when the sailor again ... leaped through the ropes ... and charged ..."

"After that, Choynski couldn't knock the sailor down. He wasn't disheartened, but he'd shot his bolt ... Sharkey, wildly anxious, ran at him more madly than ever ... The sailor knew little boxing and had forgotten what he knew. He just roughed and slammed ... as the end of the 8th round came near, Choynski was arm and leg weary and his head was spinning ... He was rushed off his feet. There was nothing to do but give the sailor the decision. Sharkey had become famous in a moment ... poor Joe ... had to take his consolation weeks later, when Sharkey roughed Jim Corbett ... champion ... the same way ... police stopped the bout half a minute early in the 4th ... to save Corbett the humiliation of being knocked out."

May 3, 1919 *Fort Wayne News and Sentinel*: "Twice Choynski hit Sharkey on the chin with the right and knocked Tom out of the ring. The first time Sharkey went between the ropes, but Choynski's 2nd right hander lifted him clear over them ... he fell on his head and shoulders on the floor outside.

Being tougher than tungsten steel ... Tom climbed back ..." Four months after the fight, Corbett offered: "From what I am told, Sharkey easily bested Choynski, and the latter acknowledged that two of his ribs were broken by one of Sharkey's blows. Choynski got the best of the refereeing, or would never have lasted the fight out." Jim gained his "information" second-hand, at best, and uttered many bombastic statements throughout his life. Two days after the fight, Sharkey said he could whip Choynski in a finish fight, and wanted to sign for one. Joe wanted to meet Tom again under the same rules as in their last clash. "The friends of Joe are confident that, but for the foul blow he received in the groin in the 1st round, he would have finished Sharkey in less than five rounds." In November, Tom said: "Didn't I make Choynski quit fighting, and were it not for the referee, who stopped the fight temporarily when I punched him so hard in the stomach he resorted to a trick to gain time, wouldn't I have knocked him out?"[8]

In analyzing the styles, assets and weaknesses of both fighters *in their respective primes*, this is how I feel Choynski and Sharkey compare: First, Joe had solid advantages in height, reach and boxing skill. Both had dynamite in either fist, capable of occasional one-punch knockouts. Tom, at his peak, tipped the scales at about 183 pounds to Joe's 168. Choynski, a boxer-puncher, experienced both an edge and a disadvantage, stylistically. Sharkey's swarming style would somewhat nullify his skillful mechanics and tactics, while Joe's power gave him a margin of superiority over a typical swarmer. Sharkey, however, was *not* a typical swarmer. In part due his stouter build, the Irish seaman could take a heavier punch. As important, he had a terrific clout. These factors should make him a close favorite over Choynski on a given night. Sharkey was not Joe's equal at the time of this fight, but would improve immensely over time.

Tom's greatest performance was the incredibly grueling, 25-round world title fight with Jim Jeffries, on November 3, 1899. Fighting under 400 arc lights, suspended over the ring in order to film the bout, the bruisers forged a brutal pace, temperatures said to have been over 100 degrees Fahrenheit. The heat was described as that from a blast furnace, and the battlers were said to have lost up to 20 pounds each and soon afterward, much of their hair, which they blamed on the inferno. Sharkey suffered broken ribs and a grotesquely swollen left ear, while Jim came in with an injured left arm. So high was the level of punishment, it is mind-boggling that it wasn't a career-ending encounter for both. In round six alone, Tom unloaded the most powerful blows his muscular body could deliver, shaking the cast-iron champion. Those punches might have taken out any other fighter.

Secondary sources claim that Joe used a novel and clever tactic against Sharkey. Seeing that "an ordinary punch wouldn't make Tom Sharkey groggy," Joe worked his foe around the ring until Tom's head was against a ring post. He drove a blow to Sharkey's chin, his head receiving an additional clout from the post, and only the latter's great stamina enabled him to survive the route. "In the dressing room ... Sharkey (about) Choynski's straight, scientific hitting: 'Why, Choynski can't hit straight, he's a round arm swinger. If you don't believe it, feel the back of me head!' Tom twisted his headpiece rearwise, exhibiting a healthy crop of full grown protuberances."[9] In a fair fight, both men competing strictly for victory, Joe should have been declared a clear and easy winner. Such agreements as went here would never be allowed in the modern game.

In a January 26, 1907 *New Zealand Truth* article, "Fighters I Have Seconded," "Spider" Kelly said: "In a mix-up the sailor tore loose a right-hand swing from his hip which sent Joe through the ropes. At that time, the gang was accustomed to fighting clean breaks, and when Tom made this rally, the crowd hissed and hooted him to beat the band. 'Foul! Foul! Foul!' they yelled. 'Never mind that,' I said to Tom when he came back to his corner; 'they would hiss the Pope. They are a tough bunch.' Sharkey was regarded as a foul fighter in those days ... never what might be called a popular

Tom Sharkey sparring with Bob Armstrong

boxer. It was not his nature to box according to the rules of the time. He was a mixer, and a grand one at that. Like Choynski and other fighters, you know, he was always at a disadvantage. Tom had a short reach, and was not as tall as most heavyweights. But there was one man whom he felt was his master, and that was Fitzsimmons. He had a wholesome respect for him. In the first fight ... Fitz handed him some body punches ... he never forgot."

"It was a pleasure to sit in the ring behind Tom, for he would do exactly as you told him. In this particular he was the best man I ever went behind ... When they got in the ring, Tom was a bit shaky. As they were putting on their gloves, I seized Tom by the shoulder, and as I shook him, said: 'What, that stiff stop you? Why, you go right over and stop him. He's got nothing on you.' My words gave Tom heart. Tom bounded out of that corner like a mad bull, and he walloped Choynski a clout on the jaw, and he flew out of that ring. Joe thought a cyclone struck him, but Joe's friends had too much money bet to allow him to lose fairly. If Sharkey had tried to box Joe cleverly that night, he would have made a poor showing, and might have been knocked out. To get inside of the opponent's longer reach, he had to rush in and fight close. Sharkey lived in fear of the newspapers! Whenever one of the boys gave him a roast, it broke his heart. I used to feel sorry for the poor sailor, for he wasn't a bad fellow at heart. When he got a boost in the papers, he would throw that big chest out and smile all over."

On April 22, Joe was off to the races. The next day's *San Francisco Chronicle* wrote, "Joe Choynski attended the races yesterday and Ed Greaney (sic) gave him several good things." What these "good things" were, isn't mentioned. April 30 *San Francisco Call*: "At the Tivoli ... To-night a testimonial benefit will be tendered the favorite comedian, Thomas C. Leary, at which the Elks will be present. A special feature of the performance will be a friendly set-to between Joe Choynski and Eddie Greany, while favorite actors from the other theaters will appear."

Next was a benefit for "Professor" Bradstreet, athletic instructor of the Fresno Athletic Club. Joe would box a six-round exhibition with Bradstreet, and "also give a ball punching exhibition, in which he is acknowledged the peer of the world, even excelling Corbett ..." A "Vaudeville and Novelty ... Display" would take place at the Barton Opera House in Fresno on the evening of May 18 to benefit E.W. Bradstreet, "Assisted by Mr. Joe Choynski and 50 other volunteers ..." Another paper called Bradstreet "the champion Indian club swinger of the Pacific Coast ..."[10]

On the 18th, the Barton was about half-filled and a few ladies were present. "The event opened with a (musical) selection by the Troubadour Club ... followed by ... bag punching by Choynski. He is considered the best puncher of the bag in the world and he gave a fine exhibition." Next was a display of club swinging and a wrestling match, preceding a three-round spar between Joe and Frank Chance. "Chance is Fresno's best boxer and he did nobly, but Choynski taught him several things. Choynski has a cool bearing on the stage. He ... never gets rattled. Chance did comparatively well, but the professional slogger was too much for him all around." Later came Court P. Edwards and his "bicycle tricks," another boxing bout and Bren Elbmirt's magic tricks. "The last on the program was a three-round sparring contest between Choynski and Bradstreet, and the latter went wild at the start and did poorly. Choynski was much the bigger and had the longer reach. Bradstreet proved himself much the more active of the two. In scientific boxing, Choynski proved himself to be a star. The pugilist returned to San Francisco on this morning's early train."[11]

The San Jose Athletic Club Pavilion hosted a special boxing programme on May 29. It featured a newly-formed troupe called "Choynski's Athletic Stars, headed by the redoubtable Joe Choynski and an array of talent." The company was managed by W.R. Daily. One of the matches on the card was between San Jose heavyweight Dan Long and Tom Kennedy, of the San Francisco A.C., two reputable fighters. On the evening of June 24, Joe refereed a fight at the Mechanics' Pavilion in Frisco, between Charles Rochette and Jack Howard, on the Jim Corbett-Tom Sharkey undercard. "Choyinski (sic) ... His decision ... 'Rochette wins!' was followed by a shout from the crowd of 'Good boy!' " Joe umpired an important fight on the card, a heavyweight clash between former opponent, Jack Davis, "Champion of the Northwest," and "Australian" Billy Smith. The latter emerged triumphant via KO2, and Choynski was again applauded. Sharkey surprised most by giving Corbett all he wanted. While crude, Tom roughed up an unprepared Corbett, en route to a four-round draw.[12]

The June 26 *Brooklyn Eagle* reported that "The Parson" had "posted $1,000 ... to match Joe Choynski against Tom Sharkey for $5,000 a side in a finish fight. If Sharkey does not desire a finish, Davies will back Choynski to stop Sharkey in eight rounds. He also offers to back Choynski against Corbett, the latter to stop Choynski in eight rounds, the entire gate receipts to go to the winner." Corbett didn't respond, and Sharkey was seeking a rematch with "Gentleman Jim," for a long-duration or finish fight. "Paul Herman, ship flag signal quartermaster of the United States man-of-war, Philadelphia, who taught Sharkey how to read and write and gave Corbett's late adversary his first lessons in boxing, says he is ready to back his protégé for $10,000 against any man in the world." On the 29th, it was announced that Choynski and Peter Maher had been matched for a six-round bout at Madison Square Garden on July 27. Joe "wired 'Parson' Davies that he would leave at once for his training quarters near Chicago."[13]

July 2 saw the new Occidental Club of San Francisco put on its first fistic carnival, at Mechanics' Pavilion. Billy Jordan was master of ceremonies. Of the bout between Jim - of Los Angeles and Dan Long of Denver, Colorado, the next day's *Call* wrote: "Amid tremendous applause, Joe Choynski was named as the referee. When he stepped into the ring with a good-natured smile illuminating his countenance, he was given an ovation ... Choynski was a hero in the eyes of the spectators." Jeffries floored his lighter adversary twice in the 1st round with booming right hands, before catching him in the 2nd with "a terrific blow on ... the jaw. Long sank to the floor and was counted out."

On July 5 at the People's Palace in San Francisco, Joe was supposed to box a four-rounder with Tom Sharkey. That didn't happen. The *Call* wrote: "The drawing card ... last night was the announcement that ... Sharkey and Choynski would spar a four-round bout. This ... had the effect of filling the building with a paying crowd. Yet ... the two braves did not face each other ... Choynski sparred with a lightweight named Leon (or Lon) Agnew, from Illinois ... the three rounds' sparring was chicken play to Choynski, who permitted the lightweight to tease him for the benefit of the audience. Not so ... the three rounds sparred by Sharkey and Needham, as Needham kept Corbett's friend in active motion ... Sharkey kept control of himself and did not deal any of his powerful punches on the body of his trainer. The entertainment ... was ... a farewell testimonial to Sharkey, who is going East." It was declared on July 7 that the Choynski-Maher fight would "take place in San Francisco instead of Madison Square Garden ..."[14]

The July 10 *Call* said "Choynski has taken his departure for Howell Mountains,* where he will rusticate for a few weeks. While Joseph is resting ... in the light and balmy atmosphere of the high altitude ... Maher will be speeding across the plains in the direction of San Francisco." A St. Louis paper said on the 19th that Joe and "The Parson" were parting ways, and disparaged the former: "I heard in Chicago that Joe ... determined to 'split' with his old manager and pal, Parson Davies ... the news surprised me. They have been such a case of 'me and Joe' and 'myself and the Parson' that I thought they would, like the brook, 'go on forever,' or at least while in the business, be 'comrades, true, tried and loyal ...' I ... if the report be true ... predict that the fighter ... will be sorry ... Choynski was never a first-rater. He is as game as a pebble and can hit like a kicking mule, but is a very poor ring general. What he may be as a man of business remains to be seen."
* A short mountain range just northeast of Napa Valley, California.

"I haven't always agreed with Davies on pugilistic matters, but I have always respected his judgment and ... diplomatic ability. He ... got Joe many good matches I don't think he could have obtained himself on his merits as a fighter, and his value in a monetary point ... has been more than the 'half' the purses ... obtained. Take the present match between Joe and Peter ... barring accident, it is 10 to one that Maher will go around Choynski like a cooper around a barrel and defeat him with ease. Nevertheless, Davies has succeeded in arranging that the purse ... be split ... no matter who wins. Maher would have been delighted (for) 'winner take all,' but Davies ... mindful of the dangers of the ring, persuaded Quinn and Maher ... to divide the purse equally. If Joe wins ... of course he will be money in by having no manager, but if he loses, where will he get another match with a drawing card?" This scribe with the anti-Choynski bias is unidentified.[15] Modern author Mark T. Dunn is probably correct in assessing that Joe split with Davies because, after the end of "Uncle Tom's Cabin" and being married, he felt he could no longer afford to split his purses with anyone.

Several Frisco clubs were vying to host the Choynski-Maher fight. One was the new Occidental Club, with Johnny Herget at the helm. That club and the Olympic A.C. were only offering a $4,000 purse, however, and the principals stated they would not fight for less than $6,000. The California Athletic Club had dissolved, and the organization deemed most likely to get the contest was the recently established National Athletic Club. J.J. Groom and Judson Gibbs of this club offered $6,000, but Gibbs recently had his request for a fight permit refused. The *Call*: "When ... Gibbs and Groom wanted to get Peter ... out here to fight Joe ... they authorized W.R. Vice of the Union Pacific to wire Maher and his two companions, Lowery and Connolly, transportation from Pittsburgh ... and back ... an obligation of $219.50 ... the fighters lost no time in leaving the smoky city for the California green fields. When the National A.C. learned there was no chance of getting a permit ... Groom and Gibbs rushed off to ... countermand their order for transportation. It was too late ... Maher and his suite were already on the way ... Maher ... is enjoying the sights ... yesterday he was ... taking in the Cliff House and ... places best calculated to afford him comfortable training quarters, in case he manages to get some ... club to hang up a suitable purse for his go with Choynski. The latter is now in the East."[16] Actually, Joe was still in the Howell Mountains.

Maher's manager, Buck Connolly, announced to the National Club on the 20th: "We came out ... on your promise of a $6,000 purse ... are ... willing and anxious to do battle if you, Mr. Groom ... will produce Mr. Choynski and a permit to spar ... You seem to be having some trouble in pulling the match off, and we do not wish to crowd you. We will wait four days longer and if you are not ready, we will open ... engagements with any other institution wishing to talk business. If the National Athletic Club cannot bring the fight off, we will not have anything to do with any other club unless the full amount of $6,000 is put up as a purse. The Olympic Club has ... offered $4,000, and I am satisfied the $2,000 lacking will be put up, to see ... Maher and Choynski come together. If ... not, we will return East where Choynski is ... we can get a match ... there. Before we leave ... we will not disappoint the public. We will give an exhibition, at which Maher will endeavor to stop the best men put against him."[17]

"Maher and ... Connolly, waited yesterday afternoon (July 26) at the Baldwin ... Choynski did not show ... 'We will go East on (the 30th),' remarked Connolly, 'unless something good turns up ...' Graney, manager for Choynski ... seen last evening ... said ... Choynski will not journey East any more ... the contest must take place (here), under ... local clubs. '$4,500 is a pretty good sum ... to fight for nowadays,' said Graney, 'Maher must be dreaming when he refuses to box eight rounds for this money ... Choynski has decided to quit pugilism and settle down to business of some kind in this City. This will be Maher's last chance of meeting him ...' "[18]

Joe was at the Baldwin Hotel on July 28, with Graney as advisor and prospective second. "Maher and ... Connolly, held a conference ... with Joe Choynski, who had just returned from Howell mountains, at which place he has been rusticating for some weeks. Connolly ... 'During our stay in this City I have received dispatches from my partner, that one of the clubs of New York would give $6,000 for ... Choynski and Maher ... I think we would be foolish to accept a lesser sum to box in this City.' Choynski agreed that Connolly was right in one particular, but added that a bird in the hand was worth two in the bush, and emphatically stated that if Maher had the remotest idea of meeting him, he must fight in this City for $4,500, and a return fight could be pulled off in New York City."

"Connolly ... said if a return match took place in New York City, the sports would not give anything like $6,000 ... Choynski smiled and said if there should be such a big demand for fighters as Connolly predicted, the New York sports would certainly give $6,000 or more for a return match. Maher entered a big 'kick' and said he was disgusted with the way ... the Californians treated him, and would take his departure for New York right away. The general opinion is that the Irishman is afraid to meet the native son in this City ..." The *Brooklyn Eagle* said Connolly's projection of a $6,000 purse in New York was based on information he received from the "well-known Eastern horsemen," the Dwyers. The Dwyers brothers said they were building a new sports venue in the "Big Apple" that would open as soon as the Horton Bill took effect in September. At least one paper said the real reason Maher decided against fighting Joe in Frisco was that Jim Corbett told Peter he would not receive fair treatment in the West, due to Choynski's close friendship with Mose Gunst.[19]

Corbett: "In my opinion, with both ... in good condition and Choynski willing to stand and fight, the probabilities are the decision will go to Maher inside of six rounds. I regard Maher the harder hitter, and one of the most formidable men in scoring a knock-out ... Choynski, on the other hand, is a systematic puncher, and can hit oftener ... but ... I don't think he will be able to reach his adversary often enough in the limited go to lower the Irishman's colors ... if it gets down to a slugging match ... will probably turn on who will 'get there' first. Honors are about even on the score of stamina. I think Choynski could go just as far as Peter ... although the latter shows improvement in each ... engagement. Choynski is undoubtedly quicker on his feet and shiftier in avoiding punishment, and if he resorted to dodging tactics instead of fighting ... probably couldn't get worse than a draw. To justify my prediction ... Maher must be in good trim ..." Corbett's words seem to imply dishonor in the use of "dodging tactics." Highly ironic, given that his own boxing style was based on this approach.[20]

"The pugilists have grown tired of waiting for fat purses ... A few days ago, Joe Choynski said he would meet Van Buskirk and Jeffries in one evening, and ... failing to stop both, he would not ask for a cent; but in case he whipped the two new aspirants to the heavy-weight championship, he must receive the entire purse." (Jeffries won a KO2 over Van Buskirk on April 9, 1897). "As soon as Joe McAuliffe learned of Joe's ... challenge, he boarded a Mission-street car ... quickly hunted up one of the managers of the National Club, and declared, 'I am ready ... to accommodate him, or any ... heavy-weight ...' When McAuliffe's statement was made known to Choynski, little Joe smiled, and after ... some thought, he sent word ... that he would fight McAuliffe under the auspices of any club that would 'hang up' a good purse ... McAuliffe ... has been training for three weeks under the supervision of Professor Barney Farley ... according to all accounts, he is getting to look like a man."[21] McAuliffe was a tanner in his "other life," but as a boxer had, in 1887 and 1888, knocked out Mike Brennan "The Port Costa Giant" and Frank Glover, each in 49 rounds. He lasted 24 heats before succumbing to Peter Jackson in 1888. Big Joe had been inactive for nearly three years, though, since an 1893 D4 with Maher.

On August 7, the two Joes met "in the club apartments over 'Young' Mitchell's saloon." The fight was to be "in the large hall at Woodward's Gardens ... leased by the new Occidental Club. About 4:30 ... McAuliffe ... and ... manager ... Barney Farley ... strolled into Mitchell's saloon. As big Joe lounged ... a marked difference in his physical aspect was observed. Joe's normal weight is about 280 pounds, and ... he is the proud ... possessor of a stomach that would make the most corpulent and self-satisfied of Aldermen ... green with envy. Now ... He tips the balance at just 230 ... the stomach has gradually disappeared. The pride of the Mission is Barney's idol. Shortly after 5 o'clock, Choynski arrived with Jimmy Carroll. His excuse for being late ... he was unavoidably detained at the Olympic Club." Others present were Billy Daly and a *Call* reporter.

" 'Well, McAuliffe,' he said ... extending his hand, 'we are here to make a fight ... and needn't let it interfere with our amicable relations.' ... McAuliffe arose and took the proffered hand ... 'That's right, Joe ...' Turning to Mitchell, Choynski queried, 'How much will the club offer us, Johnny?' 'Sixty percent of the gross gate receipts,' was the answer. Both principals ... agreed this was perfectly fair and expressed themselves as satisfied." Choynski, "who seemed to take the initiative in everything," asked how many rounds they would fight. Herget said the more, the better. Farley held out for eight rounds, more than initially planned, to give McAuliffe every chance to use his bulk to slow "The Frisco Flash" down. " 'Eight rounds suits me,' replied Choynski, laughing at Barney's vehemence."

"Eddy Graney, Choynski's manager, arrived. On being acquainted with the proceedings ... he asked a few questions, and said if his charge were satisfied, he was. Mitchell had blank forms ready, and he and Farley wanted articles ... signed then and there, but ... Graney objected. 'I promise you on my honor as a gentleman,' he said, 'that if you will appoint an hour for the signing of the articles to-morrow, we will be here ...' " All assented ... to-day at 5 p.m. ... the men ... (will) sign ... Barney went away with McAuliffe under his wing ... 'I am a good friend of yours, Joey,' he was heard to remark ... 'when old Barney goes back on you it will be snow in the Torrid Zone.' "

"Choynski ... was ... jubilant ... Hardly had the footfalls of McAuliffe and Barney ceased echoing ... when he jumped into the air, cracked his

Joe McAuliffe, undated

heels together, and proceeded to spar an imaginary opponent. 'That's the way I will take him,' he shouted, making a vicious upper-cut with his right, 'and then I will come at him with my left and dance away, so so.' ... Choynski got tangled up in a chair and proceeded to fall in a heap, upsetting a cuspidor ... As he rose with a grin, rubbing his knee where it had come in contact with the floor, he looked rather rueful and remarked: 'I will try a new tack, I think. I will get a pair of springs fixed on the heels of my shoes, and whenever I wish to reach McAuliffe's face, will sail up in the air and let drive.' " Present at the signing were McAuliffe, Farley, Herget, Carroll, Director Houston, Billy Daly, Graney and "Chauncey" Choynski. As the paper stated that McAuliffe signed for himself, but "E.M. Graney signed for Joe Choynski," the Choynski present may have been Joe's older brother, Maurice.[22]

"Choynski does his training ... at his home on Golden Gate Avenue and the Olympic Club. In the morning, he punches the bag and boxes Lou Agnew and Henry Gallagher at home, and in the afternoon, George Green and (Harry) Peppers spar with him at the club. Joe has been 'guyed' so much here lately over his ingenious idea of using spring shoes to reach his burly opponent's head, it is hard to induce him to do much talking over the ... fight." Papers said he would go East following the bout and issue a challenge to knock Corbett out in eight rounds. "Like Corbett, Choynski likes ... to have a squad of Olympic club members congregate and watch him punch the bag, twirl the wrist machines, exercise on the bars, plunge in the tanks and box with Green, Stelzner and Peppers. The 'Chrysanthemum' is in first-class condition and his flesh has a ruddy color, but he seems a trifle low in weight ... he never takes on flesh even when out of training. McAuliffe ... is now at a good weight, 225 pounds."[23] "Choynski has been doing most of his training in the basement of his home, but in the afternoon he usually puts in an hour or so at the Olympic Club. He scales 165 pounds, but hopes to put on five ... more ... against ... McAuliffe ... he wants to get ... as heavy as he possibly can. McAuliffe ... has been training ... faithfully, but it is hard ... for him to reduce. Each day he takes on three sparring partners ... a 10-mile run along the ocean beach ... and an hour or two of handball ... the full measure of his work."[24]

On the day prior to the fight, "Choynski was examined by Dr. John S. Barrett ... and found to be in perfect physical condition ... his lungs were especially strong ... (He) astonished all present by his wonderful muscular development. While men like stocky Sharkey may possess heavier muscles, no finer development has ever been seen here, even on (bodybuilder Eugen) Sandow, than Choynski presented. The chest and shoulder muscles ... are finely shown ... the three transverse abdominal muscles are simply wonderful ... more like corrugated iron than human flesh. The pectoral muscles are enormous and hard, while the intercostals are more noticeably developed than on any other pugilist. These (and) the scapular muscles, show where Choynski gets his tremendous hitting power. (Joe) can contract his scapular muscles until they stand out from under his shoulder blade like a baseball, and are fully as hard. With all this, he is not muscle bound."

"Choynski's measurements: Height, 6'; arms outstretched, 76"; biceps, 13¾"; forearm, 12"; chest, forced expiration, 37"; normal, 39"; forced expansion, 41¼"; waist, 32"; thigh, 22"; calf, 14" ... Choynski's heart ... lung ... respiration ... and his pulse, 72 ... normal. Choynski measures less than his opponent ... in every way, but he expects to make up in science, cleverness and agility what he lacks in weight and ... measurements. Choynski has a long reach, but from finger tip to finger tip McAuliffe outmeasures him 4¾" " "When unassuming Joseph cast off his habiliments ... the physician opened his eyes in astonishment, and said meekly that he had never seen such a magnificent chest and shoulders on a man of Choynski's weight. Joseph smiled as he glanced around the room at his friends ... holding his right arm in an outstretched position, he asked the boys to feel his forearm, which is as hard as steel and as brown as a berry, from exposure to the sun. Around the wrist of his left hand was a bandage which the pugilist said he had to wear, as it was slightly under the weather ... Some years ago, in far-away Australia, Joseph injured the member on Joe Goddard's hard head ... The developments of the fighter's left arm were slightly larger than those of the right." Dr. Barrett was the City Autopsy Surgeon.[25]

On the evening of August 28 at San Francisco's new Woodward Pavilion, about 5,000 saw the two Joes go to war. Captain Withman (or

Wittman) of the city's police department had a large cordon of officers on hand to "keep the peace," inside and outside the building. It was considered a "curious spectacle" that the Chinese Consul had purchased ringside seats. "Those Chinese were the most orderly people in the house." Lightweights John "Spider" Kelly, the great second, and Gus Herget, brother of John, clashed in a preliminary. At 10:20 p.m., Choynski entered the ring, accompanied by handlers, Ed Graney and E. Tillson.

"Joe smiled ... and looked confident ... McAuliffe was looked after by ...

"Big" Joe McAuliffe

Farley, Vincent White and Alexander Greggains. Australian Billy Smith ... was ... referee ... Professor Farley ... instructing his boy ... how to put his big right duke on Choynski's jaw."[26] They used five ounce gloves. Next is a blend of eight fight accounts, only one local. While three papers said the contest was scheduled for eight rounds, three others gave it as 10. The *San Francisco Call* didn't note the distance, but the previous Kelly-Herget fight went its slated 10 rounds.[27] The *Call*'s disclaimer: "It would be an injustice ... to give a technical description of the fight by rounds, as McAuliffe did not display a particle of science, and relied entirely on his push-blow ... to win ... He appeared to be clumsier than ever on his feet, and some of the reaches he made at clever Joe were quite amusing, because of their uncouthness."

Round 1 – "Choynski fiddled ... around Big Joe, and people smiled at the tactics of the clever professional ..." "Choynski assumed the aggressive from the start and hit McAuliffe when and where he pleased. Little Joe played on Big Joe's wind with his left and on the jaw with his right ..." He drove three more lefts to the breadbasket, eliciting grunts from Big Joe. McAuliffe returned the favor with three lefts to the face.

Round 2 – Choynski landed a pair of left hooks to the wind, lowering McAuliffe's guard, then pasted his head with three more from the same fist. The Irish fighter led some, but Jewish Joe evaded with superior quickness. *Call*: "McAuliffe managed, by stiffening his left hand, to keep Choynski at a safe distance, but little Joe warmed big Joe's ribs with right-hand(s) ... near the end of the round ... McAuliffe (caught him) a good stop on the nose." The *Chicago Tribune* said McAuliffe landed to the body but received a nose shot that drew blood. "Little Joe" went at him "like a demon and landed ... left on wind and right over heart." Big Joe clinched in an effort to avoid the body blows, but Choynski rushed and connected hard with lefts.

Round 3 – Choynski did more infighting, landing a series of left hooks to the body and jabs to the face. "McAuliffe was somewhat winded. He reached Choynski two or three times, but his blows lacked steam ... a vicious left swing from Choynski ... staggered McAuliffe."

Round 4 – McAuliffe was winded. More than one paper felt he had weakened himself by losing too much weight, too quickly. A left to the gut and a hard right to the face made him groggy. "The California Terror" jabbed him in the nose to draw him out. This didn't work, as Big Joe lacked the energy to counter. Choynski closed in with a two-fisted attack, finishing with his now-familiar left to the wind and right cross to the head. The "Mission Boy" "staggered backward ... against the ropes near his corner." Joe crashed a left and terrific right to the jaw, dropping McAuliffe like a ton of pig iron. The behemoth was too weak to rise before the 10-count was tolled. The *Chicago Tribune* felt he could have risen if he really cared to. The *Call* said "pandemonium reigned; everybody jumped into the air and yelled; hats were waved and canes flourished. Words of admiration for Choynski's wondrous coolness and speed were heard on all sides."

"Choynski ... appeared in fine form, not a scratch ... on his face or body. He was in the best of humor, but ... not ... inclined to do much talking. 'McAuliffe personally is a fine fellow and I like him very much, but for a prize-fighter he's entirely too slow. I knew in the 3rd round ... I had him, and made up my mind to ... finish him in the 4th.' Immediately after McAuliffe entered his dressing-room, the door was closed and admission was secured with much difficulty ... the effects of the punishment ... from his hard-hitting opponent were made ... manifest in his bruised face and swollen eyes. Directly under his left eye was a deep cut ... 'I never had the least idea Choynski was such a magnificent fighter,' mournfully admitted McAuliffe, 'or I should for no consideration met him with only five week's training. Choynski is the hardest hitter I ever went up against.' ... Barney Farley was almost overcome ... but ... was the first hand to greet him when he was led to his corner ..." Choynski stated, in 1927, of Big Joe hustling him around, "Someone said it looked like a burly farmer trying to evict a marauding urchin from his apple orchard." He tried to lift McAuliffe's bulk to his corner after the KO, but he was too massive.

The next day, the National Club's J.J. Groom approached Choynski with an offer to fight Bob Fitzsimmons for a purse of $10,000. Joe said he was "perfectly willing ... but the club has no permit for such a contest, and might not be able to procure it." He referred Groom to his manager, Eddie Graney, but the club never had Bob's consent. Joe: "Next Saturday I ... will box a limited round contest with Reddy Gallagher in Denver. I shall then go to New York ... ready to meet all comers." On the 30th, he took part in L.R. Stockwell's testimonial at the California Theater. "Actors, musicians and specialty artists ... in ... a diversified matinee performance ... about $650 for the ... actor favored by ... fellows of the profession ... Joe Choynski ... recently rejuvenated lion of local pugilism ... punched a leather bag in the most approved style ... others ... did and said clever things, but Choynski ... recently played to 5,000 spectators at fancy prices ... just plain, talented actors have no such hold upon the popular taste."[28]

Joe told the *Chicago Daily Inter-Ocean* on August 31, that he would arrive in that city by September 10 and remain two or three days. He intended to continue to New York, to clinch a rematch with Fitzsimmons. "Choynski says he wants to get at the top at once or quit the business altogether. He thinks he has been wasting enough time at the game, and unless there is an immediate ... fight with some of the big ones, he had better get into some line of work that will be of more benefit to himself. Joe ... is now one of the best known pugilists of the world and easily ranks next to Corbett and Fitzsimmons." Joe arrived in Denver with Louise on the night September 6. He stated to a Denver paper, of the June 24 Corbett-Sharkey (D4) fight: "Corbett had Sharkey nearly out in the 1st round. Sharkey's right eye was closed up so tight his face was all screwed up. Sharkey would rarely land on Jim, but he took ... the strength ... out of him in the clinches."[29]

Joe boxed a four round exhibition with "Reddy" Gallagher on the 8th. "Reddy" was given the nickname for his red hair, but his real name was Patrick or Stephan (sources vary). September 9 *Rocky Mountain News*: "Boxing at the Lyceum ... four rounds between Joseph Bartlett Choynski, the best light-heavyweight in the world, and instructor Gallagher of the DAC (Denver Athletic Club). The latter is preparing for the foot ball season, and seemed to enjoy the fast pace which Choynski set." September 17 *Brooklyn Eagle*: "Choynski's 'go' ... with Reddy Gallagher was a friendly set-to, and not a match for points, as was reported. Choynski was Gallagher's guest while there. They had a big crowd."

The *Eagle* noted that Joe stopped off at Cripple Creek, Colorado for an exhibition. "He has a little 'roast' to give Corbett for the action of the latter in Cripple Creek. Choynski boxed in the mining town two or three nights after Corbett had been there in a set-to with Billy Woods. Corbett gave a wretched exhibition – so bad the crowd hissed ... Corbett, at the end of the 1st round, went to the footlights and explained that he was so affected by the altitude that he could do no better. 'The altitude did not affect me,' said Choynski, 'when I boxed there a few nights later. But Corbett's conduct seriously affected the attendance at my set-to with Woods.' " As papers reported the Corbett-Woods spar taking place on either the 6th or 7th, it appears that Choynski boxed "Denver" Billy Woods around September 9 or 10. "Little Joe" stopped in Chicago on his way East. "One of his wrists is wrong, the result of a set-to shortly before he left San Francisco ... Davies will go East in two or three days to complete details for the match between

Choynski and Maher." Joe and "The Parson" had made amends again. September 12 London *Mirror of Life*: "Choynski's record furnished by 'Parson' Davies gives these additional victories ..." The only result not found on his boxing record is the undated, "Jem Ryan, two rounds."

September 22 *Philadelphia Inquirer*: "Apropos of Choynski, who in his closely knit self combines the traits of character that go to make up that paradoxical entity – a pugilist and a gentleman – a western sporting man has the following to say: 'I was one of a party of six at supper when the subject of heavy-weight fighters came up. The merits, personally and professionally of all the big ones, from *Denver Ed* Smith up to Corbett, were canvassed, and when the vivisection was through ... but one man ... showed a clean bill of morals and manhood ... Joe Choynski.' – *New York Journal*." Such was the consensus of his character. Davies left for New York on the 21st, Joe for Cincinnati, probably to visit his wife's family in Walnut Hills. "The Parson denies the rumor that he has done with pugilism forever ..."

Joe was a special guest at the Chicago Athletic Club on October 10: "This afternoon, Dr. Melton B. Pine, a North Side dentist and Frederick Swift, a broker, both members of the club, fought to a finish according to ... Queensberry rules. Pine won in the 2nd round, knocking Swift out with a right-hander ... a wager was made between them for $1,000 a side ... The fight was pulled off before six men on each side; George Siler ... acting as referee. Dr. Pine's weight ... was given as 190 pounds, while Swift's was 185. Joseph Biehrinski (sic), the pugilist, was in attendance, and Pine wore the tights which Choynski wore in the majority of his battles ... Pine ... hammered Swift all over the ring and finally put him out with a vicious punch on the point of the chin ... Swift was unconscious for nearly 30 minutes. What action will be taken by the officers of the club is not known, but there will certainly be much trouble over the affair."

"A great deal of secrecy ... in bringing off the fight. No newspaper men were admitted ... the affair was zealously guarded. The party privileged to witness the mill was: George Dawson ... C.T. Essig, 'Colonel' Hamburger, Joe Choynski and Al Shrosbree. Four-ounce gloves were used. The pace was hot, and both men soon began to show the lack of training. The 2nd and last round was a slugging match, in which Swift was frightfully punished. A crash to the temple sent Swift down on the polished hardwood floor, dazed and all but knocked out. Referee Siler stood over the prostrate form and counted nine seconds before Swift labored to his feet. The man was utterly defenseless and Pine ... with a full right ... to the point of the chin ... sent Swift to the floor ... completely knocked out. So forceful was the blow ... Swift's seconds feared their man had been killed, for he lay there, apparently lifeless. Vigorous kneading ... ammonia ... whiskey, and half an hour's work brought Swift back to consciousness." Thankfully, Joe did not appear to take an active part in the dangerous bout.[30]

"Choynski has been training down too fine for his battles, but claims this was the result of a total abstinence from meat during his preparatory work. He fought big Joe McAuliffe at 176 pounds, and considered himself in perfect trim. In his fight against Jim Hall last January, Joe weighed inside the middleweight limit, and was only one pound heavier ... when he came within the tick of a watch of beating Fitzsimmons ... 'My friends are afraid that Maher is too big and too strong for me,' said Choynski yesterday, 'and are warning me off. What rot! I am big enough to go against anybody.' " Joe was to arrive at Oceanic, New Jersey on the 31st, and "make the Oceanic Inn his training headquarters for his coming fight ... at the Broadway Athletic clubhouse. Maher is in training at Sheepshead Bay." Peter was born April 18, 1866, so he was in his prime, at 30 years old.[31] A humorous article read: "There are at least 20 fighters ... around New York and Philadelphia who bear Irish names for ring use, who are in reality Israelites. Jack McKeck is one ... Al O'Brien ... is another. While McKeck was boxing Kid Madden, a Hibernian remarked, 'Isn't it queer how well thim Hebrews foight when they take Oirish names. Some of thim, loike this fellow ... has no roight to thim at all, but they say Joe Co-insky is half Oirish. Now, if he was to call himself Cunningham or Cavanaugh or some of thim good old names, who knows but he moight be the champion yet?' "[32]

Joe arrived in Chicago on November 11, from his training quarters at Palos (Illinois). He was accompanied by his trainer, Al Shrosbree and Jimmy Barry. "When seen at the Tremont, Joe said: 'I feel in the best of health and am in splendid condition ... I have every confidence in defeating the *Irish Champion*. I will leave on the limited train for New York tomorrow, accompanied by my manager, Parson Davies. I will weigh about 165 pounds ... I will remain in New York to second Bob in his go with Slavin.' " "Joe ... is to train at the Chicago A.A. for ... Peter Maher ..."[33]

Davies and Choynski arrived in New York on the 14th, where Joe would finish up training for the 20 round bout "under the watchful eye of Mike Donovan at the New York Athletic Club." "(Joe) will not step into the squared circle tonight with a broken rib, as he did in his memorable victory over Jim Hall at Maspeth, which made him ... so slow of foot. Choynski has a reputation for gameness and endurance ... Maher's victories have all been short, quick and decisive. Recognized ... as the two leading heavyweights next to Corbett and Fitzsimmons ... Sam C. Austin will be referee."[34] Austin was also sporting editor of the *National Police Gazette*.

The much-anticipated Choynski-Maher battle occurred on the night of November 16, 1896. Odds were about 10 to 8 in favor of Peter. "More money has been wagered on this contest than any since Corbett-Sullivan ... Just why the odds should favor Maher (is) hard to determine ... Choynski is certainly a clever man and difficult to reach at long range. He is quick with his legs (and) hands, and it will be a part of his plan to ... avoid the terrific

Maher swings. In an even exchange of blows, Choynski realizes he would have the worst of it, although a hard hitter himself. When it comes to a mix up, Maher is not so dangerous. He can fight hard and fast at close quarters. So can Choynski, but Maher is not fond of ... rough work, preferring ... to take a chance of ... a winning blow with a rush at long range. Choynski ... feels confident he can stop Maher's rushes with a ... jab when ... not able to step out of harm's way ... Choynski will battle hard as long as he can stand, while Maher does not take punishment well and cannot fight an uphill battle. Unless the Irishman wins in four rounds, his chances of winning at all will be small. There is some doubt ... about O'Rourke being

Peter Maher, "The Irish Champion"

able to bring off this contest at his ... club. The Horton law is ... curious ... police ... allow bouts to go as far as they think the public will stand it."[35]

The March, 1901 "Famous Fights," by Londoner, Harold Furniss, wrote: " 'Now, keep your eye skinned for that right, or you'll be in trouble,' are invariably the last words of advice offered to a pugilist ... going up against ... Maher ... for ... the big fellow has one of the most dangerous right-handed punches of any of the American brigade. He depends almost wholly on a lead at the body with the auctioneer, and aims at the solar plexus, or 'mark,' as it is known in England. Possessed of great shoulder power, he is able to drive his ... blow home with terrific force, and when landed few men have been able to retain their perpendicular. Steve O'Donnell, Joe Goddard ... have all received their quietus through ... that dreaded right, and ... Kid McCoy ... was very careful to keep out of range of it. The glove seems to sneak right into the body, and with a low, gurgling gasp the stricken man falls to the floor an inert mass. With such a dangerous punch, it is at a first glance ... surprising that Peter has not more battles to his credit but ... a man depending almost wholly on a right-hander at the solar plexus must leave himself open at that most vital point, the jaw. He sacrifices everything to land his right, and very often meets a left on the point that puts him hors de combat. It is a very dangerous blow if one is not up to it, but everyone in the pugilistic world knows of it, and, consequently, Maher has few opportunities of scoring with it."

Choynski recalled, in 1930: "Fight fans shook their heads when ... I (was) matched with Peter Maher. Many thought I was daffy and did not hesitate to tell me ... But Maher's prowess did not awe me. I have always felt a sock is a sock ... I was confident I carried something potent enough to jar Maher if I could hit him. And I seldom failed to hit ... Theodore Roosevelt was Commissioner of Police at the time – and his name figures prominently in ... this momentous battle." Maher entered the ring about 9:47 p.m., followed by seconds, Pete Burns, Peter Lowry and Jack Quinn. Joe left his dressing room about 30 seconds later, attended by Tommy West, Paddy Gorman and Bob Armstrong. He looked confident, but Peter did not. Joe's hair was a bit long, papers commenting on his chrysanthemum mop and flopping blonde locks. They stood before a crowd of about 4,000. A consistent quote of the weights was about 165-166 pounds for Joe, 173-174 for Peter. Some papers gave a 10-pound advantage to the latter. Just before the bell, Maher's people insisted on Joe removing "a bandage ... firmly wrapped around his left wrist." The *Police Gazette* said the bandage covered a cut. The following is derived from multiple reports, all but one contemporary, in addition to Choynski's memoirs.[36]

Round 1 – The fight began with cautious sparring. Choynski feinted a couple of times before landing a left to the wind. Maher countered with a hard left to the body. Joe got in two or three left leads to the midsection, but as he turned in getting away, Peter caught him with a left hook to the face. Both went back to long-range sparring for the duration.

Round 2 – Peter missed a vicious swing to the head, and Joe made him pay with two hard lefts to the jaw. Maher came back with a left to the neck and a right to the body. Joe landed three consecutive left jabs to the face, then staggered his foe with a left hook; some sources said a left-right. They exchanged punches to the head as the round closed, generally in favor of Joe. He recalled, decades later, "Maher, a tremendous hitter, was much heavier than I was, and I had a deep respect for him. However, I was fast, well trained and clear headed. I let Maher swing. Then I stood off and began cutting him up." Bob Edgren (for the February 6, 1914 *Syracuse Herald*): "In the 2nd round, Choynski leaped suddenly into full speed. He made the fight at long range, avoiding Maher's furious rushes and blows that flew like lightning strikes, and jabbed him so hard that more than once Peter floundered and nearly lost his footing. Soon, Joe ... began whipping hard lefts into Peter's body, and ... Peter showed signs of distress."

Round 3 – Choynski shot three lefts to the body and a hard right to the head. Maher retaliated with a pair of lefts to the face. Joe drove a hard left to the body, then slipped to the floor, some felt, to avoid a punch. Peter forced him to the ropes and swung left and right to the body and face. He missed a vicious overhand right, the momentum dropping him to his knees. When Peter regained his feet, Joe landed a left jab to the nose. The Pride of the Emerald Isle got in two light lefts to the face at the bell, ending a fairly even round. Edgren: "Peter grazed Joe's chin with a left hook, dropping him to his knees, where he rested eight seconds before leaping up. Joe dug into Peter's body harder than ever, and more than evened the score."

Round 4 – Choynski drove a hurting left to the body, repeating the dose two-fold. Maher rushed him to the ropes and crashed a left to the face or a right to the ribs (sources vary). "The Fighting Maccabee" feinted with the left and crossed a right hard to the head that shook up Maher. Peter landed a couple of inconsequential blows to end the frame. Some of the "more unruly members of the audience" howled at the fighters to pick up the pace. Joe: "This big, powerful favorite swung and swung, but missed every other blow. The ones I stopped were full of dynamite and I knew I dared not get careless ... Just one ... in the mush, and I'd be gone."

Round 5 – Choynski assumed the aggressive, snapping the jab in Peter's face and "easily avoiding the return. Maher pasted a good left on the body, but Joe evened up with a return. Maher led for the body and brought his right round on the neck. Choynski swung his left on the face and Maher countered on the body. Peter nailed Joe on the face and they came close ... doing pretty sparring and exchanging lefts on the face." At some point, referee Austin warned Maher for using his elbow. A couple of reports called the round even, but the *Brooklyn Eagle* wrote: "Choynski toyed with his left on Maher's wind and finished up ... with a stiff punch on Maher's jaw. It seemed all over with Peter ... in the same round (he) had taken a savage straight punch on the mouth that jolted his head back."

Joe: "So I held to my steady campaign, slashing away and keeping clear ... the bout assumed the proportions of a massacre. Maher was bleeding, beaten ... in the most pathetic condition. I was still ... strong, but ... wary." Edgren: "Choynski fought with greater caution, but without letting up in the pace he had set. The end of the 5th saw ... Maher staggering and puffing, while Choynski danced around and drove in his punches ... While Joe sat in his corner at the end of that round, Mike Donovan slipped quickly around to his corner and whispered, 'Go in and mix – you've got him. Mix it up and finish him before he comes back.' Joe nodded." No contemporary account has Donovan in the arena, much less in Choynski's corner.

Round 6 – Joe rushed at Maher, smashing a left-right to the jaw that slammed him into the ropes. *Brooklyn Eagle*: "The end came unexpectedly, because on the form of the previous rounds, Choynski should have won handily ... with a left ... on Maher's jaw ... his left into the Irishman's stomach, doubling him up ... (with) a minute ... gone, Choynski threw ... his left with terrific force and caught Peter clean on the point of the jaw. The punch staggered him ... (Joe), with instructions from the corner where 'Parson' Davies was eagerly watching the course of events, was ... told to sail in. The result was disastrous ... Choynski had the battle practically won, but ... rushed blindly at Maher and received a clip on the jaw that sent him to the floor. It wasn't a knock down, and ... he got up ... only to dodge to the floor after another punch, to avoid a knockout. A hot rally ... both men smashing ... right and left at close quarters. It was a toss up ... who would get in the finishing blow. Both were weak and wild. Finally, Maher threw out his left by way of a feint. Then he crossed his right. It caught Choynski clean on the jaw ... he went down ... and lay where he fell ... when the cheering and the yelling had subsided, announcer Charlie Harvey declared the trick had been done in 2 minutes, 25 seconds ..." The *Police Gazette* said the sound of Joe's head hitting the canvas was audible.

Choynski recalled, years later: "Police got ready to stop the fight (in his favor). They were about to climb into the ring when a voice ... Roosevelt ... In his high, shrill voice, yelled: 'That man is not beaten yet. Don't stop this fight!' So we went on ... in the 6th, the slugging Harp rallied ... tearing in with his head down with no regard ... for my ... punches. I knew I had to act fast. If I let him rally ... no man ... might safely predict what would happen ... I measured Maher for a terrific wallop, put plenty of dynamite into the punch ... stepped back to watch the beef fall. But fate decreed otherwise. Instead ... Maher careened against the ropes and came bounding back – swinging a crazy haymaker. The next thing I remember, I was slumped in my corner and my seconds were drowning me with ice water. Maher's wild swing had rung my bell and I was knocked cold, thus upsetting the dope entirely. So you can see what Peter Maher and the police commissioner did to me! But it was a great scrap. I had two more sizzling battles with the tough, old walloper – with a little more glory for Choynski."

An ex-pug named Howard Carr, who fought under the name, "Kid" Howard, managed boxers and ran a gym in Chicago. He wrote (with flaws), for the July 27, 1914 *Fort Wayne Sentinel*, that Teddy stole the fight from Joe when he refused to allow it stopped, when Peter was dazed. Carr had been a second in the preliminaries, but instead of heading to the dressing room, he "slipped into a vacant box on the right ... of the ring, and ... awaited ... the big men." An usher led Roosevelt to the box and was pulling young Howard out by the ear, when the future United States President told him to remain and watch the fight. What Howard saw transpire was, in his opinion, nothing short of a rip-off. Joe "assumed a crouching attitude ... his long left stuck straight out ... Peter ... stood straight up with his right arm held high." In round two, Peter staggered Choynski with a good right, but the latter cut his man up with the left jab. Frames three and four were vicious, Joe having

Maher on the verge of a knockout several times.

"Scarcely 30 seconds were left of the (5th) round when Choynski shot a smashing left hook on the square chin of the Irishman ... a terrific right flush on the ear, and Maher sank to the floor. Slowly, the referee began to toll off the seconds ... The blue eyes of Maher were half closed and glassy ... Choynski stood over him with a half smile ... through his bloody lips the white of his clenched teeth ... The referee called 'nine' ... in another second Maher would have been counted out – bang, went the bell, and for the first time, Peter was saved. As Maher's second dragged his prostrate form to his corner, a captain of police was ... climbing up ... in the Irishman's corner. 'I am going to stop this bout' 'You are ... to do nothing of the kind,' exclaimed Roosevelt. Just then the bell rang, and Maher was pushed from his corner, fully recuperated ... Suddenly, in a fierce mix-up ... near the colonel's box, Maher shot a right hand ... on the long jaw of the Californian. Joe fell forward ... on Peter's chest. Peter stepped back, measured Choynski at arm's length, and ... let go with his famous right hand wallop. The blow landed flush on Choynski's chin point ... he fell in a limp mass ... 'You see,' said the colonel ... 'a man is never beaten until he's counted out.' "

The *San Francisco Call* said: "Police clambered into the ring, but no arrests were made." The *St. Paul Globe* and the *Decatur Review* added: "Choynski ... has ... wonderful recuperative powers, surprised everybody by regaining consciousness in less than a minute, and needed no assistance from his seconds in making his way to the dressing room." A "sporting man" told the November 29 *St. Paul Globe*: "The first time I ever saw Parson Davies rattled was Monday night. I was watching the Parson when Choynski was knocked out. The Parson is always pale, but he turned gray, dropped his watch upon the floor, and I thought he was going to faint."

The *Call* added a superstitious twist: "The sports of this City who gamble on prize-fighting ... thronged (Harry) Corbett's poolroom last evening to hear the returns of the rounds ... The general opinion ... was that Choynski would win in five or six rounds ... being rated a much more clever man than Maher, and also a heavy puncher. Choynski hit the Irishman frequently ... but his blows did not ... have the desired effect. The fight goes to prove that Choynski has lost his great hitting powers. In his great battles with Goddard, he cut great gashes in the Australian's face and frequently knocked him down. If he possessed the same power to-day, he would have knocked Maher down several times before the 6th round. A ... strange thing happened at Corbett's just about the time the 1st round ... arrived. When the rooms were crowded with sports, police were called in to disperse some of the mob, and a picture of Choynski ... hanging on the wall alongside several other pictures of pugilists, fell to the floor. A big Irishman named Ryan, who saw the photograph drop, rushed into the pool-sellers' department and placed $50 on Maher, saying he never knew ... of a picture falling from a wall that did not bring bad luck to the man or woman it represented."

Storylines the next day carried such colorful phrases as, "Ireland Bests Jerusalem in Six Rounds." At least a couple of papers, in 1905 and 1938, said Maher had gained revenge for Choynski's part in Peter's 1892 loss to Fitzsimmons. Joe supposedly rescued Fitz from certain defeat by surreptitiously ringing the timekeeper's bell, ending the 1st round early. Joe allegedly pricked Bob on the arm with a penknife, in the corner, restoring consciousness. Maher supposedly said to "Chrysanthemum" Joe, when he faced him in their 1896 clash, "Ye used a penknife on Fitz in New Orleans to bring him back, didn't ye? Begorra, whin Oi get me penknife workin', it'll be all day wid ye." Every time Peter landed a hard punch on Joe, he would say, "That's me penknife, Joe. How d'ye loike it?" After the knockout, Maher went to Choynski's corner and (purportedly) said, with pity in his eyes: "Oi'm sorry for ye, Joe, 'cause yer a good feller. But the next toime ye use a penknife on a mon, remember thot the other mon carries one thot's warranted niver to rust."[37] This is likely another "urban legend."

A 1921 column, exaggerating a wee bit, said: "Choynski, a whirlwind ... drove Maher all around the ring, dealing out a rain of savage, staggering blows ... His legs seemed to buckle ... his body one mass of fearful welts and bruises; both eyes ... practically closed; blood streamed down from ... mouth, nose ... above his eyes ... a half dozen terrible cuts on the face. A police captain ... bellowed ... 'stop the fight before Maher is killed' ... a man caught his coat tails ... yelled ... 'let the fight go on.' ... to the police captain (he) said, 'No fight should ... be stopped while a man is still on his feet and ... willing to fight.' The speaker was Theodore Roosevelt ..."[38] All things taken together, it appears a decision to declare Maher a loser by technical knockout could have gone either way. If not for the intervention of Teddy, however, Joe would have been 3-for-3 against Maher, as will be seen.

Roosevelt later said he didn't consider the bout brutal at all; in fact, "when he was at Harvard and sparred for the championship, he suffered greater punishment ... has often been knocked out at polo for a longer period than ... Choynski. He adds: 'I don't care very much for professional sport of any kind, but I ... believe in boxing as I believe in football and other manly games, and think it the greatest mistake that decent people should ... allow the hard hitting qualities which make a man a man, to be monopolized by those who don't believe in decency. Wesley said, when reproached with choosing hymns that had a swing to them, that he didn't believe in letting the devil have all the good music; and I don't believe in allowing the devil to have a monopoly of the qualities that succeed in a rough and tumble.' " While the evidence goes against Roosevelt competing for a championship at Harvard, he did box there. Counselor Ed McVey said he and "Teddie" were "classmates ... in the late 1870s, and Roosevelt was quite an ... athlete. One day ... Teddie put on the gloves with Prof. Lister, the Harvard instructor ... The professor swung real hard on Teddie's face and sent him through space, against the wall of the gym ... 'if it hadn't been for ... the wall, Teddy would be going yet ... if Maher punched Choynski any harder ... I'd hardly blame the latter if he'd called it brutal.' "[39]

Roosevelt was criticized by many for allowing the match to continue. *New York Daily Tribune*: "Mr. Roosevelt ... may be convinced ... the bouts in question were things of scientific beauty, devoid of all brutality. Those are questions of personal enjoyment ... with which the public has nothing to do. What does concern the public is that the head of the Police Department ... should ... encourage habitual lawbreakers ... to get around the statutes and indulge in prize-fighting ... Under the old law in this State, police stopped boxing exhibitions whenever they approached the line of a 'knock-out.' The ... Horton law was intended ... to restrict fisticuffs ... allowing boxing purely for exhibition in athletic clubs. Mr. Roosevelt may have received as hard blows at Harvard as any Maher gave, but he did not fire the blood of the plug-uglies there and set them scheming to get fights brutal enough for their tastes." Walter Schlichter, in the August 9, 1942 *Philadelphia Inquirer*, claimed a "sensation preacher" named Dr. Parkhurst asked Teddy to have the fight stopped. He refused, and when Peter scored his "Hail Mary" knockout, "Roosevelt jumped up ... and in his inimitable voice, yelled 'Bully.' After the bout, Maher was introduced to Roosevelt and, after he squeezed the Irish champion's hand, his ... remark was 'Dee-lighted!' "

The December 12 *Police Gazette* quoted "The Parson": "We told him not to mix ... but to keep away and jab ... in the face and wind. He lost his head ... Joe ... did a foolish thing ... with a strong, two-handed fighter like Maher." March 6, 1910 *Washington Post*: "It was asserted that the Irishman wore five yards of adhesive tape around each hand. Choynski protested ... those extremely thick bandages ... wanted ... them removed, so he could see them wound on again ... But, was notified the tape was there to stay and, if he did not like it, he could quit. So, Choynski was knocked out, but always insisted it was due to the knuckle guards worn by his adversary."

Soon after the fight, a Pittsburgh theatrical figure, Harry Davis, hired Maher and Joe to reenact their bout before his "zinematographe." This was one of the many inventions of the day used to take and show moving pictures. Reenactments were accepted in the day, while deceptive fakes were not. The film ran about 20 minutes. It was first shown publicly on February 1, 1897 at Davis' Eden Musee in Pittsburgh, and later at Bradenburgh's 9th and Arch Dime Museum in Philadelphia, New York's Huber Museum and other cinematic venues. The film unfortunately did not survive to the present; otherwise it would have afforded the only glimpse of Joe Choynski trading punches in the ring, while in his prime.[40]

Round Fifteen

The California Grizzly
(November 1896 – December 1897)

Choynski seconded Bob Armstrong on November 23 in New York, against Frank Slavin, the once-formidable Australian. Two days prior, Joe said: "He (Bob) has a remarkable reach and one of the quickest left hands I have ever seen, and can use it to perfection." Armstrong knocked out the aging "Sydney Cornstalk" in round four, softening him up with a pile-driving left jab that Frank was unable to get past. On the 27th, Choynski arrived back in Chicago. When asked about his loss to Maher, Joe had no excuses; in fact, he had nothing to say about it. Around this time, he attended a college football game: "After witnessing the late contest between the Yale and Princeton football teams, Joe Choynski ... pronounces the game more brutal and dangerous than prize fighting."[1]

A highly controversial fight took place in San Francisco on December 2, between Bob Fitzsimmons and Tom Sharkey. Infamous lawman Wyatt Earp refereed. He awarded the fight and $10,000 purse to Tom in round eight, after the sailor was rendered helpless by what nearly everyone except Earp saw as a clean body blow. Herbert Choynski was a ringside witness to the debacle, but wasn't seated in the right position to see the blow.[2] Joe defended Tom, saying: "Give a dog a bad name and it will stick to him. Sharkey has the name of ... a foul fighter ... everyone seems to have the impression he can't fight a fair round ... Sharkey is one of the fairest ... I ever stepped into the ring with. He is an awkward, rough and ready sort of fellow, always coming in with a rush, but ... fair ..."

"In spite of the fact that he did foul me accidentally, so badly the fight was stopped 20 minutes to allow me to recover ... Sharkey did not deny the foul ... the referee saw it and was willing to give me the fight. I would not accept ... because I thought I could go on and win. The blow was not a hard one, but ... below the belt, and I turned pale and sick from the effects of it. After a few minutes' rest I was all right ... When I read about people who say Fitzsimmons did not foul Sharkey, because they did not see it, although they were in a position to see, I am reminded ... that my seconds did not see Sharkey foul me, although they were in a splendid position to ... and it was ... their duty to look out for fouls. I see it is claimed ... that ... Earp is a novice in the ring. I have known Earp for a long time, and I believe he knows just as much about boxing contests as I do. I have seen Earp referee fights, and I know he has acted scores of times in that capacity. Earp may have a record, but ... is well known on the coast as a champion of fair play. Fitzsimmons is always in trouble, and a great deal ... is of his own making. When Jim Hall knocked him out in Australia, he said it was a 'fake,' admitting that he deliberately laid down for a consideration. A man that will do what he said he did should not do much yelling about fair play."

"When he fought me in Boston, I practically had him knocked out, and but for the interference of the police I would have finished him. After the bout he said he had agreed with me to go light, and I had crossed him when I got a chance. There is not a word of truth in that ... The go was on its merits, and because he got the worst of it, made that lame excuse. Fitz hit Sharkey foul and properly lost the fight." Choynski wrote in 1930 that he asked Hall about the first Fitz encounter, and Jim "indignantly denied that the fight was not on the up-and-up."[3] He believed Hall. Some of the bitterness Joe would express later was manifesting, and may have influenced him in coming to Sharkey's defense. "Choynski will leave ... for New York ... second Mike Donovan in ... bout with Mace. Donovan esteems Choynski as the greatest second and advisor ... ever ..."

At the Broadway Athletic Club on December 14, two of the legendary bareknuckle-and-glove transition fighters, "Professor" Mike Donovan and Jem Mace, the "Swaffham Gypsy," boxed a famous exhibition. Mike was 49 years old, Mace, 65. It was advertised as a six-round bout, on its merits, "showing the cleverest exponents of the English and American style(s) ... the greatest gathering of old time champions and pugilists (and) those of the present day ... At least 100 ... introduced ... many ... will participate. John Sullivan will make a speech ... his arm in a sling, while Maher, Choynski and Steve O'Donnell will cast withering glances at each other during their bouts with some of the good locals." Others listed: Sam Fitzpatrick, Billy Madden, Owen Ziegler, Dan Creedon, "Kid" Lavigne, George Dixon, Solly Smith and Jimmy Barry. Joe said (1927) that Mike only offered him the cost of transportation and $100 for expenses, but so great was Joe's desire to see old Mace in action, he accepted. "Donovan was the greatest of all boxing instructors in America ... Mace ... undoubtedly the greatest boxing teacher of all time (and) perhaps the most perfect boxer."

Joe said Donovan was worried that Mace might make him look bad, and said, "you are the greatest second in the world, and I felt I must have you in my corner." Joe "was amazed when Jem walked into the ring ... a man with coal black hair and a body as smooth and plump as a man of 30. He weighed 180 pounds ... Mike was 15 pounds lighter." Joe exaggerated, saying Donovan was 57 years old and Mace, 80! "They went three rounds ... I followed their beautiful work with deep interest. Mace was exhausted at the end of the 3rd round and unable to continue, although he had not been hit ... he was graceful, resourceful and fast. Donovan scarcely laid a glove on him squarely. Mace's head shifting was marvelously timed. He could gauge distance and slip blows by a hair. Here was Griffo and Corbett and Fitzsimmons and Jim Hall all combined in one." I suppose one could forgive Joe for some hyperbole, given that Mace was his idol.

The veterans of the prize ring went four rounds, instead of six. *Chronicle*: "Jem Mace, last of the English champions, and 'Mike' Donovan, the frost-bitten and time-hardened American pugilist, met to-night in a four-round bout that was as full of scientific points as a Christmas pudding is full of plums. Around the arena were ... many pugilistic ghosts of by-gone days ... who fought with bare-knuckles in olden times for a pot of ale or a 10-guinea prize ... one man in particular ... sat, gray-haired, silent and gloomy ... At one time the pugilistic world was at his feet ... John Lawrence Sullivan, ex-champion of the world in the knocking-out industry ... he still talks on the starboard side of his mouth with a growl like ... a grizzly bear."

"Old-timers, Billy Edwards and Arthur Chambers ... sparred ... one minute ... got tired and went to their corners without waiting for the bell. The crowd howled in serene enjoyment. Jim Corbett (and) John McVey ... sparred ... Choynski, Peter Maher and Steve O'Donnell were introduced, but refused to make speeches ... the two ancient, bald heads of Mace and Donovan loomed up on their way to the ring ... Parson Davies ... as referee, announced the receipts as $3,000, with less than $600 expenses. The rounds were only two minutes' duration ... the decision left to the spectators, who all shouted, 'A draw.' " The consensus was that Donovan "clearly asserted his superiority over the old time heavyweight champion of England."[4]

The December 15 *Davenport Daily Republican* interviewed Mace: "I am now 66 ... as healthy, hearty, rugged and strong as ever ... critics ... say I still preserve all my old time cleverness, albeit not quite as quick or enduring as of yore. Plucky Joe Choynski and clever Jim Corbett can tell you ... I put up a fair game with them in friendly bouts when they visited England. Of course, both ... could easily outlast me. There is quite a difference in the spring and autumn of life when it comes to staying power. Moderation in all things is the secret of the ... business ... An athlete in training should never ... crave for a glass of ale ... a mild smoke or ... any fruit or beverage ... its effects can be worked out of the system by exercise. But to young fellows ambitious of fistic renown, I ... give this last and special piece of advice – avoid worship at the shrine of Venus (and) of Bacchus, and you will not break down in the prime of your manhood, as many modern champions have done, a misfortune ... the old champions generally escaped."

"Parson" Davies was pegging his young heavyweight, Bob Armstrong, as another Peter Jackson. This turned out not to be the case, though Bob did become one of the most sought-after cornermen and trainers. Joe was credited as having taught Armstrong the finer scientific points of the game. In December, Joe wrote a letter to Graney, saying he was "through with the ring ... Eddie ... wired Joe that he would back him for $5,000 against Maher

... Eddie is confident that, had he been behind him, Choynski would have won. He never lost a fight when he was in his corner."[5]

It was announced in December that Joe had signed with the Siegel-Cooper Company, a New York dry-goods firm, to take charge of their sporting goods department on 6th Avenue. He would not only act as a salesman, but "as a sort of physical director and advisor. The Californian is ... well informed on the latest and best methods of training. His contract does not prohibit him from prize fighting." The contract was for one year, to commence on January 1, 1897. "Choynski has a graceful presence ... and many ... qualifications ... to make up a successful salesman." "He has ... practical experience with nearly every glove made ..." "The idea originated with Mr. Hogan, the general manager, who thinks Choynski's reputation will draw the best class of sporting people ..." It was suggested, tongue firmly in cheek, that the shrewd Hogan might recruit a former hangman to head the "gent's neck-tie department," and for the "aesthetic" Oscar Wilde to "be installed in ... the gent's underwear department."[6]

Joe told the January 7 *Logansport Pharos*: "I have quit the ring ... made arrangements with a ... sporting goods firm ... will have charge of a department, that of boxing gloves. In addition ... another department, never before heard of in a business house ... physical culture ... I will examine all patrons ... who wish me to do so, and point out ... their physical defects and how they can be remedied. Of course, I do not mean to have a gymnasium in the house and go through athletic acts ... I will have no time for that. I will simply act the part of consulting physician, and they will have to be their own home doctors. I came to the conclusion to abandon the magic circle ... after my defeat by Peter Maher ... I had met more than 100 men and had been whipped by only three – Jim Corbett, Joe Goddard ... and Peter Maher. I decided to quit the business for two reasons – First, because the public ... has no use for a loser; 2nd ... I could never get another match with the trio who defeated me or with Bob Fitzsimmons, whom I fought to a draw, as I had each one of the quartet at one stage ... nearly beaten, and consequently too 'dangerous' a man to take on again."

"These men all want the championship ... they naturally limit the entries ... shut out after Maher's victory over me, I became weary of the game, the more so as I could not get on a match with Dan Creedon of Australia, now really champion of England; Tom Sharkey, or any other good man 'near the throne.' Neither would any of the Englishmen take me on, so ... I have quit the ring ... but only as a principal. I have ever cherished its traditions and will always take the deepest interest in it. Formerly, when a pugilist forsook the squared circle, he entered the liquor business, to open up a public house in England or a café in America. I never heard of a single one of them that ever prospered. There have been men connected with the ring ... who had higher ambitions of keeping a cozy hostelry ... Fighters in bygone times

have become successful statesmen, lawyers, doctors and even preachers. There are boxers today who have the same lofty ambitions, but most of them are of a practical turn of mind, and intend with their savings to embark in business, legitimate business (I do not call acting business), and endeavor to follow Iago's* advice relative to putting money in one's purse."
* A character in Shakespeare's play, Othello.

On December 26 at the World's Theatre in Pittsburgh, Joe sparred a friendly bout with Peter Maher. "The three rounds were very lively and scientific, but nothing approaching a knockout ..." Davies had posted $1,000 to match Joe against Sharkey, Maher or Fitzsimmons, in a limited round or finish bout. For a short time, Maher became a member of Davies' stable. The team were part of a boxing show at the same venue, on the evening of January 2, 1897. Reports give seemingly conflicting information of their opponents, but provide heretofore "lost bouts" for Choynski and Maher. Multiple papers report that Joe boxed Frank Dwyer, touted as heavyweight champion of West Virginia. Joe was contracted to knock him out within four rounds or forfeit $100. He "had an easy time with Dwyer, who admitted the Californian was too much for him with the big gloves." Police stopped the bout during the 4th round. Maher next took on George Geis, who quit in the 3rd round, rather than be knocked out.[7]

The January 3, 1897 *Philadelphia Inquirer* was, from its wording, an earlier account. While mentioning the Dwyer bout, it added: "The exhibition ... tonight was rather tame. Choynski boxed three rounds with a local man named Wilson, and Maher put on the gloves ... with an amateur named O'Brien. The authorities promptly stopped any and every bout ... as soon as the men showed any signs of warming up. The romance about Joe Choynski's retirement ... and ... position in a sporting goods store didn't last long, for now Joe is asking Peter Maher for another match."

Joe told reporters: "Although I do not reckon myself a good tipster ... I am asked for my opinion ... hundreds of times a day. (On) the pugilistic ability of Corbett and of Fitzsimmons, I would like ... it understood ... I have no love for either ... I am convinced Fitzsimmons is Corbett's inferior in speed and generalship. Upon these ... I base my opinion that the New Zealander will be beat. I have frequently heard men say Corbett is not a hitter. I know he can punch hard enough to answer all purposes. As for (his) right, he can stop any man living with it, providing he can land on the jaw ... Fitzsimmons ... convinced Corbett is too clever for him, will sail in for general results, and if ... not lucky enough to land ... his freak punches ... I regard his chances ... mighty slim ... it will be all over. Fitzsimmons has a small head. Any time he is hit on the nose ... chin, over the eye or on the ear, he gets rattled. (He) has wonderful recuperative powers ... but if Corbett drops him once, he will never come back."[8] Bob was floored by a left hook in round six, rising, many accounts said, after a long count. He rebounded to take out Jim in the 14th, with a single body shot.

Dwyer related to the January 9 *Wheeling Register*: "Of reports ... the fight ... was stopped by police to save me from a knockout, I wish to brand it a fake. To vindicate myself, I would state ... Choynski stepped into the ring without a second, and as I had the best of it in the 1st round, Mr. Chas. E. Davis (sic) told Jimmy Barry to get behind Choynski and take care of him, telling Joe not to take any chances, as (Davies) saw he had no easy thing. Choynski went in to do me as fast as he could, and as I again held him even in the 4th round and Mr. Davis saw that Choynski would fail to knock me, he had the match stopped so no decision could be given ... I will fight Choynski 10 or 15 rounds for $1,000 a side ..." No contemporary report validates Dwyer's claims. It is doubtful if police would stop an even contest at the behest of a manager. "Dwyer is a physical giant, although he steps into the ring at 168 pounds ... is Scheller, the well known wrestler, although neither is his correct name. His home is in Kansas City. He ... makes no pretensions to being a world beater, but thinks he can get into ... shape and hold Choynski level for a limited number of rounds."

December 7, 1898 *Oshkosh Daily Northwestern*: "Bert Scheller, who also boxes under the name of Frank Dwyer ... has made a reputation in the east as a clever boxer." He had a WF28 in 1889 over "Cleveland Thunderbolt," Mervine Thompson, under London Prize Ring rules with skin-tight gloves. Scheller was a unique fighter, who competed well as a boxer and a wrestler. Among the famous grapplers he lost to were Fred Beell and Frank Gotch. Bert won his share, however, in both disciplines. Choynski "offered $50 for the man who could stand up before him four rounds, and $10 in the event of a failure. Scheller stood the pace ... and the referee saved Choynski by calling the bout off before the 4th round was finished." This meant that Joe's maximum payout was spared, not his hide.

"A New York sporting paper" declared: "Police prevented Joe Choynski from delivering a knock out blow on the jaw of a ringer after four rounds of hot fighting ... At the call of time Scheller went at Choynski with right and left. He made a frantic effort to land on Joe's jaw. When Choynski recovered from his surprise he ... landed on the big wrestler's stomach, Scheller's grunt could be heard above the din. He clinched ... Choynski threw him off ... and sent him to the floor. The husky wrestler was still full of fight in the 2nd, but Choynski landed on his jaw until the German's teeth rattled. Scheller came up refreshed in the 3rd but Choynski deadened him with a swing to the head and stomach. Scheller made a desperate effort to catch Choynski around the body and give him a fall, but (was) ... straightened by an upper cut. The bout stirred the crowd to a lofty pitch ... as Choynski chased the ... fighter in the 4th round and tried to knock him out. Scheller was a good sprinter, but Choynski finally cornered ... and was about to put him out when police jumped into the ring. Scheller shouted he could knock Choynski out in eight rounds or ... forfeit $1,000."

On January 14, Joe refereed a 10-round fight between Billy Leedam and "Australian" Billy McCarthy at the Brooklyn Bridge Athletic Club in Brooklyn. "Joe Choynski decided in favor of Leedam." On the 30th at the Broadway A.C., Joe, with Bob Armstrong and George Dixon, seconded Jimmy Barry against Sammy Kelly. The latter held a six pound advantage, 114½ to 108. The result was a 20 round draw. Davies told a Chicago paper: "Barry ... is still the greatest of bantams ... Kelly got him with a hard hook in the 1st ... knocked him down, and swiped him good again in the 3rd ... considering the concession of weight, Jimmy did well to stand off his man. Barry had yet got much to learn. He spars like (Harry) Gilmore, his teacher, and like him, his style is too open. Both have a way of dropping the right when the left is let go, and I saw Joe Choynski trying to correct this in Barry ... showing him the only way to guard against the counter."[9]

Peter Maher told the *Philadelphia Record* that "some 'picture company' took photographs of his fight with Joe Choynski ... and would ere now have had the whole six rounds and knock-out on exhibition in public, but for 'Parson' Davies and John Quinn, who demanded a bit of the exhibition money for the fighters. The 'picture company' refuses to give up, and there you are."[10] This sounds like a different company than Harry Davis and his "zinematographe," who hired Maher and Joe to reenact their bout.

Davies arrived in Pittsburgh on February 10, to arrange a match between Maher and Sharkey, as part of his March 15 and 16 fistic carnival in Reno, Nevada. His idea was to hold the carnival two days prior to the Corbett-Fitzsimmons title fight at Carson City, attracting attendees of that fight. Quinn accepted for Maher; it remained for Sharkey to agree to the $10,000 purse. Other fights scheduled were Bob Armstrong vs. Jim Jeffries, and a Choynski-"Denver" Ed Smith rematch. Some papers said, "The star event of the Davies' carnival will be a meeting between Peter Maher and Joe Choynski. The public is not quite satisfied with the result of their last meeting ..." Davies then took a train for New York. "Denver" Smith announced "that a fight has been arranged between himself and ... Choynski to take place at Carson, Nevada, March 17 ... The agreement was arranged yesterday by long distance telephone ... Smith has been prospecting for ore near Nenezette, Elkton County (Pennsylvania) the past three months, and ... a pick and shovel has put him in excellent trim."[11]

On February 12, it was announced that Joe had been selected as boxing instructor for New York's Knickerbocker Athletic Club, at 45th Street and Madison Avenue. The *Brooklyn Daily Eagle* noted on the 18th: "Joe Choynski is giving nightly lessons in ... boxing at the club from 7 to 10 o'clock." It didn't take Joe long to encounter adversity in his new occupation: "Joe Choynski may not be able to fight again for a while. While wrestling at the Knickerbocker ... club, he fell down and broke his collarbone." The *Police*

Gazette said he sustained the injury while grappling with the club's wrestling instructor, as he frequently had been doing. Joe felt a "sharp crack in his neck," and a physician confirmed the break. On March 1, Joe was at New York's American Sporting Club, where he, Davies, Armstrong, Tom O'Rourke and a Jack Cassidy seconded Jimmy Barry against Jack Ward of Newark, New Jersey. Barry won a 20 round decision. Fitzsimmons was quoted by the *San Francisco Examiner* as saying Maher's punching power was the greatest on the planet, followed by Choynski, then Jim Hall.[12]

While Joe's collarbone mended, the zinematographe re-enactment of the Maher fight was being shown. The primary venue was the 9th and Arch Museum, on the corner of Philadelphia's 9th and Arch Streets. It was also being shown at Havlin's Theatre in Chicago. The film was billed as an exact and correct replica of the actual fight. It was shown at 9th and Arch from about March 1 to the 20th. March 11 *Philadelphia Inquirer*: "Both Peter Maher and Joe Choynski have been frequent visitors to the 9th and Arch Museum this week. Both ... are enthusiastic over the views."[13]

Davies ordered a special train to take some 200 passengers from Chicago to Carson City to witness the Corbett-Fitz fight. It was to leave the Windy City on March 13. On board would be John L. Sullivan, Tom O'Rourke, George Dixon, Joe Walcott and Choynski. The latter was said to be writing a description of the fight for the *New York Journal*. Meanwhile, Davies, Armstrong and Barry were in Denver on March 10, to give sparring exhibitions in Denver, Cripple Creek, Victor and Colorado Springs, connecting with the train in the last-named city, en route to Carson. Davies said he needed to "leave Maher behind in Chicago, the heavyweight being too 'indisposed' to travel ... neither he nor Choynski will reach Carson City for the fight." Joe was unable to attend, perhaps due to the collarbone fracture. Peter might have imbibed too much whiskey.[14]

After seeing Corbett lose his championship on March 17, Davies' troupe continued on to San Francisco, where "The Parson" attempted to arrange matches for Choynski, Armstrong and Barry. Fitz was in the city, but had announced his retirement from boxing. He decided he was not going to defend the title just won, but would honor his wife's request and quit the ring. Bob actually boxed another 17 years! He was making many fancy horseshoes, though, and trying to find a rival to arrange a horseshoeing match with. Davies proposed a competition to crown a new heavyweight king. Managers of the top aspirants would each post a stake of $2,500 and the tournament winner would take all of the money in the pool, as well as the purses involved.[15] Like his boxing carnival, nothing came of it.

On April 4, Davies signed for a match between Joe and Dan Creedon, for 20 rounds at a limit of 162 pounds. "Choynski is rapidly recovering from a wrenched shoulder, and ... would begin training for the mill in a short time." This was likely a misconstruing of the broken collarbone. For some reason, the match was called off. It was announced April 11 that instead, a fight with "Denver" Ed Smith had been arranged. This one stuck. It was also for 20 rounds, to be held at the Broadway Athletic Club on May 11. It was also declared on April 11, that "Joe Choynski says he and 'Parson' Davies no longer have joint interests. Choynski will do his own matchmaking."[16] This was the 2nd time within a year they were said to have split up as boxer and manager. The two once again mended whatever fences were broken, and resumed their professional tandem.

Davies sent a letter on April 20 to Al Smith, in New York. Smith was a famous sportsman and stakeholder who once managed John L. Sullivan. The missive contained a $1,000 forfeit and official challenge to Fitzsimmons, to defend his heavyweight title against Joe. It proposed a finish fight for a stake of $5,000 a side, before the club offering the largest purse. "The Parson" said he would remain at the Baldwin Hotel in Frisco until April 26. Davies and gang left for New York on the evening of the 28th for the Smith fight. On the 30th, Joe was a cornerman for Ed Connolly, in a world lightweight title fight against champion George "The Saginaw Kid" Lavigne. The bout, at the Broadway Athletic Club, saw Ed, a native of St. John, New Brunswick, Canada, floored five times in round 11. Barely able to stagger to his corner, he was in danger of being badly injured or killed, if he continued. "Choynski, Connolly's principal handler ... would not permit Connolly to subject himself to any more punishment."[17]

In early May, Fitz declared, "I shall pay no attention to Choynski. He should fight ... Maher, Tom Sharkey and other heavyweights before he can expect to fight for the championship. If Joe wants to fight me, he must go ahead and lick Corbett and Maher. There is absolute (sic) no chance of any of those would-be fighters meeting me unless they ... do something. I've fought everyone and licked them all, with the exception of Goddard and Jackson. Peter is a great fighter, but has retired. Goddard ... is entitled to first chance."[18] Choynski would twice avenge the Maher defeat. Corbett, as stated previously, would never again agree to fight Joe. Fitz never fought Goddard, nor any challenger for 27 months, when he lost the crown to Jim Jeffries. In that generation, this was the standard. Bob and the other champions, with the exception of Jeff, sat on their laurels and made primary capital from stage plays, vaudeville appearances and sparring tours. One can scarcely blame them, as the law consistently persecuted top-flight heavyweights, prizefighting being still a mostly illicit activity.

Davies was still optimistic in arranging a fight for Joe with Jim Corbett. Charlie came east to negotiate the fight, for that fall in San Francisco, 20 rounds and a purse of $10,000. What made the contest seem imminent was Fitzsimmons' statement that he would only give Corbett a rematch if Jim defeated Choynski. It was well known that Joe was willing to battle Corbett again "for any amount," but Jim wasn't interested, even to earn a title rematch.[19] Joe was training at New Dorp, Staten Island with erstwhile and future ring rival, Tom Sharkey. In sparring with the Irish fireplug, he "developed quite a knowledge of rough tactics." Smith trained "at Sheepshead Bay under the direction of Pete Burns, who prepared Peter Maher for all his fights." Smith had an 1893 KO18 over Joe Goddard. He lost the November, 1896 rematch in Johannesburg, South Africa in four heats, amid rumors of a fix. It was said the "Barrier Champion" refused a rubber match with Smith, "giving the excuse that the Denver chap was too tough ... Smith had the reputation of being one of the roughest fighters in the ring ... under London (bareknuckle) rules, no pugilist now before the public would stand the ghost of a chance with him."[20]

On May 10 at Manhattan's Broadway A.C., Joe took on "Denver" Ed in a 20 or 25-rounder, "at catchweights." About 3,000 were present, including Corbett, who wore a "natty Scotch tweed," in company with "Kid" McCoy. The purse was $3,500. At 10:15 p.m., the fighters entered the ring, Joe "wearing his familiar blue trunks." His seconds were Armstrong, Sharkey, Davies and George Ross. Smith was attended by Peter Maher, Pete Burns, Buck Connolly, Jack Quinn and Dick Colyer (or Collier). The weights were 163 or 165 pounds for Joe, about 177 for Smith. It was said that Ed looked a bit flabby, despite him saying he never felt better in his life. The men were about the same height, but Choynski had a longer reach. Smith wore close-cropped hair. *New York Journal*: "He (Joe) was tall, slender legged, small eyed and hook nosed. His hair was long like a football player's. For a man so spare about the hips, his shoulders were mighty. Below the shoulders he was a discobolus; above, an Ajax." The referee was Dick Roche. The following account combines multiple contemporary reports:[21]

Round 1 – Joe danced "as if on springs," driving a hard left into Smith's stomach. After several harmless punches by each, Joe suddenly crashed a left hook to Ed's jaw and dropped him like a shot. Smith took eight or nine seconds before getting to his feet. "The California Terror" followed with a straight left, but Smith grabbed tightly onto Joe's hands and hung on for dear life, for which he was hissed by the crowd. *Syracuse Daily Standard*: "Choynski let fly a heavy right at long range, which cut open Smith's cheek for first blood, a second or two before time was up."

Round 2 – There was a lot of damage in this heat, but accounts disagree on who did what. The May 22, 1922 *Police Gazette*, probably the least reliable, said: "Smith opened the 2nd by closing Choynski's eye. He ... rushed in, but was stopped by a left to his blinker that drew blood ..." *Brooklyn Eagle*: "Smith scarcely struck a blow, while Choynski broke his ... nose, jabbed him ... about the face and punched him on the body. Smith was almost out and ... waited for a chance to land his right ... Choynski ... was very nimble ... his wily ducking tactics delighted ... as much as the terrific punishment he administered ... Toward the close ... Smith resorted to all sorts of tricks to save himself from the fusillade ... He was vigorously hissed ... for holding Joe's glove and trying to pull him in where he could hit him safely." Other reports noted that, while "Denver" did land a right to the heart and a pair of lefts to the face, "Little Joe" scored most of the clean, effective punches. He landed hard lefts to the jaw and face, staggering Smith and making him reel "halfway across the ring."

Round 3 – Smith began blatantly fouling. Joe missed a left and was countered. The California native crashed a left hook to Ed's nose, causing blood to gush in streams. One of his eyes was closed. Joe landed a series of jabs, avoiding his adversary's counters. He shot a left to Smith's "wind" and uppercut as he came in. "The two gladiators came together with a crash. The Birmingham man butted Choynski at least three times, *like a goat*, but the referee failed to even warn the offender. Joe gave Smith a thorough beating, his body ... covered with Ed's blood. Joe was content to bide his time ... confident of his ability to stop his man in short order."

Round 4 – Joe's right eye was badly swollen, but his rival's blood covered both men. Smith grabbed Joe's hand and pulled him to close quarters, butting him in the mouth. This time, Roche warned Ed not to repeat the transgression. Preferring to lose on a foul than be knocked out, Smith butted Joe in the face again. Roche sent the fighters to their corners, awarding the victory to Joe on a foul (or DQ) at 2:08 of the round. "The spectators jeered Smith until the clamor could be heard a block away ..." "Maher was so ... disgusted with Smith ... that, while the other seconds were washing blood from the big fellow's face, he stole quietly away."

San Francisco Call: "Choynski, realizing he had a slugger ... to deal with, decided to fight Smith at long range ... Joe quickly convinced the 3,000 spectators he was Smith's master in science, ring tactics and general knowledge of pugilism. The Denver fighter's methods ... were limited to dangerous swings with his right for the jaw and hook blows at close quarters with his left. Choynski, with good judgment and most skillful control of his hands, avoided nearly all of Smith's blows or broke their force ... when openings came, he deftly shot his gloved fists to vital spots until 'Denver' Smith was ... a good imitation of a punching bag." Many reports said Joe had a tooth knocked out by Smith's head butts.

Joe (1930): "Smith, one of the toughest and most unorthodox fighters I have ever met, tried to annihilate me ... Langdon Smith ... wrote: 'He was round, loggy and brutish ... a biter, eye-gouger, a thorough bruiser ... But could he fight – the man knew nothing else! You could see it in the thick overhang of the forehead, the monkey-like set of the ears ... the fierce mop of bristles that stood out above his brow.' I knew Smith's reputation ... I sailed in ... giving ... an artistic lacing ... a terrific thumping. On his face was the most ferocious expression I have ever seen in a prize ring. He had a savage temper. Every blow I landed made him furious. In the opening session I knocked him down. He got up cursing."

"Smith fought like a maniac. He rushed me and grappled. He butted me repeatedly. He used his elbows – drew his laces across my eyes! Again and again he gouged my eyes with the heel of his glove ... I staved him off and continued punching. He was bloody as a pig ... he floundered in, swearing like a sea captain. I peppered his face with rights and lefts. Twice in the 4th he butted me with his bullet-like head. This loosened several of my teeth ... the crowd, disgusted, began yelling: 'Foul! Kill him for that, Joe!' I shook him with a savage right hook to the jaw. He wobbled, then lunged forward and threw his right leg around me, bar-room style, trying to trip me. He was the roughest customer I had met since Joe Goddard ... the referee lost all semblance of patience. He ... hurled Smith back ... awarded me the fight on a foul. But to the credit of Peter Maher, I want to say he was not a party to Smith's disgusting tactics. When Smith refused to cease his foul tactics, Maher flung down his towel angrily and quit the corner."

Whereas Sharkey helped Joe pick up pointers in "rough tactics" for the Smith bout, so Joe now assisted the sailor in preparing for Peter Maher, imparting a greater degree of skill, if not finesse, to "The Irish Gob."[22] The May 19 *San Francisco Report* opined that "Choynski would take care of Jeffries in about five rounds." The rapidly improving Jeff had just stopped power-punching Henry Baker in nine rounds. "If Joe ... had been in Baker's place ... he would have chopped and stabbed Jeffries to pieces, while the big fellow was waiting to land an effective punch. As it was, Jeffries got a paste on the eye and one ... on the tip of the nose that swelled that organ and gave him something to remember for a week or so."

Graney received a letter from Choynski around this time, authorizing Ed to "challenge any man in the world to a fight on his behalf." This showed how tenuous a relationship he and Davies had. The 28th found Joe working with Tom at Boehm's Roadhouse in New Dorp, New York, with Tim McGrath and "Kid" McCoy sparring partner, Tom Lansing. Choynski told the *Police News*, still jawing about his 1894 five-round fizzle with "Ruby Robert": "The question of supremacy between us has never been settled. It has been said ... our ... encounter ... was to have been friendly ... a fake. I never 'faked' in my life ... I wanted the winner to receive all, but Fitz would not consent unless the purse ... was split in two equal parts. We were to fight eight rounds on the level, and in the 3rd ... I caught Fitz on the jaw and sent him to the floor. After that he recovered, and I'll admit he knocked me down, or rather pushed me down, in the last two rounds ... I believe the public would like to see us fight it out. I'm ready at any time."[23]

A June 2 article said: "Now Joe Choynski has taken a turn at threatening to pull Fitzsimmons' nose, or inflict some other indignity to the champion. Choynski writes a letter to his backer, 'Parson' Davies, which bristles with indignation at the fact that the Fitzsimmons party has got out a big lithograph, depicting the men whom Fitz has knocked out ... 'Everybody knows,' says Joe, 'that Fitz and I met but once, and that the police put an end to the bout. Yet in this poster, Fitz is represented as having knocked me out in four rounds. As soon as I saw it, I sat down and wrote (Martin) Julian (Bob's manager), demanding that the statement be corrected, and if it is not ... I shall call Fitz at his hotel and force him to acknowledge it is a lie. I am tired of sitting quiet while these fellows lie about me.' "[24] Joe could be excused for venting his frustrations to the press. Although Fitz admittedly came close to stopping him in the 4th and 5th rounds of their lone meeting, one didn't hear Joe (justifiably) claiming victory over Tom Sharkey, after dominating the latter in eight rounds but being declared the loser of the purse. No more was heard of the lithograph incident.

Peter Maher had recently altered his style of fighting. He no longer rushed in with abandon, but stood back and waited for openings to land his right hand. He utilized his left jab to a greater extent and was a more polished, skilled boxer, though never on the level of a Corbett or Choynski. Joe said the sailor was "becoming more clever every day." "Sharkey has learned much of the up-to-date, scientific, fast work of the roped arena, since he has been in the Californian's hands, and says he will use his newly-acquired knowledge to advantage ..." As a slugging fighter with a crushing right hand and counter-punching ability, Maher had a stylistic edge over Sharkey. He was taller, rangier and had "more ring experience and science than the sailor man." What wasn't stated was Maher's inconsistency as a performer, his predilection to avoid training and his penchant for alcohol. Also, "Choynski has been exacting and has found a willing and docile pupil in the sailor." Their camp, at Boehm's Hotel, was "situated on the beach, and the surf washes up against the gymnasium ..."[25]

On the night of June 9, at the Palace Athletic Club in New York, Tom and Peter fought before a horde of 10,000. Sharkey was handled by Joe, Tim McGrath, Tom Lansing and Solly Smith. Maher was attended by Buck Connolly, Pat Scully, Peter Lowry, Jack Quinn and Jack Cattanach. It is a great tribute to Joe that Sharkey made him chief second, rather than his normal trainer, Tim McGrath. The principals each weighed 172 pounds. Bill Brady announced that, in case of police interference, Referee Jim Colville was empowered to declare either fighter the winner, if he deemed the other incapable of winning. Otherwise, a draw would be called.

The first five rounds were tame, due to the presence of Police Inspector McLaughlin and his merry band of bluecoats, who were ready to arrest the participants at what he deemed the first sign of "brutal punching" or "breach of the peace." That all changed in the next frame as Sharkey, never one to restrain himself long, cut loose with a barrage. He swung a right to the head, pursued the retreating Maher and, landing a straight right to the mouth, sent his foe halfway through the ropes and down, in a corner of the ring. Peter took six seconds to rise, his mouth bleeding. "As Maher was getting up, Sharkey rushed toward him, but was called back by Choynski, who was afraid the sailor might commit a foul."

The 7th was nearly complete when Maher landed a hard left and smashing right that leveled Sharkey. Tom fell on his back near the ropes, struggled up at five and rushed to the safety of a clinch. The *Idaho Statesman* said that, during the clinch, Maher was driving rights to the body and head and failed to stop at the bell. "*Bang* went the bell. The crazy sailor hung on and paid no attention ... Foul after foul he rained on Maher's face, with the Irishman (Maher) going back as best he knew how." One of Maher's seconds grabbed Peter ... Sharkey punched Maher's second in the nose, drawing cries of "Foul!" from the crowd. This type of behavior in a heated moment was rather typical of Tom. At this point, Police Inspector McLaughlin ordered his men to arrest "those concerned in the fight." "The seconds swarmed into the ring. Sharkey was blind with rage. He hit Lansing and Choynski, his seconds. Police rushed over the ropes ... Clubs ... drawn. The fighters were separated ... The bout ... declared a draw. Those arrested, including the principals, seconds and referee, were escorted to the 104th Street police station, first allowing Maher and Sharkey to go to their dressing rooms and put on ... street clothes. All furnished bail."[26]

The next morning, most of those arrested appeared before a magistrate, who refused "to recognize the bout as a prize fight" and freed the men on bail bonds. Colville took much of the blame from the spectators, who said if he had separated the fighters after the bell, police would have had no reason to halt proceedings. Opinions varied as to who would have won. Joe, a biased party, stated: "Tom had him going and in another round would have put him out. Sharkey is scientific and quick ... All who saw the contest would agree he had the best of it."[27] Unable to get Fitz into the ring, Joe tried again to goad old adversary, Corbett, into a fight. June 11 *Fort Wayne News*: "Choynski has published a lot of things derogatory to his brother Californian, which may lead to making a match for the fall months." Another rivalry heating up was that with "Kid" McCoy. The June 26 *San Francisco Report* carried an interview with Joe, described as "one prolonged 'roast' of ... McCoy," who responded: "I admit I am open to criticism, and do not find fault with Joe for that, but ... he has gone beyond all bounds. I ... thought he was my friend. In future I want it understood that there cannot be anything in common between us. I will never recognize him again unless he defeats me in the ring ... he stated that he would agree to stop me in 20 rounds at 158 pounds. He offered to wager $5,000 he could do the trick. I will gladly meet him on these terms."

"He says ... Davies posted with Al Smith $5,000 to bind the match. I know positively ... Smith has no money of either Davies or Choynski ... Joe is not sincere ... It is an old game with him to sit in pleasant little parties and tell what he can do with persons who are hundreds of miles away ... Joe never intimated ... a fight ... until I posted $1,000 to fight Dan Creedon. He ... in the Gilsey House ... was the first of a party of friends to congratulate me. Then he got on a train and went to Cincinnati, where he ... made it public he wanted to fight me ... I will fool Mr. Choynski. He thinks because Creedon and I have $1,000 ... posted for a match I cannot take another ... I have been doing that all through my ... career. I usually have on several matches. I will post $1,000 at any time and almost any place, if he will ... cover it ... He is ... jealous because I am doing well, and have made more money in the past year than he ... in five ... Choynski says I talked behind his back. I will give $100 to any man who can truthfully say I ever attempted to belittle Choynski, either as a gentleman or a pugilist."

" 'What about your meeting in New York, (when) he claims to have made you look like a fright?' (McCoy) was asked. 'The only time we ever met in public was at a benefit for myself in this city. I had been laid up a week with a badly cut foot, and did not get out of bed until the night I boxed with him. It was to have been a friendly bout. He tried to *cop a sneak*. He struck me hard in the stomach and ... I feinted ... until I got him in a corner. He either slipped or went down to avoid punishment. His right leg went through the ropes and he landed on his left knee. Then police stepped in.' " July 7 *Report*: "Joe ... is coming East this week to ... arrange a bout with Kid McCoy. Choynski has expressed his willingness to bet $5,000 he can put McCoy out in 12 rounds at 165 pounds, and ... that at 158 pounds he can stop McCoy in 22 rounds." The last was likely hyperbole, as Joe could not get as low as 158 pounds, with any strength.

The June 28 *Syracuse Daily Standard* wrote unfavorably of Tom Sharkey: "He has met all the leading heavyweights, and through luck or trickery, has escaped without a decision ... rendered against him." Examples given were the four round draw with Corbett, the Fitzsimmons debacle and the eight round "win" over Choynski, when Joe failed to stop Tom. "Sharkey next met Maher, who, being afraid of the police, failed to fight for six rounds. In the 7th, Maher had Sharkey on the run when the police interfered. Despite all these inglorious bouts, Sharkey extends his chest like a pouter pigeon and announces he is champion of the world." It is fair to mention, though, that despite Tom's rough manner, nearly everyone seemed to like him outside the roped square. Fighters like Jeffries, Fitz and Choynski became close friends with Tom after their fighting days ended.

A Chicago daily said Joe would become a salesman for a cigar company, "at a salary of $5,000 a year, but this will in no way interfere with his profession as a pugilist. 'If any of the heavyweights want his game,' said Parson Davis (sic), 'I will make a match ... any time.' " The position was to be "on the road" with "a well-known western tobacco firm."[28] Graney, wiring a telegram on the 8th, said Harry Weldon, of the *Cincinnati Enquirer*, would bet $5,000 that Choynski could beat McCoy at 165 pounds, and "a $7,000 purse is offered." Joe arrived in New York City on the 4th of July, but McCoy was "out of town," so they did not meet until the 7th. "McCoy refused to shake Joe's hand. July 8 *Enquirer*: 'I suppose you came here to arrange for that fight with me?' said McCoy. 'No, I didn't,' said Choynski, laughing. 'I am not looking for any fight just now, though I would be willing to meet you to a finish or in a limited contest at 165 pounds.' 'That isn't the proposition you made in Cincinnati,' said McCoy. 'You made an offer to knock me out at 158 pounds in 20 rounds. I accept your challenge.' 'Oh, there is no use talking about that,' said Choynski. 'The only way ... I could think of meeting you would be in a regular match ... at 165 pounds.' "

"'Graney must be hitting the pipe,' was McCoy's declaration ... 'He knows ... I am a middleweight ... I am not surprised at Joe Choynski making a proposition to fight me at 165 pounds. He is only ... advertising himself, as he intimated to me. But ... Graney ... is on the square ... I am surprised he should think I, a 158-pound fighter at the limit, should agree to fight a heavyweight ... all of them appear anxious for a fight, don't they? I'll tell you what ... I will ... go outside my class ... give Joe a chance to show what he is made of, and I will test Graney's gameness,' and McCoy looked ... earnest. 'Well, I will just give those two gentlemen a quiet little call. I will meet Choynski at 160 pounds for 20 or 25 rounds, or to a finish.' "[29]

Joe wrote to Weldon: "Friend Harry: I met McCoy in a restaurant ... we ... sat at the same table and spoke pleasantly. He wanted me to meet him at 158 pounds. I said, 'Nothing less than 165 ...' He said we could not do business. We shook hands and went away. The next day's paper ... said we refused to shake. There wasn't a soul around who knew us and the meeting was ... friendly ... A lot of people want to see me licked and ... fight lower than I can. I have my own money, $5,000, that I can beat any man in the world ... it is not a bluff ... if any one thinks so, he can wire me and I will be the first to deposit $1,000 to show my good faith. I don't think it right to hound a man who has fought everybody on the calendar, black or white, and made no talk about it. Give my regards to Maciewski and all friends. I don't see why the 'Kid' should be so anxious to want a side wager, I have been boxing 10 years and never had to, but will ... at 165 pounds."

"As to ... a match at 158 pounds ... I am not after middle-weight honors ... McCoy aspires to the heavy-weight championship ... why should he not meet me at 165 pounds? I am ready to wage money ... that no man can prove Corbett defeated me more than once ... he is generally credited with having beaten me four times ... that is a great injustice, and any one that can show he got more than one decision against me can get my money."[30] The "Maciewski" mentioned was Frank Maciewski, a Cincinnati fighter who was reportedly Joe's cousin. Regarding the number of times Joe was officially beaten by Corbett, his assessment was probably correct. The one defeat was the knockout loss on the grain barge in 1889. The five-rounder the men fought on March 23, 1887 within the confines of Corbett's Olympic Club saw Jim get the better of it, but no actual decision appears to have been given. The four-rounder on July 15, 1889 at the Mechanics' Pavilion had a referee, but contemporary reports say it was a "friendly" go.

Choynski refereed a pair of fights at Staten Island's South Beach Athletic Club on the evening of July 19. First, he umpired a bout between Joe Falvey of New York and Eddie Muntzer of Staten Island. "They boxed 10 hard rounds, in which Falvey had the better of the fighting ... Choynski thought differently, however, and at the end of the 10th round he called the bout a draw. This decision did not suit the majority of those present ..." This would not be the only time Joe would be accused of rendering an inappropriate points verdict. Refereeing is a somewhat subjective role, however, and others, such as heavyweight Jack Dempsey, gained reputations for making far worse decisions. In "The Kid" McPartland-"Philadelphia" Tommy Ryan main event, Joe saw little work. Early in round one, "The Kid" floored Ryan for the full count.[31]

On the 30th, Graney signed for Joe to fight Jim Jeffries, in October at the Columbian Club. "Billy Delaney came over from Oakland ... The managers met at the old Cosmos Club ... in a few minutes the match was consummated." Although Jeff would outweigh Joe by some 50 pounds, first impressions were that "Jeffries would only be a chopping block for the agile and hard-hitting Choynski. Jeffries' only chance seems to be to get in some of his heavy smashes, but Choynski will have to lose his head to let him do it. Jeffries will have to improve greatly to even make the fight interesting." The 22-year-old was probably underestimated. While he had only engaged in seven pro fights, Jim would defeat Bob Fitzsimmons for the heavyweight title, in only his 13th bout! "The Boilermaker," as Jeff was called, due to his previous career in the manufacture of steam boilers, learned with each bout. In his last fight, on July 17, he earned a bruising, 20 round draw with fellow up-and-comer, Gus Ruhlin. This was Gus' 10th pro fight, and he would remain near the top for years. Jeff recounted later that he made the mistake of coming in lightly trained against Ruhlin, but learned his lesson and was in top fit for the Choynski fight.[32]

William Brady, former manager of Jim Corbett, but now in the same role for Jeffries, proposed on August 5 "to have the championships of all classes (divisions) settled by ... fights on the soil of Nevada the first week of October ... probably at Reno." He named a Maher-Sharkey rematch to settle a claim to the heavyweight crown that Corbett had temporarily renounced, and "In the light heavyweight division, some good man will be secured to meet Joe Choynski." After naming the other matches, all to be world championships, various papers added: "Provided Brady secures some one to meet Choynski, he will thus present seven finish battles between the leading pugilists of the world."[33] Once again, and with great consistency, the light heavyweight division was mentioned as a viable entity, and the name continually associated with it was Joseph Bartlett Choynski.

The August 5 *Syracuse Daily Journal* told of a benefit for American miners who recently began striking. The nationwide strike was initiated in Mt. Olive, Illinois, in protest of the shabby conditions and treatment miners in general faced. It resulted in the establishment of the United Mine Workers Union. The article said Joe would box the following night in Chicago for the benefit of the miners. In addition, "Mrs. Choynski, whose stage name is Louise Miller, will do her singing and dancing specialty." Joe, in a letter to Graney, confirmed he was now making Chicago his home, and was "on the road, selling cigars for a (tobacco) house of that place."[34]

Jeffries began training on August 17, at the Los Angeles A.C. He said, in going against Choynski, he was "tackling the hardest yet." Delaney would be handling him, along with De Witt Van Court, boxing instructor for the Los Angeles club. Aside from his renown as a trainer, Van Court became known for his excellent 1926 book, *The Making of Champions in California*. In 1912, De Witt said "Grizzly" Jim trained for the bout at the Reliance club in Oakland, while Joe did gym work at the Olympic club in San Francisco, running in Golden Gate Park. Joe began training, though, at the Catlin Boat Club on the north side of Chicago, before coming west. He told the *Chicago Tribune* he would again box in the Windy City to aid striking miners. This time the benefit match was held at the 2nd Regiment Armory on the 13th, an exhibition with Joe's pal, Al Shrosbree, a cornerman in the past.[35]

It was announced that Choynski would box a rematch with Dan Creedon in St. Louis, Missouri. Chief of Police Harrigan said he would "enforce the law against glove contests, and has cautioned his subordinates ... to prevent ... the five round contest ..."[36] Joe arrived in St. Louis on September 15 and visited the office of the *St. Louis Republic*. Its next-day edition read: "He spent several weeks around New York last month, and says the climate out there did not agree with him. He lost some weight during the trip. San Francisco is Joe's fancy, and he expects to land out there about November 1. 'Fitzsimmons ... is nothing but a man with two arms and two legs ... police stopped the bout before either of us had the better of it. I had just finished a 40 weeks' engagement on the road as Jackson's sparring partner, and was in no condition to do myself justice.' " He said he was robbed against Goddard in Australia, and "In this country, where he will be forced to fight clean, I can whip him sure."

The night of the 16th saw a benefit for Creedon at Armory Hall in St. Louis. No police interference occurred, probably *because* it was called a benefit. "The program consisted of boxing and wrestling ... feats of heavy lifting, etc." Many papers said the bout went three rounds, but the local *Republic* reported: "The wind-up ... was a four-round bout ... Dan stripped big and fat, while Choynski ... like a fighter in condition to fight for a $10,000 purse. All he needed was a hair cut. Creedon is still the sturdy rusher of old, and set the pace ... Choynski handled him carefully until the wind-up, when both went at it for a lively mixing. It was give and take a few seconds, and the spectators enjoyed the exhibition thoroughly. Creedon's modesty prevented him from responding to calls for a speech." No round-by-round accounts have been located. Davies said Joe had shaved off his "Paderewski" locks.[37]

Jim Jeffries, summer, 1896

It was announced that a third match between Choynski and Joe Goddard had been clinched for November, in the United States. Goddard had demanded, and been granted, 60% of the gross receipts if he won, 40% if he lost. This was called "the highest price ever offered as a losing end." "Graney said as soon as Choynski saw that a chance was offered for him to meet his old enemy, he became so anxious ... that he sent word ... he would agree to let Goddard have the entire purse if he won ... also ... the larger percentage of the purse even should he defeat the Australian." Goddard's manager, Billy Madden, accepted these generous terms.

"Choynski's friends claim he has improved greatly since (the Australia visit) and in both fights he used bad judgment ... losing his head and rushing in to receive knockout blows, when he thought his man all but gone." The National Athletic Club of San Francisco had supposedly secured the fight, but it fell through.[38] The combatants would meet one year hence, almost to the day. "The Parson," seeking fights for Joe in the interests of the miners' entertainment, was in Pittsburgh negotiating with James "Tut" Ryan, currently residing in London, England.

"Tut," a native Aussie described as "the best 170 pound man in England," would win the Australian heavyweight crown from Bill Doherty in 1901. Ryan fought three draws with Joe Goddard, over 15 and 13 rounds in 1895, and a 20 round deadlock in 1897. "Tut" arrived in the United States on October 8, but he would never fight Joe.[39]

On September 18, near Skagway, Alaska, on the Dyea Trail at Chilikoot Pass, Sheep Camp – an outpost of the Yukon Gold Rush, a landslide and washout killed as many as 18 persons. One body recovered was that of Aaron M. Choynski, first cousin of Joe. There were few witnesses and details were conflicting. Warm, heavy rains and a Chinook wind caused a thaw. "An ancient glacier," 100 feet in height and 25 feet wide, broke off the southwest side of the mountain and slid into a lake feeding the Skagway River, sending a torrent raging toward the camp.

"One of the Indian packers described ... about 160 ... at Sheep Camp ... Sunday morning ... 18 persons ... were missing." A witness said: "I was five miles away ... the terrific cannonading of that mountain of snow ... was plainly heard ... to the time my informants left, one body had been recovered ... Choynski ... bound for the Klondike. Nearly all his clothes had been torn from him, and his body was terribly bruised and mutilated. He was still living when found, but died within an hour without recovering consciousness ... carried fully a quarter of a mile by the flood ..."

"Choynski ... highly regarded for his manly qualities ... 2nd son of Isaiah ... of the *Chronicle* reportorial staff ... 24 years old last March ... lived all his life in San Francisco ... a graduate of the Lincoln Grammar and evening business schools ... an enthusiastic athlete, member of several clubs ... noted for his prowess as a boxer, his speed as a sprinter ... won a number of events on the wheel. For eight years ... in the employ of W.W. Montague & Co. as a tile setter ... highly esteemed by his employers. Choynski left here July 31st on the steamer *Willamette* ... five in the party ... joined forces to make the journey ... Besides his parents, Choynski leaves three brothers: Sol, transit superintendent of the Waters-Pierce Oil Company of Mexico; Milton, University of California, '96 ... studying law ... Harry, a clerk in the Anglo-California Bank. Mr. and Mrs. Choynski are almost heartbroken. The son they mourn was ... of high character, and his desire in seeking the Klondike was chiefly to win fortune to bestow on his parents." At 6:00 a.m. ... "A great flood of water down canyon ... near the bank of the stream, they found a man lying on his back ... groaning ... frightfully mangled by the ... avalanche. Davis raised the dying man's head to his knee and Reed pushed on toward Sheep's Camp for a physician ... the man's pain seemed to leave him ... in a lucid moment he said his name was Choynski ... a cousin of ... the prize-fighter. Before the physician and Reed returned, Choynski breathed his last ... They cared for the body and ... moved on to Sheep's Camp ... found that over 50 tents had been carried away ..."

Call: "The wave ... 10 to 20 feet in height ... carried boulders as big as freight cars ... the Stone House ... nearly 50 feet high ... 40 by 40 at the base ... top shaped like a roof ... rolled ... several hundred feet below where it ... stood. Choynski was found lying near the Stone House, bleeding and dying. His body was nearly torn asunder ... so badly lacerated that his clothes had to be cut from him. He had been ... banged against rocks, crushed by boulders and partly buried in sand. He and his partner, Flynn, had come down to the river to wash their faces and get a bucket of water to use in preparing breakfast. They ... stood up to see the torrent almost upon them, and could not escape ... Flynn ... was discovered about 300 yards down ... dead. The face was partly crushed." Sol Berliner of San Francisco: "Aaron ... was killed by ... a stone which struck him on the head. We buried him up at what we call the Scales. We saw (him) returning to his tent with a pail of water ... dashed down by the rolling rocks. He must have been killed almost instantly. I helped pull him out of the debris and bury him Sunday morning." Aaron's body was exhumed and reburied in Colma, California on October 19, at Hills of Eternity Memorial Park.[40]

September 30 *Galveston Daily News*: "Herman Bernau ... is matched with Joe Choynski for a six-round glove contest ... some time between October 11 and 16. He has gone into training under Australian Billy McCarthy. Choynski wanted the mill ... in Chicago, but ... is willing to come to Galveston, as suggested by Bernau." Joe arrived in the port city of Galveston at 1:30 p.m. on the 9th and checked into the Tremont Hotel. "Later in the evening he was visited by Mr. Brown, manager of the Texas Vaudeville Company, under whose supervision Choynski and Bernau will spar ... at the Grand opera house. Mr. Choynski looks anything but a prize fighter. The first noticeable thing about him is that he is a 'good dresser' – not a flashy dresser, but as he himself put ... 'A well dresser is a man ... so attired that it is not noticeable he has put himself out to look right.' Choynski has the appearance of a college bred man ... his conversation is that of a cultured gentleman. He uses ... select language and talks fluently and conversantly on all the topics of the day. He wore a neat, tailor made black suit, stiff bosom blue striped shirt, the latest thing in standing collars, and a gray Alpine. In fact, everything about his dress was such as would meet the approval of Eerry (Evander Berry) Wall, esq., himself."

"Choynski did not seem ... inclined to talk about his own prowess, though ... not reticent in telling reporters what he knew about ... men in the business, speaking well of some and sneeringly of others. In this particular ... alone, he showed himself to be on a level with the ordinary 'bruiser.' Mr. Brown: 'I guaranteed Choynski $1,000 to come here ...' Choynski ... stretched out in an easy chair ... discarded his shirt and lay back in an easy repose. His wonderfully developed muscles showed through his undershirt and he looked ... a specimen of ... manhood. He is about 6' tall, a blonde and clean shaven. He would be called by the ladies 'a handsome man.' "

"Corbett's name was brought up and of this gentleman ... Choynski ... said he had small regard ... as a fighter and a man. For Fitzsimmons, he ... had hardly more regard. He said Fitzsimmons was uneducated, could not hold a decent conversation and (was) a general 'dub.' The only time he ever did meet Fitz, the contest was declared a draw, but many say if it had not been for Choynski's hot-headedness, he would have knocked the Cornishman out. He ... said for the first two rounds he (Joe) had the best of it and then the fight was stopped for two minutes by the police. He claims to have been sick, and during the 3rd and 4th rounds, said Fitz knocked him to the floor any number of times, but he always got up ... Every time ... he says he remarked to Parson Davies ... 'Well, this time I go,' but Fitz didn't seem to have the ability to put him out. In the 5th round when his strength was returning and he said he felt as though he was able to fight the fight of his life, police interfered and the affair was called a draw. In the 1st round he had Fitz on the floor until nine ..." Joe's version is at odds with accounts of the day and it appears he was making excuses, as so many fighters have. When Fitz lost his crown to Jeffries, Bob claimed he was poisoned by some unknown party prior to the fight. Few believed him.

"Just then a telegram was handed Choynski from an admirer in Houston, who invited him to come up and stay with him. Choynski pronounced Houston, broadly, 'Howston,' and when the reporter entered a demurral, he argued quite belligerently as to the style of grammar in ... the pronunciation of proper names. Choynski ... accepted an invitation to go sailing on the bay this morning at 10 o'clock. He expressed a desire to see the beach, of which he had heard so much. He was just remarking that he intended to leave Tuesday when the *News* man was informed of the yellow fever rumors. Choynski expressed fear that this might delay him, but said he felt no anticipation as to the disease ... was not in the least scared of it, and ... didn't believe doctors knew what they were talking about."[41]

The Bernau fight was held on the night of October 11 at the Grand Opera House, preceded by a vaudeville show. The October 12 *Galveston County Daily News* covered the action. Papers agreed, "at no time was the local man in it" and Joe could have ended the fight any time he wanted. The set-to was shortened from six rounds to four, by the referee's intervention. Herman entered the ring at 10:00 p.m., wearing blue trunks, seconded by Charlie Porter and Charlie Brooks. Joe, close behind, wore white trunks and was attended by Tom Payne. "The crowd was asked to choose a referee ... after (much debate) ... Heiderman was chosen."

Round 1 – Choynski landed to the stomach, Bernau, a jab to the mouth. Joe came back with a left to the jaw, answering a left to the gut with a pair of his own. He floored the "Dutchman" with a left to the head. The latter quickly rose, "receives a hard one on the kidney, retaliating on Joe's mouth

... Bernau is forced around the ring, and ... Choynski landed at will, Bernau bleeding at the mouth when he went to his corner."

Round 2 – "Bernau ... side-steps and runs away ... hard in-fighting by both ... Bernau runs all around the ring. Choynski lands twice on ... stomach and face with his left ... on the kidneys with his right ..." Herman landed on Joe's face, the visitor retaliated with two to the back of the head, probably unintentionally. Joe shot in some hard stomach punches and a potent right to the jaw, sending Bernau to the floor, "and Choynski again picks him up. For the rest of the round, Choynski practically played with Bernau ..."

Round 3 – "Bernau comes up smiling and leads, but is countered ... ducks a left lead and clinches." He landed a right to the jaw, Joe countering with lefts to the kidney and head. He chased "Herman all around the ring with his left glove on mouth; he hits Bernau in the eye with a right. Bernau leads left on Choynski's stomach and clinches as time is called."

Round 4 – Joe sent rights to the kidney and head and a left to the mouth. Bernau returned fire and ducked a left. Joe landed an uppercut, but Herman the German ducked a right. Choynski tripled up with rights to the kidney, head and jaw. He forced his foe to the ropes, landing lefts and rights to the head, dropping Bernau to the floor. He rose at "eight," but was dumped again, in Joe's corner, this time taking nine seconds. Just before the bell, Joe drove a left to the stomach, and the referee awarded him the fight. Bernau had no reason to be surprised at the stoppage.

Joe said he pasted Bernau with real power, but it seems he didn't have the heart to finish the Texan before his home crowd. He added that Herman "showed no trace of the yellow feather and took his punishment like a man." Prior to the bout, Bernau told the *News* reporter he was not feeling well, and the latter agreed. "The German did look ill. After the fight he showed ... where he was full of boils on all parts of the body. He ... had only two cuts, one under his lip and the other under his eye. 'Considering my condition, I feel entirely satisfied with the showing I made and I can not understand why the referee ... called the affair off.' "

"Heiderman: 'Choynski could have sent Bernau to the 7th heaven at any time he saw fit ... when he remarked to me at the end of the 4th round, *For goodness sake, call this fight off; I don't want to hurt the man anymore*, I deemed it ... fairest ... to end the affair in favor of the Californian ...' Every man ... seemed to agree with the referee's decision ... all had a good word ... for the clever fighter from the Golden Gate city ... a general of the ring ... deserves the splendid reputation he enjoys. In the 2nd ... when he landed ... to cause the German to become groggy, he held him up ... until he could recover ... Bernau showed ... most clever in one matter ... ducking. He managed with remarkable agility to get out of the way of several viciously aimed blows ... saved himself from being more severely punished ..."[42]

On October 13, Joe left Galveston on the International and Great

Northern "refugee" train for St. Louis, en route to Chicago. It had been chartered to transport persons fleeing the yellow fever. Joe "received a telegram ... from San Francisco ... to meet Jeffries ... He was ... pleased with his visit to Galveston, but ... disappointed as to the financial outcome ... will have great tales to tell his Chicago friends of the yellow fever scare, and is glad he came, if for nothing else than to have had experiences."[43]

Joe Goddard was training in Sausalito, California, for a November 18 brawl in Frisco with Sharkey. He was asked why he wasn't recognizing Joe's challenge. "I ... whipped Choynski twice and would like to know how many times the fellow wants a drubbing before he acknowledges I am his superior. But ... if (he) ... will deposit $5,000 with your paper as a side bet, I will ... fight him in his own city." Goddard said he would take on Joe *after* the Sharkey fight, though it was said a Choynski-Goddard pairing would be a bigger draw in the city than a Sharkey-Goddard match. The November 5 Jeffries fight was postponed a few weeks, "owing to the sickness of Choynski's wife." The exact nature of her illness was not revealed. The "Parson" arrived in St. Louis on October 19; Graney and Tom O'Rourke would be in Frisco to "look after Choynski's interests."[44]

The Jeffries bout, originally for the 16th, was postponed at the request of both the National and Knickerbocker clubs. The San Francisco institutions had a clash of fight dates, and agreed it would benefit neither to go on with cards around the same night. Joe arrived by train from Chicago on November 6. The Goddard-Sharkey bout at the Knickerbocker club, initially set for November 13, came off on the 18th. This was the conflicting bout, scheduled long before the Jeffries tilt. Joe was ready "at a moment's notice, against ... all contestants, be they white, black or yellow." He said he was "until quite recently" employed by "a sporting house in Cincinnati ... His ring instincts returned and he concluded to again enter the roped arena." The *Call* noted, on the 7th: "Promoters of the Green-Ziegler fight ... selected Joe Choynski to referee ... When Green met Ziegler before ... (Joe) was ... in Ziegler's corner. Subsequently, Green and Choynski became friendly ... Neither ... objected ... the public ... will get a square deal."

November 7 *Chronicle*: "Joe Choynski, California's favorite pugilist, arrived at 7 o'clock last evening ... There was no change in the mop of hair, but ... he seemed a stronger and better man than ... a little over a year ago. His eye is clear and skin almost transparent. (He) was met in Oakland by ... relatives and Eddie Graney, and at the ferry by several more friends. Choynski was in his usual good humor, and in his free and candid manner discussed his coming fight. He is in a hurry to get back to Chicago to his wife, who is not in perfect health. Joe says his fine appearance is due to the regular training he has been doing at Washington Park race track in Chicago. He has been in condition for six weeks ... The only let-up ... the past four days he has spent on the train. Choynski went directly to his home on arrival here and spent an hour or two with his relatives. At 9 o'clock he came down town and met many ... friends at the Baldwin Hotel, where he was the recipient of many compliments on his appearance."[45]

Joe commented (honestly, if callously) on the December, 1894 death of Andy Bowen, after a KOby18 loss to "Kid" Lavigne. "He was out of training and had no one but himself and his seconds to blame for his death. I saw the ... fight ... Bowen had no earthly chance of winning after he was knocked down the 2nd time ... I would have thrown up the sponge. This idea of nerve is very good if there is a fighting chance to win. But to send a man to slaughter when ... too weak to protect himself is absolute brutality. I have heard plenty ... about the brutality of boxing ... from the early days of the London Rules ... I can't recall a case where a first class boxer ... was killed as a result of a ring encounter." Here, Joe should have acknowledged some of the more than 100 ring fatalities around the world before 1897, such as Simon Byrne, dying three days after losing an 1833 bareknuckle bout to James "Deaf" Burke. "I have been up against some pretty tough brushes ... including one ... with Corbett and two with Goddard, and I looked and felt the part of a butchered warrior at the finish. But I recovered ... in a few days ... enter(ing) the ring half trained ... is worse than not ... trained at all ... The referee ... can save many (by) compelling the groggy, disabled fighter to leave the ring when he has no show."[46]

On the night of November 10 at Woodward's Pavilion, under the aegis of the National Athletic Club, Joe refereed the Green-Ziegler bout. In the 1st round, Green drove a left to the solar plexus. "Ziegler ... went ... to his knees ... then his face ... deathly pale and groaning ... Choynski ... reached five when Ziegler ... grasping the ropes ... collapsed ... and was counted out ... (the final blow) a clean ... swing ... on a vital spot." Joe told the *San Francisco Call* he did not "think ... it was of sufficient force to cripple Ziegler ..." Graney was in Green's corner. The *Call* felt Ziegler took a dive.[47]

November 12 *Call*: "To lose a fight before the National Athletic Club ... is as profitable ... possibly more so, than to win ... one only has to recall the Sharkey-Fitzsimmons fiasco, when the loser was awarded the entire purse of $10,000 (by) Referee Earp. That affair settled for a time, the National Club, or rather Messrs. Groom and Gibbs, who comprise the 'club' as fight promoters. Nobody would have anything to do with them ... it seemed ... public opinion had permanently retired them from the game. But a year works many changes ... Ziegler dropped ... from a punch that would not have disabled a child ... Nobody ... thought Green was a party to the 'fake,' but ... thought Ziegler had permitted himself to be counted out ... Ziegler's movements yesterday fully confirmed this suspicion. A few minutes after 1 o'clock ... Ziegler staggered into the sub-treasury under the weight of a great sack ... of coin ..." This totaled about $1,000 for Owen, "a comfortable sum for the loser, with such a house as was at Woodward's Pavilion ..." Green said the knockout was legitimate, that he landed two body blows in very close, where the spectators likely didn't see them.

The Sharkey and Goddard camps selected Choynski on November 15, to umpire their clash. He refused, "on the grounds that he intends to challenge the winner." He wanted to avoid being a factor in the outcome. About mid-month, Peter Jackson was assured by Graney that, should Joe defeat Jeffries, he would give Peter a match. "Graney, who looks after Choynski's interests on this coast, stated ... Choynski will leave immediately for New Orleans after his fight with Jeffries, as he is booked to spar Alexander Greggains 10 rounds before one of the ... clubs of the yellow fever city. This will not interfere ... with his proposed contest with Jackson."[48] On the 18th, Sharkey battered Goddard, bludgeoning him to the floor in round six. The "Barrier Champion" struck his head on the floor and did not make it out of the round. He had been in many bruising battles over his career, and now, in his forties, was showing the effects.

The Choynski-Jeffries battle was slated for 20 rounds. The November 27 *San Francisco Call* gave the "tale of the tape" for the warriors:

Choynski: neck, 17"; chest, 39"; (expanded), 41"; waist, 32"; right biceps, 14"; left biceps, 14"; right wrist, 7¼"; left wrist, 7¼"; right thigh, 22½"; left thigh, 22½"; right calf, 13½"; left calf, 13½"; forearm, 11½; reach, 76"; height, 5' 11½"; weight, 170 pounds; age, 29.

Jeffries: neck, 18"; chest, 44"; (expanded), 49¾"; waist, 36"; right biceps, 17"; left biceps, 17¼"; right wrist, 8¾"; left wrist, 8¾"; shoulders, 53"; around hips, 42"; right thigh, 27¼"; left thigh, 27¼"; right calf, 18"; left calf, 18"; right ankle, 10¾"; left ankle, 10¾"; reach, 77¼"; right forearm, 14¼; left forearm, 14¼; height, 6' 1½"; weight, 216 pounds; age, 22.

Jeff prepared two months for the clash. Delaney said Jim had improved "20 per cent" since the Ruhlin fight. He contended that Joe was "a poor defensive fighter and can be hit by any pugilist who has the least knowledge of the game." The November 13 *Police News* said Joe's only advantage was experience, Jim having it all in terms of size and strength. Despite this, "if his legs do not go back on him, he (Joe) should win the money. This failing has proved a great detriment ... his only drawback to a fighting machine, otherwise perfect. He has no fear of the outcome, feeling he has the ability to down the giant from Los Angeles." November 28 *Call*: "Choynski completed his hard course of training yesterday ... What exercise he might take ... will ... consist primarily in a trot through the park to the Cliff House, returning to his father's residence, 1209 Golden Gate Avenue. Friday night Choynski was unable to sleep, owing to ... on the small toe of his left foot ... a blister. About 5:30 (p.m.) (he) walked to the residence of Eddie Graney, where he had been invited to ... dinner. Graney is an old friend ... between them ... exists a cordiality of sentiment and one purpose ... not unlike ... Damon and Pythias ... While Choynski was enjoying succulent birds, he was seized with an intense pain in the toe ... with difficulty ... he walked home. Yesterday ... went to a chiropodist (and) had ... the growth ... removed."

" 'I am feeling first rate,' said the doughty ring-general ... Choynski was aroused from a sound slumber by a member of the household ... when *Call* representatives were ushered into his presence, Joe was rubbing his eyes ... fatigue on his countenance. (He) chatted ... about his coming engagement with the Goliath of the southern citrus belt." "In all my fights I have

Jim Jeffries, circa 1900

endeavored to win ... taken punishment in order (to) knock out my man. Several ladies came in here the other evening and I was greatly amused by their talk. They had seen somebody who (had) seen somebody else who had seen Jeffries, and they commenced telling me what a great man he was; how extremely clever ... and what he contemplated doing with me. The hour was quite late, but I went down into the basement ... and took a bout at the punching-bag. I was satisfied ... I had improved somewhat in my methods, and I went upstairs and encouraged the ladies ..."

Delaney continued to talk trash about Joe, apparently trying to gain a psychological edge for his man: "I believe if Jeff begins to get the best of Choynski, a cry of foul will be raised ... When he fought Sharkey he claimed a foul and was allowed a 20 minutes' rest, though there can be little doubt the blow he received was fair." Jeff added to the diatribe: "I would rather fight Choynski than any man in the business, as I consider him the easiest mark in the heavyweight class. To my mind he has never done enough to warrant the San Francisco public in its opinion of him ..." The articles stipulated that "the fighters could strike with one arm free." The November 30 *Chicago Tribune* called the match "a case of science and agility against bone and muscle ..." but said Joe looked a bit light. "With Jim McDonald ... in charge of the ring ... fair fighting will be required."

The time for talk was over. On the evening of November 30 at

Woodward's Pavilion, under the auspices of the National A.C.,* Choynski and Jeffries met in a legendary altercation. A throng of 5,000 to 6,000 witnessed one of Joe's best performances. Weighing between 165 and 170 pounds, he conceded at least 50 pounds to his massive foe, some papers saying as much as 63 pounds. Joe (1930): "There were more leading boxers present than I could recall seeing at any previous fight. Occupying prominent seats were Peter Jackson, Fitzsimmons, Sharkey, Goddard, Joe McAuliffe ..." Jeff, who in another year and a half would win the heavyweight crown, was incredibly quick and agile for his bulk, and able to

Jim Jeffries and Joe Choynski, November 30, 1897

absorb nearly unlimited punishment. Joe entered the ring at 9:50 p.m., with seconds, Ed Graney, George Green (a.k.a. "Young Corbett") and Tom Murphy. Jeffries joined 15 minutes later, "esquired by De Witt Van Court, Billy Delaney and Jack Stelzner ... the band kept the crowd in good humor."
* Sources vary, whether the fight occurred at the National Athletic Club or Woodward's, but the best sources say Woodward's Pavilion.

Announcer Billy Jordan brought the gloves into the ring, where they were inspected by Police Captain Wittman. "Jim McDonald, the famous baseball umpire, was ... referee. Choynski was clad in blue trunks and Jeffries wore black." *Fresno Bee*: "Choynski's weight was said by his seconds to be 167 pounds, while it is said Jeffries balanced the scale ... at 230. (Jim) looked larger ... than ... ever ... while Choynski appeared ... trained to the hour. When the big Los Angeles man stepped into the ring, Choynski ... walked across ... and shook hands cordially." Next is a fusion of seven newspaper reports, Joe's and Jeff's memoirs, and other sources:[49]

Round 1 – A "feeling out" round, not a single clean blow was struck.

After a minute or two, Jeff grazed Joe's shoulder with a left. Joe cautiously gauged his man and Jim looked nervous. He told the *Sydney Referee* in 1927: "The record books show ... a 20-round draw ... but those ... at ringside ... will ever insist Joe and I fought three rounds of cyclonic battling ... the last 17 ... were of the burlesque variety. I went after Choynski from the first tap of the gong. Joe ... kept ... dodging the heavy punches for something more than two rounds." In 1910 he told the *Sydney Sportsman*: "Joe was in and out like a shadow ... keeping away from clinches, so I couldn't wear him down by using my weight and strength. He held his right back and jabbed with the left until I saw stars." Joe's 1930s memoirs also differ from the papers: "I hopped in there and began socking. But Jeff was no dumbell. He began sharpshooting with that left jab. I felt it ... but I kept socking ... I could tell he was feeling 'em. I guess the spectators expected a slow and colorless 1st round. There was plenty of action ... Jeff was like a welterweight on his feet. And ... built so solidly I doubt whether a man could have floored him with a sledgehammer. No man I had ever met could take the blows I was giving Jeff, and stand up under them. I plastered him unmercifully, but ... He blocked some ... with his long and powerful arms."

Round 2 – More cautious sparring. Joe got in a jab, Jim responding with a "tap to the ribs." The *Fresno Bee* and *Idaho Daily Statesman* said Jeff floored Joe, but other contemporary reports say that came in the 3rd.

Round 3 – The "California Grizzly" landed a few rights to the body. He suddenly smashed a left over Joe's guard, on the neck and putting him on his back. Van Court said (in 1926) that Jeff used a punch they had been working on, a left jab followed quickly by a left hook (known as "hooking off the jab"). *Philadelphia Inquirer*: "Joe stayed down five seconds and got up ... Jeffries ... did not follow up his advantage." The *Call* said he was down seven seconds and "gets up spryly just as the gong sounds ..." "I smashed him in the body with a left, then lifted it up to his chin – and Joe went down as though hit by an express train ... just then the bell sounded ..." Jeff, in 1927: "As I was moving to my corner, a crowd of police jumped up to the ring railing. They became involved in a heated debate with Bill Delaney ... I ... saw them try to jerk Bill out of the corner ... Bill managed to toss a stage whisper at me, 'Go easy, Jim – take it easy with him.' So I went out in the next round and took it easy with Joe. He was a mighty groggy fellow then – a few punches would have settled him."

Jeff's 1910 version: "He got up ... and didn't show much distress. Still, I think I could have ... finished him then, if my seconds hadn't called me to stand off ..." Delaney told Jeff between rounds, "He thinks he's got you sized up now, and he'll try to lay you out with his right. That's your queue. You slam him with the left on the jaw as soon as he wiggles that fin." Choynski, years later: "In the 3rd, I thought I saw a chance to topple him. Jeff led with a left and I ducked. Then, seeing an opening as wide as the

Ferry Building, I stepped in and shot a right as hard as any I have ever landed on an opponent. It was another of those peculiar moments, as in my fight with Corbett, when victory hung delicately poised. Jeff swayed drunkenly on the ropes. I looked for him to fall in a heap. But ... He shook his great head just as a bull does, and refused to go down."

"Just before ... this ... blow against Jeff's temple we exchanged the only remarks ... made during ... the fight. Delaney, it seems ... told Jeff to make me do the leading ... as I started a hook, Jeff beat me to it ... with a stiff right to the jaw. 'How'd you like that?' he asked. I grinned. 'I'll answer you in a moment!' ... I landed a resounding smash which Jeff afterward (said) was the hardest sock he ... ever received in the prize ring. I shook him, too, in the 10th, with a hard blow to the mouth." That Joe remembered the 3rd round as that in which he landed the legendary punch, shows that Jeffries' memory wasn't the only faulty one in later years.

Round 4 – *Call*: "Both ... land hard lefts on the body. Jeffries tries several straight lefts and Choynski jumps away each time. Both exchange hard left swings on the face. Choynski lands straight left hard on the forehead." *Philadelphia Inquirer*: "Each scored light lefts on the head and Jeffries got in a solid kidney punch. The round was rather tame."

Round 5 – Some vicious fighting took place. *Inquirer*: Joe drove several sharp jabs to the head and "backed away from Jeffries' left punches. He could not avoid the right, however, and caught three hard body punches and a left jolt in the face. Honors even." *Call*: Joe "ducks an ugly uppercut ... puts Jeffries' head back three times ... with straight lefts. Jeffries rushes and swings left several times ... lands lightly once ... throws Choynski's head back with a straight left. The first clinch in the fight occurs as the round ends." The *Chronicle* felt Joe won the round: "He landed three good lefts on Jeffries' nose ... blocked several left swings. His ducking and cleverness in getting out of corners aroused the cheers of the crowd."

Big Jim Jeffries and His 12 Great Ring Battles (1910): Joe "snapped Jeff's head back with a wicked straight left and ... saw a chance to wing him hard with the right ... but ... Jeff ... slammed him so hard in the wind with his left that he grunted. He (Joe) took another left on the jaw and staggered across the ring under a driving left and right to the body. Jeff was fighting with the skill and coolness of a veteran, but ... rushed and straightened up stiff ... the end of his nose flattened in from a rigid left ... it jarred him to his toes ... Choynski chopped a right ... on the same spot and blinded him with a volley of short lefts. Jeff fell back and crouched, and a crimson stain spread slowly over the lower part of his face ... Jeff's nose was in the way of the ... left again three times, but Choynski drew back from the mix-up with a dull, red spot low on his right side, where Jeff's left had been busy."

Round 6 – Jeffries pursued, landing a hard straight left, two more lefts to the head and a good right to the body. Joe countered with "a terrific right on the face," prompting a clinch. Jeff pounded Joe on the back twice with his right in the clinch, and closed with a hard left to the face.

Round 7 – The *Call* said Joe landed "a terrific right swing on the head," the *Inquirer*, a "heavy left arm swing to the jaw." Jeff rushed ineffectually. Joe ducked and dodged with speed and skill, countering with the left. He only took about two punches from Jim, easily winning the heat.

Round 8 – The *Call* and *Inquirer* said Jeffries took the 8th handily, landing multiple straight lefts to the face. The *Chronicle* said Joe avoided his charges, countered with the left and got the better of things. As the first two accounts were more detailed, Jeff probably won the round.

Round 9 – There was more disagreement. The friendly *Chronicle* had Joe evading his pursuer and countering with jabs. The *Inquirer* said, "Choynski was receiver again ... taking numerous hard lefts on the jaw and face. He stepped away ... the blows distressed him ... little." *Call* : "Choynski got in some good blows ... in the beginning ... plants a hard left square on Jeffries' nose. Choynski blocks several attempts (at) straight lefts,

Choynski-Jeffries, December 1, 1897 San Francisco Chronicle

and is the recipient of a hard left ... on the jaw that makes him dizzy."

Round 10 – The *Chronicle* said Joe dodged and outscored Jim with the left. The *Call* differed: "Jeffries ... rushing ... planting a hard left swing on Choynski's face. Many blows ... land on Choynski's glove guard ... Jeffries lands a hard right ... on the head." *Inquirer*: "Jeffries played both hands heavily on Joe's heart ... Joe could not land a single effective punch." The *Fresno Bee* had Joe the aggressor from rounds two through 10. The differing accounts beg the question which fight each was watching! Years later, Jeff recalled this as the round he received Joe's cosmic clout in. Time evidently confused his memory. Round 16 is the likely candidate for the event.

Round 11 – Choynski drew first blood with a hard jab to the nose, avoided a right and landed two more lefts to the same spot. He evaded an angry rush, but roughed him during a clinch. The *Call* and *Chronicle* gave Joe a slight edge. The *Inquirer* said "Jeffries flogged his man roughly about the body with both hands and landed a stiff right on the head. Honors were easy." The *Brooklyn Eagle* said Jim's nose bled from round 11 on.

Round 12 – Choynski won the round. His left stopped Jim's rushes and drew "considerable blood" from his right cheek and nose. Joe "swings his right hard on the jaw as the round closes."

Round 13 – Another "winning inning" for Joe, according to the *Call*: "Choynski throws Jeffries' head back with a straight left ... Jeffries rushes, trying right and left without success. Choynski lands on the nose again." *Inquirer*: "Jeffries ... lashed out several wicked blows, most of which were blocked by Choynski, who did some very clever ducking and side stepping, but no leading." The *Chronicle*: "The 13th, 14th and 15th rounds were not notable for heavy work. Jeffries kept pressing Choynski back, but Joe gave Jeffries but little chance to make his superior weight tell."

Round 14 – Jeffries rushed Choynski. The latter slipped to his knees, and Jim fell over him. He bulled Joe to the ropes, driving a hard left to the face and a right to the head. A powerful left to the jaw from Frisco Joe sent Jim's head flying back. They traded jabs, and Joe ducked a pair of swinging lefts. The *Inquirer* reported that, except for the single, potent left by Joe, he "took all the punishment in this round. He was chased around the ring continually and confined all his efforts to keeping out of Jeffries' way."

Round 15 – *Call*: "Jeffries ... landing a light left swing ... (a) hard one ... rushes Choynski to the other side of the ring ... lands again ... rushes ... and Choynski slips to his knees." This is the only version calling it a slip. *Inquirer*: "Jeffries ... cornered and floored him neatly with a left swing ... staggered him with hard lefts which left their mark on Choynski's face and body." "The 15th was barely two minutes old when Jeff brushed aside (Joe's) guard, and sank a killing left into his stomach. The 'native son' yell of victory made the roof beams dance, as Choynski settles down to the floor like a tired horse. But ... Choynski was young and strong, and probably the only man that ever got up after Jeff's left met his stomach square and true." Joe (1930): "A knockout ... is painless. A punch to the body is the most severe. Yet, strangely, I never felt the hardest body blows." Any contemporary report counting knockdowns said there were two, evidently coming in rounds three and 15.

Round 16 – The *Chronicle* and *Inquirer* said Joe battered Jim with the left "and soon had him bleeding from ... eyes, cheek, nose and mouth." "Jeffries fought back like a demon ... the round was the hottest of the fight ... a slight advantage for Choynski." *Oshkosh Daily Northwestern*: "Choynski's ducking was superb and his splendid work ... brought down the house ... He allowed Jeffries to force him into his own corner ... the big fellow, believing he had his opponent at close quarters, jammed him against the cable in a give and take struggle. Choynski caught the big fellow four smashing lefts on the jaw, ducked a terrific swing which threw the Los Angeles boy against the ropes, and ... flew in with his right on the side of the head – the only time he used it effectively in the ... fight. Several ... times he wriggles out of a hot situation by ... clever footwork ...” *Chronicle*: “Jeffries rushed Choynski into his corner ... (Joe) seeming to court the danger. As Jeffries was about to swing heavily, Joe let go his right, and caught Jeffries such a heavy swing on the face that he drove him back to the center of the ring.” *Call*: “Jeffries gets Choynski in his corner and plants half a dozen straight lefts on the face. Choynski gets in one right swing on the head ... a stiff left on the face ... almost closes Jeffries’ left eye ... again on the face.” This must be the round in which Jeff said Joe smashed him with the legendary right.

Round 17 – *Chronicle*: “The 16th and 17th ... clearly Choynski’s.” *Call*: “Jeffries put his left in with terrific force to the face ... Near the close of the round, Choynski lands two terrific left swings on Jeffries’ jaw.” *Inquirer*: “Jeffries tired badly ... ‘Joe’ kept up a tattoo with the left ... almost closing his left eye. Jeffries’ leads lacked steam and were neatly blocked.”

Round 18 – The “Grizzly” had his 2nd wind. He got Choynski against the ropes and landed to the jaw. Joe kept a cool head and cleverly escaped. *Inquirer*: “Joe put in a few left jabs on Jeffries’ damaged eye ... took four or five stiff body punches in return.” *Call*: “Neither scored much ... Jeffries tries ... with a straight left ... Choynski ducks away every time. Choynski throws Jeffries’ head back several times with straight lefts.” *Chronicle*: “Choynski ... two lefts on Jeffries’ jaw. Both ... blocking ... blows well ... the past few rounds, but Choynski was the neater and cleverer.”

Round 19 – The *Call* said it was the same as the 18th. The *Chronicle* and *Inquirer* differed from each other, as usual. *Inquirer*: “Jeffries still kept on the aggressive, following and landing stiff lefts on Joe’s body. Joe still looked to Jeffries’ damaged eye, which he visited two or three times with hard left jabs.” *Chronicle*: “Choynski did good work with his left, landing on Jeffries’ wounds and keeping the blood flowing. Jeffries tried frequently to land on Choynski’s wind, but the latter jumped just beyond ... reach ...”

Round 20 – They shook hands at ring center. *Inquirer*: “Both ... went at it hammer and tongs and slugged the full round ... with little or no advantage on either side.” *Fresno Bee*: “Choynski did not show a mark ... until the last round, when he was struck by the ‘heel’ of Jeffries’ glove over the right eye, which brought a little stream of blood.” *Chronicle*: “Lively, especially the last minute. Choynski ... fought cautiously. Jeffries rushed and tried to mix ... careful ... to leave no opening Choynski might fill with his fist. Jeffries ... landed his left a few times ... ineffectively, while Choynski reached Jeffries’ face ... enough to keep it bloody.” *Call*: “Choynski puts his left on the face and Jeffries rushes him around the ring, Choynski ... turns and blocks several of Jim's leads. Jeffries rushes him to the ropes ... lands a hard blow on the top of the head. Choynski lands a terrific straight left on the face toward the close of the round ... Referee McDonald ... announced ... a draw, which was received with satisfaction by the entire audience." Using a modern scoring system, Joe might have earned the nod by a miniscule margin. It was admittedly a close contest, though, and without having witnessed it, judging who won is something of a fool's errand.

Chronicle: "The principals' opinions ... are different, but interesting. 'I think I ought to have had the decision,' said Choynski ... 'I did the cleanest and ... most frequent hitting. I was in the best condition at the close. I could have finished him in a few more rounds. He has considerable cleverness and his weight of 60 pounds more ... is an important factor. I came out of the encounter with scarcely a scratch. If I am going to fight heavy-weights like him, I had better take a rest and put on flesh.' 'I think I was entitled to the decision,' said Jeffries, 'I was ... aggressive all the time. Choynski never forced the fighting once. I landed oftener than he did. I knocked him down twice. I had him running around the ring a good deal ... I signed to fight ... Queensberry rules, but the Chief of Police sent up word to my seconds and the referee that if I hit in the clinch, he would stop the fight. That is why I did not hit Choynski during the dozen or more clinches when I had a free arm and could have knocked him out ... I want ... him again. I have got his measure now and I can knock him out. I think his cleverness is overrated." Many hard punches were landed to the head without police interference. Jeff later claimed to have scored not two, but three knockdowns.

Graney: "After that 4th round, when Choynski was knocked down in using his right, I told him he ... always lost ... when he lost ... laying himself open by being too aggressive. I insisted ... he should not use his right, but ... fight ... for the decision with his left. I think ... the fight justified this. He had the better of his man in every particular, and in a very few more rounds would have had him out. When you consider the weight he gave, this is remarkable. He put up the cleverest fight ... ever seen in a ring. Choynski can beat any of them." Jeff (1910): "Joe, like Fitzsimmons, had his strength all where he could use it for punching. He had big shoulders and light legs. He was very fast and could time his punches perfectly."

"I think it was the 10th – Choynski struck me the hardest blow I ever felt ... I was walking after him, when he suddenly stopped and whipped over a straight punch ... on the mouth. My teeth are ... even and ... close together, but that was such a terrific blow it drove my upper lip ... between the two in front, wedging them apart. I held Choynski off with my left, while I put my right up and tried to pull my lip away ... At the same time I tried to force it out with my tongue, but ... no use ... it bothered me so much that a round or two later ... I had my seconds take a knife and cut away a piece of the lip to release it. I had to keep spitting the blood out as I went on ... for nothing makes a man so sick as swallowing warm blood ... Joe kept on popping his left ... to my mouth and nose ... had me smeared up, more or less." In 1943, Harry Grayson quoted Jeff as saying "he never knew a man who could jab as accurately and often with such effect as Chrysanthemum Joe."[50]

Jeff declared (1903): "I thought my head left my body. The blow dazed me, but I recovered quickly. That was the closest call I ever had in the ring." (1927): "Delaney ... cut off the piece of lip. The referee called it a

CHOYINISKI HIT JEFFRIES THE HARDEST BLOW THE BOILERMAKER EVER RECEIVED.

draw, although I thought I had won about 19 rounds ... perhaps the entire 20." This gross exaggeration was a radical departure from Jim's previous statements. (1929): "Choynski ... was all over me ... not only the cleverest boxer I had ever seen but ... a terrific hitter. He fought so fast I could not use what skill I had to best advantage, and was taking a wonderful boxing lesson ... In the 10th ... he pulled the trick ... one of the cleverest I ever saw. He was running at top speed, his back ... to me, with me in pursuit, when he ran straight into the ropes as hard as he could. The ropes gave, threw him back, and ... he turned and hit me a right hand punch in the mouth ... so hard he broke my nose and wedged my lip between my teeth. He drove my head so far back I thought my neck stretched a foot ... During the remainder of the fight I knocked Choynski down three times but ... Graney called it a draw ... I had no regrets. I had taken a boxing lesson from a master and an artist ..."[51] Jim erroneously noted Ed Graney as the referee. Contemporary accounts mention nothing about Joe using the ropes as a catapult.

Jeff (1930s): "Little Joe was the hardest hitter I ever tangled with – yes, even harder than Fitzsimmons. To this day I can't figure out how a runt like him, who was hog fat at 173 pounds, could hurt so damned bad ... a right ...

landed high on my cheekbone. I figured my whole face ... caved in ... when I tried to feel (it) with my hands, there wasn't any sensation ... my body was numb from the neck up ... had it landed a little lower, I would have been knocked out for the first time in my life. There is no question I would have quit fighting ... in those days I fought without interest and actually searched for an excuse to hang 'em up. Joe Choynski and I were always good friends. He helped me train for the Fitzsimmons fight, when I won the title. Joe taught me how to duck and block leads and cover up, and for what success I enjoyed ... much of the credit must go to Little Joe."[52]

December 2 *Fort Wayne News*: "Choynski and Jeffries ... fought one of the most vicious draws in the history of San Francisco ... while Jeffries was ... the most punished about the face, he showed great cleverness, in face of the fact that his right was damaged early in the fight ... scored two clean knock-downs, while he received only left jabs in the face." This report appears biased toward Jim, and was the only mention of an injured hand. Aside from jabs, Joe landed hefty left "swings," hard body shots and at least one terrific right. *Inquirer*: "Choynski fought against odds and ... well. After this, few will dispute Jeffries' claim (as) a possibility for ... championship. He is a clever boxer, and while little more than a novice ... fairly puzzled ... a veteran ... If any mistake was made in Choynski's corner it was in not allowing Joe to go at his big vis-à-vis at the start. Jeffries was ... rattled when he entered the ring ... not until several rounds had elapsed that he regained his natural color and began to fight with confidence."

"Choynski covered himself with glory and has never shown up to such advantage. He is as clever and as quick as ever, and last night he fought the first calculating battle he has ... been ... in. Contrary to his general tactics, he was not reckless for a minute ... A noticeable change ... is the difference in his guard and attack. He fought Jeffries with his body well open ... almost squarely in the Australian style, the old side stand he assumes in all his photographs only cropping up once or twice ... that he was not the aggressor, probably considered by McDonald when he rendered his decision, ought not to have counted against him ... with a 50 pound disadvantage ... it was the best ... generalship to keep away from rushes and to duck. Choynski ... during the last 10 rounds particularly ... stopped several mean lefts by throwing his body across Jeffries' arm."

San Francisco Call: "Joseph ... repeatedly feinted ... left ... openings in the hope Jeffries would swing ... Seeing Jeffries intended to remain ... defensive, Choynski fiddled ... like a cooper around a barrel ... plant(ed) his left glove on Jeffries' nose. Time and again Jeffries had Choynski at his mercy near the ropes, but the artful Joseph, by clever ducking and quick footwork, would ... slide out of harm's way and come up like a Jack-in-the-box, ready to resume the attack at long range ... Jeffries ... has shown marked improvement in his footwork since his fight against Gus Ruhling (sic) ... in hitting, and stopping blows aimed at his face. Choynski most assuredly scored the most points, but ... McDonald, to please the majority ... decided ... a draw. Possibly in a fight to a finish Jeffries would have outlasted his opponent, but ... Choynski certainly had the better of (it) ... scored the cleanest hits and on defensive work more than proved his superiority ..."

Chronicle: (Jim) "has entirely changed his style ... instead of ... a series of wild, elephantine swings, he guards ... head and body closely with his hands ... throws ... with considerable speed and judgment ... (but) does not seem ... to understand how far he is allowed to go in the clinches. A dozen times, when he had Choynski in a practically helpless position at close quarters with his left free ... could have pounded his man's sides and kidneys to a jelly, he stood with his glove up and made no move to punish. Had he ... he might have won the fight." The punishment Jim sustained was later credited with his development of the "Jeffries crouch." He was, however, already displaying a crude form of it in this fight. He would hunch over forward, head low and chin protected behind the left shoulder. The left arm was straight out, "like the jib boom of a ship." His right arm was held back, right glove protecting the jaw and elbow shielding the ribs.

January 5, 1898 *Sydney Referee*: "Joe tried ... to open a way for that punishing left up-swing of his, but the giant blocked him at every point. Then Joe tried straight lefts, and had better luck ... Once or twice when pressed he held his arms crosswise before his face ... Jeff got ready to throw a left dig into Joe's unprotected stomach, when down came Choynski's folded right with a chopping action. It just grazed Jeff's chin, and made him draw out quickly ... Choynski did manage to get in his right once ... about the middle of the contest ... a smash that puffed the giant's left cheek."

Joe: "After this, I tried ... everything ... to knock the mammoth out. But the Boilermaker was harder than the iron in the boilers he had turned out in the shops. I am not denying I stopped ... wallops that carried ... full share of punishment. But ... I hit Jeff at least two to one ... felt pretty sore when that umpire-referee called ... a draw! I asked ... with some heat, if he could see anything but a home run! Harry Weldon ... asked me what I thought of Jeffries. 'This man ... will be the next heavyweight champion. He can beat ... Fitzsimmons and a lot of others. I told everyone ... here was one of the greatest big men in the sock racket. Years after ... Jeffries ... discussing the hard wallops ... received ... (in) this interview ... in my scrap-book ... 'I never felt a single blow Sharkey struck ... Nor ... did Fitz hit hurt me ... Corbett ... was like the punch of a baby. But ... Choynski was the man who gave me the punch that made me see stars for a few seconds. I felt it from the roots of my hair to the soles of my feet. It ... shook my whole system ...' "

De Witt Van Court: "Up to that time, Jim was ... a swinger ... constantly hurting his hands ... had the foolish notion many young fellows have about bandaging his hands. We had a big punching bag made that weighed about

40 pounds ... convinced him it would ... improve his hitting ... He ... did a lot of skipping rope ... that increased his speed greatly ... practiced a lot of straight left-hand hitting ... short, fast sprinting ... Graney ... had ... political pull in San Francisco, and used it to good advantage on that occasion. It was agreed that the fighters could hit in the breaks ... Jeff had been practicing ... and became clever at it. Some of Graney's political friends were sitting close to our corner, unknown to myself. I always thought he had an object in doing so, and later events convinced me ..."

(Joe) "waiting ... to land a hard right ... (did) in the 5th ... Jeff ... crowded him into a neutral corner ... Joe ... side-stepping ... turned ... and let go. That terrible right ... square on Jeff's mouth ... only knocked his head back ... Jeff sat in his chair ... elbows ... on his knees and a disgusted look on his face. I asked him if the punch hurt ... he said: 'If that Jew cannot hit any harder than that, he can never knock me out.' ... he did not speak distinctly ... I ... found that Choynski ... drove his upper teeth through his upper lip ... I had to cut the lip clear with a knife ... Jim was sore at himself, to think he had been drawn into a trick ... determined to give Joe some rough work ... in the first clinch ... Jeff let go a ... hard one in the break and nearly dropped Joe. This caused a holler from Graney ... one of his friends ... touched me on the shoulder and said, 'If you don't make your man stop that ... I will stop the fight.' I did not know who he was, and asked him what he had to say about it. 'I will show you ... who I am and what I will do with you,' said he."

"I felt myself yanked over a chair by the collar, and ... was looking at a big, Irish cop, who said: 'Shut up your mouth or I will knock your head off.' I knew these 'Frisco cops pretty well ... he would keep his word if I got ... fresh. I ... found he was an old friend of mine. He smiled ... 'Do you know who you were talking to, Van? ... one of the police commissioners (Tobin) ... I have to make a bluff at thumping you ... but take my advice and don't say anything more ...' I was mum as an oyster after that. They ... made the referee stop all hitting in the breaks ... a handicap to Jeff ... Jeff won the decision ... the only correct one ..."[53] (Van Court was mistaken!)

December 1 *San Francisco Bulletin*: "Jeffries lay fast asleep in a bath house on Sutter Street at noon ... Choynski was up reading the newspapers at his home out on Golden Gate Avenue at half past 10 ... the encounter ... reflected credit on both ... Everybody would have liked a decision in favor of one or the other ... but no one is raising a howl ... Choynski evidently thinks the decision ought to have been in his favor, but ... is discreet in conversation and philosophical in temperament ... When a *Bulletin* representative called at his house this morning, he came out of the breakfast room with a cheery greeting. 'Didn't get hurt a bit, not even to my hands.' 'I see you have two black eyes.' The eyes were not really ... black, but ... the flesh under both ... a little discolored ... 'That don't amount to anything. I came straight home last night and had a good sleep. Never go to the baths after a fight ... He knocked me down once or twice, but ... I was up ... right away ... believe I could fight 30 rounds right now.' "

" 'Many ... said you never used your right, and ... it was hurt.' 'Everybody knows your business better than you ...' said the veteran, in disdain. 'The referee says he didn't give the decision to me because the other man came after me ... Well, why shouldn't he? He weighed about 60 pounds more ... But I was there all the time, wasn't I? I have no complaint ... I'll have better luck next time.' Many people wondered that he constantly took on such difficult men – generally got the worst ... in weight ... 'Well, he said in a low tone, as if speaking more to himself than his interrogator, 'I won't do it anymore.' Choynski ... intended to leave for Chicago to-morrow morning. His wife, he said, had been very ill there ... Jeffries is a better fighter than conversationalist ... Delaney, his manager, also his thinker and talker ... took his ... protégé to the baths ... this morning. Dr. Lamothe dressed Jeffries' left eye, which was ... black ... badly swollen ... Delaney ... thinks 'Choyinski (sic) fought the fight of his life. He is one of the very best ... in the world. I think the referee did the best thing ... We ought to have had the decision, as our man did most of the leading, but it's all right ... It would have meant a whole lot to either ... to have decided against him ... ' "

Bob Edgren said Joe missed his best opportunity to clinch a shot at Fitz's heavyweight crown, when he just missed his right-hand "eye-tooth punch" in the 10th. Joe's plan was not to outpoint Jeff, but outmaneuver him, until he found an opening for a knockout blow. Joe's thunderbolt crashed on Jim's face "half an inch low," squarely on the teeth. "Jeff ... tried ... to pry that upper lip from between the teeth. Joe says he looked like a cat clawing at a fishbone ... when he saw Jeffries stand up under the crushing impact of a blow that would have knocked down a mule, he decided Jeffries wasn't going to be knocked down that day. Joe had shot his bolt ... (He) jabbed hard and landed many a heavy clout, but nary ... like the polthogue ... in the 10th. Perhaps if there had been a few ounces more in that clout, Choynski ... not Jeffries, would have fought Fitzsimmons ... in that case, nobody knows who might have been champion ..."[54]

A certain knockout by Choynski in 1901 has usually been hailed as his greatest result. That contest, however, was won with a single punch, whereas the 20-rounder with Jeffries entailed an extended strategic and physical effort. Jeff retired undefeated in 1905 as champion. Had he not been hounded into making a one-fight comeback in 1910, he would have remained the only heavyweight champion, other than Rocky Marciano, to officially retire without a loss. The only blemishes on an otherwise perfect record, were the 20-round draws with Ruhlin and Choynski. Most seemed to feel he won the Ruhlin bout. "Little Joe" earned at least a tie with the Los Angeles leviathan, possibly the defining performance of his career.

Round Sixteen

Fighting At the Top
(December 1897 – December 1898)

Joe left California on December 2, taking a train over the Santa Fe route to Chicago to see his ailing spouse.[1] He arrived the night of the 8th, telling a reporter he had to cancel his bout in New Orleans with Alex Greggains. Dan Creedon's manger, "Colonel" Hopkins, engaged Joe instead to "put the finishing touches" on Dan's training for an upcoming fight with "Kid" McCoy. He would second Creedon, and ready Tommy Tracey for a clash with Joe Walcott. Tracey, Creedon and Choynski began training at Palos Springs, Orland Park, a suburb of Chicago (some sources said Palos Park, another suburb). "Since Choynski ... joined Creedon ... at Palos Springs, the Australian has been doing less bag punching and more road work and sparring." On the 13th, Choynski departed on the Baltimore and Ohio train for Coney Island, with Creedon, Hopkins and Tracey. A Chicago paper noted, "Choynski is one of the most conservative men who ever went into the ring, and one of his grievances is that he has often been misquoted, as he claims, in the newspapers. This makes him all the more cautious, apparently, in talking to reporters. 'I wouldn't undertake to predict how he (Creedon) will come out on Friday night. He is a good, stiff puncher, and can take an unusual amount of punishment.' "[2]

The party arrived in New York the evening of the 15th, greeted by a throng of sporting men. *Salt Lake Herald*: "Joe Choynski is looking like a two-year-old (racehorse) ... and expects the fight to last about 10 rounds. Creedon and his trainers will go down to a quiet place near Coney Island ..." "Never before was a prize fighter more in the pink of condition ... than is Creedon, who is spending the last two days before the battle at the Williams cottage, on the Ocean parkway ... within gunshot of the surf. Early this morning Choynski, Tracey and Benny Murphy, Dan's trainers ... started him off on a 10 mile spin on his bike ... massage treatment ... breakfast ... An hour's siesta ... then the bike ... another rubdown ... a short walk (and) hearty dinner at 12 o'clock. Shortly after 1 o'clock ... Creedon started off ... for a walk ... he will put in an hour and a half at punching the bag and later ... skip the rope ... a good rub down and Dan's work for the day is done. He usually eats a light supper ... if he feels like smoking a light cigar afterward, he does it. Dan ... lands in his couch about 11 o'clock. Joe Choynski is a great favorite at the island, where he is looked upon not alone as a star fighter, but an A No. 1 trainer, and the men he handles generally come out on top."[3] The bicycle was a new component in a boxer's training, but fell out of favor not too many years later. The alcohol and smoking many fighters engaged in would be frowned upon today!

On fight day, December 17, few were allowed to see Dan before the event. Joe was "Creedon's chief mentor" and lone spokesperson. He would only smile and say Dan was "in great trim." Creedon only did light bag punching that morning. The plan was to rush McCoy and bring the fight to close range, where Dan's superior infighting ability would carry the day.[4] These tactics often played into the hands of a skilled sharpshooter like McCoy. That night at the Coney Island Athletic Club, the 25-rounder was considered by many as for the world's middleweight championship, although former titleholder and current heavyweight champ, Fitzsimmons, never formally relinquished the crown. The referee was Sam Austin. After a few rounds, McCoy dominated with his greater speed and reach. By the 15th, Dan was bloody and reeling. "The Kid" floored Creedon, who was unable to respond for the 16th. "Choynski ... threw up the sponge ..." Graney wired a telegram from San Francisco, asking Joe to challenge McCoy to a fight in that city. The National A.C. offered $10,000 for the bout. Joe was back in Chicago on the 20th. The defi apparently reached McCoy's ears, as he "promised his first meeting will be with ... Choynski. A 20-round contest may be arranged ... near New York."[5]

On December 27 at Chicago's Winter Circus building, Tom Tracey fought a D6 with Joe Walcott. Choynski was in Tracey's corner, with Billy O'Connell and Billy Stift.[6] On the 29th, Davies posted a $1,000 forfeit for a match with McCoy. "The Kid," though he would be fighting heavyweights the next year, was currently looking to battle "for middleweight honors." That division's limit was then set at 158 pounds, and weight would be a bone of contention between he and Joe for a while yet.

At 1 a.m. on December 29, Davies and Tom O'Rourke roused Fitz's manager, Martin Julian, for an impromptu conference in Davies' room at Chicago's Tremont House. Heavyweight champ, Bob, still having claims to the middleweight title, was dictating, with Julian, which fighter McCoy had to defeat, to get a shot at Fitz's middleweight crown. O'Rourke lobbied for his charge, Joe Walcott, who recently lost a world lightweight title bout to "Kid" Lavigne, but would soon battle heavier boxers. "Julian said he had already designated Choynski as the man for McCoy to beat ... but O'Rourke begged hard to have Walcott substituted. 'If you insist ... to back Choynski, Charley, said O'Rourke ... 'I withdraw all applications for Walcott, but Choynski has not treated you right, and I do not feel you should feel obligated to back him.' The 'Parson' ... thought it was a good chance to make some money, and ... had been trying for some time to get on a match for Choynski with the Kid." Julian, manager of neither McCoy, Walcott nor Choynski, said he would be willing to name Walcott to fight McCoy, if a

Choynski match was refused, on grounds of weight differential. "Davies reproached Julian for advertising on ... posters that Fitz had knocked out Choynski in four rounds. 'It is false,' declared the 'Parson' ... Julian replied that Choynski was practically out when police stopped the fight. 'Yes, and Fitz was practically out in the 2nd round, too, when the police interfered,' replied Davies." Julian did not dispute the last point.[7]

The next day, Julian declared: "I am going to hold McCoy to his promise that he would give Choynski the next show ... He cannot get out of it by saying Choynski must get down to 158 pounds, for he knows Joe cannot do it." McCoy then asserted, "I will ... meet (Choynski) at ringside at 162 pounds, which I consider very fair ..." The "Parson" countered, "Joe ... will fight ... McCoy at catch weights at any place and ... time, for a purse of $5,000. He will agree to no particular weight."[8] Making 162 pounds would also have weakened Joe. In short order, McCoy would be fighting (and defeating) 200-pounders such as "The Akron Giant," Gus Ruhlin.

The January 8, 1898 *Fort Wayne News* said: "Mrs. Joe Choyniski (sic), wife of the ... prize-fighter, is dangerously ill at her home, and may not recover." This was only sensationalism. Yet again, the nature of Lutie's illness was not given, but she recovered, and no further mention is found of her health issues. By the 8th, McCoy had formally announced his intent of challenging for Fitzsimmons' heavyweight title. This was further indication he had been bluffing, regarding the need to fight at middleweight. Selby noted for the *Lowell Sun*, that he had boxed with Fitz on many occasions in training, and that Bob referred to him as his pupil. McCoy admitted he had already taken on heavyweights like Jim Daly and Steve O'Donnell, adding: "Foremost I am willing to cross arms with gallant Joe Choynski ... hero of a hundred battles – the clever, game fellow all the big men seem to dodge. I will meet Joe any time, at any weight, for any fair purse, and as much of a side bet as (he) may wish ... If I defeat him, as I am confident of doing, I would take on Tom Sharkey, the herculean sailor." How diametrically opposed was McCoy's stance, to that of a few days earlier!

"The Kid" gave an autobiographical account: "I was born on a farm in Rush county, Indiana, about 55 miles from Indianapolis. My father was the most athletic, industrious farmer in that section ... in the summer time, when the sun illuminated ... golden ... fields of corn and the birds chirruped ... about the farmhouse I was happy enough, but when the ... bleak winter came, I used to long to ... get a peep at the gay, beautiful world outside ... My father ... a Baptist ... religious and stern, would thrash me as earnestly as he did his wheat when he would find me thus 'wool-gathering,' as he called it ... my people sold the farm and went to Indianapolis when I was 9 years old, where my father opened a grocery store ... I did good, hard work behind the counter for three years, going to school at odd spells. I received so many thrashings from my ... muscular, yet deeply religious father, for dodging Sunday school and yielding to the fascinating game of baseball, that I determined to run away from home at the age of 12, and have been practically away ... since; although I am on the best of terms with my parents, whom I profoundly respect, and have visited them three or four times at the old homestead. When I left home, I had to hustle for fair (sic).

"Kid" McCoy in dapper mode

I first started to learn the trade of a tailor, gave it up and tried paper hanging, then painting (then) helping a surveyor to hold up a theodolite and measure distance ... a sort of jack of all trades ..."

"The name and fame of John L. Sullivan had spread through the west, and when he went to Indiana, the old (and) young grew wildly enthusiastic ... I was working for a spell at Evansville, and when John L. showed up at the principal theater ... I was ... in a front seat every night, watching every move he made in sparring with ... Jack Ashton. I grew enamored of the sport. I had always been very good with my hands and invariably thrashed every boy who endeavored to thrash me. I wanted to become a skillful boxer, so I managed to borrow a set of gloves and put them on with any one I could induce to box me. Finally, I attracted the attention of Pete Treator (Trentor?) ... one of the best amateur boxers in Indiana. He taught me a lot of points and put a number of good men up against me. I managed to beat them all and started out to fight on my own account."[9]

Norman Selby gave differing accounts of his life. While he correctly said Rush County was the locale of his birth (the town of Moscow), it is doubtful that he left home at age 12. Robert Cantwell, in *The Real McCoy* (1971), says the likely age was 16 or 17. Tales such as "The Kid" living in hobo jungles and learning dirty fighting tricks there, were all part of a public persona created to counter the fact that he was pale, slim and looked anything but a pug. But, what a fighter! McCoy would clash with Joe three more times. Davies: "I see ... the Kid wants to bring in the weight question. He says he is willing to fight Goddard and let Joe weigh a ton. Why ... is he not willing to fight Choynski?" The likely reason for McCoy's dodging tactics, was he felt he could still clinch a championship bout with Fitz, and avoid risking his ranking against opponents as dangerous as Joe.[10]

January 17 *Chicago Chronicle*: "Of all the ring athletes who make Chicago their home, none is better qualified to discuss ... pugilism than Joseph B. Choynski ... few professors of pugilism have ... attained greater skill and reputation in attack and defense ... He is a master of the game and has fought as many battles as the redoubtable champion. He exceeds the latter in intellectuality and ability to tell what he feels ... has sufficient education to talk ... on topics suggested by the squared circle ... a reporter visited Mr. Choynski yesterday ... 'How does a man feel ... confronted by a clever adversary?' 'There has been a great deal said about the crowd ... noise, etc., but ... I don't hear much ... after ... salutations to friends ... a man ... doesn't know always what his ... attack and defense will be, but he knows the principles ... his mind is full of them ... waiting for the call of time. How does he feel after he has commenced to fight? ... trying out his man ... or striving to avoid mistakes made in another contest. His mind ... intent on the man he is fighting ... watches every movement ... with catlike intensity ... or get a punch which will end the fight.' 'How do you feel when ... struck the first time?' 'If a boxer is of a hasty temper, it may make him angry. If it hurts, the ... idea is to give back as good as you get. You take the blow ... that is what you are there for, but you want to get even and bend all your energies to making the other fellow know it is not all his way.'

'What mental argument does a fighter use to sustain his courage?' 'None that I know of. He is too busy trying to get at his man to bother about courage. If he lacks pluck, he has no business there, and would not be ... some men have a stage fright on beginning to fight, but this wears off with action ... If he is getting the worst of (it) and cannot land on his man, he is apt to lose courage. But the man ... fights for prize and reputation. He hopes to win not only the purse, but a chance to get ... more good battles ... he devotes his mind ... to punishing his adversary and avoiding punishment in return. If the fighting is very fast, he thinks of his condition, and his mind unconsciously asks how long he can stand up under the hot work.' 'How does it feel to be knocked down?' 'That depends on the force of the blow ... Some times it is all off right there. But my experience has been that the man who is knocked down, unless put out, has no feeling so far as the blow ... He has his eyes on the referee, and ... one idea ... to get on his legs ... and resume fighting before the fatal 10 seconds can be counted ...'

'How does it feel to get a wallop over the heart, on ... the chin, or in the neck?' 'If a fighter is hit in the neck, he may feel the sting of impact. This blow does him little, if any, damage, provided he is in condition. It is not a knockout blow. It merely spurs him to greater exertion. But, if he gets it on the chin good and hard, he has no feeling. He is out and has lost the fight, but he don't know it for some time. A blow over the heart leaves a burning sensation ... If not enough to end the fight, it means a lot to a man who gets it. He has trouble breathing, as well as the hot feeling in the cardiac region. This blow ... is a knockout if delivered with sufficient force. It ... stops a man's breathing and ... his powers of action or resistance.' "

It was announced on the 19th that Joe was hired as boxing instructor for the new athletic club in Chicago. "The America Athletic Association ... will make its debut ... tonight with a big boxing show at its club house on 31st street. The club includes ... many Chicagoans of prominence ... The corps of famous instructors has such men as Choynski ... and instructors ... for fencing, wrestling, billiards and other ... sports. The drawing card ... tonight is a six-round contest between Choynski and Billy Stift. Choynski ... will give his entire time to building up the association. His contract ... allows him to go to other cities to engage in contests ... with the understanding ... he will return immediately ... as boxing instructor ... On the main floor is a gymnasium, with shower bath adjuncts, and a boxing room with padded walls. There are seven bowling alleys ... The boxing shows and other ... entertainment will be given in the immense auditorium on the 2nd floor ... In addition, there are large billiard parlors, a restaurant, buffet ..."[11]

Having just told the *Lowell Sun* he wanted to fight Joe, McCoy posted $5,000 on the 20th to fight either Fitz or Corbett for the championship. "When asked if he would meet Joe at catch weights, the same inducements he offered Corbett and Fitzsimmons, McCoy replied, 'No. I gave Choynski a chance to meet me at ... middleweight ... and he refused. Now I have gone out of my class to look for bigger game ... I see no reason why I should meet him. Perhaps if I cannot get a match with Corbett or Fitz ...'"

A February 11, 20-round fight was supposedly finalized for Choynski with "Tut" Ryan, at the Empire Club in San Francisco. Before leaving Chicago on January 20, he was shown a statement by McCoy, dismissing Joe's challenge, "The Kid" saying Choynski "must be looking for money" and was "mercenary." Joe replied to a reporter, "Mercenary, eh? What are we in the ring business for? I am in it for the money ... What is he in it for? Glory? If that is what he is after I will fight him for glory. I have deposited a forfeit ... I am in earnest when I say I will fight him for nothing."[12] The January 24 *St. Paul Globe* quoted "Parson" Davies: "I ... noticed a picture of Fitzsimmons and Kid McCoy standing at arm's length, in which a phenomenal reach is shown in favor of McCoy ... Choynski outmeasures the Kid in length of extended arms ... Bob Armstrong ... would pick fruit for market out of a tree under which the Kid would starve to death. One might think from the tales of McCoy's reach that he would have to keep his arms bent to avoid scraping his knuckles on the ground, a la chimpanzee." McCoy's reach measured 76", the same as Choynski's.

On the evening of the 23rd, Choynski arrived in San Francisco, going directly to his parents' home at 1209 Golden Gate Avenue. He arrived a day or two early, to take in the state's Golden Jubilee, commemorating the discovery of gold at Coloma 50 years earlier. Joe would again train at the Golden Gate residence. On January 30, he was training at the Olympic Club, while "Tut" Ryan conditioned himself "at a station near the ocean beach." Around this time, the new "Empire Club" came under suspicion, called "the notorious Knickerbocker Club reorganized." It was said, if Joe and "Tut" "would transfer their allegiance to some club in which Mr. Dan Lynch, of Fitzsimmons-Sharkey ... fame has not a finger, their prospects would be brighter. Writers ... in the East are of the opinion this city harbors the blackest gang of crooked-fight manipulators that ever dodged a penitentiary." Due to suspicions of impropriety on the part of the Empire Club, Graney and others advised Joe to withdraw from the match.[13]

On February 4, the Empire Club cancelled the fight card, due to its own dissolution. When Joe received the news, he telegraphed a challenge to McCoy, to fight him in Frisco for $5,000 a side, and wired Tom O'Rourke, "authorizing him ... making the match ..." Joe confirmed on the 5th that he and Davies were again "on the outs" (this time for good) and that he had, under his own steam, clinched a fight with Tom Sharkey. He wrote, to a Chicago friend: "I want nothing easier than my 20 round bout with Sharkey on March 17. The purse is to be divided 75 and 25 ... if I win it will put me on velvet, for there will be a big crowd. Then I will go after those other blowhards. I understand ... Davies is telling that he gave me $100 a week while ... under his management. He never gave me a cent I did not earn and was not entitled to. I made a mistake in having a manager, and hereafter will manage myself. I have gained eight pounds since coming to San Francisco and now weigh 170. I will have to reduce to be in ... shape. I am ... working hard with George Green. Tommy Ryan ... training at San Francisco for his bout with Green, boxes every day with ... Jeffries ..."[14]

The now-infamous National Athletic Club, with John J. Groom and Judson Gibbs at the helm, won the right to host the Choynski-Sharkey fight. This should have been an ominous portent for Joe. Not only had the Sharkey-Fitz fiasco taken place there, but Sharkey and Dan Lynch, his manager, were partners in the club. They had the same interest in the club for the Sharkey-Fitz bout, when they refused to approve any and every referee suggested by the Fitz camp. Articles stipulated that the club would appoint its own referee, in the "event of the inability of the contestants to agree upon the selection of the referee ..." Sharkey and gang therefore, *as* part of the club, got their choice of referee, in this case, the notorious Wyatt Earp.[15] Choynski fought at this venue before, the 20-rounder with Jeffries and the eight round "loss" to Tom, when Joe failed to knock him out, per contract. Perhaps Joe felt the club had reformed. Also, as revealed by the February 8 *San Francisco Call*, there were now only two boxing clubs in the city, "the Olympic 'Amateur' club and the National Professional Club." John Herget was trying to make a comeback with his Occidental Club.

The referee was to be selected 24 hours prior to the bout, or the National would choose the referee – again. Tom was to train at Haggerty's on the ocean beach and Joe, to "do his indoor exercise in the Olympic Club." Joe took morning runs through Golden Gate Park.[16] February 11 *Kansas City Journal*: "Bob Armstrong, the fallen Davies star, is looking for ... Choynski's scalp. The two ... have not been on the best of terms for some time, but while under the wing of the same manager ... were unable to come together. Rumor has it Bob split with Davies even before his fight with Childs ... A well known Chicago sport says: 'I think Armstrong made a wise move when he quit the Parson. The latter kept him around town starving and carrying bundles for the past year, and when he had the chance to make a little money, his manager objected to him risking his reputation. He finally decided to go against the parson's orders and take on Childs. He agreed not to knock out the latter, but Childs crossed him ... and put him to sleep. He has challenged ... Sharkey ... Maher, but would prefer Choynski.' Davies has become tired of managing pugilists ... Choynski has broken away ... again ... Davies ... spent two years working Armstrong to the front ..."

Another paper declared, "Parson Davies and Joe Choynski are no longer friends. In a recent interview in St. Louis, the Parson said: 'Joe Choynski has shut me out of the Ryan match, and I guess I will have to drop him. I have notified Tom O'Rourke to send me back the $1,000 I put up with him as a forfeit for a match between Choynski and Kid McCoy. Choynski will have to back himself in the future. I took charge of him several years ago and paid him $100 a week for 37 weeks to act as Peter Jackson's sparring partner. Jackson taught him all he knows about the scientific end of the game. Now he wants to fight poor old Jackson, who is only a shadow of his former self. This business of managing fighters is not so soft as it looks. They are a tough act to handle, and none of them know what gratitude is. I intend to wash my hands of the whole outfit as soon as I can.' "[17]

Joe wanted to take a bigger cut of his own fights, seeing his prime years slipping away. The end of a good working relationship is unfortunate to see, but often occurs before the end of a fighter's career. Joe learned a lot from "Black Prince Peter," to be sure, but he developed his skills in San Francisco and Australia, as well. Also, a match with "poor old Jackson," who was badly in need of funds, could never happen without his consent. "Choynski is charged with ingratitude, that chief sin of the latter-day pugilist, one which calls down the heartiest disdain by the manliest of men. Davies has stood by many fighters, not only with his money, but with his brains ... and sorry is the lot of the scrapper that has thrown the general manager, for many of the ingrates of the past have begged forgiveness at the Parson's feet. Choynski should quickly make friends with his old, tried and true friend, and if he is at fault he should make the amende honorable, and promise not to offend again, for Davies, and his likes, is not found on the highways, or easily to be secured for business managements."[18]

On February 13, Joe was scheduled to umpire a charity benefit baseball game for Tom Power, a retired professional ball-player from the San Francisco area who had played in the east for the "big league" teams. The game was to take place at Central Park and feature former baseball stars Joe Corbett (younger brother of Jim) and "McGinty" Carroll.[19] Noted boxing man, Jimmy Wakely, wrote: "Fitzsimmons will hold his own for another year ... But beyond that – at the dawning of the 20th century – there is another pugilist ... 'Kid' McCoy ... as yet only ... a 'kid.' 'Kid' McCoy is today the finest pugilist in the ring. He is the most skillful side-stepper, the best general, the gamiest (sic) sport and the best trained ... cool and calm and through the fight maintains this same steadiness of nerve. He fights like Choynski, with the head at one side and the eyes slanting. This gives a fighter a long-distance view ... enables him to take in the entire body of his opponent above the belt. Another advantage ... is the sway it gives the pugilist. He can avoid blows ... maintain his balance and ... deliver a blow after his opponent has ... tried to get at him."

"McCoy began ... in Louisville ... joined the Young Men's Christian Association ... and learned to box. The YMCA ... was too limited, and he transferred his ... membership to other cities ... At present, 'Kid' McCoy could not beat Fitzsimmons. The man does not live ... that could ... But ... is every bit as smart ... as good a general. I might say he is cleverer ... than Fitzsimmons. But ... lacks strength ... isn't old enough ... McCoy will meet ... Maher and Choynski, and from his present form should best both ... And ... well, I am not going to say ... more ... But I guess you know where Jimmy Wakely's money will be placed two years from now. And I think I ... know a prize fighter when I see him, for all the world knows I backed (John L.) Sullivan in the seven biggest battles he ever fought."[20] On February 25, George Green was stopped by Tommy Ryan in the 18th round.[21] Boxing referee and sportsman, "Honest" John Kelly, made a $10,000 offer for a Choynski-McCoy fight in New York. McCoy, returning to St. Louis, Missouri from Hot Springs, Arkansas, where he knocked out Nick Burley in two rounds on March 4, said: "I have $3,000 which says I stand ready to meet any man in the world. Three have accepted my defi: Maher, Choynski and Ruhlin. I ... select Ruhlin ... first ... my brother (Homer) is at Cincinnati ... ready to also make matches with Maher and Choynski ..."[22]

On March 8, sporting editors from San Francisco's "three morning papers,* by ... invitation from the National Club, enjoyed a ... ride to ... Sharkey's ... quarters ... on the ocean beach known as Haggerty's sporting rendezvous.‡ Sharkey ... in a modest way remarked, 'Well boys, I never felt finer ... and if I am not greatly mistaken, I'll make short work of my man ...

There will be no ... room ... this time for an argument about foul fighting, as I will make a clean job of it.' Fifteen minutes (later) Sharkey appeared, dressed in ... fighting clothes and ready to pose before the camera artists ... He looked a perfect Hercules when the huge bathrobe ... was cast aside by ... Tim McGrath." Tom demonstrated punches with Jack Stelzner. They followed with four rounds of heated sparring. Joe Kennedy took a turn for four light rounds. Tom had broken a rib of Kennedy's a few days earlier.

* The *San Francisco Call*, *San Francisco Chronicle* and *San Francisco Examiner*.

‡ Also known as the Golden Gate Villa, owned by Robert D. Haggerty.[23]

Comments were made of Sharkey's power, improvement in footwork, quickness in avoiding blows, and the trademark tattoo on his chest of a

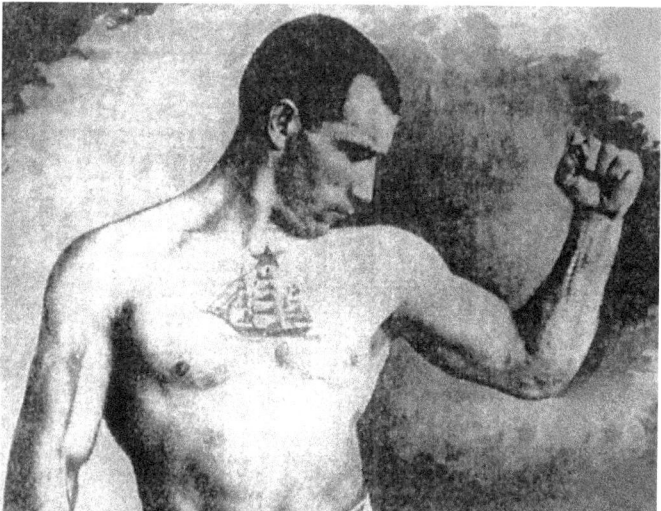 three-masted battleship, on which he served while in the Navy.

"Sharkey does not pretend to be a scientific boxer. When asked why he leaves his face open ... he replied a smash on the nose or jaw does not affect him, and his chin cannot be reached ... protected by mounds of muscle on his shoulders. 'I am always willing to take a punch if I can give one ... a few of my punches will set any man groggy if they land on the right spot.' "[24]

"Sharkey has become quite an expert at ducking ... There is method in his manner of dipping under a blow ... for he straightens up close in to his opponent and tries to send his right home across the shoulders before the inevitable clinch ..." Among the hyperbole and build-up to the fray was a claim that Tom had "perfected a new blow with his right which will knock out anything. Sharkey is muscle bound when he delivers the usual right hand blow, but this new one is at a different range and is said to be very difficult to counter."[25] Despite these claims, there were no new punches – only variations of the four (or five) basic ones – the straight left jab, right cross or straight right, left hook and uppercut.

Sharkey was expected to be as much as 15 to 20 pounds the heavier man. They were to box for 60% of the receipts and "their purse ... divided according to the California method, 75 and 25 per cent. Choynski favored the Eastern method of splitting ... evenly, but Sharkey is so confident ... he insisted winner take all. A compromise was affected ... The men have agreed not to hit in the clinches or breakaways ... a condition Choynski insisted upon ... fouls will be carefully watched. The men will meet at 8 o'clock this evening to select a referee ... The sailor's footwork and general agility have been most favorably commented on ... He is remarkably quick on his feet and has put himself through a ... course ... in dodging, ducking and side-stepping. Sharkey is also the hardest bag-puncher seen in this city.

While training (he) was clever with both hands. He no longer depends alone on his round-arm swings. He leads straight and has a neat way of landing his right on the body and quickly following with a stiff left on the jaw. He has learned to duck left leads for his jaw and has a peculiar way of coming into a clinch with his left shoulder forward."

Syracuse Evening Herald: "If the fight is on the square, as many people, considering Sharkey's reputation, will doubt, the result will be awaited with interest." Another paper likened Joe to a thoroughbred and Tom to a draft horse. It declared them models of both extremes, of the old and new styles. While Tom's build represented the "old days," "short, muscular, herculean in strength," Joe's frame was of the new school, "long, lank, lean, with clean-cut, wiry muscles."[26]

March 11 *San Francisco Call*: "Joe Choynski, otherwise known as 'Easy Going Joe,' will meet the perfect Hercules, Tom Sharkey, this evening in Woodward's Pavilion. When asked how he felt, Choynski, in his mild and unassuming way, replied: 'Never better in my life. If Sharkey whips me I shall have no excuse to offer on ... condition ... All I fear ... is that Sharkey will not fight according to our agreement, which says ... no hitting in the clinches. If he stands off and makes a clean, open fight, I shall be

Joe Choynski

the first to congratulate him if he whips me ...' Last evening Eddie Graney, in behalf of Joe ... met ... Sharkey and the managers of the National Club ...

at 8 o'clock at the Baldwin Hotel, with the object of selecting a referee." Tom asked Graney who his choices for the job were, upon which Eddie reeled off the names Jim McDonald, Hiram Cook, Charley Gagus, Ed Hofman, Phil Wand or J.M. Murphy, the racing judge.

"Graney ... hardly finished naming his men when Sharkey interrupted ... with the statement that his selections were very poor ... would not go with him, etc. 'Who are your men, Tom?' asked Graney. 'Well, they are all good people,' replied Sharkey. 'and you can pick any of them you like ... There's Billy Harrison, a dead honest fellow; Tom Lansing, Spider Kelly, Frank Carr, John Quinn, Jim Quinn and Solly Smith.' Graney objected to every

THOMAS J. SHARKEY.

person named, especially Harrison, who, Graney said, was altogether too good to act as a boxing judge. Several names were mentioned (by Ed), but Sharkey was obdurate. He wanted to go home ... have a good sleep and as a parting salute said he would dream over the matter. 'I will meet you here at 2 o'clock to-morrow and will have another list of names ...' said Sharkey, 'I think we will agree upon some good man; all I want is a fair shake.' Sharkey and ... Tim McGrath made their escape ... Graney, who felt rather put out because a referee was not selected, said he was satisfied Sharkey had not the least intention of selecting any person until to-day. 'The fellow is suspicious,' Graney remarked, 'and I am satisfied he thinks if he had named some man whom I may favor, jobbing would be resorted to. However, we will meet with the bold Sailor to-morrow ... then a referee must be selected ... that's all there is to it.' "

Whether the 2 o'clock meeting came off isn't known; no paper seemed to mention it. No referee had yet been chosen when the men entered the ring. The odds by fight time were even money. The "tale of the tape":

Choynski: Age: 30 years old; (projected) Weight: 168 pounds; Height: 5' 11¾"; Reach: 76"; Length of arm: 31½"; Biceps: 14¾" (The *Examiner* said 15"); Forearm: 11¾" (*Examiner* said 12½"); Wrist: 7¼"; Neck: 15½" (*Examiner* said 17"); Chest contracted: 38"; Chest expanded: 43"; Chest normal: 40½"; Waist: 30" (*Examiner* said 33"); Length of leg: 34"; Thigh: 21½" (*Examiner* said 23"); Calf: 14" (*Examiner* said 14½"); Ankle: 8".

Sharkey: Age: 27 years old; (projected) Weight: 190 pounds; Height: 5' 8½" (The *Examiner* said 5' 8¼"); Reach: 70"; Length of arm: 28½"; Biceps: 15" (*Examiner:* 16½"); Forearm: 12½" (*Examiner:* 13½"); Wrist: 8"; Neck:

18" (*Examiner.* 17"); Chest contracted: 42¾"; Chest expanded: 47½" (*Examiner.* 48"); Chest normal: 44¾"; Waist: 33"; Length of leg: 34¼"; Thigh: 22½" (*Examiner.* 22"); Calf: 16¾" (*Examiner.* 17½"); Ankle: 8¾".[27] (Author: Tom had long legs, relative to his height. This, along with his quick feet, a trait of swarmers, enabled him to close the distance on his foe).

On the night of March 11, a crowd of 7,000 at Woodward's Pavilion witnessed what was more of a brawl than a fight. The weights given were 178 pounds for Sharkey, 168 for Choynski. At 9:30 p.m., Joe left his dressing room to cheers, with Graney, backer Tommy Murphy and Joe Lorson (some said Charley Tasson). Sharkey was greeted by a mixture of cheers and jeers. His superior corner consisted of "Spider" Kelly, Joe Kennedy, Tim McGrath and Joe Goddard. Choynski's legs appeared much weaker and slighter than Tom's. Joe looked as cool and calm "as though their meeting was to be a friendly bout for points ..." while Tom appeared to be very nervous.

Tim McGrath

After the fighters entered the ring, the spectators had to endure nearly a full *hour* of wrangling over a referee. Once again, Sharkey's obstinacy was the primary hold up. *New York Evening Journal*: "He refused to accept any one of nearly a dozen capable men whose names were mentioned. When asked to name somebody himself, he picked out men whose relations with him have been so close that they could not be considered by the other side." "Choynski proposed Hiram Cook, Jim McDonald and Peter Jackson, but Sharkey would have none of them, and suggested Frank Carse or Billy Delaney, neither of whom pleased his opponent. Then Choynski suggested leaving the matter to the newspaper men to decide, but this was not to Sharkey's taste. Finally, Jim Chesley was agreed upon. Just as the impatient crowd was expressing its approval, that gentleman declined to serve, and the trouble commenced all over again. The matter was ultimately settled by the selection of George Green ... Time was called at 10:42 o'clock." "The selection ... gave satisfaction to all hands. Green has had experience in that line, and it was generally believed that he would fill the bill." The following is a blend of several ringside reports and Choynski's memoirs:[28]

Round 1 – Sharkey led with a left, to the head or body. Choynski countered with a vicious left hook that just missed. He forced the "swarming Sailor" to break ground, backing him around the ring. Tom missed a right swing, then fanned the air with another miss. Joe ducked,

413

then planted a sharp left to the jaw, bringing a cheer from the crowd. Both landed a few light punches before the bell. It was a close 1st round, probably even. Joe recalled, years later: "The bell rang – and there began one of the craziest exhibitions ever tolerated in a prize-ring. Talk about your gas-house brawls! Sharkey committed every foul known to mankind."

Round 2 – Choynski smiled on his stool between rounds. Sharkey rushed his opponent and scored a couple of left swings to the head. Joe blocked a left and countered with a hard left, either a jab to the head or uppercut in the stomach. He drove a right over Sharkey's heart. Tom landed a low left, drawing a cry of "foul" from the crowd and a warning from Referee Green. Joe's round. He said: "Round after round ... Sharkey clawed, butted, wrestled, and almost strangled me, and did about everything but bite me. Despite this, that efficient referee – the man who had claimed to be my best friend – let the sailor get away with it. This wasn't a boxing contest. It was more like a cross between a bullfight and jiu-jitsu."

Round 3 – Joe appeared to have the edge. He jabbed Sharkey in the mouth, Tom landing a light left to the body. The "Sailor" missed several wild swings, and Choynski countered to the head and body. He got in one especially hard body blow that Tom must have felt, then warded off a hard shot to the "wind" from the stocky Irishman.

Round 4 – Sharkey planted a powerful left to the neck, but his right was ducked. He crouched and led for the body, but Joe straightened him with a good right uppercut. He cleverly ducked Tom's punches and countered with two smart jabs to the nose. Tom countered a jab with a hard left to the neck, rushing Joe to the ropes and roughing him up. An even frame.

Round 5 – Sharkey bolted from his corner in a crouch, missed his first punch, then landed a hard left swing to the head, rushing Choynski to the ropes. The punch apparently dazed Joe, as he momentarily turned his back. He recovered, sending his foe's head back with a pair of stout left hooks to the jaw. Tom rushed into a clinch, smashing punches to the head and torso, in violation of the rules agreed upon. *San Francisco Call*: "Sharkey rushes ... Choynski ducks low and raises him in the air off his feet in the clinch. Choynski fights back, landing two straight lefts. Sharkey lands two hard ones on the chest and an uppercut on the jaw and Choynski goes down on his knees and rolls over on his back. Pandemonium reigns in the house, and almost everyone is on his feet and yelling. Choynski was up in nine seconds and Sharkey rushes him to the ropes in Joe's corner and knocks him down again. Choynski down again nine seconds, and is up only to go down the 3rd time, unable to withstand the sailor's fierce onslaughts."

"Seconds and sporting men yelling like mad. Cries of *Foul* heard from all parts ... at the way Sharkey is fighting and hitting Joe in the clinches, but the referee paid no attention, except to raise his hand for the fight to go on. Both men swinging both hands and fighting like bulldogs as the round ends

... neither heard the bell and had to be broken from a clinch by their seconds." Most papers said there were *two* knockdowns, not three, adding: "Sharkey struck Joe twice at close quarters and sent him down, and then tried to force him over the ropes, when the referee and a couple of policemen interfered." (Sandusky, Ohio) *Morning Star*: "Both men fought wild and Choynski was all but out when the gong sounded."

Round 6 – Tom repeatedly hit in the clinches; one account said Joe hit back this time. *Kansas City Journal*: "Choynski was game ... after straightening himself up, smashed the sailor in the jaw with his right until the sailor was groggy. Tom lost his head again and repeatedly fouled his opponent, but Referee Green did not interfere." The *Call* again reported a knockdown not seen by other papers, noting: "Both men rush at each other, swinging rights and lefts. Choynski, the cooler of the two and fighting hard, Sharkey backing away. Choynski lands two hard left swings and receives a stiff right on the neck. Both men landing hard in the clinches. Sharkey knocks Choynski down with a right swing on the head and Joe remains on the floor the full nine seconds. Sharkey rushes Joe to the ropes as he arises and hits him fiercely when on the ropes and in the clinches. Everybody standing and yelling 'Foul!' at the referee on account of Sharkey's tactics. Both men very tired but fighting hard as the gong sounds." The *New York Evening World* is the only other paper telling of a knockdown in the round, and it saw Joe floored not once, but twice. "Choynski woke up and punished his man severely. He was not strong enough to put him out, however."

Round 7 – "Choynski put Sharkey on the defensive with a hard left and right on the jaw which dazed the sailor." Both appeared too weak to knock the other out. Tom bulled Joe to the ropes, clinching and roughing, throwing left and right to the body and head. "Little Joe" returned fire to the head, a lot of punishment exchanged. It was clear that Joe was weakening more quickly than Tom, from all the wrestling, infighting and rough tactics. *Kansas City Journal*: "Joe jabbed the sailor time and again without return, but Tom waited until he got him against the ropes and then sent in a wild swing for the body. Choynski went to his knees, more from the force of the rush than from the effects of the blow." Sharkey continued his flagrant fouling, eliciting more excited cries of "Foul!" Green had lost any control he might have had over the brawl. He wasn't even issuing warnings to Tom, much less disqualifying him. Joe did not appear to be vocalizing complaints, perhaps being too busy defending himself. The pair "continued to fight like tigers in a clinch till the bell sounded." Choynski: "Sharkey was a mighty fellow, huge and bullish, and it wasn't long before my strength was ebbing. He had wrestled me until the spectators were yelling that he had won all falls in the category of wrestling."

Round 8 – *Morning Star*: "Choynski was weak and Sharkey rushed him all over the ring, hitting in clinches and any old way regardless of the rules. Joe was floored after a disgraceful foul, but he staggered to his feet and started in again. Sharkey was weak." *Kansas City Journal*: "Sharkey landed a left swing on the neck, but received a nasty crack on the jaw ... Joe jabbed him again and again in the face with his left, but his blows seemed weak. A left upper-swing connected with the sailor's jaw ... Sharkey rushed Choynski through the ropes, falling on the platform himself. The crowd was so thoroughly disgusted ... that the referee sent the men to their corners and declared the fight a draw. Sharkey's attitude as he rushed ... toward Green was so threatening that the police flooded the roped arena and escorted him out of it, much to his chagrin. Indeed, he wept from sheer disappointment."

Call: "Sharkey rushes Choynski across the ring to the ropes in Sharkey's corner and Joe goes clear through ... falls to the floor below, about four feet lower ... directly in front of Captain Lees. The Chief of Police ... raised his finger ... police ... clamber into the ring. The referee yelled 'Draw,' and Sharkey rushed over ... tried to expostulate, but was hustled to his corner by the police. Choynski was lifted back through the ropes by friends and walked to his corner unaided. The house was in a terrible uproar ...'"

Joe, from his memoirs: "As my resistance ebbed, he suddenly saw his chance ... in the 8th. He rushed me to the ropes and ... deliberately hurled me clear out of the ring. I fell in the audience. My head struck a chair. I was dazed. I was so weak from the crash that I had to be helped into the ring. But I wanted to continue. Then, to the amazement of every fair-minded person, the referee swaggered to the center of the ring and shouted: 'Draw! It's a draw!' I protested in vain. But they wouldn't hear me. The brawl was over. I had seen at first-hand a very fair sample of the sailor's ring trickery. There was no just reason for stopping the fight – unless it had been to award the decision to me on a foul – and this was the view of W.W. Naughton ... and others. Naughton wrote: 'There should have been a clean-cut decision. The draw business was raw. Sharkey's work was very rough. He should have lost on a foul – or been hailed a winner!' "

The 20-rounder was halted after only eight, due to the incessant fouling of Sharkey. Among papers reporting the fight, it was nearly unanimous that the "Pier Six Brawler" should have lost on a foul or disqualification. Many said Referee Green was afraid to make such a call, fearing for "his own personal safety, should he declare the battle against the wild sailor." Most felt police interference was the only reason Green felt compelled to make the stoppage. He denied this, saying he was already in the process of halting proceedings when the Chief of Police signaled for it. Green said he made the stoppage as the result of seeing Choynski in a dazed condition, the same reason police had been known to stop fights at that time.

Kansas City Journal: "Choynski clearly outpointed Sharkey in ... every round, and was only worsted when it came to wrestling tactics ... the sailor's favorite method of fighting. He would rush ... and swing his ponderous arms at random, with no seeming object in view. Choynski withstood them fairly well with straight punches in the face. It was apparent to the great majority ... that had the fight been fair on the part of Sharkey, Choynski's superior cleverness would have made him the winner. To-night's disgraceful exhibition by the sailor probably ends his pugilistic career, as far as getting another match in San Francisco ... His unpopularity has increased ever since his fiasco with Fitzsimmons ..." *Atlanta Constitution*: "Choynski showed much cleverer work than the sailor and did the harder and better fighting. Sharkey resorted to his old tactics and foul after foul was claimed, but was not allowed by the referee. Choynski was able to hit the sailor in the face when he pleased, but his blows lacked force."

Call: "George Green distinguished himself last evening ... by proving ... that he either knows not the first thing about the rules of Queensberry or had entered the ring ... with the intention of giving somebody the worst of a hard game." The *Call*, which appeared to favor Sharkey, said it was Tom who had been robbed! Its logic was that Green declared a draw in the 8th because Joe was knocked through the ropes. Green insisted, however, that he did not stop the fight and call a draw for that reason. As to the selection of a referee, it goes without saying that one should have been selected at the time the articles of agreement were signed. The spectators should not have had to endure a delay of over 60 minutes, cooped up in a stifling arena. In that day, however, there was fear of an arbiter being approached with a bribe before a fight, and the more days wherein a referee's identity was known, the greater the chance he might be "paid off."

"Sharkey: 'I have nothing to say. I was robbed. I think I ought to have got the decision as there wasn't any rule that would permit Green to decide as he did. Choynski never phased (sic) me. Why, he couldn't have hurt me if I had my hands down for a week. He went through the ropes this way: I hit him in the shoulder with my left and then put my right on the point of his jaw. My timekeepers counted 10 on him twice – he was dead out. Well, I suppose the only way to fight a fellow in this town is to have a netting around the ring so that in case I hit a man he won't fall out of the ring. I want him to rebound so I can hit him again. To show Choynski I did not want the best of it, I agreed to Green as referee, even though I knew Green had sparred with Choynski every day at the Olympic Club, and that Choynski was in Green's corner when he fought Ryan. I gave ... Alec Greggains as my choice, because he was a square man, but they did not want him. I will never fight in this town again. I have always tried to act right but have always got the worst of it. If I ever do, I will never go into the ring with a California referee." Choynski twice being "dead out" and Green showing favoritism *toward* Joe, was far from reality. Tom later said he blamed his friends for telling him to accept George Green as referee.[29]

Call: "Choynski: 'I never had such a rough fight in all my life ... when I commenced to jab Sharkey on the nose, he commenced his old-time style of rough fighting. Why, he fouled me at least 50 times, hitting in clinches and trying to break my back against the posts. I fight according to Queensberry rules, and if this ... is Queensberry rules as I understand them, then I quit the ring for good. The only injury I received was when he pitched me out of the ring by sheer force." Jim Jeffries told the *Call*, "If Choynski had fought me in the way he did Sharkey, I would have licked him in two rounds. In our fight he kept away, but in to-night's go he went right at Sharkey. I was surprised that Greaney (sic) let him do that ... Sharkey fought foul all the way through. Had Choynski kept away he would have done better. At one time he had Sharkey at a standstill. There is no one that I would rather go against than Sharkey, and as soon as my fight with Jackson is over, I am willing ... and I think I can lick him."

The *New York Evening Journal* spoke of Choynski's "nasty, cutting prods" (jabs), and his "maddening method of cutting his opponent with those incisive, smarting 'chops' of his. For a time, in the 7th round, Sharkey wobbled ... Choynski had undergone so much punishment ... he could not ... finish him." The *Journal* said Sharkey not only hit in the clinches, but sometimes after the bell. Joe: "Green should have decided ... in my favor, on account of Sharkey's repeated fouling ... When he pushed me out of the ring ... I struck my head on a chair first, then the floor. I climbed back into the ring, willing to continue ... because I felt I was yet able to land a punch that would knock him out. In the 5th round he landed several solid punches on my jaw, after the gong ... I offered no complaint. If Referee Green and the spectators saw fit to allow him to use such tactics I was willing, as I felt ... I could defeat him even at that game. The wrestling and football tactics he employed were more damaging by far than his blows. Green could have awarded me the battle many times in the earlier rounds on fouls, and I have no doubt he would have done so had I claimed them. I did not want to win on a foul, as I felt assured I could knock him out."

Brooklyn Eagle: "Ever since Tom Sharkey wrestled and roughed ... Jim Corbett ... in June, 1896, he has been a discordant element in pugilism and has done more to bring glove contests into disrepute ... than all the antagonists ... Not a single contest ... has resulted in a manner satisfactory to the public ... last night he capped ... his career ... by the most disgraceful exhibition ever seen in a prize ring in this city. Although he agreed not to strike in the clinches he repeatedly used his elbows and head, pushing, wrestling and butting Choynski against the ropes. Choynski ... did not claim a foul, but continued to jab and swing on the sailor's broad features. In the 5th round Sharkey rushed Choynski to the ropes and wrestled him to the floor and under the ropes. Choynski's seconds claimed a foul, which was not allowed by ... Green, who seemed as badly rattled as Sharkey. In the 7th, Choynski lashed out right and left ... on Sharkey's jaw and face until the latter was groggy. In the 8th ... Sharkey ... rushing and wrestling ... forced his opponent against the ropes and swung his ponderous arms like flails, until Choynski went down ... He came up and jabbed Sharkey in the face ... Tom fell back under his terrific onslaught ... Suddenly ... lowered his head and came at Choynski like a mad bull, throwing him ... through the ropes and on to the seats below. The referee ... at the direction of the police, called the fight a draw ... Choynski was bruised by his fall, but not injured by the sailor's fist. Sharkey's face was badly bruised and swollen ..."

After the fight, many papers around the country were calling San Francisco "a town where it is impossible to pull off a pugilistic contest on the square." In truth, Tom, like (heavyweight) Jack Dempsey, Rocky Marciano and a few others, was of the "rough and tumble" type; too many rules got in their way. He was more suited to London Prize Ring rules or modern Mixed Martial Arts than Queensberry rules boxing. March 13 *Salt Lake Herald*: "Sharkey comes in for a great deal of ... criticism ... even many of his staunchest backers brand him as one of the foulest fighters ... ever ... Sharkey has improved wonderfully in his boxing ... but loses all his acquired science as soon as ... given any severe punishment ... becomes like an enraged animal ... loses all control ... Sharkey ... flatly denies any foul tactics ... 'I was robbed of the purse and the honor that would go with the victory, had the decision ... been a just one. I could not have won unless I knocked him completely out. He hit me in the clinches and no one took any notice ... but they watched every blow I struck.' Choynski showed few signs of punishment when seen this morning, but ... expressed himself in very forcible terms ... criticized Green severely for calling the mill a draw."

March 13 *Nebraska State Journal*: "Last night's battle ... is the talk of the town ... Accusations of foul play, robbery ... are applied to both contestants, and ... George Green, comes in for a great deal of censure ... the majority of sporting men seem to agree ... he erred in declaring the fight a draw after having fouls committed by Sharkey. Green says: 'I think my decision was ... just ... Any fair-minded man would have decided the contest a draw. In the last round Sharkey rushed Choynski to the ropes and both men clinched. Sharkey kept punching and when one of his hands became free, he shoved it under Choynski's chin and pushed him through the ropes.' " Green acknowledged that Tom punched while in a clinch, an obvious violation of the rules. "If I had been positive Sharkey committed the foul intentionally I would have decided ... in Choynski's favor. I waited until Choynski was lifted back into the ring. I saw in an instant he was dazed, and it would have been an injustice to make him continue ..." The illogic here is twofold. Green should have declared Tom a loser on a foul for striking in a clinch. If he felt he needed to stop the fight because Joe was rendered, by fair tactics, too dazed to continue, then George should have declared Sharkey the winner. Either George was too intimidated by Tom to call against him, or was trying to save bets on both sides. In either case, he was wrong.

Joe (1927): "Those who regard Sharkey as a rough-and-tumble fighter without cunning have another guess coming. Sailor Tom was about as canny a bruiser as ever rubbed rosin on his soles. He was as cunning as Kid McCoy. I had seen Sharkey almost murder Jim Corbett with his rough-house stuff. He had Corbett beat to a frazzle when the referee stopped the fight. Jim was so weary, he had to sit in his corner a long time before he could start for his dressing room. I had also seen Sharkey knocked out in eight rounds by Bob Fitzsimmons, only to have the decision awarded to Sharkey on a foul by the illustrious referee, Wyatt Earp. The only foul thing ... was the decision. Fitz afterward got his revenge by beating the sailor almost to death in two rounds. But trusting Joe thought nothing could be handed to him in his home town. George Green, known to the sporting world as Young Corbett, was to have been my chief second, and when he did not show up on the night of the fight I thought it rather strange: the referee was to be picked at the ringside. I will connect these two facts in a moment. Later I learned that Tom remarked when he saw me: 'He looks like a sheep,' to which 'Spider' Kelly, his chief second, replied, 'and he kicks like a mule.' " Joe's memory was suffering, as that exchange occurred before the first Choynski-Sharkey bout, in 1896. He also contradicts himself, saying years earlier, that Fitz fouled Sharkey.

"Sharkey ... his affair with Fitzsimmons and tactics with Corbett had left a bad taste in the mouth, and there were more hoots than cheers ... A long wrangle ensued over the selection of referee. Sharkey pretended to be terribly suspicious and uneasy ... not a single suggestion suited Sharkey. Finally, some one in the gallery ... yelled, 'How about Wyatt Earp?' and hardly had the hisses and groans subsided when another wag called out: 'I suggest Sharkey's brother.' This caused a laugh, but the wrangle went on. The crowd began to whistle 'Home, Sweet Home.' An hour passed and Eddie Graney, my chief second, proposed that the newspaper men name the arbiter. This suggestion was refused by Sharkey also. All the while I was sitting in my corner wondering just what made Sharkey so suspicious. Suddenly some one yelled, 'How about George Green?' and instantly it was announced that Sharkey had accepted Green. I smelled a rat, but being weary from the wrangle and confident I could knock Sharkey out, I offered no objection. The truth of the matter, as I see it clearly after these years, is that I gave away too much weight to an extraordinarily powerful man who used ... rough-house tactics ... I was overconfident to the point of recklessness in match-making. It was folly enough to concede so much weight to giants who fought fairly, but ... the mauling, heeling, gouging, butting and ... slamming around of a Sharkey ... was too much."

As one paper put it: "If London Prize Ring rules ... wrestling, butting and every other variety of rough tactics prevailed in the modern arena, one

Thomas Sharkey, ex-marine, would certainly have precedence above all competitors. But as such rules are stowed away ... and as boxing is now supposed to consist of fair stand-up contests with large, fat gloves, it is difficult to understand what excuse exists for giving this Sharkey repeated chances to perform ... Such men ... do more to pile ill-repute on the boxing game than a dozen fast, clean, showy boxers can take off in 10 years." It was noted that Tom fouled Peter Maher in 1897 so often that police felt it necessary to intervene.[30] At the time of this, their 2nd fight, Tom was roughly in his prime, while Joe was slightly past his peak. One factor that should be considered in any "all-time," head-to-head comparison, is the probability that Tom would at times foul out against Choynski, as some, like "The Foul Pole," Andrew Golota, were wont to do.

Tommy Ryan, who returned to Syracuse, New York on the 12th, following the Green fight, declared: "In San Francisco ... I was a 'sucker' ... one minute after I landed ... The climate isn't conducive to work, and the natives prefer 'skinning' someone to earning their living by the sweat of their brow. That is, the sporting classes do. The minute a prize fighter with any reputation and a little money strikes town, they all try to see how much of his money they can get ... I took Henry Baker, who was training me, to a Turkish bath after my fight ... We had a bottle of beer apiece, and when I went to pay my bill, it was a few cents more than $20. That's because I was 'Tommy' Ryan. Even the 'Chinks' in Chinatown were onto the racket ... I went ... to buy some silks and things for my wife, they ... tacked on an extra price to everything ... an Eastern man has to knock out his opponent ... to get a decision. The whole trouble lays (sic) in the amount of betting ... done. The best club out there is the Olympic. I think a fight before that club is on the level ... but the others I haven't any faith in at all." "Ryan is of the opinion that if either ... got the worst of last night's fight ... Sharkey was the man. 'I scarcely believe that he fouled Choynski as they say. If he had, George Green, who is his friend and trained him for his fight with me, would certainly have given Choynski ... the decision. Besides ... Choynski is a California man and a great favorite out there.' "[31]

As a final note on the debacle, the March 17 *Syracuse Standard* quoted the *Boston Globe*: "Many of the sports who have known the inside of pugilistic affairs at San Francisco believe it was not ignorance on the part of Green, but somebody's money had to be saved. His statement that he could not judge whether Sharkey intentionally fouled Choynski is a lame excuse. If he considers that Sharkey fouled Choynski, no matter whether intentionally, he should have given the bout to Choynski."

Around the 20th, several papers reported that Joe was diagnosed with a case of blood poisoning. "The trouble has brought with it attendant infections, and Joe's heart is now in pretty bad shape. During the last few days he suffered from severe palpitations. His physician, Dr. Galway, also finds an enlargement of the cardiac organ." *San Francisco Call:* "Racked with pain and tormented by a dread illness, Joe ... is ... waiting with much anxiety for the next few days to pass. However he came by it, it is certain that Joe is now in great physical agony, and that the poison has coursed through his veins for some time. About a week before the Ryan-Green fight, while boxing with Green, Choynski tore a patch of skin off his left arm just above the elbow. They boxed for some time after the accident, clinching, wrestling and fighting at close quarters. George Green was at this time afflicted with a crop of boils, and it is thought that Choynski's open skin wound came in contact with Green's boils, and the result was blood poisoning. Joe noticed the scratch on his arm and its evident unwillingness to heal, some time prior to the Sharkey battle. At times his left arm would grow stiff, and massage was necessary to lubricate it for rapid use in bag punching. It did not pain him then, but it was a source of annoyance."

"Last Monday the left arm grew stiff, and on Tuesday night, in the presence of Ed Graney, Choynski stripped to show his bosom friend the sore on his arm. Then for the first time Joe noticed a long, black stripe on the inside of the upper left arm. Joe began to work his arm in and out, when suddenly he straightened up and fainted dead away. Graney did not lose a moment, but telephoned for Dr. Galway, who has been in attendance ever since. Not only is the left arm swollen, but the right shoulder is ... Poultices were applied to the sore places and the puss (sic) drawn to the surface. It was necessary to lance the arm and shoulder last night. The affection of the heart will demand a long rest, and the roots of the poison will have to be eradicated before Choynski can do anything physically violent. His physician thinks it a miracle that he could have fought at all with his heart in such a condition." Joe's alleged friend, Green, had caused him double grief; passing on a poor decision and an infection.

The *Brooklyn Eagle* said Joe would need six months of absolute rest, in order to "regain any sort of physical trim. It began to tell on Choynski about three weeks just previous to his last battle. He said nothing about his ailment until after the contest, when he was so weak he could hardly stand." One paper called it pyemia, a form of septicemia in which pus-producing microorganisms are present in the blood and often cause abscesses under the skin. March 22 *Philadelphia Inquirer:* "Joe Choynski will never enter the ring again; in fact, he is ... not out of danger. If he recovers he will never be able to train again. That is the ultimatum of his physician. He has undergone an operation ... it is believed ... will save his life. Choynski was suffering from blood disorder before he met Sharkey recently, but he kept the matter quiet. His physician says his condition is due to the many times he has trained for fights in his career ..." The March 23 *Omaha World Herald* opined, "Mr. Choynski should hasten to associate with Messrs. Corbett, Fitzsimmons and McCoy. It may be that the disease which has forced his retirement ... would produce tetanus in those other orators."[32]

A story on the 29th had champion Fitzsimmons saying: "Nothing on earth will induce me to enter the ring with 'Kid' McCoy until he has defeated either Peter Maher or Joe Choynski. These two ... I consider ... the only heavyweights who have any claims to the ... championship ..." April 1 *Kansas City Journal*: "Joe Choynski, in a letter from San Francisco to a friend, says the reports regarding his condition from blood poisoning have been greatly exaggerated, and he expects to make a match with Kid McCoy. Choynski hints he may join forces with Parson Davies again ... in his letter is the flat statement that Sharkey is Dan Lynch's side partner ... in the confusion preceding ... the decision, 'Spider' Kelly ... was in communication with Lynch, who occupied a box at the ringside." Where Joe received this alleged information wasn't divulged. April 16 *Police Gazette*: "John J. Quinn has received a letter from Parson Davies ... stating the report that Joe Choynski is suffering from blood poisoning to a serious degree is false" and that "a syndicate of western sporting men" offered of a $10,000 purse for a finish fight between McCoy and either Choynski or Peter Maher, "at some place west of the Missouri River in the month of July."[33]

In a piece containing as much misinformation as truth, the April 14 *Grand Rapids Herald* wrote: "Jim Corbett and Joe Choynski have been bad friends for a long while. They often abused each other in the public press. They were chums when ... boys. They went to the same school together, belonged to the same athletic club, attended the same theater, ate at the same restaurant and were never out of each other's company. They were closer than brothers. Their staunch friendship ... talked about by ... friends and relatives. While they loved ... books, they loved athletics better. Their spare hours were passed at the Olympic ... and other clubs ... One day, they fought on a barge at San Francisco and ... have not been good friends since. One day last week, Choynski and ... Graney, were seated in a restaurant in San Francisco when Corbett passed by. 'Will you make up with him?' quizzed Eddie. The question came so suddenly Joe said yes before he scarcely realized what he was doing. A second later, Graney was on the street. 'Ho, Jim; I want to see you,' he shouted. 'Joe wants to see you.' 'And I want to see Joe,' cut in Jim. Joe walked to the entrance ... they shook hands, and the bonds of friendship were rejoined. The big fellow sat down and they talked like two school boys who had not seen each other in a dog's age. Graney left them there. He was the happiest man in San Francisco ... He had accomplished what he said he would – reconcile Jim and Joe." While there was likely much truth to the reunion, the reporter did not have a firm grasp on the Corbett-Choynski connection!

Joe returned to Chicago on April 10. On the 20th, he went "to West Baden, Ind., to rest up at the springs as a result of his recent illness." He likely returned to see Louise before convalescing at West Baden Springs.

On the 26th, Joe's long-time friend, Al T. Shrosbree (sometimes, Shrosbee and Schrosbree) was shot and killed by a "cashier of a concert hall," the result of "a brawl in which several men were engaged." The locale was somewhere in Chicago, one source saying the Orpheus Saloon. Al and his brother, George E. Shrosbree, were noted boxers and seconds. Al was in Choynski's corner for the 1895 Dan Creedon tilt. Two unnamed Shrosbrees and their father, Colonel Shrosbree, attended Joe in the October, 1899 bout with "Kid" McCoy and the May, 1900 Tom Sharkey fracas.[34]

By May 1, Joe had recovered. "Friends and admirers of Joseph Bartlett

George E. Shrosbree

Choynski, Coeur de Leon of ring gladiators, as game, willing, honest and capable a boxer as ever pulled on a pair of stuffed gloves, will be glad to learn he has rounded to ... better than ever and in hot-foot after the much advertised Colonel Smooth McCoy. Choynski's name should ever stand a text for all aspirants to biffing fame ... welcome contrast to the blatant, mouthing Corbett-Sharkey-Maher-McCoy crew ... Most of Choynski's challenges have been flung to the four winds regardless of weight or reputation. Game to the marrow, he would take it as a personal insult for anyone to suggest a fake to him ... by sheer force of his iron will

and stout heart he has many a time turned the tide of defeat to ... victory ... when his esquires were deliberating on the advisability of elevating the sponge. If Joe and McCoy meet, I would be forced to hang to the Hebrew's coat-tails, but I may change my mind after I learn of the outcome of the Kid's battle with Gus Ruhlin, the German Cyclops ..."[35] McCoy won a handy, 20 round decision over Ruhlin on May 20.

"The ... Kline Cinematographe ... finest moving picture machine in America" was showing around the country, such films as "the Warship Maine and the Cuban War," as well as fight films of Corbett, McCoy, Choynski and others.[36] Joe sent a telegram from Chicago on May 14 to his Philadelphia, Pennsylvania friend, H. Walter Schlichter, nicknamed "Slick": "Slick, Match me with Goddard (in) two weeks if he is willing." He sent another letter on July 9, the day after Maher knocked Goddard out in eight rounds in New York: "Friend Slick: Can you arrange for Goddard and I any date – in Phila. Thirty per cent gross – he may go on now that Maher has defeated him. If you can arrange, send me ticket and take out of my receipts – 5606 Drexel Ave." The latter was his Chicago residence.[37]

A word on Walter Schlichter. Born in 1866, he was a noted referee and long the sports editor of the *Philadelphia Item*. Around this time, he was also promoter of Philadelphia's Arena Athletic Club. In 1902, Schlichter would organize the famous all-black baseball team, the Philadelphia Giants, with assistance from Sol White and Harry Smith. He also became President of the National Association of Colored Baseball Clubs of the United States and Cuba. Sol was an ex-Negro League player and Smith, sports editor of the African-American paper, the *Philadelphia Tribune*. Walter was first to fund the Philadelphia Giants, and in 1906 he financed White's important work, "The History of Colored Baseball."

Walter Schlichter

It was announced June 26 that Tom O'Rourke had matched Joe and "Kid" McCoy to battle the next night at his Lenox Athletic Club in New York, for 25 rounds and a purse of $10,000. It was to be followed by a 25-rounder on July 5 between Peter Maher and Joe Goddard. The latter match would occur there on July 8, Goddard stopping Maher in eight frames. The former, however, didn't happen as scheduled. On the back of the contract, signed June 7, 1898 by Homer and Norman Selby and Choynski, Joe penned: "Tom O'Rourke played one dirty trick: had me call it off to make McCoy fight before his club in N.Y. – McCoy called it off. I did so and O'Rourke immediately matched McCoy and Sharkey and I held the hat?"[38] Choynski inscribed the handwritten note some time after the contract signing, as later events showed. The animosity building between O'Rourke and Joe would escalate over the next few years.

At Dave Holland's Café in New York, McCoy met Fitzsimmons one night, apparently by accident. The conversation turned to a potential middleweight title fight between the two. June 9 *Lowell Sun*: McCoy: "I have a match on with Choynski for June 27, but owing to an accident I cannot fight on that date. I was thrown from my bike and strained a tendon in my right leg. Until that gets well I cannot even talk fight, but when it does you can bet that you will see the color of my money." A St. Paul paper said his hands were still sore and damaged from the Ruhlin bout. "McCoy will leave here in a few days for a month to be spent in the Adirondack mountains in the neighborhood of Lake Saranac." There was an attempt to move the fight to the Hawthorne A.C. in Buffalo, New York for August 27, a venue run by McCoy's brother, Homer, but referred to as "McCoy's own athletic club ..." Joe and "The Kid" supposedly signed a new agreement on June 10, for a 20 round fight in Buffalo for a $7,500 purse.[39]

Regarding the change in venue, McCoy gave the lame excuse that he was "convinced there is more money to be made in the latter place than ... in New York City." Given the comparative populations of the two cities and the popularity of boxing in The Big Apple, the statement held little water. "The Kid" commented on O'Rourke's threat to prevent the fight in Buffalo, saying his people were comfortable with the legal advice they received in their favor.[40] On June 25, Joe told O'Rourke: "I hereby promise, according to my first agreement entered into with you to box ... McCoy only before the Lenox Athletic Club ... as soon as ... McCoy is willing to meet ... I did sign to meet McCoy at Buffalo, but as I have been formed (sic) on reliable authority that he is an interested party in said club ... I have decided not to meet him before that organization. I prefer to box before a neutral club like the Lenox Athletic Club ..." This proved the kiss of death to the match, as McCoy instead signed to box Jim Corbett at the Buffalo club. That bout, scheduled for September 10 was later cancelled, owing to the tragic murder-suicide of Jim's parents in San Francisco.

Corbett's family had a history of mental illness, and his father, Patrick, had been acting erratically for some time. Around 5:00 a.m. on the morning of August 16, Patrick rose from bed, dressed in his "Sunday best," took a hidden revolver out of a dresser drawer, and shot his sleeping wife, Catherine, twice in the head. He then placed the gun in his own mouth and pulled the trigger. Jim had sent a telegram from Houston, Texas on June 27, saying he would fight Choynski at the Lenox club in New York, in place of McCoy. Jim was likely bluffing, and the match never came off. McCoy and Corbett finally duked it out on August 30, 1900, the latter winning on a KO5. It was thought by many that "The Kid" took a dive.[41] As late as July 10, a McCoy bout was mentioned, as though still scheduled. *Call*: "The ... McCoy-Choynski fight at Buffalo is to be photographed on an Edison moving picture machine, and will be exhibited ... at eight different cities, including New York, Boston, New Orleans, San Francisco and Chicago." Once again, Joe may have lost an opportunity to be filmed!

Joe composed a veritable thesis paper for the June 26 *Philadelphia Inquirer*: "Joe ... has a method of training ... that differs from that employed by most boxers. Choynski contends his system ... includes many advantages not possessed by others. He ... never begins ... a rigorous course of training for two or three months before a contest. He has always been in condition since he adopted boxing as a business, and has never been untrained, except on rare occasions, when sickness or injuries gained the upper hand. He holds that boxers should be ready to fight on short notice ... in a week he could work himself in shape to put up a creditable contest against any man. 'There is an erroneous idea held by athletes ... regard(ing) what is technically termed *wind*. They think ... a man must ... do a great deal of running to get more wind ... a man has just as much wind the day he starts to train as ... the day before he fights ... after being out of condition, as it is called, for some time, he will feel as though he could run a mile at top speed. He trys (sic) it, and soon has a burning sensation in his chest. Well, to remove that burning sensation is all training will do for the *wind*, but as to getting more wind ... a man might as well try to add to his stature. A man's lungs are the same size after as before he trains, and will only hold a certain amount of air ..."

"In regard to using dumbbells and Indian clubs and the jumping rope, I do not believe in it ... even too much bag punching should be eschewed. Such things as weights and wrist machines never find a place in my training quarters. All these ... give a ... big bunch of muscle, but do not help ... in any way. A man who trains gradually and does not do much extra work prior to a contest will not have the strong appearance of a man that does, but he will be just as good and as hard, and his muscles will respond more quickly to his efforts. Weight is a great factor in a fight, and I hold that a man should fight in the class in which nature places him, and not try to take off 10 or 20 pounds to get in a lighter division. That is what kills a man quicker than anything else. One should be able to fight as a top notcher until he is 40 years of age ... I never pay attention to weight and do not know at what figure I would tip the beam. I have not stepped on a scale in five months." Despite being considered in his day a good trainer, a fair amount of what Joe (and others) believed has been disproved today, such as the inability to increase lung capacity, and the use of weights making a fighter muscle-bound. Weight training with proper stretching is not a bad thing.

The July 14 *Call* said a Choynski-Greggains match was set for August at Woodward's Pavilion, under the auspices of the new Western Boxing Club. The bout never came off. Greggains was a useful middleweight and light-heavyweight. He stood 5' 10½", but his reach was only about 71". Alec became a leading boxing promoter in Frisco, credited with originating cards that featured only four-round bouts. The July 25 *Galveston Daily News* reported a Charles Eisenfelder arranging a fight for Joe and Jim Hall, to take place in that city on August 8. Eisenfelder said Joe wanted to train in Houston for the bout, which also failed to occur, as "District Attorney Gillespie has instructed the sheriff not to permit it." Choynski refereed a wild, six round brawl at Hanlon's handball court in Chicago on July 15, between 128-pound Joe Handler and Perry Queenan. Queenan weakened toward the finish, and Joe rendered his decision to Handler.[42]

A paper noted on July 28 that "Joe Choyinski (sic) is an applicant for the position of trainer on the Cincinnati police force." This would have moved Joe and Louise to her home town years sooner than they did, but no further mention was found. Joe was in New York City in early August, looking for a fight. "From the *World of Sport* of August 3. 'I notice that T.F. O'Rourke is attempting to belittle my bout with Corbett. O'Rourke does this because I refused to box Choynski at the Lenox Club, and I want the public to know why ... O'Rourke coolly proposed to me to put up a fake bout, something I have never done and never will do. Charles (Kid) McCoy.' " It is interesting that McCoy would comment this way, as he would be accused of throwing his bout *with* Corbett. "Choynski yesterday handed the following into this office: Chicago, August 1, 1898. 'Editor, *World of Sport* – I notice a signed statement of Kid McCoy's in Monday's *Enquirer* to the effect that the reason he refused to meet me in the Lenox Club, New York, was that he was asked to fake. I have fought for 15 years, and always honestly, and McCoy lies if he says we were to fake, as it takes two to make a fake, and I was not approached by anyone. I stand ready to take either of the men's places in Buffalo at a moment's notice, should one of them fluke.' "[43]

In late August, Joe was offered a 20 round fight with Sharkey at O'Rourke's Lenox Club. Tom was said to have given consent, but "Joe ... seen in New York last Saturday (August 20) ... declares he will not enter the ring until cold weather sets in. There is some talk of ... boxing ... Sharkey in October." Sam Austin gave his pre-fight analysis of the Corbett-McCoy match. He was editor and writer for the *National Police Gazette*, and a famous referee. " 'Corbett has not the stamina to last long, and ... of this ... McCoy intends to avail himself ...' I asked Mr. Austin whether it was true ... that McCoy is a disciple of the Corbett school of sparring. 'No ... Corbett is undoubtedly the cleverer boxer, but his style is very different than McCoy's. Corbett ... stands in the regulation position so often seen in pictures of him and generally affected by boxers for many years. McCoy, on the other hand ... leans more toward his adversary and holds his arms very far apart, so that to a novice or uncritical observer it would appear he had no guard at all, but it is a splendid pose ... and less tiring ... McCoy is, first of all, a defensive fighter, and has evolved the safest and easiest method of warding off every possible blow ... whether a cross counter with the right for his jaw, a straight jab ... for the face, or ... a punch on the solar plexus."[44]

Joe finally landed his long-sought-after 3rd bout with Joe Goddard. The match was held on the night of September 12, in the Arena Athletic Club on North Broad Street in Philadelphia. The "Barrier Champion" had his camp at Phoenixville (Pennsylvania), while Choynski had "training quarters fixed up for him at the Quaker City Athletic Club ... after his morning's run and plunge ... working at the ... club every afternoon." Goddard looked good in a six round No-Decision bout with Bob Armstrong August 29 in Philly, and was bragging about his fighting prowess, looking ahead to another fight with Peter Maher. Although nearing the end of his effective fighting days, Goddard was active and could not be called rusty.[45]

"The two upper galleries were packed ... All the boxes were filled. A large number of returning soldiers were ... scattered through the crowd. Choynski appeared first, looking a bit light. Goddard followed 15 seconds later, looking in good condition." *Philadelphia Inquirer.* "In comparison with Goddard, Choynski looked like a middle-weight, but ... demonstrated that the battle does not always go to the big and bulky." Choynski was said to be about 15 pounds lighter than Big Joe. A melding of four contemporary fight reports follows, and Choynski's memoirs from 31 years later:[46]

Round 1 – There was little fighting, as "Little Joe" gauged his man. They exchanged rights to the face and Goddard landed a light left to the chest. Joe: "Goddard was the aggressor the 1st round. I guess he thought he'd get me quick. He tore in like a mad bull. I side-stepped and, as he stepped past, nailed him with a stiff right. All through the 1st session I fought Goddard with cool savagery. I knew I'd get a square deal tonight, but I meant to fight cleverly and slash this giant to mince-meat. We finished ... in a burst of speed and I had Goddard spinning. He went puffing to his corner."

Round 2 – Choynski sent sharp left jabs in the face of Goddard, landing frequently. The latter swung wildly, unable to land much. The few big Joe did get home were reduced in impact, his retreating foe "riding" with them. The "Chrysanthemum" ducked one roundhouse right in particular, that might have decapitated him. "I came out fighting in the 2nd ... It wasn't long before Goddard was floundering around the ring. Rights and lefts were bewildering him. It would be hard for me to name my best fight, but this certainly was one of them, if not *the* one. Just before the gong ... I plastered Goddard with a series of haymakers ... the big Australian reeled and began spitting out teeth. The pace was fast and killing, but I shoved Goddard against the ring-posts and bombarded him with rights. Then, remembering what he had done to me in Australia, I said: 'It's different tonight, eh? You'll not crack my spine over the ropes, as you did before!' "

Round 3 – Goddard came out with a charge, swinging wild lefts and rights with impressive force. He tried to land an illegal right back-fist (backhand punch), eliciting hisses from the throng. The Barrier fighter landed a right to the side of Joe's head that caused his hair to fly up like a "fright wig." When the bruiser began to tire, Choynski resumed his snapping jab to the face. Goddard was temporarily punched out, barely able to raise his arms at round's end. The side-stepping, evasive tactics and formidable straight left of "Little Joe" were carrying the day. Joe: "Goddard took a fearful beating in the 3rd round. The crowd was on edge."

Round 4 – *Trenton Times*: "When he found Goddard exhausted after a wild rush, he refrained from putting it to him then and there, rather waiting until Goddard recovered a bit ... Goddard ... made a rushing fight of it in the last three rounds, but Choynski was eternally pushing disagreeable lefts into his face and bringing hard rights across." Choynski: "I never let up. I knew I couldn't afford to take a chance with this man-killer. And here it gave me satisfaction to think I was capable of it. I knew I was a better man than Goddard. It took him 13 rounds to whip Joe McAuliffe, the Mission Giant. I beat McAuliffe by a knockout in four rounds."

Round 5 – Goddard's stamina was rapidly being depleted, and he "resorted to hugging tactics." Joe: "How Goddard weathered the 4th and 5th I'll never know. I hit him so hard and so often my arms ached. My own body showed the impact. I shivered from the force of my own blows. Goddard was staggering around under a veritable hail of looping swings and stinging uppercuts. Of course, I will have to credit Goddard with gameness. No man could take this pasting unless he was game to the core. All I had against Goddard was his unfairness and unorthodox ring tactics in the Antipodes. I simply wanted to show him that an American fighter could fight fairly and still chop his huge carcass to ribbons."

Round 6 – *Duluth News-Tribune*: "Choynski was calm and banged Goddard hard on the jaw, sending him to his knees." He regained his feet, but "Choynski made a chopping block of (him) ... several times it looked as though Goddard would not be able to stay the full six rounds." *Philadelphia Inquirer*: "As soon as the men shook hands ... Goddard started to rush ... and landed with both right and left. As Choynski ducked away from one of Goddard's swings, the latter made a slight slip, and was caught by one of Choynski's lefts. Goddard stayed on the floor about five minutes (sic) (five seconds). Regaining his feet, it was evident he was in trouble, for Choynski hit him almost at will. He fought back as hard as he knew how, landing one swing on ... Choynski's jaw that came within an ace of the danger mark ... biff, bang, boom on both sides, but ... more intelligent direction behind the Californian's punches. He landed uppercuts and swings galore ... when the gong sounded Goddard had very little to spare. It was Choynski's fight." As later reports revealed, "Little Joe" sustained an injury to his right hand in the 2nd round. Choynski: "He lurched around blindly, clinching and holding, scarcely able to raise his arms. His eyes were battered shut; his face was a sight. I finished him off, receiving a tremendous ovation."

Duluth News-Tribune: "When the gong sounded, a spectator jumped into the ring and attempted to hit Goddard, but he was quickly thrown from the platform." Choynski: "I went to his corner, to see if I could do anything for him. But Goddard was in a surly temper and I started to leave. As I turned away, Dinah Sullivan, a Philadelphia boxer, climbed up to congratulate me. Goddard heard Sullivan's words and became furious. He leaned over and kicked Sullivan in the face ... Sullivan jumped into the ring and took a healthy swing at Goddard. Quick as a flash they were at it, slugging away ... locked arms and crashed to the floor ... rolled over and over. It took several policemen to get the enraged Goddard out of the ring. But my own fury had cooled. I ... was satisfied. That Australian score was balanced at last." While officially a No Decision, as were all fights in Philly then that didn't end in a knockout, Choynski was a clear and easy winner.

The September 13 *Washington Times* felt that, in the final three rounds, Choynski "seemed merciful, as few spectators did not depart believing he could have put Goddard out." Joe told a different story, though, in his memoirs: "There was one defeat – two ... in fact – which I had the supreme satisfaction of wiping out. I refer to the case of Joe Goddard. I got a raw deal in far-off Australia. But America is fairer, in many cases, and jiu-jitsu and kow-towing referees were barred when I got my final crack at (him) ... there was quite another story to tell the natives when we clashed on the soil of the good old USA! The Philadelphia Winter Circus was the scene ... For the first time in my ring career I felt like saying sharp things to an opponent. As we came out for instructions, I said: 'Well, Mr. Barrier Champion, we fight tonight under Queensberry rules. Jiu-jitsu is barred; I'm going to trim you so thoroughly your own manager won't recognize the remains.' What a terrible beating I gave Goddard that night!"

Goddard would have a more fateful run-in with a policeman on July 28, 1902. While involved with violent elements of the Republican Party, he was at a polling place (either in Pennsauken, New Jersey or Philadelphia, Pennsylvania), and became mixed up in an election riot. Joe got into an altercation with a black constable named Robert Washington. The "Barrier Champion" came at Washington with a baseball bat, and the officer shot him in the head with his revolver, in self-defense. The bullet penetrated Joe's skull and lodged in his brain. The iron-tough Aussie was transported to nearby Cooper Hospital. He lingered for six months, at one point allegedly stating, "I wasn't shot, I caught the ball and threw it away." Goddard died in Camden, New Jersey on January 21, 1903. It is said his body was later stolen by grave robbers, who sold the cadaver to a hospital or medical school. A sad end for a great and tenacious fighter.

Around the beginning of October, Choynski was appointed boxing instructor for the American Athletic Association of Chicago. Next to nothing is mentioned of his doings there, nor when he left their employ, though it likely wasn't a lengthy stay. When Joe next acted in the capacity of athletic or boxing instructor, it would be for the Illinois Athletic Club, which didn't open until 1907. "Joe Choynski ... has been asked to meet Gus Ruhlin before a new Cincinnati athletic club in five weeks." On the 24th, Joe sent a Western Union telegram from Hyde Park, Illinois, a neighborhood on the South Side of Chicago, to his friend, Walter "Slick" Schlichter. "I ... hear Ruhlin has agreed to meet me (at the) Lenox."[47]

Gus Ruhlin was born in Canton, Ohio on January 8, 1872, of Germanic descent. He fought out of Akron, and at 6' 2" was 195-to-205 pounds, much larger than Joe. The "Akron Giant" was said to have earned his nickname while playing football in that city, where his size and power impressed.[48] To this point in his career, Ruhlin had mixed results among top-flight heavyweights. In 1895, he lost to the vastly more experienced Peter Maher and "Yank" Kenny. The next two years, however, saw Gus win 10 and 20-rounders over Steve O'Donnell, a rugged 20 round draw with 22-year-old Jim Jeffries (Gus was three years his senior), and wins over lesser lights. In May, 1898, Ruhlin lost a 20 round verdict to the much lighter and speedier "Kid" McCoy, and was surprisingly knocked out in one round by Tom Sharkey. He came back with an eight round stoppage of Jim "Jack" McCormick and a 22-round halting of the humongous Ed "The Human Freight Car" Dunkhorst, the Primo Carnera of his day.

Ruhlin's last contest was a six round No Decision with Goddard.

Gus Ruhlin

October 29 *Pawtucket Times*: The Ohioan "monkeyed with Joe … knocking the big Australian down five times in the 6th round …" Gus was managed by old Sullivan pilot, Billy Madden, and trained by Madden and Henry "Pop" Blanken, the proprietor of "the Six Mile House," on Bayshore Boulevard in San Bruno. Gus had a stiff left jab, a crushing right and, at 79 inches, the wingspan of a pterodactyl. A bit awkward and erratic, he was still a dangerous boxer-puncher. Ruhlin stopped Goddard in five frames in 1899, following with a brutal 20 round draw with Peter Maher. Only six weeks later, though, Gus lost a 20-round decision to Joe Kennedy. In 1900, he knocked out a fading Tom Sharkey in 15 rounds, repeating in 11 heats, in 1902. In August, 1900, "The Akron Giant" gave Fitzsimmons a stiff argument before falling in six, a fight that saw each bloodied and floored. The talented, "on the bubble" behemoth, would now gauge his ability against the veteran Choynski.

While the Ruhlin "go" was initially set for New York's Lenox Club, the men to battle for 25 rounds and 50 per cent of the gross receipts, Choynski demanded 60 per cent, with the result that the fight there was cancelled. The venue was switched to the Arena Athletic Club in Philadelphia when Joe's buddy, H.W. Schlichter, offered the same 50 per cent of the receipts, but for a shorter, six round fight. On the morning of the fight, November 4, Joe told a *Sandusky Star* reporter that he had broken his hand during the 1st round of the Goddard fight, thus fighting in extreme pain every time he punched with it. A statement he gave after his next bout indicated it was the right. He told the *Philadelphia Inquirer* he was "likely to become a citizen of this city. He likes the way strangers are treated here, and … the training facilities are superior to any in the country. He has sent on to Chicago for his wife, and after she arrives they will go to housekeeping."[49]

Joe and Gus clashed on the evening of November 4. Just after they were introduced, Joe Goddard climbed into the ring, waving a wad of bills at the spectators, saying he was ready and willing to back himself for any amount against the winner. Old Joe just got a few hoots. Ruhlin was said to have towered over Choynski by some 2½ inches, outweighing his man by from 20 to 40 pounds.[50] Thirty to 35 would have been more accurate. The following report combines three contemporary accounts:[51]

Round 1 – Accounts disagreed on the action. *Brooklyn Daily Eagle*: "Ruhlin ... forced the fighting from beginning to end (of the fight), Choynski sprinting repeatedly around the ring in efforts to get out of his way. Toward the close of the 1st ... Joe steadied himself for the first and only time and landed several hard rights and lefts on Ruhlin's face. One of these blows broke Choynski's right forefinger." *Philadelphia Evening Bulletin*: "Ruhlin ... fought so hard the first two rounds that his strength deserted him, and ... he could not deliver somnific blows, although he was readily awarded the decision. The 1st round ... in which Joe hurt his hand, was fast and interesting ... productive of some fast work, but few blows were landed, the two men jabbing alternately." *Chicago Tribune*: "Choynski used right hand hooks to good advantage in the 1st ... meeting every rush of Ruhlin's with stiff blows." It said the fracture to Joe's hand occurred in the 2nd frame.

Round 2 – "The 2nd was lively ... but Choynski suddenly ceased fighting and began running away from his giant opponent. At the end of the round, Choynski complained that his right was broken, and at the conclusion of the contest a doctor found that the Californian had sustained a bad fracture." "In the early part of the 2nd round, Choynski fell through the ropes and landed on his head, while evading Ruhlin." "Ruhlin ... forced matters ... then was witnessed the best three-minute round ever seen in this city from heavy-weights. Gus repeatedly landed his left on Joe's face and neck, dazing him, but in the middle of the round Choynski put three lefts in Ruhlin's face in rapid succession. The last 60 seconds ... found the men tired, the giant ... too ... exhausted to place his opponent hors de combat."

Rounds 3 through 6 – "The Ohio man forced Joe all about ... the next three rounds and Choynski was shaky at the termination of each, falling ... several times to evade ... rushes. Ruhlin fouled a number of times in the clinches ... apparently due to the heat of the encounter. Both ... eased up in the final round, which was uneventful." "At the end of the 4th ... the bell must have sounded like church music to Choynski ... The last three rounds consisted of straight lefts with an occasional right swing, Ruhlin landing twice to Joe's once." *Brooklyn Daily Eagle*: "Choynski narrowly escaped being put to sleep several times ... apparently saved by the bell. The bout ... was one of the fastest seen here in a long time." *Chicago Daily News*: "Joe's hands were in bad shape ... His foot work saved him." The *Philadelphia*

Evening Bulletin gave Joe less credit, saying: "Ruhlin had an advantage of 20 pounds in weight, as well as nearly three inches in height. Choynski, however, was equal to the Akron (sic) in reach and ring generalship, but even in the latter Choynski did not show his usual skill. He would allow Ruhlin to continually jab him and ... not even attempt to side step ..." *New York Journal*: "Ruhlin punished the Californian severely. Choynski did a great deal of hugging and running away. Ruhlin was hurt very little, although at times there was some lively work at close range." It was evident that the fracture in Joe's right mitt impaired his performance a great deal. It is commendable that he finished, as some would have quit.

The *Herald Star (Steubenville, Ohio)* said "the bout was limited to six rounds and declared a draw." There actually were no decisions on points allowed by law in Pennsylvania at the time. The official decision was "No Decision," although Gus appeared to garner the majority of newspaper verdicts given. November 4 *Denver Post*: "There must certainly have been something wrong with the great California light-heavyweight ... the showing Ruhlin made in his last three fights ... showed no form which would leave anyone to believe him a dangerous factor ... against a man of Choynski's caliber. While ... the decision was not given against the Californian he was ... bested from all accounts. In the 1st ... Choynski broke the forefinger of his right hand ... at the beginning of the 2nd ... he fell off the stage through the ropes, landing on his head. Could it have been that these accidents were the cause of his poor showing ...?" (Author: ... Duh!)

November 8 *Denver Post*: "The surprise ... was the poor showing ... by Joe Choynski ... Choynski is ... such a consistent performer that his friends ... looked for the cause ... The ... letter received from him ... may explain ... 'Chicago, Nov. 6, 1898, Friend Otto: Just returned from Philadelphia, where I met Ruhlin ... I gave him a tin ear in the 1st ... had him going in the 2nd, but my hand, which I badly broke when I met Goddard, went back on me and I was afraid to use it, so I kept away as much as consistent. I will get him later for 20 rounds and ... surely put him among the has-beens. So cheer up!' Choynski will probably arrive in Denver in a week or so on his way to California, and efforts will be made to have him meet Mexican Peter before the new athletic club in this city. Otto C. Floto."

Floto was a prominent sportswriter for the *Denver Post*, and a major boxing and sports figure. Ruhlin, in truth, should have taken no more credit in "beating" Choynski than Joe would have, had he been given a newspaper verdict over a similarly handicapped and diminished Gus. A few days after their bout, the drums were already beating for a rematch. The *Sandusky Star* reported on the 11th that the Sandusky Athletic Club had them matched to fight at the Nielsen Opera House on December 5. This paper carried one of the dissenting views of the six-rounder, stating, "Ruhlin and Choynski recently fought a draw in Philadelphia which proved a surprise in more ways than one. Some papers gave Ruhlin the credit for having the best of the bout, but the *Enquirer* takes the opposite view." The *Star* may have been referring to the *Philadelphia Inquirer*. The great shame is, these two, formidable contemporaries were destined never to cross swords again.

In mid-November: "Joe ... who is to meet Ruhlin ... at the opera house in this city (Sandusky) early next month, had a funny experience at Philadelphia, while taking his daily run in the park. Several cyclers riding along the river drive recognized him and at once started to pedal a pace. Joe is somewhat of a sprinter, and, as the cyclers were not the fastest in the business, a funny race was the result. This bunch of two runners and three cyclers attracted so much attention that very soon, a big string of cyclers were following the pacemakers, and the crowd became so large that Harry Marks, Choynski's trainer, led him to one of the by-paths and the jog was finished there." Marks was a useful lightweight, but this is the only known occasion where he trained Joe. It was announced the week of November 14 that Joe had been offered employment by Philadelphia's Arena Athletic Club.[52] The exact nature of the job wasn't revealed, nor the reason he didn't accept, although it must have been as instructor or trainer.

The November 17 *Oakland Tribune* reported that the Choynski-Ruhlin rematch was "practically" set for the Lenox club in New York, the date revised from December 5 to the 26th. December 1 *Sandusky Star:* "Joe Choynski and Bob Fitzsimmons met by chance recently in one of the down-town stores at Chicago. They stood for a minute looking at each other and turned away, neither showing any signs of recognition. These men have been sore at each other since their meeting several years ago, which terminated in a draw after six rounds had been fought. Fitz's record on his lithographs that he knocked out Choynski in four rounds, does not tend to make Joe feel more amicable toward the champion."

Around the end of November, Joe had his problematic hand x-rayed. A Syracuse paper wrote, "Joe Choynski had the Roentgen rays flashed upon his bad right hand at Chicago last week. The boxer has been troubled with the injured member ... ever since he met Joe Goddard ... at Philadelphia. He smashed the knuckle of his right index finger at that time but thought that, like most injuries received in glove contests, the injured bone would harden with a little rest. He thought his hand was 'right' when he boxed Ruhlin recently, but found out differently when he tried to hit with it. The negative proof of the exposure showed a hollow triangle in the joint almost as large as a nickel. The boxer was informed that nothing could be done for him and now he expects to do 'gym' work and to callous the sore spot, so that the thick cuticle will protect it."[53] As often occurs with fighters who generate punching power belying their size, Joe damaged his hands, which were smaller than most heavyweights'. The impact was spread out over less surface area, imparting greater shock to the bones and supporting tissues.

In need of a payday, Joe ignored doctors' advice. On the 7th: "Joe ... has reconsidered ... not to box ... it is almost certain he will meet ... Ed Dunkhorst or Tom 'Stockings' Conroy ..."[54] It was Dunkhorst. Nicknamed "The Human Freight Car" because of his size, Ed was born January 1, 1877 in Syracuse, New York. By adulthood, he stood 6' 3" or 6' 3½" and

weighed at least 205 pounds. Dunkhorst often tipped the scales at 250, up to 305 pounds, though his best weight was about 230. Ed was not highly skilled, but had a good punch and could absorb great punishment. His strength and avoirdupois gave him good infighting ability. He had just fought a ND6 in Philadelphia with Peter Maher. The latter floored him in round five with

Ed Dunkhorst and Jim Jeffries, circa 1903

one of his best rights, but Ed was saved by the bell and survived.

Dunkhorst had lost a KOby22 to Ruhlin on September 19. His next fight, he had a W20 over C.C. Smith, then D10 with Bob Armstrong, and wins over "Stockings" Conroy (W10, 1897) and Armstrong (W10, 1899), drawing with Jim Hall (D15, 1897), Jack McCormick (D6, 1899) and Jack Stelzner (D20, 1899). In his career, Dunk was only stopped four times. Those who turned the trick were Ruhlin, Joe Butler (KOby6, 1899), Fitzsimmons (KOby2, 1900) and Charley Miller (KOby3, 1911), when Ed was nearly 35 and a decade rusty. The Fitz fight marked the greatest weight disparity in a bout (90 pounds) between two name heavies. While the knockout is a tribute to Bob's punching power, Ed was far overweight at 260 pounds. Dunk was disqualified in 7 against Maher in 1899, for repeated failure to break clean from clinches, having taken a beating.

Joe took on the gargantuan Ed Dunkhorst at Tattersall's in Chicago on the night of December 19. It was part of an eight-bout boxing carnival held that evening under the auspices of the Fort Dearborn Athletic Club. Sources generally agreed that Dunkhorst weighed 230 pounds, while Joe was only 160 or 162. The referee was Malachy Hogan. The following blends multiple contemporary reports. The only round-by-round description was the December 25, 1898 *Syracuse Standard*, quoting Chicago's *World of Sport*.[55]

Round 1 – "Choynski darted nimbly around the ring with his elephantine adversary in hot pursuit. Several times Dunkhorst succeeded in cornering his elusive opponent, who managed ... to slip out of danger's way on each occasion, finding time during the chase to jab a vicious left to the giant's eye, which did not improve the appearance of that organ."

Round 2 – "The 2nd round was almost a repetition of the 1st ..."

Round 3 – "A hot interchange ... followed. In a clinch, Dunkhorst fairly carried his light opponent to the ropes and seemed intent upon breaking the latter's back in the wrestling that ensued."

Round 4 – "Dunkhorst landed a right swing on the head that staggered Joe for an instant, but a moment later Choynski hooked the jaw sharply with his left and crossed his right on the big man's neck, neatly blocking all returns. Just before the gong rang, Choynski jabbed his left to the face and closing in, put a stiff right over Dunkhorst's heart."

Round 5 – "Found the Syracuse mastodon adopting a new method of attack. He took a crouching position and swung his right to the body, Choynski responding with the inevitable jab ... then the giant waxed wroth (author: became angry) ... and another foot race took place, Joe as usual proving the fleeter of the two. In the sharp rally, Choynski landed a hard uppercut on the chin and Dunkhorst crossed the right on head. Choynski put two stiff left jabs on the face and sent a stinging left hook on Dunkhorst's jaw, slipping to the floor from the recoil of his own blow."

Round 6 – "Dunkhorst sailed in savagely ... In the mixup, Choynski crossed his left to the jaw and Dunkhorst staggered. A moment later Choynski's left slid to the body and the huge carcass resounded as though he had hit a drum. But the big fellow ... continued his rushing tactics ..."

It appears Joe had the best of the fight, although one report, Ed's hometown December 20 *Syracuse Standard*, said: "The fight was not finished until 12:30 ... (a.m.). Dunkhorst clearly outpointed Choynski, but ... Hogan gave Choynski the decision. (He) took no chances of mixing ... but ran away after every lead. Dunkhorst was Joe's equal at every stage of the game, and only in the last round did Choynski fight ... Dunkhorst staggered Joe time and time again with left jabs, and once in the 3rd round sent him to the floor." Another paper said Joe fell by the impetus of his own missed punch. Other accounts used phrases like, "Choynski won in a walk." *San Francisco Call*: "Choynski ... was able to land pretty much as he liked, although the big man came back now and then with some heavy counters. It was practically impossible for a man of Choynski's size to knock out a giant like

Dunkhorst, and all that was left ... was to pepper him at long range. The decision was easily Choynski's." *Chicago Daily News*: "Not the old Joe who had something for the best of them, but the present one with a bad hand, pumped round the ring with ... Dunkhorst, a 21-year-old boy who has not yet learned to close his glove when he hits. Choynski won on points ..."

Joe (1927): "Dunkhorst was so big they had to reinforce supports under the ring when he performed ... a Chicago paper: 'Choynski ... looked like ... Gulliver against a Lilliputian. The mountain of flesh soon proved he was not as slow as appearances would indicate, and several times caught ... the elusive Joe ...' I did stay on my bicycle in the 1st round, in ... fear that Dunkhorst might step on me, but after that I unlimbered my guns and fired plenty of heavy shot. It was just like hitting a heavy bag. Sometimes it seemed my fists sunk several inches into Dunkhorst's body. He took a lacing ... but was on his feet at the close. The decision went to me."

December 25 *Syracuse Standard*: "For a man of his immense bulk, (Ed) is extremely fast, although his movements appeared slow when compared with those of the lithe-limbed Joseph." Ed left Chicago on the 20th, along with his manager, Tommy Dixon of Rochester, New York, who owned a boxing club in Syracuse. The train stopped over for a couple of hours in Buffalo, New York on the night of the 21st. While in the "Bison City," the pair spent most of their time in McIndoo's Saloon, where a *Times* reporter interviewed them. Ed felt the decision should have been a draw, while Dixon "had no fault to find with the decision. He ... was pleased with his man's work ..." "Dixon said it was the only (verdict) that could have been made. 'It was a fairly close thing, but I am satisfied Choynski outpointed Ed. We would have won ... if he had gone after Joe the way I told him to, instead of standing off, sparring ... It looks to me as if Choynski is not as good as ... some time ago.' "[56] *Chicago Record*: "Although Dunkhorst lost the decision ... he proved a revelation to Chicagoans. He moved ... with surprising agility, and, although ... sluggish and (lacking) the polish of a successful boxer, this may come later." Ed had significant experience, at least 15 pro fights against some top names, prior to the bout.

On December 29 it was announced that Joe had postponed the Ruhlin rematch indefinitely. He wired Tom O'Rourke, saying "he would be unable to fulfill his engagement owing to illness ... reports ... say he is suffering ... acute blood poisoning in the right hand and arm ... sports around town ... said Choynski ... never had any intentions of fighting ..." More than one paper, though, stated that Joe's physicians "hope to ward off serious results" from the blood poisoning. The bout was ultimately cancelled.[57]

Round Seventeen

The Real McCoy & Other Nabobs
(January 1899 – December 1899)

Gus Ruhlin's manager said Joe only requested a postponement until January 31. He had apparently agreed to that date, but eventually called the fight off, further details being sketchy. Madden intimated that Joe was afraid of his protégé, but one paper came quickly to his defense: "Billy Madden only made himself ridiculous by hints that Joe was afraid. Choynski ... has gone into scores of fights where he scarcely had a chance, just to prove his gameness." The *Lowell Sun* said Joe was already scheduled to fight Charley Lawler, in Louisville, Kentucky on January 9 and Jim Hall, at Galveston, Texas on the 16th.[1] He was still on a run of ailments, however. January 8 *San Francisco Chronicle*: "Joe Choynski may not be seen in the ring again. In addition to ... blood poisoning, he has had several misfortunes of late. A few days ago he sprained his ankle and nearly snapped a tendon in his knee in a fall that will lay him up for a month, at least."

In Galveston, on the night of the 12th, "Joe ... arrived ... from Chicago. He was tired out ... having been on the road since Tuesday, and retired early to enjoy a good night's rest. He is stopping at the Tremont House (a famous Galveston Hotel still in business). He is here on a pleasure and business trip of a few days and will probably visit other cities in the state before returning east. For the few minutes he was in the hands of his friends and a coterie of Galveston's sporting fraternity, everyone wanted to know his opinion of the Sharkey-McCoy fight. Choynski did ... consume many minutes in declaring it was Sharkey's fight ... He introduced a new slang phrase to his Galveston audience: 'McCoy would not have a look in with Sharkey.' He said in Chicago he was laughed at for arguing that the 'Kid' would meet his fate before the 'sailor.' 'They said I was prejudiced ... but ... I have seen both men and I have backed my judgment.' "[2]

The Sharkey-McCoy fight occurred on January 10. After being floored three times in the opening round by McCoy's corkscrew punches, the heavier Sharkey came back and wore down "The Kid," flattening him in the 10th frame with a resounding left hook. Referee Tim Hurst counted "The Corkscrew" out. In 1940, on the occasion of McCoy's death by suicide, Tom claimed that the latter had come into the ring with his gloves on, and the Sharkey contingent "found almost half a ton of plaster along with the heavy bandages" hidden within. He added: "McCoy was probably the hardest hitter the fight game ever knew, outside of James J. Jeffries."[3]

Joe was the center of attention within the hotel rotunda, but excused himself and "sought the quietude of his apartments on the 2nd floor." The January 13 *Newark Advocate* said Joe would "fight Jim Hall at the opera house ... Jan. 19, under the auspices of the Galveston Athletic Club ... Hall has been in training over a month down the island ..." On the 18th, Sheriff Thomas notified the club that the fight would not be allowed to take place. Two days later, the state's new Governor, Joseph Sayers, reinforced the statement, saying "the law that prevented Dan Stuart from bringing Corbett and Fitzsimmons together in this city in 1895 would be enforced." At first, the Galveston A.C. said they would proceed with the fight, expecting to circumvent the law by permitting only regular members of the club into the arena. Sayers had different ideas, sending a squad of Texas Rangers, led by Captain McDonald, to Galveston, "with instructions to stop the fight at all hazards." This they did, armed to the teeth and causing a packed house of ticket-holders to leave the opera house in disgust. January 21 *Galveston Daily News*: "Instead of boxing, the two men gave an exhibition of bag punching which the audience ... regarded as a farce."[4]

On January 24, 1899, Joe's father died of cancer at age 64. "Isidor N. Choynski ... died ... at his residence, 1209 Golden Gate Avenue ... funeral services to-morrow at 10 o'clock, at his late residence ... Interment ... by 11:30 o'clock train from 3rd and Townsend streets." I.N. was buried on the 26th in the "Ashim-Choynski Plot," of what is now Hills of Eternity Memorial Park, Colma, California.[5] The *San Francisco Call* published an article on the 28th, "Choynski's Message On A Bed Of Death, The Old Editor's Remarkable Farewell To Life. Isidor N. Choynski, the aged and eccentric, although unusually able, man whose life ended last Tuesday, dies as he lived – at war with his environment. For many years he criticized life and all life means, and when the end came, he unsparingly criticized death ... through his newspaper, *Public Opinion* he expressed his thoughts ... when he ... realized that death was upon him, he determined that his paper should die with him, and ... he would send ... his last message."

"The old man tossed on his bed of fatal illness ... A few days before the end ... finished his editorial and ... it was published in the concluding issue of *Public Opinion*. This remarkable message of a dead hand ... 'The last lines, for print, which we wrote upon this earth ... On Friday morning last, it was just 6 o'clock as we opened our eyes, there stood before us in the open doorway a tall, gray-bearded man, the very picture of Father Time, and he held a huge black sign in his hand, reaching from top to bottom of the door, upon which was written in bold, white type, German script, *Marked for death*. It was a fine greeting for a pleasant morning; but we opine that the Germans should not have been so cruel, and not have shown themselves so inhuman. We saw all the doctors the evening before, and why not have given us a chance to put our place in order? It is a cruel, wicked world; we had our struggle. Good-by.' " A poignant parting shot at the Grim Reaper, though Joe's père seems to have mellowed in his final hours. Joe wrote (1927) that he was "saddened by the news of the death of my father ... a Master Mason ... at one time Grand President of ... B'nai and B'rith."

Joe and Louise arrived in San Francisco on January 30, too late for Isidor's funeral. Various clubs were negotiating for a Choynski-McCoy fight at a local venue. McCoy was expected to arrive on the 31st. Joe told a *Call* scribe he was disgusted with the fight in Galveston being prevented, adding that "the Texas managers look upon bull fighting as clean sport, but pugilism they contend to be the most barbarous of all pastimes." "Eddie Graney will manage the affairs of Choynski during his stay in this city." Joe told another paper, "although some of the 'wise crowd' are yelling that I look like a ghost, I would like to show the sporting public that I am still good for many a hard fight. I have placed myself in the hands of the Summerfield combination, who will make all matches for me in the future. Yes, I have agreed to fight Kid McCoy in Chicago under the auspices of the Fort Dearborn Athletic club during the month of April."[6]

It was announced on February 9 that William Brady, Jim Jeffries' manager, had accepted a fight for "The Kid," with Choynski. Brady wired from "Mojave" that McCoy agreed to battle Joe "any time after March 20. He says he would rather fight Choynski than Sharkey, as he thinks Joe the better man ..." In light of Joe's recent health and the fact that Tom was in his prime, it is more likely that McCoy was choosing who he felt was the easier prospect, while throwing ballyhoo into the match. Representatives for the men signed articles on the 16th, for a March 24 fight under the aegis of Frisco's National A.C. McCoy arrived from Los Angeles with his wife on February 17 and checked in at the Occidental Hotel. That night, the couple attended the "Six-Day Bicycle Race" at Mechanics' Pavilion, where "The Kid" was scheduled to officiate the next evening as the starter.[7]

At Woodward's Pavilion on March 4, a bout between Frank Erne and Dal Hawkins took place. *San Francisco Call*: "Choynski will referee ... and a better selection could not be made." *Brooklyn Eagle*: "The appearance of Joe ... as referee was hailed with boisterous enthusiasm." Erne was an all-time lightweight and Hawkins, a fine performer noted as champion of the Pacific coast, and for a potent left hook. In the opening frame, Hawkins floored Frank for an eight count with one of these hooks. Erne evaded Hawkins' power shots thereafter. In round 7, Erne moved inside, landing a left-right combination that knocked Dal unconscious for several minutes.[8]

The March 14 *Call* reported McCoy "domiciled at Henry Leonhardt's emporium of sport, commonly known as the Casino, in Golden Gate Park. Leonhardt is a great admirer of his charge, who, he contends, was ... named 'Kid' because of his ... gentlemanly disposition. McCoy is visited daily by dozens of admirers ... Those who have seen McCoy punch the bag ... say it is worth an admission fee to any one who has a fancy for the sport." The Casino was located near the beach. The next day's *Call* quoted Ed Graney: "Why, I can't see how McCoy can best Joe. I know McCoy is faster ... but he cannot land on him as easily as he landed on Sharkey. Joe is as clever as the best of them in blocking and ducking swift blows, and when he lands ... something must hit the floor. Choynski, unlike the general run of pugilists, has never indulged in liquors ... as a consequence he can boast of a sound and healthy constitution, notwithstanding his 10 years' experience as a ring general. McCoy cannot stand heavy punishment. His armor is too light to resist heavy shot. He relies on fast traveling as a means of avoiding injury, but, although he escaped the ... shots ... aimed ... by the sailor, nearly all of which fell short ... you can rest assured Joe will aim straight and land when the clever 'Kid' least expects to receive a broadside." While the National club hosted the bout, there was a stipulation this time, that the referee would be chosen 48 hours before the fight. The articles of agreement called for no hitting in the clinches, which favored "The Kid."

The *Call*, on the 18th: "Some authorities ... contend Choynski has grown too old in the game ... (He) looks in condition ... to go 20 rounds with Fitzsimmons or any ... heavy-weight who carries a chip on his shoulder, and ... will give a big surprise to his prospective opponent if the least opening is offered ... Choynski is daily visited by numerous friends at the Ingleside House, where he is ... hard at work." The March 19 *San Francisco Chronicle* noted that, probably for the first time in his ring career, Joe would have the weight advantage over an opponent. "Nearly always has he been compelled to concede ... 10 to 50 pounds in order to get on a match ... the issue ... seems to be whether Choynski can make his advantage in weight tell in time to wear down McCoy ... sporting people generally consider this will be the cleverest exhibition of scientific boxing San Francisco has seen ..."

Homer Selby, McCoy's brother and assistant, noted that Jack Stelzner was boxing with "The Kid" and helping him prepare. Homer said his brother was looking "100% better" than during training for the Sharkey loss.[9] The March 22 *Chicago Tribune* noted that, while Joe was clever like his opponent, he was "not as lively on his feet ..." "The Kid" and Jim Corbett were perhaps the two best big boxers of the day, in the capacity to "stick and move," defend and counterpunch. McCoy, though weighing only about 160 pounds, was a potent puncher. The "corkscrew twist" he gave his jabs, hooks and crosses added serious impact to them.

The roads around McCoy's camp were damp and muddy, so "The Kid" forewent his usual 10 mile sprint on the 21st. "After dinner McCoy ... Jack Stelzner, and several friends, went out on the lawn and spent half an hour shooting at coins with small parlor rifles. McCoy proved quite as handy at this pastime as ... with the mittens. He hit several dimes square in the center and sent fragments of two or three half-dollar pieces ... skyward ... He is a wonderfully clever bag-puncher ... when he goes at the leathern sphere he makes it do everything but sing. After tossing the bag ... five or 10 minutes the 'Kid' ... sparred ... Stelzner and ... Frank Purcell. As a defensive boxer McCoy probably has no peer. He glides in and out of mix-ups, parrying blows with right and left and landing ... at the same time. Stelzner says McCoy hits harder and is harder to hit than any of the top-notch heavy-weights, and Jack has boxed nearly all of them ..." McCoy said, "while Choynski is a clever, hard-hitting boxer," he felt confident of defeating him. Of the loss to Tom: "I was winning nicely when he punched me low. The foul weakened me and ... lost me the battle."[10] If McCoy was fouled by a low blow from the sailor, current papers didn't seem to note it.

"Kid" McCoy, 1897

Homer Selby and Ed Graney, representing McCoy and Joe, met directors of the National A.C. on March 22 at the Palace Hotel, to select a referee. Several names were suggested, with neither party in agreement. Finally, someone suggested John L. Sullivan, and Selby and Graney immediately assented. Sullivan was selected more for his name than anything else. He was staying in Stockton, California at the time and notifications were sent. John was not heard from. By the 22nd, Joe had laid off training, to marshal his strength. He "walked in from Ingleside" and visited the family home at 1209 Golden Gate Avenue. Several days of heavy rains had prevented the boxers from much outdoor exercise.[11]

The March 24 *Sandusky Star* called Choynski "As game a man as ever stripped for the ring, extraordinarily clever and a tremendously hard hitter," while noting his flaw as, "a tendency to lose his head at critical moments ... to 'walk all over himself at times.' He and McCoy met in a 4-round bout several years ago, but McCoy had a lame foot and police were alert to stop the bout the instant either landed a hard punch ..." So highly thought of was McCoy and so sure were many that Joe had "slipped," most boxers and managers polled favored "The Kid."[12] Joe had been fighting since 1884, mostly with much heavier rivals, and was showing signs of decline.

The scheduled 20-rounder was held that evening at Mechanics' Pavilion. Joe was accompanied by Graney, Charley Tilson, Tommy Murphy "and the younger brother of the fighter." This was evidently the only time in which Edwin Choynski was in Joe's corner. "Choynski smiled graciously to his friends. McCoy followed, clothed in a dark sweater. When McCoy dipped through the ropes he shook hands with Choynski ... with him were Jack Stelzner, Frank Purcell and Homer Selby." "Choynski carried the box of rosin across to McCoy and sprinkled some on the floor for his adversary." Regarding a referee, "it was necessary to make a new selection and big Jim Kennedy, manager of the late six-day bicycle contest was chosen. This also caused unfavorable comment, being considered a point in favor of McCoy, though, as a matter of fact, (Jim) has long been a friend of Choynski's. Yet Kennedy was the only man available." Kennedy was also manager of the 20th Century Athletic Club in New York City. "Billy Jordan ... introduced Choynski as the popular San Francisco heavyweight and McCoy as the coming heavy (sic) champion of the world. Choynski's legs were bare to the thigh. McCoy wore loose knee pants of light material, such as sprinters wear. At 10 o'clock ... the men ... shed their sweaters. McCoy had a small American flag for a belt. Choynski had black trunks and a small silk handkerchief wound around his waist." A Houston paper said Joe wore a red sweater. The weights were about 168 pounds for Choynski, 160 for McCoy.[13] A blend of contemporary reports follows.[14]

Round 1 – There was lively sparring, each cleverly evading punches. McCoy showed superior footwork. The Hoosier ducked a left hook and countered with a hard right to the midsection, late in the frame.

Round 2 – Choynski missed a straight left to the head and ducked a vicious left swing. McCoy jabbed left to the stomach, then to the face, without a return. There was little footwork, and both were cautious.

Round 3 – They came out smiling. McCoy landed a jab to the face and escaped a return. Joe blocked a left for the head and countered hard with right and left to the body. He blocked a McCoy left for the wind. The Indiana thin man scored lightly to the head, and blocked a left to the body. Joe rushed him to the ropes, and threw a left that was around the belt line. Some in the crowd yelled, "Foul!" but the blow was not clearly low.

Round 4 – Joe rushed McCoy to a corner, blocking "The Kid's" left jabs. Joe got in a left to the body and hard right to the ribs, but McCoy gave him three stinging jabs to the face. Choynski was errant with a right to the torso, but landed to the neck. "The Kid" charged at Joe, scoring with both hands to the head and body, making his opponent a bit groggy at the bell.

Round 5 – McCoy swung a left to the head, ducked a counter from Joe, and drove a hard left to the body. Choynski forced him about the ring, landed a left to the head, but received two left swings to his head. "The Real McCoy" smashed three left hooks to the head, catching a right to the body. He landed three more portside punches to Joe's noggin, then retreated. "The Kid" crashed two hard lefts to the midsection, and a left-right to the jaw. Joe was looking old and slow. "He resorted to blocking left leads and tried to land his right, but McCoy blocked it." Joe was wobbly, the *Dallas Morning News* saying he was "saved by the gong."

Round 6 – Joe recuperated between rounds and came out strong, forcing McCoy around the ring. The "Kid" snaked out the left jab, landing repeatedly to the nose and face. The "California Terror" drove a right to the head, and a powerful left to the top of the head that nearly took McCoy off his feet. The "Kid" became more cautious. He scored with jabs, but clinched immediately after blocking Joe's attempted right cross counter.

Round 7 – Choynski forced matters and landed a light right to the body. They traded lefts. The Indiana native followed with another left to the body and a right to the head. Joe got in a straight left to the neck, then left and right to the head, the last two being glancing blows. They exchanged jabs.

Round 8 – Frisco Joe again assumed the aggressive, but only managed a light left to the body. The Hoosier came back with a left to the torso and a right stab to the head. Joe drove a hard left hook to the head that angered "The Kid," who retaliated with three quick jabs to the face. Joe got in a right to the body, but was countered with a left to the face. The "Kid" went into a crouch, landing a body shot, but when he tried to follow with a right to the jaw, Choynski got inside of it, smacking a good right to the body.

Round 9 – Joe came out determined, swinging a left-right combination that McCoy ducked. "The Kid" returned fire with a left to the body, but got a stiff left to the neck in reply. Choynski forced McCoy into a corner, but was short with a right to the head. "The Kid" scored with a left to the body and ducked a right counter. Joe snapped McCoy's head back with a smart left jab, repeated the blow and caused great excitement among the crowd. The *Chicago Tribune* said Joe attempted a 3rd, but took a steaming right hand that sat him on the mat. It added that the fall was probably a partial slip, as Joe quickly regained his feet and evaded a rush by McCoy. The *San Francisco Call* relates the knockdown occurring in the next round. The "Kid" swung a left to the face at the bell, but despite the knockdown observed by the *Tribune*, that paper still called the frame in favor of Choynski.

Round 10 – The *Call* said "The 10th ... barring the knockdown ... (was) tame ... some lively fiddling, careful sparring and pretty footwork, but no damage ... Choynski went to the floor ... from a left swing on the jaw ... He jumped up quickly, and what looked like a knockout had apparently done ... little injury." McCoy seemed able land the jab at will, "but it seemed as if he refrained ... out of pure pity. Joe's nose and lips were all puffed and swollen ... he was bleeding considerably, while the 'Kid' had not a mark ..." They sent each other's head back with good shots. "Choynski ... rushed, sending a resounding left on the ribs and right over the heart. Honors even ..."

Round 11 – Joe came out with his right cocked, but received a left to the neck and another to the body. He pursued McCoy, but took a right to the head. Joe swung for the fences with a roundhouse right, but missed and almost went down from the momentum. *Chicago Tribune*: "McCoy's footwork puzzled Choynski ... He finally sent in a left to the 'Kid's neck ..."

Round 12 – McCoy took the aggressive. He landed a left to the face, but missed a right. Joe's right to the body was blocked by "The Kid." Joe hooked to the face, McCoy countering with a left to the jaw.

Round 13 – McCoy began working his arms, shoulders and body in a series of feints, trying to draw out his foe. He sent two jabs to the face, but received one on the neck. Choynski avoided several lefts and rights to body and head by clever defense. He missed a left and was countered by a left to the face. The "Kid" rushed Joe, getting in a left swing to the neck.

Round 14 – The "Corkscrew Kid" snapped Joe's head back with two lightning jabs, ducking a return. Joe rushed McCoy into a corner and swung left and right, but the latter's clever side-stepping carried him from harm. They twice traded hard left hooks to the face. Choynski charged, but the Hoosier clinched. The "Kid" landed his left jab with amazing accuracy, with only an occasional return from Joe. Near the bell, the ex-candy maker got in a left hook to the neck, but his nose was bleeding and lips swollen.

Round 15 – McCoy missed a left to the body and Joe countered with a left to the face. He threw both hands to the jaw, "but was a trifle short." Joe tried a left to the wind, but McCoy beat him with a straight left to the face. The "Kid" sent Joe's head back with a left hook. The latter got in a harmless left to the torso, missed a hard smash for the jaw, but landed a straight left to the face, avoiding McCoy's return fire.

Round 16 – McCoy whiffed on a left to the body; Joe countered with a hook to the head. The "Kid" rushed him to the ropes, sent a left to the neck and clinched. They took turns rushing, a lot of harmless sparring in between. McCoy swung his left repeatedly at the head, Joe cleverly ducking each. "McCoy jabbed a left on the face and clinched, holding Choynski's hands ... was hooted by some of the crowd, though there was no palpable offense committed." The *Tribune* said McCoy "struck a little low."

Round 17 – Joe ducked a left for the jaw, but caught one on the neck. A quick, 3rd left landed heavily on Choynski's jaw, flooring him. Unhurt, Joe rose immediately and "sparred back at him as spry as a cricket." He landed a left high on the head, but "The Kid" answered with a pair of left jabs. Joe was unsuccessful with a right. Instead, he took a couple of lefts from McCoy to end the frame. The latter appeared the fresher of the two.

Round 18 – Joe missed a wild left and was punished with a left hook to the face. McCoy missed a left swing and was countered with a short left to the neck. The "Kid" blocked a couple of swings and scored with a pair of stiff jabs to the face. He threw a hard left for the jaw, but Joe ducked.

Round 19 – The men sparred for wind and dodged some good shots. Joe drove a left to the body, McCoy, a harmless left-right to the head. The elusive "Kid" avoided two rights to the head, then rushed Joe, who ducked a vicious left. Joe drew blood from McCoy's nose with a stiff jab.

Round 20 – They shook hands. McCoy thrust a straight left into Joe's face, blocked a left to the head and countered with a hard right to the ribs. He rushed Joe across the ring, stabbed him twice with a left to the jaw, but took a left in return. McCoy's blows "appeared hard enough to fell him," but Joe fought to a clinch. *Call*: "McCoy rushed him to the ropes ... an even exchange ... on the body. Choynski clinched ... around the neck with both hands, and McCoy smashed his right ... into the ribs. Many ... yelled 'foul,' grasping at a last chance to save the money ... bet on Choynski ... the gong sounded ... 'Billy' Jordan climbed through the ropes ... (said) 'McCoy wins' ..." The *Tribune* said McCoy struck a hard blow that seemed to land below the belt, but despite cries of foul, the referee saw it as fair.

Soon afterward, accusations were made that McCoy allowed Joe to stay the route. More than one paper felt the fix was in. *Call*: "Time and again Choynski tried to hook the 'Kid' on the chin with that famous left that ... of old sent many a hard customer to the boards, but McCoy was always on guard, and without ... apparent effort slid away from ... or ducked ... under the 'weapon of torture.' 'The Kid' apparently could have finished the game in early rounds ... but either through kindness ... or ... other reason, failed to take advantage of ... openings ..." *Syracuse Herald*: "Nearly all sporting men ... agreed the ... fight ... was fixed for the benefit of Choynski. No other explanation is possible, in light of the betting on rounds as compared with odds on McCoy. (Bill) Brady is said to have engineered the deal ... on terms that the 'pugs' ... to get 65 and 35 per cent of the gate ... should divide even, and in consideration ... of big money in the betting on rounds, McCoy agreed not to knock out Choynski. The tip was given outsiders and heavy betting ... done ... snapping up 18 round bets."

Round five in particular was referred to as evidence of a fix, when McCoy had Joe in trouble, but failed to finish him, or come out with both barrels blazing in the next round. McCoy told the *Call*: "Choynski is a strong, clever fellow and an exceptionally hard man to knock out. During the 20 rounds I landed on him several times hard enough to put an ordinary man out of business. He was making a good defensive fight, but he never seemed able to land on me effectively. Why didn't I go in and finish him? Well, I thought up to the last minute I would get him coming to me and end the battle. Choynski claimed foul several times. I never (came) anywhere near his belt." March 25 *San Francisco Bulletin*: "Kid McCoy awoke to-day with two slightly disfigured eyes and a lame shoulder. 'How are you ...?' (he) was asked ... in the Occidental Hotel corridor. 'If it were not for this shoulder I'd be all right,' he replied, raising his arm and making a horrible grimace ... 'I got that in the 5th round, when it looked so good for me. When I led, Choynski swung his left in windmill fashion, and he nearly took my right out of the socket. My shoulder pained me all night, and I slept very little. I feel no other effects from the fight.' "

" 'Did you try to stop Choynski?' 'I tried up to the 5th round, when I got that twist ... went along easily until the 15th round. After the 15th I did a lot of hard work, but ... not ... particular about knocking him out. If you get a reputation of knocking everybody out, by and by you won't ... get any matches. I prefer taking my time and outpointing my men.' 'Is it so that you and your friends bet that Choynski would stay the 20 rounds?' 'There is no truth in the report ... What money I bet, I bet on myself. If anybody bet Choynski would stay 20 rounds they did it without my knowledge.' 'How was your wind?' 'It bothered me some. But after the 15th I caught my 2nd wind and was as strong as ever. I wanted to fight as heavy as I could, so I did not work (train) as hard as I might.' " The *Bulletin* said: "The total gate amounted to not quite $10,000 ... 65 per cent went to the fighters ... McCoy and Choynski split about $6,500 between them. Choynski would not consent ... unless the purse was divided. He has not fought a battle for a couple of years without an equal division." There were often allegations of a fix in big fights, especially early in the Queensberry era.

The *Call*: "Despite the fact that his lips were swollen ... eyes puffed and discolored, the Californian seemed satisfied he had gone the route ... unmindful of the ludicrous appearance of his countenance. He grimaced at his friends and joshed them as if they were the sufferers, and laughingly asked them if he didn't look handsome. When asked to say something ... Joe hummed that tuneful ballad, 'He Has Seen Better Days,' and gloried in the fact that he was a pretty good old back number. 'McCoy hits hard enough to hurt anybody, but he did not hurt me. The blows he gave me in the groin bothered me throughout. When I told people that Sharkey hit me there they said I was 'kidding,' and to-night they seemed to have the same opinion, but ... the 'Kid' did land there two or three times, and it gave me greater pain than I received during the entire battle. I don't want to detract from McCoy's showing, nor do I want the best of it, but I do want what is coming to me. McCoy was a hard man to get at ... My ankle bothered me ... I hurt it in Chicago in one of my fights and went into the ring to-night with it bandaged, and when I fell in trying to avoid McCoy's rush earlier ... I felt a twinge of pain, and during the remaining rounds I felt the pain every time I tried for a left swing ... I would have to raise up on my toes, and the pain would shoot through my leg, causing me great suffering. As to the knuckle on my right hand, that didn't bother me at all, did it?' he jokingly queried. He ... worked his hand up and down and showed its bad condition."

Graney wanted Joe to quit the fight game, as he was now a "cripple." Ed: "For 14 or 15 years he has battled manfully, and nowadays, when he meets a youngster, he shows his age. Joe was in condition to-night, otherwise he would never have gone the distance. I did not send him after McCoy in the last four rounds ... did not want Joe to take a chance of getting knocked out before all his friends ... If he decides to stay in the business I will be his friend, but if my talk will move him, he will quit for good." The March 27, 1920 *Police Gazette* said McCoy scored the only two knockdowns, in the 9th and 14th rounds, both with left hands. The April 3 *Marion Daily Star* had the rotund referee, Jim Kennedy, stating emphatically that the bout was not a fake. He said, not only did McCoy's people not bet that Joe would last the 20-rounds, but "McCoy was a very sick man when he entered the ring ... if he had followed the advice of his physician he wouldn't have been there at all." This sounds like someone trying too hard to convince his audience, possibly to remove himself from any implied involvement. Despite any defensiveness Kennedy might have felt, there seemed to be as much evidence against a fix, as for one.

On April 4, Dr. J.C. Lewis of San Francisco examined McCoy, advising that his nervous system and heart were impaired. Earlier, Dr. J.F. Holmes of New York gave a similar assessment. McCoy's physician allegedly "said he was suffering from a fluttering heart and nerve prostration." "The Kid" told his Frisco friends he was heading for a summer resort in California to recuperate, and if he wasn't able to fully recover, would retire from boxing. McCoy sent a letter to stage impresario and boxing manager, William A. Brady, saying "He will go to Seigler Springs, California with his wife, where he will stay for three months. He will then spend three months in Lake Country. Altogether the 'Kid' will retire from the ring for six months."[15] The *St. Paul Globe* carried a story on the 10th that Joe was (yet again) retiring from the ring. "He has scores of friends in San Francisco, which city he may (again) make his home. Mrs. Choynski was a Cincinnati girl – and there was a time when she urged Joe to locate there. But Joe's early days were spent in 'Frisco, and there he desires to pass the remainder."

At least two papers claimed, in mid-April, that Joe made statements to the effect that he was not beyond throwing a fight for the right amount of money. April 12, 1899 *Sandusky Star*: "Joe ... says his fight with McCoy was on the level and the Hoosier could not have put him out, no matter how hard he tried. 'I have never faked in my life ... but I am in the business for a living and I guess if they showed me enough money to make it an object, I might lay down.' Such is the statement ... credited to Choynski, but those ... well acquainted with the clever fighter cannot believe he ever made such a declaration." "The *Pittsburgh Chronicle* (April 14, 1899) quoted ... Choynski, on his reasons for being a prizefighter: 'I can't see any glory in this business. I am in it for my bread and butter,' even to the point of throwing a match 'if there was enough inducement.' " Neither source specified where or when Joe supposedly made the avowal, detracting from their credibility.[16]

Several reports in late April implicated various persons in the fight. "Nasty rumors have been floating eastward from the Pacific coast ... since the rather one-sided contest ... These stories first involved McCoy and Choynski's seconds; then the club, McCoy and Choynski, and finally, McCoy and Eddie Greaney. The latter story carried with it a job by which young Choynski (Edwin), a brother of (Joe) was sent ... from the ringside for fresh water, when this was wholly unnecessary ... to give the jobbers time ... to substitute a bottle of whisky, 'salted' with chloral, for the bottle carried ... originally." Chloral hydrate was used in Joe's day as a sedative, and, when mixed with alcohol, as a "Mickey Finn." "Choynski was seen yesterday ... and in a guarded manner confirmed the story ... The fair-haired Californian was loath to admit any part of ... his having been jobbed. 'I dislike ... to register a kick when I lose ... but there are some things about my fight with McCoy ... which I have been unable to explain ... I noticed before the fight was very old, that the bottle ... my seconds were using between rounds was not the same which I brought to the club. This greatly surprised me, but I had no time to figure the change out ... while I was in the best condition of my life the afternoon of the bout, I felt all 'tied up' when I would try to lead for McCoy or block ... I didn't feel sick ... but ... as though my arms were being held, or ... I was muscle-bound. This was the first time I was ... troubled in a like manner, and it puzzled me.' "

"The day after the fight, McCoy was examined by a competent physician ... told he was in horrible shape and not fit to fight a round ... told ... that must have been his condition for weeks. Now, if McCoy was in such poor shape when he fought me, how must I have been, that I couldn't win ...? Still, I do not want ... any excuses ... for my defeat. The manager of the club came to me before the contest and told me I would have to 'donate' $150 to the newspapers, so they would 'boost' the show. I have never done this before, but gave up this time. One of the newspaper men, who received $50 of my $150, was the loudest in proclaiming the contest a 'fake' ... I have never engaged in a 'fake,' and fought honestly ... but ... was hampered in my efforts to whip my man, in some way ... I cannot explain at the present time. If I ever fight McCoy again, a different story may be told."

"The story goes that Joe was drugged with chloral, put in his whisky flask. It is said this drug, when used moderately ... has the effect of making the victim 'dopey.' He is able to work mechanically, but his mental capabilities are blunted. So ... Choynski could have easily gone through the fight and spectators been none the wiser. There is no more truth in this statement than in many more that have emanated from the Coast. It is sure the story is made out of whole cloth, for if McCoy was in front of a man full of dope, it would hardly have lasted ... 20 rounds." A 1921 *Reno Evening Gazette* claimed: "Choynski was slow by comparison with McCoy ... his friends ... declared he had been dosed by his opponent, who ... used some mixture on his gloves." The paper made a similar claim in 1926.[17]

Boxers of the era sometimes imbibed a little alcohol as a stimulant in their corners (some had more than a little). It was not forbidden as it is today. In Joe's case, more likely the bottle was used for water, not whiskey. While not a teetotaler, he was not known to booze it up, either. The rumors and scandal soon died away, not to be heard of again, it seems. The "tied-up," muscle-bound feeling felt by Joe might have been caused by something other than a "Mickey Finn," though if his bottle was swapped without his knowledge, what was in the "new" bottle and who was in on the conspiracy? Of Joe's three cornermen, Graney, Charley Tilson and Tommy Murphy, Graney is the least suspect, having been Joe's close friend and confidante for many years. If Choynski had any suspicions involving Graney, however, it might explain why the two had a falling out later on, which allegedly lasted a few years. Defeat can be a difficult pill to swallow, so perhaps Joe was just making excuses. That sluggish, lethargic feeling (such as Jeffries later felt against Jack Johnson) could be caused by an inability to hit the other man as one usually can do.

"The Kid" told writer Irving Wallace, a few months before taking his own life in 1940, that the term, "The Real McCoy" originated with this match. "It ... was invented by a reporter named (W.W.) Naughton. I arrived in San Francisco to tangle with ... Choynski. Just a few months before, in the ... same ring, a bum named Pete McCoy had fought and been knocked out in seven rounds. When I crawled through the ropes, someone shouted, 'Hey, what's this? Another McCoy?' I won the fight, a thrilling battle ... the following morning, Naughton's account ... began: 'Last night, the real McCoy beat Joe Choynski!' That, citizens, was how the phrase originated, and don't let anybody tell you differently ... Joe Choynski ... was the most vicious fighter that ever lived. He gave me my hardest fight."[18] He was referring to the 1900 rip-off. It is now accepted that "The Real McCoy" was coined much earlier, possibly in the 1870s.

Next for Joe was a most interesting opponent, Willard W. (Washington) Bean, known as the "Mormon Cyclone" and "Fighting Parson." Bean was born in Provo, Utah on May 16, 1868. His father, George Washington Bean, was a polygamist whose three wives bore him 30 children. Willard became a fine all-round athlete, winning awards in such diverse sports as running, high- and broad-jump, shot put, hammer throw and pole vaulting. He was also a thespian of no mean ability, having toured as a comedian, "and his talents ... extend to the teaching of physical culture and to literary work in the dryly humorous vein of the Bill Nye school." Bean boxed amateur exhibitions "by permission of my parents and the college faculty ..." He began a late professional career, his first known bout in May, 1897, at nearly 29. Bean eventually gained national renown as the middleweight champion of Utah. In February, 1915, Willard was chosen by President

451

Joseph F. Smith (a nephew of *the* Joseph Smith) to make a pilgrimage to the birthplace of Joseph Smith, Jr., in Palmyra, New York. Smith's dilemma was finding a family that would live in the Smith home, farm the land, preach and somehow make friends for the Church, in what was considered the most prejudiced place on earth against the Mormon religion, since Smith was driven out 84 years prior. Bean was largely chosen due to his previous missionary work and his fighting spirit.

Willard Bean, 1895

The mission to Palmyra, to have been for "a period of five years or more," lasted nearly 25. Early on, the townspeople dispatched a delegation of three men to the Smith farm, who declared that the couple were not wanted there and should leave. Willard attempted to pacify the men, saying they wanted to become an asset to the community. He then made it clear that they were going to stay, adding, "I'll take you on one at a time or three at a time. We're here to stay." The men weren't aware that Bean was a professional boxer, but they left, and no more was heard from the committee. Sometime later, the "Mormon Cyclone" put on a boxing exhibition, as a public relations move. He challenged all comers, taking on the toughest men in town, one at a time, until he had dispatched seven into dreamland! One afternoon, while Bean was walking the "unfriendly streets of Palmyra," a man watering his front lawn suddenly turned the hose on him. He taunted him, saying, "I understand you people believe in baptism by immersion." Willard allegedly vaulted the fence and replied, "Yes, and we also believe in the laying on of hands!"

The Beans returned to Utah as grandparents. The citizens gave them a grand farewell in 1939, saying they had grown to love the family, and would miss them dearly. One of Willard's many accomplishments in Palmyra was his negotiation of the purchase of many Church historical sites, including the Hill Cumorah. This was the spot where it is said founder Joseph Smith was given the golden plates by the angel Moroni, from which he translated the Book of Mormon. The initial asking price for the hill alone had been $100,000, but the "Fighting Parson" negotiated purchase of the hill, Grange Hall and three farms, for $53,000. Some time before his mission, Bean had been training young boxers in Utah. One of these is said to have been the young, future heavyweight champion, Jack Dempsey.[19]

Joe arrived in Salt Lake City, Utah on April 14. The next day's *Salt Lake Herald*: "Brave Joe Choynski ... accompanied by his wife, is registered at the Knutsford. (They) will remain ... several days ... Joe will give an exhibition of his art at the Grand theater, which will include a 10-round sparring match with Will Bean of Provo ... under the management of Jimmy Dixon. Choynski was entertaining a crowd of admirers in the Kenyon lobby last night ... Joe ... tells of his past experiences in the prize ring in a way that attracts and holds a crowd. He is but 30 years old, and says there are those who tell him he is a 'has been,' but he thinks it is better to be a 'has been' than never to have been at all ... if the winner of the Jeffries-Fitzsimmons mill will give him a chance, he will show he is yet ... in it ... Choynski passes the opinion that Jeffries is likely to come out (a) winner. He is quicker and more active than Fitz and yet a hard hitter, qualities ... Joe thinks will pull him through successfully ..." This was a bold pronouncement, as Bob was the favorite. Having fought both, however, Joe made the correct choice. On June 9 at Coney Island, New York, the "California Grizzly" utilized his

crouch to defend against Bob's power punches, and stopped Fitz in the 11th to capture the world crown. "While sojourning in Salt Lake, Choynski will be the guest of his old friend, Martin E. Mulvey. Choynski's arrival ... was the occasion for an informal reception in the visitor's honor ..."

April 16 *Salt Lake Herald*: "Willard Bean ... will have his first genuine try-out ... the Utah fighter will be ... 'up against the real thing.' He has a multitude of friends throughout the State who will watch with interest ... James Dixon, who has charge of the affair, said ... it will not be tame. Bean ... said he wants Choynski to let himself out ... that he may be able to judge of his ability. Dixon will ... referee. Choynski and his wife took a

Willard Bean, "The Mormon Cyclone"

trip to Saltair* yesterday afternoon and the fighter was delighted with the resort. He longed for a dip in the brine, but wisely refrained."

* Saltair (or SaltAir) – A gargantuan resort built in 1893 on the southern shore of (and on a massive pier, into) the Great Salt Lake. Billed as "The Coney Island of the West," it was destroyed by fire in 1925.

The card opened with a 10 minute bag punching exhibition by Joe and some club swinging. The April 18 *Herald* wrote: "Several hundred men and two women went to the Grand last night, to see Willard Bean, the fighting elder from Provo, and Joe Choynski, the Hebraic heavyweight, give a 10-round exhibition of scientific sparring. The crowd got its money's worth and more ... Choynski didn't let himself out ... until the last round ... Then showed ... it would have been as easy to put Bean out as to take candy from a child. Nevertheless the Provo lad gave an excellent account ... faster than ... ever ... in his life and showed ... lots of sand and ginger. He ... has a left jab that may win him something ... along with a right hook and a tasty little uppercut. Bean didn't have much chance to show what he can do in defensive work, for Choynski didn't try much leading. Bean landed with great frequency and little steam for nine rounds. In the 10th, Joe went after him, and ... could have sung him a lullaby in about three punches."

"Bean weighed 154 pounds in his green fighting trunks. Choynski scaled 163 and looked even heavier. His spidery legs, looking thinner than they really were in dark blue battle tights, were his only apparent weak point. Bean was shorter than his antagonist but his condition was of the best. He had the worst of it in reach as well as in weight. The men entered the ring at 9:40 (some said 9:55 p.m.) ... The rounds were two minutes in length with a minute rest between. The 1st round opened with 30 seconds of dancing and fiddling. Then Bean began leading with his left. He tapped Joe lightly several times without a return." The *Salt Lake Tribune* said Willard left a mark on Joe's neck with a jab, and the latter spread-eagled his arms to allow Bean a better chance at his face. "As the round ended, Joe got in a light rap that damaged Willard's nose. The organ was slightly sore to start with, and bled profusely during the balance of the contest. In the 2nd ... Bean used his left to excellent advantage, Choynski remaining on the defensive ... Willard scored half a dozen left jabs on Joe's face and as many rights on the body." Joe got in a few rib-roasters. "The 3rd round was notable mainly at an attempt at a pivot (punch) by Bean. Referee Jimmy Dixon warned him that the blow was barred and he did not repeat it. In the 4th, Choynski struck Bean below the belt. The foul was apparent but unintentional and Joe promptly apologized. The lad from Provo continued his shifty work in this, as in succeeding rounds." Bean was noted for nimble footwork, defensive ability, and quick fists. In the 5th frame, Joe drove a pair of wicked jabs to the face, his foe countering with a right hook to the jaw.

"The 6th was productive of a handsome right hook from Bean, which landed on Choynski's jaw without damage." The latter responded with two hard body shots and a nasty jab. "Joe came to in the 7th long enough to use his left a couple of times. The 2nd time he tapped Bean in a tone that could be heard all over the parquet. 'You can reach clean across the room with that left of yours' (said Bean). Joe grinned but saved his breath for sparring ... In the 8th there was a lot of scuffling and fiddling. Three times the men clinched, each time Joe winding up with his head under Willard's left arm. On (each) occasion, Bean swung his right behind him, landing on Choynski's face, to the great amusement of the audience and of Joseph himself. The 10th and last round was as lively as the fighters could make it. Choynski warmed up ... and made things exceedingly interesting for Bean. Before the round ended, Willard seemed more than a trifle groggy, for Joe hammered him with considerable vigor. Both men were in just as good shape, to all appearances, two minutes after the bout as they were before it began. In his dressing room, Choynski said Bean was a fighter of more than ordinary merit. 'But,' he added, 'a man wot don't see nothin, don't learn nothing. See?' The pugilist explained that the field for pugs in Utah was not sufficiently broad. He thought Bean should go out into the wide, wide world and go up against all kinds of men." The *Deseret Evening News* and *Salt Lake Tribune* said Joe had Bean at his mercy in the last two rounds.

On May 5 it was announced that Jack Root had agreed to fight Choynski in a six round bout at Chicago, on the 9th. The match fell through, and Joe never did fight Root, a man who would later gain recognition as the "first" light-heavyweight champion.[20] The Colorado Athletic Club supposedly clinched a match between Joe and McCoy, to be held "as soon as the new prize fight law takes effect ..." though the two would not face each other again until October 6. The fight was pushed up to June 19, for the Denver A.C., it being noted that Choynski had cancelled a June 16 bout with George Byers at the Dearborn (Michigan) A.C., in order to meet "The Kid." George Byers was a middleweight born on Prince Edward Island, Canada, of mixed black and Native American descent. He fought at from 120 to 165 pounds.[21] The July 9 *Brooklyn Eagle* said Joe was drawing the "color line" against Byers. Choynski, however, was generally considered the least prejudiced white fighter of his era, proving time and again his willingness to climb into the ring with boxers of any race, creed or color. Being of a minority group, himself (Jewish), may have been a factor in this. The same article said McCoy had cancelled all engagements and was refraining from making new ones, including ring bouts, in order to try and arrange a fight with Bob Fitzsimmons, which never occurred.

Jim Jeffries was interviewed by the *Daily Iowa Capital* on June 7: " 'Have you ever been knocked down?' 'Never in my life ... I've never been groggy, either. Choynski dazed me once with a right hand swing on the cheekbone, but it only lasted a minute.' " On June 28 in Helena, Montana, a Jake Choynski was knocked out in six rounds by Ike (or Denis) Hayes (or Hays), the "colored heavyweight ... of Montana." Articles said Jake claimed to be a cousin of Joe. An August 19 article said Jake also went by the nom de guerre, "Young Choynski."[22] Joe was in Denver, Colorado around July 2, where McCoy was, as well. The "Kid" gave a show the previous Monday at that city's Tabor Grand Opera House, and had just fired his latest manager,

Ben Benton, alias "Rob Roy." The firing was a reason McCoy gave to justify the cancellation of all the engagements made for him. July 3 *St. Paul Globe*: "McCoy went to Bailey's. He met Joe Choynski for a moment in the morning ... An appointment was made for the two to meet at 3 o'clock in the afternoon, but Choynski went out to Petersburg and did not get back until 4:30. McCoy waited for him until after 4 o'clock and then went to his train. Choynski expressed himself as disappointed over the failure to meet his old antagonist, and said he was very anxious to make the match. All negotiations are off ... until McCoy gets back to town."

On July 6, it was noted that a new athletic club had been organized at Dubuque, Iowa. The President of the club was John P. Lux, and the Secretary and General Manager was Lou M. Houseman of Chicago. The significance of this would soon be revealed. Their opening show was to be a three-day boxing carnival, scheduled for August 29-31. Jack Root and George Byers were to contest for the "middleweight championship of America," and offers were made to such fighters as Tommy Ryan, Joe Walcott, George Dixon, Terry McGovern, George Gardner, Peter Maher and Joe. Meanwhile, McCoy signed with the Westchester (New York) A.C. to "meet any two men during the month of September." One of these men was Joe, who wired his acceptance of the club's rather small $7,500 purse, for a September 2 match.[23]

Jim "Jack" McCormick

Joe arrived back in Chicago on July 17 to fight Jim "Jack" McCormick. The fight was set for the 21st at the Dearborn Athletic Club.[24] McCormick was a useful heavyweight with a good punch. Born John Forbes McCormick, in Philadelphia, Pennsylvania, "Jack" moved to Chicago around 1899. He had a spotty record, facing some of the finest competition of the day. Standing about 6' 1", he would lose over his career (1895-1905) to Herman Bernau (KOby4), Gus Ruhlin (KOby8, 1898 and 1905), Tom Sharkey (KOby2, 1899, KOby1, 1900), Joe Goddard (KOby2, 1899), "Kid" McCoy (KOby8, 1899, NDL6, 1903) and Jack Johnson (LDQ6 or 7, 1899). McCormick, however, had the biggest win of his career in his next fight, after Joe. On August 18, 1899, in Chicago, he would crash a wild right to the jaw of "Kid" McCoy in the 1st round, knocking him completely out. In an interview soon after the bout, "Jack" said Tommy Ryan showed him how to beat McCoy. McCormick said the opening in "The Kid's" defense shown by Ryan was either a low or high left guard, that he could cross a punch over. The "Kid" avenged the loss twofold. Other wins by "Jack" were over "Denver" Ed Smith (KO2, 1900) and Jack Bonner (KO5, 1900). He had several draws against top men, including Joe Goddard, Bonner (twice), Ed Dunkhorst and George Byers.[25]

On the night of July 21, about 2,000 at the Dearborn A.C. saw Joe face McCormick in a scheduled six-rounder. "Jack" appeared well trained and "strong as a lion," but Joe "looked drawn and finer than usual, if such a thing is possible." The following combines mostly contemporary reports.[26]

Round 1 – The fireworks began early. Choynski pursued his adversary about the ring, though "little hard work was done for a minute and a half." Catching Joe by surprise, "Jack" swung a wild right to Joe's left ear, dropping him to his knees. The *Hamilton Daily Republican-News* said he "stepped in suddenly, and, with a left hook and right swing, dropped his man cleanly." The *Police Gazette* said it was "a left-hand punch in the stomach" that decked Joe. As Choynski rose to his feet at "five," McCormick charged in, but ran into a potent left hook that felled him in a heap. The Hamilton paper differed: "Feinting his man at will, he let fly a terrific right that caught McCormick squarely on the point of the jaw." "Jack" got up at "nine," but was staggering and slipped to his knees again, just before the bell. This would be "Jack's" only real moment in the fight.

Joe: "McCormack (sic) and I had been in the ring less than a minute when – 'zowi!' – out of nowhere the big ruffian pulled a haymaker and it caught me solid. Down I went with the arena whirling about me. I jumped up without a count. McCormack, seeing I was dazed, rushed at me with his guard down. I braced myself against a ring post and shot a left hook to his jaw. He staggered clear across the ring, hit the ropes and bounced back into a right uppercut that sent him down for the full count (9) from Referee Malachy Hogan. After that I took no chances on wild punches from Mr. McCormack. I feinted him into knots and jabbed or hooked him for the remaining five rounds. Awarding me the decision was a mere formality."

Round 2 – "The 2nd ... was rather tame ... McCormick breaking ground." the *Chicago Tribune* said Joe forced the pace from then to the end of the fight, "jabbing ... continually and uppercutting with ... effect." Other papers agreed. The *Hamilton Daily Republican-News* dissented again, saying "McCormick was in better shape ... for the 2nd, and from that time to the end the contest was fast and furious, although little ... damage was done on either side. Choynski seemed slower than is his wont, and McCormick's blocking stood him in good stead ..." The next three rounds contain quotes repeated in nearly all the papers, evidently from a "wire service" report.

Round 3 – "Jack" swung for the fences, "but Choynski ducked and brought the Philadelphian to the floor with a right ... in the stomach."

Round 4 – Choynski had his man groggy, but McCormick survived.

Round 5 – "McCormick was knocked down ... by a left swing on the jaw, but got up ... landing a couple of good blows on Joe's chest."

Round 6 – "McCormick tried to even matters, but Joe ... easily ducked half a dozen vicious swings. The bout ended with both ... in the middle of the ring, fighting like demons." *Tribune*: "McCormick ... put in a couple of hard body blows, but Choynski would not be denied, and was forcing the fight at the call of time. The decision in Choynski's favor was well received." As usual, someone disagreed; The *Delphos Daily Herald* wrote: "Choynski ... did most of the leading, but the decision did not seem to please the spectators." The *Hamilton Daily Republican-News* said, "Choynski hurt his ankle badly in the last round while executing a side step."

Milwaukee Evening Wisconsin: "Choynski ... demonstrated ... his left ... has not lost its cunning and he is not a 'has been.' He gave Jack ... a thorough going over ..." *Tribune*: "Joe Choynski easily outpointed ... McCormick ... (who) tried rushing tactics and swung wildly, at most times with open gloves." *Hamilton Daily Republican-News*: "The eastern man showed an inclination to 'heel' ... and hit freely with the open hand." Rather than risk a chance haymaker from his larger rival, Joe was content to dominate with the jab, adding an unhealthy dose of hooks and crosses.

Joe's next opponent was the colorful "Mexican" Pete Everett, born in  Saguache, Colorado in 1875, now living in Cripple Creek (Colorado). His father was Irish, his mother, a "half-caste" of Mexican descent. "Mexican" Pete was thus, about one quarter "Mexican." A shade over 6' tall and weighing 190 pounds, he was a strong and tough, but uneven performer. Everett earned victories over Billy Woods (KO6, 1898), Bob Armstrong (KO5, 1898) and Tom Sharkey (WDQ2, 1901), but lost in 1898 to Jim Jeffries (KOby3, as he turned his back and quit), Joe Kennedy, Bob Armstrong (KOby14, 1898) and Frank Childs (L6, 1899). Pete faced Joe for $2,500 a side and a percentage of the gate.[27] The bout, set for 25 rounds, was held on the evening of August 4, 1899, at the Colorado Athletic Club in Denver. Johnny Kenney refereed.

"Mexican" Pete Everett

Denver Republican: "Peter looked like a prize steer beside a yearling ... big, strong, deep-chested ... with biceps the size of hams. He jumped into the ring ... as chipper as bobolink at daylight. He showed more confidence than usual and people began to believe he would fight. Choynski crawled between the ropes ... like a pygmy compared with his antagonist. His long hair floated about his temples and his arms and legs were like pipe-stems. One of the features ... is the electric bell ... used for the first time last night and worked perfectly. It counts ... accurately, and does away with timers. Mexican Pete was attended by Lawrence Farrell, Jerry Haley, Billy Jones and

John O'Neill ... Choynski was handled by Mose La Fontise, Bob Watkins and Mickey Dooley ... It was exactly 10 o'clock when Kenney called time." The following is based on multiple contemporary reports, including the local *Denver Republican* and *Colorado Springs Gazette*. The *Republican* had the only round-by-round account. [28]

Round 1 – *Denver Republican*: "Pete led with a light left to the ribs ... There was, from that blow to the end of the contest, (not) the slightest doubt as to the winner. The Mexican simply was not in it. Choynski's favorite tactics were left jabs for the face, and it did not take him long to have the claret flowing ... from the nostrils of the Mexican. The Californian was laying back with his right all the time, and when he did cut loose ... it jarred Pete like an explosion of nitroglycerine (sic). In the infighting, Joe worked both hands like pistons, and out of these mix-ups, Pete came decidedly the worse for wear, but anxious to fight, which mystified many ... Joe rushed in ... Pete got in a light left tap on the ribs and a right on the heart ... Joe jabbed ... with his left and bored his right in the heart. Pete fell short with ... wild swings ... frequently clinched."

Round 2 – Choynski landed a jab to the face and hard right to the heart, followed by a left to the mouth, a "light right swing in the kidneys ... a stiff right in the heart that staggered the Mexican." Joe varied the barrage, jabbing lefts to the face and hooks with both hands to the heart and ribs. Pete charged in with a right to the ribs, but fell short with his next five punches. Joe got in two jabs to the face and a "hot right rib-burner."

Round 3 – The deadly Chrysanthemum continued the attack, driving a straight left to the face and a couple of right hooks. Pete clinched repeatedly, forcing the referee to continually separate the men.

Round Four – Pete lumbered from his corner and managed a pair of light punches. Joe retaliated with another left to face and right smash to the heart. A second later, he drove an especially stiff jab to the nose that drew blood and dazed the big man. "Little Joe" landed a succession of sharp left jabs to the nose, mixing in a number of hard rights to the heart, ribs and kidneys. "Pete clinched repeatedly ... and did everything but bite."

Round 5 – *Republican*: "Choynski used Pete for a chopping block ... battered nose and mouth ... shot his right into the heart ... Pete caught him, and Joe worked corkscrews, uppercuts, hooks and jabs into the face and heart until the Mexican was dragged away by Kenney. They came together ... Joe repeated the dose, only with considerable (sic) more steam. He had Pete wavering on the brink, but the bell came to the rescue."

Round 6 – Everett appeared refreshed. He landed his own left-to-face-right-to-body combo, albeit with little force. Joe shot in three lefts, causing the blood to stream from Pete's face, then floored him with a crashing right to the head. Everett took seven seconds to regain his feet, "blinded and uncertain." "Joe ... smothered him with jabs in the face and rights to the ribs, kidneys and wind. Pete clinched ... Joe ... working in his hooks and uppercuts with both hands ... the referee separated them. Joe shoved his left into the face and swung his hard right hand to the ear, sending the Mexican to the mat. Pete was bloody and weak ... As soon as he was on his feet, the Californian ... beat him again to the mat." Joe: "In the 6th ... I floored him for seven seconds and ... nine. The bell saved him from a knockout."

Round 7 – Joe continued his combination of jab to face and right to heart. Pete clinched, then tossed Joe over his shoulder, both landing heavily to the mat. "Kenney ... gave the fight to Choynski on a foul. The decision angered the Mexican. He started towards Kenney, who ... bounded for ... safety. A half dozen blue coats sprang through the ropes and saw that Pete was safely landed in his seat ... Aside from a red spot over the heart and a couple of blotches on the ribs, Choynski did not have a mark." Joe (1927): "In the 7th I hammered the greaser until he was a sight. Suddenly, he grabbed me around the waist and threw me over his shoulder. The referee ... awarded me the decision ... the Mexican ran amuck, tried to kill the referee ... it took half a dozen policemen to quiet him down."

Denver Republican: "He ... endeavored to throw him through the skylight, but Joe held fast to Pete's body and landed on his back on the mat ... The Mexican repeatedly fouled Choynski. These fouls ... the referee wisely overlooked, as the big crowd had come to see whether Peter would actually fight or lie down, and as long as he showed a disposition to fight and Joe didn't complain, Kenney let them go on." *Brooklyn Eagle*: "Pete made a rush and struck at the referee. The police and a number of spectators jumped into the ring, and a free fight was prevented by Mexican Pete's seconds drawing him to his corner, and police assuming control of the house." The referee had to forcibly extricate Pete's arm from Joe's throat. The crowd booed and hooted Everett. Joe won every round.

Hard times had befallen Choynski's old stablemate, Peter Jackson. The "Black Prince" of St. Croix was about to turn 39. With consumption setting in, Jackson was in Victoria, British Columbia, Canada, training for a fight with Jim Jeffords (*not* to be confused with Jim Jeffries), in order to pay for food and the booze he had long since become addicted to. "Peter the Great" would not win another bout. August 5, 1899 *Sandusky Star*: "Jackson's fall from the pedestal ... he once occupied ... is one of the saddest events ... in ring history ... he was ruined by prosperity. He lived at a fast clip even ... under Davies' management with Joe Choynski as a sparring partner ... when he was supposed to be at his best and capable of beating any man in the world. But, unlike the majority of convivial knights of the stuffed glove who make themselves ... conspicuous ... under the influence of the 'cup that cheers,' Jackson ... at all times of a quiet and retiring nature, kept to himself, and the public at large knew little of his mode of living ... The big Australian is ... but a ... shadow of his former self. Withal, he has been such a prince of good fellows and made so few enemies ... that nothing but sympathy is expressed for him on all sides." Peter returned to Australia, where he succumbed to tuberculosis on July 13, 1901.

On August 13, Joe's cousin, "Sol Choynski, eldest son of Isaiah and Fannie ... died in Vera Cruz, Mexico ... native of San Francisco, (age) 28 ... graduate of Lincoln Grammar ... and ... Commercial High School ... Five years ago he went to Mexico ... connected ... with some of the largest business firms (there) ... visited his parents ... two years ago ... formerly a member of the Naval Militia of California ... President of the Alpine Athletic Club ... favorably known ... a young man of sterling qualities. His death is a severe blow to his parents, who ... mourn a younger son ... killed ... in a landslide, less than two years ago ... two brothers survive ... Milton ... and Harry ..." Kin today were unaware of "lost" relatives, Aaron and Sol.

On the 17th, Joe seconded former cornerman, Mose La Fontise "of Montana," in a bout against Frank Bartley. The scheduled 20 round contest was held at the Colorado A.C. The men were 140-pounders and the referee, former Choynski victim, Billy Woods. A quick note on Mose (courtesy of Tracy Callis): "LaFontise was a mute. He may have been deaf too. All his brothers were mutes (four of them boxed)." The men were to break clean, but La Fontise had a volatile temper. In the 12th, After being cautioned by Woods for hitting in the clinches, Mose got Bartley's head in a headlock. He punched Frank in the jaw with his free hand, before Woods pried him off and awarded the fight to Bartley on a foul. When Bartley walked over to shake hands, La Fontise jumped from his chair, swinging. "Their seconds rushed in and separated the men before any damage was done."[29]

Choynski wrote a letter from Denver, saying he had "decided to fight in the middleweight class from now on ... I understand 'Jim' Ryan wants to meet me in Louisville. I will meet him at 158 pounds, give or take two. I am trying to get 'Jack' Stelzner to meet me here." In 1930, Joe claimed, "Only twice in my life, when I clashed with the mighty Joe Goddard (in Australia), was I able to bring my weight up to 168. And ... that by forced feeding! Otherwise, I might have been refused a chance at ... the terrifying Barrier Champion. On other occasions announcers 'boosted' my weight. When I fought Jeffries ... I weighed 159 pounds. I knocked out Jack Johnson when I weighed but 160. In my ... finish fight with Corbett ... only 155."[30]

The *Syracuse Herald* noted that another fight with "Kid" McCoy had been postponed. He "was originally billed to meet McCoy," but begged off, due to a sprained ankle he suffered during the Everett fight. It was announced August 3 that Joe was matched to face Jim Hall at Louisville's Nonpareil Athletic Club, on September 5. This contest would come off as planned. Did Joe's ankle heal so quickly? It seems more likely that he felt able enough to defeat Hall, but needed more time to ready for "The Kid." Rumblings for another bout were heard, with welterweight Joe Walcott. Choynski said he wanted the fight, and Walcott's manager, Tom O'Rourke was already hurling insults, in an effort to anger Joe into signing.[31]

Joe's next fight was with "Australian" Jimmy Ryan, in Dubuque, Iowa, where that city's Athletic Association was holding a three day fistic carnival.

The primary guiding force behind the event was Louis M. Houseman. Born in New Orleans, Louisiana in September, 1863, to German Jewish immigrants, Lou relocated to Chicago in 1886. There, he became a famous boxing promoter and manager. A 1900 article said, "As a sportsman he is honest ... and dead game. He would never take the blue ribbon at a beauty show ... Houseman is a little over five feet in height and broad of girth ... He came to Chicago the day of the Haymarket riot ... began work as a police reporter for the *Inter-Ocean* ... made sporting editor."[32]

Lou Houseman

Lou is generally considered the first to promote the new light-heavyweight division, a bridge between middleweight and heavyweight. This had long been needed, as most 160-pound men cannot compete against true heavyweights. The Ryan fight was billed by Houseman, the Dubuque

Athletic Association, and many papers across the nation, as for the "light-heavyweight championship of the world." It was a 20-rounder set for August 29, first night of the three night carnival, replacing a match between Jack Root (of Houseman's stable) and George Byers. Joe began training in Denver, Colorado, while Ryan set up quarters in far away Bath Beach, Coney Island, New York.[33] Many sources referred to Choynski as the current "light-heavyweight champion of the world."[34] The fledgling class had been mentioned for some time, but until Joe, no one had been declared its champion (as far as is known). He had long been given that title by the media, and even if he didn't proclaim himself as such, owing to the division's relative obscurity, he was, in this author's view, its initial titleholder. The purse was to be split, $3,000 to the victor, $500 to the loser. Six bouts were scheduled, George Siler to referee all. In 1930, Joe called Jimmy "one of the most dangerous hitters in the sock business."

John L. Sullivan, the American bareknuckle king who fought primarily with gloves, under Marquis of Queensberry rules (despite what some believe), is credited by a number of historians as the first world heavyweight champion of the Queensberry code. This is due to a fight he had in 1885 with Dominick McCaffrey, which had been billed (somewhat obscurely) as for just that. McCaffrey, while a good heavyweight, was far from the best contender around, and had not done anything remarkable to earn a title challenge. I find it ironic that Joe Choynski, billed often as the world light-heavyweight champion, and defending that distinction more than once, has not been accepted by most of these same pundits. Jack Root, recognized today as the first world light-heavyweight champ, had no more to recommend him for that title than did Joe. In fact, the same Lou Houseman, who was a promoter, newspaper scribe and Root's manager, advertised Choynski, and later, Root, as light-heavyweight champion.

August 27 *Dubuque Herald*: "Joe gets in from Denver this morning. He will go to headquarters ... out near the Monastery. Ryan is doing his work on the hill-tops ... near Eagle Point ... mostly hill-climbing and short sprints. Choynski, already in shape, will do nothing but light roadwork ..." The "Monastery" was probably the New Melleray Abbey, in the rolling farmland of Peosta, Iowa, about 15 miles southwest of Dubuque. The event would be held in the old Saengerbund Auditorium, which had been refurbished and renamed the Dubuque Athletic Club. The carnival was coordinated to coincide with the city's annual horse-racing competitions. The day prior to the fight, Joe told a reporter, "I'm as sound as a rock, and expect to win ..." Neither did Ryan lack confidence, saying: "Choynski may have a little the better ... in weight, but I think I have the edge ... in all other respects."[35]

Called the greatest boxing carnival ever held in the west, Houseman's production got under way about 10 p.m. on the night of August 29, with a bantam preliminary. All fights took place in a stakeless ring.[36] Choynski was a 3 to 2 favorite over Ryan, whose résumé included wins over Nick Burley (KO1, 1895), "Mysterious" Billy Smith (WDQ7, 1896), James "Doc" Payne (KO7, 1898) and George Byers (D25 or W25, August 12, 1899). Ryan's spotty record included at least 15 losses, but he was a dangerous puncher with good endurance. As usual, there was a discrepancy in the weights. At least one paper said Joe weighed 158 pounds, Ryan 152. These appear too light to be plausible. Another source said Ryan weighed slightly less than Choynski; yet another, that he was "much heavier" than Joe. The *Dubuque Herald* said Ryan looked "a bit flabby." 6,000 people attended, and shortly after 11:00 p.m., the fighters entered the ring. Joe and his handlers, Harry Peppers and Pat Hurley, were followed by "Australian" Jimmy Ryan and cornermen, Frank Early and Jack Thornby. The combined report melds multiple contemporary accounts, including three Iowa papers:[37]

Round 1 – They began cautiously. Joe landed several lefts to the head and one to the gut, while Ryan countered with a single left hook to the jaw.

Round 2 – Ryan cleverly ducked two lefts. Choynski landed a pair of jabs, the Australian countering with a quick right to the neck. Joe scored with a jab to the nose and right to the chest. Joe ended with a left-right to the nose and chest and a left hook to the jaw, winning the round.

Round 3 – Joe got in left to the ear and right to the neck. One paper said Jimmy landed a right to the kidneys and a stiff left to the nose. Joe drove a left to the ear and a right uppercut. Ryan sank a left to the stomach, but was countered with a pair of left hooks to the mouth. Joe neatly blocked a left for the jaw and landed a light right to the ear at the bell.

Round 4 – Joe snapped two quick straight lefts to the face, but Jimmy countered with a right to the chest and a light left to the ear. The "California Terror" sent Ryan into the ropes with a left-right to the jaw. Jimmy got in a left hook to the jaw and ducked Joe's follow-up blast. They traded hard lefts to the head. Joe drove a straight left to the chin and a left hook to the ear, followed by a jab on the nose and a right to the ear.

Round 5 – Choynski landed a succession of punishing lefts to the head and a hard right cross. Jimmy swung a heavy right under Joe's ear, but the *Dubuque Herald* said "in the early part of this round, Ryan was severely beaten up by the clever Californian. Blood was issuing from Ryan's nose when the round ended." *Davenport Leader*: "The Australian landed a terrific right just under the heart, raising a welt on Choynski's side. Choynski had a particularly clever way of protecting himself in breakaways."

Round 6 – Joe landed a left to the cheek and Jimmy went into a crouch. He traded a straight left for an uppercut. Ryan landed a left swing to the cheek, Joe retaliating with a straight right to the mouth, then a left-right to the head. He was throwing the right more than in previous rounds.

Round 7 – Jimmy ducked a right swing and drove a right to the ribs, but was countered with a shot to the nose. He landed another, to the body or head. Joe got in a left-right to the mouth and ear, then repeated the combination. The Aussie pounded his right to the head or shoulder, forcing Joe to clinch. He slugged Ryan to the head with a pair of hard rights.

Round 8 – Jimmy slammed a right to the body, Joe, with a pair of left hooks to the mouth. As he started another, Ryan beat him with a right to the jaw. Joe landed several lefts to the head, and Jimmy clinched. They exchanged lefts, and Joe drove in two body shots, making Ryan grunt.

Round 9 – The *Dubuque Herald* and *Grand Forks Herald* had Choynski and Ryan trading about evenly. Each landed lefts and rights (mostly rights), to the body and head, mixing their punches well.

Round 10 – Choynski came out aggressively, landing three hard lefts to the jaw. They traded rights to the neck, but Joe got the best of the next sequence, scoring heavily with left-rights to the head. Jimmy responded with a right to the torso. "Frisco Joe" finished with an ugly jab that brought the blood in a spurt from Ryan's nose, splattering all over Choynski.

Round 11 – Once more Joe came out swinging, landing a half dozen left and right swings to the head. Ryan responded with a left to the stomach or a right to the head. Joe smashed a potent left hook to the jaw and a heavy right to the wind that sent Jimmy staggering. He ducked a swing for the head and sent in another stiff jab to Ryan's bloody mouth.

Round 12 – Ryan came out fresh, but Choynski shot in a series of hurting left jabs to the mouth and a hard right. Jimmy's left eye sustained damaged, but he answered the barrage with a right to the mouth. Joe connected with a stiff uppercut, a left hook to the head and a straight left to the jaw. Another right by Joe, then Jimmy got in a blow to the head and another to the body. The *Davenport Leader* said "Ryan claimed Choynski had something in his left glove, but Referee Siler examined the mitt and found nothing." This was perhaps Ryan's best round, though he still lost it.

Round 13 – Joe landed a left hook to the neck, a heavy right to the ear and a short left to the stomach. Ryan answered with a straight left and a heavy right to the jaw. Choynski traded a left to the kidney for a right uppercut. He started the blood flowing again with a sharp jab to the proboscis. Joe ducked a vicious roundhouse right, countered with a good right to the wind, then got in a left-right to the head. The Australian closed with a right to the ear, but was bleeding profusely from the nose.

Round 14 – "The Frisco Flash" scored three consecutive left jabs to the chin, then a right and left to the head. Ryan got in a right to the chest, but Joe assaulted him with a pair of left hooks under the ear. Jimmy clinched repeatedly, but managed a left uppercut. Joe landed a left-right combination to the neck and a jab to the mouth. Ryan caught him with a right to the ear, but Joe retaliated with a left to the cheek. Jimmy feinted with the left and hammered a heavy right to the head. Ryan tried for a knockout, but failed.

Round 15 – Choynski crashed a short right to the jaw and two straight lefts to the mouth. Ryan hugged to avoid punishment, but got in a heavy left to the ribs. Joe put a little distance between Jimmy and himself, landing a pair of jabs to the face. He cracked home a pair of powerful left hooks, skinning Jimmy's cheek and causing his left eye to swell.

Round 16 – Choynski smacked a heavy right to the jaw and a left under the ear. Ryan connected with a pair of rights to the neck. They exchanged short rights to the ribs, then Joe forced Ryan to the ropes with a left-right. He ducked a heavy right and countered with a left to the neck. Jimmy smashed two heavy rights to the kidneys, sending Joe to the ropes.

Round 17 – The "California Terror" was all over Ryan. Jimmy ducked a left hook, but the American landed left to the head and two rights to the jaw. He followed with a right hook to the ear and a stiff left to the ribs. Joe got in another left hook to the head, and Jimmy replied with a right to the chest. Joe smacked a pair of left hooks to the jaw, causing his foe to clinch.

Round 18 – The men traded hard. Choynski cracked one to the chin and Ryan swung a left to the jaw, Joe coming back with a hard right to the mouth. He got in another right to the jaw, but Jimmy answered with a left to the ribs. Joe landed a straight right to the mouth and a left-right to the jaw. He ducked a vicious right and countered with right and left shots to Ryan's eye, ducking Jimmy's follow-up. The round was Joe's.

Round 19 – Choynski drove a straight left to the jaw, causing Ryan to clinch. Another jab to the mouth. Ryan pounded a right cross to the head, but Joe landed a series of jabs to Jimmy's swollen left eye. The latter came back with two lefts and a right to the neck. Now it was Joe's turn, driving two jabs to the eye, cleverly blocking a counter and bashing a heavy right on the nose. He blocked a left and cracked a right uppercut to the jaw.

Round 20 – Jimmy came out determined to score the knockout he needed to win. They exchanged rights to the neck. Joe kept up the fusillade of jabs to nose and mouth. He ducked away from a left feint, and Jimmy threw a wicked right swing that went around Joe's back. He answered with a left to the jaw and a heavy right to the forehead. Joe drove another left and blocked Ryan's counterpunch. George Siler gave the decision to Joe, "and there were no mutterings of disapproval ..."

Choynski showed he could still go 20 full rounds at a rapid pace, finish strongly and easily outpoint an opponent. After the gunshot and other bone injuries to his left hand, Joe was measuring his punches more than in his youth. He didn't often cut loose with full power in either fist, so as not to risk becoming a one-handed fighter. In this fight, Joe displayed a nice mixture of aggression and caution; enough of the former to damage and outscore his rival, but sufficient in the latter not to place himself egregiously at risk. The *Milwaukee Evening Wisconsin* said Joe would have won with a certainty in a finish fight. The *Omaha World-Herald* noted that "Choynski was trained down like a greyhound ... too fine for the long, hard chase the tough Australian gave him." Joe's propensity to overtrain still plagued him. The *Davenport Daily Leader* wrote that, when he entered the ring, "Choynski looked like a sick man, his eye being dull and his flesh flabby."

The September 5 *Dubuque Daily Herald* quoted Joe: "You know, most boxers are superstitious, but I was never troubled that way. They talk about a corner being unlucky if it happens to have been occupied by a beaten man. But in Dubuque ... All the losers in the preliminary bouts and the winners in the main events sat in the same corner. For instance, I took the corner used by Suffield, who was defeated by Forbes ... And Tommy Ryan had Sellers' place, the coon who quit with Kerwin." Even if not a bigot, Joe was not beyond using a racial epithet common to his era. "I don't place any stock in hoodoos. The only thing that hoodoos a man in the ring is a pair of stuffed gloves, when one ... happens to get to the point of his jaw."

"Australian" Jimmy gave an angry rebuttal to comments by Joe after the bout: "Choynski is quoted as saying the real reason he did not knock me out ... was he thought I would quit after I got well jabbed. Choynski seems to forget that he may be accused of quitting, too. I think I made a game fight with him ... when ... far from in good condition ... When he was in Australia he quit most deliberately against old Joe Goddard. I saw the fight ... he held out his hands to his seconds to have the gloves pulled off at the end of the 5th round ... after he had knocked Goddard down a couple of times the round before. I am prepared to bet $1,000 that Choynski cannot stop me in 20 rounds ... next time I will be in good shape. If he cannot whip me out of condition, he certainly has no chance when I am myself."[38] Ryan got a chance to back up his boast on October 20, but failed. (Both Goddard fights ended at the end of four, not five, rounds).

In an article on "Boxing Trusts," Choynski "admits he is in the business only for the money he can earn. Pugilistic honor and fame are tarnished baubles to him." Joe's attitude might have been due to his being unable to get a shot at the biggest bauble, the world's heavyweight championship. The paper quoted Joe: "And the men ... powerful enough to keep alive a business, against which the reformers of the various communities are continually charging, do a great favor for the pugilists. Of course they make money, but without them, the pugilists would gain but little."[39]

Next for Joe was a rematch with his old stablemate, Jim Hall, on September 25 in Louisville, Kentucky. It was announced in early September that he had also been matched to face middleweight, Tommy Ryan, the following October 6 at Chicago's Dearborn A.C. Tommy felt confident enough after seeing Choynski go the route against "Australian" Jimmy, to request a six-rounder with him. He announced in late September, though, that he was unable to fight. Ryan was replaced by "Kid" McCoy for the same date, in Chicago. Joe set up training camp for the Hall match at West Baden, Indiana, and Jim, in Memphis, Tennessee. Joe moved operations to

Louisville on September 18. A local paper noted: "The Californian was up bright and early yesterday morning (the 22nd). He took a few spins through the Western Park and along the river bank near Fountain Ferry (Park). Upon his return to Fountain Ferry, he worked with various ... apparatus and finished up with a few rounds with the punching bag ..."[40]

"In the afternoon, Choynski took a run up town ... to a local gymnasium, where he met three of the best amateur boxers in Kentucky. His boxing was a revelation ... very fast on his feet and showed great cleverness in blocking, side-stepping and ducking. After three long, fast bouts, Choynski spent nearly an hour with the dumbbells and other gymnastic paraphernalia, and finished up without a long breath. Instructor Gearhart of the YMHA (Young Men's Hebrew Association) ... had rarely seen a boxer in better condition. 'Joe is stronger and bigger than when I saw him last,' said Mr. Gearhart, 'and his wind is in fine shape. His muscles stand out like whipcords and yet ... pliable. His forearms are almost as hard as iron.' Choynski will rest ... with the exception of long walks ... forenoon and afternoon ... to keep 'on edge.' " One of the bouts was against an unidentified, "huge Negro from Tennessee," introduced by the referee, a "baldish little man in a wrinkled tuxedo," as the heavyweight champion of Tennessee. A young Edmund Rucker, who later fought professionally as "Kid" Rucker, saw Joe knock out his humongous opponent in the opening round of a slugfest, with a single right hand to the ribs. Rucker, who sparred a rattling bout with Jim Corbett at West Baden Springs in 1898, when the latter was preparing for Tom Sharkey, said the venue for the Choynski exhibition(s) was the Buckingham Theater. On the 23rd, Joe said he was in the best condition he'd seen in the past five years.[41]

On the 24th, Hall arrived in Louisville with a party of friends. They "went to Kenwood Park ... where quarters had been engaged ... The Australian did little training today (the 25th), only punching the bag ... He ... has many admirers in this city, where he once lived. He says Choynski has but one blow, and he knows what that is."[42] The contest was held the night of September 25 at the city's Music Hall, under the auspices of the Nonpareil A.C. Several papers said, "The fight was for the light-heavyweight championship, limited to 20 rounds ..." before a crowd of 2,000 to 2,500. In Joe's corner were Tom Williams, of England, Lawrence Fitzpatrick and Jim Watts. Behind Hall were Frank Kelly, Patsy Grubbs, "Doc" Hottun (or Dick Hattum) and "Australian" Jimmy Ryan. Reports from most papers agreed, and gave the weights as 168 pounds for Hall, 160, Choynski. Next is a consensus of contemporary accounts:[43]

"The fight was lively ... possibly in Hall's favor ... the first two rounds ... in the 3rd, Choynski used his right and left effectually ... when but half a minute ... remained ... landed several rights and lefts in succession, sending Hall to the floor, where he remained until carried to his corner ... there were cries of 'farce' ... a right hook on the jaw sent Hall down ... from spectators' standpoint ... not delivered with sufficient force to have put the Australian out." Joe wrote, in 1930: "Hall was quoted at 10 to 6 to beat me. But ... All he could accomplish was a neat smash in the opening round, ... in the mouth. I will admit it hurt and made things spin, but it was the final gesture ... (for) Hall ... In the 3rd, I knocked him so silly it took his seconds an hour to set his mental house in order ... he mumbled, 'Where am I?' Poor Jim! ... his end was sad. He died in Wisconsin, in a farmer's field where he had dragged his broken body from the roadway. It saddens one to think of great fellows like ... Hall and Peter Jackson fading away to nothing."

"In the 3rd ... Choynski ... ducks wicked lead for jaw. Hall calls referee's attention to alleged foul below the belt. Not allowed. Hall lands ... several rights and lefts before they clinch. Choynski rushes ... landing right and left on face several times in succession, Hall going to the floor ... remained face downward, resting on one arm, apparently making an effort to regain his feet, while Referee Rucker counted ... cries of 'fake' ... the blow ... did not seem to possess sufficient force to ... put out a bantam weight ... 'With a competent referee,' said Hall ... 'my claim of foul would have been allowed ... The blow ... in the first part of the 3rd ... took all of the fight out of me ... made me dizzy ... I was unable to guard against Choynski's swings.'"

As Jim regained consciousness a minute or two later, he supposedly raised himself to one elbow and sleepily said to a reporter, " 'Oh, I'm tired; lemme sleep a little longer. 'Tain't time to get up.' He thought he was back in Memphis, in his own ... bed, and his landlady was calling him in the morning. 'It did not hurt ... I just dropped off into dreamland, and imagined I was back home, as I began to regain my senses.' 'Something like hitting the pipe, isn't it?' suggested E. Gray, the Louisville sport and pugilistic promoter. 'Yes,' was the reply, and then Jim went out to a neighborhood high ball joint, and saturated himself with snowball straights."[44]

Joe was matched to box Steve O'Donnell in a 20-rounder at the Music Hall on October 11, as part of the annual Elks Club Fair. He was back in Chicago, set to arrive in Louisville the following Monday. "He will complete his training ... at Fountain Ferry ... The match didn't occur until the 27th, and Joe participated in three more before then. On October 6, at the Windy City's Fort Dearborn Athletic Club, Joe and nemesis, "Kid" McCoy, agreed to battle six rounds, a draw if both finished on their feet. The *Chicago Tribune* wrote that this agreement possibly "saved Referee Hogan from a dilemma, for the fighting was fairly even." Most papers, though, said McCoy had the better of it. While the majority said the fight came off at the Fort Dearborn A.C., the local *Chicago Tribune* and *Oshkosh Daily Northwestern* said it was held at the Star Theater. McCoy occupied his "unlucky corner," the same he sat in during his surprise loss to McCormick the preceding August. He was attended by Homer Selby, Jack Leonard,

Harry and Sammy Harris. "Choynski came in accompanied by two boyish-looking seconds, N. and G. Shrosbee. He looked far better than ... with Ryan at Dubuque a month ago, having more color and a brighter eye." The following account blends several contemporary reports.[45]

Round 1 – After a mutually cautious start, McCoy landed a right to the ribs and escaped a return. He was mindful of the McCormick punch that cold-cocked him two months earlier. Choynski blocked a left to the face. The "Kid" drove left to face and right to ribs, but Joe countered with a stinging left to the ear. McCoy beat a tattoo on the ribs with the right in a clinch, then brought it up to the ear. Joe unsuccessfully tried to draw him out with a myriad of feints. At least two papers said Joe drew blood from McCoy's nose, others saying it happened in the 2nd frame.

Round 2 – After a McCoy left to the head, the men clinched. Each landed short-arm shots to the body and head, "but Choynski brought first blood with a short hook on McCoy's nose." "Choynski's left was cleverly blocked, and McCoy jabbed his face three times in quick succession. Several good exchanges ... Choynski twice backed away from McCoy's onslaughts."

Round 3 – The "Corkscrew Kid" slammed a left to the mouth and right to the ear. Joe retaliated with a right to the ear, but took a left to the mouth. The "Kid" got in two jabs to the face and one to the ribs, working his foe against the ropes. He shifted, ala Fitzsimmons, feinted with the right and crashed a left hook to the mouth, sending Joe to the mat. He got up immediately, his mouth bleeding heavily, this before the advent of the protective mouthpiece. McCoy advanced, looking to finish Joe, but the latter roared back, snapping his foe's head back with a left-right.

Round 4 – McCoy struck with two sharp lefts to the face, but Joe got even with a hard left hook to the mouth, bringing a cheer from the crowd. Joe scored with a left hook to the ear, but McCoy snapped his head back with a pair of straight lefts. "Choynski evened matters with right and left, hard to the jaw." The "Kid" landed a left-right to the head, but Joe staggered him with a nasty right counter on the neck.

Round 5 – Joe blocked a McCoy left and drove a hard left to the eye. The "Kid" returned fire, staggering his rival with a crashing right over the ear. The light-heavyweight champion covered his left ear with his glove. Both landed hard lefts and rights to head. In a clinch, the Hoosier rapped Joe on the ear with a left, then wrestled him to the floor at the bell.

Round 6 – McCoy snapped the jab to Joe's nose and started the blood flowing. Choynski missed a right to the chin and Selby sank a right to the kidneys. In a clinch, he reddened Joe's ribs with short, pounding rights. Choynski sent a left to the neck and a hard right to the ribcage. The "Kid" scored a left to the mouth, but Joe shook him with a right to the jaw before the gong. Joe's lips were a bit swollen, McCoy escaped without a mark. As agreed beforehand, referee Malachi Hogan declared the fight a draw.

Chicago Tribune: "Even battle ... Hoosier scores only knockdown, but no decided advantage ... McCoy may have had a shade of advantage ... but Choynski's friends would have denounced such a decision ... no question the arrangement of a draw if both men were on their feet detracted from the vigor of the contest, for while both ... apparently fought earnestly, a bout of such limited duration was hardly sufficient for either to emphasize his superiority. It would have been more satisfactory ... had such an arrangement been made public in advance. Both men did a fair share of the aggressive work. McCoy did some clever work ... once or twice had Choynski guessing. McCoy's lightning left was often in action, and although Choynski cleverly blocked some ... many ... landed. Some ... delivered while the 'Kid' was on his toes. In the clinches, McCoy did the better work ... Choynski showed great reluctance at times in breaking."

The *Oshkosh Daily Northwestern*'s exaggerated account: "The Indianan landed three blows to Choynski's one and twice sent the latter to the floor. At the end ... neither ... had much more than scratches to show ... although McCoy had a slightly blackened left eye from ... Choynski's right hand ... early (in) the fight. McCoy was easily the cleverer ... Choynski took more chances and put in blows ... a trifle harder. McCoy frequently used a short, snappy left ... while Choynski made some good swings and blocked cleverly. Both ... were in ... condition, although Choynski seemed short on wind after the 3rd ..." The *Atlanta Constitution* and *Brooklyn Eagle* said "McCoy ... clearly outpointed the Californian ... took no chances ... stabbing Choynski with his left. He used his right ... seldom, but it generally counted ... when he did ... Choynski scored many times ... with his right." The *Sandusky Star* of the 12th said McCoy claimed it was Joe's demand that they draw if the bout went the limit, and added that Joe was better than when the pair last tangled.

The Chicago Athletic Club announced on October 11 that they had selected Choynski to referee their bouts during the winter, beginning on the 14th. On the 12th at Louisville's Monarch Athletic Club, Joe was to have fought Steve O'Donnell in a 20 round contest. "The men were to box for a part of the gate receipts, which only aggregated $200. Choynski was not willing to go into the ring for so small an amount. O'Donnell sparred six rounds with Beech Ruble of Ohio, and the small, disgruntled audience went home." While top fighters in their weight class were getting paid purses of from $5,000 to $10,000 for such fights, Joe could hardly be blamed for refusing to risk his reputation for a measly $200, or go 20 rounds for that amount. Joe seemed to be doing well for himself, acting as his own manager. On the 16th and 17th, three bouts were in the works for him.

Boxing referee and baseball umpire, Tim Hurst, said he had arranged a fight for Joe with Dick Moore, at the St. Louis Athletic Club. Joe was also matched to box in Cincinnati with New Yorker, Tom Carey. Carey was already in Cincinnati to train. An Ohio paper added: "This is in a manner,

(Joe's) home. Joe married a Cincinnati young lady and spends a great deal of his off-hours in this city." Carey had a win over Joe Butler. The *Brooklyn Eagle* said Choynski was trying to arrange a match with "Kid" McCoy in New York, feeling he could win in a long fight..[46] First, he had a scheduled 25 round rematch with "Australian" Jimmy Ryan, at the Broadway (New York) Athletic Club on the night of October 20, before 3,500 spectators. Many who thought Joe was a "back number" were astonished at his dominance. Five contemporary reports comprise the following:[47]

Round 1 – Joe got in a left hook to the jaw and landed at least a dozen times with his accurate jab. Ryan's right eye was discolored and starting to swell. He was on the defensive, only getting in one left to Joe's face.

Round 2 – Joe kept the jab going and began throwing the straight right behind it, landing three times to the head. Ryan tried to inflict damage during the infighting, but clever Joe blocked every punch. He bored in throughout the frame, connecting at least 20 times with lefts and rights to the face. Again, Jimmy managed one clean left to the jaw, at close quarters.

Round 3 – Ryan determined to land a knockout with the right. Joe blocked all attempts, but wasn't idle, either, landing at least a dozen stinging jabs to the eye and two right crosses to the jaw, staggering his adversary.

Round 4 – Ryan shot from his corner in a furious rush, landing a roundhouse right to the jaw. Joe was shaken, and wisely clinched until the referee parted them. Jimmy started a left for the body, but Joe beat him to it, straightening him with a hard left uppercut. Ryan was unable to land again in the round, although he did some clever dodging. Choynski continued to dominate with the smart jab, winning the heat.

Round 5 – "Australian" Jimmy opened again with a gritty charge, connecting with a heavy right to the ribcage. As before, it was the only punch he got through Joe's guard. Ryan tried to follow up, but a snapping jab stopped him. Joe controlled his rival, leaving Ryan's nose a bloody mess.

Round 6 – This was Ryan's best round, although he lost it. He came roaring out as usual, driving a straight left to the face. They exchanged lefts to the jaw, then Joe drew blood again with a hard jab to the nose. Jimmy kept trying, twice visiting Choynski's body and face with left and right. Joe outpointed Ryan, the latter's face being badly bruised and bloodied.

Round 7 – In a dying effort at victory, Ryan stormed after Choynski and crossed a hard right on the jaw. This incurred Joe's wrath. He drove his foe into the ropes with a flurry of lefts and rights, pummeled him into a corner and felled him with a powerful right hook to the jaw. Jimmy took a nine-count before regaining his feet. Joe plowed in again and dropped him with another crashing right to the same spot. Ryan somehow managed to stagger again to his feet. This time, Choynski approached with caution, having in the past been knocked out with a "Hail Mary" punch at such a juncture. He feinted, saw an opening, and hammered a right to the jaw. Ryan dropped to his hands and knees, and was counted out at 2:35 of the round.

Joe (1930): "Ryan ... did his best ... to add my scalp to his list. But I was ... banging away with both hands ... in the first five rounds ... in the 6th ... I hammered him unmercifully." "The Days of Finish Fights": "Ryan landed on his hands and knees, as if ... looking for a collar button, until the 10 seconds had flitted by. Then he was lifted to his feet by Choynski." The *Milwaukee Evening Wisconsin* on the 21st said: "Choynski was at his best, light as a feather on his feet, quick as a flash and heady withal." *Philadelphia Inquirer:* "Ryan was outpointed from the first tap of the gong, and when the knockout came, Choynski was as fresh as when he began." *Brooklyn Daily Eagle:* "Jab after jab landed repeatedly on Ryan's left eye, and that organ was closed tight long before Joe put on the finishing touches." The *Melbourne Sportsman*, drawing from New York papers, said Choynski weighed 12 stone (168 pounds) and Ryan, 174 pounds. They fought at catchweights, therefore Joe's light-heavyweight crown may not have been at stake.

There was no rest for Joe, as he took on St. Paul, Minnesota's Dick Moore on October 23 at the St. Louis Athletic Club, in St. Louis, Missouri. The fight was slated for 20 rounds, but Joe dispatched Moore in 3. The referee was Tim Hurst. Joe had the edge in height, weight and reach. The following blends four contemporary accounts:[48]

Dick Moore

Round 1 – Moore threw lefts and rights to the body, forcing his foe to retreat. Joe landed a stiff jab, jarring his adversary. This was it for Dick, as Joe dominated the remainder of the fight.

Round 2 – Choynski had him sized up. After a brief exchange, he floored Moore with a right to the jaw. Soon after, Dick was dropped by another right to the jaw. This time, on regaining his feet, he made a ferocious charge. The round ended in the midst of a heated exchange.

Round 3 – Joe bludgeoned Moore with a jab and a right to the side of the head, leveling the St. Paul slugger a 3rd time. Dick bravely took to his feet, but was sent to the mat with another right to the jaw. He rose a 4th time, but Joe floored him again with a bombing right. Moore gallantly tried to pull himself up, but was counted. November 11 *Police Gazette:* "Moore ... made a desperate effort to regain his feet ... barely succeeded ... toppled over again from weakness and gave up the ghost."

October 25 *Denver Post*: "All around town ... everybody who takes any interest in boxing ... was pleased to hear of Joe Choynski's victory ... When Joe was here during the summer, he made ... many friends by his gentlemanly behavior, and ... can retain a friend ... a man who has never fought above 165 pounds, to mix ... with giants like Jeffries, Maher, Goddard, Sharkey, etc., was relying on ... cleverness ... his courage ... in excess of his physical resources. Joe is ... entitled to more credit than many more noted boxers, and deserves the well wishes of boxing patrons who ... admire courage." On the same night, in Syracuse, New York, Peter Maher failed to put out Ed Dunkhorst in seven rounds. Bob Fitzsimmons was one of the few to turn the trick. Fitz, in the build-up to this bout, was credited with the phrase, "The bigger they are, the harder they fall."[49]

Only three days after the Moore fight, Joe saw action again, against Steve O'Donnell. The set-to was only for six rounds, but Joe put out his larger rival. O'Donnell, who had been Jim Corbett's sparring partner and known as a clever boxer, was also something of a "gym" fighter. He looked

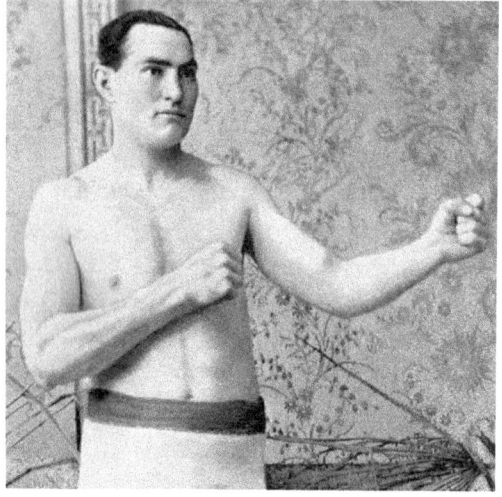

Steve O'Donnell, of Australia

great in training, but erratic in real fights. Still, Steve defeated Frank Craig (W4 1893), Herman Bernau (KO15 1895), Jake Kilrain (KO21 1895, TKO5 1899), Billy Woods (TKO15 1895), Owen Sullivan (TKO10 1896), Frank Slavin (TKO5 1896) and Alec Greggains (KO8 1897). About 6' tall, he tipped the scales at some 180 pounds, but was known more for boxing skill than punching force. The *Chicago Tribune* said Steve appeared to be 20 pounds heavier than Joe, but "a trifle soft." The match occurred on the night of October 27 at the Star Theater in Chicago, under the auspices of the Fort Dearborn Athletic Club. The following is from ringside accounts:[50]

Round 1 – Choynski put a left in the stomach. Each blocked a left. They exchanged left jabs, and Joe got warmed up. He sent in four stiff jabs to the face, sending Steve's head back each time. Joe smashed a hard left hook to the jaw, drove a straight left to the face and sent his man to the canvas. Steve took six seconds before rising. Joe feinted several times, then landed a pair of lightning left hooks to the jaw. O'Donnell ducked a 3rd, but the

"California Terror" followed with a short, straight right to the mouth that dropped Steve again. Three seconds later, the bell saved him. The Australian groggily regained his feet and staggered to his corner.

Round 2 – Joe sent a jab and hard left hook to the jaw. Steve shot a right to the kidneys in a clinch. His "efforts to counter were ... laughable, Choynski ... being a foot out of range before his opponent's blow was delivered. (Joe) opened a cut on O'Donnell's upper lip, which bled freely the rest of the contest ... Choynski hardly used his right ... (Steve) did some clever ducking ..."

Round 3 – O'Donnell led more and did slightly better work in the clinches. Joe continued sticking the jab at mid- and long-range, and by mid-round had his adversary's nose and mouth bleeding profusely.

Round 4 – O'Donnell's best round. He stabbed Joe with the left, ducked a wicked right, then drew applause by mixing

Joe Choynski, 1899

with Joe for several seconds. His punches lacked force, though. Joe "had a trick of getting in sideways in the clinches and sending his right to the ribs and body in quick succession, and O'Donnell seemed unable to reply ... Choynski ... sending in three hard left jabs to the face."

Round 5 – O'Donnell came out "game, but weak." Joe eased up, and Steve made a good showing early on. He tired, though, finishing in poor condition. Some papers said Joe ended the fight here, scoring several knockdowns. Many clearly indicate, though, that the bout ended in the 6th.

Round 6 – After a series of jabs, Joe drove O'Donnell to the ropes. He shot a right and left to the head, then hammered a left hook to the jaw.

Steve crashed to the floor in a heap. The *San Francisco Call* and *Brooklyn Eagle* said this was the 2nd of two knockdowns in the round, giving no details of the first. Choynski audibly told Steve to "Stay down – stay down." "O'Donnell was badly beaten, both eyes ... closed ... his lips cut," and his nose badly swollen. The *Chicago Tribune* said the knockout came just after the two minute mark. Most sources said Joe could have ended the fight any time after the knockdown in round one, but "went at it easily" thereafter. Joe (1927): "After knocking the big Australian down repeatedly, I floored him ... in the 6th round with a stiff right hook. I did not want to hit him again and urged him to stay down. It was doubtful if he really could have got up. Anyway, he took my advice and was counted out."

Choynski had just scored three knockouts within a week. Papers said he was fighting better than in "many years."[51] As Tom Sharkey would soon be an opponent again, a nice description of his fighting methods and ability follows. November 3 *Biloxi Daily Herald*: "Sharkey is low in stature, with wonderful knots of muscle over his body. His chest protrudes like the chest of a pouter pigeon. His short, heavy arms are knotted from toil while he was a common seaman on board the United States cruiser, Charleston. He has the shortest reach of any of the big boxers. His ... hips seem weak under the great bulk of muscle above. But it is the hips and legs of Sharkey which have given him his victories. He is one of the fastest men on his feet in the ring, and uses his legs like a lightweight ... maneuvering for a position."

"Sharkey is a vicious ... foul fighter ... can take punishment. He merely looked surprised ... when Peter Maher dropped him with a terrific right-hander." Sharkey took terrific punishment against Fitz and "Kid" McCoy, coming back to knock out the latter. He had improved a lot over the past couple of years, but sustained terrible damage in the Jeffries smack-down. William Inglis, author of "Champions Off Guard" (1932), saw Tom in his dressing room after the fight, saying he lay in a stupor on the rub-down couch, unresponsive, both eyes closed and swollen, white styptic power (to stop bleeding) giving his face a ghastly pallor. The attending physician, Dr. Butler, found Tom had two broken ribs, two others with "green twig" fractures, and "at the spine two or three ribs ... knocked out of their sockets." Jim's power and Tom's toughness were both in evidence.

In early November, Choynski said he had purchased a residence in La Grange, Illinois, about 12 miles from Chicago. "He will do what he can in the ring during the coming year and then engage in some quiet business in Chicago." While the location of the home is uncertain, his street address in 1905 was 117 Madison Avenue. A house at 117 South Madison still stands. The two-storey home, built in 1891 or 1892, is 2,500 square feet, with a lot of 8,100 square feet.[52] If this was the location of his poultry farm, it was a small one. Joe's next bout was the evening of November 4, against Tom "Jabber" Carey. It was held at Robinson's Opera House in Cincinnati, under the aegis of that city's Olympic Athletic Club, part of a "grand boxing carnival." The bout was set for 15 rounds, but a meager purse of only $600. Joe arrived in Cincinnati on the 2nd. Tom had just finished two weeks of hard work and was in fine fettle.[53] Reports said "Carey was thoroughly outclassed ... utterly unable to defend himself" and "Carey ... went down from a love tap ... allowed himself to be counted out. Carey became frightened in the early part of the 1st ... ran around the ring during the rest ... went to the floor from a ... punch, and remained ... while the referee counted 10. The large crowd left the club yelling 'fake.' " A 3rd paper said the angry horde wanted to mob Carey. The end came in round 2.[54]

On November 11, Joe refereed the Clarence Forbes-Danny Dougherty fight at the Chicago A.C. Danny was floored some 15 times, before Joe counted him out in the 6th round![55] Several papers announced (again) that "Joe Choynski has decided to retire from the ring ... has managed to save ... enough to buy a home and keep ... comfortable ... the remainder of his life. Choynski's last fight will probably be with Tom Sharkey. The Sailor has agreed to meet in a limited round bout in Chicago, just as soon as his sore shoulder will permit ..." Joe "has almost all the time had the misfortune of meeting the really good ones just as they were coming to the surface. Hence he has been termed the 'champion trial horse.' "[56]

Tom's L25 to Jeffries was perhaps the most grueling fight in history. Fought at an inhuman pace, under a battery of arc lights raising temperatures to over 100 degrees Fahrenheit, the war began taking on legendary status the day after, aided by hyperbole and the principals' penchant for exaggeration. Jeff said one of Sharkey's three ribs that he caved in, was protruding from the skin! Neither objective eyewitness accounts nor photographic evidence validate this. Still, Tom waged a brave, epic battle, which might have been called a draw. The trauma took a heavy toll; he was never the same. How they endured is difficult to fathom.

Tom O'Rourke was negotiating again with Choynski, for a fight with Walcott. Virtually everyone in the boxing world thought Tom was crazy, biting off more than his fighter could chew. The latter only stood about 5' 1½" tall, but was built like a squat Mike Tyson. He won the welterweight crown in 1901, defending it several times. The *Pawtucket Times* said: "O'Rourke figures ... Walcott ... being so much smaller than Choynski, will have a chance to do more straight body punching than ... with a man of his own height ... also ... his man will be a much smaller target to shoot at, and Choynski will have to hit downward ... a great disadvantage." It was announced December 15 that the Dubuque Athletic Association had signed the fighters for the Saengerbund Auditorium the first week in January. The fight would not occur until late February, though, as Walcott broke his hand on December 14 while training.[57]

Round Eighteen

The Great Swindle
(January 1900 – December 1900)

The year 1900 opened with a reversal of fortunes for the world of Boxing. Whereas Theodore Roosevelt had always favored "the manly art" as New York City's Police Commissioner, he now opposed it. As New York State Governor, Roosevelt was more concerned with the political hot issues of his constituents, to the point where he recommended repeal of the Horton Law. This law, enacted in 1896, legalized boxing in the state. With future United States President Roosevelt's help, the Lewis Law would soon be voted in, repealing the former, and making pugilism illegal in New York. "Teddy" said: "Boxing is a fine sport, but this affords no justification of prize fighting, any more than the fact that a cross-country run or a ride on a wheel is healthy, justifies such a demoralizing exhibition as a six-day race. When any sport is carried on primarily for money – it is in danger of ... acquiring some exceedingly undesirable characteristics. In ... prize fighting ... the exhibition has a demoralizing and brutalizing effect ... the gross abuses in its present administration makes (sic) its existence on the statute books of the Empire State an offense against decency."[1]

As the Horton Law was in effect until the end of August, even more importance was lent to Joe's next tilt, with "Kid" McCoy, in Brooklyn, New York. The clash was scheduled for 25 rounds. McCoy had just knocked out Peter Maher in five frames, on January 1. Joe left for New York on the 9th, arriving the next day. McCoy would train at William Muldoon's famous "health farm" in White Plains, New York, as he had for Maher.[2] Former Greco-Roman wrestling champion Muldoon, known as "The Solid Man" and "Iron Duke," built his first camp at his birthplace, Belfast, New York, moving to White Plains in 1894. Later in 1900, he relocated to Purchase, New York and named the fitness center, "The Olympia." He would die there in 1933, after serving as New York State Athletic Commissioner.

Joe would referee boxing matches long after he retired as an active fighter. The January 10 *Daily Iowa Capital* quoted him: "I always carry a watch in my hand when I'm refereeing. You can't tell me a referee won't lose time in counting the nine seconds, without one ... I've seen men down ... nearly 14 seconds in a championship fight, just by slowing (sic) counting of a referee. You count 10 as some of these referees do and have some one hold a watch ... see how far off you are." Joe was considered one of the better referees of the era. *New York Sun*: "The fight may be interesting ...

because of Choynski's remarkable cleverness and ring experience. He outclasses Maher as a scientist, which leads many ... to believe McCoy will not find him ... an easy mark ... The Californian fights much after McCoy's style. He is light-footed, uses his left often ... and knows how to work at long range. He is not rough and believes in taking his time. As regards hitting ability, McCoy has quite an advantage. He is faster ... getting in and out and has received credit for being the Californian's master in science. Choynski ... is sure of staying the entire route and feels ... he has a fine chance of securing the large end of the purse. He has been training hard for nearly a month and is in good condition. Since he ... arrived ... he has been working in a local gymnasium ... weighs about 168 pounds and expects to enter the ring at about 170. McCoy will weigh about 168."

Joe: "I have been looking forward to this match ... and have prepared accordingly. I know ... McCoy ... is a shifty fellow, speedy on his feet ... but he has never knocked me out. I may be getting old and all that, but it is not so long ago that McCoy and myself went 20 hard rounds in 'Frisco. I am going to retire after this year, and if I can add any luster to my record by defeating McCoy, I am going to do so." "The Kid" had been training the past six weeks, including the four weeks he put in for the Maher bout. He told the *Sun*: "Some people have an idea Choynski is a soft mark ... I don't think so, and have trained as hard as I ever did. He is clever and shifty and I will not hold him cheap ... to win ... will compel Sharkey and Fitzsimmons to recognize me. I want to knock him out. I wasn't in good health when we met in 'Frisco, but ... there will be another story ... tomorrow night." Indeed there would be. Joe was experiencing something of an "Indian Summer" in terms of late career performance, while Selby was about 10 pounds heavier than their last meeting. Odds on McCoy were about 3 to 1.[3]

A quick assessment of McCoy's record to this point (the Choynski bouts aside) shows victories over Jim Daly (TKO3 1896), Bill Doherty (KO9 1896), Nick Burley (KO3 1897, KO2 1898), George LaBlanche (KO1 1897), Dan Creedon (TKO16 1897), Gus Ruhlin (W20 1898), Steve O'Donnell (KO6 1899), Jack McCormick (TKO8 1899), Billy Stift (KO13 1899) and the KO5 Maher. He had come close to stopping Tom Sharkey, before the "Sailor" dispatched him in the 10th. Joe, in 1927, said McCoy tried to intimidate him, or "get his goat," prior to the fight. "I received a visit from McCoy's brother, Homer Selby. I surmised at once that the scare racket was to be employed. Homer must have read my thoughts, for he choked in the middle of his opening sentence. 'The Kid wants to know—' he began and hesitated. 'Well,' I growled as roughly as good health would permit, 'what does the Kid want to know?' 'The Kid – er – wants to know – er – if you would like to fight winner take all, in case of a knockout.' I laughed. 'You go back and ask the Kid which of my goats he prefers – Nancy or Billy,' I said, and Homer eased himself away."

On the night of January 12, 1900, at the Broadway Athletic Club in New York, Joe competed in what would be one of the biggest heists in sports history. The referee for the scheduled 25 round match was Johnny White. Choynski's seconds were Owen Ziegler, Dan Dougherty and Fred Hausman, while McCoy's were Homer, Jimmy De Forest and Frank Hart.

"Kid" McCoy, 1899

Joe wore "a blue breechclout, American colors around his waist." Receipts were said to exceed $15,000. The following is a blend of primary source accounts:[4]

Round 1 – McCoy shot a left hook to the jaw. Joe slipped in his own corner. He rose and sent a left to "The Kid's" jaw. The Hoosier landed two lefts to the face and a right over the heart. The round was his, according to the wire service report. Choynski differed, saying in 1927 and '30: "I was determined he should not outsmart me as he had tried to do with Tommy Ryan and Peter Maher. I had no intention of boxing him. My previous fights with him proved how futile this would be. I decided on a radical change in fight strategy. I would make it a slugging bee from the tap of the gong, and keep ... slugging until one of us dropped. I knew I could outhit McCoy and I was just as fast as he ... I tore into McCoy like a bulldog after a tramp cat. It brought the crowd to their feet, yelling like lunatics. I saw McCoy was unprepared for my terrific offensive ... I plastered him with rights and lefts ... He rallied ... about the middle of the 1st round ... and was soon back-trading and resorting to his clever left to stab me off. But I bored in. Four times he speared me with that left. Then he asked, in that insulting way of his: 'Say, don't those hurt?' I grunted: 'Surely, you're not trying to hurt me, are you, Kid?' By the end of the 1st round I scented a knockout ... I had reached his body several times with sickening smashes, and had jarred him down to his toes with a couple of hooks to the head. I had not been hit effectively. Sometimes a fighter knows when he is about to win – feels a sudden, reassuring rush of power. And I think McCoy sensed this, too. He had a weird look on his face as he slunk to his corner."

Round 2 – "Choynski sent the Kid to the floor with a right on the jaw.

McCoy took nine seconds ... Choynski sent him down again with a left on the neck. Twice more McCoy was floored ... he went to his corner bleeding badly from the nose and mouth." *Brooklyn Daily Eagle*: "Three times ... the Kid had been sent to the floor with right hand smashes on the jaw, and was rising ... when the timekeeper's bell rang." Choynski: "Not for an instant was there to be any rest ... until one of us was stretched on the floor, helpless. McCoy started a blow ... a left to the kitchen bent the Kid forward ... swift as light, I feinted with a left hook for the head and, as he raised his right to block, crossed my dependable old right ... to his chin. Bang! Down went McCoy – lifeless ... with a crash that shook the ring posts ... an impact that loosened Tom O'Rourke's diamond shirt stud. He was finished ... the place was a madhouse. McCoy had been the favorite in the betting, and the betting was heavy. The fast pace made me blow, but I had plenty of fight left." Choynski and Edgren misidentified the referee as "Charlie White," another famous ref of the period. Joe: "As the referee ... started counting ... I smiled at my seconds. That smile was premature. Perhaps it would be more convincing to let an unprejudiced observer tell it."

"Bob Edgren wrote: 'Choynski got a vicious right over to McCoy's jaw. He was down 18 seconds. But the referee was there to see McCoy win, not lose. He counted in a most peculiar manner: *One – two – Choynski, get back there – three – Choynski, go to your corner or I'll stop this count. You've got to stand further away – four – I told you to go to your corner – five,'* and so on. When the count was finally up to 10 – it must have been 18 – McCoy got up. Choynski went after him, eager to give him the finishing blow. McCoy went down two or three times. Once he stayed down 12 seconds by the timekeeper's watch. It had been the custom at the Broadway club to ring the bell after a knockout, just as it is rung at the end of a round. Thinking he was finished, the timekeeper rang the bell. Then they dragged McCoy to his corner – after only two minutes of the round had passed. Thus, McCoy was given the full benefit of the other minute, and the regular minute's rest, as well.' Edgren's account is substantially correct, with the exception of his suggestion that the shortening of the round was a mistake. If that was a mistake, so is the city hall. And now, in the face of this travesty, I was forced to come out for the 3rd time and start cutting McCoy down all over again." Referee Johnny White, in a *Police Gazette* interview, said, at 1:45 of the round, the timekeeper tapped his bell several times; the succession of taps being used to signify the end of the fight, not the round.

Round 3 – "McCoy fought like a crazy man when he rushed out of his corner, and Choynski was equally erratic ... McCoy got the better of the Western man at close quarters. Choynski rushed McCoy, but the Kid was too spry on his feet, and Joe slipped to the floor in a vain attempt to land a swing. When Joe got up, he ran into a clinch, from which the referee had to separate them. Then ... landed a right swing on the jaw and McCoy went down, taking nearly seven seconds ... When McCoy got up, Choynski rushed ... his legs gave way and he fell to the floor, but regained his feet in an instant. McCoy was queer in his leg movement, but went in and mixed ... McCoy hooked his right to the jaw, Choynski landing his left at the same moment, and both men went down ... got up ... the bell rang while they were mixing ... Neither ... evidently heard the gong ... McCoy whipped his right over on the jaw and Choynski fell. There were wild cries of 'Foul, foul,' as Choynski was carried to his corner, and ... unable to respond when the bell called him for the 4th. Choynski's seconds threw up the sponge as McCoy rushed from his corner ... and McCoy was declared the winner." Thus, the foul haymaker by McCoy rendered Joe unable to answer the bell for a 4th round which never should have been necessary.

Joe: "It was the consensus that I got the rawest deal in the history of fighting – outside of the double-cross given Bob Fitzsimmons by ... Wyatt Earp." "Every newspaper in New York denounced the referee and blasted the officials to high heaven. Even John L. Sullivan ... was disgusted: 'Choynski ... knocked McCoy out in the 2nd round, and if a knockout counts for anything, Choynski should have been given the fight. McCoy was my choice and I bet on him, but he was defeated by ... Choynski. Joe got a raw deal all around.' And Bob Fitzsimmons, also a witness, testified: 'To deprive Choynski of the fight after he had scored a clean knockout was nothing short of theft. This kind of work is an outrage on the fighters and the spectators, and if allowed, it means the death of fighting.' I have met some weird ring characters in my time, including Sharkey, Denver Ed Smith and the erratic Mysterious Billy Smith, but I take my hat off to McCoy when it comes to ... ring travesties ... it would be interesting to know just what goes inside the cranium of a split personality like McCoy."

"A word about the corkscrew punch. McCoy himself was astonished when he read in the papers one morning that he had invented a new blow ... the corkscrew. The Kid had knocked some fellow out with a left hook, or rather, a series of left hooks, for that was his style. Several days later, he was telling ... reporters how he did it. In slow-motion picture style, he illustrated the left hook. It was observed that the Kid's fist turned at the wrist as his knuckles neared the jaw of his imaginary foe ... reporters concluded this was the deadly feature – the twisting of the wrist – which all American boxers practice with the left hook, and they gave it the name of the corkscrew. Fighters smiled over the yarn, but the ... punch became a prize-ring legend." Joe said he utilized a form of McCoy's punch as an amateur, as related by writer Joe Williams in the April 29, 1925 *Ogden Standard-Examiner*.

Norman Selby/McCoy, did often change his story, further confusing the legend of "The Real McCoy." On September 4, 1924, while sitting in a prison cell, on murder charges, Selby was asked by a reporter how he invented the punch. He said a worker at a shooting gallery told him the spiral grooving inside a rifle imparted more speed and force. McCoy got the idea to add a quick twist to his punch, and saw that it did more damage than a regular blow. "I tried to teach ... boxers how to deliver the corkscrew punch, but they could not learn. Some twist their hands too much or not enough, or too soon or too late. The hand has to be twisted just as the blow is delivered. The impact is increased and the blow given terrific force by the effect of the twisted arm, with its turning muscles."

McCoy, recapping his career in 1904, could only speak of his bout with Joe. "Although I have been boxing ... some 12 years and ... over 200 ring battles ... I can without hesitation ... point to my 3rd fight with Joe Choynski ... as the hardest trial of my ring career ... crowded into those nine minutes was more real action than two fighters have ever produced in a similar time in a ring ... I ... am sure no two men will ever again fight with gloves as we did. I went into the ring with features as perfect as the day I was born, and came out with a countenance ... which resembled anything but a human face. My nose was broken, my flesh slashed and cut, and blood dripped from ... everywhere. When I reached my dressing room ... I wondered how I ... who had always prided myself on ... defense, could have been pounded into such a sight, and could never ... to this day, account for the unusual manner in which I fought. Friends told me ... we battled like men whose bodies and souls were controlled by the devil ... threw science and guard to the winds ... in a wild, insane fusillade of blows which felled us both to the floor, time and again. I had fought Choynski twice before ... and believed I knew his every move, but after the first hard blow I gave him near the end of the 1st round, he seemed a different man ... no longer the cool ... shifty boxer ... I sparred with at San Francisco and Chicago. He became a demon, with seemingly one purpose ... my total annihilation."

"I knew by the wicked glitter in his eyes ... for the 2nd round it was to be a terrible fight ... He was in the center of the ring almost before the clang died ... and rushed me to the ropes with a vicious right ... in the stomach. As he bent over me I tried to jab him off, but he clung to me with a strange strength ... with ... difficulty I shook him loose ... raised my guard ... too late ... Choynski's left ... came crashing into my face, his wrist striking me under the nose and almost erasing that feature from my face. I felt the bones crack and the cartilage tear as his arm was raised, and I knew my nose had been broken. The pain ... was terrific. No blow I ... received in my career ... bruised my very heart as that had, and I sank to my knees ... The whole front of my face seemed gone ... as I reclined upon one knee I rubbed my glove across my bleeding features and smiled through my pain, as I realized that there was no part of my physiognomy missing. John White ... tolled off the seconds while I spat blood ... what I suffered in those few seconds no one will ever know ... I ... confess the sound of the gong was ... welcome. As I arose to go to my chair there was a great uproar and confusion ... I did not know what ... caused the sudden outburst until my brother, Homer ... told me one of the Choynski crowd ... reached over and hit the gong with his cane before ... time expired ... we were given a minute and 32 seconds' rest ... to keep the time straight ... at its conclusion my strength ... returned, and I determined to finish Choynski in the next round."

"Choynski ... swung both hands for my head. I easily avoided ... for they were wild, and ... a short-arm jolt ... reached Choynski's chin and felled him in a heap ... I knew I had him, for he tumbled on me as soon as he regained his feet, and we both went down ... When we ... both struggled to our feet, the persistence of Choynski's hugging told me I had but to throw him off and put in the final blow. As I loosened up, he straightened up and brought around his right in a final effort. It grazed my battered nose. The blow was Choynski's last ... his head sank momentarily on his breast. I jabbed him lightly with the left, and as he raised his chin ... I poised the right. At that moment the bell clanged ... but it was too late. I had started the blow and could not stop it. My glove crashed into Choynski's jaw and he fell prone on the floor like a dead man. As his seconds ... dragged him to his corner, the great assemblage went crazy with excitement. There were wild cries of 'foul,' but the referee appreciated the fact that I started the blow almost simultaneously with the ... bell, and there had been no foul ..."

"Choynski's handlers ... were unable to bring their man to his senses for the 4th round. As they released him, he pitched forward from his chair and fell ... upon his face ... the sponge was tossed into the ring ... There was some dissatisfaction with the sudden termination ... but all fair-minded men appreciated that Choynski had been fairly knocked out, despite the howls of some who wished to deprive me of the glory of victory ... I was prepared to go on and Choynski was not. What other course could an honest referee have taken? The Choynski today is not the Choynski of four years ago, but were I to fight until I am 50, I do not expect ever to encounter a man who will inflict upon me the punishment the long-haired western fighter gave me in 1900." January 4, 1905 *Oakland Tribune*: "Choynski gave me the toughest fight I ever had ... I'd swear he gave me more punishment than all the others together. He knocked me down eight times before I got him, and all the time I was saying to myself: 'Oh, you lobster! You lobster! Just wait.' Well, he waited and I got him all right. One was enough."[5]

January 13 *Rocky Mountain News*: "One man was robbed of a prize fight and 8,000 ... were robbed of $15,000 to-night ... 50 policemen saw the robbery committed ... The men who got up the fight wanted McCoy to win ... their money was on him ... so the fight was given to him ... McCoy was knocked out ... At ... a minute and 45 seconds of the 2nd round, Choynski landed a death-dealing right-hand ... full in McCoy's face, and knocked him under the ropes at the south side of the ring. 12 seconds elapsed, and the gong was rung – first one tap, as is customary at the end of a round ... then a succession of taps ... the fashion in which the end of a battle in the ... ring is announced. McCoy was helped to his corner, so weak he could hardly stand. He had fought two minutes of a three minute round."

"Instead of being the end of the fight ... the gong rang again at the end of a two-minute rest, and McCoy went wabbling ... to the center. By as unfair an advantage as was ever taken of another fighter, the manager gave McCoy two minutes instead of the one he was entitled to, in which to recuperate. To cap the climax of crookedness at the end of the next round, after the bell rang and Choynski had dropped his hands, McCoy ... struck his antagonist in the face, knocking him out. Twice ... Choynski was robbed of the decision. The audience howled for five minutes, hissing McCoy, the referee and the club. It was the worst exhibition of thievery ever seen in the New York prize ring. Choynski's cleverness out-pointed and out-shadowed all of McCoy's clever ring work. Colonel Mike Padden, timekeeper for McCoy, said afterwards that the round was clipped by 40 seconds ... After the bout, Choynski and McCoy signed articles to meet again under the same conditions ... at the Broadway Athletic club on February 20. Whatever popularity Kid McCoy ... gained in defeating Peter Maher was scattered to the winds last night ..." Imagine how groggy Joe must have been, to have signed for a rematch with McCoy at the same venue!

While virtually every paper in the country agreed that Choynski was robbed of an enormous victory, they disagreed on many details. Most sources correctly blamed the club's official timekeeper, Joe Dunn, with striking the gong early (2nd round), but a few thought the fault was with Joe's timekeeper, C.A. Liebeskind. "Choynski's timekeeper claimed the Kid had been counted out, and in his excitement reached over and pulled the official timekeeper's arm, releasing the bell." This seems unlikely, at best. Liebeskind, himself, attested that Dunn rang the bell. (Wire service report): "Timekeeper Dunn refused to discuss the fight. He closed his watch and left the building, but he was seen to protest to the referee at the end of the 2nd round, that he was right." Normally, only the referee could declare a knockout, and indeed, should have. Some papers absolved the ref of any culpability. Bill Brown, later a member of the New York State Athletic Commission, witnessed the fight. In 1943, he called it "the most flagrant foul and boldest job of robbery he ever saw in the ring."[6]

"Johnny White ran to the timekeeper's box and called for the bell to be rung for the continuance of the (2nd) round, but his order was not obeyed. Choynski also realized that the round was short, and tried to protest, but was held in his corner by his seconds ... spectators ... filled the building with wild shouts of 'foul.' Time was then called for the 3rd round ... McCoy was still weak, but Choynski was almost exhausted from nervous excitement ... He sent McCoy down again ... just as the bell rang ... McCoy hooked his right to the jaw and put Choynski out so completely that he was unable to respond for the 4th. Again cries of 'foul' were shouted, but the blow was started with the bell, and as Choynski had done the same thing in the 2nd round, the referee took no notice of it. The crowd ... refused to leave the building for a long time. Cushions were hurled into the ring, and for a time it looked as though there would be trouble, but when the lights were turned out, the crowd slowly left the building." January 13 *New York Times*: "Capt. Chapman and his men succeeded in partially restoring order."

Johnny White told the *Oregonian*: "McCoy was not knocked out. I counted nine and McCoy got up just as I counted 10. Then the bell rang, and I and the fighters thought the round was over. The timekeeper had taken it upon himself to count (out) McCoy, and rang the bell. He had no business to do it. It was my place ... The punch McCoy struck Choynski as the bell rang was unpremeditated, and while it knocked Choynski down, did not affect the result (?!) Choynski was very sick from a punch in the stomach when the bell rang for the 4th. He refused to come from his corner, and I was compelled to give the fight to McCoy." Even if White honestly felt McCoy had beaten his long count, there was no justification for the rest period to be extended. As to "The Kid's" late punch "not affecting the result" and the allusion to a stomach punch no one else saw, being the culprit, this appears to reveal White as an accomplice to the crime. Several papers claimed, afterward: "Choynski, while feeling rather sore, said he had no fault to find with the referee, and in a conversation with the latter in the office of the club, expressed himself freely, but exonerated ... the referee, of all blame. 'I had him licked good and sure ... 'and had the timekeeper acted right, I had McCoy out. However, I am satisfied nothing was done by either the referee or official time keeper with an intention of doing me a wrong.' " Either it took Joe some time to feel he had been cheated, or he was in fear of incurring the wrath of certain parties before being paid at least the loser's end of the purse. In more than one of Joe's fights, it seems a referee robbed him of victory.

As to the early termination of round two: "Choynski's seconds protested vigorously, but Referee ... White ... knowing the round was short by several seconds ... ordered the men to continue ... for the opening of the 3rd round ... the blow ... which sent Choynski down and out, was delivered almost two seconds after the bell rang for the completion of the 3rd round. There was a great deal of noise in the building ... and undoubtedly neither man heard it." McCoy stated to the *San Francisco Call* on the 13th: "I don't know ... about the timekeeper's watch showing I had been down 12 seconds, but ... I was on my feet when the referee counted nine ... I purposely waited to hear the referee count nine before I got on my feet. If I had been declared out on the timekeeper's count, it would have been an injustice to me, as I was listening to the referee. About the blow delivered by me after the bell ... I want to say I did not hear the bell ring. I delivered the blow in good faith, and do not think I should have been disqualified ... I think I beat Choynski fairly." Well put and truly said ... if it all had been that simple.

Joe: "I was the victim of the most unjust ruling ever rendered against a boxer in competition. I beat McCoy fairly and squarely and should have been declared the winner. According to ... the official timekeeper ... McCoy was down 12 seconds of the 2nd round, and ... therefore out ... the Kid later dealt me a foul blow ... I was robbed of victory twice." Joe told the *Denver Times*: "In the 3rd round, McCoy knocked me down after the bell rang. I am a little deaf, but I heard the bell. McCoy did not." The paper's final word on the larceny: "The majority of the scribes declare the whole thing ... a case of rotten thieving engineered by the men who had their money on McCoy." Bill Brady witnessed the fight, only saying: "Choynski went at McCoy in the Kid's own style – wide-open guard, with a long left. Each man was fanning at the other, and Choynski landed first."[7]

July 21, 1911 *Syracuse Herald*: "According to McCoy: On the afternoon of the fight, McCoy met Jere Dunn in a Broadway café ... Dunn expressed the hope that McCoy would whip Choynski, saying he would give the 'Kid' a new hat if he won. That night, Jere ... sat ... by the corner into which the ducking, blocking 'Kid' retreated when charged by Choynski in the 2nd round. As McCoy came opposite Dunn, the latter called ... 'Don't forget you've got to win that hat, Kid,' to which McCoy replied: 'Don't you fret; I'll win the hat, all right.' ... he turned his head slightly in Dunn's direction, speaking out of the corner of his mouth, as he usually did. Choynski saw the opportunity and shot out his fist ... in time to catch McCoy on the jaw, knocking him flat on his back. He was almost out. His brother Homer ran along the side of the ring, imploring him to get up."

The *Herald* said, of Joe being floored after the end of the 3rd: "Choynski was dragged to his corner. His chief second, Owen Ziegler, walked out to Referee White and claimed a foul. They argued ... nearly three-quarters of a minute, the referee refusing to allow the claim. Finally, Ziegler went back to the corner and, stooping over, whispered in Choynski's ear. He had scarcely straightened up when Choynski, who had been sitting ... in his chair and rapidly recuperating to all appearances, slumped ... to the floor. Although it looked suspiciously like an attempt to gain sympathy ... as likely it was the after-effect of the blows ... Five seconds after ... the gong ... for the beginning of the 4th ..." Joe either could not or would not continue.

It appears Choynski had one of his biggest career victories stolen from him, in not one, but *five* different ways! First, when he cleanly knocked McCoy out at about 2:20 of round two, "The Kid" was given a long count by White. Then, the round was cut short, to save "The Kid" from a certain loss. Next, the 40 to 60 seconds that were clipped from the frame were added to the one minute rest between rounds! If what Joe related a bit later is correct, McCoy's corner entered the ring (in clear violation of the rules) and doused the "Corkscrew" with a bucket of water, another infraction. The 5th transgression? McCoy cold-cocked Joe after the bell ended round three. It seems clear there was skullduggery afoot.

January 21 *Omaha Bee*: "Men who are devotees of pugilism because they look upon it as the prime exponent of manly art, and believe the chief element ... in perpetuation of the sport is fair play ... denounce the McCoy-Choynski fiasco ... followers of pugilism have not in a long time been so stirred up over any matter ... discussion of future pugilistic ... championship honors ... have been abandoned in consideration of this most remarkable of affairs. 'Kid' McCoy, who, prior to January 12 was idolized by many a true sportsman, is today viewed most unfavorably by many of his former staunch admirers. That he was defeated fairly and squarely by Joe Choynski, there seems ... no reasonable doubt in the minds of a vast majority of the sporting world ... yet he defiantly asserts he won a clean victory ..."

The Bee levied an accusation, unconfirmed by any other source and likely untrue: "January 12 he (Joe) was matched to meet Joe Walcott at the Broadway club in New York. Walcott was unable to ... and rather than lose the big money promised, the managers of the club arranged for an exhibition between McCoy and Choynski. It is related that the fight was pre-arranged to be purely an exhibition ... with Choynski 'fixed' to go down at a certain, specified time. Only with such an arrangement would the 'Kid' consent ... But in the heat of the battle, Choynski forgot all about such an arrangement. He found that 'Kid' McCoy had either been greatly over-rated or was not himself ... and the opportunity seemed present for him to turn the tables on the 'Kid' for the defeat administered him early last year ... McCoy money went a-begging at the ring-side that night. Heavy odds were offered on him, and there were but few takers ... Is this the solution of the mysterious actions of ... Johnny White, and the flagrant robbery from Choynski of a decision he so richly deserved?"

Several papers quoted Joe: "I won the fight three times ... Not only was McCoy permitted to remain on the floor many seconds over the limit and enjoy the benefit of a two-minute rest, but his brother ... was allowed to go through the ropes and throw water over the 'Kid' in an effort to revive him. This ... is a foul and McCoy should have been disqualified. I am satisfied my timekeeper ... counted McCoy out, but will let the matter rest for the present. I have two or three matches on ... before I meet the 'Kid.' I am feeling in my old-time form just now ... never fighting better. I will do my training for these battles at Lakewood, where I have secured quarters in conjunction with Corbett." The matches mentioned were with Jack McCormick, "Stockings" Conroy and Jack Bonner. McCoy: "I have been wrongfully condemned since my fight with Joe Choynski ... It was nothing but a mistake of Choynski's timekeeper, for which I am not accountable. I have always fought to win, I have always fought fairly. There was no money bet on this fight that I know of, and if I had not started to knock him out in a few rounds, he would never have knocked me off my feet."

He told the January 17 *Davenport Republican*: "If he (Joe) is anxious for another meeting ... he can have it." Joe's timekeeper, Charles Liebeskind: "McCoy accuses me of making a mistake. What mistake could I have made? ... a silly statement ... No one but the official timekeeper has anything to do with the bell.' " As to McCoy's claim of always fighting fairly, he was several times accused in detail of pulling a fast one on opponents. He claimed, for instance, that he threw tacks on the mat in South Africa, while fighting a massive, bare-footed native. It is a terrible injustice that Joe's official record still bears the result, "KOby3" (or "KOby4"). If there was any doubt of the Horton Law being repealed, the larceny on January 12 sealed its fate. Adoption of the scoring system of a referee and two judges was said to have come about as a result of this fight.[8]

Two days after the donnybrook, the smoke was still clearing from the flames of the scandal. The *Morning Herald* attempted to explain the fiasco, not by any crooked work done, but simply because timekeeper Dunn and Referee White were rattled. It said neither man had any reputation for being less than honest. This is not entirely true, as indicated by a fight on October 13, 1899, at the same club. Top lightweights Owen Ziegler and "Kid" McPartland fought a 25 round bout, refereed by Johnny White. The *Chicago Tribune* wrote (on the 14th) that McPartland had the better of the first nine heats, but "Zeigler (sic) slammed the 'Kid' all over the ring" in the final 16. The crowd expected Owen to receive the decision, but Referee White gave it to McPartland. Soon after, "Eddie Connelly and 'Matty' Matthews clashed at the same club and Connelly beat his man handily, but a draw was the best 'Eddie' could do. 'Johnny' White refereed the contest."

At least one paper said Joe's purse was $2,400. If so, it was but a pittance. "McCoy was around town today, waiting to get his share of the purse and nursing a broken nose. Choynski deposited $500 to bind a match with McCoy for 25 rounds ... before the Broadway Athletic Club. Up to a late hour, McCoy had not covered the money. Joe ... and C.A. Liebeskind ... were seen by a reporter today. Choynski was much disgusted ... said, 'I have a $500 deposit up ... to make a match with McCoy on Feb. 20. If he does not meet me I will retire from the ring. Today I canceled three bouts that I arranged ... in Chicago ... Youngstown, O., and ... Milwaukee. I am satisfied the last blow McCoy hit me on Friday night was struck fully three seconds after the end of the round. It was a foul blow if ever there was one. Everybody admits the 2nd round was cut at least 30 seconds. I could have finished McCoy easily during that time, considering the condition he was in.' Choynski left for his home in Chicago to-night."[9]

The January 24 *Mansfield News* cited the *Chicago News*: "Joe Choynski has demanded that Kid McCoy cover his forfeit of $500 binding another match

... If it is not done, Choynski will fight his three matches ... A great deal of surprise is being expressed at Choynski's willingness to fight at the Broadway, after the open-and-shut deal tendered him in his last fight there." Not surprisingly, George Considine, manager of the Broadway club, defended Johnny White. Also not a shocker was that Tom O'Rourke, never much of a friend to Choynski, agreed with White's actions: "I think the decision was a fair one ... McCoy was in trouble in the 2nd round and appeared to be out, but that is the business of the referee to look after. The blow struck by McCoy in the final round was not foul. The fact that the men have signed to meet again shows they are satisfied."

As a final postscript to the fight, according to a 1955 article: "One day just before World War II, Kid McCoy happened to be in Cincinnati, and he dropped in on Choynski, who was sick in bed with the flu ... This was their first meeting in 40 years, and Joe was so happy to see McCoy that he got out of bed and hugged him around the waist. 'It's wonderful to see you again, Kid, after all these years' ... 'That goes double for me,' replied McCoy, his voice choked with emotion. 'How do you feel?' 'Oh, not bad,' sputtered Choynski.' 'You know, Joe, I never knew how you took that thing we pulled on you at the Broadway A.C. – when they gave you a short round and me a long rest ... many a time I wanted to write to you and apologize, but I never had the nerve.' Joe looked McCoy square in the eye and roared with laughter. 'Kid,' he said. 'I was out of shape for the first time in my life, and my bank balance was plenty low. I figured to lose that night, and so I took $1,000 and bet it on you to win at ... 2½ to 1. Of course I was out to win, but when I saw you drop in that 2nd round, I nearly died. I knew they cut the round ... I'd been around too long not to know what was going on ... I was never so happy in my life to get the 'Business.' "

A 1960 version: "Do you remember how I knocked you out that night, Kid?' Joe asked. He pulled the covers up around his chest. In bed with the flu, he wheezed ... 'Do I remember!' McCoy said, as he held a glass of water up to the old man's lips. 'I remember *how I won* that fight, too! And, Joe, I want to apologise. I would have, a long time ago, but I just didn't have the guts.' They shook hands ... 40 years later, Joe was forgiving. Tears came to Kid McCoy's eyes as Joe's frail hand closed around his. He was ... relieved there was no lasting vengeance in Joe's great heart. The two old fighters looked at each other fondly ... eyes misty. The Kid ... walked to the door. 'All right, then, get over this cold ... when you come up to Detroit, we'll put the gloves on for a round or two. I'm going to give you a chance to get even for that *short* one, Joe. Okay?' Joe waved weakly. 'Okay, Kid – I'll be on the lookout for your tricks.' "[10] A nice finish to the story, but its veracity is unproven. "But Kid McCoy played his last trick in April of 1940, when he committed suicide ... now Joe Choynski was all but alone. Jeffries and ... Sharkey were to outlast him by 10 years, but they lived out on the coast and

... in another world, so far as Joe was concerned."

Another bout between Joe and "The Kid" never occurred, apparently because McCoy didn't want it. He declared, *after* signing to fight Joe again, that he would only do so, "winner take all." While this sounds confident and noble – in actual practice, few boxers fought "winner take all." As men like Corbett and Jeffries revealed, the public were told many ring affairs went under this agreement, but a particular split of the purse was negotiated "on the sly." Joe said he cancelled all three of his engagements, then announced he would wait until noon on the 16th, and if McCoy did not accept his challenge, he would honor the bouts. Acceptance never came, but Joe cancelled the matches, anyway, for reasons unclear.[11]

Tom "Stockings" Conroy LF5 to Peter Maher on March 9. McCormick LKOby1 to Tom Sharkey on March 15., while Bonner L6 to Frank Childs in Chicago. "The Kid" didn't fight again until May, when he stopped Dan Creedon in six rounds in New York. In August, McCoy engaged in another allegedly fixed fight, when he was halted by Jim Corbett in 5, in the "Big Apple." It was accused that he took a "dive" in a gambling coup, which Jim may or may not have known about. Corbett stopped in Chicago around the middle of January, en route to his training site in Lakewood, New Jersey. Jim said "he was greatly impressed with Joe's fine showing against Kid McCoy, and congratulated Choynski on the good fight he had made, sympathizing ... over the injustice done him by the referee. Choynski shook Corbett's hand warmly. Corbett has invited Choynski to go down to Lakewood and train with him. Joe ... accepted the offer ... Jim and Joe will spar and wrestle ... at the cottage in Lakewood, where the former champion will try and get into condition for his battle with Jeffries in March." The men arrived in Lakewood around January 18.[12]

Fitzsimmons was offered a six round bout with Choynski in Chicago, for February 3 or 8. He declined, "owing ... that his left hand is not in good enough shape."[13] Bob's hands had been broken several times and were bothering him tremendously at this stage of his career. What is not to his credit, however, is that he never gave Joe another crack at him, after their 1895 clash. That the light-heavyweight division was still not universally recognized, was illustrated again, by the *Fort Wayne News* of January 20 and March 8: "Billy Madden, Sam Fitzpatrick and a number of others interested in boxing were discussing the scale of weights recently, and all admitted that, as now arranged, the weights were unjust and had been shifted to suit the whims of certain champions. After considerable argument, it was the unanimous opinion that the following scale of weights would be a decided improvement over the system, or lack of system, that prevails at present:
Paperweight ... 105 pounds (Later renamed "Flyweight")
Bantamweight ... 115 pounds
Featherweight ... 125 pounds

Lightweight   ... 135 pounds
Welterweight ... 145 pounds
Middleweight ... 155 pounds
Intermediate weight ... 165 pounds (generally called "Light-heavyweight")
Heavyweight, all over 165 pounds
By arranging the scale so that 10 pounds separates each ... all classes will ... be placed on an equal footing. By establishing the Intermediate heavyweight class ... men, like McCoy, Choynski ... who cannot rough it with such heavy fellows as Jeffries, Ruhlin and Sharkey, will have a chance at a ... reasonable weight ... it would be optional if they entered the heavier class."

A boxer named Ike Burrows, the "Black Turk," fought in the Dawn Athletic Club's "smoker" on January 24 at the Broadway A.C. It was reported by that date's *Philadelphia Inquirer* that Burrows some time previously, had fought "Jack McCormick, Joe Choynski and a few others." This would be an additional fight on Choynski's record, if verified. Joe said he had a date at one of the Chicago theaters all that week.[14] This entailed his next two boxing bouts, the first against Marshall Woods, on February 8: "Marshall Wood, a local colored fighter, tried to get Joe Choynski's $50 forfeit by staying four rounds ... last night at the Park theater. He was knocked out in the 3rd round with a short, right-hand jolt on the jaw, which rendered him unconscious for more than five minutes." His next fight was a rematch with Peter Maher, on February 16 in Chicago.

On the 8th, Choynski and Maher began training. Peter, "near the Gravesend race track in the east, and Choynski in a Chicago gymnasium."[15] Joe and Louise had celebrated their 5th wedding anniversary on January 25. February 11 *San Francisco Chronicle*: "Joe ... recently celebrated his wooden wedding ... showered on him and his wife by admiring friends: Two washtubs, 29 ironing boards, 17 washboards, one wooden horse, eight wooden buckets, 15 wooden spoons, six mincemeat bowls and three miniature express wagons." Otto Floto of Denver predicted: "Although Joe Choynski does not state so, he will be under the management of Parson Davies again in the near future. Joe realizes ... had the Parson ... charge of his interests in the ... fight with McCoy, he would have received the decision instead of losing by a fluke."[16] Floto was probably mistaken. Joe and Davies did not reconcile, and, as the fix was in for that fight, no intervention by the good "Parson" would likely have made a difference.

One paper wrote, on the 12th: "Choynski, who never complains when he falls a victim to another man's fists, has never said that Maher's former victory over him was due to an accident or a chance blow, but he has waited for ... the Irish champion ... the 2nd time ... in the fall of 1896 ... Choynski, according to all accounts, had the best of the fighting for five rounds. Maher, who is always dangerous, reached the Californian's jaw for a knockdown in the 6th round, and two or three more blows put him out.

Choynski has been anxious ever since to retrieve that defeat. He is in better form now than ... for several years, and his friends think he will be returned as the victor this time. Maher is training at Westchester, N.Y., and he will not reach Chicago until Wednesday. Choynski is doing his work in Chicago ..." Maher arrived in the Windy City the night of the 15th. It was said he would enjoy a 10 pound advantage in weight over Joe, who had weighed in that day at 165 pounds. Peter planned on finishing Choynski "in jig time," in order to force a rematch with "Kid" McCoy.[17]

The long-awaited fight came off on the night of February 16 at the 2nd Regiment Armory in Chicago, sponsored by the Fort Dearborn Athletic Club. It was carded for six rounds and held before a crowd of about 5,000. Joe was first to enter the roped square and seconded by the Shrosbree family, father and two sons. He was greeted by a loud cheer. Maher climbed through the ropes, clad in a blue sweater. His handlers consisted of his brother, Jim Maher, Peter Lowry and Danny McMahon. Malachi Hogan was the referee. Four different round-by-round accounts were used in the amalgamated report, several other papers adding details:[18]

Round 1 – Maher feinted and Joe backed away, evading a left swing. Peter scored with a good left to the ribs, but Joe countered with a heavy punch to the cheek. Maher put in a right and left to the jaw, prompting the Californian to come back with hard lefts to the ribs and the right eye, reddening it. Joe planted a heavy left hook to the face, but Peter countered with a similar punch. He charged at Joe, missing three consecutive lefts. A second before the bell, Choynski smashed a terrific left hook to the jaw, that sent Maher staggering like a sailor on shore leave. The latter was badly dazed and lurched back to his corner. Papers agreed that, had the round lasted a few seconds more, Joe would have won right then.

Round 2 – Peter came out a bit groggy, but Joe, remembering their first fight, danced warily around his rival for a minute, then planted two lefts to the face. Maher cleverly blocked the next few. Joe drove a hard straight left to the nose, but Maher got back with a heavy right to the ribs. Next, the "California Terror" landed a series of stinging jabs to the face, targeting the sore and swollen right eye. Maher closed in and smashed two potent left swings to the chin, dropping Joe to his haunches. Some sources said Joe purposely dropped for a respite. He jumped up immediately and snapped a left jab to the face. Peter landed left and right to the ribcage, and Choynski broke ground. It was the only round that Maher won.

Round 3 – Joe came out jabbing, landing a trio to Maher's face. Pete replied with lefts to the ribs and right ear. "Little Joe" got a solid left to his foe's stomach and escaped a return. He connected with another hurting jab to the nose, but Peter retaliated with a crashing right to the ribs. He rushed at Joe, who stopped him in his tracks with a steaming left to the mouth. Maher hooked a hard left to the mouth, but Choynski charged, landed a short, straight left to the face, and avoided a counter.

Round 4 – Joe landed two lefts to the head. The Irish slugger rushed, but Joe met him with a "terrific left jolt to the face." Peter came back with a powerful right to the gut. Joe straightened him with a hard left hook to the jaw and got inside to escape a roundhouse right. Maher sank a heavy right into the ribs. He rushed again and dazed Choynski with a pole-axing left to the chin, another right to the chin and several body blows. Joe got back with a terrific left on the chin, and just before the bell repeated the dose, staggering Peter. Both were tired from the extremely rugged action. The right-hand body blows taken by Joe in this round and later are possibly responsible for breaking his ribs, as will be seen in the Walcott fight.

Round 5 – Joe landed to the mouth, and planted right and left on Peter's sore right optic. Maher feinted, slammed a quick right and left, and a solid right to the ribs. Choynski countered with a hard, straight left to the mouth and another to the stomach. Peter got a light right in on the ribs, but Joe landed a pair of stinging jabs to the face just before the bell.

Round 6 – The men came out smiling and shook hands. Joe shot two jabs to the face, Maher plunging his right into the ribs. Joe danced around his opponent like an early-day Muhammad Ali, snapping another jab into the face. Peter's left swing glanced lightly off Choynski's neck, but Joe sent his adversary's head back with a stiff jab. Maher got in a left-right to the ribs, but Joe countered with a powerful right to the face that staggered the "Irish champion." He planted two more rights, first to the mouth and then to the rapidly closing right eye. Maher made a desperate rush, but Joe clouted him with a hard right to the ear that spun him around. Another charge by the Celt was stopped by a sharp jab. Choynski hooked him hard in the gut with left and right. The latter made a dying effort, forcing Joe to the ropes and getting in a few body blows. Choynski jabbed him off and crossed his swaying opponent with a right to the jaw. Maher was groggy, staggering around, but the bell rang before Joe could finish him off.

Joe wrote, in 1930, his memory a bit flawed, that the bout took place at Tattersall's in Chicago, adding: "This time I took no chances. I was wise to his savage attack, and I knew plenty about his amazing recuperative powers. The fellow was superhuman. He had to be, to stand up under what I gave him in New York, and then come back and floor me. In the Chicago fracas, I devoted the first three rounds to speed and science. I wanted to knock Maher out, which was a difficult thing to do, and I understood quite well that I must be careful. No man who had felt Maher's huge paw, as I had, would care to taste its sting a 2nd time. The Chicago sport writers said I went around Maher like a gamecock ... around its rival, and ... agreed I gave him an artistic shellacking. One fellow said I trimmed him so badly the police couldn't even identify him by his fingerprints. I was awarded the six-round decision ... but I wanted ... to knock Peter Maher out ... I was eager to rectify that clumsy mistake ... in New York!"

New York Evening World: "The big Irishman was not knocked out, but only because the authorities do not permit boxing bouts of longer than six rounds' duration. Maher ... was so badly muddled he hardly knew when the bell rang ... the end of the fight. In other rounds ... he was in bad shape, but the merciful gong always came to his aid. The vicious left-hand jab onslaught ... had anything but a pleasing effect on Maher, who, in the 2nd round, became so angry he indulged in a little 'rough-house' work, and by a chance blow sent Joe to the floor with a right on the jaw, which was the only clean score Maher counted in the game." Many journalists of the day made less competitive fights appear closer and more active than they were. Joe dominated the short match. They would face each other one more time.

Further efforts were made by a club in Chicago to entice recently-deposed heavyweight champion Bob Fitzsimmons to "cross swords" with Joe. The offer was a choice of 50 per cent of the gate or a guaranteed purse of $5,000, for a six-rounder. Bob refused, saying he could get twice that at a New York club. Upon hearing this, Broadway Athletic Club manager George Considine offered 60 per cent of the gate receipts. The offer was still rejected and the fight never occurred. On February 21, at the same Broadway A.C., there was a boxing benefit for former world featherweight champion, George Dixon. Joe boxed Fred "Cyclone" Morris as part of the show. Also included were Jim Corbett, sparring a pupil named Lester, and Gus Ruhlin vs. featherweight Dave Sullivan, in a disparity of 60 pounds. Other bouts saw "Kid" McCoy with Joe Falvey and Tom Sharkey box Bob Armstrong. The wind-up featured "Terrible" Terry McGovern, who had taken the crown from Dixon the past January 9, and the man of the hour, Dixon. He was said to be receiving $7,000 to $8,000 from the benefit, despite "many vacant seats" in the house. No detail was given of Joe's bout with Morris, a good black middleweight who was nicknamed (William) "Muldoon's Cyclone," and nearing the end of his career.[19]

Next came an event which colored Choynski's career with a blotchy stain he would never completely eradicate. Joe arrived in the "Big Apple" on the day of the Dixon benefit for a 25 round contest at the Broadway Athletic Club with great welterweight (and later, middleweight champion), Joe Walcott. A Kentucky paper quoted the *Louisville Times* as presciently stating, "Walcott ... has a chance and a good one. The 'Black Demon' is a wonderful fighter. His conformation and general ruggedness give him invulnerableness to attack to a large degree. His stomach is about the only point where he is susceptible to damage, and being of low stature he is hard to reach, especially as he is always boring in on an opponent. His low size also gives him full play on an opponent's middle works, and he goes for the body with a hurricane aggressiveness. He is a terrific thumper, too, and it takes a wonderfully good man to withstand him. Although a middleweight,

O'Rourke, his manager, thinks he can whip most of the heavies, and he is probably right. Walcott is a heavyweight in everything but height, and his low stature, contrary to the general rule, gives him an advantage in some points of the fistic game. Choynski is a heavyweight of the lower register (in terms of weight), and will not have … much the better … in the matter of heft. Despite the assertion by some that Walcott is over-matched, it will be an achievement for Choynski to land him."[20]

Joe Walcott, the "Barbados Demon"

As Walcott only weighed around 145 pounds, he was not generally expected to do well against a foe who was 10" taller and 20 pounds heavier. Still, Walcott would prove to do well against larger foes, while, perhaps counter-intuitively, have more problems with fighters his own weight. George "Kid" Lavigne defeated him in both of their bouts, Tommy West beat Walcott in two clashes, and "Mysterious" Billy Smith won a 20 round verdict over him. On the other hand, Walcott beat Dan Creedon several times, and kayoed light-heavyweight, Billy Hanrahan.

On the night of February 23 at the Broadway Athletic Club, before 2,500 people, it was "Little Joe" versus "Littler Joe." The odds were about 3 to 1, Choynski. The weights at ringside were 163 pounds for Joe, 147 for Walcott. Choynski said, in 1927, that he weighed 161, ringside. While this signifies a dearth of 14-16 pounds for Walcott, it also indicates that, once again, Choynski had overtrained. 163 was too light to maintain his strength. O'Rourke, who strongly disliked Choynski and was given to hyperbole (and often, lies), claimed in 1924 (for the November 7 *Manitoba Free Press*) that *his* Joe "tipped the beam at exactly 134 the night he fought Joe Choynski," and "the white man was 40 pounds heavier …" That would put "white Joe's" weight at 174 pounds, which was sheer nonsense.

Strangely, Choynski agreed to Johnny White as referee, once again! February 24 *Brooklyn Daily Eagle*: "Before the men entered the ring, Tom

O'Rourke ... had an argument with Choynski ... regarding the division of the money. Choynski was obdurate and insisted on getting 75 per cent of half of the gross gate receipts, and O'Rourke had to comply ... Walcott wore that ever present smile of his, while Choynski looked very serious." The articles of agreement called for 75 per cent to the *winner*, 25 per cent for the loser. *Philadelphia Inquirer*: "It was said before the battle that the Californian was suffering from an injured rib, while Walcott complained of an injured foot." Hitting in the clinches was allowed. *St. Louis Republic*: "Walcott was far from ... in good condition ... suffering for a week or more from a severe attack of hemorrhoids. John L. Sullivan, who evidently had been playing court to Bacchus, was in a box near Choynski's corner, and just as the gong sounded for the beginning of the 1st round, he adjured Choynski to 'go in and knock the block off the black lobster.' " One drunken bigot's rantings aside, the crowd seemed well behaved. The "play-by-play" account blends multiple contemporary reports and other sources.[21]

Round 1 – The "Barbados Demon" rushed out and forced Joe to the ropes, driving a hard left to the torso. The *St. Louis Republic* observed that Choynski's guard was unusually low, "seeing which, Walcott leaped at him like a tiger and landed his right ... on his jaw." After Choynski got in two lefts to the face, Walcott rushed again. Joe slipped to the boards in avoiding a punch. As he rose, Walcott smashed a hard left hook to the jaw, but was countered with a hard left to the mouth. Infighting and a heated exchange followed. Upon breaking away, the black Joe floored his foe with a wicked right to the jaw. Choynski took nine seconds and dragged himself up, using the ropes. He scarcely stood upright before the smaller man knocked him back on the mat with another right. Frisco Joe climbed to his feet after an eight-count, somewhat dazed. This time, he rushed at "Barbados Joe" and sent two hard lefts to the mouth, cleverly evading a vicious right hook. "Walcott made a wild swing for Choynski and it landed on his posterior. It slammed him up against the center stake on the Broadway side of the ring with such force that he fell to the stage. He was up in an instant ... badly dazed ... His legs shook and he missed four or five jabs which didn't ... have enough steam ... to make a dent in a pound of butter. Walcott ... abounded in the air, bringing his right with fearful force against Choynski's jaw. The white man was stretched full length on the carpet."

At the count of seven, the bell saved Joe from a knockout. Accounts generally indicate three or four knockdowns, if the first slip is counted, but the wire service report described five: "The first time ... he was hit under the right eye. Another hard right in the vicinity of the solar plexus put him down a 2nd time, a right cross on the jaw was the cause of his 3rd fall, and a left on the jaw put him down for the 4th time. Walcott was very nimble and danced around while Choynski was regaining his feet. Choynski came up very groggy from his 4th knockdown, only to go down from a right on the point of the chin, which sent him flat on his stomach to the floor ... It looked ... as if Choynski was out for good, but three seconds after he went down, the bell rang and he was helped to his corner." The crowd expected Choynski's corner to throw in the towel, but the diligent work of his seconds enabled Joe to come out in reasonable condition.

Round 2 – Despite the punishment, Choynski came out "with a jaunty step." The *New York Evening World* said he "sailed into the negro. With stiff left jabs he had Walcott dazed, and then he sent the colored boy half way across the ring and against the ropes with a right-hand swing on the jaw. Choynski entered the ring with a badly swollen left side. Walcott knew this, and he pounded away at the sore spot at every opportunity. Walcott met him with a stiff left in the face ... got in his left to the body and right to the jaw ... put his right into Choynski's ribs and his left hard on the jaw. Another left to the jaw ... dazed Choynski. Choynski landed a fearful right-hand swing on Walcott's jaw, sending him staggering against the ropes. Walcott sailed into Choynski and received a bunch of lefts and rights on the jaw that made him groggy. Walcott, with a left-hand swing, nailed Choynski full on the jaw, dazing him as the bell sounded." *Philadelphia Inquirer*: "Walcott was again the aggressor, and soon staggered the heavyweight with right and lefthanders. Terrific infighting followed, during which Choynski sent Walcott reeling to the ropes. They were fighting at a terrific rate when the bell rang, and Walcott appeared distressed."

Round 3 – Walcott began landing a combination of left to the kidney and right to the head. Choynski was weak. The smaller Joe kept in close, slamming his left hook to the jaw of the taller man, who looked like a rank amateur under the onslaught. Choynski shook his antagonist with a few stiff lefts to the face and a good left to the body, but Walcott dominated. He landed flurries of lefts and rights, from the hips up. *The Washington Post*, in 1910, said "Choynski doubled over to save his body and held the black terror off, getting only a few glancing blows on the head."

Round 4 –Walcott forced the fighting and landed multiple lefts to the body and head. "Chrysanthemum" Joe got in a few good punches, two jabs to the face and a pair of rights to the stomach. Walcott was especially effective with the left hook to the jaw. *Washington Post*: "Walcott jumped in harder than ever and made try after try, until at last he landed squarely on the broken rib again. Choynski, in distress, could not straighten up. His jaw was in easy reach now, and Walcott hammered him around the ring until the white man was groggy and spattered with gore."

Round 5 – The Barbados dynamo slammed into Joe with lefts and rights, the short left to the jaw still being most effective. One to the right eye raised a big, dark lump underneath. *New York Evening World*: "When the bell sounded, Choynski staggered to his corner, hopelessly beaten."

Round 6 – Choynski came out aggressively, landing a heavy right to the ribs. Walcott got back with interest, striking with three hard, right swings to the jaw, getting away each time without a return. The *New York Evening World* said "Walcott countering with his right on Joe's fractured rib. The Californian was so weak and groggy that he could hardly raise his hands." He continued to land with a potent left to the head, sometimes snapping back Choynski's head. The *Brooklyn Daily Eagle* said "he cut Choynski's right eye with a left hand swing." Once, while trying to land a haymaker, "The Barbados Demon" missed a swing and fell to the canvas.

Round 7 – Frisco Joe started well, despite his wobbling legs, but was put on the defensive by two left hooks to the jaw. Walcott rushed and slammed hard lefts and rights to the torso and cranium. A right to the wind and two potent lefts to the face sent Choynski staggering. Finally, a strong left and a crushing right to the jaw dropped him in a heap. Joe climbed bravely to his feet at "five." Walcott swarmed all over him, landing right and left smashes all over Joe's face, jaw, stomach, kidneys and ribs. So hopelessly beaten was he, that Referee White intervened and declared "The Barbados Demon" the winner. He stepped between the men, shoving Walcott back to his own corner, simultaneously catching Choynski around the body and dragging him to his corner. "White said afterward that he felt another good punch would have put Choynski out ..." *New York Evening World*: "Choynski was in a pitiable condition, and the services of a physician were necessary."

A February 25 Chicago paper revealed the story behind the scenes: "Joe Choynski ... was utterly unfit to fight on Friday night. That fact is known, and it is charged that thousands of dollars were made by certain men. Choynski was practically forced to fight, despite the protests of unfitness. That is the reason Walcott, so much lighter and shorter, severely beat Choynski, had him blinded, staggering around the ring, helplessly groping for the ropes, while the blood poured from him, when but two minutes and 38 seconds of the 7th round had passed. Choynski went into the ring with a broken rib; around his body was tightly wrapped surgeon's tape to support the rib. But, every time he breathed, Choynski suffered excruciating pain. And when he tried to protect his jaw, the 'black demon' smashed him on the ribs. Walcott alternated his tactics, one round playing for the jaw, the next for the body. Tom O'Rourke was in Walcott's corner. Men near that corner distinctly heard O'Rourke ordering Walcott to direct his blows at Choynski's body. And O'Rourke knew that Choynski's rib was broken. Choynski had shown the fracture, bound up, to O'Rourke and to Tim Sullivan, in proof of his statement that he was unfit to fight."

"Choynski has the reputation ... of being as 'square' as he is 'game.' He knew he had no more chance than a 3-year-old sick child would have against the gutta-percha black from Barbadoes (sic). For, besides his broken rib, the Californian had a severe attack of the grip. These statements are not the excuses of a defeated man. Dr. Joseph Muir, 41 West 36th street ...

confirms them. Choynski was and is Dr. Muir's patient. Dr. Muir is treating him for his fractured rib, a floating one on the left side, and for the grip. 'Choynski never should have gone into that ring last night,' said Dr. Muir today. 'I strongly advised him against it, for I think a great deal of him.' The management of the ... club knew Choynski's exact condition. Choynski asked ... before the fight to declare all bets off. It was not done. But all those 'on the inside' quietly took the odds of 5 to 1 on Choynski, the ... odds if (he) was in condition. Tom O'Rourke bet $2,000 to Al Smith's $1,000. Al Smith is a 'square' man, his experience told him that the 'black demon' had no chance against Choynski in condition."

"Choynski was forced to fight. He showed his broken rib to the managers of the club, and they agreed to give him 75 per cent of the gate receipts to take a licking. One argument of the management that weighed heavily with Choynski was that his non-appearance would hurt the Horton Law by disappointing the spectators, that 'his own game would be queried,' if he did not show 'as advertised.' And then the management held a $500 forfeit of Choynski's, which he had put up to show his good faith in making another match with McCoy. Choynski couldn't get the $500 back. These and similar reasons, urged on Choynski, caused him to go into the ring ..." The *Washington Post* quoted Dr. Muir as stating, "He ... was under my treatment for his broken rib and also for an attack of influenza."

The February 26 *New York Evening World* published an interview with Choynski: "After beating Maher in Chicago last Saturday, I slipped on an icy pavement and fell. I struck a post and broke my rib. I wrote the Broadway Athletic club people I had a broken rib and couldn't fight. They ... told me how much it would hurt the Norton (sic) Law if I didn't. Besides, I wanted to get back the $500 McCoy forfeit they were holding. They insisted. I came on, showing my rib and insisted I couldn't fight. They argued with me, and at last, on their agreeing to give me 75 per cent of the gate, I fought. Of course, I knew I'd be licked, because I couldn't defend myself. I asked the managers to declare all bets off before I went into the ring. They promised to do so." "The Broadway club, as well as every other club operating under the Horton Law, is obliged to have a physician to examine every fighter before he goes in the ring, and if his condition does not warrant his fighting, it is the doctor's duty to say so, and the club must not permit the fighter to go on. If a doctor was not engaged ... then they violated the law; and if a physician did report the men in condition when other conditions prevailed, he is unfit to be employed ..."

"Al Smith ... one of the most honest of sports, declared that if Choynski's story is true, the club ought to have done as Choynski claims he asked – declare all bets off. 'But ... Choynski should never have entered the ring if ... not in shape, for when he did, he threw all his friends down.' Tom O'Rourke told an *Evening World* reporter ... the ... fight was strictly on the level. 'That story's all rot,' he said. 'Same old take. When a man's licked, he never comes out like a man and says so. I'll tell you what I'll do ... I'll bet $500 that Choynski did not have a broken rib when he entered the ring. He may have a few ... now, but not then. I'll make another match ... as soon as he wants it.' O'Rourke wiped the perspiration from his face and more coolly said he was willing to match Walcott against Fitz, if (he) desired ..."

February 28 *Dubuque Herald*: O'Rourke: "Anyhow (sic) who saw the Californian spar at Dixon's benefit can judge whether he was all right or not. The club did not insist

Walcott JUMPED RIGHT OFF THE FLOOR TO REACH CHOYNSKI!

Choynski-Walcott, Jan. 18, 1908 *New York Evening World*

upon Choynski's fighting, and would not, if it were aware he was not in proper shape." February 28 *Brooklyn Daily Eagle*: Walcott "is emphatic in his denial that there was anything the matter with Choynski ... during the fight, excepting ... from the punishment he received. 'He handed me enough stiff ones in the 2nd round,' said Walcott, 'to prove ... beyond a doubt that he was at his best.' " That month's *Police Gazette*: "He was simply unable to hit the Senegambian demon ... judgment of distance was defective ... unable to uppercut effectively ... blows went over Walcott's head, around his neck, over his shoulder ... every place ... but the right place."

The March 1 *Philadelphia Inquirer* quoted O'Rourke: "This fellow Choynski ... deliberately offered to fake a fight at the Lenox Athletic Club with Gus Ruhlin a year ago, and I have still got his letter in which he made the proposition. He was matched to fight Ruhlin at my club, and after I wired him that the match was arranged he wired back, asking if I would put up his forfeit of $250. I consented to do so, and a week before the fight came off, he sent me a letter saying he was sick and could not go on. I immediately wired him, telling him that, as I had $250 posted for him that I would lose it unless he fought. He thereupon sent me the letter to which I refer, and in which he stated that he would come on and fight in order to save my money, but would quit in the 1st round and get the loser's end of the purse. I was not satisfied with his suggestion and declared the contract off. I offered Billy Madden, manager of Ruhlin, the forfeit of $250, but he refused to take it." This does not have the ring of truth to it. Joe would not likely throw a fight, and he stood to lose the money, not O'Rourke, as the latter would fully expect Joe to reimburse him for that amount.

Joe: "Tom O'Rourke knew my rib was fractured before the fight, for I told him so in the presence of Bob Smith, Jim Corbett and Bob Considine. As soon as I struck New York I saw Dr. Muir, and he ... declared I was troubled with influenza and ... in no condition to fight. I said, 'Doctor, my side is troubling me – will you look at it?' I ... showed ... him ... he declared it to be fractured. I went down to the club ... showed them Dr. Muir's statement and told them I was in no shape to go on ... when they refused to give up the $500 forfeit money, I said I would go on for a round and do the best I could, and after that tell the crowd I was in no shape to fight and declare all bets off ... George Considine gave me a paper that called for 75 per cent of the 50 per cent gross, which did not amount to $500, and it was agreed I was to go on ... fight the one round, and make the announcement." "Choynski's face is swollen at the lips and his eyes blackened. The broken rib on the left side sticks out an inch and a quarter fully, and can be felt through his coat. He called on Dr. McNamara this morning to have it patched up, and it will be two months before he will be able to fight. Joe says he told several ... friends at ring-side he was in no condition to go on, and O'Rourke promised to make the announcement."

May 17, 1911 *Syracuse Herald*: Referee Charlie White claimed, "The result ... pleased ... O'Rourke, exceedingly ... A few years before, O'Rourke had matched George Dixon to fight Jack Skelly at New Orleans ... at Davies' request, Choynski was chosen as one of Skelly's seconds (as) he needed very much the $75 or $100 he would get for ... the duties of a chief second. In those days, managers had the say as to who would be the seconds, and it was through O'Rourke that Choynski was given a job. When the referee called Dixon and Skelly to the center of the ring for ... Choynski said to him: 'Mr. Referee, I want you to watch Dixon closely during this fight. He is a foul fighter and hits low.' Little Dixon, who was as fair a fighter as ever pulled on a glove, was dumfounded. 'Joe, don't you think I have a hard enough time of it down here without your trying to make it harder ... by saying such things?' poor little Dixon asked Choynski."

"Dixon afterward told O'Rourke what Choynski said to him and O'Rourke went up in the air ... 'Look here, Joe ... there was ... no reason ... you should have said that, George has never done you any harm, and you know ... he never fought a dirty fight in his life. The only reason you were allowed to be a second was because Davies told me you needed the money badly. Now ... I won't rest until I get you licked good and plenty, and ... by a negro, at that.' " Whether there is any truth to the tale is a matter of conjecture. Certainly, a second telling a prominent umpire like "Professor" John Duffy that he needs to watch a famous and respected champion, is unlikely, as watching fighters was obviously Duffy's job. It also seems out of character for Joe. Tommy West, the welterweight who had been Joe's second and trainer in the past, was quoted by the November 5, 1913 *Janesville Gazette*: "Joe Choynski got $1,790 for another man's reputation. That is what Tom O'Rourke paid him to meet Joe Walcott ... Choynski was sick and wouldn't fight until he was given all the money. Walcott whipped him and then made money on the reputation he got."

The Oshkosh Daily Northwestern added, on the 1st: "Choynski came back from the east last night. He now says he broke his rib before the Maher fight, and fought the Irishman with one smashed slat. Joe did not act like a man with a broken rib in front of Peter. He still declares that he asked the Broadway club people to call all bets off, which was not done, although Choynski was in the ring when the announcing was done, and he could have insisted upon the bets being called off if he had wished to." March 4 *St. Paul Globe*: "The general public will likely give Choynski the benefit of any doubt that may exist. O'Rourke's ability to jeopardize his reputation for truth-telling is so notorious, that what the Boston ex-carpenter says is always sifted for facts, with poor success." Even if O'Rourke didn't contrive the story of the "Choynski dive proposal," Tom did his sport a great disservice, as those who sought to repeal the Horton Law would welcome this ammunition, pointing to the dishonest and crooked elements in the sport. Although the entire truth will never be certain, Joe's credibility was historically better than O'Rourke's. Joe apparently contradicted himself in some areas, however, and if events proceeded as he specified, he certainly damaged his boxing reputation for a measly sum.

Choynski wrote a letter from La Grange to the Sporting Editor of the *Chicago Daily Inter-Ocean*: "Dear Friend: You, who know me for a number of years, know that I am not a chap to squeal and do much talking, but ... to show that I am right when I say I had a broken rib before I fought Walcott: I showed the fracture to Jim Corbett, Sam Austin of the *Police Gazette*; Bob Smith, manager of Erne, and the officials of the Broadway Athletic club. They were satisfied I was suffering from a fracture. As an inducement to go on, they gave me 75 per cent of the receipts. It certainly was unheard of ... when they had $500 of my money as a forfeit, which they could have claimed. I asked them to declare all bets off. Instead of doing so, "Shylock" O'Rourke went out and got his money down at 5 to 1. Can you divine, in the face of this, why they did not claim my forfeit, but offered me extra inducements to go on? Can you see the betting angle?"

"Since my contest with McCoy, they have been having Charley White as referee, a man they could not approach, but lo and behold! When I fought Walcott, they rang in my old friend, Johnny White. Dr. McNamara of the Cook county hospital staff, and also one of the county medical board, set my fractured rib. Will anyone ... claim that I broke my own rib ... to confirm my story ...? There is not a dishonorable mark on my record. I have fought men of all sizes and colors. I have never dodged an honest challenge, and have always followed my much-abused profession along honorable lines ... if possible, I will wipe out the black mark ... on my record. The phoenix never dies. I received nearly $2,000 for my portion with Walcott. The reason the fight did not draw was because the papers ridiculed it as a farce. Walcott 5 feet and your humble servant nearly 6. The papers before the fight cartooned it with Walcott on stilts and ladders."[22]

Further testimony came from Jim Corbett, though a mixed offering. In a 1906 piece, he said, "The ... big house that was expected never materialized ... all thought Walcott never had a chance. Choynski, when he saw the crowd, demanded his 75 per cent of the receipts before going on. Choynski entered the ring as confident as a bull terrier. Walcott was prepared and coached especially for Choynski (and) admitted after the fight that he had never been in such excellent condition ... in his life." Writing for the *Atlanta Constitution* in 1915, however, Jim wrote, "Another thing not evidently known by those who prate about Wolcott (sic), and especially his defeat of Choynski, is that the latter was a sick man when he entered the ring with the coon. Joe should never have been permitted to box that night ... it was only a question of how long he could stand on his feet ... he didn't want it said he was afraid of a man 25 or 30 pounds lighter. I was one of the few who advised him to call the bout off, but other pressure brought to bear ... overruled me, and Choynski went down to a quick defeat."

Joe wrote, in 1930: "O'Rourke appealed to Corbett. And Corbett, thinking I had only a little fever, urged me to go on. He said: 'Walcott's a little chap ... Your little touch of fever evens things up. Just go on out there, rip into him, and finish it quick. So, I consented. Corbett, who always regretted that he had urged me to go in there, later wrote: 'In the 1st round Choynski showed no life at all ... no spring to his feet; no snap in his blows ... He ... acted like a man in his sleep, just going through ... motions from instinct or habit. I have never forgiven myself for it. It was one of the worst cases of bad judgment I have ever shown in my life – my talking Choynski into entering the ring that night. Besides, I had not watched Walcott work – and I did not know how good a fighter he was.' I leave you to figure out for yourself the reason for Walcott's failure to meet me again."

Corbett added, in 1919: "Choynski, by fighting a man nearly a foot shorter than himself, had to assume a crouch entirely unnatural to him ... Choynski couldn't jab with real effectiveness ... couldn't put real power into his swings ... a downward swing. It's the straight punch or the overhand into which a fighter can put all the terrific strength ... Walcott was benefited by being able to use the effective straight punches or the overhand swings. Walcott, always a great body puncher, was in his glory against Choynski, because Joe's heart was in a direct line with his straight blows and Joe's jaw was just high enough to be reached with the overhand 'haymakers.' " In 1931, a *Ring* magazine scribe who was not at the fight, claimed that Johnny White gave Choynski a long count several times, trying to amend for the raw deal he gave Joe in the January 12 McCoy fiasco. [23]

Bob Edgren (July 1, 1918): "Walcott didn't perform any miraculous feat in knocking out Choynski. The black demon was a wonderful fighter, but never good enough to beat Joe ... on his merits. Choynski was a sick man ... a prominent New York doctor ... found he had two badly broken ribs. Choynski asked the doctor to plaster him up so he could fight Walcott. The doctor told him it was impossible for him to fight, and if he insisted on fighting he would have to get some other physician to look after him. Choynski's chief second begged him to have the match postponed, saying his friends would bet their money on him and lose, but Choynski obstinately insisted that he could beat Walcott, ribs or no ribs. He thought he could keep the injury a secret until after the fight."[24] Once again, there are contradictions as to whether Joe went in the ring knowing he would lose, fighting for 75 per cent of a meager purse, if he expected to fight as best he could for one round, then quit, or if he felt he could win despite his injury. Although Bob wrote of a bout 18 years earlier, he attended nearly all major bouts and was probably an eyewitness.

Joe arrived in Des Moines, Iowa on March 9. That evening, he was to referee all matches for a fistic carnival at the city's Mirror Theater. He would also read wire service report bulletins from the Terry McGovern-Oscar Gardner world featherweight title fight taking place the same night in Brooklyn, New York, explaining each boxing term to the audience. The *Des Moines Daily News* said "two dummies will be used by Choynski in explaining the fight as reports indicate by rounds." He was also to address the crowd on the Walcott fight. The *Dubuque Daily Herald* called him, "Joe Choynski, the most popular pugilist in the world," another Iowa paper referring to him as "undoubtedly the most popular man in the prize ring today." *Daily Iowa Capital*: "Choynski will prove even more of a drawing card than Siler, because he is himself a fighter as well as a referee."

"The attraction of the evening was ... Joe Choynski, who had been secured to referee the bouts. As soon as the curtain went up, the crowd began to call for Choynski, for it was understood he was to make an address. The big Californian was suffering from a bad cold and did not care to respond to the repeated calls from the audience. The first contest ... and Choynski leaned back in the corner of the ropes and calmly watched the fight. Choynski was dressed in a black frock coat and striped trousers, and appeared very much at home in the ring. Like Siler, he made very little fuss over arrangements, said very little to the fighters, but refused to let the bouts go on when it was seen that the end was only a question of a few seconds, and that needless punishment was being inflicted. After ... there was a lull ... calls for Choynski were more frequent, and at last (he) stepped out before the footlights and said: 'Gentlemen, I was in no condition when I fought Walcott. I was suffering from a fractured rib ... However, I hope to meet Walcott again in a few weeks, also hope to defeat him.'"[25]

A March 12 article out of Chicago involving Charles Essig, Secretary of the Fort Dearborn Athletic Club, noted: "While playing with a revolver, Richard Essig, seven years old, shot his mother in the abdomen. Mrs. Essig is at the Lakeside hospital, where it is feared the wound will prove fatal. The child's father, Charles T. Essig ... is ... manager of Joe Choynski. When the boy expressed the desire for a revolver, his father took home a 32-calibre revolver. A box of cartridges accompanied the gift and the son was cautioned to be careful in handling the weapon." Giving a seven year-old a revolver! It makes Joe's recklessness with a gun look mighty careful by comparison![26] Whether Essig was ever his manager is unverified.

Heavyweight champion Jim Jeffries was to face three men in the ring, one at a time, on the night of April 5 in Chicago. He would attempt to knock out, in six rounds or less, Jack McCormick and Jim Barnes. It was hopeful the 3rd adversary would be Choynski, but if Jeffries objected to Joe as an opponent, the sacrificial lamb was expected to be George Lawlor.[27] Joe did not face "The California Grizzly," nor McCormick or Barnes. Jim instead flattened Jack Finnegan in 55 seconds, in Detroit, Michigan.

In mid-April, several papers stated the current monetary value of some of the top boxers, giving Choynski's worth as $20,000 and Fitzsimmons at $15,000. Featherweight champion "Terrible" Terry McGovern was said to be worth a whopping $40,000, and Tom Sharkey's financial value, given as $50,000! "Kid" McCoy was said to have amassed $25,000, while the estate of Peter Maher was valued at only $5,000. While the source was not divulged, it indicates that Joe was well-to-do at this time. A Texas paper quoted Lou Houseman on Joe and Charles Davies parting ways: "Choynski and Davies divided the Californian's money, share and share alike, until Choynski rebelled and refused to fight longer under these conditions ... Billy Brady and Jim Jeffries are partners on the basis of 70 per cent to Jeffries and 30 per cent to Brady. The same is true of Sharkey and O'Rourke. Big Gus Ruhlin and Billy Madden cut the Akron giant's earning clean in two."[28] Joe was signed on April 22 to fight Sharkey, at Tattersall's in Chicago on May 8. It was said that Joe's broken ribs had completely healed. By May 4, he was training for the fight at his home in La Grange, Illinois.[29]

Sharkey was slightly past his peak and Choynski, very much on the decline, but the match held intrigue for the public. The bout would be six rounds at catchweights. The referee would be Malachi Hogan and the fight to be decided on its merits, no draw agreed to if it went the limit. On the morning of the contest, the *Dubuque Daily Herald* said, "Choynski ... has trained for 10 days ... which is about all the time the long haired fighter ... needs to fit him for the fastest six rounds he ever fought. Joe has done little work since his ... fight ... with Joe Walcott. His ribs were caved in ... his hands injured on the hard skull of the black man, and Joe decided ... to take a long rest ... lying idle ... at his country home and enjoying life. He took on about 12 pounds weight while doing nothing, but his health was perfect ... Choynski is a fiend for work. He overdoes it most of the time, but he allowed himself just training enough this time to get into perfect shape. He does a little road work, but most of his labors are at the bag and with the skipping rope. Joe is training for speed more than anything else. He realizes he will have a rough journey ... with the sailor fighter, and wants to be at his best for the bull dog rushes of Tom O'Rourke's champion."

"Sharkey ... is training for strength and endurance ... at Forbes' quarters at Leavitt and 22nd streets ... Like Choynski, Sharkey is not paying much attention to road work ... most of his training is ... with the bag and sparring bouts with Bob Armstrong ... The black man was led a merry chase yesterday afternoon, in a bout lasting about a half hour ... Sharkey worked like a demon ... and when they quit, both were limp and tired out. Armstrong is a good foil for the rushes of the white man, and gives Tom the best sort of practice. He thoroughly understands Sharkey, having helped him train for most of his important fights in the last year."[30]

At Tattersall's that night, the finale of the Choynski-Sharkey trilogy was played out. Joe had thrashed a young, inexperienced Tom in 1896, the latter only receiving the "verdict" due to a pre-fight agreement. The 2nd bout (1898) was declared an eight round draw, although "The Shark" probably should have been disqualified for foul tactics. This 3rd fight saw about 10,000 in attendance, who witnessed a short, but brutal encounter. The weights were generally given as 165 pounds for Choynski, 180 to 185 for Sharkey. The "Sailor" entered the roped enclosure first, accompanied by O'Rourke, Armstrong, Jack Root and Harry Forbes. Joe followed a few moments later, squired again by the three Shrosbrees, the Colonel and two sons. The following blended report is culled from primary source accounts. The only local report was by George Siler, for the *Chicago Tribune*.[31]

Round 1 – Sharkey came out storming. Joe stopped him in his tracks with a hard left to the jaw, but not for long. They mixed it, and the "Sailor" caught his foe partially behind the neck with a powerful left hook that knocked Joe to the mat. He rose at once, and Tom, obeying shouted instructions from O'Rourke to go to the body, smashed Choynski with a vicious left to the torso. Joe backpedaled, taking the force out of a follow-up left-right to the head. He countered with a hard left hook and stepped out of danger. Tom roared in, throwing punches in bunches. Some landed, most were wide of the mark. The boxers converged, clinching and trading frequently. Sharkey was the primary aggressor, but Joe caught him with a left hook that raised a lump near the right eye. When Tom tore in again, the Californian measured him, hooked another left and floored him. Sharkey bounced right up and charged in, swinging both hands wildly. Joe side-stepped and clocked Tom with a right hook to the jaw that sent him to the mat a 2nd time. They traded heavily and Sharkey tried to land a pair of illegal pivot punches. The first missed Joe's face, but the 2nd went around his neck, sending him off balance and down. Some said it was a left hook to the jaw. Joe stood up, tired from the frantic pace. The *Daily Nevada State Journal* said Sharkey floored him a 3rd time with a right to the jaw; other papers disagreed. Tom smothered him with a flurry of wild punches. The men exchanged potent shots to the bell. Sharkey's body attack was heavy and ferocious. He was obviously targeting Joe's newly-healed ribs.

Round 2 – Tom resumed his rushing tactics, compelling his opponent to break ground. The fireplug drove Joe to the ropes, forcing him to trade. While Choynski generally hooked with both fists to the head, Sharkey used a combination left to body, short right to head. About mid-way through the frame, Joe put together a series of two lefts and a short right cross, that rattled "The Shark." When flustered, Tom swung wildly, as he did now. He recovered, though, and sparred for wind. Choynski escaped the ropes on occasion, spinning away and dancing to ring center, with Sharkey in pursuit. Tom held off, slapping with a left that bore little power. Toward the close of the round, Joe evidently expected nothing more was coming before the bell. He was wrong. After getting Joe on the ropes, Tom tossed another left slap, suddenly slamming in a crushing right hand. The torpedo crashed flush on the jaw, and it was lights out. As Joe dropped to the mat, such was the impetus of Sharkey's final effort that he nearly fell through the ropes and out of the ring. The time: 2:53 of the round. *Oshkosh Daily Northwestern*: "Choynski fell in a heap, turned partially over and curled up like a man who had put his head under a sledge-hammer. He was ... put to sleep with a blow that would have annihilated the best man that ever put on the gloves. Every man of the 10,000 in the building rose and yelled." Hogan counted over the unconscious Choynski, but at "eight" the gong sounded, ending the round. At this time, a fighter could be "saved by the bell," and his cornermen allowed to drag him back to the corner to revive him.

The *Daily Nevada State Journal* was alone in saying that Sharkey decked Joe early in the 2nd with a right to the back of the neck, and again at the end of the round. The wire service report claimed that a left took him out. *Oshkosh Daily Northwestern*: "The seconds were painfully slow, but it mattered little ... They ... pulled Choynski toward his corner and tried to put him on his feet. He sank to the floor and was allowed to remain where he had fallen, while a weak and ineffectual attempt was made to bring him back to his senses. Choynski made a heroic effort in his blindness, but was hardly able to more than lift his head. There was no water to aid in his slowly returning strength and he fell backward, thoroughly defeated as the gong rang for the opening of the 3rd round. Sharkey ... advanced for battle while Choynski's seconds were still rubbing his body and limbs. Referee Hogan took a glance at the prostrate pugilist to see that all was over, then led Sharkey to the front of the ring and announced him the winner ... The sailor, in glee over his quick victory, performed an Irish jig in the center of the ring." The *Chicago Tribune* said, as Sharkey was expected to win, the victory didn't add much to him in the way of credit, and his gloating "war dance" drew adverse comments from spectators.

Sharkey told the *Oshkosh Daily Northwestern*: "Just as I expected. Couldn't have happened any other way. Choynski ... was too light to do any damage. He was very fast for a while, and I was rather surprised at the way he started in at me." Joe: "Those body blows did the business. I am more than willing to admit Sharkey was too fast for me. The two rounds were, however, fast for both of us, and I have nothing to regret. I trained hard ... and really expected to last the six rounds." The March 11 edition said Tom confronted George Siler after the bout, saying: "I suppose if you had refereed 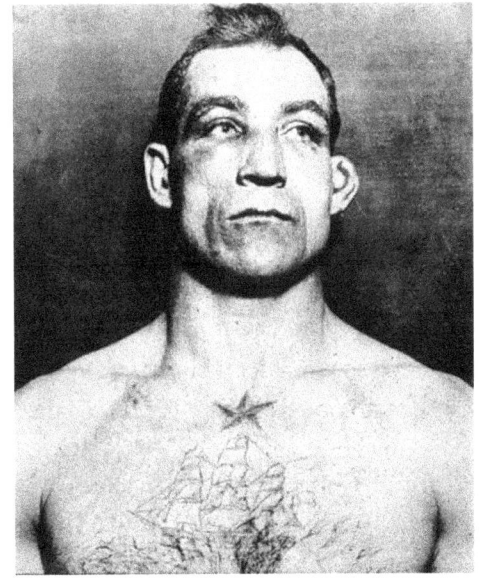 tonight you would have declared against me on a foul." Siler's joking reply was, "Of course I would." He had given Jeffries the decision over Tom in 1899. May 13 *St. Paul Globe*: "Sharkey has improved wonderfully in the past year ... besides showing an ability ... in infighting, he ... gave as pretty an exhibition of left-hand jabbing, hitting and getting away as one would wish to see. Those who think Sharkey is not clever will be mistaken ... One ... mistake Choynski made ... his customary method of having two little boys for his seconds ... such ... should never be allowed in the ring ... it was plain ... when Choynski came to his corner a bit shaky at the end of the 1st (sic) round, the boys were unable to do much to revive him ... Older and stronger seconds might have aided Joe in prolonging the contest."[32] He was allegedly set for a rematch with Walcott, but it never occurred. Despite Joe passing his fighting prime, some of his best results were still ahead.

"The Frisco Flash" started an exhibition tour with a theatrical company, with a sparring partner named Frank Marshall. Aside from a three-round exhibition with Marshall, Joe participated in a "fighting satire" called "The Razzler." It was someone's poor idea to put him in a comedic role, wisecracking jokes, which, according to a June 12 paper, were greeted with an ominous silence from the audience. The sparring was received in a much better light, although it was said of Joe, that "He booted Marshall around like an old carpet and made the latter look like two cents worth of dried prunes." The tour was booked for 12 weeks, but only lasted about eight. Choynski was keeping himself in general boxing trim. Jim Corbett, following an unsuccessful May 11 title go with Jeffries, paid a visit to Walter Watson's gymnasium in New York and found Joe training there.[33]

The July 14 *Police Gazette* said Joe was looking to return to the ring, particularly to fight Frank Childs. On July 24, at Tattersall's in Chicago, he acted as a cornerman for Jack Root in a six round bout with Tommy Ryan. Ryan floored Root in the 1st with a right hook to the jaw, but Jack landed heavy rights to Tommy's ear in the 2nd, that "brought the blood in streams. After that, the contest appeared more like a sparring exhibition ... spectators gave vent to their disapproval in cries of 'Fake' and 'Take them off.' During the 5th ... several hundred left the hall, so disgusted had they become ... Root had about 10 pounds the better of the weights."[34]

On August 2 it was announced that Joe had posted $500 to face two heavyweights on the same night, one after the other. He contracted to defeat both; these were no sparring exhibitions, though the scheduled distance was not specified. The venue would be the Casino Club of Dayton, Ohio and the fighters originally chosen by the club were "Big" Jim Smith of Cincinnati and John Matthews, "The Black Demon," of Baltimore, Maryland. The event occurred on the night of August 7, but Jim Smith was replacing by "Frank Taylor, a colored man of Dayton." Both of Joe's foes were African-American, again demonstrating that he did not draw the "color line." The paper reporting the affair said: "Matthews lasted three rounds and refused to go farther. Frank Taylor did not last two rounds, being knocked out." Matthews was a spotty fighter, his only other recorded bouts being three losses and a draw. He would, however, in 1920, become owner and manager of the superb Dayton Marcos of the Negro Baseball Association.[35] In truth, both of Joe's opponents were inferior boxers.

Joe arrived in New York City on August 24, to begin training for a bout with Peter Maher, at the Broadway Athletic Club. He set up training quarters at New Dorp, Staten Island, where he had prepared for the 1897 "Denver" Ed Smith bout. On the evening of the fight (August 28), Joe went to his room at the Colonnade Hotel, next door to the club. Around

7:00 p.m., he complained of stomach trouble. A physician was hurriedly summoned, who "pronounced Choynski totally unfit to take part in the contest." The malady wasn't said to be of a long-term nature, but serious enough to prevent Joe from meeting Maher before the Horton Law expired.[36] Club Manager Michael Padden called the fight off. Joe laid low until early October, when he told several papers he had retired from boxing "for good," and would in 30 days be the head of a physical culture establishment in La Grange, Illinois. While Joe did retire from boxing about as often as Muhammad Ali, he was not done yet. He set himself up as boxing instructor in his own little gym. October 1 *Milwaukee Evening Wisconsin*: "It will be a resort for fagged-out businessmen and aspiring athletes of means, and will be something on the lines of 'Muldoon's farm' in White Plains, N.Y. Even Choynski's enemies acknowledge that he is one of the cleverest pugilists, and his long experience in training and handling many renowned glove men should stand him in good stead when he opens his school for the development of brawn and muscle."[37]

On the night of November 2, at the Colorado Athletic Association in Denver, Colorado, Joe fought local heavyweight Fred Russell. When Russell battled Tom Sharkey the following year, he was referred to as champion of Colorado. Prior to Choynski, Fred came off two wins over "Mexican" Pete Everett, in Cripple Creek, Colorado. Over the course of his career, Russell stopped such heavyweights as "Klondike" (John Haines) and Jack McCormick. He stood about 6' 4", weighing from 200 to 255 pounds, and was known as a strong, but dirty

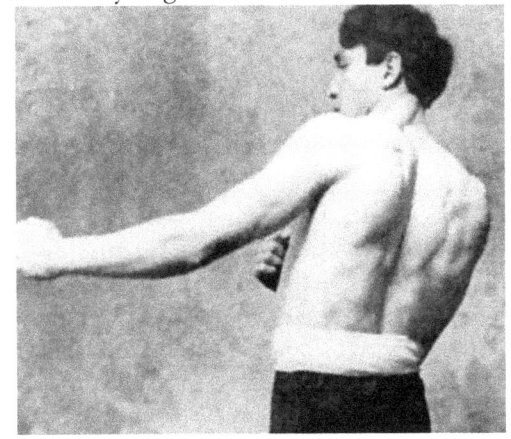

Fred Russell

fighter.[38] Soon after facing Walcott, "The Giant Killer," Choynski would have to play giant-killer, himself. Frank Cullen refereed, before about 2,000 spectators. Colorado produced or cultivated some very tough fighters, others being "Denver" Ed Smith, "Mexican" Pete Everett, "Fireman" Jim Flynn and, of course, "The Manassa Mauler," Jack Dempsey. Next is essentially the wire service report, featured in many papers:

Round 1 – "Just after the fight started, Joe went to the floor with his hands on his groin and showed evidence of pain. He struggled to his feet and Russell nearly threw the referee out of the ring in his efforts to get at Joe, which brought a storm of hisses ... There was a great deal of wrestling and clinching all through ... Joe was thrown to the floor several times, and in return, threw Russell clear over his head once. Russell's superior strength gave him the advantage in this style of fighting, and he undoubtedly would have worn Joe down and knocked him out, had the fight continued."

Rounds 2 and 3 – "The fight was the most vicious ever witnessed in Denver. Russell's great weight and strength were more than Joe could stand ... he was frequently rushed off his feet and against the ropes. He clinched repeatedly to save himself, and in breaking received some hard punches on body and head. Joe got some hard jabs to Russell's head and body as the latter bored in ... cut through the flesh over both of Russell's eyes ..."

Round 4 – "With blood streaming from deep cuts over both eyes and a savage expression on his countenance, big Fred Russell ... broke from a clinch as the gong sounded ... and with two terrific punches to the body, sent (Joe) flying through the ropes and on to the floor ... where he remained nearly five minutes, stretched at full length. A couple of policemen lifted him to his feet and assisted him into the ring. Joe ... walked up ... and squared off in front of Russell. Referee ... Cullen stepped between the men ... about to mix it up again, and holding Joe's arm in the air, declared him the winner on ... Russell's fouling ... intense excitement among the handlers, club officials and spectators ... when Joe had been seated in his corner and his seconds were fixing him up, the timekeeper sounded the gong for order. Joe, thinking it was the call of time, got up for business again, and was only restrained by the repeated shouting of the crowd that he had won."

Joe returned to Chicago soon after. On November 8, it was reported that he sustained a badly-injured hand in the fight. "This may make it impossible ... to ... fight at Tattersall's November 27 with Joe Walcott." Indeed, not long afterward, an "indefinite postponement" of the bout was declared. At least one paper, however, said it was due to "the unsatisfactory contest between (Joe) Gans and (Terry) McGovern" on December 13, not because of Joe's hand injury. The McGovern-Gans match-up was considered a fixed fight.[39] A benefit was to be held in Chicago on December 14 for consumptive Jim Hall, featuring exhibitions by Choynski, Jim Corbett, McGovern, Gans, Eddie Santry and Tommy White. It is not confirmed if the benefit occurred.[40] Hall did die of tuberculosis, but not until March, 1913. Joe had no inkling that the coming year, 1901, would bring with it the most famous triumph of his boxing career.

Round Nineteen

The Galveston Giant
(January 1901 – January 1902)

January 1 of the new year saw Joe and Louise visiting her family in Walnut Hills, Ohio. Promoters in nearby Cincinnati were trying to sign him and "Kid" McCoy, as a preliminary bout on the Jeffries-Ruhlin heavyweight championship card at that city's Saengerfest Athletic Club, scheduled for February 15. The club would be unable to seal the deal, and the Jeffries-Ruhlin match wouldn't occur until November 15, in San Francisco. Joe had tangled with both men, and, though Gus was coming off a recent 15 round stoppage of Tom Sharkey in June, 1900, Joe chose Jeff to win the fight. Joe and his spouse, meanwhile, had decided to go into vaudeville together. To that end, they had a short, 30-minute play written for them by Charles W. Murphy, sporting editor of the *Chicago Enquirer*, called, appropriately enough, "The Sketch Factory." It was reported in early January, that theater impresario William A. Brady, manager of heavyweight champion Jeffries, had arranged for Choynski to box Jeff's younger brother, Jack, in a preliminary to the Ruhlin bout. Joe insisted that "he would not entertain any proposition for" it, owing to his vaudeville obligations.[1]

January 4 *Oshkosh Daily Northwestern*: "Joe Choynski is going into vaudeville. More ambitious than Jeffries, who speaks only eight words in 'The Man From the West,' Joe will take part in a rapid-fire dialogue. He will be assisted by his wife, who did a song and dance stunt before she married Joe. The pugilist has had some experience on the stage, having traveled two seasons with a burlesque show, giving exhibitions of bag punching and sparring with his partner. Whether he will make a hit or not when he elocutes is a question yet unanswered. In speaking of his sketch, Joe said: 'Don't think for minute this ain't on the square. I don't do any heavy act and I don't save any lives. This is funny, it's all comedy. I don't ring in anything about the ring, don't even punch the bag. I'll have to act, on the level, although my wife will help out. She's a peach dancer and can warble some. No, I go off the track when the band plays, although I bet I can beat some of these fellows who come out in dress suits and ring in the *mother* songs with red and blue pictures of the old home. But I'm going in as a comedian; if they don't like me, all they've got to do is say so. I'm booked till June, and if I make a go of it I'll never go back in the ring again.' "

On February 6, Lou Houseman attempted to murder his wife, by shooting her. He was caught kicking and beating her near Chicago's

Morrison Hotel. Lou attempted to shoot the men who came to her rescue, as well. Although further details are sketchy, he was eventually restrained and arrested. The police court, in its "infinite wisdom," merely fined Lou $5 "and costs" for the transgression. His spouse was probably Clara, born in 1857 in Germany. By 1930 he was married to Adelaide M. Houseman.[2] Joe had another set-to scheduled with Tom Sharkey, for March 11 in Louisville, Kentucky. It was announced as early as February 19, however, that Sharkey was pulling out of the fight. Tom arrived in Louisville on the 18th, but left for New York shortly after midnight on the morning of the 19th, having "decided that his match with Choynski would not draw enough money to justify his training." He was heading for his home in Sheepshead Bay, New York to train instead for a bout with Peter Maher.[3]

Next up was, what appeared to be a bout of minor significance for Choynski. It was anything but. A gentleman named Albert Lasker, raised on Galveston Island, Texas, and later referred to as "the founder of modern advertising," offered Joe $500 and transportation to and from the island. Joe, decades later, recalled it as an offer of $800 and two round-trip tickets. Lasker began promoting boxing matches in a little club he had established. Prizefighting was illegal in Texas then, as in most states. The law, however, had been circumvented by the boxing crowd, who billed these fights as "exhibitions" or "scientific demonstrations" and conducted them within private clubs.[4] Traveling down to Galveston under the guise of a boxing professor demonstrating the sweet science, Joe had a fight arranged with a young, black heavyweight by the name of John Arthur Johnson. Johnson, who went by the name, Jack, was born and raised on the island and had 26 recorded fights by this time, spread over seven years.

His results against top opponents included: Jack (Jim) McCormick (D7, WF7, 1899; KO2, KO7, 1900), "Klondike" (John Haines) (KOby4 or 5, 1899; D20, KO14, 1900). In the first "Klondike" battle, in Chicago, the undernourished Jack was worn down by body blows, until, weakened and discouraged, he allegedly quit. Jack had improved immensely by the time he faced Joe, though he had a ways to go to become a great boxer and the first black heavyweight champion. Legend has it that Lasker paid Johnson only $25 for the Choynski fight. Galveston was still recovering from the horrific disaster of the previous year. On September 8, 1900, the island was devastated by a tremendous hurricane. Estimates of the loss of human life range anywhere from 6,000 to 10,000, making it the deadliest storm in United States history. Johnson was there, not quite 22 years old. While Jack was a notorious storyteller and embellisher of facts, his tale of helping to rescue many from the raging waters likely has much truth to it.

As Joe recalled, in 1912, he arrived in town a week before the fight "and took a few turns over the beautiful beach to keep in trim – the city was still desolate, due to the recent tidal wave and storm, and the hall in which we appeared looked moth-eaten. However, a big house greeted our appearance, with no inkling of trouble, no casting of shadows. I had never seen my opponent in action, but he ... looked formidable."[5] The match took place at Harmony Hall, at the corner of Church and 22nd streets, under the auspices of the Galveston Athletic Club. A tarp was stretched over the ring to keep water off in the event of rain, as the roof still had not been replaced. The law against prizefighting in Texas was enacted in 1895, to prevent the Corbett-Fitzsimmons heavyweight title fight. Following that, it had not been enforced with any vigor. Governor Joseph Sayers, however, decided that prizefighting would be a detriment to the recovery of the community. The legal loophole with prizefighting allowed that, as long as neither participant was paid in money, "or other thing of value," no wagers made nor fees charged for admission, the fight would be

Jack Johnson, circa 1901, photo from his wife, Mary

considered an exhibition. Joe was to be paid $500 a month as the club's boxing instructor, the exhibition simply a manifestation of his duties, for which he would not actually be paid – or so the story went.

Sayers dispatched an incognito Company of Texas Rangers, led by Captain John A. Brooks*, to ascertain if there was any money involved. Failing in this, the Rangers were ordered to arrest the boxers at the conclusion of the set-to, if the local county government neglected to do the deed. This, in hope that the courts would convict the "perpetrators" of prizefighting, anyway. Brooks was one of the most decorated and esteemed members of the Rangers, a crack shot with a shotgun or six-shooter, who had been involved in "pulling in" many a wanted desperado.[6] Choynski, in his memoirs, said, "When I reached Galveston, I learned that the Texas governor had ordered out the Texas Rangers, with orders to 'arrest all concerned, if the law is violated.' The promoters ... assured me confidently that there would be nothing serious done, that the Rangers would simply preserve order in the event of any racial trouble, if the black man won."

* Some sources name the leader of the Rangers as Captain Bill McDonald or Captain Luke Travis, but it was Captain Brooks.

On the cold, wet night of February 25, the pair fought before a packed hall. There, seated at ringside, in disguise, were Brooks and four other Rangers. The referee was former Choynski opponent and local athletic instructor, Herman Bernau. Johnson, in his memoirs, said he was extremely happy he was finally going to fight a real "champion," one whose great experience and skills could not help but benefit him. "I do not think I was nervous when I entered the ring to face the celebrated Californian heavyweight, but I must confess I was a bit anxious. It was the beginning of the end for which I had been striving, my first fight with a really 'big' fellow, and I felt that a great deal depended on the outcome. I do not think the possibility of beating Choynski ever occurred to me for a single moment. At the very best I hoped to ... stand up to him for a few rounds, and I made up my mind that when he knocked me out I would be right on hand to see how he did it." He said Joe asked some of Jack's friends questions before the fight, trying to get a line on him. Joe was told it was pointless to try and wear Jack down, due to his strength and stamina. It was best to strike early, before Johnson had a real chance to get started. Albert Lasker supposedly pleaded with Choynski before the contest, "Just let him stay a round or two – don't kill him the first moment."[7]

Joe: "I discovered that Johnson was clever and far from a set-up. In fact, I had never met a better defensive fighter. He was black and sleek, trained to the minute, and ... wild to make a great showing by trouncing the warhorse, Choynski. Still, when we got in the ring, there was a trace of doubt in Johnson's demeanor. I noted this – and wondered – but his later actions explained it." The confrontation was scheduled for 20 rounds – not, as some have said, a fight to the finish, illegal in Texas at the time. The preliminaries were rather unusual. First, there was "singing by a party of colored minstrels and a quartette from Houston. Two colored boys, who had been each deprived by accident of a leg, gave a fistic event." Choynski entered the ring at 9:34 p.m., accompanied by Billy McCarthy "and his other supporters." Johnson followed five minutes later. The following is comprised of contemporary reports and Joe's memoirs:[8]

Round 1 – Time was called at 9:47 p.m. After several seconds of cautious sparring, Joe led with a light right. Jack ducked a follow-up left and landed a left counter to the neck or jaw. The punches came quickly from both men. Johnson adroitly evaded a few Choynski left jabs, and they clinched. The young "Galveston Giant" drove a left to the body, "The California Terror" countered with light jabs. The *Galveston Daily News* said

Joe "put a considerable blow on the chin of Johnson," then another on the forehead, and just before the bell, grazed Jack's head with a third. The *Chicago Daily Tribune*, citing an unnamed Galveston paper, said, "The gong sounded with Round One easily Choynski's." Joe: "Johnson boxed with extreme caution. He seemed to have great respect for my hitting. He looked surprised when I whacked him. His eyes rolled. I could see their whites. Somebody – a southern partisan – yelled: 'Choynski, kill that smoke. If you don't, we'll kill you.' Johnson grinned uneasily. But, I discovered one thing quickly. Here was a man who would put up a wonderful defense. Johnson was shifty. I kept remembering something: 'You can't knock a black man down by hitting him on the head.' But this wasn't my idea. It was only the common report. But, legend or no legend, I banged away at Johnson's black head. With the 1st ... fairly even, I returned to my corner pretty confident. I had the feeling that I was going to topple this clever fellow."

Round 2 – The men traded several blows to the forehead. Johnson drove a left to the wind, but Choynski countered with a sharp straight left to the nose. Jack tried again for the breadbasket, but Joe blocked him and landed a light counter to the jaw. The bell ended an even round. Choynski (1927): "In the 2nd round, when his advisors urged him to cut loose, Johnson called back rather hotly, 'Dis ain't no Jack McCormick I'm fightin.' I'm gwine to be keerful tonight – sho 'nuff keerful.' However, toward the close of the round, Jack did loosen up, and we had several peppery exchanges. His close-shaven head was hard to hit." Joe contradicted himself in 1930, saying: "Johnson must have received some stiff instructions during the rest. He trotted out for the 2nd round and began mixing with me. He shouldn't have done this. I drove in the old sledges, battering him around the ring. Then, just to see how much, or how little, he knew, I purposely dropped my guard, to open him up. He bit, but I let that pass. Again, he opened up. And still I waited. But now I knew what to do. Only ringcraft teaches a man this. We have to learn it by bitter example."

Round 3 – Jack assumed a crouch and his clever footwork elicited applause. The fighters exchanged lefts and rights. Suddenly, Joe feinted with a right and hooked a paralyzing left to the jaw. Johnson fell forward, eyes closed, landing in Choynski's arms briefly, before slipping face-first to the floor. He rolled onto his back and lay there, as Referee Bernau completed the 10-count. The *Call* called the final punch "a right-hander to the pit of Johnson's stomach," while the *Galveston Daily News* said it was a right to the jaw, followed by a left cross over the heart. Bernau told reporters that the finishing sequence "was a feint with the left and a strike with the right on the jaw ..." Indeed, most accounts say Choynski feinted with the left and crashed in a right hook. Joe, however, on more than one occasion called it a left hook to the head. Old Joe contradicted himself shortly before his death in 1943, though, referring to the haymaker as a right.[9]

Suddenly, five men wearing 10-gallon hats stormed the ring. One of them shouted that he was Captain Brooks of the Texas Rangers, and placing both fighters under arrest. At this point, Johnson began regaining his senses, as the Rangers helped him to his feet. Joe walked to his corner, where one of the Rangers arrested him, then escorted him to his dressing room on the floor below. As the boxers were ushered from the main hall, the crowd cheered them and jeered the Rangers. Brooks was quoted: "You boys are going to the cross-bar hotel." The boxers were allowed to dress, and later that night, locked up in the Galveston County Jail, located near the wharves.[10]

Choynski KO3 Johnson cartoon by TAD, February 25, 1901

Referee Bernau recalled, for the January 17, 1905 *Galveston Daily News*: "Two hooks to the jaw put an end to the contest, and it was one of the prettiest knockouts I ever saw ... the Galveston boy was defeated fairly and squarely and ... did not on that occasion sell out." Choynski: "I trotted out for the 3rd round, thinking hard and keeping the old eye peeled for the opening I craved. The round had been underway about two minutes, with the fighting fairly even. Then, thinking I had laid the foundation for the finale, I turned my trick again. Suddenly, I dropped my guard. Johnson bit, opened up for a lead, and I nailed the old convincer solid to the top of his skull. Johnson's huge bulk hit the floor with a thud they could have heard down to the Gulf. He was cold as a mackerel ..."

"When they revived Johnson, he rubbed his head ruefully, glanced toward me and muttered: 'I done told you-all I wasn't fightin' Jack

McCormick dis time. Dis Joe Choynski has got dynamite in them hands of his.' Johnson had enough of Choynski. He never craved another match with me. That was his old inferiority complex at work again! Then, the Rangers escorted me to the hoosegow ... now began the legal battle. The governor and a county judge felt that the dignity of the sovereign State of Texas had been insulted. Therefore, Johnson and I were thrown in jail for conducting a prizefight in the Lone Star State. And there we lingered for 30 days, with the cheerful prospect of going to prison for an indefinite stay – provided the district attorney could induce the grand jury to hang the proper ... legal indictment on us. My happiness in jail was not lessened ... by the fact that my partner in crime was also there. Jack and I were not much company for each other, for he was sloughed away in a dungeon, deep down in the bowels of the earth, below the jail basement. The keeper explained that Jack was so accustomed to jail life, he would be bored by an ordinary cell." So went another example of the day's extreme bigotry.

"The sheriff treated me as a distinguished guest. Every night for a week, he and some friends took me ... to a roadhouse several miles out of Galveston, and we enjoyed fried chicken and champagne. But the papers got on to the racket ... and my night rides ceased. Thinking to make me more comfortable, the sheriff promoted me to the insane ward on the top floor ... I was associated with more or less harmless 'nuts,' who accepted my standing without question." At another (less lucid?) time, Joe recalled he and Jack sharing the same cell: "We were supposed to go 10 heats ... five husky Texas Rangers leaped into the ring, flashing big, blue six-shooters. We were locked up in the same cell for 28 days before a Governor's pardon finally unlocked the door. I consider my KO victory over him the highest point of my career – there can never be another Johnson."[11]

Jack: "No, I shall never forget that fight ... I was 22 years of age ... in prime condition to take punishment, but about as awkward in the ring as anybody could be. From the moment he ... chucked out of his bathrobe, I never ceased studying him until I passed into temporary dreamland as the result of one of his scientific taps. First, I took a rapid inventory ... I decided promptly that I had the advantage in weight, height, reach, and strength. But Choynski had something I knew I lacked – 'class' expressed it as well as anything ... That was 10 years ago ... I have learned a lot since ... I believe I acquitted myself fairly well in the 1st and 2nd rounds. It was early in the 3rd and something – it came so quickly I didn't see it coming – reached my jaw with an accuracy that left no doubt ... I learned afterwards it was ... a 'right hook.' I sometimes use the little persuader myself nowadays, but on that ... day ... I was not interested in further proceedings for a while."

"When I was able to sit up and take notice again, I found that Joe and I were behind bars. Governor Sayers ... not an admirer of the manly art ... determined to make an example of us. The days that followed were mighty disagreeable ... They had us in court every day for two weeks. No sooner would we be released ... on one charge than we would be met at the door by the Rangers waiting to arrest us on another. Sheriff Henry Thomas was a fine fellow, and he treated Joe and me royally. Boxing gloves were sent to the gaol from the (Galveston A.C.) club-house, and we boxed every day in the gaol yard, with a lot of county officials and invited guests looking on. Joe developed a great liking for me, and to show his goodwill volunteered to teach me all the fine points of which he was the master ... I learned more in those two weeks than ... ever ... before. There was nothing ... for us to do but eat, sleep, talk, and box. I took good care that boxing was not neglected. It was a mighty lucky thing ... I spent that two weeks in gaol. Of course our arrest put the club out of business, and I had to go elsewhere to practice my profession; but it was ... the earnest tuition at the hands of Joe Choynski that made it possible for me to become a champion." Jack later said, "He hit the bulb (eye) so hard I couldn't close it."[12]

April 8, 1928 *Galveston News*: "While he (Brooks) and two of his men looked after Choynski and kept the crowd from jumping through the 2nd-story (sic) windows, two of the Rangers stood guard over Johnson, who lay in the middle of the ring, unconscious of the new show. His awakening from a deep sleep, with ... nightmares of having been in a storm, was startling to behold. He pictured in his befuddled brain that the two young athletes standing over him were his opponents ... but was soon persuaded ... he had entertained an hallucination. He was introduced to Captain Brooks ... The idea was to permit the contest to proceed in order to avoid any legal technicality about (it) having been 'spoken of,' 'proposed' or 'about to take place' ... We waited until something did actually happen." The February 21, 1954 *Galveston News* noted that the men sparred on the grass of the jail yard, behind the jail. Its February 23 edition said "Johnson was ill in his first few days of imprisonment, probably ... the after-effects of his defeat ..."

The time the fighters spent in jail has been quoted at from 14 to 30 days, but was actually parts of 26. They were incarcerated late on February 25 and released the afternoon of March 22; 1901 was not a leap year. While there, Choynski tutored Johnson, particularly in defensive technique. At some point, Joe allegedly told him, "A man who can move like you should never have to take a punch," and, "Don't try to block – you're fast enough to get clear out of the way." If true, then Jack didn't take all of Joe's advice. He became possibly the greatest blocker of punches who ever lived.

Around 1944, while paying a visit to New York's Madison Square Garden, Johnson told The *Ring*'s Nat Fleischer, "Blond Joe socked me with a left-hander that staggered me, and then he let fly a left hook that caught me on the point of the chin, and the floor came right up and kissed me. I came to my senses just as the referee was finishing the count ... I didn't get up like a lot of our present day fighters do, to make the public believe that they want to fight some more. I'd had enough and was willing to admit it." Jack (1936): "He hit me on the eye so hard I thought a tornado had ... landed on my head."[13] Johnson developed a style that involved stopping an opponent's blow before it started, picking punches out of the air or avoiding them with a slip or clever sidestep. He cruised along at a slow, leisurely pace, content to counter-punch and frequently clinch, using a left jab and magnificent uppercut. After his adversary was softened up, Jack would pelt him with a rapid assortment of punches from either hand. A tactic Jack was said to have used in the Choynski fight, was to parry an antagonist's punch by driving his own blow to the biceps of his opponent. It was very painful to the recipient, as Joe attested.[14]

Depending on his mood, over the years, Johnson would either admit or deny that Joe knocked him out. An example of the latter is from the November 4, 1911 *Grey River Argus*: "Jack Johnson, the world's heavyweight champion, talked ... to an English interviewer the other day ... 'I have never been knocked out in my life, and ... the hardest punch that ever came my way, I received from Joe Choynski in a match ... police stopped in the 3rd round.' " Choynski, for the March 8, 1910 *Boston American*: "In the nine years ... since my battle with him, I can to-day see little change in Johnson. Then, as now, he was extremely clever ... at all times he was a wonderfully strong fellow, for he swung me around a couple of times in our battle much as if we were children, playing the old game of crack the whip."

"But ... one wonderful change ... accounts in great part for his being champion ... the confidence ... attained by whipping Tommy Burns and others made him the most dreaded of men in the ring to-day ... Johnson jumped around a lot more in those days ... to-day ... when he faces an opponent, he is not alarmed at the slightest feint. I knocked Johnson out with a left hook to the right eye ... just below the temple ... He fell upon his back, wallowed around and attempted to get up, but was counted out. Johnson weighed 192 pounds that day, I only 159. In the opening round, we both did a lot of dancing ... He kept dancing away and there was scarcely a punch struck ... The 2nd ... about the same ... we were both full of fancy flourishes. 'This won't do,' I thought ... 'This is likely to go the 10 rounds, and I might lose a hairline decision. I'll ... take a chance ...' I walked out for the 3rd ... with my guard held high, to tempt him to lead for my ribs. He bit like a hungry bass ... as he tried to reach my body, I lashed out with all my weight for his jaw with a left hook, which, pardon me for the little bouquet, was the equal of any man's punch, bar none. I wanted the jaw, but he dropped his head just a bit, and it landed just back of his eye. The force with which I landed jarred me, too, and I knew I had him. Incidentally, I never got one penny for whipping Johnson. I was promised $500 and a percentage of the house. I never knew what became of my part."

Joe told Nat Fleischer, "some years" before 1939 (in an undated *New York Telegram*), "it was not until the count of 8 that he (Jack) attempted to get up, but he couldn't make it." When Joe was mentioned as an opponent, "Johnson, who had seen me fight, declared I was too small. Well, I got the match anyway." Nat considered Jack the greatest heavyweight of all time, possessing the best right uppercut, was the best feinter, the greatest defensive fighter in history, as good as any on the attack, with the exception of Jeffries and Joe Louis. "Johnson boxed on his toes, could block from almost any angle, was lightning fast on his feet ... could feint an opponent into knots ... possessed everything a champion could hope for – punch, speed, brains, cleverness, blocking ability and sharp-shooting."[15]

Choynski and Johnson were taken the next morning (February 26) to police headquarters, where Recorder Allen set bonds at $5,000 each. If convicted of prizefighting, the boxers faced between two and five years in the state penitentiary at hard labor.[16] With neither able to afford bail, their defense attorney, Marc McClemore, that day called at the residence of Judge R.M. Franklin of the 56th District Court, presenting a petition for a writ of habeas corpus. Judge Franklin said that, as Judge A.C. (or Noah) Allen, scheduled to preside over the trial, was away in Houston, he would pass the petition on to him for consideration. There was a much respected rabbi living on the island, Henry Cohen. So highly thought of was he, that Joe allegedly asked to see him first, rather than a lawyer.

Rabbi Henry Cohen was born in London, England on April 7, 1863. He came to the States in 1885, and moved to Galveston three years later. Cohen's relief work after the hurricane of 1900, his wonderful personality and other charitable works made him "the foremost citizen of Texas," in the words of Woodrow Wilson (U.S. President, 1913-1921). He aided black, white, Jew and Gentile alike. Henry could be tough when the situation demanded. The diminutive, 5' 1" rabbi was once confronted by a pair of angry toughs who threatened violence and demanded money, in front of his wife and children. Cohen sent one of the men flying down the stairs with a single uppercut to the chin, and both fled the scene.[17]

Joe protested to Rabbi Cohen that the bail was too high. Cohen met with Sheriff Henry Thomas and suggested that Choynski and Johnson be allowed to spend their days outside of the County Jail. The rabbi would see that the fighters returned to their cells every night. Supposedly, the sheriff agreed, if the boxers observed an 8:00 p.m. curfew. It was said that, each day, Jack spent time with family at his home, while Joe stayed at a hotel. The two slept in their cells at night. When the boxers made their departure

Galveston County Jail, 1901: l-to-r, Deputy Sheriff Wallers Burns, Choynski, Johnson, Sheriff Henry Thomas, Jailer Frank Schreiber

from Texas, Cohen told his wife that Sheriff Thomas threw a farewell party at the jail, and it could only happen in Texas! Parts of this account don't jive with contemporary reports. On February 27, several friends visited Choynski in prison.[18] On March 5, Judge Allen set the case before the Grand Jury, instructing them in the law relative to prizefighting. On the 8th, while Joe, Jack and attorneys were in the court room, the jury submitted a written report, saying, after considering the facts of the case, they failed (or refused) to find a "true bill" against Choynski or Johnson.

Special State Counsel, Lovejoy, was going to have Sheriff Thomas serve a new warrant, based on charges prepared anticipating the Grand Jury's action. Only Recorder Allen had legal right to levy new charges, and he was out of town. The fighters were ordered back to jail, pending Allen's return, despite heavy protests by their attorneys. As a stalling tactic, Lovejoy contended that "no person shall be discharged upon failure of the Grand Jury to find an indictment, until after the Grand Jury had adjourned for the term." He declared this was only the beginning of the term, and the Grand Jury would not be discharged until the court decided there hadn't been some mistake made in its decision. Judge Allen backed him, stating "he had obtained information from a reliable source, that the Grand Jury did not understand the case as ... presented ... he was going to again instruct them on the subject." Bond was reduced from $5,000 to $2,500, still more than either could afford. The case would now go before the court of criminal appeals. A man in the same prison, convicted for murdering his wife, was released after a sentence shorter than theirs.[19]

There was a large crowd in the courtroom during proceedings, which began shortly after 8:00 a.m. Judge Allen called for an adjournment until 2:00 p.m. During the wait, Choynski "conversed with his friends and Johnson did not lack attention." Joe told a humorous tale involving Eddie Foy, "the comic opera comedian" and Jim Corbett, denigrating to Corbett. During "The habeas corpus hearing ... Choynski was placed upon the stand. He testified that he did not own any property in the city, county or State ... was far from ... a rich man ... unable to give a large bond. Upon cross-examination by Lovejoy, Choynski said he resided at La Grange, Illinois ... owned no property in that State, except his home." When asked when he arrived in Galveston, Joe said, about the 22nd or 23rd of February.

Lovejoy asked when Joe came to Galveston before that time, and for what purpose. "Mr. Lovejoy said he proposed to show the defendant's earning capacity and that he had friends to make his bond, if he so desired. 'I want to show ... that he came to Texas two years ago to violate a State law, and was only prevented from ... it by the State Rangers.' " Judge Allen overruled objections. "Choynski said that two years ago, he came to Galveston to act as physical instructor for the Galveston Athletic Club. When asked if he did not come to meet Jim Hall, he replied in the negative. Choynski further stated that he was to receive a salary of $500 a month, and ... was subject to the orders of the club ... as to whether he did not know at that time it was a violation of the State law to engage in prize fighting, he said the only information he received was that the Governor wanted the proposed contest between himself and Hall stopped."

"Choynski stated that ... the Galveston Athletic Club ... (brought him) in addition to ... boxing instructor ... also to give exhibitions, demonstrate the science of boxing. He said he had not stated to Captain Brooks ... that he was going back to Illinois immediately after the exhibition with Johnson, and ... wanted to get his ... money ... He said he knew the club charged fees to members ... did not remember being told two years ago it was against the law to have a fistic exhibition ... said his main reason in coming ... was not to meet Johnson, and the $500 a month tendered him by the athletic club was not solely for ... an exhibition ... His appearance ... with Johnson ... was for ... instruction in the art of self-defense. Attorney Lovejoy asked him if

$500 was not a good figure for giving instructions for a month, and Choynski said he had many times made more ... than that."

"When asked if he was not considered a good man in his line, Choynski smiled and said he was now a 'has been.' 'Is it not a fact ... you knocked Johnson down and out?' 'No sir ... he just found a soft spot and laid down. I have given exhibitions with other people and had them do the same thing.' Referring to the proposed exhibition with Jim Hall two years ago ... he said this was to be a prize fight ... with Johnson ... a scientific exhibition ... to demonstrate ... the different blows. 'Who explained them?' inquired Mr. Lovejoy. 'I don't know that any one did ... The people ... are supposed to see them as they are delivered.' 'Is it not a fact that when you struck (Jack) you told Referee Bernau that would do?' 'I might have ... because I have seen other people quit in exhibitions when they got tired, but ... I am positive Johnson could have gotten up if he had wanted to.' 'Isn't it a fact that you knew when you struck him, he would not get up?' ... 'No, sir ... The blow was not hard enough to hurt a child.'"

"Choynski ... said he was furnished a railroad ticket by club management ... for a round trip ... the returning portion was produced ... showed a limit of 21 days. The point was made ... that Choynski testified he had been engaged for a month, and yet the ticket expired within that time. The defense suggested the ticket might be extended, if necessary ... Brooks ... told of tickets on sale for the contest, although he had not bought them ... Walker said for the sake of saving time, the defense was willing for the Court to assume the defendants ... guilty of prize fighting, and let the Court fix the bond, as in other ... cases of similar degree. He said the case was not of such ... nature that the bond should remain at the present figure."

"Captain Brooks ... said he saw Johnson after the contest, and it was his opinion that he had been knocked out. He ... did not arrest the men before the fight ... because he was instructed by Mr. Lovejoy that to constitute a prize fight, a blow must be struck. When asked why he did not arrest the men before the 3rd round, he said the men merely danced around ... no damage was done ... there were other amusements before the exhibition ... singing and clog dancing ... a sparring contest between two one-legged men. When asked if he had arrested the one-legged men for sparring, he said he had not. 'What did the people pay to see, the boxing exhibition between Choynski and Johnson, or the singing and dancing?' asked ... the defense, and the Ranger ... admitted he did not know ... Brooks said he had been before the Grand Jury ... and ... was excused from further testifying."

"Lieutenant Baker of the Ranger force ... testified about the tickets ... purchased ... he had expended $14 ... he stood over Johnson ... after Choynski struck ... it was fully five or 10 minutes before Johnson recovered. He was of the opinion that Johnson was unconscious ... had to be helped out of the hall after the contest ... prior to the contest ... Johnson stated that

$500 and a portion of the gate receipts was to go to the winner, and the loser was to receive the small end ... Mary Johnson, wife of Jack ... testified that her husband was a poor man ... not able to give the bond required. The case was ... submitted ... and Judge Allen announced he would fix the bond at $2,500 each. The defense gave notice of appeal. It is expected a decision ... will be reached within 10 days or two weeks. Choynski and Johnson have not given bond and are still in custody of the Sheriff." March 9 *Brooklyn Daily Eagle*: "The Grand Jury ... failed to indict the pugilists ... As soon as the fighters were released, Governor Sayers had them re-arrested ... says he will continue ... until a jury is found that will indict the two men."

On the 9th, Judge Allen recommitted the case to the Grand Jury, giving his interpretation of Texas prizefighting law. Attorneys for Joe and Jack were John C. Walker and Marsent Johnson. Marc McClemore was absent. They contended that their clients were illegally restrained. Judge Allen told the jury, "organizations ... had boxers employed to give exhibitions in private to members only, and if no outsiders were permitted and no admission fee charged ... if ... not (for) championship money ... such would not be a prize fight." He instructed that if the jury found any of these elements had been present at the match, they must find both men guilty. The term would not end until the 30th, and the Grand Jury "need not report ... on your action ... until the latter part of the term."[20]

The March 11 *Galveston News* wrote a sympathetic, if maudlin, article: "Good natured Joe Choynski, whose name in fistic annals is a synonym for honest and fair dealing, still languishes a prisoner at the County Jail. He bears his confinement with good grace. He has no word of criticism for those who placed him under lock and key. Texas people he admires, but some of the laws he fails to understand. His attorneys tell him he is illegally restrained of his liberty, that the State ... has no right to keep him in jail, but the rattle of the turnkey's implements ... suggest a different tale. Choynski is a dreamer. With half-closed eyes he sat in jail yesterday afternoon and thought of those he had left behind. He thought of a vine-clad cottage 1,500 miles away ... of great iron bars that rise to cruel heights, shutting him off from one he loves ... of a time when he would once again return to that home, where some one is waiting, where there is also a tiny Scotch terrier, ready with welcome bark to greet his master. And then he awoke. One of those rapid boys in uniform, who go around on bikes to consume more time, disturbed his slumbers. He had a telegram from Choynski's wife, which read: 'La Grange, Ill., March 10 – County Jail, Galveston, Tex.: Leave for Galveston Tuesday, Can stand suspense no longer. Louise.' "

" 'It's just like her,' was Choynski's only comment ... Cramped quarters are tiresome. The only exercise he obtains is in walking from one end of his quarters to the other ... Jail experience is a new thing for the Californian ... He has always had a horror of courts and jails, and ... remarked to a *News* man ... yesterday, 'I never ... cared to go around courts. I never was curious about hearing testimony ... a jail has always been to me a nightmare.' Such is the irony of fate. The Salvation Army came ... yesterday afternoon, to hold ... Sunday ... services. 'Do you know,' said Choynski, 'people as a general rule don't understand those people. They do more good in one minute than all of those preachers in the world ... driving about in their fine carriages ... six days of the week, and preach one sermon on Sunday to a fashionable congregation. I never understood the Army or its mission until a few years ago. I know now they ... help the needy, feed the hungry ... clothe the naked, and ... there are ... thousands of people in the United States who would be in absolute want, if it were not for those boys in the red shirts. They can get my money any day, and ... need not tender any account for it.' Choynski ... grew eloquent in discoursing upon this subject."

"Choynski played a prominent part at a Salvation Army meeting, not many years ago ... at San Francisco. The Salvationists were calling on sinners to repent ... requesting those who did not want to commune with the devil, to join in prayer. Choynski was standing on the outside of a great crowd that circled about ... near him was an objectionable fellow who repeatedly interrupted the services. All efforts of Salvation Army members to silence him proved ineffectual. 'Where do you want to go to when you die?' asked a sweet-faced Army lassie, addressing the man, and his reply was that he wanted to go to a place where hot air was dispensed without charge, and he wanted to go there quick. 'Well, you won't have to wait,' came from Choynski, and the meeting ... progressed without further interruption. Some friends called to see Choynski yesterday. He also received several letters, one from a brother in San Francisco who is a practicing attorney ... Choynski expressed the belief that he would soon be out of the trouble ... Someone loaned him a copy of the Texas Statutes, and about half the day, his time is occupied in reading that portion relating to prize fights."

On March 14, Attorney-General Robert John began proceedings against the Galveston Athletic Club for breach of charter, relating to prizefighting charges. Concluding the Choynski quagmire, on the 20th, Marsent Johnson received a telegram from the Court of Criminal Appeals at Dallas, stating the bond of the men had been reduced to $1,000 each.[21] At 2:00 p.m. on March 22, Joe and Jack posted bond and were released from the Galveston jail. Joe took a train that evening for his home in La Grange, while Johnson availed himself of the next locomotive for St. Louis, Missouri. He'd had enough of the strict prizefighting laws in his native Texas and would now, on the advice of Joe, seek his fortune in more remote parts. Jack took with him his newly-acquired boxing knowledge, and soon earned a reputation as a great defensive fighter. He wouldn't be knocked out again until April 5, 1915, when the 37 year old heavyweight champion was stopped in round 26 by the hulking Kansas cowboy, Jess Willard! Joe's feat in knocking out

Johnson in 1901, despite the fact that the latter had yet to reach his prime, is considered quite an accomplishment. "Li'l Artha" has been touted by some boxing historians as the greatest heavyweight of all time.

Before Joe departed, he told the *Galveston Daily News*: "I shall never enter

Choynski and Johnson released from Galveston County Jail, March 22, 1901

the ring again, even to engage in a friendly exhibition. I shall retire and devote my time to other pursuits. My wife ... at La Grange, has begged me to forsake my ring life for some time, and ... after each contest I have ...

assured her I would retire ... it is hard to break away from a game I have followed so long. But ... Choynski's name will not figure in ring history in the future. To ... Sheriff Thomas and Deputy Will Thomas and Jailers (Deputy Sheriff, Wallers) Burns, (Frank) Schreiber and Lott, I am grateful for many favors. Prison life is especially irksome to an active man, and a fellow, after being in prison 24 days, feels like a 2-year-old on a fast track, when given his liberty. A man who has never been detained ... don't know the value of freedom. It was a new experience, but one I shall profit by. Joe Choynski wants no more ... with Texas ... I may make frequent trips to Galveston, but ... to see my friends ... There are a whole lot of good people in Galveston ... I have many warm friends here." "Choynski said he would return ... to answer any charge ... growing out of the contest ... Johnson says he was treated kindly during his imprisonment, but is glad to be free again. Choynski had an offer from Louisville and ... the Memphis Club, to engage in a limited round contest with local celebrities, but he declined."[22]

Joe stopped off at Louisville, and at the YMHA gymnasium, gave some tips to a young boxer named Ed Rucker. Rucker said he was having great difficulty losing weight, despite running five to eight miles and "an hour's drill" each day. Joe told Rucker he could dry out three or four pounds by abstaining from any liquid for three or four days prior to a fight. Joe said, "You get hellish thirsty. Gargle with cold water." Like Jim Jeffries, Choynski believed depriving oneself of water could be a good thing. We know today it is detrimental to health. Rucker: "The sheriff treated Joe as a guest, gave him a comfortable bed ... good food and even permitted him to go out at night. 'What about Jack Johnson?' I asked. 'They're kind of tough on darkies in the South,' smiled Joe. 'They kept him in a dungeon on bread and water.' "[23] Thus was repeated the tale where Jack was confined to the cellar, rather than a cell near Joe's. The truth on the matter is elusive.

By March 27, Joe was home in La Grange, but "weary and worn." In absentia, he learned of events transpiring in Texas. April 1 *Laredo Times*: "Another Grand Jury ... has failed to find an indictment against Choynski or Johnson ... The Governor will ... have to give up his effort to prosecute those men. It is probably not very becoming to criticize the jury, but it does appear singular that they could not get such evidence before them as would show that the now famous mill was a prize fight." It seems clear that the citizens of Galveston were not fond of the Governor's dictates.

Joe told the April 4 *Oshkosh Daily Northwestern*: "I have gone through enough to make me foreswear the fighting game. When they set the bond at $5,000, it was, of course, prohibitory, and I stayed in jail. There, however, I received the best of treatment. The sheriff, as well as everyone else, with the exception of Judge Allen and one or two other gentlemen, were kindness personified ... Allen ... did everything in his power to make it unpleasant as possible for me. When the Grand Jury failed to find a true bill ... he was forced to reduce the bonds to $2,500, and later on these were reduced again to $1,000. I sent home for this amount, and am now ... with my mind fully made up, regarding the fighting game in quarters where it is not wanted. Would you believe, I gained five pounds while in jail, and acted as the barber for a few days, while that worthy was sick? I had friends on the outside who provided me with food, and my enforced stay was really not unpleasant, everything considered." Joe (in a 1950s article): "Even at that early stage of his career, Jack Johnson showed signs of the fabulous ability which was to make him the greatest fighter of all time. His perfect stance, mastery of defense and uncanny knack of slipping blows."[24]

On October 20, Joe appeared at Hopkins' Theater in Chicago, in a vaudeville sketch entitled, "An Engagement Ring." A review the next day: "Whenever a boxer determines to go on the stage, he secures a play or a sketch which allows him to knock out some heretofore invincible fighter. That's what Joe Choynski does ... in a sketch ... which introduces him as a vaudeville performer. But there is some relief in the fact that he ... disposes of the villain behind the scenes. For the rest, he is a college athlete – and the comparison isn't so bad. He falls in love, and when he wins the fight he also wins a bride. Mrs. Choynski is the chief of his stage companions. She sings, and so does a little girl, the niece of the fighter." This "niece of the fighter," Edna Spence, must have been a niece of Louise. Joe would only have three nieces. Herbert's daughter, Janet, wasn't born until 1908; Edwin's eldest daughter, Florence, in 1914, and youngest daughter, Harriet, in 1926.[25] In mid-November, Joe signed for a 20 round match with Jim Jeffords. Jim was a large, young heavyweight who just had a D6 with Peter Maher. So much for Joe's intent to retire from the fight game, although this contest fell through. Just why is uncertain.[26]

Choynski strived to juggle a vaudeville tour and the remainder of his boxing career. Much was written of the former in the papers. The week of November 18-23, Joe and Louise played at the Howard Athenaeum in Boston, Massachusetts, in the Wang Doodle Comedy Company. "Joe Choynski leads the house olio ..." November 19 *Boston Journal*: "With a huge chrysanthemum (prop) in the lapel of his up-to-date frock coat, Joe ... smiled at reporters when they asked him about his acting. Joe used to be known as Chrysanthemum Joe by some of his pugilistic friends, because he always wore his hair that way. When asked how he happened to start in as an actor, Joe said Mrs. Choynski advised it. Mrs. Choynski ... has been on the stage since she was 4 years old, and played Topsy in the Uncle Tom's Cabin Company ... Unlike other boxers who have gone to the stage, Choynski does not box. There is some reference to a bout in which Hamilton, a young college man (Choynski), takes the place of one of the principals and whips an English pugilist. Choynski said he is in trim all the time ... ready to go back to the ring at a moment's notice ... said he weighed

187 pounds, and ... ran a mile in 4:30 the other day. Choynski is very good as an actor, has a good comedy sketch, and very sensibly does not try to make a speech, but goes ahead and does his part."

The next day's *Pawtucket Times*: "Choynski ... playing in Boston in his vaudeville sketch, 'A Tangle of Ropes and Diamonds,' says his histrionic effort would not prevent him ... entering the ring again, and if Jeffries were willing, he would not hesitate to don the mitts with the champion. 'It was a shame,' he said ... 'to put poor Ruhlin up against Jeffries. Ruhlin simply wanted the money, and took his beating to get it. He is not a scientific boxer, although personally he is all right, and it was only a question of how few rounds Jeffries would take to beat him. Ruhlin brought discredit on the ring by quitting, and he would have quit before the 5th round, had there not been so many people there." While Joe's words were harsh, his opinion of Gus had a fair amount of support in the boxing community.

Joe: "Fitzsimmons has retired, Sharkey has no license to meet Jeffries, Ruhlin is out of it ... I do not see but Jeffries will have to meet me next. There is no heavyweight among younger men capable of tackling Jeffries I ... believe I have the best right to him. I have a good pair of hands left me, and I know Jeffries can be whipped. He ... scared Ruhlin before they had been in the ring a minute. The man that will keep away ... and hit him when he gets the chance will beat him. Jeffries is not a fighter, except he manages to hit the other man when the other gets too close ... I mean he is not scientific, as Corbett was. I have kept in good condition for the past 18 years. I take my gymnasium exercise regularly ... would not need ... much training if I had a fight ... Walcott defeated me, but I had a couple of broken ribs ... I notice (he) has kept away ... since ..."

During the last week of November, Joe and Louise continued "A Tangle of Ropes and Diamonds" at the Howard Athenaeum.[27] On the afternoon of December 27, he and Tom Sharkey climbed into the ring at Wood's Gymnasium, 6 East 28th Street in Manhattan, New York. They traded punches in a heated, impromptu, "friendly" three round bout. "The two ... met by chance at Wood's gymnasium, where Sharkey is training for ... Maher. Choynski ... makes it a practice to take daily exercise ... he readily consented to put the gloves on ... for a friendly bout. The sailor was kept busy knocking the Californian's jabs and swings that came from all directions, and several times the pair came together as though they really meant to do damage ... those who had the good fortune to be present were satisfied they had witnessed a real fight." This is the only sparring found between the pair that week, although an Iowa paper noted, "Joe Choynski is said to have been boxing in some rugged bouts at a New York gymnasium with Tom Sharkey. The latter is ... getting into ... condition for ... Jeffries. Joe is working simply because he likes it."[28]

On December 30, Joe arrived back in Chicago. Evidently, the short "go" with Sharkey acted like a bellows to the embers of his fighting impulse. He told George Siler, "I have got quite a little time on my hands at present, and am just aching to crawl through the ropes with some one.' 'Not Jeffries?' inquired one of his friends. 'Yes, Jeff or anyone else. I am not picking them, and they can trot them along at any old weight.' 'How about Jack Root?' 'He'll suit first-rate, and there will be no difficulty in arranging the weight, either. I do not know how low Jack can fight at, but I will agree to make any weight he names. They tell me I am getting old ... If some of these youngsters think I am on the down grade, I ought to be easy picking, eh? I see Wild Bill Hanrahan snuffed Marvin Hart's candle with a whiff. Now, why wouldn't Bill and I make a good team to swap punches? Too heavy ...? I'll bet ... I can get as low as (Kid) Carter, or ... within a couple of pounds ... I'll accept the first man that comes along.' Light exercise daily, with an occasional bout 'with the mitts,' keeps (him) ... ready for a scrap at short notice." Joe made a broad challenge through the papers, "To box any man in the world, whether heavy or any other weight, and he prefers a meeting with James J. Jeffries, the present champion of the world."[29]

Among those Joe challenged was George Gardner. In a recent win over "Kid" Carter, Gardner was said to have captured the "middleweight championship of America." He would win general recognition as world light-heavyweight champion in 1903, stopping Jack Root in 12 rounds. In his next fight, George lost the title to 39½-year-old Bob Fitzsimmons. What he wouldn't do, it seems, is fight Choynski. A match between the two was scheduled for October, 1902, but later cancelled. While he was throwing down the gauntlet, Joe didn't neglect the middleweights. He offered, "for the sake of getting a match," to train down to 158 pounds, a feat likely impossible without rendering him weak as a kitten. Joe said he would stop two top middleweights, in four rounds each on the same night, with no intermission between. The boxers named were Jack Moffat and Australian, Tim Murphy. Joe "has begged for matches with Marvin Hart, 'Wild Bill' Hanrahan, 'Kid' Carter, George Gardner and Jack Root, without avail." Directors of the Chicago Athletic Association felt the highest offer they could make would not meet with his approval. Joe weighed 163 pounds on January 7, and felt he could lose another five without weakening himself. On the 9th, Moffat's manager, Sam Pooler, said he would accept the "handicap match" for any purse Joe might name.[30]

A report on the weight classes said: "The ... situation appears ... muddled. Walcott ... (is) welterweight champion ... the others are in some doubt. A ring follower has attempted to classify the leading fighters ... 154-pound class – George Gardner ... 177-pound class – Bill Hanrahan ..." Bill's ranking was based on his recent 1st-round knockout of Marvin Hart, who would win partial recognition as heavyweight champion, after Jeffries retired in 1905. "The idea of dividing the heavyweight class has been often discussed. To place a limit of 175 pounds on some matches would make matters interesting for fighters of the McCoy, Choynski, Maher, Hanrahan and Sharkey class, though Fitzsimmons could whip ... all ... at that weight. Jeffries, Ruhlin and Corbett appear ... the only men in the 200-pound class ... It would not be out of the way for ... boxing authorities ... to get together and arrange a definite scale of weights."[31] Heretofore, the limit of a division was often set by its reigning champion, for his convenience in making weight. It is notable that the "champion" of the light-heavyweight division named was Bill Hanrahan, as he was Joe's next opponent.

His broad challenge over three divisions and such, got Joe plenty of bites. "Choynski ... the target of more challenges than are usually sent at a champion, since ... his offer to whip several men in one night, will probably have his first encounter with Jim Jeffords at Philadelphia early in February. Choynski says he will meet Jeffords before taking up the challenge ... by Chicago boxers ..." The Jeffords bout fell through. It was noted on the 18th, "Choynski has made a success of his theatrical venture. His sketch, 'An Engagement Ring,' has proved ... a good drawing card on the road."[32]

Harry Corbett, Jim's older brother, was trying to arrange a match for Joe with the winner of the January 31 world light-heavyweight championship in San Francisco, between George Gardner and Jack Root. Harry handled many of the city's boxing bets in his saloon. January 26 *St. Paul Globe*: "Should Gardner win, the return match will take place Feb. 24, but in case Root is the lucky one, a contest between him and Choynski is problematical. Root's manager has repeatedly refused to give Choynski a chance at his protégé, in spite of the fact that Joe has volunteered to do 158 pounds, or any ... weight suitable to the West side Bohemian. In the meantime, Choynski is to meet 'Wild' Bill Hanrahan ... at Louisville, Feb. 14. Hanrahan, since his jig-time win over Marvin Hart, is being touted as the coming heavyweight. He weighs in the 90s and is a terrific hitter."

Ironically, Root (born Janos Ruthaly, in Bohemia, Czechoslovakia) declined to fight Joe on the grounds that he weighed too much. Jack's manager, Lou Houseman, wished to establish him as a light-heavyweight *because* he was too heavy for middleweights and too light for heavyweights. The *San Francisco Call* said on the 30th: "Choynski will meet the winner of the Gardner-Root fight ... will start for the coast immediately. The officials of the Yosemite Athletic Club have the promise of Root and Gardner, that whichever man wins will take on Choynski at catchweights on February 28." Neither Gardner nor Root would ever trade punches with Joe. They are recognized today as the first two world light-heavyweight champions. Joe was a few years too early, in terms of general public acceptance.

Round Twenty

Dueling the Young Guns
(February 1902 – March 1903)

By February 4, Choynski had resigned himself that he would not get a match with the winner of the Gardner-Root clash. He had "partially declared off his meeting with Hanrahan," in order to get a bout with one of them. Al Cook, matchmaker for the Monarch Athletic Club of Louisville, Kentucky, visited Chicago for a couple of days, trying to convince Joe to keep his fight with "Wild" Bill on the 14th. Hanrahan had just lost on a 4th round knockout to Frank Childs on February 3 in Chicago. At his suburban home in La Grange, on February 6, Joe signed articles for a bout at catchweights on the 18th. Referring to Joe as "The La Grange farmer" (for his small chicken farm there), the *Davenport Daily Leader* quoted him on the 4th: "They say I am too old to battle. That is a queer statement, when it is known to everybody that Fitzsimmons is well past 40 years of age. Jim Corbett is 36 – that I know, *because I went to school with him* (emphasis is mine) ... I am only 33 ... Does that make me too old? What have I done that would indicate I am too old to box? It's the most foolish thing that has been said in a long time. Just give me the chance and I will box as well as any of them."[1] The Hanrahan match would not occur until March 7.

The February 6 *Brooklyn Daily Eagle* had heavyweight king Jim Jeffries claiming: "Choynski almost licked Fitz at Boston, and I think he has a chance ... again. I killed the proposed (Choynski) meeting at Philadelphia, because I was afraid Fitz would get licked, and I want him ... *I broke up that bout myself.*"[2] (emphasis is again mine). Yet another example of the regard held for Joe, but likely a burst of hyperbole, as Jeff probably didn't have the clout to "break up the bout." In the July title fight, Bob cut Jim up terribly, before succumbing to the younger, larger man's heavy artillery in round eight. A boxing show was held at Douglas Hall in Chicago, on the night of February 15. Choynski refereed the main event, a featherweight battle between local product, Young Mowatt (real name, Tommy Moore) and Ned "Kid" Broad, of New York. The contest went the six rounds, Joe declaring a draw. Many dissented with his verdict, feeling that Broad held a slight edge, and that Joe favored the local man.[3]

Joe had been training for Hanrahan, at his home in La Grange, since about the 2nd week in February. On the 27th, it was announced the match would be transferred to the Music Hall of Louisville, under the auspices of the Empire Athletic Club. On March 5, Joe arrived in Louisville. He said "he weighed 165 pounds, stripped, and never felt more like boxing in his life. 'I'll do a little training here ... Just punch the bag a bit, do a little road work every day.' With Choynski is George Schrosbree (sic), a Chicago boxer."[4] "Wild" Bill was the type who either knocked out an opponent or was knocked out, himself. All nine of his recorded victories came by way of stoppage, and of his 11 losses, nine were knockouts. Hanrahan's greatest triumph was probably the 1st-round kayo he scored the previous December 17 over future heavyweight champion, Marvin Hart. He also knocked out "Kid" Carter twice in 1900, by KO12 and KO10. Bill possessed remarkable stamina, as seen by his late-round victories. This was contrary to most sluggers, who spend their energy early by throwing so many bombs.

The writer using the pseudonym, "Old Timer," for the pulp, *Fight Stories*, described Hanrahan: "Pound for pound, I don't believe there were many better punchers in the ... history of the game. Not enough control, true enough, but steam, zip, the whisper of sudden death ..." "Wild Bill" was born in Louisville on January 1, 1882. The fine manager-trainer, Jimmy DeForest, was said to have discovered him fighting on the streets, in the area of New York City known as "Hell's Kitchen." DeForest guided the Louisville slugger through an amateur career, capped off by the national middleweight championship, and through his early pro career.[5] Joe: "At the time I met Hanrahan, he was about 21, (barely 20, actually), 12 or 13 years younger than I was, and weighed around 185 or 190 pounds. He stood 6' in

"Wild Bill" Hanrahan, Chicago, 1901

height, had enormous shoulders, a long reach, and fists like Armour hams. They called him 'Wild Bill' because of his ring tactics and contempt for punishment. It was his habit to paw around the ring like an infuriated bull. The moment the bell rang, he would rush out and hurl himself at his antagonist like a thunderbolt. He was more like the modern Jack Dempsey than any man I can think of. 'Wild Bill' was regarded by many fistic experts as the most promising heavyweight of his time. Hart was one of the toughest heavyweights that ever took a punch. Hanrahan knocked Hart as dead as a mummy with one, terrible heave to the whiskers."[6]

The referee was George Siler. Most papers said the altercation was slated for 25 rounds, a few said 20. Bill was in fine condition, despite his penchant for avoiding a disciplined regimen. His manager, Joe Sullivan, "never left the pugilist while he was training for Joe ..." "Wild" Bill did some trash talking in the lead-up to the fight. He was quoted in the December 17, 1901 *Louisville Courier-Journal*: "Speaking of Choynski, I feel that I have something on him. When he was training for his bout with Joe Walcott ... I boxed with him and loosened his ribs with a wallop." Joe, weighing 168 pounds, entered the ring at 10:20 p.m.; Hanrahan weighed 189.[7] The following is taken from primary source accounts and Joe's memoirs:[8]

Round 1 – Soon after the bell, "Wild" Bill connected with a smashing punch to Choynski's neck, dropping him to his knees. Joe wasn't badly hurt, and rose quickly. Probably because of this, Hanrahan didn't rush and follow up. The rest of the frame saw the boxers cautiously circle each other. Siler recalled, in the *Chicago Tribune*, the knockdown occurring in the next inning. He said Joe avoided Hanrahan's haymakers to the head, but some caught his blocking left shoulder, jolting him off balance. Choynski tried to score with the jab, but Bill's guard was too effective. Joe: " 'Wild Bill' came at me ... both hands driving at my head. I was so busy picking off his blows that my head swam for a moment. His style was the most confusing I had encountered. One never knew where his licks were coming from or where they would land. They plopped all over the ring ... I felt the weight of his terrible blows several times. I managed to avoid their full impact, but even what was left ... jarred me terribly. The pace was as fast as in my fights with Goddard in Australia. He (Bill) caught me a bender, after about 30 seconds of fighting, and I understood ... how he had rolled up his swift knockout record. I didn't go down, but ... into a shell, and ... did some intensive thinking. As the round ended, he dropped into his seat, grinning wickedly and slashing his long arms. I think he was sorry the bell had rung."

Round 2 – Siler said Hanrahan landed his "Mary Ann" (Bill's nickname for his right fist) to Joe's neck early on, flooring him for a two-count. The Cedar Rapids paper said the round was in Joe's favor. The *Trenton Times* said "Honors were even." Joe: "He began trying to sink those huge paws into my stomach, but I kept going away ... a moment later, as I was trying for my famous crusher, Bill plastered me one in the stomach; the blow just about bent me double. How that punch hurt! A few seconds later, he banged a straight left to my kisser ... I felt as if my neck had been broken. Blood flowed from my lips. The power behind (his) blows was terrific. I decided to begin sharpshooting at his head. I managed to even things up a bit by crashing a right to Hanrahan's ear ... For 50 seconds I battered his jaw and ears. But he took them like a good fellow and came in bellowing for more ... he tore into me with greater fury. Wild Bill was wild, all right."

Round 3 – The discrepancies continued. *Chicago Tribune*: Hanrahan kept his guard high, as coached by his corner, and only used his left. He made Choynski look rather amateurish, driving the left into his face. Bill also roughed Joe up in the clinches and sent him to the canvas for a 3-count. *Cedar Rapids Republican*: "The 2nd and 3rd rounds were in Choynski's favor, and in the latter ... Joe landed on Hanrahan's jaw four times without return." *Trenton Times*: "Hanrahan knocked Choynski down with a straight left to the face. The round ended with a furious rally, and was Hanrahan's." It appears to have been a close frame, probably clinched for Bill by the knockdown. Choynski: "I hoped things would get better in the 3rd ... they grew worse. Wild Bill battered me around like a punching bag. I got in a solid whack now and then, but was unable to stop his rushes."

"Bill hammered me to the floor with a series of jarring jolts. True, most of them landed on my shoulders, but ... the impact was crushing. One bounced against my ear, and I took a count. As I came up ... Wild Bill thought he had me. I saw that wild light in his eyes. He forced the milling ... seemed bent on ending it quickly, I fought fiercely. There were several exchanges in the next minute that thrilled the huge crowd. Hanrahan ... landed three terrible body blows that hurt ... would have ended the hopes of the average fighter. But, I weathered the tempest. He seemed chagrined. I went to my corner with the conviction that I must ... change my pace or be battered out of the picture by this hard-hitting Kentuckian. Up to this time, I had been fighting ... at long range ... I decided to ... keep inside his long swings, and see what I could accomplish at close quarters."

Round 4 – Siler said Joe was getting leg weary, "and it was not, 'who would win, but how many more jabs Joe could take before going down and out.' Hanrahan, seeing Joe's condition, foolishly shifted from straight lefts to right hand swings. This change was a relief to Joe, and also gave him an opportunity to connect with his left, which he did quite frequently. Still the tide of battle was slowly but surely going against him, and at the end of the round he looked for all the world like a loser. Vigorous work by his seconds brought him around in good shape for round five ..." Joe: "There came some pretty rough work in the clinches. Bill seemed determined to break me down in the hind-parts. But, I noticed one good thing. I wasn't stopping so many of his longshoreman rights. Hanrahan missed several hard swipes, and I jabbed him on the nose with force enough to shake him. The ring, already rich in claret, now received plenty more. We fell into a clinch, but I shook out of it. As we broke clear, I sent home a fearful right to the big fellow's jaw. He fell back on his heels. Then I shot over a hard right hook and followed it with a straight left to the chin. I was finding him, but he refused to fall. The bell found us exchanging killing rights."

Round 5 – The fighters were both wary and weary. So spent appeared Joe at the end of the 4th, many thought he wouldn't last out the 5th. As it turned out, he didn't have to. The dueling duo punched furiously. Hanrahan landed several straight lefts to the mouth, but "The Frisco Flash" drove hard jabs and two potent rights to the jaw. Near the end of the round, he ripped a staggering left uppercut to the jaw. As "Wild Bill" staggered, Joe swung a short, powerful right behind the left ear, and Bill crashed to the floor. Siler counted over him. Amid the din of the crowd, all that was heard, finally, was the bell. *Tribune*: "The knockout came so close to the end of the round that Hanrahan's seconds had their doubts as to the correctness of the count ... lugged their subject to his corner, and began working on him, to bring him to the scratch for round six."

"Meanwhile, Choynski was receiving the congratulations of his friends ... explaining how poorly he fought. After ... about 30 seconds, Joe Sullivan, Hanrahan's manager, noticing the crowd preparing to leave ... suspected something amiss ... the contest was over. Immediately after I (Siler) counted Bill out, I asked the official time-keeper how long after the count out had he tapped the gong ... he replied, 'About half a second.' I thought it was hardly that long, as I was just ... reaching down to tap Bill on the shoulder, when clang went the gong. It was a close call for Joe. Bill, however, was out for keeps. What the minute's rest would have done for him, or ... the outcome ... had time been called a second earlier, is beyond me."

The winner was challenged by Marvin Hart and "Kid" Carter. The wire service report said, "It is understood, however, that Choynski's next match will be with Tom Sharkey, in this city (Louisville) on May 3, Derby night. The *Chicago Tribune* said Joe complained of feeling ill before entering the ring, and said he waged a poor fight. The contest had been clean throughout, neither ... engaging in "rough work." The paper felt a lucky punch by Choynski ended it. Whether Joe's pre-fight comment on feeling ill was to save face in the event of a loss cannot be known. The *Cedar Rapids Republican*, however, wrote, "Choynski had the best of the fight all the way through, and his feinting and dodging was too much for the New Yorker, whose vicious swings failed to land." The *Oakland Tribune* agreed: "Choynski was at all times master of his opponent, his feinting, dodging and smart foot work playing havoc with the vicious swings of the 'wild' man ... and tired Hanrahan." The BBBC (British Boxing Board of Control) 2005 Yearbook said Joe laid claim to "the American 170 pounds title."

Joe (1930): "The 5th was a massacre. I kept in close, working hard, and this ... bothered Bill. Like a gunner, he had lost the range ... I saw a chance for my dependable left, and rammed it home. The blow staggered Bill. I caught him another on the point ... followed with a right to the ribs and another in the stomach. He grunted ... But ... came back and slashed me with two lefts on the head. Fortunately, they were badly timed. Then, Bill ...

put everything into ... a wild, right swipe. Happily for me, it missed ... before he could recover ... I clicked him with a paralyzing left hook back of the ear. He dropped like a stone. It was one of the hardest punches I have ever landed. It not only finished that fight for Wild Bill, but virtually finished his ring career. It was a clear-cut triumph of science and ring generalship over brute strength. That fight made me realize I was no longer a youth as athletes are reckoned, and, while I had beaten a dangerous foe, it had been a narrow escape." Joe once stated, "I hate to get hit, but as soon as I am I fight better than ever."[9] That held true here. "Wild Bill" died of pneumonia in Chicago on April 18, 1902, only 20 years old.

On March 9, C.H. Dickens, matchmaker for Louisville's Empire club and manager of Marvin Hart, brought his protégé to Chicago to be placed under Joe's tutelage. While "The Fightin' Kentuckian" had strength, grit and punching power, he was badly in need of skill and science. Joe arrived back in the Windy City the day before, and attributed his poor performance to weakness from dysentery. He admitted "he could not solve Hanrahan's defense ... the latter fought along more scientific lines than he expected. 'I looked for wild and wooly ... swings, such as he indulged in with Frank Childs ... (he) surprised me with his straight left ... jabs. When I got to him with several hard lefts in the (4th) ... I knew I had him.' Joe said he would ... handle (Sharkey) as he did Hanrahan." On the 14th it was said Joe was to fight in June at the athletic carnival in England, put on by the National Sporting Club (NSC) of London. Dr. Ordway of the NSC "made an offer to Ed Horman, Choynski's manager, for a match between Choynski and some ... good man. The offer was forthwith accepted. Jack Root ... or George Gardner ... will in all probability be chosen ..."[10] This is the first and only time an "Ed Horman" was mentioned as a manager of Joe.

Next was Eddie "Kid" Carter. Born Edward Blazwick in Zagreb (now Agrem), Austria, on January 1, 1880 to Croatian parents, Carter moved with his family to Brooklyn, New York at age five. Like Joe, Eddie had blond hair. At age 15, he commenced his boxing career under the fighting name, "Young Olsen," and was nicknamed "The Gangling Swede." Starting as a featherweight and filling out to middleweight, "The Kid" battled many of the top light-heavyweights and heavyweights of his day. Up to now, Carter had beaten men like Hanrahan (KO10, 1900), Jack Bonner (W20, 1900) and Joe Walcott (WDQ19, 1901, KO7, 1901). Losses came at the fists of "Philadelphia" Jack O'Brien (L10, 1898), Matty Matthews (L20, 1899), Bill Hanrahan (KOby12, 1900), George Gardner (LDQ 19, 1900, KOby18, KOby8, 1901), Tommy Ryan (L6, 1900) and Jack Root (LDQ 15, 1901). Many felt he was robbed of a knockout win in the Root tilt, the crowd not seeing the knockout punch to the body as a foul blow. Carter also fought 20 round draws with Hanrahan and Bonner (twice). He had engaged in at least 47 bouts up to 1902. The "Kid" was a deadly puncher, with the uncanny ability to snatch victory "from the jaws of defeat." He was "a robust fighter with a long reach, clever in an unskilled way, capable of receiving and delivering unlimited punishment ... not as cool and calculating as (Tommy) Ryan, (nor) as cunning and shifty. But ... a dangerous rival at all stages ... possessed of the stuff that goes to make champions."[11]

The fight was held on the night of the 24th, at the American Athletic Club in Chicago. The referee was Malachi Hogan, and the bout set for six rounds. Although weights were not given, Joe appeared heavier than "The Kid," and was said to be a couple of inches taller. Carter is listed at 5' 10". The crowd witnessed a short, explosive and controversial encounter, one of the most sensational in the history of the Windy City. The hybrid report uses contemporary and (a few) secondary sources:[12]

Eddie "Kid" Carter

Round 1 – The fighters came out swinging. Joe slammed into "The Kid" with a furious onslaught that had him badly dazed and reeling, blood spurting from his nose. Reports said Joe "reached Carter's jaw with both hands at least 20 times." In a "clinch, Joe pinioned Carter's right against his body, and ... smash with his left. Carter knew the trick and it failed. They stood toe to toe like a couple of longshoremen and slammed away. Joe had the better of it and they mauled ... all over the ring." Carter was out on his feet from the fusillade of lefts and rights, mostly to the head. Choynski, seeing an opportunity to finish his man, charged in recklessly, his guard down. he was caught by a desperation, powerful right in the pit of the stomach, doubling him over. Before he could straighten up, "The Kid" crashed a roundhouse right to the head, "a trifle high," and dropped Joe to his knees.

"The latter regained his feet at "four," but was staggering and barely able to lift his arms. (Some reports said the count was seven or eight seconds). Instead of clinching, Joe unwisely chose to slug. Carter, quickly recovering and seeing his chance, charged in. After missing several desperate swings, "The Kid" landed a smashing right to the jaw. *Idaho Daily Statesman:* "The blow had such force that it lifted Choynski clear off his feet, and he went down on the top of his head. It was thought for a time he had been seriously injured, but with the assistance of a physician, his handlers brought him to his senses, after he had been unconscious for fully 10 minutes. The round lasted two minutes and 35 seconds."

April 19 *Police Gazette*: Joe cut "The Kid's" eye with a potent right. The final punch "put Joe to the floor, his head striking with a thud. Up to the count of six, Choynski lay on his back ... eyes ... popping from his head ... with a groan, he rolled over on his face and was counted out. After coming to, Joe informed his seconds it was the hardest wallop he had received in his long ... career. Carter left the ring reeling like a drunken sailor ..." March 27 *Syracuse Post-Standard*: "Carter would hardly have lasted more than two or three rounds ... had not the accidental blow got in ... Even (so), the defeated man almost saved himself. Few ... will give Carter credit for being a better man than Choynski." *Davenport Daily Leader*: "It took about five minutes for Joe to realize what had happened. His first words were: 'I had him licked, didn't I?' ... looking around the ring dreamily ... Joe went to his dressing room, and thence to the farm at La Grange, there to ponder over the folly of being in too much of a hurry. They saw Eddie dash to his corner with a little jig step and soak big Jack McCormick playfully in the ribs."

"Choynski was broken-hearted in his dressing-room. He said: 'He's a tough, young fellow and he can stand a lot of punching. I thought I had him ... for I could hit him as I pleased, but he was lucky enough to get in a couple that brought me down. All I can hope is that I get another match before anybody else gets a chance at him.' Carter was wildly jubilant ... could scarcely contain himself while dressing. 'He did not hurt me at all, except with a couple of punches in the nose. I could have gone along 20 rounds at the same pace, for he was merely stinging me, and I was satisfied that in a short time, I could get in a winning punch ... I saw the chance when he tried to cross me with a right. I got inside and planted a right into his ribs. I felt him weaken, and then it was easy.' " I suppose Carter could be forgiven some exaggeration and braggadocio, given his youth and unexpected upset victory. All accounts agreed that "California Joe" looked a sure winner, before the "Hail Mary" punch to the body turned the tide. Carter came up with a similar performance on December 3, when power-punching Peter Maher floored and badly hurt him, only to see Carter rise and smash his much heavier foe unconscious in round two. The British Boxing Board of Control's 2005 Yearbook says that, as a result of this fight, Carter claimed Choynski's "American 170 pounds title."

The April 4 *St. Paul Globe* reiterated that Joe had been "selected to take part in London's sparring match, apropos of the Coronation ... one of the stars in the galaxy of fistic talent now being gathered from everywhere, to compete for world's championship in June." This was the coronation of Albert Edward, Prince of Wales, as Edward VII, King of England, succeeding his mother, Queen Victoria. Due to an attack of appendicitis, his coronation was postponed until August 9, 1902, and held at Westminster Abbey. Joe did not travel to England, as it turned out.

His next foe was Al Weinig. Born and raised in Buffalo, New York, Weinig stood about 6' 1", and in addition to being a boxer, had also been a noted cyclist. Although described as a light-heavyweight, Al met and defeated a number of good boxers, up through heavyweight. In 1927, Choynski described him as a "game and hard-hitting slugger with no small amount of skill." His résumé included wins over Dan Creedon (KO10, 1900, WDQ6, 1901, KO9, 1902), Billy Stift (W6, 1901), Jim Jeffords (KO8, 1900, KO3, 1902), Dick Moore (KO4, 1901), Jim Scanlon (KO6, 1901) and Jack McCormick (KO10, 1902). He lost to such as Dick O'Brien (KOby2, 1899), Dan Creedon (KOby10, 1900), Billy Stift (KOby1, 1900, KOby2, 1901), Marvin Hart (KOby11, 1901) and "Kid" Carter (L6, 1902). Weinig's loss to Carter was described as a close, terrific battle. Joe fought Al in Louisville, Kentucky on May 2, the night before the Kentucky Derby. It was slated for 20 rounds, and the referee was George Siler. The principals were to arrive on April 29, to finish their training in Louisville.[13]

The fight was held at the Music Hall, under the auspices of the Empire Athletic Club. One paper said, "the Southern Athletic Club." Harry Myers and Billy Robinson were behind Weinig, while Marvin Hart, Jimmy Barrett, Pete Treynor and Jimmy Urell seconded Joe. Time was called at 10 o'clock. The following combines ringside reports from the *Louisville Courier-Journal* and *St. Paul Globe*, with input from other contemporary papers:[14]

Round 1 – From the tap of the gong, the men went at each other. Joe started off the fun with a left hook to the face. Al replied with a hard right to the body, a short, left stab to the nose, and blocked a left-right. "The Frisco Flash" hooked left and right to the head. Following a clinch, Weinig pumped three or four jabs to the face, but "Joe hooked hard with right and left to the jaw. There was a hot mix-up, both landing rights ... Weinig ... went to one knee from a right to the jaw. Both did some clever ducking. Al sent a hard, straight left to the mouth just before the bell."

Round 2 – The round started with close-in work by both fighters. Choynski made use of his eccentric, "long, hooking left, which he kept jabbing into Weinig's face." They traded lefts and rights to the ribs, then the battle went to long-range, where both did some good work. Joe connected with a sharp right hook to the head, Al countered with a hard left to the ear. More infighting followed, thudding body blows on both sides. After exchanging rights to the head, Weinig landed "half a dozen lefts to the face." The *St. Paul Globe* only said, "honors were about even and no damage ... done, owing to the clever blocking and ducking."

Round 3 – The pair resumed rugged infighting. The *Louisville Courier-Journal* said Choynski landed a right hook to the jaw that dropped Weinig on his backside. Strangely, the local paper seemed the only one that saw the knockdown. Al rose quickly, and Joe went after him, scoring several hard lefts to face and body. He staggered Weinig with a cracking left-right to the jaw, landing more stiff lefts there. The men traded jabs and did some clever outfighting, or long-range work. They came together in a wild flurry of punches, which Joe had the best of, landing lefts and rights to the jaw. Weinig appeared groggy, but "just as the gong sounded" (per the *Louisville Courier-Journal*), he connected with a sensational right hook to the jaw that floored Joe. He required help from his seconds to get to his corner. *St. Paul Globe*: "The 3rd ... nearly proved disastrous to Choynski, for Weinig landed again and again on his face and jaw, and just before the end of the round, sent Choynski to his knees with a hard right to the jaw. Choynski seemed unable to rise, but the gong sounded just in time to save him."

Round 4 – Joe's corner did skillful work between rounds. Again, the fighters slammed into each other with body punches at close quarters. Choynski got in a good left and right to the face, Weinig shot several stiff left jabs to the mouth. He connected with a hard right to the jaw, but Joe countered with a left hook that slammed his opponent into the ropes. The groggy Buffalo man clinched and held on. Al was hurt, but both he and Joe were very tired from the hellacious pace. Just as the bell rang, Weinig again landed a staggering right to the jaw, but Joe remained upright.

Round 5 – Al seemed the fresher of the two, and starting with a rush. He landed body shots that hurt, and several lefts and rights on the jaw. Joe looked groggy and tired, but got in a good right to the ribs. Weinig gave the perfect counter, staggering Joe with a hard left to the jaw over his low right. Each landed jabs, and Choynski scored with a pair of uppercuts. Weinig rushed and landed a left-right. Joe timed his next rush and caught Al coming in, with a right to the jaw. Al shot in a series of jabs to the nose, and, on breaking from a clinch, staggered Joe with a fierce left hook to the jaw. This was the 3rd heat in a row where he was caught with a blistering shot at the end of the frame, and Joe should have known better. Perhaps his mind was cloudy. At this stage, the bout was a bit in Al's favor.

Round 6 – Choynski came out fresh, and forced the fighting. He hooked a hard right to the jaw and staggered Weinig. After an exchange of jabs, Joe stepped in and hooked left and right to the head, shaking up his foe. He went hard at Al, driving in short lefts and rights. The Buffalo man showed terrific gameness and stamina. Joe floored him three times with clean shots, but Al struggled to his feet each time. The first knockdown was an eight-count, the 2nd, for nine. Finally, Joe rushed his foe to the ropes and pounded him with his right to the head, until Al toppled over. He fell in a prone position, helpless, one arm hanging on the lower rope. He was clearly out, and Siler, rather than counting, motioned for Weinig's seconds to drag their brave charge to his corner. *Louisville Courier-Journal*: "It was several minutes before Al could be convinced that the fight was over. After the crowd rushed into the ring, Joe crossed over to shake his opponent by the hand. Al jumped up and squared away in fighting posture, for he did not realize the decision had been given against him."

The May 3 *St. Paul Globe* wrote: "Bicycle Fighter is Knocked Out by the Blonde-Haired Chicken Raiser." It said Weinig was floored twice in the final round, but the *Louisville Courier-Journal* said he was decked three times, adding: "It was one of the fastest and most scientific glove contests ever seen in this part of the country between big men. For five rounds honors were practically even, each ... giving a superb exhibition of the ability to hit, side-step, block and get away. In the mix-ups he (Al) showed up as clever as Choynski ... this ... coupled with his youth and vitality ... made him look like better than even-money ... But, about the middle of the 6th ... after a fast mix-up ... the blonde-haired boxer ... landed a short, vicious left hook squarely to the point of the jaw. This staggered the Buffalo bicycle rider ... Choynski ... saw his advantage ... and shot a right hook to the proper spot. He followed ... with lefts and rights to the jaw so rapidly it was almost impossible to count them, but Weinig's superb condition, ability to withstand punishment and his stamina, prevented a knockout for at least a full minute. Twenty times at least, the Chicago man timed his blow and shot a terrific blow to the exact spot, and for a time it seemed as if Weinig could not be knocked out. Choynski finally landed a left uppercut to the chin, and as Weinig staggered backward, put a short, right swing flush on the point of the jaw. The Buffalo man toppled forward as if ... to fall on his face, but his right arm caught on the lower rope and he dangled there helplessly."

Although the Louisville paper said Siler stopped the bout without a count, the *Globe* wrote that "He (Al) remained practically unconscious while Referee Siler counted him out." The *New York Evening World* agreed with the *Courier-Journal*, saying "Siler stopped the fight as the police were about to enter the ring." The *World* said Al was dropped four times in the 6th, the *Kansas City Star*, that he was out for 10 minutes after the finish. Al was cheered by the crowd for his gritty display of will and courage.

On May 5, Joe was still in Louisville. That night, at the Southern Athletic Club, a bloody, brutal fight took place between local bruiser, Marvin Hart, and Eddie "Kid" Carter. Choynski was in Hart's corner. More than one source said he made the difference. May 5 *Newark Advocate*: "Hart ... was ably handled and advised by the veteran, Joe Choynski. Carter, on the other hand, had much ill-timed advice poured in his ear, and in the 7th round, changed a style of fighting that was telling on his opponent." Each round saw both battered all over the ring. Amazingly, there were no knockdowns until round nine, when Hart smashed Carter to the canvas twice, the 2nd time for keeps. It was probably the fastest and most exciting bout seen in Louisville to that time. In 1905, Marvin won a KO12 over Jack

Root, in a fight billed as for the heavyweight crown vacated by Jeffries.

On May 19 in Philadelphia, two "kids" fought – "Kid" McCoy and "Kid" Carter. "McCoy ... out-generaled Carter in the 1st ... However, in the 2nd ... Carter floored McCoy for what should have been a definitive kayo. Martin Julian, brother-in-law of ... Fitzsimmons, promoted the show ... The bell was rung to save McCoy. Philadelphia Jack O'Brien ... helped carry McCoy to his corner, where he was worked on ... to answer the bell for the 3rd round. On three occasions during the 3rd ... McCoy hit the floor and received the benefit of another (short) round ... to save a knockout. The 5th ... found Carter flooring McCoy for the 5th time. Strange, but true, McCoy won the 6th ... Referee (Crowhurst) and ... O'Brien admitted the rounds had been cut short at ... Julian's orders."[15] The official verdict: ND6.

The July 5 *Police Gazette* ran a story, "Choynski, the War Horse: Eddie Greaney ... to referee the ... battle between Jeffries and Fitzsimmons, is an old friend of Joe Choynski's. Choynski is responsible for the statement that when they were kids together, they used to stand around on the corners talking boxing. The coppers got after them ... and broke up the outdoor sessions, and they joined an athletic club. They boxed at tournaments together, and Choynski still has a gold watch and several diamond-studded medals he won as an amateur. 'Do you know why so many people call me the old war horse?' said Joe ... 'I have been boxing since I was 14 years old, and, as I am now 33, you can see that the public naturally has an impression that I am an old man. I am still as good as ever ... have always taken the best care of myself, and have my own ideas about training. I'll bet right now I can go out and beat any man my weight ... for 160 yards."

"I was champion of the Pacific Coast when I was 17. One of the first men I ever boxed was Con Reardon (sic), who died in the East after boxing Bob Fitzsimmons. The first pair of tights I ever wore were presented to me by a big fellow who just came off the high seas. He was a sailor, and they called him the Tipton Slasher. When I whipped him, he pulled off the tights and handed them to me. He said I would some day make a great fighter. The funniest part ... was that I did not think I could fight at all, when I was an amateur. I guess I must have knocked out half a dozen young fellows before I realized it was my punching ability that did it. At the beginning, I ... thought some one had fixed my opponents to fake knockout ... to make me believe I was a world-beater. But, after awhile, I got on to the fact that it was all on the square, and I could not sleep at night, thinking what a great fighter I would be if I could keep it up. When I fought Jim Corbett on a barge ... there were 250 spectators ... At the end, all had left but 10 ... one of the hardest fights ... I've been in as many as any man in the game."

In mid-August, Joe was at "a Chicago headquarters of the fighters," perusing "a couple of journals devoted to the poultry business." The August 16 *Deseret News* said he had "made up his mind to quit the boxing game," to become a full-time breeder of poultry. "About everybody has written me out of the ring, and I suppose I must bow to the critics. True, I've been fighting for 18 years, but ... never dissipated, except in the mildest ... way ... as a preventive of staleness. I would like ... one more fight ... Carter, the man who last whipped me. I haven't the slightest ... recollection of what happened. I distinctly remember I forgot all I ever knew. My left hand, usually the best thing I have, might as well have been cut off, for all the good it did me, and I rushed right into the punch that knocked me out. Maybe he could do it again, but I do not think so. It would be sweet revenge ... to get one more shot at him. Then back to the chickens ..."

"I trained differently ... from other fighters. I used my own ideas. I didn't run 10 miles just because I saw some other fighters do it. I wanted to know first why they did it. They told me ... it took off ... weight and made their wind good. That's nonsense. A man can get better results by breaking off ... 50 yards or so at top speed ... the average fighter knocks his digestive apparatus out completely by frequent changes of diet. What a man has been used to all his life he should relish ... more when ... training ... It will do him no good to keep shifting his food about, because books on physical exercise and ... trainers tell him he must not have this or that. I'm going out to La Grange to look after the poultry. Tell Carter what I said ..." Joe was ahead of his time, in terms of sprinting as a key component of training.

It was noted on August 19, that Joe had "signed articles to box Jim Driscoll and Jack Beauscholte ... at Douglass Hall (in Chicago), on the 29th. Choynski is already training ... Each bout is ... six rounds. Jack O'Brien, of Philadelphia, recently got a decision over these two ... if the Californian is as successful, he will be matched to box the Quaker. The contests will be under the auspices of the Illinois A.C. of Chicago." Joe said he would stop both men. "Choynski is ... training ... at his home in La Grange, where he enjoys the long runs in the country. He has his gymnasium ... at home ..." The matches were cancelled on the night ... by the city's mayor, "at the 11th hour ... just as the doors of the clubhouse were about to be thrown open to ... a crowd of over 1,000 people." One paper said club manager Paddy Carroll, "violated police rules in using flaring lithographs in advertising ..." The *Police Gazette*, though, said "Objection to glove contests by residents of the district is said to have been the cause of the trouble."[16]

On September 22, Joe refereed a six round fight between lightweights Jack O'Keefe and Tommy Mowatt, at Chicago's American Athletic Club. Joe rendered his verdict in favor of Mowatt, to the consternation of the wide majority of spectators. George Siler called it a terrible decision: "Even a draw might have been an injustice to O'Keefe. He had the better of every round, and I cannot see how Choynski could pick Tom as the winner, in the face of the peppering he received." While most decisions have dissenters, this one generated a lot of controversy. A Wisconsin paper said, on the 24th, "Joe Choynski has been repudiated as a referee by the American A.C., on account of the peculiar decision made by the Lagrange fighter ... the final action of the club will probably end Choynski's career as a ring official about Chicago."[17] This was, in large part, hyperbole. Joe would, in fact, be a valued referee. The next day's *Salt Lake Telegram* announced that Alec Greggains, manager of the San Francisco A.C., had made multiple fight offers for October. He telegraphed "Philadelphia" Jack O'Brien and Tommy Ryan to fight before his club, "or battle with George Gardner for the middle-weight and light-heavy-weight championships of the world. Greggains also sent Choynski an offer to battle Gardner ..." a guarantee of $1,000, win or lose. Joe didn't fight in Frisco that year. Perhaps someone forgot to clear the match with Gardner.

Around late September and mid-October, Joe was helping Chicago welterweight Martin Duffy prepare for a bout against the great, black welterweight, Joe Gans. While sparring, Duffy hurt one of his hands on Joe's skull, and the match had to be cancelled. At this stage of his career, the fading Choynski had become a "trial horse" for the young blood. He was an experienced, dangerous opponent, whose speed and reflexes had diminished with time. He had lost some punching power, as well. Joe's next engagement was against "Philadelphia" Jack O'Brien (real name, James Francis Hagen, born in January 1878), the middleweight and light-heavyweight who fought out of the city he was nicknamed for. It was reported on September 26, that "Kid" McCoy had been training and instructing O'Brien at French

"Philadelphia" Jack O'Brien, 1906

Lick, Indiana the past two weeks.[18] O'Brien was a fast, scientific boxer, but a light puncher. He had the reputation of being directly involved in several fixed fights. Jack had 97 recorded bouts to this time, his most notable wins coming in 1902, against George Cole (KO4), Yank Kenney (KO3), Jim Driscoll and Jack Beauscholte (W6 and W6, same night) and Billy Stift (W6). His only losses were L4 Bobby Dobbs in 1897 and KOby13 to

"Young Peter Jackson," after O'Brien was far ahead on points.

The O'Brien match was held on the night of September 29 at Chicago's American Athletic Club. George Siler refereed, and McCoy was in Jack's corner, along with Billy Stift and a "Philadelphia" Tommy Ryan.[19] Joe's cornermen were not named. When O'Brien entered the ring, Joe objected strenuously to his hand wraps. After a brief argument, Jack, who had about a yard of tape on each fist, tore off the wraps and had them reapplied, to suit Joe. "Siler called them up at 10:25 (p.m.) ... Choynski seemed ... more favored in the preliminary applause, despite the weak decision he had made in the O'Keefe-Mowatt bout the week before. (He) appeared nervous and sported a fine, black eye. O'Brien was quietly confident." Old West legend, "Bat" Masterson, acted as timekeeper for O'Brien, while a Fred Kammerer performed in that capacity for Joe. The *Oshkosh Daily Northwestern* had the only round-by-round description. What follows is a blend of three fight reports. The *Brooklyn Daily Eagle* carried a wire service account.[20]

Round 1 – O'Brien showed superior speed and quickness. He was 23 years old, Choynski, nearly 34. Jack was in and out like a flash, landing a sharp left jab and occasional right cross to the jaw. He suddenly stepped in with a staggering straight left to Joe's nose that made him blink. He was sniffling and his eyes appeared red. While Joe blocked some jabs, several got through. O'Brien slipped down briefly, and just before the bell, Joe tasted the canvas. Whether it was a knockdown or a slip is in dispute.

Round 2 – The frame began with furious trading, Choynski just missing a powerful right. *Police Gazette*: "Both men proved themselves past masters in the art of hit, stop and get-away. The speed, youth and shiftiness of the Philadelphia fighter carried him along at a pace too fast for the veteran." Jack staggered him with a nice jab and straight right to the jaw. He flurried with several hooks from each hand, leaving Joe "tired and worried ..."

Round 3 – Choynski tried to land hooks to the head, but O'Brien cleverly stepped inside, the punches to going around the back of his neck. Jack forced the pace, combining skillful boxing and aggressive follow-through. A heated exchange of lefts ended the round.

Round 4 – The action slowed a bit, due to the frantic pace. The crowd called for the fighters to step it up. "Both smiled sadly at this." Joe looked spent and did not have his old-time speed. O'Brien sent Joe back time and again with straight lefts to the face, causing him to hang on.

Round 5 – Choynski was unable to land a meaningful punch, though neither was overly active. Suddenly, Jack closed the distance and slugged. This caused alarm in his corner, who warned their charge to stay out of danger. Before the bell, Joe narrowly missed a "wicked swing."

Round 6 – The final round was the best of the fight, rousing the crowd to a frenzy. The Frisco fighter, seeing his last chance to "pull the fat out of the fire," roughed it with O'Brien. He cracked home a stiff right, inflicting a deep cut on the forehead and infuriating Jack. Joe tried to finish his foe, but soon tired. They traded hot and heavy for a time, before Jack took over. He landed "half a dozen blows on the jaw" that left Joe nearly helpless. *Brooklyn Daily Eagle*: "O'Brien ... made every effort to finish Choynski, but time was too short, though the final bell found Choynski barely able to stand." The spectators cheered wildly. Siler gave his decision to "Philadelphia."

The *Police Gazette* called the bout "one of the cleverest ever seen in that city," and said "neither man bore visible marks of injury." *Oshkosh Daily Northwestern*: "O'Brien ... gave Joe ... an artistic and thorough beating last night ... Choynski's master at all knicks and knacks of the fighting game, and that he did not take more than one or two chances of ... slugging with Joe is ... to his credit. He had the decision won nicely on points and let it go at that. Jack ... out-boxed, outhit, outgeneraled and out-strengthed (sic) the ... veteran ... O'Brien is about 25 per cent faster than Choynski, and while maybe he does not possess the hitting powers that Choynski once had – it is doubtful if he has them now – his extreme speed and wonderful feinting and blocking, show a man of Choynski's present ability up in a mediocre light. There never was a stage of the contest that O'Brien was in danger. Perhaps in the closing round, when he staggered back from a left straight in the chin, there was a chance for Choynski, but the chance passed as quickly as Jack winked his eyes a couple of times and got his bearings."

Joe (1927): "Yes, my career was in its twilight ... I realized the end was near. For some time I had been troubled with neuritis. Continuous training and fighting for 18 years had taken their toll of my vitality." Of the fight, he only said: "We met for six rounds in the Quaker City. I simply could not get started, and the decision went to O'Brien. Some of the papers intimated that I had not tried to fight." Here, his memory fails him, as the venue was Chicago, not Philadelphia. Had it been the Quaker City, the verdict would have been a No Decision, as dictated by local law. In 1930, he said: "My collaborator asks me to name the cleverest man I ever met. Many ... were clever, but I think Philadelphia Jack O'Brien was the shiftiest. He was fast and game, but not a very hard hitter. I met Jack in short bouts. In a long fight I think I could have 'taken him into camp.' Oddly, on both occasions ... I was suffering intensely. It was dysentery, which was the bane of my existence." A six round rematch was scheduled for November 20 at the Penn Art Club in Philadelphia, but was cancelled.[21]

Choynski climbed into the ring on the night of December 1, at the Lyceum Athletic Club in Chicago, against the tough black fighter, Frank Childs. Both were Chicago men and stiff punchers, so locals were excited over the match. Joe said the result would test whether or not he would continue his vocation as a fighter.[22] Childs, known as "The Crafty Texan," was born in the Lone Star State on July 17, 1867. Frank was generally a middleweight, although his weight fluctuated between 165 and 185 pounds, and he fought middleweights to heavyweights.

Over his career, Childs had wins over "Australian" Billy Smith (KO12, 1893), Bob Armstrong (W6, 1897, KO10, 1898, KO6, 1899), "Klondyke" Haines (KO6, 1898, W6, 1899, KO3, 1899), Henry Baker (KO3, 1898), Tom "Stockings" Conroy (W6, 1898), Ed Dunkhorst (W6, 1899),

Frank Childs, 1902

"Mexican" Pete Everett (KO6, 1899, W10, 1900), Fred Russell (W6, 1900, W6, 1900, W10, 1900), Joe Butler (KO6, 1900), Billy Hanrahan (KO4, 1902) and Joe Walcott (KO3, 1902). He lost to Bobby Dobbs (KOby3, 1892), Dan Creedon (L3, 1894), George Byers (L20, 1898) and "Denver" Ed Martin (L6, 1902). Frank was kayoed in 12 by Jack Johnson on October 21, but was still good enough to knock out "Klondyke" in eight rounds, in 1904. At least one paper said he held the edge in weight over Choynski, but the consensus was that Joe was too much of a ring general for him. The referee was Malachy (or Malachi) Hogan. An amalgam report follows:[23]

Round 1 – Joe commenced hostilities with a nasty, hooking jab to the jaw and hard right to the gut. Frank rushed Joe to the ropes, but he cleverly escaped. Soon after, Childs drove a heavy right to the jaw and "rushed into a mix-up, forcing Joe all over the ring." Joe got in a good left to the jaw, to end an even round.

Round 2 – About midway through the round, Childs drove a hard left to the stomach, but was countered. Joe floored him with "a short, fierce hook on the jaw." (Two papers said a left and right did it). Frank was up in an instant, but ran into a left-right that sent him staggering. He answered with a good right to the body, but his lips were cut up and bleeding.

Round 3 – The best round of the fight. Childs came out with a rush and got in several stiff punches. Choynski stopped the charge with a cracking left-right to the jaw. Frank was right back, connecting with his own right and left to the jaw. Then, Joe rushed, and "showered blows on his head and face ..." The *New York Evening World* said that, before the bell, Childs was getting much the worst of it. The *Oshkosh Daily Northwestern* disagreed, saying: "Choynski puffed up Childs' left eye with a right hook, but Childs was the stronger, and apparently nearly had Joe out at the end."

Round 4 – Frank was drained from his exertions, and came out warily, trying to avoid exchanges. Joe threw and landed most of the punches, but was careful not to open himself up to counters. Both were recouping their resources. Choynski's jabs were mostly unanswered. He crossed the right over a couple of times, but his blows were lacking in force.

Rounds 5 and 6 – Essentially repetitions of the 4th, with Childs making slow rushes, easily avoided by Choynski. In round five, Frank landed one flurry of "stiff body blows." Joe dominated the final two heats, landing several left and right hooks to the body and head. Hogan quickly rendered his verdict in Joe's favor, which was popular with the crowd.

The papers conflicted on many points, some calling it was a fast bout dominated by Joe, others saying he put in a disappointing performance. *The Oshkosh Daily Northwestern* said Childs "entered the ring fat and in poor condition." The *New York Evening World* said Joe "had a majority of points in every round ... outfought (Frank) at every stage of the game," and both were tired at the finish. The *Milwaukee Evening Wisconsin* said Choynski "received the decision ... due to his gameness ..." On December 6, Joe reportedly signed articles to fight George Gardner, "at Chicago on Dec. 22 ... for six rounds. Gardiner (sic) has just arrived in Chicago ... in superb fettle." Instead, George battled on the 29th with "Kid" Carter, who he decisioned in six rounds. As 1903 opened, Choynski claimed that, of the estimated $40,000 he had earned in his 15-plus years in the ring, he managed to save about $30,000. This was about $775,000 in 2009 dollars. If so, Joe was much better then at saving money, than in later years. The *Washington Times* quoted him as saying the $30,000 was "invested in Chicago real estate for a cold day," that he would "engage in two more battles and then retire." Joe said he had figured in over 200 fights to date. These would have included the matches against "all comers" that he contracted to stop in four rounds or less, and perhaps his amateur bouts, as well.[24]

An "11th-hour" fight was scheduled with Peter Maher on January 19. It was postponed until the 26th, due to Joe's inability to reach the Quaker City in time. The bout was for six rounds, part of Philadelphia's "No Decision" era.[25] If a knockout was not scored, no points decision would be allowed, although many papers rendered their own, unofficial "newspaper decisions." Maher, over the course of his career, had improved from a raw slugger to a somewhat skilled boxer. While defense would never be his strong suit, Peter developed a good left jab and became more adept at straight punching, thereby making better use of his reach.

The final installment of the Choynski-Maher series took place at the Washington Sporting Club in Philadelphia, on the night of January 26. The "record-breaking crowd" of 3,000 witnessed a short fight. By 9:00 p.m., every seat was occupied, and some 500 persons were compelled to find standing room. The referee was William H. "Billy" Rocap. In addition to a respected referee, Rocap was also sports editor of the *Philadelphia Public Ledger*, and recognized as America's first amateur featherweight champion. In 1923, he became the first Chairman and Commissioner of the Pennsylvania State Athletic and Boxing Commission.[26] The men boxed under modified Queensberry rules, meaning they would not hit upon separating from a clinch. Both appeared in good condition. January 31 *Fort Wayne News*: "Just before ... Choynski left his dressing room ... a messenger boy handed him this telegram: 'It's just eight years ago tonight. Do you recall it? Give Maher a good blow for me.' It was from his wife, and recalled the fact that it was his wedding anniversary." Louise was probably just romantically poetic; one would hope Joe had not forgotten his 8th anniversary! *Police Gazette*: " 'Kid' McCoy and 'Philadelphia' Jack O'Brien were introduced ... Choynski, clad in a bath robe, climbed through the ropes ... followed ... by Maher, who wore a big sweater." The following blends contemporary accounts and a few secondary sources:[27]

Round 1 – Accounts disagreed. Using clever, nimble footwork, Joe evaded and blocked the vicious swings of the "Wild Irishman," spearing him in the face with quick jabs. Maher appeared somewhat gun-shy. Seeing this, Joe stepped up the assault with the straight left. Peter was confused and "unable to return the fusillade." The *Oshkosh Daily Northwestern* said the jabs "raised a lump as large as a walnut over his ... right eye. The Irish champion ... caught the Californian coming in ... causing the blood to start from Choynski's nose (first blood). It was a beautiful battle of left hands ... Maher landing more often ... possessing the longer reach. All the right-hand counters excepting one were blocked by both men. This ... almost ended the contest ... Maher catching his opponent as he was trying to sidestep, after a left lead. The Californian was retreating, however, and the blow had spent its force ... The 1st round closed with Choynski swishing his left in a short, half-arm swing, catching Maher on the point of the jaw. It staggered (him) ... the bell rang with him clinching ... to save himself from further punishment." *Police Gazette*: Joe at one point "stopped and feinted Maher into a state of bewilderment. Peter scowled and rushed again. The blonde-haired fighter crossed him with the right. Maher toppled back and Choynski followed instantly with a series of jabs. They were fighting viciously along the ropes, when Maher let loose the left hook that turned the tables for a moment. The ... crowd was all with Peter in a second."

The *New York Evening World* echoed most papers, while mostly disagreeing with the *Northwestern*: "Maher was completely outclassed by the clever Choynski. Peter tried time after time to get in his famous right swing ... but the Californian was too shifty, and the blow only scattered the smoky atmosphere. The only good blow Maher landed was a short left hook to the jaw. It ... made Choynski's knees knock together ... Choynski, by good ring generalship, avoided ... Realizing the easiest way to beat Maher was ... jabbing him, Choynski (shot) his long left into Peter's face ... every time he landed, Peter's head was sent back as if it had been jerked from behind. The jabs came so fast that Maher was tired and bewildered before the 1st ... was finished." *Washington Times*: "The ... round ... was as pretty an exhibition of straight, effective hitting as one could wish to see. Choynski was a little bit the better at long-range work, but every time he landed, he was in reach, and Maher never forgot to send back the best punch he had. Choynski made Peter's right eye look watery before the fight was a minute old with a straight left, and ... reached Peter's nose frequently ..."

Philadelphia Inquirer: "There was but one man in it ... Choynski. He feinted and sidestepped Peter until the latter did not know whether he was afoot or ahorse-back (sic) ... yet ... The 1st ... was almost over when he walked right into one of Peter's left handed swings ... but ... sent in a straight left against Peter's face that ... gave Choynski a chance to get himself together." *Philadelphia Evening Bulletin*: "What advantage there was ... belonged to Choynski ... landing on Maher's jaw just before the bell ... The punch was a trifle too high to end the fight ..." A 1920 *Police Gazette*: "Both were bleeding toward the end of the round, Maher from the mouth and nose and Joe from the ear and right eye. Choynski was groggy as he stumbled over to his corner." In 1927, Joe said Peter landed a "steaming left hook that made me see angels in the Milky Way."

Round 2 – Maher's face looked red; Choynski's, set and determined. Peter tried to spar for wind, putting out a tentative left jab, but Joe crossed a powerful right over it and Maher staggered back. "The California Terror" smashed a hard left to the mouth that sent Peter into the ropes. The son of Erin wasn't done, though. Joe walked right into a stiff-arm, straight left, causing him to reel backward. Maher drove four straight lefts at his tormentor, but Joe ducked several right-hand bombs. Choynski landed a good right to the ribs. Peter held on for dear life, but "Little Joe" shook him off and waded in. After trading a few hard rights, Peter stuck out another left, and Joe countered again with a potent right, just inside the left. Maher clinched, but let go almost immediately and wobbled away. After clearing his head, the Irishman charged, and Choynski broke ground. He stopped Maher's rush with hard left jabs and a few rights. Finally, Joe slipped in a quick, light jab, then feinted for the body. Quick as a flash, as his opponent dropped his guard to block, Joe drove a downward, smashing right to the chin and floored his rival heavily. Maher was counted out at 2:10 of the round. *Washington Times*: "His head was in his own corner ... and, while he writhed a little, showed no disposition to get up until Referee Rocap had counted the fatal 'ten.' ... Peter's seconds lifted the ex-Irish champion to his corner, and he seemed little the worse for wear. Many seemed to think Peter had quit, and hooted as (he) left the ring."

Some sources, like the wire report carried by the *Massena Observer*, said the finishing punch was a left. Most independent reports called it a right. *New York Evening World*: "Choynski ... had his revenge on Peter Maher. He knocked the erstwhile champion out ... 50 seconds before the end of the 2nd ... Maher was never in it. His knockout came so suddenly ... many ... thought the Irishman ... quit. This was not so. Choynski's short right-hand ... did the job neatly and quickly ... Each ... received $450 as his share ... While ... Rocap was ... counting Maher out, an orchestra could be heard playing the grand march at the ball of the Ancient Order of Hibernians of Philadelphia ... in Industrial Hall, which adjoins the club-house of the Washington Sporting Club. Maher is one of the prominent members of this organization, and ... at his request Matchmaker Johnny Kelly started the show half an hour earlier than usual so Maher could attend the ball." January 27 *Police Gazette*: "The blow ... was planned by a master of ringcraft, delivered on the most vulnerable point with mathematical exactness, and hard enough to have floored a longshoreman."

The *Philadelphia Inquirer's* lyrical offering: "His ... form measured its length on the ... floor ... The ever-faithful Peter Lowry threw some cold Schuylkill* upon the recumbent form. The touts in the corner beseeched Peter to git (sic) up. But ... Peter was communing with the stars." Following the bout, McCoy and O'Brien challenged the winner. "Philadelphia" Jack would get the fight. A curious "bystander" asked Joe how long he had been fighting. "With a smile, Choynski replied, 'Just 19 years ... I have always lived a good life, retiring early each night. I never drank a drop of intoxicating liquor ... don't chew nor smoke, and never was sick an hour in the 19 years I have been fighting. That is the secret of my success.' "[28] Joe was proud of his fitness and longevity, so he might be forgiven the exaggeration, regarding his total abstinence and never having been sick. Bob Edgren, for the July 1, 1917 *Fort Wayne Journal-Gazette*: "I saw Choynski hit ... Maher a right-hand blow on the chin that turned Peter completely over in the air and knocked him out for several minutes." Joe (1927): "Maher had a unique, free, loose style of hitting. This was due, I believe, to the fact that he never did bag-punching, which tends to shorten blows."
* Schuylkill is both a township and a river near Philadelphia. The river is a tributary of the mighty Delaware River, hence, a noted source of water.

February 9 *Pawtucket Times*: "Choynski and George Gardner were matched ... for six rounds at Philadelphia on Feb. 16. The two were to have met a few weeks ago, but Choynski's hands went back on him and he was compelled to cancel ... Choynski is also contemplating a match with the winner of the Root-McCoy contest ... to be decided at Fort Erie next month. Choynski will post a forfeit with Al Smith this week ..." The set-to never occurred, and the reason was soon revealed. On the 10th and again on the 13th, reports divulged that: "Joe Choynski is lying seriously ill with pneumonia at his home in La Grange. Shortly after his battle with ... Maher ... he contracted a severe cold, which has settled on his lungs, and he has been ill for over a week ... Choynski was matched to meet George Gardner ... who holds the light-heavyweight championship of the world, to fight February 16, but this ... has been cancelled, owing to his illness."[29]

Joe fought a rematch with "Philadelphia" Jack O'Brien on the evening of March 30, 1903. The setting was again the Washington Sporting Club in Philadelphia. The former candymaker did his training at West Baden Springs, Indiana, a spot he had used twice in the past. He arrived in Philly on the night of the 28th.[30] The referee was again Billy Rocap, and the distance, six rounds. On this night, the storm in progress outside the building was scarcely worse than the one brewing inside, among the crowd. Evidently, something strange was going on in the ring, as more than one report saw it. The following is drawn from four contemporary reports, though little is written of the first four frames:[31]

Round 1 – *Worcester Daily Spy*: "Choynski started well, but appeared to lose heart under O'Brien's unceasing rain of left jabs."

Round 2 – *Worcester Daily Spy*: "From the 2nd until the last round, Choynski's only object seemed to be to stay the limit."

Round 3 – *Worcester Daily Spy*: "The 3rd and 4th rounds were particularly tame, and the referee warned the men."

Round 4 – Here is where things started getting weird. *Washington Times*: "The bout last night ... had a very bad look. There's no question as to the sincerity of the principals until the beginning of the 4th ... when Choynski let slip by many chances that, had he tried, he could have done considerable damage to Jack. But ... he invariably drew his arm back, when the blow was already on its way. The crowd was quick to see something was wrong, and hissed Choynski time and again for not following up his leads."

Round 5 – *Washington Times*: "The 5th round was worse than the preceding ... Choynski did not even try to land ... On the other hand, O'Brien jabbed, uppercut, and hooked as he pleased, but his blows were rather weak. The referee ... stopped the men long enough to caution them. O'Brien said that he was doing his best. Evidently he was, as he hit Choynski three to one ... clearly outpointed him ... and could have no reason to enter into an agreement with (Joe) having bested Choynski ... some time ago. After the referee cautioned the men, Choynski let out a few links and went after O'Brien right and left, but Jack danced nimbly out of harm's way, and hooked his left to the face when the bell rang." *New York Sun*: "It became so painfully obvious Choynski was not trying, that ... Rocap stopped the bout and warned him to extend himself."

Round 6 – *Washington Times*: "They ... cut out a terrific pace. O'Brien ... was much ... quicker and landed oftener ... but his blows lacked ... steam ... Again ... Choynski, after his spurt, let up, and it looked as though he was not trying to fight. The crowd again started hissing and yelling to stop the bout, and kept up ... Choynski paid no attention to the hissing, and only smiled. After the bout was over ... spectators ... gave vent to their feeling in very strong language." *Worcester Daily Spy*: "O'Brien was more aggressive and subjected his opponent to a severe drubbing ..." *New York Sun*: "In the 6th round he (Joe) did extend himself, and O'Brien was visibly tired. In the middle of the round, however, he again started to take things easily."

Although Jack clearly outpointed the aging warrior, the "scrap" was a No Decision, as required by state law. *New York Sun*: "The bout ... had all the ear marks of a fake, so far as Choynski was concerned. It was evident from the start that he was not taking advantage of the many openings presented ... and ... the spectators became demonstrative." The *Fort Wayne News* found nothing fishy about the set-to, its reporter simply attributing the lack of a knockout to the dearth of force behind O'Brien's punches. As strange as Joe's lack of follow-up may have seemed, it is entirely possible an injury was responsible. The April 16 *Mansfield News*, though, wrote: "The fellows faked, and it is now asserted that O'Brien refused to go on unless Choynski consented to a mere exhibition, and no saucy slaps."

On March 31, at Mechanics' Pavilion in San Francisco, "Tuxedo" Ed Graney, known for the trademark tux he wore in the ring, umpired the world featherweight title fight between "Terrible" Terry McGovern and "Young" Corbett II (William Rothwell). The result was a KO11 win for Corbett. April 1 *San Francisco Chronicle*: "Graney ... the Beau Brummel of ringdom, in spotless shirt and smart evening clothes ... looked like a blacksmith, and he had stripped to his dusky undershirt. In the 2nd round, while pulling the men apart, he received a beautiful splotch of blood right in the center of his broad shirt ... from Corbett's left eye, which was bleeding profusely. He looked disconsolately at the shirt. The next round, the fighters clung to each other repeatedly, and Graney had a trying time in effecting breakaways. Perspiration seemed to stream from every pore, and his face had assumed a carmine tint from his strenuous exertions. For several rounds it grew worse, until Graney ... pulled off his coat and threw it to a friend in the crowd. Next round, he savagely jerked off his vest and collar and tie ... Next round, he threw off his white vest ... wet through with perspiration. When he came out of the ring after the finish, he did not have a dry rag on him. He said next time ... he would wear a sweater."

The April 11 *Police Gazette* noted: "Joe Choynski is in receipt of a letter from an Australian who wants him to visit the Antipodes and meet some of the heavyweights there. The writer says Choynski can have a match with Billy McCall, who is looked upon as one of the best of the big fellows in Australia." Joe was about to visit another land, but it wouldn't be Australia.

Round Twenty-One

Seeking Fortune in the Yukon
(April 1903 – January 1904)

The first rumblings from the Far North were heard at this time, as far as Joe went. The May 2 *Omaha Sun* said, "Joe Choynski ... has received an offer from Dawson City Athletic Club of Dawson City, to meet Nick Burley, the pride of the mines ... $2,000 purse for a 10-round bout ... on June 20." Four days later, the fight was upped to June 30. Matchmaker Burns of the Dawson A.C. received the assent of both boxers, so Joe prepared to depart for the Yukon. A May 6 article noted: "Burley has fought Tom Sharkey, Denver Ed Smith and other prominent big men. He has been in Alaska some years and is a favorite of the miners, who will back him heavily ..."[1] Joe, in his memoirs, called Burley, "the heavyweight champion of Alaska." On May 20, "a number of Choynski's Lagrange friends gave him a banquet, assuring him a hearty welcome on his return to Chicago. Mrs. Choynski accompanied the pugilist to Dawson City." They departed on the 22nd, aboard the train, the Northwestern. About 50 of Joe's friends were there to see the couple off. Later that day (or night), Joe and Louise passed through Omaha, Nebraska, en route to San Francisco.

The May 23 *Omaha World-Herald* reported (incorrectly) that the fight had been pushed up to the 4th of July, and that he would battle "Dick (sic) Burley ... at Dutch Harbor."* "While waiting for their train to start for the west, Mr. and Mrs. Choynski sunned themselves on the platform at the union station in the morning. Choynski ... announced he would challenge the winner of the Jeffries-Corbett fight (August 14, Jeffries won, KO10) ... 'I am the only man Jeff has never whipped, he said, 'and I think I can hold out against him for 10 rounds. If I can do that, it is a good proposition, and I am in for it.' His shoulders are the only significant feature about him. His legs are thin, and appear unstable, but he stands erect, and walks with a lithe, powerful swing. Mr. and Mrs. Choynski will spend about three months in Alaska, camping and fishing. They will return in August ... in San Francisco in time to deliver his challenge at the ringside to Jeffries or Corbett, as the case may be." Joe correctly picked Jeff to defeat Corbett.[2]
* Dutch Harbor is the port located in the city of Unalaska, Alaska.

They reached Frisco on the 26th, when Joe visited the Olympic Athletic Club to see old friends. The couple also visited his family. It was a quick stopover, as they left "The Paris of the West" the following day, the next stated stop being Nome, Alaska.[3] It is doubtful if they traveled to Nome, as it is far northwest of any logical route from Seattle to Dawson. The June 6 *Daily Alaska* (Juneau) *Dispatch*'s late report read: "Choynski is expected to arrive in Dawson about June 1 ... two or three weeks ... to get ready for ... Nick Burley. Should the river be open, that should land him here the first week in June. Choynski ... is said to be in good condition for his daily exercise in the club. The money for round trip tickets between Chicago and Seattle for Choynski and his trainer was telegraphed to a Chicago bank ... A Seattle bank will ... supply tickets ... from Seattle to Dawson and return. Expense money was also sent in care of the banks."

As Joe had no trainer, the other ticket was for Lutie. From his memoirs: "The journey was interesting and delightful. The Dawson sports allowed me $1,000 for expenses and two round-trip tickets. Arriving at Seattle, I received a visit at my hotel from a representative of the Seattle branch of the Canadian Bank of Commerce ... to enquire if anything further in the way of funds were needed to complete my journey ... by boat to Skagway, rail to White Horse, and boat to Dawson. The scenery was wonderful. I had seen nothing like it, even in Switzerland. At Dawson we were greeted like visiting royalty. Joe Boyle, who had the timber concessions at Bear Creek, one of the wealthiest men in the Yukon, placed his finely equipped home at our disposal. This Joe Boyle was a remarkable man, the most versatile fellow I ever met. He was a boxer, wrestler, runner, musician and business man. He could sing or tell a story as well as any professional entertainer. A big, handsome fellow weighing 230 lb., with plenty of money. He was once a poor, Chicago booze fighter. During the World War he organized and financed a regiment of Canadian soldiers."[4]

Dawson City, Yukon, Canada was the major focal point of the Klondike Gold Rush, which lasted from 1896 to 1899. During that time, it was known as "The Paris of the North." From 1896 to 1898, future legendary boxing promoter, George "Tex" Rickard, was working as a bartender, faro dealer and "front man," at such gambling houses and saloons as "The Northern" and "The Monte Carlo." Dawson City was the capital of the Yukon from 1898 until 1955, when the capital was moved to Whitehorse. In 1902, Dawson was incorporated as a city, the population when Joe arrived being a bit under 5,000. Although the Gold Rush had ended, an entrepreneur named Joe Boyle was dredging the rivers for gold using a series of special dredging machines, while also making money entertaining the locals. The following year, 1904, Boyle, who backed and promoted the local Dawson City hockey club, had them travel across Canada to the nation's capital, Ottawa, making the trek by coastal steamer, sled dog, bicycle, train and on foot. There, they made a challenge for the Stanley Cup, symbolic of North American hockey supremacy. The team arrived exhausted in Ottawa, in January, 1905, where they were pounded by the reigning Stanley Cup champions, the Ottawa Silver Seven. The Yukon side, known alternately as the Dawson City Nuggets or the Klondikes, were crushed by scores of 9-2 and 23-2, in a two-game, total goal series. This was the only challenge for the Cup by a team from Alaska, and their harrowing journey was far more of a story than the series itself.

Joseph Whiteside Boyle was born in Canada in November, 1867, but became a long-time United States resident. For a time, at least in 1891, he managed the Hoboken (New Jersey) Athletic Club. Boyle took over the career of the aging Frank Slavin, and shortly thereafter, they made a boxing tour. This venture proved unsuccessful, due mostly to laws against prizefighting. Living a hand-to-mouth existence, the duo made their way across the Northeastern United States. In 1897, they migrated to San Francisco, where Slavin lost to Joe Butler. Nearly penniless, Boyle had an idea. The broke blokes made their way north to Juneau, Alaska, where they rented a hall and scheduled a boxing show, to fight each other. The local military commander, acting as the law in Juneau, refused to allow the prizefight (they had failed to purchase a boxing permit from the town's sheriff). Slavin instead put on a bag-punching exhibition, while Boyle played the piano, sang, told jokes and stories, all with surprising proficiency. The crowd not only refused to ask for its money back, they offered to pay Joe an additional $5 each, to continue performing. Boyle did so, but for free.[5] The money they earned paid their way to Dawson City, Yukon.

The June 20 *Daily Alaska Dispatch* announced that the new (and correct) date for the Burley fight would be June 25. "The date was arranged while Choynski was in Skagway, and the latter was notified by wire the day he left here." Joe therefore did stop off in Juneau, though the exact dates he was there isn't known. The logical route would have taken him from Seattle to Juneau, then to Skagway, Alaska. A brief description of a boat trip along the coast to Skagway around 1903 is included for background: "The scenery for a thousand miles ... is magnificent ... evergreen hills, snow-peaks, and glaciers to no end. The men for the most part wore flannel shirts, broad hats, riding breeches and long Strathcona boots, and one could see the shape of a revolver sometimes in their hip pockets. Skagway, at the head of the Lynn Canal, which is really a big fjord, was the most unusual place ... with its shack-like houses ... and its crowded, bustling streets. Tents were put up wherever there was room ... Filth lay around everywhere. Men with packs on their backs, pack-trains of horses and mules, and many dog teams, were going about. Indians and squaws were scattered among the crowd, and all languages were being spoken. The sidewalks were raised about two feet above the churned-up mud and muck of the roadway."[6]

At least one version of Choynski's record shows him boxing a four round exhibition in Dawson City on June 15 with a Charley Carroll.[7] The match has not been verified by this author. There was at least one exhibition that day, however – Boyle engaged in a spirited three round bout with Frank Slavin. It was reportedly the last time he actively boxed.[8] The June 29 *Boston Daily Globe*, with late news from the Frozen North, wrote, "Nick Burley, who some years ago made this city his home ... has done well since he went to Dawson City, and the miners there think he is invincible. If Choynski should win, and there is no reason why he should not, he will pick up a pot of money, for the miners will bet their all on Burley."

Nick Burley was born Nicholas Barovich, on May 17, 1875, in either Austin, Nevada or San Jose, California. He moved to the Yukon sometime

Nick Burley, "Champion of the Yukon"

between 1900 and 1902, winning its heavyweight championship on April 24, 1902 by KO9 over the old "Sydney Cornstalk," Frank Slavin. By his time, Burley already had a long career. Significant wins included Frank Craig (KO2, 1893), "Scaldy" Bill Quinn (KO3, 1895) and "Australian" Jimmy Ryan (W10, 1898). Losses came at the fists of such as Peter Maher (KOby1, 1893), Jack Bonner (KOby4, 1897, KOby3, 1898), Dan Creedon (KOby2 or 3, 1897, KOby1, 1897), "Kid" McCoy (KOby3, 1897, KOby2, 1898) and Jim Jeffords (KOby1, 1899). Nick stood about 5' 11¾" and, while in the Yukon, weighed about 165 pounds. He was a game, stiff puncher, fairly clever and quick on his feet.[9] While always a dangerous foe, Burley's chin could be dented.

The Choynski-Burley fight was held in Dawson on June 25, at the DAAA (Dawson Amateur Athletic Association) Rink, under the auspices of the Dawson A.C. It was for 20 rounds and a purse of $5,000, contradicting that given earlier, $2,000 and 10 rounds. Joe Boyle, who helped promote the bout, refereed. Choynski took his brief training at Boyle's Gold Bottom camp. Boyle's brother, Charley, assisted the Californian in his training. Because of this, Burley objected to Boyle as referee, feeling he was too close to Choynski to be impartial.[10] Joe (1927): "I trained at the Dawson Athletic Club, a big, wooden structure seating 4,000. The floor was covered with ice all the year. The ice was covered with sawdust when fights were held, and used for skating at other times. The prices charged for my fight with Burley were 5, 10 and 15 dollars. The house was sold out. Alaska and the Yukon were full of tough fighters in those days – glove fighters, fist fighters and gun fighters. It was a he-man country and the fittest survived ... Nick Burley was a rugged champion of a rugged fighting country. His last battle before the match with me was ... with Frank Slavin, and Burley beat the Australian in one round."[11] The DAAA arena was a three-storey edifice erected the previous year. The 100' by 40' building housed not only a regulation hockey rink, but also a two-sheet curling rink. It had such amenities as steam-heated dressing rooms, a well-outfitted lounge room and private club with bar, upstairs. These were "the only enclosed rink surfaces west of Winnipeg." Winnings were paid "in the form of a gold brick."[12]

The only good coverage was supplied by the *Sunday Alaska* (Juneau) *Herald*, with its late report of July 12: "In less than two rounds, Nick Burley knocked out Joe Choynski ... The knockout was clear and decisive, and Burley proved that when he cut loose, there is power and steam behind his long right and left swings. The battle lasted one round, two minutes and 29 seconds. Almost at the beginning of the 2nd round, Nick sent a terrific left swing to Joe's jaw, which staggered the world-famed fighter. From the shock of that long swing, Choynski was unable to rally, and while by clever work, he was able to stave off the great climax, he grew steadily weaker. Three times he went to the floor, but managed to regain his feet and return to the battle. With his right eye battered and swollen, but fiercely aggressive, Nick went after the famous light heavy-weight, and the end was in sight. With a long right swing, Burley smashed his opponent on the jaw and sent him tumbling to the boards ... Game as ever, Joe tried his best to get to his feet at the 6th count. He reached his knees, and then, unable to stand the strain any longer, fell flat on his face. Standing by the prostrate form, Joe Boyle slowly counted Choynski out. All the time, the crowd yelled and cheered, and when Boyle flung up his arm as a signal that it was all over, a scene of indescribable enthusiasm filled the big arena."[13]

"The fight was fast and scientific from the start. In the 1st round, Choynski seemed to have a little the best (sic) of it, but Nick took punishment in a way that surprised his friends. Both were wonderfully quick on their feet ... when a blow reached home, it was with telling effect. As a result of his victory, Nick Burley jumps to a higher plane in the prize ring, and is entitled to consideration at the hands of good fighters ... Before the fight, Burley expressed dissatisfaction with Boyle as referee, on account of reports ... of intimacy between Choynski and the Boyles. After the battle ... he expressed satisfaction with the work of the referee, and remarked that he had been given a fair deal throughout the contest. Needless to say, Nick was well pleased ... He spoke highly of Choynski. 'I didn't win. That's all there is to it,' said Choynski when seen in his dressing room after the fight. There was no accident in it. Burley was in the ring to knock me out and did it. When he sent that left swing to the jaw, I lost my speed.' " An undated

July *Police Gazette* said, "The men fought for a purse of $2,500, of which the winner received $2,000. In the 2nd ... Burley knocked Choynski groggy with a swing on the jaw, and, as quick as a flash, crossed him with his right, dropping him to the floor, where he was counted out. After Choynski recovered consciousness ... he turned to his seconds and said: 'When a dub like this fellow, Burley, can beat me, I think it is about time I retired from the ring.' Choynski declared he would never fight again."

Joe (1927): "Over-confidence was probably my greatness weakness as a fighter. I mentally pictured ... shifting away from Burley's lunges, making him miss, working him into position for the old slam, then 'bang!' to the button and the referee starts to count. Well, it didn't turn out that way. In the 1st ... Burley pulled a Jack McCormick haymaker out of the air. I got a crack on the jaw and was all but put out. Burley apparently did not realize how badly hurt I was, or ... may have thought I was stalling. I managed to keep going until near the close of the 2nd round, when I got another clout, went down, and was counted out. I figured it out the next day ... my timing was getting a bit off. The smallest fraction of a second may mean the difference between a miss and a knockout, when two hitters are shooting at each other in a ring. But for a slight miscalculation in that 1st round, I felt sure I would have battered Burley to the floor in a few rounds."[14]

The *Yukon Reader*, a 1990s magazine, said Burley's youth gave him the edge. Nick waited several minutes for Choynski to recover, before shaking hands. Joe "was carried to his dressing room, where he was heard to complain he didn't have enough time to acclimatize to Dawson's Spring weather. Yet he was gracious in receiving Burley's wife, when she visited with Frank Slavin to express her sorrow." Joe's reasons for his retirement from boxing the next day, were a thumb he'd sprained prior to the fight, which would take too long to heal, and Joe's feeling that he "was already too old."[15] July 2 *Trenton Times*: "The veteran ... did not show a semblance of his old-time form and was outclassed at every stage. In the 2nd round Burley got to Choynski's stomach ... (he) was finally knocked out with a right on the jaw. Choynski ... says that he is through with the boxing game for good ..." June 28 *San Francisco Call*: "Choynski ... leaves to-morrow for Chicago to resume his training-school." This was a knee-jerk reaction, as Joe stayed another two months in the Yukon. He wrote a letter to "a Chicago friend," saying he lost to Burley because "he broke one of his hands in the *fifth* (sic) round and had no chance to win."[16]

Gardner and Root clashed at Fort Erie, Ontario, Canada on July 4, George halting his foe in 12 rounds. "The battle will be for the light heavyweight championship of the world, a title which Joe Choynski long held undisputed possession of."[17] Why Choynski's name hasn't entered the "official" ledger as the first light-heavy champ, yet Root's has, is hard to reconcile. July 13 *Washington Times*: "When George Gardner defeated Jack

Root ... he won ... a new title, light heavyweight champion. With his victory there went ... a belt, which signifies in his own class, Gardner was as much a champion as Jeffries in his. The new ... classification makes the 7th. There is heavyweight, light heavyweight, middleweight, welterweight, lightweight, featherweight and bantam. Fifteen years ago, there were only three recognized divisions. The four new ... are the outgrowth of the realization that it was unfair to cheat of careers ... clever and able boxers ... too light for one class and too heavy for another." This time, though, a championship belt lent more recognition to the light-heavyweights. This was not the only source of the day, calling Gardner the "first light heavyweight champion." Jack Root lobbied The *Ring* office years later, for recognition as an earlier world light-heavy titleholder, and received it.

Joe changed his mind about leaving Dawson, and was seeking revenge. According to a 1974 biography of Joe Boyle: "By providing encouragement and the hospitality of his summer home on the Klondike River to Choynski, Boyle persuaded the defeated fighter to accept a rematch."[18] It seemed, though, that Nick was trying to dodge the issue. July 17 *Dawson Record*: "It looks a little like Nick Burley wants no more trouble with Choynski. He seems to be looking for an excuse to get out of his present bargain, and gives as his sole objection that he will not box while Joe Boyle officiates as referee ... says Boyle and Choynski are together too much ... Boyle says he knew Choynski several years ... but only very slightly ... and since the latter arrived in Dawson, he has rented a house from Mr. Boyle. Choynski and Boyle have walked upon the public highways a few times ... In fact, Burley and Boyle have been known to walk along the street together, yet Choynski has never objected to a match with Burley on that account ... *Morning Record*: The negotiations ... between the DAAA and ... Burley ... have now been at a deadlock for some time ... The articles are ... the same as ... under which the men met before ... Burley gives as his excuse for not signing ... that he objects to myself acting as referee. While his ... reasons ... are of a most flimsy nature and not worthy of notice, I think it only fair to the club and to Choynski to publicly state that under no consideration would I ever again act as referee in a contest in which Burley took part. If Burley really means business he will have no further excuse. Yours truly, J.W. Boyle, Dawson, July 16, 1903."

On August 6, reports came out of Seattle, Washington, that "George Gardner, the light heavyweight champion of the world, arrived yesterday on his way to Dawson to meet Joe Choynski. The contest ... will take place this month. He and Choynski have been anxious to meet ... for years. The club at Dawson recently sent Gardner his traveling expenses, and he has been prompt in starting." As so often was Joe's misfortune, it was announced only one day later, that "The club offered to hang up a purse of $7,500 ... but Gardiner (sic) figured Dawson City too far away and declined the offer."[19] Having made it all the way to Seattle, it is so strange that George would reject the fight at the 11th hour. Had he accepted, it would have been an intriguing opportunity for the aging "Chrysanthemum."

Burley finally agreed to a rematch. The fight was held August 7 at the DAAA arena, and turned out to be "the hardest contest ever seen in Dawson." As promised, Boyle refused to referee the match. The (Juneau, Alaska) *Daily Record-Miner* said, "There was a great wrangle over the referee, and for awhile pandemonium prevailed." Barney Sugrue was finally selected. "Burley was seconded by Kreling, Larry Gleason and Stewart Baggerly. In Choynski's corner were Prof. Zeno, Ralph King and 'Kid' Owen." The lone detailed account was the August 8 *Dawson Record*.[20]

Round 1 – Time was called at 10:51 p.m. Joe came out determined, though Nick got there first with a right to the head. He landed a left-right. Joe drove a hard left hook to the body. Nick scored with a left jab to the face, a stiff right to the body and back up to the face, sending Joe into a corner. He got in another left-right to the face, and a combination left to ribs and right to face. Joe answered with a pair of straight lefts to the head. Suddenly, "with the speed of chain lightning, he hooked his left to Nick's jaw and knocked him sprawling ... Burley got to his knee instantly and rose on the 9th count." Joe rushed, drove a left-right to the face and blocked a counter. He pressed in with ramrod jabs. Burley responded with a left hook to the head, had a roundhouse right blocked, but thumped a hard left to the kidneys. When he tried another right, Joe beat him to the punch with a fierce left to the body. The Yukon heavyweight champion overcame his distress and sent a right and left to the head. Joe hammered a left hook to the head. Nick came back with a good left to the body at the bell. *Dawson Record*: "Choynski ... His left seems to be landing hard on Burley and doing damage. Though Burley kept leading and forcing matters, he was getting the worst of it. Cheers ... as the men took their corners."

Round 2 – Burley drove a pair of lefts to the head, Joe replied with a nasty left uppercut to the face. Nick thumped two hard ones to the body and a left-right to the head, but retreated when Joe gave him a feint. "Joe lands a terrific left on Burley's jaw. Nick hooks left to kidneys and right to belly." The men traded to the body and head. Nick hooked a left to the stomach, then up to the head. He repeated the combination, and Joe appeared in trouble. He wisely clinched. They traded jabs. Burley's left to the head was countered by a right body blow, then a left to the kidney, just before the gong. *Dawson Record*: Burley "rallied and came up in the 2nd strong. With tigerish agility, he dodged right and left, and began to systematically beat down his opponent. Shooting out his wonderful left like a piston, Choynski managed to inflict considerable punishment, however, and the round ended with Choynski still a little to the good."

Round 3 – Burley landed a straight right to the face, a "nasty left to Joe's wind" and another to the body. Choynski crashed a left to the face. Nick returned with a right to the body and left hook to the jaw. A left to the body and up to the face. Joe shot a left to the stomach, but his tormentor chopped lefts to the face and over the kidneys. Joe ducked a right to the head and artfully blocked two lefts. Burley drove in a left and chased Joe to the ropes. There, he attacked with a double left, to face and stomach, and another to the stomach. The electric light overhead malfunctioned and dimmed, but didn't go out. Joe slammed a right to the stomach. Burley blocked two lefts, landed a left to the face and a right to the wind. Choynski drove in a pair of left jabs, but took a left to the body just before the bell. *Dawson Record*: "Nick ... would drive in some mighty blows. From this time to the ... finish, Burley's friends were confident of his winning, and cheered wildly between every round. Whenever Choynski got in close enough to do damage, he was sure to get as much as he gave. Burley is bleeding from a cut over his left eye and from both nostrils. The effects of Joe's terrific left jabs are apparent, as Nick's whole face is badly bruised."

Round 4 – Burley landed a short left to the gut and ducked a straight left. Joe used clever and lively footwork. He connected to the neck, then evaded a left and right for the stomach. "The Frisco Flash" delivered a right to the head and a left in the stomach, taking a hard left to the gut. They traded lefts and rights, then Joe speared his foe with two sharp jabs to the nose. The Dawson resident sent a right to the body, blocked a hook and drove a jab to the right eye. Joe missed a right cross, and Nick countered with a three-punch combination, all lefts – to stomach, head and stomach. Joe took two jabs and a hook to the jaw, but smacked a right to the face. They were winded. Choynski was bleeding badly from the nose. He landed a left to the head and Burley countered with a right to the body. Joe missed a haymaker left that likely would have ended the fight. Nick whiffed on a left to the body, and caught a hard right to the head at the gong. This was a big round for Burley, and the betting swayed his way.

Round 5 – They traded lefts, then Burley took over. He cracked a left to the face, right to body, left to jaw, then two more lefts to the face. Joe seemed to have lost his defense. Nick stepped in with a left to the body and hard right to the face. He missed several punches, as Joe used swift footwork. Choynski missed a left, and Burley got him with two jabs and a hooking right to the head. Joe tried to counter a jab with a right cross, but was blocked by Burley. After trading "love taps" in a clinch, Joe landed a left swing to the head. His nose continued to bleed, as he missed a left and had another blocked. Nick slammed a right and left to the body, left to the jaw and a straight left to the head. Joe clinched to avoid punishment. It was not looking too good for him. He landed a hook to the jaw, but was countered by a left to the body. Another winning canto for Nick.

Round 6 – *Dawson Record*: "Joe advances smiling ... sends left to Burley's head. They do some lively foot work and spar for an opening. Nick sends a right to stomach and Joe ducks left … Nick sends a left to stomach and a hard right to head … drives his left to Joe's chin. Joe appears dazed … tries left hook to head, but misses. Tries another and lands hard. Nick lands hard right on stomach. Nick sends hard left to the stomach …" Burley missed a "vicious swing for Joe's jaw. Both men are tired, especially Burley." He landed several punches to Choynski's body and head, forcing him to clinch. They traded shots before the bell. Burley's nose is bleeding heavily, but the consensus is, it is his fight to lose. There is a tumultuous cheer at round's end, as the spectators realize they are "witnessing a mighty struggle."

Round 7 – They advance slowly, the pace having taken a toll. Once they engage, both cut loose. Burley lands a left, Choynski misses one. After a clinch, he lands a right. Nick hammers a succession of shots to the face: left, right, left, left. Joe retaliates with a right and left to the head. His nose is bleeding freely. They trade lefts to body and head, but Burley gets the better of it. Nick's nose is bleeding in rivulets. There is no thought of defense now. Both are slugging, all out. Nick smashes two lefts to the face, Joe answers with a hard left-right. They exchange right and left to the head, and Joe drives a right to the wind. He is coming on. *Dawson Record*: He "swings … terrific right on Nick's chest and a hard left to … wind. Burley falters and is groggy. Joe thrashes hard left and right on jaw, followed by another right and left to head, and has Burley going. Burley surprises Joe with swings of left and right of wonderful force … Joe staggers and is dazed, as he rushes Burley with two hard jabs, right and left to head. Both men are covered with blood and bleeding freely from the nose. Joe lands a long left swing on jaw. Burley's arms drop, and he is moving without purpose. He is badly dazed, but trying desperately to stay the round. Joe sees his advantage, and … throws right and left to Burley's chin as hard as he can. He is landing right and left on head at will. He lands a full left swing on the jaw. Nick is wobbling on his feet, and though he sees Choynski clearing his left for the knockout, is helpless. With a cleverly vicious left hook to the point, Joe drops Nick to the mat. Nick is not conscious of the count and rolls over in pain, as Sugrue's hand drops for the last time."

In the DAAA arena and at the *Dawson Record* and *Bonanza Record* offices in Dawson City, where reports of the fight were being wired, pandemonium reigned. Joe Choynski was the man of the hour, both to those who bet on him to win, and to the fickle. Joe had slipped badly from the pinnacle of his prime. In what became a war of attrition, however, his experience may have led him to pace himself better. Nick landed the greater number of punches prior to the 7th, but as he admitted, the vim and vigor left him with extreme suddenness. The only knockdowns were suffered by Burley – in the 1st and 7th rounds. Joe carried his punch into the last part of the fight. This would, in fact, be the final knockout victory of his career. *Dawson Record*: "Up to within two seconds of the knockout, from the beginning of the 7th, Burley's friends were expecting to see him drop Choynski ... at any time. Then, all at once, Nick seemed to lose all his strength and was gasping for breath. He swung wildly, and ... was caught by the ... left in Joe's corner ... the cheers were deafening and prolonged for several minutes. The ring was overrun with men ... to congratulate the victor. With sportsmanlike instinct, Choynski disregarded the hands proffered him and turned to the fallen man. He helped Burley to his feet and half carried him to his corner. When he climbed over the ropes, he was literally taken from his feet by the crowd. He was happy, as was plain when he shook his moppy 'chrysanthemum' locks and beamed a good natured grin on the spectators."

"In his dressing room, Choynski complimented Burley without restraint. 'A mighty hard fight,' he said between breaths. 'If Dawson ever witnessed a harder or prettier contest than that, I would like to hear about it.' As proof of the strength of Burley's blows, Joe displayed the stumps of two back teeth, broken off when a hard swing landed." Joe's teeth being snapped off at the gums is likely a gross exaggeration. That said, he fought before the advent of the protective mouthpiece, when extensive damage to the lips and teeth was not uncommon. " 'Though I am feeling pretty good now,' Choynski continued, '... Burley gave me hard punishment. I was in prime enough condition, but ... a little shaky on account of my weight. Just think of it! I weighed a scarce 160 pounds! This worried me greatly before I entered the ring ... A few minutes sparring showed my fears were right, for ... I didn't seem to have the ... weight to put behind my blows. Otherwise I was ... in great shape ... My wind was perfect. Had it not been, I don't like to think what the consequences might have been, for Burley landed terribly on my kidneys ... It must have been a wonderful contest from a spectator's standpoint, for there was not a suspicion of a wrong act during the whole time ... Nick Burley is a gentleman. This I want to emphasize ... as things have come to my ears that ... there was enmity between us. This is not so, for I had and still have the greatest respect for the man I beat.' "

"Burley was terribly downcast. The punishment he took was simply marvelous. Beaten and bruised, he could hardly see or speak when he went to his dressing room. He did not seem to realize what a game battle he had put up ... Naturally, he had no excuse to put forward. 'I wonder if I could have stood some more of that man's punishment,' he said, as he pulled on his clothes. 'I was desperate in that last round, for I had begun to feel my strength and energy slipping away ... I can't explain it, but I seemed to lose strength all of a sudden, just as if something in me had snapped. The only way I can account for it is I must have overtrained and become stale.' "

"After he was dressed, Choynski went to Burley's dressing rooms ... he laid his hand on the other's shoulder ... 'Nick ... You are a game fighter and a fine fellow. I want you to feel that I think well of you, for I do. You have treated me like a gentleman.' Then, lugubriously poking a big finger to his heart, Joe, smiling, exclaimed, 'And that's not any kidding, either, it's from in here.' Burley smiled wearily in return and shook Joe's hand heartily, as he assured him he treasured not a particle of ill feeling on account of his defeat. 'That's all right,' said Joe as he went out the door. 'When you come to my town, you'll get the best treatment I know how to give a gentleman.' Barney Sugrue refereed the go in a most satisfactory manner. Choynski's plans at present include an early departure for the outside. Mrs. Choynski has been engaged to work at the Auditorium next week, and of course, he will be in town until the end of the week. When asked if he would be willing to meet Gardner, Choynski said he would, if George appeared in the country soon enough. He pointed out, though, that he had been working hard for two months, and, as it was getting late in the Northern season, he was anxious to get back to his home in Chicago."

Joe (1927): "Without offering any excuse, I asked for a return match. I gave Burley such a terrible beating, ending it with a clean knockout in the 7th round, that a cry was set up that my first fight with him had been a fake. I never faked a fight. I was simply clouted on the jaw with a wild swipe in the first fight, and did not possess the old-time recuperative power to shake it off. This experience made me realize the time was near, when I would have to hang up the gloves ..." Joe Boyle, it was said, "was so overjoyed at the result of the contest that he could scarcely keep from dancing."[21] "Joe Choynski has become the fistic idol of the Klondike. The exploits of the aged heavyweight pugilist in the ring in Dawson City have made Joe a great favorite with the mining contingent in the gold district ..."

Dawson News: "Nick Burley added another knockout to his credit last night (August 12) ... A big, husky individual who towered over the pugilist, seized ... and threatened him. Like a flash, Nick landed a short arm jolt on his ... chin ... the latter collapsed and did not come up for 10 minutes. The man lost $20 on Burley ... saw Burley on the side walk, and ... seized him by the lapels of his coat. He was angry, and demanded Nick give him $20 ... a ... jolt ... Nick helped to carry his assailant into a saloon." Louise entertained the Dawson public a short time: "Mrs. Joseph Choynski in High-Class Specialties for one week, commencing Monday, August 10."[22]

Joe Boyle dredged for gold in the Yukon until 1917, when he traveled to Russia, to reorganize that country's railroad system. In December, 1917, "The King of the Klondike" successfully petitioned Russia's new Bolshevik government to return currency and archives to Romania. In the Spring of 1918, he rescued some 50 high-ranking Romanian officials from captivity in Odessa, Ukraine. At the 1919 Paris Peace Conference, Boyle helped Romania obtain a $25 million credit from the Canadian government. He gained much influence in the royal court and was bestowed the title, "Saviour of Romania." He maintained a close friendship with British-born

Marie of Edinburgh, Queen of Romania. Some say he was her paramour. Boyle was decorated by the governments of Romania, Russia, England and France for varied achievements. He died in Hampton Hill, Middlesex, England in 1923. In 1973, his body was reburied in his home town of Woodstock, Ontario, Canada. From 1923 until 1938, when Queen Marie died, a mysterious "woman in black" brought flowers to his grave on the anniversary of his death. Naturally, many believe this was Marie.[23]

Although it is not known just when he left the Yukon, one of Joe's keepsakes from the trip was a lunch menu from the steamer, *Dolphin*, dated August 25. The September 1 *San Francisco Call* read: "Joe Choynski is in town ... proudly displaying a handsome 'gold brick' presented him by admirers in the Klondike regions. The brick is the real thing, and valued at $300. Joe is delighted with the reception he received in Alaska." *The Kansas City Star* quoted Joe: "I don't believe there is a finer lot ... on the face of the globe. Their generosity and hospitality is charming. I could not have been treated better had I been a prince of the blood royal. Mrs. Choynski and myself left San Francisco on June 3 ... when we arrived at Dawson they met us with a full military band ... when we came away, the same band escorted us to the pier, playing 'Good-by, My Lover, Good-by,' and all sorts of tunes ... calculated to make a fellow feel there was regret at his departure."

"Of ... Burley, Choynski had but little to say, merely ... in the first contest he broke the bones of his wrist in the 1st ... and was ... unable to successfully finish a one-handed contest ... about the place in which the fight was pulled off ... the conduct of the club management towards the participants ... especially himself ... 'I think I have seen every fighting arena in the country of any prominence,' said Joe, 'and ... none ... can equal the arrangement in Dawson City. The match was under the auspices of what is known up there as the D. Three A. club, or ... Dawson Amateur Athletic Association ... a magnificent clubhouse ... The place will seat 4,000 people, and the lighting and the ring arrangements are the best I have ever seen anywhere. Aside from the main auditorium, the building is fitted up as a gymnasium, with up to date paraphernalia and most conveniently arranged baths. The auditorium is used in winter time as an ice rink, and a curious fact in this connection is that the ice floor is preserved throughout the summer. When I fought there, there were 14 inches of ice on the floor, covered with sawdust, for the double purpose of preservation, and, as I imagine, to keep the fighters and others from having cold feet. The effect of this was to make the place delightfully cool, although it was midsummer ... the seats are built up over this solid foundation of ice.' "[24]

In August, an undated *Police Gazette* ran a tribute to Joe, by Sam Austin: "When you wish to point to one man who has adorned the profession of prizefighting, you pick out Joe Choynski. Abstemious in his habits, honorable, conscientious, truthful and grateful, five qualities which are rarely combined in men, and rare indeed, among the exponents of pugilism. For 19 years, Choynski has been conspicuous in pugilistic affairs ... How he has managed to retain his strength and vigor all these years and still be a factor in ... pugilistic honors ... he takes the best of care of himself, neither drinks nor smokes, and to this ascribes the fact that he is as good to-day as ... in the middle of his career. His father was a pioneer, a member of the famous 2nd Vigilance Committee of 1856 ... a man of much learning. Young Joe Choynski became a well-educated prize fighter ... Choynski was the medium through which Jim Corbett reached the goal of his ambition."

On October 11: " 'This is my last appearance in Dawson, and when the Casca* pulls out of here next week, I will bid good bye to the town forever,' said Nick Burley ... after he ... defeated Billy Bates. 'I am going to the coast and will look for Choynski. I think yet that I can defeat him, and will follow him until I get a match.' The contest with Bates was the 16th that Burley has had in Dawson. He has won them all, with the exception of the 2nd contest with Choynski. Burley will go first to Seattle, where he has offers either to become boxing instructor of one of the clubs, or to wait for a match with one of his own weight."[25] Nick would remain and have fights in Dawson until September, 1906, finishing his career in December, 1907. He went on a downward spiral following this interview, and would not face Joe again.

* The Casca was a steamboat that regularly navigated a route on the Yukon River between Whitehorse and Dawson, until 1952.

On October 27, it was reported that John Dewey, "champion wrestler and noted athlete" who "formerly traveled with the Choynski Athletic company" had been fatally shot that day.[26] It is not known when he was a member of the Company, and any details about Joe's combination seem lost to history. In his final ring combat of 1903, Joe took on Marvin Hart, "The Kentucky Plumber," whom he had trained but a short time earlier. It would also be Joe's last great performance. The fight took place on the night of November 16, before a large crowd at the Washington Sporting Club in Philadelphia. It was scheduled for six rounds, and would be declared a "No Decision" if no knockout occurred. The referee was Billy Rocap. The following blends multiple contemporary reports, including the local *Philadelphia Inquirer*, and Choynski's memoirs.[27]

Round 1 – The battlers slammed lefts and rights into each other at a terrific pace and with telling effect, targeting the body and head. Joe sank a left into Hart's wind and ducked a counter right to the head. As Marvin tried to rush, Choynski met him with a straight left that sent his head back. Joe dodged two more roundhouse rights and countered with a jab. They came to a clinch, where the heavier Hart got the better of the infighting. Upon breaking, Marvin thumped Joe in the body with a heavy right. A fast mix-up followed, Hart again having the edge. The wire service report, though, said "there was no perceptible difference in the men during the first two rounds." So furious was the action and so much energy expended, the *Philadelphia Inquirer* opined that "After the 1st round, either man would have been a cinch for most any of the good light heavyweights." Joe (1930): "The 1st round was full of gloves ... Hart taking mine and giving plenty in return. He had learned a lot, this upstanding Kentuckian, and I had to use all my ringcraft to offset his attack ... we had the spectators yelling wildly as a result of our spectacular mix-ups ..."

Marvin Hart

Round 2 – "Beginning with the 2nd ... neither showed any speed (nor) footwork. Choynski landed ... left and right round Hart's body ... his right on (the) jaw ... woke up the Louisvillean, who rushed Joe and carried him to the ropes ... a fierce exchange at close quarters, Hart landing several ... right ... uppercuts that did Choynski no good ... caught (Joe) on the face with his right ... both ... swinging wildly (at) the bell ..."

Round 3 – The wire service account saw a knockdown the *Philadelphia Inquirer* didn't: "Hart sent Choynski to the floor with a terrific punch on the jaw. Choynski remained ... until Referee Rocap counted eight ... rose ... and came back vigorously ... but (Hart) managed to hold his own." *Philadelphia Inquirer*: "Choynski ... got two stiff right handers round the body from Hart. After Joe ducked ... from another pair ... there was (a) mix-up. No attempt was made to box by either man. They simply swung ... sometimes for the head, sometimes ... the body. Both landed frequently, but the blows were pushes ... They fairly wobbled to their corners when the bell sounded."

Round 4 – The men were tired; the inning, "rather tame." *Inquirer*: "As usual, Choynski started ... with a left to the body. Hart got back with his right to the jaw, and there was a clinch, in which Choynski was slammed to the batting. He wisely took all that was coming to him. The little rest appeared to do ... some good, for he rocked Hart with a straight right. The finish ... was the same as ... the 3rd, both men throwing their arms about in aimless fashion ... landing about as often as they missed." Two other Philadelphia papers, the *Press* and the *Record*, told a different story, one of heavy exchanges, the fighters taking turns rocking each other. Hart had a nosebleed and Joe sustained a bad cut over his left eye.

Round 5 – The pair blasted with terrific shots from both hands. *Inquirer*: "After a minute's work ... the men became so tired all they could do was fall up against each other ... resting ... they would lunge ... only to fall on each other's shoulders again. For a brief period, it looked as though Hart's legs were going to go back on him ..." Joe was bleeding from the nose and over both eyes, but seems to have connected with more skill and accuracy.

Round 6 – *Inquirer*: "*Last round!* was announced ... They shook hands warmly, and went at it. Hart was dominant in the early portion, until Joe sank a left to the wind that turned things in his favor. Marvin's defense was porous, as he was arm-weary. Joe took advantage, landing a half dozen times on his jaw, but there was only enough steam behind the punches to wobble Hart's head. They were mixing ... in a wild sort of way when the bell sounded. Anything worse than a draw would have been unfair." *Worcester Daily Spy*: "Hart hit Choynski almost at will. The latter was weakening rapidly and ... a little groggy until 30 seconds from the end ... when he rallied. He rushed at Hart and smashed him frequently with his right. Hart, weakened by his own exertions ... was unable to withstand Choynski's onslaught, and the latter kept punching him until the bell ... Notwithstanding the ... punishment received, neither ... was badly hurt. Choynski appeared to be in better condition than Hart. The latter looked as though he weighed 15 pounds more than his opponent."

Choynski (1930): "From first to last I battled this great heavyweight to a standstill ... Sport authorities acclaimed it the most savage fight ... yet one of the most scientific ... ever witnessed." Joe (1927): "A fight that had enough action ... for 20 rounds ... sports writers agreed ... the fiercest ever seen in Philadelphia. One paper described ... 'Hart had a great advantage in weight. Choynski was pinched and drawn. There were blue rings under his eyes, and his legs, always thin, were drawn to a fineness that made appropriate the title of *greyhound*, which tradition attaches to him. Both were cheered to the echo as they left the ring. The greatest applause was Choynski's. In the twilight of a great career he had given an exhibition of courage and desperation that will never be effaced from memories ...' "

Joe (1930): "Hart had both my eyebrows hanging ... plastered my kidneys time and again, but I didn't feel the blows. After the fight, a physician ... couldn't find a trace of injury ... my body was neither red nor welted by the terrific blows. So much for perfect condition." *San Francisco Call*: "The bout was fast, both ... taking severe punishment ... at the close ... Hart's nose was bleeding, and ... mouth, while Choynski had a slight cut over the right eye." *Inquirer*: "With the exception of ... Fitzsimmons and Ruhlin ... it is doubtful if two big men ever boxed six harder rounds than ... Hart and Choynski ..." As the Fitz-Ruhlin brawl was a supremely punishing bout that nearly killed Gus, that is saying a lot. "There were stages ... when it looked as though Choynski must succumb, but just when he appeared to be going, he would ... rally, and ... it would look as though Hart would be the one to go out. The fat lay in rolls over (Hart's) capacious abdomen, and this handicap told after the first minute ... in each round. He would start in with a rush, hoping to finish the job with a punch, but he invariably shot his bolt, while Choynski always came a little toward the finish. At the end of the 6th ... Joe was a shade ... livelier in his legs than ... Hart." While officially a No Decision, every paper called the fight a draw, and it was discussed for days, around the country.

On the 19th, Joe visited older brother, Maurice in Pittsburgh, accompanied by a Mr. Calvert, the city clerk of Dawson City. He was making a tour of the States and had returned with Joe from the Klondike. After a few days with "Chauncey," Joe returned to La Grange. He was seeking a rematch with Hart, and had received an offer from the Criterion

Joe Choynski, 1903, at La Grange, IL home

Club in Boston for a match on December 23.[28] It did not occur. Still vacillating between retirement or continuing his career, Joe told the November 21 *Police Gazette* he would retire when Fitzsimmons did, not before. This shows the rivalry Joe had with Bob. Commenting on the impending world light-heavyweight title bout on November 25, between Fitz and champion, George Gardner, Joe unhesitatingly picked the latter.[29] Bob was a fading veteran, while George was in his prime and recently stopped Marvin Hart and Jack Root in 12 rounds each. Choosing Gardner would probably be deemed logical, but his caution led to a points win for Bob, who captured his 3rd world title in three weight classes. Fitz would engage in fights and exhibition bouts into 1914. Joe would not.

A fight with Jack Root before the Chicago Athletic Association, was called off. The club offered a $1,000 purse for the bout, but although Joe accepted terms, Root's manager said the purse wasn't large enough.[30] Into January, 1904, multiple papers announced that Joe and "Kid" Carter were going to engage in a *3rd* fight. "Joe Choynski ... and 'Kid' Carter, the strong, rugged and cyclonic light heavy-weight of South Brooklyn, will have another tussle ... within the next three weeks. *The men have already fought two great fights* (emphasis is mine). Carter has begun training ... at West Baden Springs, and Choynski is rounding into condition at his home at La Grange, Ill. In a letter to a friend in this city, Carter says the baths at West Baden have made a new man out of him, and ... he will be stronger and in better physical condition than ... for any fight in over a year."[31] The pair first clashed on March 24, 1902 and were about to meet again in January, 1904, but this was only their 2nd recorded battle. The reference to a 2nd bout in the recent past and the upcoming match being their 3rd, is an enigma.

The January 19, 1904 *Washington Times* claimed: "Kid won the first bout ... the other was decided a draw ... tonight ... Carter and Joe Choynski meet for the 3rd time ... The two previous battles were of the hurricane order, in which there was not a moment of idleness on the part of ... Carter or Choynski. In the first bout ... in Chicago less than two years ago ... Swings, straight jabs, uppercuts, and all the other pet blows ... were turned loose in bewildering order, with the result that Choynski was the first to succumb ... in the 1st round. Their 2nd battle was a six-round affair in Philadelphia, recently, which went the limit ... both were completely tired out, and it is doubtful if the bout could have gone much further."

Joe fought Jack O'Brien on March 30, 1903, was in the Yukon until the end of August, and battled Hart in Philly on November 16. A Boston paper said, on October 15 that "Choynski and ... Carter will meet in Philadelphia, October 26," a New York publication adding on October 22 that "Choynski intends to come East for the purpose of arranging all details for his six-round bout with 'Kid' Carter ... postponed from October 26 to Nov. 2."[32] It is conceivable that they fought around these dates, but no account of the fight has been located, nor a date for it. Neither did Joe mention a 3rd fight in his memoirs. Perhaps reports referred to the Hart bout in November, or a missing bout on Joe's record has yet to be discovered.

On January 8, Choynski received a telegram confirming a scheduled 15 round fight with Eddie "Kid" Carter at catch-weights, at Boston's Criterion Club. Joe was training at two different locations, alternating between Summerfield & Essig's gymnasium in Chicago and his own, private gym at his La Grange home. He rested on the day preceding the bout. Carter set up quarters at West Baden, Indiana, where he had prepared for some time. He returned to Philadelphia for a while, after which he trained some in Lakewood, New Jersey, with a noted boxing trainer named Joe Macias. Beantown awaited eagerly, another short, but memorable fight.[33]

Round Twenty-Two

Retirement
(January 1904 – April 1910)

The anticipated Carter rematch occurred on the evening of January 19. The referee was Jimmy Colville. Choynski's seconds were Andy Daly, Danny Dougherty and Billy Kennedy, according to the *Washington Times*. The *Lowell Sun* said they were Joseph Daly, Hugh Kennedy, James F. Feefe and "Jack" Cattanach. The latter source said Carter's seconds were Stephen J. Mahoney, Michael E. Sears, Harry E. Williams and Danny Dougherty. The following uses 13 contemporary reports, and Joe's memoirs:[1]

Round 1 – Carter tore in with a stiff right to the ribs, trying futilely to reach Choynski's head. Joe answered with two hard rights to the stomach and a sharp jab that snapped "The Kid's" head back. He continued dispensing, but Carter replied with a good left to the head. They swapped punches furiously. The *Philadelphia Inquirer* said, about a minute in, Carter rushed Joe, who, in trying to avoid, "tripped and fell headlong, striking the ropes with his face. The fall started Choynski's nose going a little ... (Joe) with a stiff right opened Carter's left eye. The work of Choynski ... had the crowd on edge, and the consensus ... was (he) had the better of it."

About two minutes in (the *Police Gazette* said two and a half minutes), came the finish: Joe feinted "The Kid" into throwing a lead right. He stepped to his own right to evade, and as Carter followed, Joe came in. Carter was already throwing a powerful left (some said a right) to the body. It crashed home with tremendous force, but caught Choynski "flush in the groin." Joe doubled up like a jackknife, with a cry of pain. He sank to the floor, writhing and clutching his groin. Colville, instead of acknowledging the foul, began counting over the prone Choynski. Joe rolled onto his back and tried to rise, but fell back again. His seconds jumped into the ring, claiming a foul, but the referee waved them aside. Colville tolled off the 10 seconds and motioned "The Kid" to his corner. Moments later, the announcer awarded the fight to Carter. The *Decatur Daily Review* said the fight ended "after two minutes and 55 seconds ..."

Some papers said Joe was incapacitated nearly four minutes, others, "several minutes," but the *Philadelphia Inquirer* said "it was fully 15 minutes before the latter was able to hobble to his corner. The majority ... agreed the decision was an unjust one." Papers seemed unanimous in stating that Joe had the better of the bout until the final blow, which a few sources called a punch to the stomach, rather than the groin. An undated January *Police*

Gazette wrote: "In all fairness to Carter it must be said that the foul was unintentional ... and Choynski was partially to blame, in that stepping in towards Carter he made it possible for the blow to land where it did. Carter expressed his regret at the abrupt ending ... in so unsatisfactory a way. Up to the (end), Choynski had all the advantage, and had been forcing matters. He repeatedly forced Carter to break ground. He had all his old-time speed and ... ability to sidestep Carter's rushes ... Carter led for the head several times, but ... Choynski cleverly avoided his leads."

New York World: "Notwithstanding the fact that he was dealt a foul blow ... Joe Choynski was adjudged the loser ... victim of the unintentional foul ... For some time, the ... crowd sat spellbound, and then broke into a storm of hisses, catcalls and jeers. The action of the referee was unexplainable, for there was no question in the minds of the spectators about the Chicago man being hit low. Referee Colville said, after giving his decision and as the crowd was leaving the building, that he did not see any infringement of the rules and did not believe a foul had been committed. He intimated that Choynski, while having been hit very low, wanted to quit. After the bout, Carter admitted hitting his opponent lower than the rules permitted, but maintained it was entirely unintentional, and they shook hands and became as friendly as ever. Choynski was cheerful, even in the face of all the adverse circumstances. 'Of course,' he said, 'the injury robbed me of the bout. However, it was entirely an accident, and I do not blame anyone, although I think the referee made a mistake in giving Carter the decision.' "

"As the principals left the ring, they ... with their seconds and attendants, were placed under arrest by a squad of detectives under the direction of Captain O'Lalor ... and Chief Inspector ... Watts. The principals were accompanied to the dressing-rooms and under strict surveillance ... allowed to dress, and ... taken in close carriages to Station 5, where Choynski and Carter were booked on a technical charge of mutual assault and battery. The seconds were charged with aiding and abetting a prize fight. The men were all allowed to go, after bail of $200 ... had been furnished ... officers went to the club armed with warrants ... admitted ... as special guests of the Board of Directors ... police admit the action was ... a test case ... The Police Department has resorted to almost any means to stop boxing in Boston, without success ... The Criterion Club is the most important in the city, and officials have several times been hauled to court ... but ... never convicted." The *Colorado Springs Gazette* said Joe, after the fight, appeared ... "in great distress ... eight other men, including seconds ... referee and managers of the club were also arrested ... Each was released in $2,000 (sic) bail."

The case came up for trial in municipal court on the morning of the 21st. So interested was the public, wrote the *Lowell Sun*, that "A throng ... which would have filled three courtrooms sought entrance ... Perhaps the most interested ... was Judge William H. Emmons, chairman of the Boston police board, who has declared his purpose of putting a stop to all boxing exhibitions or prize fighting in the city ... chief witness of the prosecution was Head Detective Watts. He said the blows struck ... were severe and the contest warm, until Choynski fell to the floor, where he moved as if in great pain. He was carried to his corner by his seconds. The bout was concluded by a foul blow, which ... Watts thought was an accident."

Another witness, Inspector Houghton, when asked to compare the bout with a football game at Soldier's Field, said he had seen more brutality on the gridiron than in the ring. Attorney Sweeney ... for the Defense, called to the stand ... Emmons. He asked ... if any prior warnings had been given the Criterion Club, that they must stop hosting boxing contests, to which he replied in the negative. *Philadelphia Inquirer:* "The court, after hearing the arguments, declined jurisdiction ... the defendants were held for the grand jury in the sum of $500 each ... released on the understanding that they would file a bond to-morrow. Choynski left for Philadelphia to-night to take in the Ryan-O'Brien fight." Before leaving the courthouse, Joe jokingly told a *Boston Globe* reporter that "he was seriously thinking of changing his name from Joe to Jonah," so bad had his fortunes become. The boxers were found to be "probably guilty" of "mutual assault."[2] After what happened in Galveston, one cannot blame Joe for fleeing Boston! He headed home to Chicago, however, not Philadelphia.

All defendants filed bonds the next day, January 22. If convicted, Joe and Carter were subject to a prison term of up to 10 years or a fine not to exceed $5,000. The others involved were subject, under Massachusetts law, to a prison term of up to five years or a fine not to exceed $1,000. The local Central Athletic Club put on a boxing show the following night, refusing to admit authorities. They had no trouble. Once again, Joe announced that he was finished with the game. In fact, he would engage in only one more pro contest. Papers said Joe was "credited with great thrift" and had saved enough of his ring earnings to securely retire on.[3]

The January 22 (Christchurch, New Zealand) *Star* (ironically, quoting the *Boston Police News*), wrote: "A good second or adviser ... has often changed the aspect of a seemingly hopeless battle. Modern pugilists realize the importance of this, and make it their business to have only experienced men in their corners. The methods of present day handlers ... are vastly different from those employed years ago. Such expedients as smelling salts, oxygen, electric fans or attending physicians were practically unknown. Seconds invariably depended on ... water and muscular exertion to revive their men. Joe Choynski and Tommy Ryan are regarded the best seconds in the country ... their services are much in demand. Choynski is credited with aiding many pugilists to victory ... a fighter, himself, he is able to recognize a pugilist's weakness at a glance (He) says a fighter is a very sensitive person and must be humored and cajoled while ... in an important mill."

"Choynski said, 'Of course, if a fighter hasn't the necessary ability, courage and stamina, it is a hard task to help him much. Yet, I have known fighters who were really cowards, but who won because they were properly handled. Between rounds, especially after a man has received severe punishment and shown signs of impending collapse, is the time when the second's art does the most good ... the first thing to do after a boxer has become groggy or dazed is to revive him with cool water. A little application, such as spraying him, will work wonders ... I am not a physician, but I understand respiration to some extent. When you notice a pugilist breathing heavily ... he is either exhausted or growing weak ... he needs all the air he can inhale. There is a knack in waving a towel that will help. You must flourish it in a way that will give him plenty of air without distressing him. I bring smelling salts into (it) as a last resort only."

On the night of the 22nd, Joe and Louise arrived back in Chicago. Shortly after they left the Illinois Central Station, a man dashed toward the couple, grabbed the satchel Joe was carrying, and ran off. The bag contained $150. Rather than chase the robber, Joe reported the theft at the local police station. The details of various papers varied, the *Fort Wayne News* writing: "Accompanied by his wife and two children on the way from the ... depot shortly after midnight, Joe Choynski ... was attacked by three highwaymen at 12th street. One of the robbers felled Mrs. Choynski with a severe blow. Another ... struck the prize fighter ... in the face, but Choynski's attention was taken more in the care of his family than in fighting the bandits, and the three got away. A purse containing a small sum of money was taken from Mrs. Choynski." The satchel was generally reported as belonging to Louise, Joe carrying it at the time. This was the only report of three men involved or of punches thrown. The *Aberdeen Daily News* also mentioned Joe and Louise with "family." The "children" must have been the Pon boys. More on them later.[4]

It was announced February 6 that Choynski, Carter, et al., had been discharged by the Suffolk County Superior Court, the grand jury failing to indict. Joe said he was retiring, at the request of his wife. "There are fighters who had more fights," said Malachy (or Malachi) Hogan, "but I do not think ... a boxer living ... (is) as well preserved ... after 20 years of fighting." A February *Police Gazette* sarcastically wrote, "For the 64th time, Joe Choynski has announced his retirement from the ring." In early February, a representative of Dawson City's Athletic Association showed up in Chicago and offered Joe a 20 round match with George Gardner. The purse was $5,000 and traveling expenses. "Choynski ... is willing ... When asked if he had not stated ... that he had retired ... he laughed and said: 'I was in a state of mind that night to ... say almost anything. No, I am in the fighting game for all there is in it ... when good money ... is offered, I am going ... after it. Gardner does not look ... harder ... than any of the others ...'"[5]

Joe's Bull Terrier, Sappho; Louise with 5 Boston terrier pups, La Grange, IL; Joe with Boston Terrier, Staten Island dock. His Boxer, Brindle, Astor Library, New York City.

A great lover of dogs, Joe owned canines of various breeds over the years. March 26 *Mansfield News*: "When last heard from, Joe Choynski was shining at kennel shows, a bulldog he owns being a high-class one and prize winner." Among those he owned was a Staffordshire Bull Terrier named Sappho, who had at least one litter of pups. Joe described her as "a great dog." A photo, circa 1899, shows Louise holding a bushel basket of five terrier pups. Choynski also had a male boxer named Brindle. He acquired a Malamute called Skookum (Chinook for "biggest, best") in Alaska at four

weeks old, in 1903 or '04. Joe said, "Finest dog ever, had Rin Tin Tin beat from a pup." He owned pet dogs from at least the late 1890s through the 1930s. Joe was soon training boxers again. A late February *Police Gazette* shows a dark, blurry photograph of "Kid Coxey – A 105-pound boxer of New York ... one of Joe Choynski's promising pupils." Whether this was his friend of later years, George Coxey, is uncertain. George was a noted boxer; later, a well-known insurance agent for New York Life. Joe bitterly told a reporter in May: "There is nothing more in the fighting game for me ... purses are small and do not pay for the trouble and annoyance ... the following of the sport gives ..."[6]

(Above) Joe's malamute, Skookum, and a pup of Sappho; (Below) Sappho, all taken at La Grange, IL

A story came out of an injury to Joe in 1896, at the New York Athletic Club. "About seven years ago, ("Professor" Mike) Donovan's powers of endurance received a genuine test. At that time, his best pupil was Fred Winthrop. Winthrop ... stood 6' ... weighed ... 175 pounds. He was an ideal athlete and had won the middleweight and heavyweight championships of Harvard. Donovan is popular with professional pugilists and many seek his advice regarding training and the ... delivery of effective blows. One day, Joe Choynski ... came to see Donovan at the old building ... 6th Avenue, and asked for ... putting on the mitts with Donovan's best pupil. Winthrop was in the room ... Mike introduced him to Choynski. The latter had a match on with Jim

Hall ... and ... wanted some lively exercise. Winthrop and Choynski came together for four rounds. The Californian evidently thought he had a novice before him, and began to play with his man ... he soon realized Winthrop was no neophyte, for the latter cleverly blocked all his punches and retaliated with some stiff ones, himself"

"After the bout, Choynski complained of a pain in his side. He gave it no further thought until he returned to his training quarters. Then, the pain became so intense a physician had to be summoned. The doctor diagnosed ... a broken rib, and Choynski had to lay off training for a week. He entered the ring with the rib still broken, but managed to whip Hall by sheer grit and courage. Winthrop broke Choynski's rib with a right hand drive. Two days after ... Jim Corbett sparred with Donovan's pupil, and the ex-champion had to hustle to keep ... from being punished ... Corbett was enthusiastic over Winthrop's cleverness and wondered why he did not become a professional ... Donovan had done a hard day's work instructing ... pupils and was pretty tired. Winthrop, too, was weary, but seemed fresher than Donovan. Nevertheless, the older man managed to keep the youngster in check, although the going was as lively as one would care to see."[7] This supports the November 16, 1896 *Brooklyn Daily Eagle*, that Joe had a broken rib for the Hall fight. Choynski only said he received a scratch over one eye while boxing Mike Donovan, likely because he didn't want to reveal a weak spot that might be exploited. Broken ribs heal slowly.

The July 16 *Police Gazette* said Joe "wants to enter the roped arena again, and is doing light training at his home in LaGrange, Ill." The September 25 *Washington Post* commented on the mannerisms of boxers prior to fights. It said Peter Jackson was especially nervous in the hour or so before a contest, when he would drink a glass of brandy. Tom Sharkey, on the contrary, was fidgety and cranky in the days leading up ... but would relax about an hour prior to the bout. Bob Fitzsimmons, like Rocky Marciano after him, sometimes fell asleep before a match. Choynski "would not recover his natural demeanor until he entered the building and saw the crowd. (He) became confident when ... friends would ... grasp his hand. He was happy when they asked him a lot of questions and wished him good luck. Choynski always fought better ... under these circumstances."

The October 17 *Trenton Times* reported Jim Jeffries' "intimate friend," Jules Hurtig, arranging a multi-fight event. "The California Grizzly" was to take on three well-known heavyweights on the same night. "Hurtig is willing to bet $10,000 that Jeffries will come out of the fray unscathed, provided the men he names are selected ... Hurtig ... a boxer ... himself, thinks Gus Ruhlin, Sandy Ferguson and Joe Choynski would prove easy victims ... Of course ... the men must stand ... and fight, not run away." Jules thought Jim could turn the trick on all three in less than 30 minutes. "I suggest Jeffries take on each man one after the other, without rest. Should a man go down to avoid punishment, he must forfeit the battle. I will post a forfeit of $500 with Al Smith ... to show my sincerity." Although intriguing, the event did not occur. Over the years, much has been written about Joe engaging in an exhibition with Jeffries in San Francisco in 1904. References fail to mention when, and over what distance. If the bout took place, it was likely a four-rounder, and would have been the 2nd time Joe boxed a reigning heavyweight king, the other being Sullivan, in 1892. There is no definite record of the Jeffries exhibition, nor of Joe in California in 1904.

Around the 3rd week in October, another match with "Philadelphia" Jack O'Brien was announced, for St. Louis, Missouri's West End Club, on October 9. It was slated for 15 rounds at the light-heavyweight limit, generally 168 (in modern times, 175) pounds. Joe trained three weeks for the bout in La Grange. Suddenly, the fight was off. On October 20, telegrams from Joe to fight promoter Charley Haughton and the West End Club, read: "Will not fight Thursday night. Have decided to quit game," and "Call fight off. Am out of the game for good." The *Milwaukee Free Press* said he had requested an additional week of training, weeks earlier. The club felt this meant that the aging veteran was unable to develop the stamina for a long battle in three weeks. Not wanting to embarrass himself, Joe declared retirement. On November 4, it was announced that he had reconsidered. Joe "accepted terms for a bout with 'Philadelphia' Jack" on November 14 in Philadelphia.[8] The O'Brien match quietly went by the wayside; it turned out that Joe received a more acceptable offer. The October 27 *Washington Times* said Joe had $40,000 saved, in addition to the property in La Grange, and could retire to a life of ease, if he wished.

The replacement for the O'Brien match turned out to be Choynski's final pro bout. It was announced on the 11th: "Jack Williams, the light heavyweight of Philadelphia, and Joe ... for six rounds at catchweights on November 16, before the Gentleman's Boxing Club of Philadelphia, for its initial show. Williams is a coming man in his class ..." He was called a "first-rate performer ... thought highly of in the Quaker City ... a strong, healthy young fellow with a punch in either hand ... a protégé of Jack O'Brien."[9] The distance was six rounds instead of 15, and Jack was expected to trade with Joe, giving the latter more openings. O'Brien was an elusive target, too difficult at this stage for "The California Terror." Jack Williams was described as a middleweight, at about 160 pounds. Photos show him as rangy and muscular. His biggest wins came in 1904, over Peter Maher (KO1, June, KO2, July) and "Kid" Carter (KO3, October). The match was held November 22, in the new Washington Sporting Club. As usual, no decision would be rendered if it went the distance. Jack Root and Lou Houseman were among those present. No referee was named, but it was likely Billy Rocap. The following combines seven contemporary papers:[10]

Round 1 – *Boston Journal:* "For a brief interval ... it looked as though

Williams was going to carry Choynski off his feet. Joe broke ground and twice went to the ropes, but suddenly caught Williams with a straight left-hand ... on the nose, putting that member out of commission."

Round 2 – *Pawtucket Times*: "Choynski landed a straight left to Williams' nose that brought blood and shook (him) up ... near the bell, however ..."

Round 3 – Joe cleverly ducked, sidestepped, jabbed and countered.

Round 4 – *New York Evening World*: "For four rounds he blocked ... making Williams appear a novice. He had blood streaming all down Jack's face ... once in a while sent in a stiff jab or stinging heart blow. Williams was wild and uncertain ... annoyed at his inability to inflict any real damage ... the men ... clinched, feinted and jabbed. Against a slow man, Williams might have made a better showing, but he tired himself trying to reach Joe's face. The latter played a foxy game ..." *Pawtucket Times*: Joe "kept closer ... roughed it, showering short rights and lefts to Williams' body ... without doing much harm." The *Wilkes-Barre Times* said Jack "cut loose," landing straight lefts to Joe's nose.

Jack Williams

Round 5 – Joe staggered his adversary with a smashing right to the jaw. A good right to the stomach had Jack in distress, and he received two potent shots to the jaw. Showing a resilient chin, the Quaker City fighter came back and the two went at it "hammer and tongs" to the bell. The *Trenton Times* said Joe had his foe bloodied up again.

Round 6 – *New York Evening World*: "Choynski opened with a left jab on the nose. Williams swung wild, and Joe sent his left into the stomach and crossed his right on the jaw. He went right after Williams and was all over his man. When the gong sounded, Williams was hanging on to save himself." *Pawtucket Times*: "Choynski kept ... after Williams ... landed several good rights, but Williams was always willing to mix it up, and toward the close gave more than he received." *Trenton Times*: "In the last round the ropes saved Williams from a knockdown, and so rapid were the exchanges that he was forced to clinch to save himself." *Baltimore Sun*: "Choynski had Williams at his mercy and, had the Western boxer been a few years younger, would have undoubtedly put the down-town lad away."

Although no official decision was allowed, five of the seven papers here gave their nod to Joe. *New York Evening World*: "Only in two rounds did Joe show flashes of his old-time form, but this was sufficient to give him the verdict if decisions were allowed in the Quaker City. Williams was expected to make a show of the old man ... but experience told against youth and vigor, and Choynski not only held his own, but was entitled to the decision. Jack O'Brien, who was at ring-side and challenged the winner, could have defeated both ... in one night ... judging by his showing last night, Choynski did well to sidestep O'Brien ..." The *Boston Journal* agreed: "Had a decision been permissible it must have gone to the grand old man."

Trenton Times: "Joe ... proved ... the cleverer ring general and able to administer greater punishment ... for all-round work ... would have been entitled to the decision ... (The) evasive tactics of the Californian bewildered not only Williams, but many in the crowd ... At times Williams must surely have felt he was leading at a phantom. Twice, after desperate ... swings, he went sprawling on the floor, so clever was Choynski at side-stepping." *Baltimore Sun*: "It was about ... even ... up to the last round (when) Choynski had Williams at his mercy ... Williams was the aggressor all through ... but showed a lack of knowledge ... His leads ... were weak ... it appeared as if he was ... pulling back his blows as he let them out. Time and again Choynski side-stepped ... Once ... Jack slammed up against the ropes, and another time ... fell headlong to the floor ... unable to get out of his own way." Two dissenting voices were the *Pawtucket Times* and *Racine Daily Journal* (quoting the *Times*): "Jack Williams ... had the better ... was too fast for Joe, who has gone back very fast in the past year, and although he tried to use the good right, was never able to land ... owing to Williams' quickness." In the concluding battle of Joe's career, he gave at least as good as he got, not going out with a loss, as so many fighters have.

In late November, Choynski was in New York City, for reasons uncertain. He left on the 25th for La Grange, saying he wanted to meet Jack O'Brien in the west, "as he thinks the clubs are more liberal in their purses and bouts can go a further distance." Near the end of 1904, the Illinois Athletic Association was established. Their clubhouse on Michigan Avenue, "two doors from the Chicago Athletic Association," however, would not open until 1907.[11] Joe would be appointed that year as its first athletic instructor. In his 1930 memoirs, Choynski said his smallest career purse had been only $208, for the five round classic with Fitzsimmons, and his largest purse, a mere $5,000, for knocking out Billy Woods in 34 rounds!

Here, both Jeffries and Fitzsimmons told the boxing public that the hardest and most hurtful punch they ever received came from the fist of Choynski. Fitz qualified the statement, saying a clout to the jaw from Joe was one of the two most powerful he ever received, the other being a brutal left to the gut from Jeff.[12] It was high praise, as the era was chock full of heavy punchers. "The California Grizzly" said he often wondered how a man of Joe's size could punch so hard without breaking his hands.

On the other side of the coin, a New Zealand paper listed "Little Joe" as among the boxers possessing a "glass jaw." "There is no more scientific pugilist in the country than Joe Choynski, but the Californian has a weak jaw. He can stand plenty of grueling on the body, but when a rival succeeds in reaching his face, Choynski becomes dazed, and is in a position to be put to sleep easily. When Choynski met Joe Walcott ... several years ago, he was getting along famously until Walcott landed a light blow on the Hebrew's countenance. The blow made Choynski groggy, and Walcott had no trouble in defeating him." Other notables on its "china chin" list, were "Kid" McCoy, Jim Corbett, "Wild Bill" Hanrahan, "Young Griffo" and Joe Gans. Not bad company to be with, although I would not rate Choynski's mandible so fragile as to rate in the glass jaw category.[13]

In the April, 1955 *Boxing and Wrestling* (magazine), Jim Corbett said: "Choynski was the best all around fighter I ever fought with but one exception, Peter Jackson ... had Choynski carried the same weight as Jackson, he would have been Peter's equal and perhaps mine, too." Jim had a way of qualifying comments to present himself as the best of the bunch. Fitz said of Joe: "We boxed a five round draw in Boston. In the 3rd he caught me with a left hook on the chin. I saw the blow coming; it was an overhand, snaky looking thing. I didn't think it packed much steam, but when it struck my jaw I lost all sensation and my head filled with sparkling stars. I remember nothing more about the fight, although they told me later I just beat the count of 10 and held my own for the remaining two rounds. Choynski and I never hit it off well together as friends, but he was the most devastating puncher I ever faced. The man was remarkable in every sense of the word." "Joe Choynski was an odd yet handsome man. Like Henry Armstrong, the upper part of his body was ... that of a light heavyweight, while his legs and understructure were so spindly that even a broken down featherweight would be ashamed to own them. His hair ... always parted straight down the middle, was a dirty blond color and generally hung low below his ears. Standing straight up, the way he fought, Joe was 5' 10" tall, his best fighting weight ... between 165 and 173 pounds. His eyes were a striking blue, alive with excitement and obvious intelligence."

"Choynski, unlike most of his high-living associates, was not a free-living hell-raiser. He enjoyed the quiet of the training camp, classical music, especially scores composed by Beethoven, and his idea of a wild night was scanning the *Police Gazette*'s suggestive pages. Joe was a hopelessly modest sort with a dry, subtle sense of humor; much too keen an observer of human nature to grow swell-headed by the praise lavished on him. It wasn't until he approached his 60th year that Joe took an honest inventory of himself and concluded that he must have been one hell of a man, after all, and despite his age could still step a fast 10 with the best of 'em."

Corbett wrote, in early March: "Choynski ... never overlooked a chance to get the money ... one of the greatest fighters ... ever ... when it came to meeting the type of fighter ... Sullivan was continually knocking out while traveling over the country, Joe was not far behind the great John L. One of the toughest scraps Joe ever had was with a man of this type. He was lying on a couch one day in a club that was then flourishing at Portland, Ore. There was at that time a big laborer who had gained somewhat of a reputation for knocking out sailors and would-be pugilists. He weighed well over the 200-pound mark ... a very strong fellow. When Choynski stood along side of him, he looked like a mere boy. Joe was deeply interested in an article he was reading in the paper, when the backer of the big dock laborer ... wanted to know if Joe would meet his man. Choynski looked up in an unconcerned way and said, 'Sure, if he will bet enough money.' The backer ... After making the rounds ... on the docks, managed to scrape up $300 ... and the fight was arranged. Six carriages took the party out into the country from Portland, and Joe and the big fellow went at it on the turf. Near the end of the 9th round, Joe landed one of those awful jabs, which I remember well ... which ... Fitzsimmons and ... Jeffries will ... vouch for, and the big stevedore went down like a ton of brick. The fight was over, and Joe pocketed the money, and upon returning to the club, picked up the paper and continued to read where he had left off."[14] Jim didn't name the "dock laborer," but the match occurred in early 1890.

An item by Joe in the March 30, 1905 *Chicago Daily Tribune*, read: "Lost: Brown Eskimo Dog. Reward. Jas. (sic) B. Choynski, 117 Madison-av., La Grange, Ill." Whether he located the lost pet isn't known. Sam Austin of the *Police Gazette*, acknowledged Joe's retirement, on April 1: "Joe Choynski has enjoyed as many farewells as Patti; we have chronicled his retirement before, many times and oft; but it looks as if the end were at hand, and the popular big fighter quit the game. A match between Choynski and George Cole was on the tapis recently, and it looked as if ... we would have the pleasure of seeing a good bout between (Joe) and the clever colored middleweight. Now ... Jack Diamond, the Chicago handler of boxers, who has made a host of friends since he located in Philadelphia, got a letter ... from Choynski, saying he could not see ... boxing Cole. Joe ... believed his days in the ring were over, as he had a chance for a good position ... with a Colorado mining corporation ... had practically accepted ... and would have to renounce his former profession ... it was unlikely he would ever don the gloves again, except in a friendly bout. Choynski leaves the ring with a stainless record ... has made an army of friends all over the country. It is safe to say there was never a suspicion of crookedness or underhanded work in all of (his) contests ... Joe was always out to win if he could, and when he was beaten, the man who bet on him always had the satisfaction of knowing he got a full return for his money ..."

April 2 *Los Angeles Times*: "Joe Choynski, the 'trial horse' of champions, announces his retirement from the hit-and-get-away game. Choynski's friends and admirers run into the thousands, and all will wish him success in his new vocation of traveling salesman." Either Joe reconsidered the mining position, or it fell through. The same day's *Fort Worth Star-Telegram* wrote: "A friend of Joe Choynski ... in Philadelphia recently, received word from (Joe) ... that he had retired ... his battles are fresh in the mind of every fan ... the world, for where is the shore on which Joe has not set foot? It was Joe who came nearest to getting the scalp of Jeffries." It was clear that papers around the nation were accepting and validating Joe's final departure from active ring combat. They were chiming in from all directions, praising him as one of the best and most honest glove fighters of all time.

Now, however, there came aspersions of scandalous activity having taken place in the two Choynski-Burley fights in Dawson. Several papers quoted an undated *Seattle Times* article, that said Jack "Twin" Sullivan would be fighting Burley in Dawson shortly (Sullivan knocked out Nick in the 2nd round in Nome, Alaska on May 24). "Sullivan ought to make easy work of Burley, who cannot hit hard enough to dent a dab of butter ... if he does he will clean up ... for 5th-rater, as the Sound sports know Burley to be, he has a great reputation in Alaska, and never has any trouble in getting backing. Perhaps this will be a repetition of the two fights ... with Choynski ... in which the two men cleaned up a satchel full of gold. Burley knocked Choyniski (sic) out in jig in their first battle, 'as previously arranged,' as the Japs have it ... there was a talkfest of several weeks, while the 2nd match was ... arranged. Burley got so chesty because he had whipped Choynski that the old timer got a bit sore ... he chopped Burley's countenance up until it looked like a Hamburg steak, and won as he pleased. There are still sports in Dawson who will say the fights were on the square. The 2nd one probably was, for Joe was sore and knew there was no more money in sight. But that first fight – fudge!" The allegations, if true, were never proven, and those attending the fights raised little or no stink at the time.[15]

An April 13 New Zealand paper paid tribute: "There are many representatives of the Hebraic race (says the *Boston 'Police News'*) who have gained renown ... In pugilism, we have had, it must be confessed, a paucity of prominent boxers ... The grandest Hebrew performer in the ring was undoubtedly Joe Choynski, although ancient history tells us of the desperate battles Dan Mendoza was wont to indulge in ... Choynski proved of great moment in establishing the worth of the Hebrew as a pugilist. He always had the worst of the weight, and conquered more by gameness than any other attribute. Choynski would talk from the ring after a fight, but does not do so now, because, he says, he is growing old."[16]

Joe, in his new occupation as a "commercial traveler" for a Chicago felt goods company, was at the Hotel Racine in Racine, Wisconsin on the evening of June 6. He said, with high-sounding words: "Never again will I consent to taking a pounding and beating to make an American holiday. There is nothing in fighting ... financially or any other way. I suppose I must have made considerable money in my career, but that doesn't get me anything now. I can't lay my hands on a penny of it at the present ... However, I find the prominence I gained through pugilistic efforts helps me to some extent in selling goods." For Joe to have made so much capital from boxing, then say, "there is nothing in it," was an early display of the bitterness he felt at times, at the sport by which he made his name. He was also contradicting recent statements that he had saved $40,000 from his ring years. That weekend, Joe visited friends in Janesville, Wisconsin. On July 4, he was a guest at a San Francisco brokers convention at Tonopah, Nevada.[17]

Joe Choynski, 1905

Choynski's brother, Herbert, was the defense attorney for Ed Graney. "The Honest Blacksmith" was suing the city of San Francisco for $2,171.75, owed for horseshoeing the Fire Department's horses from August to December of 1904. During the hearing, the City Attorney said "bids for shoeing were so advertised as to preclude everyone except Graney from accepting the contract." This, Herbert denied.[18] He won the case and Ed was paid, but the latter's position as farrier was soon terminated.

"Colonel" Choynski had a pair of automobile mishaps soon after the case. On August 17, while taking a party of friends for a moonlight ride in his "horseless carriage," on the road between Fairfax and San Anselmo, the right front tire exploded. The vehicle careened and flipped, throwing the party onto the roadway. Luckily, they sustained only slight injuries. Also that month, Herbert was arrested for driving at a "dizzying speed ... exceeding four miles per hour," in Ross, California, about 18 miles north of San Francisco.[19] On October 5, he was back in court, defending boxing promoter "Sunny Jim" Coffroth, Jimmy Britt, Willus Britt and the Moto-Photo motion picture company. World lightweight champion, Oscar

"Battling" Nelson, charged the former with defrauding him out of his cut of (film) profits from his September 9 title bout with Jimmy Britt. Herbert's counterpart for the prosecution was the flashy-dressing, flamboyant attorney, Charles M. Shortridge. October 5 *San Francisco Call*: "Choynski ... looked with alarm upon the array of opposing counsel, but, as a brother of the once great Joe Choynski ... is prepared to fight to the knockout."

An August *Police Gazette*: "In all probability, Joe Choynski's popularity will remain intact as long as he lives. Choynski is a member of several lodges, a thorough family man, and admits he is a fighter simply for the money ... one of the few pugilists who can command ready cash at any time. He is the first ... to give his opponent all the credit in defeat, and just as accessible to strangers as to friends." Joe was back in Janesville on the evening of October 20, conducting business for the Western Felt Company. The *Police Gazette* described his job with the Chicago firm as "handling a line of tailor's trimmings."[20] The October 22 *Waterloo Times* wrote of forgotten heavyweight, Frank (or Phil) Mayo. It claimed Mayo once replaced Joe as sparring partner for Peter Jackson. The paper may have meant Will Mayo, who sparred Joe in November, 1895. Frank Mayo was a physical instructor in Iowa at the time of the piece, earlier a noted boxer, with wins over "Yank" Kenny, Frank Craig and Dan Creedon. "The last fight of real importance Mayo engaged in was a 17 round draw with Joe Choynski. Since ... he has been athletic instructor in various gymnasiums and Y.M.C. associations." Nowhere else is a bout with Frank Mayo mentioned.

The February 15, 1906 *New York Tribune* told of famed whaling Captain George Fred Tilton, making a cruise to the North Pole in a steam brig. Tilton, of New Bedford, Massachusetts, had won fame and glory in the winter of 1898, when he purportedly traversed 2,600 miles of Alaskan wilderness on foot! His whaling ship, the *Belvedere*, had become imprisoned in ice off the shore of Alaska, prompting Tilton's six-month trek across the state, to fetch a rescue party for his crew. Allegedly, the Captain tried more than once to reach the North Pole; most recently in 1904, when his steam whaler lost its propeller, entering the Arctic. The determined Tilton used the ship's sails to buck its way through the ice pack, returning with "a rich cargo of oil and bone ... another story his friends like to tell of the doughty skipper is ... his rough and tumble victory over ... Joe Choynski. A company of whalemen were lined up along the bar of a San Francisco saloon, when a big, brute of a man under the influence of liquor swept all the glasses off the bar. 'Fill them again,' said Captain Tilton, approaching the stranger. The latter was about to repeat the performance when Tilton picked him off the floor and flung him on his back. Choynski, as the sailors afterward found the man to be, took the full count." This is quite a fish story. Many have posed as famous fighters, to gain notoriety and special consideration. The actions of the "Joe Choynski" of the Tilton tilt are contrary to that of the historical Joe. If he did engage in the fracas, Joe would have been inebriated to the point where the Captain's "feat" was rendered effete.

1927 *American Mercury Magazine*: "As a symbol of its former glory, (New Bedford) maintains at one of its deserted wharves, an authentic whaler, fully equipped and captained by George Fred Tilton, last of the buccaneers. Captain Tilton, a great bull of a man ... for all his years, with enormous hands, a massive head, and a booming laugh that can be heard as far as Nantucket, is ... a legendary hero. Besides ... the most fearless whaling skipper who ever sailed out of New Bedford, he is reputed to have walked 1,000 miles in the Far North to obtain relief for shipwrecked companions, to have broken Joe Choynski's jaw in a fight over a girl in a San Francisco dance-hall, and, during the late war ... as commander of a barge ... carrying ... explosives to and from ... near New York City."[21] *If* Tilton made his way across 2,600 (or 1,000) miles of Alaskan Tundra over a six-month period, with no assistance, supplies or shelter, it puts to shame modern survivalists, "Survivorman" Les Stroud and Edward Michael "Bear" Grylls.

In March, 1906, Herbert Choynski served as counsel for "the fight trust," Ed Graney, Billy Roche, James Coffroth, Willus Britt and Mark Shaughnessy, as well as the Yosemite Club. The aforementioned were brought up on charges in the death of boxer Harry Tenny (real name Sam Tennenbaum). The latter died after being knocked out by bantamweight champion Frankie Neil, in San Francisco's Mechanics' Pavilion on February 28. Graney was president of the Associated Athletic Clubs, under whose auspices the fight occurred. A Coroner's jury determined Tenny's death the result of gross negligence. The fighters had not been examined prior to the bout by "a regularly registered physician," as required by law. "Spider" Kelly, Tim McGrath, Frankie Neil and his manager-father, James Neil, were represented by attorney R. Porter Ashe, the same politician, gambler and sportsman who was a former backer of Jim Corbett. Ultimately, all charges were dismissed. The next time Joe's barrister brother and his friend, Ed Graney, were involved together in court, it would be on opposite sides.

The Great Quake and Fire, a City Laid Waste

At about 5:12 a.m. on April 18, 1906, a massive shift in the San Andreas Fault caused a violent earthquake in San Francisco. It measured a magnitude of about 8.0 on today's Richter scale, among the most powerful in recorded history. Buildings crumbled, streets were rent asunder and gas lines in various parts of the metropolis ruptured, causing a fire of immense scope. Modern estimates of the death toll are generally in excess of 3,000 persons. Miriam Choynski recalled stepping outside the family residence at 1209 Golden Gate Avenue in the morning, and seeing the fronts of neighborhood houses crumbled. The Choynski home was damaged to the extent that they relocated shortly afterward, to 1679 Oak Street. The amount of damage isn't known, but only two months later, on June 19, a Joseph D. Bell is shown living at the 1209 address. By 1909, the widowed Harriett and Edwin were living at 61 6th Avenue.[22]

Among the many buildings destroyed in the disaster were the Palace Hotel, the *Chronicle, Examiner* and *Call* buildings, the Orpheum Theater, Columbia Theatre (formerly Stockwell's Theatre), City Hall and the Hall of Records. Mechanics' Pavilion was converted into an emergency hospital and the Presidio became a tent city.[23] One of the few large buildings to remain standing was Temple Sherith Israel. Joe was living in Chicago at this time, and any comments he had on the event have not been found. The *San Francisco Chronicle* managed to get out an edition on April 30, publishing an article by Waldemar Young. It included a short poem, which told of the crumbling of the Tenderloin, or "Red Light" district.

Young wondered what became of the fight crowd, such as Harry Corbett and Jimmy Coffroth: "I did see Eddie Graney ... at his blacksmith's shop, an improvised frame structure at the foot of Van Ness Avenue. The map of the city has so changed within the past 10 days ... he didn't seem out of place ... Eddie's smiling face appeared at the door. 'Want a job shoeing horses?' was his greeting ... we fell to talking of the fight trust ... He was as cheerful as ever ... though his biggest asset, the Belvedere, is ... nothing but crumbled walls and unrecognizable debris. Harry Corbett's place ... for years the headquarters of fight fans, is level with the ground. No more will a choice bunch gather ... and discuss great fighters past and present ... The old scales, which have weighed more great pugilists than any dozen other scales in the world, are gone with the place."

On May 14, it was reported that "Little Joe" would be helping to train newly-crowned heavyweight champion, Tommy Burns. Burns, a Canadian (real name Noah Brusso), had lifted the disputed heavyweight title from Marvin Hart on February 23 at Los Angeles, on a 20 round decision. Tommy, who only stood about 5' 7" but weighed some 175-180 pounds, was a very good boxer-puncher. He was scheduled to face old Bob Fitzsimmons on Memorial Day at the Tuxedo Club, near Philadelphia. Burns had been training on a farm at Waukegan, Illinois, but was soon to depart for Chicago. While there, the champion was to "work with Choynski and Klondike, taking the latter East with him."[24]

The proximity to boxing activity evidently stirred the coals and lit a fire under Joe, as he expressed the desire to get back in the ring. *Kansas City Star*: "Joe Choynski ... living quietly at his farm ... for some ... time past, felt the old fever return recently, and straightaway declared he was feeling as young as ever and could whip 'em all, especially Jack Root. Jack is willing, but no match has yet been made." A Maine paper took a dimmer view, saying, "Joe ... does not like to be classed as a 'has been,' and he is out with a challenge to ... Root ... sports do not take the challenge seriously. They figure old Joe is taking that means to keep his name before the public."[25]

In the last week of June, Joe wrote a letter to the Indianapolis Athletic Club, requesting a fight with one of the young lions. Those he wanted to meet were Young Mahoney, Hugo Kelly and Dave Barry, the last two being formidable opponents. He was not seeking soft touches. Joe also wrote the *Police Gazette*, saying he had been keeping in shape and would "shortly don the mitts again." This time, the prospective foes named were Al Kaufman, "Philadelphia" Jack O'Brien and Jack Root. Joe was reported on July 29 as saying he was looking for a fight with anyone, not "particular who gives it to him. He says he is stronger than ever, has lost none of his ring generalship or hitting powers, and if any of the fighters in his division doubt him, they can have a match on a winner-take-all basis any time ..."[26]

On August 8, Herbert Choynski married Ethel Berger. The wedding took place at Tait's Café in San Francisco, at the corner of Van Ness Avenue and Eddy Street. As Ethel was the older sibling of Sam Berger, it was a case of "a pug's brother wedding a pug's sister." It was a mostly private affair, though "a wedding of unusual interest." The groom was famous boxing promoter, James W. Coffroth. In attendance were Harriett, Edwin and Maurice (referred to as Chauncey Choynski of Pittsburgh), Maurice's wife, Sarah, Nat and Maurice Berger. Joe wasn't able to attend. Soon after, Herbert was nominated in local primaries as a Democratic delegate for Congress, although he wasn't elected.[27]

The September 29 *Racine Daily Journal* claimed that Bob Fitzsimmons and Joe had finally made amends, or "kissed and made up." "The pair of old timers have been on the outs since their scrap at Boston in 1894, but ... according to what happened yesterday, they are as warm friends as ever." No further details were given, and exactly "what happened yesterday" may never be known, but Joe never truly forgave Fitz for the slights he received at his hands, nor the fact that Bob never gave him a rematch.

Around this time, Herbert became involved in the Abe Ruef scandal. Ruef (born Abraham Rueff), was a corrupt lawyer and political boss during the administration of San Francisco mayor, Eugene Schmitz. The October 14 *Oakland Tribune* declared: "Choynski ... is a mustang politician. He bucks in and out of all parties. He used to do politics with McNab, then with the Horses and Carts, with a little Republican business on the side. More latterly he has been training under Ruef's banner, but has revolted ... because Ruef took a fat fee that Choynski wanted. Ruef has a way of taking fat fees ... Choynski ... says Ruef's ancestors didn't drown when Christ chased the swine into the sea. The Colonel ... charges ... that Ruef gave certain Supervisors $4,000 apiece to vote for Pat Calhoun's trolley ordinance ... (that) Schmitz and Ruef equally divided $500,000."

The Belvedere Dance Hall, located on O'Farrell Street, had Herbert,

Graney and Jimmy Coffroth among its original stockholders. Herbert believed it would become as successful as Hammerstein's Olympia in New York. Upon discovering this was not the case, he sold his interest in it. Later, Ruef tried to shake down owners of the Belvedere "for ¼ of the earnings and stock ... to hold it immune from police interference ..." Even after a fire burned down the building, Ruef tried to secure ¼ of the $15,000 in insurance money. This is when the courts became involved, and the Grand Jury summoned Coffroth, Graney and Herbert to testify.

On November 21, "All ... witnesses ... claimed if such payment was made, it was done by Eddie Graney. This attempt to place the entire responsibility (on) Graney has warmed his wrath to white heat ... Belvedere was run in violation of city ordinances ... to safeguard public morality ... to conduct such a resort, it was necessary ... to pay Ruef. ... to keep Graney from testifying ... The boss detailed Henry Ach, chief counsel, and a detective to hold close to Graney until the horseshoer enters the jury room ... today." Graney wanted to "spill the beans" and avoid the penitentiary, so he ultimately gave evidence against Abe. Herbert said the 25 per cent had been set aside from the beginning "as promotion stock ... to be used in some way to help the company," specifically, to bribe Abe Ruef.

Probably the most heinous example of Ruef's corruption was his collusion with Mayor Eugene Schmitz, in the refusal to grant the Fire Department the city-wide pumping system they requested. City Fire Chief Dennis Sullivan lobbied hard for a system to pump salt water from the Bay to combat fires. He also requested more fireboats, and for the 57 massive cisterns beneath the city to be filled with water. Had he received these things, most of San Francisco likely would have survived the conflagration that followed the earthquake of 1906. What he got was an administration that took bribes from contractors who wanted to fill the cisterns with construction debris. They undercut the fire-fighting budget, supplying minimal resources and pocketing the "surplus" money.

Graney clearly feared Ruef, as on November 26, he was reported to be retracting his testimony. On the one hand, there was the threat of perjury charges and worse, if he recanted; on the other, the wrath of Ruef. The December 4 *Call* revealed that, once good friends, Herbert and Ed were now embittered enemies. "Herbert: 'Because I told the truth to the grand jury, Graney has been running around town, telling everyone he will put it onto me. I know a few things about Graney. I have been doing his legal work for six years and he has been in trouble most of the time; but ... I never got a cent from him. I am going to sue him for an accounting ... The facts ... will show that his title of the 'honest blacksmith' is one he never won. He is the crookedest man that ever refereed a prizefight. He has been crooked in fights my brother has been in." What part of these allegations might have been a manifestation of Herbert's anger, is unknown. Graney never established a reputation for crookedness. It must be said, as well, that, although Herbert could be a hard man with a sometimes caustic nature, he was not known as a teller of tales. On December 29, he filed a $6,000 suit against Ed, for legal fees. "The suit ... will establish ... the extent of Graney's holdings in the Tuxedo, the saloon at Fillmore and O'Farrell ..."[28]

Joe (1927): "I finally realized the end had come ... I quit fighting forever. Do I regret it all? Well, if I had to do it over again I doubt if I would choose fighting as a profession." He would have. "But I had a wonderful time. I saw the world. I knew the greatest athletes the human race has produced. The number of men who have fallen under my blows must run into hundreds. I am sure no other ... has knocked out so many. John L. Sullivan ... made them spin cartwheels when he landed, but nowhere near so much as I. Fitzsimmons? A marvelous knockout artist ... but his ... record is meager, compared to mine." (1930): "I wish to make full acknowledgement of the defeats as well as victories. No human being who went to the wars as often as I ... could hope to return without a few defeats. But if you scan ... my 18 years of fighting, I think you will be amazed at the results. There are few decisive upsets ... against my record, and these came in the twilight of a tempestuous career. And now, my merry gentlemen, the wars are over and the old gladiator withdraws from the scene of the carnage. It was a jolly old joust, this hectic business of meeting and clouting the hard heads of the iron men of the ring, but it is ended and I am glad. The gong may clang, but not for me. Let the young men go forth to battle."

Late IBRO member, Mike Paul, developed a system of rating fighters on a month-by-month and year-by-year basis. He graded a boxer's results, both on the caliber of opponents and margin of victory. Based on this, Joe Choynski, not even a true heavyweight, was rated in the top 10 of that division an amazing 13 straight years, from March, 1890 through February, 1903! He was the number three-ranked heavyweight in 1892, 1893 and 1894, holding the number two spot for a few months.

On December 28, it was announced that Joe had been appointed boxing and athletic instructor for Chicago's new Illinois Athletic Club. Its directors chose him over several other "veterans of the prize ring." Joe's duties were to begin when the club opened its doors in the Spring of 1907. His salary would be a tidy $5,000 per year. The *Salt Lake Evening Telegram* joked, "How the mighty have fallen!" The cost of the 12-storey club was about $500,000. The gymnasium was located on the 10th and 11th floors, encircled by a running track. The boxing, wrestling and fencing rooms were on the 7th floor, where Joe would instruct his pupils. There were racquetball, handball courts and bowling alleys. The natatorium, or swimming facilities, occupied most of the cellar, basement and 1st floor. Swimmer Johnny Weissmuller joined in 1920. He won three gold medals in the 1924 Olympics, and two more in 1928. He later starred as Tarzan in several films.[29]

In early 1907, "Philadelphia" Jack O'Brien was to travel to Australia and take on that country's top heavyweight, Bill Squires. He pulled out at the "11th hour," saying Australians "appeared to regard professional athletes as little better than rogues and vagabonds," and so, he would remain at home. He was castigated for it. Joe wrote the *Sydney Referee*: "O'Brien's cable is ... of a disordered brain, due to 'Nouveux Rich,' which is prevalent in this hemisphere. A few years ago O'Brien was driving a sand waggon in Philadelphia. ... he is to be commended for his rise, but has no claims to aristocracy. He struts around and puts on airs like one to the 'manner born.' I suppose ... in this age of commercialism the public demands it. He apes all the manners of a gentleman, and is much cut up if ... not recognized as such; But, I found long ago that a pugilist is a pugilist. I never claimed anything else; people can take me as they find me, and had I ... to begin life over again, my decision would be the same. O'Brien's ... attack on sports and athletes is from the end of his tongue ... not borne out by facts. Australia treated me like a native, and ... I never should forget it."[30]

Around May 1, it was announced that the Illinois A.C. planned to stage its first boxing programme, a four-day tournament, from June 15 through 19. The bouts were to be six-rounders, and Joe was to box "Philadelphia" Jack O'Brien. Mayor Busse of Chicago, however, said he would not tolerate boxing matches in the Windy City.[31] June 13 *Pawtucket Times*: "Choynski is boxing instructor of the new Illinois A. C. ... has made many new friends since filling the position. Joe will meet Jack Root ... at the ... club ... the latter part of this month." This match also failed to occur.

On July 29, Herbert Choynski requested a warrant for the arrest of Bernardo Yerba Shorb, a "young society man, on a charge of obtaining by false pretenses a locomobile from the General motor company, in which he went on his wedding tour." R.P. Troy, representing Shorb, said, " 'Didn't you tell me last Saturday ... if you were paid $500 you would drop the matter?' 'That's a deliberate lie,' retorted Choynski. 'I did nothing of the kind.' 'I say you tell a deliberate lie,' angrily shouted Troy. 'You are a loud mouthed faker. All you want is your pound of flesh and you think nothing of humiliating this young man by having him arrested. I warn you that you will render yourself liable for damages.' 'I don't want any advice from you,' shouted Choynski, 'and I am ready to back up my reputation, physically or otherwise, whenever you feel inclined.' The judge called a halt ..." The Choynski males were no strangers to combative situations.

This was further proven on October 17. *San Francisco Call*: "The dogs of war were unleashed in automobile row yesterday when ... Herbert Choynski ... settle(d) ... differences with former associates in the General motor car company. Some time ago, 'Billy' Harrington severed ... with the ... company ... accompanied by Chief Mechanic Miller ... The Colonel, while driving down Golden Gate Avenue ... with Bernard Shorb as his chauffeur (he had evidently forgiven Shorb) ... seeing Miller ... alighted from his car and ... asked him what he had done with some tools he had stolen from the ... company. For a moment, the men gazed at each other and then clinched ... fell to the ground, Miller breaking loose ... running around a pile of debris, with the Colonel in hot pursuit. Farther down the avenue, the Colonel met Harrington ... asking him about a voucher for $35 for an expense account of a year ago. Words flew, curses followed and Harrington started the fun by lashing out a straight left, which fell plumb on the Colonel's proboscis, drawing the claret. The Colonel, still game, let fly a right ... on Harrington's left ear, giving it the appearance of a cauliflower. Harrington came back with a straight jab ... hitting the Colonel's left eyebrow, cutting the flesh ... friends and spectators parted the combatants."[32]

On August 10, Joe was at the old Polo Grounds in Upper Manhattan, taking part in the annual Charity Field Day, to benefit the Home for Destitute Crippled Children. A crowd of about 5,000 witnessed, first, a baseball game between managers and actors, including George Cohan and Jim Corbett. Following a 100-yard dash for theatrical agents and a chase after a greased pig, "A pie-eating contest for colored gentleman resulted in a dead heat. Boxing bouts came next, each of three one minute rounds." Among those participating were Jack Johnson, Bob Fitzsimmons, Tommy West, George Dixon vs. Terry McGovern, Mike Donovan against Ed Dunkhorst and Joe Choynski swapping punches with "Young" Griffo. "A battle royal among eight colored gentlemen ..." and "a serious ball game between Cohan's Yankee Doodle team and the Comedy Club team ... The cowboys and Indians from the Wild West show at Brighton Beach ... gave exhibitions of fancy riding and ... throwing lassooes (sic) ..."[33]

Joe: "Hitting is a knack that perhaps must be born in a man. Few ever acquire it, even with diligent years of practice. I could hit as hard when a mere boy as I can today ... To hit correctly ... there must be a ... stiffening of the muscles ... The entire frame must be rigid just at the moment the punch lands." "My best blow would be hard to pick out ... when I saw a proper opening, I used my left hook with deadly effect. However, variety is the spice of the business ... on stage or in the ring. When ... an opponent was anticipating that left, I surprised him with a corking right. Speed, an essential overlooked by many, was one of the things I cultivated. In addition to being strong, I was naturally fast, and I made it my business to improve these gifts. I always tried to see how quickly I could hit and then withdraw my hand. It does not require so much speed if you learn to time an opponent's punches, then beat him to it. But this calls for gameness. One must be prepared to take it ... I dropped many big men with one punch ... due to my speed and the shortness of the blow. The farther the ... punch travels the less ... weight it carries. But my knuckles always hit squarely. I learned *how* to hit ... Nothing less will suffice ..."[34]

Joe was to participate in a testimonial for George Siler, on September 21 at the Coliseum in Chicago. Also listed were Abe Attell, Jimmy Barry, Tommy Ryan, Jack Root and George Shrosbree. It is not confirmed if the programme took place.[35] Meanwhile, Joe had been filmed boxing a five round, friendly match with pugilist Harry Gilmore of Chicago. The cinematic short is first mentioned being shown in Anaconda, Montana, on or about February 7, 1907, at the American Theater. It was called "The Hoosier Fighter": "In this remarkably good film, we present the celebrated, all-around (sic) favorite in the pugilistic world, Joe Choynski. In the title role of a nicely arranged story ... Mr. Choynski ... is seen in a fast and rapid five-round contest, with Harry Gilmore ... not altogether a prize fight film ... there is a beautiful story of heartfelt interest ... through the whole subject, something that will interest every one. Price ... 10 Cents." The film was shown again the week of April 15, at Priester's Amusement Park, White City, Belleville, Illinois. The brief advertisement said, "Kinodrome Moving Pictures: Hoosier Prize Fight – Joe Choynski and Harry Gilmore."[36] The footage of this five round spar does not appear to have survived.

The February 28 *Anaconda Standard* noted: "Jim Jeffries ... (Bob) Fitzsimmons ... Jack Johnson ... All the big fighters say Choynski had the hardest punch." Johnson told the *San Francisco Bulletin*: "Was I ever soaked? My goodness, that man, Choynski, caught me ... and I thought he opened the top of my head. He hit me on the forehead over my right eye, blackened that eye and almost broke the jaw on the other side. My golly, he simply knocked the brains, wind and ambition out of me. I don't think anyone in the world was ever hit so hard. That Choynski boy was the hardest hitter that ever lived, bar none. There's no use bluffing about not being licked, like a lot of these fellows do."[37]

Joe wrote an article on the value of body punching, and compared John L. Sullivan to Jeffries. March 22 *Los Angeles Herald*: "I have sparred with ... both ... seen both fight. Jeff is stronger, much cleverer, and fully as game. In Sullivan's time, the big men he met were cowards – Cardiff, Ryan, Slade and the rest. Sullivan had a hard time with the little men who were clever – Mitchell, Burke and Tug Wilson." Joe was mostly referring to an aging Sullivan, but his words disparage John to the point where one suspects he was retaliating, for some of the unkind things an old, bitter "Strong Boy" had said about Joe and his contemporaries. Joe: "When Jeff went east on his first visit (to New York) he was coached wrong – bent over – and all he could do was swing his left hand. That stooping posture indulged in by our present-day men is only good for short-arm work. You can't lead a straight punch. When Jeff fought Corbett in San Francisco – also Fritz (sic) – he stood straight up, and they didn't last long."

"Sullivan's favorite blow ... not generally known, was a right swing between the shoulder blades ... not on the jaw ... men ... were afraid of him and resorted to clinching ... John would ... punch them in the back – a very effective blow (author: illegal, however) ... that 'back lung' punch. In ... Boston, he rushed 'Prof. Donovan' and clubbed him across the back so hard Donovan was knocked flat ... on his face, breaking his nose and knocking him out. Fitzsimmons probably was the greatest of the body punchers. While meeting all comers, he was advised to use body blows ... he hit so hard he was apt to kill some untrained man with a smash to the chin. He developed the 'solar plexus' punch ... used it to win all his big fights ... he had an original knack of landing it. Tom Sharkey flailed away in all directions, but it was ... a body blow that nearly broke McCoy in two ... Jeffries ... studying Fitz ... became a terrible body puncher. He knocked Corbett out ... with a body blow. He hammered Sharkey in the ribs until he cracked them ... Sharkey never entirely recovered ... was never able to take so much body punishment afterward ... with a long left, almost straight body punch ... Jeffries beat Fitz in their last ... fight. Jeff is naturally left handed, and can control that left arm ... like a fencer using a foil."

Old John L. had "a few jolts for Buttinski Joe Choynski" in short order: "Joe ... says that all of the big men I fought were cowards. I'm not going to stand for anybody calling good men like Ryan and the rest a gang of cowards ... I'd like to know who filled Choynski with the punk information he's getting out of his system, now that a lot of them are dead and can't talk back. I admit some of the men I fought were afraid of me ... but they had the sand to go against what was coming, and that isn't cowardice. A man who would get into a ring in the bare knuckle days, when he had to fight off blackjacks in the hands of thugs at ringside, take a chance of getting done up before he got out of the woods, if the cops didn't get him ... was anything but a coward. If Mr. Choynski will pardon me ... I beg to differ, and if he won't ... I'll jam it down his yawp just the same ... any fighter that got a hearing in my time had to have sand to burn ... men who tried for my title when I was good, were fit to fight to the limit, and ... did it like men ... any Jo-Jo ... tries to splash them with mud for the sake of saying something that looks smart, can have me to argue the question any way he wants. Buttinski Choynski never would have taken a chance of telling any of (them) they were cowards, and he's no coward at that."

On April 11 in Colma, California, great Chicago lightweight, "Packey" McFarland, knocked out former lightweight champion, Jimmy Britt, in six rounds. McFarland dominated, flooring Britt three times in the final frame and putting him to sleep with a succession of straight, right hands. Afterward, "Packey" said, "I owe a lot to Harry Gilmore and Joe Choynski for what they have done in teaching me the game."[38]

August 28 *Des Moines Daily News*: "That awful Mr. Anthony J. Drexel Biddle of Biddle-delphia. Ever since Tony got himself knocked out by Mr. Faking John O'Brien ("Philadelphia" Jack) ... (he) wants to ... beat up everybody ... another rich fellow ... wants to fight him, for the Boodleweight championship of the world ... George Lytton of Chicago ... described as social leader and millionaire secretary of the Illinois Athletic Club. He is said to carry a punch as big as a coal-scuttle in each fist, and ... such a ... polite way of delivering ... that no gentleman ... could possibly take offense at being jarred into somnolence. Lytton has boxed with Joe Choynski, and alleged to have jolted Mr. Choynski severely ... now he has challenged T. Hyphen Biddle. Gee! Think of blue, millionaire blood squirting around like mixed-ale gore! But maybe they won't fight. Lytton's fighting weight is about 200 pounds, Biddle's only 175. Mrs. Biddle ... an ... admirer of her husband's fistic prowess, will probably hear about this ... will she let ... Tony ... go up against that 200-pound Mr. Lytton? Not if she is the careful lady we think her to be." Lytton pops up again in Chapter 26.

A September 9 article called Daniel Mendoza, the English-born pugilist of Spanish-Jewish descent, the first Hebrew fighter to win a world championship. More accurately, he has been recognized as the Champion of England, as close to a "world" champion as there was in that era. Daniel was probably the best "knuckle fighter" in England from 1792 to 1795, despite standing only 5' 7" and weighing but 160 pounds. He was a highly skilled and elusive boxer with great endurance, defeating much larger men by evading their blows, and landing straight lefts and counterpunches. He became a celebrated figure, and is today a legend. Lightweight bareknuckler, "Dutch Sam" (born Samuel Elias), an overlapping contemporary of his, was considered the next great Jewish boxer. "In the first half of the last century, prize fighting decayed. When it came to the front again ... under ... Queensberry rules, another Jew soon attracted attention ... Joe Choynski, who just missed being champion more times than any fighter that ever lived. Choynski, like Mendoza, was a little too small to beat a Jeffries, and lost many tough fights by an eyelash."[39] Saying that Joe "just missed being champion" is misleading. One must be granted a title shot to win a title, and I feel he was the first world light-heavyweight champion.

Mendoza was born in London around 1765 and died in 1836. With the dexterity of his fists, he helped dispel some of the negative stereotypes of his people in England. Like many prominent bareknucklers, Daniel opened a boxing academy, instructing pupils in the art and science of fisticuffs. Due to his success and popularity, youths in the Jewish community began to develop boxing skills, resulting in less abuse among their number. Mendoza wore his hair long, as Choynski sometimes did. This led to Daniel's defeat in 1795 against "Gentleman" John Jackson. The latter ungentlemanly grabbed Mendoza's locks with one hand and pummeled him into oblivion with the other. While not technically illegal, the tactic was looked upon with disdain. Choynski is the next great "heavyweight" in the lineage of Jewish pugilists, and the first great American fighting Jew.[40]

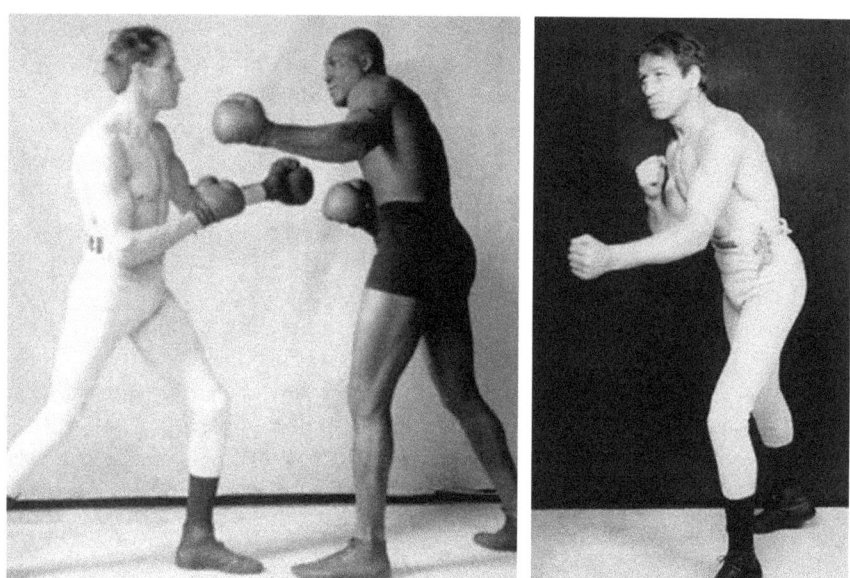

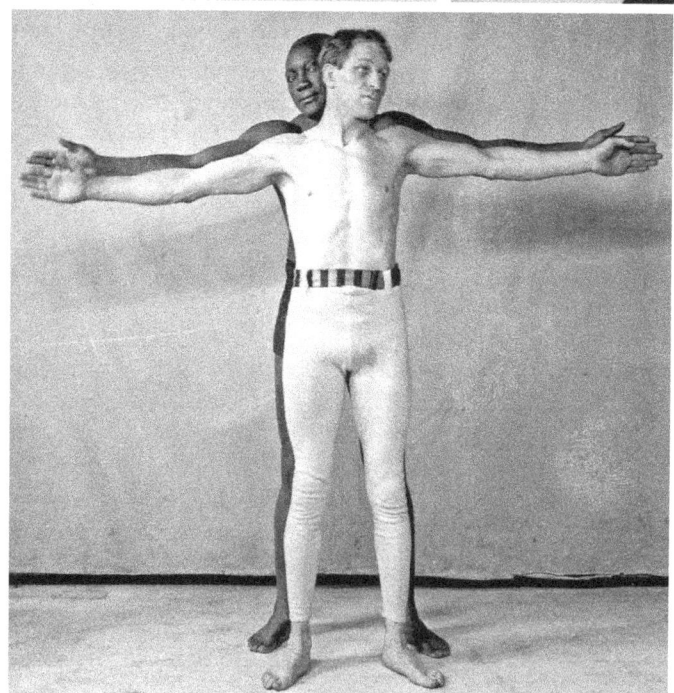

Joe Choynski and Jack Johnson, Chicago, 1909

In October, Joe opened a "physical culture emporium" in downtown Chicago, as co-proprietor with a William Gelder. The address was 185 Dearborn Street, Room 214, although it wasn't specified North or South

Dearborn. If the former, Joe's facility was located on the bank of the Chicago River, near Wolf Point. The latter would place it about eight blocks south, in the Loop area of Chi-Town. September 12 *Chicago Tribune*: "School of Physical culture – Baths – Joe Choynski, an athlete for 25 years – and still at it." Joe's brother, Maurice, moved from Pittsburgh to Chicago in January, 1906, establishing the Windy City's 2nd nickelodeon theater.* In 1907, he operated the Halsted Theater (181 S. Halsted Street) and another at 607 Blue Island Avenue. By 1910, only one, at 318 South Halsted.[41]

* The 1905 and 1907 Pittsburgh City Directories give his final business listing there only as, "amusements, 330 Diamond Bell."

On November 8, Joe celebrated his 40th birthday. A Chicago paper wrote that he wanted to celebrate it "in a most peculiar manner," by climbing back in the ring and showing up "the Burnses and Johnsons and Kaufmans." Choynski felt that present day fighters would be fodder for him, and that "a growl from a really, truly fighter of the old guard" would make them run for cover. Joe was still boxing instructor at the Illinois Athletic Club, and claimed to be in as fine condition as ever. One publication said he, having reached the 40th milestone, wished to take on the winner of the Burns-Johnson heavyweight championship fight. " 'I'll meet anybody in the ring today,' said Joe, as he did a little shadow boxing, and seemed as nimble on his feet as he was 10 or 15 years ago."[42]

On the final day of 1908, it was announced that Joe was chosen to referee the Marvin Hart-Mike Schreck heavyweight bout, at the Lexington, Kentucky Opera House that night. Joe received a telegram at noon from the promoter, asking if he would umpire the bout, and he immediately wired back his acceptance. He was to leave for Lexington that night. The winner was to tackle either Jack Johnson, or the victor of a Jim Barry-Al Kaufman battle.[43] It was reported on January 2, however, that the fight had been called off. *Salt Lake Evening Telegram*: "Joe Choynski, who was engaged to referee the fight, has called all bets off." The parties involved were evidently chased out of the city by "reformers."

On December 26, at Rushcutters Bay, New South Wales, Australia, Jack Johnson took the heavyweight crown from the head of Canadian, Tommy Burns, on a 14th round stoppage. The victory made Jack the first boxer of African descent to annex the championship. Earlier, Peter Jackson held the Australian and British Empire titles, but neither Sullivan nor Corbett wanted anything to do with him after they won a share of glory. A paper wrote, on January 3: "That Jack Johnson is much better than Peter Jackson ever was in his palmiest days is the belief of Joe Choynski, who was Jackson's sparring partner for years. Choynski said last evening that he believed Johnson was in a class by himself at present, and there is no hope he will ever be defeated unless James J. Jeffries returns to the ring. Choynski says the only living heavyweight ... who has a chance with

Johnson is Sam Langford." That Joe would pick Johnson over Jackson is a bit surprising, given that Peter traveled and sparred with him for so long. The reference to Jeff coming out of retirement to face Jack was a portent of things to come. Contradicting Joe was Sam Fitzpatrick, who had managed both Jackson and Johnson. That same year (1909), while still piloting "The Galveston Giant," Sam told British author Frederick Hornibrook, "Peter Jackson was the best man in the world and would have beaten Johnson. Peter was ... like a featherweight on his feet. Johnson, on the other hand, is a flat-footed boxer who makes men come to him, and ... possesses this wonderful defence. Peter's left hand would have been too quick for that defence, and he would have made Johnson come to him."[44]

Joe was evidently in a generous mood, as, on January 8, he complimented Jim Corbett: "Choynski, who was to box Marvin Hart in Lexington, Ky. ... when the owners of the opera house called off the Hart-Schreck bout, says he would have taken part only in a short exhibition, and ... has no ... intention of re-entering the ring. 'Corbett, in his day, was about the ideal boxer,' Joe said ... 'Yes, running my eye back over the entire list of the last 25 years, I can recall none better fitted to carry off the title, at least, of champion boxer. But Jim could fight, too, let me tell you. Remember that I caught him when he was young and fresh and full of ambition, and I can truthfully say that Jim always had that fighting spirit, whether it was inborn or not. He was pugnacious enough at all times ... although not at all endowed with natural physical strength or ruggedness."[45] Indeed, Corbett was the epitome of speed, agility and boxing smarts in his day.

A benefit was put on for Chicago's 7th Regiment on the night of January 20. It consisted mainly of a boxing show, but also featured a prima donna, a pie eating contest and a few wrestling matches. Despite many name fighters being involved, public turn-out was rather sparse. This was due to the insistence of Mayor Busse, that only "debrutalized sparring" would take place, with big gloves. Choynski "simply played with" his pal, George Shrosbree. In a wrestling bout, Choynski's gym partner, William Gelder, defeated Tim O'Neil in two and a half minutes, despite the latter at one point losing his temper and viciously punching Gelder in the eye. It turned out that Tim O'Neil was a boxing protégé of Joe's.[46]

Around this time, lightweight Oscar "Battling" Nelson, "The Durable Dane," told of the "left half scissors hook," that made him a champion. Nelson, whose forte was to soak up all his foes could dish out, and outlast them, said this blow, a quick hook to the top of an opponent's liver, had been taught him by Joe: "Men ... would crumple up ... in a heap. The pain is intense. Often the blow is not seen by spectators, and they have the idea the fighter ... is quitting ...' I discovered how to use this deadly punch from ... Choynski. He had a wicked habit of placing his fingers on an opponent's breast, while in the clinches ... as if to talk to him. With the tips of his fingers touching the other fellow's right nipple, he would say, 'Now, old fellow, you want to be good.' Then, before a word could be said in reply, by the mere movement of the wrist, he would plunge the heel of his right hand into the man's liver. When a man doubled up from the unexpected pain, Joe would whang him in the jaw, and the fight would be over ... I got a chart of a human body and saw ... where the liver was located. I improved on Choynski's scheme and developed the left half scissors hook ... in the early part of 1903 ... I began to use (it) with deadly effect."

December, 1912 *Pearson's* magazine: "One slow afternoon, when ... (Nelson) could not get a match with anybody, he sat in the rear room of a road house and watched Joe Choynski spar with a young heavyweight. The youngster was rougher and bigger and stronger ... it looked as if one punch ... ought to annihilate the wispy old hero of the ring. Yet, suddenly, in a manner that would be apparent ... only to those intimate with the tricks of the game, Choynski, without any seeming effort, dealt a deadly blow. The young heavyweight dropped his arms, rolled his eyes and fell to the floor, writhing in agony. He was right again in half a minute, but, for the time being, he was utterly 'out.' Nelson was powerfully impressed. He sought Choynski and begged to know the secret ... Joe taught him what, after months of practice, Nelson developed into his celebrated 'left half-scissors hook,' the blow that won him the championship and converted him from an awkward second-rater into a boxer of first-rate, 'class.' "

"First Choynski brought out an anatomy chart and taught Nelson the location of the liver. Then he showed him how to deliver a ... twisting blow on the tip of the liver. Such a blow, if placed at a moment when the abdominal muscles are relaxed, sends agonizing pains throughout the nervous system, and, if of sufficient force, will ... paralyze temporarily. The spot of its best efficacy is about half an inch under the lower right rib and two inches toward the middle from the side. The blow must be sent in ... downward from the right, so that it can only be given with the left hand. A straight blow with the back of the fist has but an ordinary effect. It must be a glancing blow with the heel of the fist, or better still, with the thumb and forefinger ... this ... verges perilously near to a violation of the rules, which prohibit 'gouging and back-heeling.' However, the liver is ... above the belt and a man ... usually places it with a swing of a few inches and a twist so that neither the referee nor ... spectators is likely to know ... whether he hit with the back or side of his glove ... Nelson found that nature had curiously equipped him for its ... delivery ... Choynski pointed out to him that his left elbow had a crook, a deflection from the normal which naturally turned his left hand in an inch or more. This may seem a trifling matter, but ... vital in the swift height of action ... when, if one turned his wrist obviously and prepared ... he would be but serving warning of his intent."[47]

While on the subject of battling Danes, the February 23 *Eau Claire*

Leader noted that "Joe Choynski, the old boy, will go on in an exhibition bout with Ed Skaring, the Fighting Dane, at an entertainment at La Grange, Ill." It is not known when, or if, the bout occurred. On April 18, in his *Chicago Tribune* column, Jim Corbett said he had been asked his opinion on the best ever fighters in the light-heavyweight class, and who the greatest gloved "little heavyweight" was. Without hesitating, Jim picked Joe. He said Choynski had more fighting ability than about any fighter he had ever known, and, had Joe weighed 40 pounds more, keeping all of his ability and speed, he "would have been a wonderful man," having already given many champions the hardest battles they ever had. Corbett said Joe not only had the kick of a mule in his fist, but also a particular manner of landing the punch that bamboozled so many opponents. He added that "Little Joe" possessed more science and "fighting nerve" than any of the current light-heavies. Jim felt that a prime Joe would have whipped Tommy Burns and "Philadelphia" Jack O'Brien, only Stanley Ketchel having about an even chance ... Corbett even gave the opinion that a vintage Choynski would have given a real "cleaning" to a prime Jack Johnson! Although unlikely, this reveals how highly Jim respected his former foe.

On the night of April 19, Joe refereed an eight round lightweight contest at the open-air Phoenix Club of Memphis, Tennessee, between Danny Goodman and Julius Stein. It was the inaugural card of the new arena. The match went the distance, Joe calling it a draw, which was popular with the crowd. On May 3 at the same venue, Joe refereed two eight-rounders, both going the full route. Neither verdict met with disapproval. Three days later, a United Press report insisted that old Joe would "return to the ring before a local club," facing two men on the same night in a pair of four round bouts. The report added that Joe, if he could stand the training and passed the test set before him by the two boxers, would face world champion, Jack Johnson. Rumors persisted through the month of May, one paper stating that Choynski would take on the two opponents around June 1 in Memphis. It said he was "training hard at a gymnasium near Chicago ..." The pugs were said to be of Joe's own selection, though no names were given.[48] If this sounded a bit improbable, it was.

Joe had been training with bantamweight champion, Johnny Coulon, "The Chicago Spider," helping him prepare for a defense of his title against Monte Attell on June 12 at Colma. Coulon had been suffering from a strain in his side for some time, and this may have been the reason the fight didn't come off. Instead, Monte faced Frankie Neil at Jimmy Coffroth's Arena in Colma on June 19, where he won the vacant world bantamweight crown. This win made siblings Monte and Abe Attell (the world featherweight champion) the first brothers to hold world titles simultaneously.[49]

By early June, Joe had viewed the film of the Johnson-Burns fight, and, as the June 19 *Tanaki Herald* noted: "In the *Chicago Evening Journal*, Joe

Choynski ... says: 'I felt the views did not give the full effect of blows delivered ... Burns ... did all the leading, with the exception of three rounds, when Johnson rushed for about 10 seconds each time. Burns' apparent knock-downs seem to be *push-downs*, as he gets up as lively as ever. Only once does the referee count ... where police step in. Burns does not appear ... greatly punished. A tuft of hair standing up gives the appearance of a bloodstain from the pictures, and they say negatives never lie. Burns was entitled to the decision when police stepped in, as he did all the leading, and a knock-down does not win a contest.' " While in the minority, Joe is not the only party feeling that Tommy fared better than given credit for.

One pupil Joe "took under his wing" was a lightweight named Walter Parker. Ever the optimist, regarding boxers he tutored, Joe believed he would lead Parker to the lightweight and welterweight championships. His confidence is difficult to fathom, as Parker's listed record to this point showed 10 wins and a draw, with seven losses, five coming by knockout. His record only shows one more fight, a knockout loss in three rounds on February 8, 1911.[50] Walter couldn't even be considered a flash in the pan. Joe found time to draft and propose his own revision of the Marquis of Queensberry code, finding some fault with the old rules. Notable variations he proposed: 4) "If either man is knocked down ... the other ... to move about 10 feet away, so as to give the man who is down a chance to arise." Existing regulations allowed a fighter scoring a knockdown, to stand over his foe until he regained his feet, when he could nail him. This preceded the "neutral corner rule" of the early 1920s, which figured prominently in the 1927 Gene Tunney-Jack Dempsey "Long Count" fight.

6) "Any second ... entering the ring during the rounds shall be ejected ... the contest shall continue, and no foul allowed ..." This was an apparent reaction to the Corbett-Sharkey match of November, 1898, when Corbett's second, McVey, climbed into the ring when it appeared Tom was about to knock Jim out. A disqualification was considered less damaging than a knockout loss, though in that particular case, the damage to Jim's reputation was likely worse than if he had been manfully knocked out. 7) "Should the contest be stopped by police interference, the referee has full power to render a decision." Far too many fights were halted by police, often ruled "No Contest" or a mandatory draw, regardless of who was winning.

8) "Five-ounce special gloves, furnished by the club, to be used in all contests." Up to this time, the size of gloves varied greatly, some clubs specifying two-ounce mittens, others mandating four or five-ouncers. 16) "If a contestant commit a foul, which in the opinion of the referee is unintentional and does not incapacitate his opponent from continuing, he shall be warned, but if the foul incapacitates his opponent ... or ... destroys his chances of winning, he shall be disqualified." This was an improvement, as a fighter often lost on a foul for a lone, accidental blow, even if the

punch caused no grievous harm. Not until Max Schmeling won the vacant heavyweight championship in 1930 on a low blow from Jack Sharkey, were Boxing's rules changed, whereby no boxer could ever again lose a fight on a single foul punch. 19) "If a second throws up the sponge, when it is apparent to the referee that the principal can continue and have a winning chance, the contest shall not be stopped, but the second so offending shall be ejected from the building and not allowed to act as second again, at any future time, before any club." Wow! A tough stance, but done to help prevent double-dealing, i.e., a second skying the sponge to ensure that his boxer loses, in order to save a bet he has on the opposing fighter.

Duluth News-Tribune: "Choynski ... says (hand) 'bandages should be barred' ... figures if a principal is possessed of bad hands, he should be forced to wait for a match until his hands heal. 'A man may set up a claim that his nose is broken,' says Choynski. 'Should he be allowed to wear a nose guard as football players do?' Choynski considers a principal hanging on the ropes in helpless state, with toes off the ground as 'down' " (the same holds true today). "All bouts that go the limit should be decided on points, declares Choynski. A point, the veteran says, is a clean hit, which ... must be delivered with the back of the knuckles. Willingness to mix, the force of blows, cleverness of footwork, and general all around work should enter into a referee's duty in separating the principals, if the bout should travel to the limit. The referee's instructions ... to hit with one arm free, and not to hold and hit, and break 'when I tell you,' is rather incongruous. How can a man hit with one arm free and not hold, or if his opponent holds, then the opponent is perpetrating a foul, and what right has the referee to order 'break,' after admonishing the contestants to hit with one arm free?"[51] Joe was always questioning the rules, and had valid points. Joe's comments are seen in his handwriting, on articles of agreement that he signed with such opponents as Peter Maher and "Kid" McCoy.

Former heavyweight champion James J. Jeffries had announced his retirement from the ring in May of 1905. As a reaction to the years of grueling training he hated so much, Jim had "let himself go," ballooning to some 300 pounds. After Jack Johnson gained the crown in 1908 and cleared the scant field of all but the best black contenders, the racially prejudiced public hounded Jeff relentlessly, to (as writer Jack London put it) "emerge from his alfalfa farm and restore the honor of the white race." Taciturnly refusing at first, Jim's resolve was slowly beaten down, and, in 1909, he hired former Olympic Games heavyweight champion Sam Berger as his manager and sparring partner. Jeffries lost weight, as he and Berger took their sparring and training show on the road. Around this time, Sam and his brothers, Nathaniel and Maurice (along with baby Janet Choynski), were living in the Herbert Choynski household at 3427 Clay Street in San Francisco, as delineated by the 1910 Federal Census. (Sam and Nat later ran the Berger's Clothing and Haberdashery on Market Street).

August 11 *Otago Witness*: "Jeffries ... believes he will be quite ready to enter the ring with the long black about March 17 of next year. Jeffries recently appeared in a sort of 'try-out.' Those present, instead of seeing a man ... totally unfit for battle, saw a perfect athlete, a Jim Jeffries as good as he was four years ago. The majority expressed ... that Jeffries was ready to fight now ... Joe Choynski ... was ... present. He ... thought Jeffries was almost fit for the battle on the spot. 'Will he win?' (he) was asked ... Choynski replied, 'Will a duck swim? Had I not seen it with my own eyes, I would never have believed that a man out of the ring so long could get back to his present shape.' " Joe proposed his new rules to govern the upcoming Johnson-Jeffries contest. A paper added, on December 30: "Taken as a whole, the Queensberry rules are out of date, and Choynski's substitution is worthy of note, according to many followers of pugilism."[52]

Around the 3rd week of August, an article entitled, "The Funny Side of Pugilism" carried humorous tales of fighters: "After winning an important fight years ago, an admirer asked Joe Choynski if his father was proud of him. 'Yes,' was the joshing reply. 'He's very proud of me. He thinks I'm a bank burglar.' Choynski ... used to tell a story about an old fellow who dropped into his father's cigar store in 'Frisco. 'Well, Mr. Choynski, how is your son?' was the greeting. Joe's father pondered a moment and then blurted out" 'Which son do you mean? The prize fighter or the loafer?' "[53] A cryptic notice in the October 1 *Anaconda Standard* probably refers to Joe. If so, it indicates that he worked, at least a short while, for the *Police Gazette*. If not him, the article may have referenced Jake Choynski, an alleged relative of Joe's: "Jack Choynski, western representative of the Richard K. Fox publications of New York, is in the city looking after business matters. Choynski probably knows as much about boxing and boxers as any man living and he is at his best when discussing the coming Ketchel-Johnson scrap. He entertained a number of Anaconda sports yesterday, discussing the boxing game." (Fox published the *Police Gazette*).

The October 17 *Nebraska State Journal* gave an excellent assessment of Choynski's punch: "Joe had an awkward punch that was used by few boxers, hard to block and of terrible force. He had the knack of dropping it down when least expected, and it generally had the label, 'turn off the gas' ... when it landed fairly. It was a full arm, downward swing, with the right for the nose or jaw, generally a counter. He would wait for you to lead for his face with a straight left or a left hook, preferably the latter. He would let you go along a few minutes, when suddenly down it would come with all his strength, plumb over your left lead and the right which you might have crooked on your chest, using as a guard. The only drawback to the punch was that he couldn't time it well or judge distance carefully with it, because it was ... a 'wild' punch. Oftentimes it landed on the forehead or on top of the head, and its effectiveness was lost."

One interesting character who had sparred with Joe, was O.E. Kenyon. A real estate man out of Spokane, Washington, "who ... turned to evangelism last winter ..." Kenyon was said to be "hale and hearty ... having been in strenuous training for his chosen field of expounding the doctrine of muscular Christianity ..." "I went for a long time last summer on but one meal a day, and during that time, I had daily wrestling lessons with a professional and boxing bouts with the pugilist Joe Choynski in Chicago. Result: I'm hard as nails right now ... I met some fine men while I was in the East. But, the finest man I think I met was an old preacher who knows the bible through, backward and diagonally. He's the father of Jim Jeffries, and is a wonderful old man." "He (Kenyon) announced his conversion to a religious life during the Billy Sunday meetings last winter."[54]

Around the 1st of December, a tall, muscular black man walked into

George "Kid" Cotton and Jack Johnson, 1910

Joe's gym. He went by the name George Cotton, and told Choynski he wanted to become a professional fighter. Cotton stood a little over 6' tall, tipped the scales around 195 pounds and had an 18½" neck. Joe agreed to give him a try out. The prospect was born Sylvester Cotton in New Orleans, Louisiana, in 1888 or 1889 (some sources say Baton Rouge, Louisiana). *Colorado Springs Gazette*: "It is seldom that Joe gets enthusiastic about anyone in the fighting line, but he is carried away about this one. Joe intends to carry the young man along and get him some battles with men of his color ... until he has proved his worth. Then, he will go after bigger and better game." Choynski soon went as far as to claim that, with a little experience, Cotton would be ready to tackle Jack Johnson.

Soon Johnson, himself, would come calling at Joe's gym. Jack, now preparing for a title defense against Jeffries, asked Choynski if he had any likely-looking material for a sparring partner. Joe unselfishly told him about his new protégé and Jack asked if he could "borrow" Cotton, to employ at his training camp. Choynski agreed. "The Galveston Giant" was living at this time in a nice home on Wabash Avenue in Chicago. It has been written that Johnson gave Sylvester the new moniker, "George," but contemporary reports show he was referred to by this name at the time he entered Joe's gym.[55] The fledgling pugilist soon took the nom de guerre, "Kid" Cotton, and became Jack's chief sparmate, along with Marty Cutler.

Jim Jeffries was raking in the money on his tour with Sam Berger, making an average of $4,000 a week. Jim Corbett ventured the opinion that Jeff only need increase his endurance and judgment of distance, in order to vanquish "Li'l Artha." Choynski was vocally boosting Jeff, as well, saying he would regain his old form and defeat Johnson.[56] Joe wrote his memories of the Johnson fight for the March 8 *Boston American*. He said it would be difficult to pick a winner, based on what he knew of both men. "I didn't see Johnson again until a few months ago, when he was boxing in a Chicago theater with a partner. He is a great boxer, a keen fighter, and a bad man ... in the ring. I hope to be at the ringside when the great clash is started, but it is possible I will ... be on the road with a vaudeville engagement. I am now rehearsing a monologue they tell me will be a big go." Joe didn't know it, but he would have a special ringside view, indeed.

The first indications of Joe's involvement in the big fight came out by March 30, when it was revealed that Jeffries was "issuing a call for 'human punching bags.' Mike Schreck should volunteer his services at once. So should Marvin Hart. Jeff has already secured Bob Armstrong, Joe Choynski, James Corbett, 'Farmer' Burns, Roger Cornell and Frank Gotch."[57] April 2 *San Francisco News*: "Sam Berger, J. Jeffries' manager, arrived on the overland train last evening from the East, where he has been for the past week perfecting arrangements for Jeffries' camp life. Berger will leave either today or tomorrow for the Santa Cruz mountains, where he will direct final preparations at the training camp at Rowardennan. When Jeffries arrives in this city Monday ... everything will be planned ... said Berger ... 'In regard to the men who will assist Jeff at the camp, our force is practically complete. I had a long conference with Joe Choynski, and it is likely he will be on hand. He is very anxious to help condition the big fellow."

Jeffries, "The Alfalfa King," arrived at the Rowardennan camp (Ben Lomond, California) on the 5th. He had been retired more than five years, and had bloated to well over 300 pounds on his farm. He had already taken off much of the weight, however, doing some training for the past year, including his exhibition tour. Martin "Farmer" Burns had beaten Japanese wrestling champion, Sorakichi Matsuda, in 1891 to gain recognition as world "all-around" grappling champion. He defeated Evan "Strangler" Lewis in 1895, to annex the American "Catch-as-catch-can" (Freestyle) crown. Burns, referred to here as chief trainer, would grapple with Jeff and act as conditioning coach. Current world wrestling champion Frank Gotch, who had trained under Burns, was also supposed to join the camp, after defending his title against Stanislaus Zbyszko, possibly sooner. Berger, who was to spar with Jim several times a week, acted as manager, trainer and press agent. Choynski was being sought for his knowledge of Johnson's skills, and for the respect Jeff had for Joe's boxing strategy and acumen.[58] Big Jim was to add hiking, hunting, fishing, rowing, jumping rope, handball and baseball to his training itinerary, although he would get carried away with the hunting, fishing and baseball. He wanted to train outdoors, with a roofless gym, as well as eat and sleep outdoors.

"The California Grizzly" was putting off putting on the gloves, and still hadn't begun to spar by April 8. He had been hiking over the mountains and fishing, but that was all. Berger told the press that Jim was worn out by the 25 mile hike to the village of Boulder Creek and back, while his retinue of trainers claimed they were happy that Jeff had slowed up in his preparation, having lost so much weight, so soon. At this stage, they probably had a good point. On the 8th, Berger "sent a hurry call by wire to Joe Choynski, to come to the training camp. Jeffries ... wants to secure a fast boxing partner, as he knows Johnson is very quick." He telegraphed a "good offer," seeking an immediate reply, so Sam could make "other arrangements" if Joe decided not to come. The camp gymnasium was still being prepared, and Jeff was using this as an excuse to postpone sparring a few days more.[59] On April 9, Joe telegraphed his acceptance. He had been waiting for "a definite financial offer," and said he would leave for Ben Lomond in one week. Joe had to cancel several theatrical engagements in order to join camp. He said he had been running several miles a day and currently weighed 162 pounds, adding, "I figure what (Jeff) needs most is plenty of ... energetic boxing, and none of that fancy sparring ... when we begin our training stunts, it will be the real thing, let me tell you."[60]

Round Twenty-Three

4ᵗʰ of July Pyrotechnics
(April 1910 – July 1910)

Jim Jeffries sparred for the first time on April 12, a fast three rounds with Sam Berger. The final frame was cut to 1½ minutes, after Sam took some smashing left hooks from the former champion. Berger, while a fine amateur heavyweight, was only a mediocre professional. Jeff said, "I never felt better in my life." Following the bout, Jim shadow-boxed for 10 minutes, punched the bag for six, and grappled a short time with "Farmer" Burns and Bob Armstrong. He finished with a 10-mile run.[1] "Kid" Cotton signed on as Johnson's sparring partner on the 10ᵗʰ. Jack had this to say, looking back from mid-1911: "On April 11 I had a six-round boxing bout with Kid Cotton, just to prove to myself that I was not in need of any very long training ... Kid is one of Joe Choynski's finds ... only 19 years of age, and a superb specimen of an athlete. He was tall, broad-shouldered, deep-chested, splendidly muscled, and as light and springy on his feet as a panther. Choynski had been teaching him for about a year, and he had developed into a first-class boxer. I made up my mind that Kid Cotton would be a mighty useful man to have in my training camp, and although it was rumored even then that Choynski was going to attach himself to the camp at Rowardennan, I determined to get hold of his protégé at any cost. He was just the lad I needed to help me do my heavy work, and a far better boxer than Al Kauffman (sic), who afterward joined my camp ..."[2]

Around April 15 or 16, Joe met up with old stablemate, Tommy Ryan. The two conversed on the Johnson-Jeffries fight. The middleweight was thought likely to be in Jack's corner the night of the contest. His opined that the first clinch would also clinch the win. "There'll be a feint or two and they will drop into a clinch. Before they are pulled apart, one ... will know he is the weaker man. That practically will settle the fight right there." Choynski agreed, adding that the match would then be decided by gameness alone. " 'It is true the average fighter of brains can tell almost instantly when he takes hold of an opponent, whether he can beat him or not ... as far as my experience goes, that comes out right in 19 cases out of 20. One thing I am sure of, I have discovered the secret of Jeffries' crabbedness and if they will let me alone, I'll get him out of it in 48 hours. Just watch me,' and the veteran waved a hearty farewell."[3]

On the night of April 16, Choynski left Chicago for California. Many of the nation's papers, in listing the reasons why he was chosen by Jeffries' camp, cited the obvious – that he was the only fighter who rendered Jack Johnson unconscious, his status as a cornerman and strategist, etc. Another reason given, was that Joe was related to Sam Berger by marriage. It is true Sam was the brother-in-law of Joe's older brother, Herbert, but the primary reasons were likely related more to his skills. "The Frisco Flash" had a fine reputation as boxing instructor and physical culturist. The *Dunkirk Evening Observer* believed he would be appointed chief second, and that Jim Corbett was too hot-headed and excitable to be of much use to Jeff.

Joe told a couple of papers that, upon arrival in the west, he would nail down how much authority he would have in camp. If he had it his way, Joe would "not allow anyone in the camp to talk fight to Jeffries at any time," as the pressure of "redeeming the white race" was making Jim overly nervous and irritable. Choynski also felt that if Jeff won the fight, the added prestige gained by training the victor would bolster Joe's vaudeville career. Jeff turned 35 on April 15, and Jack Johnson sent him a birthday telegram the next day. It was anything but happy for Jim at first, as his ailing wife had been transported to Oakland for an operation. When he got word that Frieda's procedure had been successful, Jeff brightened up. As for Johnson, who was training at Seal Rock House at Ocean Beach (near the Cliff House), he was a bit overweight, but was getting down to work.[4]

Joe's train made a stop on April 18 at La Junta, Colorado, where he was interviewed by that town's *Evening Post*. The former "California Terror" said: "While making good time on a very interesting trip back to my native state ... I have had much time to ponder some plans for working with ... Jeffries at Rowardennan. Music, art, psychology, painting, poetry, literature – all of these are going to be tried on the former champion at his training camp ... providing ... as chief boxing partner and superintendent of training, I am given the latitude I should have. I shall permit no one to indulge in fight talk or pugilistic fanning with Jeffries when he is at the training table, or when in the evening he elects to rest on the porch as a reward for strenuous road and gymnasium work ... I have my theories on how to dissipate his nervousness and tendency to develop grouches. When we are out on the road, no automobile or rig will be permitted to accompany us. I'll try to be with him every minute. If he wishes to slow down to a walk, loaf under a tree or even ruminate in some beautiful nook in the country, over which I rode a mustang in my younger days, and before anyone ever thought of putting in a Summer resort or camp, he can do so."

"I would have anyone who cares to talk fight with Jeffries, do so until his tongue is sore – the more ... the better. But, music art, painting, etc. must be the subjects of conversation at the training table. I have theories about the nerve centers and their effect upon a pugilist in training ... commended and corroborated by a number of Chicago physicians (and) some of the highest medical authorities. I'll stake my life on them ... upon my ability to get Jeffries into a pleasant frame of mind ... in grand physical condition. I have in my trunk a bit of paraphernalia for ascertaining nervous faults, and will use the appliances on the big fellow. I have a new form of therapeutic lamp ... useful in diagnosis and remedy. For years I remained stationary in weight, and only weigh 167 pounds today. But ... have applied the nervous-centre treatment upon myself, despite ... that I thought I was about the healthiest man in the world ... resulting in a gain of flesh. There will be no malice or grudge work ... but I'll try to hit him, and he will try to hammer me. I will not wear a pneumatic pad over my heart. It will be my task to keep him from landing those crushing blows." More than one paper ridiculed Joe's "culture above the punching bag" or "tutelage of a Munsterberg or a Howison, rather than the attentions of Farmer Burns and the towel brigade." The *San Francisco Call* depicted Jeff reading Shakespeare and poetry while listening to love tales of Hoffmann, communing with the lilies and being led by Joe through fine art museums.[5]

On April 19, the great middleweight, Billy Papke, joined Jeff's camp as a sparring partner. He would make Jim work for speed, and train for his own bout with Joe Thomas. Papke won the world middleweight title by knocking out the legendary Stanley Ketchel in September, 1908. Ketchel got revenge two months later, defeating Billy again on July 5, 1909. Papke, "The Illinois Thunderbolt," would stop Joe Thomas in 16 rounds, on May 19. Tragically, he would lose his grip on sanity in 1936, first shooting to death his estranged wife, then turning the gun on himself.[6]

Choynski's train arrived at the San Francisco depot on April 20, where he was met by his brother, Herbert, and Berger. *Call*: "Joe could hardly express his surprise when he took a look at Market Street. He had not seen it for a dozen years or more, and admitted he would have lost his way, had not his friends been on the job to pilot him around. It was all new to old Joe. Choynski has ... new ideas and ... theories which he hopes to work out on the big fellow ... If he gets away with some of the stunts ... he must be put down in the book as a wonder, for nobody else ever has accomplished such feats. Choynski is a great student of the ... game ... a constant reader and a deep thinker. He believes in the higher ideals, even in the fighting line, so the result can easily be imagined when he tries ... some of the Shakespearian stuff on that bear of a man in the Santa Cruz mountains. If Joe switched his talk from art, literature and science to bears and mountain lions, he will get along much better with James J. For several years past, Choynski has conducted a boxing school in Chicago ..." Joe was due in camp the following afternoon. Jim, meanwhile, went three hard rounds with Armstrong, and swung a pick and shovel at the San Lorenzo River, where laborers were creating a small lake for Jeff to swim in.[7]

Sam and Joe arrived at camp on the evening train, April 21. One paper noted: "Choynski is one of the intelligent products of the prize ring. As boxing instructor, he has no peer and is a great trainer. It has often been declared by pugilists, referees and critics, that Choynski is the best handler of fighters in the world. He is well educated, knows every angle of the boxing game and is a good fellow personally, but whether he possesses a sufficient ... iron will to compel Jeffries to follow his instructions to the letter remains to be seen." There was a lot of skepticism regarding Joe's, or anyone's, chances of getting Jeff into top condition, due to his reputation for being surly and difficult in training. Jack Johnson was expected at the coast on May 1, stopping for exhibitions in Nebraska, Utah and Los Angeles, California.[8] On the 22nd, Jeff sparred three rounds with Armstrong, and two with Berger. Sam continually threw a right uppercut, trying to mimic "The Galveston Giant's" style, and coaching Jim to block it. Joe watched, saying his fighting togs wouldn't arrive until the next morning, when he would be ready to spar. He ran with Jeff that morning. "Farmer" Burns measured Jim for posterity: Height: 6' 1½",

Joe Choynski, dated April 22, 1910

Weight: 228 pounds, Neck: 18", Chest (normal): 45", (expanded): 50", Waist: 36", Biceps: 16", Forearm: 13", Wrist: 8¼".[9]

Jeffries was vacillating in the intensity and nature of his workouts, one day sparring, running and punching the bags; the next, baseball, boating and fishing. This he did on the 23rd, though the temperature was 96 degrees (Fahrenheit) in the shade. Choynski dressed in boxing gear, expecting his first go with Jeff, but Jim, after rowing two hours, was not in the mood to spar. His younger brother, Jack, was to join the camp on May 1. Joe now said he would get into top condition, himself, before boxing Jeff, which might take two weeks. Berger felt that Jim was too light, needed to ease up on training and *add* weight. It was becoming evident that Jeffries' retinue of trainers were less than stern taskmasters. They more or less allowed Jeff to call the shots and work at his own pace. Bob Armstrong, while considered by some the "greatest sparring partner of all time" because of his ability to mimic any style, was rather timid in his sessions with Jeff. Wrestling champion Frank Gotch was valuable for roughing with Jim, but was not at camp much. "Farmer" Burns, at age 49, was really too old.[10]

By this time, it was clear that Joe was the "physical director," or trainer-in-chief at Jeffries' camp. He said "he wished to be absolute boss of the training of Jeffries, or he would pack his trunk and leave for Chicago." Joe added that, despite the appearance of good health, Jeff "required much hard work to get into his old condition." An astute observation, as Jim was far from being fight-ready. A large boil had formed on the small of his back, Joe diagnosing it as the result of severe blood poisoning. Feeling the condition was brought on by Jeff "working too arduously since he went into training," Choynski advised him to lay off strenuous exercise until further notice. That afternoon, Jim took an automobile trip to Santa Cruz, where he "had a dip in the surf and ... a hot salt water tub bath." The big fellow was back at it on April 26, however. He arose at 5:00 a.m., and ran 10 miles with Choynski, Armstrong, Burns and Papke. "In the middle of the forenoon," he worked the medicine ball, chest weights, skipped rope and played handball. In the afternoon, Jim was scheduled to box, but this was cancelled. He heated up, and it was feared his condition would worsen. Instead, he put in some rowing on the river.[11]

On the 28th, the boil was lanced, as it wasn't healing as quickly as hoped. Jeff was again told to ease off, which displeased the now-ambitious fighter. It was announced the next day that having spectators at Jeffries' camp was upsetting him, so future training bouts would be behind closed doors. Joe declared that all fight talk in Jim's presence would now be banned.[12] Speculation came from many quarters, that a power struggle would ensue between Choynski and Corbett, when the latter arrived at camp. It was a common feeling among the press, cognoscenti and boxing public, that Joe and Jim were has-beens, antediluvians, too old and washed-up to be of much help to Jeffries. Factoring in the 49-year-old "Farmer" Burns, many were dubbing Rowardennan, "the old man's home."

Racial prejudice was a major and unfortunate element leading up to the July 4 confrontation. It would be the most racially-charged boxing match of all time. Aside from the obvious, Johnson being black and Jeff, white, much was made of the fact that a black man, Bob Armstrong, played a significant role in Jim's training, while white men were expected to perform a major part in Jack's camp. Two former Jeffries trainers, Billy Delaney and Tommy Ryan, were rumored as about to be hired by Jack. The irony should have been that these men were once so loyal to Jeff, not about skin color. Billy had guided Jeffries through his championship reign, but it was said that, at the beginning of Jim's comeback, his wife objected to him as trainer, so Jeff chose Sam Berger. Early reports had Johnson starting in with a vengeance, but he was training in a leisurely manner, "shunning the gymnasium" and driving his touring car around town with his wife.[13] Jack's condition, however, would not be in question when the time came.

May 3 *Lincoln Evening News*: "To an outsider, the training camp looks like a midway in a country fair – run to make money, and not to make Jeffries a champion. They charge for everything. Berger, the 'boy manager,' has the concessions. He even sells 'exclusive news' about the ... camp. Jeff stands for this because he hates being interviewed and photographed. He leaves everything to Berger, who takes advantage of it to the limit. Fans are hoping Jeff will ... go into real training. Art, literature and music never helped a man swing a sleep producing right hook ... though Choynski has introduced such novel training methods. Billy Delaney could handle Jeff, and as long as he was at the helm, Jim was the fighting wonder of the age." There was a lot of truth to this. Delaney could be a wonderful trainer. Choynski was a terrific cornerman and coach, but he wasn't an ideal *head* trainer – at least, not with a difficult, stubborn and moody subject like Jeffries.

On the evening of May 3, Jeff traveled to Oakland to bring his wife back to camp. This cheered him up immensely. On the 5th, Choynski put on the gloves with Jeffries for the first time. Just prior to this, though, Jim took on middleweight Billy Papke. The big man shook him severely in the 2nd round with a right over the eye, raising a lump. After the set-to, Papke said, "Not once did he hit me hard intentionally, and a fellow like me can learn a lot boxing with him. I am a pretty strong fellow ... but I was a mere baby in his hands. When he leaned his weight on me a couple of times, I thought he was going to break my back." The *Titusville Herald* quoted him: "Jeffries is the king of boxers. I have been in training here for several days, and I consider my wind good, yet I came out of my round with Jeffries blowing as if I had not trained a minute. He is so fast that he is bewildering." It was evident that, to some extent, at least, Jim's sparmates were suppressing their own egos in the interest of stoking his confidence.

Next up was "Little Joe." He and Jim smiled pleasantly as they raised their gloves. *Morning Oregonian*: "Choynski is evidently in better condition than any of the other boxers in the Jeffries camp. He displayed much of his old time agility and prowess and came out of the contest without being distressed. They went at it with a will, Jeffries favoring Joe all the way, being even more gentle ... than with Papke. Choynski was tickled to death with himself, as well as with Jeffries, and declared that after a few more days of sparring, he would show to much better advantage ... Jeffries delighted his trainers by displaying a lot of the old time ginger. He romped around the ring like a boy who loved the game. After the boxing, he went through a couple of handball games at top speed." The pair completed three rounds. Afterward, Joe told the *Brownsville Daily Herald*: "Jeffries' foot work, his wonderful speed, his idea of distance, is perfect. I will stake my judgment Jeffries will be in shape for his fight with Johnson inside of a week. Few people realize (the) splendid condition he is in at present ..."[14]

"The California Grizzly" rested on May 6. Joe predicted: "Jeffries will win in about seven rounds. I have figured this out carefully and it has nothing to do with my being attached to the Jeffries camp. Remember this and see if I didn't call the turn." On the 7th, Jeff sparred six rounds with Papke and three with Joe. "Jeffries jolted (Joe) amidships with several smashing lefts ... The point of Jeffries' chin Choynski's objective ... He landed often ..." Papke left for San Francisco shortly afterward,

saying he would return after the Thomas bout. Jeffries had taken a liking to Billy, and was sorry to see him go.[15] Joe countered Berger's claims of Jeff being in top condition. He said Jeffries was overweight and slow, a long way from being fit. He now said his charge should take at least another month before beginning "the really strenuous exercises." "He needs gradual seasoning to harden his muscles and perfect his wind. He has not indulged in the proper kind of boxing ... is in need of some hard fighting."

Jack Johnson stated on the May 8: "I can block all of Mister Jeff's blows and my reach will beat him. I don't intend to take any chances in the early rounds, because he'll be trying his best. But, I think my left hand will ... gradually tire him out. I will be ready to go 45 rounds ... but I don't think Mister Jeff can last that long. He never licked a man of his own size, for he outweighed Fitzsimmons, Corbett, Sharkey and others by many pounds. I always thought Mister Jeff was over-rated and now I'm going to prove it. He's got to be better than he ever was in his life, to beat me. I'll have him down and out before we have gone 25 rounds." A "prominent eastern sporting writer" felt that Jeffries and his trainers did a foolish thing when they added rowing to his ... regimen. "Rowing ... develops ... the opposite set of muscles a man needs in boxing. The pulling muscles are of little use to a fighter, excepting in a rough-and-tumble bout. He will lessen both his speed and hitting power ..." Jim Corbett said, the same day: "I believe Jeffries made no mistake when he engaged Choynski to work in his training camp. Joe may well be regarded as one of the best handlers ... in the world ... He is always clear-headed, cool and resourceful, a clever boxer himself and a horse for work. 'Parson' Davies used to say that Choynski used to fight the preliminary rounds of his battles in his training camp."[16]

On May 9, Jack Jeffries, "Tex" Rickard and their spouses arrived at Rowardennan. The sparring Jeff took part in that day with Armstrong and Joe comprised seven, bruising rounds in the handball courts. The *Washington Post* said Jim was hit harder and more often than at any other time since the beginning of training camp. First, Armstrong scraped skin off Jeff's forehead with a sharp uppercut, bloodied his lip, then cracked Jim over the left eye with a hard right. He would have quite a shiner in the morning. The rest of the day's workout entailed an eight mile run, weights, shadowboxing, punching the bag, and several games of handball.[17]

"The Boilermaker" sparred three "rattling" rounds each with Armstrong and Choynski on May 10. He weighed about 225 pounds and his speed was improving. On the 11th, Jeff went another three with Joe and Bob, showing improved aerobic condition. W.W. Naughton observed that the handlers were mirroring the mood of Jeff. When he felt depressed, "the men around him scowl in sympathy and have not a word to throw to a dog. When he feels fine and goes to his work like a killer, one gladsome smile pervades the nook in the redwoods." Jim denied he was a grouch, saying the intense roadwork and general grind had "disarranged" his stomach. From now on, said Jeff, roadwork would play a relatively minor role in his training, and all would be goodness and light.[18] If only that were the case.

The 12th saw Jim spar four hard rounds with Joe and three with Armstrong. He showed "ginger in his boxing," and practiced infighting and combination punching. It was Choynski's turn to get a black eye, the result of a high left hook from the preacher's son. Jeff also bloodied Joe's mouth and scraped off skin from under Armstrong's left eye. Jim said, " 'That makes four black eyes in camp now.' 'How's that?' questioned Choynski. 'Well, you have one, I have one and Bob Armstrong has two,' answered Jeffries, with a grin. Bob Armstrong laughed at the reference ... and answered, with some animation: 'Yes, but mine don't hurt.' " Others in Jim's entourage, besides his wife, were: Jack Wooley, Jeff's partner in the saloon business and a trusted crony, Dick Adams, the "court jester of the Jeffries stronghold" and Walter C. Kelley, "of Virginia, judge fame, who keeps the party in excellent humor with his droll stories." Most of Jim's training was to be done in the morning, with the exception of Sundays, when he would spar at 3:00 p.m. to satisfy the public, who arrived by train to see him box. Wednesdays were designated as days of rest.[19]

The May 14 *Lincoln Evening News* told of internal strife in the camp. It spoke of the "recent cropping out of jealousies among Jeff's handlers," and that "Corbett is expected ... the latter part of the month. Although he has not said so officially, he has intimated to his friends that he expects to assume charge in Jeff's camp. When Joe Choynski arrived ... he boldly announced that he was going to run things, but up to date, he has only done so in print. Burns has been the real court ... his decisions ... subject to revision only by the big fellow himself. Corbett and Choynski are believed to be none too friendly, and it is feared there will be a clash between these two." The writer feared a case of "too many cooks spoil the soup."

Old West figure, W.H. "Bat" Masterson, wrote: "While Jeffries was in London last fall he ... arranged to have Corbett join him at his ... camp, and assume full charge of his preparation. Corbett agreed to put in the last four or five weeks preceding the battle ... Since these arrangements were made, Sam Berger got busy with Joe Choynski ... (who) ... has ... been looked upon as commander-in-chief ... Corbett and Choynski have not been on the friendliest terms for ... many years, and the presumption is that Corbett will refuse to play 2nd fiddle to Joe ... who ... supported by ... Berger, his brother-in-law, will be a hard man to dislodge ... the prospect for a clash between the two is particularly bright. The probabilities are ... when it comes to a show-down, Jeffries will stand for Corbett, which will no doubt mean exit, Mr. Choynski ... bringing Choynski into camp was a foolish move ... as he could not be of any possible service to the big fellow. The only conclusion ... to account for Berger's action, is that he was anxious to push Corbett aside ..." One thing is certain: "Bat" had strong feelings against Joe.[20]

On May 17, Roger Cornell, known as "a condition expert and masseur," joined the team and immediately assumed charge of "the rubbing room." In order to join Jeffries' staff, Cornell "deserted" the Portland professional baseball team he had been in the employ of. He said there would be no more boils forming on Jim's back; the previous eruptions had been "due to errors in massaging." Choynski suffered a strange mishap while jogging with Jeff. During the final sprint, Jeff's little fox terrier ran between Joe's feet, causing him to trip and crash to the ground. Joe came out of the ordeal with "a badly lacerated hand and a huge lump on his head." "In the handball, Jeffries played ... brother Jack ... Choynski and Armstrong. He took the trio into camp in two straight games."[21]

Jeff took May 18 off, leading an all-day fishing excursion on Monterey Bay, near Santa Cruz. That night, as the party returned to Ben Lomond, Choynski was said to have discoursed learnedly on the subject of astronomy, "with Halley's comet as a text ... in pursuance of the aesthetic uplift movement that he threatened some time ago to inject into Jeffries' training operations. If Jim were edified ... he did not let on. His rumored comment was, 'Close your yap, Joe, you're scaring the fish!' Motoring home, the party kept a sharp lookout aloft for the comet. Farmer Burns was unusually silent, and his commonly serene brow was puckered and corrugated ... 'What's the matter with you, Farmer?' someone inquired. 'Me? Oh!' stuttered Burns ... 'Say, fellows, what makes a comet's tail?' Choynski was framing a scholarly answer, but a general 'What?' chorus cut him off. 'Because the comet,' said Burns, 'is 400,000,000 years old. That's why it's stale.' He was not much hurt when he landed by the roadside." While the writer's "account" is tongue-in-cheek, it portrays the likelihood that Joe's cultural offerings were unappreciated by the dour Jeffries.[22]

On the 20th, the team exhibited in Santa Cruz, before the Knights of

Choynski, Berger, Jeffries, "Farmer" Burns - May 8, 1910 San Francisco Call

Pythias convention. First, Jeffries bounced Armstrong off a wall with a left hook in the 3rd and final round of their set-to. Next, "Joe was tossed about recklessly for three rounds. He emerged from the scuffle with a bruised ear and a blackened eye." It was said that Choynski nearly "took the count" in round two. Jack then made his camp sparring debut. Jim, feeling his brother was not yet in proper condition, took it easy, the pair going two or three frames. Next, Jeff wrestled three rough rounds with "Farmer" Burns, after which, he shadowboxed, skipped rope and played handball.[23]

On May 22, Corbett left New York for California, saying he intended "to introduce no rivalries" into camp. To avoid a clash with Joe, Jim would stay 10 miles away at Santa Cruz, taking an automobile each day to Rowardennan. He said he "will box with Jeffries … and … give such advice as he thinks is needed, but Choynski will keep his titular honors." That day, Jeff put on his best boxing exhibition thus far in camp. It was held before 50 members of the Olympic Club of San Francisco, in addition to "a number of prominent San Francisco sporting men." He went three rounds each with Jack, Choynski and Armstrong. Jeff also took on his nephew, Tad Boyer and Choynski in a game of handball, and was said to have beaten them handily. Choynski was to co-umpire a pro baseball game in the "Three C League" at Santa Cruz on May 22. The two "bottom-feeders" of a six-team league, "Santa Cruz" and "Gantner & Matterns," would play. A Jim

Jeffries and Choynski, with WW Naughton (left), Corbett (center) and others

Nealon was to umpire, and Choynski was to support. Whether Joe "co-umped" on the day in question, is in question. No report has been found to confirm it, and he was in camp that day.[24]

On May 24, in the sun-heated handball court, Jeff went three rounds each with Armstrong and Jack, both perspiring and breathing heavily at the end. Berger fought Jeff hard for two rounds, but was used up afterward. The fiercest go was with Choynski. Jim went at him in brutal fashion. "The California Terror" needed all of his quickness and savvy to stave off heavy damage. In the 2nd heat, Joe "shot in three sharp blows to Jeffries' body in rapid succession … Jeffries … rushed Choynski from one corner … to the other. Joe defended bravely, but Jeffries' powerful arms … inflicting blows … that put him plainly in distress. Joe was repeatedly hurled to the walls …

He occasionally returned a stinging blow, but ... was kept busy warding off the rapid-action blows of his huge opponent."

Several reports said Joe emerged from the set-to with a broken tooth, a "bad ear" and a damaged nose. At some point, Jim winced as he took a blow to his left thumb. " 'I sprained it the other day,' he explained to Choynski, 'and when you caught me there, it hurt. I guess it will be all right, though, in a couple of days.' ... blood came from Jeffries' upper lip ... Sharp edges on his teeth are responsible ..." The May 31 *Des Moines Daily News* went much further, claiming: "Last Tuesday ... Jeffries knocked out Joe Choynski so cold that it took some time to bring him back ... Jeffries' handlers kept the story quiet, for they did not want it noised about that the big fellow is beating up his training partners."

"It was a real fight. The two ... went at it nip and tuck for four rounds. Suddenly, Choynski swung a vicious left to Jeffries' jaw and twisted the big fellow's head ... Jeffries waded in. Choynski's ears were smashed into cauliflower shape, his nose crushed, a tooth knocked out and his lips split. Another swing and Choynski went to dreamland." As nothing was noted on May 24 by witnesses, the tale is somewhat dubious. A kayo by Jeff would boost his reputation, so a deliberate cover-up seems silly. *Waterloo Daily Courier*: "Today, Jeffries and Choyinski (sic) laughed when they heard the story was out, and declared they have been chuckling in their sleeves whenever people tell Jeffries he ought to do more roughing work."

Billy Delaney accepted the offer to assist Johnson. Not only would he provide the champion with about 40 years of ring experience, but also had great familiarity with Jeffries' style. The latter was back at it on the 26th, running with Choynski and Burns to the Toll House, one mile beyond Felton, and back, a 12 mile round trip. He took his usual gym work in the afternoon. On May 27, Jim and gang put on a public exhibition at Dreamland Rink in San Francisco. An astounding cheer greeted Jeff. As planned, Corbett was at the rink to meet the Jeffries ménage, along with a crowd of about 10,000. They climbed into the ring as one, and the first thing Corbett did was walk over to Choynski and throw his arm around Joe's shoulder. The two old rivals "laughed in each other's face and skayed (sic) around in a mock clinch, and the crowd cheered harder than ever."[25] After all that was written in the papers about the bad blood that would come to the fore when "Gentleman" and "Chrysanthemum" got together, this was a smart way to defuse and debunk the matter.

Jeff and Joe went three rounds, showing excellent mobility and speed, but clearly pulling their punches. Jeffries went another three lively cantos with brother, Jack; Berger refereed both bouts. Heavyweight Al Kaufman, who was about to join Johnson's camp, made a surprise invitation for Jeffries to spar with him. The request was denied. John L. Sullivan, just returning from his European honeymoon, made a valid point, telling reporters that Jeff was making a mistake, in not getting a number of younger and faster sparring partners. While knowledgeable, men like Choynski, Corbett, Armstrong and Burns were no longer quick enough to press Jim with speed and make him faster. Corbett said he would spend the next week jogging and playing handball, as the transcontinental train ride had taken a toll on his stomach. He would soon take his turn in the sparring rotation, emulating Johnson's boxing style: jabbing with the left, uppercutting with the right and blocking punches.[26]

The May 30 *Washington Times* gave Joe fervent (and humorous) praise for his use of psychology at the camp: "If Jeffries doesn't win the big mill, it will not be for the lack of scientific training. He has placed himself largely in the hands of that apostle of culture ... Choynski, who outlined his regimen ... The big fellow was to have 'roadwork and sprinting and plenty of my psychology

Berger, Choynski and Jeffries at training camp, 1910

prescription – art, literature, and science for the leisure hours.' As Mr. Choynski delicately intimates, physical exercise is all very well in its way, but success depends so much on being able to land an uppercut at the psychological moment, that psychology is really of paramount importance. The sprint along the open road ... hardens the muscles and gets the system in condition, but it is the intellectual bath immediately following which really does the work. Give a man an hour or so of the 'Critique of Pure Reason' and he can go out and whip his weight in wild cats. What could be a finer preparation for a set-to with 'Jack' Johnson than three or four sittings with 'The Descent of Man?' A lecture by Mr. Choynski on the influence of the impressionist school of art would furnish inspiration for a 40-round battle. Psychology has too long been overlooked as a factor in training ... and thanks ... go out to Mr. Choynski."

On May 30, Corbett paid an unannounced visit to the camp. He got in a workout, despite heat of 90+ degrees (Fahrenheit), heading back to Santa

Cruz prior to Jeff's return. Jeffries had been on a fishing excursion with "Tex" Rickard and Jack Wooley, and expressed disappointment at missing Jim. Several papers felt "Corbett's refusal to take up his abode in the quarters prepared for him here is attributed to his wife's desire to remain at Santa Cruz."[27] On June 1, Jeffries told his sparmates to hit him hard. Armstrong came out aggressively for three rounds, but Jim doubled him over just before the final bell with a shot to the midsection. Choynski gave three clever stanzas, "displaying even more skill than usual. The main event ... was a two-round go with Sam Berger ... in slam-bang fashion ..." Corbett showed up again. Jeff lost a game of handball to him, punched the bag half an hour, skipped rope, did abdominal exercises and jogged seven miles. That evening, an outdoor ring was erected in front of the gym, a duplicate of the one to be used on July 4th, at Corbett's suggestion.

Also on the 1st, United States examining surgeon of San Francisco, Dr. Charles V. Cross, visited camp and gave Jeffries a thorough examination. Afterward, Cross, one-time physician of Jack Johnson, pronounced Jim the most impressive specimen he'd ever examined. He said he possessed wonderful strength and condition, his brain, heart, lungs, stomach, kidneys and liver perfectly sound. Comparing Jeffries and Johnson, Cross said both were roughly the same in terms of fitness, except Jack currently had more "excess flesh." On June 2, on the alleged May 24 knockout of Joe, "Bat" Masterson wrote: "Choynski admits being defeated after four rounds of vigorous slugging. There may be nothing in the story, of course. It may be the work of a press agent. All I know ... is what I read in the papers ... If Choynski did give out the story, he must be getting modest in his old age. A few years ago Choynski would not be found admitting he had been knocked out ... even by Jeffries ... without making some sort of an excuse to account for the disaster. But, if ... it really took Jeff four rounds to put Choynski out ... I can't figure how the big fellow expects to beat Johnson. How Jeff could expect to give himself a test by engaging in a bout with a man whom everybody, or nearly everybody, has beaten, is a mystery to me."[28] Masterson's bias against Joe showed once again.

Joe said, in the June 2 *Portsmouth Daily Times*: "Don't ever believe Jeffries is not as good as he ever was. He is better. Last Tuesday ... he and I had a real finish fight. We fought four rounds and I collapsed. Jeffries smashed my nose, crushed both my ears, split my lips and broke a tooth. In the 4th ... I caught him a vicious swing on the jaw. It woke the big fellow up, and I received a crashing smash that almost knocked my head off ... He followed with a swing to the body, which knocked me out." One might be forgiven if he said this sounded like a press agent. Joe parrots the exact description of the May 31 accounts. Jeffries continued to intersperse days of hard training with his beloved fishing trips. June 4 saw him go an unspecified number of quick, aggressive rounds with Choynski and Jack Jeffries. On June 5, he sparred three fast frames with Joe before 500 spectators, adding rope jumping, bag punching, shadowboxing and chest weights to the program. An added surprise was a friendly, three-round set-to between Choynski and Corbett. The latter was short of breath at the finish.[29]

On June 6, Corbett continued the tendency of Jeff's handlers to heap inordinate praise on him. He was rather out of character, writing: "When I look back now, I wonder at the fact that I was able to give him a hard, 23-round fight at Coney Island, for I know Jeff could have beaten me on the best day I ever saw. He's the greatest fighting man ... since the game was invented." "Pompadour Jim" normally expressed himself as second to none. In later years, he continued to claim that he knocked Jeffries silly while Corbett was training at Carson City for Fitzsimmons, and that Jeff was lucky to defeat him at Coney Island. He sparred with "The California Bear" on June 10. As Corbett was not yet fit enough to go full-bore, Jeffries restrained himself. Afterward, Jeff went three with Joe, and "showed dazzling speed and an assortment of accurately placed punches."[30]

Corbett and Joe headed that night for San Francisco, where they would box each other in an exhibition at "Louis Blot's new arena at 8th and Howard streets" the following afternoon. Originally, a policeman from the city requested that Jeffries box for a benefit there, but he declined, saying it would disrupt his training schedule. The old rivals agreed to go on, instead. June 10 was a happy day for Jeff, who sang while he trained. His favorite tunes were "I Wonder Who's Kissing Her Now" and "Has Anybody Here Seen Kelly?" Camp attendants joined in. After warming up on the wrist machine, big Jim sparred three rounds with Armstrong, under the skylight in the middle of the new gym. Bob mimicked Johnson, blocking lefts and stepping in with right uppercuts. "The Boilermaker" covered his chin with the right hand. He worked with the pulleys, wrestled two 10 minute rounds with "Farmer" Burns, skipped rope and punched the bag. Finally, Jeff watched Choynski and Corbett play two games of handball.[31]

On June 11, Joe and Corbett appeared at Blot's arena. "Young Mitchell" was the referee. Said the *Call*: "He looked as though he could devour both ... in jig-time in a rough house battle. Herget has filled out and has a pompous look. Corbett and Choynski have got rid of their superfluous flesh and only carry around ... enough to make them feel comfortable." Corbett wore white knee breeches, blue stockings and a pink, armless shirt. Joe wore all white, except for black stockings. While "Choynski, his fuzzy hair unkinking itself in the breeze, stood with a hand on the ropes," announcer Billy Jordan introduced the boxers. The spectators witnessed a mild reenactment of the duo's fray on the barge ... 21 years earlier. "They ... danced around ... and exchanged tit for tat. 'Gentleman' Jim did show some of his oldtime cleverness in getting away from Choynski's swings, but ... felt duty bound to let old Joe hit him nearly every time he shot in a wallop to

Joe's head or body." The old-timers went three rounds, and "The show was given under the auspices of the local Eagles ..." The *Oakland Tribune* estimated the sparse attendance at from 500 to 600 persons.

W.W. Naughton: "What followed was a clever display of hitting and blocking, interspersed with imitation slugging spells at close quarters. The crowd kept the opponents laughing with its reference to the fight on the barge, but ... failed to arouse ... resentment in (either). They went three rounds, and toward the end of the 3rd, Corbett used that old double left on the body and face that was a standby of his in ... spars at the Olympic Club. They wound up ...

Choynski-Corbett spar - June 12, 1910 San Francisco Call

Corbett hitting at the head, Choynski at the body, and when time was called they hugged each other in a good natured way, to prove the bitter fight in the late '80s had mellowed into a memory."[32]

On June 12, Jeffries took an eight mile run to Boulder Creek and back, in the blazing heat. A throng of anywhere from 1,000 to 5,000 watched him take on Corbett and Choynski for three rounds each. "Tex" Rickard, Tim McGrath and comedian Willie Collier were among the crowd, which saw a cheerful Jeffries engage in "bantering chatter" with his sparmates. He dominated Corbett, blocking most of his punches and snapping the latter's head back with straight lefts. The "actor-fighter" tried to emulate Johnson's right uppercut. Jeff blocked and avoided many, but "Gentleman Jim" managed to land several to the chin, and connected with a "business-like left," that didn't faze the big man. Corbett injured his right thumb at some point. Joe fared worse, blocking several quick lefts from Jeff with his face. One nearly took him off his feet in the 2nd round, but Joe battled back

626

gamely. "The Grizzly" followed with two rounds of grappling with "Farmer" Burns. Johnson, meanwhile, tossed the medicine ball with "Kid" Cotton and sparred with Cotton, Al Kaufman and Dave Mills.[33]

The unpredictable Jeff was up with the birds the next day, completing his morning regimen before his handlers had risen. Afterward, he went three, hustling cantos with Armstrong, and alternated six rounds with Choynski and Berger, taking no rest in between. "Little Joe" "waded in, whaling away with his justly celebrated right cross," which Jeff blocked and dodged. Next, the "bear" did stomach exercises, worked the wall machines, did 15 minutes of vigorous shadowboxing. As Jeffries was heading to play handball, Corbett suggested that any more work that day might be counterproductive. Jeff took his advice, gathered up his fishing gear, and headed for the trout stream with his brother, Jack.[34]

Word came on June 15 that California Governor Gillett was working to prevent the fight within the state. He sent a letter to Attorney General Webb, who petitioned the Superior Court for a restraining order against the principals and promoters. Church leaders were primarily responsible for the movement to kill the bout. "Tex" Rickard: "We will not contest ... the court if the first ruling goes against us. It will then be Reno, Ely (Nevada) or Salt Lake." As Promoter "Sunny" Jim Coffroth noted, Gillett represented both the civil and military authority in the Golden State, so the contest would likely be quashed. Rickard, after speaking with Webb, still held out hope that the match might be held there. Webb promised Rickard an official statement within two days, due to expenses already incurred by the venture. "Tex" met with promoter Jack Gleason and their attorney, Herbert Choynski. Any legal defense would hold until Webb made his report. Gleason felt the fight was legal and could not be stopped.[35]

On the 18th, Berger gave orders that the camp equipment be packed up and the retinue prepare to move operations to Reno, Nevada. The action was prompted by news that Governor Gillett had ordered out the militia that day, to stop the Sam Langford-Al Kaufman fight in San Francisco. Jeffries remained upbeat, ready to fight at any venue Rickard decided on. "I am more sorry for Rickard than anyone ... I think the action of the Governor, taken at this late day, is not at all fair ... Do they call it religion to allow a man to risk his every penny on a business proposition, only to grab his game at the 11th hour? If they do, I'm afraid the definition of the word has changed considerably since my daddy used to teach it to me."

At 3:30 p.m., Jeff went for a hike up Ben Lomond Mountain with Jack Jeffries, Cornell, Burns, Choynski and a Dave Lewishon. The turn-around point was at an elevation of 2,000 feet and four miles distant. Cornell, who "wrestled 42 professional matches throughout Nevada and knows the country thoroughly," said Jim would benefit from being acclimated to the altitude. Johnson had been training at the beach. The June 19 *Oakland*

Tribune said Cornell and Corbett "are two of Jeff's trainers who wield most (sic) influence with the big fighter. By means of cajolery and diplomacy they have frequently made the big fellow work when he scarcely felt inclined ... Jeff's skin is ... tough as leather. He is brown as a berry and could easily pass as kin to his dusky opponent ... Jeff had his body saturated daily with a pickling process which toughens the skin ... to prevent cuts ... spreading, in case his face or body is laid open during the fight ..."[36]

Jeffries gave a sparring exhibition with Choynski and Corbett at Santa Cruz on June 19. Jeff, Joe and gang bade farewell to the camp at

Corbett, Choynski, Jeffries and Bob Armstrong

Rowardennan and took the 10:00 a.m. train for Oakland, en route to Reno. The townsfolk of Ben Lomond took the day off from work in order to give them a proper sendoff. Jeff and his staff arrived in Oakland about 6:00 p.m.; he had whiled away the trip playing cards with Joe, Dick Adams and a Colonel Kowalski. They would take a 9:00 p.m. train for the new quarters at Moana Springs, Nevada, about three miles south of Reno. Nevada Governor Denver Dickerson assured Rickard there would be no interference in that state. The fight site would be "a rock-strewn field in East Reno ... scene of the Hart-Root contest of July 4, 1906." An open-air arena of about 300 square feet would be ready two or three days prior to the big battle. It was announced that Rickard would also referee the bout, as the two camps couldn't agree on a regular, established ref.[37]

The elevation at Moana Springs was about 4,500 feet. The party arrived in Reno around 10:00 a.m. on June 22, to a rousing cheer. John L. Sullivan was on the train, also receiving a loud ovation. Shortly after the group reached the hotel, "The Golden," Jeffries, Berger and Rickard motored out to Moana Springs to inspect the camp. Choynski, Corbett and others, after shaking hands with old friends in the lobby of The Golden, followed on the Reno-Sparks trolley. The next day, attendants set up camp. Rickard and Jack Gleason were there. Frieda Jeffries took up residence in a chair by the main cottage, while Jeff and Berger were on the porch. Joe donned a pair of trunks and joined others for a dip in the large pool nearby. Corbett watched from the gallery. "Choynski will devote some attention to young Hackenschmidt, who will wrestle Edwards next Sunday at the springs." This was George Hackenschmidt, "The Russian Lion." In 1902, he won the Greco-Roman wrestling crown from Brit Tom Cannon. In 1905, he defeated American freestyle grappler Tom Jenkins, becoming the first generally recognized world heavyweight wrestling champion.[38]

June 25 saw a reunion of historic proportions. Joe, Rickard and old William Muldoon each claimed credit for the event. John L. Sullivan had been hired by the *New York Times* to give his opinions on the fight and respective fight camps. He said some uncomplimentary things about Jeffries and crew, which was not taken kindly by "Gentleman Jim." Corbett chased Sullivan away from the Moana Springs site on the 24th, but he was invited back the next day. The peacemaker was, according to Nat Fleischer and other sources, Joe Choynski. It appears that Joe and Muldoon each deserve credit as diplomats. "The Solid Man" (Muldoon) spoke with Corbett at camp, about a reconciliation. Several photos exist of the peace conference, reenacted later in the day by a movie camera. The clip shows the white-haired John L. displaying his quick fists. First, "The Strong Boy" shakes hands with Jeffries. He makes a few feints at Corbett, before the pair also shake hands. This was mostly for the press, as all was not truly forgiven until years later, when John L.'s sentiments softened in his final days. He noted: "Good old Joe Choynski was so happy over the whole morning's work that I think he hugged all of us. I know I saw him hugging Corbett. Joe is a good old scout, the salt of the earth."[39]

"Kid" Cotton was making an immense contribution to Johnson's camp, and not only as a sparmate. He was "the joy and favorite with the training squad," his wit and humor keeping the camp loose. June 26 was one of the hottest days of the year. Jeff's only "training" was a short baseball game, him and his staff against the "war correspondents," or news scribes. Corbett pitched and Armstrong played first base. The other players and positions weren't noted, but Choynski played. Jim was not the pitcher his younger brother, Joe Corbett, was. His tosses were hit all over the field, the final score after only two innings being either 15 to 2 or 9 to 3, for the newsmen. The roles in Jeff's corner on fight night were not yet clearly established, with one exception. Roger Cornell was to be chief cut man, and in charge of massaging Jeff's legs between rounds.[40] Jim was back at it on the 27th: "Jeffries boxed three rounds with Choynski, three with Berger, three with Armstrong and two with Corbett." "Joe's long hair floated in the breeze, and his thin legs flashed about as he tried to keep clear of the retired champion's wallops." Afterward, "Farmer" Burns tussled for 10 minutes with Jeff, who said his wind was better than at Rowardennan.

June 28 *Oakland Tribune*: "The boxing with Choynski was not ... fast and furious ... for Choynski seemed afraid and Jeffries did not press ... hard. At times, Joe would bound in with a left hook or right cross, and several times landed with all the force he possesses. The punches did not seem to bother (Jim) ... Choynski is an adept at the art of side stepping, and each time he tried to ... from a rush, Jeffries was always ready to deliver a punch as he straightened up. His wonderful speed on his feet and good balance make it possible ... to be right on top of the man when he side steps ..." His old friend from Los Angeles, DeWitt Van Court, was now assisting in camp. At Johnson's quarters, Al Kaufman did his imitation of Jeffries, enabling Jack to hone his skills at infighting and stifling left hooks.[41]

While Jeffries disliked having crowds witness his workouts, Johnson, who was something of an exhibitionist, thrived on it. June 28 *Reno Evening Gazette*: "Jim Corbett is to be Jeffries' chief second ... to play the largest part in ... backing up the white fighter. Jeffries has already given an order that no one is to shout orders or advice ... while he is fighting, or make suggestions ... between rounds, but Corbett. The other seconds are to convey their ideas to the chief second, and if he approves he will pass them on to Jeffries."

"Roger Cornell will carry the ... medical case. If the big fellow's face is cut ... his nose bloodied ... muscles cramped ... joints twisted or ... internal organs injured, Cornell will administer ... Van Court, Jack Jeffries and ... Choynski will ... after each closing gong and with rough towels ... rub down their fighter. Farmer Burns is to have charge of the water buckets and sponging off of Jeffries' face. According to the ... plan, Manager ... Berger will not figure ... as a regular second ... (his) attention will be ... occupied with the business end ... Bob Armstrong will probably be also sent from Jeffries' corner. Jeffries is known to have as much confidence in Bob and ... affection for him as any ... but it is likely the black sparring partner with the rare tact he has always displayed, has chosen of his own accord to be elsewhere ..." The statement was not explained, but it is likely that someone mistrusted Bob because, like Johnson, he was a black man.

The June 29 *Reno Evening Gazette*, on Johnson: "His chief characteristic is his unfailing good nature ... even temper that nothing seems to ruffle. His 'golden smile' is seldom out of evidence, and not even the coarse and insulting jibes that frequently greet him from fight spectators seem to ... disturb him. Even when ducking a storm of blows ... (he) never loses his poise ... His eyes ... appraise everything that transpires ... That his good nature does not indicate a low order of intelligence ... has been clearly shown by his clever business methods and his rather well done ringside speeches. Men ... say he simply has no nerves ...''

"Johnson ... regards his ... staff ... as the best he ever had ... Tom Flanagan ... a well-known Canadian athlete and sportsman ... has developed ... prominent long-distance runners ... Walter Burns, in charge of the rubbing and massage squad, is a negro who has been with Johnson ... the last eight years ... an expert in his line. Barney Furey, a negro who had charge of roadwork ... before Flanagan ... with Johnson the last eight years ... sparring partners, Marty Cutler (white), George Cotton and Dave Mills (colored) ... have given ... admirable service ... Kauffman (sic) ... dons gloves with the champion ... these ... furnish the real excitement at camp.''

William Muldoon and W.W. Naughton wrote (June 29 *Syracuse Post-Standard*) that Jeff was not sparring enough. An example was the 28th. A large throng gathered in the morning to see Jeff box, but he had other ideas. Contrary to the wishes of Choynski and Corbett, the big man decided to take an eight-mile jog with "Farmer" Burns. At least he wasn't fishing. When someone pleaded with "The Grizzly" to spar, saying, "Look at the crowd," Jim retorted, "I didn't invite anyone here." Corbett later told the crowd that Jeff had promised to "take on all of his sparring partners between 4 and 5 o'clock this afternoon." That was another false alarm, and the group that was there in the afternoon left disillusioned, as well. Johnson put in a good day, sparring multiple rounds with Kaufman, Cotton, (Walter) Monahan and (Dave) Mills.

In addition to the massive purse the principals would receive (the winner, $85,750, loser, $35,250), they sold their movie rights, constituting $66,666 for Jeffries and $50,000 for Johnson. That they had already been paid this, was fortuitous for them, as movies of the bout would soon be banned in the States. Governor Dickerson was in attendance on June 29, in addition to Captain Cox of the State Police, Warden Maxwell of the State Penitentiary, 1,000 spectators and "the whole sporting fraternity." A motion picture machine was on hand to record the training sequence for posterity. Jim did not disappoint. First, in blue ring attire, he skipped rope, punched the bag and shadowboxed with light dumb-bells. Then, Choynski put on the gloves with Jeff. Some of the footage exists today. It shows Joe on his toes, dancing lightly on his feet and getting in and out on his larger opponent. Joe holds his left far out, as a feeler, and to parry and jab. He keeps his right close to his body, about six inches from his chin. Jeff steps quickly after him but does not appear to land much. Joe, at 41 years old, was very spry and agile. "In all, Jeffries did six rounds ... two with Joe Choynski, two with 'brother' Jack and two with Sam Berger."[42]

Captain Cox said he would have armed men at the fight, to protect Jack Johnson, should he emerge victorious. A preacher wrote to Choynski, pleading with him to convince Jeff not to enter the ring on July 4. Whether the preacher's motive was racial or anti-boxing, is uncertain. Johnson trained each day while facing the bright, hot sun, in preparation for conditions on fight day. Joe Woodman, manager of the great black boxer, Sam Langford, showed up at Jack's training quarters on June 30. He had been pursuing a title shot. Jack would have none of it, instructing a policeman to tell Joe to leave, then politely repeating to Woodman. Joe departed, frustrated.[43] Langford is generally considered the greatest "uncrowned champion" of all time, and would not be granted another bout with Jack. The two had fought in 1906, when Johnson was a prime, 190-pounder and Langford, some 40 pounds less. Sam, only an inexperienced welterweight or junior-middleweight, was floored twice by Jack, but put up an argument. It was said that, after Sam gained 30 to 35 pounds of muscle and more experience, Jack avoided him like the Black Death.

On July 1, Muldoon and Corbett said it was a serious mistake that Jeffries hadn't boxed more, but were quick to say that he would win, nonetheless. That day, trains began pulling into Reno, laden with passengers from all over the nation. There were champions and ex-champions, contenders of all weight classes, famous sportsmen and scribes. Former heavyweight champ Tommy Burns and wrestling king Frank Gotch went to Jeff's camp. Burns was a visitor, while Gotch was an assistant. The principals were now idle, gathering their energy.[44]

On the day prior to the fight, though security was tight and only close associates allowed into camp, "The Michigan Assassin," Stanley Ketchel, a great middleweight champion, slipped in. He began taking photos, when Jeffries noticed and told him to leave. Ketchel had fought Johnson on October 16, 1909. Well behind on points, he floored the champion in round 12 with a wild right. Jack rose and knocked him completely out. They established a friendship born of mutual respect. This bond, and the fact that Ketchel was to be Johnson's timekeeper, made Stanley unwelcome in Jeff's camp. Though no one could know it then, Ketchel would be shot dead on October 15, the victim of a jealous farm hand named Walter Dipley.

Many made predictions on the battle, among them Choynski: "I have never seen as finely a conditioned athlete as Jeffries. If there be any flaw in his physical fitness, it can only come to the surface in the fight ... I boxed ... Jeffries and Johnson when they were novices. Johnson will find himself pitted against a man much faster, cleverer and stronger than himself, and he'll surprise me if he lasts longer than seven rounds." Billy Delaney arrived at Johnson's camp on the 3rd, none too early. He gave Jack a quick visual inspection and was satisfied with his condition. That night, while Jeff slept at camp Moana Springs, a dozen friends and attendants kept vigil, to make certain no one tried to harm him or sabotage his chances in any way. Such was the level of paranoia. Joe, Corbett, Cornell, Armstrong and "Farmer" Burns, kept watch outside Jeff's sleeping quarters.[45]

On July 4, 1910, a horde of 20,000 packed the gargantuan, outdoor stadium. It was hot day in the Silver State, scarcely any clouds adorning the azure sky. Billy Jordan introduced celebrities in attendance. Choynski was

Billy Jordan, Jim Jeffries, Joe Choynski and others in Reno ring, July 4, 1910

among those taking a bow. There were no preliminaries, only the main event, set for 45 rounds. At 2:30 p.m., Johnson entered the ring, smiling and displaying no nerves. He wore a silk robe and was attended by Delaney, Kaufman, Cotton, "Doc" Furey, "Professor" Burns and Dave Mills.

A somber-looking Jeffries entered soon after, with Choynski, Corbett, Berger, Cornell, "Farmer" Burns and timekeeper, Billy Gallagher. Per Jeff's order, only Corbett and Berger were to give verbal instructions. Rickard was refereeing his first fight, not an ideal situation. His inexperience, thankfully, would not prove a major factor. As Jordan shouted his classic, "Let 'er go!" the seconds left the ring. Jeff and Jack did not engage in the customary handshake; the gong simply rang to commence hostilities.[46]

Several papers (and Joe) said Johnson appeared nervous and worried at the start. Round one began with a feint from Jeff. Johnson glided backward, but the men soon came together and clinched. A few half-hearted body punches were thrown, but little else was done. Round two saw Jim come forward in the "Jeffries crouch," hunched over with the left arm straight out. Already, though, Jack's confidence had increased, as he forced the fighting and landed an uppercut during infighting. A few papers, though, said he appeared worried throughout the first three rounds.

They wrestled, Johnson showing he was as strong as Jeffries. He found "The California Grizzly" more grizzled than grizzly. Jack blocked and avoided pretty much whatever Jim threw, from rounds two through seven. It wasn't until the 6th that he really began using uppercuts; his left doing the most damage. A left uppercut, though, closed Jeff's right eye. Only in the 4th did Jeff land a telling blow, crashing a left to the body that made Johnson wince. Jim reopened a cut on Jack's lip that he sustained in training, gaining the dubious honor of "first blood."

After seven rounds, Jeff became tired, throwing fewer and fewer punches. Corbett kept up a shameless diatribe, hurling insults at Johnson in an attempt to get him riled and lose his plan of battle. It failed miserably, as Jack laughed and countered with clever retorts of his own. "Gentleman" Jim finally saw the futility of these tactics and ceased the chatter. Johnson flippantly taunted Jeffries, calling him an old man and telling him it was "all over but the shouting." He was adept at blocking most of Jeff's body blows with his forearms or pulling back from them, although Jim did manage a couple of good ones in the 9th. They did not faze the champion, who mixed punches to the body and head. Johnson punished his foe in the 11th with lefts and rights to the head. Jeff dripped blood from the nose and mouth, but made a nice rally, landing in a fast series of exchanges. At the close of the next round, he spat a mouthful of blood. Jim took a beating in round 14, his face looking as if it had been passed through a threshing machine. The end came in the 15th. Johnson, seeing his man ready to go, waded in with a flurry of powerful lefts and rights, flooring Jeffries for the first time in his career. Jim fell on his haunches, halfway through the ropes, and appeared to have lost a sense of his surroundings. Jack stood over him, waiting to strike if Jeff regained his feet before the count completed. The neutral corner rule would not take effect for several years. At this moment, Corbett could be heard pleading with Jack not to hit Jeff any more.

"Jeffries painfully raised ... to his feet. His jaw had dropped. His eyes ... nearly shut ... his face covered with blood. With trembling legs ... he tried to put up a defense, but could not stop a terrible right ... on the jaw, followed

by two left hooks. He went down again. Jeffries' physician and other friends jumped into the ring. 'Stop it,' they cried, 'Don't put the old fellow out.' "
"The Boilermaker" staggered up at nine, and Berger told Bob Armstrong to throw in the towel, signaling defeat. Jeff suffered a 3rd and final knockdown, struggling to rise once more. Rickard counted to seven or eight, when Berger climbed through the ropes and gestured to stop the contest. "Tex" waved the fight off and placed his hand on Johnson's shoulder, in token of victory. (Others said he raised Jack's arm or merely pointed at him). Jim had to be half-dragged to his corner. After clearing the cobwebs, the beaten man took his head in his hands and groaned, "I was too old to come back." "Corbett and Choynski and brother Jack and the others were ready to cry, but ... united in trying to cheer the defeated man. 'Cheer up, we'll go fishing to-morrow,' said Frank Gotch ..." When the crowd realized the fight was over, they stormed the ring and disassembled it for souvenirs.[47]

The fireworks on this day were not so much from the action in the ring, but rather, the explosive outcome and aftermath. Jack Johnson was masterful in victory over the former undefeated heavyweight champion; boxing brilliantly, if in boring fashion. He maintained almost perfect control of his bulky antagonist, wielding a brutally effective left hand. Jack commanded both the infighting and outfighting, surprising many. When news of the result reached the nation, the effect in several states was race riots, brawls, and in some cases, deaths. This would have far-reaching consequences; one would be the barring of black men from competing for the heavyweight title for many years. Not until Joe Louis captured the crown in 1937, was another African-American allowed to fight for Boxing's biggest prize.* In the immediate future, it resulted in banning of the fight films from around the country. It must be said, however, that in the arena at Reno, Johnson was treated fairly by the officials.[48]
* The lone exception is December 19, 1913, when Johnson fought a D10 in Paris, France, with fellow black, "Battling" Jim Johnson.[49]

Sometimes the truth is an elusive quarry. In the years following his defeat, Jeffries would swear he had been drugged, and that this accounted for his loss. It was surprising how quickly his endurance failed, this "empty shell" of a fighter, as he was referred to for this performance. Perhaps tellingly, though, he mentioned nothing about being drugged, in the first 24 hours after the match. Other fighters used the same excuse for losing big contests – Bob Fitzsimmons, for example, when he lost his title to Jeffries in 1899. There was never any hard evidence in either instance. That night, at Moana Springs, instead of a victory banquet, Jim had a bit of soup. Frieda, Roger Cornell and "Farmer" Burns ministered to him most of the night, tending to his wounds and consoling him. It was stated later, from many quarters, that Jeff thought he had a firm agreement from Johnson, for Jack would "take a dive" and lay down for money, giving Jeff his title back. As the unconfirmed story goes, Jack was to have gone down for the count in round 12, but he told the Jeffries camp about 20 hours prior to the contest, that he changed his mind. When big Jim heard he would have to win the fight on his own merits, he supposedly lost his nerve.[50]

Corbett said Jeff was "whipped before he left Moana Springs for the ringside. He felt he was to fall before the negro, and it was too much for him to face. As the hour approached, his nervous condition became such that his mind lost all control over his body. It began Saturday and indicated itself in various ways. Sunday night he did not sleep a wink, but walked around his room and looked out his windows. When he sat in the corner of the ring, Choynski, as he wrapped his hands, exclaimed, 'Why, Jim, your hands are as cold as ice and clammy.' We thought even then that he was only a little nervous, and ... would get over it in the fight. When I asked him today what he remembered from the time he entered the ring, he replied: 'Well, I remember sitting in the corner ... getting up and not ... able to get my arms upright. I ... don't remember much about what I did.' "

William Muldoon echoed this theme, visiting Moana Springs the day after the fight. *Syracuse Post-Standard*: "Joe Choynski and the chauffeur for Mr. Jeffries ... were the sole occupants of the front yard, save now and then a waiter ... picking up debris. Choynski informed me that Jeffries and Corbett had walked down the road and would soon be back. Dr. Porter, the family physician ... from Los Angeles ... dropped in. Then Jeffries and Cornell came strolling in. The ex-champion shows no physical marks ... But ... seems stupid and dull, his head hangs down and no one can make him talk. 'Yes' or 'no,' is about all you can get out of him." What Muldoon gleaned about Jeffries' mental and emotional state:

Jeffries' handlers noticed on July 3, that he was becoming extremely irritable and nervous. He was trying to play cards, but paid no real attention ... He made many misplays and seemed annoyed by everyone who came around. Dr. Porter found no physiological problems, but was unable to get Jeffries to speak. Jim ate little for supper, retired early ... Frieda said he was restless and slept little. Porter told Muldoon he felt Jeffries was "suffering from a severe attack of nervous prostration." No one other than Jeff seemed to think he had been drugged. "Corbett, Choynski and Burns ... never saw a man so completely prostrated before entering the ring. His arms were ... limp and he shuffled his feet along ... The trainers did not know what to do, for in all ... their experience, they had never seen anything of the kind. He only answered: 'I'll be all right when I get started.' And when he came to his corner after the 1st round, Choynski offered some advice, and the only response was: 'I can't see. I have no judgment of distance and my arms won't work. But, I'll be all right in another round or two. This fellow can't lick me." The cornermen scarcely got another response from Jeff the rest of the contest. Jim later told Muldoon: "I was weak and ... played out from the very moment I entered the ring." On the night of July 5, Jeffries and his wife took a train out of Nevada, en route to his farm near Los Angeles, by way of San Francisco.[51]

In 1930 ("I Fought 'Em All"), Joe recalled: "Jeffries was in great shape – *physically* ... not ... *mentally* ... The man's long retirement had shaken his confidence. What he ... should have done – was meet several minor heavyweights before tackling the big black. This would have restored his confidence ... just 10 minutes before Jim left his dressing room ... I realized he had lost confidence. Jeffries, like myself, had no use for bandages. We both felt ... (they) were a handicap ... as they have a tendency to retard blood circulation in the hands. Therefore, when Jeff asked me to get him some ... I was dumfounded. Only a few days before he had boasted that he never used bandages! ... I realized ... that my great friend was in a bad way. Psychologically, he went into that ring a beaten man before he ... raised a hand in battle! Those ... who have seen moving pictures of the ... fight will ... recall that Jeffries made no effort to try a lead. He was always on the defensive. Trying to snap him out of this, I spoke sharply to Jim as he came to his corner. I said: 'Start something, Jim! Try all your best stuff. You know enough to beat this fellow in no time at all! Lead!' And each time I pleaded with him, Jeff, with a blank expression, would respond: 'Yes, yes, Joe – that's right. I must get him. I'll go after him the next round.' But he ... continued his defensive tactics! For the first three rounds, the Galveston black was in a sweat, for fear Jeffries would rip his head off. Then, realizing Jeff was incapable of putting up a fight, Johnson sailed in."

All of this time in the midst of boxers had stirred the old fighting spirit in Joe. He wrote former opponent, Willard Bean. July 6 *Salt Lake Evening Telegram*: "Willard Bean is in receipt of a letter from Joe Choyinski (sic) ... who is anxious to come to Salt Lake and meet any two or three men in an exhibition bout." Joe's letter might have been a temporary cathartic for his newly-revived thirst for combat, as nothing came of the idea.

Around July 7, rumors came out that Jeffries had been doped in the fight. Gossip on the streets of San Francisco was that his food had been drugged, and the unfortunate target of the accusations was Bob Armstrong, apparently because he was black. Jeffries had taken a 6:30 p.m. train for Los Angeles and was unavailable for comment, but Choynski had traveled with the party and was still in the city. He refuted the rumor, saying it was "practically impossible for Armstrong to have been a party to any such scheme and ... the colored boxer was one of the strongest supporters Jeffries had." *New York World* sporting editor, W.P. McLoughlin, in an editorial on the 8th, said Joe told him: "It's the old fright that ... comes to a man ... out of the ring for a long time. It has even happened to me. I can remember once ... after a prolonged absence from the ring. As soon as I got back, I had a terrific fear of the man I was going to fight. In other words, I needed a fight in me. It was the same way with ... Jeffries."

The point was made – correctly – that, had Johnson's team lost the fight and claimed afterward that their man was rendered ineffectual by "nervous prostration," boxing critics and the public would have called it a manifestation of the supposed "yellow streak" possessed by Jack. This was just another expression of the day's racial bigotry. News scribes criticized Jeffries for his lack of sparring.[52] Jim should have taken an approach more like former heavyweight champion, George Foreman. The latter, in his 1980s and '90s comeback, after being retired for nearly a decade, fought a series of 24 tune-up bouts over four years, before battling for a championship. Jeffries had zero actual fights in preparation for the Johnson debacle. He had no one but himself to blame. It was evident that Jeff realized he was probably going to lose. Whether a prime Jeffries would have beaten "vintage" Johnson is a valid question, one which has spawned much debate. Certainly, in this fight Jeff's punches lacked force, as attested by Johnson, and his old-time stamina was lacking.

Choynski left on July 9 for Chicago, but not before telling a reporter he was going to challenge Johnson! He said he felt as good as ever, and would defeat Jack as he had in 1901, but would only make the defi if his wife gave her consent. Frank Gotch, a great wrestler who proved a mediocre boxer, also challenged Jack. Neither he nor Joe backed up their "thrown gauntlet" with cash, however. The controversy occasioned 31-year-old younger brother, Edwin, to speak out: "If Joe ... gets too serious about wanting to assume the responsibilities of the white race and do battle with ... Johnson, his relatives will come to the fore and check his progress. They seem to realize that, however game and once great a fighter Joe was, it was all in the past, and he has not the youth that would make him a formidable challenger ... 'I think, at that, Joe would give Johnson a good fight if he should happen to be good on the day of the contest,' said Ed Choynski, a brother of the old-timer. 'But we won't let him fight. He is too old and out of the game too long. He would likely have a good and then a bad day, like all of them, and the result would be evident ... in training ...' "[53]

The former "California Grizzly" went on a long hunting and fishing trip, trying to recover from the devastating loss. The fight itself was proving a greater loss for black boxers around the nation, as many areas were banning bouts between blacks and whites. Thankfully, things would begin to open up again, starting in the lighter divisions. Joe arrived in Chicago on July 18. He had harsh words for Jeffries, telling the *Chicago Daily Tribune* and other papers that he had written a letter to Jim, urging him to put up $50,000 and have another go with Johnson. Joe said it wasn't Jack's punches Jeff feared, but the thought of losing. He explained, the big man had received hundreds of letters from admirers each day, imploring him to defeat "The Galveston Giant." They told Jim he was "the hope of the white race," and this preyed on his mind, ultimately causing a mental collapse. Then, Joe became caustic, saying Jeff was a coward, because he was "not a fighter by instinct." He claimed the only way Jeff could redeem himself "in the eyes of the white race" was to fight Johnson again, that Jim would have nothing to lose in a rematch, and would therefore be more confident.

Choynski: "That doping yarn was about the funniest ever pulled. But ... there is always some wild story ... after every big fight. There is a medical term for what happened to Jeff ... but for fear you might think me too wise, I won't spring it on you ... if he had been a fighter by instinct, he wouldn't have had to be coaxed and cajoled and fairly dragged into the ring ... A real fighter ... would have welcomed the chance to get at the black man ... and wouldn't have questioned for a minute ... the financial reward ... Remember, they had to break all records in the way of purses before Jeff finally consented to fight. Yes, sir, properly handled, he can do a lot better, and I believe he has an excellent chance of whipping Johnson. But, he must fight, fight, fight; fairly live on it all the time ... I begged him to take a punch in order to give one, to get close and slam away at the negro's ribs. He was forced to take the punch, any way, so why not fight back? Berger pleaded that this would be a confession of weakness. What rot!"

"If I had anything to do with Jeffries again, I would want it all or nothing. There would be no staff around him like ... before. They all jollied him into thinking he was great ... for their own aggrandizement ... when that eye was closed, there wasn't a man but me in the corner who knew what to do ... And it wasn't part of my duties to attend to such hurts. Wasn't that a fine situation? They say Johnson quit once, but he got over it ... and there isn't a trace of yellow in him. So can Jeffries ... I'd like to see him try." The function of cut man had been entrusted to Roger Cornell. The August 20 *New Zealand Truth* wrote of Joe's impromptu role: "Choynski massaged the useless eye while the other handlers got busy with liniment and fans, and Corbett whispered counsel in (Jeff's) ear during the minute's rest. When he came out for the 12th ... he seemed to have a new ... purpose."

August 13 *Anaconda Standard*: In a letter to "a friend," Joe said: "Jeff repulsed any attempts at gaining his confidence, and it was necessary to throw away the germs of culture ... prepared so carefully." "As a final fling at the noble Judas Corbett, Abraham Attell ... Berger and other dignified retinue, Choynski says if he hadn't been there, Jeffries wouldn't have lasted six rounds, for the others were in a quandary what to do. Joe kept the claret running from the bear cat's nose in order to prevent his eye shutting completely." Johnson said he would fight Jim again, for about $75,000. Many said Jeff's management and trainers had failed him.[54] Getting Jim to do anything he didn't want to do, though, was impossible.

An October 23 *Nebraska State Journal* article can be taken as a last word on the Jeffries camp. It noted that training methods of the "modern boxer" had become ridiculous, savoring of excessive "limelight and circus show business. In the old days, when champions prepared for ring battles, they selected some resort in the backwoods where fight fans couldn't find them and where they could work from three to six months getting hard as nails. At these quiet training quarters ... there was ... no band of camera fiends, no crowd of war correspondents to chronicle every little incident, and no daily attendance of admirers and experts to offer foolish advice and carry tales. Only a few close friends and the backers of the principals were allowed ... a first class fighter seldom had more than two or three men ... a chief trainer ... usually an old, retired fighter ... knew the game from A to Z. Next ... a sparring partner who boxed every day with the star and ... went with him on hard road runs. The outfit was rounded out by a 3rd man ... known as a 'rubber' ... who had to do all kinds of chores around the camp."

"It seems ridiculous to recall the numerous trainers and camp followers ... at Reno. Each pugilist had nearly a dozen men at his heels, and it must have cost $1,000 a week to keep each camp going, more ... for one week's training than some of the old ring champions received for a bare knuckle fight of 50 or more rounds. We never believed any fighter could successfully train himself, or ... be the boss of his own quarters. He had to knuckle down and obey ... the man ... placed in charge ... There was no ... 'Well, I guess I won't box today, I'll go fishing' ... if he was lazy or dodged his ... training, the boss of the camp reported ... to his backers ... the backers went to the quarters and called the slothful pug down in raw style. He made a serious mistake ... failing to box in private ... such hardy young men as ... Ketchel, Sam Langford Al Kaufman or Jim Barry. If he had engaged two or three of these scrappers instead of the ancients ... Jeff could have ... learned just how far he had gone back. Lack of speed was the chief cause of Jeff's defeat." The point was well made and pertinent, but many modern camps would be similar to Jeff's, such as that of Muhammad Ali.

The July 29 *Anaconda Standard* wrote disparagingly (if humorously) of Choynski: "When he reopens his fisticulturist academy in Chicago, it will be in order for Joe Choynski to announce that highbrow talk on music and art will be dropped from the course, and the concomitants of swat lore will be dope on ragtime and silhouettes." The *Kansas City Star*, looking back on Jeffries' training camp, opined: "Choynski should have been a poet or a composer of sonatas and nocturnes, but his mischievous destiny made him a fighter."[55] Perhaps so. Joe never mentioned the "highbrow" or "cultured" approach again. He would resume his position as instructor of boxing and physical fitness, but soon, in a state other than Illinois.

Round Twenty-Four

The Sage of East Aurora
(August 1910 – December 1915)

On September 27, Miles McLeod (pronounced "McCloud") of Albany, Missouri, arrived in Chicago. He was the latest of the "White Hopes" aspiring to dethrone Jack Johnson. He went to Gilmore's Gym at 1604 Ohio Street the next morning, where he met "Professor" Choynski by appointment. This was the facility run by Harry Gilmore, whom Joe developed a friendship with over the years. McLeod was born in Gentry County, Missouri on July 13, 1883, stood 6' 5" and weighed 225 pounds. He possessed little ring experience and was commencing a boxing career at a very late age. Miles, however, refuted a lack of knowledge and practice: "I feel reasonably sure I can beat that fellow, for I have boxed since I was 10 years old, and know something about the fine points of the game. I believe I can hit as hard as Johnson and know I can take a deal more punishment. I do not have to enter this profession to make a living, as I have a farm in Albany ... I am glad to have the opportunity to box with a fighter like Choynski. I am sure he can ... (teach) me some of the finer points, and a defense which will block most of Johnson's blows. I want to meet at least three men before I battle Johnson, for there is not going to be a repetition of the Johnson-Jeffries fight, with me playing the role of Jeffries." Joe was "elated over the appearance of the Missourian," and if McLeod could fight at all and would face Jack, he would train Miles for all of his fights.[1]

Joe and Miles sparred two rounds on the 28th. McLeod's reach was given as 82" (fingertip to fingertip), waist, 39", chest, 45" expanded, and biceps, 16".[2] The *Montreal Daily Herald* said Choynski "declared McLeod to be one of the most promising novices he had ever boxed ... with two month's proper handling, McLeod would be able to give any of the heavyweights a stiff argument ... (he) has a left which is phenomenal, and as soon as he is taught how to use it, will develop into one of the best two-handed fighters in the game." The September 29 *San Francisco Call* had a different take: "McLeod ... tried out by ... Choynski this afternoon ... returned to his Missouri home badly bunged up. His experience probably ends his pugilistic ambitions." This was incorrect; Joe was not done with Miles yet.

The October 4 *Evening Standard* ridiculed McLeod's chances as a serious challenger for the title. It said the whole thing was good for a laugh, but McLeod and his pretensions "should go to the discard." Another paper noted: "Joe Choynski and his wife will make a swing around the vaudeville circuit this winter. Joe has a clever little sketch ... he thinks will go well ... he is a clever talker and can give an entertaining monologue relative to the white man's hope." He took Miles on the road. They were seen in Davenport, Iowa's American Theater on November 21, in Joe's new sketch, "His Last Battle." "He made a hit when he introduced Miles McLeod, the man whom he claims will whip Johnson in a year."[3]

Miles' brother, Walter, who lived in Chicago, had spoken with Jim Corbett months earlier about his sibling's pugilistic ambitions, and a meeting was arranged. Jim: "In Davenport, Iowa, I was given the opportunity of watching Miles McLeod in ... an interesting set-to with Joe Choynski, who has the young giant in charge. McLeod is there with the looks and size, and I was surprised at the speed he showed ... with a little more experience under the capable wing of ... Choynski, the Missourian will be ready to start ... as a professional ... That he has a goodly punch his instructor will swear to. In one of the rallies, big Mac gave Joe as pretty a 'blue' eye as I ever saw. Choynski has that rare gift ... to impart his knowledge ... to beginners, and (Miles) ... has proved an apt pupil. Choynski has his eye on Tommy Ryan's protégé, Con O'Kelly ... (Ryan) entertains the idea that he has a comer in the big Irishman, and a bout between the ... giants ... may result in ... a ... candidate for the championship ..." O'Kelly was a 6' 4", 220 pound freestyle wrestler, who won the heavyweight gold medal at the 1908 Olympics in London, England. Corbett was looking at a prospect from Oklahoma named Carl Morris, who would become a top heavyweight contender of the 1920s. The plan was for Joe to spend the winter telling in his vaudeville show, "how a certain little affair at Reno came about," while training Miles between shows.

By the 14th, Ryan proposed to Joe that his protégé, O'Kelly, McLeod and Corbett's new charge, Morris, fight it out in a round-robin tournament to determine who might get a crack at Johnson's world title. Jack was at the Labor Temple in Pittsburgh, Pennsylvania on December 20, to second Walter Monahan against George "Kid" Cotton. Johnson and Cotton had a falling out after the Jeffries fight, "Kid" allegedly resenting the abuse he suffered in camp at the hands of the champion. Cotton gained a measure of revenge against Monahan, beating him soundly in six rounds and exposing him for the unschooled, though brave, pug that that he was.

Joe admitted that McLeod did not possess sufficient experience to take on Con O'Kelly. He turned down Ryan's offer.[4] O'Kelly wouldn't amount to much as a boxer, though, with a ND10 with Dan "Porky" Flynn on January 17, 1911 and a KOby11 in 1913 to "Battling" Jim Johnson. The *Syracuse Post-Standard*, covering the "white hopes," said "Nobody seems to take McLeod seriously except Choynski, and he is securing a meal ticket with Miles in vaudeville." Indeed, the farmer from the "Show Me State" never had a recorded boxing match, only sparring sessions with Joe.

After their vaudeville tour, it was said that McLeod and Choynski split the proceeds. A pair of articles gave closure to the episode. The first was by prominent Chicago fight manager-promoter, "Doc" Reid, for the January 22 *Duluth News-Tribune*: "Miles McLeod was ... loudly heralded as a white man's hope, and after being boosted through the press, went on a theatrical tour under the management of Joe Choynski ... Of course ... McLeod never had a fight in his life, never saw a set of gloves, nor even knew how to hold up his hands. But that didn't make any difference to Joe when he needed money ... Joe used McLeod until the public began talking about matching the latter with some other hope, and when the talk got too strong, Joe and his hope parted. This will in all probability wind up Miles."

The December 15, 1912 *Oakland Tribune* said: "Joe slipped a pair of mitts on the farmer's fists ... and showed him how to pose. The reporters got flashlight photos of him; Joe told 'em how Miles nearly killed him with a punch while they were sparring ... and the McLeod boom was launched ... Joe secured a nice vaudeville engagement ... He managed to teach McLeod how to put up his hands and go through a sort of denatured boxing exhibition. It was pretty poor stuff, but it went O.K., because the announcement was always made ... that McLeod had challenged for the ... championship, and intended to wipe out the disgrace of Jeffries' defeat. Of course, McLeod never meant to go into the ring ... When the ... course was over, he took it on the lam for his farm, where I suppose he'll be telling the boobs for the rest of his days about the time ... he was a 'famous fighter.' " Miles went back to Missouri and was not heard from again.[5]

On January 9, 1911, it was announced that Choynski had been appointed boxing instructor of the new Pittsburgh Athletic Club. The recently-completed facility, located at 4215 5th Avenue in "The Smoky City," was reported to have cost $1,500,000, and called "one of the finest clubhouses in America." The magnificent structure houses the club today. Joe was chosen over candidates from around the country. He cancelled the vaudeville tour he had scheduled for the rest of the winter. Joe signed a contract with the Pittsburgh Athletic Association, and returned to Chicago on the 9th. He immediately set about the task of selling his La Grange property "and moving his lares and penates* to Pittsburgh." Joe said his friends advised him to apply for the job, and did so on a lark, but "It was taking a shot at the moon." Joe said he was "tickled to death" to have the job.[6] He was to report for duty at the club's opening on February 22, but that date would be pushed back. Joe had ended his connection with the Illinois Athletic Association some time after 1908.

* Lares and Penates – Originally, ancient Roman gods of the household; a family's treasured possessions, household goods.

February 10 *Mississippi Daily Herald*: "Some years ago, Choynski appeared before the Chicago Athletic Club ... against a promising amateur.

'Go after me as hard as you please,' said the pugilist. Depend on me to take care of myself. We will give the spectators something to see.' The amateur was a husky youth, and went after Choynski with such vim that for three rounds, he had the best of the argument. The go was ... for four rounds, and when time was called the 4th time, there were some expecting to see Choynski knocked out. Hardly had the men stepped into the ring, than Choynski landed a punch on the amateur's jaw that put him to sleep for 10 minutes. Choynski afterward apologized for the blow. 'I had to do it,' he said, 'for you put up such a stiff fight that if I had not knocked you out, my reputation would have been ruined.' " The identity of the "amateur" isn't known, and no exact fit for the bout is found in Joe's record. The closest match is the three-round knockout of an "M. Woods" on February 11, 1900 in Chicago, so this might be the set-to in question.

On January 28, a wealthy oil magnate named F.B. Ufer took over the management of "white hope," Carl Morris. Ufer wired Choynski, requesting that he travel to Tulsa, Oklahoma, along with Bob Armstrong, and develop Carl to challenge Jack Johnson. While flattering, Joe had already accepted the prestigious and lucrative position in Pittsburgh, and had to decline. "He is getting a line on ... fighters around the country, and plans to stage a good show about a week after the club's opening." In "getting a line," Joe sparred on the 10th with a Chicago lightweight contender named Mickey Sheridan. He was favorably impressed and declared Sheridan "a comer" with the makings of a champion. Although never a champion, Mickey did have a rather successful career, covering at least 46 fights over nine years.[7]

"Lying on a bed in a small room on the 3rd floor of the Hotel Albany" in New York City, an ailing Charles "Parson" Davies told the March 13 *Colorado Springs Gazette* that his ideal fighter was Jackson. He testified that Peter was "a cripple" in his match with Corbett, having been thrown from a buggy and badly injured four weeks prior to the bout. "The Parson has seen little or none of the local boxing shows. He can't get around without help, and without Kid McCoy, or as the Parson calls him, Dr. Selby, he would lie in bed continuously. The Kid manages to get around daily to cheer the 'old sport' up. He dresses him at times, and gets him down to the hotel's café, where the Parson can sit and talk with old friends ..."[8] The erratic trickster, McCoy, had a caring and humanitarian side – that much is clear.

On March 5, Nick Burley died of a heart attack in Seattle, Washington. He was only 35. His obituary in the March 14 *Daily Juneau Dispatch*, quoting the *Tacoma News*, claimed his real name was Nicholas Berinavitch, rather than Barovich. "The Champion of the Yukon" had his last recorded fight in December, 1907 in Victoria, British Columbia, Canada, knocking old Frank Slavin out in two rounds. "Nick was a nifty looking fellow when ... at his best ... a neat dresser ... well built ... a rugged constitution. In the past three years he aged a lot and at the time of his death, his hair was almost white ...

he still imagined he was in good enough shape to enter the ring ..."

Jack Johnson told a reporter, "Now that I've got this 'color line' business out of my system I feel better ... There was such a prejudice against dark-skinned fighters that everybody wondered how Joe Choynski happened to go into the ring with me down in Galveston. Some went so far as to say that Joe must have been under the influence of 'wealthy water' when he agreed to meet me. The fact was, Joe did not size up a man by his color. Joe was on the look out for muscle, and he didn't care anything about the color of the package it was wrapped in."[9]

Joe still hadn't got the fighting bug out of his system at age 42. Notices came out on March 22 that he was seriously considering taking on "Kid" McCoy, in a six or 10 round contest. The venue would be either the new Pittsburgh A.C. or "Philadelphia" Jack O'Brien's new American Athletic Club in Philly. "The Kid" had just "made a poor showing against a preliminary fighter" named Jack Fitzgerald in Philly on March 20. Choynski received a letter on the 21st from O'Brien, asking if he would be willing to meet McCoy in a six-rounder, the date to be named later. Joe was undecided, but asked O'Brien what terms might be worked out. That very day, Joe "put up a stellar bout" with a tennis player named John C. Neely, Jr. at Gilmore's Gymnasium, and demonstrated that he was still as clever as ever. He let Neely force matters, adroitly slipping and evading blows, countering judiciously, so as not to discourage or hurt his opponent.[10]

Promoters were attempting to organize an international amateur boxing tournament. It was expected the heavyweight class would have "entries from England and France ... against (such) American exponents ... as Warren Barbour, Tony Biddle and the pick of the division from the west." William Warren Barbour won the 1910 National AAU heavyweight championship the previous year. Rather than turn pro, he pursued a career in politics, serving as a New Jersey Senator from 1931 to his death in 1943. "Tony Biddle" was Anthony Joseph Drexel Biddle, Sr., a millionaire who pursued a range of interests, including "athletic Christianity." The 1967 Walt Disney film, "The Happiest Millionaire," was based on his life. Biddle frequently sparred with "Philadelphia" Jack O'Brien, Jack Johnson and Gene Tunney, in a boxing ring on his property. *Oakland Tribune*: "Choynski has a pupil in Chicago whom he thinks superior to ... Barbour or Biddle. He will be ... in the elimination trials to decide ... the American title defender."[11] The name of Joe's mysterious pupil wasn't mentioned.

Joe got the last of his affairs settled in Chicago on March 28, and left the next day for Pittsburgh. He was to be present the first week in April for the opening of the new "Millionaire Athletic Club," as the new facility was referred to. Shortly after Joe's arrival, he established a domicile at 228 Coltart Avenue,* about two blocks from the club. The address of the clubhouse, built in the Venetian High Renaissance architectural style, was

3430 Forbes Avenue, where Joe was listed as "Instructor."[12] The club's formal event was held on the evening of April 20. *New York Times*: " 'A half dozen prominent society women jumped up from their seats ... at the first boxing show ... for society at the $2,000,000 Pittsburgh Athletic Association clubhouse, and appealed to the referee to stop the fight ... when Madole brought the blood from Goodman's mouth with a right-hand jab. Referee Joe Choyinski (sic) ... had to send the boys to their corners and beg the women to keep their seats. It is estimated that $40,000,000 of Pittsburgh's wealth was represented by the 1,000 present. Engraved invitations were sent out to 1,200 society women and men. It was also a full dress affair. Even Referee Joe Choyinski was in full dress. The women were attired in beautiful gown ... management ... intends inviting 'Tony' Biddle and Jack O'Brien here in the near future for a six round fight. Since Jack O'Brien had Philadelphia society at his exclusive club to witness a boxing bout some time ago, Pittsburgh society has been clamoring for society fights.' "
* The 1914 Pittsburgh City Directory lists Joe's residence as 228 Coltart Square, but no such location exists today.

On the night of June 30, Joe was at Pittsburgh's new 18th Regiment Armory's housewarming show. The Enlisted Men's Club included in its program "gymnastic exercises by Prof. Roth's class of athletes, popular songs by individuals and a quartet, two wrestling bouts and two three-round boxing matches, with Joe Choynski as referee." The boxing bouts were between amateurs from K Company, M Company and neighborhood locals. On November 10, "Joe Choynski ... now giving boxing instructions here to wealthy amateurs, demonstrated that he had 'come back' before an audience of club women today by skipping the rope 212 times."

While sparring with his young students, the former "Frisco Flash" got the idea he still had the stamina to face a prime lion of the ring. On the 11th, it was announced that Joe was making a comeback, preparing to take on a young, local fighter by the name of Albert "Buck" Crouse. The clash was to be a six round affair, held in Pittsburgh sometime the following month. Choynski recently gave his assessment that "present day fighters are a lot of sluggers without science. He ... figures they would have little chance to outpoint any level-headed man with a nifty left jab. Crouse ... is one of the most promising heavyweights in the ring today, and is apt to upset Joe's ... pugilistic aspirations." Joe felt he wouldn't have much trouble "slipping over the sleep producer on his opponent." Typical of many retired boxers, he felt the new crop were "counterfeits," who couldn't hold a candle to his contemporaries ... or to him. An Iowa paper claimed that Choynski "does not drink even tea or coffee and has long been careful of his diet." Crouse stood 5' 10" and went about 170 pounds. He had some 73 pro fights, including 48 wins (38 knockouts) and only one loss.[13] He would have presented a formidable first opponent in a comeback attempt. It is just as well that Joe changed his mind once again about a serious bout.

Next came mention of Joe's friendship with George Coxey. He wrote, from the Pittsburgh club: "Dear George: It is true I am contemplating a return to the ring. I have seen all the newcomers ... they are a lot of real dubs, such as I would give $100 to if I couldn't stop 'em in three rounds. I am in better shape than ever. People will laugh at this ... but ... I do 10 miles at a run three times a week, where I never could run a quarter in my career. I will get on here later on, and if I fail, it will give the croakers another chance to vindicate, 'I told you so,' but, as I live, I'll fool

Joe with George Coxey, January, 1913

'em ... my hands – my strong point – are intact, and I can meet the big men. And who knows – I am the most confident man alive."

Coxey was born George Weinstein, in Russia, September, 1883, but immigrated to the States and became a professional boxer. The January 21, 1912 *Atlanta Constitution* said bantamweight Harry Harris, "the human hairpin," and George M. Cohan, famous actor, singer, dancer and playwright, boxed "almost daily with George Coxey ... a very clever boxer of the Attell type." Coxey was a sparring partner of the great Abe Attell, years earlier. On October 20, 1899, he was involved in a tragic bout with a Jim Hill (or Hall, no relation to the Choynski foe). George was a 10-1 underdog in the Covelo, California fight. Hill "punished Coxey mercilessly in each round." George came back to stop his opponent in the 6th ... with "a right-hand uppercut on the jaw and a left-hand heart punch." Hill did not regain consciousness and died shortly thereafter. The October 22, 1899 *San Francisco Call* said "Coxey claims relationship with 'General' Coxey of Coxey army fame." The event likely prompted George's retirement from the ring. He later became a highly-noted life insurance agent for New York Life, at their 51 Madison Avenue headquarters in New York.

In 1926, he was referred to as "George W. Coxey, the newsboy who made a fortune selling insurance." He wrote policies for Charlie Chaplin,

Jack Dempsey (heavyweight), Al Jolson, Jim Corbett and Cohan. A 1930 columnist wrote: "New York has several spectacular champ life insurance solicitors reputed to do a combined business of many millions a year. One is George Coxey, who specializes in ... writers, cartoonists and figures in the sporting world. He angles for new business through a free press clipping bureau. His readers clip, file and index articles about his ... prospects. Coxey rarely makes a personal or telephone call. Instead, from time to time he mails ... clippings to those on his list. He merely inquires if they have seen the printed matter and expresses a hope they are enjoying life. A policy is never suggested. A clipping from an obscure paper in the Orient about Tex Rickard resulted in the contact which sold a huge policy to the fight promoter." Coxey had been selling insurance since around 1898, and was still collecting and posting articles from "unheard-of sources" as late as 1948. That year, the *Lowell Sun* noted: "George Coxey, the Broadway insurance man, who has been keeping Big Street's improvident characters out of jams for 50 years, maintains the largest one-man newspaper clipping service in the world. It is almost impossible to get your name in the papers without receiving a cutting ... from the roly-poly veteran."

A 1925 article: "You would think him a cold-blooded, disinterested individual, like 'insurance agent' sounds. But, some day when Coxey appears before the Judgment Seat, the Master is going to say, 'George, you're not an insurance agent, you're a friend to man – a guardian of lives. I've a list of hearts you have saved from breaking.' And, George, surprised, will shuffle uncomfortably and murmur, 'Why, that wasn't anything. I couldn't see those folks lose out, that's all.' ... Coxey ... keeps eternally after the fellows who 'mean to provide for the wife and kids, but don't just get 'round to it.' George prods and pokes ... follows them ... into elevators ... the subway ... theatres ... taxis and on 42nd Street. 'Now, Tom,' Coxey will say, 'you know you ought to fix up that insurance. What would Kittie and Tom, Jr. do if–' 'Oh, I know, I know, I'll do it tomorrow, George, positively I will.' 'No – You'll do it now,' says George. 'If you're short, I'll fix you up till next month. Only, you got to take out a policy, and a big one.' We know one little woman in the theatrical business whom George saved from the doorstep wolf, just by a hunch. He saw that her husband was burning the candle at both ends, he coerced him into doubling his insurance, and he saw to it that 24 hours after the poor chap dropped dead, the wife was paid her due. You will meet George on a front seat in the Celestial Regions."

A 1958 bio reads: "Somewhere in Southern Russia ... a little baby boy ... named George Weinberg. His father and mother were among the downtrodden ... through a kind Providence, 10 years later ... this Russian-Jewish boy was selling papers in New York ... about the time Coxey's army of tattered men* tramped the country. Little George's clothing was so tattered the other newsies called him 'Coxy' ... George Coxey. This title insulted his pride ... The misery of his poverty became an enemy to be avenged. Strolling up Broadway almost any day, one might meet him, two benevolent eyes set deep in a rough face, button-holing the Broadway boys and preaching a personal religion. Those who knew him best called him 'The Reverend George.' And gladly they listened, for he was preaching the gospel of cheer and opulence. One day, a great calamity befell a poor family in the neighborhood where George lived. The breadwinner ... met with a fatal accident ... no one remained to provide ... He ... presented the widow with a fully paid insurance policy, which he had continued on the life of the unfortunate husband and father. (Coxey) numbered among his 'converts,' many Broadway celebrities, but his largest flock was among the lesser lights ... a host of widows and orphans ... who would be in despair only for his generous and quiet way of never letting a life insurance policy lapse."[14]

* The populist, Jacob Coxey. In 1894, he led a march of unemployed workers (nicknamed "Coxey's Army") on Washington, D.C., in an effort to force Congress to allocate more funds toward the creation of jobs.

Coxey sold many high-profile policies. June 14, 1927 *Ogden Standard-Examiner*: "Payment of $25,000 to Mrs. Beatrice Houdini, widow of Harry Houdini, magician, by the New York Life Insurance company ... for accidental death ... disclosed the company's acceptance of the claim that he died as the result of a blow. Houdini's death on October 30, 1926, according to George Coxey, an agent for the company, followed a week after he had challenged a McGill University student in Montreal to strike him a hard blow. He did this to prove his excellent physical condition, Coxey explained, adding that the blow landed in the region of the appendix and caused a rupture." (*New York Times*, July 13, 1927).

An incident allegedly occurred in Chicago sometime in 1911, when a bevy of famous heavyweights were in the city at the same time. John L. Sullivan and Bob Fitzsimmons were with their vaudeville companies, while Choynski was teaching the "sweet science" on the South Side. Jack Johnson, who had a house at 3344 South Wabash Avenue, was also in town, and Jake Kilrain was touring with Sullivan. A "resourceful press agent" felt it would be a great idea to get the fighters together for a photo, but he hadn't accounted for the venom that existed between them. Fitz had some sort of vendetta against Johnson, while Sully felt similarly toward "Ruby Bob." Jack supposedly said he "couldn't get a pleasant look from one of dem white trash fossils when he was in hawd luck, an' now they wants me to hop along an' do a brudder act wif dem." It is unlikely Johnson made such a statement, and the writer "quoting" him in the era's so-called "darky lingo," further detracts credibility. At any rate, the celebrated boxers chose not to celebrate together. "Choynski was the only one of the bunch, with the possible exception of Kilrain, who appeared to be unprovided with a grouch against ... the proposed combination."[15] In his old age, Joe did harbor bitter feelings toward some of his old rivals.

Joe Ruddy is a water polo legend. He won gold medals at the 1904 St. Louis Summer Olympics in the 4 x 50 yard freestyle (swim) relay and Men's Water Polo. Born Joseph Aloysius Ruddy, Sr. in 1878 to a family of swimmers, he became a member of the New York Athletic Club Water Polo team that won gold in 1904. Joe's underwater leg scissors was deadly, whether to the waist or legs. On March 14, 1912, the Pittsburgh Athletic Club hosted the United States AAU championships, featuring Ruddy's team against the Chicago Athletic Club's squad. Choynski was involved in the match, called "the roughest water polo game on record." Ruddy, nicknamed "The Human Fish," who could hold his breath underwater for 3 minutes 19 seconds, was in a similar match four years earlier. On March 28, 1908, the same two teams met in the national AAU final at New York.

March 29, 1908 *New York Times*: "A terrific game ... Rough play and charges of foul tactics marked the bitter contest from first to last, and because of the disabling of players on two occasions play was interrupted ... and men were ruled out or suspended while substitutions ... made ... at the end of ... two periods ... the score ... 1 to 1. (With only) 3 min. 16 seconds to play, Joe

Water Polo master, Joe Ruddy

Ruddy, NYAC, took the ball ... the length of the tank underwater ... tackled ... by 3 Chicago men, and fought them off ... At the Chicago goal, was tackled by Healy, 6 foot 4, 220 pound goaltender, who got him with back strangle and scissors hold ... outlasted Healy, came up, scored winning goal with 4 seconds to go ... after being underwater, fighting, 3 minutes 12 seconds." Following this match, the AAU temporarily removed Water Polo from its sanctioned sports, and the United States did not send a team to the 1908 London Games.

Back to March, 1912: *Time* magazine, April 1, 1935, claimed Choynski was coach of the Chicago team, although, as instructor of the Pittsburgh club, he had no business coaching the Chicago crew. Joe (in 1935), and Ruddy both refuted his role as coach, though Choynski recalled the event taking place in 1911. *Time*: "After four men had been carried out of the pool unconscious, Pugilist Choynsky (sic) hit Swimmer Ruddy on the jaw. Swimmer Ruddy then hit Choynsky in the eye. A riot ensued. Dr. W.L. Savage, the Pittsburgh physical education director, stopped the game (before half-time) and announced that several of the contestants would be barred from the Pittsburgh club house and pool. Among the spectators were Mrs. Ruddy, Anna Held. Both fainted. The Amateur Athletic Union promptly dropped water polo from its schedule until a year ago (1934)." As a result of the events of this day, the United States did not send a water polo team to the Stockholm Olympic Games of 1912.

Time magazine, May 6, 1935: "Sirs: I do not know whether it is intended for a joke but it is ill timed; on p.42 of your prized magazine dated April 1 is a squib about Ruddy, an amphibian of parts who claimed to have punched my optic ... I was boxing instructor at Pittsburgh Athletic Association. The club had just been inaugurated and a night set apart for the opening of the beautiful pool. The elite of Pittsburgh were in attendance. I was merely a spectator on the side lines. Ruddy punched an opponent on the nose and a reciprocal punch from his ... antagonist caused Ruddy's nose to bleed ... I ordered the swimmers out of the tank and they knew their master's voice. Like a lot of sardines they crawled to the dressing room ... Joseph B. Choynsky (sic), The Cincinnati Club, Cincinnati, Ohio."

From the book, "Letters," Ruddy's June 10, 1935 rebuttal: "Choynsky (sic) ... denies participating in fisticuffs with me during the ... game ... which marked the opening of the Pittsburgh Clubhouse some 25 years ago ... (said he was) a spectator on the side-lines at this memorable water polo game. However, later on he says he ordered the swimmers out of the pool ... As none of the participants ... came from Pittsburgh, let alone from the Pittsburgh A.A., it is absurd to ... believe these players (obeyed him) ... Choynsky came after me to tell ... what he felt like doing to me, and I told him in no uncertain terms what I intended to do to him if he started anything. I am sure there was no man present ... prizefighter or not, who could hit me and not get it back. If Mr. Choynsky says he did not strike me, and I didn't strike him back, I am willing to believe him now. All is forgiven and all is forgotten. Joseph A. Ruddy – New York City."

Ruddy won his first swimming race in 1893. He married champion swimmer Mary Donahue and the couple had five children, Mary, Dorothy, Joe, Jr., Ray and Donald. "Ruddy children were taken for their first swim at 11 months. At 2½ years, they were carried to the ocean, dumped into the breakers. At three, all were expert in the crawl. Girl Ruddys were trained until they won all the swimming prizes at their summer camps, then permitted to bathe for pleasure only. Ruddy boys received more rigorous instruction." Joe coached the New York A.C.'s water polo team in the 1920s and '30s, and his three sons were key players. A prime Ruddy, at approximately 170-pounds, with his lack of boxing experience, would be seriously handicapped against even a 43 year old, 1912 Choynski. "Joe Ruddy, famed water polo coach of the New York Athletic Club, insists that he not only hit Pugilist Choynsky (sic) in the eye but ... could have hit him two or three times. He firmly denies that anyone hit him on the nose. Ten years after the Pittsburgh incident Ruddy met Choynsky in Chicago and Choynsky challenged him to a public fight. Ruddy said he was willing if they could make any money out of it. Nothing happened."[16]

On the night of April 16, 1912, the Pittsburgh club hosted the Western Pennsylvania AAU boxing trials, and "Little Joe" refereed all bouts. In early August, he made a short visit to Chicago. Joe said he already felt like a native of Pittsburgh, having lived there only 15 months.[17] In September, opined "The Chrysanthemum": "The modern fighters have retrograded – especially in the heavyweight division – about 500 per cent in the last 10 years. Far be it from me to pose as a knocker, but I'm out of the game. I haven't even a white hope to manage, and I've watched 'em come and go ... at present ... there isn't even a bunch of good material in sight. Periods of depression happen in the boxing game, as in any ... sport or business. In a few years there will be a new crop of splendid fighters ... (there isn't now) a white man who can put up even a decent bout with Johnson ... who is 34 years old ... Imagine Johnson confronted by the fighters of the past – Corbett, Fitzsimmons, Slavin, and that crowd ... where would he be? I omit John L. Sullivan, because he drew the color line."

"In his own race, there would be Peter Jackson to meet him – and to beat him, sure and certain. Too bad Johnson hasn't the qualities of Peter Jackson. If the black fighters of today were like Jackson, there would be no color line and no racial prejudice in the ring. Jackson was a splendid gentleman, despite his color. To know him was to admire him and respect him. Bob Armstrong came nearest him in gentlemanly ways, but poor Bob never got up far enough to make a deep impression on the public. Were I but young again – oh, well, why blow my own trumpet? Still, I knocked Johnson out once, didn't I? And in my time, there were several heavies who were much larger and stronger than I – how would Johnson fare against (them)? Commercialism and crookedness have hurt the game and turned from the ring a lot of game lads who might have been champions, but who wouldn't stand for trickery. The fighters who were truly great and who live longest in the memories of the crowd were the honest ones ... However, if they succeed in discovering a duplicate of our old friend Bob Fitzsimmons, they may feel assured of developing a new world's champion."[18] In picking Jackson to defeat Johnson, Joe contradicted earlier statements. As regards bigotry relying on one man's behavior, this was self-delusion.

Joe penned a September 18 letter to Sydney, Australia: "Writing to the 'Referee's' old friend, Mr. F.E. Diamond ... Choynski says: 'Jim Barry ... asked me to second him against Luther McCarthey (sic), which I did. (Author: heavyweight Jim Barry, not the bantamweight). He made a miserable showing. Mac showed well for a novice, and is magnificently built ... whether he improves any is to be seen. How Barry ever stood up to Langford (whom I never saw in action) beats me, unless Sam is overrated, like the rest of them, for I have yet to see a man of this decade handle himself in an orthodox manner. Johnson's wife did the correct thing. Women are the limit. I hope it has a salutary effect on the hundreds of other white girls in the big cities of the North who have colored lovers. They all ought to be strung up.' "[19] Joe's harsh reference to Jack involved the suicide of his Caucasian wife, Etta Duryea, that same month. She shot herself in the head with a revolver, apparently suffering from clinical depression. Strange words, for one who was not known as a bigot.

In the years to follow, came fighters who assumed Joe's name as their "nom de guerre." At least two other boxers had the moniker, "Joe Choynski." It is doubtful if this was their real name. Jake Choynski claimed to be Joe's cousin. Some notable imitators, between 1900 and 1930, were "Sailor Joe Choynski," Bill Choynski, Jack Choynski, Pete Choynski, Steve Choynski ("The Milwaukee Iron Man" and "South Side Pole") and as many as seven who used the name, "Young Choynski" (or "Young Joe Choynski"). There was also a Bozo Choyinski and Simon Choyinski (sic). Most or all took their inspiration from "The California Terror."[20]

In January, 1913, Joe said of young, Cleveland, Ohio boxer, Tommy Gavigan: "He is one of the most promising middleweights I have seen in a long time ... cool-headed ... good tempered, and appears to have two good hands. In my opinion, Gavigan will be a topnotcher in a short time."[21] Comments like this would pass right under the radar, if not for the fact that Joe would soon be managing Gavigan. Tommy fought a ND6 against future champion, George Chip, on January 4 at the Old City Hall in Pittsburgh. This is probably where Joe first saw him. By October, Tommy already had 26 recorded pro fights, mostly wins.

The rise of 19-year-old Luther McCarty to the fabricated title of "White Hope Heavyweight Champion," following a KO18 of Al Palzer, resulted in yet another wave of young, would-be pugs. The February 5 *Grand Forks Herald* said Joe had discovered (yet again), his own, new "white hope," "able to crowd aside McCarty and (Jess) Willard as soon as Choynski turns him loose. The veteran says his discovery has frequently knocked him down in training bouts ... he is not wasting his time on a dead one. Choynski refuses to reveal the name of the new wonder, who he says is the son of a wealthy man who will not give his consent to the youngster's ... career in the ring, unless he is sure to become the champion. Another month or two ... to put on the finishing touches ... and ... challenges to McCarty and Willard will be in order." This young "phenom" was apparently not Gavigan.

A heavyweight prospect being compared to Joe and Jim Corbett was Bob McAllister, of Frisco's Olympic Athletic Club. With some 19 amateur fights, he was described by a knockout victim, as "a mighty clever man ... fast as lightning" "In ... appearance ... ring work ... a counterpart of old Joe Choynski ... the coolness and judgment of an old ring veteran, his judgment of distance is splendid ... blows ... accurate ... hard as a trip hammer." "A dancing master ... employs the same tactics (as) Corbett ... He shoots his left straight from the shoulder ... counters ... with his right ... well versed in side stepping, keeping inside of leads and landing on the body at will."

McAllister won the Pacific Coast amateur championships in the middle- and heavyweight divisions and had yet to lose a fight. The club brought in Jim Corbett to watch him spar. Although Jim found points to improve upon, he felt Bob had the right stuff. He especially liked his balance, quickness in countering and punching to the ribs while infighting. On March 2, while Bob was training at the Wheelman's Club for his first pro tilt, against "Sailor" Willie Meehan, Joe's brother, Edwin Choynski, who lived in Oakland, was "giving McAllister what pointers Joe did not steal from the family locker. He is as much interested in the game as was the former champion, although he did not make the mark in the squared arena that his brother did." Edwin was a member of the Olympic Club at this time, along with eldest brother, Herbert. On the 12th, Edwin was in McAllister's corner for his pro debut against "Fat Boy" Meehan. He won a handy 10 round verdict over the short (5' 9") "wee" Willie. Bob (6' ½") floored his man in the opening frame and outboxed him down the stretch.[22] Meehan was a tough choice for a pro debut. He went on to win a pair of four round nods over a young Jack Dempsey, adding a couple of four round draws, and only losing to "The Mauler" once.

Around March 20, Tommy Gavigan signed a managerial contract with Joe. He had just come off a knockout loss to George Chip on February 24. Although losing to Chip was no disgrace, it signaled a decline in Tommy's career. On the 29th, Gavigan said he had already been taught a lot by Choynski and expected to win a March 31 bout in Pittsburgh against Walter Monaghan. It was not enough, as Gavigan came out on the wrong side of a six round "newspaper decision" (ND6).[23] On August 1, Bob McAllister put on a boxing show for his fellow "Winged O's" at the Olympic A.C. The *Oakland Tribune* said one his sparmates was to be "Eddie Choynski."[24] Bob lost his first bout on January 12, 1914, a KOby7 to legendary middleweight Mike Gibbons, but not another defeat until his 33rd pro fight, the vast majority of results being decision wins. The most important bout of his career was a L4 to future heavyweight champion, Jack Dempsey. While McAllister never gained a shot at a world title, Edwin's protégé fought some top names, and did not dishonor himself.

On October 16, Joe refereed a middleweight scrap at Elmwood Place, Ohio (a tiny suburb of Cincinnati) between Gus Christie of Milwaukee, Wisconsin and "Young" Clark (or, Grant "Kid" Clark) of Columbus. In round two, Clark fell to the floor, claiming a foul. Choynski saw no foul, and instructed Clark to continue. The latter refused, so Joe awarded the fight to Gus and called all bets off. The last act allegedly enabled Joe to spoil a betting coup. Promoters of the fight received a letter a short time later from the sporting writer of a Middletown, Ohio paper, reporting that several Middletown friends of Clark had taken part in a scheme, whereby he would "emerge victorious" by crooked means, thus gaining them a windfall on bets. Joe remarked, "I am glad I called all bets off."[25]

Sometime shortly before October, 1913, Joe Choynski first met and befriended Elbert Hubbard. Elbert Green Hubbard was born June 19, 1856 on a farm in Bloomington, Illinois. His father was a country doctor and farmer. At age 16, Elbert left for Chicago, where he worked as a newspaper writer. In 1875, he moved to Buffalo, New York and began as a salesman for soap manufacturer, J.D. Larkin and Company, becoming prosperous. Hubbard felt unfulfilled, however, and wanted a literary career. He sold his interest in the Larkin Company, and, in 1895, established an Arts and Crafts community in the little village of East Aurora, New York,  where he made his fame. Located 15-20 miles southeast of Buffalo, East Aurora was home to former United States President, Millard Fillmore from 1826 to 1830. Upon founding his artisan colony, Elbert gathered a number of very talented (and some eccentric) artists and craftsman together. He named the movement or community, the Roycrofters, after the 17th-century London printers, Samuel and Thomas Roycroft. The name (Roycroft) had an additional significance to Hubbard, as it meant "King's Craft." In early European guilds, craftsmen earned the right to make things for the King, by achieving a high degree of proficiency at their craft.

Hubbard set up a small printing press, known as the Roycroft Press. He took his inspiration from the Kelmscott Press, established in England by William Morris in 1891. The Roycroft community would employ some renowned individuals. One was the young author, Stephen Crane (1871-1900), whose most noted work was the classic Civil War novel, "The Red Badge of Courage." Crane died in Germany of tuberculosis at the young age of 28. His writing style was a great inspiration to Ernest Hemingway and others. Another celebrated Roycrofter was illustrator, W.W. (William Wallace) Denslow (1856-1915). Denslow got his start creating minor illustrations for various journals, and was employed for a time by the *Chicago Herald*. In 1896, upon hearing of the first book produced by the Roycrofters, "Song of Songs," Denslow sent samples of his art to Hubbard, which led to his prompt hiring. He created many fine illustrations for Hubbard's magazines over the years, but in 1899, fashioned a business alliance with L. Frank Baum. Denslow illustrated Baum's 1899 children's book, "Father Goose," but achieved his greatest fame the following year, when he created the classic imagery for Baum's instant blockbuster, "The Wizard of Oz." He died of pneumonia in 1915.

Elbert became famous as an author, orator, philosopher, publisher and salesman. His guild produced fine books from handmade paper, wooden furniture and items of iron, copper, stained glass and leather. Similar to the bookstore and home of I.N. Choynski, the Roycroft community, which Hubbard sometimes referred to as "The Society of Philistines," became a place for freethinkers, radicals, reformers and suffragists. "The Master of Roycroft" gave many opportunities for women in his business, not a given in that era. He also became a popular fixture on the lecture circuit, his "homespun philosophy" said to have evolved from "a loose William Morris-inspired socialism," to a fervent defense of American free enterprise, know-how and perseverance. Hubbard began referring to himself as "Fra Elbertus" (Brother Elbert), a tongue-in-cheek affectation meant to "emphasize the aura of medieval monasticism surrounding the Roycroft Campus ..." The two long-running magazines published by Elbert became famous for their wit, whimsy, philosophy and satire. The 1st was "The *Philistine*," bound in brown butcher paper, because, as Hubbard quipped, "there is meat inside." It ran from 1895 until his death in 1915. The other was "The *Fra*," first published in 1908, but continued after Elbert's death by his son, Elbert Hubbard II, until 1918. Although his "Little Journeys" book series of biographical sketches was wildly popular,

Elbert Hubbard, circa 1914-1915

Hubbard's most famous and enduring single work was probably his inspirational essay, "A Message to Garcia."[26]

If "Elbert Hubbard" or the surname, Hubbard, rings a bell (aside from the Old Mother of nursery rhyme fame), it can be told that L. Ron did have a quasi-relationship to the former. Lafayette Ronald Hubbard, the late science fiction writer, author of the book, Dianetics and founder of the Church of Scientology, was born March 13, 1911 in Tilden, Nebraska, to Harry Ross Hubbard and Ledora Hubbard. His father, Harry, born Henry August Wilson in Fayette, Iowa, was orphaned as an infant. He was later adopted by Elbert's brother, James, who lived in Fredericksburg, Iowa. L. Ron Hubbard, though not related by blood to Elbert, became his nephew by adoption. He was barely four years old when "The Fra" met his untimely demise in 1915. The two may have never met. Elbert was a Rosicrucian, believer in big business, and much more. Opinions of him and his legacy run the gamut. Detractors called him an egomaniac, but if nothing else, the man should be credited for organizing and maintaining a prosperous community and business, contributing to the American culture.

Just when and where Joe met Elbert Hubbard does not appear a matter of record. It may have been during one of the trips "The Sage of East Aurora" made while lecturing, or on other business, as he was frequently in such cities as Chicago and Pittsburgh. Certainly, there were qualities possessed by Hubbard that led to his becoming a good friend of Joe's. Although one was from "Sun-up" (east coast) and the other, "Sunset" (west coast), they shared many common traits. Both were versed in and sought out art and the beauty in life. Elbert believed in honest, hard toil and exercise outdoors, fresh air and wholesome, simple meals, food that had been organically grown outside. Further, he believed in big business, but at the same time, in abstemious habits and "poverty of the soul," as the path to happiness. The fact that Hubbard undertook and survived William Muldoon's full, six-week spartan and grueling health course at his Purchase, New York camp, or "Hygienic Institute," speaks volumes of his fortitude.[27] In Hubbard, Joe seems to have found a kindred spirit – one who, while very much a part of free enterprise, also had a side which was independent, free-thinking, anti-establishment and non-conformist. Joe made the trip to "Sun-up" (a nickname Elbert had for the East Aurora community) on at least three occasions. The known visits are the one mentioned next, a 2nd in 1917 and the 3rd in 1918, the last two after Hubbard's death.

The only known photo of Choynski and Hubbard together appeared in the October, 1913 "Fra," in an ad for James S. Coward Shoes. It shows them conversing and smiling broadly: "Joe Choynski and Fra Elbertus discussing old times. When Professor Joe Choynski spent a few weeks at Roycroft, incidentally giving daily readings from the writings of Ibsen* ... he said: 'Lookee, my boy! When you walk, see to it that you are rightly shod.

You must have shoes ... neither too tight nor too loose ... heels ... not too flat nor too high. It is a matter of anatomy and foot-ease. When training for my debates, my principal exercise was walking ... on the good old Open Road – a bunch of us – 5, 10, 15, 20 miles and back. Walking is man's

natural exercise.' So says Joe Choynski, and Joe knows. Joe is 45 and 'fit' yet. Well-being traces to the feet ... reflect the condition of your underpinning. If you would be at peace with yourself and your neighbor ... It is essential your sole-mates be on good terms with your pedals. The next thing to having your path through life strewn with American Beauty roses is ... Coward Shoes."

*   Henrik Johan Ibsen (1828-1906), a famous Norwegian

Elbert Hubbard and Choynski, East Aurora, NY, 1913

poet and playwright. That Joe would recite such a literary figure is another example of his cultured persona and interest in the fine arts.

Although Joe's quoted words seem contrived, they give further insight into the man and his era. It is probable that the term "debates" here, is a euphemism for his fights. Hubbard was known for his ribbon bow tie, wide-brimmed Stetson hat, long, Buster Brown-style hair, baggy corduroy pants and long, caped overcoat. He spoke highly of the Elks (BPOE), of which Joe became a member. Although Hubbard said he was not a "jiner" (joiner), he said he would begin and end with the Elks, if he were, and, "The Elks stand for a certain intellect and ethics ... has no quarrel with God. Your Elk never weeps over his own troubles, but for the stricken souls of earth his tears of pity are near the surface. The Elk loves children, respects old age ... To do good is the first prong in an Elk's creed."[28] He never seems to have spoken so positively of any other organization.

1914 began with Pittsburgh promoters negotiating with Fitzsimmons for a six round fight at the city's Duquesne Gardens arena. Fitz recently challenged the current white hopes, as Joe had, earlier. This prompted local fight architects to bombard Bob with offers. Choynski was not overly enthusiastic about a match with Bob, as he was a prosperous boxing instructor and not in need of publicity, but papers said promoters had "practically landed him." They expressed the belief that Joe was "perhaps in better trim than any of the old timers." Amazingly, fight fans appeared interested in such a clash. If Joe was in financial need, it would be put behind him in a short time, as he was about to receive an unexpected windfall. The proposed match went by the wayside. Sometime in 1914, Joe and Louise moved to 4 Olympia Place, a few blocks further from the Pittsburgh club, where Joe also taught boxing. He was listed as "Instructor" and "Physical Director." There they would reside until at least 1917.[29]

The February 10 *New York Times* told of a recent raid by police on Tom Sharkey's saloon, on 14th Street in Manhattan. Tom was convicted of "being the proprietor of a disorderly resort," awaiting sentencing without bail. In that era, boxing, saloons and such fell in and out of favor with the law, depending on such factors as public sentiment, which political party ruled and who they owed favors to. Sharkey's Café had long been a notorious watering hole, though, and he remained in confinement until March 17, also paying a fine. Tom had lately developed an interest in light harness horses, and "He and his fast horse have been familiar figures on the Speedway for several years." A photo circa 1930 shows Sharkey and Choynski standing at a racetrack. The ex-rivals maintained a friendship to the end.

In early March, one paper claimed: "Interest in amateur boxing in Pittsburgh has been aroused to its highest point by the announcement that Joe Choynski ... had been engaged to coach the students of Pitt university in the manly art of self-defense."[30] If this happened, Joe either performed the task on the side, in addition to his instruction at the Pittsburgh A.C., or he taught students *at* the Pittsburgh club. Meantime, Joe wasn't giving up hope of discovering *his* "hope." He was quoted on March 13: "I have the coming champion of the world under my wing – George Hauser. He stands 6' 1" in height, does not smoke or drink, not even tea or coffee. He has already won six knockout bouts. He's as game as a pebble and nice to look at. Hauser runs an ice wagon in the summer and a blacksmith shop during the winter." The name George Hauser never illuminates the ledger of "pugilistic greats," his existing (and probably incomplete) record showing three wins and two draws before the article, eight consecutive losses after. Hardly compelling stuff. As late as June 28, however, Joe was still crowing about his "great find": "My man Hauser scored another KO recently. He is improving wonderfully, but will not let him show in New York until next winter ... until he's fit, as I cannot stand sarcasm, and I'm very vain. So, believe me when I tell you he'll make good. We will not demand all the money ... Will act just like the old school. Get what we draw. Pittsburgh is the best town on the map for bouts, but we've had such rotten shows that the fans will not attend. If they would only allow decisions."[31]

On March 25, Joe discovered he had inherited $10,000. A Chinese restaurateur in Chicago named Jim Pon passed away a few days earlier, and his two sons, Ned and Bert Ying, sent for Joe by telegraph, as directed earlier by their late father. The young men had been unable to open their father's safe. Choynski arrived in Chicago on the 25th with a safecracker, at "The Garden of the Seven Lilies," the 22nd Street restaurant the father had owned. Within a few minutes, the "safe expert" opened the steel safe, and Mr. Pon's will, inside, was read in the presence of "the family lawyer." Joe was named executor of the estate, the guardian of Jim's two sons, and left $10,000, a goodly portion of Pon's amassed fortune.

"Choynski ... became accustomed to hiring Chinese help in his house; so, when in Chicago he needed a 'boy,' he usually applied to Moy Sing ... one of the Windy City's prominent citizens in Chinatown. About nine years ago, Mrs. Choynski informed Joe that a new servant would have to be obtained. Moy Sing immediately got in touch with Yian Pond, who had two sons in China ... he was anxious to bring to the United States for educational purposes. Choynski agreeing to house the youngsters, they were sent for. These boys were Yian Ying Song ... now 25 – and Ying Ngow, 18. Their family name is Yian, but according to the Chinese custom, boys cannot assume this until they become of age. Ying Song, having reached man's estate, is known as Yian Ying Song to his Chinese friends, and to his Yankee acquaintances as Ned Ying. Ying Ngow has three years to go before he can take the family name. He is better known as Bert Ying."

Joe extended many kind acts toward Pon over the years, and the latter never forgot. First, Joe sent the boys to school. He said they were apt students, and they remained with him "until he came to Pittsburgh several years ago. They quickly became Americanized, and are now up to the minute. 'Both these boys,' said Joe, 'are good Americans. They speak excellent English, are well educated, can ride, box, shoot and do everything boys of this country are taught to do.' " The Chinese restaurant owner became wealthy and sent his oldest son, Ned Ying, to China, where he married. Upon Ned's return to the States, leaving his wife and a young son behind, he was halted at Seattle, Washington by immigration officials. The officials questioned his identity and status as a citizen, and were preventing Ned from re-entry. Joe came to the rescue, when his urgent letter to the immigration department explained that Ned Ying had been born in America. Ned was re-admitted, and Choynski arranged for his little boy to join him in the States. Jim Pon's real name was said to be Yian Pond. In accordance with Pon's will, Joe arranged for the care of Ned Ying's wife and mother in China. The remains of Jim Pon were sent to "the Yian burial grounds in a small province in western China."[32]

Elbert Hubbard told a less accurate version. He related an incident

Jackie Wilson, Jim Corbett & Joe, Atlantic City (NJ) boardwalk, August 14, 1914

several years earlier in Chicago: "It seems that Col. Joe Choynski, prize fighter and ambidextrous, charming, bookish gentleman, about 20 years ago was working the Wire Grass Circuit with a variety show ... one of those well-to-do county seats where sons of the best citizens at times transform themselves into hooligans and hoodlums. A Chinaman had come to town and opened (a) laundry; one night the hoodlums gathered and were sending dead cats and other delectables through the front windows. Joe ... on his way from the theater to his hotel ... stopped, sized up the situation, gently chided the

hoodlums for their actions ... begged they would go along peaceably and leave the Chinese to his textile ablutions ... the hoodlums transferred their attentions (to) 'the dude actor.' ... Colonel Choynski only smiled ... waded in, gave out upper cuts ... short-arm jabs and ... long-armed swings, all without prejudice. The hoodlums hit the dirt, and suddenly ... there was no one on the spot but Joe and the Chinaman."

"Joe ... left town the next day on the 9:40 and duly forgot the incident. And the years passed. The Chinaman made money in his industrious and economical fashion. A few weeks ago he was taken ill ... sent for a lawyer ... made his will, and left all of his money, about 10,000 dollars, to Joe Choynski. Then, the Chinaman died. The lawyer ... found ... Joe ... acting as director of the Pittsburgh Athletic Club. The Chinaman, it seems, had written Joe's name out on a piece of butcher's paper with a stick and kept it all these years. The money was sent to Joe ... He really did not know what to do with it, and explained ... since he ... never earned it, it wasn't really his, and all he could do was accept it as a trustee. And now ... Choynski has decided what he will do with the 10,000 dollars. He has started a school in San Francisco to give lessons to Chinese in physical culture."

Choynski was "teetotally flabbergasted" at the windfall, adding, "I never met a finer man in my life than was old Yian Pond. He was dead in love with those two sons ... to do them a good turn was to win the father's undying gratitude. While I knew the old fellow liked me, I never dreamed of him remembering me in his will." Joe "said ... his newly-acquired riches will not have any effect on his present mode of life. He will remain with the P.A.A. (Pittsburgh Athletic Association) and go along ... as though nothing happened."[33] The ethnic stereotypes (a "Chinaman" and a laundry) and other errors (confusing Joe with "Colonel" Herbert, etc.) aside, Elbert's article suggests he and Joe were as yet only so well acquainted.

April 11, 1914 *New Zealand Truth* (Neville Forder): Joe was "the first American to wear his hair long in the ring, under the impression it was a protection to his head; a myth also ... believed ... by American-rules football players. A fair-haired, blue-eyed, lazy, lounging sort of a lad, Joe became an immense favorite in Sydney." Abe Pollock, noted boxing referee and scribe, wrote of the cultivated jabs thrown by fighters like Corbett and Fitz. "Joe Choynski used his left almost entirely in all his hardest battles, and was known as the hardest hitting boxer ... to get around. His opponent always ran into that jabbing, stinging left ... and nine times out of 10, gave up sore and discouraged." An October 10 story out of Chicago told of a visit Joe made there a short time earlier. He believed a lack of versatility by boxers in attack and defense did more to shorten careers than any other single factor. "It has beaten more champions than high living or ... general decay." He said, if a versatile boxer couldn't get his opponent one way, he would apply other tactics until something worked. This was echoed by "Manassa" Jack Dempsey, years later, when he said most fighters who had a rock-hard chin were less able to take it to the body, and vice-versa. If he couldn't soften up a foe with body blows, he cranked his punches to the chin.[34]

Joe was asked to pick the winner of the April 5 world heavyweight title go in Havana, Cuba, between Jack Johnson and former Kansas cowpoke, Jess Willard. He believed the huge, 6' 5½", 245-265 pound Willard was too large and lumbering to get out of his own way. Choynski said his own, easiest fight had been against the much larger Jim Jeffries. He quipped, "What's the last thing a fighter loses? Well, I should say his alibi." On the day before the fight, Joe said the only way Johnson could lose was if he "quit cold." While acknowledging that Jack was "hog fat" due to his "mode of life," Joe said Jess lost the previous year to Tom "Bearcat" McMahon (officially ND12), and couldn't possibly have improved

Joe Choynski, November 8, 1914 (46th birthday)

much since then.[35] Not for the first time, he was wrong. Johnson, having fought only three real fights in the five years since the 1910 Jeffries bout, was old and rusty. He handily outpointed his foe over the first 15 rounds, but Willard gradually wore him down in the blistering heat and knocked Jack out in round 26. While massive men often lack the speed and coordination to deal with lighter rivals, exceptions have been such as the Klitschko brothers and Lennox Lewis.

A January 4, 1915 article reported that "Joe Choynski ... has developed quite a string of clever amateur scrappers." Sadly, nothing is found of most of these boxers or their accomplishments. He felt that some of his amateurs were good enough to defeat Johnny Kilbane, the clever but light-punching world featherweight champion. Kilbane fought a six-rounder in Pittsburgh, January 1, against Patsy Brannigan, which left Joe unimpressed. He said boxing was a lost art, and was unable to see Kilbane as a good boxer. "He has nice footwork, a fair feint and an abstract left hand, that's all." Tommy Ryan, now a boxing promoter in Syracuse, New York, disagreed. He said Kilbane was "one of the cleverest boys" he had ever seen, and there was no one around who could beat him at his own weight.[36]

On February 22 at Duquesne Gardens, Joe refereed a six round quarrel between middleweights George Chip and Albert "Buck" Crouse. A war ensued, Chip smashing Crouse on the jaw in the 1st, sending him reeling into the ropes, nearly out. "Buck" managed to hold on and clear his head, surviving to the bell. From here on, both traded thunderbolts, causing spectators to stand on their feet and roar. The official verdict was a No Decision. Choynski was the arbiter for all matches on the card.[37]

On the 28th, the *Rocky Mountain News* did a feature on Tim McGrath, the Irish immigrant who was an early manager of Joe's, then a trainer of Tom Sharkey and others. "Probably one of the most eccentric (and) best liked ... Tim's long suit was training boxers, wrestlers, baseball teams, wild animals ... anything from a flea to an elephant ... He was a walking dictionary and directory on sporting events ... an Irishman of the old school and proud of it ... endowed with all the natural wit and humor of the Emerald Isle. Very few people in the world can boast of having no enemies, but if ... one ever lived, it certainly was Tim McGrath. He could tell stories in a manner that would make the Egyptian Sphinx laugh. Around training camp he was as good as a circus, keeping everyone in good humor all the time."

Choynski was at Duquesne Gardens again on the night of March 1, refereeing a heavyweight bout between Carl Morris and Tom McMahon. As in many events in which Joe was involved, it was not without incident. The next day's *New Castle News* said: "The referee quit – he didn't like the fight, for fight it was, and not an exhibition ... as it had been scheduled. (They) wrestled, slugged, clinched, bled and listened to ... several lectures, from Referee Joe Choynski ... last night, and at the end of five and a half rounds the bout was given to McMahon ... Neither ... deserved the verdict ... The two men ... liked their own rules too well to pay any attention to ... Choynski, who was being paid ... to give the patrons a run for their money. Choynski (did), but ... in the nature of a vaudeville performance and not a fistic bout. Choynski also gave the crowd a little talk in which he pointed out ... that he had 'refereed boxing bouts for 35 years, but this is the worst bout I ever saw, for the men don't know a thing about rules.' "

"Before the battle ... Choynski announced that the men were not to hit in the clinches and ... to break clean at the word of command. And then the fun – or fiasco – started. The men ... hit in clinches, whether or not the referee was shouting ... 'break, break!' ... the 1st round passed with Choynski rushing around the ring, doing his best to keep the two men apart, but with little avail. The 2nd ... was worse. The ... men grabbed each other's arms ...

and while McMahon tried to work himself loose, the big Oklahoman ... continue(d) to hit in the clinches. And before the round was over, both ... pummeling each other in the clinches ... And then Choynski quit. Throwing up his arms and shouting, 'the fight is off – the fight is off' ... climbed through the ropes and started towards the door while McMahon and Morris hesitated near their corners ... club members ... pleaded with Choynski to continue ... then ... Choynski made his impassioned oration about the ethics of fighting and the brains of boxers – some in particular; and you know, kind reader, that man Choynski can become quite sarcastic when he wants to. And he wanted to, last night."

"The next four rounds were little better, although the two men began to obey the injunction of the referee to 'break' about the time the last gong sounded. In the four rounds ... McMahon walloped the Oklahoman hard enough and often enough ... to be given the verdict ... (they) looked as if they had been in a real mixup. Had not both ... lost their heads and refused to listen to the referee, the bout would have been a humdinger, as both men could hit and both were quick enough for heavyweights. Morris ... showed a punch and quickness which were noticeable, but also ... an inclination to get in close, so as to evade McMahon's sledge hammer swings to the body and ... hooks to the head. As a result ... Choynski became disgusted and the crowd interested. It was something new to Pittsburgh – a vaudeville performance, lecture and fight in the same ring." In this epoch of heavyweights that saw so many farmers, cowboys and strongmen in the ring, slugging and infighting with one arm free seemed to be the order of the day. It was something Joe could not accept.

Around mid-March, Jim Corbett made a long-desired visit to Australia, signing a two-month contract with promoter Hugh McIntosh, to perform a monologue at Sydney's Tivoli Theatre. Jim chatted with writer Neville Forder on the 16th. He said the late Australian writer, W.W. "Bill" Naughton, told him about Australia when the two boxed together in Jim's youth. Jim considered Peter Jackson the greatest fighter that ever came to America from the island-continent, "Young Griffo" the cleverest. Finally, Corbett told Forder: "Goddard! Now there was some rough fighter for you! A good man to side-step! If he hadn't got diseased he would have been champion of the world ... when he came over ... he ... asked me to fight him. I knew he had beaten up Joe Choynski in four rounds, and I confess I didn't like the look of him, anyway. So, I spoke sort of soothingly ... making a gesture as though smoothing down a man's coat sleeve – 'Now, you run along and fix up with somebody else. There are several men with much bigger reputations and much easier to beat, that'll do me.' "38

On May 7, 1915, off the coast of the Old Head of Kinsale, Ireland, near County Cork, an historic and tragic event occurred. The RMS *Lusitania*, an ocean liner on a journey from New York to Liverpool and carrying 1,959 people, was torpedoed and sunk by the German U-Boat (submarine), *Unterseeboot 20*. Also aboard the doomed vessel were 159 Americans, including Elbert Hubbard and his wife, Alice. The attack hastened the United States' entry into World War I. There is a poignant tale behind this, as well. In 1912, following the sinking of the RMS *Titanic*, Hubbard wrote a portentous commentary about two of that vessel's casualties, Isidor and Ida Straus. Isidor, a co-owner of Macy's Department Store, and his wife, Ida, were inseparable. Legend has it, when on April 14, 1912 the *Titanic* had collided with an iceberg and was taking on water, an officer loading passengers on a lifeboat told Straus he could join his wife in the boat. The 67-year-old Isidor reportedly refused, saying he would not go before younger men. Ida Straus also refused to enter the half-filled lifeboat, stating, "I will not be separated from my husband. As we have lived, so will we die together." The couple perished with the sinking luxury liner.[39]

Hubbard: "I envy you that legacy of love and loyalty left to your children and grandchildren. The calm courage that was yours all your long,

Hubbard on deck of *Lusitania*, May 1, 1915

useful career was your possession in death. You knew how to do three great things ... live ... love and ... die ... there are just two respectable ways to die ... of old age, and ... by accident. All disease is indecent. Suicide is atrocious. But to pass out as did Mr. and Mrs. Isador (sic) Straus is glorious. Few have such a privilege. In life ... never separated ... in death they are not divided." Though he couldn't have known it then, Hubbard would, by a bizarre fate, have that "privilege." Shortly before departing, Elbert stood on the deck of the *Lusitania* and said, amidst a crowd of reporters: "From a strictly personal point of view, I would not mind if they did sink the ship. It might be a good thing for me. I would drown with her, and that's about the only way I could succeed in my ambition to get into the Hall of Fame. I'd be a regular hero and go right to the bottom."

Just six days later, the ship was sunk. A survivor, Ernest Cowper, sent a letter to Elbert Hubbard II, dated March 12, 1916. He said he witnessed the couple emerge from their port side room and calmly walk on deck, arm in arm. He heard Elbert exclaim, "Well, Jack, they have got us. They are a damn sight worse than I ever thought they were." Walking toward the opposite side of the ship, "in preparation for a jump when the right moment came," Ernest asked Hubbard what he planned to do. Elbert just shook his head, but Alice Hubbard smiled and said, "There does not seem

Choynski with the Roycrofters, August, 1918

to be anything to do." At this, Elbert turned with Mrs. Hubbard, his "White Hyacinth," entered a room on the top deck and closed the door behind them. "It was apparent his idea was that they should die together, and not risk being parted (in) the water."[40] Unlike Isidor Straus, their bodies were never recovered. About 3,000 people attended the May 23, 1915 memorial

service for Elbert and Alice Hubbard, held in East Aurora, New York.

"*Roycroft*" magazine, which replaced "*The Fra*" in September, 1917, posed the question, in 1918, "Did the Kaiser kill Elbert Hubbard because he wrote, 'Who Lifted the Lid Off Hell?': Some say the Kaiser in his blind wrath sent the U-Boat to sink the *Lusitania* because Elbert Hubbard was aboard. Elbert ... named the Kaiser a 'Mastoid Degenerate' and told about his withered arm and leaky ear. When Hubbard was called to Europe to write from first-hand information for the American People, the Kaiser knew what to expect. Then ... a Sub slipped out from Kiel and the *Lusitania* never reached port! Elbert ... died, but his indictment of the German tyrant lives!"[41] Among the scathing tidbits Hubbard included, was: "Caligula, the royal pagan pervert, was kind compared with the Kaiser."

It is clear that Joe Choynski not only thought highly of Elbert Hubbard,

Joe (and Louise ?) Choynski with Roycrofters, August, 1918

but was influenced by him. Whereas Joe wore standard ties with his suits, before Hubbard's demise, he took to wearing "The Fra's" distinctive ribbon tie thereafter, clearly a tribute to his departed friend. On September 21, 1915, the Roycrofters published a 350-page tribute to Elbert and Alice, entitled, "In Memoriam." In it are quotes from friends and key figures, of diverse occupations and areas. William Muldoon: "No other man, since the days of Colonel Robert Ingersoll, has been able to coin the words that fit the situation and give the definition so briefly and so thoroughly as Elbert Hubbard. I knew him well; he was a man, physically and mentally, capable of taking care of himself in just such an emergency as that in which he lost his life; but he was a man who would not spare his own life if those in his care might perish. Like ... thousands of his friends, I look about me for his successor, but can find no one. I am afraid we shall never see his like again. Elbert Hubbard, the man with the wonderful productive mind – hundreds of thousands of people are better off for his having lived."

Choynski: "To know Elbert Hubbard was to love him: kindly, unselfish and just, with a cheery word for all. Before me on my desk is a photo – of the Fra and me – taken at East Aurora (under the shade of an old apple tree), with his sad, sweet smile beckoning. When he visited Pittsburgh, he always called, and my trips to East Aurora were always fraught with pleasure. His like we shall never see again. I shall miss him – I shall miss him. Long may his spirit hover over the village of his dreams! Pittsburgh Athletic Association, Pittsburgh, Pa." Joe also wrote of him: "Your photo is framed and has the place of honor in my Hall of Fame." As will be seen, Elbert's influence may have caused Joe to become a chiropractor. Another boxer, Freddie Welsh, appeared in more than one of Hubbard's publications, and both spoke highly of each other. In September, 1914, Elbert wrote that Freddie was a "Roycrofter-at-large" and had trained at the East Aurora establishment, passing the medicine ball and running cross-country. Born Frederick Hall Thomas in Wales in 1886, Welsh was a great lightweight boxer who won the world championship from Willie Ritchie in 1914.[42]

Joe with Dr. Frank Crane, East Aurora, NY, August, 1918

Welsh: "During the 13 years I was familiar with Elbert Hubbard and his writings, I grew to love ... the ... wholesomeness, kindness and courage of the man. In our strolls through the woods of East Aurora ... he would relate many good stories, and ... laugh when the joke was on him. He worked hard mentally ... kept himself physically fit ... He had more working energy than any ... man I ever met. He always found time for exercise and sport, whether ... hiking over hills, wood-chopping, horseback-riding or baseball. He would discuss the boxing situation with me with the enthusiasm of a fan, and he wound up one of his last letters to me ... 'So here are love and blessings to all good sports, and if there is no squared circle in hell, you and I will arrange one.' ... the ... world lost a friend and leader when the Sage of East Aurora was taken away." While it is true that "Fra Elbertus" had many virtues, it is only fair to mention the infidelity. Elbert married his first wife, Bertha Crawford, in 1881. The couple moved to East Aurora in 1884, with young Elbert II. Around 1887, "Fra" fell in love with a local schoolteacher named Alice Moore, and had an affair with her for several years. Bertha finally left him in 1901, and Elbert married Alice in 1904.

C.S. Carr, M.D., offered: "Three things Hubbard did as no other ... has ... for which I am truly grateful. First, he was ... against the political doctors who wished to establish a compulsory vaccination and other forms of legal surgery. He was opposed to that great, powerful, omnipresent, formidable association of doctors known as the American Medical Association. He was a friend of the drugless healer as against that autocratic doctor of drugs bolstered up by tyrannical laws. Hubbard gained no fame or financial support from (it)." A chiropractor from Oklahoma named Dr. Willard Carver was another friend of Elbert's. In 1918, he gave a dissertation for *Roycroft* magazine, on chiropractic. In July, 1917, Carver gave a lecture at the Roycroft Convention on the topic, a gathering which Choynski attended.[42] Carver was probably a key element in Joe becoming a chiropractor.

On the evening of May 17, Joe took a train from Pittsburgh's Union Depot for Cincinnati, along with members of the Natural Gas Association of America, who were holding their annual convention on May 19 and 20 at the Gibson House, a music hall. Joe refereed, "by special request," several bouts at a boxing carnival the Association put on. The ring was set up in an area above the pipe fittings exhibit. Though the year was 1915, the card featured a "diversion" from the past, known as a "battle royal." This involved a ring full of young black men duking it out, often wearing blindfolds, and the last man standing won. This one included five "dusky gentlemen from the Queen City." Of Joe, it was said: "His style made a wonderful impression on the crowd, and he received a great ovation."[44]

Hugh Fullerton reported that Joe was planning yet another comeback. Fullerton (1873-1945) played a key role in founding the Baseball Writers Association of America, in 1908. He blew the whistle on the infamous 1919 "Chicago Black Sox Scandal," and in 1929 wrote the renowned Jim Jeffries biography, "Two Fisted Jeff." While Hugh got a few facts wrong in his piece on Choynski, two interesting claims were made: 1st, that "the other day, he stopped a husky youngster, so he's coming back at 47," and, that two things had been with Joe "for 20 years, hard luck and rheumatism."[45] It is not found elsewhere by this author, that Joe had "rheumatism," a now-antiquated term, nor who the "husky youngster" was. The May 30 *Duluth News-Tribune* gave a more detailed report, quoting Joe: "Being vain of my prowess has kept me young. When one loses vanity, he deteriorates," and that his knockout victim was "a young heavyweight of 24 years."

"After all these years – an even dozen ... it seemed like a new experience to re-enter the ring – until I heard the gong. Then, like the old fire horse ... latent memories were aroused, and it was like old times. I have added speed and an increased punch, but ... when the big guy ... bumped into me, it hurt. Did I care to enter the ring in real earnest, a week of rough work would ... enable me to stand the rough going, which ... is a good way to describe the present-day style ... I train every day and I am as strong as a Hercules, but I'm not training for rough stuff. It's different from the ordinary run of training." The comeback thankfully went by the boards.

Referee and sportswriter Abe Pollock, for the June 8 *Rocky Mountain News*, commented on the overabundance of seconds in a corner in many fights, and how this hindered, rather than helped, a boxer. Abe rendered his opinion that (John) "Spider" Kelly and Joe Choynski were "the greatest seconds of them all ... as they would never allow more than three men in a corner at any time, and never allowed yelling during rounds."[46]

Choynski went on a rant in late July, in which he castigated three heavyweights. Joe was in San Francisco, taking in the Panama Pacific International Exposition with Louise. "Jess Willard is a joke as a champion. He could not stand up for four rounds before any of the mixers of the old school. He knows absolutely nothing about boxing and was lucky in beating Jack Johnson. Johnson, like Jim Jeffries in Nevada, quit like a dog in his fight. He could not train, for he has what is known among conditioners as 'fatty' heart. He took a chance, and after 10 rounds found that he was tiring, and started to

Joe Choynski, 630 Lake St., San Francisco, 1915
"The Chrysanthemum losing its petals"

lead ... something he never had to do before, and the more fatigued ... the more anxious he was to quit ... when the opportunity arrived, he picked a soft spot and flopped. Any of the pictures of the knockout will show that Johnson was shading his eyes as he was sprawled out on the mat, and his legs were not stretched out. If two men ... are fighting, one man will be knocked out within four rounds. I toured the United States and Australia for a year and fought as many as three men a day, and each man who lasted three rounds was to receive $100. I never had to pay a fighter."

"I never liked Johnson since I knocked him out in Galveston, Texas ... He was a dirty-talking fighter in the ring and he said a good many things to me in the short time he was awake. But, the people do not give the big, black fellow credit. In the first place, he has plenty of money. Jack Johnson will buy liquor for friends, if they are close to him, but he seldom drinks, himself. Lack of sleep and eating have been the downfall of Johnson." The reporter called Joe "the greatest light-heavyweight that ever lived," adding, "Joe Choynski is credited with having the heaviest straight left ever turned loose in the roped arena." Joe allegedly said he "was unable to leave his bed for three weeks and could not see a thing for 14 days" following the barge fight with Corbett, and that he had been floored 14 times in the Billy Keneally fight before Joe came back to knock Billy out. Like many retired fighters, Joe sometimes exaggerated when recalling the past.[47]

Australian boxer Mick Dunn, who had been Choynski's second for the 1894 Fitzsimmons bout, said he had witnessed the first Goddard brawl. At that time, with Joe allegedly ordering Sam Fitzpatrick to sky the sponge after the 4th round, Mick felt that Joe was a cur, or coward. His sentiments underwent a marked change after the five round Fitz match, in which Dunn saw Joe "terribly knocked about." "I always had a good opinion of Fitzsimmons as a fighter and a hitter, but I never knew half what a terrible man he was ... till that night. Well, I went home, and to bed, but I could not sleep for thinking of what a game chap Joe Choynski was, and how many there were in Sydney, on the night he fought Goddard, that thought he was one of the biggest curs in the world, to stop after the way he had cut Goddard to pieces. A man might fight good to-night and bad to-morrow night; or one man's style might suit you better than ... another."[48]

A smattering of papers covered Joe's 47th birthday on November 8. A week later, on the 15th, it was announced that he had been re-engaged as boxing instructor at the Pittsburgh A.C.[49] 1915 ended on a tragic note. Ed Dunkhorst passed away in Chicago on October 25, at the young age of 38. "The Human Freight Car" succumbed to Bright's disease, a severe ailment of the kidneys. At the time of his death, Ed was said to have weighed as much as 500 pounds. In later years, starred in a vaudeville act, dressed as a baby and nicknamed "Little Willie." On December 30, Henry "Pop" Blanken died of peritonitis at 77. His "Six Mile House" in San Bruno, California had been a famous training resort for Choynski and many other luminaries. Blanken immigrated to the States from Germany in 1857. His establishment on Bayshore Boulevard, which he opened in 1876, had provided food, drink, lodging, bowling, shuffleboard, a livery service, and trap and rifle shooting.[50] Soon, Joe would face his own mortality.

Round Twenty-Five

A New Opponent: Pneumonia
(January 1916 – December 1919)

Choynski began the new year as a special speaker at a dinner of the new Traffic Club of Pittsburgh, on the evening of January 17. After a 6:00 p.m. dinner, Assistant General Passenger Agent of the Baltimore & Ohio Railroad of Baltimore, Maryland, W.E. Lowes, gave an "illustrated lecture" on the "Evolution of Transportation in America." Following this, Joe gave a talk, to "relate some of his personal experiences." On January 20, old ring rival Tom Sharkey added his voice to that of Jeffries, Fitzsimmons and Johnson, stating that Joe "was the hardest hitter that ever placed a wallop on his jaw." Having taken the most powerful punches of Fitzsimmons, Jeffries and Peter Maher, Tom certainly gave a valid frame of reference.[2]

Joe Choynski, circa 1915-16

On February 26 at the Orpheum Theater (some say Palisades Rink) in McKeesport, a small city just southeast of Pittsburgh, lightweight Ray (Charles Raymond) Pryel garnered a 10 round "newspaper decision" over "Steel City" resident "Young Goldie." Joe Choynski had just taken over the reins of Pryel, and was grooming him toward a championship. Ray had a listed amateur record of 48-4, wins to losses, and three professional fights, comprising two newspaper wins and a draw. The 5' 8" Pryel, while never gaining a shot at a title, proved a useful boxer, whose career lasted until 1924, with far more wins than losses. It is not known for certain that Ray ever lost a bout under Choynski's guidance, but Joe only handled him a short time. Pryel had several pilots during the course of his profession. Meanwhile, Joe's stable of amateur scrappers were devastated in a tournament around March 1, one paper stating, "Joe Choynski ... was forced to witness the defeat of all his pupils, accept (sic) one, whipped in a

New York amateur tourney last week."[3] The first week of July saw Joe in East Aurora, for the 22nd annual "Philistine or Roycroft Convention." It is not known if Joe attended the conventions of 1914 through 1916, but here he was in 1917, mingling with those who had known and admired Elbert Hubbard. At this time, Joe was still wearing a conventional tie with his suit. Debates and discussions took place and music was provided.[4]

Choynski's duties at the club were soon increased: "He has just been made athletic director of the Pittsburgh Athletic Association, and begins his duties September 1. He will have general charge of all branches of sports. He has been in charge of boxing there for some time."[5] There was talk that boxers in general, and heavyweights in particular, displayed a "lamentable lack of cleverness," compared with the previous generation. Joe laid the blame with the rules in vogue: "Have the Queensberry rules strictly adhered to and there will be a big change ... because the 'rasslers' will be eliminated. It always amuses me to hear the announcer shout: 'These bouts will be straight Queensberry rules, hitting in the clinches with one arm free' – when, as a matter of fact, the ... rules strictly prohibit hitting in the clinches. The rules in use today are nothing more or less than the old London prize ring rules with the wrestling cut out, and it is laughable to hear a referee tell the contestants to hit with one arm free and break at his word. What authority has the referee to tell boxers to break after telling them to hit? If one man is holding and the other has arms free, they must break, anyhow. The referee earns his money and looks wise as he expends his strength breaking them. In the old days boxers knew the rules and the referee never had to touch them. If they persisted in clinching they were disqualified."

"Joe Choynski: Folks not afraid of an idea," *Fra* magazine, January, 1917

"Another thing that has hurt boxing is the no-decision bout. No one loses and no one wins. The boxing public wants action for its money. I think decision bouts is (sic) the only answer for the uplift of the game, and I believe referees could stamp out a great amount of the betting by announcing all bets off at the ringside. Nowadays, any man with hair on his chest and big muscles is a fighter. Cleverness is overlooked ... Mr. Atkinson, the real man behind the Queensberry rules, was a friend of mine, and he explained how the rules were drawn up ... gave me the whys and wherefores ... It was to eliminate wrestlers and put ginger and science into boxing that the rules ... were drawn up." Actually, what had been in popular, general use since the Queensberry era began, was a modification of the original code drawn up by John Graham Chambers (not the mysterious Mr. Atkinson, whoever he was) in 1865 in London. This variation allowed hitting in the clinches, as long as one arm was free. It had to be approved by both camps, but is something that occasionally still sees use today.[6]

The August 6, 1917 *Tacoma Times* noted that four of the seven titleholders in the recognized boxing divisions were currently held by "Hebrew," or Jewish, fighters. They were Benny Leonard (lightweight), Ted "Kid" Lewis (welterweight), Al McCoy (middleweight) and "Battling" Levinsky (light-heavyweight), real names, Benjamin Leiner, Gershon Mendeloff, Alexander Rudolph and Barney Lebrowitz. All except McCoy are now in the Boxing Hall(s) of Fame. Along with this quartet was mentioned "Joe Choynsky (sic), then (sic) whom there was never a gamer or greater fighter at his weight ..." Great Jewish pugilists, along with Abe Attell, Leach Cross, Charlie White, "Kid" Herman and Harry Lewis. Joe was the pioneer of them all in the United States.

On August 29, it was announced that Jim Corbett had been appointed chairman of the U.S. War Department's "committee on athletic instruction." The board was organized to teach boxing to soldiers at Army encampments across the country, and to consist of Corbett, Norman Selby ("Kid" McCoy), "Professor" Mike Donovan and "Professor" Richard Nelligan of Amherst College, with Bob Edgren as Secretary. The team of instructors acting under their direction was to include Benny Leonard, Johnny Dundee, Packey McFarland, Mike Gibbons, Ted "Kid" Lewis, Abe Attell, Tommy Ryan, Freddie Welsh and Joe Choynski.

It was noted, on September 1: "All these distinguished savants cheerfully donate their services to the cause. They will be distributed among the various cantonments ... knowledge of boxing will be of invaluable service to the men in the use of the bayonet, teaching them especially quickness of eye and rapidity of movement. Moving picture men in New York are now very busy making films of Mr. Corbett engaged in boxing. After the pictures have been exhibited, the boxers delegated ... will begin instructing classes of about 30 soldiers each ... When this class has learned thoroughly ... the soldier pupils will ... instruct the other soldiers in the same camp. A big hall in New York City has been hired for a meeting which will be held within the next two weeks that will bring together all the boxers ..." "Motion pictures will be taken of Corbett and Selby going through the boxing movements of use in bayonet work, and these will be shown at the various camps, and serve as a guide for the work of the pugilists."[7] How many of the ex-boxers actually took part in the program isn't known, but the military training video still exists, featuring a choreographed sparring session between Corbett and McCoy. It is evident by the dearth of further mention, that Joe did not participate. The exact reason for this is uncertain.

On October 22, former Choynski friend and adversary, Robert James Fitzsimmons, died of double lobar pneumonia in Chicago. He was 54. Bob collapsed four or five days earlier, while involved in his vaudeville act. In his final years, Fitz had become an evangelist, traveling the country with his spouse, Temo. He was buried on the 24th in Chicago's Graceland Cemetery, where, less than 200 feet away, Jack Johnson would join him in 1946. Bob Edgren was told many things over the years, by several heavyweights. Sharkey said, while he'd have been willing to fight Jeffries again, he wanted no more of Fitzsimmons. "Say! I'm not a quitter ... but I don't want his game. Last time he hit me on the jaw, I didn't remember what happened for a couple of days, and then I thought a mule had kicked me."

Of his 2nd go with "Ruby Robert," Jeffries exclaimed, "If I'd known what a beating the old man would hand me in that fight, I wouldn't have taken it for $100,000. He broke every bone in my nose ... loosened every tooth in my head and nearly tore my ears off. He closed both my eyes. For a week after ... I thought my jaw was broken." "Kid" McCoy never met Fitz in a real fight, only sparring sessions. Said Edgren, "One day, 15 years ago, he told me why. 'I can outguess all the others ... but nobody knows what old Fitz has in the back of his mind. When you think you know every move he can make, he springs something ... you never dreamed of. I wouldn't fight that old guy if he was a hundred years old." Mike Donovan is credited by Edgren for inducing "Speckled Bob," in 1891, to punch to the body more, as head punches nearly resulted in a fatality. Gus Ruhlin said, "For two weeks after he (Fitz) hit me in the body, I felt sure I was going to die. I wouldn't fight him again for all the money in the world."[8] Fitz's punch did lead to the death of at least one fighter. A world champion in three weight divisions, Bob was called "probably the greatest fighter of any weight that ever lived." The world would never see another quite like him.

The November 7 *Lincoln Daily Star* ran a "mini-bio" of Choynski on the eve of his 49th birthday: "in his day, (he) was considered the greatest of light-heavies." Exactly how Joe celebrated his birthday isn't recorded, but he appears to have spent it in Pittsburgh. He may have already been in ill health, though. The November 27 *Philadelphia Inquirer* reported that Joe was battling for his life with pneumonia. A number of other papers around the country followed soon afterward. This was big news, especially in the wake of Fitz's death from the same malady. On December 5 he was said to be at home with "pleuro-pneumonia," an inflammation of the lungs and pleura, the chest cavity membrane surrounding the lungs. Pleuropneumonia is caused by a bacterial infection. It was not only life-threatening, but very painful. Pleurisy alone causes extreme chest pain. It was added, "physicians at his bedside are working strenuously to pull him through."

December 5 *Philadelphia North American*: "He ... has made thousands of friends among the upper class of business and professional men. Choynski has also developed a lot of fine young boxers, some of whom won championships in the middle-Atlantic district of the AAU. He has been manager of Ray Pryel ever since the latter entered the professional ranks ... After taking charge of athletics at the Pittsburgh association, he was called on to referee all inter-city bouts, and only three weeks ago was the arbiter in the Cleveland-Pittsburgh tournament." Its next-day edition noted that Joe was "at least holding his own." "Choynski's many friends the country over are pulling hard for him to win his present battle with Death. A fairer and squarer man never pulled on a glove than the Hebrew lad of California, who fought them all in the days of real fights and real fighters." A La Crosse, Wisconsin rag wrote: "Choynski groggy! Pneumonia may win. Having scored a knockout over Bob Fitzsimmons, Kid Pneumonia has tackled another veteran ... Joe Choynski, who ... is in a critical condition ... his opponent having the better of the bout. Joe ... trained the boys that whipped the amateur boxers from Cleveland here a few weeks ago."

The *North American* declared on the 8th that Joe had "passed the crisis of the disease ... now on his way to recovery. Choynski's rugged constitution has stood him well ... his physicians say in a few weeks he will probably resume his duties as athletic director of the Pittsburgh A.A." Joe had defeated an opponent that "Ruby Bob," could not. His superior physical condition helped save him, as stated by physicians at his Pittsburgh home. Sadly, Bob hadn't kept in such fine trim. The *Lethbridge Herald* said on the 20th that Joe was still "stricken with pneumonia," adding: "Choynski is a careful liver and has saved considerable money out of his ring earnings." It noted that Joe, during his fighting career, visited France, as well as England and Australia, and "In 1892, when Choynski visited London, he ... settled down for a while to enjoy easy life. He is a very close observer, and through his acquaintance with many odd characters in London, he gained a fund of interesting information and hundreds of clever stories."

"Choynski went to Dawson City in 1903 ... to appear at the Ice Palace there. The fight took place at 12 o'clock midnight, but no artificial lights were required, as it was twilight at that hour. Joe knocked Nick (Burley) out in the 3rd round. Previous to taking up his home in Pittsburgh, Choynski was a resident of Evanston, Illinois."[9] The publication was incorrect on at least one point, as Joe settled accounts with Burley in seven stanzas. It has not been validated that he ever lived in Evanston, Illinois. Joe won his battle with pneumonia and would live another quarter-century. By 1918, Joe and Louise were living at 2 Olympia Place, beside their previous 4 Olympia address, and he was still listed as "Physical Instructor."

Choynski held a subscription to the Australian, *Sydney Referee*. He dispatched a "chatty" letter to the paper's editor, Will Corbett, dated May 29, 1918: "The good old *Referee* came this a.m., and pleased was I to receive it, as were others who are considered fortunate to peruse it after I am finished. I remember Jack Hall very well when he appeared in San Francisco in the late '80s, and was much impressed with his speed and cleverness and wonderful endurance. It was his never-stand-still tactics that I plagiarized and enabled me to be successful in my small way. My last letter was somewhat garbled by your linotype artist; perhaps he was suffering from strabismus, myopia, or some kindred ailment. Re. Jackson's bout with Slavin. Jackson often told me that Slavin was a cocktail, and when I seconded him against Slavin at the National Club in London, Peter told me he knew he was Slavin's master, and would make him quit."[10]

A rebuttal was forthcoming, in the August 21 *Referee*: "My old friend, Billy Maher of the Victorian Club, Melbourne, knows ... thoroughly what he writes regarding old sporting things ... To-day Billy takes up the cudgel in ... Slavin's behalf ... 'I am sure any fair-minded old-time sport would do as I am doing ... take exception to certain parts of ... Choynski's letter ... wherein he writes that Peter Jackson told him Slavin was a cocktail, and that he would make him quit ... Anyone knowing Jackson would think as I do ... it is an absolute untruth, for Peter was too manly a fellow ... to give rant to assertions of that kind. As for the making quit part of the business, boxing writers chronicle their scrap as being ... the greatest and fiercest ever witnessed between two heavies. Slavin ... was beaten, down and out. Again, Frank's deeds in the ring before he met the redoubtable darkie, shows he was a rare plucked 'un (translation: very courageous), and ... a rare exploit or two on the battlefield lately stamps him what I have dubbed him.' "

" 'Choynski ought to remember the old saying about people who live in glass houses, for I well recollect how he yellow-streaked in his go with Joe Goddard in July, 1891. However, we all know Goddard was practically unbeatable that time ... I have a vivid recollection of Choynski getting a rare drubbing from a 10-stone welter ... Joe Walcott. The latter administered such a hiking to his heavy opponent ... that Choynski wouldn't show up for some time afterwards.' I am sorry Billy Maher decided to abuse the other side ... But, nevertheless he has a case, and a strong one. Choynski ... was Jackson's chief second that night. But why abuse Choynski? He said Jackson told him Slavin was a cocktail. The charge is not Choynski's invention. Though I agree with Billy Maher that Slavin was anything but a cocktail, Peter Jackson had every reason to consider him such, before they fought in London. The manner in which Slavin backed and filled and side-stepped ... while the pair were in Australia, made it appear that Slavin feared the black. The incident at Foley's White Horse Hotel, when Slavin attacked Jackson without any warning and while Jackson was under the influence of drink, was the act of a bully, and a bully is a coward any time."

Will Corbett, writing under the pseudonym "Amateur," continued: "I write emphatically now, as I have so often written ... that Choynski was not a coward the night he capitulated to Goddard. He was a badly battered and broken man, and his intelligence prompted him to stop, where a beetle-browed, bull-headed person, dead from the shoulders up, might have continued. Joe Walcott, the Barbados Demon, did to Choynski what he invariably did to taller and bigger men than himself ... tall men experienced exceeding difficulty in finding Walcott. Manager Tom O'Rourke would not let Tom Sharkey meet Walcott, and Sharkey himself had no appetite at all for the demon. The pair had been in the same stable together. Choynski proved as game as any other man. He showed uncommon grit in his battles with Jim Corbett – especially that at Benecia – and in a terrific fight with Peter Maher, during which both men were cut to pieces ..."[11]

Joe left Pittsburgh at the end of June for a week's visit to East Aurora, New York, home of the Roycrofters. Here he is seen relaxing and appearing jovial; standing and sitting beside assorted "Philistines" (as "Fra" Hubbard called his fellow kindred spirits, he said, because they were going after the 'Chosen People' in literature). While it is not stated that Louise accompanied Joe, in all likelihood she did. A bespectacled woman sitting beside him on a hill in one of the group photos looks like it could be her. On July 6, Joe arrived in nearby Buffalo, and gave a brief interview to the *Syracuse Herald*. "Fifty-one years young (actually, 49), looking as spry and athletic as the best-preserved man of 30 or 35, with locks as thick and curly as the most popular matinee idol, a carriage that would grace a dancing master, arms and legs as firm and solid as mahogany and a stomach as ribbed as the old-fashioned washboard, Joe Choynski dropped into Buffalo after a week's vacation and rustication in East Aurora, and mingling with a group of fans at the Iroquois, had things most interesting to say ..."

"Joe says ... modern fighters, Jack Dempsey and Billy Miske are the only ones who hit as the old-timers used to. Joe never could see the tappers and swingers. In his day, men like himself, Jim Corbett, Tommy Ryan, Joe Gans ... never swung or hit with the back of the hand. It was straight-from-the-shoulder stuff ... 'It's a case (now) of rush in, wallop ... and hope a good punch lands. In the old days a man knew where he was hitting, and ... if ... any good ... about where the other fellow's punches would land. I've slipped off enough punches with my left shoulder to win a championship. Dempsey hits straight and true ... is a natural fighter and so is Miske. So was Corbett. When he started to box, he picked up the fine points so fast that he soon outboxed his teacher ... I was his teacher.' Choynski leaves this morning (July 7) for Pittsburgh to resume his duties. He has a featherweight down there who he boosts very highly, and promises to send him up here for a trial soon at the Queensbury (sic) club."[12] One suspects Corbett would take issue with the notion that Joe taught him how to box.

"Kid" McCoy was interviewed by a July 24 paper. He reiterated that his toughest fight was the 1900 go against Joe, but claimed he had been dropped nine times in the match. "Nine times in three rounds is taking a few, to say the least." The statement is at odds with contemporary accounts. "It is hard to say which was the best man. Corbett, Maher, Goddard and Choynski were all great fighters." What an age of great fighters it was, but Frank L. O'Connell of the *New York Herald* probably went too far when he wrote: "Joe Choynski is almost forgotten to the present generation of boxing fans, but to the old timer there would not be a better bill than a bout between him and Jack Dempsey if the two of them were of the same age. Some boxing writers call Dempsey one of the best heavyweights that this country has ever developed. That is more or less of a joke. No one who ever saw Choynski fight can believe that Dempsey would have stood a chance with him. Dempsey has nothing to brag about outside of the fact that he knocked out Fred Fulton."[13] In all likelihood, Joe was too light to have handled the magnificent "Manassa Mauler."

Around November 5, 1918, Joe began studies at the chiropractic school in Pittsburgh. Some time that year, the Universal Chiropractic College (UCC) of Davenport (Iowa) merged with the Pittsburgh College of Chiropractic, becoming the UCC of Pittsburgh. What the official name of the college was upon Choynski's enrollment is uncertain, but he would graduate from the Universal Chiropractic College of Pittsburgh on May 5, 1920.[14] Joe wrote a letter to Will Corbett of the *Sydney Referee*, dated September 22. He attended the previous day's 10-round Billy Miske-Harry Greb fight at the city's local ball park, a clash between two all-time greats. "It was very cold, and only a small crowd turned out. It seems any event advertised as for the benefit of the Red Cross, etc., is always a fizzle, the fans thinking it will merely be an exhibition. For six rounds, Greb danced around and tapped Miske lightly. After that, Miske hit him in the stomach, and ... Greb was a punching bag for him. Another round and Greb would undoubtedly been outed. Miske was pounds heavier, not very slow, and his knowledge of the game was nil. You would think he only had one arm, his left was never in evidence. Pittsburgh is now a war zone, and all aliens must now leave the vicinity. We have barracks on all unoccupied fields, all the men of high-class – aviators, engineers, mechanics, etc. Boxing will be the only game after the war. The schools in California are taking it up. It has taken a long time to come into its own. Certainly, it is a man's game."

"Re. the Jackson-Slavin battle ... I cut Peter's tights short, previous to the battle, which made him awful wroth. He usually wore long tights. I cut them off above the knee, and he was furious. I told him it was a hot night, and he would be thankful. Peter broke the knuckle of his right hand ... and found it impossible to knock Paddy down, although he had him helpless. I told him to push Slavin up to the ropes, and when I said 'Now,' to shove Slavin, and the rebound would throw Slavin to the floor, and he would not get up. After the contest he thanked me, and said the cutting of the tights was a great relief." Will: "Like a good many more visitors ... Choynski had to thank Australia for something learned. In his first match at the old Sydney amateur Gymnastic Club, in York-street, he wore 'long tights,' and they were cut short after the opening round, just as he treated ... Jackson's tights." Joe wrote again to Will on the 28th. He referred to Billy Maher's defense of Slavin, saying that he (Joe) had only been quoting Peter. Joe added that he had never seen Frank quit, had only seen him fight that one time, but Slavin "was afraid of Pete ... when they met in London. Our cold weather is about due, and I dread it. Some day me for the land where the sun shines in Winter, and swimming is the vogue."[15] He was apparently referring to Australia, though he would never visit again.

Another Corbett, "Gentleman Jim," interviewed Tom Sharkey for a November installment of "In Corbett's Corner." He asked Tom who the hardest hitter was that he ever faced, and "The Shark" said: "Choynski could get more power into a punch than any man that ever lived. Every time he landed, he rocked his man from head to foot; every time he put one against the ribs, it seemed that he caved them in. Choynski perhaps would be ranked now as the greatest fighter that ever lived if his legs had been only a little more powerful. He had dynamite power in his shoulders and arms, but ... his legs ... were too thin to support his heavy upper body, making Joe top-heavy. If a fellow kept rushing Joe, it soon tired him, and Joe's legs would begin to wobble. Then, a heavy punch to the jaw would send Joe down. But that boy wouldn't stay there with one punch. I guess you know that, Jim – you fought him often enough. That boy was game – right through. He had to be beaten to a pulp before he would stay down, even though he knew each time he got up, it was only to go down again; that his legs had failed him. But, if Joe's underpinning had been powerful like Jeff's, or like Fitz's, or like mine, Joe would have been the heavyweight champion of the world – and I guess he would have kept the title longer than anybody else ever had kept it. That boy was a wonder of wonders, not only as a hitter, but as a ring general and a boxer."

Corbett next posed the query, "Who would you rank next to Choynski in punching power?" Tom: "I guess I'd hand it to Kid McCoy, giving 3rd place to Fitzsimmons and 4th place to Jeffries. The Kid was a marvel. The ring game has known but few superiors as boxers and only one or two in braininess. And that fellow could hit with the power of a piledriver. I don't know where the Kid got the steam he put into his punches. His body always seemed frail. But he had it. The Kid shot one to my jaw ... and ... I thought somebody had thrown a brick at me. He didn't hit me often ... because he played the 'hit and get away game.' But, when he did ... he made me see stars. If the Kid could have taken the beatings that Jeff, Fitz and the rest of us took, he would have been unbeatable in ... his prime. Fitz was another great hitter, but one peculiar thing about Bob was that he could put the real damaging power only into his body wallops. He won some fights with punches to the chin, but it was these short, driving wallops, delivered from the waistline into the pit of the other fellow's stomach that made Bob world-famous. He knew just where to land on the body to knock the wind out of a man, long enough to keep him out of the fight for more than 10 seconds. Jeff could hit, and he certainly carried steam in his blows. But, great as was Jeff, he couldn't hit in a class with either McCoy or Fitz. And, Choynski had it on all of them – a dozen ways."[16]

On Friday, November 8, 1918, Choynski reached his 50th milestone. The occasion was noted by papers around the country. The editor of the wire service report declared that "he wouldn't care to take on Joe, even at 50."[17] No report is found of his doings. The world-wide Influenza Pandemic that exploded in August, 1918 was still raging, and would through the following year. Secondary, but also taking many lives, was pneumonia. A report came out in January, 1919 that "Joe Choynski is likely to become boxing instructor at Carnegie Tech, where boxing will be instituted." Located in Pittsburgh and known today as Carnegie Institute of Technology (CIT), Carnegie Technical Schools did have a boxing program for a short time when Joe lived there. They would not, however, be his employer. He remained athletic director of the Pittsburgh club, but baseball legend, Honus Wagner, was appointed "athletic instructor" at Carnegie.[18]

The June 1 *Galveston Daily News*, in the build-up to the Willard-Dempsey clash, called the young "Mauler," "one of the best heavyweights uncovered during the past 20 years," and "Dempsey certainly compares favorably with any of the old-timers, with the possible exception of Fitzsimmons. Although not quite as big as Jeffries, Dempsey is a better hitter and a faster man. Judging by the way rough Sharkey slammed Corbett around the ring, Dempsey would have been too much for Gentleman Jim. Dempsey is bigger than Sharkey was, and a more accurate and deadly hitter. Whether he can eat up punishment as the sailor could, never has been demonstrated as yet. Dempsey certainly is a better man than Ruhlin was in every respect. He is faster, tougher, hits far harder and is just as clever. Dempsey probably would have outgamed (sic) the slow-thinking Peter Maher and knocked him out in quick time, for Peter was afflicted with a glass jaw. Joe Choynski and Kid McCoy, both light men who were fast and very clever, probably would have caused Dempsey more trouble than the big fellows. Fitzsimmons might have been too good for Dempsey. The old fellow hit so hard and knew so much about fighting the only thing that could beat him was a jaw tougher than his brittle fists ... if Dempsey were lucky enough to land early as Jeffries did, he would have finished him in quicker time than it took

Jeffries to win the title." The author didn't consider that Corbett was rusty and in poor condition when he first tangled with Sharkey. History would show that Dempsey could take punishment to the nth degree.

When the world crown was contested on July 4 in Toledo, Ohio, Choynski had a $50 seat. "Bushy hair and all," Joe stood up and shook hands with all his friends in that section. Everyone stood when the panorama camera took a picture from the ring, for posterity. Jim Corbett was present, but "preferred the shade under the stand to exposure in the arena." The heat was upwards of 90 degrees (Fahrenheit) in the shade. Journalist Al Spink claimed the thermometer read 120 degrees in the arena! He sat within three feet of Willard's corner, Corbett was one seat from him, and "Just behind Jim was Joe Choynski ..." Also nearby were Mose Gunst, "Bat" Masterson, Bob Edgren, actor George Cohan, and sports artists "TAD" Dorgan and George McManus. Spink said "Choynski sat still as a mouse while Dempsey was putting it over Willard, but the nervous Corbett could not keep still for a minute, and every time Dempsey landed on Willard, Jim would shout, 'Oh, you big boob!' " The *Duluth News-Tribune* said "Joe sat beside Corbett (and) they talked of their own battles."[19]

The throng of 80,000 saw the 1st-round-knockout-artist, Dempsey, floor Willard seven times in the opening frame, only to have the bell save him. The gong was inaudible over the tumult, even Referee Pecord raising Dempsey's arm in token of victory. The official timekeeper advised the referee the round had expired just before the full count was tolled, so he yelled for Jack to return. Somehow, the champion's corner revived the brave Willard and sent him out for round two, which saw him land a few powerful right uppercuts on his arm-weary foe. Dempsey administered another beating in round three, after which Jess's handlers threw in the towel. Jack mixed in a beautiful assortment of lefts and rights to body and head, with speed and accuracy. The first "Kid Dynamite" held the championship throughout most of the "Roaring Twenties."

Corbett, on July 30 at his Bayside, Queens, New York home, criticized Dempsey for not pacing himself better, though Jim was probably unaware that Jack's manager, "Doc" Kearns allegedly bet $1,000 on his charge at 10-1 odds to win in the 1st ... Jim: "Kid McCoy or Choynski would have given Dempsey a merry time ... when they were good. They could hit hard and like lightning. They would have stalled him off for a few rounds, and then you would have seen a fight ... Jeffries? Dempsey and Jeff would have been a bloody mess. If this Dempsey ever learns to control himself, he's going to be the best heavy we've ever had. As yet, he's only a boy at the game. He has to learn to save a little for the next round ... his only fault ..."[20]

Joe visited San Francisco. While there, he reconciled with "Tuxedo" Ed Graney, ending a "parting of the ways" that was never well-documented. August 22 *New Castle News*: "Eddie Graney and Joe Choynski ... once the closest of pals ... later, the bitterest of enemies – 'kissed and made up' on Market Street ... And, it wasn't one of those prearranged affairs, such as we frequently have in the boxing game. It was a 'natural,' and ... though it happened several days ago, was slow to break into joint. The Graney-Choynski feud has been so long outlawed ... people have forgotten there was any trouble. Suffice it to say that for some years this Damon and Pythias ... refused to speak as they passed by ... Graney, Sam Berger and a 3rd party stopped ... to discuss fighters. The ... Blacksmith ... enthusiastic over the fistic ability of Choynski. 'The new talent never would have stood a chance with Joe' he declared ... along came Choynski ... here visiting

Joe Choynski, Edwin, Edwin, Jr. (Tim) and Florence Coe, 630 Lake St., San Francisco, California, circa August, 1919

relatives. 'Come here, Joe,' shouted Berger, who had either forgotten or never was acquainted with the feud. 'I want you to meet Eddie Graney again.' The two squared off, looked each other in the eye, and shook hands. Followed an old-fashioned talk and reconciliation. So, still another of our pugilistic heirlooms has gone by the boards." The bad blood may have stemmed from the Graney-Herbert Choynski trouble in 1906.

Graney told the September 10 *New Castle News*: "Jim Corbett stood out over all the rest of the fistic fraternity as a searchlight ... over a flivver tail light. I'm talking about the Corbett of 1889 ... 23 years old. Choynski was a great fighter, wasn't he? Corbett beat him two out of three times. He (Jim) had more brains than a carload of the greatest fighters ... He fought as you'd play checkers ... did certain things for a reason. He could outfeint the greatest lightweights we have today. His footwork was immense and his ducking reminds me of Griffo. People have an idea Corbett couldn't hit. He was a great hitter. That wasn't his style, though. He usually made a monkey out of the man who faced him ... Tommy Ryan knows Corbett could hit ... knows Corbett was a master fighter ... Ask Bob Armstrong if he could hit. Bob trained him for many a battle. When you saw Corbett fight, you saw the kingpin of the ring." "Jim Coffroth blew down to Sheepshead Bay the other day for a breath of salt air, and bumped into that jolly old tar, Tom Sharkey ... 'Who hit you the hardest punch you ever received?' Jim asked ... 'Joe Choynski ...' 'Well,' chirped Coffroth, 'Bob Fitzsimmons hit you so hard that he knocked you out, didn't he, Tom?' Sharkey pulled down the peak of his cap and bawled, 'Yes, he did, *but I*

Joe, Edwin and Florence, San Francisco, 1919

didn't feel that one.' " As hard and hurting as Joe's punch was, it was just short of the annihilating quality Fitz's howitzers possessed. The most devastating blows consistently produce unconsciousness.

Jim Corbett, October 8 *Oakland Tribune*: "*Amateurs 25 years ago did things professionals of today can't do*. (emphasis was his). There were two amateur lightweights at that time in San Francisco, Tommy McCord and Frank Cooley ... the best I ever watched. They never turned professional ... had footwork and feinting down to a science. It would be a treat to see them meet some of the lightweights of today. They'd show them up. Another ... ring marvel ... Tommy Ryan. Oh, I don't think there's a man of his weight ... today who would have stood a chance with him. Couldn't he hit? Ryan could feint and know why he did it. Feinting is a lost art ... But my greatest? ... Peter Jackson. Mind you, I don't say he towered over the other fighters I've ... mentioned, but ... as a ringster, he was the star."

"I saw an exhibition with Fitzsimmons at the old California Athletic Club, and it was like a professor giving his pupil a lesson. *He just made*

Fitzsimmons look like a sucker. No wonder (Fitz) challenged the world, bar Jackson. I saw Jackson spar four rounds with Choynski, too, and it was the same. Joe couldn't touch him with a basket full of clothespins. You know, Jackson stood 6' 1½" tall, and weighed 205 pounds, stripped ... his speed ... footwork ... feinting ... punch. He had everything. He knocked out Frank Slavin, the greatest slugger of his time. Just outslugged him. Clever fellows were the same ... He'd outbox them. He was a student." Corbett added how surprised he was to see Jackson keep up with him, in May, 1891. Jim was bewildered, needing all of his wiles and ability to get by. How Peter might have done if he hadn't injured an ankle in training! Corbett said he was tired for six months after the 61-round contest! "Jeffries. A wonderful fellow ... for a man without the fighting spirit. Jeff, naturally left-handed and with tremendous power behind it, was tough; but, I can look back and see that Jackson, with everything ... was my ideal fighting man."

A topic cropping up many times over the next two years, evidently began at the Dempsey-Willard fight, when "several of the boys" told Joe the modern boxer had it on those of his era. Joe retorted: "That's ... ridiculous ... it can't be ... men of today have a thing we didn't have. There are just seven blows that can be used with effect ... anything else a man tries is merely a variation ... One ... may crouch, another ... stand up straight and another ... turn his right side to the foe, but once a blow is started ... it is one of these seven." An October 24 paper: "Choynski ... declared boxing had reached its ultimate because there are only seven possible punches. Mr. Corbett intimates that there is in these seven, an infinite variety."

Joe: "One punch fighters of today do not know how to use is the kidney punch. To us old timers it is amusing to sit at a fight and hear remarks about the kidney punch when some 3rd rater reaches over the shoulder of the man he is fighting and slams him with the open hand on the back. The man who introduced the kidney punch was Danny Needham, and there's never been another man who could use the punch as Danny could. The kidney punch is a jab ... not a swing. And it doesn't land on a man's back. It lands on the soft part of the side – just above the belt. One kidney punch or two, though painful, will not be very effective. Needham specialized on the punch and sometimes landed it as often as a dozen times in a round. He'd keep using it until the other fellow's side was blood raw and he caved in. And all the time, remember, it was a jab, just a poke and a twist of the wrist and the sinking of the fist a few inches into the soft flesh."

"Joe Choynski ... is afraid the mitt game is degenerating into a pink tea and chiffon proposition ... before many years, boxers will be apologizing every time they hit an opponent. Choynski used the (kidney) punch against Corbett, according to the latter's admission, although it did not serve to stop Corbett. It rendered his side quite lame for several days after the battle."[21] The four basic blows, classified by form, are: left jab, right cross, left hook and uppercut. Defined by location, the seven basic blows *should be*, in my opinion: left jab to head, right cross to head, left hook to head, left hook to body, right to body, right (or left) uppercut to head, uppercut to body. Joe essentially agreed, as on September 29, 1923, he said they were "The left lead or jab; right cross; right to the heart; left to the stomach; left hook to the stomach; left hook to the head; right upper cut to the chin." He only differs in citing a 2nd left to the body, instead of a right uppercut.

Joe's talk involving "Paddy" Slavin reached the latter's ears in Canada, where Frank returned after being wounded, fighting in Europe during World War I.[22] The tough, old codger was not long in responding. November 1 *Lethbridge Herald*: "Anyone who knows Frank Slavin knows he is no quitter, and the 'old war horse' is pretty well known. It is no wonder the veteran ring champion should feel a little peeved over the story recently appearing in the *San Francisco Bulletin* and other papers, in which Joe Choynski is represented as accusing Frank Slavin of failing to keep a contract with him, and claims he made him back down. 'Back in 1892 ... we were both beginners in our pugilistic careers.' Slavin: 'Of course, Joe has a poor memory, as ... a great many paper writers have ... Before 1892 I had met and defeated many Americans ... big Joe McAuliffe, Jake Kilrain, Jack Burke, the Irish Lad, and Martin Costello ... So, if I were only a beginner ... as Joe puts it, where did I lick ... before coming to America, the best men of the British Isles, Australia and New Zealand."

"I never had a chance to meet Joe Choynski, as he was always looked upon as a second-rater ... Choynski lies ... I was in New Orleans in March, 1892. Mitchell and myself had ... a preliminary to the Fitzsimmons-Maher bout. We boxed two big fellows ... sparred four rounds between ourselves and got $5,000 for so doing. I think there is an ulterior motive behind the attempt at this date to show the public that I cannot be relied upon.' " Frank was stung enough by Joe's words to hurl a bitter diatribe; Joe was never considered a second-rater. Also (see chapter 7), a six-rounder was proposed between Joe and Frank for the California A.C. in February, 1892, but Charley Mitchell claimed "Slavin's schedule would not allow it."

In his November 6 column, Jim Corbett called Choynski "the tough luck champion battler of all time." "Joe (was) one of the most remarkable gladiators ever ... a super-hitter, one of the most scientific ... of all time; and ... of splendid courage ... also the most jinxed of heavyweights. Choynski lost many fights because of freak rulings of referees ... flukey punches, and ... reasons that did not mitigate against his greatness ..." Jim used as his prime example, the June, 1894 Fitzsimmons bout, Corbett claiming that Joe had been robbed of a victory by Referee Bill Daly's long count.[23]

Round Twenty-Six

Joseph B. Choynski, DC
(January 1920 – December 1929)

On March 15, the *Bridgeport Telegram* reported (dateline Pittsburgh): "Hans Wagner, former Pittsburgh shortstop ... and Joe Choynski ... were appointed members of a boxing commission to regulate and govern boxing bouts in this city." Johannes Peter "Honus" Wagner, born February 24, 1874 in Pittsburgh, earned the nickname, "The Flying Dutchman," for his stellar speed. During his 20-year Major League Baseball career, which ended in 1917, Wagner won eight batting titles and led the league in stolen bases five times. To this day, many baseball historians consider him the greatest shortstop ever (along with names like Cal Ripken, Jr. and Derek Jeter) and among the best all-round players. Ty Cobb called Wagner "maybe the greatest star ever to take the diamond." Honus would be elected into the Baseball Hall of Fame in 1936, one of the first five members. What the retired baseball superstar knew about boxing, however, is in question. Wagner was appointed to the Pittsburgh City Boxing Commission, although it is not confirmed whether Joe was.[1]

As mentioned, Willard Carver was probably crucial in Joe's decision to become a chiropractor. On June 12, 1905, he graduated from the Charles Ray Parker School of Chiropractic, in Ottumwa, Iowa. This was among the earliest chiropractic schools, the first being the Palmer School and Cure, founded in 1896. Willard was an early pioneer in this form of alternative therapy. He co-founded his own school in Oklahoma City in 1906. D.D. Palmer and his son, B.J. Palmer, established the Chiropractic philosophy, based on the premise that "Inflammation was the essential feature of disease ... caused by displaced anatomic parts, such as arteries, veins, nerves, muscles, ligaments, bones, and joints." The focus later shifted to nerve irritation "due to subluxation of spinal joints as the source of illness."

Carver was, at first, a good friend of D.D. Palmer, offering the latter a faculty position at his new school. D.D. instead founded the Palmer-Gregory College of Chiropractic in Oklahoma City. In later years, Carver and the Palmers developed an adversarial relationship, which seemed to start in 1910, when Willard made known his intention of including "suggestive therapeutics" into Chiropractic. Wanting to keep Chiropractic pure and separate, D.D. wrote: "Friend Carver: Mind does not control the functions. There is an Intelligence that controls the mind and its functions, as well as the functions of the body. You ought to know by this time that I do not treat disease, even by suggestion. Therein Chiropractic differs from all other methods. Suggestion, if it is anything, is a treatment."

On July 15, 1919, B.J. Palmer wrote to W.C. Schulze, MD, DC, National School of Chiropractic (Chicago): "In getting your Lyceum Program ... I noticed Willard Carver ... on the same afternoon as I. I will not be on your program as scheduled. Had I known ... Carver was ... I should never have accepted your invitation ... Carver has been ... deliberately misrepresenting me, in ways ... so apparent to the ... profession that he has lost their friendship, confidence and business. Willard ... preaches 'Chiropractic' and deliberately teaches Orificial Surgery, has ... diverted his ideas from the fundamental principles of Chiropractic laid down by my father in 1895 ... these are injurious to the present or future welfare of Chiropractic ... I cannot have my name connected, or affiliated with any meeting which might give credence, or value to him or his ideas, which would tend to destroy real Chiropractic ... Carver has been refused ... even upon his personal solicitation, a place on any of our Lyceum Programs."[2]

While I am by no means qualified to render an expert opinion as to who might have been more "correct" here, it can be said in defense of Willard Carver, that his heart was in the right place. In his speech before the Roycroft gathering in 1918, he declared it inexcusable for a physician to misdiagnose: "The mistakes in diagnosis are in exact ratio to the anatomic ignorance of any school of doctors. The best of the medical doctors admit making mistakes in 55 per cent of diagnoses. In other words, admit their diagnosis is but an advised guess." He said physiology wasn't being taught properly in schools; descriptions of organs, yes, but not their function. Carver concluded, "If I was guilty, as a Chiropractor, of more than five per cent of mistakes in diagnosis, I would take down my sign in shame for my ignorance and would hie me hence to the most secluded jungle, and ... finish my days alone, where I could do no one harm."[3]

On March 5, 1920, Joe graduated from the Universal Chiropractic College,* located at 1940 5th Avenue in Pittsburgh, on the corner of 5th and Jumonville Street. The school was situated three blocks north of the Monongahela River and the tracks of the Baltimore & Ohio Railroad, about one mile west of Choynski's 311 Coltart Avenue (or "Coltart Square") residence.[4] Although Universal closed its doors in 1944, as of 2013, the structure still stands. Joe's had been an 18-month course, the norm for many such schools of the time. Others, notably the National Chiropractic College (today, the National University of Health Sciences), had a course of four years, which is more or less the standard today.* Choynski received a diploma, granting him the degree of D.C., or Doctor of Chiropractic. From November 5, 1918 to March 5, 1920, he evidently alternated as instructor at the Pittsburgh A.C., and a student at the college There is no indication he had severed connections with the club; Joe is listed in the City Directories

of 1919 through 1921, as "Athletic Director, P.A.A."
* Thanks to James Winterstein, DC – President of the National University of Health Sciences (NUHS). (See Endnotes for more).[5]

One of the men who attended the Universal College with Joe, was Frank Grady, of Ashland, Schuylkill County, Pennsylvania. Grady was a terrific amateur boxer in his youth, it being said that if it weren't for his aversion to

Universal Chiropractic College, Pittsburgh, Pennsylvania, circa 1924

having his features marked up, he would have been the greatest boxer ever to come out of Schuylkill County. The former boxers met at Universal, graduated together and became friends. As of 1935, Grady was still a practicing chiropractor, at his Centre Street location in Ashland. He had an Elks Club membership in common with Joe, as well.[6]

On June 28, Charles "Parson" Davies died in the town of Bedford, Virginia, a week short of his 69th birthday. The cause of death was cerebral hemorrhage. He had been in poor health a long while. The manager, promoter and sportsman had given at least one recent interview, and seemed at peace. Bedford is the location of the Elks National Home, where Charlie spent his final days. He had for many years been a member of the BPOE (Benevolent and Protective Order of Elks), and was elected Grand Exalted Ruler in 1879. Davies is, to this day, the only former Grand Exalted Ruler buried in the Elks Rest Cemetery in Bedford.[7]

The Jack Dempsey-Georges Carpentier heavyweight title fight at Boyle's Thirty Acres, Jersey City, New Jersey took place July 2. It was boxing's first million dollar gate, courtesy of promoter George "Tex" Rickard. The day prior, Joe said "the ... scrap is to be the greatest in the history of the game, and he has made arrangements for a seat at the ringside." It is not verified if he attended. By the end of the first week in August, Joe and Louise were vacationing in Chicago. A reporter for the *Chicago Daily Tribune* met Joe on the street on the 8th, noting that, in addition to instructing at the Pittsburgh A.C., he was "a practicing chiropractor in the Smoky City."[8] Exactly where Joe hung his shingle is uncertain; probably at his home.

From now on, Edwin, his wife Florence, and Joe's older sister, Miriam, would no longer be known by the surname, Choynski. On September 15, at Superior Court in San Francisco's City Hall, they applied for a legal change of name. After advertising the name change for four weeks in the local *Sunset Journal,* the three became, on November 29, 1921, Edwin Walker Coe, Florence Carmelita Coe and Miriam Coe. Why the name change? Although the answer is uncertain, David Fleishhacker, grandson of Herbert Choynski, said: "When Herbert died, my grandmother (Ethel) changed her

"Parson" Davies, early 1900s

name, too – I figure she just got tired of people not being able to pronounce Choynski. But my sister (Delia) remembers her second thoughts ... saying, 'When Herbert looks around, somehow, in the afterlife, he's going to say, *Who is that broad buried next to me?*' "[9] Today, there are none left from Joe's branch of the family, bearing the name Choynski.

On September 16, columnist Frank G. Menke gave a dissertation on the art of body punching, saying its use could make the difference between a mediocre and a truly great fighter. Even light-punching classic boxer Jim Corbett developed a good body attack, particularly with the left hook. Punching to the face in a fight is an instinct from youth, but cultivating a smash to the torso takes effort, practice and intent. Conversely, it is natural for an adversary to guard his face, anticipating a blow there. Body punching scores points, lowers an opponent's guard, exposes his chin and slows him down. He cited great midsection thumpers (heavyweight) Jack Dempsey, John L. Sullivan, Fitzsimmons, Jeffries, Terry McGovern, Stanley Ketchel, Joe Walcott and Joe Choynski, adding: "Choynski, regarded by many as the most terrific hitter of ... all, was a body clouter par excellence."[10]

An April 29 paper said that Ray Pryel, from Homestead, Pennsylvania, "is ... so good, a lot of older and wiser boys are side-stepping him. Joe Choynski ... is steering Pryel toward the title. The Pennsy boy ... had a match lined up with Sailor Friedman ... contender to Leonard's crown, but ... Friedman was taken into custody in connection with a shooting scrape. Pryel is to get his chance in New York within the next few weeks, and hopes to meet Leonard* during the summer." [11] This is the last heard of Joe being involved in Pryel's career. On January 1, 1923, a streak of wins ended when Ray was stopped in six by Eddie Shevlin.

* world lightweight champion, Benny Leonard, "The Ghetto Wizard."

One paper called Ed Graney, the "leading sportsman of San Francisco, veteran billiard room keeper ... owing to his fairness in the ring, he was called on to referee billiard matches and other sport happenings on the coast and soon, no sporting event of any consequence was complete ... without Graney ... (as) referee. (He) ... in a three-day amateur tournament ... handled a total of 232 matches ... a record. Mr. Graney started refereeing in 1889 ... has seen all the great fighters ..." He called Jim Corbett the best boxer, regardless of weight, and Choynski "the hardest puncher ... Every time he landed a blow it hurt, whereas hard punchers like Bob Fitzsimmons were wild and did not connect every time ... The three greatest scrappers ... that I knew were negroes ... Pete Jackson, Joe Walcott and George Dixon ... Jackson was a greater heavyweight than Johnson ..."[12]

Around March 17, 1923, Tim McGrath saw Choynski, apparently in New York. He said Joe "looked so young and athletic when I met him on the train, I really thought he was a four-rounder of the present day, who I might have overlooked ..." "Joe is in town here now (San Francisco) and plans to open up a health institute, with a little chiropractic on the side. The stuff they are handing out ... here for booze is awful, and I think Joe will do well in his new venture, as a health institute on every street would not be overdoing it." A May *Ring* magazine article noted, "Dr. Joseph Bartlett Choynski ... is the sign that has been placed in a window on a neat San Francisco residence. Joe ... until a few weeks ago ... athletic director of the Pittsburgh A.A., resigned that position and went to the Coast to pursue Chiropractics. He is a close student of this branch of medicine and has decided he can make more money practicing ... than ... as an athletic instructor." An August issue said Joe "has attained prominence as a chiropractor ... established a gymnasium and chiropractic offices at 358 Sutter street, Rooms 203 and 204, where he will rejuvenate business men. Choynski's long years in the ring ... gave him a knowledge of the human body, which combined with his latter day studies, fits him better, perhaps, than any ... man in America to do the work he has undertaken."[13]

Next, an account of a Choynski fight that, to this point, has not been validated. May 23, 1922 *Fort Wayne News-Sentinel*: "I'm reminded of (a) battle between Sam Pruitt, a gigantic gentleman of color in San Francisco in the old days, and Joe Choynski. Sam was a world's champion in the gym, but liked to take his time and box ... along to a clever victory. Joe ... knowing

Sam's love for boxing, discarded his own cleverness and for several rounds forced his way close to big Sam and used only one short arm blow, landing it every few seconds on Sam's nose. At last Sam went down, and while the referee counted, turned his face up to the official and said peevishly: 'Boss, I don't call this no scientific fighting. Why don't you make that man scatter his blows some?' When Sam got up, Joe peppered him on the nose again, using the same crowding tactics, and Sam dropped. The referee counted nine, and ... holding his arm raised before the fatal 'ten,' asked: 'Sam, ain't you going to fight any more?' 'Sure, I am,' said Sam, 'but not tonight!' " If the match occurred, it was probably early in Joe's career.

In August, Joe decided he didn't "think so much of Jack Dempsey ... he can be whipped by the first big man ... who can both fight and box." "Perhaps Joe is wrong – but this much is certain: Choynski, in his prime and only weighing 161 pounds, would have given Dempsey ... 188, a royal battle!" Tom Sharkey chimed in: "Dempsey has to come to his opponent to be effective ... 'Jeff' ... slaughtered everyone who did it. Another ... I think could easily have beaten Dempsey was Joe Choyinski (sic). He fought like Jeffries ... there is only one of the old-timers whom Dempsey could have beaten ... Jim Corbett. I think he would have knocked out Corbett as easily as Jeffries would have beaten him. I am not underestimating Dempsey. I won $2,500 the day he whipped Willard, and I seconded Jack the day he stopped Carl Morris. The trouble with boxers today ... when they gain the championship they become actors and let their strength ebb away at some soft job."[14] It is typical of boxers to favor contemporaries and disparage those coming later. Dempsey was one of the great ones, a fighter's fighter. And, Tom only needed to take off the blinders to see that men of his own generation, Corbett and others, had "become actors and let their strength ebb away ..." I have found no source to validate Tom being in Jack's corner for the 18-second starching of Carl Morris on December 16, 1918.

An unidentified former amateur boxer (possibly Harry Pegg) related the following, regarding the 1889 barge fight: "Many years later (in 1922) I found myself ... in Motor Square Garden in Pittsburgh, opposing Harry Fay in an AAU Meet. Choynski refereed the fight. At this time Joe was boxing instructor at nearby Duquesne University. Later in the dressing room, he told of this sensational battle. Corbett, using an uppercut, struck Choynski on the bottom of his nose, tearing the part that separates the nostrils from his upper lip, causing a heavy flow of blood that could not be stopped, and he had to quit beyond his desire to continue. For many years the famous old barge remained tied up near Benecia, gradually rotting, parts being taken as souvenirs. The photo of the remains was taken in 1946, at which time I received a paper-weight made from a piece of lumber from this relic of long ago."[15] No record is found to confirm Joe as boxing instructor at Duquesne University. In late October, papers announced that he had "retired from active participation in athletics" and was "going into pictures in Los Angeles." On November 13, Joe was near Santa Monica, California, looking for a site "on which to establish a gymnasium health farm."

Choynski said: "One of the fundamentals of boxing ... is the ability to feint an opponent, draw a lead ... block ... then hit him," insinuating that none of the "moderns" did this. After calling Stanley Ketchel and "Young Corbett" two of the most overrated in ring history, Joe was castigated by sportswriter, Damon Runyon. The latter said that "Honest" John Kelly, a renowned referee of yesteryear, once opined that "Choynski was a good, game fellow with a glass chin." This was more of an insult than a valid rebuttal, as the "glass jaw" label has been applied over the years (by some) to Joe Louis, Roy Jones, Jr. and Lennox Lewis. The resiliency of one's mandible relates little to an ability to draw a punch and counter. It was said of Runyon, that for many years he was on the take; that is, took bribes from managers and promoters, that they might get adequate coverage for their fighters in his syndicated column. He allegedly skimmed off gate receipts from the annual Hearst Milk Fund boxing benefit in New York, which he ran for several years. It was further claimed that Damon had New York City gangsters as close friends.[16] He clearly was not on Joe's payroll.

Damon was at it again on January 5, 1923, quoting a letter sent him by old Choynski nemesis, Tom O'Rourke. "Reading your article about Joe Choynski brought to memory a saying of little Jimmy Barry, once bantamweight champion ... in ... Davies' stable during the same period as Joe ... Barry often remarked that Choynski could show a man more ways to whip another fighter and hit the boards himself oftener than anybody living." Runyon: "Barry's remarks have been ... true ... often ... a man who has no great personal ability to the matter of execution is a great teacher. He knows how things ought to be done, though he may not be able to do them himself. Choynski ... is a good instructor, a poor judge of pugilistic greatness."[17] Of the latter, so was Runyon. Whether Barry actually made the comments about Joe, whom he was supposedly friends with, is uncertain, coming as they did from a questionable source like O'Rourke.

A February 13 paper stated: "Dr. Joseph Bartlett Choynski is to become a permanent resident of San Francisco. Joe, who moved to the Pacific Coast from Pittsburgh a short while ago, was advised to settle in Southern California. He ... looked over the situation and decided that San Francisco, his home town, is good enough for him. So, Joe is back. Just ... what he will start has not been decided. He is a practicing chiropractor – a noted one in Pittsburgh and other Eastern cities. He may lease offices in one of the big buildings and hang out his shingle or he may start a big physical culture institute. He ... will decide in a few days." Joe, in the Bay area since November, 1922, was mulling over a return to his native city. It didn't happen, but it is fairly evident that he continued as a *part-time* chiropractor.

He continued as a referee and boxing instructor, but Janet Choynski Fleishhacker said that her Uncle Joe "was a chiropractor until he died. But ... never terribly successful ... one of the gentlest human beings I have ever met." Chiropractic was still not widely understood nor popular.[18]

Choynski refereed a six-fight card at the Auditorium in Modesto, California on March 22. The referee and two judges scored a fight if it went the distance. He rendered a verdict in the first four bouts, the last two ended in knockouts. "Joe ... an added attraction as referee ... gave exceptionally fair decisions, despite the howls of a few fans who thought they knew more about the art of self defense than one of the greatest exponents of the game ..." Although it isn't known when Joe became a member of the BPOE (Benevolent and Protective Order of Elks), he was apparently one by now. *Modesto Evening News*: "Joe Choyinski (sic), considered the greatest man of his inches who ever donned a padded mitt, was the guest of honor at a dinner party at the Elks'

Joe and brother Edwin Coe, San Francisco, 1923. Courtesy, Western States Jewish History Archives

club last evening, before Joe refereed four-round bouts at the auditorium. Manuel Borba(?) (illegible), an old friend of Joe's, was the host." At some point, Joe sparred at the Olympic Club with a "young boxer," and was called "a very trim figure at the age of 55."[19]

On May 2, he was in the corner of 21-year-old "Spider" Kelly protégé, Pat Lester, along with Kelly and Tim McGrath. The fight took place at San Francisco's Association Club, against Mel Smith. Although Lester scored a KO2, he was unimpressive. McGrath was the trainer of note, although it was added, "He's (Lester) receiving his boxing experience against Joe Choynski ..." McGrath boasted that Lester was receiving the "old-time training system," that Tim gave Tom Sharkey in his heyday. He wanted Pat to prove "the methods of yesteryear surpass today's." Lester was born Frank Myron on December 23, 1901, stood 6' 4" and weighed 220 pounds, with an 81" reach. His best punches were a straight left and right cross; he was a slow starter with a lot of heart. Joe was still working with Lester in

September, 1924; how much longer is not certain. Pat wound up his career in 1928 with 23 wins (14 knockouts), 11 losses (3 by knockout) and 3 draws. He proved a useful, but not exceptional, heavyweight.[20]

Joe wrote a September 25 letter to TAD. He named, among the greatest fighters of all time, the previously-discounted Stanley Ketchel and Billy Papke, middleweight champions: "Both good men, but sluggers. After seeing them box for the first time I stated one was just as likely to win as the other and subsequent events bore me out. But what chance would either have had with Tom Ryan or Fitz? It is true, the men of today are in better condition than the old-timers, due to the many chances to display their wares. But there are no new blows ... no improvement. I cut the following ... from the *Examiner* this a.m.: 'Jack Dempsey ... they say is easy to hit, and ... leaves himself wide open ... Have you ever noticed how a tiger, a lion and other ferocious animals leave themselves wide open to the attack? Well, then you have an idea how the champion resembles them.' A bit of sophistry. The writer does not know his natural history. The tiger stalks his prey or springs from ambush. I wonder, did he ever see four or five dogs worry a lion and get him, or a mongoose get a snake. Not in the open, I'm sure."[21] TAD, a famous cartoonist and journalist, was born Thomas Aloysius Dorgan on April 29, 1877, in San Francisco. He died May 2, 1929, but left a legacy as the greatest creator of American slang. He is credited with such terms as "for crying out loud," "cat's meow," "hard-boiled" and "as busy as a one-armed paperhanger."

Joe left San Francisco and by February 14, 1924, was in Chicago, joining friend and former second, George Shrosbree. *Kingston Daily Freeman*: "Joe Choynski ... has come to Chicago and plunged into the work of beautifying the big city in its changes now going on. He joined a construction firm with George Schrosbree (sic), brother of Al, another former fighter, now dead, and is ... moving houses to make several streets wider. The houses are moved scientifically. The families are not asked to move, and in five hours the water, gas and electric lights are again hooked up and life goes on under the new conditions. Some brick houses have the front cut off as if with a big cheese knife. Joe is superintendent of the construction gang doing this work and enjoys it. It is out of doors and he occasionally swings a pick-ax to get through some tough cement and finds it exhiliarating."[22] Apparently, Joe was feeling unsettled at this period in his life, perhaps suffering from retirement blues. The April 9 *Manitoba Free Press* reported that he had "entered the insurance business" in Chicago.

At this time, Choynski began training a 6' 3", 210 pound heavyweight from Trieste, Italy, named Arturo Del Monte. He was tutored by Joe until early 1925, when he had his first professional fight. Del Monte, whose real name was probably either Arturo Del Monte or Arturo De Kuhacevich (a 1933 article calls him Curtino Del Monte), would go on to box as Arthur

De Kuh, a good heavyweight of the mid-1920s to early '30s.[23] Like most Joe trained, however, an experienced manager soon assumed control of De Kuh's career. Young, talented heavyweights were not excessive in this period, and Joe would never bring a boxer to great heights.

In the Dempsey-Firpo heavyweight championship of September 14, 1923, Luis, after dropping Jack with an early right, was floored seven times in the 1st round, but knocked the champion through the ropes and out of the ring. Jack landed on a journalist's typewriter, badly cutting the back of his head. He managed to re-enter the ring, assisted by a push from the Press. Upon his return, the referee had counted to four, but many with stopwatches saw 14 seconds elapse. "The Mauler" knocked out the huge "Wild Bull of the Pampas" in round two. Joe held the view that "the Queensberry rules were designed for ... rings at floor level. There, if a man were knocked out of the ring, the count should start at once ... in the elevated ring ... conditions are changed, and commissions should recognize the right of the boxer to have ... time to get back into the squared circle. Elevated platforms are ... recent innovations, made necessary by the great crowds ... If a fighter is pushed or knocked out of the ring, he receives extra punishment through a fall to the ground ... not contemplated by the Marquis of Queensberry, and he should not be disqualified for being set back on the raised platform."[24] Choynski's take holds merit, though the code was never modified as he recommended. He may have been the only one to voice this idea.

On June 7, 1924, Joe's mother, Harriett, died in San Francisco at the age of 81. She was buried on the 9th at the Hills of Eternity Memorial Park in Colma, in the Ashim-Choynski Plot. She lies next to Isidor, and near her parents, Morris and Rachel Ashim.[25] Joe had been close to his mother, and his grief must have been immense. The morning of August 13 saw a tragedy of a different sort occur in Los Angeles, involving Norman Selby, alias "Kid" McCoy. Selby shot to death his live-in lover, Mrs. Theresa Mors. Shortly afterward, in the Mors' antique shop, after being

Harriett Ashim-Choynski, 1920s

told that Mr. Mors wasn't there, he ordered several men to remove their trousers and hand over their money. Norman shot and wounded two men and a woman, before turning himself in to police. After Selby was arrested for murder, Choynski and other boxing figures recounted memories of him for the papers. They were kinder than were the papers, themselves.

As testimony in the trial unfolded, many papers began tearing down the legend that was McCoy, saying he had never been a "ring idol," that he was always a deceitful, conniving individual; never a great boxer, only a "showman." There was some truth to these words, but much was unfair and untrue. One paper claimed, "he was distinguished by a certain rapidity of blows that attracted considerable attention. He delivered them in such a manner as to deceive and bewilder many better men, as in the instance of his fight with Joe Choynski at San Francisco. He resorted to any means he could devise to defeat his opponent other than blows, and never possessed a true fighter's punch. His foot-work ... was not notable in any way. In fact, it gave the impression of clumsiness at times, and he never depended on it, but used instead sudden circus-like shifts ... from his hips up."

McCoy's defense attorneys formed their case around his "unbalanced mental condition." Billy Elmer, a "well known sport and theatrical promoter ... associated with McCoy in the Consolidated Athletic Club in

"Kid" McCoy, 1924

New York in 1903 and 1904" and was prepared to testify that "McCoy had not been right since 1900, when he took a terrific beating from Joe Choynski." Given the public's uncertainty of the exact nature of Selby's psychological profile and guilt, if the death of Theresa Mors had been the only point of contention, Selby likely would have been acquitted. Instead, his violence toward others figured into the jury's perception, even if his marriages to nine different women and accusations of being a "love pirate" did not. Ultimately, a sympathetic jury, after 78 hours of deliberation (mostly in an attempt to distinguish between the legend of McCoy and the real Norman Selby), found him guilty of manslaughter in Mrs. Mors' death. McCoy was sentenced to 48 years in San Quentin Prison – 10 for manslaughter and 38 for the shootings of three bystanders in his follow-up rampage. Selby was released from prison in the summer of 1932 on "good behavior," and given a job by Henry Ford at the employees' vegetable gardens, at the Ford Motor Company plant in Detroit.[26]

In September, a *Police Gazette* article entitled, "Joe Choynski: Boxer and

Gentleman," said he "was an ornament to the game. He was honorable, clean in his habits and his morals." Joe "conducted himself with the same grace of manner, and always displayed a skill and bearing within the roped arena that made him a reputation even among those who seldom, if ever, visited the fighting rings. He was a type apart from most of the fighters of those roseate days, and there is little but good that can be said about him. Until a couple of years ago he was the athletic director of the Pittsburgh Athletic Association. Leaving that position he went to San Francisco, where he opened up an office to practice chiropody (sic). Apparently this business wasn't a great success, for in April of this year he entered the insurance business in Chicago."[27] The reporter mistook chiropody (podiatry, treating conditions of the foot and ankle) for chiropractic.

Joe Williams humorously wrote, on October 30: "Joe Choynski, old-time fighter, has declined to enter the presidential race ... 'Imagine one of the Choynski boys sitting next to a pork barrel!' he exclaims."[28] While it is not known that Joe trained any more big-name pugs, he did instruct Eddie Garvey, a member of the "Fighting Irish" football team from 1920 through 1922. Garvey was turning heads at the close of 1924 by his performance as an amateur boxer. December 9 *Lincoln Star:* "The speed in which Eddie Garvey, heavyweight, knocked Hugo Pukat kicking in the heavyweight elimination contests in New York City (possibly an AAU tournament) has centered attention on the former Notre Dame left tackle ... Garvey, christened Arthur Aloysius, was born in St. Louis, Missouri in 1900, but lived all his life in Holyoke, Massachusetts, where he played baseball and football on the high school 11. He graduated in law, but that sedentary profession sent his weight up from 215 to 287, so he hied himself to Chicago and got a job at the Hawthorne race track, where the famous old timer, Joe Choynski, took him in charge and taught him how to fight. He has many of Choynski's tricks in the ring. Lincoln fight promoters are angling for Garvey's appearance in a local ring engagement." How far Garvey went in the New York bouts isn't known.

Joe's "kid" brother, Edwin Coe, officiated on September 24 at a Pacific Athletic Association boxing tournament, at the Olympic Athletic Club. On at least two other occasions that year, Coe refereed important amateur matches at the Olympic, on Post Street. He would be used the following year as arbiter for the Far Western AAU championships. Jim Corbett, now a stage actor and part-time columnist, said he still saw Joe occasionally, "and we never cease talking about those 28 rounds on the fish boat in the Bay." On November 10, there was "an unconfirmed report afloat that the New Jersey Boxing Commission is planning to ratify a fight between Harry Wills and old Joe Choynski, for George Washington's birthday."[29] Wills was a great black heavyweight and top contender from about 1915 through 1925. At around 6' 3" and 220 pounds, he towered over most of the field, figuratively and literally. He was variously nicknamed "The Brown Panther," "Black Panther" and "Black Menace." A former stevedore, Wills was a monstrously strong infighter who liked to hold and hit, especially with a right to the body. He had a strong left jab and stout right to the head. Matching him with any long-retired boxer was ridiculous.

Bob Edgren wrote, for the December 6 *Fresno Bee*, that he sat with McCoy on the train to Philadelphia for the latter's May, 1902 tilt with "Kid" Carter. McCoy "was anxious to talk about Carter. He was, I think, a little jealous of the blond Norseman's growing ... reputation. Carter was a savage fighter who took any and all risks in a fight, for ... putting over a knockout punch. He ... was knocked out ... by Billy Hanrahan, George Gardner and Marvin Hart. But, he knocked out Hanrahan later and by knocking out Joe Walcott in seven ... and Joe Choynski in a round had established a unique reputation. Walcott up to that time had been considered punch-proof ... 'I'm going to show this slugger up, said McCoy. 'You watch me. I won't hit him anywhere but on the left eye.' Sure enough, for nearly two rounds, McCoy, sneering derisively at the plunging Carter, corkscrewed him ... on the left eye until Carter's lamp was completely closed. Carter was swinging wildly and McCoy seemed to have no trouble ... avoiding his punches. Just at the end of the 2nd round, Carter let go a terrific right, and landed squarely on the point of McCoy's chin, knocking him cold."

"As the count reached 'eight,' the bell rang. It was ... claimed ... the bell was rung several seconds too soon, to save McCoy from a knockout. The ... seconds ... began to drag him toward the corner. McCoy recovered ... enough to cross the ring when the bell rang. McCoy was knocked down six times in five rounds, and took a terrific beating. He came to enough to make a furious finish in the 6th and last round ... sent Carter spinning ... into the ropes with a desperate right hand punch ... the next day ... He was still dazed, and he told me he couldn't remember anything about the fight, except he had started the 1st round by hitting Carter on the left eye ... I think there is a strong possibility that all of McCoy's mental eccentricities of later years and the trouble he is in now, might have been avoided if he had been counted out at the end of that 2nd round with Carter, instead of being sent back after a cold knockout ... and take more punishment ..." While possible that brain damage caused Selby's violent behavior in later years, it was more likely a combination of alcohol and Selby's nature.

Jim Corbett wrote that he had still not seen a boxer who "hit with more terrific power than Joe Choynski." He "thought, each time Joe hit me, that he was using a slab of iron. In the later years ... Joe's punches carried even more crushing force and I came then to regard him as the greatest hitter of them all." Jim, in discussing the merits of various fighters, said the lone point upon which there was never any dissent was when anyone said, "Joe Choynski was the greatest hitter. Choynski could hit with either hand with almost the same power. And it made no difference whether he hit to the jaw or the body, he crushed or crumpled his man – or left some ghastly imprint – whenever he landed. Joe loved the fight game ... Oftentimes I feel that his sheer love for fighting, which eclipsed the normal eagerness to win, caused him to toss away innumerable chances for knockout triumphs in battles which he merely won on points or ... went to a draw. Choynski could ... annihilate a foeman with one punch ... one of the few one-punch knocker-outs that ever lived. But (he) rarely chose to end a fight in a hurry. He liked to play around with the scientific feature of it. If the going did get rough, and Joe was in danger of being put away ... he didn't take many chances. Peter Maher attempted to get rough with Joe in Philadelphia. Joe hit him once – and that ... was over. He knocked out one man who didn't recover for 30 minutes. Another was in a coma for 15 minutes. Almost every man Joe ever faced ... was knocked out or down ..."

High praise, but this author gets the sense that Jim was giving his greatest kudos now, through guilt at never granting Joe his long-requested rematch. Choynski did have a love for the game when young, but seemed to lose it toward the end of his career, when he became increasingly bitter at the hand fate had dealt him. With a little more weight and perhaps, good fortune, he might have won the heavyweight crown. In my opinion, Fitz and Maher carried a slight edge in terms of one-punch knockout force. Corbett: "Then there's an epistle from Carroll Van Court, whose late father knew all the old-time boxers ... Carroll: 'Here is how Choynski came to have such power in his hands and arms. By trade, for a time, Joe was a candy-puller, and as this was long before automatic candy machines were used, Choynski used to lift and pull candy over those big hooks several hours a day. He also tried the brine trick (on his skin) and would sometimes chop wood with two hatchets or hand axes. He got speed with the hands by playing with a cat and studying its motions, as he would feint at it and watch it jab and slap at him.' " Carroll may have been thinking of "Kid" McCoy, regarding the cat. Corbett was perhaps becoming senile. In 1928, he said the hardest hitter he ever faced was not Joe, but two men, Mike Cleary and Denny Kelliher! "Cleary was the hardest natural hitter ... ever ... Kelliher ... could knock a man stiff with a three-inch punch. They could make all the other hitters ... look like powder puffs ..."[30]

In 1926, *Ring* magazine found Peter Maher working on the Hoboken docks in New York. When asked who the greatest fighter he ever saw was, without hesitating, the old war-horse said, "Joe Choynski."[31] Around this time, Joe began to write an abbreviated biography, published in 30 weekly installments. The chapters began on December 31, 1926 in Canada's *Manitoba Free Press*. The mini-bio, entitled, "The Days of Finish Fights," ran through February 19, 1927. Each chapter was published a few days later by the Australian newspaper, the (Adelaide) *Advertiser*.

In Chapter 1, Joe related: "In fact, I was only a middleweight, if classified according to the weight divisions of the present. When I began fighting, the middleweight boundary was 154 pounds. There was no light-heavyweight division in those days, and any man weighing over 154 pounds was a heavyweight. When I fought Jeffries a 20 round draw, I weighed only 158 pounds; I knocked out Jack Johnson when I beamed just 161, and my weight in the famous finish fight with Corbett was only 153. Only twice in my life – when I met Joe Goddard in Australia – was I able, by forced feeding, to bring my weight up to 168. To-day at the age of 58, after a retirement of 22 years, I weigh only 164 stripped. Imagine Tiger Flowers, the current middleweight champion ... thrown into the ring with Dempsey, Wills, or Firpo, and you can appreciate the weight handicap under which I almost invariably fought. The middleweights ... would have nothing to do with me, and I had to give away gobs of weight to get work ... It was not until such ... as Bob Fitzsimmons, Kid McCoy and Jim Hall ... appeared ... that I could get matches with men of my own weight. But although much lighter than the heavyweights of my day, I was at no disadvantage with most ... in strength or reach. Indeed, I was often-times surprised to find myself stronger than much heavier opponents. Like Fitzsimmons, I acquired my strength in a blacksmith shop ... developed a freakishly powerful torso, with long arms like horses' legs, and huge, strong fists. Two years swinging a 20-pound sledge 10 hours a day developed me from a stripling at 16 into a Hercules at 18. I had the slender but sturdy legs of a racer."

"My reach, 76", was greater even than that of Bob Fitzsimmons. I also worked in a candy factory, where for many months my daily exercises were rolling 300-pound barrels of sugar upstairs from the basement, one step at a time, and 'pulling' 50-pound batches of candy. Is it any wonder I could sock so hard? Having adopted prize fighting as my trade, I never refused any reasonable offer ... and never asked the other fellow's weight, record, or color ... I was always in action, either fighting the greatest men of my day or meeting all comers in four-round stage exhibitions when no important match was at hand. I was never content to be idle ... I am unable to understand the reluctance of modern champions to do their stuff. As the result of the length and activity of my ring career and my mastery of knockout technique, I believe I have knocked out more men than any other fighter, ancient or modern. Of course, the vast majority of these victims of my wallops were dubs who were lured by an offer of money to stay four rounds with me, but many ... were fighters of real ability."

The January 4, 1927 *Brooklyn Daily Eagle* gave the opposing views of two experts on the relative merits of Boxing's "old and new schools." Former heavyweight wrestler, William Muldoon, took the stance that moderns held an edge over old-time pugs, while Choynski supported the earlier fistic warriors. Muldoon, a famous conditioner, was the inaugural Chairmen of the New York State Athletic Commission, from 1921 to 1924. While he obtained his observations primarily as a trainer, Joe formed his opinions in swapping punches with great boxers. Muldoon, born in 1852, 16½ years prior to Choynski, was the only man able to force John L. Sullivan, in training, from going on an alcoholic binge. "The Solid Man," or "The Iron Duke," accomplished this by wresting Sullivan into immobility, gaining his respect. He was a key factor in John defeating Jake Kilrain in 1889.

The author used analogies based on horse racing and said no incontrovertible avowel of supremacy could be made for either view: "It can't be done. Track conditions, soil and the construction of the various courses are entirely different. In the years dead and gone, endurance was the chief asset of a race horse; today it is speed." It was noted that the size of gloves had changed, with five-ounce or heavier being the norm in the 1920s. Muldoon opined that, of the old guard, only Peter Jackson was good enough to compare with Gene Tunney, Jack Dempsey and Jack Sharkey. It wasn't believed, however, that Muldoon ever witnessed Fitzsimmons and Jeffries fight. Shortly after his appointment as Chairman of the New York Commission, William said he didn't know why he'd been selected, as he hadn't seen a fight in 13 years. Joe didn't feel Tunney could have withstood the blows of Jeff, Fitz or Sharkey, but he did believe the best current kings of the lighter divisions compared well with those of his era.[32]

Joe: "Tommy Ryan was the most cautious fighter that ever lived. He would take 60 rounds to lick a man he could beat in five or six ... Some of the funniest incidents of my ring career occurred when I was serving as second. In London one time, I was in the corner of Timmy Burke, a local scrapper. Burke's opponent kept jabbing him in the nose. I yelled ... 'Why don't you stop some of those punches?' In a moment he looked over the shoulder of his foe at me and yelled back, 'You don't see many of them going by me, do you?' On another occasion I was in the corner of an English bruiser who was just holding his own, but getting disgusted. At the close of a rough round he came back to the corner with the announcement that he had decided to quit. 'Why, Gawd blime me, man,' I said, imitating the Cockney accent in an effort to encourage him, 'why do you want to quit? Why, you are the winner.' 'Well, Gawd blime me,' he grunted, 'then I'll quit a winner.' And he tore off his gloves."

"I was training in New Jersey for a fight with Peter Maher ... running alongside a railroad track when some track workmen sat a handcar on the tracks ahead of me and started pumping down the track. Thinking to use them as a pacemaker, I sprinted a bit to overtake them. They took a look at my long legs and flying hair and speeded up their handcar. The faster they went the more speed I put on. The fellows were amazed to see me running along mile after mile. Apparently, they took me for an escaped lunatic. Finally, I put on another sprint and seemed about to overtake them, when

... they abandoned the handcar, leaped over a fence and ran for a house several hundred yards ... from the road. Brandishing the cane I was carrying and yelling lustily, I also leaped the fence, ran a few yards as if in pursuit, then turned back to the road. The sight of those terror-stricken boobs ... gives me a laugh every time I recall it. On another occasion, I was telling George Ade about the big fighter I knocked out as an amateur, and who demanded to know my real name, when I told him I was Joe Choynski. Ade: 'You should have said to him, do you think if I had any other name I would call myself Choynski?' I live a quiet life now in Chicago. I am the manager of a motion picture theatre. I still love the fight game, and sit ... ringside now and then. Occasionally I act as referee. I go into a gymnasium daily to play handball, swim or put on the gloves. I believe in keeping fit – even at 58. Indeed, I feel like 28. It doesn't seem such a long time since the days of finish fights." Joe was probably in partnership with Maurice in the motion picture theatre, though not for long.

Joe Choynski, March 1, 1927, age 58

Joe was granted an Illinois state referee license sometime in early 1927. On March 26, at the Coliseum in Chicago, he refereed the vacant National Boxing Association (NBA) bantamweight title fight between Charles "Bud" Taylor and 19 year old Tony Canzoneri. The furious, 10 round match was declared a draw by Joe and the two ringside judges. Taylor, "The Blond Terror of Terre Haute," gained the crown in a rematch on June 24, via 10 round decision. Choynski refereed that one, too. Canzoneri, at his peak, won world titles in the featherweight, lightweight and junior welterweight divisions. He also won the rubber match with Taylor, in 10 rounds on December 30.[33]

Associated Press Sports Editor Charles W. Dunkley noted: "Looking more like a musician or a poet than a pugilist, he (Joe) has become the ace of referees licensed by the Illinois athletic commission ... Choyinski (sic) is now 58 years old but he doesn't look it. He is in marvelous physical condition. His grey streaked hair, now creeping back on his forehead, is worn long, with a fluff in the back. No lightweight moves around the ring with more speed or grace than Choyinski ... He never becomes confused in an emergency." On June 30, Joe was ringside at Chicago's Comiskey Park, to witness several heavyweight match-ups, including: Jim Maloney vs. Bud Gorman, "Seal" Harris vs. Roy "Ace" Clark and Arthur De Kuh against "Farmer" Lodge. About a month later, Joe told a reporter that what he observed was disheartening. He saw clear proof that the current generation had lost many of the rudiments of boxing. Punches were telegraphed, footwork, feinting and defense were sorely lacking. None of the fighters he observed at Comiskey Park showed any ability to feint. "Yes, I wish I might go back 25 years. I would be a millionaire within a year."[34]

Gene Tunney, "The Fighting Marine," had lifted the heavyweight crown from the aging head of Jack Dempsey on September 23, 1926, on a 10 round decision. The rematch was coming to Chicago's Soldier Field a year later, September 22. Speculation was hot as to who the referee would be. Joe was on the short list, along with Benny Yanger, Dave Miller, Dave Barry, Phil Collins, Ike Bernstein and a few others, from an application list of over 100. According to Illinois state law, the referee was required to be a resident of the state, and could not be named until a few minutes before the fight began, such was the corruption involved in gambling. The law was primarily an effort to prevent anyone bribing the referee. While some of these arbiters, Yanger and Collins, for instance, had been criticized for recent decisions rendered, it was said: "Choynski is one of the colorful figures of the ring and has been consistently good as a referee." "Choynski ... is the 'ace' of the commission's list of referees. He has handled more windups in Chicago than any other official. His decisions have met with popular approval." As late as September 17 it was said, "There is much talk to the effect that Joe Choynski ... may be called in as the 3rd man ... He is said to be acceptable to both camps."[35] Ultimately, Dave Barry was selected, in the "Battle of the Long Count." Dempsey, far behind on points, floored a badly dazed Tunney in round seven, but refused to go to a neutral corner until some 5 seconds had elapsed. Gene used the extra time to clear his head, backpedal and recover. He even dropped Jack in the next frame for a short count, winning another 10 round verdict.

On September 2, Joe umpired the Tony Canzoneri-"Cowboy" Eddie Anderson fight at Chicago's Mills Stadium. In a strange turn of events, he was overruled by the ringside physician. Anderson claimed in both the 1st and 2nd rounds that Tony fouled him, but Joe refused to allow the claim. Though the nature of the alleged breach wasn't specified, it was probably a low blow. After the end of the 2nd heat, "a physician for the boxing commission examined Anderson and found that he had been fouled." If Eddie had been fouled, it would necessarily have been a severe one, to be visually evident. At any rate, the commission was not amused, suspending Canzoneri for 90 days and revoking his boxing license! A December issue of The *Ring* mentioned that "Joe Choynski ... has taken quite an interest in Jack Norris, Toledo light-heavyweight. He sees quite a future in the ring for (him). Norris ... expects to see plenty of action here this winter." No record of Norris was found, online or in record books.[36]

A February 21, 1928 paper called Joe: "One of the best referees in the country ... a former light-heavyweight champion ... in some of the most important bouts ever ... in the Windy City. Choynski was a popular choice for the Tunney-Dempsey title go. He, Dave Barry and Phil Collins were the three chosen from among a large number ... As a 3rd man in the ring, he has an outstanding reputation." Joe was at the Coliseum in Des Moines, Iowa on the night of April 10 to referee a main event between Mike Mandell of St. Paul, Minnesota and local boy, Kenneth Hunt, in what was billed as the light-heavyweight championship of the Mid-West. Mandell won via KO4. Joe umpired a main event at the Coliseum in Davenport on May 3, between heavyweight contenders Chuck Wiggins, "The Hoosier Playboy" and Cecil (or Ceil) "Seal" Harris. Harris went about 6' 3" and 220 pounds, whereas Wiggins was only 5 10½" and 190 to 195. Chuck bragged of flaunting the rules of training, but fought so often, he kept in shape. He was a very good "bar-room slugger" with a tough chin. Training rules weren't the only ones he held in contempt. Chuck alternately kneed and head-butted, adding low blows and back-hand punches. In round five, after multiple warnings from Choynski and a flagrant knee by Wiggins, Joe declared "Seal" the victor. The 2,500 in attendance had begun to resemble a lynch mob, and Joe called a pair of policemen in, to escort the loser out. Matchmaker Henaghan held up Wiggins' $750 purse. The May 3 *Davenport Democrat and Leader* noted, "Al Bellevue, Moline arbiter of the ring, is an old buddy of Joe Choynski, the 3rd man in the ring ... Bellevue helped condition Joe for some of his major bouts, including ... with Fitzsimmons at Boston."[37]

In June, sportswriter-cartoonist, Ed Hughes, for the now-defunct Bell Syndicate, gave tribute to Choynski, in his article, "The Above-the-Belt Brigade ..." Some that he listed were Joe, George Dixon, Joe Gans, Fitzsimmons, Jeffries, Corbett, Tommy Burns, "Kid" Lavigne, Sam Langford, Gene Tunney and Tommy Loughran. A few he named are questionable, like John L. Sullivan, Jack Dempsey, Stanley Ketchel and Harry Greb. Hughes specified that Greb and Ketchel never threw *low blows*, though he admitted Harry "frequently fouled with other rough-stuff." Ed noted that Joe was "100% game" and never fouled an opponent.[38]

Jim Jeffries was in San Mateo, California on July 22, set to embark on a theatrical tour with his brother, Jack. He gave his opinion on the upcoming Tunney-Tom Heeney title fight, correctly picking Tunney to win and saying that Gene, while an excellent boxer, was not in the class of Jim Corbett. He said Gene would have been defeated by middleweight Tommy Ryan, who "at his best, was the most skillful ring general and ring wizard I ever saw ... and he could hit ..." Then, repeating what had become his mantra, Jeffries said: "The hardest punch I ever got in my life was from Abie Jacob's friend, Joe Choynski! They tell me ... Choynski didn't hit me with a club, but I still insist he did, and ... I believe Abie loaned him the club ... Choynski ... turned on his heel as I was going full speed ahead ... poked me with that famous right of his, and ... I thought the roof dropped down on me ... but I was so big and strong I weathered that blow ... At that time I believe they could have hit me with a crowbar without hurting me." Almost a virtual representation of "irresistible force versus immovable object," with the latter barely surviving the encounter. Of Jacobs, the *San Mateo Times* wrote: "Abie Jacobs, the 'Sacramento Flash,' who once boxed with the great Joe Bowker ... (is) now in training to take off weight. Five or six years ago, Jacobs, although well past his prime, could put the gloves on with any of the champions and give them a tussle in a limited round bout."[39]

Around September 1, Ed Graney suffered a stroke. At Ed's 2850 Lake Street home, his physician, Dr. Louis X. Ryan, said the stroke was "aggravated by the fact that Graney has been a semi-invalid for the past eight months." Eddie owned a billiard hall at 61 Eddy Street, called "The Graney." He had been in "ill health" for several years. One article said he "has wielded power in municipal affairs from the days when he ran a blacksmith shop at 4th and Howard streets. His interest in boxing ... dates from that time, and many the bout, informal or matched, took place behind that blacksmith shop. His billiard hall ... is headquarters for boxers, fight managers and others interested in sport in San Francisco."

On September 7, Graney died at the age of 61. Bob Edgren said he "made the tuxedo popular in San Francisco ... elevated boxing and made the Mechanics' Pavilion or Woodward's Gardens as much a society center as the National Sporting Club in London. Before Graney's time a referee officiated in his shirtsleeves – usually rolled up. His shirt was likely to be pink, decorated with blue and green stripes. If he had on a collar and a tie he removed them before the first bell and tossed them to someone in the press box to guard until the fights were over. He wore trousers with a four inch check, and light yellow shoes. Sometimes a referee wore a sweater and a cap. There was no class ... until ... Graney made his first ring appearance in his little 'tux,' with stiff while shirt, high collar, hand tie black bow, three of the best pearl studs on Larkin Street." Among Ed's criticisms: "Did it ever strike you that not one referee in a hundred knows the rules? ... the rules say a boxer must rise within 10 seconds, unassisted ... he's assisting the boxer to get up ... Just the sight of the referee ... over him, waving his hand and counting in a loud voice, has aroused many a beaten boxer who never would have gotten up in 10 seconds if left to himself."

"The Honest Blacksmith" was described by the *San Francisco Call* as "A man of commanding presence, quiet demeanor ... has the respect and confidence of all in his private and public life." Prior to the Fire of 1906, Ed "had the largest horse shoeing establishment in the country ... many shops ... in different sections of the city." He once described the difficulty of being a competent ring arbiter: "Take ... a case in court involving, say, $50,000 ... testimony is heard ... Each day newspapers print their opinions ... After six or seven days the judge takes the case under advisement, before instructing the jury. He goes home ... consults the authorities, perhaps his wife. He gets a broad idea of what others think ... Then ... the decision, and the man who loses has recourse to a higher court, with an appeal. Now ... the referee in an important boxing match ... has to decide off perhaps millions wagered on the result – not $50,000. Sitting around the ring are thousands in a jury that listens for the referee's verdict. The referee must give that decision immediately ... the next morning he will know what the newspapers and the public think of his ruling." One point Ed seems to have lost, is that a person charged with such rulings needs to ignore outside influences and opinions – of course, easier said than done.

Of Graney's funeral: "A great multitude ... responded with deep emotion to the tributes to his loyalty, courage, charity and reliance. All ... faiths and nationalities were represented ... Father Oliver Welch ... 'It is not customary for the Catholic Church to eulogize ... its children who have departed, but I cannot but say a few words on the passing of my good friend Edward Graney. It has been a friendship of 45 years and one of the sweetest and noblest ... in my life. His kindnesses in life and his honest purposes have been mine to know. His charities – you know. But all the sorrows and secrets of the broken friendships of his life are still locked up in his heart.' Mr. Graney is survived by his widow, Mrs. Florence Graney, of 1800 Broadway, San Francisco, and by one sister, Mrs. John P. Culley. Mr. Graney married in 1918 Miss Florence Clifford ..."[40]

In late 1928, Joe was spotted by Chicago writer, Ed Carey, in "Kid" Howard's Gym on Chicago's West Side. "I noticed a lithe, broad-shouldered figure skipping rope in a far corner ... a queer looking guy who looked as out of place among the 16 and 17 year old punks ... shadow boxing ... as a cigar in Cal Coolidge's mouth. There was something familiar about his face and especially ... his flowing sandy hair, which bounced up and down like a flap-jack every time he took a jump. 'Who's that guy jumping rope?' I asked Kid Howard. 'Why, that's old Joe Choynski doing his daily dozen. But, whatever you do, don't tell him how good he looks. He's already challenged Dempsey, winner take all and to a finish ... with a little encouragement he's likely to slug Jack on the street.' 'I was amazed at the way he looked, it appeared as if his body had been embalmed when he was about 30 years old, but he kept right on living. The skin was stretched tight over his boney frame; there wasn't the slightest trace of hanging flesh. Could this be the same man who fought Jim Corbett 40 years ago?"

"He sensed my curiosity, as if people staring at him was a daily routine, and he stopped jumping. Before I could introduce myself, he said in a shrill, bored voice, 'Yes, I'm Choynski and I fought Fitzsimmons, Jeffries, Corbett and the rest.' 'How old are you, Joe?' I asked. 'Just stepping from 59 to 60,' he replied, with a boyish grin spread across his face. I tried not to show my astonishment, although I knew here indeed was a new wonder of the world. 'What would you do against your old rivals if you fought them today – say, Jeffries or ... Sharkey?' I asked. 'Oh, it would be a shame to take the money ... both have grown old and gone to seed, as it were. Poor old Jeff has a touch of gout and hardening of the arteries, and he's taken enough beating to kill 10 mules. The man is entitled to a rest. But, without blowing my horn, I will say that I could put both Jeff and Sharkey out with a couple of punches ... You see, I'm much too young for them. Do you know who I would really like to fight? Jack Dempsey. I think I can take him. When he tries that weaving, crouching stuff of his, I'll do what I did to Jeffries; you know I taught the big guy how to do it.' " Joe was obviously feeling good about himself, and relishing the attention. He was also a bit delusional, wanting to tangle with "The Mauler," at nearly 60 years old!

Carey asked Joe how he would fare against Corbett, if the pair tangled again. "Choynski looked down at the floor and ran his fingers through his long hair. 'Jim is a dead leaf nowadays, but still clinging to the vine,' said Joe. 'I wouldn't have the gall to hit him now.' Carey started to ask him about Jack Johnson, who at the time was in just as good condition as Choynski, but before he could spit out all the words, Joe broke in again. 'You know who I'd love to get a crack at right now? Gene Tunney. Now, there's a guy I know I can spot 30 years and flatten for sure. These new fellows lack the stuff the old boys had, and they can't think fast enough to figure a way out of the hot spots when the going gets rough. Tunney is supposed to be real cute, but I'd like to see him out cute Kid McCoy or Tommy Ryan or me.' Choynski started to laugh and tears filled his eyes. 'Sure, I'd like to fight Dempsey and Tunney, but suppose I challenged them, why the boxing commissioners would fall off their plush chairs and say, go back to your rocking chair, Choynski, you're too old for this business. And so you see, that lets me out.' With that he turned on his heels, flung the jump rope over his head and nimbly skipped away, leaving Ed Carey with his mouth hung open and his eyes looking like a pair of brown saucers. Choynski's fabulous punching power was the product of perfect timing and faultless coordination, a rare combination which cannot be acquired ... Coordination can be refined, to be sure, but the basic seed must be planted at birth ... Choynski was endowed with the magic gift by his parents, and had they known their son was to become a fist fighter, they couldn't have chosen a more valuable heritage."[41]

Joe was sighted at Howard's Gym again in late 1929. The *Ring* wrote: "During our brief little visit to Chicago, and in Kid Howard's gym de luxe, we were surprised one day when we strolled in and saw 63-year-old Joe Choynski ... stepping around quite lively with a Filipino protégé inside the ring. The old fighter's perfect defense and shrewd deliveries brought many favorable remarks from the onlookers. After his three-round set-to, we enjoyed a ten minutes pow-wow with the genial Joe."[42]

The June 17, 1928 *Appleton Post-Crescent* announced a "series of ... eye-witness adventures ... by famous referees ... and prominent members of the fistic fraternity," entitled, "My Greatest Thrill." They would "tell of the one greatest 'kick' they got out of ... watching fighters from inside the ropes." Fifteen men were chosen to tell their stories, including trainer Jimmy De Forrest, announcer Joe Humphries and referee Joe Choynski. On June 26, the paper published Joe's piece, called, "A Draw When Fighters Knock Each Other Out ... (as told to Kiddy Romano)": "In over 40 years of refereeing, I have experienced what some might call thrills, but ... having participated in events which I was told were thrilling, I learned to repress my emotions. Forty years ago, Sam Fitzpatrick ... called the 'Australian Comet' ... was matched to fight Tom Cleary of New York in a finish fight with 2-ounce gloves ... staged by the Golden Gate Athletic Club of San Francisco. I was the referee. Fitzpatrick and Cleary relied on their right hand wallop, which carried a sleep potion. In the 3rd round, both men shot their right hand simultaneously for the jaw. Both landed and measured their length on the canvas floor of the ring. I counted both out. When they had returned to their corners, I told them the contest was a draw."

"The fighters were not satisfied ... and insisted on continuing. In the 7th, Cleary landed his right and Fitzpatrick was unable to continue ... Every year, a bunch of sports used to congregate in San Francisco. The Butte crowd once brought along Jim Bates, middleweight champion of the northwest, to clean up Tom Cleary. Tom Fitzgerald ... gun at his side, was timekeeper for Cleary. A two-gun man was timekeeper for the Montana scrapper. In the 3rd round, Cleary dropped Bates with a right hand swing, and the official timekeeper counted him out, not audibly. Bates' timer said the count was too fast. Fitzgerald insisted the timing was correct. Quite an argument ensued and guns were drawn. Being neutral and wishing to play fair with both sides, I went to the official time-keeper, took his watch and permitted the contest to be resumed. In the 7th round, Cleary got over another sleep producer and I counted the Montanan (out). All hands were satisfied ..." A wire service report claimed that Joe was "now in the theatrical business in Chicago," but this has not been substantiated. It may refer to his brief management of, or co-venture in, a nickelodeon theatre.[43]

Round Twenty-Seven

Final Home – Walnut Hills
(January 1930 – January 1943)

Joe spent only a few years back in Chicago. Sometime in late 1929 or early 1930, the couple relocated to Cincinnati, Ohio. They resided in Flat number 2, 2640 Kemper Lane, where Joe was a "Physical Director." Some time later, they moved to the neighborhood of Walnut Hills, where Louise grew up. Joe was already working as an athletic or boxing instructor at "The Cincinnati Club." One might assume this was the Cincinnati Athletic Club, but *The History of the Cincinnati Athletic Club, 1853-1976* chronologically lists all staff. At no time does it mention Joe employed there. He is only named when they declined to send their boxing team to Pittsburgh in March, 1925, to meet the Pittsburgh Athletic Association team. "Gym President Morry Longenecker is not enthusiastic ... he thinks they got the worst of the decisions several years back ... 'in one bout, Joe Choyanski (sic) cast the deciding vote against me, but Joe always was a home umpire. At that the bout was very close.' " A 1936 paper said Joe was "hanging out around Cincinnati, where he has interest in a small athletic club."[1]

The modern Cincinnati Club, built in 1923 at 30 Garfield Place as a private club and grand hotel, is a catering facility. It is not clear that it was ever an athletic venue. The Phoenix Club, built in 1893 at 812 Race Street, as "the first Jewish Businessmen's organization in this region of the country," was purchased in 1911 by the Cincinnati Club as a sports annex. The basement had a full-length "lappool" and bowling alley. The second floor held the Billiards Room, filled with some 25 billiards tables. On the third floor was a basketball court, with a balcony on three sides for spectators. The building closed in 1983, renovated and reopened in 1988. Along with the Cincinnati Club, the Phoenix Club functions as among Cincinnati's "finest private dining and restaurant facilities." It was almost certainly at one of these locations where Joe taught.[2]

The *Ring* wrote, in 1930: "Joe Choynski ... is Cincinnati's latest addition. Joe recently made application for a referee's license ... the time is not far distant when Joe will be third man in Queen City rings." A fight for Milwaukee on April 11 between local white fighter, Henry "King Tut" Tuttle, and Bruce Flowers, a black man from New Rochelle, New York, was to be the first "mixed bout" in Milwaukee in 20 years. Promoter Tom Andrews said the last mixed bout there was between Joe Choynski and Klondyke, of Chicago. This was John "Klondyke" Haines, a Jack Johnson opponent. Haines does not appear on Joe's record. Tom Andrews, though, was seldom incorrect about such matters. He was the same T.S. Andrews who compiled the famous Sporting and Boxing record books, from 1903 through 1934 and again in 1938. Andrews, born in Canada, later became Sports Editor of the *Milwaukee Evening Wisconsin*.[3]

On June 28, Damon Runyon covered the June 12 Max Schmeling-Jack Sharkey bout for Tunney's vacated heavyweight crown. The championship was awarded to Max on a low-blow foul in the 4th round. "Joe Choynski, to this day accounted the greatest Jewish heavyweight of all time, remarks brusquely of foul claimers: 'They are all cheating when they plead they cannot walk from the ring.' Which ... is my own contention. Old Joe took pen in hand out in Cincinnati, where he is now an athletic instructor ... after the ... fight, and, gleaming with indignation, wrote to George Coxey, an old pal of his big town days. George Coxey is a pudgy man, whose facile fist has jotted down life insurance policies on most of the Broadway mob. George used to be a boxer before he got tangled up with the New York Life, and he still keeps in touch with all the veterans."

" 'Too bad the big go ended so disastrously ...' comments Joe. 'Not a man today ... knows how to deliver a left-hand body punch. Nearly every fight, someone has to be cautioned about a low blow, and ... when that fellow is hit, he carries on awful.' Old Joe sniffs at the custom ... in some sections of having a foul claimer examined in the ring by a doctor. In fact, Joe seems inclined to blame the medicos for fouls. 'They pull a man's tights back ... look at the area struck, and shout foul ... when ... there is nothing to show ... a foul has been committed. It takes several minutes for congestion to appear. Schmeling had to be carried from the ring. What for? There is no sympathetic connection between the motor nerves of the legs, and that part of the anatomy when a foul occurs. A man should be given 15 minutes rest when unintentionally fouled, and two rounds taken from his opponent. That would make the erring one work hard to overcome the handicap.' " Choynski was old school, believing a fighter's corner had to claim a foul, for a referee to declare one was committed.[4] (Author: After viewing stills and video, I believe the Sharkey clout was below the belt. Max was allegedly told by his manager to embellish, however. It is good the rules were amended to disallow a boxer from winning on a single low blow).

Sometime in late 1930, Joe had "an operation at the Jewish Hospital, for bladder trouble." Although not specified, this probably occurred in Cincinnati. On February 4, Tim McGrath asked Corbett what his hardest fight had been. Jim replied that, although the battle on the barge with Choynski had been tough, the knockout loss to Jeffries in 23 rounds was his toughest and hardest fight. This was a complete course change from his previous claims. It was announced that Corbett would "recall his boyhood scraps and his first meeting with Joe Choyniski (sic), the school 'bully' ...

during the premier of the Howard Dandies program, over WABS and the Columbia network ... September 14." Referring to Joe as "the school bully" doesn't jive with anything else ever stated about him. One paper gave a financial "exposé" on Joe's career purses, saying the smallest amount he ever received was a mere $208 for the Fitzsimmons match, the largest, $5,000 for the Billy Woods go, and the most offered him, $20,000 by the California Athletic Club in 1889, fought instead for a fraction of that amount, on the barge anchored at Benecia.[5] On June 22, 1931, Lou Houseman died in Los Angeles, age 67. Lou had left Chicago for California around 1903, becoming a noted figure in the theatrical field.[6]

Over the years, many famous boxers have been impersonated, either by the mentally ill or by those desiring special treatment. A man claiming to be John L. Sullivan was living in my birthplace, Massena, New York, in the summer of 1900. It was said that "his family had a home in Massena Springs," next to the railroad tracks and near the old, Victorian, Hatfield House, which he frequented "for entertainment and socializing." He probably got many a free drink out of the ruse. The real John L. turned 42 that October and was running a saloon in Manhattan. His parents were long dead, and he was no longer with his first wife, Annie Bates Bailey, after 1884. Sullivan's only child, John L., Jr., died of diphtheria in 1886, age 2½, and "Jawnell" didn't marry his 2nd and final spouse, Kate Harkins, until 1910. The photo of the faux John L. who spent a summer in Massena bears no resemblance to the authentic ex-prizefighter.[7]

Joe had at least one impersonator, the most notable showing up in 1931, at the Salvation Army Home in Dallas, Texas, where he was recovering from "double pneumonia." The February 15 *Dallas Morning News* printed his photo, which bore little resemblance to the real Joe. "Joe is 66 now, but looks only 40. He is of Scotch and Polish ancestry ... a strong booster for Gene Tunney ... whom he met ... when they were in France together during the World War, Choynski as a Salvation Army chaplain. Joe claims he taught Gene the art of punching and was in Tunney's corner when he fought Dempsey, both at Philadelphia and in Chicago. His daughter, Bonnie Choynski, arrived ... from Los Angeles, Cal., and will accompany him to their home on the coast ... Choynski now plies the trade of a chef." No more was heard until, in Santa Ana, California, roughly 1,400 miles from Dallas, the December 13 *Fresno Bee* noted: "An aged and broken man, who claimed to be Joe Choynski, 69 ... had a job to-day, after he was almost counted out by the depression. Broke and jobless, the man came into the police station here and asked for food. He said his last job was in Indio, California, a few months ago. He gave a fictitious name, but Desk Sergeant Frank Lutz, an old army man, thought he recognized the once great fighter. 'Aren't you Joe Choynski?' asked Lutz. After some hesitation, the aged man said he was ... The *Santa Ana Register* carried a story that the famous Joe ...

was in the city in need of work, and offers of employment ... came in ... the man selected a job as a cook in Fullerton, California."

The next day, the cat was out of the bag. *Bee*: "Joe ... is comfortably situated at Cincinnati ... but local sports ... maintain that the elderly itinerant, who ... last week ... represented himself to be Choynski, had enough boxing skill to make the claim plausible. The traveler, who carried a sack of potatoes and onions and said he had been cooking his meals at roadside fires for many weeks, left for San Francisco after staging boxing exhibitions at the Salvation Army Hall in return for meals and shelter. Those who saw his footwork and heard his yarns of olden ring days believed he was Choynski, until relatives of the former ... contender denied it." The *Oakland Tribune* did a follow-up story on the 16th, which contained inaccuracies, but had interesting points: "Joe must have received quite a surprise when he read the story in his palatial Philadelphia home ..." It erred further, saying Joe had been an instructor for many years at the Philadelphia A.C., and still lived in that city. "On this (sic) side he has an investment business, and is said to be worth quite a sizeable fortune."[8]

Old-Time Fighter Here

—News Staff Photos.

JOE CHOYNSKI.

Joe Choynski imposter, Feb. 15, 1931
Dallas (TX) *Morning News*

Tom Lewis, who co-wrote "I Fought 'Em All" with Joe in 1930, visited his home on November 8, 1931. February 7, 1932 *Philadelphia Public Ledger*: "Sometimes these old battlers fool you. I found Chrysanthemum Joe Choynski at his home on his 63rd birthday. However, if I expected to come upon him huddled in the family rocker or cuddling his feet in bedroom slippers, I was woefully off my reckoning. I was directed to the rear of the Choynski ménage. Long before I saw the San Francisco Whirlwind, I caught the steady rat-tat-tat of businesslike apparatus. Joe was in the garage doing his daily dozen. He was making that old punching bag say 'uncle.' His condition surprised me. 'But it needn't,' said Joe, 'for I've always been in good shape. That was my business. Is there any logical reason why I should neglect it now?' This amazing, long-haired, hard-hitting Polish-American was born to be a scholar. Instead, he developed into ... a mighty son of sock ... double poison to most behemoths and a triple threat to ... champions ... Yet ... scarcely more than a ...

middleweight. He knocked out ... Johnson ... hit Bob Fitzsimmons so hard ... Lanky Bob fell like a log ... hammered Sharkey until ... Tom was shaken from head to foot. He fought the dazzling Corbett to a standstill before Choynski ... fell ... held Jim Jeffries to a 20 round draw ... gave ... the stiffest clout Jeffries ever received ... How did he do it?"

" 'Practice ... plus natural endowment. A man has to be born with something ... I guess I had a little ... I developed what I had, and ... got some more. As for my best punch, I played no favorites, for I felt that a man should always have something in reserve. I practiced all my blows ... until I perfected them ... I stood straight up ... This gave me the full swing of shoulders and added ... body weight to my punch. Today we find many of our million-dollar fighters telegraphing their punches. That's pathetic. It shows they don't know how to hit. The best blow ... should never travel more than four or five inches. This is only acquired by long practice.' ... his toughest fight. Oddly, it was with Marvin Hart ... who died recently ... 'Both my eyes were virtually closed,' said Joe, 'ring critics said ... Hart and myself delivered some of the hardest blows ever seen in a Philadelphia ring.' Choynski attributes his own

Joe Choynski, November, 1931, age 63

strength to hard training and work he did in boyhood and young manhood. This ... included candy-pulling and day labor in a blacksmith shop. He could lift 300-pound barrels of sugar with ease." By 1932, Joe and Louise had moved to 1509 Blair Avenue, listed there through at least 1934.

Jim Corbett continued to display mental decay, quoted in November, 1931 as saying he didn't originate the left hook during the fight on the barge, but after, and because of it. Jim was unable to punch the bag in the aftermath of the Benecia Bay brouhaha, having smashed up his hands. "The knuckles of my left hand were still too sore ... to take a straight shot at the bag ... to ... practice without suffering ... I began to hook with that left ... to avoid landing dead-on ... The hook was regarded a freak punch exclusively my own then, but ... effective and the ... boys ... developed it and now the left hook is perhaps the most effective of all ring deliveries, because it is hard to duck or block and ... liable to bat you to sleep."[9]

On November 28, 1932, Joe wrote to *Ring* magazine founder, Nat Fleischer: "Much surprised; nay, dumfounded, to read, 'California's Golden Age of Boxing' in Dec. issue ... I could have composed a better article solo ... with a collaborator it would have been a wow. Will send you a story soon that will be of interest? Tell me where I get off on this story racket. Lacking verbiage, who gets the emolument \$?" Joe was joking about the article, since he was the author of it, weaving a lyrical sketch of old San Francisco. The December 5 *Time* ran a story on George Lytton. His father, Henry, opened a successful chain of Chicago clothing stores. He turned the business over in 1917 to George, whose true interest was boxing. Now 58, George still worked out at the gym he installed years earlier, near his office. For some years, Lytton was considered the amateur heavyweight champion, having boxed Fitzsimmons, Corbett and "Battling" Joe Choynski. Upon the opening of the Illinois Athletic Club in 1904, he swapped punches with Jack Johnson, whereupon Jack said he would "back Lytton against anyone in the world." George was a judge at the Tunney-Dempsey "Long Count" fight. He died the next year, 1933. His father, Henry, reassumed ownership of the business until he died in 1949, at the age of 103!

Another celebrity Joe boxed with was Bernard Baruch (1870-1965), a famous statesman, philanthropist, financier, and economic advisor to two American Presidents. Baruch: "I used to be a pretty good boxer. I got some pointers ... from ... Choynski and ... Fitzsimmons ... at Woods' Gymnasium, 28th Street ... (Manhattan)." "Among the 'pros' who worked out at Woods' were ... Choynski ... Sailor Sharkey and Tom Ryan ... If in a gracious mood, the pros might show us our shortcomings ..."[10] In February, 1933, Jim Corbett was in the last stages of terminal cancer at his home in Bayside, Queens. Many stories covered his career in the ring and theater. W.W. Naughton knew Jim well. That month, he wrote that Joe and Jim used to have "grudge fights ... at school," prior to their first clash at the Olympic Club. W.W. said, "Choynski did not seem to know the first thing about boxing. He rarely made a swing at Corbett that he did not throw himself to the floor, and a slight thrust ... put Choynski off balance."

On the 14th, Joe said: "When Corbett and I were kids, we lived about a mile apart in San Francisco. I wouldn't go to school, so my parents put me to work in a blacksmith's shop. I got so strong, I could throw all the other men in the neighborhood." He said their first set-to lasted only 30 seconds, "because the stable in which the bout was held was unsuitable." "Two weeks later, Choynski and Corbett went to a woods to renew their scrap. After a few minutes, a solid blow knocked Corbett to the ground. When he got up, he refused to go on with the fight. When they met again, at the Olympic club, Corbett outboxed Choynski, but the latter amazed spectators with his powerful punches." After the barge fight, Joe said, "We were offered $20,000 for a return match, but Corbett would never fight me again."[11] On February 18, 1933, Corbett passed quietly into eternity.

Joe attended the March 26, 1933 fight at Chicago Stadium, between Barney Ross and Tony Canzoneri, recognized as for both the world lightweight and junior welterweight championships. "He was accompanied by Al Bechtold, secretary of the Cincinnati boxing commission."[12] Ross won a close, 10 round split decision, in a bloody, grueling and excellent fight. The men would split their two later meetings.

The 1930s saw, for the first time, multiple heavyweights of Jewish extraction battling at the top. It has often been thought the best of these was Max Baer, who knocked out Italian, Primo Carnera, on June 14, 1934 to gain the world crown. He held it only one day short of a year, losing on points to "The Cinderella Man," James J. Braddock. Baer, however, is not generally considered Jewish. His paternal grandfather was a Jew, but Orthodox Jews require, to be Jewish, one's mother being born into Judaism, or converted to it before the child's birth. Max's mother, Dora, was a gentile of Scotch-Irish descent, who evidently never converted to Judaism. Neither did Max. Choynski fell into a similar category, in that his maternal grandmother, Rachel Bartlett, was a Protestant. She did, however, convert to Judaism prior to the birth of Joe's mother, Harriett.

Top contenders of the 1930s were Art Lasky (born Arthur Lakofsky), "King" (or "Kingfish") Levinsky (Harris Krakow),[13] and Bob Pastor, who twice gave Joe Louis a stiff argument. He, however, with Max and Buddy Baer, were said to be Jewish only on their father's side. Another good one was hulking Abe Simon, who twice faced Louis for the championship. Natie Brown, a Max Schmeling sparring partner, lost a tough, 10 round decision to "The Brown Bomber" in 1935. He tangled with "Joltin' Joe" again two years later, but was kayoed in four. Another useful heavyweight of the '30s was Jack Gross, who had mixed results against top-flight boxers like Primo Carnera and George Godfrey (not "Old Chocolate"). Another worth mentioning was Abe Friedman, who defeated "Two-Ton" Tony Galento. For reasons mostly economic, "Hebrew heavies" flourished in this decade like none before or since. The greatest of them all was Joe.

Early in his career, Joe sometimes entered the ring with several days' growth of whiskers, as Dempsey did in "The Roaring Twenties." A 1934 paper said "Choynski ... was the first to go into a fight with a heavy growth of beard ... so he could give his opponent a wire-brush painting ... in the clinches." A 1943 periodical claimed he "was the first to insist on fighting with three days' growth of beard."[14] *New York Daily Mirror*, in celebration of Joe's 66th birthday on November 8, 1934: "It is doubted if any heavyweight ever equaled his record of facing six men who held the heavyweight championship." These were John L. Sullivan, Corbett, Fitzsimmons,

Jeffries, Johnson and Marvin Hart. Also might be added Peter Jackson, who arguably merited much consideration, to the title of "world's champion." Joe battled other champions, like "Philadelphia" Jack O'Brien, who defeated light-heavyweight king Fitzsimmons in 1905, middleweight titleholder "Kid" McCoy, who received some recognition as light-heavyweight champ, and welterweight boss, Joe Walcott.

The *Daily Mirror* carried an indignant rebuttal from Joe, for an article the tabloid ran at the time of Corbett's death: "A friend in New York sent me the *Mirror* on February 14, in which you have a somewhat garbled account of my bouts with the late Jim Corbett. Many times have I written to sports writers ... a correct version of our meetings, but not belonging to the racket, I was ignored. I never knew Corbett or saw him until I was 16 years old. My brother, a frail lad, worked alongside of Corbett's brother in City Hall. After some banter, they agreed we should meet in Corbett's stable, where we were surrounded by his pals in a space 14 feet square. In lieu of ropes were the nether parts of several equines. We sparred one minute, I judge – no judge. Fearful of the horses, I stopped, never having had a pair of gloves on previously, while Corbett was the amateur champ. A week later, my brother told me I had to fight Corbett again. So, on Sunday morning I accompanied my brother and a pal to a dog pound in the hills. Jim had his gang ... with him. No officials, he belted my nose and I knocked him down. One of his pals yelled, 'Time.' My pal said you haven't got a chance here."

"Two weeks later, Corbett came to my shop (candy), and asked me to box him in the Olympic Club, where he was a member. He said a professional had flunked at the last minute and he would provide tights, etc. I was alone. We boxed five rounds to no decision; I had no seconds, there was no referee. I joined a club and learned how to box and, being abnormally strong, soon had a reputation. The California Athletic Club offered us $20,000 to meet. But, Corbett insisted we meet in private for $1,000 a side – draw your own conclusions! The fight was stopped after four rounds. A week later we fought again and he defeated me in 28 rounds. Surely ... as there was no recrimination, I must be believed. Never could get him to meet me again. Harry Smith, of the *San Francisco Chronicle*, will verify these statements. Another thing, why do they always say the Jew-boy. If one is fighting, one should never say a word of the religious beliefs of his opponent. Surely, if I am to be chronicled, may I have the right to have the truth told?" Joe insinuated that Corbett's plan to ensure victory was to fix things in his favor, away from prying eyes.

Norman Selby, now working for the Ford Motor Company in Detroit, said "the hardest battle of his career was with Joe Choynski, who broke his nose and knocked him down 16 times before falling victim to the famed McCoy punch." Selby was either telling tales or had a failing memory, as no account has Joe flooring him 16 times in any of their four encounters. He made similar claims in 1939, saying Joe busted two of his ribs. McCoy told many other tall tales, stating, for instance, that with his "corkscrew punch," he had knocked out 170 men. He variously attributed his development of that blow to watching a cat play with a ball, or realizing the spiral groove inside a rifle barrel added impetus to a bullet, and would do the same with a punch. On December 18, in what was evidently a case of mistaken identity, Associated Press writer Andy Clarke wrote: "Joe Choynski, the big belter of better days, is on relief at Staten Island." As Joe was living in Cincinnati, it was highly unlikely that he was on relief in New York."[15]

On April 29, 1936, Joe's brother, Herbert, died in San Francisco. Obituaries read: "Colonel Herbert Choynski, 73-year-old Spanish-American War veteran, publisher, attorney and one-time auto salesman, who gained fame by firing the opening gun in (the) famous graft investigations of 30 years ago ... was active in the ... law until two weeks ago, when he was stricken. He died at Dante Sanitarium ... His only child is Mrs. Mortimer Fleishhacker, Jr., of the banking family." "After serving in the ... War, Choynski took over editorship of *Public Opinion* ... and vigorously attacked the Ruef regime. He later relinquished editorship and turned to the practice of law." "A request that his funeral be as simple as possible was disclosed ... 'I want no prayers, no fuss, no funeral, and I direct that the cheapest and most expeditious be made of my remains,' his will directed. His wishes were carried out in simple military services at the Presidio ..." Herbert was buried May 2nd at the Presidio's National Cemetery. A municipal journal carried a memorial on May 4: "The Grim Reaper, Death, has called ... prominent attorney, brilliant soldier and ... clubman, Herbert Choynski who, for over a quarter of a century has been ... favorably known to many ... sorrow at the demise of this popular ... San Franciscan ..."[16]

On May 22, Joe Williams, sports columnist for the *New York Evening Telegram*, interviewed the 67 year old Joe at his home in Cincinnati (probably either 1509 Blair Avenue or 2524 Chatham Street). "Everything about the gentleman suggested a Shakespearean ham. He was tall, gray and sparse. He wore a flowing silk bow tie. A heavy gold chain dangled from his waistcoat. He walked with conscious dignity, and there was the roll of thunder in his voice, as he spoke of the days when he fought Corbett, Fitzsimmons, Jeffries and Johnson. For this gentleman was no relic of the ancient drama; he was Joe Choynski, first and last of the great Jewish heavyweights. He has a vague connection with one of the local athletic clubs. He has a hacking cough, is not altogether well, but mentally alert. Like most of the old timers, he hasn't much respect for the moderns, though he admits Joe Louis, the young Negro, may be good. He has never seen him in action. Jack Dempsey is the only modern fighter he would give you a quarter for. He insists Gene Tunney was no better than fair, says he couldn't come forward, couldn't feint, knew nothing about weaving with his head."

"But, if Choynski is critical of the moderns, he sings no lasting rhapsodies to the old timers. Not all of them, anyway. To him, Fitzsimmons

Tom Sharkey and Choynski at racetrack, 1930s

was a cur. That's the word he used. And he didn't smile when he used it. I asked him to explain. 'It is something that needs no explanation,' he snapped. It was evident that for some reason, Choynski did not hold the freckled walloper in high esteem ... my suspicion was his bitterness stemmed from a personal matter. Certainly there is nothing in Fitzsimmons' record to suggest he lacked a fighter's heart. He came off the floor or ... from behind, to score some of his most notable victories. No better yardstick for measuring human courage in the ring exists. The bell saved him in the 1st round ... with Tom Sharkey at Coney Island. He ... stiffened the sailor in the next round. Jim Corbett had him on the floor at Carson City, before ... the ... solar plexus punch. And Mr. Choynski – sh! That's it. Choynski had him out, dead to the world in a Boston ring when the bell rang and cops stormed the arena. There is no record of the two ever having met again, and this may explain why the Jewish gentleman still carries an active enmity for him."

"Choynski ... was that rare combination ... a clever boxer and a tremendous hitter. He undoubtedly would have won the championship if he had been a bigger man. He was a middleweight mingling with heavyweights ... he flattened Fitzsimmons, had Kid McCoy on the floor, knocked out Peter Maher, Jim Hall and Jack Johnson, held Tom Sharkey and Jim Jeffries even. 'As a matter of fact, I beat Jeffries,' insists Choynski.

'A baseball umpire by the name of Jim McDonald refereed ... I thought I had won easily on points. When McDonald raised Jeffries hand (the fight was actually ruled a draw), I said ... *Does a fellow have to hit nothing but home runs to win with you?* Choynski laughed reminiscently. It was evident he considered this a very neat crack. I asked him about the time he knocked out Johnson in three rounds at Galveston, Texas, and in his sharp, quick tones, he said, 'There is nothing to say ... I just knocked him out.' But after a few seconds he explained somewhat." Choynski rehashed the Johnson knockout and the interview concluded.[17] It is clear that the elderly Joe was becoming bitter and probably a bit senile by this time.

On May 26, a reader calling himself "An Old Timer" claimed he had witnessed the 1894 brawl between Fitz and Choynski, although with a flawed memory: "Under the new deal, bouts were limited to four rounds, and were exhibitions ..." The fight was scheduled for eight rounds, and not as an exhibition. He recalled Joe's knockdown of Fitz in the 2nd frame, but it was the 3rd. "The round still had 20 seconds to go, but someone rang the gong, and there's no doubt it saved Fitz. But Fitz was all right when the gong rang for the 3rd, and he came out sneering and calling Choynski a double-crossing this and that. For the first minute ... he deliberately cut Choynski to ribbons. He didn't want to put him away ... just ... to beat him up. This kept up until you could see one more punch would have dropped Choynski, and then the coppers closed in and stopped it. Choynski took the worst walloping of his career in this abbreviated round." The bout actually went into the 5th before it was halted. Williams apparently accepted all at face value, as he finished: "My thanks to the Old Timer, and a severe rebuke to Mr. Choynski for violating a gentleman's agreement. This was very naughty of him. A number of other letters have also been received, reproving Mr. Choynski for calling Ruby Robert a cur."[18]

On June 19, a bout of great historical importance took place at Yankee Stadium, Bronx, New York, between Max Schmeling of Germany and America's "Brown Bomber," Joe Louis. Max scored a monumental upset, handing Joe a methodical beating and stopping him in 8 rounds. (Louis won the epic 1938 rematch, annihilating "The Black Uhlan" in the opening frame). In Schmeling's dressing room prior to the fight, he received a visit from Tom O'Rourke. After conversing with Max, Tom suddenly slumped down on the bench where he sat, and attended to by others. Schmeling's handlers, not wanting him to be rattled before the critical match, told him O'Rourke was ill, but would be okay. Max said later, though, that he knew Tom had passed away. He was dead of a heart attack, at age 83. For Max to perform as brilliantly as he did, is a tribute to his mental toughness.

It was looked on with irony by some that O'Rourke, who had managed several great black fighters, allegedly gave advice to Schmeling as the way to defeat Louis, a black American heavyweight: "Louis always feints twice with his left before jabbing. He holds his head too high when he comes in and his left glove too low. It leaves him set just right for you. Keep far away from him, make him feint and lead, and then send in a smashing right."[19] Tom's tactical advice was superb, but in truth, Max told reporters at least a day before the bout, that he had "seen something" and knew how to beat Louis. He had observed the same flaws in the young Louis' style, and had been practicing his right-hand counters for weeks.

Max, who died in 2005, just short of 100 years old, had been boycotted in America during the 1930s, accused of being a Nazi. He was not one. He had many Jewish friends, among them, his manager, Joe Jacobs. Max got

himself in trouble with Adolph Hitler and Nazi Propaganda Minister Joseph Goebbels, for refusing to fire Jacobs. Max risked his life by hiding in his apartment, the two sons of his friend, David Lewin, during the Kristallnacht pogrom of November, 1938. The boys escaped and made their way to the States. In 1989, one of them, Heinz "Henri" Lewin, then president of the Sands Resort Hotel in Las Vegas, held a special tribute dinner for Schmeling. Against Max's wishes, Lewin revealed what the former champion had done for him and brother, Werner. Schmeling and

Joe Choynski, December 23, 1937, Cincinnati, Ohio

Joe Louis became friends after the War. Max, who became the Coca-Cola distributor for West Germany, gave money on several occasions to assist Joe, when the latter's health was failing.

An amateur boxer Joe was training at this time was Don Koons, of Hamilton, Ohio. His protégé, a "sensational Hamilton light-heavyweight," made it to the finals of the Los Angeles Golden Gloves tournament in December, 1936. His opponent in the semi-final, Georgie Hughes, was the favorite and "hailed as a 2nd Joe Louis." Koons "weathered numerous low blows to win a unanimous decision in three rounds." No more seems to have been heard of him, however. Sports scribe Dan Parker noted in February, 1937, that "Old Joe Choynski, still a fine physical specimen as a result of vigorous exercise, including long daily walks, regales all listeners in Cincinnati with stories of his famous battles." In 1937, Joe joined 3,000 others at the 2nd annual Veteran Boxers Banquet, at Philadelphia, Pennsylvania's Convention Hall. It was said to be, at the time, "the largest get-together of ex-ringmen the world has ever known."[20]

At the same venue, the Veteran Boxers Association held their "Carnival of Champions" dinner, on March 29, 1938. A magnificent silver trophy for "the most deserving and courageous boxer" in the country, was presented before 41 champions and famous boxers. Joe said, "I look forward with pleasant anticipation ... The wife read in my tea leaves only a day or so ago that I was going to attend an immense gathering of celebrities in a distant city. I have always had the happiest recollection of Philadelphia ... it will certainly be a treat to meet ... my old friends again." Jack Dempsey presented the trophy to "The Cinderella Man," Jim Braddock. Choynski was seated beside old opponent, Peter Maher. Others in attendance: Benny Leonard, "Battling" Nelson, Tommy Loughran, Abe Attell, Tony Canzoneri and "Philadelphia" Jack O'Brien. Proceeds were to benefit needy former boxers.[21]

"Battling" Nelson and Joe (top) outside Veteran Boxers Association building, March 29, 1938. With other famous boxers (below, Joe in middle)

Speaking of which, on April 30, Tom Sharkey checked in at San Francisco's Laguna Honda Home for the destitute. He was once said to be worth about $250,000. A combination of horse racing bets, a failed saloon and other investments cleaned him out. A 1939 paper said: "20 years ago, it was the general custom of fighters to get 60 per cent of the gate, and split the purse any way they liked. Sometimes they fought on a winner-take-all basis, although the usual practice was 75 per cent to the winner and 25 to the loser. The first real business man of the ring was Joe Choynski. Though little more than a middleweight, Joe was ready ... to go on with the best big men in an era that had no equal, as far as star heavyweights ... (Joe) enjoyed fighting, but looked on his business as ... uncertain ... Though he could whip 90 per cent of the fellows ... Joe always insisted on a 50-50 split in advance. Other managers and fighters began to see ... sound sense in Choynski's method ... there began to be more demand for guarantees and equitable splits ... The old bare-knuckle men, who took terrible beatings and received nothing ... save bruises ... were out-moded, and the big business era of the prize ring was ... launched."[22]

In March, papers noted that Joe was a collector of antiques, photos showing him proudly holding a carved, antique ivory tusk. He also collected

"Peaceful Pursuit": Joe, 1939, with scrimshaw, Inuit-carved walrus tusk cribbage board

ornate souvenir spoons, from his travels around the globe.[23] Joe had, in his lifetime, passed through or visited 11 other nations. In 1890 and 1891, he visited Hawaii (then a Kingdom and separate nation from the United States), and a brief stop at New Zealand en route to Australia. On the return trip, he stopped at the Samoan Islands. In 1892, Joe visited England, Germany, Switzerland and France, passing through Belgium, as well. He embarked on a ship at Glasgow, Scotland to return to America. In 1903, he visited Canada.

By 1939, Joe and Louise were living at 2524 Chatham Street, Walnut Hills, Ohio. In an April 13 letter, Walter Schlichter sent Joe two tickets to the Veteran Boxers dinner, for the Penn Athletic Club on May 1. The dinner was apparently cancelled, as a return epistle from Joe on September 30, read: "I look toward you: The illness of one's wife is a source of distress hard to combat – and moving? requires a dual nature, of a Job? But, if you whistle: O.K.? Most people have forgotten me? They are interested only in tonight's meal? Too bad the veterans' gathering is to be discontinued ... glad to attach my John Robinson to photo – I am to tell Joe Williams Tues. of Ghouls club." The final reference is obscure, but Joe spoke of his move to Cincinnati and of Louise being ill. He put question marks at the end of many sentences, for reasons unclear. He also exchanged many letters with Nat Fleischer. In one, dated May 3, 1939, Nat requested a pair of skin-tight gloves, such as were used early in Joe's career.[24] Another, from November 11 (translating Joe's nearly unintelligible scribble):

Joe with malamute, LaGrange, IL home, Dec. 25, 1938

"I attended ... Buddy Knox and (Paul) Pross (Joe's birthday, Cincinnati, November 8, 1939). Pross, a protégé of Dempsey? ... out in two rds. Wherever they get the idea they can box? Ben Leonard was referee ... did OK. After I beat Hall, Donovan asked me to second him against Mace ... thought I was the greatest ever, offered to pay my expenses and ... $100 ... thought Mace was trying to get his job? I told him he was foolish, Mace could not box but he insisted so I intimidated Mace before the event, talked to him psychologically and agitated his nerves. They met in Old Broadway A.C. ... near Boone looking on Wash. Sq.? I was want (sic) to live in hotel next door. The Colonade? (sic)."

"The 1st round Mace landed his left unexpectedly early on Mike's nose ... I told Mike, remember he does not know how to hook left hand; collect yourself and lead for stomach, his left will go over your head ... he did just that and found himself. I had to admonish him that Mace was 72 years old or more. Mace had to remove his false uppers. Two rounds, no decision. They both received $1,300. Mace cried when the promoter refused to take part of his money. Donovan counted all the tickets? and when I asked him for my expenses he told me a hard luck tale and ran out on me? A lie detector can prove my assertion. When I first started to box a man told me ... you could only trust a boxer a far as you could sling a bull by the tail? Joe. There is no solar plexus punch. The plexus is behind stomach a bundle of nerves. Fitz punched Corbett in liver. I taught it to Bat Nelson, ask him."[25]

September, 1939 saw the start of World War II, with the invasion of Poland by Nazi Germany. America's involvement would begin in late 1941, with the Japanese bombing of Pearl Harbor, Hawaii. Joe, born after the end of the Civil War and living through the Spanish-American War and World War I, would not see the end of this one. On February 22, 1940, Norman Selby was in El Paso, Texas, visiting former contender, "Australian" Billy Smith. McCoy told *El Paso Herald-Post* reporter, Betty Luther: "I'm on my way back to Detroit and my job in the personnel department of the Ford Motor Company. I left the story of my life, 'Ten Lives in One' with Warner Brothers in Hollywood. They are thinking of making a picture from it, with James Cagney as the 'Real McCoy.' " Selby's "9th wife" had just wired from Detroit, saying, "Drive carefully, darling, I'm dying to see you."

McCoy, described as "soft-spoken, erect, gentle in manner," stated: "Today's boxing is a sloppy affair. They don't have enough road work, only two or three miles a day. I did 10 and 12. There's nobody to teach the old ways, they copy each other. They are trying to use both hands, instead of using one for feint and the other for punching. They seem to ignore speed – the greatest asset in the boxing game ... Joe Louis ... fights flat on his feet. He's the best, of course." When asked where he got his speed from, Selby replied, "Hoboed five years. Learned it reaching for the train. See?" "He demonstrated a movement of feet and hands, reaching to hop the freight." "I learned the knack of hitting from Bob Fitzsimmons ... My hobby is teaching youngsters to learn how to co-operate with nature. Masticate your food. Don't drink with meals and you'll make great headway. Erect posture ... to live a long, healthy life. Give your heart a chance to work."

On April 18, Selby checked into the Tuller Hotel in downtown Detroit, and took an overdose of sleeping pills. He scrawled a suicide note, headed "to whom it may concern," stating: "For the past 8 years I have wanted to help humanity ... I wish you all the best of luck. Sorry I could not endure this world's madness. Norman Selby." A 2nd note, addressed to the "youth of America," told them to "keep your bodies clean and be always in condition for any emergency." The former "Kid" was 67. He had lately been expressing angst over the war in Europe, and had become addicted to sleeping pills. His widow, the former Sue Cobb Cowley, Homer Selby, and early fight manager, Jack Rush, arranged for removal of the body. The next day, Tom Sharkey was less than gracious when learning of McCoy's suicide. "Kid McCoy was the slickest, meanest fighter that ever pulled on a glove." While sorry to hear of the death of a great fighter, he was in no mood for eulogies. "McCoy ... was fast, cold-blooded, a good feinter and fine boxer. But ... He never missed a chance to cut up his man, even after he had the fight in his pocket. But, he couldn't take a punch ... well. The Kid was a character. His main hobby was pretty women. All his wives were beautiful, and I believe ... had money. He was a sarcastic sort of fellow to talk to."

"Sharkey ... is Irish and sentimental, but his lips tightened involuntarily around his cigar when he was told that Norman Selby ... had committed suicide ... with $17.75 in his pocket. 'I'm sorry to hear about McCoy's death ... but you'll have to excuse me if I can't say nice things about him.' ... the Lenox Club ... 1899. Neither was champion, but it was the fight of the year. 'He came into the ring that night with his gloves on,' Sharkey said bitterly. 'Tommy O'Rourke, my manager, ordered the gloves removed. We found almost half a ton of plaster along with the heavy bandages. Had the plaster stayed on, McCoy probably would have knocked me out for keeps. Do you wonder why I didn't have ... pleasant memories of McCoy? ... probably the hardest hitter the fight game ever knew, outside of ... Jeffries ... when the Kid knocked me down in the 1st round, the ringside went wild ... But I weathered the storm and ... 10th round. I couldn't box him – he was too slick, so I went for his stomach. That finished him.' "[26]

On July 22, Peter Maher passed away at the home of his son, Peter, Jr., in Baltimore, Maryland. "The Irish Champion" was 74.[27] Maher worked in his final years as a "dock walloper"* in New York City. In June, 1941, George W. "Biddy" Bishop, previously a fight promoter, manager, referee, second and sports editor of the *Tacoma Daily News*, said, of the late Bob Fitzsimmons: "I ... handled the Cornishman in more than half a dozen battles, and I saw him in all of his many moods. He was a master-fighter – but, emphatically he did not fancy the idea of being hurt."
* One who loads and unloads seafaring vessels; longshoreman or stevedore.

"I handled Fitzsimmons' corner in his fight with Philadelphia Jack O'Brien ... Dec. 20, 1905. Fitz quit in the 14th round, refused ... to go out when the gong rang and continue on. He was not seriously hurt ... nowhere near being finished. When Fitz boxed Peter Maher in New Orleans, March 2, 1892, he won in 12 rounds, yet he insisted on quitting in the 6th. It was all his seconds Jimmy Carroll, Alex Greggains and Joe Choynski could do to get him up for the next round. In the 6th round of his memorable battle with Jim Corbett, whom he knocked out in the 14th, Fitz ... was being counted out on one knee when he was forced to get up, only in response to the frantic screams of his wife, Rose Julian ... Fitzsimmons, boxing men much heavier than himself, did take terrific punishment on numerous occasions, but these other incidences ... are recited just to let the ring fan judge for himself." Bishop's testimony validates some things Choynski said about "Ruby Bob" in the past – and in the near future.[28]

Joe wrote to Nat Fleischer, August 31: "Eyes Front: Am to write Warner Brothers, that if they refer to Corbett having beaten me four times, I will sue? Aloha, Joe."[29] The 2524 Chatham Street address would be the final residence of Joe and Louise. They rented, sharing a duplex with 2526 Chatham. The 1940 U.S. Census says "the highest grade of school completed" for both Joe and Louise was grade 5, which is highly unlikely,

Joe having left school at age 16. Louise was listed as tending house, while Joe was "unable to work."[30] Joe referred to Warner Brothers filming the movie "Gentleman Jim," based loosely on Corbett's autobiography, *The Roar of the Crowd*. It is said that, after Joe complained about multiple points the studio planned to include in the film (many fictional), Warner Brothers paid him to be a silent "advisor," that is, to shut up and keep the facts to himself. An October 1 paper: "No wisecracks, but Errol Flynn's next picture will be ... the screen biography of Prizefighter Jim Corbett. So far, Warners have located three men who actually fought (Jim) ... Sharkey, Jim Jeffries and Joe Choynski. All will be asked to work as technical advisors on the picture." Armond Fields wrote in 2001: "Aged, angry and senile, Joe Choynski got $1,000 to keep his mouth shut."[31]

Another missive to Nat was dated October 11, 1941.[32] Here, Joe's bitterness really came to the fore: "Heads up: Came a young fellow to my house, a cub rookie ... Cin. 'Enquirer,' from a small burg in Tennessee; had never seen a boxing match – very pert, at first? I soon sized him (up): he acknowledged he never seen any sport in Tennessee. I told him it would be hard work to make him understand and was about to send him on his way, but I thought – his first assignment? – be tolerant. I told him I did not care to be in papers. I was (illegible) etc. and he would not put my words in papers. Well, I told him and he did the best he could. Came the next day – showed me proof and wanted me to have witness – turned out, he was sincere. Can you imagine anyone being honest these days? Do you know, Nat: only two people have asked me why I fought Corbett for $1,000.00 in private – when club offered us $20,000? My wife and Chinese boy I raised in Chicago? Damn fool says he? Corbett was afraid of me and he did not want to be whipped by me; so in the open, with his mob he could wrangle the fight was he being worsted, and a draw would ensue; he had sergeant police in S.F. who sat alongside to stop Sharkey from licking him."

"And in N.Y., his cat's paw(!) Connie McVeigh – not a bad fellow, but anybody's cat's paw, step in ring in the Garden so he could lose on foul? Sharkey was licking him again; one punch from Jeff and he quit. Fitz hit him one punch and he quit, at that it was a hand punch. He ran away from Peter Jackson for 62 rounds. How in the world they could ever see him I do not know. No education – no up bringing? Fight here to-morrow night, may go if my body guard comes? I am so hoarse from complaining: maybe I am stenciled, Nat? Even (Hype) Igoe knows I did not have much chance to beat Corbett: he wrote that Corbett came to my corner and offered Nonpareil Dempsey a bet of $500.00 and Dempsey, his friend, smiled and said 'I am only getting paid to second him? I have no interest?' Aloha.
I just got up 12 A.M. – breakfast. Joe. (P.S.) Nothing can be done to stop Warners saying Corbett beat me four times: I do not know if they will: but their authenticity is Corbett's book: auto-biography?

(¹) cat's paw - a person used by another for an unpleasant or distasteful task – from the fable of unknown origin in which a monkey uses the cat's paw to retrieve hot roasted chestnuts from the fire."

The letter brings up many questions. Who was the "cub" reporter from the *Cincinnati Enquirer* who interviewed Joe? This may have been the interview mentioned on August 10, 1942. What was the meaning of the brief rant, "My wife and Chinese boy I raised in Chicago? Damn fool, says he?" Did this regard a comment allegedly made by Corbett? As curt as Jim could be at times, It is difficult to fathom him remarking that Choynski was foolish in raising a "Chinese boy," a son of Jim Pon. The reference to Joe's wife is cryptic. Evidently, he was suffering the effects of senility. Finally, did insomnia cause Joe to rise for breakfast, not at noon, but midnight?

73-year-old Joe was the subject of a radio show on December 3, 1941. Mason City, Iowa's AM station, KGLO, 1300 on the dial, broadcast a "wake-up" show hosted by Bob Lewis. Choynski was interviewed by Lewis on his "Today's Profile" feature, but the content of the show is lost to history. On December 21, Joe sent Nat Fleischer "a 1930 portfolio of famous sporting prints by the Studio in London."[33] It is the last known communication between the two. In April, 1942, Joe's story entered popular culture in comic book form. "The True Life Story of Joe Choynski" was published by Fiction House in the pulp periodical, Fight Comics #18. The artwork was good, by Lou Fine and perhaps also by Alex Blum and/or Rudy Palais. The original pages were labeled as part of an

Joe Choynski at his Cincinnati home, May 22, 1942

Eisner & Iger, Ltd. Studios production (Will Eisner and Jerry Iger). This marks it as a likely reprint of an earlier-published work, as that studio, also known as Syndicated Features Corporation (a comic books "packager"), only existed from 1936 to 1939. The entertaining, five-page story contained multiple errors, not the least of which was the depiction of "Old Chocolate," George Godfrey, as a huge white man.

Walter Schlichter wrote, on August 9, after stating in error that Joe was "now a police official in Cleveland, Ohio," that "Choynski has promised to come to the next annual dinner of the Veteran Boxers' Association, where he will renew old associations ..."[34] Joe never made it back to the Quaker City. United Press scribe Jack Cuddy noted the next day: "Joe Choynski, last of the old-time heavyweight greats, still lives, and – at 74 – warns modern youngsters in war time not to be knocked out psychologically because they see a boxing glove or a bayonet thrown at them. The longevity and lucidity of Choynski was emphasized over the weekend that saw Jack Dillon, a well known fighter of only 50 years, pass on to the paradise where a boxer can get a 'big-money' fight each week without a manager cutting in."

"Joe Choynski ... may be old, but he's not giving in – not until America wins this war, at least. Choynski, son of a German-Jewish father who came to America when he was 14, warns everyone in service or out that F-E-A-R causes most defeats in physical combat. He says, 'The boxer sees the punch coming. He gets frightened and the blood leaves his head and goes to his stomach. More boxers have been scared stiff than have been put out because of a nerve short circuit ... that must be particularly true in bayonet fighting, although I never fought with a bayonet. But, I could tell every American with (one) – go in to rip 'em up intelligently and never lose your head, regardless of how close the Nazi steel may come. Remember the other fellow is more scared than you – because he hasn't had the advantage of our contact sports.' If Choynski thought differently ... he would say so, because he's outspoken in his likes and dislikes. For example, old Joe ... still considers Corbett a 'bum.' ... 'He wasn't a great fighter ... I'm not saying that because he always outweighed me many pounds. Actually, Corbett never met more than three good men in his life. When they put the bum in there with anyone who could hit, he got knocked out.' "

"My Cincinnati agents ... quote old Joe as saying that Corbett and Jim Jeffries were pawns of Diamond Jim Brady (Author: presumably Bill Brady), and that Brady manipulated (them) any way he thought they would make the most money. But, we had the greatest admiration for that old-time warrior ... because of the things my agent left unsaid. We asked him particularly to report whether Choynski – who at 74 must be senile and useless, as far as earning a living was concerned – was in want. Our agent replied, 'Joe probably is the only fellow who made a lifetime living off boxing. He fought professionally 20 years, and taught boxing at the Cincinnati club until five years ago. He's too damned proud to say ... what his financial situation is. I know he's not earning anything. There are rumors that his family – a reportedly successful family – is supporting him. But, I think someone ought to look into Choynski's situation.' Right! We agree ... Someone should find out ... how this old man is getting on. There are any number of war-time industrialists who could charge off a quick trip to Cincinnati and a bit of a gift – if necessary – against their income taxes. We would be delighted to accompany said industrialist on his charitable trip and to let the world know of his gesture ... it would be a lasting shame if this old man were permitted to reach the end of the trail – in want."[35] Events following Joe's death revealed that he had little or nothing left from his "salad days." Where the money went is uncertain.

The Hollywood biopic, "Gentleman Jim," premiered November 26, 1942. While it received mixed reviews, it is remembered today as a most entertaining flick. The December 10 *Ogden Standard-Examiner* offered that, of all the miscast roles in the film, "Farthest out of line ... is the over-sized wrestler Sammy Stein's impersonation of Joe Choynski, who ... always looked frail."[36] Several noted boxers had involvement, as stand-ins, or, in the case of "Mushy" Callahan, a trainer for Errol Flynn. Others were Billy Conn, Freddie Steele, Jack Roper and pro wrestlers Ed "Strangler" Lewis and Mike Mazurki. Warner Brothers certainly took more than its share of "artistic license," (including, for example, Victoria Ware, a fictional love interest for Corbett). Choynski obsessed over the faulty presentation of facts. Burdened by an accumulation of bad memories spanning decades, Joe seems to have become an embittered soul. A cynic might say he had become a misanthrope – in a sense, he had become his father. Having campaigned and fought so many years to gain an opportunity at the heavyweight crown, only to be denied, the "Chrysanthemum" had withered and wilted, leaving a dour, old man, seemingly consumed by anger. This change in personality is also common with the onset of senility.

Fleischer, in his 1942 biography, "Gentleman Jim": "When writing the story of the Corbett-Choynski fight, I sent a message to Joe at his home in Cincinnati, requesting him to give me his version of the feud. Choynski, from a sick bed to which he had been confined for many months, wrote: 'The true story of our fights has never appeared in print. It seems that every time someone wants to write a story about Corbett's career, he takes the liberty to tell how Jim beat me. The facts are that only once did Corbett defeat me. The other bouts in which we fought were not to Corbett's credit, by any means. If it were left to Corbett, his record would have been dotted with several more contests, because every time he looked at me, he was wont to call it a fight. He was a wrestler – strong as Hercules – a wagon blacksmith. I was asked to box Corbett at a time when I never had a boxing glove on my hands before. I did not know him, though I had heard of him in our district. I was 16 and he was 18 when we first met, but he already had considerable experience from boxing in a barn back of his home."

"In our first fight we had only fought a few minutes when the bout was halted by interference ... the space allotted ... only 10 or 12 feet, as the mob ... pressed in ... and gave us little opportunity to move about. I fought him with bare hands in a sand lot a 2nd time. I knocked him down. We had no referee ..." After relating the interrupted skirmish in the Sausalito hay loft and the barge smack-down, Joe added: "We fought once at the Olympic Club in a four round bout. Contrary to statements ... by Corbett that he won that affair, there was no referee. That was my first contest in a ring. We faced each other five times and not four, as all the record books have it, and with the exception of the fight on the barge, I could never understand why Corbett said he had beaten me ... I gave him as much as he gave me."[37] The failing Joe contradicted himself, as he'd had prior ring contests, the George Bush and Frank Glover fights being two examples.

An article reported Joe "battling for his life with pneumonia." He had been treated for various ailments by his physician, J. Reizler, since April 9,

Joe Choynski's final residence - 2524 Chatham St., Walnut Hills, Ohio

1942.[38] On January 10, 1943, Joe Williams showed up at 2524 Chatham Street. The tired ex-fighter submitted to another interview, his last. The dialogue rehashed some from the one in May, 1936, but was far more extensive. Its publisher noted, in 1956: "A few weeks before he died in 1943, Joe Choynski ... granted an exclusive interview ... printed here for the first time": "The old man sat on a faded green couch facing the window; naked from the waist up so that the inpouring sun bathed his chalky skin. He was tall, white headed and lean, surrounded by an air of sublime dignity. His classic Barrymore profile and the long cut of his hair ... Every so often he would raise slowly to his feet and pace restlessly around the room ... straining against the inevitable pitfalls of old age ... I listened to him relive his fights with Corbett, Jeffries, McCoy, Johnson; fascinated by his vivid, sometimes biased accounts; intrigued by his reasoning and convictions."

"Choynski ... has a vague connection with one of the local athletic clubs, although no one is quite sure exactly what it is. He also has a hacking cough

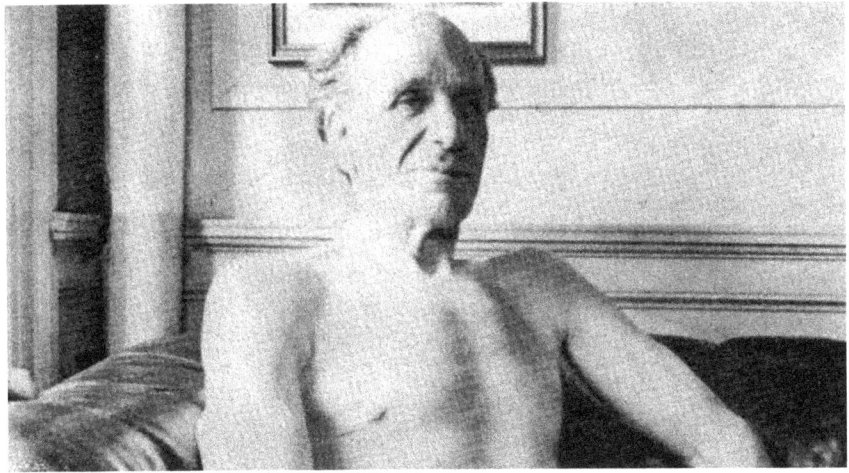

Joe Choynski, January 10, 1943 - 15 days before his death

and his fingers are tortured by crippling arthritis, but his mind is sharp and his words have the bite of a tough teenager. Like all old-timers, he belittles and resents modern-day pugs – the exception being Joe Louis. His compliment to the Brown Bomber? 'If he were around 50 years ago, I'd have let him carry my water bucket.' Choynski was more generous to Jack Dempsey – 'He is the only heavyweight since Johnson ... worth his salt.' But modern fighters are not alone in feeling Choynski's harassing. To him, Bob Fitzsimmons was a cur. Naturally, I was curious ... what ... made Joe sour on the freckled wizard. I knew he had boxed Fitz and later toured thousands of miles with him on exhibition jaunts, and that Fitz cut him in for 50 percent of his purses." (Author: The statement is false).

"Why this animosity? I pressed him for an explanation! 'If you could give me some hint why you condemn Fitzsimmons.' He raised his square chin. His eyes blazed as they must have years before when he was one of the most feared fighters in the world. 'That is what I don't like about you reporters,' he snapped. 'I made a point ... told you it needs no explanation, but still you insist I give reasons.' I tried to apologize, but he refused to let me. 'Fitzsimmons wasn't the kind of person you could trust. He'd tell you one thing to your face and then stick a knife in your back. It happened to me many times. He did the same ... to Kid McCoy and Tommy Ryan. Of course, I don't like to say these things publicly ... Bob is dead and can't talk back. I know if our positions were reversed, with me buried under six feet of dirt and (Bob) here by this window relishing the warm sun, I would expect him to hold his tongue about me. But those are personal things.' "

"Choynski picked an old book from the table. 'Let us look at Bob's record ... through the thin line of type in Tom Andrews' record book. Take ... his fight with Gus Ruhlin. The book shows Ruhlin was stopped in the 15th round. (Note: it was the 6th round). But it doesn't say what condition Fitzsimmons was in at the time. I was there and I know. He was bathed in his own blood. His eyes were swollen into slits and his nose was smashed. Ruhlin was ... getting ready to knock him out when Fitz let go a desperation punch which, luckily for him, landed squarely ... with Sharkey ... Fitz was saved by the bell in the 1st round because his manager had a deal with the timekeeper, who pulled the handle some 30 seconds before he should have. And Jim Corbett had him on the floor at Carson and was winning in a cake-walk when Fitz tagged him with the solar-plexus punch."

" 'And ... And ... And.' Choynski stuttered for a moment. All he could say was 'and.' 'And what, sir?' I asked anxiously. 'And what about my fight with Fitzsimmons?' he finally sputtered. 'The record book shows that we boxed a five round draw in Boston. I hit him with a short, inside right to the mouth, and he dropped like he was dead. I walked back to my corner, knowing that he wasn't going to get up. The round wasn't a full minute old when all of a sudden the bell rang. I spun around and to my amazement, saw Martin Julian, Bob's manager, picking Fitz up. Police swarmed into the ring and their chief waved his arms over his head. That was the signal that the bout had been stopped. (Author: Joe's account is off the mark, and primarily demonstrates Fitz's courage in coming back from the brink of defeat). To this day, I still wonder if the fight would have been stopped if it were I, not Fitzsimmons, laying on the floor.' "

"Choynski had been up on his feet throwing imaginary blows as he described his skirmish with Ruby Robert. Now he was seated again, breathing hard from the strenuous motions. There was a glass of wine on the table. He picked it up and wet his lips. I asked him about the time he knocked out Jack Johnson ... 'How did a little fellow like you ever manage to knock out the greatest heavyweight champion of all time?' The old man grinned. 'So even you know how great a fighter he was. That shows you're on your toes, young man,' Choynski said curtly. 'But ... I must be honest ... Jack was only a kid ... and he made a mistake leading into me. I watched him do that for a couple of minutes ... then I pulled back, quickly like this,' Choynski was on his feet once again, taking his fighting stance, left hand far out in front, right hand cocked away back like a sling shot. I cracked him over the temple with a right smash ... the ... target I had in mind from the second the fight started. He dropped like a stunned ox.' He took another sip of wine ... 'I should have had more sense than to hit him hard, but when

I saw the opening, I just couldn't resist ... Jack and I spent 30 days in jail, talking to reporters and posing for photographers. The food was terrible; wormy bread and moldy beans. We were dog sick most of the time.' "

"When I asked Joe who was the best ... he ever faced, he threw his arms into the air. 'I knew that was coming,' he said bluntly. 'It never fails. Everybody wants to know who was the best. That is a tough one to answer and frankly, I don't like to be pinned down. But if I were forced to give an opinion, I'd have to say Corbett. You asked me who was the best ... I ever fought, not ... the best I ever saw. Had that been the question, I'd say the black giant from Australia, Peter Jackson. Although I never met him in a real bout, I did spar against him in numerous exhibitions. You people today think Joe Louis is a great fighter. Know what ... Jackson would have done to Louis? He'd have chewed him up and spit him out.' Choynski snapped his fingers. 'Like that ... without breaking a sweat.' What made Jackson so great? 'Everything. The way he boxed and punched and picked off blows in the air. In my opinion he was the perfect prize fighter. I respected Jeffries as a great war-horse, but Jackson was vastly superior ... in every department save brute strength. There is no question he would have slaughtered Jeffries and knocked him out ... over a 25-round distance.' I asked ... who was the best fighter pound for pound ... regardless of weight."

"Again the old man's face lit up, as he dug back through the years. 'Another Australian ... A dopey kid who fought under the name of Young Griffo. He was a tiny shaver. A featherweight with a funny build. A terrible drunk. I saw him chop up George Dixon, Joe Gans and Kid Lavigne, and I still don't believe what my eyes saw. They talk about *once in a lifetime* miracles. This Griffo was remarkable. It is my opinion that the world will never again see a boxer who approaches Griffo's genius. If he were heavier, say ... 160 pounds, he could easily have held the heavyweight championship ... that may sound like a ridiculous statement, considering 225-pound Jim Jeffries held the title ... But Griffo was great enough to offset Jeff's 65-pound weight advantage and stab him to pieces.' Choynski looked at the big, ancient railroad watch which hung from the mantle. 'I see I've been talking for over an hour,' he said. 'That's the time limit I set for interviews nowadays.' He started to walk toward the door and I followed. Just as I was about to set outside, he put his massive hand gently on my shoulder and said: 'I am flattered that you visited me, young man. Flattered to know people still want to read about the old-timers. I realize your head has been filled with ... many confusing stories about Sullivan, Jeffries, Corbett and the rest of us. Sports writers have a way of drifting ... from facts ... to make a good story. If you are suspicious of what you have heard, I honestly can't blame you. But, this one point I want to make clear. For all those weird stories there was a solid, factual basis. They were a master race of fighting men. I'm proud I was one of their generation.' "[39]

Early on the morning of Monday, January 25, 1943, at 12:25 a.m., Joe Choynski took his last breath. Louise contacted his physician, Dr. Reizler, she being listed as the "Informant" on Joe's death certificate. Dr. Reizler wrote: "I hereby certify that I attended deceased from April 9, 1942 (to) Jan. 25, 1943. I last saw him alive on Jan. 24, 1943 ... The principle cause of death and related causes ... in order of onset: Pulmonary Edema, Cardiac Dilation (January 23, 1943). Contributory causes ... not related to principal cause: chronic bronchitis and bronchiactasis, arterial sclerosis, senile changes." Joe succumbed to cardiopulmonary troubles. He was 74. A 1960 article said: "One day in 1943, Joe Choynski got lonesome for the old gang. He didn't awaken one morning and when they found him, he had a smile on his face and his hands were slightly clenched. It seemed as though the last thing he tried to do before going to sleep was to make a fist."[40] By a strange coincidence, Joe's death came on his 48th wedding anniversary. This must have made his passing doubly poignant for Louise.

The Cincinnati Elks Lodge Number 5 held a service for him, on the 26th at 8:00 p.m., at the funeral home of Busse & Borgmann, on Central Parkway. His funeral service took place there on the 27th at 3:00 p.m. Joe

was buried later that day in Walnut Hills Cemetery, interred in Section 30, Row 56, Grave 446. The cemetery is about 5 blocks northeast of 2524 Chatham Street, and coincidentally, next to the Harriet Beecher Stowe House. It is not known when Joe became a member of the BPOE (Elks Club), but one of his membership cards survives. He paid dues on April 2, 1930, and was already a member. He belonged to the Pittsburgh, Pennsylvania Lodge Number 11, member number 3126.[41]

Beginning the 25th, obituaries came out across the globe. There were many errors, as usual. Various obits said Joe was "last of the bareknuckle fighters" and had fought Jake Kilrain. "One of the saddest episodes ... occurred in Chicago ... shortly after boxing had become legalized in Illinois. Choynski applied for a referee's license, and had been duly appointed. In the summer of 1927 he refereed some bouts in an outdoor arena, and his decisions did not meet with universal approval. One disgruntled fan, who evidently wagered on the wrong man, wrote the State Athletic Commission a red-hot letter, demanding that Choynski's license be revoked. 'It's about time the commission got hep to itself ... What is the idea of appointing old men who never saw a boxing glove, as referees?' (Author: The crank obviously had no idea who Joe was!) Old Joe didn't work many bouts after that. His pride was hurt. Like many an old-timer, he lived in the fond belief that every fight fan remembered (him). That letter ... by an insignificant gambler ... led to Choynski's voluntary retirement as referee."[42]

"He was in no sense a killer, like Dempsey. Rather ... the forerunner, as was Corbett, of the Tunney type, depending much on mind and little on muscle. Most boxers, outside the ring, remain boxers, tough, truculent and considerably on the uncouth side. Choynski, to the contrary, was a polished man of the world, who invariably wore beautifully tailored clothes and manifested the manners of a cultured gentleman. He was an intelligent conversationalist in almost every field ... a witty, clever ... much-sought after dinner speaker. When he came to Cincinnati, (about) eight years ago, he had difficulty convincing persons he ... had been a fighter. He was especially well informed about the stage, and one of his hobbies was a study of great masterpieces of painting. In 1938, Choynski was employed as boxing instructor at the Cincinnati Club. He could still move as fast as students 50 and 55 years his juniors and could still throw punches. Of his disciples, he demanded perfection. The natural slugger was not to his liking. He preferred the scientific type ... who went in for footwork rather than ... haymakers. If they didn't bear down, he ... dropped them from his class. Choynski is survived by his widow and a brother, Maurice, who for many years has been in the motion picture business in Chicago. Funeral services will be arranged after the brother's arrival in Cincinnati."

January 26 *San Francisco Chronicle*: "Old-timers claim that Joe Choynski was the sharpest hitter of all time. Not the hardest ... for Joe was little more than a middleweight. But he could put every ounce of his 172 pounds behind a precision punch that had been prepared through rounds of maneuvering his opponent. As a kid, he was the champion of Fillmore Street, and when the Corbett family moved from south of the slot to Hayes Valley, there was a rival for his laurels. Surviving are his widow ... brothers, Edwin Coe, 1135 Ulloa street, San Francisco (who simplified his name), Morris Choynski of Chicago, and a sister, Miriam Coe, 630 Lake Street, San Francisco ... Tom (Sharkey) was sorry to hear of Joe's death when called on the phone last night. 'We was great friends ... The first time we met, he agreed to stop me in eight rounds. He didn't, so lost. The 2nd time, I knocked that little guy clear out of the ring and he came back to get referee ... Green's decision (Author: It was a draw) ... in 1900, I ... knocked him out in two rounds ... by that time he was an old timer, as fighters go. I fought Jeffries and Fitzsimmons, but they couldn't hit any harder than that skinny Choynski. He was ... a sharp-shooter.' " Tom was quoted in Joe's memoirs: "Choynski was a great fighter and a game one. He was a clean-cut man ... I have seen him hit a man so hard that he shook all over as with a chill."[43]

Two bouts were referenced that Joe allegedly had with Ed Dunkhorst: "Sharkey saw Joe's fight ... in Chicago in 1898 ... Choynski 173, Dunkhorst ... 260 (Author: Some said 300 pounds). Choynski cut him to pieces in four rounds. The next time Joe did the same ... in six, but Dunkhorst was ... too big for him to kayo." The lone confirmed fight was a W6 on December 19, 1898 at Chicago. A ND6 fight is claimed by some to have occurred December 9, 1898 in Philadelphia. That bout was between Ed and Peter Maher.[44] On Joe's 1887 bout with Billy Keneally, The *Chronicle* wrote: "Choynski won ... by a kayo in the 4th. The late, beloved Captain Keneally of the San Francisco Fire Department would explain that 'lucky punch' on the least provocation. Choynski last visited his home town about 1923 ... he made his first and only appearance at the Olympic Club ... put on the gloves and worked out with some young boxer. He was a trim figure at ... 55."

One paper wrote, on the 26th: "He had been in ill health, but as recently as four years ago was 'lightning fast,' friends said, as he instructed young hopefuls in boxing at the Cincinnati Club." This indicates Joe being an active teacher as late as 1939. He recounted: "I used to stick my fists into a pickling vat, maybe for hours, just to toughen 'em up." Several dailies mentioned Joe's "vinegar-hardened dukes," calling him "barrel-chested with pipe-stem legs ... a ring freak on the order of Bob Fitzsimmons." "Described by close friends as an esthete at heart, he had a penchant for beauty – be it a painted picture, the subtle turn of a phrase or the glory of a sunrise. An intense student of the stage, he appeared at conversational ease whatever the subject ..." The 1897 draw with Jeffries, "brought forth one of the first references to Choynski as the 'California Terror.' " Al Santoro of the *Los Angeles Examiner* said Joe had the most mispronounced name in pugilism, then gave the proper pronunciation as "Ko-in-skee not Choinski, as popularly supposed." An obituary by Hugh Fullerton, Jr. of the *Raleigh Register*, noted that Jim Corbett had said of Joe, "The salt of the earth, an all-around good fellow, gentleman ... always on the level, and ... no gamer man ever answered ... the gong!" Another paper called Joe's Battle of the Barge with Jim, "the most celebrated grudge fight in ring history."[45]

A recurring theme throughout, was Joe's extreme gameness as a fighter.[46] He was also noted for his longevity, though the length of his career was probably shortened by so many bouts with heavier opponents. Had Joe fought men of his own weight more often, the results he achieved would have been even better. Late in his career, especially, the losses he suffered resulted, in part, from the wear and tear of battling adversaries of much greater mass. Still, his results are impressive.

The day after Joe's death, legendary boxing trainer and second, Tim McGrath, said: "Ah, lad, there was a man. I knew him for 50 years, and no finer fighter and gentleman ever came out of San Francisco." The United Press said, "McGrath met the great Jewish puncher when they worked in a San Francisco candy factory more than 50 years ago. 'I had just come over from Limerick,' he said, 'and Choynski was already the hero of the Hayes Valley Jewish colony and the despair of the Irish.' Choynski was handicapped by small legs ... forced to support a huge, deep-chested body. Many of his friends thought he trained too hard and claimed his legs gave out early in fights because of long gymnasium sessions, McGrath said." The April, 1943 *Ring* magazine added, "For the last 15 years he resided ... in Cincinnati, Ohio. Until his health began to fail, he gave private boxing lessons. He was happily married, no scandal ever clouded the serenity of his domestic life, he died respected and liked by all who knew him." Being free of marital scandal isn't something that could be said of Corbett or "Kid" McCoy. Florence Dibert Coe, wife of Edwin, recalled Joe as a "kindly, soft-hearted, truly great personality whom everyone called a marvelous man," his "tall, handsome slenderness and ... compassionate blue eyes." An anonymous "old fight friend" recalled Joe's musical ability with mirth, as he recalled "hearing battling Joe ... play a waterlogged piano."[47]

The *London Stars and Stripes* of the 27th said: "He (Joe) was the chief rival of ... Corbett, of whom he hadn't a very high estimation. 'Who'd he ever beat but me?' he was quoted as cracking." A paper, the next day, quoted Jack Johnson: "Choynski was a great fellow, and what a puncher. I've been in auto wrecks, have had cars turned over on me – but nothing hurt me like Choynski!" "But Choynski ... could box, too ... a keen student of the game. At one time he sought to 'mentally influence' his opponents ... a sort of mental telepathy angle." A January 31 article called him "Boxing's most famed proponent of the right cross ..."[48] In an undated letter to Nat Fleischer, shortly before Joe died, he "related how he met thousands of people who saw him fight Jim Corbett on the barge. 'Only 25 adherents were permitted on a side ... and when I attended school in San Francisco, 25 and 25 made 50.' " A 1943 article said: "For years it's been a trick of old timers on the coast to let some gent say he was one of the privileged few to view that ancient classic, and lead to comment upon how dark it was when they finished. If he fell into the trap, they knew he wasn't there."[49] (The fight occurred in broad daylight). If as many were on the barge as claimed to have been, it would have sunk beneath the waves!

An article by Harry Grayson alleged that Joe and Corbett never spoke to each other while training Jeffries for the 1910 Johnson fight, nor cast a glance in the other's direction. This is not true. The men sparred on several occasions and greeted each other in a friendly manner when Corbett first joined camp. There was, however, some animosity still harbored in the heart of at least one of them. "Enmities are things of the earth and not of the great beyond, but those who knew them best surmise things will be different in the case of Choynski and Corbett. They never got along here and it is doubtful they will there." Most of Joe's top opponents credited him with the hardest blow they ever felt. Even Corbett gave tribute. When he was preparing to face Sullivan for the heavyweight championship, Jim "recalled a match ... with Joe ... in which he had been hit on the bridge of the nose. This made his eyes water and his nose bleed. It bothered him more than any ... punch he had received ... he thought: 'I'll punch John L. ... on the nose at the first opportunity. If it bothers him like it did me, the fight will be easy. I'll keep him busy, be careful not to get hit, and use my left hand.' " Corbett nailed "The Strong Boy" with a straight left to the nose, drawing plenty of blood.[50] Jim went on to victory.

A friend from Joe's youth, George P. Webster, recalled: "I first met Joe when he was 10, at his father's bookstore on ... Geary Street. I was going to the old Lincoln Grammar School on 5th, and was 16. Later, I went on the stage and formed a partnership with William A. Brady, who took Corbett East to spar for the '... show called *After Dark*.' " George shared a 1930 letter from Joe, "in which Choynski recalls friends he made when he made his stage debut in 'The Sea of Ice' at the Academy of Music on Market Street." Choynski signed it, "Intrinsically, Joe B. Choynski."[51]

Jack Johnson told reporters: "Choynski was the only man ... who hurt me" "Jeffries had a solid wallop and Fitz could knock your head off but ... Choynski could paralyze you even when he didn't catch you flush. In my opinion, he was the hardest hitter, pound for pound, of the last 50 years ... I think his left hook was much more effective than ... Dempsey's or Louis's"[52] On June 10, 1946, Jack was driving his car at high speed near Franklinton, North Carolina, having angrily left a diner that refused to serve him because he was black. He was on his way to see the June 19 title rematch between Joe Louis and Billy Conn, but went off the road and crashed into a tree. He died in hospital a short time later.

In 1945, the number of Jews taking up the sport decreased dramatically, as a new generation pursued occupations in commerce, art and other areas. As generally applies to all ethnic groups, only in tough economic times do they, in numbers, endure the punishment that Boxing requires. In the April, 1943 *Ring*, "The Veteran" wrote: "To those who might dispute the ranking of Choynski as the premier heavyweight of his race because Max Baer once won the ... championship ... Choynski was a far better and greater all-around fighter than ... Baer, who ... was only partly Jewish."

On the night of April 27, 1943, a benefit was held at the Pittsburgh Athletic Club (in Pittsburgh), for Joe's widow, Louise. This lent further evidence that he died destitute. About 400 attended the show, which featured amateur boxing and boxers from the Dutch Athletic Club of Moundsville, West Virginia. The take at the gate was announced as $1,000.[53] The June 17 *Ogden Standard-Examiner* carried a piece on the zoot suit, the male garment popularized during the jazz and swing eras of the 1930s and '40s. The writer said former *San Francisco Chronicle* scribe, Jack Lawlor, noted: "This freak outfit, as a whole, is new and originated in New Orleans, but, piece-by-piece, the get-up is as old as the hills."

"The current, knee length zoot coat is a throwback to the 'Frisco box coats in the middle 80s ... The garment was cream in color, with black or brown velvet collar and big pearl buttons. They were worn as overcoats by all the sports ... and the first two I saw were on Joe Choynski and Eddie Graney about 1888, who used to come down to our neighborhood to see the same girl – on different nights. She was a cooper's daughter, and didn't marry either one ... Those old zoot coats couldn't be worn in the rain, howsomever, and were strictly a fair weather piece of goods."

On June 11, 1944, at his home in Chicago, Joe's brother, Maurice, "Chauncey" from their childhood, died at age 78. He was a member of BPOE Chicago Lodge number 4, under whose auspices the memorial service was held at the funeral home at Eric and Wabash Avenue. This was the same Lodge "Parson" Davies belonged to and helped establish. Maurice was buried at Rosehill Cemetery on the 14th. *Boxoffice* magazine's June 24 obituary read: "Maurice A. Choynski, pioneer showman ... started in show business on the west coast 35 years ago. He was head of a Chicago theatre circuit when he retired two years ago ... the first president of the Exhibitors League of America ..."[54] Maurice and Sarah visited San Francisco in 1940 to see the Golden Gate International Exposition (popularly known as the San Francisco World's Fair) at Treasure Island. There, they had a reunion with Miriam, Edwin, and Edwin's youngest daughter, Harriet.

On November 18, 1944 at 4:45 p.m., less than two years after her husband's death, Louise Choynski passed away at the 2524 Walnut Hills residence. This was 10 days after what would have been Joe's 75th birthday. It might not be too poetic to say the former "Lutie" Miller died of a broken heart. She was 73 or 74. Her former occupation was listed as "Housewife." Evidently, her death was sudden, as attending physician, Richard W. Vilter, M.D., inscribed on her death certificate that he only attended her on the 18th. The cause of death was coronary occlusion (blockage of an artery feeding the heart). The embalmer was Robert Bamber and the Funeral Director, John Bamber, whose funeral home was located at 3011 Woodburn Avenue. Louise Anderson Choynski was laid to rest on November 22 in Walnut Hills Cemetery, directly beside Joe.[55] A description of the burial site was given me by Mark Palmer, who visited the graves in October, 2008: "It is ... about a mile south of Xavier University ... Much of the cemetery covers a large hill, with some graves at steep angles, some very close to the narrow, one-lane roads that crisscross the property. There are numerous big, old trees shading the grounds. This area is ... flat and doesn't have many trees ... different than the rest of the cemetery ... Most of the stones in ... the Choynski section, date from the 1940s."

More than one ex-pug claimed to have fought Joe at one time or another, but isn't found in his record. July 14, 1948 *Wisconsin State Journal*: "Jack (actually George) Gunther, the 78-year-old French-Algerian Negro who fought more than 600 ring contests ... fought ... Jack Blackburn nine times and won six ... fought Joe Choynski, Sam Langford and stopped Georges Carpentier before the Frenchman met Dempsey ... at his best never topped 172 pounds and stood 5' 9"." Gunther boxed pro from the turn of the 20th century to the early 1920s. He did tangle with Carpentier, Langford and Blackburn, but his record shows 1 win, 5 losses and 3 draws against Blackburn and two 15 round losses to Georges. It doesn't show him meeting Choynski. Another fighter who was claimed to have not only fought, but defeated Joe, was the useful black middleweight, Bob Scanlon, who fought from about 1904 to 1920, later joining the French Foreign Legion. A 1996 book said, "In civilian life he had whipped Mar-Robert, Marthenon, and Joe Choynski – even the Boche shells respected him!"[56] In Bob's 1925 memoirs, "American Volunteers in the French Foreign Legion, 1914-1917," he does not mention any bout with Joe.

On January 25, 1949, the Helms Athletic Foundation honored "Northern California's athletic heroes of the past and present" by selecting 64 men and women as athletes of the year, beginning with 1890. The very first winner was Joe Choynski, followed by John Herget ("Young Mitchell") (1891) and Jim Corbett (1892). "The selections were made (by) sports editors of San Francisco and Oakland newspapers ..." A 1952 editorial revealed that the home of Jim Corbett's youth, at 518 Hayes Street, site of the livery stable, still stood. "The old Corbett residence should be ... on the itinerary of the sightseeing buses." The building was eventually razed, as had occurred with Joe Choynski's boyhood homes at 118 Natoma Street and 1209 Golden Gate Avenue. (Author: A 1976 article by Tro Harper said the Corbett residence in 1889 was at 307 Hayes Street).[57]

Joe's sister, Miriam, died February 2, 1953 in San Francisco, age 88. She never remarried after her divorce from Captain Williams, and had been living at 630 Lake Street, where her mother, Harriett, lived until her death. On March 3, Jim Jeffries died of a heart attack in Burbank, California, age 77. He had often been morose since his wife, Frieda, was struck and killed by an automobile in 1941. Upon hearing of his friend's death, Tom Sharkey reportedly quipped, "Well, I finally beat him." Just a month later, on April 17, 79 year old Tom died in his sleep at San Francisco County Hospital. On January 1, 1958, Joe's last remaining sibling, Edwin, died at his home at 95 Patricia Drive in Atherton, California. He was 78.[58]

Epilogue

As a final assessment of Joe Choynski, the boxer, here are some opinions and testimonials: December 23, 1911 *Denver Post*, a story by W.A. Phelon: "Peter Maher is credited with having as hard a right-hand punch as any heavyweight that ever lived. Peter could flash it in fast ... and did little telegraphing before he shot it over. Bob Fitzsimmons, though, had it on Peter and all of them, because he could hit hard with either mitten. Old Bob had an awkward cleverness, a queer foot-shuffle and a trick of humping up his shoulders to guard the jaw. Add to that a startling shift, and it wasn't hard for Bob to put either hand into the framework of an adversary. Robert, however, broke those hands all to pieces with his mighty swipes, and had no fighting tools at all in later years. Joe Choynski, so those who fought him say, had a right-hand kick as heavy as that of Bob Fitzsimmons, and delivered even more suddenly. Joe hadn't the weight, and his legs lacked the endurance ... so he never was a champion."

"Jim Jeffries ... ought to have been a dreadful hitter, but his usual style – letting the other man come in ... then impaling him on a defensive punch – never showed how hard Jim could hit if he wanted to. He did let out some on Jack Muroe (sic), and seemed to have a wallop quite in proportion to his stature. Jack Johnson, too ... preferred to hold back the punch and let the other man harpoon himself on it. People who have been hit by Mistah Johnsing say he has a lovely whack if he wants to use it – a nice K.O. in either hand. Probably the best combination of boxer and ... hitter ... ever ... was Tommy Ryan, whose footwork was equal to that of any featherweight, and who could hit a jarring knockout punch with either hand ... Most of the sluggers, however, have been slow footed, and most of the boxers ... gentle hitters. Tommy Ryans come only once in a generation."

Old Joe had his adherents. February 28, 1912 *Colorado Springs Gazette*: "Although Joe Choynski never weighed over 176 pounds in fighting condition, I believe if he could step into the ring today in his old-time form, he would ... clean up ... our big army of so-called 'white hopes,' said Bug Slattery at the Victor Athletic Club ... Choynski ... was like Tommy Ryan in ... many respects – a cool head ... hit hard with either hand ... one of the best ring generals of his time. I saw Joe in several ... bouts ... (he) used a sort of downward chop for a left hook ... a very effective blow, for he had the knack of putting all of his power into the blow."

In Allen Bodner's 1997, *When Boxing Was a Jewish Sport*, Choynski is rated the best of Jewish heavyweights, ahead of Bob Pastor, Art Lasky, Abe Simon, "King" Levinsky, Natie Brown, Bill Weinberg, Abe Feldman, Bill Poland and Jack Gross. Overall, regardless of weight class, Joe was ranked the 9th greatest Jewish boxer of all time, ahead of Louis "Kid" Kaplan, but preceded by, in order, number one through eight: Benny Leonard, Abe Attell, Ted "Kid" Lewis, Harry Lewis, Barney Ross, Lew Tendler, Charlie White and Jackie "Kid" Berg. The list was compiled by boxing historians Hank Kaplan, Mike Silver and Vic Zimet.

Joe was posthumously elected to the *Ring* magazine Hall of Fame in 1960. This was the first recognized Hall of Fame for Boxing, instituted in 1954 by Nat Fleischer.[1] More vestiges of Joe's past crumbled with the passage of time. The *Galveston Daily News* referred in 1965 to the pile of rubble at 16th and Water Street that once was the Galveston County Jail. Two articles claimed that Joe and Jack went at it again (in 1901) in a six round bout in the jail's courtyard, "with Johnson again taking the count." On September 20, 1970, 30 old-time pugs were inducted into the California Boxing Hall of Fame. The first California Old-Timers Boxing Convention was held in Fresno. The inductees read like a "who's who" of "Fistology." Besides Choynski, contemporaries inducted were Corbett, Jeffries, Sharkey, Herget, George Green, Abe Attell, Ed Graney and Alec Greggains, Billy Delaney, Tim McGrath, "Spider" Kelly, promoters Jim Coffroth and Tom McCarey and announcer Billy Jordan. Joe was in good company![2]

By this time, virtually anyone who ever knew Joe Choynski had passed from the mortal plane. While a huge compliment, it was beyond the bounds of reality when Billy Nolan, former manager of lightweight champion Willie Ritchie, called Joe "the greatest heavy weight of all times ..." Nolan: "He only weighed 160 pounds, but with his cleverness, possessed a wonderful punch. He ... performed ... wonderful ring feats, although ... always greatly outweighed." In 1975, it was said that "Choynski's career offered the first major opportunity for the stereotype of the Jew to be extended from the world of trade to the world of sports, from storekeeper to athlete. When the image of the Jew was broadened by activities so typically American as athletics, the Jewish presence in America was further naturalized ... Joe Choynski emerged as a symbol of how American a Jew might be, given a new frontier upon which to plant an ancient culture."[3] In 1991, Joe was voted into the International Jewish Sports Hall of Fame, along with Sam Berger, Max Baer, "Ruby" Goldstein and Howard Cosell.

On June 14, 1998, Joe was inducted into the International Boxing Hall of Fame in Canastota, New York. Founded in 1990, it was the most prestigious of the boxing halls. The other deceased members of the Class of '98 were: Sammy Angott, William A. Brady, "Professor" Mike Donovan, Frankie Genaro, George "Kid" Lavigne, Benny Lynch, Sammy Mandell and Herman "Bud" Taylor. Living inductees were: Miguel Canto, Antonio Cervantes, Lou Duva and Matthew Saad Muhammad. A crowd of 2,000 witnessed the ceremonies, following an afternoon parade. In attendance were such boxing celebrities as "Smokin' " Joe Frazier, Ken Norton,

"Marvelous" Marvin Hagler, Carmen Basilio, Pernell "Sweet Pea" Whitaker, Floyd Patterson, Alexis Arguello, Aaron Pryor, Eddie Futch, Emanuel Steward, Gerry Cooney and Christy Martin.[4] Author David Bezmozgis wrote an article on Joe's induction for the *Canadian Jewish News*, saying that Herbert Goldman read out the names of each boxer and a short summary of their accomplishments. Choynski was first to be inducted, in the Old-Timers category. After Herbert listed Joe's achievements, "a ceremonial ringbell was struck in the boxer's honor." While it is customary to present the induction certificate to a living relative of a deceased member, no surviving kin were found for Joe.[5] He and Louise had no children, and surviving relatives may not have been aware of the event.

Joseph Bartlett Choynski: His was an interesting life, a useful life – one not only of "tolerance," but of acceptance. During the course of Joe's 74-plus years on this planet, he made very few, if any, enemies. On the contrary, Joe left a legacy of more friends and admirers than many of his profession, despite his rather low-key and private nature. It may sound cliché, but it is true: Joe never asked what religion his fellow human belonged to, not the pigmentation of their skin, nor their ethnic origins. In an era of gross bigotry, he treated his fellow man (and woman) with dignity and respect. It is probably this, as well as his accomplishments in the ring, that Choynski should be most remembered for. As a final word, this author feels that Joe's legacy should not be that he "*fought* them all" ... any journeyman trial horse can do that – but rather, how well he *performed* against the greatest of his time. He was known by those who knew him best, as a great light-heavyweight – though today he would be a super-middleweight, a full three weight divisions below heavyweight. Yet, Joe essentially held even the greatest dreadnoughts of his day, the first heavyweight "golden age" of the Marquis of Queensberry Era. He should be remembered as a great pound-for-pound fighter, a master boxer and devastating puncher; the first light-heavyweight champion, a fine ambassador of the sport – and a *mensch*. Joe Choynski deserves to be up where he is – a first magnitude star among the fistic firmament.

Boxing Record of Joe Choynski:

My amended and updated version of the fighting record of Joe Choynski follows:
(Using records from cyberboxingzone.com, Boxrec.com and my research; Special thanks to Tracy Callis)
+++ - My addition   ### - My correction   ??? - Unconfirmed

MANAGERS : Charles E. "Parson" Davies, Ed Graney, Tim McGrath
***** Amateur Bouts *****
1884 (undated bouts)
Jim Corbett	San Francisco, CA	ND 1 (informal bout in Corbett livery stable)
Jim Corbett	San Francisco, CA	ND 1 (informal bout at the "Dog Pound")

1887
Mar 23	Jim Corbett	San Francisco, CA	NDL5
	Pat O'Sullivan (or Sullivan)	San Francisco, CA	W2 or W3
	J. O'Connell	San Francisco, CA	?(possibly Joe Connolly/Connelly)
	Jack Lynch	San Francisco, CA	KO1 +++
Jul 22	Tom Moran	San Francisco, CA	TK2 ###
Sep 7	Joe Connelly	San Francisco, CA	KO3 ###
Nov 29	William Keneally	San Francisco, CA	KO4

-Amateur Heavyweight Championship of the Pacific Coast

1888
Feb 14	Jack (or John) McCauley	San Francisco, CA	EX3
Apr 13	Joe Bowers	San Francisco, CA	EX3
Jun 26	Peter Jackson	San Francisco, CA	EX4
Aug 7	Edward Cuffe	San Francisco, CA	EX3 or 4
Aug 14	George Bush	San Francisco, CA	EX3
Sept 28	Jim Hall (colored)	San Francisco, CA	W3
Oct 26	Frank (or Jim) Cantwell	San Francisco, CA	TK4
Dec 26	J.E. (or Jem, Harry) McDonald	San Francisco, CA	EX3 ###

***** Professional Bouts *****
1888
Nov 14	George Bush	San Francisco, CA	KO2

1889
Feb 26	Frank Glover	San Francisco, CA		KO14
Apr 26	Con Riordan	San Francisco, CA		EX3 or 4
May 30	Jim Corbett	Fairfax, CA		ND4
Jun 5	Jim Corbett	Benecia Harbor, CA	(1:47:00)	LT27

-This bout was fought on a barge; (some sources say LT 28)
Jul 15	Jim Corbett	San Francisco, CA	L4
Aug 6	Gus Keen	San Francisco, CA	sparred 4
Aug 27	Billy McCarthy	San Francisco, CA	EX4
Sep 24	Thomas McCarty	San Francisco, CA	EX ?

(*San Francisco Chronicle*, September 25, 1889, which didn't note the duration)
Sep 30	Billy Hennessy	San Francisco, CA	sparred ?

(*San Francisco Chronicle*, October 7, 1889. Exact date of spar uncertain)
Oct 14	Fred Woods	San Francisco, CA	EX3
Nov 16	sparred unnamed opponent(s)	San Francisco, CA	EX ? +++
Nov 24	sparred unnamed opponent(s)	San Francisco, CA	EX ? +++
Nov 26	sparred unnamed opponent(s)	San Francisco, CA	EX ? +++
Nov 30	Billy Hennessy	San Francisco, CA	sparred ?

1890
Jan 25	Frank (or James) McClarney (or McLarney)	Portland, OR	KO2
Feb ?	(a lumberjack)	?, Oregon	KO1 +++

Joe Choynski, "I Fought 'Em All" (1930), "The Days of Finish Fights" (1927)
Mar 26	Billy Wilson	San Francisco, CA	KO2

May 26 "Omaha" Jack Davis   San Francisco, CA   KO9
Jul 9 Bob Fitzsimmons   San Francisco, CA   ND4
Aug 3 Ed Lynch   San Francisco, CA   EX ? +++
Aug 14 Evan "Strangler" Lewis San Francisco, CA   Lost, 1 Fall, 8 min. (Boxer vs. Wrestler)
Aug 30 ? Wilson (or Charles Hopkins) Honolulu, Oahu, HI KO2 ###
Aug 30 unnamed opponent   Honolulu, Oahu, HI   EX ? +++
Nov 24 Jim Fogarty   Sydney, NSW, Aus   KO10
Nov 26 Jack Fuller   Sydney, NSW, Aus   sparred ? ###
1891
Feb 10 Joe Goddard   Sydney, NSW, Aus   LK4
May 25 Mick Dooley   Melbourne, Vic, Aus   KO2
Jun 3 Martin "Buffalo" Costello Melbourne, Vic, Aus   EX4 or ND4
Jun 20 Owen Sullivan   Melbourne, Vic, Aus   KO2
Jul 20 Joe Goddard   Melbourne, Vic, Aus   LK4
Aug 22 Dave Green   Melbourne, Vic, Aus   EX ? +++
Sep 14 Joe Goddard   Melbourne, Vic, Aus   sparred 3
Nov 13 Bob Fitzsimmons   San Francisco, CA   sparred 4
Dec 17 Billy Woods   San Francisco, CA   KO34
Dec 20 John L. Sullivan   San Francisco, CA   EX3
1892
Feb 28 Bob Fitzsimmons   San Francisco, CA   sparred 4
Feb 29 Bob Fitzsimmons   San Francisco, CA   sparred ?
Mar 1 Bob Fitzsimmons   San Francisco, CA   sparred ?
Mar 10 Bob Fitzsimmons   New Orleans, LA   sparred ?
Mar 10 Alec Greggains   New Orleans, LA   sparred 4 +++
Mar 29 Jim Hall   Detroit, MI   EX4
Apr 2 Jim Hall   Chicago, IL   EX3 or 4 ?
Apr 2 John (or Jack) Dalton   Chicago, IL   EX3
Apr 9 Joe Godfrey   Philadelphia, PA   TK1
Apr 11 Jim Hall   New York, NY   EX3
Apr 13 Jim Hall   New York, NY   EX3
Apr   -Choynski and Hall sparred (almost) nightly at New York, NY (Niblo's Theatre)
Apr 19 Jerry Slattery   New York, NY   KO2
Apr 21 Charles McCarthy   New York, NY   KO2
Apr 22 Tom Ryan   New York, NY   KO2
Apr 30 "Denver" Ed Smith   Philadelphia, PA   TK4 ###
       -Police intervened; Some sources report "W 4"
May -Choynski and Jim Hall gave boxing exhibitions in London, Eng (Novelty Theatre) during May
May 25 Jack Hart   London, Eng   TK3
May 26 William Patmore   London, Eng   TK2
May 28 Morris (or Mike) Horrigan   London, Eng   TK1
May ? Albert Hall ? (Canning Town) London, Eng (Joe's memoirs)TK3? ???
Jun 1 -Choynski challenged Jem Smith to a bout; It was never held.
Jul 30 -Jem Smith challenged Choynski to a bout; It was never held.
Aug 25 - Sep 2 Choynski and "Parson" Davies sailed back to the USA.
Oct 13 unnamed boxer   Atlantic Highlands, NJ   EX ???
Oct 29 Jack Cattanach   Navesink Highlands, NJ   EX3
Oct 31 George Godfrey   Coney Island, NY   KO15
Nov 21 C.C. Smith   Philadelphia, PA   TK4
Nov 23 Denny Kelliher   Philadelphia, PA   TK2
Nov 26 Jack Fallon   Philadelphia, PA   TK4
Nov 26 Joe Butler   Philadelphia, PA   EX3
Dec 3 Jack Fallon   Brooklyn, NY   ND4
Dec 29 Bob Ferguson   Chicago, IL   TK4 ###
Dec 29 Mike Boden   Chicago, IL   W4 ###
1893
Jan 2 Frank Fitzgerald   Salt Lake City, UT   EX4 +++
Jan 10 Peter Jackson   San Francisco, CA   EX10
Jan 11 Peter Jackson   San Francisco, CA   EX3 ???

Feb 6 Tom West	Portland, OR	WDQ3
Joe Butler		D4 ???

The following exhibitions with Peter Jackson were held between acts of the play, Uncle Tom's Cabin:

Mar 17 Peter Jackson	San Francisco, CA	EX3 +++
Mar 19 Peter Jackson	San Francisco, CA	EX3 +++
Apr 4 Peter Jackson	Cheyenne, WY	EX3 +++
Apr 8-Apr 14 Peter Jackson	Kansas City, MO	EX3 +++
Apr 20 Peter Jackson	Omaha, NE	EX3 +++
Apr 21 Peter Jackson	Omaha, NE	EX3 +++
May 1-May 6 Peter Jackson	St. Louis, MO	EX3 +++
May 7 Peter Jackson	Chicago, IL	EX3 +++
May 14-May 20 Peter Jackson	Chicago, IL	EX 3 +++
Jul 10 Solly Smith	Roby, IN	EX
-This was a wrestling session of 30-60 minutes.		
Aug 31 Peter Jackson	Newark, OH	EX3 +++
Sep 4-Sep 7 Peter Jackson	Cincinnati, OH	EX3 +++
Sep 14 Peter Jackson	Olean, NY	EX3 +++
Sep 18-Sep 20 Peter Jackson	Syracuse, NY	EX3 +++
Oct 2 Peter Jackson	Kingston, NY	EX3 +++
Oct 15-Oct 22 Peter Jackson	New York, NY	EX3 +++
Oct 24 Peter Jackson	Lawrence, MA	EX3 +++
Oct 27 Peter Jackson	Bangor, ME	EX3 +++
Nov 3 Peter Jackson	New Brunswick, ME	EX3 +++
Nov 4 Peter Jackson	Lowell, MA	EX3 +++
Nov 14 Peter Jackson	Holyoke, MA	EX3 +++
Nov 15 Peter Jackson	New Haven, CT	EX3 +++
Nov Peter Jackson	Hartford, CT	EX3 +++
Dec 4 Peter Jackson	Philadelphia, PA	EX3 +++
Dec 14 Peter Jackson	Worcester, MA	EX3 +++
Dec 15 Peter Jackson	Worcester, MA	EX3 +++
Dec 18-Dec 23 Peter Jackson	New York, NY	EX3 +++
1894		
Jan 1 Peter Jackson	Worcester, MA	EX3 +++
Jan ? Peter Jackson	New York, NY	EX3 ???
Feb 3 Peter Jackson	Logansport, IN	EX3 +++
Feb 4 Peter Jackson	Milwaukee, WI	EX3 +++
Feb 5 Peter Jackson	Milwaukee, WI	EX3 +++
Feb 13 Peter Jackson	Kalamazoo, MI	EX3 +++
Mar 4-Mar 9 Peter Jackson	Washington, DC	EX3 +++
Mar 15 Peter Jackson	Richmond, IN	EX3 +++
Mar 17 Peter Jackson	Decatur, IL	EX3 +++
Mar 18-Mar 24 Peter Jackson	St. Louis, MO	EX3 +++
Apr 30 Peter Jackson	Boston, MA	EX3 +++
May 1-May 6 Peter Jackson	Boston, MA	EX3 +++
Jun 15 Tommy West	Worcester, MA	sparred 2
Jun 15 Martin Whalen	Worcester, MA	sparred 2
Jun 17 Bob Fitzsimmons	Boston, MA	D5
-Police intervened		
Sep 15 Harry Miller	Cincinnati, OH	W3
Sep 17 Mike Boden	Chicago, IL	TK3
Nov Tommy Ryan	Chicago, IL	EX
-Choynski and Ryan gave public exhibitions every day during the first week of November		
Nov 5 Billy Stift?	Chicago, IL	EX ???
Dec 13 Tommy Ryan	New Orleans, LA	EX ???
Dec 19 Tommy Ryan	Chicago, IL	EX
-Choynski and Ryan began a sparring engagement in Chicago		
1895		

Jan   -Choynski sparred daily with Tommy Ryan at the New York, NY (New Manhattan AC) Athletic Club the first two weeks in January

Feb 25 Jack Douglass	Chicago, IL	W3 +++
Mar 11 Mike Madden	Kansas City, MO	TK4 ###
Mar 21 Dan Creedon	Chicago, IL	D6

-Technical verdict was a "draw, " as both were standing at end; Joe hammered Creedon around ring

May ? Tommy Ryan	Dead Lake, NJ (near Asbury Park)	EX
Jun 3 Jack Cattanach	Baltimore, MD	KO2
Jun 8 Bob Armstrong	New York, NY	EX3
Jun 27 Bob Armstrong	New York, NY	EX6
Aug 20 Dick Wilson	Louisville, KY	KO2
Nov 3 Will Mayo	Chicago, IL	EX ? +++
Nov 3 Will Mayo	Chicago, IL	EX ? +++

-Above two bouts occurred on same night, against same fighter

Nov 6 Tom Silverthorn	Chicago, IL	EX3 +++
Nov 9 Al Tulrock	Chicago, IL	EX3 +++
Nov 13 Billy Stift	Chicago, IL	EX ? +++
Nov 14 Charley O'Connor	Chicago, IL	EX ? +++ ???

-Above bout was scheduled; The outcome is not known

Nov 14 Frank Childs	Chicago, IL	EX 3 +++
Nov 16 Billy (William A.) Phelon	Chicago, IL	EX 3 +++

-Above bout against Phelon was scheduled; The outcome is not known

Dec 27 Spider Kelly	San Francisco, CA	sparred ? +++

1896

-Sparred daily with "Professor" Mike Donovan at the New York Athletic Club (Jan 13-19?)

Jan 19 Dody Schwangler/George Schwegler and/or Fred Winthrop NYC		sparred ? +++
Jan 20 Jim Hall	Maspeth, NY	KO13
Mar 21 Charles "Kid" McCoy	New York, NY	ND4
Apr 9 Theodore Van Buskirk	San Francisco, CA	EX2 +++
Apr 16 "Sailor" Tom Sharkey	San Francisco, CA	L 8

-Sharkey lasted and claimed win, although he took a beating.

Apr 30 Ed Graney	San Francisco, CA	EX ? +++
May 18 Frank Chance	Fresno, CA	EX3 +++
May 18 "Professor" E.W. Bradstreet	Fresno, CA	EX3 +++
July 5 Leon (Lon or Lou) Agnew	San Francisco, CA	EX3 +++
Aug 28 Joe McAuliffe	San Francisco, CA	KO4 ###
Sep 8 "Reddy" Gallagher	Denver, CO	EX4 +++
Sep 10? Billy Woods	Cripple Creek, CO	EX4? +++
Nov 16 Peter Maher	New York, NY	LK6
Dec 26 Peter Maher	Pittsburgh, PA	EX3

1897

Jan 2 Frank Dwyer (Bert Scheller)	Pittsburgh, PA	W4
Jan 2 (last name, Wilson)	Pittsburgh, PA	W3

-Above two matches were stopped by police

May 10 "Denver" Ed Smith	New York, NY	WF4
May Tom Sharkey	Staten Island, NY (Southfield)	EX

-Joe sparred often with Sharkey from early May to June 8, helping Tom train for Peter Maher

Aug 6 Bob Armstrong	Chicago, IL	EX ???
Sep 13 Al Shrosbree (or Schrosbee)	Chicago, IL	EX
Sep 16 Dan Creedon	St. Louis, MO	EX4 ###
Oct 11 Herman Bernau	Galveston, TX	TK4 ###
Nov 30 Jim Jeffries	San Francisco, CA	D20

1898

Mar 11 "Sailor" Tom Sharkey	San Francisco, CA	D8

-Police intervened; Most sources said Sharkey was fouling and should have been disqualified

Sep 12 Joe Goddard	Philadelphia, PA	ND-W6
Nov 4 Gus Ruhlin	Philadelphia, PA	ND-L6
Dec 19 Ed Dunkhorst	Chicago, IL	ND-W6

1899

Mar 24 Charles "Kid" McCoy	San Francisco, CA	L20
Apr 17 Willard Bean	Salt Lake City, UT	D10 ###

Jul 21 Jim "Jack" McCormick	Chicago, IL	W6
Aug 4 "Mexican" Pete Everett	Denver, CO	WF7
Aug 29 "Australian" Jim Ryan	Dubuque, IA	W20 ###

-This bout was promoted as the Light Heavyweight Championship of the World

Sep 23 Unidentified Kentucky amateur	Louisville, KY	EX ###
Sep 23 Unidentified Kentucky amateur	Louisville, KY	EX ###
Sep 23 Unidentified black Kentucky amateur	Louisville, KY	EX KO1 ###
Sep 25 Jim Hall	Louisville, KY	KO3
Oct 6 Charles "Kid" McCoy	Chicago, IL	D6 ###

-It was pre-arranged that verdict would be a draw if both finished on their feet

Oct 20 "Australian" Jim Ryan	New York, NY	KO7
Oct 23 Dick Moore	St. Louis, MO	KO3
Oct 27 Steve O'Donnell	Chicago, IL	TK6
Nov 4 Tom Carey	Cincinnati, OH	KO2

1900

| Jan 12 Charles "Kid" McCoy | New York, NY | LT3 (KO2) |

-Joe was robbed of a knockout victory in 2nd round

Feb 8 (or 11) Marshall Woods (colored)	Chicago, Il	KO3 ###
Feb 16 Peter Maher	Chicago, IL	W6
Feb 21 Fred "Cyclone" Morris	New York, NY	EX ###
Feb 23 Joe Walcott	New York, NY	LT7
May 8 "Sailor" Tom Sharkey	Chicago, IL	LT2

-Beginning mid-June, Joe went on a sparring exhibition tour with Frank Marshall for about 8 weeks

Aug 7 John Matthews "The Black Demon"	Dayton, OH	W3
Aug 7 Frank Taylor "colored man of Dayton"	Dayton, OH	KO2 ###
Nov 2 Fred Russell	Denver, CO	WF4

1901

| Feb 25 Jack Johnson | Galveston, TX | KO3 |
| Dec 27 "Sailor" Tom Sharkey | New York, NY | sparred 3 +++ |

-called a heated, but "friendly" three round bout

1902

Mar 7 "Wild" Bill Hanrahan	Louisville, KY	KO5
Mar 24 Kid Carter	Chicago, IL	LK1
May 2 Al Weinig	Louisville, KY	KO6
Sep 29 "Philadelphia" Jack O'Brien	Chicago, IL	L6
Dec 1 Frank Childs	Chicago, IL	W6

1903

Jan 26 Peter Maher	Philadelphia, PA	KO2
Mar 30 "Philadelphia" Jack O'Brien	Philadelphia, PA	ND-L6
Jun 15 Charley Carroll	Dawson City, YT, Can	EX4 ???
Jun 25 Nick Burley	Dawson City, YT, Can	LK 2 ###
Aug 7 Nick Burley	Dawson City, YT, Can	KO7
Nov 2 Kid Carter	Philadelphia, PA	D6 ???
Nov 16 Marvin Hart	Philadelphia, PA	ND-D6 ###

1904

| Jan 19 Kid Carter | Boston, MA | LK1 |
| Nov 21 Jack Williams | Philadelphia, PA | ND6 |

***** The following bouts are reported but not confirmed *****

1904

| Jim Jeffries | San Francisco, CA | EX |

Undated

Jack Cattanach	San Francisco, CA	EX4
C.A.C. Smith		D
Steve O'Donnell	Sydney, NSW, Aus	L4

-This bout possibly took place during 1890-1891

*** Assistance and some data was provided by Sergei Yurchenko and Mark Dunn ***
www.cyberboxingzone.com/boxing/choynski.htm

Endnotes

Introduction:

[1] April 14, 1888 *Daily Alta California*: "The following-named non-commissioned officers, 2nd Artillery, were reduced to the ranks for neglect of duty: Corporal Joseph B. Choynski, Company G ..."

Round 1:

[1] Janet Choynski Fleishhacker said in a 1974 interview that per family tradition, the children were all born at home, as was true almost everywhere in the United States in that period; The 118 Natoma family address in 1866 is taken from the 1866 IRS Tax Assessment, www.ancestry.com; *Weekly Gleaner*, April 17, 1857; *Jewish Voices of the California Gold Rush* by Ava Fran Kahn, 2002.

[2] *San Francisco, a Guide to the Bay and Its Cities* by Works Progress Administration of Northern California, 1940 and 1973; History of San Francisco, California – en.wikipedia.org, and other websites.

[3] *North to California: the Spanish Voyages of Discovery, 1533-1603* by Paul A. Myers, 2004; sandiegohistory.org and several other sources; *San Francisco, a Guide to the Bay and Its Cities*, 1940 and 1973; *North to California: the Spanish Voyages of Discovery, 1533-1603* by Paul A. Myers, 2004; inn-california.com and other sources; *San Francisco, a Profile With Pictures* by Barnaby Conrad 1959; *Lights and Shades in San Francisco* by Benjamin E. Lloyd, 1876.

[4] *Adventures of a Forty-Niner* by Daniel Knower, 1894; *San Francisco, A Guide to the Bay And Its Cities* by Works Progress Administration of Northern California, 1940 and 1973.

[5] *Mark Twain, A Life* by Ron Powers, 2005; *San Francisco, a Guide to the Bay and Its Cities* by Works Progress Administration of Northern California, 1940 and 1973; *Adventures of a Forty-Niner* by Daniel Knower 1894; maritimeheritage.org/vips/vigilance.html and other sources.

[6] *Lights and Shades of San Francisco* by Benjamin Estelle Lloyd, 1876.

[7] *The Barbary Coast, an Informal History of the San Francisco Underworld* by Herbert Asbury, 1933.

[8] *San Francisco, a Guide to the Bay and Its Cities* by Works Progress Administration of Northern California, 1940 and 1973.

[9] *Our City, The Jews of San Francisco* by Irena Narell, 1981; *New York Times*, March 27, 1922.

[10] October 10, 1894 letter to I.N. Choynski from Ambrose Bierce, David Fleishhacker; *San Francisco, a Profile With Pictures* by Barnaby Conrad, 1959; *Disaster!: The Great San Francisco Earthquake and Fire of 1906* by Dan Kurzman, 2002; *San Francisco, a Guide to the Bay and Its Cities*, 1940 and 1973; several other sources. For Jack London's *The Game* influencing the retirements of Tunney and Marciano, see *The Boxing Filmography* by Frederick V. Romano, 2004.

[11] *San Francisco Call*, October 22, 1868, and several other sources; *Davenport Daily Gazette*, November 9, 1868; "Mega Disasters: The San Francisco Earthquake" (2006) (A History Channel documentary).

[12] *San Francisco Call*, October 22, 1868; Manuscripts Collection for I.N. Choynski – receipt from Howard & Folsom streets Property Union, payment of $30.00 for one share (no. 12), March 2, 1869. The address is 524 Howard Street. North Baker Library San Francisco, California. (ark.cdlib.org); *The Great Register of San Francisco, 1867*: gives I.N. Choynski, "Occupation: Bookseller" as "Last Residence," 118 Natoma. In 1873 & 1874, their dwelling was 524 Howard St., according to the *San Francisco Directory*. From Albert J. Draper – Choynski, I.N. Importer of books, 34 Geary. Residence, 127 O'Farrell. (Harriet Draper's father, Edwin W. Choynski, was born here in 1879); "I Fought 'Em All" by Joe Choynski, *Fight Stories*, Oct.-Nov. 1930; "The San Francisco Journalism of I.N. Choynski ...," 1997.

[13] *Dubuque Daily Herald*, November 8, 1868; *Davenport Daily Gazette*, November 9, 1868.

[14] *San Francisco, a Profile with Pictures* by Barnaby Conrad 1959.

[15] kolpack.com/packnet/prussia.html; infoplease.com/ce6/world/A0860564.html; en.wikipedia.org/wiki/Prussia; *Canadian Journal of History, December, 2001* by A.B. Pernal; *The Other Prussia: Royal Prussia, Poland and Liberty, 1569-1772* by Karen Friedrich, 2006; findarticles.com/p/articles/mi_qa3686/is_200112/ai_n9004488; *Cambridge Studies in Early Modern History*, Cambridge University Press, 2000.

[16] "The San Francisco Journalism of I.N. Choynski, He Flatters None and Displeases Many" by Robert Singerman, 1997; *History of Modern Europe (1792-1878)* by C.A. Fyffe 1880; *Systems of Land Tenure in Various Countries, a Series of Essays*, edited by J. W. Probyn, 1876.

[17] "The San Francisco Journalism of I.N. Choynski ...," 1997; "Family, Business, and the San Francisco Community," California Jewish Community Oral History Series of the Judah L. Magnes

Memorial Museum, 1975; *Sports & the American Jew* by Syracuse University Press, 1998 states, "His father Isadore (sic), the son of a rabbi ..."; Correspondence with Mortimer Fleishhacker (III), August 2007.

[18] United States Federal Census, 1880, 1900; San Francisco Directories, 1874, 1898, 1900 and 1909; Jewishgen.org shows Isaiah's death in 1919, but the 1915 *San Francisco City Directory* lists his spouse, "Choynski, Fanny (wid. Isaiah)," as a widow, at their 404 Ashbury residence. The *Financier* (New York), January 15, 1918; "San Francisco's Fighting Jew," *California Historical Quarterly*, Fall, 1974; California Death Index (1940-1997); familysearch.org; Isaiah and Fanny Choynski headstone at findagrave.com.

[19] itd.nps.gov/cwss; fold3.com; genealogybank.com; Robert Singerman wrote in "The San Francisco Journalism of I.N. Choynski ...," 1997: "Without knowing in which state he (Isaiah) enlisted, it is impossible to verify his service from Civil War military records..." In the August 20, 1886 *American Israelite*, Isidor (under the pseudonym, "Maftir") said he had a brother who fought in the Battle of Bull Run. In the September 25, 1880 *Antiquarian*, he stated that this brother served under General Rosecrans.

[20] *Los Angeles Daily Star*, Fall, 1874; *Western States Jewish Historical Quarterly*, Volume 14, 1981 by Southern California Jewish Historical Society; U.S. Civil War Soldier Records and Profiles, New York: Report of the Adjutant-General; ancestry.com; civilwardata.com; ftp.rootsweb.com/pub/usgenweb/ny/state/military/civilwar/service/firstnyengineers-ak.txt; Washington State and Territorial Censuses, 1857-1892; Seattle, *Washington City Directories*, 1888-1890.

[21] Albert and Harriet Draper; "The San Francisco Journalism of I.N. Choynski ...," 1997. The 1935 birth date is also found at online.dralex.com/jberlowitz/mainn.html, Judith's Extended Mishpatchah.

[22] "The San Francisco Journalism of I.N. Choynski, He Flatters None and Displeases Many," 1997.

[23] *A Brief Description of the System of Education Adopted in the Celebrated Common Schools of Prussia* by Victor Cousin, 1838; *German University Education, or the Professors and Students of Germany, To Which Is Added a Brief Account of the Public Schools of Prussia* by Walter C. Perry, 1846. Isidor being able to speak 17 languages, from a small clipping, dated August 6, Stanley Weston collection, University of Notre Dame libraries. The year is uncertain, but perhaps 1914. It is mentioned that the writer believed Joe was still a boxing instructor at the Pittsburgh Athletic Club; "The San Francisco Journalism of I.N. Choynski, He Flatters None and Displeases Many," 1997; *Los Angeles Times*, August 11, 1942.

[24] www.maritimeheritage.org/ports/naEastcoast/newyork.html

[25] "The San Francisco Journalism of I.N. Choynski, He Flatters None and Displeases Many," 1997; *American Israelite*, October 28, 1881, December 17, 1886.

[26] In January, 2008, Daniel Hartwig, Records Services Archivist of Manuscripts and Archives for Yale University advised me that he was unable to find any indication that any Choynski had attended Yale. Robert Singerman corresponded in the 1970s with Yale's Chief Research Archivist, Judith Schiff and in 1996 with Yale Archivist Nancy Lyon. Each combed the records covering 1846 to 1860 and reported that I.N. neither attended nor graduated from Yale. Director of Alumni Records for Yale, Wesley Polling, in 1978, validated the same findings.

[27] Bob Petersen, in personal correspondence with this author, 2009.

[28] "The San Francisco Journalism of I.N. Choynski, He Flatters None and Displeases Many," 1997.

[29] *Police Gazette*, May 7, 1921; *Report by Oregon Office of the Secretary of State*, 1899.

[30] "The San Francisco Journalism of I.N. Choynski, He Flatters None and Displeases Many," 1997; *San Francisco City Directory*, 1860; "San Francisco's Fighting Jew," 1974.

[31] United States Library of Congress, American Memory website; *Oakland Tribune*, March 26, 1904.

[32] "The San Francisco Journalism of I.N. Choynski, He Flatters None and Displeases Many," 1997; *Alta California*, August 30, 1863; Official document in possession of Al and Harriet Draper.

[33] *Jewish Voices of the California Gold Rush* by Ava Fran Kahn, 2002; "The San Francisco Journalism of I.N. Choynski, He Flatters None and Displeases Many," 1997.

[34] *Daily Alta California*, June 3, 1866, May 26, 1867, May 2, 1868; *San Francisco Chronicle*, November 19, 1867; I.N. Choynski letterhead, December 10, 1871; *Common Sense* by William N. Slocum, 1874; I.N.'s 1864 I.R.S. Tax Assessment shows he was taxed $2.00 for a piano.

[35] "The San Francisco Journalism of I.N. Choynski ...," 1997; 1874 *San Francisco City Directory* (R.L. Polk & Company); For details of the position of President of District Grand Lodge No. 4, see "San Francisco's Fighting Jew," 1974: The *Hebrew* (San Francisco), January 23, 1874, January 29, 1875; Janet Choynski Fleishhacker, Pioneer File, California Room, California State Library, Sacramento.

[36] *San Francisco Chronicle*, June 6, 1868; *Des Moines Daily News*, December 1, 1912; *Anaconda Standard*, December 8, 1912; *Booksellers of Early San Francisco*, 1953; *Rowell's American Newspaper Directory* by George P. Rowell & Company, 1887; "The San Francisco Journalism of I.N. Choynski ...," 1997.

[37] *The Annual Report of the Library Company of Philadelphia for the Year 1984* by Library Company of Philadelphia, 1985; Locations of bookstore are from Albert J. Draper; 1875 *San Francisco City Directory*; The ad for I.N.'s bookstore is from *The Magazine of American History with Notes and Queries* by John A.

Stevens, Benjamin F. Decosta and others, 1879.

[38] *Congressional Serial Set, Issue 1722* by U.S. Government Printing Office, 1887; for I.N. Choynski blaming railroad monopolies for the ruination of California, see "The San Francisco Journalism of I.N. Choynski, He Flatters None and Displeases Many," 1997.

[39] *Jewish Voices of the California Gold Rush* by Ava Fran Kahn, 2002.

[40] "Wayward Etchings, I.N. Choynski Visits Southern California, 1881," Robert Singerman and Elinor Grumet, *Western States Jewish Historical Quarterly*, 1979; I.N. was described by David S. Hirshberg and Robert Singerman; *Ellis Island to Ebbets Field* by Peter Levine, 1992; *Family, Business, and the San Francisco Community*, 1975; Julius Eckman letter to Harriett Choynski, September 3, 1872; *Western States Jewish Historical Quarterly*, October, 1974; Mrs. Edwin Coe, *Western States Jewish History*, April, 1992; freepages.genealogy.rootsweb.ancestry.com/~rawls/CCFWC/clubs2.html.

[41] *Booksellers of Early San Francisco* by Robert Ernest Cowan, 1953.

[42] "Wayward Etchings, I.N. Choynski Visits Southern California, 1881," 1979.

[43] "The San Francisco Journalism of I.N. Choynski, He Flatters None and Displeases Many," 1997.

[44] The *American Israelite* article, from Al and Harriet Draper, is dated circa November 27, 1885, as he referred to the Thanksgiving holiday and his mother, Rosalie, being 76 years old.

[45] "The San Francisco Journalism of I.N. Choynski ..." 1997; The 1886 *San Francisco Directory* lists the bookstore at 39 6th Street, while 33 6th is shown in *Farley's Reference Directory of the Booksellers, Stationers and Printers in California* by A.C. Farley, 1886; The 1889 location is from *Caspar's Directory of the American Book, News and Stationery Trade* by C.N. Caspar, 1889; For *Public Opinion*'s address, see the 1888 *Directory*.

[46] Unidentified newspaper article dated October 30, 1886, from Al and Harriet Draper.

[47] "The San Francisco Journalism of I.N. Choynski, He Flatters None and Displeases Many," 1997; The *Menorah* by B'nai B'rith, July-December 1899; *Family, Business, and the San Francisco Community*, 1975.

[48] Some sources, such as Janet, give Harriett's birthplace as London, England. Others, like data.jewishgen.org, as Liverpool, England; 1860 and 1870 United States Federal Censuses; *Proceedings of Annual Session* by B'nai B'rith, District number 4 Grand Lodge, 1864; *San Francisco Evening Bulletin*, August 29, 1857; ancestry.com, ark.cdlib.org.

[49] *Jews in Nevada* by John P. Marschall, 2008; *Our City, The Jews of San Francisco* by Irena Narell, 1981; Magnes Collection of Jewish Art and Life, University of California, Berkeley; January 12, 1924 *San Francisco Bulletin*, "Petter Is Better Than Girl Of Old, Is Belief." " 'The modern flapper, despite her petting parties, her hip flask, and motor freedom, is *not so worse*,' in the opinion of Harriet Ashim Choynski, member of the first class to graduate from the San Francisco General High School in '61. Mrs. Choynski, who is 82 and still spry, rises to defend the San Francisco girl from the charge of wholesale petting which has burst out of a clear blue sky. 'They are no worse today than they were in 1861,' says she. 'The youngsters of today seem different because we are living in new conditions. But at heart they are the same. The world is getting better – not worse. Where now the great prohibition is *petting*, in 1861 it was other things ... I used to be reproached for spending too much time on clothes. The big fuss then was whether or not a girl was going to be ruined by going to high school. I am proud to say that San Francisco decided against that nationwide prejudice and pioneered in girl's education.' Mrs. Choynski marched with 1,000 other children in San Francisco's first May Day parade in 1853. (She) is the mother of Herbert Choynski, San Francisco attorney, Maurice Choynski, Chicago movie theatre magnate; Joseph Choynski heavyweight fighter; Edwin Choynski, San Francisco broker, and Miriam Choynski, now in Paris." She passed away the following year. David Fleishhacker told me, "Concerning the conflicting stories of the Ashim family coming west (1) fighting Indians on the overland route or (2) coming via Panama. I think both are true: I theorize that the recollection of the trip west overland was of the trip TO Kentucky, which was almost as far west as one could go at the time, the Mississippi being the U.S. boundary until 1848. Of course, that would not explain the recollection of events happening near Salt Lake City, but I take that part of it with more than a grain ... of salt."

[50] "Harriett Ashim Choynski, An 1850 Western Arrival" by Norton B. Stern – *Western States Jewish History*, April 1992; *Chronicles of Emanu-El* by Jacob Voorsanger, 1900; *The Jews of California, from the Discovery of Gold Until 1880* by Dr. Rudolf Glanz, 1960.

[51] *Charleston Courier*, April 19, 1847; *Charleston Mercury*, September 22, 1858.

[52] *Weekly Gleaner*, March 19, 1858; *Jews in Nevada* by John P. Marschall, 2008 has the Ashim store located in 1862 and 1863, above Aaron Fleishhacker's General Store at 202 North Carson Street, Carson City. David Fleishhacker said "this cannot be correct, for the store did not have a 2nd floor, apparent from a later photograph. It would not likely be located at 202 North Carson Street because that is ... where Aaron's store was located, but at the time, advertisements put it at Carson and Musser streets."

[53] 1862 Nevada State Census; dmla.clan.lib.nv.us/docs/nsla/archives/appeal/a-an.htm, *San Francisco Bulletin*, August 25, 1873; *Carson Appeal* Newspaper Index, 1800s; *Jews in Nevada* by John P.

Marschall, 2008, Unidentified June 1, 1878 Nevada paper; rootsweb.com/~nvgenweb/nvtax.txt; Early tax lists for Nevada Territory, beginning 1862; For the Fleishhackers as bankers, see *Financial California, an Historical Review* by Le Roy Armstrong, J.O. Denny, 1980; rainesmarket.com, robertwynn.com/Eureka.htm; *Jewish Women Pioneering the Frontier Trail* by Jeanne E. Abrams, 2006; *Eureka and Its Resources* by H. Keller, 1879; Nevada Historical Society Quarterly, Spring 1982; *Eureka Daily Republican*, October 19, 1877; *Eureka Sentinel*, April 20(?), 1879; *Salt Lake Tribune*, April 26, 1879.

[54] *The Great Register of San Francisco*, 1867; JewishGen Online Worldwide Burial Registry (JOWBR); *Daily Alta California*, May 29, 1886; The *Nevada State Journal*, 1870-1900, shows Rebecca marrying Duncan McNichol on October 3, 1871 in Eureka, Nevada; Union County, South Carolina records, September 17, 1850; Charleston, *South Carolina 1855 Directory*; *Daily Alta California, San Francisco Call*, August 19, 1888; worldconnect.rootsweb.com; United States Federal Censuses, 1860, 1870, 1880, 1900.

[55] *Jews in Nevada* by John P. Marschall, 2008, and several other sources.

[56] *Darwin, California* by Robert F. Palazzo, 1996; *Jews in Nevada* by John P. Marschall, 2008; *Silver Stampede* by Neill Compton Wilson, 1971; www.croatians.com/french.htm; *Yugoslav Survey of California, Nevada, Arizona, and the South, 1800-1900* by Adam S. Eterovich, 1971; *Yugoslavs in Nevada, 1859-1900* by Adam S. Eterovich, 1973; *The Croatian Immigrants in America* by George J. Prpic, 1971; members.aol.com/dierdorff/darwin/dar-1.html;

[57] jwfgenresearch.com/SFCall/6900-05.htm, *Call* vital records for 1869-1891; Barach's death date is from JewishGen Online Worldwide Burial Registry (Ancestry.com) and California Genealogical Society (CGS) Probate Index; *San Francisco Evening Bulletin*, April 26, 1859, December 24, 1863, June 24, 1864; 1861 *San Francisco City Directory*; *Daily Alta California*, April 28, 1860, December 7, 1860, January 17, 1862; Death dates of Rachel and Morris Ashim, see *Proceedings of Annual Session, District Grand Lodge* by B'nai B'rith District Number 4 Grand Lodge, 1864; data.jewishgen.org.

[58] Family, Business, and the San Francisco Community, 1975; *Daily Alta California*, May 2, 1861; San Francisco Historic Record and Genealogy Bulletin, April 1965; "Harriett Ashim Choynski, an 1850 Western Arrival" by Norton B. Stern – *Western States Jewish History*, April 1992; *Western States Jewish History* lists their first home at 237 Tehama Street; Various editions of *Daily Alta California* and *San Francisco Bulletin*, dating from January 30, 1863 to January 12, 1864.

[59] For the death notice of Rachel Ashim, see *San Francisco Evening Bulletin*, December 24, 1863; skepticfiles.org; *San Francisco Call*, Jan. 25, 1899, Jan. 28, 1899; *Brooklyn Daily Eagle*, Jan. 26, 1899; *Booksellers of Early San Francisco* by Robert Ernest Cowan, 1953; ancestry.com.

[60] "The San Francisco Journalism of I.N. Choynski, He Flatters None and Displeases Many" by Robert Singerman, 1997; *Family, Business, and the San Francisco Community*, 1975.

[61] *A Debonair Scoundrel* by Lately Thomas, 1962; *San Jose Mercury Herald*, January 17, 1918; *New York Supplement, 1906* by West Publishing Co.

[62] *Family, Business, and the San Francisco Community*, 1975; Interview with Janet's daughter, Delia Ehrlich by Elisabeth Laurence, *San Francisco Examiner*, February 17, 2007.

[63] *Daily Alta California*, January 10, 1889; *San Francisco Call*, May 13, 1900, May 22, 1900, October 26, 1900, June 20, 1901; *Oakland Tribune*, November 6, 1900, June 20, 1901; *San Francisco Evening News*, June 21, 1901; *San Francisco Chronicle*, July 16, 1901, July 25, 1901.

[64] *Family, Business, and the San Francisco Community*, 1975; Harriet and Albert Draper.

[65] Albert and Harriet Draper; Various years, United States Federal Census; *San Francisco Directory*, 1891-1892: Morris Choynski, Clerk; *San Francisco Directory*, 1909: Morris Choynski, Attorney At Law, 1434 Merchants Exchange. Residence, 404 Ashbury (the *Directory* may have mistaken attorney Milton Choynski for Maurice/Morris); 1909 Chicago City Directory; *Nickelodeon Theatres and Their Music* by Q. David Bowers, 1986; "Jazz Age Chicago, Movie Theater Index," chicago.urban-history.org/sites/theaters; *The Moving Picture World, October – December 1916* by Moving Picture Exhibitors' Association, October 7, 1916: "Film Men Firm Against Censorship" by W. Stephen Bush.

[66] *Moving Picture World, July 29, 1916, January-March 1917* by Moving Picture Exhibitors' Association; *Reports of Cases Determined in the Appellate Courts of Illinois* by Illinois Appellate Court, 1917; www.ilsos.gov/GenealogyMWeb/IDPHDeathSearchServlet, Illinois Death Index, 1916-1950.

[67] Various *San Francisco Directories*; *Members of Olympic Club, By-laws and List of Members of the Olympic Club*, March 1, 1913; Correspondence with Harriet and Albert Draper, September 2009.

*** For more on Joe Choynski's family, see "Joe Choynski's Combative Clan" by Christopher J. LaForce, *Western States Jewish History*, Volume 46, Number 1, Fall 2013.

Round 2:

[1] This was attested to by I.N. in his writings for the *American Israelite*, *Weekly Gleaner* and other publications. Joe verified the visits by various celebrities and writers, in "I Fought 'Em All," *Fight Stories*,

June-July 1938, *Ring* magazine, December 1932, "California's Golden Age of Boxing" by Joe Choynski; for Joaquin Miller's description, see *The Biographical Review of Prominent Men and Women of the Day* by Thomas W. Herringshaw, Benno Loewy, 1889.

² *Mark Twain, A Life* by Ron Powers, 2005; *San Francisco, a Guide to the Bay and Its Cities*, 1940 and 1973; *Cosmopolitans, a Social and Cultural History of the Jews of the San Francisco Bay Area* by Fred Rosenbaum, 2009. I.N. Choynski's 1864 I.R.S. Tax Assessment shows he was taxed $2.00 for a piano, residence 540 Mission; undated clipping from the Choynski file in the newspaper morgue.

³ *Syracuse Daily Standard*, October 7, 1887; *Wheeling Sunday Register*, October 9, 1887; The Robert Schalkenbach Foundation presents *Who Was Henry George?* by Agnes George de Mille, January 1979. She is the grand-daughter of Henry George. Also, wikipedia.org and gettysburg.cdmhost.com. David Fleishhacker told me in 2012, "The story that Henry George composed his book in the back of Choynski's store has no basis besides family recollection and is probably an exaggeration. He certainly might have known I.N. ... but Singerman's exhaustive chase of this rumor got nowhere. The same, I believe, is true of the allegation that I.N spoke 16 or 17 languages. No evidence of this except family memory, which could derive from an impressionable child recalling a father say 'hello' or 'thank you' in many languages. That's my theory, nothing more."

⁴ Letter from Joe Choynski to I.N. Choynski, June, 1878, sent to the author by David Chesanow.

⁵ A letter from Edwin Walker Choynski to Joe Choynski dated May, 1891, a photocopy of which was sent to me by Albert and Harriet Draper in 2008. The information regarding Aunty and Uncle Walker also came from Albert and Harriet Draper in 2008.

⁶ 1880 United States Federal Census; Janet Fleishhacker, May 24, 1964 letter to Rudolf Glanz, on family tradition that I.N. Choynski had a daily breakfast of champagne and gefilte fish. YIVO Institute For Jewish Research Archives, Rudolf Glanz Papers, Record Group 1133.

⁷ An 1883 *Public Opinion* article by "Maftir" (I.N. Choynski) reveals their residential address is still 127 O'Farrell, whereas the 1884 Federal Census shows them at 1209 Golden Gate Avenue.

⁸ According to Al and Harriet Draper, the Choynski family story is that Edwin Walker Choynski/Coe started school at Lincoln and finished at Lowell. Information on the schools attended by Maurice and Miriam is taken from *29th Annual Report of the Superintendent of Public Schools for the School Year Ending June 30th, 1882* by the Department of Public Schools, City and County of San Francisco, 1882.

⁹ *San Francisco Chronicle*, September 25, 1897.

¹⁰ "I Fought 'Em All" by Joe Choynski, June-July 1938; *Waterloo Courier*, December 6, 1919.

¹¹ Ned Goldschmidt article, a 1927 *Jewish Tribune, Jewish Boxers Hall of Fame* by Ken Blady, 1988.

¹² "I Fought 'Em All" by Joe Choynski, *Fight Stories*, June-July 1938; *Baltimore Sun*, March 15, 1897.

¹³ Ibid.

¹⁴ 1874, 1876-1890 *San Francisco City Directories, McKenny's Pacific Coast Directory*, 1880-81; "San Francisco's Fighting Jew," 1974; Ron Jackson suggested in a 2008 telephone conversation that this might have been Graney's blacksmith shop. For information on Graney's father, see *California and Californians, Volume 4* by Dr. Rockwell D. Hunt, 1926, 1930.

¹⁵ *Daily Messenger* (Canandaigua, New York), February 15, 1922.

¹⁶ "I Fought 'Em All" by Joe Choynski, *Fight Stories*, 1930; "The Days of Finish Fights," *Adelaide Advertiser*, January 7, 1927.

¹⁷ *Brownsville Daily Herald*, September 16, 1892; *Syracuse Herald*, August 8, 1913; *The Roar of the Crowd* by James J. Corbett with Robert G. Anderson, 1925; *Freeman's Journal and Daily Commercial Advertiser* (England), but, according to the article, originally taken from a publication called *Sport Today*.

¹⁸ "I Fought 'Em All" by Joe Choynski, *Fight Stories*, June-July 1938; The Corbett interview is from the *Freeman's Journal and Daily Commercial Advertiser*.

¹⁹ *Syracuse Herald*, June 15, 1917; *Daily Alta California*, May 5, 1887; *Our Jim, the World's Champion* by Crown Publishing Company, 1892, thanks to Rob Snell.

²⁰ *The Roar of the Crowd* by James J. Corbett with Robert G. Anderson, 1925.

²¹ "I Fought 'Em All" by Joe Choynski, *Fight Stories*, June-July 1938.

²² *San Francisco Morning Call*, April 12, 1892; *Daily Alta California*, March 24, 1887.

²³ *Police Gazette*, July 22, 1887, *Daily Alta California*, July 23, 1887.

²⁴ *Police Gazette*, December 15, 1888.

²⁵ *Police Gazette, Daily Alta California*, September 8, 1887.

²⁶ "Tubal Cain" was, according to various pseudo-biblical works, the 7th-generation offspring of Adam's son Cain. Essentially a blacksmith, a forger of iron and brass, Tubal-Cain was said to have great physical strength and was a master of martial, or fighting, arts. Tubal, like Cain and many of his ancestors, was said to be known for "acting unjustly, and doing injury for gain." This description is from Flavius Josephus, among other sources. "Tubal Cain" has often been indicated as the "secret password"

of a Master, or 3rd -Degree, Freemason. I.N. Choynski had been a Freemason.

[27] *Transactions of the 38th & 39th Annual Reunions of the Oregon Pioneer Association, 1910 & 1911*, published 1914 from diaries 1852-54; *Conversations With Bullwhackers, Muleskinners, Pioneers, Prospectors, '49ers, Indian Fighters, Trappers, Ex-barkeepers, Authors, Preachers, Poets & Near Poets & All Sorts & Conditions of Men: Voices of the Oregon Territory* by Fred Lockley and Mike Helm, 1981.

[28] *Daily Alta California*, October 8, 1887, November 26, 1887; *Daily Alta California*, May 28, 1888.

[29] *Police Gazette*, week of November 29, 1887; *Daily Alta California*, November 30, 1887; *St. Louis Dispatch*, November 15, 1889.

[30] *Police Gazette*, November 27, 1887; *Daily Alta California*, November 30, 1887 and the *St. Louis* (Missouri) *Dispatch*, November 15, 1889, reminiscing about the November 1887 fight. Weights for the fight were also given by the *Bismarck Daily Tribune*, January 5, 1915.

[31] "I Fought 'Em All" by Joe Choynski, *Fight Stories*, June-July 1938.

[32] *Daily Alta California*, February 15, 1888, April 14, 1888; *James J. Corbett, a Biography of the Heavyweight Boxing Champion and Popular Theater Headliner* by Armond Fields, 2001.

[33] *Daily Alta California*, May 28, 1888.

[34] *Sydney Referee*, July 10, July 17, July 24, 1918; *San Francisco Examiner*, March 3, 1889; Photos of Choynski and Jackson sparring at Barney Farley's, circa March, 1889 by Eclipse Studios, 5 Stockton Street, San Francisco, from Joe Choynski's personal collection – JO Sports, Inc.; *Daily Alta California*, June 27, 1888; *Kings of the Queensberry Realm* by W.W. Naughton, 1902.

[35] *Daily Alta California*, July 21, 1888, August 8, 1888, August 14, 1888, August 15, 1888.

[36] *Daily Alta California*, September 29, 1888.

[37] *Alta California, San Francisco Chronicle*, October 27, 1888; London *Mirror of Life*, September 12, 1896; *Fresno Bee Republican*, January 28, 1944.

[38] *Daily Alta California*, October 29, 1888; *In The Ring with James J. Corbett* by Adam J. Pollack, 2007.

Round 3:

[1] *San Francisco Chronicle*, November 15, 1888.

[2] *Police Gazette*, December 15, 1888; "The Days of Finish Fights," *Adelaide Advertiser*, February 10, 1927, Chapter 4. The December 15 *Police Gazette* called Joe's seconds Paddy Gorman and Young Granger, although the November 15 *Alta California* called the latter second "George Greaney" and the *San Francisco Chronicle* of the same date referred to this handler as "Smithy."

[3] "I Fought 'Em All" by Joe Choynski, *Fight Stories*, June-July 1938; *Jewish Boxers Hall of Fame* by Ken Blady, 1988; "San Francisco's Fighting Jew," 1974, William M. Kramer and Norton B. Stern's interview with Florence C. Dibert Coe.

[4] *Daily Alta California, San Francisco Chronicle*, November 15, 1888; *Police Gazette*, November, 1888.

[5] *Daily Alta California*, November 30, 1888; *The Legendary Mizners* by Alva Johnston, 1953.

[6] *Daily Alta California*, December 27, 1888.

[7] *Daily Alta California*, February 25, 1889. Joe Choynski did call the Frank Glover fight his first in the pro ranks, in a November, 1894 article in the *Philadelphia Item*. Glover's real name is given in his obituary in the *Chicago Herald*, September 23, 1892. *Francisco Daily Evening Bulletin*, February 27, 1889; "I Fought 'Em All" by Joe Choynski, *Fight Stories*, June-July 1938.

[8] *Daily Alta California*, February 26, 1889.

[9] *Daily Alta California, San Francisco Call, Fresno Daily Republican*, February 27, 1889; *Police Gazette*, February, 1889.

[10] *Police Gazette*, March 30, 1889.

[11] *Fresno Daily Republican*, March 14, 1889.

[12] *The Freeman's Journal and Daily Commercial Advertiser, San Francisco Examiner*, April 10, 1889.

[13] *The Tumult and the Shouting, My Life in Sport* by Grantland Rice, 1954.

[14] *Gentleman Jim* by Nat Fleischer, 1942; *The Roar of the Crowd* by James J. Corbett with Robert G. Anderson, 1925.

[15] *The Roar of the Crowd* by James J. Corbett with Robert G. Anderson, 1925, various other sources.

[16] *Alta California*, May 14, 1889.

[17] "I Fought 'Em All" by Joe Choynski, *Fight Stories*, June-July 1938; *San Francisco Examiner & Chronicle*, August 8, 1976, "One of the Great Ones," by Tro Harper; *The Roar of the Crowd* by James J. Corbett with Robert G. Anderson, 1925.

[18] *Daily Alta California*, May 13, 1889; *San Francisco Chronicle*, May 27, 1889, May 29, 1889.

[19] "I Fought 'Em All" by Joe Choynski, *Fight Stories*, June-July 1938; *Sunset* magazine by Southern Pacific Company, Passenger Department, December 1925 - January 1926, Volumes 54 & 55; *The Making of Champions in California* by De Witt Van Court, 1926.

[20] *San Francisco Daily Bulletin*, May 30, 1889; *Daily Alta California, San Francisco Chronicle*, May 31, 1889.

[21] *Daily Alta California*, May 31, 1889.

[22] *San Francisco Chronicle*, article undated but circa 1949; *High Points in Boxing's Long History: Choynski vs. Corbett, Jeff vs. Johnson by Harry B. Smith*; "I Fought 'Em All," *Fight Stories*, June-July 1938.

[23] *Roar of the Crowd* by James J. Corbett, Robert G. Anderson, 1925; *San Francisco Call*, May 11, 1897.

[24] *San Antonio Light and Gazette*, February 17, 1910; *San Jose Evening News*, December 11, 1916.

[25] *San Francisco Call*, May 11, 1897, June 29, 1913, May 31, 1897; *Daily Alta California, San Francisco Daily Evening Bulletin*, May 31, 1897; *Syracuse Herald*, June 25, 1917.

[26] *San Francisco Chronicle*, February 8, 1933.

[27] *San Francisco Evening Post, San Francisco Chronicle*, May 31, 1889.

[28] *Daily Alta California, San Francisco Daily* (Evening) *Bulletin*, May 30, 1889.

Round 4:

[1] *The Roar of the Crowd* by James J. Corbett with Robert G. Anderson, 1925; *San Francisco Post*, June 6, 1889; *Syracuse Herald*, June 27, 1917; *Des Moines Capital*, August 24, 1924.

[2] *Westways* magazine by Lawrence Clark Powell, *Automobile Club of Southern California*, January 1957; *San Francisco Chronicle*, June 6, 1889, February 8, 1933; *Sacramento Daily Record-Union*, October 10, 1884, October 29, 1884; *Woodland Daily Democrat*, September 14, 1894; *The Roar of the Crowd* by James J. Corbett with Robert G. Anderson, 1925, and "I Fought 'Em All" by Joe Choynski, *Fight Stories*, June-July 1938; *Tombstone Epitaph, Daily Alta California, San Francisco Chronicle, San Francisco Evening Post*, June 6, 1889; *Annual Report of the Chamber of Commerce of San Francisco, 1889*; *The Federal Reporter* by District of Columbia Court of Appeals, 1897; *Annual List of Merchant Vessels of the United States* by Department of Commerce, Bureau of Navigation, 1913; *The Legendary Mizners* by Alva Johnston, 1953.

[3] *San Jose Mercury Evening News, Oakland Evening Tribune*, June 5, 1889; *San Francisco Post*, June 5, 1889; *Woodland Daily Democrat*, September 14, 1894; *Syracuse Herald*, June 29, 1917; "One of the Great Ones" by Tro Harper, August 8, 1976 (from the *San Francisco Examiner and Chronicle*).

[4] *Westways* magazine by Lawrence Clark Powell; *Automobile Club of Southern California*, January 1957; *Washington Post*, November 28, 1909; In January 21, 1931 *Niagara Falls Gazette*, Tim McGrath claimed he was in Choynski's corner, and that Joe's two ounce gloves had been stolen by a souvenir hunter. He added that, when Corbett approached Choynski with $1,000 given him by Porter Ashe to bet with Joe, Mose Gunst shouted that he would cover the bet. As a giveaway, though, that Tim was somewhat of a fabricator, he also claimed that it was he, not "Nonpareil" Dempsey, who pleaded to Graney to throw in the sponge, causing Choynski to protest. McGrath said it was round 24, but this occurred in the 20th round. He quoted many things written over the years in various newspapers, many inaccurately.

[5] *Sunset* magazine by Southern Pacific Company, Passenger Department, December, 1925 - January 1926, Volumes 54 & 55.

[6] *San Francisco Call*, June 29, 1913; *Syracuse Herald*, August 8, 1913, June 29, 1917; *Decatur Review*, September 8, 1892; *Janesville Daily Gazette*, November 9, 1916; *The Roar of the Crowd* by James J. Corbett with Robert G. Anderson, 1925; "One of the Great Ones" by Tro Harper, August 8, 1976 (from the *San Francisco Examiner and Chronicle*).

[7] *Wilkes-Barre Times-Leader* of March 13, 1914; *Oakland Tribune*, March 19, 1914.

[8] *Oakland Tribune, San Francisco Daily Evening Bulletin, San Jose Mercury Evening News, San Francisco Evening Post, Daily Alta California, San Francisco Examiner*, June 5, 1889; *San Francisco Chronicle, Chicago Herald, Philadelphia Inquirer, Tombstone Epitaph, Daily Alta California, Fresno Daily Morning Republican*, June 6, 1889; *Police Gazette*, circa June 5, 1889, *Perry Daily Chief*, December 6, 1894; *San Antonio Gazette*, January 30, 1905; *Oxnard Daily Courier*, December 3, 1924; *The Roar of the Crowd* by James J. Corbett with Robert G. Anderson, 1925; *Chillicothe Constitution-Tribune*, January 12, 1931; *San Francisco Chronicle*, February 8, 1933; "I Fought 'Em All" by Joe Choynski, *Fight Stories*, June-July 1938; *San Francisco Chronicle*, January 28, 1940; *Police Gazette*, January, 1943; *Westways* magazine, January, 1957, undated *Police Gazette*, circa 1969; *Crown of Thorns* by Norman Giller and Neil Duncanson, 1992.

[9] *Sport Tales and Anecdotes* by Frank G. Menke, 1953.

[10] *Manitoba* (Winnipeg, Canada) *Morning Free Press*, May 17, 1911; *Syracuse Herald*, August 8, 1913.

[11] *San Francisco Chronicle*, undated article, circa 1949, Harry Shaffer, Antiquities of the Prize Ring.

[12] "One of the Great Ones" by Tro Harper, August 8, 1976, (*San Francisco Examiner and Chronicle*).

[13] *Evening Democrat* (Warren, Pennsylvania), March 21, 1895; *Police Gazette*, June 5, 1919; *Gentleman Jim* by Nat Fleischer, 1942; *Sport Tales and Anecdotes* by Frank G. Menke, 1953.

[14] *Oakland Tribune*, March 19, 1914.

[15] *Jewish Boxers Hall of Fame* by Ken Blady, 1988; *Daily Alta California*, June 6, June 8, 1889; "I Fought 'Em All" by Joe Choynski, *Fight Stories*, June-July 1938.

[16] *San Francisco Chronicle*, June 7, 1889; *Daily Alta California*, June 10, 1889; *Syracuse Herald*, July 10, 1917; *Des Moines Capital*, September 7, 1924; *Westways* magazine, January, 1957.

[17] *San Francisco Call*, May 21, 1891; *San Francisco Chronicle*, June 7, 1889; *Duluth News-Tribune*, August 12, 1921

[18] *Sacramento Sunday Union*, June 9, 1889; *Daily Alta California*, June 20, 1889.

[19] *Daily Alta California*, June 28, 1889.

[20] *Daily Alta California*, July 13, 1889.

[21] *San Francisco Chronicle*, July 15, 1889; *Daily Alta California*, *Fresno Daily Republican*, July 16, 1889; *Dallas* (Texas) *Morning News*, March 9, 1933.

[22] *The Roar of the Crowd* by James J. Corbett with Robert G. Anderson, 1925; "I Fought 'Em All" by Joe Choynski, *Fight Stories*, June-July 1938.

Round 5:

[1] *Daily Alta California*, August 3, 1889.

[2] *San Francisco Chronicle*, *Daily Alta California*, August 7, 1889. In the *Alta California*, the Cribb Club members indicated they would soon be changing the name of the club to the Eureka Athletic Club.

[3] *Daily Alta California*, August 20, 1889, September 25, 1889, October 15, 1889, October 17, 1889; *San Francisco Chronicle*, September 25, 1889, October 7, 1889.

[4] *Daily Alta California*, October 26, November 17, November 25, November 27, 1889.

[5] *Daily Alta California*, December 1, 1889.

[6] *San Francisco Chronicle*, December 24, December 25, 1889; *Daily Alta California*, December 21, 1889.

[7] *Portland Oregonian*, December 27, 1889; *James J. Corbett ... by Armond Fields, 2001.

[8] *Philadelphia Inquirer*, January 5, 1890; *Daily Alta California*, January 22, 1890. This newspaper contradicted itself, first stating the fight was scheduled for eight rounds, then, for 10 rounds.

[9] *San Francisco Chronicle*, February 11, 1890; *Milwaukee Evening Wisconsin*, February 14, 1890.

[10] *San Francisco Chronicle*, *Sacramento Daily Record-Union*, February 21, 1890; "I Fought 'Em All," *Fight Stories*, June-July 1938.

[11] *Daily Alta California*, February 22, 1890.

[12] *San Francisco Chronicle*, February 27, 1890; *Alta California*, March 8, 1890, March 22, 1890. The March 8 *Alta* said bail was set at $2,000.

[13] *Sacramento Daily Record-Union*, February 27, 1890; *Alta California*, *San Francisco Chronicle*, March 25, 1890; *Chicago Inter-Ocean*, March 27, 1890.

[14] *Daily Alta California*, March 25, 1890; *San Francisco Evening Bulletin*, *Chicago Inter-Ocean*, *Sacramento Daily Record-Union*, *Chicago Herald*, March 27, 1890; Unknown paper (*Police Gazette?*), March 28, 1890.

[15] *Daily Alta California*, April 6, 1890, May 5, 1890; *St. Louis Republic*, April 1, 1890.

[16] *Daily Alta California*, April 26, *Newark* (Ohio) *Daily Advocate*, April 28, 1890.

[17] "The Days of Finish Fights," *Manitoba* (Winnipeg, Canada) *Free Press*, January 8, 1927; "I Fought 'Em All," *Fight Stories*, June-July 1938.

[18] *Louisville Commercial*, November 21, 1898.

[19] *Daily Alta California*, May 12, 1890; *New Orleans Times-Democrat*, January 16, 1891. Special thanks to Adam J. Pollack for this source information; also, *Lanky Bob* by K.R. Robinson, 2008.

[20] *Daily Alta California*, May 24, 1890; *San Francisco Morning Call*, May 25, 1890; *Omaha Daily Bee*, May 27, 1890.

[21] *San Francisco Morning Call*, *San Francisco Chronicle*, *Daily Alta California*, *Omaha Daily Bee*, *Rocky Mountain News*, May 27, 1890.

[22] *Kansas City Star*, March 30, 1891, and other sources.

[23] "The Days of Finish Fights," *Manitoba Free Press*, January 8, 1927; "I Fought 'Em All," *Fight Stories*, June-July 1938.

[24] *Daily Alta California*, June 2, 1890, June 30, 1890, July 8, 1890; *Oakland Tribune*, June 14, 1890; *Wheeling Sunday Register*, June 15, 1890.

[25] *San Francisco Chronicle*, July 8, July 10, 1890; *San Francisco Call*, *Daily Alta California*, July 10, 1890.

[26] *Daily Alta California*, July 18, 1890, July 19, 1890, July 26, 1890, August 13, 1890; *San Francisco Bulletin*, July 22, 1890, July 26, 1890, August 12, 1890.

[27] *Boston Globe*, July 29, 1890; *San Francisco Morning Call*, August 4, 1890.

[28] "The Days of Finish Fights," January 8, 1927, *Manitoba Free Press*; "I Fought 'Em All," *Fight Stories*, June-July 1938.

[29] *Alta California*, August 7, 1890; *San Francisco Call*, August 9, 1890; *New Zealand Truth*, April 11, 1914; for more on Captain Morse, see *The Earth Girdled* by Thomas De Witt Talmage, 1896; *Ambassadors in Pinstripes: the Spalding World Baseball Tour and the Birth of the American Empire* by Thomas W. Zeiler, 2006.

[30] *San Francisco Chronicle*, August 14, 1890.

[31] www.wrestlingclassics.com/wawli/REDUXNos.31-40.html, Wikipedia article on Evan Lewis.

Round 6:

[1] *Report on Internal Commerce of the United States*, United States Bureau of Statistics, 1891; freepages.genealogy.rootsweb.ancestry.com/~nzbound/zealandia1876.htm; theshipslist.com/ships/lines/oceanic.htm; *Daily Alta California, San Francisco Chronicle, San Francisco Morning Call*, August 24, 1890; *Daily Bulletin* (Honolulu, Hawaii), August 30, September 1, 1890; *Hawaiian Gazette*, September 2, 1890; *San Francisco Call*, September 17, September 30, 1890; November, 1894 edition of *Philadelphia Item*; "The Days of Finish Fights," *Manitoba Free Press*, January 8, 1927; freepages.genealogy.rootsweb.ancestry.com/~nzbound/zealandia1876.htm; *Zealandia* ship's manifest, dated September 20, 1890.

[2] "The Days of Finish Fights," *Manitoba Free Press*, January 8, 1927; *Chicago Daily Inter-Ocean*, September 26, 1891.

[3] "I Fought 'Em All" by Joe Choynski, *Fight Stories*, June-July 1938.

[4] *Heroes of the Fancy* by Arnold Thomas, 1999.

[5] "I Fought 'Em All," *Fight Stories*, June-July 1938; *Melbourne Sportsman*, September 24, 1890.

[6] *New Zealand Truth*, September 28, 1890; *Lanky Bob* by K.R. Robinson, 2008.

[7] *Maitland Mercury*, November 29, 1890.

[8] *New Zealand Truth*, January 29, 1916, August 26, 1916; *Peter Jackson* by Bob Petersen, 2011. There were four Thompson brothers (sons of Samuel Solomon, of London, England): Barney, Jack, Joe and Phin. They were noted bookmakers, boxing and sportsmen. For more, see *New Zealand Truth*, April 11, 1914; Australian Dictionary of Biography, Joseph Thompson.

[9] www.easystreetretreat.com.au/australianroyalty; Boxing Records at www.boxrec.com

[10] "The Days of Finish Fights," *Manitoba Free Press*, January 8, 1927; undated clipping from an unknown, contemporary newspaper; clipping from Harry Shaffer.

[11] *San Francisco Chronicle*, November 26, 1890; *New Zealand Truth*, November 30, 1890; *Grey River Argus*, December 16, 1890; *Wellington Post*, December 22, 1890; *Philadelphia Inquirer*, December 23, 1890; *Miami Leader, Sydney Referee*, December 26, 1890; *Police Gazette*, January 24, 1891.

[12] *Wellington Evening Post*, December 22, 1890.

[13] *Wellington Evening Post*, December 23, 1890.

[14] Undated clipping from an unknown contemporary newspaper; from Harry Shaffer.

[15] *Wanganui* (New Zealand) *Herald*, December 31, 1890.

[16] *Alta California*, September 26, 1890; "The San Francisco Journalism of I.N. Choynski ...," 1997.

[17] *San Francisco Morning Call*, January 15, 1891, January 18, 1891.

[18] *San Francisco Morning Call*, January 15, 1891.

[19] *Barrier Miner*, January 11, 1891; *San Francisco Morning Call*, January 18, 1891. The *Call* also quoted a contemporary *Sydney Referee* article, regarding Goddard's fighting style.

[20] A Special Thanks to Tony Barton of Australia for this information. His uncle is the grandson of Joe Goddard and has in his possession Goddard's birth certificate (now posted on Wikipedia), in addition to other documentation and family anecdotes.

[21] *Australian Star* (Sydney, Australia), February 10, 1891; *Chicago Tribune*, May 9, 1892.

[22] *New Zealand Truth*, February 10, 1891; *Barrier Miner, Melbourne Sportsman*, February 11, 1891.

[23] *New Zealand Truth*, February 10, 1891; *Barrier Miner, Melbourne Sportsman, St. Louis Post-Dispatch, Sydney Referee*, February 11, 1891; *Brisbane Courier*, February 12, 1891; *Wanganui Herald*, February 21, 1891; *South Carolina State, Tacoma Daily News*, March 20, 1891; *Johannesburg Star*, March 23, 1923; *In The Days of the Giants* by William J. Doherty, 1931; "I Fought 'Em All" by Joe Choynski, *Fight Stories*, June-July 1938; undated, contemporary edition of the *Sydney Referee* from Joe Choynski's scrap-book, within the article; "The Days of Finish Fights," *Manitoba Free Press*, January 15, 1927.

[24] Undated article, Harry Shaffer, from unknown February 1891 paper, most likely the (Boston, Massachusetts) *Police News*. For the alleged Goddard quote, *Lincoln Daily Star*, October 29, 1917.

[25] *St. Louis Post-Dispatch, San Francisco Morning Call, St. Paul Daily Globe*, March 20, 1891.

[26] *San Francisco Chronicle*, April 18, 1891.

[27] *Wellington Evening Post*, May 15, 1891.

[28] *St. Louis Post-Dispatch*, May 25, 1891.

[29] *Wanganui Herald*, May 22, 1891.

[30] *Melbourne Sportsman*, May 25, 1891.

[31] *Melbourne Sportsman*, May 25, 1891; *Oakland Tribune*, May 26, 1891; *Melbourne Sportsman, San Francisco Chronicle*, May 27, 1891; *Police News*, June 6, July 25, 1891; *Police Gazette*, June, 1891.

[32] *Melbourne Sportsman*, June 9, 1891; *Heroes of the Fancy* by Arnold Thomas, 1999.

[33] "I Fought 'Em All," *Fight Stories*, June-July 1938; "The Days of Finish Fights," *Manitoba Free Press*, January 15, 1927; *South Australian Register, Barrier Miner*, June 22, 1891; *Barrier Miner*, June 22, 1891; *Melbourne Sportsman*, June 24, 1891; *Australian Town and Country Journal*, June 27, 1891.

[34] "The Days of Finish Fights," *Manitoba Free Press*, January 15, 1927.

[35] The *Ring* (magazine), April, 1943.

[36] Weights given by *Sydney Referee*, July 22, 1891 and *Wanganui Herald*, August 8, 1891; *Sydney Referee*, July 22, 1891 said Choynski's cornermen were Sam Fitzpatrick, Jack Fuller and Jack Bateman, while *Melbourne Sportsman*, July 20, 1891 indicated them as the Costello brothers and Harry Thompson. *South Australian* (Adelaide) *Register* also said the seconds were Martin "Buffalo" and J. Costello; *Centralia Enterprise and Tribune*, July 25, 1891.

[37] *Melbourne Sportsman*, July 20, 1891; *Melbourne* (Australia) *Argus*, July 21, 1891; *Sydney Referee, Morning Olympian, St. Louis Post-Dispatch*, July 22, 1891; *South Australian Register*, July 23, 1891; *Centralia Enterprise and Tribune*, July 25, 1891; *New Zealand Truth*, July 26, 1891; *Wellington Evening Post*, July 28, 1891; *Wanganui Herald*, August 8, 1891; *Dallas Morning News, San Francisco Morning Call*, September 6, 1891; *San Francisco Chronicle*, September 7, 1891.

[38] "I Fought 'Em All" by Joe Choynski, *Fight Stories*, June-July 1938.

[39] *Reno Evening Gazette*, August 6, 1891; *San Francisco Bulletin, New Zealand Observer and Free Lance*, August 22, 1891; *Chicago Daily Inter-Ocean*, September 6, 1891.

[40] *Barrier Miner*, August 20, 1891, August 24, 1891; *Adelaide Advertiser*, August 28, 1891.

[41] *Dallas Morning News*, August 25, 1891; London (England) *Sporting Life*, August 26, 1891.

[42] *Dallas Morning News*, September 6, 1891; *Morning Olympian, San Francisco Chronicle*, October 3, 1891; *Auckland Star*, October 9, 1891; *New Zealand Observer*, October 17, 1891; *Morning Olympian*, October 31, 1891.

[43] *San Francisco Examiner*, October 30, 1891.

[44] *San Francisco Morning Call*, October 31, 1891.

[45] *John L. Sullivan, the Career of the First Gloved Heavyweight Champion* by Adam J. Pollack, 2006.

[46] "The Days of Finish Fights," *Manitoba Free Press*, January 15, 1927; "I Fought 'Em All" by Joe Choynski, *Fight Stories*, June-July 1938; "Joe the Giant Killer," *Boxing and Wrestling* magazine, April, 1955; Wikipedia article on Malietoa Laupepa; *The Imbroglio in Samoa* by Henry C. Ide, *North American Review*, June 1899; guide2womenleaders.com/Samoa.htm, worldstatesmen.org/Samoa.html

Round 7:

[1] *San Francisco Evening Bulletin, San Francisco Chronicle, San Francisco Examiner*, October 30, 1891; *Wheeling Register*, October 31, 1891. All papers said the steamer arrived "yesterday," but the *Wheeling Register* was incorrect; *San Francisco Chronicle*, October 30, 1891.

[2] *Chicago Daily Inter-Ocean*, September 6, 1891; *Morning Olympian*, October 27, 1891; *San Francisco Morning Call*, October 31, 1891.

[3] *St. Louis Post-Dispatch*, November 12, 1891; *Boxing in San Francisco* by F. Daniel Somrack, 2005; *Jewish Boxers Hall of Fame* by Ken Blady, 1988; *San Francisco Examiner*, October 30, 1891.

[4] *Wheeling Register*, October 31, 1891; *San Francisco Morning Call*, October 31, November 5, 1891.

[5] *San Francisco Chronicle*, November 6, 1891; *San Francisco Call*, November 7, 1891.

[6] *San Francisco Morning Call*, November 25, 1891.

[7] *Morning Olympian*, November 25, 1891; *San Francisco Chronicle*, December 14, 1891; *Police News*, December 21, 1891; *Oakland Tribune*, December 10, 1910.

[8] Unknown paper, likely *Police Gazette* or *Police News*, December 17, 1891, from Harry Shaffer; *Rocky Mountain News*, December 18, 1891.

[9] Unknown publication from Harry Shaffer, December 17, 1891; *Rocky Mountain News, Colorado Sun, Daily Nevada State Journal, Denver Republican, Fresno Weekly Republican, San Francisco Morning Call*, unknown paper from Stanley Weston collection at Hesburgh Library, University of Notre Dame, December 18, 1891; *Galveston Daily News*, December 19, 1891; *Davenport Daily Leader*, December 20, 1891; *Police Gazette*, December 16, 1922; "The Days of Finish Fights," *Manitoba Free Press*, January 15, 1927; "I Fought 'Em All" by Joe Choynski, *Fight Stories*, June-July 1938.

[10] "The Days of Finish Fights," *Manitoba Free Press*, January 15, 1927; "I Fought 'Em All" by Joe Choynski, *Fight Stories*, June-July 1938; *San Francisco Examiner*, December 21, 1891; *John L. Sullivan and His America* by Michael T. Isenberg, 1988; *John L. Sullivan, The Career of the First Gloved Heavyweight Champion* by Adam J. Pollack, 2006; "Joe the Giant Killer," *Boxing and Wrestling* magazine, April, 1955.

[11] *Morning Olympian*, December 22, 1891; *Omaha Sunday World Herald*, January 17, 1892.

[12] *Philadelphia Inquirer*, January 20, 1892; *San Jose Mercury Evening News*, January 27, 1892.

[13] *San Francisco Morning Call*, October 21, 1890.

[14] *Milwaukee Evening Wisconsin*, January 6, 1892.

[15] *San Francisco Morning Call*, January 17, 1892. For Flanigan's support of Joe McAuliffe, see *San Francisco Morning Call*, September 21, 1890.

[16] *San Francisco Morning Call*, February 3, 1892, *Oregonian*, *San Francisco Morning Call*, February 5, 1892.

[17] *San Francisco Morning Call*, February 18, 1892; *San Francisco Chronicle*, February 19, 1892; *Morning Olympian*, February 27, 1892.

[18] *Morning Olympian*, February 27, 1892; "The Days of Finish Fights," *Manitoba Free Press*, January 15, 1927; "I Fought 'Em All," *Fight Stories*, June-July 1938; *New York Sun*, February 29, 1892, March 1, 1892; *In The Ring With Bob Fitzsimmons* by Adam J. Pollack, 2007.

[19] *New Orleans Daily Picayune*, *St. Paul Daily Globe*, March 3, 1892; *Topeka Weekly Capital*, March 10, 1892; *Philadelphia Inquirer*, March 14, 1892; *Newark* (Ohio) *Evening News*, April 27, 1892; *In The Ring With Bob Fitzsimmons* by Adam J. Pollack, 2007.

[20] *King News, an Autobiography* by Moses Koenigsberg, 1941.

[21] *Alaska Citizen*, December 2, 1912; *Duluth News-Tribune*, August 9, 1914; *Salt Lake Telegram*, November 4, 1917; *New Castle News*, November 22, 1917; *Oakland Tribune*, July 5, 1925; *Syracuse Herald-Journal*, February 15, 1943.

[22] *San Francisco Chronicle*, April 4, 1892, *Syracuse Herald*, November 20, 1917; *New Zealand Truth*, July 6, 1918; *Anaconda Standard*, January 26, 1922; *Brownsville Herald*, March 16, 1944; *Boxing and Wrestling*, September, 1956; *Lanky Bob* by K.R. Robinson, 2008; *The Fighting Blacksmith* by Gilbert Odd, 1976.

[23] "The Days of Finish Fights," *Manitoba Free Press*, January 15, 1927.

[24] *Davenport Sunday Leader*, March 6, 1892.

[25] *Cedar Rapids Evening Gazette*, *St. Louis Post-Dispatch*, March 4, 1892.

[26] *Cedar Rapids Evening Gazette*, *Morning Olympian*, *St. Louis Post-Dispatch*, *St. Paul Daily Globe*, March 5, 1892; *Davenport Sunday Leader*, March 6, 1892; *Waterloo Daily Courier*, March 8, 1892; "The Days of Finish Fights," *Manitoba Free Press*, January 22, 1927.

[27] *New Orleans Times-Democrat*, March 11, 1892; *In The Ring With Bob Fitzsimmons* by Adam J. Pollack, 2007; "The Days of Finish Fights," *Manitoba Free Press*, January 15, 1927; "I Fought 'Em All" by Joe Choynski, *Fight Stories*, June-July 1938.

[28] Correspondence with Mark Dunn, and *Chicago's Greatest Sportsman, Charles E. 'Parson' Davies* by Mark T. Dunn, 2011. It is the only biography to date, of this famous manager and sports figure.

[29] *The Political History of Chicago From 1837-1887* by M.L. Ahern, 1886; *The Biographical Review of Prominent Men and Women of the Day* by Thomas W. Herringshaw, Benno Loewy, 1889, (Decatur, Illinois) *Daily Republican*, June 13, 1895; *Denver Post*, January 11, 1907; *Salt Lake Telegram*, August 16, 1907; *Denver Times*, February 26, 1910 (an autobiography by Davies); *Washington Post*, September 25, 1910; *Atlanta Constitution*, April 23, 1916; *Cincinnati Times-Star* obituary by William A. Phelon, dated June 28, 1920; *Bridgeport Telegram* obituary, dated June 30, 1920; *Sydney Referee*, September 22, 1920, featuring an article from a July 1920 *Police Gazette*; Correspondence from Mark T. Dunn of Chicago to Bob Petersen of Lane Cove, Australia, dated May, 2002; legacyofwrestling.com/Kohler.html

[30] *Chicago Daily Inter-Ocean*, March 14, 1892.

[31] *Recollections of Life & Doings in Chicago* by Charles H. Hermann, 1945.

[32] *Wheeling Register*, March 15, 1892; *Tacoma Daily News*, March 17, 1892.

[33] *Chicago Sunday Inter-Ocean*, March 20, 1892.

[34] *Chicago Inter-Ocean*, March 29, March 30, April 3, 1892; *San Francisco Chronicle*, April 3, 1892.

[35] *Philadelphia Inquirer*, April 6, 1892; *Philadelphia Inquirer*, April 4, 1892, April 5, 1892.

[36] *Philadelphia Inquirer*, April 6, 1892 April 9, 1892, April 10, 1892; www.cyberboxingzone.com; *Chicago Daily Inter-Ocean*, April 8, 1892; "I Fought 'Em All" by Joe Choynski, *Fight Stories*, June-July 1938.

[37] *Chicago Tribune*, April 11, 1892.

[38] *Morning Olympian*, April 12, April 14, 1892; *Chicago Daily Inter-Ocean*, *Kansas City Star*, *New York Herald*, April 14, 1892.

[39] *Philadelphia Inquirer*, Apr. 21, , April 22, 1892; *Philadelphia Item* (Jewish paper), April 20, 1892, April 22 1892, thanks to Tracy Callis. The venue information (Clermont Rink) came from www.boxrec.com.

[40] *Philadelphia Evening Item*, April 23 1892, thanks to Tracy Callis; For the possibility of Tom Ryan being "Philadelphia" Tommy Ryan, see *The Irish Champion, Peter Maher* by Matt Donnellon, 2008.

Round 8:

[1] *Middletown Daily Press*, *San Francisco Chronicle*, May 5, 1892; *Germanic* ship manifest, May 13, 1892; ancestry.com; norwayheritage.com.

[2] *San Francisco Morning Call*, May 13, 1892 said they arrived May 12, *Sporting Life* of London, May 21,

1892 said it was on May 13. The most likely date was May 12, as various manifests show it took the *Germanic* just over seven days to make the voyage. Note – The *Germanic*'s route took it from New York City to Liverpool, England, but it stopped in between at Queenstown (modern name, Cobh), Ireland.

³ *San Francisco Morning Call*, May 13, 1892; *Sporting Life* of London, May 21, 1892 (Tony Gee); *Chicago Tribune*, May 22, 1892; *The National Sporting Club, Past and Present* by Arthur Frederick (A.F.) Bettinson and William Outram Tristram, 1901, 1902; *Morning Olympian*, May 18, 1892; *The Yellow Earl: the Life of Hugh Lowther* by Douglas Sutherland, 1966.

⁴ *Chicago Tribune*, May 31, 1892; *Indiana Democrat*, June 2, 1892; *Fresno Republican*, June 3, 1892; "Famous Fights," number 91, May 30, 1892.

⁵ *Peter Jackson, a Biography of the Australian Heavyweight Champion, 1960-1901* by Bob Petersen, 2011; *St. Louis Post-Dispatch*, January 21, 1893.

⁶ *Wheeling Sunday Register*, June 5, 1892.

⁷ *Chicago Tribune*, June 6, 1892.

⁸ *Chicago Tribune*, June 6, 1892; *Gentleman Bruiser, A Life of the Boxer Peter Jackson* by Bob Petersen, 2005 by Croydon Publishing.

⁹ *Wheeling Sunday Register*, July 3, 1892; *Chicago Tribune*, July 12, 1892.

¹⁰ *San Francisco Morning Call*, July 7, 1892.

¹¹ "The Days of Finish Fights," *Manitoba Free Press*, January 22, 1927; "I Fought 'Em All" by Joe Choynski, *Fight Stories*, June-July 1938; The copy of *The Scapegoat*, inscribed "Joe Choynski, London, 1892," is in the possession of Al and Harriet Draper.

¹² *San Francisco Morning Call*, July 19, 1892; *Chicago Tribune, Brooklyn Eagle*, July 20, 1892.

¹³ *Peter Jackson, a Biography of the Australian Heavyweight Champion, 1960-1901* by Bob Petersen, 2011; *Chicago Tribune*, July 27, 1892; *Hamilton Daily Democrat, Tacoma Daily News*, July 30, 1892. That Choynski accepted a challenge from Smith was confirmed by the *Daily Huronite*, August 1, 1892.

¹⁴ *Wheeling Register*, August 6, 1892.

¹⁵ *Music Hall and Theater Review* (London, England), August 5, 1892, August 19, 1892 (Tony Gee); *Chicago Daily Inter-Ocean*, August 16, 1892.

¹⁶ "The Days of Finish Fights," *Manitoba Free Press*, January 22, 1927; "I Fought 'Em All," *Fight Stories*, June-July 1938.

¹⁷ "The Days of Finish Fights," January 22, 1927; *New Haven Evening Register*, August 8, 1892; *Kansas City Star*, December 4, 1893.

¹⁸ *Chicago Tribune*, August 28, 1892.

¹⁹ *New York Times*, June 27, 1881, April 21, 1882.

²⁰ *Oshkosh* (Wisconsin) *Daily Northwestern*, August 25, 1892; *San Francisco Chronicle*, August 15, 1892.

²¹ *Chicago Tribune, Chicago Inter-Ocean, Idaho Daily Statesman, San Francisco Call*, September 3, 1892.

²² norwayheritage.com and other internet sources.

²³ *San Francisco Chronicle*, September 4, 1892; *Idaho Daily Statesman*, September 5, 1892; "The Days of Finish Fights," *Manitoba Free Press*, January 22, 1927; "I Fought 'Em All," *Fight Stories*, June-July 1938.

²⁴ *Williamsport Daily Gazette and Bulletin*, September 4, 1892; *Chicago Daily Inter-Ocean*, September 5, 1892; "The Days of Finish Fights," *Manitoba Free Press*, January 22, 1927; "I Fought 'Em All" by Joe Choynski, *Fight Stories*, June-July 1938.

²⁵ *Sporting Life* (Philadelphia), November 11, 1892.

²⁶ *Columbus* (Georgia) *Daily Enquirer-Sun, Hamilton Daily Democrat*, September 7, 1892.

²⁷ *Oshkosh Daily Northwestern*, September 22, 1892; *Chicago Tribune*, September 26, 1892.

²⁸ *New York Times*, July 27, 1890; *Trenton Times*, September 27, 1892; Undated *Police Gazette* article.

²⁹ *Wheeling Sunday Register*, October 2, 1892; *Chicago Daily Inter-Ocean*, October 2, 1892.

³⁰ *Brooklyn Daily Eagle*, October 8, 1892, October 9, 1892, October 16, 1892.

³¹ *Brooklyn Daily Eagle*, October 17, 1892; "I Fought 'Em All," *Fight Stories*, June-July 1938.

³² *Decatur Daily Republican, Brooklyn Eagle*, October 17, 1892, *Sandusky Register*, October 18, 1892.

³³ *Brooklyn Daily Eagle*, October 26, 1892, *Buffalo Express*, October 29, 1892.

³⁴ *New York Times*, October 31, 1892.

³⁵ *Buffalo Express*, October 29, 1892.

³⁶ *Colorado Springs Republic and Telegraph, Brooklyn Eagle*, October 31, 1892.

³⁷ *Philadelphia Item* (Jewish paper), October 31, 1892; *Grand Forks Herald, Salt Lake Herald, San Francisco Call, Chicago Tribune, San Francisco Chronicle, Rocky Mountain News, Brooklyn Eagle, Colorado Sun, Tyrone Daily Herald*, November 1, 1892; *New York Clipper, Sporting Life* (Philadelphia, Pa.), November 5, 1892; *Police Gazette*, October 31, November 12, 1892, circa 1933; *Black Dynamite* by Nat Fleischer, 1938.

³⁸ *San Francisco Chronicle*, November 1, 1892.

³⁹ "I Fought 'Em All" by Joe Choynski, *Fight Stories*, June-July 1938.

40 *Brooklyn Eagle*, November 3, 1892.

41 *Brooklyn Eagle*, November 12, 1892.

42 *Elmira Daily Gazette*, November 12, 1892: "Joe Choynski's head must have been affected by the punching of George Godfrey. He imagines he can act and is thinking of having a play written for him."

43 "The Days of Finish Fights," *Manitoba Free Press*, January 22, 1927; "I Fought 'Em All" by Joe Choynski, *Fight Stories*, June-July 1938; *Peter Jackson, a Biography of the Australian Heavyweight Champion, 1960-1901* by Bob Petersen, 2011; *Philadelphia Inquirer*, November 22, 1892; *Black Dynamite, Volume 4* by Nat Fleischer, 1939; *Baltimore Sun*, November 25, 1892.

44 *Chicago Daily Inter-Ocean, Omaha Sunday World Herald, Philadelphia Inquirer*, November 27, 1892.

45 *Kansas City Times, Daily North Carolina* (Charlotte?) *Observer, Lowell Sun*, November 29, 1892.

46 *St. Louis Post-Dispatch*, November, 1892 (exact date unknown), December 3, 1892; *San Francisco Chronicle*, December 4, 1892.

47 *Brooklyn Eagle*, December 5, 1892.

48 *Worcester Daily Spy*, December 9, 1892.

49 *Chicago Inter-Ocean*, December 21, December 25, December 27, 1892.

50 *Chicago Sunday Inter-Ocean*, December 25, 1892.

51 *Chicago Tribune*, December 29, 1892.

52 *Chicago Inter-Ocean, Chicago Tribune*, December 30, 1892; *Fort Worth Star-Telegram*, April 30, 1905.

53 *Milford* (Iowa) *Mail*, January 12, 1893; *Idaho Daily Statesman*, December 31, 1892; *Salt Lake Herald*, January 1, 1893.

54 *Buffalo Express*, January 2, 1893.

55 *Salt Lake Herald*, January 3. 1893; *Ogden Standard*, January 1, 1893.

56 *Morning Olympian*, January 5, 1893; *Brooklyn Eagle*, January 12, 1893.

57 *Oshkosh Daily Northwestern*, January 7, 1893; *St. Louis Post-Dispatch*, January 9, 1893.

58 *St. Louis Post-Dispatch, San Francisco Examiner*, January 11, 1893.

59 Thanks to Bob Petersen, from *Gentleman Bruiser, A Life of the Boxer Peter Jackson* by Bob Petersen, 2005 by Croydon Publishing.

60 *South Carolina State*, January 16, 1893.

Round 9:

1 Full title, *Uncle Tom's Cabin; or, Life among the lowly. Chicago Tribune, St. Louis Post-Dispatch*, January 21, 1893. For Stockwell cutting ties with the Alcazar Theater, see the *New York Clipper*, June 9, 1888.

2 *San Francisco Examiner*, January 22, 1893.

3 *Gentleman Bruiser* by Bob Petersen 2005.

4 "Up Against the Ropes, Peter Jackson As Uncle Tom In America" by Susan F. Clark, 2000.

5 *Oregonian*, February 6, 1893.

6 *San Francisco Morning Call, San Francisco Chronicle, Oregonian*, February 7, 1893.

7 *Boxing and Wrestling* magazine, April, 1955.

8 *New York Times*, April 20, 1906; *San Francisco Telephone Directory*, February 1893; www.vialibri.net; *San Francisco Morning Call, San Francisco Chronicle*, February 13, 1893, February 19, 1893; *Galveston Daily News*, February 14, 1893; *Boston Globe* (probably), February 24, 1893.

9 *Chicago Tribune*, February 26, 1893 said Choynski left Chicago February 25, 1893 for New Orleans. *Galveston Daily News, South Carolina State*, February 27, 1893; *Chicago Tribune, Chicago Inter-Ocean, San Francisco Chronicle, San Francisco Examiner*, February 28, 1893; *Ogden Standard-Examiner*, February 26, 1943.

10 *Frederick* (Maryland) *News, Philadelphia Inquirer*, March 3, 1893.

11 *Galveston Daily News*, March 4, 1893.

12 *Kansas City Times, Omaha Daily Bee*, March 8, 1893.

13 *Philadelphia Inquirer*, March 10, 1893, *Kansas City Times*, March 12, 1893; "I Fought 'Em All" by Joe Choynski, *Fight Stories*, June-July 1938.

14 *New York Times*, March 10, 1893.

15 "The Days of Finish Fights," *Manitoba Free Press*, January 22, 1927; "I Fought 'Em All" by Joe Choynski, *Fight Stories*, June-July 1938.

16 *San Francisco Call, San Francisco Chronicle, St. Louis Post-Dispatch*, March 12, 1893; *San Francisco Examiner, Decatur Republican*, March 14, 1893.

17 *San Francisco Morning Call*, March 20, 1893; *Galveston Daily News*, March 21, 1893, *Salt Lake Herald*, March 26, 1893.

18 *San Francisco Morning Call*, March 20, 1893.

19 *Salt Lake Herald*, April 1, 1893.

20 Thanks to Mark T. Dunn for this information; *Kansas City Star*, April 8, 1893.

[21] *American Citizen* (Kansas City, Kansas), April 14, 1893.

[22] *Omaha Daily Bee*, April 16, 1893.

[23] *Omaha Daily Bee*, April 21, 1893.

[24] *Who's Who On the Stage*, edited by Walter Browne and Frederick Arnold Austin, 1908; imdb.com; *New York Times*, October 16, 1987.

[25] *Omaha Daily Bee*, April 21, 1893.

[26] From Mark T. Dunn; *St. Louis Post-Dispatch*, May 1, 1893, May 2, 1893; *Chicago Inter-Ocean*, April 30, 1893; *San Francisco Call*, May 3, 1893.

[27] *Philadelphia Inquirer, Chicago Daily Inter-Ocean*, May 8, 1893.

[28] *Chicago Tribune*, May 7, May 8, 1893.

[29] *Chicago Inter-Ocean*, May 14, 1893; *Oswego Daily Times*, May 16, 1893.

[30] *San Francisco Chronicle*, May 22, 1893.

[31] *Chicago Daily Inter-Ocean*, June 7, 1893, *Omaha Daily Bee*, June 13, 1893.

[32] *San Francisco Morning Call*, June 11, 1893.

[33] "The San Francisco Journalism of I.N. Choynski, He Flatters None and Displeases Many," 1997.

[34] *Milwaukee Evening Wisconsin*, June 16, 1893.

[35] *Philadelphia Inquirer*, June 26, 1893; *Manitoba Free Press*, June 28, 1893; *Oswego Daily Times*, June 29, 1893 (quoting the *Buffalo Commercial*).

[36] *Warren Evening Democrat*, June 20, 1893; *Chicago Tribune*, June 27, 1893, *Trenton Times*, June 29, 1893; *St. Louis Post-Dispatch*, November 18, 1897.

[37] *Chicago Inter-Ocean*, July 9, 1893.

[38] *Chicago Daily Inter-Ocean, Helena Independent*, July 10, 1893; *Salt Lake Herald*, July 11, 1893; *Washington Post*, February 5, 1911; Thanks to Mark T. Dunn for details of the Smith-Griffin fight and the Columbian Exposition tragedy.

[39] *St. Paul Daily Globe, Chicago Daily Inter-Ocean*, July 16, 1893.

[40] *San Francisco Chronicle*, July 22, 1893; *Dallas Morning News*, July 23, 1893; *Daily Huronite*, July 24, 1893.

[41] *New York World*, July 25, 1893; *Chicago Tribune*, July 26, 1893; *Police Gazette*, July 29, 1893, quoting an edition of the *Chicago Sporting Gazette*.

[42] *Chicago Inter-Ocean*, July 30, 1893, July 31, 1893; *Portrait Gallery of Pugilists of America and Their Contemporaries* by Billy Edwards, 1894; *Williamsport Gazette & Bulletin*, August 1, 1893. Mark T. Dunn, for Davies and gang to Roby; *Newark Advocate, New York Times*, August 15, 1893.

[43] "The Days of Finish Fights," *Manitoba Free Press*, January 22, 1927; "I Fought 'Em All," *Fight Stories*, June-July 1938.

[44] *Daily Bulletin* (Honolulu, Hawaii), September 18, 1893.

[45] *Newark Daily Advocate, New York Times*, August 31, 1893; *New York Spirit of the Times*, August 12, 1893, information from Mark T. Dunn; *Olean Democrat*, September 12, 1893, September 14, 1893.

[46] *Syracuse Courier*, September 19, September 20, September 27, 1893; For Choynski portraying Simon Legree, *Perry Daily Chief*, September 16, 1902.

[47] Thanks to Mark T. Dunn; *Hawarden Independent*, November 16, 1893.

[48] *Lowell Daily Sun*, November 13, 1893; *San Francisco Chronicle, Brooklyn Eagle*, November 17, 1893.

[49] Mark T. Dunn, Bob Petersen; Park Theatre playbill, October 16, 1893; *Philadelphia Inquirer*, October 17, 1893; *Charlotte News*, October 18, 1893; *Chicago Sunday Inter-Ocean*, October 20, 1893; *New York Dramatic Mirror*, October 21, 1893; *Lowell Sun*, October 31, November 3, November 4, 1893; *Police Gazette*, November 4, 1893; *New York Times*, November 12, 1893; *New Haven Evening Register*, November 15, 1893.

[50] Journal of Lancaster County Historical Society, Volume 79, Number 3, 1975; The troupe's itinerary is thanks in part to Bob Petersen and the *New York Dramatic Mirror*; the Grand Horse Show was covered by the *New York World*, November 15, 1893.

[51] Thanks to Mark T. Dunn; *Kansas City Star*, December 4, 1893.

[52] *Philadelphia Inquirer*, December 5, 1893; *Maitland Mercury*, December 12, 1893; *Worcester Daily Spy*, December 16(?), 1893, date uncertain.

[53] Undated *Sydney Referee* from 1894, probably February.

[54] *New York Herald*, December 19, 1893; *New York Dramatic Mirror, New York Clipper*, December 23, 1893; *Out of Sight, The Rise of African-American Popular Music, 1889-1895* by Lynn Abbott and Doug Seroff, 2003; *Chicago Inter-Ocean, St. Louis Republic*, December 22, 1893; *Wheeling Register*, December 23, 1893.

[55] *Brooklyn Eagle*, January 16, 1894; *Atlanta Constitution*, January 24, 1894. Worcester, Massachusetts show from *Sydney Referee*, March 28, 1919, quoting from the *Worcester Telegram* of January 2, 1894.

[56] Thanks to Mark T. Dunn.

[57] *Chicago Tribune*, January 26, 1894; *Logansport Pharos*, February 1, 1894; *Milwaukee Evening Wisconsin*, February 3, 1894; *Philadelphia Inquirer*, February 13, 1894; *Kalamazoo Gazette*, apparently February 14, 1894, courtesy of Mark T. Dunn; *Washington Post*, March 4, 1894.

[58] *Washington Post*, March 6, 1894.

[59] Mark T. Dunn; *Decatur Daily Republican*, March 14, 1894, March 15, 1894; *Decatur Daily Review*, *Decatur Morning Herald*, March 18, 1894.

[60] *Sydney Referee*, March 19, 1919.

Round 10:

[1] *Boston Journal*, May 2, 1894.

[2] *San Francisco Chronicle, Kansas Weekly Capital and Farm Journal, St. Louis Post-Dispatch*, May 10, 1894; *Oswego Daily Times*, May 17, 1894.

[3] "I Fought 'Em All" by Joe Choynski, *Fight Stories*, June-July 1938.

[4] *Milwaukee Evening Wisconsin*, June 9, 1894; *Brooklyn Eagle, Buffalo Express*, June 14, 1894; *Worcester Daily Spy*, June 16, 1894, June 18, 1894.

[5] *Decatur Weekly Herald-Despatch*, June 23, 1894.

[6] *Syracuse Herald*, June 15, 1911.

[7] *Chicago Tribune, Police Gazette, Boston Herald*, June 18, 1894; *Rochester Democrat and Chronicle, Boston Daily Globe, Boston Post, Kansas City Star, New York Herald, New York World, Brooklyn Eagle, Lowell Daily Sun, Manitoba Free Press, St. Louis Republic, Syracuse Evening Herald*, June 19, 1894; The *Sporting Life* (Philadelphia, Pennsylvania), June 23, 1894; *Police Gazette*, June 30, 1894, June (undated) 1919; *Syracuse Herald*, June 16, 1911; "The Days of Finish Fights," *Manitoba Free Press*, January 22, 1927; "I Fought 'Em All" by Joe Choynski, *Fight Stories*, June-July 1938.

[8] *Syracuse Herald*, June 15, 1911.

[9] *Salt Lake Herald, Wheeling Register*, June 20, 1894.

[10] *Police Gazette*, July 7, 1894.

[11] *Brooklyn Daily Eagle*, March 25, 1895.

[12] *South Carolina State*, May 5, 1895.

[13] *Brooklyn Eagle*, July 27, 1894; *Waterloo Courier*, July 28, 1894; *Decatur Herald-Despatch*, August 4, 1894; *Janesville Gazette*, February 4, 1914.

[14] *Omaha World Herald*, July 28, 1894; *Daily* (Winnipeg, Manitoba, Ca.) *Nor'wester*, August 25, 1894.

[15] *San Francisco Call, Chicago Tribune, Milwaukee Evening Wisconsin, Omaha World Herald, Bangor Daily Whig and Courier*, September 18, 1894; *Galveston Daily News*, September 19, 1894.

[16] *South Carolina State, Brooklyn Eagle, Delphos Daily Herald, Milwaukee Evening Wisconsin*, September 22, 1894. The *Columbia State* said the men were in Jackson, Mississippi, but the *Brooklyn Eagle* and *Delphos Daily Herald* said Jackson, Michigan. The *Milwaukee Evening Wisconsin* had it as Jacksonville, Illinois. As Joe Tansey fought a Frederick Cox on November 3, 1894 at the Clinton House in Cox's home town of Jackson, Michigan, I believe this is the locale where Choynski and Davies were, on the day in question.

[17] *Fort Wayne News*, October 4, 1894; *Police Gazette*, October 13, 1894; *Chicago Tribune*, October 25, 1894.

[18] *Chicago Tribune*, October 14, 1894; *New York Illustrated News*, October, 1894, otherwise undated.

[19] *Milwaukee Evening Wisconsin, Oakland Tribune*, November 1, 1894; *Dallas Morning News, Milwaukee Evening Wisconsin*, November 7, 1894.

[20] *Brutes in Suits, Male Sensibility in America, 1890-1920* by John Pettigrew, 2007; *Chicago Tribune*, November 11, 1894; *New York Journal*, October 26, 1895.

[21] *New York World*, November 12, 1899. Thanks to Adam J. Pollack, from *In the Ring with James J. Jeffries*, 2009, for locating the quote.

[22] *Morning Oregonian*, December 26, 1918. The article, "Ring Summary is Complete; F.J. Tomassuly Tells How Fighters Made Start In Life," said Joe Choynski had been a "Cash boy in a bank in San Francisco." It also notes that Jim Corbett "Started out as a messenger in a San Francisco bank," which alleviates any concern of the writer having confused Choynski with Corbett. *Duluth News Tribune*, September 9, 1919: "In San Francisco when only a little lad Joe worked as a cash boy in a large department store as a salesman of sporting goods." It adds that when Joe left the store's employ, he had shown such excellent ability as a salesman, that "he received a position on the road with a well known western tobacco firm ..." The journalist may have confused his facts and recollections, as Choynski's latter occupation became a reality well into his boxing career.

[23] *Perry Daily Chief, Sandusky Register*, December 14, 1894.

[24] *Brooklyn Eagle*, December 19, 1894; *Kansas City Star*, December 24, 1894.

[25] www.cyberboxingzone.com/boxing/barry-j.htm

[26] *Black Dynamite, Volume V, Sockers in Sepia* by Nat Fleischer, 1947.

[27] *Police Gazette,* January 6, 1895.

[28] *Chicago Daily Inter-Ocean,* January 7, 1895.

[29] *Philadelphia Inquirer,* January 19, 1895.

[30] *Chicago Daily Inter-Ocean,* January 12, 1895.

[31] *Philadelphia Inquirer,* January 17, 1895.

[32] *Sioux Valley* (Correctionville, Iowa) *News,* January 18, 1895.

[33] *Cedar Rapids Daily Gazette, Oshkosh Daily Northwestern,* January 18, 1895.

[34] *Brooklyn Eagle,* January 19, 1895, January 22, 1895.

Round 11:

[1] Louise Miller death certificate, Mary S. Miller death certificate; ohiohistory.org; ancestry.com; walnuthillscemetery.org; fold3.com; United States Federal Census, from 1850, 1860, 1870, 1880; Cincinnati, Ohio City Directory, 1895 showed Louise's brother as Thomas H. The wedding date of Thomas S. Miller and Mary Susan Gossen comes from the July 13, 1895 *New York Clipper.*

[2] *Boston Journal,* November 19, 1901.

[3] *New York Clipper,* November 10, 1877, November 5, 1881, February 11, 1882, March 17, 1894, July 7, 1894; museumcollections.in.gov. The Golden Troupe was based in New Harmony, Indiana. They toured the country from 1875 to 1891. Martin Golden was manager of the Troupe, but the star was his wife, Bella. Their four offspring all participated, Martin Jr., William, Grace and Frances. They brought the "Superb Silver Band and Orchestra" and from 15 to 20 actors and actresses on tour with them. The Troupe disbanded after Bella was injured while on tour in 1891.

[4] *New York Clipper,* January 13, 1885, January 17, 1885.

[5] *New York Clipper,* November 28, 1885, December 19, 1885.

[6] *New York Dramatic Mirror,* January 23, 1886; *Newark Daily Advocate,* December 9, 1886.

[7] *Newark Daily Advocate,* December 11, 1886.

[8] *Newark Daily Advocate,* December 13, 1886; *New York Dramatic Mirror,* January 1, 1887.

[9] *Newark Daily Advocate,* January 13, 1887, January 14, 1887; January 15, 1887.

[10] *Newark Daily Advocate,* January 17, 1887, January 18, 1887.

[11] *Newark Daily Advocate,* January 21, 1887; January 25, 1887.

[12] *New York Clipper,* September 17, 1887.

[13] *Chicago Daily Inter-Ocean,* October 3, 1887; *New York Dramatic Mirror,* October 8, 1887.

[14] *Newark Daily Advocate,* November 9, 1887, November 11, 1887, November 14, 1887.

[15] *Newark Daily Advocate,* November 18, 1887, November 19, 1887.

[16] *Milwaukee Daily Journal,* January 28, 1888; *New York Dramatic Mirror,* January 30, 1888; (Kansas City, Missouri) *Evening News,* February 14, 1888; *Kansas City Journal, Kansas City Times,* February 17, 1888, all courtesy of the February 25, 1888 *New York Clipper.*

[17] *New York Dramatic Mirror,* March 24, 1888.

[18] *Utica Sunday Tribune,* May 20, 1888; *New York Clipper,* July 7, 1888; *New York Dramatic Mirror,* March 26, 1888, July 14, 1888; July 21, 1888.

[19] *Pittsburgh Leader,* (Pittsburgh) *Post, Chronicle Telegraph* (Pittsburgh, Pennsylvania), *Dispatch* (Pittsburgh), *Pittsburgh Press,* September 4, 1888, courtesy September 15, 1888 *New York Clipper.*

[20] *Newark Daily Advocate,* January 24, 1889.

[21] *Wheeling Register,* February 9, 1889, February 24, 1889; *New York Dramatic Mirror,* March 1, 1889.

[22] *New York Clipper,* April 27, 1889; *Wheeling Register,* February 6, 1890; *Hamilton Daily Democrat,* February 21, 1890.

[23] *New York Clipper,* February 23, 1890; *Washington* (D.C.) *Critic,* May 13, 1890.

[24] *New York Dramatic Mirror,* November 22, 1890.

[25] *Dallas Morning News,* February 12, 1892.

[26] *New York Times,* May 15, 1892, May 21, 1892, May 24, 1892.

[27] *Chicago Tribune, Chicago Daily Inter-Ocean,* January 26, 1895.

[28] *Kansas City Star, San Francisco Chronicle, Chicago Daily Inter-Ocean,* January 27, 1895; Cincinnati, Ohio City Directory, 1895 and 1896 editions. Thomas S. (Louise's father, is listed in 1895 as a salesman for C. Crane & Co., in the 1896 edition as a "Cutter").

[29] Oberlin Alumni magazine, Volume 2, 1905; Sydney Dix Strong papers, swarthmore.edu/Library/peace; *History of the Walnut Hills Congregational Church of Cincinnati (1843-1935)* by Almon M. Warner, 1935; *Notable Women of China: Shang Dynasty to the Early Twentieth Century* by Barbara Bennett Peterson, 2000; *Notable American Women, Volume 4* by Barbara Sicherman, Carol Hurd

Green, 1980; historylink.org; Anna Louise Strong papers, Special Collections, University of Washington Libraries, Seattle, Washington; lib.washington.edu.

[30] *History of the Walnut Hills Congregational Church of Cincinnati (1843-1935)* by Almon M. Warner, 1935; Information related to me by Harriet Marie (Coe) Draper and her husband, Albert. Harriet is the youngest child of the late Edwin W. (Choynski) Coe, Joe's brother.

[31] *New York Clipper*, October 1, 1898, August 3, October 5, 1901, March 8, 1902; *Bourbon News* (Paris, Kentucky), February 19, 1901.

[32] *New York Clipper*, July 27, 1895.

Round 12:

[1] *Milwaukee Evening Wisconsin*, January 31, 1895.

[2] *St. Louis Post-Dispatch*, February 4, 1895, February 11, 1895; *Portrait Gallery of Pugilists of America and Their Contemporaries* by Billy Edwards, 1894; boxrec.com.

[3] *St. Louis Post-Dispatch*, February 11, 1895; *Brooklyn Daily Eagle*, February 14, 1895.

[4] *Chicago Inter-Ocean, Chicago Tribune, Omaha World-Herald, Sandusky Register*, February 26, 1895.

[5] *San Antonio Light*, March 1, 1895.

[6] *Kansas City Star*, March 7, 1895; *Kansas City Times*, March 8, 1895; *Portrait Gallery of Pugilists of America and Their Contemporaries*, 1894.

[7] *Chicago Daily Inter-Ocean, Kansas City Star*, March 11, 1895.

[8] *Chicago Daily Inter-Ocean, Idaho Daily Statesman*, March 12, 1895.

[9] *Chicago Daily Inter-Ocean*, March 13, March 14, 1895; *Police Gazette*, March 16, 1895; *Syracuse Herald*, August 8, 1913.

[10] *St. Paul Daily Globe*, March 21, 1895.

[11] *Boston Herald, Idaho Daily Statesman, Omaha Morning World-Herald*, March 22, 1895; *Manitoba Free Press*, March 23, 1895.

[12] *Boston Herald, Idaho Daily Statesman, Milwaukee Evening Wisconsin, Omaha Morning World-Herald, Chicago Daily Inter-Ocean*, March 22, 1895; *Manitoba Free Press*, March 23, 1895.

[13] *Sioux Valley News*, March 29, 1895.

[14] *Chicago's Greatest Sportsman, Charles E. 'Parson' Davies* by Mark T. Dunn, 2011; *St. Paul Daily Globe, Chicago Tribune*, March 26, 1895.

[15] *Chicago Daily Inter-Ocean*, March 27, 1895; *Chicago Daily Inter-Ocean*, March 30, 1895, April 7, 1895.

[16] *Kansas City Times*, March 31, 1895; *Chicago Inter-Ocean*, April 7, 1895; *Brooklyn Eagle*, April 8, 1895.

[17] *Chicago Daily Inter-Ocean*, May 2, 1895; *Philadelphia Inquirer*, May 6, 1895.

[18] *Brooklyn Daily Eagle*, May 10, 1895; *Chicago Inter-Ocean*, May 19, 1895; Publication only identified as "*Gazette*," June 1, 1895, from David Chesanow; *Peter Maher, the Irish Champion* by Matt Donnellon, 2008.

[19] *San Antonio Daily Light*, May 19, 1895.

[20] *Brooklyn Daily Eagle*, May 26, 1895; cyberboxingzone.com/boxing/choynski.html

[21] *Chicago Daily Inter-Ocean*, May 28, 1895; *Atlanta Constitution*, May 29, 1895.

[22] Boxing Records at www.boxrec.com; *Baltimore Sun*, June 3, 1895.

[23] *Milwaukee Evening Wisconsin*, June 3, 1895; *Omaha Morning World-Herald, Brooklyn Daily Eagle, Daily Kennebec Journal*, June 4, 1895.

[24] *Brooklyn Daily Eagle*, May 27, June 5, 1895; *Fresno Bee*, June 9, 1895; *Bangor Daily Whig and Courier*, June 10, 1895.

[25] *Newark Daily Advocate*, June 9, 1895.

[26] *Red Bank* (New Jersey) *Register*, June 19, 1895; *Dan Stuart's Fistic Carnival* by Leo N. Miletich, 1994; *New York Times, New York Herald, Olean Democrat, Salt Lake Herald*, June 28, 1895; Joe Choynski record, Cyber Boxing Zone.

[27] *Salt Lake Herald*, June 30, 1895.

[28] *Chicago Sunday Inter-Ocean*, July 7, 1895; *Galveston Daily News*, July 7, 1895.

[29] *Wheeling Register*, July 8, 1895.

Round 13:

[1] *Biloxi Herald-Weekly*, August 17, 1895; cyberboxingzone.com/boxing/choynski.html; boxrec.com. Dick Wilson's record shows 29 wins, 3 losses, 3 draws going into the fight. The only other recorded bout for Wilson, however, was a 3rd round KO loss to Yank Kenney on July 12, 1897.

[2] *San Antonio Daily Light*, August 28, 1895; Unknown paper dated August 29, 1895; *Bangor Daily Whig and Courier*, August 30, 1895.

[3] *San Francisco Call*, August 24, 1895; *Chicago Daily Inter-Ocean*, August 26, 1895, August 29, 1895.

[4] *Chicago Daily Inter-Ocean*, September 26, 1895; *Philadelphia Inquirer*, October 2, 1895.

[5] *Daily Republican* (Decatur, Illinois), October 2, 1895; *Galveston Daily News*, October 21, 1895.

[6] *Minneapolis Journal*, October 10, 1895; *Chicago Daily Inter-Ocean*, October 19, 1895.

[7] *Chicago Daily Inter-Ocean*, November 1, November 3, 1895; November 4, November 7, 1895.

[8] *Chicago Tribune*, September 30, 1895, *Salt Lake Herald*, *Chicago Sunday Inter-Ocean*, November 6, November 10, 1895.

[9] *Chicago Inter-Ocean*, November 12, 1895; *Peter Maher, the Irish Champion* by Matt Donnellon, 2008.

[10] *Chicago Daily Inter-Ocean*, November 14, 1895, *Davenport Daily Republican*, December 12, 1895.

[11] *Chicago Daily Inter-Ocean*, November 15, 1895, November 16, 1895.

[12] *Chicago Daily Inter-Ocean*, November 16, 1895.

[13] *Daily Capital Journal* (Salem, Oregon), May 20, 1910.

[14] *Chicago Inter-Ocean*, November 26, November 28, 1895; *San Francisco Chronicle*, December 1, 1895.

[15] *Philadelphia Inquirer*, July 5, 1895.

[16] *Chicago Daily Inter-Ocean*, December 10, 1895.

[17] *Tacoma Daily News*, December 28, 1895.

[18] *Galveston Daily News*, December 28, 1895.

[19] *Brooklyn Daily Eagle*, January 8, 1896, January 14, 1896; *Milwaukee Evening Wisconsin*, January 11, 1896; *Omaha World Herald*, January 12, 1896; *Sioux City Herald*, January 16, 1896.

[20] *Sioux City Herald*, January 16, 1896; *San Francisco Chronicle*, January 18, 1891.

[21] *Fort Wayne Evening Post*, January 20, 1896; London *Mirror of Life*, September 23, 1896; *New York Sun*, June 26, 1904; "I Fought 'Em All" by Joe Choynski, *Fight Stories*, June-July 1938; The *Ring* (undated, but circa 1960); *Reared in a Greenhouse* by Dorothy B. Wexler, 1998.

[22] *Boston Herald*, January 20, 1896; *New York Sun*, *Salt Lake Herald*, *San Francisco Call*, *Brooklyn Daily Eagle*, *Colorado Springs Gazette*, *Denver Times*, January 21, 1896; *Daily Huronite*, January 22, 1896; *Chicago Daily Inter-Ocean*, January 23, 1896; *St. Louis Republic*, January 27, 1896; *Mirror of Life*, (London, England), February 8, 1896; *Police Gazette*, undated but circa 1921.

[23] *Chicago Daily Inter-Ocean*, *Chicago Tribune*, *Denver Post*, January 23, 1896.

[24] *Davenport Daily Leader*, January 24, 1896; *St. Paul Daily Globe*, January 26, 1896.

[25] *St. Louis Republic*, January 27, 1896.

[26] *Chicago Sunday Inter-Ocean*, January 29, 1896.

[27] *Fort Wayne Evening Post*, *Syracuse Daily Standard*, February 3, 1896.

[28] *Galveston County Daily News*, January 31, 1896.

[29] *San Francisco Call*, *Omaha World Herald*, February 1, 1896; *Milwaukee Evening Wisconsin*, *Lowell Daily Sun*, February 3, 1896; Unidentified publication from February, 1896, from David Chesanow.

[30] *Chicago Sunday Inter-Ocean*, February 8, 1896; *Brownsville Daily Herald*, February 11. 1896; *Fort Wayne Evening Post*, February 11, 1896.

[31] *San Francisco Call*, March 7, 1896.

[32] *San Francisco Call*, *Philadelphia Inquirer*, March 19, 1896.

[33] *Police Gazette*, March 21, 1896; *Knoxville Daily Journal*, *Atlanta Constitution*, *Brooklyn Sunday Eagle*, *Dubuque Sunday Herald*, March 22, 1896.

Round 14:

[1] *San Francisco Call*, April 5, 1896.

[2] *Chicago Daily Inter-Ocean* , April 6, 1896; *San Francisco Call*, April 11, 1896.

[3] *San Francisco Call*, April 10, 1896.

[4] *San Francisco Chronicle*, April 15, 1896; *San Francisco Call*, *Kansas City Star*, *Milwaukee Evening Wisconsin*, April 16, 1896.

[5] "Fighters I've Met" by Tom Sharkey, 11 clippings from "The *Evening Herald*" (exact location of newspaper is unknown), beginning September 1917. While usually given as one of nine children, Tom Sharkey was actually one of 10. From, *I Fought Them All*, 2010 by Greg Lewis and Moira Sharkey.

[6] "A Comment on the Evolution of Punching Technique from the Gaslight Era Forward" by Christopher J. LaForce, IBRO newsletter number 69, March 23, 2001. Two of the manuals referred to were *Scientific Boxing* by James J. Corbett, 1912 and *Donovan's Science of Boxing*, 1996 reprint by Doyle Studio Press, of original 1893 book by "Professor" Mike Donovan.

[7] *Police Gazette*, April 16, 1896; *San Francisco Call*, *San Francisco Chronicle*, *St. Louis Republic*, *Rocky Mountain News*, April 17, 1896; *Wilkes-Barre Times*, *Daily Nevada State Journal*, April 18, 1896.

[8] *Philadelphia Inquirer*, April 19, 1896; *Omaha World Herald*, August 16, 1896; *San Francisco Call*, November 10, 1896.

[9] *Syracuse Herald*, May 10, 1914; *Oakland Tribune*, June 13, 1914; *Waterloo Courier*, March 27, 1920.

[10] *Fresno Bee*, April 22, 1896, May 7, 1896; (Advertisement in) *Fresno Morning Republican*, May 15, 1896; *San Francisco Call*, May 17, 1896.

[11] *Fresno Morning Republican*, May 19, 1896.

[12] *San Jose Mercury Evening News*, May 27, May 28, May 29, 1896; *San Francisco Call*, June 25, 1896.

[13] *Salem Daily News*, June 26, 1896; *Milwaukee Evening Wisconsin*, June 30, 1896.

[14] *San Jose Mercury Evening News*, *San Francisco Call*, July 2, July 6, 1896; *Daily Huronite*, July 7, 1896.

[15] *St. Louis Republic*, July 19, 1896.

[16] *San Francisco Call*, July 20, 1896.

[17] *San Francisco Call*, July 21, 1896.

[18] *San Francisco Call*, July 27, 1896.

[19] *San Francisco Call*, *Brooklyn Daily Eagle*, July 29, 1896.

[20] *Philadelphia Evening Bulletin*, August 1, 1896; *Chicago Tribune*, August 16, 1896.

[21] *San Francisco Call*, August 7, 1896.

[22] *San Francisco Call*, August 8, 1896, August 9, 1896.

[23] *San Francisco Call*, August 15, 1896, August 22, 1896.

[24] *San Francisco Call*, August 25, 1896.

[25] *San Francisco Call*, August 28, 1896.

[26] *San Francisco Call*, August 29, 1896.

[27] *Kansas City Journal*, *San Francisco Call*, *St. Paul Globe*, *Chicago Tribune*, *Davenport Republican*, *Denver Post*, *Denver Republican*, *Denver Times*, August 29, 1896.

[28] *Chicago Sunday Inter-Ocean*, August 30, 1896; *San Francisco Call*, August 31, 1896.

[29] *Chicago Daily Inter-Ocean*, September 1, 1896; *Rocky Mountain News*, September 7, 1896.

[30] *Lexington Morning Herald*, *Chicago Daily Inter-Ocean*, *Knoxville Journal*, October 11, 1896.

[31] *Chicago Daily Inter-Ocean*, October 12, 1896; *Brooklyn Daily Eagle*, October 25, 1896.

[32] *St. Paul Globe*, November 1, 1896.

[33] *Chicago Daily Inter-Ocean*, November 12, 1896; *Salt Lake City Herald*, *Idaho Statesman*, *Philadelphia Evening Bulletin*, November 13, 1896.

[34] *Salt Lake City Herald*, November 15, 1896; *Brooklyn Daily Eagle*, November 16, 1896.

[35] *Perry Daily Chief*, November 17, 1896.

[36] *Brooklyn Daily Eagle*, *Decatur Daily Review*, *San Francisco Call*, *St. Paul Globe*, November 17, 1896; *Denver Post*, *New York Daily Tribune*, November 18, 1896; *Fitchburg Sentinel*, November 27, 1896; *London Sportsman*, by way of the *Wanganui Herald*, January 8, 1897; *Philadelphia Inquirer*, November 29, 1938; "I Fought 'Em All," *Fight Stories*, June-July 1938.

[37] *Salt Lake Herald*, *San Francisco Call*, November 17, 1896; *Pawtucket Times*, June 13, 1905; *Philadelphia Inquirer*, November 29, 1938.

[38] *Idaho Daily Statesman*, May 9, 1921, column by Frank G. Menke.

[39] *Brooklyn Daily Eagle*, November 18, 1896; *Lowell Sun*, November 19, 1896.

[40] *The Emergence of Cinema: The American Screen to 1907*, by Charles Musser, 1994; *Fight Pictures: A History of Boxing and Early Cinema*, by Dan Streible, 2008, in addition to various other sources.

Round 15:

[1] *Brooklyn Daily Eagle*, November 21, 1896; *Black Dynamite, Volume V* by Nat Fleischer, 1947; *Chicago Daily Inter-Ocean*, November 28, 1896; *Hazel Green* (Kentucky) *Herald*, December 3, 1896.

[2] For Herbert at the Sharkey-Fitzsimmons fight, see *The Earp Decision* by Jack DeMattos, 1989.

[3] *Chicago Inter-Ocean*, *St. Louis Republic*, December 11, 1896; "I Fought 'Em All," *Fight Stories*, 1938.

[4] *Brooklyn Daily Eagle*, December 14, December 15, 1896; *San Francisco Chronicle*, December 15, 1896.

[5] *Philadelphia Inquirer*, December 20, 1896; *St. Paul Globe*, December 21, 1896.

[6] *Milwaukee Evening Wisconsin*, December 23, 1896; *San Antonio Light*, December 24, 1896; *Printers' Ink, the Journal for Advertisers*, article dated December 26, 1896 (but strangely, found in issue dated *October 7*, 1896); *Police Gazette*, January 16, 1897; *Sioux City Journal*, January 17, 1897.

[7] *Kansas City Journal*, December 27, 1896; *Steubenville Herald*, December 28, 1896; *Fort Wayne Sentinel*, January 2, 1897; *Philadelphia Inquirer*, *St. Paul Globe*, January 3, 1897; *Boston Globe*, January 5, 1897.

[8] *Oakland Tribune*, February 5, 1897; *Syracuse Daily Standard*, February 6, 1897.

[9] *Brooklyn Daily Eagle*, January 15, 1897; *Philadelphia Inquirer*, *Fort Wayne Journal*, January 31, 1897; *Chicago Tribune*, February 8, 1897.

[10] *Philadelphia Record*, February 7, 1897.

[11] *Galveston Daily News*, *Oakland Tribune*, February 10, 1897; *Fort Worth Register*, *Lowell Sun*, February 11, 1897; *San Antonio Light*, February 21, 1897.

[12] The *Iron Era* (Dover, New Jersey), February 12, 1897; *Brooklyn Daily Eagle*, February 18, 1897;

Philadelphia Record, February 20, 1897; *Milwaukee Evening Wisconsin*, February 27, 1897; *San Francisco Examiner*, March 1, 1897; *Philadelphia Inquirer*, March 2, 1897; *Police Gazette*, March 13, 1897.

[13] *Philadelphia Inquirer*, February 25, 1897, February 28, 1897, March 4, 1897, March 7, 1897, March 9, 1897, March 19, 1897; *Philadelphia Record*, March 4, 1897; *Chicago Tribune*, March 7, 1897.

[14] *Salt Lake Herald*, March 11, 1897; *Omaha World Herald*, March 12, 1897.

[15] *San Francisco Call*, March 20, March 22, 1897, March 26, 1897.

[16] *Fort Wayne News*, April 5, 1897; *San Francisco Call*, April 6, 1897; *Milwaukee Evening Wisconsin*, April 11, 1897; *Daily* (Decatur, Illinois) *Republican*, April 13, 1897.

[17] *San Francisco Call*, April 22, 1897; *Fort Wayne Gazette*, April 23, 1897; *Galveston News*, May 1, 1897.

[18] *Tacoma Daily News*, May 4, 1897 and May 6, 1897.

[19] *Daily Iowa Capital*, May 6, 1897; *Minneapolis Journal*, May 10, 1897; *Scranton Tribune*, May 12, 1897.

[20] *Brooklyn Daily Eagle*, *San Francisco Examiner*, May 10, 1897; for rumors of a fix in the Goddard-Smith rematch, see *Lincoln Daily Star*, November 25, 1915.

[21] *San Francisco Call*, *St. Paul Globe*, *Philadelphia Record*, *Brooklyn Daily Eagle*, *New York Journal*, *San Francisco Examiner*, *Syracuse Daily Standard*, May 11, 1897; undated *Police Gazette*.

[22] *Scranton Tribune*, May 19, 1897.

[23] *San Francisco Report*, May 25, 1897; *Fort Wayne News*, May 28, 1897; *Police News*, May 29, 1897. The letter by Choynski was referenced and sold by Christie's Auction House in 1994. The statement mentions that the lot "consists of a handwritten letter dated May 8, 1897."

[24] *Chicago Tribune*, June 2, 1897.

[25] *San Francisco Call*, June 3, 1897; *Philadelphia Inquirer*, June 6, 1897; *Brooklyn Daily Eagle*, *Idaho Statesman*, *Philadelphia Inquirer*, June 9, 1897.

[26] *Newark Daily Advocate*, *Idaho Statesman*, *Salt Lake Herald*, June 10, 1897; *Greatest Sports Stories From The Chicago Tribune*, 1953.

[27] *San Francisco Chronicle*, June 11, 1897.

[28] *Chicago Tribune*, July 9, 1897; *Milwaukee Free Press*, April 17, 1904.

[29] *San Francisco Report*, July 13, 1897.

[30] *San Francisco Report*, July 23, 1897; *San Francisco Bulletin*, July 31, 1897.

[31] *Brooklyn Daily Eagle*, *New York Times*, July 20, 1897.

[32] *San Francisco Bulletin*, July 31, 1897; *San Francisco Chronicle*, August 1, 1897; *Two Fisted Jeff* by Hugh Fullerton, 1926.

[33] *Idaho Statesman*, *Waterloo Daily Courier*, August 5, 1897.

[34] *San Francisco Bulletin*, August 10, 1897.

[35] *San Francisco Call*, July 18, 1897; *Chicago Tribune*, September 8, 1897; *Anaconda Standard*, August 11, 1912.

[36] *Police News*, September 8, 1897; *Duluth News-Tribune*, September 12, 1897.

[37] *San Francisco Bulletin*, *St. Louis Republic*, *Oakland Tribune*, September 17, 1897.

[38] *San Francisco Chronicle*, September 19, 1897; *Cedar Falls* (Semi-Weekly) *Gazette*, September 24, 1897.

[39] *Oshkosh Daily Northwestern*, September 24, 1897; *Steubenville Herald*, September 25, 1897; *Trenton Evening Times*, October 9, 1897.

[40] *Oakland Tribune*, *Woodland Daily Democrat*, September 24, 1897; *San Francisco Chronicle*, *Fresno Bee*, *Dallas Morning News*, *Naugatuck News*, *Waterloo Reporter*, September 25, 1897; *San Francisco Call*, *Fresno Bee*, *Galveston Daily News*, September 26, 1897; *Waterloo Courier*, September 27, 1897; *Sioux Valley News*, September 30, 1897; *Daily Iowa Capital*, October 19, 1897; *Galveston Daily News*, November 16, 1897; skagwayfolklore.blogspot.com.

[41] *Galveston County Daily News*, October 10, 1897.

[42] *Galveston County Daily News*, *Brooklyn Daily Eagle*, October 12, 1897.

[43] *Galveston Daily News*, October 13, 1897; *Ferris Wheel* (Ferris, Texas), October 16, 1897.

[44] *San Francisco Call*, October 16, October 20, 1897; *Brooklyn Daily Eagle*, *Syracuse Herald*, *Oakland Tribune*, November 1, 1897.

[45] *San Francisco Call*, November 2, 1897, November 6, 1897; *Salt Lake Herald*, *San Francisco Call*, *San Francisco Chronicle*, November 7, 1897.

[46] *Centralia Enterprise and Tribune*, November 27, 1897.

[47] *Oakland Tribune*, November 10, 1897; *San Francisco Call*, *Brooklyn Daily Eagle*, November 11, 1897.

[48] *San Francisco Call*, November 16, November 19, 1897; *Newark Daily Advocate*, November 17, 1897; *Police News*, November 20, 1897.

[49] *San Francisco Call*, *Oshkosh Northwestern*, *Brooklyn Eagle*, *Fresno Bee*, *Idaho Statesman*, *Trenton Times*, December 1, 1897; *Fort Wayne News*, *Philadelphia Inquirer*, December 2, 1897; *Sydney Referee*, January 5, 1898; *Jim Jeffries and His 12 Great Ring Battles*, 1910; *Jim Jeffries, My Life and Battles*, 1910; "The Days of

Finish Fights," *Manitoba Free Press*, January 29, 1927; "I Fought 'Em All," *Fight Stories*, 1938; *Jim Jeffries, A Man Among Men* by Kelly Richard Nicholson, 2002; *Ultimate Tough Guy* by Jim Carney, 2009; *In the Ring With James J. Jeffries* by Adam J. Pollack, 2009; *The Making of Champions in California*, D. Van Court, 1926.

[50] *Ogden Standard-Examiner*, February 4, 1943.

[51] *San Francisco Call*, August 16, 1903; *Sydney Sportsman*, September 21, 1910; *Sydney Referee*, August 10, 1927; *Two-Fisted Jeff* by Hugh Fullerton, 1929.

[52] Article by Ed Smith in the *San Francisco Chronicle*, as quoted by "Joe the Giant Killer," *Boxing and Wrestling* magazine, April 1955.

[53] *Anaconda Standard*, August 11, 1912.

[54] *Syracuse Herald*, February 12, 1914.

Round 16:

[1] *San Francisco Call*, December 3, 1897.

[2] *Trenton Evening News*, December 9, 1897; *Chicago Tribune*, December 14, 1897; *Des Moines Daily News*, December 15, 1897.

[3] *Philadelphia Inquirer, Salt Lake Herald*, December 15, 1897; *Brooklyn Daily Eagle*, December 16, 1897.

[4] *New Haven Evening Register, Brooklyn Daily Eagle*, December 17, 1897.

[5] *Oshkosh Daily Northwestern, Galveston Daily News*, December 18, 1897; *Massillon Independent, New Haven Evening Register*, December 20, 1897.

[6] *Daily Iowa Capital*, December 28, 1897.

[7] *Philadelphia Inquirer, Chicago Tribune*, December 30, 1897.

[8] *Brooklyn Daily Eagle, Cedar Rapids Gazette*, December 31, 1897; *Fort Wayne Journal*, January 1, 1898.

[9] *Lowell Sun*, January 8, 1898. The Selby/McCoy background is included here, as it doesn't appear in *The Real McCoy, the Life and Times of Norman Selby* by Robert Cantwell, 1971, nor in any other biographical article on his life, as far as is known.

[10] *Trenton Evening Times*, January 11, 1898.

[11] *Des Moines Daily News*, January 19, 1898.

[12] *Des Moines Daily News*, January 18, 1898; *Syracuse Evening Herald*, January 21, 1898; *Kansas City Journal*, January 22, 1898; *Sioux City Journal*, January 23, 1898.

[13] *San Francisco Chronicle*, January 24, 1898; *San Francisco Call*, January 30, 1898; *San Francisco Examiner*, February 3, 1898.

[14] *Kansas City Star*, February 4, 1898; *Trenton Evening Times*, February 5, 1898; *Milwaukee Evening Wisconsin*, February 22, 1898.

[15] *Lanky Bob, the Life, Times and Contemporaries of Bob Fitzsimmons* by K.R. Robinson, 2008.

[16] *San Francisco Call, Oakland Tribune, San Francisco Chronicle*, February 9, 1898.

[17] *Lowell Sun*, February 11, 1898.

[18] *Daily* (New Orleans) *Picayune*, February 13, 1898.

[19] *San Francisco Call*, February 12, 1898.

[20] *Duluth News-Tribune*, February 13, 1898.

[21] *Syracuse Evening Herald*, February 21, 1898; *San Francisco Call*, February 22, 1898.

[22] *New York Evening Journal*, March 5, 1898; *Philadelphia Inquirer*, March 6, 1898.

[23] *San Francisco Call*, November 14, 1895; *San Francisco Examiner*, March 9, 1898.

[24] *San Francisco Call*, March 9, 1898.

[25] *San Francisco Examiner*, March 9, 1898; (Sandusky, Ohio) *Morning Star*, March 9, 1898.

[26] *Syracuse Evening Herald*, March 10, 1898; *Lowell Sun*, March 10, 1898.

[27] *Lowell Sun*, March 10, 1898; *San Francisco Examiner, Syracuse Evening Herald, Tacoma Daily News*, March 11, 1898.

[28] *Kansas City Journal, St. Paul Globe, Naugatuck* (Connecticut) *Daily Times, Atlanta Constitution, San Francisco Call, New York Evening Journal*, (Sandusky, Ohio) *Morning Star, Brooklyn Eagle*, March 12, 1898; *Salt Lake Herald*, March 13, 1898; "The Days of Finish Fights," *Manitoba Free Press*, February 5, 1927; "I Fought 'Em All" by Joe Choynski, *Fight Stories*, June-July 1938.

[29] *Perry Daily Chief*, March 15, 1898.

[30] *Kansas City Journal*, March 14, 1898, quoting the *Chicago News*.

[31] *Syracuse Daily Herald*, March 13, 1898.

[32] *Salt Lake Herald, San Francisco Call*, March 20, 1898; *Brooklyn Daily Eagle*, March 21, 1898; *Portsmouth Daily Times, Philadelphia Inquirer*, March 22, 1898; *Omaha World Herald, Argus and Patriot* (Montpelier, Vermont), *Hamilton Daily Republican News*, March 23, 1898.

[33] *Waterloo Daily Courier*, March 29, 1898; *Lincoln Evening News*, April 4, 1898.

[34] *Milwaukee Evening Wisconsin*, April 14, 1898; *Kansas City Journal*, April 20, 1898; *San Antonio Light*,

April 26, 1898; *First in Violence, Deepest in Dirt, Homicide in Chicago, 1875-1920* by Jeffrey S. Adler, 2006.

35 *Omaha World Herald*, May 1, 1898.

36 (Fort Wayne, Indiana) *Sunday Gazette*, May 8, 1898.

37 Postal Telegraph-Cable Company telegram dated May 14, 1898, from Harry Shaffer.

38 *Hamilton Daily Republican-News*, May 26, 1898. The note by Joe on the reverse of the June 7, 1898 contract, courtesy Lelands Auction site.

39 *Lowell Sun*, June 9, 1898; *St. Paul Globe*, June 10, 1898; *Milwaukee Evening Wisconsin*, *Oakland Tribune*, June 11, 1898.

40 *Lowell Sun*, June 17, 1898; *Syracuse Evening Herald* , June 27, 1898.

41 *Trenton Evening Times*, June 28, 1898.

42 *Milwaukee Evening Wisconsin*, July 16, 1898; August 4, 1898.

43 *Portsmouth Daily News*, July 28, 1898; *Brooklyn Daily Eagle*, August 8, 1898.

44 *Lowell Sun*, August 26, 1898; *Kentucky Irish American*, August 27, 1898; *Fort Wayne Journal*, September 4, 1898.

45 *Philadelphia Inquirer*, September 8, 1898, September 11, 1898.

46 *Duluth News-Tribune* (wire service report), *Philadelphia Evening Bulletin*, *Philadelphia Inquirer*, *Trenton Evening Times*, September 13, 1898; "I Fought 'Em All," *Fight Stories*, June-July 1938.

47 *Sandusky Star*, October 5, 1898; *Milwaukee Evening Wisconsin*, October 20, 1898; October 24, 1898 Western Union telegram, from Harry Shaffer.

48 *Los Angeles Herald*, August 15, 1907.

49 *Lowell Sun*, October 29, 1898; *Philadelphia Item*, October, 1898, from Harry Shaffer; *Sandusky Star*, *Philadelphia Inquirer*, November 4, 1898.

50 *Chicago Tribune*, November 5, 1898.

51 *Brooklyn Daily Eagle*, *Chicago Tribune*, *Philadelphia Evening Bulletin*, November 5, 1898.

52 *Sandusky Star*, November 12, November 16, 1898; *Milwaukee Evening Wisconsin*, November 15, 1898.

53 *Syracuse Standard*, December 5, 1898.

54 *Milwaukee Evening Wisconsin*, December 7, 1898; *Sandusky Star*, December 9, 1898.

55 *San Francisco Call*, *Chicago Daily News*, *Nebraska State Journal*, *Syracuse Standard*, December 20, 1898; *Trenton Evening Times*, December 21, 1898; *Syracuse Evening Herald*, December 22, 1898; *Syracuse Standard*, December 25, 1898.

56 *Syracuse Evening Herald* , December 22, 1898, citing reports from *Chicago Chronicle*, *Chicago Record*, *New York Evening Journal* and *Buffalo Times*.

57 *Lowell Sun*, *Eau Claire Leader*, December 30, 1898; *Centralia Enterprise and Tribune*, December 31, 1898.

Round 17:

1 *Naugatuck Daily News*, *Lowell Sun*, January 3, 1899; *Mansfield News*, January 7, 1899.

2 *Galveston Daily News*, January 13, 1899.

3 *Naugatuck Daily News*, April 19, 1940.

4 *San Jose Mercury News*, January 18, 1899; *Naugatuck Daily News*, January 20, 1899; *Galveston Daily News*, January 21, 1899, referenced in *Galveston News*, January 21, 1949.

5 *San Francisco Call*, January 25, 1899; JewishGen Online Worldwide Burial Registry.

6 *San Francisco Call*, *Sandusky Star*, January 31, 1899.

7 *Fresno Morning Republican*, February 10, 1899, February 17, 1899; 6dayracing.ca/resources/start-lists-results.html, *San Francisco Call*, February 18, 1899.

8 *San Francisco Call*, March 3, 1899, March 4, 1899; *Brooklyn Daily Eagle*, March 4, 1899.

9 *Mansfield News*, March 20, 1899.

10 *San Francisco Call*, March 22, 1899.

11 *San Francisco Call*, *Chicago Tribune*, *Milwaukee Evening Wisconsin*, March 23 1899; *Denver Post*, March 24, 1899.

12 *Syracuse Evening Herald*, March 24, 1899.

13 *Chicago Tribune*, *Houston Daily Post*, March 25, 1899.

14 *Chicago Tribune*, *Dallas Morning News*, *San Francisco Call*, *Brooklyn Eagle*, *Denver Post*, *Denver Times*, *Nevada State Journal*, *San Francisco Bulletin*, March 25, 1899; *Denver Post*, *Syracuse Herald*, March 26, 1899.

15 *Sandusky Star*, April 5, 1899; *Lowell Sun*, April 8, 1899; *San Antonio Daily Light*, June 8, 1899.

16 *Pittsburgh Chronicle*, April 14, 1899, cited in *The Professionalization Of Prizefighting: Pittsburgh At The Turn Of The Century* by Thomas M. Croak. Western Pennsylvania History, Number 4, October, 1979.

[17] *Minneapolis Journal*, April 28, 1899; *Police Gazette, Police News*, May, 1899, *Reno Evening Gazette*, June 27, 1921, December 1, 1926.

[18] "I Was the Real McCoy," found in *Irving Wallace, a Writer's Profile* by John Leverence, 1974.

[19] willardbean.com; *Willard Bean: Palmyra's 'Fighting Parson'* by Vicki Bean Zimmerman, *Ensign*, June 1985; *San Francisco Call*, March 18, 1900.

[20] *Trenton Evening Times*, May 5, 1899.

[21] *Fresno Morning Republican*, May 21, 1899; *Lowell Sun*, May 22, 1899; *Milwaukee Evening Wisconsin*, June 2, 1899.

[22] *Anaconda Standard, Butte Weekly Miner*, June 29, 1899; *Helena Daily Independent*, August 19, 1899.

[23] *Dubuque Daily Herald*, July 6, 1899; *Portsmouth Daily Times*, July 10, 1899.

[24] *Milwaukee Evening Wisconsin*, July 18, 1899.

[25] *San Francisco Herald*, August 21, 1899; www.boxrec.com; For McCormick's birth name, see boxrec.com and McCormick's grand-daughter, Peggy McCormick of San Ramon, California.

[26] *Chicago Tribune, Anaconda Standard, Delphos Daily Herald, Dubuque Daily Herald, Hamilton Daily Republican-News, Milwaukee Evening Wisconsin*, July 22, 1899; *Police Gazette*, August 12, 1899; Unidentified, undated article, likely from *Police Gazette*, Stanley Weston collection, Notre Dame Libraries.

[27] Boxing Records at www.boxrec.com; *San Jose* (California) *Mercury News*, August 4, 1899.

[28] *Brooklyn Eagle, Colorado Springs Gazette, Denver Republican, Milwaukee Evening Wisconsin*, August 5, 1899; *Fresno Republican*, August 10, 1899.

[29] *San Francisco Call*, August 17, 1899.

[30] *San Francisco Evening Herald*, August 17, 1899.

[31] *Newark Daily Advocate*, August 23, 1899; *Rocky Mountain News*, August 24, 1899.

[32] 1870, 1900 and 1930 United States Federal Censuses; *St. Paul Globe*, May 13, 1900.

[33] *Rocky Mountain News*, August 24, 1899.

[34] *Waterloo Daily Courier, Daily* (Illinois) *Republican*, August 24, 1899.

[35] *Dubuque Sunday Herald*, August 27, 1899; *Milwaukee Evening Wisconsin*, August 28, 1899.

[36] *Dubuque Sunday Herald*, August 29, 1899.

[37] *Des Moines Daily News, Grand Forks Daily Herald, Milwaukee Evening Wisconsin, Omaha World-Herald, New York Times, Davenport Daily Leader, Dubuque Daily Herald*, August 30, 1899; *Trenton Times*, August 31, 1899. Round-by-round accounts: *Grand Forks Daily Herald* and *Dubuque Daily Herald*.

[38] *Denver Times*, September 22, 1899, quoting an unspecified edition of the *Chicago Chronicle*.

[39] *Stevens Point Daily Journal*, August 31, 1899; *Lima Daily News*, September 4, 1899.

[40] *Atlanta Constitution*, September 2, 1899; *Philadelphia Inquirer*, September 6, 1899; *Louisville Courier-Journal*, September 23, 1899; *Ohio Herald-Star*, September 29, 1899.

[41] *Kentucky Irish American*, September 16, 1899; *Louisville Courier-Journal*, September 23, 1899; "A Prizefighter in the Nineties" by Edmund Rucker, *Harper's* magazine, November, 1939.

[42] *Atlanta Constitution*, September 25, 1899.

[43] *Columbus* (Georgia) *Daily Enquirer, Kansas City Star, Newark Daily Advocate, Salt Lake Herald*, September 26, 1899; *Racine Daily Journal*, September 27, 1899.

[44] *Cedar Rapids Evening Gazette*, August 17, 1901; *Philadelphia Inquirer*, August 16, 1903.

[45] *Louisville Courier-Journal*, October 4, 1898; *Chicago Tribune, Oshkosh Daily Northwestern, Atlanta Constitution, Brooklyn Eagle, Rocky Mountain News*, October 7, 1899.

[46] *Milwaukee Evening Wisconsin, Brooklyn Eagle*, October 12, 1899; *Des Moines Daily News*, October 13, 1899; *Fort Wayne Journal-Gazette*, October 16, 1899; *Hamilton Daily Republican-News, Brooklyn Daily Eagle*, October 17, 1899.

[47] *Brooklyn Daily Eagle, New York Times, Philadelphia Inquirer*, October 21, 1899.

[48] *Pawtucket Times, Fort Wayne Journal-Gazette, Rocky Mountain News*, October 24, 1899; *Police Gazette*, November 11, 1899.

[49] *Rocky Mountain News*, October 24, 1899.

[50] *San Francisco Call, Chicago Tribune, Tyrone Daily Herald, Brooklyn Daily Eagle, Daily* (Wisconsin) *Gazette*, October 28, 1899.

[51] *Tyrone Daily Herald*, October 28, 1899.

[52] *San Francisco Chronicle*, November 4, 1899; *Milwaukee Evening Wisconsin*, November 18, 1899; *Hamilton Daily Republican*, November 21, 1899; *Chicago Tribune*, March 30, 1905; redfin.com; zillow.com.

[53] Article from unidentified paper, Stanley Weston Collection, Libraries, University of Notre Dame.

[54] *Duluth Sunday News-Tribune, Morning Herald* (Lexington, Kentucky), November 5, 1899; *Milwaukee Evening Wisconsin*, November 6, 1899.

[55] *Kansas City Journal*, November 12, 1899; *Mansfield News*, November 23, 1899.

[56] *Philadelphia Inquirer*, November 16, 1899; *Sandusky Star*, November 30, 1899; *Mansfield News*, December 3, 1899.

[57] *Pawtucket Times*, December 11, 1899; *Dubuque Daily Herald*, December 15, 1899; For the postponement of the Walcott fight, see *Mansfield News*, December 20, 1899.

Round 18:

[1] *Brooklyn Daily Eagle*, January 4, 1900.

[2] *Daily Iowa Capital*, *Denver Post*, January 10, 1900.

[3] *Daily Iowa Capital*, *Brooklyn Daily Eagle*, January 11, 1900; *Milwaukee Evening Wisconsin*, *New York Sun*, *Oshkosh Daily Northwestern*, *San Francisco Call*, *San Francisco Chronicle*, January 12, 1900.

[4] *Oregonian*, *San Francisco Call*, *Bangor Daily Whig & Courier*, *Brooklyn Daily Eagle*, *Denver Republican*, *Denver Times*, *Portsmouth Herald*, *Rocky Mountain News*, *New York Times*, January 13, 1900; *Chicago Tribune*, *New York Times*, *Oregonian*, January 14, 1900; *Baltimore Morning Herald*, January 15, 1900; *Omaha Bee*, January 21, 1900; *Durango Democrat*, February 6, 1900; *Syracuse Herald*, July 21, 1911; "I Fought 'Em All" by Joe Choynski, *Fight Stories*, June-July 1938; "The Days of Finish Fights," February 5, 1927; "The Case for Choynski" by Christopher J. LaForce, IBRO newsletter #61, June 1999.

[5] *Des Moines Capital*, September 7, 1924; *Butler County* (Ohio) *Democrat*, May 26, 1904.

[6] *Brooklyn Daily Eagle*, *Chicago Tribune*, January 14, 1900; *Cumberland Evening Times*, February 5, 1943.

[7] *Oshkosh Daily Northwestern*, January 24, 1900.

[8] *Boxing in San Francisco* by F. Daniel Somrack, 2005.

[9] *Chicago Tribune*, January 14, 1900; *Bangor Daily Whig & Courier*, January 26, 1900.

[10] "Joe the Giant Killer," *Boxing and Wrestling* magazine, April 1955; "The Remarkable Joe Choynski" by Johnny Brannigan, *Boxing Illustrated – Wrestling News*, January 1960.

[11] *Milwaukee Evening Wisconsin*, January 15, January 17, 1900; *Bangor* (Maine) *Daily Whig & Courier*, January 29, 1900; *Mansfield News*, January 18, 1900; *Bangor Daily Whig & Courier*, February 13, 1900.

[12] *Bangor Daily Whig & Courier*, January 9, 1900; *Mansfield News*, January 18, 1900.

[13] *Mansfield News*, January 19, 1900.

[14] *Dubuque Daily Herald*, February 1, 1900; *Daily Iowa Capital*, February 6, 1900.

[15] Un-named paper, February 9, 1900, from David Chesanow; *Daily Iowa Capital*, February 9, 1900.

[16] *Oshkosh Daily Northwestern*, February 12, 1900, quoting from the *Denver Post*.

[17] *Oshkosh Daily Northwestern*, February 14, 1900, quoting *New Orleans Picayune*; *St. Paul Globe*, February 16, 1900.

[18] *Columbus Daily Enquirer-Sun*, *Dallas Morning News*, *New York Evening World*, *Lincoln Evening News*, *Oregonian*, *Rocky Mountain News*, February 17, 1900; Two articles from unknown publications, undated, probably *Police Gazette*, from Stanley Weston collection, Libraries of University of Notre Dame; "I Fought 'Em All" by Joe Choynski, *Fight Stories*, June-July 1938.

[19] *New Haven Register*, *Pawtucket Times*, February 21, 1900; *New York Evening Telegram*, *Springfield Republican*, February 22, 1900.

[20] *Pawtucket Times*, February 22, 1900; *Morning Herald* (Lexington, Kentucky), February 23, 1900.

[21] *Philadelphia Inquirer*, *New York Evening World*, *Brooklyn Daily Eagle*, *Lincoln Evening News*, *Oakland Tribune*, *San Francisco Morning Herald*, February 24 1900; *Chicago Tribune*, *St. Louis Republic*, February 25, 1900; *Washington Post*, February 27, 1910.

[22] *Chicago Daily Inter-Ocean* , March 6, 1900; Quoted in *Des Moines Daily News*, March 7, 1900.

[23] *Fort Worth Star-Telegram*, December 7, 1906, *Atlanta Constitution*, February 7, 1915; *San Antonio Evening News*, March 19, 1919; Undated *Ring* magazine, but from May, 1931, from David Chesanow.

[24] *Sydney Referee*, September 11, 1918.

[25] *Daily Iowa Capital*, March 6, 1900, March 9, 1900; *Dubuque Herald*, *Des Moines News*, March 7, 1900; *Des Moines News*, March 8, 1900.

[26] *Grand Forks Herald*, March 13, 1900.

[27] *Racine Daily Journal*, March 27, 1900; *Oshkosh Daily Northwestern*, March 28, 1900; *Oshkosh Daily Northwestern*, March 30, 1900.

[28] *Elmira Daily Gazette*, April 16, 1900; *Oshkosh Daily Northwestern*, April 19, 1900; *Galveston Daily News*, April 29, 1900.

[29] *Milwaukee Evening Wisconsin*, April 23, 1900; *Dubuque Daily Herald*, May 3, 1900; *Oshkosh Daily Northwestern*, May 4, 1900.

[30] *Dubuque Daily Herald*, May 8, 1900.

[31] *Daily Nevada State Journal*, May 8, 1900; *Chicago Tribune*, *Milwaukee Evening Wisconsin*, *Oshkosh Daily Northwestern*, *Brooklyn Daily Eagle*, *Rocky Mountain News*, May 9, 1900.

[32] *St. Paul Globe*, May 13, 1900.

[33] *Oshkosh Daily Northwestern*, June 12, 1900; *Police Gazette*, June 16, 1900; *James J. Corbett, a Biography of the Heavyweight Boxing Champion and Popular Theater Headliner* by Armond Fields, 2001.

[34] *Des Moines Daily News*, *Anaconda Standard*, July 25, 1900.

[35] *Milwaukee Evening Wisconsin*, *Pawtucket Times*, August 2, 1900; *Pawtucket Times*, August 8, 1900; *The Dayton Marcos* by Margaret E. Peters, Dayton Area Sports History website; www.boxrec.com.

[36] *Milwaukee Evening Wisconsin*, August 10, 1900, August 21, 1900; *San Francisco Call*, August 25, 1900; *Newark Daily Advocate*, *Cedar Rapids Republican*, August 29, 1900; *Marshall Expounder*, August 31, 1900.

[37] *Milwaukee Evening Wisconsin*, October 1, 1900; *New York World*, *Lowell Sun*, October 4, 1900.

[38] *Pawtucket Times*, October 22, 1900; *Papa Jack* by Randy Roberts, 1983.

[39] *Milwaukee Evening Wisconsin*, November 8, 1900; *Police Gazette*, December 8, 1900; for the postponement being due to Gans-McGovern, see *Austin* (Minnesota) *Daily Herald*, December 17, 1900.

[40] *Van Wert Times*, December 14, 1900.

Round 19:

[1] *Des Moines Daily News*, *Salt Lake Herald*, January 1, 1901; *Philadelphia Inquirer*, January 2, 1901, January 4, 1901; *Auburn Bulletin*, January 3, 1901; *Oshkosh Daily Northwestern*, January 4, 1901; (Lexington, Kentucky) *Morning Herald*, January 6, 1901; *Pawtucket Times*, January 11, 1901.

[2] *Sandusky Daily Star*, February 6, 1901; 1900 and 1930 United States Federal Censuses.

[3] *Ohio Times Democrat*, February 19, 1901; *Buffalo Express*, February 20, 1901; *Oshkosh Daily Northwestern*, February 22, 1901.

[4] *Galveston, a History of the Island* by Gary Cartwright, 1998.

[5] *Waterloo Times-Tribune*, February 4, 1912.

[6] *Captain J.A. Brooks, Texas Ranger* by Paul N. Spellman, 2007.

[7] *New Zealand Truth*, March 11, 1911, *My Story of My Life's Battles, by Jack Johnson*, Chapter 8; *My Life and Battles by Jack Johnson* (translated from "Vie au Grand Air," 1911) by Christopher Rivers, 2007; *Taken at the Flood* by John Gunther, 1960.

[8] *Milwaukee Evening Wisconsin*, February 25, 1901; *San Francisco Call*, *Denver Post*, *Galveston Daily News*, *Trenton Times*, February 26, 1901; *Chicago Daily Tribune*, July 2, 1912; "The Days of Finish Fights," *Manitoba Free Press*, February 5, 1927; "I Fought 'Em All," *Fight Stories*, 1930.

[9] "Joe the Giant Killer," *Boxing and Wrestling* magazine, April 1955; For Joe calling the punch a right hand, see "A Great Fighter Confesses" by Joe Choynski, *Boxing and Wrestling* magazine, August 1956.

[10] *Black Champion* by Finnis Farr, 1964; *The Man Who Stayed in Texas, the Life of Rabbi Henry Cohen* by Anne Nathan Cohen and Henry Isaac Cohen, 1941.

[11] *Jewish Boxers Hall of Fame* by Ken Blady, 1988.

[12] *New Zealand Truth*, March 11, 1911, *My Story of My Life's Battles, by Jack Johnson* Chapter 8; *Beyond the Ring* by Jeffrey T. Sammons, 1990.

[13] *Hitters, Dancers and Ring Magicians: Seven Boxers of the Golden Age* by Kelly Richard Nicholson, 2010; *Logansport Pharos-Tribune*, April 18, 1936.

[14] *Jack Johnson & His Times* by Denzil Batchelor, 1956.

[15] *Black Dynamite, Volume IV, Fighting Furies* by Nat Fleischer, 1939.

[16] *Trenton Times*, *Tyrone Daily Herald*, February 26, 1901; *Galveston Daily News*, February 28, 1901.

[17] *Kindler of Souls, Rabbi Henry Cohen* by Henry Cohen II, 2009; *Lone Stars of David, the Jews of Texas* by Hollace Ava Weiner and Kenneth Roseman, 2007; tshaonline.org/handbook/online/articles/fco13

[18] *Kindler of Souls, Rabbi Henry Cohen* by Henry Cohen II, 2009; *Lone Stars of David, the Jews of Texas* by Hollace A. Weiner and Kenneth Roseman, 2007; *The Man Who Stayed in Texas, the Life of Rabbi Henry Cohen* by Anne N. Cohen and Henry I. Cohen, 1941; *Galveston Daily News*, February 28, 1901.

[19] *Sandusky Daily Star*, March 5, 1901; *Des Moines Capital*, March 8, 1901; *Idaho Daily Statesman*, *Galveston Daily News*, *San Francisco Call*, March 9, 1901; The convicted murderer leaving prison before Joe and Jack, is from *Beyond the Ring* by Jeffrey T. Sammons, 1990, and many other sources.

[20] *Galveston Daily News*, March 9, 1901, March 10, 1901.

[21] *Lowell Sun*, March 14, 1901; *Galveston Daily News*, March 21, 1901; *Milwaukee Evening Wisconsin*, March 22, 1901.

[22] *Galveston Daily News*, March 23, 1901.

[23] "A Prizefighter in the Nineties" by Edmund Rucker, *Harper's* magazine, November, 1939.

[24] *Oshkosh Daily Northwestern*, March 27, 1901; *Galveston Daily News*, May 29, May 30 1901; Undated article from an unidentified 1950s newspaper.

[25] The review from an unidentified Chicago newspaper is from Mark T. Dunn, in a letter he wrote to Bob Petersen on April 21, 2002.

[26] *Mirror of Life*, November 13, 1901; *Police Gazette*, November 16, 1901.

[27] *New York Dramatic Mirror, New York Clipper,* November 23, 1901.

[28] *Pawtucket Times,* December 28, 1901; *Davenport Weekly Leader,* January 3, 1902.

[29] *Chicago Tribune,* December 31, 1901; *Police News,* December (undated) 1901, and other sources.

[30] *Lowell Sun,* January 4, 1902; *Chicago Tribune,* January 8, 1902; *Davenport Leader,* January 10, 1902.

[31] *Oshkosh Daily Northwestern,* January 11, 1902.

[32] *Davenport Daily Republican,* January 18, 1902; *Mansfield News,* January 18, 1902.

Round 20:

[1] *Davenport Daily Leader,* February 4, 1902; *Chicago Tribune,* February 7, 1902.

[2] *Brooklyn Daily Eagle,* February 7, 1902.

[3] *Davenport Daily Leader,* February 16, 1902.

[4] *Davenport Daily Leader,* February 27, 1902. (The *Trenton Times* said the match was at the Southern Athletic Club, not the Empire Athletic Club); *St. Paul Globe, Daily Iowa State Press,* March 7, 1902.

[5] "Famous Fights I Have Seen—Hanrahan and West" by Old Timer, *Fight Stories,* October, 1930.

[6] "The Days of Finish Fights," *Manitoba Free Press,* February 19, 1927; "I Fought 'Em All" by Joe Choynski, *Fight Stories,* June-July 1938.

[7] *Sandusky Daily Star,* July 11, 1902.

[8] *Milwaukee Free Press, Chicago Tribune, Cedar Rapids Republican, Oakland Tribune, Daily Journal, Trenton Times,* March 8, 1902; "The Days of Finish Fights," *Manitoba Free Press,* February 19, 1927; "I Fought 'Em All" by Joe Choynski, *Fight Stories,* June-July 1938.

[9] *Salt Lake Telegram,* September 3, 1906.

[10] *Chicago Tribune,* March 9, 1902; *Pawtucket Times,* March 14, 1902.

[11] The *Veteran Boxer,* November, 1952, Veteran Boxers' Association; *Only a Game* by Bill Littlefield, 2007; *Trenton Times,* September 15, 1902.

[12] *Davenport Daily Leader, Idaho Daily Statesman, Oshkosh Daily Northwestern, Racine Daily Journal, Utica Herald-Dispatch,* March 25, 1902; *Syracuse Post-Standard,* March 27, 1902; *Police Gazette,* March, 1902, actual date unknown; *Durango Democrat,* March, 1902, actual date unknown; The *Veteran Boxer,* November, 1952 by the Veteran Boxers' Association; July, 1955 *Ring* magazine, actual date unknown.

[13] *Kansas City Star,* March 3, 1902; *Milwaukee Evening Wisconsin,* April 15, 1902; *Davenport Daily Leader,* April 29, 1902.

[14] *New York Evening World, Paducah Sun, St. Paul Globe, Anaconda Standard, Kansas City Star, Louisville Courier-Journal,* May 3, 1902.

[15] The *Veteran Boxer,* November, 1952.

[16] *Philadelphia Evening Bulletin,* August 19, 1902; Article from unknown paper, dated August 28, 1902, from Harry Shaffer; *Racine Daily Journal,* August 29, 1902; *Milwaukee Evening Wisconsin,* August 30, 1902; *Police Gazette,* (circa) September 1, 1902.

[17] *Chicago Tribune,* September 23, 1902; *Idaho Statesman, Racine Daily Journal,* September 24, 1902.

[18] *Police Gazette,* undated, but from October, 1902; *Fort Wayne News,* September 26, 1902.

[19] *Trenton Times,* September 29, 1902; *Oshkosh Daily Northwestern,* September 30, 1902.

[20] *Brooklyn Eagle, Oshkosh Daily Northwestern,* September 30, 1902; *Police Gazette,* October 25, 1902.

[21] *Wisconsin State Journal,* November 20, 1902.

[22] *Milwaukee Free Press,* November 30, 1902; *New York Evening World, Milwaukee Evening Wisconsin,* December 1, 1902.

[23] *New York Evening World, Milwaukee Evening Wisconsin, Milwaukee Free Press, Oshkosh Daily Northwestern,* December 2, 1902.

[24] *Pawtucket Times,* December 6, 1902; *Washington Times,* January 4, 1903; *Salt Lake Telegram,* January 24, 1903; *Lincoln News,* May 12, 1903.

[25] *Milwaukee Free Press,* January 20, 1903.

[26] *New York Evening World,* January 27, 1903; *Remembering Bob Fitzsimmons* by Pember W. Rocap and William H. Rocap, 2001.

[27] *Milwaukee Free Press, Philadelphia Bulletin, Philadelphia Inquirer, Washington Times, New York Evening World, Anaconda Standard, Oshkosh Daily Northwestern, Police Gazette, Rocky Mountain News,* January 27, 1903; *Massena Observer,* January 29, 1903; *Police Gazette,* January 24, 1920, June 26, 1920.

[28] *Milwaukee Evening Wisconsin,* February 7, 1903.

[29] *Milwaukee Evening Wisconsin,* February 10, 1903; *Daily Nevada State Journal,* February 13, 1903.

[30] *Philadelphia Evening Bulletin, Washington Times,* March 30, 1903.

[31] *Washington Times, Worcester Daily Spy, New York Sun, Milwaukee Free Press,* March 31, 1903.

Round 21:

[1] *Milwaukee Evening Wisconsin*, May 6, 1903.

[2] *Milwaukee Free Press, Omaha World-Herald*, May 23, 1903; *Washington Times*, May 25, 1903.

[3] *San Francisco Call*, May 27, 1903.

[4] "The Days of Finish Fights," *Adelaide Advertiser*, February 27, 1927, Chapter 28.

[5] *Joe Boyle, King of the Klondike* by William Rodney, 1974; "Boxing in the Klondike" by Darrell Hookey and the Yukon Reader, 1998 (yukonalaska.com/klondike/boxing.html).

[6] *I Was There, a Book of Reminiscences* by Mary Edith Carey Tyrrell, 1939.

[7] www.cyberboxingzone.com, record by Tracy Callis.

[8] *Joe Boyle, King of the Klondike* by William Rodney, 1974.

[9] *Tacoma News*, September 15, 1908; www.boxrec.com; www.cyberboxingzone.com.

[10] *Boxing in the Klondike* by Darrell Hookey and the Yukon Reader, 1998 (yukonalaska.com/klondike/boxing.html)

[11] "The Days of Finish Fights," *Adelaide Advertiser*, February 27, 1927, Chapter 28.

[12] *Boxing in the Klondike* by Darrell Hookey and the Yukon Reader, 1998 (yukonalaska.com/klondike/boxing.html)

[13] *Joe Boyle, King of the Klondike* by William Rodney, 1974.

[14] "The Days of Finish Fights," *Adelaide Advertiser*, February 27, 1927, Chapter 28.

[15] "Boxing in the Klondike" by Darrell Hookey and the Yukon Reader, 1998 (yukonalaska.com/klondike/boxing.html)

[16] An undated article from a July, 1903 issue of *Police Gazette*.

[17] *Police Gazette*, undated, but likely the beginning of July, 1903.

[18] *Joe Boyle, King of the Klondike* by William Rodney, 1974.

[19] *Daily Alaska Dispatch*, August 7, 1903; *Wilkes-Barre Times*, August 7, 1903.

[20] *Daily* (Juneau, Alaska) *Record-Miner, Dawson* (Yukon) *Record*, August 8, 1903.

[21] *Yukon Sun*, August 8, 1903; *Oshkosh Daily Northwestern*, September 2, 1903; "The Days of Finish Fights," *Adelaide Advertiser*, February 27, 1927, Chapter 28.

[22] *Daily Alaska Dispatch*, August 24, 1903, quoting the *Dawson News* of August 13, 1903. The handbill was provided by David Chesanow.

[23] Boyle's biography at the Dictionary of Canadian Biography Online (biographi.ca); *Joe Boyle, King of the Klondike* by William Rodney, 1974; en.wikipedia.org/wiki/Joseph_W._Boyle

[24] *Kansas City Star*, September 9, 1903. Luncheon menu from steamer, *Dolphin*, by David Chesanow.

[25] *Sunday Alaska Dispatch*, October 11, 1903.

[26] *Waterloo Daily Courier* (article by Associated Press), October 27, 1903.

[27] *Columbus Daily Enquirer, Philadelphia Inquirer, Philadelphia Press, Philadelphia Record, Worcester Daily Spy, San Francisco Call*, November 17, 1903; *Police Gazette*, November 28, 1903.

[28] *Wilkes-Barre Times*, November 20, 1903; *Oshkosh Daily Northwestern*, December 3, 1903; *Kansas City Star*, December 5, 1903.

[29] *Lincoln Evening News*, November 24, 1903.

[30] *Oshkosh Daily Northwestern*, December 15, 1903.

[31] *New York Evening World*, December 26, 1903; *Kansas City Star*, December 31, 1903.

[32] *Boston Globe*, October 15, 1903; *New York Evening World*, December 22, 1903.

[33] *Fort Wayne News*, January 7, 1904; *Syracuse Post-Standard*, January 9, 1904; *Bellingham Herald, Boston Journal, Oshkosh Daily Northwestern*, January 18, 1904; *Pawtucket Times*, January 19, 1904.

Round 22:

[1] *New York Evening World, Washington Times, Colorado Springs Gazette, Pawtucket Times, Philadelphia Inquirer, Decatur Review, Fort Wayne Journal-Gazette, Lowell Sun, Oshkosh Daily Northwestern, Syracuse Post-Standard*, unnamed paper, January 20, 1904; *Police Gazette*, (undated), January, 1904.

[2] *Lowell Sun*, January 21, 1904; *Philadelphia Inquirer, Worcester Daily Spy*, January 22, 1904; *Boston Daily Globe*, January 25, 1904.

[3] *Pawtucket Times*, January 23, 1904; *Chicago Tribune*, January 24, 1904; *Grand Forks Herald*, February 17, 1904.

[4] *Fort Wayne News, Oakland Tribune*, unnamed paper, Stanley Weston collection, January 23, 1904; *Philadelphia Inquirer*, January 24, 1904; *Aberdeen Daily News, Boston Daily Globe*, January 25, 1904.

[5] *Oakland Tribune*, January 25, 1904; *Mansfield News*, January 26, 1904; January, 1904 *Police Gazette*; *Oshkosh Daily Northwestern*, February 1, 1904; *Washington Times*, February 2, 1904. *Paducah Sun*, February 4, 1904; *Pawtucket Times*, February 6, 1904; *Daily Kennebec Journal*, February 8, 1904.

[6] *Idaho Statesman*, May 9, 1904; Joe Choynski's notes and photos from John E. Rogers collection.

[7] *New York Sun*, June 26, 1904; *Reared in a Greenhouse* by Dorothy B. Wexler, 1998.

[8] *Syracuse Post-Standard*, October 20, 1904; *Decatur Review, Milwaukee Free Press*, October 21, 1904; *Decatur Review*, November 4, 1904.

[9] *Oshkosh Daily Northwestern*, November 11, 1904; *Boston Journal*, November 21, 1904; *Trenton Times*, November 22, 1904.

[10] *New York Evening World, Pawtucket Times, Boston Journal, Wilkes-Barre Times, Racine Daily Journal, Trenton Times*, November 22, 1904; *Baltimore Sun*, November 23, 1904.

[11] *Milwaukee Free Press*, November 26, 1904; *American Gymnasia and Athletic Record 1906*.

[12] *Racine Daily Journal*, December 30, 1904; *Lincoln Evening News*, January 9, 1905; *St. Louis Republic*, January 22, 1905.

[13] (Christchurch, New Zealand) *Star*, January 10, 1905.

[14] *San Antonio Gazette*, March 8, 1905, for the Newspaper Enterprise Association syndicate.

[15] *Daily* (Juneau) *Alaska Dispatch*, April 11, 1905; *Oakland Tribune*, April 14, 1905.

[16] (Christchurch, New Zealand) *Star*, April 13, 1905.

[17] *Racine Daily Journal*, June 7, 1905; *Janesville Daily Gazette*, June 12, 1905; *Tonopah Sun*, July 4, 1905.

[18] *San Francisco Call*, July 27, 1905.

[19] *San Francisco Call*, August 19, 1905; townofross.org.

[20] *Janesville Daily Gazette*, October 21, 1905; *Police Gazette*, November (undated).

[21] *New York Daily Tribune*, February 15, 1906, repeated in *Washington Post*, March 25, 1906; *American Mercury Magazine*, September to December 1927, *An American Master* by Thomas Craven.

[22] For the Choynski family living at 1679 Oak, see the 1907 Crocker Langley's San Francisco City Directory; *San Francisco Call*, June 19, 1906; 1909 Crocker Langley's San Francisco City Directory.

[23] *New York Times*, April 20, 1906.

[24] *Milwaukee Free Press*, April 27, 1906; *Pawtucket Times*, May 14, 1906.

[25] *Daily Kennebec Journal*, May 16, 1906; *Kansas City Star*, May 23, 1906.

[26] *Boston Journal*, June 23, 1906; *Police Gazette*, June (undated); *Milwaukee Free Press*, July 29, 1906.

[27] *San Francisco Call*, August 8, August 15, September 23, 1906; *Oakland Tribune*, August 9, 1906.

[28] *Oakland Tribune*, October 21, November 26, December 9, 1906; *San Francisco Call*, November 17, November 21, November 22, November 23, December 30, 1906.

[29] *Trenton Evening News, Milwaukee Free Press*, December 29, 1906; *Grand Forks Daily Herald*, January 2, 1907; *La Crosse Tribune, Police Gazette*, January 19, 1907; *Salt Lake Evening Herald*, March 6, 1907; geostan.ca/bio.html; *American Gymnasia and Athletic Record, Volumes 1 and 2*, 1905.

[30] (Christchurch, New Zealand) *Star*, January 3, 1907.

[31] *Racine Daily Journal*, May 1, 1907; *Daily Kennebec Journal, Washington Post*, May 3, 1907; *Salt Lake Evening Telegram*, May 4, 1907; *Oakland Tribune*, May 7, 1907.

[32] *San Francisco Call*, August 1, 1907; *San Francisco Call*, October 18, 1907.

[33] *New York Dramatic Mirror*, August 10, 1907.

[34] *Milwaukee Evening Wisconsin*, September 2, 1907; "I Fought 'Em All," *Fight Stories*, 1938.

[35] *Lake County Times*, September 21, 1907.

[36] *Anaconda Standard*, February 7, 1908; *Belleville News-Democrat*, April 15, 1908.

[37] *San Francisco Bulletin*, undated issue, by way of the *New Zealand Truth*, April 25, 1908.

[38] *Elmira* (New York) *Morning Telegram*, March 15, 1908; *Racine Daily Journal*, April 13, 1908.

[39] *Mansfield News*, September 9, 1908.

[40] Tony Gee, 'Mendoza, Daniel (1765?-1836),' *Oxford Dictionary of National Biography*, Oxford University Press, 2004; *Big Book of Jewish Sports Heroes* by Peter S. Horvitz, 2007.

[41] *Daily Kennebec Journal*, October 21, 1908; Chicago City Directories, 1907 – 1911; *1910 Chicago City Street Guide*; 1910 U.S. Federal Census.

[42] *Chicago Daily Tribune, San Francisco Call*, November 14, 1908.

[43] *Winchester News*, December 31, 1908; *Reno Evening Gazette*, January 1, 1909.

[44] *Salt Lake Herald*, January 3, 1909; *The Lure of the Ring* by Frederick Arthur Hornibrook, 1946. *Gentleman Bruiser*, by Bob Petersen, 2005.

[45] *Salt Lake Telegram*, January 8, 1909.

[46] *Chicago Daily Tribune*, January 21, 1909; *Racine Daily Journal*, January 29, 1909.

[47] *San Francisco Call*, February 5, 1909; *Pearson's* magazine, Volume 28, December, 1912.

[48] *Cedar Rapids Tribune*, April 16, 1909; *La Crosse Tribune*, April 19, 1909; *Milwaukee Evening Wisconsin*, April 20, 1909; *Des Moines News*, May 4, 1909; *Des Moines News, Dunkirk Observer*, May 6, 1909; *Boston Journal*, May 7, 1909; *Reno Evening Gazette, Lethbridge Herald*, May 18, 1909; May, 1909 *Police Gazette*.

[49] *Colorado Springs Gazette*, June 2, 1909; *Bisbee Daily Review*, June 23, 1909; *Jewish Boxers Hall of Fame*

by Ken Blady, 1988.

[50] *Waterloo Reporter*, July 17, 1909; *Police Gazette*, undated July issue; www.boxrec.com.

[51] *Fort Wayne Journal-Gazette*, July 25, 1909; *Duluth News-Tribune*, August 22, 1909.

[52] *Warren Evening Mirror*, December 30, 1909.

[53] *Police Gazette*, August 21, 1909; *Anaconda Standard*, August 22, 1909.

[54] *Morning Olympian*, November 27, 1909.

[55] *Racine Daily Journal*, December 16, 1909; *Colorado Springs Gazette*, December 19, 1909; *Syracuse Herald*, January 6, 1910; *Police Gazette*, January 22, 1910; *Cedar Rapids Tribune*, January 28, 1910; Boxing Records at boxrec.com, cyberboxingzone.com and other sources.

[56] *Waterloo Semi-Weekly Courier*, January 4, 1910.

[57] *Portsmouth Daily Times*, March 30, 1910.

[58] *Oshkosh Daily Northwestern*, April 6, 1910.

[59] *Indianapolis Star*, April 8, 1910; *Billings Daily Gazette*, April 9, 1910.

[60] *Des Moines Daily News, Milwaukee Evening Wisconsin*, April 10, 1910.

Round 23:

[1] *Indianapolis Star*, April 12, 1910; *Nevada State Journal*, April 13, 1910.

[2] *Waterloo Evening Courier, Nebraska State Journal*, April 11, 1910; for Johnson on "Kid" Cotton, see *New Zealand Truth*, June 24, 1911.

[3] *Salt Lake Herald-Republican*, April 24, 1910.

[4] *Dunkirk Evening Observer*, April 16, 1910; *Milwaukee Evening Wisconsin, Milwaukee Free Press, Nebraska State Journal*, April 17, 1910.

[5] *New York Times*, April 19, 1910; *San Francisco Call*, April 20, 1910.

[6] *Washington Post*, April 20, 1910.

[7] *San Francisco Call, Washington Post, Lincoln Evening News, Lowell Sun*, April 21, 1910.

[8] *Syracuse Post-Standard, New York Times, Eau Claire Leader*, April 22, 1910.

[9] *Nebraska State Journal, Nevada State Journal, Syracuse Post-Standard*, April 23, 1910.

[10] *Washington Post, Morning Oregonian*, April 24, 1910; *Des Moines Daily News*, April 25, 1910; *Nevada State Journal*, April 26, 1910.

[11] *San Francisco Call, Anaconda Standard*, April 26, 1910; *Oakland Tribune, Lowell Sun, Racine Daily Journal, Fort Wayne News, Nebraska State Journal*, April 27, 1910.

[12] *Lowell Sun*, April 28, 1910; *Brownsville Daily Herald*, April 29, 1910.

[13] *Anaconda Standard, Lima Daily News*, May 1, 1910; *Nevada State Journal, Syracuse Post-Standard, Lincoln Evening News*, May 3, 1910; *Police Gazette*, May 7, 1910.

[14] *Brownsville Daily Herald, Morning Oregonian*, May 6, 1910; *Titusville Herald*, May 7, 1910.

[15] *Anaconda Standard*, May 7, 1910; *San Francisco Call*, May 8, 1910.

[16] *Nebraska State Journal, Morning Oregonian*, May 8, 1910.

[17] *Racine Daily Journal, Washington Post*, May 10, 1910.

[18] *Nevada State Journal, Reno Evening Gazette*, May 11, 1910; *Syracuse Post-Standard*, May 12, 1910.

[19] *Warren Evening Mirror*, May 12, 1910; *Warren Evening Mirror, Syracuse Post-Standard* May 13, 1910.

[20] *Reno Evening Gazette, Lincoln Evening News*, May 14, 1910; *Atlanta Constitution*, May 15, 1910.

[21] *Salt Lake Herald-Republican*, May 18, 1910.

[22] *Ogden Standard, Lowell Sun*, May 19, 1910.

[23] *Galveston Daily News, San Francisco Call, Syracuse Post-Standard*, May 21, 1910.

[24] *San Francisco Call*, May 15, 1910; *Nebraska State Journal*, May 22, May 23, 1910; *Fort Wayne Journal-Gazette*, May 23, 1910.

[25] *Fort Wayne Sentinel, Galveston Daily News, Nevada State Journal, Washington Post*, May 25, 1910; *Syracuse Post-Standard*, May 26, 1910.

[26] *Reno Evening Gazette*, May 27, 1910; *Lincoln News, Syracuse Post-Standard, Washington Times*, May 28, 1910; *Galveston Daily News*, May 29, 1910.

[27] *Ogden Standard, Syracuse Post-Standard*, May 31, 1910.

[28] *Ogden Standard, Syracuse Post-Standard, Kansas City Star*, June 2, 1910.

[29] *Indianapolis Star, Waterloo* (Iowa) *Times-Tribune*, June 5, 1910.

[30] *Galveston Daily News, Washington Post*, June 6, 1910; *Salt Lake Telegram*, June 10, 1910.

[31] *Fort Worth Star-Telegram, Lowell Sun, San Francisco Call, Syracuse Post-Standard*, June 11, 1910.

[32] *San Francisco Call, Oakland Tribune*, June 12, 1910.

[33] *Brownsville Daily Herald, Nevada State Journal, San Francisco Call, Syracuse Post-Standard, Washington Post*, June 13, 1910.

[34] *Anaconda Standard, Syracuse Post-Standard*, June 14, 1910.

[35] *Lincoln Evening News, Nebraska State Journal, Nevada State Journal,* June 16, 1910.

[36] *Nevada State Journal,* June 18, 1910; *Oakland Tribune,* June 19, 1910.

[37] *Titusville Herald,* June 20, 1910; *Lincoln Evening News,* June 21, 1910; *Nebraska State Journal, Nevada State Journal,* June 22, 1910.

[38] *Fort Wayne Sentinel,* June 22, 1910; *Nevada State Journal,* June 23, 1910.

[39] *Indianapolis Star, New York Times, Washington Post,* June 26, 1910.

[40] *Indianapolis Star, Lincoln Evening News, Ogden Standard, San Francisco Call,* June 27, 1910; *Santa Fe Employees'* magazine, Volume 4, 1910.

[41] *Anaconda Standard, Nebraska State Journal, Nevada State Journal, Washington Post,* June 28, 1910.

[42] *Indianapolis Star,* June 29, 1910.

[43] *Portsmouth Daily Times, Reno Evening Gazette,* June 30, 1910.

[44] *Idaho Daily Statesman, Lincoln Evening News,* July 1, 1910; *Nebraska State Journal, Syracuse Post-Standard,* July 2, 1910.

[45] *Morning Oregonian, Nevada State Journal,* July 4, 1910.

[46] *Galveston Daily News,* July 5, 1910.

[47] *Hamilton Daily Republican-News, Galveston Daily News, Nebraska State Journal, Syracuse Post-Standard,* July 5, 1910; *Nevada Evening Gazette,* July 4, 1960.

[48] *Hamilton Daily Republican-News,* July 5, 1910.

[49] *Battling Jim - The Johnson Who Fell Just Short* by Christopher J LaForce, August 19, 2012. www.cyberboxingzone.com/blog/?p=11386

[50] *Palestine Daily Herald,* July 5, 1910; *Anaconda Standard,* September 12, 1915.

[51] *Lowell Sun, Syracuse Post-Standard,* July 6, 1910.

[52] *Los Angeles Herald, New Castle News,* July 8, 1910; *Nebraska State Journal,* July 10, 1910.

[53] *San Francisco Chronicle,* July 11, 1910, July 12, 1910.

[54] *Chicago Daily Tribune, Lowell Sun,* July 19, July 22, 1910; *Syracuse Post-Standard,* July 27, 1910; *San Francisco Chronicle,* undated article from July, 1910, Stanley Weston collection.

[55] *Grand Forks Herald,* September 14, 1912.

Round 24:

[1] *Waterloo Evening Courier,* September 28, 1910; *Williamsport Gazette and Bulletin,* December 9, 1910; *Oakland Tribune,* December 11, 1910.

[2] *Oakland Tribune,* December 11, 1910.

[3] *Montreal Herald, San Francisco Call, Waterloo Courier,* September 29, 1910; *Evening Standard* (Ogden, Utah), October 4, 1910; *Poverty Bay* (Gisborne, New Zealand), October 11, 1910; *Lethbridge Herald,* October 17, 1910; *Milwaukee Evening Wisconsin,* October 1, 1910; November 22, 1910.

[4] *Ohio Evening Telegram,* November 25, 1910; *Williamsport Gazette and Bulletin,* December 9, 1910; *Anaconda Standard, Oakland Tribune,* December 11, 1910; *Syracuse Post-Standard,* December 14, 1910; *Naugatuck Daily News,* December 19, 1910.

[5] *Unforgivable Blackness: The Rise and Fall of Jack Johnson* by Geoffrey C. Ward, 2006.

[6] *Chicago Daily Tribune, San Francisco Chronicle, Washington Post,* January 10, 1911; *New York Times, Titusville Herald,* January 11, 1911; *Stevens Point Daily Journal,* February 23, 1911.

[7] *Washington Post,* January 30, 1911; *Milwaukee Evening Wisconsin,* March 2, 1911; www.boxrec.com.

[8] *Colorado Springs Gazette,* March 13, 1911.

[9] *New Zealand Truth,* March 18, 1911.

[10] *Des Moines News, Milwaukee Evening Wisconsin, Chicago Tribune, Indianapolis Star,* March 22, 1911; *Eau Claire Leader,* April 2, 1911.

[11] *Oakland Tribune,* April 3, 1911.

[12] *Fort Wayne News,* March 28, 1911; *New York Times,* April 21, 1911; 1912, 1913 Pittsburgh, Pennsylvania City Directory; *Janesville Daily Gazette,* August 16, 1922.

[13] *Pittsburgh Press,* July 2, 1911; *Milwaukee Free Press, Lowell Sun,* November 11, 1911; *Middletown Daily Times-Press,* November 22, 1911; *Waterloo Evening Reporter,* December 1, 1911; Albert "Buck" Crouse's online boxing record from the Cyber Boxing Zone, courtesy of Tracy Callis.

[14] *Syracuse Herald,* January 10, 1912; *Goldfield Chronicle,* February 15, 1909; *Idaho Statesman,* December 10, 1910; *New Castle News,* July 2, 1915; *Death under the Spotlight: The Data* by Joseph R. Svinth, ejmas.com/jcs/jcsart_svinth_b_0700.htm; boxrec.com and ancestry.com; *San Francisco Call,* October 22, 1899; "New York Day By Day" by O.O. McIntyre, *Logansport Pharos-Tribune,* March 19, 1926; *Chester Times,* October 10, 1929; *Ogden Standard-Examiner,* November 20, 1930; *Tucson Daily Citizen,* August 15, 1943; *Lowell Sun,* October 22, 1948; "Zoë Beckley's Corner," *Poughkeepsie Eagle-News,* February 25, 1925; "This Morning's Matchbox" by Clover Culver, *Morning Herald* (Uniontown, Pennsylvania), July 2, 1958.

[15] *Mansfield News*, January 13, 1912.

[16] *Time* magazine, April 1, 1935.

[17] *New York Times*, April 17, 1912; *Milwaukee Evening Wisconsin*, August 6, 1912.

[18] *Anaconda Standard*, September 15, 1912; *Lexington Herald*, November 17, 1912.

[19] *Sydney Referee*, October 23, 1912.

[20] Thanks to Boxing Records at boxrec.com, in addition to an assortment of newspaper articles in the possession of the author.

[21] *Duluth News-Tribune*, January 10, 1913; *Racine Journal-News*, January 24, 1913.

[22] *Morning Oregonian*, January 26, 1913; *Oakland Tribune*, March 3, 1913, March 13, 1913, April 10, 1914; *Miami Herald*, February 25, 1913; *By-laws and Members of the Olympic Club*, May 1, 1913.

[23] *New Castle News*, March 21, 1913, March 22, 1913; March 29, 1913.

[24] *Oakland Tribune*, July 31, 1913.

[25] *Indianapolis Star*, *Racine Journal-News*, October 17, 1913; *Lincoln Daily Star*, October 26, 1913.

[26] roycrofter.com, roycroft.org, freenet.buffalo.edu, Wikipedia articles on "Elbert Hubbard" and "Roycroft," *Medievalism in North America* by Kathleen Verduin, 1994, and many other sources.

[27] *Muldoon, the Solid Man of Sport* by Edward Van Every, 1929; *Selected Writings of Elbert Hubbard* by Elbert Hubbard, Bert Hubbard, 1922.

[28] *Elbert Hubbard of East Aurora* by Felix Shay, 1926.

[29] *Oelwein Daily Register*, January 2, 1914; *Duluth News-Tribune*, January 26, 1904; *Pittsburgh City Directories*, 1914 through 1918.

[30] *Oelwein Daily Register*, March 6, 1914.

[31] *Lexington Herald*, March 13, 1914; *Duluth News-Tribune*, June 28, 1914; boxrec.com.

[32] *Hamilton Journal*, *Morning Oregonian*, *New Castle News*, March 26, 1914; *Williamsport Gazette and Bulletin*, March 27, 1914; *Lowell Sun*, March 28, 1914.

[33] *Williamsport Gazette and Bulletin*, March 27, 1914; *Fort Worth Star-Telegram*, May 6, 1914.

[34] *Rocky Mountain News*, August 4, 1914; *Fort Wayne News*, October 10, 1914. For Jack Dempsey on the subject of diverse tactics, see *Championship Fighting Explosive Punching and Aggressive Defense* by Jack Dempsey, Prentice-Hall, 1950.

[35] *The Day* (New London, Connecticut), January 4, 1915; *Salt Lake Tribune*, April 5, 1915.

[36] *Elyria Chronicle*, January 4, 1915; *Syracuse Herald*, January 18, 1915.

[37] *New Castle News*, February 23, 1915.

[38] *New Zealand Truth*, March 20, 1915.

[39] *Titanic – An Illustrated History*, by Don Lynch, 2010.

[40] *Lusitania* by Diane Preston, 2002; *The Tragedy of the Lusitania*, by Frederick D. Ellis, 1915; *In Memoriam, Elbert and Alice Hubbard* by John Thomas Hoyle, 1915, among many other sources.

[41] *Roycroft* magazine, August, 1918, Volume 2, Number 6.

[42] *Elbert Hubbard of East Aurora* by Felix Shay, 1926; *Fra* magazine, September, 1914; boxrec.com.

[43] The *Fra* magazine, August, 1917.

[44] *Municipal Journal*, number 24, 1915; The *Iron Age*, issues 13-25, 1915; *Gas Record*, June, 1915; *Gas Journal*, June, 1915.

[45] *Fort Wayne Sentinel*, June 7, 1915.

[46] *Rocky Mountain News*, June 8, 1915.

[47] *Ogden Standard*, July 24, 1915; *Morning Oregonian*, August 8, 1915; *Anaconda Standard*, August 15, 1915.

[48] *New Zealand Truth*, August 21, 1915.

[49] *Lincoln Daily Star*, November 8, 1915; *Lethbridge Herald* November 13, 1915; *Syracuse Herald*, November 15, 1915.

[50] *Morning Oregonian*, *Washington Post*, December 30, 1915; *San Francisco's Visitacion Valley* by Visitacion Valley History Project, 2005; The *Overland Monthly* by Bret Harte, July, 1917; *Memories of Early California* by M.L. Cook; Boxing Records at boxrec.com.

Round 25:

[1] *Traffic World* by Traffic Service Corporation, Volume 17, January 15, 1916; *Wilkes-Barre Times-Leader*, January 20, 1916.

[2] *Miami Herald-Record*, November 28, 1916.

[3] *Lima Daily News*, February 27, 1917; Boxing Records at www.boxrec.com; *Wilkes-Barre Times-Leader*, March 8, 1917.

[4] The *Fra* magazine, August, 1917.

[5] *Logansport Pharos-Reporter*, June 12, 1917.

[6] *Logansport Pharos-Reporter*, July 28, 1917.

[7] *Orange County* (New York) *Times-Press*, August 31, 1917; *Anaconda Standard*, September 1, 1917; *New York Times*, September 28, 1917.

[8] *Oakland Tribune, San Antonio Light, Syracuse Herald, New York Times*, October 22, 1917; *Fort Wayne Journal-Gazette*, November 4, 1917.

[9] *Philadelphia Inquirer*, November 27, 1917; *Milwaukee Evening Wisconsin*, December 5, 1917; *Philadelphia North American*, December 5, December 6, December 8, 1917; *La Crosse Tribune and Leader-Press*, December 6, 1917; *Lethbridge Herald*, December 20, 1917; *Syracuse Herald*, December 22, 1917.

[10] *Sydney Referee*, August 4, 1918.

[11] *Sydney Referee*, August 21, 1918.

[12] *Syracuse Herald*, July 7, 1918.

[13] *Evening News* (San Jose, California), July 24, 1918; *New York Herald*, August (unknown day), 1918; *Wilkes-Barre Times*, November 28, 1918.

[14] 2008 correspondence with James Winterstein, DC, President of the National University of Health Sciences, and Tracy Litsey, Public Relations Specialist, National University of Health Sciences. They advised that, in 1944, the Universal Chiropractic College consolidated with Lincoln Chiropractic College in Indianapolis, Indiana. In 1971, Lincoln College closed its doors and National College of Chiropractic (now National University of Health Sciences) became the repository of record for Lincoln and its associated schools – which included Universal Chiropractic College.

[15] *Sydney Referee*, October 30, 1918; January 8, 1919.

[16] *Syracuse Herald*, November 13, 1918.

[17] *Fort Wayne News and Sentinel*, November 30, 1918; *Milwaukee Free Press*, December 1, 1918; *Grand Forks Herald*, December 10, 1918.

[18] *New Castle News*, January 3, 1919; *Honus Wagner: The Life of Baseball's 'Flying Dutchman'* by Arthur D. Hittner, 1996.

[19] *Modesto Evening News*, July 4, 1919; *Hamilton Daily Republican-News*, July 21, 1919; *Duluth News-Tribune*, September 9, 1919, June 16, 1920; *Fort Wayne Journal-Gazette*, February 20, 1921.

[20] *Olean Times*, July 30, 1919.

[21] *Lincoln Evening Star, Kansas City Times*, October 24, 1919; *Fort Worth Star Telegram*, October 30, 1919. *Lincoln Evening State Journal and Daily News*, November 1, 1919.

[22] *New Zealand Truth*, July 26, 1919.

[23] *Fort Wayne News and Sentinel*, November 6, 1919.

Round 26:

[1] *Honus Wagner: The Life of Baseball's 'Flying Dutchman'* by Arthur D. Hittner, 1996; *Honus: The Life and Times of a Baseball Hero* by William Hageman, 1996.

[2] philosophyofchiropractic.com/wp-content/uploads/2012/04/Carver-College-of-Chiropractic-History.pdf

[3] *Roycroft* magazine, August, 1918, Volume 2, Number 6.

[4] Thanks to James Winterstein, President of the NUHS and Tracy Litsey, Public Relations Specialist, NUHS, for Joe's graduation date; 1923 map of Pittsburgh, images.library.pitt.edu.jpg

[5] James Winterstein advised in 2008, that records from the time Choynski attended the Universal Chiropractic College are minimal. It is only known that he studied for 18 months, graduated on May 5, 1920 and received a diploma. Tracy Litsey searched their repository of records, but found nothing from Universal from that time period. (See also, Endnote 26, Chapter 26). Thanks also to Tracy McHugh, M. Collins and the other NUHS staff members, who forwarded my emails to Mr. Winterstein.

[6] *History of Pottsville and Schuylkill County* by Joseph Henry Zerbey, 1935; *Ashland Daily News*, December 26, 1930.

[7] The *Mixer and Server*, (Hotel, Restaurant and Bartenders' Journal), Number 8, August 15, 1920 (quoting the *Cincinnati Times-Star*); *Oakland Tribune*, June 29, 1920; *Bridgeport Telegram*, June 30, 1920; elkshistory.org; *Chicago's Greatest Sportsman, Charles E. 'Parson' Davies* by Mark T. Dunn, 2011.

[8] *Kansas City Star*, May 20, 1921; *Kingston Daily Freeman*, June 1, 1921; *Wyoming State Tribune*, June 30, 1921; *Racine Journal-News*, July 2, 1921. For Choynski's advocacy of straight punching, see *Duluth News-Tribune*, March 22, 1922; *Chicago Daily Tribune*, August 9, 1921.

[9] Courtroom minutes taken on September 15, 1921, given the author by Al and Harriet Draper. The opinions and information regarding the Choynski-to-Coe name change is from correspondence between this author and David Fleishhacker in 2007.

[10] *Idaho Daily Statesman*, September 16, 1921.

[11] *Olean Evening Herald*, April 29, 1922.

[12] *Lincoln Star*, May 14, 1922.

[13] Unidentified publication, probably *Ring* magazine, dated March 17, 1923; *Ring* magazines, undated, but from May, 1923 and August, 1923, all from David Chesanow.

[14] *Lethbridge Herald*, August 18, 1922; *Casa Grande Bulletin*, September 9, 1922.

[15] Article from unidentified and undated paper, from Bob Petersen of Lane Cove, Australia; The *Veteran Boxer*, February, 1941, from David Chesanow.

[16] *Duluth News-Tribune*, October 26, 1922; *Philadelphia Inquirer*, November 7, 1922; *San Jose Mercury Herald*, November 14, 1922; *San Antonio Evening News*, December 21, 1922; *Syracuse Herald*, December 27, 1922; *Tunney* by Jack Cavanaugh, 2006.

[17] *San Antonio Evening News*, January 5, 1923.

[18] *New York Evening Telegram*, February 13, 1923; *Family, Business, and San Francisco Community*, 1975.

[19] *Modesto Evening News*, March 23, 1923; boxrec.com; *San Francisco Chronicle*, January 26, 1943.

[20] *Boxing Blade*, May 19, 1923; *Appleton Post-Crescent*, July 25, 1923; *Oakland Tribune*, September 3, 1924; boxrec.com.

[21] Unknown paper (likely the *New York Journal*) dated September 29, 1923, Stanley Weston collection, University of Notre Dame Libraries.

[22] *Kingston Daily Freeman*, February 14, 1924.

[23] *Elyria Chronicle-Telegram*, March 25, 1924; *New York Sun*, April 5, 1926; *Ironwood Daily Globe*, October 20, 1926; biography and (incomplete) boxing record at boxrec.com. Arthur De Kuh was referred to as Curtino Del Monte in *San Francisco Chronicle*, February 8, 1933.

[24] *Waukesha Daily Freeman*, April 10, 1924; "The Days of Finish Fights," *Adelaide Advertiser*, Chapter 30, February 9, 1927.

[25] ancestry.com, including the JewishGen Online Worldwide Burial Registry.

[26] *Fresno Bee*, August 15, 1924; *Reno Evening Gazette*, December 9, 1924; *Oxnard Daily Courier*, December 11, 1924; *Ogden Standard-Examiner*, December 15, 1924; *The Real McCoy, the Life and Times of Norman Selby* by Robert Cantwell, 1971.

[27] *Police Gazette*, October 11, 1924.

[28] *Modesto Evening News*, October 30, 1924.

[29] Letters sent me by Al and Harriet Draper, penned by James J. Richardson, Boxing Commissioner of the Olympic Club. They were dated October 26 and November 2, 1926; Three articles from unnamed California papers, Al and Harriet Draper. The first was dated September 25, 1925, the other two, undated; *Oneonta Daily Star* , October 26, 1925, 1924; *Ogden Standard-Examiner*, November 10, 1924.

[30] Unknown paper and date, from Stanley Weston collection, Libraries of Notre Dame University; *Van Wert Daily Bulletin*, July 2, 1928.

[31] *Peter Maher, the Irish Champion* by Matt Donnellon, 2008.

[32] *Brooklyn Daily Eagle*, January 4, 1927.

[33] *Beloit Daily News*, probably March 27, 1927 but possibly as late as March 30, 1927; *Modesto News-Herald, Syracuse Herald*, March 27, 1927; *The Terror of Terre Haute, Bud Taylor and the 1920s* by John D. Wright, 2008; boxrec.com.

[34] *Lewiston Daily Sun*, April 25, 1927; *New Castle News*, July 30, 1927; boxrec.com.

[35] *Athens Messenger, New Castle News*, August 17, 1927; *Oakland Tribune*, September 1, 1927; *San Antonio Light*, September 17, 1927.

[36] *Syracuse Herald*, September 7, 1927; December, 1927 *Ring* magazine, from David Chesanow.

[37] *Waterloo Evening Courier*, April 9, 1928, May 4, 1928; *Davenport Democrat and Leader*, February 21, May 1, May 3, May 4, 1928; *Mason City Globe-Gazette*, May 2, 1928.

[38] *Portsmouth Times*, June 23, 1928.

[39] *San Mateo Times*, July 23, 1928.

[40] *Oakland Tribune, Woodland Daily Democrat*, September 7, 1928; *California and Californians, Volume 4* by Dr. Rockwell Dennis Hunt, 1926, 1930; *San Francisco Call*, June 29, 1913; *Fort Wayne News and Sentinel*, July 24, 1920.

[41] "Joe the Giant Killer," from "Boxing and Wrestling" magazine, April, 1955.

[42] *Ring* magazine, undated, but from December, 1929, from David Chesanow.

[43] A wire service report published in *Oshkosh Daily Northwestern*, August 9, 1929.

Round 27:

[1] Williams Cincinnati Directories (1930 to 1932); *Wisconsin State Journal*, June 28, 1930; *Fresno Bee*, December 14, 1931; *The History of the Cincinnati Athletic Club, 1853-1976* by Jonathan Dembo, 1995. Other contemporary papers said Joe was boxing instructor "at the Cincinnati club," and the June 13, 1936 *Las Vegas* (New Mexico) *Daily Optic* wrote that he had an interest in a small athletic club there.

[2] thephx.com/about/history; en.wikipedia.org/wiki/Phoenix_Building/Cincinnati_Club

[3] *Ring* magazine, undated, but from January, 1930, from David Chesanow; *Stevens Point Daily Journal*, April 7, 1930; Thanks to Pete Ehrmann of The Sweet Science website.

[4] *Wisconsin State Journal*, June 28, 1930; *Ring* magazine, undated, but March, 1930, David Chesanow.

[5] *Ring* magazine, undated, but from October, 1930, David Chesanow. (Madison, Wisconsin) *Capital Times*, February 4, 1930; *Monessen Daily Independent*, September 11, 1930; *Chester Times*, October 10, 1930.

[6] *Chicago Daily Tribune*, June 23, 1931.

[7] *Images of America, Massena* by Theresa S. Sharp, David E. Martin, 2005; *John L. Sullivan and His America* by Michael T. Isenberg, 1994.

[8] *Dallas Morning News*, February 14, 1931, February 15, 1931; *Fresno Bee*, December 14, 1931; *Oakland Tribune*, December 16, 1931.

[9] Cincinnati Directories, 1932-1934; *Tyrone Daily Herald*, November 17, 1931.

[10] multiculturalcanada.ca; *Life Sketches* by John Hersey, 1989; *Baruch, My Own Story* by Bernard Mannes Baruch, 1957.

[11] *San Antonio Light*, February 7, 1933; *Oshkosh Daily Northwestern*, February 14, 1933.

[12] *Chicago Tribune*, June 23, 1933.

[13] *Max Baer, Glamour Boy of the Ring* by Nat Fleischer, 1970; *Lowell Sun*, June 18, 1934.

[14] *Chronicle Telegram*, September 26, 1934; *Long Beach Independent*, September 30, 1943.

[15] *Dallas Morning News*, May 29, 1935; *Wisconsin State Journal*, September 20, 1939; *Jefferson City Post Tribune*, December 18, 1935.

[16] *Oakland Tribune, San Mateo Times, Fresno Bee*, April 30, 1936; *San Mateo Times*, May 7, 1936; Burial record at Ancestry.com website; *Journal of Proceedings, Board of Supervisors, City and County of San Francisco*, Volume 31, Number 18, May 4, 1936.

[17] *Syracuse Herald*, May 22, 1936.

[18] *El Paso Herald-Post*, May 26, 1936.

[19] *Chicago Jewish Star*, November 6-19, 2009; auschwitz.dk/schmeling.htm; *Daily Globe* (Ironwood, Michigan), June 30, 1936.

[20] *Hamilton Daily News-Journal*, December 11, 1936; *San Antonio Light*, February 1, 1937; The *Veteran Boxer*, February, 1941, from David Chesanow.

[21] *Chester Times*, March 28, 1938; *Wisconsin State Journal*, March 30, 1938.

[22] *Albuquerque Journal*, May 1, 1938; *Wisconsin State Journal*, May 7, 1938; The *Referee* (San Francisco, California), January 23, 1939.

[23] *Billings Gazette*, March 12, 1939; *Wisconsin State Journal*, March 28, 1939; Antique spoon collection owned by Al and Harriet Draper.

[24] From David Chesanow: 1939 letters, Walter Schlichter to Choynski, March 26 and April 13, 1939, a November 30 letter from Joe to Walter; Swann Auction Galleries, Lot# 81, Auction Date, 1997.

[25] Three-page letter from Joe Choynski to Nat Fleischer, November 11, 1939, from Harry Shaffer.

[26] *Sheboygan Press, Wisconsin State Journal*, April 18, 1940; *Dallas Morning News, Wisconsin State Journal*, April 19, 1940; *Straits Times* (Singapore), October 27, 1957; *The Real McCoy, the Life and Times of Norman Selby* by Robert Cantwell, 1971.

[27] *San Antonio Express, San Antonio Light*, July 23, 1940; *Reno Evening Gazette*, July 24, 1940; *The Irish Champion, Peter Maher* by Matt Donnellon, 2008.

[28] *Montana Standard*, June 8, 1941, quoting Bishop's column, "Boxing Bulletin," unnamed paper.

[29] One-page letter from Joe Choynski to Nat Fleischer, dated August 31, 1941, from Lelands.com.

[30] 1940 United States Federal Census; Address on envelope of the August 31, 1941 letter from Joe Choynski to Nat Fleischer.

[31] *Las Cruces Sun-News*, October 1, 1941; *Winnipeg Free Press*, October 7, 1941; *James J. Corbett, a Biography of the Heavyweight Boxing Champion and Popular Theater Headliner* by Armond Fields, 2001. I attempted to contact Armond for further detail on Joe's participation in "Gentleman Jim." Alas, I was two weeks too late. His widow, Sara Fields, informed me on September 6, 2008, that Armond had died of cancer on August 17.

[32] Three-page letter from Joe Choynski to Nat Fleischer, October 11, 1941, from Harry Shaffer.

[33] *Mason City Globe-Gazette*, November 29, 1941; Christie's Auction House, Lot 258, sold in New York on October 5, 1995.

[34] *Philadelphia Inquirer*, August 9, 1942.

[35] *Wisconsin State Journal*, August 10, 1942.

[36] *Ogden Standard-Examiner*, December 10, 1942.

[37] *Gentleman Jim* by Nat Fleischer, 1942.

[38] Unknown paper and date, Libraries of Notre Dame University; Joe Choynski's death certificate.

[39] "A Great Fighter Confesses" by Joe Choynski, *Boxing and Wrestling* magazine, August 1956.

[40] "The Remarkable Joe Choynski," *Boxing Illustrated-Wrestling News*, January 1960.

[41] Joe Choynski's death certificate; walnuthillscemetery.org; Joseph Choynski tribute at findagrave.com; *Cincinnati Enquirer*, January 26, 1943; Joe's 1930-31 BPOE membership card, thanks to David Chesanow. On May 11, 2011, Arlene M. Pauly, Secretary of the Pittsburgh Lodge Number 11, replied: "Dear Mr. LaForce: I regret to tell you that I have searched for information on Joe. Unfortunately, we moved to this location in 1984. Before this, the Elks were located in about 4 different buildings. We have the records on members that have joined since we have been in this building."

[42] Unknown paper and date, from Stanley Weston collection, Libraries of Notre Dame University.

[43] "I Fought 'Em All" by Joe Choynski, *Fight Stories*, Oct.-Nov. 1930.

[44] The Cyber Boxing Zone website; Ed Dunkhorst's record at www.boxrec.com.

[45] *Morning Herald* (Gloversville/Johnstown, New York), *Cincinnati Enquirer*, *Los Angeles Examiner*, *Raleigh* (WV) *Register*, *Huntingdon Daily News*, January 26, 1943; *Gentleman Jim* by Nat Fleischer, 1942.

[46] *Los Angeles News*, January 26, 1943.

[47] *Nevada State Journal*, January 27, 1943; "San Francisco's Fighting Jew," 1974, William M. Kramer and Norton B. Stern's interview with Florence Carmelita Dibert Coe; Undated clipping from Choynski file in *San Francisco Examiner* newspaper morgue.

[48] *Los Angeles Evening Herald and Express*, January 28, 1943; *Abilene Reporter-News*, January 31, 1943.

[49] *Berkshire Evening Eagle*, February 2, 1943; *Cumberland Evening News*, February 19, 1943.

[50] *Coshocton Tribune*, February 4, 1943; *Ironwood Daily Globe*, February 10, 1943.

[51] Undated (1943) article from unidentified newspaper, obtained from Antiquities of the Prize Ring.

[52] *Binghamton Press*, February 24, 1943; *Jewish Boxers Hall of Fame* by Ken Blady, 1988.

[53] *Gettysburg Times*, Charleston (West Virginia) *Daily Mail*, April 28, 1943.

[54] *Dallas Morning News*, January 16, 1944; The 1930 United States Federal Census shows Maurice and Sarah living at 854 North Clark Street, Chicago. *The Certified List of Domestic and Foreign Corporations, Volume 1* by Illinois Office of Secretary of State, 1944, shows them still living at same address; Cook County, Illinois Death Index, 1908-1988, File 17153; *Chicago Daily Tribune*, June 13, 1944; *Boxoffice* magazine, March 11, 1944, March 18, 1944, April 8, 1944, June 24, 1944.

[55] Louise Choynski's death certificate.

[56] *American Volunteers in the French Foreign Legion, 1914-1917* by Paul Rockwell, 1925; *Negro, an Anthology* by Nancy Cunard, 1996; boxrec.com.

[57] *Fresno Bee Republican*, January 25, 1949; *Modesto Bee and News-Herald*, September 13, 1952; For the 518 Hayes Street address, see *James J. Corbett ...* by Armond Fields, 2001; "One of the Great Ones," August 8, 1976 *San Francisco Examiner and Chronicle*.

[58] *Modesto Bee and News-Herald*, March 4, 1953; *New York Times*, April 18, 1953; The *Ring*, February, 1994; *San Mateo Times*, January 3, 1958.

Epilogue:

[1] *Pacific Stars and Stripes* (Tokyo, Japan), December 7, 1960; *Ring Record Book*, 1979 edition.

[2] *Galveston Daily News*, January 27, 1965 (quoting a paper called *News-Tribune*), August 11, 1965; *Fresno Bee Republican*, September 21, 1970.

[3] *Salt Lake Evening Telegram*, May 14, 1913; William M. Kramer and Norton B. Stern, California Historical Quarterly, Number 3, Fall, 1974.

[4] *Syracuse Herald-Journal*, June 11 and June 12, 1998; *Syracuse Post-Standard*, June 11 and June 15, 1998.

[5] *Canadian Jewish News*, July 16, 1998; cjnews.com/pastIssues/98/july16-98/sports/sports.htm

Bibliography:

A Brief Description of the System of Education Adopted in the Common Schools of Prussia by Victor Cousin, 1838

A Debonair Scoundrel by Lately Thomas, 1962

Adventures of a Forty-Niner by Daniel Knower, 1894

American Gymnasia and Athletic Record, Volumes 1 and 2, 1905

American Gymnasia and Athletic Record, 1906

American Handy Book of Brewing and Malting by Wahl and Heinus, 1902

American Volunteers in the French Foreign Legion, 1914-1917 by Paul Rockwell, 1925

Annual List of Merchant Vessels of United States by Department of Commerce, Bureau of Navigation, 1913

Annual Report of the Chamber of Commerce of San Francisco, 1889

Annual Report of the Library Company of Philadelphia for the Year 1984, 1985

Autobiography of Sol Bloom by Sol Bloom, 1948

Automobile Club of Southern California

Baruch, My Own Story by Bernard Mannes Baruch, 1957

Beyond the Ring by Jeffrey T. Sammons, 1990

Big Book of Jewish Sports Heroes by Peter S. Horvitz, 2007

Big Jim Jeffries and His 12 Great Ring Battles by J.W. McConaughy, 1910

Biographical Review of Prominent Men and Women of the Day by T.W. Herringshaw, Benno Loewy, 1889

Black Champion by Finnis Farr, 1964

Black Dynamite, Volume I by Nat Fleischer, 1938

Black Dynamite, Volume IV, Fighting Furies by Nat Fleischer, 1939

Black Dynamite, Volume V, Sockers in Sepia by Nat Fleischer, 1947

Black Prince Peter by A.G. Hales, 1931

Blue and Gold by University of California, Berkeley, Zeta Psi Fraternity, Iota Chapter, 1895

Booksellers of Early San Francisco by Robert Ernest Cowan, 1953

Boxing in San Francisco by F. Daniel Somrack, 2005

Brutes in Suits, Male Sensibility in America, 1890-1920 by John Pettigrew, 2007

California and Californians, Volume 4 by Dr. Rockwell Dennis Hunt, 1926, 1930

Cambridge Studies in Early Modern History, New York, Cambridge University Press, 2000

Captain J.A. Brooks, Texas Ranger by Paul N. Spellman, 2007

Canadian Journal of History, Dec 2001 by A.B. Pernal

Champions Off Guard by W.O. Inglis, 1932

Chicago's Greatest Sportsman, Charles E. 'Parson' Davies by Mark T. Dunn, 2011

Chronicles of Emanu-El by Jacob Voorsanger, 1900

Congressional Serial Set, Issue 1722 by United States Government Printing Office, 1887

Cosmopolitans, a Social and Cultural History of the Jews of the San Francisco Bay Area by Fred Rosenbaum, 2009

Dan Stuart's Fistic Carnival by Leo N. Miletich, 1994

Darwin, California by Robert F. Palazzo, 1996

Disaster!: The Great San Francisco Earthquake and Fire of 1906 by Dan Kurzman, 2002

Donovan's Science of Boxing by Mike Donovan, 1893

Elbert Hubbard of East Aurora by Felix Shay, 1926

Ellis Island to Ebbets Field by Peter Levine, 1992

Eureka and Its Resources by H. Keller, 1879

Famous Fights by Harold Furniss, London, England

Fight Comics by Fiction House

Fight Pictures: A History of Boxing and Early Cinema by Dan Streible, 2008

Fight Stories by Fiction House

Financial California, an Historical Review by Le Roy Armstrong, J.O. Denny, 1980

First in Violence, Deepest in Dirt, Homicide in Chicago, 1875-1920 by Jeffrey S. Adler, 2006

Galveston, a History of the Island by Gary Cartwright, 1998

Gentleman Bruiser, a Life of the Boxer Peter Jackson by Bob Petersen, 2005

Gentleman Jim by Nat Fleischer, 1942

Gentleman Jim Corbett by Patrick Myler, 1997

German University Education, Or the Professors and Students of Germany, To Which Is Added a Brief Account of the Public Schools of Prussia by Walter C. Perry, London, 1846

Greatest Sports Stories from the Chicago Tribune, Edited by Arch Ward, 1953

Heavyweight Champions by W.W. Naughton, 1910

Heroes of the Fancy by Arnold Thomas, 1999

History of Modern Europe (1792-1878) by C.A. Fyffe 1880, reissued 1895

History of the Walnut Hills Congregational Church of Cincinnati (1843-1935) by Almon M. Warner,

1935

Hitters, Dancers and Ring Magicians: Seven Boxers of the Golden Age by Kelly Richard Nicholson, 2010

I Was There, a Book of Reminiscences by Mary Edith Carey Tyrrell, 1939

Images of America, Massena by Theresa S. Sharp and David E. Martin, Arcadia Publishing, 2005

In Memoriam, Elbert and Alice Hubbard by The Roycrofters and John Thomas Hoyle, 1915

In The Ring with James J. Corbett by Adam J. Pollack, 2007 & 2008

In The Ring with Bob Fitzsimmons by Adam J. Pollack, 2007

In The Ring with James J. Jeffries by Adam J. Pollack, 2009

Irving Wallace, a Writer's Profile by John Leverence, 1974

Jack Johnson & His Times by Denzil Batchelor, 1956

James J. Corbett, a Biography of the Heavyweight Boxing Champion and Popular Theater Headliner by Armond Fields, 2001

Jewish Boxers Hall of Fame by Ken Blady, 1988

Jewish Voices of the California Gold Rush by Ava Fran Kahn, 2002

Jewish Women Pioneering the Frontier Trail by Jeanne E. Abrams, 2006

Jews in Nevada by John P. Marschall, 2008

Jim Jeffries, a Man among Men by Kelly Richard Nicholson, 2002

Jim Jeffries, My Life and Battles, 1910

Joe Boyle, King of the Klondike by William Rodney, 1974

John L. Sullivan, the Career of the First Gloved Heavyweight Champion by Adam J. Pollack, 2006

John L. Sullivan and His America by Michael T. Isenberg, 1988 & 1994

Journal of Proceedings, Board of Supervisors, City and County of San Francisco, Volume 31, Number 18, May 4, 1936

Kindler of Souls, Rabbi Henry Cohen by Henry Cohen II, 2009

King News, an Autobiography by Moses Koenigsberg, 1941

Kings of the Queensberry Realm by W.W. Naughton, 1902

Kings of the Ring by Wilfrid Diamond, 1954

Lanky Bob, the Life, Times and Contemporaries of Bob Fitzsimmons by K.R. Robinson, 2008

Life Sketches by John Hersey, 1989

Lights and Shades of San Francisco by Benjamin Estelle Lloyd, 1876

Lone Stars of David, the Jews of Texas by Hollace Ava Weiner and Kenneth Roseman, 2007

Lusitania by Diane Preston, 2002

Mark Twain, A Life by Ron Powers, 2005

Max Baer, Glamour Boy of the Ring by Nat Fleischer, 1970

Medievalism in North America by Kathleen Verduin, 1994

Members of Olympic Club - By-laws and List of Members of the Olympic Club, March 1, 1913 by Olympic Club

Muldoon, the Solid Man of Sport by Edward Van Every, 1929

My Life and Battles by Jack Johnson (translated from "Vie au Grand Air," 1911) by Christopher Rivers, 2007

Negro, an Anthology by Nancy Cunard, 1996

Nickelodeon Theatres and Their Music by Q. David Bowers, 1986

North to California: The Spanish Voyages of Discovery, 1533-1603 by Paul A. Myers, 2004

Notable American Women, Volume 4 by Barbara Sicherman, Carol Hurd Green, 1980

Notable Women of China: Shang Dynasty to the Early 20th Century by Barbara Bennett Peterson, 2000

Our City, the Jews of San Francisco by Irena Narell, 1981

Our Jim, the World's Champion by Crown Publishing Company, 1892

Out of Sight, the Rise of African-American Popular Music, 1889-1895 by Lynn Abbott and Doug Seroff, 2003

Oxford Dictionary of National Biography, Oxford University Press, 2004

Papa Jack by Randy Roberts, 1983

Peter Jackson, a Biography of the Australian Heavyweight Champion, 1960-1901 by Bob Petersen, 2011

Peter Maher, the Irish Champion by Matt Donnellon, 2008

Portrait Gallery of Pugilists of America and Their Contemporaries by Billy Edwards, 1894

Printers' Ink, the Journal for Advertisers

Proceedings of Annual Session District Grand Lodge by B'nai B'rith, District number 4 Grand Lodge, 1864

Reared in a Greenhouse by Dorothy B. Wexler, 1998

Recollections of Life & Doings in Chicago from Haymarket Riot to End of World War I by C.H. Hermann, 1945

Records of California Men in the War of the Rebellion, 1861 to 1867 by Brigadier General Richard H. Orton, published 1890 and transcribed by Kathy Sedler, 2004

Remembering Bob Fitzsimmons by Pember W. Rocap and William H. Rocap, 2001

Report by Oregon Office of the Secretary of State, 1899

Report on the Internal Commerce of the United States by United States Bureau of Statistics, 1891

Rowell's American Newspaper Directory by George P. Rowell & Company, 1887

San Francisco, a Guide to the Bay and Its Cities by Works Progress Administration of Northern California, 1940 and 1973

San Francisco, a Profile with Pictures by Barnaby Conrad, 1959

Selected Writings of Elbert Hubbard by Elbert Hubbard, Bert Hubbard, 1922

Silver Stampede by Neill Compton Wilson, 1971

Sport Tales and Anecdotes by Frank G. Menke, 1953

Sports & the American Jew by Syracuse University Press, 1998

Sunset magazine by Southern Pacific Company, Passenger Department

Systems of Land Tenure in Various Countries, a Series of Essays, edited by J. W. Probyn, 1876

Taken at the Flood by John Gunther, 1960

The Barbary Coast, an Informal History of the San Francisco Underworld by Herbert Asbury, 1933

The Biographical Review of Prominent Men and Women of the Day by T.W. Herringshaw, Benno Loewy, 1889

The Boxing Filmography by Frederick V. Romano, 2004

The Certified List of Domestic and Foreign Corporations, Volume 1 by Illinois Office of Secretary of State, 1944

The Croatian Immigrants in America by George J. Prpic, 1971

The Earp Decision by Jack DeMattos, 1989

The Emergence of Cinema: The American Screen to 1907 by Charles Musser, 1994

The Legendary Mizners by Alva Johnston, 1953

The Federal Reporter by District of Columbia Court of Appeals, 1897

The Fighting Blacksmith by Gilbert Odd, 1976

The History of the Cincinnati Athletic Club, 1853-1976 by Jonathan Dembo (1995)

The Iron Era (Dover, New Jersey)

The Jews of California, from the Discovery of Gold until 1880 by Dr. Rudolf Glanz, 1960

The Lure of the Ring by Frederick Arthur Hornibrook, 1946

The Magazine of American History with Notes and Queries by John Austin Stevens and several others, 1879

The Making of Champions in California by De Witt Van Court, 1926

The Man Who Stayed in Texas, the Life of Rabbi Henry Cohen by Anne N. Cohen and Henry I. Cohen, 1941

The Moving Picture World by the Moving Picture Exhibitors' Association (various volumes and years)

The National Sporting Club, Past and Present by A.F. Bettinson and W.O. Tristram, 1902

The New York Supplement, 1906 by West Publishing Company

The North American Review, June, 1899

The Old Jewish Cemeteries at Charleston, S. C. by Barnett Abraham Elzas, 1903

The Other Prussia: Royal Prussia, Poland and Liberty, 1569-1772 by Karen Friedrich, 2006

The Political History of Chicago from 1837-1887 by M.L. Ahern, 1886

The Real McCoy, the Life and Times of Norman Selby by Robert Cantwell, 1971

The Roar of the Crowd by James J. Corbett with Robert G. Anderson, 1925

The Terror of Terre Haute, Bud Taylor and the 1920s by John D. Wright, 2008

The Tragedy of the Lusitania by Frederick D. Ellis, 1915

The Tumult and the Shouting, My Life in Sport by Grantland Rice, 1954

The Yellow Earl: the Life of Hugh Lowther by Douglas Sutherland, 1966

Three Years in America, 1859-1862 by Israel Joseph Benjamin, 1862

Titanic – An Illustrated History by Don Lynch, 2010

Traffic World by Traffic Service Corporation, January 15, 1916

Transactions of the 38th & 39th Annual Reunions of the Oregon Pioneer Association, 1910 & 1911 published 1914

Tunney by Jack Cavanaugh, 2006

29th Annual Report of the Superintendent of Public Schools for the School Year Ending June 30th, 1882 by the Department of Public Schools, City and County of San Francisco, 1882

Two Fisted Jeff by Hugh Fullerton, 1929

Ultimate Tough Guy by Jim Carney, 2009

Unforgivable Blackness: The Rise and Fall of Jack Johnson by Geoffrey C. Ward, 2006

Voices of the Oregon Territory by Fred Lockley and Mike Helm, 1981, 1996.

Who's Who on The Stage, edited by Walter Browne and Frederick Arnold Austin, 1908

Yugoslav Survey of California, Nevada, Arizona and the South, 1800-1900 by Adam S. Eterovich, 1971

Yugoslavs in Nevada, 1859-1900 by Adam S. Eterovich, 1973

Newspaper (and magazine) sources:

Where a newspaper is alternately a daily, evening, weekly or Sunday paper, I generally have kept the name as generic as possible, ie., *Trenton* (New Jersey) *Times*, instead of *Trenton* (New Jersey) *Evening Times*.

Aberdeen (South Dakota) *News*
Abilene (Texas) *Reporter-News*
Adelaide (Australia) *Advertiser*
Alaska Citizen
Alaska (Juneau) *Dispatch*
Alaska (Juneau) *Herald*
Albuquerque (New Mexico) *Journal*
American Citizen (Kansas City, Kansas)
American Israelite
Anaconda (Montana) *Standard*
Antiquarian
Appleton (Wisconsin) *Post-Crescent*
Argus and Patriot (Montpelier, Vermont)
Ashland (Pennsylvania) *Daily News*
Athens (Ohio) *Messenger*
Atlanta (Georgia) *Constitution*
Auburn (New York) *Citizen*
Austin (Minnesota) *Daily Herald*
Australian Star (Sydney, Australia)
Baltimore (Maryland) *Morning Herald*
Baltimore (Maryland) *Sun*
Barrier Miner (Broken Hill, NSW, Australia)
Bangor (Maine) *Daily Whig and Courier*
Belleville (Illinois) *News-Democrat*
Bellingham (Washington) *Herald*
Beloit (Wisconsin) *Daily News*
Berkshire (Pittsfield, Massachusetts) *Evening Eagle*
Billings (Montana) *Gazette*
Biloxi (Mississippi) *Herald-Weekly* (also, *Sun-Herald*, *Daily Herald* and *Mississippi Daily Herald*)
Binghamton (New York) *Press*
Bisbee (Arizona) *Daily Review*
Bismarck (North Dakota) *Daily Tribune*
Boston (Massachusetts) *American*
Boston (Massachusetts) *Globe*
Boston (Massachusetts) *Herald*
Boston (Massachusetts) *Journal*
Boston (Massachusetts) *Post*
Bourbon News (Paris, Kentucky)
Boxing and Wrestling magazine
Boxing Blade (Minneapolis, Minnesota)
Boxoffice magazine
Bridgeport (Connecticut) *Telegram*
Brisbane (Queensland, Australia) *Courier*
Brooklyn (New York) *Daily Eagle*
Brownsville (Texas) *Herald*
Buffalo (New York) *Express*
Butler County (Ohio) *Democrat*
Butte (Montana) *Weekly Miner*

Capital Journal (Salem, Oregon)
Capital Times (Madison, Wisconsin)
Carson (Nevada) *Appeal*
Casa Grande (Arizona) *Bulletin*
Cedar Falls (Iowa) *Gazette*
Cedar Rapids (Iowa) *Gazette* (also, *Cedar Rapids Republican*)
Cedar Rapids (Iowa) *Tribune* (also, *Centralia* [Wisconsin] *Enterprise and Tribune*)
Charlotte (North Carolina) *News* (also, *Charlotte Observer*)
Charleston (South Carolina) *Courier*
Charleston (South Carolina) *Mercury*
Charleston (West Virginia) *Daily Mail*
Chester (Pennsylvania) *Times*
Chicago (Illinois) *Daily Inter-Ocean*
Chicago (Illinois) *Jewish Star*
Chicago (Illinois) *Record* (also, *Chicago Times, Sun-Times* and *Times-Herald*)
Chicago (Illinois) *Journal*
Chicago (Illinois) *Tribune*
Chillicothe (Missouri) *Constitution-Tribune*
Cincinnati (Ohio) *Enquirer*
Cincinnati (Ohio) *Times-Star*
Colorado Springs (Colorado) *Gazette* (also *Colorado Springs Republic and Telegraph*)
Colorado Sun (Colorado Springs, Colorado)
Columbus (Georgia) *Enquirer* (also *Daily Enquirer-Sun*)
Coshocton (Ohio) *Tribune*
Cumberland (Maryland) *Evening Times* (and *News*)
Daily Alta California (San Francisco)
Daily Bulletin (Honolulu, Hawaii)
Daily (Huron, South Dakota) *Huronite*
Daily Iowa (Des Moines) *Capital*
Daily Iowa State Press (Iowa City, Iowa)
Daily Messenger (Canandaigua, New York)
Dallas (Texas) *Morning News*
Davenport (Iowa) *Gazette*
Davenport (Iowa) *Leader* (also, *Democrat and Leader*)
Davenport (Iowa) *Republican*
Dawson (Yukon, Canada) *News*
Dawson (Yukon, Canada) *Record*
(The) Day (New London, Connecticut)
Decatur (Illinois) *Morning Herald* (also, *Herald-Despatch, Decatur Review*)
Decatur (Illinois) *Republican* (also, *Daily Republican*)
Delphos (Ohio) *Herald*

Denver (Colorado) *Post* (also, *Denver Times*)
Denver (Colorado) *Republican*
Des Moines (Iowa) *News*
Dubuque (Iowa) *Herald* (also, *Telegraph-Herald*)
Dubuque (Iowa) *Times*
Duluth (Minnesota) *News-Tribune*
Dunkirk (New York) *Evening Observer*
Durango (Colorado) *Democrat*
Eau Claire (Wisconsin) *Leader*
El Paso (Texas) *Herald* (and *Herald-Post*)
Elmira (New York) *Daily Gazette*
Elmira (New York) *Morning Telegram*
Elyria (Ohio) *Chronicle* (also, *Chronicle-Telegram* and *Ohio Evening Telegram*)
Emporia (Kansas) *Weekly Gazette*
Eureka (Nevada) *Daily Republican*
Eureka (Nevada) *Sentinel*
Evening News (San Jose, California) (in 1927 it was called the *San Jose Evening News*)
Ferris Wheel (Ferris, Texas)
Fitchburg (Massachusetts) *Sentinel*
Fort Wayne (Indiana) *Evening Post*
Fort Wayne (Indiana) *Gazette* (also *Fort Wayne Journal* and *Journal-Gazette*)
Fort Wayne (Indiana) *Sentinel* (also, *Fort Wayne News* and *News-Sentinel*)
Fort Worth (Texas) *Register*
Fort Worth (Texas) *Star-Telegram*
Frederick (Maryland) *News*
Freeman's Journal and Daily Commercial Advertiser (England)
Fremont (California) *Argus*
Fresno (California) *Bee* (also, *Fresno Bee Republican* and *Fresno Republican*)
Galveston (Texas) *Daily News* (also *Galveston County Daily News*)
Gettysburg (Pennsylvania) *Times*
Goldfield (Nevada) *Chronicle*
Grand Forks (North Dakota) *Herald*
Grand Rapids (Michigan) *Herald*
Grey River (New Zealand) *Argus*
Hamilton (Ohio) *Daily Democrat* (and *Daily News-Journal*)
Hamilton (Ohio) *Daily Republican* (and *Daily Republican-News*)
Harper's magazine
Hawarden (Iowa) *Independent*
Hayward (California) *Daily Review*
Hazel Green (Kentucky) *Herald*
Helena (Montana) *Independent*
Hendricks (Minnesota) *Pioneer*
Houston (Texas) *Post*
Huntingdon (Pennsylvania) *Daily News*
Idaho (Boise) *Statesman*
Indiana (Pennsylvania) *Democrat*
Indianapolis (Indiana) *Star*
Ironwood (Michigan) *Daily Globe* (also, *Daily Globe* [Ironwood, Michigan])
Janesville (Wisconsin) *Gazette*

Jefferson City (Missouri) *Post Tribune*
Kalamazoo (Michigan) *Gazette*
Kansas (Topeka) *Weekly Capital and Farm Journal* (and *Semi-Weekly Capital*)
Kansas City (Missouri) *Journal*
Kansas City (Missouri) *Star* (and *Kansas City Times*)
Kennebec (Augusta, Maine) *Journal*
Kentucky Irish American (Louisville, Kentucky)
Kingston (New York) *Daily Freeman*
Knoxville (Tennessee) *Journal*
La Crosse (Wisconsin) *Tribune* (also, *Tribune and Leader-Press*)
Lake County (Indiana) *Times*
Laredo (Texas) *Times*
Las Cruces (New Mexico) *Sun-News*
Las Vegas (New Mexico) *Daily Optic*
Lethbridge (Alberta, Canada) *Herald*
Lewiston (Maine) *Daily Sun*
Lexington (Kentucky) *Herald*
Lima (Ohio) *Daily News*
Lincoln (Nebraska) *Star*
Lincoln (Nebraska) *News* (also, *State Journal and Evening News*)
Logansport (Indiana) *Pharos* (also, *Pharos-Tribune* and *Pharos-Reporter*)
London Stars and Stripes (Middlesex, England)
Long Beach (California) *Independent*
Los Angeles (California) *Daily Star*
Los Angeles (California) *Examiner*
Los Angeles (California) *Herald* (also, *Los Angeles Evening Herald and Express*)
Los Angeles (California) *News*
Los Angeles (California) *Times*
Louisville (Kentucky) *Commercial*
Lowell (Massachusetts) *Sun*
Maitland (NSW, Australia) *Mercury*
Manitoba (Winnipeg, Canada) *Free Press* (became the *Winnipeg* [Manitoba, Canada] *Free Press* in 1931)
Mansfield (Ohio) *News*
Marshall (Michigan) *Expounder*
Maryland Sun
Marysville (California) *Daily Appeal*
Mason City (Iowa) *Globe-Gazette*
Massena (New York) *Observer*
Massillon (Ohio) *Independent*
McKean Democrat (Smethport, Pennsylvania)
Melbourne (Australia) *Argus*
Melbourne (Australia) *Sportsman*
Menorah (monthly newsletter of B'nai B'rith)
Miami (Florida) *Herald*
Miami (Piqua, Ohio) *Leader*
Middlesboro (Kentucky) *Daily News*
Middletown (New York) *Daily Press* (also, *Daily Times-Press*)
Milford (Iowa) *Mail*
Milwaukee (Wisconsin) *Evening Wisconsin*
Milwaukee (Wisconsin) *Free Press*

Minneapolis (Minnesota) *Journal*
Mirror of Life, (London, England)
Modesto (California) *Bee* (also, *Evening News* and *News-Herald*)
Monessen (Pennsylvania) *Daily Independent*
Montana (Butte) *Standard*
Montgomery (Alabama) *Advertiser*
Montreal (Quebec, Canada) *Herald*
Morning Herald (Gloversville and Johnstown, New York)
Morning Herald (Uniontown, Pennsylvania)
Morning Olympian (Olympia, Washington State)
Music Hall and Theater Review (London, England)
Naugatuck (Connecticut) *Daily Times*
Naugatuck (Connecticut) *News*
Nebraska (Lincoln) *State Journal*
Nevada (Reno) *Evening Gazette* (also *Nevada State Journal* and *Reno Evening Gazette*)
New Castle (Pennsylvania) *News*
New Haven (New York) *Evening Register*
New Orleans (Louisiana) *Picayune* (also *New Orleans Times-Democrat*)
New York (New York) *Advertiser*
New York (New York) *Clipper*
New York (New York) *Daily Mirror*
New York (New York) *Dramatic Mirror* (also *Dramatic Mirror & Theatre*)
New York (New York) *Evening Telegram*
New York (New York) *Herald*
New York (New York) *Illustrated News*
New York (New York) *Journal*
New York (New York) *Sun*
New York (New York) *Times*
New York (New York) *Tribune*
New York (New York) *World*
New York (New York) *Spirit of the Times*
New Zealand (Auckland) *Observer and Free Lance*
New Zealand (Auckland) *Truth*
Newark (Ohio) *Advocate*
Niagara Falls (New York) *Gazette*
North Carolina (Charlotte?) *Observer*
Nor'wester (Winnipeg, Manitoba, Canada)
Oakland (California) *Tribune*
Ogden (Utah) *Standard* (also, *Examiner* and *Standard-Examiner*)
Oelwein (Iowa) *Daily Register*
Ohio (New Philadelphia) *Democrat*
Olean (New York) *Democrat* (also, *Olean Evening Herald*)
Olean (New York) *Times*
Omaha (Nebraska) *Bee*
Omaha (Nebraska) *Sun*
Omaha (Nebraska) *World-Herald*
Oneonta (New York) *Daily Star*
Orange County (Middletown, New York) *Times-Press*
Oregonian (Portland, Oregon)
Oshkosh (Wisconsin) *Daily Northwestern*

Oswego (New York) *Daily Times*
Otago (New Zealand) *Witness*
Outing magazine
Oxnard (California) *Daily Courier*
Pacific Stars and Stripes (Tokyo, Japan)
Paducah (Kentucky) *Sun*
Palestine (Texas) *Daily Herald*
Pawtucket (Rhode Island) *Times*
Perry (Iowa) *Chief*
Philadelphia (Pennsylvania) *Bulletin*
Philadelphia (Pennsylvania) *Inquirer*
Philadelphia (Pennsylvania) *Item*
Philadelphia (Pennsylvania) *North American*
Philadelphia (Pennsylvania) *Press*
Philadelphia (Pennsylvania) *Public Ledger*
Philadelphia (Pennsylvania) *Record*
Pittsburgh (Pennsylvania) *Chronicle* (also, *Chronicle Telegraph*)
Pittsburgh (Pennsylvania) *Leader*
Pittsburgh (Pennsylvania) *Press* (also, *Dispatch*)
Police Gazette (technically, the *National Police Gazette*) (New York, New York)
Police News (Boston, Massachusetts)
Portsmouth (Ohio) *Times*
Portsmouth (New Hampshire) *Herald*
Poughkeepsie (New York) *Eagle-News*
Poverty Bay (Gisborne, New Zealand)
Racine (Wisconsin) *Daily Journal* (also, *Journal-News*)
Raleigh (West Virginia) *Register*
Record-Miner (Juneau, Alaska)
Referee (San Francisco, California)
Ring magazine, various issues
Rochester (New York) *Democrat and Chronicle*
Rocky Mountain News (Denver, Colorado)
Sacramento (California) *Daily Record-Union* (also, *Daily Union, Daily Record and Union*)
St. Louis (Missouri) *Post-Dispatch*
St. Louis (Missouri) *Republic*
St. Paul (Minnesota) *Globe*
Salem (Ohio) *Daily News*
Salt Lake (Utah) *Herald* (also, *Herald-Examiner* and *Herald-Republican*)
Salt Lake (Utah) *Telegram* (also, *Evening Telegram, Deseret* [Salt Lake City, Utah] *News* and *Deseret Weekly*)
Salt Lake (Utah) *Tribune*
San Antonio (Texas) *Evening News* (also, *San Antonio Express*)
San Antonio (Texas) *Light*
San Francisco (California) *Bulletin* (later, *San Francisco Call, Evening Post, Post, Chronicle, Examiner, News*)
San Francisco (California) *Report*
San Jose (California) *Mercury Herald* (also, *Mercury News*)
San Mateo (California) *Times*
Sandusky (Ohio) *Star*
Sandusky (Ohio) *Register*

Index

Quinn, John J. (or Jack), 311, 316, 344, 356, 368, 371, 374, 412, 423
Rickard, "Tex" George, 558, 617, 623, 625-628, 632, 634, 647, 689
Riordan, Con, 71, 81, 118, 173, 198, 203, 306, 745
Rocap, William, 217, 552-555, 570, 571, 582, 775
Roche, Billy, 186, 589
Roche, Dick, 371, 372
Roosevelt, Theodore, 356, 358-361, 478
Root, Jack, 6, 7, 455, 456, 462, 463, 507, 510, 532-534, 539, 545, 554, 562, 563, 573, 581, 590, 591, 594, 596, 627
Ruddy, Joe, 649-651
Ruef, Abe, 44, 83, 591, 592, 718
Ruhlin, Gus, 12, 378, 387, 397, 400, 403, 409, 424, 425, 431-436, 438, 439, 456, 479, 492, 495, 501, 502, 506, 513, 531, 533, 572, 580, 675, 681, 732, 733, 748
Russell, Fred, 511, 512, 550, 749
Ryan, "Australian" Jimmy, 7, 164, 462-468, 471-473, 560
Ryan, Jem, 353
Ryan, Paddy, 173, 189, 310-313, 315-317, 327
Ryan, Tom (not Tommy Ryan), 195, 746, 760
Ryan, Tommy, 6, 10, 90, 180, 189, 227, 233, 270, 273, 276-280, 295-304, 307, 309-317, 329, 335, 407, 409, 417, 421, 422, 456, 457, 467, 480, 510, 539, 540, 547, 548, 877, 578, 596, 610, 614, 641, 663, 674, 678, 684, 694, 702, 705, 708, 715, 732, 742, 747, 748
Saengerfest Athletic Association, 513
Sage, Tony, 178, 200, 221, 222
Sayers, Governor Joseph, 440, 515, 519, 526
Scanlon, Bob, 741
Schlichter, Walter, 196, 361, 424, 431, 432, 723, 728, 783
Schmeling, Max, 605, 711, 716, 721
Schmitz, Mayor Eugene, 591, 592
Schreck, Mike, 600, 601, 608
Sea Queen (tug), 94, 95, 110-112
Seaside Athletic Club, 280, 300, 302
Selby, Homer, 409, 425, 442-444, 469, 479, 480, 484, 487, 725
Sharkey, Tom, 6, 9, 12, 101, 113, 147, 182, 308, 309, 317, 328, 330-337, 339-344, 349, 352, 362, 363, 365, 366, 368, 370, 371, 373-376, 378, 385-389, 398, 403, 407-425, 428, 432, 439, 441, 442, 448, 456, 458, 468, 473, 475, 477, 479, 482, 491, 492, 495, 506-509, 511, 513, 514, 531-533, 538, 539, 557, 580, 597, 604, 605, 616, 658, 663, 672, 675, 678, 680-682, 684, 692, 694, 702, 708, 711, 714, 715, 719, 722, 725-727, 733, 736, 737, 741, 743, 748, 749, 767, 768
Sherith Israel, Temple, 33, 38, 590
Shrosbree, Al, 299, 353, 354, 379, 494, 748
Shrosbree, George, 424, 596, 601, 695

Siler, George, 242, 246, 299, 300, 353, 463, 465, 466, 505-507, 509, 532, 536-538, 542-544, 546, 548, 549, 595
Silverthorn, Tom, 312, 313, 748
Slattery, Jerry, 195, 746
Slavin, Frank, 12, 146, 153-155, 159, 177, 179, 181, 187, 188, 196-198, 200-205, 207, 208, 297, 298, 312, 354, 362, 474, 559-562, 643, 651, 677, 679, 680, 685, 686
Smith, "Denver" Ed, 192, 195, 196, 213, 229, 234, 246, 251, 368, 370-372, 457, 510, 511, 746, 748
Smith, Al, 213, 307, 320, 370, 375, 500, 554, 580
Smith, "Australian" Billy, 139, 343, 350, 550, 725
Smith, "Mysterious" Billy, 232, 270, 278, 301, 302, 463, 482, 496
Smith, C.A.C., 213, 214, 223, 436, 746, 749
Smith, Jem, 134, 199, 203, 204, 206-208, 746
Smith, Paddy, 114, 115, 117, 118, 245, 246
Smith, Solly, 244, 248, 363, 374, 412, 747
Spreckels, J.D., 136, 138, 144, 201, 264
St. Louis Athletic Club, 471, 473
Stelzner, Jack, 331, 348, 389, 410, 436, 442-444, 461
Stift, Billy, 270, 274, 314, 402, 406, 479, 542, 547, 548, 747, 748
Stockwell, L.R. (Lincoln), 230, 231, 233, 235, 236, 241, 247, 250, 290, 351, 762
Stowe, Harriet Beecher, 230, 236, 239, 240, 244, 250, 293, 735
Strong, Sydney, 291-293
Stuart, Dan, 325, 326, 440, 766
Sullivan, John L., 9, 12, 46, 56, 66, 76, 81, 122, 146, 159, 165, 167-169, 171, 173, 176, 181, 182, 189, 190, 212, 213, 224, 226, 231, 232, 269, 278, 279, 298, 305, 310, 311, 313, 316, 327, 333, 369, 370, 404, 443, 463, 482, 497, 593, 596, 621, 627, 628, 648, 651, 690, 701, 705, 712, 716, 746, 759, 783
Sullivan, Owen, 144, 152, 157, 158, 168, 474, 746
TAD (Thomas Aloysius Dorgan), 98, 682, 694, 695
Taylor, Frank, 510, 749
Thomas, Sheriff Henry, 440, 520, 523, 529
Thompson, Harry, 155-157, 160, 759
Tillson, Charley, 65, 123, 128, 335, 350
Tipton Slasher, 69, 545
Tracey, Tommy, 242, 244, 272, 297-300, 401, 402
Tulrock, Al, 313, 748
Tunney, Gene, 24, 81, 82, 149, 604, 644, 702, 704, 705, 708, 711, 712, 715, 718, 736, 751, 782
Turner, Charlie, 71, 114, 117, 125
Twain, Mark (Samuel L. Clemens), 12, 24, 40, 51, 750, 754

Finally ... the Back!

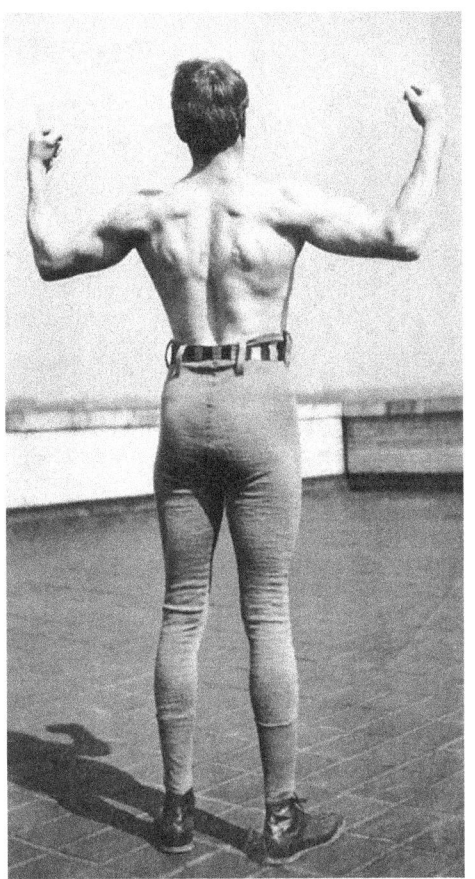

Joe, rooftop, circa 1900

Milton Keynes UK
Ingram Content Group UK Ltd.
UKHW011318140524
442696UK00004B/20